HANDBOOK

OF

WORLD EDUCATION

A Comparative Guide to Higher Education
& Educational Systems of the World

HANDBOOK

OF

WORLD EDUCATION

*A Comparative Guide to Higher Education
& Educational Systems of the World*

WALTER WICKREMASINGHE
B.S., M.B.A., Dr. Ing.
Editor-in-Chief

AMERICAN COLLEGIATE SERVICE
HOUSTON, TEXAS

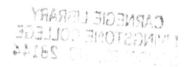

American Collegiate Service
P.O.Box 442008
Houston, Texas 77244, U.S.A.

Library of Congress Catalog Card Number: 90-080955
ISBN: 0-940937-03-4

Printed in the United States of America

Second Printing, May, 1992

CONTENTS

PREFACE

The *Handbook of World Education* is the outcome of three years of cooperative efforts of over 130 distinguished scholars from all over the world. It is an attempt to present, in a single handy volume, major aspects of the educational systems in different countries, with focus on higher education. The *Handbook* is also unique in another respect: the book devotes, for each country's educational system, one chapter written by a scholar native to that country.

The primary function of the book is to serve as a concise source of up-to-date information for both the academic community and the general public who have an interest in international education. The broader goal is to facilitate international understanding by promoting transnational fluidity in education – the same idealistic objective that influenced some of the pioneering scholars of comparative education. The most practical aim is to serve the needs of students, teachers, and researchers who seek information on foreign educational systems as a prelude to study or research work in countries other than their own.

This ambitious project for preparation of the *Handbook* was prompted by three conditions. First, recent years have witnessed a growing sense of global interdependence and a need to educate the citizens to meet the challenges of a new global era of cooperation and understanding among nations, thus moving international education to a period of lively ferment. Compelling evidence of this need is well documented in many U.S. studies and reports, the most recent and the most eloquent of which include the 1988 report, *Educating for Global Competence*, of the "Bartlett Committee", a nationally distinguished group appointed by the Council on International Educational Exchange, and the 1990 study, *A National Mandate for Education Abroad*, of the National Task Force in Undergraduate Education, a panel formed by the Council on International Educational Exchange, the Institute of International Education, and the National Association for Foreign Student Affairs.

At the grass roots level too, there is a growing thrust on internationalism among students in U.S. colleges and universities. For example, a 1990 survey conducted at my own alma mater, Harvard University, reported, "...20.5 percent of the Class of 1990 planned to spend their first postbaccalaureate year abroad, more than double the 10.1 percent who planned the same in 1980 and a step up from 19.8

percent a year ago. All told, 58.8 percent of the Class of 1990 either spent time abroad as undergraduates, planned to spend their postgraduate year abroad or both – a 3 percent increase over the Class of 1989." (*Harvard University Gazette*, November 1990)

Second, there is a critical need for a single reference volume of convenient size and price, with up-to-date information on national systems. This *Handbook* is designed to fulfill that need. Reference works on the subject fall into three categories: essays in comprehensive educational encyclopedias; year books and guides; and publications on single nations or specific geographical areas. The encyclopedias come in multiple volumes and have been published many years ago. At the time work commenced on this book, the most current encyclopedias which had entries on national systems of education were already several years old: *The International Encyclopedia of Higher Education* edited by Knowles was published in 1977 in ten volumes (Jossey-Bass Publishers) and *The International Encyclopedia of Education* edited by Husen & Postlethwaite was published in 1985, also in ten volumes (Pergamon Press). Although these sources continue to be historically valuable, time has now come to take stock of recent developments and trends. The year books and guides, including the ones published by UNESCO are primarily sources of statistical records or have a limited focus. The publications on single nations or specific geographical areas cover only a single system or systems in a single region. In general, they are of limited distribution and do not serve the readers looking for a ready comparative reference that provides a global perspective.

Third, it is important to provide a historical record of the state of knowledge on the educational systems, as seen at this particular period of time. The author's note in the chapter on East Germany illustrates the point: "Since this article was first written, Germany has undergone dramatic political changes. The reunification of the two Germanies became a reality in 1990 and the educational system will consequently undergo change, following the example of West Germany. The forty-year endeavors by the German Democratic Republic will be part of history. Time will tell which positive factors in the development of the educational system will prevail and what needs to be discarded. This article, however, will be of interest as a historical discourse. The German Democratic Republic phase cannot be eliminated from history."

This *Handbook* devotes one chapter for each country. The chapters are arranged alphabetically by the names of the countries. As Editor-in-Chief, I must acknowledge that my own experiences in a variety of educational settings in Asia, Africa, Europe, and North America have influenced my approach to the structure, organization, and editing of the book. All credit for individual chapters, however, must go to contributing authors.

At the very outset, when we started the book in 1988, we contacted over 600 distinguished educational leaders and scholars from various parts of the world. Consultations with potential authors resulted in the invitation of 150 authors to prepare articles on their national educational systems, with emphasis on higher education. The principal authors are listed at the beginning of the book. They are established scholars from a variety of backgrounds: presidents of universities, deans of faculties, chairpersons of departments, heads of institutes, professors, director generals of national education, and other academics and educational professionals. A recommended outline for the contributions was sent to each participating author. A limit of 5,000 words was established for each chapter. The editorial process included review of every article for both content and clarity. All articles were prepared exclusively for the book.

Each chapter provides a concise discussion of a given country's educational system, with emphasis on higher education. The book was planned to be descriptive and informative giving an overall view of the topic. Completeness of treatment or details of the minutiae were not designed. This would hardly have been possible given the limitation imposed on the size of the book to make it widely available to the broadest range of institutions and individuals. Going into more details would have defeated the purpose of providing a concise single volume handy reference. Breadth of coverage is intended, rather than depth. However, the bibliography listed under each country will enable the interested reader to pursue the subject in depth. All chapters are written in simple language, in a way that the text is meaningful to the lay person as well.

In general, a chapter is organized into four sections: background, primary and secondary education, higher education, and issues and trends. The section on background is an introduction to the historical perspective of educational development in the country, with focus on higher education. Primary and secondary education section includes information on educational administration, primary education, secondary education, curriculum, examinations, funding, and policies pertaining to teachers. The section on higher education describes institutions, governance, undergraduate study programs, advanced study programs (graduate/-postgraduate study), research, fields of study, admission policies, duration of studies, student facilities, costs, funding, faculty, and other important aspects. Issues and Trends cover contemporary issues facing education in the country and discernible trends.

While most authors have followed the general format we outlined, the chapters differ in emphasis, detail, and degree of sophistication depending on authors' inclinations. This difference is particularly evident in the arrangement of material within sections. For example, in the case of Malaysia, the historical perspective of higher education is treated under the section "higher education" whereas most other chapters include this aspect under the section "background". Similarly, some chapters address the topic of teaching staff under "institutions", whereas the topic is discussed under a separate section, in some of the other chapters.

A major concern of mine was our decision not to include any essays, as an introduction or otherwise, on comparative analysis of educational systems within major geographic regions or among countries. This decision was made, after considerable thought, primarily because we did not want to deviate from the main purpose of providing information and facts, leaving inferences to the reader, although it is well recognized that the possibilities for and the value of such analyses, are great.

An international endeavor of this magnitude cannot be expected to be accomplished without running into unexpected hurdles. Some of these hurdles were so unique, we would like to briefly share our experiences with the readers.

1.   Communication: Our biggest hurdle was communication. Coordinating the contributions of a multitude of authors spread around the globe was a major challenge. Airmail letters took anywhere from three weeks to three months to receive a reply, depending on where the country was located. Telex and facsimile modes helped ease the problem but regular airmail was the backbone of our communication. Editing and rechecking with the contributing authors took many months, at each round. For example, a manuscript mailed from Mongolia took almost three months to reach Houston.

2.   World Political Order: Since the commencement of the project in 1988, many political changes have taken place in several parts of the world; and most often these changes had a direct impact on the progress of the book. For example, the move towards democracy in Eastern Europe (Czechoslovakia, Poland, Romania etc.) and the Soviet Union became an agent of change in the educational structure of these countries. Some changes have already taken place and others are on the way. What final form, education in these countries would take, is yet uncertain. Although the systems are in a state of flux, we could not possibly wait until the changes have been completed.

Authors from some of these countries thought it was best not to include their articles because of the significant changes that were taking place. Others made an effort to revise their texts to recognize the changes. A case in point is the chapter on Czechoslovakia, which was withdrawn by the author. In addition, political unrest in some countries either totally prevented the authors from completing their articles as in the case of Lebanon or the authors did not get the opportunity to review their manuscripts after editorial work, due to disruption of mail service as in the case of Liberia. The extreme cases were the war situation in the Persian Gulf and the reunification of East and West Germanies.

The Gulf crisis affected the articles on both Kuwait and Iraq. Although the first draft of the articles had been completed earlier, we lost contact with both the authors, since the eruption of the crisis and had to forgo consultations with the authors, during the editorial process. Nevertheless, we made a decision to include both the articles. In the case of the Federal Republic of Germany and the German Democratic Republic, the two countries became one and the developments we have seen so far indicate that the system in the former German Democratic Republic is yielding to the West German system. Before the reunification, we already had a chapter written on the German Democratic Republic. In consultation with the author, it was decided to retain the article for its historical value, although, in reality, there is only one Germany now. The article is listed under "East Germany". Even labor disputes (e.g. postal strike in Greece) had a negative effect on the progress of the book.

3.   Manuscripts: For the most part, the authors who were commissioned to contribute to the book were able to complete their manuscripts, revisions, and proofreadings in a timely fashion. However, there were exceptions and in fact we had to make the difficult decision of leaving out some countries for a number of reasons. This situation occurred when a completed manuscript was not received in time or when a manuscript did not meet the standards desired and there was not enough time left to conduct discussions with the authors to rewrite the text. Hence we recognize there is a certain degree of incompleteness in this *Handbook* with regard to coverage of all countries. In addition, we would like to have had greater breadth and depth of coverage of certain sections in some chapters but if we waited to have the broadest possible coverage and the perfect book, it is unlikely that we could have sent the book to production anytime soon. We do count on addressing these aspects in the next edition of the book planned in about 3 years from now. Unlike information in a multivolume education encyclopedia, the size and price of this *Handbook* make it quite practical to issue such revised editions every few years, not only to make the book complete but also to take account of periodic changes in educational systems, as they adjust to social, political, and economic trends over time.

4.   Semantics: Given the cultural diversity of the authors, the problems of semantics, sentence structure, and style of writing were not uncommon, particularly in the case of countries, where English is not the medium of instruction. The problems were compounded as there were many articles that had to be translated from foreign languages (mostly French, German, and Spanish). Although we have attempted to bring all manuscripts in line with the general style of the book without making major changes, some chapters still retain a certain cultural flavor and uniqueness. Also, the articles being signed contributions, we have retained any value judgments the authors may have expressed, particularly under issues and trends. It is useful to note, however, that a good number of the authors have had international contacts (several hold graduate degrees from institutions in the United States and Europe) and their views do portray an international perspective. We have also made a conscious effort to reduce the likelihood of misinterpretation of terms used by individual authors, by changing certain terms to "neutral" words. For example, "graduate" education in the United States is referred to as "postgraduate" education in many parts of the world. So, we deliberately named that section in every chapter as "advanced education" but left the word "graduate" or "postgraduate" in the descriptive part of the section, as used by the author.

The completion of this book brings to a close three years of incessant efforts on the part of a variety of people; most importantly of our contributing authors to whom we owe a deep debt of gratitude for their painstaking work and positive response to our comments at diverse stages of preparation of the manuscripts. If not for the commitment, competence, cooperation, and understanding of our contributors, this work would not have been possible. Bringing the idea of this *Handbook* to fruition has not been a smooth endeavor but it worked, and worked well. We believe that international cooperation in academic pursuits is very much alive and can be nurtured for the benefit of all peoples of the world: this book demonstrates the point.

Houston, Texas   Walter Wickremasinghe
January 1991   Editor-in-Chief

PRINCIPAL CONTRIBUTORS

MANZOORUDDIN AHMED (Pakistan) is Vice-Chancellor of the University of Karachi, Pakistan. Previously he has been Professor of Political Science and Dean of the Faculty of Arts at the University of Karachi. He holds the M.A. degree from Allahabad University, India, and M.A. and Ph.D. degrees from Columbia University, U.S.A. He has published three books including *Contemporary Pakistan: Politics, Economy, Society* (1980), and has written contributions to five other books. He is Editor of *Pakistan Political Science Review* and two other journals. He has been a visiting professor at the University of Alberta, Canada, and Columbia University, U.S.A.

GIASUDDIN AHMED (Bangladesh) is Professor of Education and Director of the Bangladesh Institute of Distance Education. Previously he has served as Dean of the Faculty of Education at the University of Rajshahi and Principal of Teacher Training College, Rajshahi, Bangladesh. He holds the Master of Agriculture degree from Dhaka University, Bangladesh, and M.A. in education from Michigan State University, U.S.A. His publications include many articles on education and several text books.

JORGE ALEGRIA A. (Chile, coauthor) is Director of the Department of Curriculum and Instruction, and Professor in the Faculty of Education, Humanities, and Arts at the University of Conception, Chile. He holds the M.Ed. degree. His background includes several years of teaching experience at primary and secondary schools. His fields of special interest include theory of education, curriculum, and teaching methodology for history and geography.

MANUEL LOUIS ESCAMILLA ALFARO (El Salvador) was Professor of Education at the National University of El Salvador and at several other universities including the University of Havana, and the National Autonomous University of Honduras. He received his M.A. degree from the University of Chile and holds a doctorate from the University of El Salvador. His publications include many papers on educational reforms in El Salvador. He has previously held several higher education positions as Dean of the Faculty of Humanities at the University of El Salvador; President of the National Commission of UNESCO; and a consultant for UNESCO. He is a corresponding member of the Royal Spanish Academy.

SAAD JASIM ALHASHIL (Kuwait) is Associate Professor and Dean of the College of Education at Kuwait University. Previously he has served as Director of the Educational Research Center at the Kuwait Ministry of Education. He holds the B.A. degree from Kuwait University, and M.A. and Ph.D. degrees from Michigan State University, U.S.A. He has written several papers in the areas of teacher education, educational research, and educational leadership. He is a member of the National Board for the Public Educational System and the Advisory Council for the Educational Research Center, Kuwait.

KASHI 'IYADA AL-MA'ADHIDI (Iraq) is Assistant Professor in the Department of History and former Dean of the College of Education at the University of Baghdad, Iraq. He holds the B.A. degree from the University of Baghdad; and M.A. and Ph.D. degrees from the University of Cairo, Egypt. He has authored or coauthored eleven books, including several university text books in history and education. He has also written many articles and research papers published in academic journals or presented at national, regional, and international conferences.

AKIRA ARIMOTO (Japan) is Professor of Sociology and Education in the Research Institute for Higher Education at Hiroshima University, Japan. Previously he has served as Chairman of the Department of Education at Osaka University of Education. He holds the B.A., M.A., and Ph.D. degrees from Hiroshima University. He has authored or coauthored fourteen books including

Education in Japan (1981), and *What is University Education* (1988), and published many articles on topics in sociology of science, academic productivity, and comparative education. He is Chairman of the Editorial Board of the journal *Daigaku Ronshu* (Research in Higher Education).

SOULEYMANE K. BASSABI (Benin) is Rector of the National University of Benin. He holds the Doctor of Medicine degree from the University of Dakar, Senegal; and the Certificate of Specialization from the University of Paris, France. Previously he served as Professor of Ophthalmology at the National University of Benin and Director of the National Medico-Social Institute, Benin. He is a member of numerous professional organizations including French Society of Ophthalmology and Pan African Society of Ophthalmology.

ABDELALI BENTAHILA (Morocco, coauthor) is Professor and former Head of the Department of English at Sidi Mohamed Ben Abdellah University, Morocco. He holds the *licence* degree from Mohamed V. University, Morocco, and M.A. and Ph.D. degrees from the University of Wales, U.K. He has authored the book *Language Attitudes Among Arabic-French Bilinguals in Morocco (1983)* and has written several research papers, articles, and chapters of books on bilingualism, foreign language teaching, interaction of language, and culture. His most recent contribution is a chapter entitled "Aspects of Bilingualism in Morocco" contributed to the *International Handbook on Bilingualism and Bilingual Education* (1988).

FRANCINE BEST (France) is Inspector General at the Ministry of Education and former Director of the National Institute of Pedagogical Research, France. She holds the *license* degree, the Diploma of Advanced Studies, and the Higher Education Teacher's Certificate (*agregation*) in philosophy. She has authored or coauthored eight books including *L'Adolescent dans la vie scolaire* (1976) and *Naissance d'une autre ecole* (1984) as well as numerous articles on education. Her background includes service as Director of two Teacher Training Schools in Normandy. More recently she has served as a consultant to the Council of Europe (on education) and as an expert of the UNESCO Consultative Committee of Education for Peace, Human Rights, and International Understanding.

KEVA MARIE BETHEL (The Bahamas) is Principal of the College of The Bahamas. She holds the B.A. and M.A. degrees from the University of Cambridge, U.K.; and the Ph.D. from the University of Alberta, Canada. Previously she has served as Chairman of the Division of Humanities and Dean of Academic Affairs in the College of The Bahamas. She has presented papers at seminars and conferences sponsored by organizations such as the Organization of American States, the Caribbean Network od Educational Innovation for Development, and the American Vocational Association. She won the 1986 Chamber of Commerce (The Bahamas) Award for Government.

SURENDRA BISSOONDOYAL (Mauritius, coauthor) is Pro-Chancellor and Chairman of University Council of the University of Mauritius. He has previously served as Director of the Mauritius Examinations Syndicate and as Education Officer at the Ministry of Education. He holds the B.Sc. (Honors) degree from the University of London, U.K., and the Diploma in Educational Administration from the University of Leeds, U.K.

PAUL V. BREDESON (United States of America, coauthor) is Associate Professor of Educational Administration at the Pennsylvania State University and Executive Director of the Pennsylvania School Study Council, U.S.A. He holds the B.A. degree from Northern Illinois University, U.S.A, and earned his M.A. and Ph.D. degrees from the University of Wisconsin (Madison) U.S.A. He has authored or coauthored over twenty publications including chapters for books. The books to which he has contributed include *Encyclopedia of School Administration and Supervision* (1988), *An Introduction to Teaching* (1988), and *School Leadership* (1989). His articles focusing on school administration, teacher selection, interpersonal communications, and educational leadership have appeared in journals such as The *Journal of Research and Development in Education*, and the *Educational Administration Quarterly*. He has presented more than forty papers (authored or coauthored) at a variety of state, national, and international professional meetings. He is President of the National Council of Professors of Educational Administration and has served as Chairman of the Faculty Council, College of Education, Pennsylvania State University.

ZIYA BURSALIOGLU (Turkey) is Professor of Educational Administration and Chairman of the Department of Educational Administration and Planning at the University of Ankara, Turkey. His background includes service as Deputy General Director of Manpower Training, Ministry of Education, Turkey. He earned his M.A. and Ph.D. degrees from the University of Illinois (Urbana), U.S.A. He has authored seven books including *New Structures and Behavior in School Administration* (revised edition 1987), and forty articles and papers. He was visiting professor at Saskatchawan University, Canada.

ALICIA S. BUSTOS (Philippines) is President of Baliuag College, Philippines. She has previously served as Dean of the Graduate School of Education and Dean of the College of Education at the University of the East, Philippines. She earned the B.A. and M.A. degrees from the University of the Philippines, and the Ed.D. from Indiana University, U.S.A. She has written five books including *Psychological and Sociological Foundations of Education* (1986) and has authored twenty-two papers and articles on topics in teacher education, higher education innovations, and educational planning. She is Chairman of the Philippine Association of Colleges and Universities - Commission on Accreditation, and President of the Philippine Association for Teacher Education.

MA. DE LOS ANGELES CAVAZOS (Mexico, coordinating author) is Director of the Division of Educational Sciences and Humanities at the University of Monterrey, Mexico. She holds the B.A. and M.A. degrees from the Institute of Technological and Higher Studies, Monterrey, Mexico. She pursued specialized studies in educational investigation at the Ibero-American University, Mexico. Her papers have focussed on educational statistics.

C. E. M. CHIKOMBAH (Zimbabwe) is Senior Lecturer and Dean of the Faculty of Education, University of Zimbabwe, Zimbabwe. He has served as Chairman of the Department of Educational Administration (1982-89). He holds the B.A. from Lincoln University, Pennsylvania, U.S.A.; M.Ed. in Curriculum Studies from Queens University, Kingston, Canada; and M.Ed. and Ph.D. in Educational Administration from University of Alberta, Edmonton, Canada. He has authored two books and several articles on education in Zimbabwe. He was a visiting scholar at the School of Education, Michigan State University, U.S.A. (1985-86); and at the University of Graz, Austria (1990). He is Chairman of the Editorial Board of the Zimbabwe Journal of Educational Research.

LEONG YIN CHING (Malaysia, coauthor) is Associate Professor and Head of the Department of Development Education at the University of Malaya, Malaysia. She holds the B.Ec. and M.Ed. degrees from the University of Malaya and Ph.D. from the University of London (Institute of Education), U.K. She has authored or coauthored over twenty research papers and publications on topics in curriculum reforms, secondary schooling, and school library development. She has served as team leader of Fourth Education Project in Malaysia under the aegis of the World Bank (project which evaluated Miri Teacher Training College, Sarawak, industrial training institutes, primary schools, and education resource centers).

DIEGA ORLANDO CIAN (Italy) is Professor of Education and former Head of the Department of Educational Sciences at the University of Padova, Italy. She is Director of the Center for Child Education and heads the program for the *licence* degree in education. Her fields of interest include child education, didactic methodology, linguistic education, child-adult relationships, teacher training, and history of education. She has published over twenty scientific publications including books and articles on these topics.

URBAN S. DAHLLOF (Sweden) is Professor of Education at Uppsala University, Sweden. He holds the *Fil.kand* (B.A.) and *Fil.Lic.* (M.A.) degrees from Uppsala University and the *Fil.dr.* (Ph.D.) from the University of Stockholm, Sweden. He has authored or coauthored over thirty publications including the book *Reforming Higher Education and External Studies in Sweden and Australia* (1977). His publications have addressed topics in school reform, curriculum and teaching, educational research and development, regional universities, and evaluation in higher education. He has served as President of the Swedish Psychological Association; and Chairman of the Government Committees on School

Research, and Upper Secondary Education. He was a visiting professor at the University of Melbourne, Australia, and the University of British Columbia, Canada. He is a member of the Royal Swedish Academy of Sciences and the Royal Swedish Academy of Letters, History and Antiquities.

EIRLYS E. DAVIES (Morocco, coauthor) is Lecturer in the Department of English at the Sidi Mohamed Ben Abdellah University, Morocco. She holds the Ph.D. degree from the University of Wales, U.K. She has authored the book *The English Imperative* (1986). She has also authored or coauthored over twenty-five articles on topics including stylistics, pragmatics, bilingualism, foreign language teaching, and cross-cultural communication.

LAZARE DIGOMBE (Gabon) is Director of Higher Education and University Affairs at the Ministry of Higher Education and Scientific Research, Gabon. He holds the *licence* degree from the University of Louvain, Belgium; and earned his master's and Diploma of Advanced Studies from the University of Strasbourg, France. He also holds the doctorate in archaeology. Previously he was Dean of the Faculty of Letters and Humanities at the University of Omar Bongo, Gabon.

H. DUGER (Mongolia) is Director of the Scientific Research Institute of Pedagogics, Ulan Bator, Mongolia.

F. JAVIER DUPLA (Venezuela) is Director of the School of Education at the Catholic University of Andres Bello, Venezuela. He holds the *licenciado* degree in philosophy from the Catholic Pontifical University of Ecuador; the *licenciado* in education from the Catholic University of Andres Bello, Venezuela; and a specialist qualification in educational research from the Center for Educational Studies in Mexico. He has authored a number of school text books and several publications that focus on socio-political aspects of education.

M. HELMY EL-MELIGI (Egypt) is Professor of Educational Psychology and Dean Emeritus of the Faculty of Education at the University of Alexandria, Egypt. He received his B.Sc. degree from the University of Alexandria, and his M.A. and Ph.D. from the University of London (Institute of Education), U.K. He has authored three books including *Contemporary Psychology* (7th print 1985) and *Psychology of Creativity* (4th print 1985), and has presented over twenty papers on topics in educational psychology, distance education and socio-psychological issues, and educational policy.

LAUREANO GARCIA ELORRIO (Argentina) is Director of the National Center for Educational Information and Documentation, Argentina.

JOSE FUICA F. (Chile, coauthor) is Adjunct Professor in the Faculty of Education, Humanities, and Arts at the University of Conception, and Rector of the Conception College, Chile. He holds the M.A. degree from Columbia University, U.S.A. He has served as Head of the Department of Psychology, Director of the School of Education, and Dean of the Faculty of Education, Humanities, and Arts at the University of Conception. He has presented papers at several national and international conferences.

CHARLES FARRUGIA (Malta) is Head Professor of the Department of Educational Studies, and Dean of the Faculty of Education at the University of Malta. He holds the M.Ed. degree in education from Concordia University, Canada; and Ph.D. from the University of London (Institute of Education), U.K. His research interests are development of teacher education programs and educational problems of small states. He has published extensively on both subjects and his latest work is a handbook on educational administration and management in small states, commissioned by the Commonwealth Secretariat in London. He has also carried out consulting work for UNESCO.

IRMA ACOSTA DE FORTIN (Honduras) is Rector of the University of Jose C. del Valle, Honduras. She holds the M.S. degree from the Catholic University of America, U.S.A; and earned her civil engineering degree from the National Autonomous University of Honduras. She was the first woman engineer of Honduras. Her background includes service as Director of the University Center for

General Studies, National Autonomous University of Honduras; and Coordinator of International Cooperation for Development at the Ministry of Foreign Affairs, Honduras, in the rank of ambassador.

JORGE TINGA NAMBURETE FRANCISCO (Mozambique, coauthor) is staff member in the Center for African Studies at Eduado Mondlane University, Mozambique. He holds the B.A. degree from Eduardo Mondlane University. Previously he has served as a secondary school teacher and has held several economic staff positions in the government.

ESTHER GARKE (Switzerland) is Staff Officer in the Division of Higher Education at the Federal Office for Education and Science, Switzerland and also serves as Liaison Officer for the UNESCO-Center for Higher Education (CEPES). She studied at the Universities of Basel, (Switzerland) and Aberdeen, (U.K.) and earned her Dr.Phil. degree. The responsibilities of her division include the preparation of the Swiss national policy of higher education, the implementation of the University Promotion Act, and the advancement of international academic cooperation. Her publications have focussed on Swiss higher education and on women in universities.

FODIO GBIKPI-BENISSAN (Togo) is Assistant Professor of Sociology and Educational Science and Director of the National Institute of Educational Sciences at the University of Benin, Togo. He holds the *licence* degree from the University of Lyon, France; and earned his master's degree, diploma in advanced studies, and doctorate from the University of Paris V, France. His current research focuses on French colonial educational policy in Togo.

POL GEORIS (Belgium) is honorary Professor of School Organization at Brussels Free University, Belgium. He holds the *candidate* (B.A.) and *licentiate* (M.A.) degrees from the Brussels Free University, as well as from Liege State University. He earned his doctoral degree from Brussels Free University. Previously he has served as Dean of the Faculty of Psychology and Education at Brussels Free University. He is author or coauthor of eleven books and thirty articles on topics in education, and guidance and counselling. His present research focuses on holistic education and school guidance.

EDRICK H. GIFT (Trinidad & Tobago) is Senior Lecturer and former Dean of the Faculty of Education at the University of the West Indies, St. Augustine, Trinidad and Tobago. He holds the B.A. (Honors) and Diploma in Education from the University of the West Indies, and M.Ed. and Ph.D. from the University of Otawa, Canada. His work has focussed on curriculum theory and teacher education, in which fields he has authored several publications and two monographs.

G. B. GUNAWARDENA (Sri Lanka) is Director of the Research Division, National Institute of Education, Sri Lanka. His background includes service as Director of Teacher Education, National Institute of Education, Sri Lanka; Chief Education Officer, Ministry of Education, Sri Lanka; and Principal of Katukurunda Teacher's College, Sri Lanka. He obtained his B.A., Dip.Ed. (postgraduate), and M.A. in Education from University of Ceylon; and earned the M.Ed. and Ph.D. degrees from Monash University, Australia. He has authored several research reports, papers, and publications on topics in teacher education, curriculum development, and educational administration.

BENICIO VIRGILIO GALDO GUTIERREZ (Peru) is Principal Professor at the National University of San Cristobal de Huamanga, Peru. Previously he has served as Head of the Department of Education and Human Sciences, Dean of the Faculty of Educational Sciences, and Rector of the University of San Cristobal de Huamanga. He holds the B.A. degree in educational sciences from the National University of San Cristobal de Huamanga and the Diploma in Anthropological Studies from the Catholic Pontifical University of Peru. He contributed the chapter "History of Education in Peru" for the book *Historia General del Peru* (5th edition 1984). He has also authored or coauthored thirty-two other publications covering topics in Peruvian education, history, anthropology, and culture.

KACEM BEN HAMZA (Tunisia, coauthor) is Director of the Bourguiba Institute, at the University of Tunis, Tunisia. Previously he has served as Head of the Department of English at the Bourguiba Institute, Associate Professor at the University of Tunis, and Assistant Professor at California State University (Los Angeles), U.S.A. He holds the *licence* degree from the University of Tunis, and M.A.

and Ph.D. degrees from Indiana University (Bloomington), U.S.A. His publications have focussed on various facets of anthropology and language teaching.

ISAHAK HARON (Malaysia, coauthor) is Professor of Education and former Dean of the Faculty of Education at the University of Malaya, Malaysia. He holds the B.A. (Honors) and Dip.Ed. degrees from the University of Malaya; M.Ed. from the University of Sydney, Australia; and Ph.D. from the University of Chicago, U.S.A. He has authored or coauthored over twenty publications and research papers in higher education, educational planning, evaluation of language teaching, and curriculum development. He has served as a member of the Central Curriculum Committee of the Malaysian Ministry of Education, and the Committee to Review the System of Public Examinations in Malaysia.

WILFRIED HARTMANN (Federal Republic of Germany) is Professor of Education and former Dean of the Faculty of Education at the University of Hamburg, Federal Republic of Germany. He pursued higher studies at the Universities of Hamburg and Tubingen and obtained the Dr.Phil. degree in general linguistics. His publications include books and articles on the role of linguistics with emphasis on semantics, general didactic, and comparative education. He was a member of the international study committee of the International Association for the Evaluation of Educational Achievement (IEA) for a fourteen country study on written composition and is chairing the German National Study Committee for the IEA study on reading literacy.

BRIAN V. HILL (Australia) is Foundation Professor of Education and former Dean of the School of Education at Murdoch University, Australia. He earned his B.A., and B.Ed. (Honors), degrees from the University of Western Australia; M.A. (Honors) from the University of Sydney; and Ph.D. from the University of Illinois, U.S.A. He is also a fellow of the Australian College of Education. He has authored over 100 articles and seven books including *Education and the Endangered Individual* (1973), *Choosing the Right School* (1987), and *Values Education in Australian Schools* (1988). He is a past editor of the *Journal of Christian Education.* He has been a visiting scholar in England, U.S.A., India, and Singapore.

SUNG-YUN HONG (South Korea, coauthor) is Professor and Dean of the Graduate School of Education at Chung-Ang University, South Korea. Previously he has served as Dean of the College of Education at Chung-Ang University. He earned his M.A. degree from Chung-Ang University; M.Ed. from Loyala University, U.S.A.; and Ed.D. from Chung-Ang University. He is President of the Korean Teacher Education Council. He has authored six books including *Process of Learning and Instruction* (7th print 1986) and *Behavior Modification for Primary School Teachers* (1987), and presented over fifty papers on topics in curriculum and instruction.

ZHONGWEN HUANG (China, coauthor) was Professor, Chairman of the Department of Foreign Languages and Literature, and Director of Research Institute of Foreign Literature at Nanjing University, People's Republic of China. He is presently in Canada conducting research on Caribbean anthology. He had his education at the South-China Institute of Literature and Art, Harbin Institute of Foreign Languages, and Nanjing University in China. He has been a visiting scholar at the University of Toronto, Canada. His publications include two books on Canadian literature. He was a member of the National Committee for Compiling and Editing Foreign Languages Text Books.

ENRIQUE E. BATISTA JIMENEZ (Colombia) is Professor and Dean of the Faculty of Education at the University of Antioquia, Colombia. He obtained his B.S. and M.S. degrees from the University of Oregon, U.S.A.; and Ph.D. from the University of Illinois, U.S.A. He has published numerous articles on topics in educational psychology, evaluation of college teaching, and distance education, and has authored or coauthored five books including *School and School Promotion* (1989). He also served as Head of the Center for Research, in the Faculty of Education, University of Antioquia, and now functions as Head of Admissions and Registration at the University of Antioquia.

GARETH ELWYN JONES (United Kingdom, coauthor) is Professor of Educational Research at the University College of Wales, Aberystwyth, U.K. Previously he has served as Reader at the University College of Swansea, U.K. He is author of six books and editor of eight books. He has also written over thirty other publications including articles in major academic journals and chapters of books. Among his more significant books are *Modern Wales* (1984), *Controls and Conflicts in Welsh Secondary Education* 1889-1944 (1982), *Which Nation's Schools: Direction and Devolution in Welsh Education in the Twentieth Century* (forthcoming 1990).

KARL OYVIND JORDELL (Norway) is Research Coordinator in the Institute for Studies in Research and Higher Education at the Norwegian Research Council for Science and the Humanities, Norway. Previously he has served as Advisor to the President of the University of Oslo and Associate Professor of Education at the University of Tromso, Norway. He holds the *cand.paed.* (master's) and the *dr.philos.* (Ph.D.) degrees in education.

BRAGI JOSEPSSON (Iceland) is Associate Professor of Comparative Education at the Icelandic College of Education, Iceland. He earned his B.A., M.A., and Ed.D. degrees from Peabody College of Vanderbilt University, U.S.A. His papers and publications have focussed on topics in educational system in Iceland, comparative education, school administration, and social systems. Previously he has served as Associate Professor, Western Kentucky University, U.S.A; Head of the Department of Instruction, Ministry of Education, Iceland; representative of Iceland to the General Assembly of the United Nations; and first alternate member of parliament in the District of Reykjavik, Iceland.

RIGOBERTO JUAREZ-PAZ (Guatemala) is Dean of the School of Humanities at the University of Francisco Marroquin. He is also founding Vice-President of the university.

JOUKO KARI (Finland) is Professor and Director of the Institute for Educational Research at the University of Jyvaskyla, Finland. He holds the *Paed.Cand.* (master's), *Paed.Lic.* and Ph.D. degrees from the Jyvaskyla University. He has authored or coauthored more than 100 publications (books, research reports, and articles). His publications have addressed topics in school reform, learning materials, teacher training, and educational research and development. He is a member (national editor) of the Editorial Board of the *Scandanavian Journal of Educational Research.* Previously he has served as Associate Professor of Education and Director of the Department of Teacher Training at the University of Jyvaskyla.

MICHAEL KASSOTAKIS (Greece) is Professor of Education at the University of Athens, Greece and Vice-President of the Greek National Institute for Education. Previously he was Professor of Education and Dean of the Faculty of Letters at the University of Crete and Director of the School for the in-service training of secondary school teachers in Heraclion (Crete). He earned his B.A. from the university of Athens, and Ph.D. from the University of Sorbonne (Paris V). His publications include books and articles on topics in school evaluation, vocational guidance, and training of teachers.

ADOUM KHAMIS (Chad) is Assistant Professor of African Linguistics and Phonetics and former Dean of the Faculty of Letters and Humanities at the University of Chad. He holds the *licence* as well as master's and doctoral degrees.

EPHRAIM D. KADZOMBE (Malawi) is Associate Professor in Curriculum and Teaching Studies and Principal of the Malawi Institute of Education, Malawi. Previously he has been Dean of the Faculty of Education at the University of Malawi and Dean of the School of Education at Chancellor College. He earned his B.Sc. degree from the University of Nigeria and M.Sc. from the University of London, U.K. His publications include books and articles on topics in geography curriculum, and the teaching of geography. He is a member of the Malawi Government Examination Council and has served as a member of the National Advisory Council on Education.

JURGEN KNOOP (East Germany, coauthor) is Professor at Humboldt University of Berlin, East Germany.

JAN K. KOPPEN (The Netherlands) is Director of the Higher Education Research Program in the Center for Educational Research (SCO) at the University of Amsterdam, The Netherlands. He earned his doctoral degree from the State University of Utrecht, The Netherlands. He has served in a number of research posts in both secondary and tertiary educational research at the Research Institute for Applied Psychology and the Center for Educational Research. His recent publications include an evaluation study of the newly introduced two-tier structure in higher education.

LYA KREMER-HAYON (Israel) is Head of the Center for Educational Administration and Evaluation at the University of Haifa, Israel. She obtained her B.S. degree from the University of Minnesota, U.S.A.; M.A. from the University of Tel Aviv, Israel; and Ph.D. from the Hebrew University, Israel. She has authored or coauthored sixty-seven articles on various facets of teacher education, curriculum planning, and professional development. Books and booklets written by her include *Educational Deliberations in the Process of Teaching* (1985). She has been a visiting professor at the John Hopkins University, U.S.A.; and the University of Utrecht, The Netherlands. She has previously served as Head of the Department of Education at the University of Haifa.

RYSZARD KUCHA (Poland, coauthor) is Professor, Head of the Institute of History of Education and Vice-Dean of the Department of Pedagogy and Psychology at Maria Curie-Sklodowska University, Poland. He completed his pedagogical studies at Maria Curie-Sklodowska University, and earned the Ph.D. and the *docent* degrees. He is author of the book *Elementary Education in the Kingdom of Poland in the Years 1864-1914*. He has also edited several books including *Polonia Education: Selected Problems*, and has authored a number of publications on topics in the history of education. He spent an academic year in U.S.A under a fellowship from the Kosciuszko Foundation (U.S.A.).

GI-WOO LEE (Korea, coauthor) is Research Director of the Child Research Division of the Korean Institute for Research in the Behavioral Sciences. He holds the B.A. and M.A. degrees from Chung-Ang University, Korea. He is also a doctoral assistant in the Graduate School at Chung-Ang University. He has served as secretary of the Division of Educational Psychology of the Korean Society for the Study of Education.

ERICH LEITNER (Austria) is Professor at the University of Educational Studies in Klagenfurt, Austria, and Chairman of the Department of Higher Education. He holds the *Mag.Phil.* (M.A.) and *Dr.Phil.* (Ph.D.) degrees. He has published extensively on topics in history of higher education, higher university pedagogics, and comparative higher education. His publications include *Politics and Higher Education* (1978), *Basics of Higher Education* (1984), *Higher Education* (1984), *The Pedagogical Challenge of the University* (1980), and *Research and Teaching at Universities* (1990).

HSIN-HAN LIU (Taiwan) is Dean of the Graduate School of Education at the National Chengchi University. He holds the Ed.D. degree.

MOHAMED MAAMOURI (Tunisia, coauthor) is Professor in the Faculty of Letters of Manouba, University of Tunis, Tunisia. He earned his *licence* degree from the University of Tunis, and M.A., and Ph.D. degrees from Cornell University, U.S.A. He has authored or coauthored several books including *The Influence of the Teaching of Foreign Languages on the Arabic Language* (1983). He was a visiting lecturer at Hosei University, Japan, and University of Venice, Italy. He has received many awards and honors including the titles of Commander of the Order of the British Empire (U.K.), Officier de L'Ordre du Merite National (France), and Pushkin Gold Medal (U.S.S.R.).

EBERHARD MANNSCHATZ (East Germany, coauthor) is Professor and Director of the Pedagogical Section at Humboldt University of Berlin, East Germany. He holds the *Dr.habil* degree.

YONG MAO (China, coauthor) was Deputy Director, Office of the President of Ninjing University, Vice-Director of the Research Institute of Higher Education, Nanjing University, and Editor of the quarterly *Research on Higher Education*. He graduated from Ninjing University, China. He has written many articles on education and administration of universities.

MELVIN J. MASON (Liberia) is President of Cuttington University College, Liberia. Previously he has served as Dean of Instruction at Cuttington University College and as a general educator at UNESCO (Paris). He earned his B.A. degree from Cuttington University College; M.A. from Yale

University, U.S.A.; and Ed.D. from Michigan State University, U.S.A. His publications have focussed on post-primary education and teacher training.

ZUSI A. MATSELA (Lesotho) is Associate Professor of Education and Dean of the Faculty of Education at the National University of Lesotho. His background includes service as a primary school teacher, education officer, the first Director of the National Teacher Training College, and the Principal Secretary for Education. He holds the B.A. degree from the University of South Africa and Ed.D. degree from the University of Massachusetts, U.S.A. He has written four books for primary schools (science and language) and three books of Sesotho poetry; and five books in the areas of secondary and tertiary level Sesotho language usage, methods of teaching Sesotho, and Sesotho culture.

GAONTATLHE MAUTLE (Botswana, coauthor) is Lecturer in Education at the University of Botswana. He holds the B.Ed. degree from the University of Botswana and Swaziland and earned his M.Ed. and Ph.D. degrees from Ohio University, U.S.A. He has intermittently served as acting Head of the Department of Education at the University of Botswana. He is Chairman of the Botswana Foundation for Education and Vice-Chairman of the Botswana Educational Research Association. He is also Chairman of the Departmental Instructional Affairs Committee. He has published technical articles covering topics on school curriculum, social studies, and research development.

MOHAMED MILIANI (Algeria) is Professor in the Institute for Foreign Languages and Vice-Rector for Pedagogy at Es-Senia University, Oran, Algeria. He received his first degree from the University of Oran, Algeria, and completed his M.Ed. and Ph.D. degrees at the University of Wales, U.K. He is also Director of Postgraduate Studies in Linguistics and Teaching of English as a Foreign Language. He was previously Head of the English department. Articles authored by him have appeared in several academic journals.

MOHAMED MONIR MORSI (Qatar) is Professor of Education and Director of the Educational Research Center at the University of Qatar. Previously he has served as Associate Professor in the Faculty of Education at Ain Shams University, Egypt. He earned his M.A. degree from Ain Shams University, and his Ph.D. from the University of London (Institute of Education), U.K. He is author of over thirty books and many papers on Arab education and culture.

HERME JOSEPH MOSHA (Tanzania) is Professor and Dean of the Faculty of Education at the University of Dar Es Salaam, Tanzania. He obtained his B.A., and M.A. degrees from the University of Dar Es Salaam, and Ph.D. from the University of Alberta, Canada. His publications include the book *The Quality of Primary Education in Tanzania* (1987), several articles, papers, and research reports on educational policy planning and administration, curriculum design, and program evaluation.

NYANGO MPEYE (Zaire) is Professor at the University of Kinshasa, Zaire, and acting Inspector General of Higher Education and Scientific Research, Zaire. He studied at the Lovanium University, Zaire, and at the State University at Leige, Belgium. He holds the Doctor of Applied Science degree. He has served as Rector of the University of Lubumbashi; Rector of the University of Kinshasa; and Administrator of the University Foundation of Zaire. He is also the President of the Council of Administration of the Higher Technical Institute of Zaire and a member of the Royal Overseas Academy of Belgium-science section.

MAFORI CHARLES JULIUS MPHAHLELE (South Africa) is Professor and Dean of the Faculty of Education at the University of the North, South Africa. At the time he was elected Dean (1984) he was the first black faculty member to occupy a deanship in any South African university. He holds the B.A., B.Ed., M.Ed., and Ed.D. degrees. He is author or coauthor of several books in Northern Sotho (language); a series of history textbooks for standards 5-7; and the book *Reform or Revolution*.

DANIEL G. MULCAHY (Ireland) is Professor of Education at Eastern Illinois University, U.S.A. Formerly, he was Professor of Education and Head of the Department of Education at the University College, Cork, U.K. He earned his B.A. (Honors) degree at the University College, Cork; M.A. (Honors) at the University College, Dublin; and M.Ed. and Ph.D. at the University of Illinois, U.S.A.

He has authored three books including *Curriculum and Policy in Irish Post-Primary Education* (1981) and, as coeditor, *Irish Educational Policy* (1989) and has written forty-eight articles and research papers in the areas of curriculum reform, staff development, and teacher education. He is a member of the editorial board of *Irish Educational Studies, Educational Theory, Aspects of Education, and The European Journal of Teacher Education.* He is a past President of the Educational Studies Association of Ireland.

IBRAHIM A. O. NASSER (Jordan, coauthor) is Assistant Dean of the Faculty of Education at the University of Jordan. He earned his B.A. at Alexandria University, Egypt; M.A. at the University of Jordan; and Ph.D. at Georgia State University, U.S.A. He has written several books, research papers, and articles on topics in educational sociology. He has also developed cultural and educational programs for Jordan Broadcasting Service. He is President of the Jordan Society for Educational Studies.

HOANG DUC NHUAN (Vietnam) is Professor of Biology and acting Director General of the National Institute for Educational Science of Vietnam. His background includes service as a teacher at teacher training colleges and Head of the Contents and Teaching Methodology Department of the National Institute for Educational Science. He holds the Doctor of Biology and Ph.D. degrees from the U.S.S.R. Academy of Science.

JORGEN L. NIELSEN (Denmark, coauthor) is Associate Professor of Social Sciences (sociology of education) and Chairperson of the Institute of Communication Research, Educational Research, and Theory of Science at the Roskilde University Center, Denmark. He is also Associate Dean for the Humanities. He earned his Ph.D. degree at the University of Copenhagen, Denmark. He has authored or coauthored seven books including *School in Society* (1979), and *Education in a Time of Crisis* (1984), as well as thirteen articles on topics in sociological aspects of education, distance education, and the use of information technology in education. He has been a visiting Fulbright scholar at the University of Oregon, U.S.A.

NORBERT NIKIEMA (Burkina Faso) is Associate Professor and past Dean of the School of Liberal Arts at the University of Ouagadougou, Burkina Faso. He holds the *licence* degree from the University of Ouagadougou; M.A. from Ohio University, U.S.A.; and Ph.D. from Indiana University, U.S.A. He has been a visiting scholar at the Universities of Iowa and California, U.S.A. He has authored or coauthored twenty-four articles with emphasis on linguistics. He is a member of the National Commission of Burkina Languages.

DOMITIEN NIZIGIYIMANA (Burundi) is Director General of the Ministry of Higher Education and Scientific Research, and former Dean of the Institute of Pedagogics at the University of Burundi. He earned his *licence* degree from the University of Burundi and doctorate from the University of Paris III, France. He has served as lecturer and researcher in the Faculty of Letters and Humanities at the University of Burundi. He is author of many articles on African oral literature and linguistic phenomena in Africa.

ILSA ESTHER PINO DE OCHOA (Panama) is Professor and Head of the Department of Educational Administration in the Central American Institute of Educational Administration and Supervision at the University of Panama. She obtinaed her first degree from the University of Panama and master's degree from the University of Santa Maria La Antigua, Panama. Her studies and writings have focused on the evaluation of structure and functioning of regional university centers and educational administration. She also serves as acoordinator of ICASE-UNESCO adult education programs in Panama.

JAKAYO PETER OCITTI (Uganda) is Professor and Dean of Education at Makerere University, Uganda. He earned his B.Ed. from the Universty of East Africa; M.A. from Makerere University; Ph.D. from the University of Dar Es Salaam, Tanzania; and Certificate in Higher Education Management from the University of Manchester, U.K. He has published two books and over twenty articles on various topics in education and geography; and two novels in the Luo language. His research interest include geography education, teacher training, and non-formal indigenous education. Previously (1987-90) he has served as a member of the Uganda Education Policy Review Commission.

FRANK D. OLIVA (Canada) is Dean of the Faculty of Education and Professor in the Department of Educational Policy and Administrative Studies at the University of Calgary, Canada. He obtained his B.Ed. and M.Ed. degrees from the University of Alberta, and Ed.D. degree from the University of Oregon, U.S.A. He has authored or edited several books, and published over twenty articles on topics in educational administration, adult literacy, teacher education, and organizational communication. He has been a member of numerous boards and committees including the Board of Teacher Education and Certification of Alberta, and Research and Development Review Board of the Alberta Human Resources Research Council. He has also served as President of the Alberta Council on School Administration.

NATHANIEL KOFI PECKU (Ghana) was Dean of the Faculty of Education (1985-87) and Dean of Student Affairs (1984-85) at the University of Cape Coast. He obtained his B.A. from the University of London, U.K.; M.Ed. from the University of New Hampshire, U.S.A.; and Ed.D. from Indiana University (Bloomington) U.S.A. His publications include the book *Introduction to Guidance for Training Colleges* (1980) and a number of articles on educational planning, school curriculum, and counselling. He recently served as Consultant in Counselling to Ghana's Ministry of Mobilization and Social Welfare.

ALAN W. PERSICO (Guyana) is Dean of the Faculty of Education at the University of Guyana and Head of the Department of Languages and Social Studies Education. He holds the B.A. degree from the University of the West Indies; M.A. degree from the University of Texas at El Paso, U.S.A.; and Ph.D. from the University of Illinois at Urbana, U.S.A. He has published articles in scholarly journals and has presented papers at conferences, on topics relating to, educational administration, foreign language learning, guidance, and distance education. He is a member of the Caribbean Examination Council National Committee and has served on various committees in the Ministry of Education, Guyana.

ARPAD PETRIKAS (Hungary) is University Professor and Head of the Department of Pedagogy at Kossuth University, Hungary. He obtained his diploma as a teacher of Russian from Lajos Kossuth University; and *candidate* degree (Ph.D.) in education from Zdanov University, U.S.S.R. He has authored or coauthored 140 publications. His research areas include problems of community education, personality formation of high school and primary school children, and comparative pedagogy. He has been a member of the pedagogical committee of the Hungarian Academy of Sciences and serves as Head of the Educational Team of the Debrecen Section of the Academy.

JOSE ANTONIO REBUCHO ESPERANCA PINA (Portugal) is Professor in the Faculty of Medical Sciences and Rector of the New University of Lisbon, Portugal. He completed his degree in medicine at the University of Lisbon, and also received the *agregation* from the same faculty. He has published seventy scientific papers and given over 200 lectures at various conferences and institutions. He has served as president of numerous academic bodies including National Council of Teaching and Medical Education of the Order of Doctors (Portugal). He is a member of the National Council for Higher Education. He has received many awards and honors including the French Order of the Honor Legion (awarded by the President of France), and Great Officer of the Public Instruction Order (awarded by the President of Portugal).

KAROL POZNANSKI (Poland, coauthor) is Professor in the Institute of Pedagogy at Maria Curie-Sklodowska University, Poland, and Rector of the Higher School of Special Education in Warsaw, Poland. He completed his pedagogical studies at the Catholic University of Lublin, Poland, and earned his Ph.D. and *docent* degrees. Previously he has served in the History of Education Institute of the Polish Academy of Science in Warsaw. He is coauthor of the text book *History of Education* and author of the book *Educational Reforms in the Kingdom of Poland in 1862*. He has written many articles and papers covering topics in the history of education.

WALI MOHAMMED RAHIMI (Afghanistan) is Professor and Chairman of the Department of Ethnography at Kabul University, Afghanistan. He earned his M.A. degree from Teacher's College at Columbia University, U.S.A. Currently he teaches social science courses. He is a member of the faculty academic council, university academic council and the university research council. He also serves on the university curriculum and program committee. Previously he has served as Director of the Kabul University Research Center. Professor Rahimi has authored and translated a number of publications including three text books and several articles.

JOSE A. ACOSTA RAMOS (Puerto Rico) is Associate Professor in the Faculty of Education at the University of Puerto Rico. previously he has served as Associate Dean of Academic Affairs at the Utuado Regional College of the University of Puerto Rico. He holds the B.A. degree from the Inter American University, Puerto Rico; M.A. from the University of Puerto Rico; and Ed.D. from Lehigh University, U.S.A. He has authored several publications on topics in curriculum development, educational supervision, and teacher development. He has served as President of the Association of Supervision and Curriculum Development, Puerto Rico Chapter.

T. S. RAO (India) is Professor of Education and Dean of the Faculty of Education at Banaras Hindu University, India. He holds the M.A., M.Ed., and Ph.D. degrees. His publications include *The Bilingual Child* and articles in education and psychology journals.

ROY RATHAN (Grenada) is Chief Education Officer at the Ministry of Education, Culture, and Fisheries, Grenada.

CHRIS J. RENNER (Sierra Leone) is Planning Officer of the University of Sierra Leone and Lecturer in the Postgraduate School of Education, Fourah Bay College (one of the three constituent colleges of the university). He holds the B.A. (Honors) and M.Ed. degrees from the University of Sierra Leone, and Ph.D. from the University of Sussex, U.K. His publications include many articles and research papers on education presented at national, regional, and international conferences.

WILLIAM L. RENWICK (New Zealand) is Senior Research Fellow in the Stout Research Center for the Study of New Zealand Society, History, and Culture, Victoria University of Wellington, New Zealand. He holds the M.A. degree of the University of New Zealand, and the Honorary D.Litt. of Deakin University, Australia. He was Director General of Education for New Zealand, 1975-88. His various publications on New Zealand education include *Moving Targets: Six Essays on Educational Policy* (1986). He was Chairman of the New Zealand National Commission for UNESCO, 1983-90, and is a member of the Governing Board of the Commonwealth of Learning. He was a Fulbright Senior Research Scholar at Teachers College, Columbia University, U.S.A. in 1986. In 1988 he was awarded the ANZAAS Mackie Medal for distinguished work in education in Australia.

JEANINE RAMBELOSON-RAPIERA (Madagascar) is President of the EESR (Faculty) of Arts and Humanities at the University of Antananarivo, Madagascar. She obtained her *licence* degree from the University of Paris (Sorbonne), and master's degree from the University of Bordeaux III, France. She also holds the *agregation* in modern languages. Her writings include contributions to secondary school text books and malagasy literature in French language, as well as papers on literature studies.

CHARLES-POISSET ROMAIN (Haiti) is Dean of the Haiti Institute of African Study and Research. He holds the *licence* degree from the State University of Haiti and the doctorate from the University of Paris III (Sorbonne), France. He has authored and coauthored several books. His articles have been published in a number of Haitian and foreign journals. He has served as a consultant to the Haiti Ministry of Education and as President of the Committee of Administration of the Baptist Theological Seminary in Haiti. His research interests are sociology of development, sociology of religion, and sociology of education.

GERALD ST. C. ROSE (Barbados, coauthor) is Lecturer in the Faculty of Education at the University of the West Indies (Cave Hill Campus), Barbados. He earned his B.Sc. and Dip.Ed. degrees from the University of the West Indies and M.Sc. from the University of Keele, U.K. He has authored or coauthored a number of papers and articles primarily on topics in mathematics education and educational evaluation.

ELVIRA MARTIN SABINA (Cuba) is Director of the Center for the Study of Higher Education, University of Havana, Cuba. She obtained her doctorate from the University of Havana. She has published over twenty articles and presented many papers on topics in higher educational development. She is a member of the consultative committee of CRESALC-UNESCO and was the Cuban delegate for the 39th (1984) and 41st (1989) international educational conferences of UNESCO.

HANI ABDUL RAHMAN SALEH (Jordan, coauthor), is Professor of Educational Administration and Dean of Students at the University of Jordan. He holds the B.A. degree from Cairo University, Egypt; M.A. from the University of Chattanooga, U.S.A.; and Ph.D. from Tennessee University, U.S.A. He has published five books including *Educational Administration and Organizational Behavior: Individual and Group Behavior Within Systems* (1986). He has also written several articles and research papers on topics in educational administration, teacher training, and higher educational issues.

ROBERT ARTHUR SARGENT (Swaziland) is Senior Lecturer and Dean of the Faculty of Education at the University of Swaziland. He holds the B.A., B.Ed., M.A., and Ph.D. degrees from Dalhousie University, Canada. He also holds the M.Ed. degree from Saint Mary's University, Canada. He has presented papers at many international conferences and seminars on topics in student profiling and assessment, historical research, and education in Africa; and has published several articles on the same topics.

ALEXANDER YAKOVLEVICH SAVELYEV (Union of Soviet Socialist Republics) is Director of the Moscow State Research Institute for Higher Education, U.S.S.R. He graduated from N. Bauman's Moscow Higher Technical School. He holds the degrees of Doctor of Engineering and *Candidate*. His research interests have focussed on the development of higher and secondary specialized education with emphasis on computerization of education and learning systems. He won the 1984 U.S.S.R. Council of Ministers Prize for his work in these fields. He is author of 149 scientific publications including eight monographs and five books.

LEONARD L. SHOREY (Barbados, coauthor) is former Senior Lecturer in the Faculty of Education at the University of the West Indies (Cave Hill Campus), Barbados. Currently he is an education consultant. He earned his B.A. and Dip.Ed. degrees from the University of the West Indies and Ph.D. from the University of Toronto, Canada. Previously he has served as coordinator of a joint University of the West Indies-USAID primary education project in Barbados, and Deputy Director of the Department of Educational Affairs of the organization of American States. He has written widely on various aspects of education, particularly in relation to the Caribbean. In 1986, he was appointed to the Barbados Senate.

KEDAR NATH SHRESTHA (Nepal) is Member Secretary of the Council for Higher Education, Nepal. Previously he has served as Chief of the Curriculum, Textbook, and Supervision Development Center of the Ministry of Education and Culture, and as Dean of the Institute of Education at Tribhuvan University, Nepal. He obtained his M.A. degree from California State University, U.S.A. and Ph.D. from Southern Illinois University, U.S.A. He has authored a number of books, booklets, and articles covering topics in educational administration and teacher education. He is a member of the National Education Committee.

ALIRIO F. BARBOSA DE SOUZA (Brazil) is Associate Professor in Education at the Federal University of Bahia, Brazil. He earned his B.A. and M.A. degrees from the Federal University of Bahia, and Ed.D. degree from Pennsylvania State University, U.S.A. His publications have focussed on educational development in Brazil.

ROBERT A. STEWART (Fiji & the Islands of British Oceania - coordinating author) is former Head of the School of Humanities and Professor of Human Development at the University of the South Pacific (USP). He has also served a two-year term as pro Vice-Chancellor for Academic Affairs at the

USP. Presently he is Executive President of Scientific Journal Publishers, Society for Personality Research, Inc. He obtained his B.A. degree from the University of New Zealand; M.Ed. from Harvard University, U.S.A.; and Ph.D. from Massey University, New Zealand. He is coeditor of the book, *Toward a World of Peace: People Create Alternatives.* He has written or edited five books, fifty-six chapters of books and journal articles, and has presented twenty-three papers to conferences. He also edits the international journals *Social Behavior and Personality,* and *Psychology and Human Development.*

ABDOU SYLLA (Senegal) is Assistant Professor in the Fundamental Institute of Black Africa at the University of Cheikh Anta Diop of Dakar, Senegal. He earned his *licence* degree from the University of Dakar, Senegal; and master's and doctorate degrees in philosophy from the University of Paris (Sorbonne), France. He has authored three books including *L'Ecole future, pour qui?* (1987) and *L'Ecole Senegalaise en gestation: De la crise a la reforme* (1991) and has written a number of papers, articles, and contributions to books (chapters) in the areas of school reforms, youth issues, religious education, and higher education.

LANCINE SYLLA (Ivory Coast) is Professor in the Department of Sociology at the National University of Ivory Coast. He has previously served as Director of the Department of Sociology and Dean of the Faculty of Letters and Humanities at the National University of Ivory Coast. He holds the Doctor of Letters degree from the University of Paris, France. He has authored many publications on topics in sociology. He is the founding President of the Ivory Coast Association of Sociologists, and Mayor of the commune of Tieme, Ivory Coast.

GULAMO AMADE TAJU (Mozambique, coauthor) is Research Officer in the Center for African Studies at Eduardo Mondlane University, Mozambique. Previously he has served as a teacher and director of secondary schools. He holds the B.A. degree from Eduardo Mondlane University.

JOSIAH S. TLOU (Botswana, coauthor) is Associate Professor of Education at Virginia Polytechnic Institute and State University, U.S.A. He holds the B.A. degree from Luther College, U.S.A.; M.A. degree from Illinois State University, U.S.A.; and Ed.D. from the University of Illinois (Urbana), U.S.A. Previously he has served as Senior Lecturer, University of Botswana and as social studies specialist for the Botswana Primary Education Improvement Project of the University of Botswana. His publications include several articles and book chapters on African education, teacher education, and international educational issues.

CHO-YEE TO (Hong Kong) is Professor and Director of the School of Education at the Chinese University of Hong Kong. He obtained his M.A. degree from Washington University, U.S.A., and Ph.D. from the Southern Illinois University, Carbondale, U.S.A. He has authored or coauthored over eighty research reports, books, articles, and reviews on philosophy of education, educational and social research, and cross-cultural studies. His papers have appeared in many academic journals such as *Comparative Education Review, and The Journal of Asian and African Studies.* His books include *Philosophy, Culture, and Education* (1988) in Chinese, and *Religion and Education* (1991). Previously he served as Professor of Education and Chairman of the Department of Social Foundations of Education at the University of Michigan, U.S.A. He serves in the board of directors of the Higher Education Association of China.

NOPADOL TONGSOPIT (Thailand) is President of Khon Kaen University, Thailand, and Associate Professor of Cardiothoracic Surgery. He holds the Doctor of Medicine degree from Mahidol University, Thailand, and had graduate residency training in surgery at New York University, U.S.A. He has served as Head of the Department of Surgery at Khon Kaen Hospital, Director of Khon Kaen University Hospital, and Vice-President for Student Affairs, Khon Kaen University. He has held membership of numerous bodies including American College of Surgeons, International College of Surgeons, and National Research Council of Thailand. His publications include several books on surgery and higher education administration, and articles on topics in medicine, educational administration, and human resource development.

THEOPHILE TOUBA (Central African Republic) is Dean of the Faculty of Letters and Humanities at the University of Bangui, Central African Republic. He earned his *licence* and master's degrees from Paul Valery University, France, and doctorate from the University of Aix-en-Provence, France. Previously he has served as Director of *Ecole Normal Superieure de Bangui*, and Professor of Linguistics in the Faculty of Letters and Humanities.

MUHYIEEDDEEN SH. TOUQ (United Arab Republic) is Dean of the College of Education at the United Arab Emirates University. Previously he has served as Professor and Chairman of the Department of Psychology of the University of Jordan, and Assistant Professor at the University of Wisconsin, U.S.A. He obtained his B.A. degree from the University of Jordan; M.A. from Ball State University, U.S.A.; and Ph.D. from Purdue University, U.S.A. He has authored several books including *Educational Psychology* and over twenty-five articles and papers on topics in teacher effectiveness, juvenile delinquency, socio-economic influences on education, and continuing education.

MAMADOU TRAORE (Mali) is Professor at the Higher Institute of Applied Research and Training (ISFRA), Mali. Previously he has served as Professor and Director General of the Teacher Training School, Mali. He obtained his Diploma of Advanced Studies (D.E.S.) and doctorate from the University of Dakar, Senegal. He directed the preparation of an atlas of Mali (1981).

TZEKO I. TZEKOV (Bulgaria) is Professor in the Faculty of Law and Chairman of the Department of Criminal Law at Sofia University, Bulgaria. He holds degrees from Sofia University and the European University Center in Nancy. He has served as Director at the Council of Higher Education in the Ministry of Public Education, Bulgaria, and Vice-Rector of the Sofia University. He has been the Bulgarian representative at CEPES and is a member of the Consultative Council of CEPES-UNESCO in Bucharest. He is author of many books on law and has written a number of papers and articles on higher education.

JAIME ORTIZ VEGA (Puerto Rico, coauthor) is Dean of the Catholic University of Puerto Rico at Mayaguez. Previously he has served as Associate Professor and Director of the Department of Education at the Inter American University, Puerto Rico. He holds the B.A. degree from the University of Puerto Rico; M.A. from Inter American University of Puerto Rico; and Ed.D. from New York University, U.S.A. He has authored or coauthored a number of publications on topics in curriculum development and educational administration and has served as President of the Association of Supervision and Curriculum Development, Puerto Rico chapter.

DEVI VENKATASAMY (Mauritius, coauthor) is Deputy Director of the Mauritius Institute of Education. She was formerly the Head of the Department of Humanities and Social Studies at the Mauritius Institute of Education. She holds the B.A. (Honors) degree from the University of Leeds, U.K.; and Ph.D. from the University of Liverpool, U.K.

COLOMER VIADEL VICENTE (Spain) is Rector of the University of Cordoba, Spain. Previously he was Professor and Chairman of the Department of Physics at the University of Cordoba. He earned his first degree as well as his doctorate at the University of Complutense, Spain. He has written six books and authored or coauthored several scholarly publications. He has published over sixty scientific papers in plasma physics and electromagnetics. He was a visiting scientist at the Massachusetts Institute of Technology, U.S.A., and a visiting professor at the University of Paris-Sud, France. He is a member of the Royal Society of Physics-Special Committee on Electromagnetism.

SERGIO VIEIRA (Mozambique, coauthor) is Director of the Center for African Studies at Eduardo Mondlane University, Mozambique. He attended the Faculty of Law in Lisbon, Portugal, and the Institute of Political Studies in Paris, France. He has been at the forefront of the Mozambique liberation movement and collaborated in the preparation of the book *The Struggle for Mozambique*. In 1975 after Mozambique's independence, he held a series of appointments in the government: Director of the Cabinet of the President of the Republic; Governor of the Bank of Mozambique; Minister of Agriculture; Vice-Minister of Defence; and Minister of Security.

MICHEL VILAIN (Belgium, coauthor) is Professor of Continuing Education Methods at Brussels Free University, and Director of the State Economic Institution in Tamines, Belgium. He obtained his *candidate* (B.A.), *licenciate* (M.A.) and doctoral (Ph.D.) degrees from Brussels Free University. Previously he was Professor of Psychology, Pedagogy, and Methodology at the state pedagogic institutes of Mons and Couvin, Belgium. He is author or coauthor of several books and articles on education.

JESUS UGALDE VIQUEZ (Costa Rica) was Professor and Dean of the School of Education at the University of Costa Rica. He obtained his first degree from the University of Costa Rica; Master's degree from Harvard University, U.S.A.; and Diploma in Educational Administration from the University of Reading, U.K. He has authored over eighty publications on topics in science teaching, curriculum, educational administration, and educational research. He has previously served as consultant to OAS, UNESCO, and to the Ministry of Education, Costa Rica.

WASSEF AZIZ WASSEF (Bahrain) is Professor of Science Education at the University of Bahrain. Previously he was Chairman of the Department of Curriculum and Instruction and Vice-Dean of the Faculty of Education at the University of Tanta, Egypt. He earned his B.Sc. degree from the University of Alexandria, Egypt; M.Ed. from the University of Ein Shams, Egypt; and Ph.D. from the University of London (Institute of Education), U.K. He has published several technical articles and ten books on topics in science education and in teaching practise.

THOMAS W. WEBB (Denmark, coauthor) is Professor of Sociology of Education at the Roskilde University Center, Denmark. He has also served as President of the Roskilde University Center. He holds the B.A. degree from Baldwin-Wallace College, U.S.A. and Ph.D. in sociology from the Ohio State University, U.S.A. His publications include thirteen papers on topics in sociology of education, distance education, and information technology in education. His current research focus is on the use of computers in distance education courses for adults.

MICHAEL THOMAS WILLIAMS (United Kingdom, coauthor) is Professor of Education, Head of the Department of Education, and Dean of the Faculty of Educational Studies at the University College of Swansea, U.K. His research work has been in the broad fields of curriculum development and evaluation and educational policy making, and has been reported in more than fifty publications. His books include *Designing and Teaching Integrated Courses;* and *Teaching European Studies, Geography, and the Integrated Curriculum.* His articles have appeared in such journals as *Research in Education, British Journal of Educational Research, School Organization, and Educational Review.*

DONALD J. WILLOWER (United States of America, coauthor) is Distinguished Professor of Education at the Pennsylvania State University, U.S.A. Previously he has served as Chairman of the Graduate Program in Educational Administration. He holds the B.A., M.A., and Ed.D. degrees from the University of Buffalo (now State University of New York at Buffalo), U.S.A. He has authored or coauthored over 130 publications on topics in educational administration. The books to which he has made invited contributions include *Handbook of Research on Educational Administration* (1988), *and Thoughts and Research in Administrative Theory* (1986). His articles have appeared in such journals as *Journal of Educational Research* and *Journal of Educational Administration.* He has served on the editorial boards of *Educational Administration Quarterly,* the *Journal of Educational Administration,* and the *Alberta Journal of Educational Research.*

RICARDO YEVENES M. (Chile, coauthor) is Professor in the Faculty of Education, Humanities, and Arts at the University of Conception, and Rector of the Sacred Hearts College, Chile. He earned his M.A. degree from the University of Conception. His background includes several years of experience as principal of high schools. Previously he has held faculty positions at the Catholic University of Chile, the Technical University of Federico Santa Maria, and the University of the North.

MAKONNEN YIMER (Ethiopia) is Associate Professor and former Dean of the Faculty of Education at Addis Ababa University, Ethiopia. He holds the B.A. degree from Addis Ababa University, Ethiopia; M.A. from the University of Wisconsin (Madison), U.S.A.; and Ph.D. from the University of Illinois

(Urbana-Champain), U.S.A.   He has authored or coauthored several publication on topics in educational evaluation.

COLVILLE N. YOUNG (Belize) is former President of the University College of Belize. He holds the B.A. degree from the University of West Indies and Dr.Phil. from York University, U.K. Previously he has served as Principal of St. Michael's College, Belize, and has Lectured at the Belize Technical College. He has published verse as well as material on language and folk-lore.

AFGHANISTAN

by
Wali Mohammed Rahimi
Chairman, Department of Ethnography and Professor
Kabul University, Afghanistan

BACKGROUND

Modern education in Afghanistan really began in the 1920s with the founding of several primary schools and high schools during the rule of Amir Amunnullah Khan. It was Amir Sher Ali Khan who had established the first formal primary school in the country in 1830. Before his rule, the Muslim mosques and *madrases* formed the centers of education. Teaching was conducted by religious leaders, the Mullahs, and the curriculum primarily consisted of aspects of Islam and Arabic language and literature. Education lacked organization and central administration. It was during the rule of King Amanullah that a Ministry of Education was established. Also foreign Western influence and cooperation during this period accelerated educational development and lead to significant exchange of students and teachers with foreign countries such as France, Turkey, Germany, and India.

The foundation of higher education in Afghanistan can be traced back to the founding of the Faculty of Medicine in 1933 at Darul-Aman near Kabul City under a technical and cultural cooperation arrangement with Turkey. The faculty had an enrollment of eight students and its teaching staff consisted of foreign scholars and specialists. The administration of the faculty was headed by a Turkish dean, a medical doctor named Refqi Kamal Beig. Until 1947 the faculty had affiliation with Turkey and later with France. In 1953 a fundamental change occurred and young Afghan doctors took the responsibility of teaching and administration of the faculty, with foreign specialists continuing their assistance and services only in those areas and fields of study for which no trained Afghans were available.

The founding of the Faculty of Medicine was followed by the opening of other faculties: the Faculty of Law and Political Sciences in 1939 with an enrolment of five students, the Faculty of Natural Sciences in 1943 with an enrolment of sixteen students, and the Faculty of Letters in 1945 with ten students. Each faculty was headed by a dean and functioned as a semi-autonomous institution under the direction of the Ministry of Education. In 1946 a fundamental change occurred, and with the issue of a government decree, the concept of a university as an administrative complex composed of various faculties came in to fruition. The faculties that existed as separate units were combined to form the Kabul University. The minister of education was still the link between the university and the

1

government but the ministry's administrative hold on the university weakened and the university became an autonomous entity. The new institution began directing its efforts towards promotion and expansion of its academic units. The period 1951-61 became the decade of university development. More faculties were added. In 1951, the faculties of Islamic laws, engineering, agriculture, economics, and veterinary sciences were opened. In the same year, the Institute of Education came into existence, as a multipurpose institution for training of in-service school teachers and supervisors as well as for curriculum and textbook development. The opening of the women's section in the Faculty of Medicine in 1957 paved the way for women to enter higher education and seek specialization in addition to teaching. Other additions included the Faculty of Pharmacy, the Faculty of Education, and a separate polytechnic school, The Kabul Polytechnic Institute in 1963.

In the decade since 1964 the government also paid more attention to teacher education programs and instituted "higher teacher's colleges" in provinces. The political changes of 1974 then brought many changes in the education institutions, specially reorganization of faculties.

The year 1980 marked the beginning of another progressive step in higher education: the founding of evening schools/ faculties for those who were unable to follow university education. Evening programs were initiated in the fields of history, economics, law and political sciences, jurisprudence, Dari and Pushto languages, and journalism. In addition, graduate degree programs became available at the Kabul Polytechnic in 1983 and at Kabul University in 1987. The 1980s also saw the opening of more universities: one in Balkh and another in Herat, and other higher education institutions such as the faculties of social sciences, journalism, and fine art. The first university to be located in a province was the Nangarhar University established in 1967 which is now called the University of Bayazid Roshan.

Administration and control of higher education in Afghanistan is highly centralized and falls basically under the Ministry of Higher and Vocational Education, though the Ministry of Education and the Ministry of Public Health run their own institutions of higher education.

The president of a university (or institute) is elected from among the institution's academic staff holding higher academic ranks. He is assisted by two or three vice-presidents handing key functional areas. The president is sometimes named rector or chancellor. Each university or institute has an academic council composed of the president, vice-presidents, deans, two elected representatives of each faculty, chief of research unit, and the librarian (the last one is included only if the person is a professor). This council oversees coordination of instructional, academic, and research activities. Key decisions are made by the council but require approval of the minister. Boards and committees in the ministry review the policies, programs, plans, and budget allocations before they are submitted for approval of the minister. At a still higher level, the deputy prime minister in charge of education, science, culture and public health, and the Office of Cultural Affairs and Social Services in the President's office look into major issues of higher education. The Law of the Institutions of Higher and Vocational Education enacted in late 1989 regulates the functioning of higher education institutions.

By law, education in Afghanistan at all levels (elementary, secondary, technical, vocational, and higher) is offered free of charge to both the citizens and any foreign students accepted to education institutions in Afghanistan. Funds to support education come from the general revenue of the state through the budgets of three ministries: Ministry of Higher and Vocational Education, Ministry of Education, and Ministry of Public Health. Students are provided free tuition, free board and lodging, free medical care, free books, and even a modest amount of pocket money.

At a national level, higher education policies are formulated by the Higher Education Council which is composed of seven ministers besides representatives of higher education institutions. This council is empowered by the Law of the Institutions of Higher Education to coordinate formulation of general objectives, policies, and laws affecting higher education institutions. Curriculum development is carried out keeping in mind the scientific, technological, socio-economic, and cultural needs of the country. Training is also geared to meet the annual plans in various scientific and industrial sectors. Curriculum for each field of study is developed by the relevant department with the consent of the faculty academic council. The final approval of the curriculum must come from the Ministry of Higher Education.

PRIMARY AND SECONDARY EDUCATION

Primary education forms the first cycle of general education in the country. Its duration in the present planned structure (6-3-3) is six years. Children enter school at the age of 6-7 years. The curriculum of the first stage (1-3) covers religious studies, languages, mathematics, and general knowledge. In the second stage, social studies and science are added. The first stage is teacher centered while the second one is subject centered. All students are entitled to enter middle schools after successful completion of the primary level. Primary education is coeducational and free.

At present two different structures, ten and twelve years, are in existence for the primary and secondary education cycle. Plans are now underway to redefine the cycle (in 1991) to a twelve-year system.

The curriculum for secondary education generally includes religion, languages, mathematics, physics, chemistry, biology, social sciences, work education, and calligraphy. Primary and secondary education is provided free of charge. The two official languages, Pushto or Dari, are the mediums of instruction depending on the location of the school. Completion of secondary education is marked by the award of the secondary school certificate, the baccalaureate, which is a basic requirement for entry to higher education institutions.

Extracurricular activities at secondary education level have been expanded in the recent years as a complement to students' moral, intellectual, social, and physical development. The schools have associations and clubs and an assistant principal is usually in charge of these activities. Main extracurricular activities consist of cultural and artistic meetings, dramas, variety shows, festivals, literary days, knowledge contests, field trips, sports and games, voluntary work to assist the needy, and gardening.

Teachers are appointed either by the ministry or by the education departments of the provinces mainly from among the graduates of higher teachers' colleges and from university graduates who have followed teacher education programs, based on the availability of vacancies. There is no specific selection process or criteria.

HIGHER EDUCATION

Institutions

Higher education in Afghanistan is provided by several universities, the polytechnique institutes, higher teachers' colleges and vocational schools. These institutions come under three ministries.

The Ministry of Higher and Vocational Education oversees Kabul University in Kabul, Kabul Polytechnic Institute in Kabul, Nangarhar University of Bayazud Roshan, Balkh University in Balkh province, Herat University in Herat province, University of Islamic Studies and Research in Kabul, and several technical and vocational institutions including the technikums.

The Ministry of Education oversees Kabul Institute of Pedagogy in Kabul, Provincial Institutes of Pedagogy in several provinces, Sayed Jamaluddin Higher Teachers' College in Kabul, Faculty of Roshan in Kabul, and Higher Teachers' Colleges in several provinces.

The Ministry of Public Health oversees Kabul Institute of Medical Sciences in Kabul, Faculty of Medicine in Nangarhar province, Balkh Faculty of Medicine in Balkh province, and the Institute of Medical Education.

Undergraduate Studies

All universities in the Republic of Afghanistan offer bachelor's degrees. Duration of study in the schools of engineering and veterinary sciences is five years, while in all other schools it is four years. Equivalent degrees are offered by the institutes of pedagogy, in the fields of arts and sciences, under various teacher training programs. Institutions offering two-or three-year courses or programs, award diplomas. Graduates of these institutions are entitled to enter universities and other institutions offering bachelor's degrees or postgraduate programs, after taking a special entrance examination administered by the Ministry of Higher and Vocational Education.

All citizens of the Republic of Afghanistan who complete secondary school education irrespective of their national, racial, linguistic, tribal or social status; religious beliefs; political conviction; occupation; wealth; or residence are entitled to enter higher education institutions provided they are successful at the entrance examination. A small portion of high school graduates who complete military service are admitted to higher education on the basis of government resolutions and decrees. They get admitted to schools of their first choice based on an evaluation of their high school examination records (last three years). This privilege is limited for those who apply for admission only after completion of military service for one year. Age limit for entry to undergraduate studies is 35 years.

The entrance examination for admission to first degree studies (*conqouor exam*) vary in form and content depending on the type of secondary school which the students attend (high schools, vocational schools, and technical schools). The examination is administered by a special department in the Ministry of Higher and Vocational Education with the cooperation of teaching staff and under the supervision and control of a committee appointed by the minister. The intake of various faculties and institutions is planned in advance by the government and is influenced by the need to strengthen certain fields. Foreign nationalities residing in the country and proficient in the languages of instruction (Pushto or Dari) are privileged to study free of charge in all education institutions in this country.

The academic year in the universities consist of two semesters, and each semester lasts seventeen weeks. Other institutions of higher education follow somewhat similar schedules. At the undergraduate level, the curriculum for each semester includes a fixed number of courses (7-9) covering an average of thirty two hours per week. There are no optional or elective subjects. Students are required to attend classroom lectures in all the required courses and any laboratory sessions specified for the courses. Besides completion of courses, students are also required to submit a monograph prepared independently, or take a comprehensive written or oral examination entitled "State Examination" in their fields of specialization. In the Polytechnic Institute, where the studies lead to a master's degree, students devote the last semester to complete a research project called "diploma work". They are awarded the degree after successful presentation and defence of a thesis before a jury.

The duration of undergraduate programs can be three, four, five, or seven years depending on the field of study and the type of institution. In most faculties in the universities, an undergraduate degree requires four years; in the institutes of "intermediate medical education" it is three years; and in engineering and veterinary sciences it takes five years. Medical degrees require seven years.

Kabul University, the oldest and the largest institution, grants bachelor's, master's, and doctoral degrees in various branches of arts and sciences as well as in agriculture, engineering, veterinary sciences, and pharmacy. The University of Nangarhar offers bachelor's degrees in the fields of agriculture, engineering, languages, and education. The Polytechnic Institute offers master's degrees (five-year program) and doctorates in the fields of construction, electro-mechanics, geology, and mining. The University of Islamic Studies and Research grants bachelor's degrees in the fields of law and jurisprudence, Islamic education, preaching, and guidance.

The Abu Ali Sena Institute of Medical Sciences located in Kabul and its branch campuses at two other provinces offer Doctor of Medicine degrees in curative medicine, pediatrics, stomatology, and military medicine. The Institute of Medical Education grants diplomas in five areas at intermediate level (2-3 years at postsecondary level) in medical technology, stomatology, pharmacy, radiology, and epidemiology.

The Institute of Pedagogy grants bachelor's degrees under the auspices of the Ministry of Education. Higher teachers' colleges offer diplomas equivalent to a bachelor's degree. In the sphere of extracurricular activities, students at higher education institutions are active participants in students' annual conferences, art exhibitions, teaching (literacy courses), voluntary work (construction, cleaning etc.) for their institutions and residences, sports and games, students' festivals, knowledge contests, plays, dramas, and concerts.

The medium of instruction in all institutions of higher education is one of the two formal national languages: Dari or Pushto. Students learn the second national language in primary and secondary schools. Students of all institutions are also required to learn one foreign language from among English, French, German, and Russian.

In recent years, particularly after the Saur Revolution, cultural and social activities became more organized and intensified with the creation of "cultural councils" within each institution. Students also actively cooperate with main social organizations in the country like Youth Organizations and the Womens Council.

Since education is free by law, students at higher education institutions do not pay any tuition or fees. Even textbooks are given free of charge. Living accommodation at all residential institutes of higher education are also provided free of charge to students who demonstrate need.

Teaching appointments to higher education institutions are governed by the Law of State Personnel. All teachers are civil servants appointed by the government. University teaching staff is classified as professor *(pohand and pohanwal)*, associate professor *(pohandoy and pohanmal)*, instructor, and assistant *(pohyalie and pohanyar)*. With the exception of *pohand* all others are appointed by the Ministry of Higher Education, on the proposal of the head of department, the faculty and the university. The *pohand* is appointed by the prime minister on the proposal of the ministry. Minimum academic qualifications for a teaching position is a bachelor's degree. A master's degree is required for a *pohanyar* position.

Foreign nationals not residing in Afghanistan, who wish to study in Afghan universities, either apply directly or they are introduced through their respective embassies in Kabul to the Ministry of Higher and Vocational Education through the Ministry of Foreign Affairs. The Ministry evaluates their academic record and in turn refers them to the universities, mostly Kabul and Nangarhar. These students first learn the language of instruction for at least two semesters and then enroll in the faculty of their own choice. They are not subject to entrance examination. They study free of charge. Their board and lodging costs are paid by the Ministry. Fields of study popular among foreign students in Afghanistan are medicine, pharmacy or engineering.

Advanced Studies and Research

Postgraduate studies and research programs leading to higher degrees are available at Kabul University (master's degrees and doctorates), Polytechnic Institute (master's degrees and doctorates), and Institute of Social Sciences (master's). Postgraduate studies are carried out within individual departments of the university, rather than in a separate graduate school. Individual departments prepare the curriculum for its postgraduate programs and the curriculum is reviewed and assessed by the university's committee of postgraduate programs. Approval of the academic council of the university and the Ministry of Higher and Vocational Education is also required. A master's degree requires five semesters (110 hours) of studies, including a thesis in the field of specialization. A doctoral program requires three years of work under the supervision of an academic advisor. It can extend to four years for employed persons and in some cases to five years. This program does not require course work or class attendance.

Admission to master's degree programs is based on an entrance examination. Candidates are required to hold a bachelors degree with grades of 75 percent or more and they must not exceed thirty years of age. Candidates for doctoral programs must hold a master's degree, have a grade of 75 percent or more, possess work experience of at least two years, and pass a doctoral qualifying examination administered and supervised by the postgraduate committee composed of senior professors from relevant fields of study.

Postdoctoral and other research work is carried out to a limited extent at various research centers or units at some universities and institutions. Research units are in existence at Kabul Polytechnic Institute, Kabul Institute of Medical Sciences, University of Islamic Studies and Research, Institute of Pedagogy and at Kabul University. Doctoral, postdoctoral, and research studies are recent developments in the country. Research is funded by the government, and the programs generally funded are the programs which are included annually in the "Science and Technology Development Plan".

ISSUES AND TRENDS

Generally the trend at all levels of education is to train all-round students with a sense of responsibility towards development of the Afghan society.

The changing socioeconomic conditions in Afghanistan have made it necessary to organize education institutions and curricula to meet the drastic and rapid changes being witnessed now. Afghanistan's reconstruction needs skilled workers and well trained scientific and technical cadres. This need has resulted in the present emphasis on technical and vocational education. Higher education, which was a privilege of a few, is needed to be made available to an increasing number of high school graduates from all walks of life. Within this background, there are several issues and trends that dominate the present day education in Afghanistan and they include the following: at preschool, expansion of nursery and kindergartens (at residence and at work places); changing the structure of the school system by increasing the duration of study from eleven years to twelve years, along with a change in the curricula of primary and secondary education; expansion of higher education by establishing new universities, institutions, and medium level vocational and technical education programs to spread higher education from center to provinces; advancement of higher education by expanding master's and doctoral degrees; widening the scope of extracurricular activities at all levels; and emphasizing development oriented research at universities and at research centers, and avoiding scattered and individualized research activities.

The most important educational problem in the country is the realization of universal, compulsory, and free primary education. The problem is partly economical and partly due to present unsettled conditions in the country. There is an imminent need for reconstruction and revival of schools and their equipment which have been destroyed or damaged. The destruction of a considerable number of schools as a result of the war has caused a serious shortage of classrooms, space, and equipment. The main problems blocking the quality of education, particularly in higher education, has been the paucity of resources. Although funds are allocated, the amount of resources available is not enough for full mobilization of higher education. Of course, even if all facilities and resources were available, a major difficulty is the lack of a peaceful atmosphere due to the present war.

From an international perspective, Afghanistan, has a history of advocating the value of international cooperation. It has consistently strived to strengthen its international ties in the efforts towards country's development. As a member of UNESCO, the country has benefited from many programs organized through the Afghan National Commission for UNESCO. Also under bilateral cultural and educational exchange programs, Afghanistan has benefitted from scholarships, fellowships, and exchanges of scholars. During the past four decades, exchange programs have enabled Afghans to receive education in foreign countries at both undergraduate and postgraduate levels. Afghanistan has also hosted many scholars and specialists from Western as well as Eastern countries at the Polytechnic Institute and other institutions like the Kabul University. There were times when students from fifteen countries were studying at the Kabul University. At present, foreign students are studying in the fields of agriculture, engineering, medicine, pharmacy, languages, and literature. Afghan scholars are active participants in international conferences, and function as members of teaching staff at many universities in the Western and Arab countries.

BIBLIOGRAPHY

Arezo, M. *Kabul University: A Short Glimpse.* Kabul: Kabul University Press, 1986.

Central Statistics Office. *Statistical Year Book: 1986.* Kabul: Central Statistics Office, 1986.

Habib. A. "Kabul University in Forty Years of its Service in Training Specialists and Scientific Research" *Social Sciences.* Special Issue (in Dari). 1 (1986).

Kabul University. *Education in Afghanistan in the Last Fifty Years: Higher Education Volume II* (in Dari). Kabul: Education Press, 1968.

Rahimi, W. M., ed. *Kabul University in the Last Ten Years* (in Dari). Kabul: Kabul University Publication, 1988.

Rahmati, M. *Human Geography of Afghanistan* (in Dari).   Kabul: Kabul University Publication, 1985.

Science and Technology Commission.   *National Seminar on Administration and Management of Education* (in Dari).   Kabul: Kabul University Publication, 1980.

Wahidi, A. N.   "On the Curriculum of General Education Schools", *Erfan*, (1981): 11-22.

Wahidi, A. N.   *The Law of Higher Education Institutions*.   Kabul: Ministry of Higher and Vocational Education, 1989.

ALGERIA

by
Mohamed Miliani
Vice-Rector of Pedagogy and Professor
Es-Senia University, Algeria

BACKGROUND

Before the French occupation in 1830, Algeria had its own system of education composed of Koranic schools, primary schools *(medersas)*, and secondary schools *(zaouias)*. The primary objective of these schools was to form good citizens and to disseminate Islamic culture. In addition, pupils studied jurisprudence, geometry, philology, physics, astronomy etc. Higher education institutions, however, did not exist and for advanced studies, students went to universities in the neighboring countries (Zitouna in Tunisia, Karaouine in Morocco, and El-Azhar in Egypt.)

Since independence, education became a major preoccupation of the government of Algeria for two reasons: first the Algerian population consisted predominantly of youth (in 1989, 65-70 percent of citizens were younger than twenty-five years) and second, it was important to shed the vestiges of 132 years of colonialism and build a socialist society that would move vigorously to the twenty-first century. The government formulated educational policies taking into consideration general guidelines provided by the National Charter, the Constitution, and the resolutions adopted at the congresses of the National Liberation Front (the ruling party).

Education in Algeria is funded exclusively by the government. Almost 40 percent of the government budget is devoted to education. Even this expenditure, however, does not fully meet the needs of Algerian universities as they struggle to fully develop their potential. Of course it is also true that the available resources have not always been utilized in an optimal fashion, and students bear only a negligible portion of the cost of their education, compared to government expenditure. With the decline in revenues from petroleum resources, it is becoming increasingly important to look for other sources of funding to supplement government contribution to education.

Institutions of higher education have a fair degree of autonomy. Central administration at ministry level coordinates the activities of the institutions under the ministry and is in regular contact with individual institutions. Teachers, students, and workers are being given an increasingly important role in the management of the institutions.

PRIMARY AND SECONDARY EDUCATION

Primary Education

The objective of primary education is to give the children an increasingly "polytechnical" education by blending theory and practice and introducing them to the multiple problems of the twenty-first century with a view to producing citizens who are capable of adapting themselves to socioeconomic and cultural transformation taking place in the country.

Primary education lasts nine years and is compulsory. It consists of three cycles (stages): first cycle or the basic stage; second cycle or the awakening stage; and the third cycle or the training stage. At the end of the third cycle the students take the final *brevet d'enseignement fondamental* exam which, if they pass, allows them access to secondary schools (general or technical) or technical training *programs (formation professionelle)*.

Secondary Education

Secondary education is of two types: technical and general. The first type, from the point of view of student enrollment, is far from achieving its objectives. Thus, in 1987-88 only 20 percent of the students opted for "technical" secondary education in spite of the addition of new fields of studies (information technology, applied biochemistry, etc.), extension of agricultural education, and addition of optional subjects (foreign languages, design, etc.). Technical stream provides students with two options: industrial option and commercial option. Teaching staff is largely Algerian but the percentage of expatriate staff (about 12 percent) is higher than in the general secondary education.

Admission to secondary schools is based on two measures: first the student quota for each institution is fixed by the ministry, and second the students are selected competitively based on their grades. The allocation of students to fields of studies depend on how well they have done in the primary subjects relevant to the field.

After three years of studies, students appear for the *baccalauréat* examination which determines their admission to higher education institutions. This examination is conducted at a national level. Students who fail the examination either enter the job market based on the skills they acquired or pursue other avenues of technical training.

General secondary education, which is the traditional preparation for studies perceived as prestigious (medicine, law, etc.), offers several streams including humanities, mathematics, and sciences and is valued by parents as much as by students. The curriculum consists of experimental sciences, mathematics and humanities. The medium of instruction is universally Arabic but French is a supplementary language used in instruction in the case of technical secondary education. General secondary education also ends with the *baccalauréat* examination.

The academic year for all secondary education is from September to July with a fifteen-day break in December and in March. Free education is guaranteed by the Constitution and students do not have to bear any costs. Students' living is supported by parents or scholarships offered by the government. Extracurricular activities play an important role in students' lives (choirs, sports, painting, etc.). These activities are financed and organized either by the school or by parents' associations. It must be noted that physical education, sports, music, and art form part of the school curriculum, taught by teachers who specialize in these areas.

HIGHER EDUCATION

Institutions and Undergraduate Studies

The higher educational system in Algeria consists of two types of institutions: level five which lasts five semesters, and Level six which lasts 8-12 semesters. The aim of these institutions is to produce well educated citizens with adequate knowledge and skills to meet the sociocultural and economic development needs of the society. The institutions that come under the Ministry of Education produce about 90 percent of the graduates (bachelor's degree level). There are also several institutions that come under other ministries.

The type of degrees awarded depend on the duration of the course of studies and the type of institution. Generally the shorter duration level five (five semesters) leads to qualifications as a technologist and longer duration level six (8-12 semesters) may lead to a first degree (licence), higher education diploma *(Diplôme d'études supérieures)*, or other professional degrees in medicine, dentistry, pharmacy, and engineering. Both Arabic and French are used as languages of instruction. Arabic is used mostly in humanities and social sciences. French is usually the medium of instruction in applied sciences, technology, architecture, and medicine. The academic year lasts from September to July and consists of two semesters with a twenty-one day break in January.

Institutions under the control of the Ministry of Higher Education fall into four categories:

1. Universities which comprise thirteen institutions:universities in Algiers, Annaba, Constantine, Tlemcen, Blinda, Sidi Bel Abbes, Tizi Ouzou, Batna, Setif, and Oran; Islamic University of Constantine; and universities of science and technology in Algiers and Oran. Each university consists of several institutes each of which coordinates a number of departments. The areas most popular in the universities are letters and languages, juridical and political science, medical sciences, technology, and fundamental sciences.

2. Engineering schools *(grandes écoles)* which comprise seven institutions: *Ecole nationale polytechnique, Ecole nationale vétérinaire, Ecole polytechnique d'architecture et d'urbanisme, Institut nationale agronomique, Institut national de formation en informatique, Institut des Télécommunications d'Oran,* and *Institut des sciences de La Mer et de L'Aménagement du Littoral.*

3.   Teachers' colleges *(écoles normales supérieure* and *ecole normale superieure d'enseignement technique)*, the objective of which is to train teachers for secondary schools (both general and technical).

4.   National institutes of higher education *(instituts nationaux d'enseignement supérieur - INES)*. These came into being as a result of renaming of the previous university centers (centres universitaires) and about fifty INES are in existence now. These are institutions much smaller than universities. These institutions offer degree programs in a variety of fields including archeology, architecture, physical education, history, language, music, philosophy, education, applied sciences, commerce, sciences, information sciences, economics, mathematics, religious studies, medical sciences, and technology.

Institutions coming under other ministries primarily cater to the needs of specific sectors of the economy which the ministries oversee. These offer study programs of 5-10 semesters:

-          Ministry of Education and Training: Institutes of education that train teachers. Institutes of public works and electro-mechanical maintenance that train technicians.

-          Ministry of Health: Institutes of public health that train public health workers.

-          Ministry of Postes and Telecommunications: *Ecole Centrale* that produce telecommunication inspectors at junior and senior levels.

-          Ministry of Interior and Environment: Police training schools that train police officers.

-          Ministry of Hydraulics: Institutes of hydraulics that train technicians and engineers.

-          Ministry of Information and Culture: School of Fine Arts, Institute of Drama, and Institute of Hotel Management and Tourism.

-          Ministry of Heavy Industries: Institutes of mechanical engineering, and electrical and electronic engineering that produce technicians and engineers.

-          Ministry of Light Industries: Institutes of manufacturing, food technology, and construction materials that produce technicians and engineers.

-          Ministry of Energy and Petrochemical Industries: Petroleum Institute, and Institute of Hydrocarbons producing technicians and engineers.

-          Ministry of Agriculture: Institutes of agronomy, agriculture, and fishing that produce technicians as well as engineers.

-          Ministry of Commerce: Institutes of commerce and refrigeration that produce technicians as well as graduates in commerce.

-          Ministry of Public Works: Institutes of public works that produce technicians as well as engineers.

-          Ministry of Construction: Institute of Building Construction.

-          Ministry of Transport: Institutes of transport that produce technicians, engineers, and merchant shipping officers.

-          Ministry of Youth and Sports: Institutes of sports technology, and youth formation that produce instructors and counsellors.

Each university is administered by a rector who is assisted by three vice-rectors (postgraduate studies, research and exterior relations; academic affairs; and planning). Institutes with n a university are each headed by a director. There are department heads who oversee the activities of individual departments within an institute.

Minimum requirements for admission to undergraduate programs is the *baccalauréat* or an equivalent qualification *(cours préparatoires aux études supérieures, capacité en droit,* etc.). Certain fields of study have additional requirements like the entrance examination for medical sciences. Foreign students are also admitted to Algerian higher education institutions if they meet the admission requirements and their parents are resident in Algeria or if they receive an Algerian scholarship.

Residential accommodation and board for students are arranged by the *Centres des Oeuvres Scolaires et Universitaires,* which also administer scholarship awards for needy students (whose parents are unable to bear the cost). The increase in the number of students in the recent years has put the available facilities under considerable stress.

Teaching staff at Algerian higher education institutions, for many years, consisted primarily of expatriate personnel but in the recent years the Ministry of Higher Education *(Ministère Delegue aux Universités)* has initiated a policy of total Algerianization by the year 2000. At this time more than 85 percent of the *maîtres assistants* level teachers (assistant professors) are Algerian but at the *maitres de conferences* level (professors) the number is relatively low. Entry level teachers at the universities require at least the third cycle master's level qualification.

Advanced Studies and Research

Three factors influenced the launching of graduate programs at Algerian universities: first the need to solve the problem of Algerianization of teaching staff; second the need to use Arabic in teaching; and third the importance of getting universities involved in the country's development effort.

Graduate education in Algeria is not yet fully developed and the programs presently available fall into two categories: master's level programs *(magister)* and doctorate level programs *(doctorat d'état).* Admission to master's level programs require a first degree *(licence)* or equivalent, and candidates for doctoral level studies need a master's degree *(magister)* or equivalent. Additional requirements may be specified by individual institutions.

The first graduate degree *(magister)* takes four semesters (two years). The first two semesters are devoted to course work, directed research, seminars, and the study of one foreign language (generally English). The second year is spent in writing a dissertation. Both Arabic and French are used during postgraduate studies. The fees are nominal (about US$10). Foreign students may enroll provided they are authorized by the Ministry of Higher Education. Students at graduate level may receive grants. In the academic year 1988-89, there were 11,987 graduate students, an increase of 998 percent from 1974-75.

ISSUES AND TRENDS

It is becoming more and more evident that the old educational structure is not responsive to the present and future needs of the country. Education reform is a dominant issue facing the party (in power), the government, and the universities themselves. In recognition of the urgency of this issue, the government appointed a National Commission just recently, in January 1989, with the principle objective of finding satisfactory solutions, giving due consideration to the Constitution of 1989, the National Charter of 1976, and the 1988 central committee resolutions of the National Liberation Front (ruling party). Some of the relevant issues are outlined below.

Policy of Arabization, Democratization, and Algerianization

Arabization, the use of Arabic language as a medium of instruction, is no longer a wish but a reality. In the area of humanities and social sciences, Arabic is the only language of instruction but in the scientific fields there are still many difficulties in adopting this policy. Examples of successful programs as in the case of Jordan which uses Arabic for scientific areas since the eighties are often cited in support. However, the Algerian situation is much more complex. An Arabic Language Academy has only just been established. The bilingual situation (Arabic/-French) and the rift between local dialects and literary Arabic calls for fundamental studies on the language. "How can Arabic be made to respond to the needs of teaching science subjects?" is a question facing many of the Arab countries.

The democratization of education has been one of the important policies of the government since independence. The result of such a policy is the quantitative development of education to mitigate the limited and selective opportunities provided by colonial masters. The benefits included the replacement of an elitist system with equal opportunities for all and reduction of social stratification. However, the expansion carried with it a corresponding reduction in the quality of education. It also created problems of handling the large numbers of students and staffing requirements.

Algerianization, which aims at replacing expatriate staff with Algerian personnel (locally or foreign trained) remains an important objective. As a whole, about 65 percent of the posts were Algerianized by 1979, 85 percent by 1987, and it seems possible to achieve the 100 percent level by the nineties.

Quality of Higher Education

After years of focus on quantitative development of education, the stage is being set now for improving the quality of education. One of the objectives assigned to graduate study programs in Algeria is the training of manpower demanded by different sectors of the economy. A major problem facing university authorities is the lack of any graduate programs in scientific fields, conducted in Arabic. Development of research is also beginning to be seen as a necessary vehicle to rid of total dependence on foreign sources.

In essence, it is naive to assume that a program of reforms, as planned, will put the education on right tracks. There are many problems still to be resolved:

- The policy of Arabization could be in conflict with the need to use foreign languages which in reality provide a window to the outside world of science and technology.

- The democratization as put into practice has demonstrated its limits on the quality of education. There is a new thinking that a system based on competition may offer better solutions.

- The polytechnical approach to fundamental education provided some hope but it does not seem to have resolved the problem of disparity between training and employment opportunities or the problem of orienting the students towards technical education.

BIBLIOGRAPHY

Ageron, C. R. *Histoire de l'Algérie contemporaine* (1830-1982). Paris: Presses Universitaires de France, 1983.

Colonna, F. *Instituteurs Algeriens, 1883-1939.* Algiers: Office des Publications universitaires, 1975.

Colonna, F. "Le système d'enseignement de L'Algérie coloniale" *Archives Europeennes de Sociologie.* Vol. XIII, no. 2 (1972).

Glasman, D. and Kremer, J. *Essai sur l'université et les cadres en Algerie.* Paris: CNRS, 1978.

Grandguillaume, G. *Arabisation et politique liguistique au Maghreb.* Paris: Francois Maspero, 1983.

Mazouni, A. *Culture et enseignement en Algeria et au Maghreb.* Paris: F. Maspero, 1969.

Micaud, C. A. "Bilingualism in North Africa: Cultural and Socio-political Implications" *The Western Political Quarterly.* (1974): 92-103.

Mignot-Lefebvre, Y. "Bilinguisme et système scolaire en Algérie" *Tiers Monde.* Vol. XV. no. 59-60 (1974): 671-693.

Necib, R. *Industrialisation et système educatif Algerien.* Algiers: Office des publications universitaires, 1986.

Souriau, C. "L'Arabisation en Algerie" *Introduction a l'Afrique du Nord Contemporaine.* Paris: CNRS, 1975.

Taleb Ibrahimi, A. *De la decolonisation à la revolution culturelle, 1962-1972.*
Algiers: SNED, 1976.

ARGENTINA

by
Laureano Garcia Elorrio
Director
National Center for Educational Information
Ministry of Education and Justice, Argentina
(Professors M. Martinez, R. Brambilla and M. Guiberto of the National Center for
Educational Information have assisted in the preparation of the text)

BACKGROUND

The only university that existed during the colonial period within the territory of the present Argentinian Republic was the University of Cordoba. This institution opened its doors in 1614. In 1622, Pope Gregorio XV granted it authorization to award degrees, and the university status of the institution was ratified by King Philip III of Spain. In fact the permanent authorization was granted only in 1634 by Pope urbano VIII, as the original authorization was provisional and was valid only for ten years.

The next institution, the University of Buenos Aires, was a project planned since the colonial times, but it was realized only when the government of General Rodriguez promulgated an edict on 9 August 1821 creating this institution. The founding of this university made it possible to bring under one administration, all the academies and schools which depended on ecclesiastical chapters or the state. When the city of Buenos Aires became a federal city, the university received national status in 1881. In 1885 this university as well as the University of Cordoba came under the "Avellaneda Law" (named after the senator and ex-president who proposed it) which regulated the functioning of national universities. Subsequently, over twenty other universities, both state supported and privately owned, have come into existence.

PRIMARY AND SECONDARY EDUCATION

Primary education in Argentina consists of seven years of study for children of 6-12 years of age and it is compulsory. The administration of primary education is mostly decentralized. Each province develops its own curriculum within national guidelines and policies. Schools run by private enterprises coexist with those managed by the state. Children who complete primary schools (age 12-13 years) are admitted to secondary education which is also referred to as middle level.

Secondary education consist of two cycles: a basic cycle covering general subjects, and a superior cycle in which students receive specialized training as well as preparation for entering higher education. Although secondary education is not compulsory, the trend is to encourage the maximum number of students to pursue this level of studies by providing free education and scholarships to ensure that capable students are not deprived of opportunities.

There are a variety of avenues available at the secondary level: general education (*bachillerato*), commercial education, agricultural education, artistic education, and technical education. Period of study varies from four to six years, at the termination of which students receive a certificate or title depending on the field of studies.

The bachillerato program provides a general education and prepares students to enter higher education institutions. The duration is five years consisting of a basic cycle of three years and a superior cycle of two years. On completion of the basic cycle, students have several options of which they can select one. The options include common bachillerato program; specialized bachillerato program with specialization in letters, biological sciences, or physical and mathematical sciences; and bachillerato with focus on agriculture or teaching. These are the bachillerato programs available at the majority of institutions but other bachillerato programs are also available with different curriculums like administration, communication, sports and recreation, languages, commerce, etc.

Commerce programs prepare students for administrative careers associated with business and lead to the title of *peritos mercantiles* through day or night studies. The day school consist of a three year basic cycle and a two year superior cycle. The night school for adults take four years. Private schools also provide programs leading to *bachillerato comercial* and *bachillerato mercantil*.

Agriculture programs are aimed at preparing technical specialists at various levels depending on the needs of agro-industries and consist of a basic cycle of three years and a superior cycle of three years.

Artistic programs provide the opportunity to develop students' artistic abilities in many areas such as fine arts, ceramics, decoration, dancing, and music. Programs are offered at secondary as well as at higher levels. In general, students specialize in artistic fields while following simultaneously *bachillerato* studies. To obtain the title of *maestro nacional* in a given speciality, it is necessary to have completed five years of secondary studies.

Technical education consists of two distinct structures: training of technicians, and training of professionals. Training of technicians aim at preparing students for middle level technical positions in industry where as training of professionals strive to produce well qualified persons to meet the demands of various occupations (trains persons who serve as assistants to university trained professionals). Programs leading to the title of "technician" consist of a three year basic cycle (four years for night students) and three years of superior cycle (four years for night students). Programs with a shorter superior cycle are available for auxiliary technician titles. Dual programs that combine practical work in industry and study at school are also available. Technical education includes a variety of fields some of which are electronics, electricity, hydraulics, automotive mechanics, naval construction, refrigeration and airconditioning, metallurgy, design, ceramics, carpentry, graphic arts, telecommunications, etc.

There are also secondary schools specifically meant for adult students, who can work towards obtaining a *bachillerato* or specialized qualifications in technical, artistic, or commercial fields. Successful completion of three years of studies can provide the opportunity for adults to enter higher education.

HIGHER EDUCATION

Institutions

Higher education is provided at both the university and non-university levels. There are twenty-nine state universities, twenty-five recognized private universities, and a state supported technological university. Non-university higher education is generally offered at teacher training institutions.

The state universities include the national universities of Cordoba, Buenos Aires, La Plata, Litoral, Entre Rios, Northwest, Tucuman, South, Cuyo, La Pampa, Catamarca, the center of the province of Buenos Aires, Comahue, Jujuy, Patagonia, Lomas de Zamora, Lujan, Mar del Plata, Misiones, Rio Cuarto, Salta, San Juan, San Luis, Santiago del Estero, Rosario, Formosa, Qilmes, and La Mataniza as well as the National Technological University and the Provincial University of the Rioja. In addition, there is a police academy (Advanced Academy of Police Studies) under the jurisdiction of the Ministry of the Interior and an engineering school (School of Aeronautical Engineering) under the jurisdiction of the Ministry of Defence.

The primary objective of establishing the universities in the North, Center, and South of the country was to make these institutions the technical and professional centers for supporting regional development through exploitation of regional resources, so that youth of the region did not have to emigrate to other regions in search of new horizons.

The year 1959 saw a profound change in the policy on establishing of universities: legislation was passed (Law 14.557) authorizing private universities to grant degrees and titles. This resulted in the official recognition of the Catholic University of Santa Maria de Los Buenos Aires. This university aimed at disseminating higher humanistic-Christian cultural values, scientific research, and preparing students for professional careers. Other private institutions recognized by the government since then include the Center for Advanced Studies in Exact Sciences, University School of Theology, Technological Institute of Buenos Aires, Argentine University of Business, Argentine University "John F. Kennedy", Catholic University of Cordoba, Catholic University of Cuyo, Catholic University of La Plata, Catholic University of Salta, Catholic University of Santa Fe, Catholic University of Santiago del Estero, University of Belgrano, and several others.

In 1956, the National Worker's University (which was established in 1948 under the Law 13.229 for providing postsecondary engineering training to members of the working class) was renamed and received autonomous status as the National Technological University. The objectives of this university include the training of professionals in specialized technical areas, developing in students an appreciation of humanistic culture; promoting of scientific research and studies necessary for improvement of industry; consulting with public as well as private organizations; and establishing a close relationship with other universities, technical and cultural institutions, industry, and economic forces of the country.

The structure and organization of universities conform to the Decree-Law 6403 of 23 December 1955. Article 1 of the law gives considerable administrative and financial autonomy to the national universities. Article 2 sets guidelines for the governing roles of different authorities and organs of the university including deans who head the faculties, directive councils *(consejo directivo)* which oversee faculty activities, directors who head the departments; rector who heads the university, and superior council *(consejo superior)* which consists of professors, students and some staff and forms the highest governing body.

Higher education for training of school teachers is given at non-university institutions which are directly administered by the National Directorate of Higher Education (and the Ministry of Education). The normal schools *(escuelas normales)* train teachers for preschools and primary schools in programs lasting two and one-half years. The national institutes for secondary teachers *(institutos nacionales del profesorados)* train teachers for secondary schools, in programs having a duration of four years. Students can obtain their teaching qualifications in a variety of fields including languages, economics, juridical sciences, political and social sciences, natural sciences, philosophy, psychology and pedagogy, exact sciences, mathematics, informatics, and administration. A rector functions as the administrative and academic head of each national institute for secondary teachers. Normal schools (teacher training schools) are headed by a director. Some specialized teacher training programs are provided by other authorities such as the National Directorate of Artistic Education and the National Directorate of Physical Education, Sports, and Recreation.

Programs and Degrees

University education generally consist of three cycles: basic cycle, professional cycle, and graduate cycle.

Admission to universities is open to students who have completed secondary education.

Foreign students are admitted on the same basis as Argentinian students. They must hold a qualification equivalent to the completion of the Argentinian secondary education (on the basis of existing conventions with Argentina or as determined by the Ministry of Education and Justice).

In the first year, all students who enroll follow the one year basic cycle consisting of two semesters (of four month each). Some fields do not require the students to take the basic cycle. Students who successfully complete the basic cycle proceed to the second year to follow their specialized fields of studies.

The curriculum for the professional cycle differs for each field and varies between four and seven years for degree programs. There are programs leading to the first degree *licenciado* for non-professional studies in arts, science and humanities and to professional titles of engineer, physician, etc. In addition there are programs of a shorter duration, lasting 1-4 years, leading to qualifications that are at a lower level than degrees (intermediate level professionals etc.). Courses may be offered on an annual or semester (four months) plan and promotions are made on the basis of one or more assessment criteria: class attendance, examinations during the course without a final exam, examinations during the course with a final exam, written and oral final exams, research reports, etc.

Fields of studies offered at the universities generally include basic sciences and technology (agriculture, architecture, engineering, pharmacy, etc.), social sciences (economics, administration, law, political science, etc.), humanities (philosophy and letters, education, fine arts, music, etc.), and medical sciences (medicine, dentistry, allied health, etc.).

In the area of graduate studies, programs leading to doctorates as well as specialized courses for advanced training are offered at the universities. Doctorate is the highest degree and requires defence of a thesis based on rigorous scientific research under the guidance of professors opted by the candidate. Doctorates are not available in all fields of studies but are generally considered important in scientific areas. Research is conducted within the universities, at private institutions, and by government entities such as the National Council of Scientific and Technical Research (under the Ministry of Education and Justice).

Financial assistance offered to students come mainly from the universities. For example, assistance offered by the University of Buenos Aires fall in to several categories: scholarships that offer a monthly stipend from the funds at the disposition of the faculties and other academic centers; scholarships for meals at university restaurants; scholarships for final year of studies; scholarships for students coming from other Latin American countries; and grants for purchase of books and supplies.

ISSUES AND TRENDS

Key issues facing education include decentralization of education, community role in education, improvement of the teaching profession and interrelationship between different levels of education. The challenge is to develop education within the context of the realities of sociopolitical transformations facing the country.

BIBLIOGRAPHY

Centro Latinoamericano de Documentación e Informática y Electrónica. *Directoria de base de datos en ciencia y tecnología en Argentina.* Buenos Aires, 1986.

Klubitschko, Doris. *El origen social de los estudiantes de la Universidad de Buenos Aires.* UNESCO, 1980.

Marquez, Angel Diego. *Una nueva educación superior para un nueva proyecto nacional; las oportunidades educativas a nivel superior.* Rosario: Universidad Nacional de Rosario, 1986.

Ministerio de Cultura y Educación. Subsecretaría de Cienciay Tecnología. Dirección National de Planificación Científica y Tecnológical. Departamento de Información y Estadística. *Relevamiento de recursos y actividades en ciencia y tecnología. zona nordeste: Informe de los resultados obtenidos.* Buenos Aires, 1981.

Presidencia de la Nacion. Secretaría de Planeamiento. Subsecretaría de Cicncia y Tecnología. *Relevamiento de recursos y actividades en ciencia y tecnología: Informe de los resultados obtenidos.* Buenos Aires, 1983.

Rodriguez, Deolinda y otros. *Demanda educativa de nivel universitario en el área del Gran Buenos Aires, una aproximación al tema.* Buenos Aires: Ministerio de Educación y Justicia, 1986.

Secretaría de Educación. Centro Nacional de Información, Documentación y Tecnología Educativa; *Estadísticas de la Educación: educación superior, universitaria, cifras provisionales.* Buenos Aires, 1985.

AUSTRALIA

by
Brian V. Hill
Foundation Professor of Education
Murdoch University, Australia

BACKGROUND

The dominant role in Australian education has been played by government, although 25 percent of primary and secondary schools are under private, mainly Roman Catholic, auspices. In the first half century of Australia's existence as a British colony, several schools were set up by various Christian denominations, but the creation of government departments of education in each state gradually tipped the balance to the public sector, as policies were implemented which provided schooling that was "free, secular, and compulsory".

In the second half of the nineteenth century, these departments grew rapidly, though their concern was mainly with primary or "elementary" schooling, while secondary education remained the preserve of church schools. It is therefore ironical that the first wave of universities, created in this period, were all under state government auspices. Sydney (1851) and Melbourne (1853) were later followed by Adelaide (1874) and Tasmania (1890). With the creation of Queensland (1909) and Western Australia (1911), the initial pattern of one university in each of Australia's six states was complete.

The separate states of Australia agreed to federate as one nation in 1901, with the federal capital in Canberra. Constitutionally, education was to be the responsibility of the states, and not a federal matter.

In the first half of the twentieth century, state education departments extended the provision of universal state schooling into the secondary level, streaming students by ability into high (academic), technical, and commercial schools. The general pattern became six years of primary schooling, four of junior secondary, and two of senior secondary, leading to university entrance at about the age of eighteen. Curricula were generally derivatives of English and Scottish educational patterns and ideas. Meanwhile, institutions of technical education at school and college level were developing in each state, catering especially for part-time and mature-age students.

After the Second World War, the American idea of the comprehensive high school was adopted. More students qualified for higher education, and a second wave of university development occurred with the creation of new state universities in the capitals of New South Wales, Victoria, and South Australia. Others began in the Australian Capital Territory and several regional areas. Then, in 1975, a third wave occurred with the foundation in 1975 of Deakin, Griffith, and Murdoch Universities.

The postwar expansion in university provision was due to the increasing growth and industrialization of the Australian society, and the view that access to postsecondary education should be more democratic and according to ability. At federal level, the Liberal Government of Robert Menzies, taking the view in 1958 that universities were central to the national effort, broke with tradition by supplementing state funding of universities. At the same time, and for the same reasons, many teacher training institutions, technical and agricultural colleges, and institutes of technology were coming into being, and from 1964 and the Menzies Government extended federal funding to this sector, designated "colleges of advanced education" (CAEs).

In 1972, with the Labor party under Gough Whitlam in power at the national level, the federal government took over the whole responsibility for funding higher education, although the granting of charters for tertiary institutions continues to be the legal responsibility of state governments. Until 1989, all the Australian universities had been created and funded by government. The first private university has only just appeared, with the opening of Bond University in Queensland. Where others will follow remains to be seen.

PRIMARY AND SECONDARY EDUCATION

Each state of Australia operates its own school system. Most follow a 6-4-2 pattern with an optional kindergarten or pre-primary year at the beginning. (For the sake of accuracy, it should be noted that Queensland and Western Australia extend their primary schools to Year 7, so that the junior secondary stage lasts only three years. Standard nomenclature across Australia is to number the years of schooling from 1-12, with six year olds in Year 1).

Approaches to curricula vary. In most primary school systems the regular basic subjects in language, reading, writing, number work, social studies, health and physical education, natural science studies, art, music, and craft are part of the compulsory curriculum, internally examined. Elective studies utilizing community resources are occasionally provided through local option for older students. Religious instruction is given by the classroom teacher and/or visiting representatives of religious groups (mainly Christian). The primary teacher is a generalist, though the number of specialist teachers is slowly increasing, usually on an itinerant basis.

At the junior secondary level, there is usually a core of required subjects embracing English, mathematics, social studies, and science, surrounded by optional studies chosen from such areas as art, home economics, languages, manual arts, media studies, music, physical education, and technical studies. Religious studies, usually of a mainly Christian but partly comparative kind, are available in some states as part of the general curriculum, while in others they are provided by visiting representatives of religious groups.

Some states, notably Western Australia, are experimenting with a "unit curriculum" approach in which students may select a range of levels at which to study different subjects, provided that they take a minimum from each of several broad categories, e.g. science and technology. Whatever the approach, junior secondary studies in Australia are examined internally, and any student leaving school at the statutory minimum age of fifteen receives a school certificate recording progress to that point. State schools are not allowed to charge tuition fees, but it is not uncommon to find a number of charges being imposed, including the cost of purchasing textbooks. In such cases, most schools have provision for giving financial assistance to needy cases.

At the senior secondary level, all states assume that one of the school's functions is to prepare students for admission to tertiary institutions. At the same time, a general rise in retention rates has brought many students into Year 11 who do not have tertiary aspirations. A distinction has developed in some states between pre-tertiary courses and more general courses which count for school graduation but not tertiary admission. In the former category are subjects such as biology, chemistry, economics, English literature, geography, history (Australian, Asian, European, etc.), languages (Chinese, French, German, Indonesian, Italian, Japanese, etc.), mathematics (at advanced levels), and physics. The second category is much more varied, often reflecting prevocational and general life-style studies.

All states base at least part of their assessment for tertiary admissions on internal school assessment, and most combine this with external final examinations. There are no national examinations as such. Students receive the high school certificate recording their achievements at the point of leaving school. Admission to tertiary institutions usually requires an additional score, derived from marks obtained in those courses recognized as pre-tertiary. In calculating this score, several states also include performance on the Australian Scholastic Aptitude Test (ASAT) designed by the Australian Council for Educational Research. Students coming from interstate or overseas to seek entry to tertiary education are usually judged by what their comparative standing in their home state would be.

Most states are moving to a school year of two semesters (four terms), totalling about forty teaching weeks, with two-week breaks during the year and a six-week vacation from Christmas through January. State school staff are appointed by state authorities, and are required to have had three or four years of initial teacher training which, for secondary teachers, includes a degree in their special teaching area. There is great variation in the extent to which schools provide extracurricular activities in such areas as sport, music, recreational clubs, and voluntary religious groups. Boarding schools are probably the ones which make the most effort in this regard.

Fee-paying "independent" schools, mostly under the sponsorship of christian denominations, and mostly in metropolitan areas, are strongly oriented to achievement at the upper secondary level. The majority include facilities for boarders as well as day students, and some have large foreign student enrollments. State schools do not usually have facilities for student boarders, except in some country centers away from the capital cities. Foreign students may enrol in Australian State schools provided they have family residence in Australia.

HIGHER EDUCATION

Institutions

Until 1989, institutions of higher education in Australia could be classified as follows:

(i)   The seventeen universities previously described, with staff appointed to undertake research and provide studies from undergraduate to doctoral degree level and varying in size from roughly 3,000-18,000 students.

(ii)   Institutions in the "advanced education" sector. These included a few large institute of technology (two of which had become universities), and a number of smaller colleges of advanced education (CAE) which had grown out of what were formerly teachers, agricultural, technical and art colleges. They offered undergraduate diploma and degree courses, with some developing master's degrees and research activities.

(iii)   The technical and further education sector (TAFE), consisting of a variety of other postsecondary institutions, providing post-school, diploma and, in some cases, first degree courses in a large range of vocational areas.

Though federally funded, public universities and colleges obtain their charters from their respective state governments. Around 1989 pressures from the federal government obliged all states to make arrangements for all campuses in the "advanced education" category to become amalgamated with either a traditional university or a consortium of colleges thereafter to be called a university. This process is now nearly complete. The original seventeen universities retain their names, but the process of renaming the new conglomerates has yet to be completed.

These institutions are government-run, except for some accredited private teachers' colleges. Most are now multi-purpose institutions, offering programs in a variety of fields. There is also a growing number of private institutes, mostly in the capital cities, catering for business studies and students of English as a second language. The latter have multiplied greatly since the Federal Government in 1986 initiated a policy of encouraging full-fee paying students from other countries, especially in the Asian region, to enrol at Australian institutions. Also, some students continue to receive assistance for study in Australia under Australia's programs of aid to developing countries. Students of Asian origin, whether now resident in Australia or on student visas, are today a significant and valued part of the student body on many campuses.

In addition, some professional institutes and industries, particularly banks, conduct training courses of their own. Arrangements to transfer credit between government educational institutions are common, and were formalized in the 1988 White Paper on higher education. It is less common for credit to be granted for study in the private sector. Some professions, such as accountancy, engineering, law, and medicine have requirements for membership or fellowship which may involve special studies outside the higher educational system, but the trend is to nominate particular public qualifications for this purpose rather than to conduct in-house courses. Similarly, recent years have seen a nationwide movement in the nursing profession away from hospital-based training to degree programs offered by colleges of advanced education.

The administrative structure of higher education institutions tends in general towards a participant model, where academic and resource decisions are made by committees with faculty representation. A majority of university staff belongs to the Federation of Australian University Staff Associations, with similar bodies active at the advanced education and TAFE levels to secure better industrial conditions and protect members from discriminatory employment practices. Salaries are fixed by an industrial tribunal at federal level, and are subject to automatic cost-of-living adjustments.

Universities are autonomous institutions governed by a university council which generally consist of representatives of academic, professional, and industrial communities as well as some faculty members and students. The council selects the chief executive, the vice-chancellor. The position of chancellor is largely a ceremonial one. A grouping of academic departments (disciplines) form faculties headed by a dean who is appointed by the university council or elected by the faculty professors. The heads of departments and generally tenured appointments are made by the council. The administrative structure at colleges of advanced education (CAEs) follows a similar pattern with the chief executive being the director or principal.

Undergraduate Studies

In general, Australian universities offer three-year first degrees such as the B.A., B.Sc., and B.Econ. The first two cover a wide range of potential specializations, of the kind common in Western multi-purpose educational institutions. The general language of instruction is English. Many CAEs offer similar degrees, and also provide three-year undergraduate diplomas and two-year "associate diplomas" in a number of applied fields such as accountancy, engineering, food catering, health and textiles.

Selection for entry to institutions of higher education is competitive within the programs nominated, based on the tertiary aggregate obtained by school leavers as described in the previous section, or on the particular mature age entry conditions laid down by each institution. In the former case, most states have central authorities which collate aggregates, match them with applicants' declared program preferences, and coordinate offers of places. In 1988 there were over 400,000 students nationwide in the higher educational system.

Degree structures vary widely, but Australia stands between the highly specialized English model and the widely elective American model. Students develop a "major" area of study which typically commits from a third to a half of the courses they take, leaving room for elective choices in other areas, usually quite close to the major (e.g. in the humanities, or social sciences, or physical sciences). Degrees at "honors" level usually require a fourth year, and have till now only been offered by universities. The fourth year involves further course-work in the major area, together with a small, original research dissertation.

The academic year comprises 26-34 teaching weeks plus final assessment periods, and runs generally from late February to late November. Some institutions still teach subjects through a three-term year, but the majority split the academic year into two semesters. Some professional programs, such as medicine and teaching, utilize additional periods in the calendar year for field experience. Running intensive courses for credit during summer is not common, but several universities have a long tradition of "extension" courses and "summer schools," offering the general public courses for interest rather than academic credit.

Tuition fees for Australian residents were re-introduced in 1989, using the principle of a deferred payment or graduate tax which takes effect when the student's salary in later working life reaches a specified level. This is called the Higher Education Contribution Scheme, and the typical charge is currently US$190 for each unit in an eight-unit year. Students may be eligible in whole or in part for government financial assistance, known as Austudy, subject to a means test. Otherwise they depend on parental support and earning from vacation work. Alternatively, some government departments and private firms provide cadetships for promising employees. Students from overseas countries have, since 1986, being required to pay full fees at enrolment. The charge for an individual unit in an eight-unit year ranges from US$7,000 in areas such as arts and economics to US$20,000 for medicine and veterinary studies. Most universities and several former CAEs have a limited amount of residential accommodation available, ranging in type from traditional halls or colleges to self-contained flats, but the dominant pattern is for students to commute from home each day. The average weekly cost for full board and lodging ranges from US$4,800-7,000, the higher prices being in Sydney and Melbourne metropolitan areas.

Several professional programs require either one or two years of general study in arts or science before professional studies begin, or a minimum initial training of four to six years before award of the first degree(s). A minimum training of four years is common for such fields as dentistry, engineering, law, psychology, and theology. Secondary teaching usually involves taking a Diploma in Education after an appropriate first degree. A five-year minimum applies to veterinary studies, while medicine simultaneously awards the M.B. and the B.S. after six. Interesting variants are the programs (Murdoch University) which awards a B.Vet.Biol. in the veterinary sciences after three years, and the B.V.M.S. after a further two. Another university (Newcastle) presents a medical program oriented to general practice lasting five years. The finer details can be studied in the *Commonwealth Universities' Yearbook* produced in London by the Association of Commonwealth Universities).

Traditionally, selection of staff in universities has been by open international advertisement, and other tertiary institutions have increasingly followed this example. The staff of most multi-purpose institutions in Australia is therefore noticeably multicultural. The usual levels of academic appointment are tutor, senior tutor; lecturer, senior lecturer; and associate professor, professor. Most positions from lecturer upwards are tenurable. Internal promotion can occur within the tutor and lecturer ranges, but not between them. Except for personal chairs, professorships are filled by open advertisement, not internal promotion. Australian academics have traditionally been expected to take sabbatical leave, now approximating six months every six years, in order to interact with scholars in their disciplines in other places.

Advanced Studies and Research

Universities offer research opportunities in all fields and training to Ph.D. level. It is now common practice in many fields to offer two kinds of master's degrees. The first is based on a research dissertation. The other is based mainly on course-work with a smaller research project, and is usually geared to professional development. Most Ph.D's are highly specialized and based on original research. Access to research degrees is usually dependent on very good results at honors level. The fields of study available may be ascertained by consulting the *Commonwealth Universities' Yearbook.* Institutions in the CAE sector are currently expanding their programs in research and higher degrees.

Most higher degrees can now be taken in either the full-time or part-time mode. Selection for both is competitive. Good Australian applicants can seek support for full-time study through the Commonwealth Postgraduate Research Award (CPRA) scheme. Several institutions administer comparable scholarship schemes internally, many of which are open to foreign students as well as nationals. The Australian International Development Aid Bureau assists many postgraduate students from developing countries to study in Australia.

Sometimes it is possible, particularly in fields which attract large research grants, typically in the physical and medical sciences, to obtain a research assistantship which allows time for a part-time research degree enrolment. Postdoctoral fellowships are also available in many universities, but they are usually non-tenurable because they depend on the soft money of research grants.

Traditionally, the research activities of higher education institutions have been generated by individual staff or small teams, rather than by institutional nomination or government requirement. Historically, only two Australian universities, Sydney and Western Australia, have had access to substantial benefactions outside the government funding system. Most of the available funding has come from government sources, and recently there have been moves on the part of the federal (Labor) government of Robert Hawke to indicate national priorities that will cause those applications which are deemed to be more relevant to them to be viewed more favorably than others.

Also, in 1988, the federal government abolished the practice of funding universities and colleges of advanced education at different levels and put them on the same financial footing, diverting the funds released by this move into a common pool for research purposes. Any institution may now bid for research grants through the Australian Research Council. In keeping with this new entrepreneurial approach, higher education institutions are being urged, as in Britain, to become more active in seeking financial support for research from private business and industry.

ISSUES AND TRENDS

The most noticeable trends in Australian education at the present time are tighter economic management and an emphasis on national goals and vocational preparation. These are familiar leitmotifs to readers in other industrially advanced Western countries, where, like Australia, population growth has been slowing, and the economy has been undergoing reorganization to cope with the technological competition of other countries. In higher education particularly, a special Australian variation on the theme is growing tension between the goals of the National government and the aspirations of state governments who resent the strong centralism of the former.

In regard to schools generally, where as an older generation of policy makers spoke of the liberal education of the whole person and championed more progressive and individualized methods, the present generation uses the language of management and accountability. There is much talk about "getting back to the basics", though local research does not support the claim that "standards" have been deteriorating.

There is frequent reference to the "youth problem". Adolescent delinquency, drug culture, and high unemployment tend to be blamed on the victims rather than on their elders. Politicians respond by working for higher retention rates in high schools, more vocationally-oriented training, and job creation schemes, without acknowledging that the real problems are a declining sense of community and family stability, and a common view that young people have nuisance value only in a capital intensive economy which has less need for their labor. The overall percentage of unemployed has been reduced to single figures after a blow-out in the early eighties but the 16-21 cohort is still in double figures.

Research on a wide range of educational issues springs constantly from higher education institutions and the Australian Council for Educational Research. Internationally, Australia has participated actively in studies by UNESCO and the Organization for Economic Co-operation and Development. Fraternal links exist between the Australian Association for Research in Education and kindred bodies in other countries, and a number of internationally recognized educational journals emanate from Australia, including the *Australian Journal of Education, Curriculum Perspectives, Educational Philosophy and Theory,* and the *Journal of Christian Education.*

BIBLIOGRAPHY

Austin, A. G. *Australian Education, 1788-1900.* Melbourne: Pitman, 1961.

Beswick, David G. "The Role of Government in Higher Education in Australia". Research Working Paper 87.16. Center for the Study of Higher Education, University of Melbourne, 1987.

Harman, G. S., et al., eds. *Academia Becalmed: Australian Tertiary Education in the Aftermath of Expansion.* Canberra: ANU Press, 1980.

Harman, Grant, and Smart, Don. *Federal Intervention in Australian Education.* Melbourne: Georgian House, 1982.

Higher Education: A Policy Statement. Circulated by the Hon. J. S. Dawkins, MP, Minister for Employment, Education and Training. Canberra: Australian Government Publishing Service, 1988.

AUSTRIA

by
Erich Leitner
Chairman, Department of Higher Education and Professor
University of Educational Studies in Klagenfurt, Austria

BACKGROUND

The history and growth of higher education in Austria has been greatly influenced by the political and spiritual developments in Europe. The opening of the first Austrian university in Vienna in 1365 is a classic example. It was indeed a reflection of the struggle of the then Austrian dynasty headed by Rudolf IV of Habsburg to win the political rivalry with the King of Bohemia, who in 1348 founded the first university in a German speaking area in Europe. Then in the sixteenth and the seventeenth centuries additional universities came into being under the influence of the spiritual leadership. The Jesuit order established one university in Graz in 1585 and another in Innsbruck in 1669. The Order of the Benedictines opened a university in Salzburg in 1622, which however remained only as a theological faculty from 1850 to 1962.

As the nineteenth century unfolded, higher education institutions expanded rapidly, prompted by the needs of an aspiring industrial society for highly qualified technical and business professionals. Institutions established during this period include the University of Engineering *(Die Technischen Hochschule)* of Vienna in 1815 and of Graz in 1811, the University of Mining *(Die Montanistischen Hochschule)* of Leoben in 1840, the University of World Commerce *(Die Hochschule fur Welthandel)* of Vienna in 1898, the University of Veterinary Medicine *(Die Veterinarmedizinische Hochschule)* of Vienna in 1767, and the University of Agriculture *(Die Hochschule fur Bodenkultur)* of Vienna in 1872.

As Europe went through its biggest expansion in higher education, in the sixties and the seventies, Austria did not lag behind. New institutions were established to meet the increasing demand for higher education: the University of Salzburg was re-established in 1963, the University of Linz was founded in 1964, and the Klagenfurt University of Educational Studies was established in 1970. Today, Austria has twelve universities.

Structure of Education

The conceptual basis of the Austrian higher education institutions is the philosophy of Humboldt. The unity of research and teaching, "education by scholarship", freedom of teaching, and freedom of learning have been very basic to the functioning of the Austrian university. Where Austrian institutions deviate from

Humboldt's philosophy is in the inclusion of professional studies as part of the university's role and also in the relationship between the state and the university (autonomy).

The Austrian universities function on the basis of laws enacted by the National Council of the Republic of Austria. All Austrian Universities are centrally governed federal institutions and have little autonomy in financial and personnel matter. The authority for nominations and appointments of professors including tenure decisions rest with the secretary of science and research who implements the relevant procedures established by the government. The secretary of science and research coordinates the functioning of the universities, in consultation with other public agencies such as the Conference of University Presidents, the Federal Conference of Scientific Personnel and the Austrian University Student Organization.

Advancement of science and research forms a vital element in the development priorities of the present Austrian government and it is one area that has received increased funding in the recent years, inspite of the government's general austerity measures. This increased funding has been earmarked especially for innovative projects in the field of "technology of the future" and for development of new courses of study. The federal ministry is required, every three years, to present a comprehensive report to the National Council of the Republic of Austria on the achievements and problems of the Austrian higher educational system.

Austrian universities and colleges are financed predominantly by the government from tax revenues. The expenditure for "science and research" in 1986 was 16.2 billion schillings, or about 3 percent of the Austrian national budget. Of this amount, 4.5 billion schillings (27.5 percent) went towards the operating costs of the universities, 3.4 billion (21.5 percent) for university and hospital construction, 7 billion schillings (43 percent) for personnel expenditures and 1.2 billion (7.7 percent) for science and research projects. University related expenditure per student was about 42,000 schillings. In addition to public funding, the Austrian universities and colleges also received 527 million schillings as grants, gifts, and foreign student tuition. No tuition is charged from native students. The Austrian government encourages universities and professors to carryout scientific research projects for various public and private enterprises as a means of generating additional revenue for their institutions.

SECONDARY EDUCATION

Two streams of secondary education prepare students for the upper secondary diploma *(matura)*, which is a precondition for university admission. First group of high schools prepare students for work emphasizing technical and economic qualifications and is attended for five years (ages 14-19) immediately following compulsory schooling. Second group of high schools teach general education and is attended for eight years (ages 10-18) after elementary school. From the school year 1988-89 there are in fact three types of upper secondary, each emphasizing a different curriculum: secondary school (emphasis on languages), non classical secondary school (emphasis on mathematics and science), and commercial secondary school.

Working Austrians who are employed during the day have the opportunity to attend upper secondary at night and obtain the upper secondary diploma *(matura)*. Adults who have special professional or non-professional qualifications also have the option of taking a special university entrance exam, although the subjects offered in this exam are somewhat limited. About 1 percent of the students at Austrian universities have gained admission in this manner. In addition, any Austrian has the right to attend individual classes of his choice as a guest auditor (not necessarily the right to complete a university or academic degree).

HIGHER EDUCATION

Institutions

Twelve universities and six art academies form the nucleus of higher (tertiary) education in Austria. They are all public institutions under the jurisdiction of the Federal Ministry of Science and Research. There are no private universities. Four universities are in Vienna, and others are spread out in the country: University of Graz in Graz, University of Innsbruck in Innsbruck, University of Salzburg in Salzburg, University of Linz in Linz, Technical University of Graz in Graz, University of Mining in Leoben, and University of Educational Studies in Klagenfurt. Universities in Vienna include the Technical University as well as universities of agriculture, veterinary science, and economics.

Of the six art academies, three (academies of fine arts, applied arts, and music and theatre arts), are in Vienna. There is an Academy of Music and Theatre Arts in Graz, *Mozarteum* in Salzburg, and Academy of Artistic and Industrial Design in Linz. Some universities and academies have research study facilities more than others.

In addition to the universities and art academies, there exists a number of public post secondary institutions for the education of public school teachers (primary and lower secondary level), social workers, military officers, and medical professionals other than physicians. These institutions are independent of the universities or art academies both organizationally and administratively, and are not under the jurisdiction of the Federal Ministry of Science and Research. They are administered by the Federal Ministry of Instruction, Art, and Sport. Also there is an Academy of Administration for training of public servants and it falls within the jurisdiction of the Federal Chancellory. Many professional agencies and private organizations provide continuing educational opportunities with a variety of good quality programs. This aspect of adult education is experiencing a great demand and expansion at this time.

Parallel to the academic administrative structure, the universities and academies also have a government administration which is responsible for legal and other matters relating to finance, curriculum, personnel, and campus facilities. At the head of this administration is a civil servant knowledgeable in law and appointed by the secretary of science and research. He has authority to act independently and reports to the Central Administration Office for Science of the Federal Government.

In spite of the central control by the federal government and limited autonomy in administration, finance, and personnel matters, the Austrian universities enjoy a large degree of discretion in research and teaching. This is ensured by the special status of the professors who have full responsibility for their respective areas. The professors can use their full discretion in the selection of research projects and on the content and method of teaching. A new set of regulations which came into operation in 1988 define the roles of teaching staff:

1. Professors with a teaching certificate (teaching certificate or *venia docendi* is an academic degree acquired within the university system based on special research achievements after the doctorate). This group include the following: (a) Full professors, who are top ranking academics selected by the secretary of science and research from among three candidates recommended by the university and are appointed for life. They are responsible for research in their respective fields and a teaching load of six hours per week. They retire from teaching at the age of sixty-eight but can continue their research skills with full salary for life. (b) Associate professors, who are appointed by the secretary of science and research based on the recommendation of the university and are required to be natives of Austria possessing a certificate of teaching. Their teaching responsibilities are generally eight hours per week. They retire at the age of sixty-five. (c) Assistant professors, who are professors who have a certificate of teaching and tenure. They have only research responsibilities, but can be called on for teaching. They retire at the age of sixty-five.

2. Professors without teaching privileges, falling into the following categories: (a) University assistants who are required to have a degree when entering employment, assist in research and teaching. They are employed under contract for a limited time (2-4 years). They may be considered for permanent employment on completion of a doctorate. (b) Study assistants, who are students assisting in research and teaching on a year's contract. (c) Upper secondary teachers in college employment. They have a qualification to teach (upper secondary level) including an academic degree in a special teaching field (e.g. linguistics). Their teaching requirement is thirteen hours per week.

With the exception of the upper secondary teachers in university employment, most university teachers begin their careers at the university primarily in research activities, and their professional advancement is a reflection of their achievement in research, with teaching playing only a secondary role. This bias for research, a part of the Humboldt University concept, permeates the entire Austrian university system, and has lead to some neglect of the teaching role. Recent years, however, have seen recognition of this deficiency and a shift towards teaching is now becoming noticeable. In the case of art academies, research is not a factor.

Although centrally controlled by the government, the Austrian universities and academies have considerable autonomy in matters of research, teaching, and administration. The professors, assistants, and students participate in various committees generally in a ratio of 2:1:1. The universities are headed by presidents who are elected from among the full professors for a two-year term. Universities having several faculties (Universities of Vienna, Graz, Innsbruck, Linz and Salzburg and the Technical Universities of Vienna and Graz) have a dean as head of each faculty.

The smallest administrative unit of a university is an "institute" which is responsible for the management of research and teaching assignments in a given area. Some institutes are sub divided into departments. Each institute is governed by a board of directors elected for a two-year term by the professors associated with the institute. In 1987, there were 814 such institutes at Austrian universities. Besides these, there is a small number of pure research institutes and two inter-university institutes. Annually, the universities present to the ministry, a projection of their financial and personnel requirements (budget and position roster) for the following three years, based on expected research and teaching needs. They also submit proposals for hiring personnel and for the renewal of employees' contracts. In the academies of art, the focus is on the development of arts and the training of the artistic generation. Teacher qualifications in this case is not tied to performance in research.

In 1987, the teacher population in university employment consisted of 1,152 full university professors, 580 associate professors, 5,168 university assistants and about 600 high school teachers. Of the 5,168 university assistants, about 1,500 have the full licence to teach. Teaching staff is recruited from among assistant professors, university assistants, and external candidates from industry, administration, etc.

In 1966, the General University Studies Act outlined the aims of Austrian university education in the following manner:
- Development of the sciences and education of the nextgeneration of scientists.
- Scientific training of students, which include introducing university students to the scientific approach and to the tasks of research, training of students in the scientific methodology, and development of students' critical thinking and capacity to act independently.
- Education by scholarship. Developing students' understanding of significance of his field of study in relation to science in its entirety, significance of scholarship in relation to the culture in general, intellectual integrity, tolerance, and responsibility.

Admission to Austrian universities is open to upper secondary degree *(Matura)* holders. Certain specific requirement may apply to students desiring to major in some areas (such as knowledge of Latin for philology or knowledge in demonstrative geometry for technical studies). These may be fulfilled by taking additional courses during the first year of university. Only art academies limit the number of students for admission and require corresponding admittance tests.

Programs and Degrees

Austrian universities offer over 100 different courses of study and several combined inter-disciplinary programs, which may be taken aside from the regular courses of study. A number of additional courses, focusing on new professional fields, are being explored. Austrians also have the opportunity to enroll for correspondent courses at the distant university in Hagen (West Germany). The correspondent students are counseled in Austria at the student centers in Vienna, Bregeuz, and Klagenfurt.

The length of studies at Austrian universities vary, depending on the subject, and is about 8-10 semesters (winter semester from the beginning of October to the end of January, summer semester from the beginning of March to the end of June). However, it is not uncommon for the allotted time of study to exceed the minimum requirements by up to 50 percent. Every field of study is divided in to at least two parts. Some subjects (for example medicine, veterinary medicine, and technology) consist of three parts and students, after passing any of the parts, may seek a transfer to another university and receive full college credit. All university studies lead first to a master's degree and then to a doctorate excepting in medicine. In medicine, the first degree is a doctorate.

The master's degree studies are divided into two or three sections. The first section usually takes about four semesters and ends with the first master's examination. The next section takes two to four semesters and lead towards the academic degree of *magister*. In technical fields, the academic degree is "graduate engineer". The academic degree is awarded on the basis of a dissertation as well as a final examination. Throughout their studies, students have to demonstrate their progress by passing examinations at various stages of their courses.

The courses at Austrian universities are centrally regulated by legislation *(Rahmenplan)*. However, within these regulations, individual universities can still set up guidelines covering duration, course content, and examination requirements for specific courses. Study commissions, autonomous groups of professors, assistants, and students have an input in the determination of the structure of studies. Even though the intent of the legislation was to bring uniformity to studies and to ensure comparable level of qualifications, the Austrian system of studies is extensively influenced by the professors' teaching at individual universities, their scientific orientation, and the standard of testing. The concept of academic freedom, thus, leads to substantial regional deviations in the curriculum as well as differing standard of testing.

In the case of independent scientific studies leading to doctorates, and the corresponding preparation at master's level, professors have considerable latitude in designing the curriculum. For each case, the curriculum is established on an agreement between the doctoral candidate writing the thesis and his professor. Doctoral studies in Austria take at least four semesters, and is substantially exceeded in most cases. Doctoral candidates are required to prepare a thesis which has to be approved by at least two professors and a testing commission chaired by the president of the university. The degree of "doctor" (Dr.) is conferred on successful candidates.

The universities in Austria carryout the scholarly and theoretical preparation of students for academic professions. The practical aspect of the training process takes place on the job by pursuing an additional period of training, usually controlled by professional bodies. The graduates of medicine (M.D.) can therefore only practice on their own after they have completed an internship of three years subsequent to their university studies. A graduate of law has to practice at least nine months in court and five additional years in a law office before being eligible for an attorney's examination, to become an independent attorney. Teachers at schools of upper secondary require one year of probation with simultaneous studies in education. Comparable requirements exist for graduates of other technical fields who plan to work on their own.

The language of instruction at the universities in Austria is German. Recently some subjects are offered in English, mainly in doctoral programs.

University students in Austria are free to choose any subject or university of their liking. They have considerable freedom in organizing their study programs and in changing their fields of study. This invariably places a great premium on self discipline and the ability to organize oneself. A great deal of information is made available to the student on the curriculum and regulations affecting examinations but no timetable is specified for completion of individual sections for final examinations. As a consequence, the dropout rate is exceedingly high (about half of all university students do not graduate).

Austrian universities do not charge any tuition from Austrian students but the students must take care of their own living expenses. The biggest part of a student's expenditure is for housing and food. The cost for books and other educational materials is less significant. Austrian universities are generally located in large cities and have little influence on the lifestyle of the students. In many university towns, private and public dormitories are available to the students at reasonable cost. However, only 20 percent of the student population live in them with the rest of them depending on private housing or living at home when they attend a hometown university. The use of public transportation from living quarters to the university is free for college students in Austria. Every university has a cafeteria which offers student meals for comparatively low prices.

Most university students are supported by their parents and the parents receive public assistance for children under twenty-five enrolled in college. In the recent years, the number of university students who receive an income from some kind of employment has greatly increased. The government also grants scholarship assistance to university students whose parents cannot fully finance their children's education, provided the students maintain requisite grades. In 1987, 9 per cent of the Austrian college students received such scholarships. Students who excel in their studies receive achievement scholarships irrespective of the financial situation of the parents. Certain organizations, corporations, and foundations also award scholarships.

A considerable number of foreign students are enrolled at Austrian higher education institutions. In the winter semester of 1986-87 the number rose to 15,126. They form about 9 percent of the total student body, and their enrollment is especially high at the art academies. Numberwise, most of the foreign students are at the University of Vienna and the Technical University of Vienna. Any foreign student who has the qualifications to attend a university in his homeland may study in Austria. Numerous bilateral and international agreements exist relative to transfer of academic credits for study or study sections. The tuition fee for foreign students is 4,000 schillings. However, students from third world countries, conventional refugees, and recipients of scholarships from public corporations are exempt from this fee. All universities offer classes to foreign students for learning the German language.

Research

Austrian Universities are establishments of research and teaching. The conceptual idea of the university, "education by scholarship", is that research is very basic to the existence of the university and teaching is seen as a means to achieve a goal by preparing the student for scientific research (participation of the student in the process of acquiring knowledge). Thus independent scientific research (dissertation) is a necessity excepting in the case of studies at an art academy or in medicine.

The principal bearers of the torch of research are the professors, who by themselves or in teams formulate and deal with scientific enquiry and publish their work, make up the biggest part of the Austrian research establishment. A significant contribution to research is also found in the dissertations of the university students.

The professors at the institutes and departments coordinate the research activities at their institutions. Participation in research by the faculty is on a voluntary basis. Development of scientific research and scholarship is supported by the Ministry for Science and Research through special funds. A non-profit entity funded through taxation supports research plans of individuals or groups of researchers including publication of scientific material. There is also a similar research development fund for industry, specifically designated for the promotion of scientific development work in the industrial sector.

Austria has been striving for several years to intensify scientific research links between universities and the industry. Efforts in this direction include regular publishing of research work, arrangements for university assistants to work for a period of two years in the development of industrial research, and financial assistance as well as business development advice to scientists who desire to start new businesses based on research ideas. To enhance the transfer of technology between university and industry, universities have established special contact stations, the so-called "external institutes".

An important goal of the Austrian university and research system is strong interaction between Austrian universities and the international scientific and research community. International mobility of Austrian university teachers and students is very much encouraged and there are several bilateral agreements with many nations on scientific and cultural exchanges and on other aspects of higher education and research.

Austria is also a signee of the UNESCO convention with respect to recognition of curriculum, diplomas, and academic degrees of the European states; and the European agreement on the length of university studies, equivalence of academic degrees, and university grades.

ISSUES AND TRENDS

At the moment, the development of research at the universities receive a lot of public attention and recognition because of its importance for supporting the industrial growth of the country. The most pressing problem is the large increase in the number of university students that tax the limited resources of the university. The number of university students in the Austrian university system has risen rapidly within the last thirty years, increasing from 25,000 in 1957-58 to 173,000 in 1987-88. Women comprise 44 percent of the student body. About 18 percent of an age group (cohort) enter university. This development, even with the extensive effort of the universities, far surpassed the growth of teaching staff and facilities. Originally, the university system had been designed to oversee a smaller student body giving the students sufficient freedom in setting up their curriculum. The tremendous influx of students in the recent years has defeated that purpose and resulted in student anonymity and insufficient counseling. The student dropout rate has reached about 50 percent and there are complains from employers that the graduates are not fully equipped for the real world. Of course the lack of practical experience which is especially targeted by industry for complains does really reflect a deterioration in the quality of university education as "scholarship" remains the basic goal of the university. Professional knowledge is largely to be acquired in an "on the job" situation.

The future demand for individual study fields vary to a great degree. At the moment there is a great oversupply of academically qualified upper secondary school teachers, medical doctors, lawyers, and graduates in the liberal arts. At the same time there is a noticeable shortage of graduates in the technical fields. The information given to freshmen about future job potential has not made the expected shift of students toward study fields for which there is a demand. The result is a considerable number of jobless college graduates, who cannot find employment to suit their education. Students are free to choose their field of studies, but if the choice is out of line with the market demand, their career options become very limited.

BIBLIOGRAPHY

Bundesministerium für Wissenschaft und Forschung. *Hochschulbericht 1969, 1972 (Bd 1, 2), 1975, 1978, 1981, 1984, 1987 (Bd 1, 2).* Wien, 1969-1987.

Bundesministerium für Wissenschaft und Forschung. *Das Österreichische Hochschulsystem.* Wien, 1986.

Clement, W., Ahamer P. F., and Kaluza, A. *Bildungsexpansion und Arbeitsmarkt.* Wien, 1980.

Drischel, O. *Die Internationale Abkommen uber Gleichwertigkeiten.* Wien, 1987.

Engelbrecht, H. *Geschichte des Österreichischen Bildungswesens.* Bd 1-5. Wien, 1983-1988.

Hollinger, S.   "Planning Communication Between University and Practice. University Studies and Professionalization of Study Courses in Austria". *Western European Education* 19, 1, (1987): 32-41.

Leitner, E.   "Current Trends in Austrian Higher Education: The Call for a New Reform". *European Journal of Education* 14, 1, (1979): 59-67.

Leitner, E.   "University and Professional Education: The Case of Austrian Universities". *International Journal of Innovative Higher Education* 4, 1/2, (1987): 27-31.

OECD. *Die Hochschulen in Österreich.* Bd 1, 2. Wien, 1975.

OECD.   "Reviews of Educational Policies for Education: Austria".   *Higher Education and Research.* Paris, 1976.

THE BAHAMAS

by
Keva M. Bethel
Principal
College of The Bahamas, The Bahamas

BACKGROUND

In The Bahamas, the provision of higher education on any comprehensive and sustained basis has been a relatively recent development. Although throughout the twentieth century, and even earlier, sporadic attempts were made to introduce some forms of education or training beyond the level of secondary schooling, it is only in the past thirty years that consistent measures have been taken to incorporate postsecondary programs into the country's educational system.

The development of education at the postsecondary level has been driven largely by the Bahamian government's recognition of the need for better educated, more highly skilled citizens to meet the demands of a rapidly expanding and increasingly sophisticated economy. Further, the provision of such opportunities has been essential to support the effective implementation of the government's policy of "Bahamianization", i.e. the replacement, wherever possible, of foreign nationals in the work force by appropriately qualified Bahamians. This reduction of an excessive reliance on outside expertise at almost every level of the labor force is deemed crucial to the full participation of Bahamians in their nation's economic development and in the shaping of their own destiny.

Traditionally, the provision of higher education has been the responsibility of the Bahamian government. Recently, however, there have sprung up numerous private institutions offering, particularly, courses and programs in business related subjects.

PRIMARY AND SECONDARY EDUCATION

In The Bahamas, children begin their primary schooling at the age of five. The primary level of education spans a period of six years, and aims at developing in all children skills of literacy and numeracy, an understanding of the physical and social environment, and a sense of cultural identity.

There are government and independent primary schools distributed throughout the islands of The Bahamas. In addition, there are a number of all-age schools (located for the most part in the island outside of New Providence), which offer both the primary and secondary level of schooling.

Secondary education, which is normally begun at the age of eleven, is compulsory to age fourteen and is provided in public and private high schools. It

45

is interesting to note that, despite the legal school leaving age, most Bahamian students remain in secondary schools to the end of the senior high level, i.e. to age sixteen or seventeen.

Government supported secondary schools are found in most of the major islands of The Bahamas, while private high schools are located primarily in Nassau and in Freeport.

Almost all the private secondary schools are affiliated with religious denominations, and there are schools supported by the Anglican, Baptist, Catholic, Evangelical, Lutheran, Methodist, and Seventh-Day Adventist churches. There is, however, one non- sectarian private high school in New Providence.

The secondary school curriculum in both private and public schools covers the usual range of academic subjects as well as art, music, physical education, and a variety of practical and vocational courses. In certain of the public high schools, considerable emphasis is placed upon vocational preparation via programs in agriculture, industrial arts, secretarial studies, hotel and catering subjects, and the like. In all Bahamian high schools the language of instruction is English, except in foreign language classes where part or all of the teaching may be given in the language concerned.

The duration of secondary schooling is generally six years in public and some private schools, and five years in certain other private institutions which offer an optional sixth year for College bound students. In both public and private systems, students sit overseas examinations at the end of their secondary school careers. They generally include the British General Certificate of Education Ordinary Level examinations, Royal Society of Arts and Pitman's examinations. In some schools, students also sit the U.S. Scholastic Aptitude Test.

In government secondary schools there are no tuition fees. In private high schools, fees can range from approximately US$350 to US$1,500 per term. The school year, which runs from September to June, is divided into three terms. Fee-paying students are generally supported by their parents. Financial aid and scholarship assistance are available in some schools for needy children.

Teachers for both public and private high schools are recruited both locally and from abroad. Positions are advertised in the national and foreign press, applicants are screened and, when possible, interviewed before appointment. Teachers for public high schools are appointed by the Bahamas Public Service Commission. Most teaching staffs in both public and private high schools are international in composition, with teachers coming from The Bahamas, The Caribbean, North America, Great Britain, and other Commonwealth countries.

Foreign student enrollment is generally small in both public and private high schools. As there are no boarding schools in The Bahamas, most foreign students are children of foreign nationals residing locally.

Postsecondary education preparing students for university admission did not exist in Bahamas till the 1950s. Persons wishing to pursue university degrees had to leave The Bahamas for universities abroad (in the United Kingdom, U.S., Canada or the West Indies) and entrance into those universities required examination passes at Higher School Certificate or General Certificate of Education Advanced Level (U.K.), i. e. at a level beyond that of the final year of regular high school in The

Bahamas. Many individuals were obliged to prepare for those examinations at schools outside The Bahamas.

In 1951, an abortive attempt was made to introduce higher school certificate programs at one of the private high schools in Nassau. Later in that decade, however, a small Sixth-Form was established at the then sole public high school (known simply as the Government High School). Work leading to the University of London General Certificate of Education Advanced Level examinations was further expanded at that institution when, in 1960, it acquired new facilities with laboratories adequate to accommodate the teaching of science subjects at that level.

In the late 1960s, a generous scholarship scheme was introduced by the newly elected Progressive Liberal Party government. This government, the first in The Bahamas's history to be representative of the majority of the population, saw the need to encourage more high school students to undertake Sixth- Form work in order to proceed to higher levels of education. As numbers of such students increased, other high schools added Sixth-Form programs of their own.

In 1975, the Advanced Level programs of the Government High School were incorporated into the curriculum of the College of The Bahamas and were offered through the divisions of humanities, natural sciences, and social sciences.

HIGHER EDUCATION

Programs and Degrees

The College of The Bahamas is the main institution through which higher education is provided in The Bahamas. This institution was established in 1974 by Act of Parliament and brought together under one central administration the work of four existing institutions: two teacher's colleges, a technical college and the Sixth-Form of the Government High School.

The College was founded to serve as the apex of the Bahamian educational system, and was intended to "meet the special needs of The Bahamas in education, training, and national development" (Ministry of Education 1972:10). Its main campus is located in Nassau but there is also a center in Freeport. In addition, the college maintains a network of adult education (evening) institutes throughout the major islands of The Bahamas.

The college is publicly financed, and is community oriented in its offerings. The private sector, however, provides important support in a number of ways. These range from the funding of special projects aimed at improving facilities and learning resources, to the provision of scholarships for needy students.

Courses and programs at the College of The Bahamas are offered on a modular basis. The academic year, which runs from September to July, consists of two sixteen-week semesters and an eight-week summer session.

There are six teaching divisions which embrace a wide range of academic and vocational disciplines. These are the divisions of business and administrative studies, education, humanities, natural sciences, social sciences and technology. In addition, there is a Division of Continuing Education and Extension Services and a Library Division.

Although plans are currently underway for the extension of certain programs to the bachelor's degree level, the college is still essentially a two-year institution offering, through full or part-time study, programs leading to Associate of Arts or Associate of Applied Science degrees which may be used for university transfer or job-entry purposes. There are also a number of diploma and certificate programs in specific professional or vocational areas such as banking, social work, public administration, word processing, and computer data processing.

A three-year University of the West Indies Bachelor of Education degree program for serving teachers is taught through the Education Division, and a variety of programs are offered in cooperation with government ministries or community agencies. These include (a) programs leading to professional banking qualifications, offered in conjunction with the Bahamas Institute of Bankers; (b) Associate of Arts degree programs in nursing and environmental health offered jointly with the Ministry of Health; (c) programs in social work offered in association with the Department of Social Services; and (d) programs in public administration offered jointly with the Training Division of the Ministry of Public Personnel.

The Division of Continuing Education provides specially designed short courses, programs, seminars, and workshops for organizations in the public and private sectors, as well as a wide variety of general interest courses for the community at large. The division also administers the network of evening institutes, and has been a participant in a regional project in distance education funded by the Organization of American States.

The college maintains ongoing relationships with the public and private sectors through a variety of instructional programs and other joint projects. These relationships are further strengthened by a cooperative education program, which makes a period of on-the-job experience an integral part of many of the vocational and career oriented programs. In addition, representatives of government ministries, professions, business, and industry serve on the college's many program advisory committees, and assist through this involvement in the planning and monitoring of the institution's work.

The college is governed by a nine-member council whose members are appointed annually by the Minister of Education. Authority to approve academic policies, programs, and courses has been delegated by the council to the academic board which is made up of divisional chairpersons, senior administrators, and representatives of the student government. The senior administrative officers of the institution are the principal, vice-principal, registrar, bursar, academic dean, and assistant registrar. The divisions are administered by chairpersons and assistant chairpersons who are elected from among divisional members. They are assisted by program and subject coordinators.

Admission to the college's associate degree programs, requires five General Certificate of Education "Ordinary" Level subject passes at grade C or better, or the equivalent. Passes in English language and mathematics must be included. Candidates for admission are also required to take an entrance/placement examination in English and mathematics. There are provisions for mature student entry, and for the making up of academic deficiencies. Diploma and certificate programs generally require slightly lower qualifications for entry. Admission to an advanced certificate or postgraduate diploma programs normally requires possession of a bachelor's degree or the equivalent. Candidates for admission to the University of the West Indies Bachelor of Education program must possess an Associate of Arts degree and/or appropriate teacher's certificate, and must perform at an acceptable level on an entrance examination set by the university. The language of instruction for all programs is English, although foreign language courses may be conducted in the languages concerned.

At the College of The Bahamas, tuition fees are currently charged at the rate of US$25 per credit, for Bahamian students, and US$50 per credit for non-Bahamians. There are some additional charges in the form of lab fees, student activities and insurance fees, and identity card fees. For students experiencing financial difficulties, there exists extensive financial aid through government scholarships, bursaries or grants, private scholarships, or a college-financed work/study program.

The college is not a residential institution. A limited number of college-subsidized residential units are available, however, for students from other islands and from abroad.

In the fall semester of 1988, there were approximately 2,000 full-and part-time students enrolled at the college. These ranged in age from fifteen to over fifty, with females outnumbering males two to one. Of students enrolled only thirty-four were non-Bahamian.

There is a wide range of clubs and organizations providing extracurricular activities for students. In addition, all enrolled students are automatically members of the College of The Bahamas Union of Students (COBUS), which each year elects a student government whose representatives sit on all major boards and committees of the institution.

The college's teaching staff is made up of individuals from a variety of countries and backgrounds. Approximately one-half of the 135 full-time lecturers are Bahamian nationals. The rest are drawn from countries in the Caribbean, from the United States, Canada and Great Britain, and from countries in Africa and Asia. The college also employs a large number of part-time instructors drawn from the Bahamian community. Through their instructors, therefore, students are exposed to a rich cultural and ethnic mix.

Generally, members of faculty are recruited through advertisements placed in Bahamian and foreign journals. Applicants are screened and shortlisted by relevant divisions and then are recommended by an Appointments Board to the College Council.

It was in the field of teacher education that the earliest higher education initiatives were taken in The Bahamas. As far back as in 1835, a school commission appointed by the governor of the period recommended that a training program be introduced to raise the standards of teachers in the schools. The resultant attempt at establishing a "Normal School" for this purpose, however, proved unsuccessful as did other initiatives taken in the following decades, and little was actually achieved.

Subsequently, several attempts were made to establish a teacher training program but it was only in 1950 that a government-funded training college was opened. The college was closed (after seven years of operation) due to severe problems in the organization and administration of the institution but was reopened in 1958. In 1968, a second residential, government-supported teachers' college was opened on the island of San Salvador. In 1974, the two colleges were merged to form the Education Division of the newly established College of The Bahamas.

It should be noted that since the 1960s, by mandate of the Bahamian government, programs of teacher training offered in The Bahamas have fallen under the control of the Joint Board of Teacher Education of the Faculty of Education, University of the West Indies, and they lead to certification awarded by that body.

In addition to the College of the Bahamas and the University of West Indies, several U.S. universities are also engaged in the delivery of degree-level studies and/or research programs in The Bahamas. These include, notably, the University of Miami, which conducts an M.B.A. program in Nassau on a biennial basis, Florida International University which has collaborated closely with the College of The Bahamas in offering bachelor's degree programs in technology, as well as a variety of professional development activities for persons in the public and private sectors, and St. John's University and the College of St. Benedict of Minnesota, which conduct programs leading to bachelor's degrees in education, for the benefit of full-time employed teachers.

Technical and vocational education in The Bahamas at postsecondary level received a boost in 1961 when the Nassau Technical Institute was established by the Bahamian government. This was supplemented by a Technical Center which was opened in 1968 to provide vocational training to pupils aged sixteen and over. In 1971, the two institutions were merged to form one establishment which later became one of the constituent parts of the newly formed College of The Bahamas. In the new structure introduced in 1975, the programs formerly offered at those institutions (except those related to hotel work and catering) formed the basis of the divisions of applied sciences, business and administrative studies, and technical and vocational studies.

In the 1980s, with the establishment of an industrial training center, many of the programs of the college's Technical and Vocational Studies Division were transferred to that body, and the remainder were combined with the offerings of the Applied Sciences Division to form the college's present Division of Technology.

Besides the College of The Bahamas, there are a number of other postsecondary institutions which provide specialized training for specific spheres of work. The Bahamas Hotel Training College, established by the Bahamas Hotel Training Council, offers programs leading to diplomas and certificates related to the hospitality industry. The college is currently accredited by the Commission on Occupational Education Institutions of the Southern Association of Colleges and Schools (U.S.A.) and delivers its programs in both Nassau and Freeport. The Bahamas Hotel Training College is well known throughout the Caribbean and attracts students from other parts of the region. Its entry requirements vary according to the program for which the student applies. Generally, however, these include high school completion, with two or three passes in the General Certificate of Education examination at Ordinary Level, and satisfactory performance on an entrance examination.

The college currently has an enrollment of 300, is administered by a director, and is staffed by some forty full-and part-time lecturers most of whom have had significant experience in the hotel industry. The college also offers industry-based training to approximately 850 hotel employees. Several College of The Bahamas lecturers teach academic courses on a part-time basis at the Hotel Training College. This sharing of human resources reflects the cooperative relations which continue to exist between these two institutions which are likely to become even more formally linked in the future.

The second and third year of a three-year Bachelor of Science degree program in hotel or tourism management are also offered in The Bahamas by the University of the West Indies. Students who have completed the first year of the bachelor's program at one of the other campuses of the university (in Jamaica, Barbados or Trinidad), or who have completed an Associate of Arts Degree program in business administration at the College of The Bahamas, may complete part II of the program at the center in Nassau. Provisions also exist for diploma graduates from The Bahamas Hotel Training College to enter the program after completing specified supplementary courses at the College of The Bahamas.

The Bahamas School of Nursing trains nurses and midwives and over the years a number of postbasic training programs have been added to the curriculum of the school including programs in community health nursing, psychiatric nursing, and in maternal and child health care. Since 1984, the School of Nursing and the College of The Bahamas have offered jointly an Associate Degree program in nursing.

In 1970, a Public Service Training Center was formally opened offering training for clerical personnel, supervisors, administrators, middle managers, and technical officers employed in the public service. Training courses are offered free of charge, and vary in duration and approach depending upon the nature of the clientele and their needs. Trainers are drawn from the Bahamian Public Service itself, and from overseas as needed for special purposes.

A special program in public administration for senior officers is offered through and in collaboration with the College of The Bahamas, and recently a number of training courses which were formerly the sole responsibility of the center have been carried out by relevant sections of the college.

In 1980, an Industrial Training Center was established to provide basic job entry skills to unemployed youth and high school graduates possessing no marketable skills. As an inducement to young people to pursue the training offered, tuition was free and students of the center were (and are still) paid a weekly stipend.

The center took over the craft-level and apprentice-type programs in the construction, engineering, and service trades formerly offered through the Technical and Vocational Studies Division of the College of The Bahamas. Instructors were drawn from among the college personnel, who were transferred to the service of the center, from the schools and from industry. A few were recruited from abroad.

Programs of one year's duration integrate center-based periods of instruction with on-the-job work experience, and are offered both in Nassau and in Freeport.

Professional education in The Bahamas is largely a function of the professional organizations. For example, legal eduction in The Bahamas has been provided through a program of clerkship, which requires the student to be articled for a period of up to five years in the chambers of a master to study, serve continuous apprenticeship, and write a series of examinations locally set and marked. Teaching of the articled students for Bar examinations has normally been undertaken by serving attorneys.

Similarly, The Bahamas Institute of Bankers, an autonomous association of banks and trust companies established in 1975, assists in the education and training of employees of member institutions, in conjunction with the College of The Bahamas.

ISSUES AND TRENDS

In common with many other countries of the world, The Bahamas is committed to producing through its educational system citizens who are literate, numerate, and well-informed, who possess skills which make them employable within the context of their country; and who are able to survive and compete in a highly technological world. There is, moreover, serious concern that the educational system should produce graduates capable of making a meaningful contribution to national development through productive participation in the country's major industries, through entrepreneurial activity, and through greater involvement in the production of food for the nation. Increasingly, too, there is emphasis on the need to develop among young people a greater sense of national pride, and a consciousness of important moral and ethical values, as a means of counteracting the many social ills which beset the country, such as violence, drug abuse, pregnancy among teenagers, and the like.

Due to its proximity to the United States, and its almost unlimited access to the films, television, video recordings, satellite programs, and all other forms of mass media emanating from the U.S., a continuing major challenge facing The Bahamas is that of preserving its own cultural identity. This challenge, along with the promotion of greater awareness of the need to conserve and preserve the natural environment, is a further issue of high priority for the Bahamian educational system as a whole.

The higher educational system of The Bahamas has, in a comparatively short time, made considerable strides in affording to significant numbers of Bahamians the opportunity of equipping themselves to play active roles in the shaping of their country's future. There is now a need to provide an even wider range of options in training at this level, and greater access to at least bachelor's degree studies at the College of The Bahamas. Plans are currently being formulated in this regard.

There is also a consciousness of the need to integrate and articulate more fully, the somewhat fragmented efforts of the various public postsecondary institutions, in order to create a more rational and efficient higher educational system capable of responding effectively to the educational and training needs of the Bahamian society. The fulfillment of this need continues to be a major goal of those entrusted with the planning and development of Bahamian education.

BIBLIOGRAPHY

Craton, Michael. *A History of The Bahamas.* 3rd ed. Waterloo, Ontario: San Salvador Press, 1986.

Dupuch, S. P., et al. eds. *Bahamas Handbook and Businessman's Annual.* Nassau, Bahamas: Etienne Dupuch Jr. Publications, 1988.

Houghton, H. "Report on Education in The Bahamas." Unpublished report, Colonial Office, London, 1958.

Leys, C. T., et al. "Report of the Development of a College of The Bahamas." Unpublished report, University of the West Indies, Kingston, Jamaica, 1968.

Massiah, Erna. "A Study of the Development of Higher Education in The Bahamas and its Relationship to National Goals." Unpublished doctoral dissertation, The University of Houston, 1979.

Ministry of Education and Culture, Bahamas. *Focus on the Future.* White Paper on Education. Nassau, Bahamas: Bahamas Government Printing Department, 1972.

Marshall, Lincoln H. "A Study of the Goals of The College of The Bahamas as Perceived and Preferred by Faculty, Students and Administrators." Unpublished doctoral dissertation, American University, 1982.

Roach, Arthur Leon. "The Development of a Continuing Education System for the College of The Bahamas with Implications for Third-World Countries." Unpublished doctoral dissertation, Andrews University, 1985.

Watson, Rose Thomas. "Education and National Development in The Bahamas." Unpublished doctoral dissertation, University of Miami, 1981.

BAHRAIN

by
Wassef Aziz Wassef
Professor of Science Education
University of Bahrain, Bahrain

BACKGROUND

Educational policy in Bahrain is based on the Constitution of 6 December 1973. The state is responsible for providing educational and cultural services to all inhabitants. Education is compulsory and free in the elementary levels designated by the Laws. Three main laws outline the framework of the educational structure and policy in Bahrain.

(i)   The Law of Education, enacted in July 1985: It defines the philosophy and objectives of education in Bahrain and lays down guidelines for curricula, methods of teaching, evaluation, examinations, etc.

(ii)   The Law of Private Education, enacted in 1985: It defines the objectives of private education and states guidelines for establishing and supervising private schools.

(iii)   The Law of Illiteracy and Adult Education: This is still under study.

The Ministry of Education is the official body responsible for formulating and implementing the educational policy. It supervises all education institutions at all levels in Bahrain. It supervises private education as well as mass illiteracy.

University education includes the Arab Gulf University established by the Gulf states under the auspices of the Gulf Cooperation Council. There is also the University of Bahrain governed by its council of trustees. However, the minister of education is the upper authority responsible for the administration of both universities; hence he is the chairman of the councils of both universities.

A Council for Educational Planning and Coordination which includes education officials functions under the auspices of the minister of education. This council has the responsibility for establishing educational programs and plans to fulfill the educational policy of the ministry, and for following up their implementation. The council also reviews and approves the curricula, the annual budget of the ministry, and the draft laws and plans. The council also carries out evaluation of the educational system in Bahrain on a regular basis to ensure continuous development.

The undersecretary of state administers the functional activities of the ministry and is supported by four assistant undersecretaries who oversee the areas of planning and educational information, curricula and training, general and technical education, and financial and administrative affairs.

Vocational education in Bahrain comes under the jurisdiction of the Higher Council for Vocational Training consisting of the minister of labor and social affairs (chairman), representatives of the ministries concerned with vocational training, and representatives of workers and owners of enterprises in different industrial and vocational areas. The council oversees national plans for vocational training for manpower in different economic sectors, conducts research on measurement of skills, and arranges seminars and regional conferences. The Department of Development of Manpower in the Ministry of Labor and Social Affairs supervises the implementation of the decisions of the Higher Council for Training.

PRIMARY AND SECONDARY EDUCATION

Traditional education in Bahrain was based for many years on Al-Kuttab, a one-class school. Study was coeducational, and included religious instruction and basic education. It was run by Al-Mullas (religious educators) and was found almost everywhere (at mosques, shops, and street corners, etc.).

The first modern public school in Bahrain was inaugurated in 1919. It was a school for boys, which started first as a primary school, called Al-Hidayah School. It was supervised by a council of leading personalities who financed its costs. The first primary school for girls was started in 1892 by the American Mission (Reformed church). It adopted the Western system of education. Education came under the direct auspices of the state in 1928. The first public school for girls was established in 1938. Students used to come from all the Gulf region to study in Bahrain.

Primary education in Bahrain is compulsory and takes six years. Students enrol at the age of six. It constitutes the first stage in the system of education. The main objective of primary education is to develop the basic skills of students in reading, writing, and arithmetic, and to assist children to develop their attitudes and mental abilities such as those of observation, listening, systematic thinking, and curiosity; and to develop their interests and desire to continue their education individually. Primary education aims also at developing the values of students and their attitude towards work, production, and manual labor. All government primary schools in Bahrain follow a common curriculum. Subjects studied include Islamic religion, Arabic, English, mathematics, science and technology, social science, art education, physical education, songs and music, and family education (for girls). The first three years in primary education constitute a cycle in which a single teacher, "level teacher" or "class teacher" teaches all subjects. There are schools for boys and schools for girls.

Bahrain has taken a lead among Arab countries in establishing a teacher training program for "class teachers" at the primary level. The training is conducted by the University of Bahrain, under the auspices of the Ministry of Education. The plan of study for teachers is a balanced schedule consisting of academic, vocational, and cultural subjects as well as teaching practice. The medium of instruction is Arabic. Educational subjects include important fields such as curriculum, methods of teaching (for each subject), evaluation, and administration. Computer training has also been introduced.

Middle schools, called "preparatory schools", are of three years duration under a 6-3-3 system introduced in 1961. Again, all government middle schools follow a common curriculum. Students learn religion, Arabic, English, mathematics, social science, science, practical studies, fine arts and physical education. In addition, girls are taught home economics.

Teacher training for the middle level of education is conducted at the University of Bahrain. Teachers specialize in a given subject, conforming to the policies outlined by the Ministry of Education.

The first secondary school in Bahrain was established in 1939. Now there are a number of well equipped modern secondary schools for both boys and for girls. Admission to secondary schools is based on the needs of the state. These needs are reflected in the Plan of the Ministry of Education as outlined by the Ministerial Decree No. 1970 of 19 March 1984. The first article of the decree maintains that "the concerned organs of the ministry determine the number of students admitted to each branch of secondary education in accordance with the needs of the country for different specializations fulfilled at a due time."

The duration of secondary schools is three years. The school year is divided into two terms. Secondary education comprises several branches: general secondary education; commercial secondary education; industrial secondary education; catering secondary education; textile secondary education; animal husbandry education; health secondary education; printing secondary education.

General secondary education is divided into two divisions: The arts section and the science section. Students of the arts section begin study with common subjects, covering religion, Arabic, English, social science, mathematics, general science, physical education, and statistics or French. After the first year, students choose one of four branches: language branch; economics and clerical branch; home economics branch; fine arts branch. Students of the science section also begin study with common subjects covering religion, Arabic, English, social science, mathematics, physics, chemistry, natural history, and physical education. After the first year, students choose one of two branches: physics and mathematics, or chemistry and biology. Students can choose one optional subject (three hours per week) from the following subjects; typewriting, fine arts, French, artistic and technical drawing, electronics, electricity, social subjects, music, and home economics. Secondary school students spend thirty-eight hours per week at school, including three hours for optional subject, and one hour for activity.

Two important developments are taking place in secondary education now. the first is the introduction of the credit system on an experimental basis, with "subjects" being replaced by "courses". The second is the introduction of computer literacy in all schools.

The 1989-90 statistics show that 96,400 students were enrolled in primary (60 percent), middle (21 percent) and secondary (19 percent) schools. Males and females were almost equally represented in the student population. At the secondary school level 41.4 percent took science subjects, 39.2 percent literary subjects, and 19.4 percent commercial subjects.

Vocational education is given in either commercial or industrial schools for both boys and girls. The program at commercial schools lasts three years. Students in the first and second years study general subjects including religion, Arabic, English and physical education, as well as commercial subjects such as accounting, secretarial work, and typewriting. In the third year students select one of two branches: accountancy or secretarial work.

Industrial schools are also of three years duration. There are ten specializations: machine shop, blacksmithing and welding, auto-mechanics, auto-electricity, diesel, refrigeration, electricity, radio and television, industrial electronics, measurement and control. Only male students are admitted, and they are divided into three main specializations: mechanics, electricity, and electronics. Bahrain attaches great importance to this type of education. There are also vocational programs for agricultural and animal husbandry, textiles, printing and catering.

Private schools have also played a very significant role in the history of education in Bahrain. The American Mission established a small school for girls in 1892 in Bahrain. It was the first school in all the Gulf area. In 1901, there were sixteen students. Then it adapted its education and system to traditional needs and customs of girl's education. It developed steadily since them, and later adopted the national system of education. The Bahrain school established in 1968 is a private school which follows the American system of education and is one of the top schools. St. Christopher's School established in 1961 follows the English system of education. There are also Indian, Pakistani, Persian, Urdo, Korean, Philippino, Japanese, French and Cypriot schools in Bahrain. These schools reflect the structure and harmony of the community, and the foreign population. Out of 10,307 students in private schools, 1,843 are Bahrainis, 3,712 Indians, 1,959 Pakistanis, 1,053 British, and 220 Egyptians.

HIGHER EDUCATION

Institutions

There are two universities in Bahrain that provide undergraduate education: The Arab Gulf University and the University of Bahrain.

The Arab Gulf University was established by Decree of the Fifth Conference of the Ministers of Education of Arab Gulf States (held in Kuwait in 1980). The Conference agreed on the establishment of a common Arab Gulf University and Bahrain was chosen for locating the institution. The Amiri Decree No. 19 of 1980 approved its establishment. The General Council is considered the highest authority of the university. It has the right to stipulate all decisions concerning its work. The university has a board of trustees comprising members having experience in higher education and representing the seven Gulf countries, as well as the chairman of the executive board and director of the Arab Educational Bureau and three Arab persons of international experience in higher education.

There is also a university council, headed by the president of the university, vice-presidents, deans, directors of the university centers, and representatives of staff members.

The Arab Gulf University includes the following colleges: the College of Medicine and Medical Science, the College of Education, and the College of Applied Sciences. This university is the only Arab university serving at a regional level. According to the 1986/87 enrollments, the College of Medicine and Medical Science enrolled 193 students, of which 72 were males. The distribution of students according to nationality reveals its regional objective: Bahrainis 29 percent, Arab Emirates 19 percent, Qataris 15 percent, Kuwaitis 7 percent, Saudis 8 percent, Omanis 17 percent and the balance coming from other countries. Enrollment in the other two colleges is very low, with only nine students enrolled in the College of Applied Science. These students of whom six are Bahrainis study for M.Sc. in Desert and Arid Land Science. Students enrolled in the College of Education are just five, all of whom are Bahrainis.

The university is running into financial difficulties and debts due to the general decline in funding by member Gulf States. Economic measures, however, are being undertaken. The Gulf ministers of education in their last meeting in Bahrain, on 24 March 1989, decided to continue the functioning of this unique university.

The University of Bahrain has been newly established by the Act of 1986. It came out of merging the previously existing two colleges: the University College of Arts, Science and Education, and the Gulf Polytechnic College. It was reorganized subsequently into four colleges, two from each of the previous establishments: the College of Science and Arts, the College of Education, the College of Commerce and Business, and the College of Engineering. The total enrolment of the university in 1988-89 is 5,192 students of whom 54 percent were females. About 32 percent of the students study engineering and another 25 percent study science and arts. A significant percentage, 26 percent, study commerce and the remaining 17 percent is in education.

It has been decided in 1990 that the College of Arts and Science be split into two colleges: the College of Arts and the College of Science starting 1990-91.

Undergraduate Programs

The University of Bahrain (College of Arts and Science) offers B.Sc. in mathematics, physics, chemistry, biology, and computer science. It offers B.A. in Arabic and Islamic Studies, English, and general studies. Students specialize in a major of those fields and a minor field, which may include, in addition to those fields, education, and psychology. Duration of study is 4-5 years.

The College of Education offers B.Sc. degrees in physical education and education for primary schools (class teacher). Duration of study is 4-5 years. It provides also a minor in education. A future middle or secondary school teacher has to specialize in a major in addition to a minor in education. The College of Education also provides a one-year postgraduate diploma in education, and a 2-3 year Master in Education for college graduates. A new Diploma in Learning

Resources and Information has been started in 1989-90 to train librarians and those working in audio-visual .

The College of Business Administration offers a four-year B.Sc. in accounting, business management, and office management, as well as a graduate program leading to Master in Business Administration degree. The college also offers a part-time program, and a continuing management education program (COMEP) lasting for about three semesters.

The College of Engineering offers B.Sc. in civil, electrical, and mechanical engineering. These programs normally require four and one-half years of study consisting of about 170 credits. The college also offers two-year associate diplomas in a number of fields including chemical engineering technology, civil engineering technology, building and construction, civil work, surveying, computer technology, electrical engineering, electronics and telecommunication technology, mechanical engineering, air conditioning, production, and power. These diplomas are intended to prepare graduates for jobs as assistant engineers and specialists in occupations. Students who complete the associate degree programs may continue towards the B.Sc. degree. Other programs offered by the college includes a continuing engineering education program (CEEP).

The college also formulates special programs to meet the needs of industry for specialized instruction and training outside the regular college programs. Recent special programs include special program in telecommunication, power plant certificate program, introduction to technology program, and process plant certificate program.

The University of Bahrain has offered recently an orientation program of two semesters to all full-time students. Students may be exempted from part of it after passing an admission examination to the orientation program. The program intends to orient students towards university life and includes academic as well as social subjects. Arabic, English, mathematics and science form the core curriculum of this program. Computer training is also offered to all students.

Advanced Studies

The Department of Education of the University of Bahrain was the first to provide graduate studies in Bahrain. The first graduate degree, a master's degree in education, was awarded in 1986. The work dealt with a typical environmental subject, marine biology. Two other master's were subsequently awarded. At present twenty-four students follow graduate programs in education. They are all in the field of curriculum development (in areas of Arabic, mathematics, and science). There are plans to diversify the areas of study. A comprehensive program including the study of ten courses of three credits each precedes the preparation of a master's thesis.

The Department of Education also provides a Postgraduate Diploma in Education, started in 1979. At present ninety-six students (half of whom are females) are enrolled.

The College of Business Administration started an M.B.A. program in 1987. The enrolment in this program is fifty-four students, ten of whom are females.

ISSUES AND TRENDS

1.   Education in Bahrain is presently at a stage of steady development. The Ministry of Education has ruled that all "class teachers" (level teachers) who teach a full compliment of subjects in the first three years of primary education are required to be university graduates holding bachelor's degree in education. The University of Bahrain has instituted a special program to meet this need. Another program is planned to be implemented in 1990 for providing training for "area teachers", i.e. teachers specialized in related areas of subjects, who will teach fourth, fifth, and sixth forms of primary schools. These training programs are expected to improve the quality of pre-university education significantly.

2.   Preparatory schools have now become an extension of the first six years of primary education, forming nine years of basic education.

3.   The new credit system will also change the nature of secondary education. Repeated failures due to difficulties encountered by some students in certain subjects will no longer lead to repetition of a whole year. Bright students too can benefit from the advantages of this system, being able to go faster.

4.   One of the most important developments in secondary schools has been the optional activity subjects. These attract students. Students in the humanities are seen registering in electronics, computer studies, and some typical scientific specializations. Specialists are appointed for teaching these activities.

5.   The Ministry of Education has plans to stipulate a master's degree requirement for all curriculum advisors and head teachers as part of a continuing effort to improve the teaching level.

6.   Most recently, a new development took place in August 1990. As a result the of the unsettled condition in Kuwait and in the Gulf region, the University of Bahrain offered to accept students from the University of Kuwait to ensure continuation of their studies. Staff members from Kuwait were also welcomed, particularly in areas needing their expertise. The Arab Gulf University accepted students of medicine. Bahrain will also cope with more than 1,500 Kuwaiti pupils to be integrated into government schools when the new term starts late September. The youngsters have been stranded with their families in Bahrain following the Iraqi invasion of Kuwait in August 1990. The educational system in all Gulf States is similar in duration, curriculum, and textbooks. Thus the students can be assimilated with little or no problems.

7.   The Arab Gulf University will start, beginning 22 September 1990, three higher diplomas in the Colleges of Medicine, Education, and Applied Science. These are the programs of nutrition, special education for the gifted, and higher diploma in analysis.

BIBLIOGRAPHY

Al-Hamer, Abdul-Malik Youssef. *An Analytical Study of the System of Education in Bahrain, 1965-70.* Bahrain: Oriental Press, 1969.

Hamoud, Rafika S. *Education in Bahrain* (in Arabic). Riyadh: Arab Bureau of Education for the Gulf States, 1987.

Jain, Jiya Lal. *A Brief History of Education in Bahrain.* Bahrain: Ministry of Education, 1986.

Muscati, Anisa Ali, and Faika, Said Al-Saleh. *Education in Bahrain - Between Development and Innovation* (in Arabic). Bahrain: Ministry of Education, 1985.

Teacher Education in the Arab Gulf States - Proceedings of the Conference on Teacher Education, Doha, State of Qatar, Jan 6-9, 1984. The Arab Bureau of Education for the Gulf States, Riyadh; The University of Qatar, Doha; the International Council of Education for Teaching, Washington, 1984.

BANGLADESH

by
Giasuddin Ahmed
Professor of Education and Director
Institute of Distance Education, Bangladesh

BACKGROUND

The history of the present structure of education in Bangladesh can be traced back to the British colonization of the Indo-Pakistan-Bangladesh subcontinent over two hundred years ago. Prior to the British occupation, an indigenous system of education existed in the villages, under which children received their basic and spiritual education. The Christian missionaries initiated the introduction of the British system of education and the subsequent British rulers sustained the system primarily as a means of achieving their religious and colonial objectives. The system was mainly designed to train public servants for local administration, revenue collection, and for running the bureaucracy. Bangladesh became a sovereign state in 1971 but its educational system still reflects the basic characteristics of the colonial system although it has undergone many changes over the years.

PRIMARY AND SECONDARY EDUCATION

Primary education in Bangladesh is of five years duration (grades 1-5). About 36,000 primary schools are managed, controlled, and financed by the government and another 7,500 are privately managed and are funded through public donations and subsidies. About 11,000,000 children or 55 percent of the total school going children were enrolled in primary schools in 1983. The proportion of boys and girls is about 53:36. Over 190,000 teachers are engaged in teaching. Most of the teachers are high school graduates with a year's training in teaching methodology (some teachers are university graduates and holders of master's degrees in education). The Directorate of Primary Education with a director general as head oversees primary education activities.

Secondary education in Bangladesh consists of three stages: grades 6-8 form the lower secondary stage, grades 9-10 form the secondary stage, and grades 11-12 form the higher secondary stage. Secondary education begins at the age of ten years and continue till the students are about seventeen years of age.

Lower secondary and secondary education curriculum includes Bangla language, English, general mathematics, and geography as compulsory subjects. The students are required to take four additional subjects selected from integrated physics and chemistry, biology, elective mathematics, home science, religious education, history, geometry and technical drawing, and folk music. Students take a public examination at the end of the tenth grade. This examination is conducted by the region's Board of Intermediate and Secondary Education. There are four such boards in the country. Successful students are awarded a secondary school certificate. Only about 200 schools out of a total of over 8,000 are managed directly by the government secondary education directorates. The rest is privately managed. However, government bears 70 percent of the salary cost of the private schools (on the basis of salaries comparable to those paid to government school teachers). Students of both the government and private schools pay tuition fees, which in the case of private schools vary depending on the institution. Students who obtain 75 percent or more marks at the secondary school certificate examination receive scholarships.

Higher secondary studies (grades 11-12) are open to students who perform well in the secondary school certificate examination. Higher secondary program is offered at a number of colleges (mostly private) and the curriculum consist of two compulsory subjects (Bengali and English Language) and three other subjects selected from elective mathematics, physics, chemistry, biology, geography, history, civics and economics, statistics, advanced English, and advanced Bangla. At the end of the two years, students take a public examination conducted by the respective Board of Intermediate and Secondary Education. Successful candidates are awarded a higher secondary certificate, which makes them eligible to seek admission to undergraduate studies. Some scholarships are awarded by the government and respective Boards but the majority of the students are supported by their parents for tuition and living expenses.

Bangla is the medium of instruction for all the stages of secondary education. A public board (National Curriculum and Textbook Board) plans and develops curriculum and publish necessary textbooks.

Students at the secondary stages of education take part in a variety of extracurricular activities. Games like football, volleyball, and cricket as well as debates and cultural activities are very popular among students.

Selection of teachers for the government secondary schools are made by the Public Service Commission. The basic requirement for entry is a bachelor's degree. For higher secondary level, a master's degree is required. In the private secondary schools the selection is made by the managing committee of the school.

Only 8-10 percent of the students who enter grade one complete grade twelve.

HIGHER EDUCATION

Undergraduate Studies

Higher education (tertiary) in Bangladesh is provided by constituent colleges of universities, universities themselves, and specialized institutes like medical colleges, engineering colleges, and agricultural colleges. Majority of the constituent colleges are privately managed but are administered conforming to regulations enacted by the government. Two types of first degrees are available: a two year pass degree and a three year honors degree. In the case of professional programs the duration is longer: four years for degrees in agriculture or engineering and five years for degrees in medicine or architecture. Medicine also requires one year of internship.

Admission to undergraduate programs is based on the higher secondary certificate examination. Competition, particularly for professional programs, is severe. Students may also be required to take special entrance examinations conducted by the respective institutions or faculties. Admission to arts and social science programs is relatively less competitive. Also there is stiff competition for admission to colleges which have a high reputation. Officially the medium of instruction is Bangla but English is almost a necessity to successfully complete a degree program.

A University Grants Commission is responsible for planning higher education within the framework of economic development and for allocating financial resources to universities. It consists of a chairman, two permanent members, and two vice-chancellors (heads of universities) elected for a period of two years by the fellow vice-chancellors. Like in other stages, the Ministry of Education has no direct control in the administration of higher education other than the annual allocation of government funds through the University Grant Commission. The Association of Universities of Bangladesh facilitates communication among the institutions, coordinates their activities, and acts as a liaison between the universities and the top level of the ministry. The association is composed of three representatives from each university: the vice-chancellor and two members nominated by the academic council to serve one year.

At present there are six universities along with a number of constituent institutes and affiliated colleges offering programs in higher education. The University of Dhaka established in 1921 is the oldest and has faculties of arts, social science, science, biological sciences, commerce, law, education, and medicine offering bachelor's, master's and doctoral degrees. It has an enrollment of over 10,000 students. About 200 colleges are affiliated to the university. Other universities include University of Rajshahi (1953), University of Chittagong (1966) Jahangernagari University (1961), Bangladesh Agricultural University (1970), and Bangladesh University of Engineering and Technology (1961). There are four medical colleges affiliated to the Dhaka University, two medical colleges are affiliated to Rajshahi University and two more medical colleges are affiliated to the University of Chittagong. Also four degree-granting engineering colleges (BIT) exist at Rajshshi, Chittagong, Khulna, and Dhaka. Three agriculture colleges and one post graduate agricultural institute are affiliated to the Agricultural University.

All the universities in Bangladesh are corporate autonomous bodies (University Act of 1973) which maintain academic and administrative control of constituent departments, institutes, and affiliated colleges. Other than Jahangirnagar University, all other universities are both "academic" and affiliating universities. The universities set academic standards for their affiliated institutes and colleges. They are also responsible for establishing standards for physical facilities and teaching staff, for determining curricula and syllabi, and for administering common examinations for their affiliated colleges which are managed by the government or private bodies. The affiliated colleges, most of which are private, generally offer undergraduate programs. Some colleges also offer honors and postgraduate studies. University departments and institutes conduct some undergraduate and most of the postgraduate programs. Two more universities, one at Sylhet and one at Khulna, are under construction.

The syndicate is the executive body of the university while the senate ratifies proposals of the syndicate and approves its annual reports, annual accounts, and budgets. The university vice-chancellor, as principal executive officer, is the chairman of the syndicate, senate, and academic council. The president of Bangladesh, who is the chancellor or titular head of all universities appoint vice-chancellors for a period of four years from among three nominees selected by the university senate. Deans of the faculties are elected by the teaching staff. The students send six representatives to the senate. Since 1973, students are also represented in certain committees dealing with regulations and examinations. The academic council is composed of deans, professors, representatives of the teaching staff, and representatives of the affiliated colleges. The academic council is the supreme authority for academic purposes. But all decisions of this council require approval of the syndicate.

All universities, professional colleges, and general colleges provide student accommodation. The demand far outweigh the supply of rooms. The situation is particularly acute in the case of female students. Tuition fees are charged by all institutions but many students who score high marks at the higher secondary certificate examination receive scholarships from the government and the Boards of Intermediate and Secondary Education. Majority of students, however, are supported by their families.

The higher educational institutes in Bangladesh provide a variety of programs in medicine, engineering, technology, agriculture, business administration, journalism, teacher education, fine and applied arts, home science, physical sciences, and social sciences in programs leading to bachelor's degrees.

The selection of teaching staff for universities is done by a selection committee appointed by the syndicate. In the case of government colleges, teaching appointments are made by the Public Service Commission. There are a limited number of foreign students at higher education institutions in Bangladesh, particularly at agricultural and engineering universities and medical colleges.

Teacher education for primary school teachers is conducted at fifty-two primary training institutes of different levels spread over the country. A National Academy for Primary Education control the academic aspects of these institutes. Ten teacher training colleges and the Institute of Education and Research at the University of Dhaka provide training to secondary school teachers. Several of the teacher training colleges provide bachelor's as well as master's degree programs in education. Two physical education colleges, one at Dhaka and one at Rajshahi, train physical education teachers. One Technical Teacher Education Institute trains teachers of vocational subjects. The National Institute of Educational Administration, Extension, and Research arranges training for educational administrators.

Vocational education is provided by the seventeen polytechnic institutes and fifty-five vocational institutes in the country. Polytechnic institutes offer technical training in civil, mechanical, chemical, electrical, metallurgical, and water resource engineering. The vocational institutes offer trade courses. There are thirteen agricultural training institutes which offer courses for mid-level extension and research workers in agriculture. Three commercial institutes (at Rajshahi, Chittagong, and Khulna) offer trade courses. Bangladesh Institute of Distance Education provides teaching aids for primary and secondary schools. This institute also prepares radio and television programs for school children and teachers.

Advanced Studies and Research

Master's degrees are awarded after two years of course work beyond regular bachelor's degree or one year after an honors bachelor's degree. Master's degree candidates are evaluated at the end of the academic year by essay examination and viva voce. Some selected students prepare dissertations under the supervision of senior teachers. Candidates for Ph.D. degree do not pursue regular course work but must study independently with a professor. The doctorate degree is awarded on submission of a dissertation to be judged by a committee of professors. The committee also includes two external examiners. A Ph.D. degree needs approval of the advanced study committee, academic council, and syndicate of the university.

The universities of Dhaka and Rajshahi offer courses for the doctorate degree in many areas. Normally the candidates take three years for completion of a dissertation. A maximum period of five years is allowed for submittal of the dissertation. Doctoral students are generally supported by scholarships from various research institutions. Bangladesh Council of Scientific and Industrial Research in Dhaka is the premier institution coordinating research work. Other institutes include the Rice Research Institute, Jute Research Institute, and Forest Research Institute. These institutes work in close liaison with the universities which award some degrees based on student's research work done at the research institutes.

ISSUES AND TRENDS

There is a mass awareness in the country about education as an investment. The enrollment in education institutions at all levels has been increasing very rapidly. Particularly the rapid expansion of enrollment at postsecondary levels is making it difficult to provide adequate facilities and competent staff. It is also true that a significant "braindrain" is occurring with many of our young college and university teachers leaving the country for more lucrative positions in the Middle East and industrial countries of the West. To compound this problem, a great number of Bangladeshi scholars studying abroad are not keen to return to the country. Private sector has not kept pace with the demand for expansion of educational facilities. As a result, the responsibility for education is falling more and more to the lap of government officials, who are less than enthusiastic about this development.

The country has a great need for technical personnel to meet the needs of industry and agriculture as well as to generate self-employment opportunities. Hurried revisions to curriculum has not provided the required vision or the desired results. The enrollment in science streams at the secondary, higher secondary, and university level has increased rapidly in the recent years but opportunities for students to continue beyond this level is very limited. Higher education institutions providing technological education are few in number and the severe competition for admission does not allow many of the aspiring young students to become part of the mainstream of technological development of the country. The resources of the country are too limited to provide for the necessary expansion.

In the area of staffing, there is a severe, shortage of qualified teachers, particularly at the secondary level. The salary structure and social status of teachers are less than attractive for talented students to enter the teaching profession, compared to other employment avenues (for example in the bureaucracy). In addition, ten teacher training colleges in the country can hardly cope with the teacher training needs of a population of 110 million people. To alleviate the situation, some arrangements have been made recently to provide pedagogical training (B.Ed.) to secondary school teachers through distance education under the auspicious of the University of Rajshahi.

The examination system presently in place in the country falls short of making adequate assessment of students' knowledge and skills. the system is open to abuse with unscrupulous students adopting unfair means. This has resulted in a deterioration of the quality of education. Student unrest and political activism at the universities has also deviated student's minds from the central theme of "learning", thus further affecting the quality of education. The challenge is therefore to overhaul the system to improve the quality of education.

BIBLIOGRAPHY

Bangladesh Bureau of Educational Information and Statistics. *Primary Education in Bangladesh.* Ministry of Education (Bangladesh), 1987.

Bangladesh Bureau of Educational Information and Statistics. *A Profile on Primary Education in Bangladesh.* Ministry of Education (Bangladesh), 1989.

Bangladesh Bureau of Statistics. *Statistical Yearbook of Bangladesh, 1983-84.* Govt. of the People's Republic of Bangladesh, n.d.

Bangladesh Bureau of Statistics. *Statistical Yearbook of Bangladesh, 1987.* Govt. of the People's Republic of Bangladesh, n.d.

Ministry of Education (Bangladesh). *Bangladesh Education Commission Report.* *1974.*

Ministry of Education, Government of Pakistan. *Report of the Commission on National Education. 1960.*

BARBADOS
WITH SOME REFERENCE TO THE CARRIBEAN

by
Leonard L. Shorey
Education Consultant
and
Gerald St. Rose
Lecturer in Education
University of the West Indies, Barbados

BACKGROUND

Education is highly prized in the Caribbean and most of the countries spend between 18 percent and 22 percent of their annual budgets on education. Similar structures and provisions in education are to be found throughout the region among those countries which once were or still are colonies of Great Britain, since they all share a common legacy from their colonial period.

In the Caribbean, education is under the control of the respective governments all of which accept it as their responsibility to provide education for children of primary age, 6-11 years. However, such "total" provision has not yet been achieved in all countries in the region. Tremendous improvements have taken place during the past two or three decades but the problems identified by Shirley Gordon in the early sixties have not been entirely solved. As Gordon put it:
West Indian governments are struggling to provide postprimary education for all; extended secondary education to meet the need for better educated people in teaching, administration, social work and personnel management, and for specialists in industrial and agricultural development; more vocational instruction to provide skilled workers, a measure which will help to beat the increasing problem of adolescent unemployment; an expanding university; and for all these, to provide competent teachers with some training as well as education to prepare them for the ever more exacting requirements of their profession. (Gordon 1963).

In Barbados free public schooling exists for all primary-age children but there are also fee-paying private schools available for those who want to make use of this option. Nonetheless the national government, like others, accepts responsibility for ensuring that the education provided at all levels, whether in government or in non-government institutions, is of satisfactory quality and is suited to the maturity level and needs of the children concerned.

PRIMARY AND SECONDARY EDUCATION

Education at secondary and postsecondary levels is also provided by the government of Barbados, but at both these levels there are also other institutions which cater to persons who do not wish to use these facilities and prefer instead to pay directly for the education services they require.

The secondary program typically extends to the age of sixteen years but the opportunity exists for students to continue at school for a further two or three years up to a maximum age of nineteen years. Those who pursue this extended program generally do so with a view to gaining admission requirements to the University of the West Indies or to other universities.

At the end of the normal five-year secondary program, secondary school students generally sit the exams of the Caribbean Examinations Council (CXC) in a wide range of subjects. The number and variety of subjects offered by this examining body at a level equivalent to the General Certificate of Education (G.C.E.) Ordinary Level (O-Level) examinations of Cambridge University continue to increase, but they do not yet include all the subject areas studied in the region's schools. Students are therefore permitted to write the Cambridge examinations in subjects not yet available from the Caribbean Examinations Council.

These CXC examinations are conducted at two levels of proficiency: General and Basic. The General Proficiency level is intended for those students who expect to study the subject or closely related subjects beyond the secondary level while the Basic Proficiency level is intended for students who do not envisage pursuing the subject further. The intent behind this two-tier system is to allow students a mix suited to their interests and abilities instead of forcing them to opt for a course of study in an area in which they may not reach the highest levels. The General Proficiency level therefore carries greater prestige than the Basic Proficiency level and as a result many students prefer to write exams at the General rather than at the Basic level.

Students continuing at school beyond the age of sixteen years generally sit the Advanced Level examinations of the General Certificate in Education (G.C.E.) set by the University of Cambridge, England, while private candidates frequently sit the examinations set by the University of London's Examinations Syndicate.

In Barbados there are twenty-one government secondary schools, the majority of which are coeducational institutions, but there are three single sex schools, one for boys and two for girls. The total enrollment in 1988 was 21,184. Private (fee-paying) secondary schools cater to one-or two-thousand additional pupils, a large number of whom are in receipt of government bursaries to assist with the payment of fees.

Moreover, since the Caribbean Examinations Council does not yet provide examinations in subjects beyond the G.C.E. Ordinary Level standard, students must of necessity take the Cambridge and London Advanced Level subjects at the end of their two-year program of study beyond the Ordinary Level.

Extracurricular activities are usually wide-ranging and include indoor and outdoor sports such as chess, dominoes, hockey, soccer, cricket, volley ball, lawn tennis, music, dance, athletics, and table-tennis. Also to be considered are the

Inter-Student Christian Fellowship, literary and debating clubs, as well as hobby clubs/groups relating to philately, photography and the like.

In Barbados and indeed throughout the region, the academic year is divided into three terms beginning in September of each calendar year. There is little foreign student enrollment in Barbados since there is only one boarding school, but there are small numbers of non-national students who reside with friends/relatives during the school terms.

Admission to secondary level education is through an island-wide examination, the Secondary Schools Entrance Examination (SSEE), set by the Ministry of Education in May of each year. The examination is open to youngsters of ages of 11-12 years. This examination is of critical importance since the school to which pupils are admitted depends in large measure on how well they have performed in this examination.

As in the other English-speaking countries the medium of instruction is English.

HIGHER EDUCATION

Institutions

Higher education (tertiary) can, for convenience, be divided into two broad categories: education provided within a university, and education offered by non-university institutions which provide formal education to meet the needs of those who have completed secondary or equivalent level education.

Teacher education is normally provided at two levels by different agencies: teachers' colleges, to be found in individual countries of the region, and the faculties of education of the University of the West Indies and the University of Guyana.

In Barbados, training for classroom teaching at primary level and for non-graduate teachers at secondary level is provided at Erdiston Teachers' College which is administered by a board of management appointed by the Minister of Education.

Training of graduates for classroom teaching in secondary schools and in other institutions is provided by the University of the West Indies through its Faculty of Education which, since 1973, has mounted a training program for teachers at its Cave Hill Campus in Barbados. Similar training programs are available at the other two campuses in their respective Faculties of Education, and at the University of Guyana.

There were several attempts to establish institutions of higher education in the region, but such education in the English-speaking Caribbean is most frequently associated with Codrington College (Barbados), Jamaica College (Jamaica), The Imperial College of Tropical Agriculture (Trinidad), the University of the West Indies at its three campuses, and the University of Guyana.

Codrington College, in Barbados, began as a Grammar School "since there were no schools in the island to instruct boys up to a standard necessary for entrance into a college as envisaged by Christopher Codrington" (Simmons, 1977) who had made the bequest to the Society for Propagation of the Christian Religion in Foreign Parts. In 1830, after a number of vicissitudes, it was transformed to become "the first institution of higher education in the English-speaking Caribbean", (Ramesar 1977) and the intention was that it should train persons to serve as medical missionaries.

The College became affiliated to Durham University, England, in 1875 and was thus "the first institution outside of Great Britain to grant a residential degree of a British university". (Simmons 1977) This affiliation was later terminated following the establishment of the University of the West Indies (UWI), and the College now provides theological training to meet the academic requirements of this University.

Jamaica College, established in relation to the already existing Jamaica High School, began in Jamaica in 1890 with the objective of offering B.A. and M.A. degrees from the University of London, England, but it had only a short life, ending in about 1908 as a university college. The High School component has continued under the name of Jamaica College.

The Imperial College of Tropical Agriculture was established in 1922 to focus attention on and to provide training suited to the needs and requirements of agriculture in the tropics. As the undersecretary of state for the colonies stated:I attach the highest possible importance to the foundation of the new Agricultural College in Trinidad. It is impossible for any industry to compete successfully in the modern world unless it has easy access to the bestscientific advice upon practical questions that arise inthe course of the daily routine. The College will provide a center for the prosecution of research and for the gradual propagation of scientific ideas, not only in Trinidad, but throughout the colonies from which its students will undoubtedly be drawn in increasing numbers. (Gordon 1963)

Following the establishment of the University of the West Indies, the Imperial College of Tropical Agriculture was incorporated within that institution as its Faculty of Agriculture.

The University of the West Indies began in Jamaica in 1949 as the University College of the West Indies, a college of London University, and was established as a result of the Asquith Commission of 1943 which had been appointed to enquire into the needs of higher education in the colonies. It became the University of the West Indies in 1962 with the first campus in Jamaica, other campuses being subsequently established in Trinidad and in Barbados.

In 1963, the Government of Guyana opted to establish its own university, the University of Guyana, offering degrees in arts, natural sciences, and social sciences. Some years later that university and the University of the West Indies set up a special relationship to prepare candidates for the L.L.B. degree of the latter university. Under existing arrangements, students may pursue the first year of the law degree program at any one of the campuses of the University of the West Indies, or at the University of Guyana. However, the second and third years of the course must be completed at the Barbados Campus of the University of the West Indies.

The University of the West Indies with campuses in Jamaica, Trinidad, and Barbados, and a Division of Hotel Management in the Bahamas, is jointly funded by the governments of the English-speaking Caribbean, except for Guyana which, as previously indicated, has its own university. The contribution to be made by a given territory is determined by a formula which takes into account both the size of its population and its economic level.

Although the economic costs of the University of the West Indies are met by the governments of the region, the institution is essentially autonomous, having the right to make its own appointments to the academic and non-academic staff, determine the courses to be offered and the content of such courses, award its own degrees, etc.

Initially the university's administration was highly centralized, largely as a result of its early beginnings as a college of London University, since for many years there was, in fact, only one campus (in Jamaica).

With the subsequent establishment of campuses in Trinidad and Barbados, the need for some measure of decentralization became apparent and the present structure places considerable autonomy in the hands of each campus administration. As a result of this devolution of authority and responsibility, the administrative structure of the university has necessarily changed. As the Marshall Report (Marshall 1986) clearly indicated, the new administrative provisions give greater influence to the governments of the countries in which campuses are sited.

As indicated above, course development remains within the prerogative of the university. So, too, does curriculum development, and each faculty is responsible for constant monitoring and reassessment of its offerings to ensure that they keep abreast of developments in the respective fields so as to meet more effectively the needs of students.

In between the university and secondary level institutions are other tertiary level institutions with varying functions indicated by names such as polytechnics, community colleges, state colleges, teachers' training colleges and labor colleges, all of which cater to the varying educational needs and requirements of persons many of whom have completed a secondary level program of study.

Details of provisions differ across the Caribbean region, but the situation in Barbados is reasonably typical. At the tertiary level, the institutions include the University of the West Indies Cave Hill Campus, and its affiliate, Codrington College, a "community college" similar in many respects to like-named institutions in Canada and the United States of America, a polytechnic, and a teachers' training college. There are also several non-governmental education and training institutions particularly in the secretarial and computer technology fields.

Linkages between the university and other tertiary level institutions tend to develop to meet specific needs. Thus during the past few years the university has liberalized its provisions to permit the community college to teach students for its preliminary science program. As a consequence, both the college's students and those students pursuing the preliminary science course at the university itself sit the same examination.

Among the other tertiary level institutions themselves there is somewhat greater collaboration. Thus, in secretarial training there is a logical progression from the initial training at the polytechnic to the more advanced training provided by the community college and collaboration between the staffs of the two institutions minimizes duplication of effort while at the same time ensuring better dovetailing of the two programs. Similar collaboration is to be found between the community college and the teachers' college where both institutions share responsibility for certain programs.

Another set of interrelationships exists between the community college and the community itself, as well as between the polytechnic and the community. These interrelationships are typified and facilitated by the advisory committees appointed by both institutions which include among their members persons drawn from business and industry; in this way the institutions seek to ensure that their programs of study remain relevant to current needs and in line with the best of practice in the country.

Although these three tertiary level institutions (community college, polytechnic, teachers college) are entirely funded by the government of Barbados, they all have a considerable degree of autonomy with respect to their day to day operations. Each is administered by a board of management which acts as a buffer between the Ministry of Education on the one hand and the principals and their administrative staff on the other. Members of staff of the institutions are appointed by the respective boards of management.

The three institutions offer programs leading to quite different academic qualifications. Persons successfully completing the program of study at the teachers' college qualify as trained teachers and receive the college's certificate. A sufficiently high grade further entitles such persons to have their certificates endorsed by the university's Faculty of Education; this gives the certificates regional currency.

Students completing courses at the polytechnic qualify for the award of the institution's certificates and those completing programs of study at the community college may qualify for a college certificate, for a Cambridge General Certificate of Education (Advanced Level), or for the award of an associate degree.

While the teachers' college concerns itself solely with the training of teachers for the primary schools in the country, the polytechnic and the community college have broader objectives. Both institutions offer programs aimed at preparing their students for direct entry into the work market in a variety of technical and commercial fields and, in addition, the community college also provides academic options in liberal arts and natural sciences.

Undergraduate Studies

Except for theological education provided at Codrington College, an affiliate of the University of the West Indies, university education in Barbados is provided by the Cave Hill Campus of the University of the West Indies. This campus offers degree programs in the general range of university-based fields of study in liberal arts (history, modern languages, English, mathematics); natural sciences; mathematics, physics, chemistry, biology; social sciences (economics, sociology, political science); law; and education.

Degree programs in medicine are offered at the Mona Campus in Jamaica, and are in the planning stage for the St. Augustine Campus, Trinidad, which already offers agriculture and engineering. Both these campuses also provide the usual range of degree programs similar to those identified above for the campus in Barbados.

Admission to the university's campuses is generally on the basis of performance in the Cambridge General Certificate of Education examination, in the exams of the Caribbean Examinations Council, or by means of an appropriate combination of both. In some cases, faculties may stipulate admission requirements over and above those required for general matriculation.

Qualifications for admission to the university's undergraduate programs are of three types:

1.   Normal matriculation permits a student to graduate in three years. In this case students must have passes in either five subjects (including English language) of which at least two must be at Advanced Level of the General Certificate of Education (G.C.E.) or equivalent; or four subjects of which at least three must be at Advanced Level or equivalent.

2.   Lower level matriculation allows students to embark on university studies with passes in at least five subjects at the equivalent of O-Level standard in the General Certificate of Education. To this end, the University of the West Indies recognizes the General Proficiency Certificates of the Caribbean Examination Council at Grades 1 and 2. While faculty requirements vary slightly, all require a pass in English language.

3.   Opportunity is available for admission of mature or experienced persons who may not fulfil the precise requirements for normal or lower level matriculation. In such cases individuals are required to present satisfactory evidence of their academic or professional attainments.

In addition to the general university admission requirements indicated above, all faculties and some departments have their own entry requirements. These are indicated in the various faculty handbooks which also contain information about the goals and philosophies of the respective faculties, as well as details of courses offered.

The university academic year normally begins in October and ends in June when examinations are completed, but there are some certificate and diploma courses which extend beyond this period. Supplemental examinations are conducted after June but before the beginning of the following academic year. Previously the University of the West Indies, like most universities in Great Britain, followed the traditional pattern of three terms with examinations being held during the second half of the third term. However this structure is likely to be changed with effect from October 1990, to follow the North American semester system.

Degree programs of study normally extend over a period of three academic years. The medical course is longer (five years) and requires an internship in an approved teaching hospital while the prospective attornies-at-law is required to spend an additional two years in internship with an approved law firm before they can be admitted to the Bar. With respect to the field of education, qualification as a trained teacher normally requires an additional year of study beyond the first degree unless the first degree itself contains education as a major component.

All governments in the region give some measure of assistance to nationals wishing to pursue a university program, though the degree of assistance varies, as do the terms on which such assistance is provided. In some cases, students (and/or their parents) are required to meet part of the cost of university education but a number of students benefit from the scholarships and other kinds of assistance offered by international or regional organizations, or from assistance given by local bodies.

In Barbados, the national government meets the economic (tuition and examination) costs of nationals gaining admission to the university's campus in Barbados, as well as the costs of university courses overseas where such courses of study are not available at the Campus in Barbados.

In general, part-time students are required to pay their own tuition fees, and all students are normally required to meet the expenses of caution-money and books. Where nationals of Barbados attend other campuses of the University of the West Indies, their costs are paid by the government.

About half of the students attending the campus in Barbados are non-nationals and a small proportion of them find accommodation in the hall of residence on the campus, but the great majority have to find accommodation off campus; in this they are assisted by the university authorities. The Cave Hill Campus (of the University of the West Indies), since its establishment in Barbados in 1963 has grown from 118 students to 1900 students in 1985-86.

Appointment to the staff of the University and/or admission to its student body is without reference to sex, race, political affiliation or religious belief. The language of instruction at all campuses of the university is English.

Advanced Studies

Students who satisfactorily complete a suitable first degree at the university or who have acquired degrees of an acceptable- standard from recognized universities may be admitted to postgraduate study for which the first degree constitutes a suitable prerequisite. In some cases supplementary qualifications may have to be acquired before admission to the particular degree program is granted.

The typical master's program extends over two years of full-time study and, in general, completion of a doctoral program requires not less than two years' study beyond the master's level.

ISSUES AND TRENDS

As in other school systems, education in Barbados and in the region as a whole remains plagued by certain problems most of which stem from the way in which the educational systems have developed.

Typical of such problems are the following:

1.   Existing procedures for allocation of pupils to secondary schools tend to place the higher performers in certain "high prestige" schools while the lower level performers find themselves placed in different schools with lower prestige. One of the results of this differential allocation is that both the low performing pupils and their teachers tend to acquire low self-perceptions. This in turn creates a debilitating effect on the teachers' performance in their classroom

activities leading to an undesirable cycle which tends to result in undesirably low performance by both teachers and pupils.

2.   There is an increasing proportion of pupils at primary level who reach the end of the primary school stage without having acquired desirable competence in language skills and who have not reached a satisfactory numeracy level.

3.   There is need for more effective student assessment on a continuous basis; this remains a constant concern to which increasing attention is being directed.

4.   There is the question of whether or not specialization in subject teaching should become a regular feature at primary level. For this reason, a pilot project on this matter was begun and is being closely observed. It focuses attention on the effectiveness or otherwise of specialization among teachers at primary level in the teaching of English and mathematics.

5.   Attention is also being given to review and possible modification of the existing procedures for on-the-job assessment of teachers.

6.   Specific attention needs to be given to the way in which education resources are distributed among schools in the island since it is very evident that this distribution is undesirably uneven.

7.   There is need for greater attention to and support for educational research in the region.

BIBLIOGRAPHY

Goodridge, Rudolph V., and Layne, Anthony. *A Digest of UNESCO Studies and Documents on the Democratization of Higher Education.* Paris: UNESCO, 1984.

Gordon, Shirley C. *A Century of West Indian Education.* London: Longmans, Green and Co. Ltd., 1963.

Harvey Ellis, Joan, and Symmonds, Patricia. eds. *Barbados Functional Competencies Survey.* Barbados: Ministry of Education, 1986.

Inniss, John. *Primary School Reading Survey.* Barbados: Ministry of Education, 1984.

IOP/UWI/ISS. *Project of Cooperation in Teaching and Research in Women and Development Studies.* Barbados: University of the West Indies, Institute of Social Studies, 1985.

Layne, Anthony. *Higher Education in Barbados.* Caracas: CRESALC-UNESCO, 1989.

Marshall, Sir Roy, et al. *Review Report on the Cave Hill Campus.* Barbados: Ministry of Education, 1986.

Miller, Errol. *Educational Research: The English-Speaking Caribbean.* International Development Research Center, 1984.

Ramesar, Esmond D. "Recurrent Issues in Higher Education in the Caribbean - A Critical Appraisal." *In Perspectives in West Indian Education,* edited by Norma A. Niles, and Trevor Gardner. Michigan: Michigan State University, 1977.

Shorey, Leonard L. "Education in the Caribbean Context: Challenge and Opportunity" *In Perspectives in West Indian Education.* edited by Norma A. Niles, and Trevor Gardner. Michigan: Michigan State University, 1977.

Simmons, George C. "Foundations of the Legacy of Classical Learning in the Commonwealth Caribbean." *In Perspectives in West Indian Education,* edited by Norma A. Niles, and Trevor Gardner. Michigan: Michigan State University, 1977.

BELGIUM

by
Pol Georis
Honorary Professor of School Organization
Brussels Free University, Belgium
and
Michel Vilain
Professor of Continuing Education Methods
Brussels Free University, Belgium

BACKGROUND

Two important revisions of the Belgian Constitution occurred in 1970 and 1980 and along with them, the unitary system of education that existed before came to be replaced by a community based system under which the national government shares power with the regions, provinces, and communities. Since January 1989 the power in educational matters and, for a large part, in scientific research has been transferred to the communities. The central government retains responsibility only for three matters: setting limits for the compulsory school attendance period; defining minimum conditions for the conferment of diplomas; and overseeing the pension system.

Education in Belgium is structured along linguistic, political, and religious lines and is a clear reflection of the complex identity of the country. So we now have three different languages of instruction; schools belonging to the Communities (French, Dutch, and German) the provinces, and the local communities; and non-denominational and church-associated organizing bodies. The system is destined to become more and more decentralized with possible structural changes to correspond to local realities.

PRIMARY AND SECONDARY EDUCATION

Primary schools are organized in six classes for the age group 6-12 (nursery schools accept children from 2 1/2-6 years). Schools may call up on the services of remedial teachers who are trained to help pupils having any learning difficulties. Guidance is provided at psycho-medico-social centers. Primary education is tuition free.

Secondary education in Belgium begins at the age of twelve and continues for six years. School attendance is compulsory until the age of sixteen. Compulsory schooling requirement may also be fulfilled by part-time attendance in certain programs or by other specified training, in which case the compulsory requirement extends to eighteen years.

Secondary education is of two types, both of which have the same admission and graduating requirements. Psycho-medico-social centers provide guidance to students in the selection of the type of secondary education stream to suit their individual needs.

The most prevalent and developed type of secondary education consists of two major streams: the transition stream which prepares pupils for higher education, and the qualification stream which prepares pupils for careers whilst allowing them the opportunity of continuing their studies in higher education. The first two years of studies have a common curriculum. From the third year the pupils select one of the following options: general academic education, "transitional" technical or artistic education, "qualification" technical or artistic education.

The second type of secondary education which is somewhat less flexible requires the pupils to make choices very early in the secondary education. They have to choose from general academic education (seven sections: Latin-Greek, Latin-mathematics, Latin-sciences, mathematics A, mathematics B, economics, human sciences) or technical education. Vocational education exist in both types of secondary education and begins from the second year.

Pupils have access to secondary education after having earned the "Certificate of Basic Education." A special first year exists for pupils who encountered difficulties in elementary education.

Higher school certificates and diplomas certifying completion of secondary education are awarded by individual schools and must be ratified by an assessment committee (Homologation Committee). These certificates and diplomas may also be awarded by a state jury. Students following technical, artistic, and vocational streams receive qualification certificates from a mixed jury of the school, consisting of teachers and representatives from the community.

Compulsory education is tuition free for Belgian citizens. The Communities also pay part of the cost of basic school supplies. Foreign pupils are required to pay a tuition fee of 35,000 Belgian francs.

Teachers at lower secondary level generally receive three years of training at the *ecoles normales* (non-university). At higher secondary level, teachers are required to have a university degree (4-5 years of study).

HIGHER EDUCATION

Higher Non-University Education

Belgian higher non-university education has a long tradition. In the last part of the nineteenth century, the industrial development of Belgium required highly specialized technicians in different fields such as mechanical technology, iron and steel, and electrical technology, and non-university courses and training met this vital need. Gradually, the number of schools providing such education grew and today there are over 300 institutions in existence providing training in applied sciences and technical fields. Non-university education is organized or subsidized by the Communities.

Higher non-university education is provided under eight categories: technical higher education, higher education in economics, agricultural higher education, paramedical higher education, higher education in social studies, artistic higher education, pedagogical higher education, and maritime higher education.

Short term higher education lasts one cycle of two, three, or four years and trains students to obtain a variety of qualifications such as nurse, social worker, librarian, archivist, elementary school teacher, and lower secondary school teacher.

Long term higher education last two cycles of about two years each and leads to qualifications such as licenciate, industrial engineer, commercial engineer, and architect.

Admission to most non-university programs require the Certificate of Higher Secondary Education.

Tuition fees vary with the type of studies and can reach 40,000 Belgian francs. Foreigners pay 40,000 Belgian francs for short term type and 60,000 Belgian francs for each of the two cycles of the long term type non-university programs. Living and other expenses for students vary from about 130,000-180,000 Belgian francs, depending on whether students live independently or with their families. The higher cost is for students living independently. (Data valid for 1989-90).

University Education

Belgium has a long tradition in university education. The Catholic University of Leuven dates back to 1436. The universities of Ghent, Liege, and Brussels were founded at the beginning of the nineteenth century. The Communities now finance seventeen university institutions.

University studies are divided into two main categories: studies leading to degrees called legal degrees for which conditions of access, program, and duration of studies are determined by law; and studies leading to degrees called scientific degrees for which conditions of access, programs and duration of studies are determined by universities.

University education is offered in universities, university centers, university faculties, and groups of faculties. University education is also offered at the Faculty of Protestant Theology in Brussels and Heverlee, the Royal Minitary Academy, the Luxembourg University Foundation, and the University Center in Charleroi.

The Universities of Brussels, Louvain-la-Neuve, Leuven, Liege, and Gent also have constituent schools and institutes offering specialized study programs. Most universities offer graduate programs leading to doctorates. Fields of studies available include applied sciences, agronomy, economics and social sciences, law, medicine, philosophy and literature, psychology and education, sciences, and theology.

Admission requirements for universities is the Diploma of Suitability for Higher Education or Certificate of Access examination. Foreign students are required to have equivalent qualifications. The "international baccalaureate" and the "maturity diploma" awarded by the SHAPE school in Casteau (Belgium) are also considered equivalent.

The academic year is divided into two periods of 14-15 weeks, from September/October to July. Generally four years of study are required for an undergraduate degree but professional degrees require additional years: five years for law, dentistry, pharmacy and engineering; six years for veterinary medicine; and seven years for medicine.

Tuition charged at the universities vary from 14,000 Belgian francs per year in the Dutch-speaking universities to 18,000 Belgian francs per year in the French-speaking universities. For certain categories of foreign students additional fees are required: they vary with the type and the level of studies and range from 89,000-271,000 Belgian francs per year. (Data valid for 1989-90).

At state universities, teachers are appointed by royal decree. At free universities, they are appointed by the administration board of the university. The access to teaching posts is limited to persons holding doctorates or those who have earned the degree of professor in higher education.

Scientific research in Belgium is coordinated by the National Council for Scientific Policy and the special law of 8 August 1988 defines the responsibilities of regions, communities and national authorities for scientific research.

A great part of research work is carried out in the universities and about 31 percent of the researchers are working at this level. Scientific research in universities is financed by public institutions (90 percent), private institutions, and international public and private institutions (mostly European).

The Inter-University Council of the French-Speaking Community (CIUF) and the Inter-University Council of the Dutch-Speaking Community (VLIR) act as advisory councils in matters relating to inter-university cooperation.

ISSUES AND TRENDS

Since 1959 Belgium has focused on strengthening its efforts in education by developing a very dense infrastructure, allowing subsidies to the organizing bodies, and financing universities. The cultural emancipation of youth whilst maintaining the requirements of education at a high level continues to be a major aim of the educational effort. Between 1960 and 1984 the secondary student population has grown sixfold and the non-university sector has grown fourfold.

The political preoccupations such as European integration, democratization of education, and equality continue to dominate the thoughts of the educational community. The authorities of the French-speaking Community is planning several measures: organization of priority educational zones *(Zones d'education prioritaire)* with the aim of focusing efforts on disadvantaged school communities; support to pedagogical innovations; and improvement of teacher training with the objective of reducing failures and drop outs.

In the Dutch-speaking Community, the priorities are: decentralization by creating (from 1 January 1989) an autonomous council which will organize official education *(Autonome Raad van het Gemeenschapsonderwijs)* and (from 1 April 1991) local education councils, more rational geographical distribution of university education, and generalization (from 1 September 1989) of a single type of secondary education which will keep the positive aspects of the present two types.

The authorities of the German-speaking Community emphasize the geographical situation of their region (between the French-speaking community and Germany), and the need to organize bilingual education which respects the cultural identity of the pupils.

In each Community scientific research is considered as a priority.

Universities are confronted with new realities. The financial means are gradually diminishing for both education and scientific research. There is a flood of diplomas in some fields of study and a saturation in some sectors of the labor-market. Soaring unemployment of over 10 percent is a matter of concern.

The University Foundation has begun, in 1986, an analysis of university education as it relates to matters of current concern such as the size of the student body, demands of the labor market, failures, financial means, and efficiency.

BIBLIOGRAPHY

Baeck, L. *Enseignement et recherche scientifique: les options prioritaires.* Bruxelles: Fondation Universitaire, 1987.

Crisp. *Université et recherche.* Bruxelles: Crisp, 1987.

De Bock, A., et Mertes, P. *Coûts et allocations d'études supérieures.* Bruxelles: Crisp, 1988.

De Potter, R. *L'Université et sa tâche pédagogique.* Bruxelles: Fondation Universitaire, 1988.

Formation universitaire et marché de l'emploi. Bruxelles: Fondation Universitiare, 1988.

Mandy, P. *Formation universitaire et perspectives d'emploi.* Bruxelles: Fondation Universitaire, 1988.

Ministere de L'Education Nationale. *Education development in Belgium.* Brussels, 1988.

Philippart, A., et Janne, H. "Universities in Belgium: Balance Between Public Policy and Company Influences." *Privatization of higher education: international trends and issues,* edited by R. L. Geiger. Pennsylvania State University, 1988.

BELIZE

by
Colville N. Young
ex-President
University College of Belize, Belize

BACKGROUND

The earliest record of public education in Belize is the Honduras Free School, established by voluntary public subscription in 1816 and supplemented by annual allowances from the public treasury. (The early settlement was generally called Honduras). Management was entrusted to the established Church of England; this early pattern of state-community-church involvement in education continues to this day.

By the end of 1915, there were fifty-eight government-aided church-run primary schools in Belize, staffed by seventy-seven teachers. The total average enrolment was 5,528 but average daily attendance was only 3,912. In that same year a compulsory attendance ordinance was passed (a law whose enforcement put pressure on the then inadequate school facilities). Also compulsory schooling entailed release of the obligation of parents to pay fees as they had done since 1855. Secondary education began in the late nineteenth century and, like primary education, was dominated by the churches.

The educational system of Belize provides education at the preschool, primary, secondary, sixth form or junior college, and university levels. The age levels are approximately 3-5 years for preschool, 6-14 years for primary, 14-17 for secondary, and 17+ for post secondary.

At the primary level, education is universal and compulsory; its extension to fourteen years reflects the fact that a significant part of the student population do not have access to secondary schools.

National educational policy is the ultimate responsibility of the minister of education. To advise him is a National Council of Education (established in 1967) consisting of the chief education officer and fifteen members appointed by the government. While responsibility for the administration of the system lies with the permanent secretary in the Ministry of Education, the chief education officer functions as a professional and technical advisor in the implementation of policy. there are two principal education officers, one responsible for the primary system, the other for secondary and postsecondary. In addition there are fourteen other education officers with various functions and responsibilities (e.g. curriculum development, agricultural education, examinations).

As previously stated, there is a dual system of state-church involvement in education. Government schools and colleges are controlled by the Ministry of

Education. Church or community schools and colleges are managed by the relevant denominational church (principally Roman Catholic, Anglican, and Methodist) or a board or council of community representatives.

Primary education is free except for three private schools charging fees ranging from US$4 to US$50 per month. Church schools receive government grants of 50 percent capital expenditure for building, maintenance, equipment, and furnishings. Recurrent and supplementary grants cover all salaries. Churches provide their own management. Church secondary schools and sixth forms receive government grants of 50 percent of all approved capital expenditure and 60 percent of recurrent expenditures and salaries including faculty and support staff.

As an indication of government's commitment to education, the 1984-85 national budget allocated 21 percent to education; this amounted to US$18,150,000. The first building to be erected at the new University College of Belize campus now nears completion (September 1988) at a cost of over US$1,000,000. This is exclusive of classroom, laboratory and office equipment, and library volumes (over 3,000 valued at about US$120,000; the holding is projected to triple in a year).

PRIMARY AND SECONDARY EDUCATION

At the primary level, education is free and every Belizean child of 6-14 years of age has access to primary schooling. In 1987 there were 40,000 students in 226 primary schools staffed by 1,575 teachers. Only about 119 of the schools are government run. Others are government aided denominational schools.

Studies at primary level terminate with a country wide examination, the Belize National Selection Examination. Some 220 scholarships as well as bursaries for secondary school studies are annually awarded by the government on the results of this examination, based on merit and need.

At the secondary level, only few schools exist and only about 60 percent of primary school leavers continue to secondary school. At present there are twenty-five secondary schools of which eight are managed by the government. Of these eight, the Belize Technical College provides eduction mainly in the sciences and mathematics, business, building construction, engineering and home economics, offering some of these subjects up to associate degree level (sixth form or junior college). Two junior secondary schools offer three-year postprimary courses in academic and vocational subjects. Other technical schools are established in Benque Viejo (west), Orange Walk and San Roman (north), and Belize City, the former capital and the largest urban center. The other seventeen secondary schools are private institutions almost all managed by various churches.

Most Belizean secondary schools have four-year courses leading to the British Royal Society of Arts (RSA) examinations or the General Certificate of Education (GCE) Ordinary Level, of the Cambridge University Syndicate. The latter examining body is being gradually replaced by the Caribbean Examinations Council (CXC), a regional body subscribed to by, and serving, the English-speaking Caribbean. It approximates in scope and level the British examinations but is designed to be more relevant to the needs and environmental realities of its Caribbean contributing territories.

The Stella Maris School for physically handicapped and the Lynne School for the mentally retarded were amalgamated in 1982 to become the Stella Maris School which serves the needs of all students with special learning disabilities. The enrollment in 1984 was 100. In addition to government funding, assistance is provided by service institutions like Rotary. there are also four other special education units, two in Belize City and one each in the south (Dangriga) and north (Corozal).

Secondary school enrolment in 1987 was 7,155 at twenty-four schools, staffed by 522 teachers. About 36 percent of the teachers had university degrees and 20 percent had diplomas or certificates from teacher colleges.

Postsecondary (higher secondary) education in Belize has traditionally been offered at the St. John's College sixth form and the Belize Technical College sixth form. For almost forty years these colleges, the former private (Roman Catholic) and the latter government, have been offering academic courses leading to the associate degree level in the sciences, arts and business. As with sixth forms in most former British colonies, their students sit the overseas General Certificate of Education, (Advanced Level), of the Cambridge University Syndicate. Two subject passes plus a pass in the General Paper of this examination has been the minimum entry requirement for the University of the West Indies (UWI), to which Belize is a contributing territory and to which most of her undergraduates have gone (and still go). In 1985, the sixth form enrollment totalled 403.

In addition, two new sixth forms were established in 1987, one at Dangriga in the south, the other at Corozal in the north.

The Belize Teachers' College awards a trained teachers diploma based on a two-year intra-mural program followed by a one-year teaching internship. This program is moderated by UWI and graduates about 80 annually.

Other institutions involved in professional adult education are the Bliss School of Nursing and the Belize College of Agriculture (both operated by government), The Belize Institute of Management, and the Extra-Mural Department of UWI. The latter has been involved over the years with a variety of cultural and academic activities and offers challenging examinations in law, social sciences, arts, and general studies taken locally after a one-year course. Successful candidates are then permitted to complete a full degree in one year less than usual in one of the campus territories (Jamaica, Barbados, Trinidad and Tobago).

HIGHER EDUCATION

In 1979, the Belize College of Arts, Science, and Technology (BELCAST) was founded by the government to coordinate tertiary education (the sixth forms, the Teachers College, the School of Nursing, and the College of Agriculture), to provide needed technical and professional skills, and to offer courses one year beyond junior college or sixth form level. After an appropriate period of preparation and experience, BELCAST was targeted to evolve into Belize's first national university.

In 1986, government decided to restore the autonomy of the constituent institutions of BELCAST and, to serve the undergraduate needs of Belize, established the University College of Belize. This was a two-year institution accepting students with transfer credits from an associate degree course. Accreditation was formerly ensured by a partnership arrangement with Ferris State University in Michigan.

The initial program offered was a B.Sc. in business, and UCB has its first baccalaureate graduation in May 1988. The young institution has gone on to accept, in September 1988, undergraduates for a new degree, B.Sc. in secondary education. Projected development envisages new degrees in arts, sciences, and social sciences in a few years. In addition, the University College of Belize offers diploma courses in English as a Second Language (ESL) and cooperates with the Ministry of Health in the training of nurses, pharmacists, and medical technicians. Belize, as a bilingual country in Spanish-speaking Central America, has unique opportunities and advantages in the field of ESL and this program, though small, is expected to develop rapidly over the next few years.

University College of Belize operates on a three-term system and fees are US$300 per term (US$900 per year) for full-time students, or US$25 per credit hour. Classes are mostly held in the afternoon and night, enabling students to work during the day and still work towards their degrees. Another advantage of having late classes is that it enables qualified faculty who work elsewhere during the day to contribute part-time services; without such part-time contribution, the range of courses offered by UCB would be greatly curtailed.

The language of instruction at the University College of Belize is English. As in most countries where a Creolized variety coexists with the standard language, there is an urgent need for new and more effective strategies and approaches to language teaching at all levels of the educational system.

University College of Belize is not a residential institution but the establishment of dormitories, especially for rural and foreign students, will proceed as funding becomes available. The fees for foreign students in the University College of Belize degree programs are US$62 per credit hour.

University College of Belize is a chartered institution governed by a council. Members of this council represent a cross-section of the community (business, law, trade unions, government). The charter fully guarantees academic freedom. It has a strong program of cooperation and faculty exchange with several American universities: Ferris State, Murray State, Western Kentucky and North Florida. It is expected that a consortium of these U. S. universities and higher education institutions in Belize has been established. It is expected that the University College of Belize will also establish links with regional institutions in Central America and the Caribbean.

ISSUES AND TRENDS

Education in Belize faces many problems and challenges. There is, for example, the challenge of multilingualism. And although English is the official national language, the variety in common use (called "Belize Creole") is quite different. Another serious problem is the high cost (and, in too many instances, inappropriateness) of foreign textbooks. There is the problem of democratizing education (making education accessible to more of its citizens) without at the same time sacrificing quality.

BIBLIOGRAPHY

Belize in Figures 1988. Government Information Service and the Central Statistical Office of the Ministry of Economic Development, Belmopan, 1988.

Bennett, Joseph Alexander. "Some Aspects of Educational Development in Belize, 1915-1935." In *Journal of Belizean Affairs.* June 1973.

"Educational Development in Belize, 1935-1965." In *Journal of Belizean Affairs.* December 1973.

Nembhard, J. A. "The Educational System of Belize." Ministry of Education, Belmopan, 1984.

Nembhard, J. A. "Overview of Education 1988." Ministry of Education, Belmopan, 1988.

BENIN

by
Souleymane K. Bassabi
Rector
National University of Benin, Benin

BACKGROUND

August 1960 marked the end of nearly a century of colonization of Benin by France. A turbulent period followed after a series of "coup d'etats" but after the revolution of October 1972, the country has returned to a period of relative stability. The colonial educational system that was in place in Benin no longer served the development needs of the newly independent country. The first educational reform was attempted in 1971 under the banner "Gross Tete-Dossou Yovo Reform" (named after the then Minister of Education, Mr. Dossou Yovo, and a French advisor to the Ministry, Mr. Grosse Tete). The reform, as it was being implemented, met with much resistance and in 1975 it was replaced by a new program *Programme National d'Edification de l'Ecole Nouvelle.*

The principal features of the new program of education include: democratization of education by providing education free of charge and without elitism; development of a "new citizen" devoid of "neocolonialist" influences and devoted to development of the country; equality of educational opportunity to every child and equal geographical distribution of educational infrastructure throughout the country; and integration of the school with the society to meet the needs of national development. The realization of these noble objectives, however, ran into many obstacles, notably uncontrolled growth of manpower; the burden of financing the education (about 37-40 percent of the national budget); chronic shortage of qualified teachers; and poor planning and administration. As a result, the quality of education suffered a set back. In 1981 a review of the education brought in some new strategies to make the reforms effective.

Under on the new guidelines, the education is still free at all levels. The only criteria for selection (to different levels) is academic or competitive examinations where the number of places is limited. Parents make a small annual financial contribution towards the schooling of their children: between US$30-100 at the primary level; US$100-170 at secondary level; and about US$180 for higher education. Student's living expenses are borne by the parents.

The Party of the Popular Revolution of Benin, PRPB, (the party in power) and the government set the educational policy for the country, define educational programs, organize the exams and award diplomas. However, if the government so desires, private organizations may assist in the implementation of the educational policy. National education in Benin comes under the administration and control of two authorities: The Ministry of Nursery and Basic (primary) Education which oversees education of children of ages 3-11 years; and the Ministry of Middle (secondary) and Higher Education which oversees education of children over eleven years of age.

The medium of instruction at all levels of education is French. The school year lasts nine months from the beginning of October to middle of June excepting in the case of agricultural education where the academic year is from February to October, to avoid the rainy season.

Teacher recruitment is done by the Ministry of Work and Social Affairs on behalf of the ministries of education. Career advancement is based on the criteria established by the general statute for public servants and specific statutes applicable to the teaching professions.

In 1987, the government expenditure on education was allocated on the following basis: nursery and basic (primary) education 40 percent; middle level (secondary) education 20 percent; middle level technical and professional education 16 percent; and higher education 24 percent.

SECONDARY EDUCATION (MIDDLE LEVEL)

Children who complete primary (basic) school enter secondary education which caters to the age group 11-18 years. Secondary (middle) schools are of two types: general, and technical and professional.

General secondary education lasts for seven years and consists of two levels: Level one that leads to the certificate *(brevet)* of the first cycle (BEPC) after four years of studies; and level two lasts for three more years leading to the *baccalaureat* with different specializations (L-literature, languages and philosophy, B.G.- chemistry, biology and geology, and S.T.-mathematics, physics, and chemistry). This type of education is offered today at 151 public schools with an enrollment of 85,671 students and has grown rapidly till about 1985 (with near doubling of students and facilities in the prior ten years) but is on the decline now. From 1986 to 1988 the student enrollment decreased by 14 percent. This decrease is not a phenomenon unique to Benin but has been a general trend in African schools, primarily due to economic hardtimes facing many countries in the African continent and the resulting decrease in expenditure for education.

The results of the final exams, BEPC and *baccalaureat*, have been deteriorating till about 1987 due to shortage of qualified teachers and teaching material, but corrective measures taken since then have resulted in a significant improvement: 30.7 percent passed the BEPC in 1988 compared to 18.1 percent in 1987, and 26.1 percent passed the *baccalaureat* in 1988 compared to 12.0 percent in 1987.

Training of teachers for general secondary schools take place at the Teacher Training School of the University of Benin and takes five years for certified teachers and three years for assistant teachers (after *baccalaureat*).

Technical and professional secondary education in Benin aims at producing technical workers. There are fifty-five institutions falling into this group, of which thirty-five are private institutions. In 1987-88 there were 6,307 students and represents a slight reduction from the level in 1984-85 (7,871). This sector of education has not always been a priority item on the economic agenda of the country.

Technical and professional secondary schools fall into several categories: agricultural, commercial, industrial, and health related. Agricultural institutions which are all public, trains students at two levels. At level one students entering after primary school receive the Certificate of Tropical Agriculture (BEAT) after three years of studies. Students who do well at level one, as well as those possessing the certificate of the first cycle (BEPC) from general secondary school (on the basis of a competitive examination) have the opportunity of studying for a further period of four years to receive the Diploma of Tropical Agriculture (DEAT). Commercial institutions, some of which are private, trains students for careers related to commerce (accounting, secretaryship etc.) and also has two levels: level one lasting three years and level two requiring an additional three years. Industrial institutions are all public excepting one. They prepare students for different trades (construction, automobile mechanics, industrial design, etc.) at two levels similar to agricultural institutions. Health related institutions (National School of Nursing and the National Medico-Social Institute) are public and trains professionals for health care (nursing assistants' diploma takes three years after middle school and nurses' diploma takes three years after the certificate of the first cycle).

There is a severe shortage of qualified teaching personnel at the technical and professional secondary schools. In 1988, there were only eleven certified teachers and fifty-eight assistant teachers in a teaching staff of 642. The rest were simply *baccalaureat* holders with no teacher training. The teacher shortage in this sector is a matter of serious concern for the government and two new teacher training schools have been opened in 1987-88.

During the colonial period as well as in the years soon after independence, technical and commercial secondary education received very little encouragement from political leaders as well as from parents who preferred the traditional form of general secondary education. As a result, the educational system fell short of producing the skilled manpower to meet the employment needs of the country. The present government has recognized this shortcoming and has, in recent years, focussed attention to this sector of education, given the manpower needs arising from the planned agricultural and industrial development of the country. In view of this, the Ministry of Secondary and Higher Education has authorized in 1988-89, opening of twenty new technical and professional schools compared to four general secondary schools. Also students will be required to spend at least 70 percent of the time for practical work.

HIGHER EDUCATION

Institutions

All higher education institutions in Benin come under the umbrella of the National University of Benin, which is the only university in the country. The objectives of higher education were laid down in 1972 (following the revolution): "It is imperative to establish a democratic and patriotic education system which will provide training in science and modern technology to serve the interests of the people.... to open our university to every form of knowledge and to contemporary scientific learning ... reserving a privileged place for mingling of accumulated experiences of sister universities."

The National University of Benin, established in August 1970 has its beginning in the *Institut d'Enseignement Superieur du Benin* which was founded in 1965 in collaboration with the Republic of Togo. In 1970, this institution was divided into two separate national universities and the University of Dahomy (Benin was known as Dahomy at that time) came into existence with three departments (medicine, science and technology, and letters) and an institute of administration. The university had an enrollment of 350 students. In 1975, it was renamed the National University of Benin and the departments became faculties. Also a university polytechnic college was created. After 1978, based on the needs of the national economy, "professional training institutes" were added (now eleven in number) alongside the traditional faculties. In 1987-88 there were 8,883 students enrolled in the university including 356 foreign students from other African countries.

The university comes under the Ministry of Secondary and Higher Education and is funded entirely by the government. The rector, secretary-general, and directors of academic affairs, administration, and finance form the top echelon of administrators at the university and they are appointed by the council of ministers. The deans of faculties are elected for a period of three years (once renewable) and confirmed by the council of ministers. A National University Council was created in 1982 but has not started functioning yet. The "management committee" consists of the rector; deans and directors; and representatives of teaching staff, trade unions, people organizations, and students. The university has six campuses. The main campus is at Abomey-Calavi and others are at Cotonou, Porto Novo, Lokossa, Parakou, and Natingou.

Teaching staff consists of two categories conforming to public service statutes: assistant professors who have successfully completed the doctorate of the third cycle; and professors who possess the state doctorate *(doctorat d'etat)* and "aggregation" (in medicine, law, pharmacy etc.). In 1987-88 there were 229 assistant professors and 56 professors. In addition there were 306 "assistants" who hold the master's *(maitrise)* or engineer's diploma *(diplome d'ingenieur)* but who have not yet completed a doctorate. The teaching staff included fifty-six expatriates. The African and Malagache Council for Higher Education oversees promotional matters related to teaching staff.

Admission to the university requires a minimum of *baccalaureat* diploma or equivalent. In addition, admission to professional programs where the openings are limited is based on competitive exams. For candidates who do not hold the *baccalaureat*, there is a special examination. In general only a very few candidates pass this special exam (about 150 per year). Admission of candidates without a *baccalaureat* but holding another similar or higher qualification is determined by the *Commission Universitaire d'Orientation.*

Students from Benin pay a nominal fee of about US$20 per year but foreign students are charged about US$430 for non-science programs and about US$500 for science programs.

Undergraduate Studies

With regard to educational programs, the institutions of higher education (all coming under the University of Benin) can be grouped in to three categories: institutions of professional education, institutions of general education, and para-university institutions.

The institutions of professional education provide training leading to a professional career. Admission is based on a competitive exam (after *baccalaureat*). Candidates must be less than thirty years of age. In general students are required to obtain 60 percent of the marks for promotion from one year to the next. There are two levels: level one requires three years of study and leads to "technician" diploma, and level two requires five years of studies and leads to a "higher level" diploma. The exceptions are the "agronomist engineer" program which consists of a single cycle of five years and the medical degree which takes seven years. Major institutions falling into this category include *College Polytechnique Universitaire* (CPU) which has the level one in the areas of medical laboratory work, radiology, natural sciences, civil engineering, electrical engineering, etc.; *Ecole Normale Superieure* (ENS) which offers secondary teacher training programs at both the levels; *Ecole Normale Integree* at Lokosa, Parakou, and Natitingon that trains secondary school teachers at level one; *Ecole Nationale d'Administration* (ENA) which offers programs in public administration at both the levels; *Institut National d'Economie* which trains economists and management personnel at both levels one and two; Faculty of Agronomy which offers the *diplome d'ingenieur* in agronomy, after five years of studies; Faculty of Health Sciences which awards the doctorate in medicine after seven years of studies and offers a four year post graduate specialist training in several fields.

The institutions of general education are the traditional type faculties which admit students on the basis of a baccalaureate, without any competitive exam. They do not prepare students for any specific profession. Here too, there are two levels of studies. Level one takes two years and level two takes additional years (after level one). The faculty of science and technology provides programs in a variety of disciplines: mathematics, physics, chemistry, biochemistry, biology, geology and zoology. Level one leads to a university diploma in scientific studies *(diplome universitaire d'etudes scientifiques)* and level two awards the masters *(maitrise)* in four years. The faculty of juridical, economic, and political sciences prepares students, in two years, for a university diploma in general studies *(diplome universitaire d'etudes generales)* and in four years for the masters *(maitrise)*. The faculty of letters, arts and humanities offer programs in modern literature, languages, linguistics, philosophy, sociology, and geography. A *license* is awarded after three years of studies and a *maitrise* after one more year.

The para-university institution category presently consists of only the Benin Center for Foreign Languages, which provides courses in French.

Advanced Studies and Research

The University of Benin does not offer any doctoral programs at this time (excepting the doctorate in medicine and medical specialist programs). However a program for offering a diploma in advanced studies *(diplome d'etudes approfondies)* has just been established at the *College Polytechnique Universitaire* in the field of mechanics, in collaboration with the *Institut National Polytechnique de Lorraine* (in France) for training twelve of the college's teachers. This type collaboration would probably be a necessity for further expansion of postgraduate education.

Research activities at the university is still very much at an embryonic stage. Shortage of funding and facilities has been the main obstacle but there is also a lack of motivation and initiative on the part of the staff as well as an absence of a proper organizational structure for research. Some research work is being carried out within the academic programs of the African and Malgache Council of Higher Education for aggregation or for the third cycle doctorate and state doctorate *(doctorat d'etat)*. Also many degree students engage in introductory research work, particularly in their final years preparing various studies on topics related to their disciplines. A university scientific council and sectoral scientific committees are in existence but they have not proven to be very effective. A revitalization effort is on the way.

Student Facilities

Student lodging, meals, and transport are subsidized by the government. Student housing is provided at different campuses but sufficient accommodation is not available for all students. Some reside outside the campus. Many cultural, artistic and sports activities are open to students. The *Centre National des Oeuvres Universitaires* at the university coordinates all student activities and assist them materially and morally. There is a scheme of scholarships and financial aid for students, under which the government makes grants varying from US$75-130 per month and give aid up to US$330 per year. Conditions of award vary from year to year depending on the government's ability to set apart necessary funds. In 1988, scholarships were awarded to 2,649 students and aid was given to 601.

ISSUES AND TRENDS

In poor countries, education is of foremost importance because it is the education which produces the principal actors of development. This is so well understood in Benin that education has become a major preoccupation of political authorities who make the policy decisions. The country now spends about 37-40 percent of its national budget for education for providing free education at all levels.

The key user of the end product of education is also the government which is the principal employer in the country. In fact, education is very much oriented towards meeting the manpower needs of the government and, until recently, all students who received scholarships had to serve the government for ten years on completion of their studies. Today, however, the government is no longer able to recruit all graduates coming out of the educational system and the result is unemployment of educated youth for whom the limited resources of the government have been spent without any returns. To resolve this problem it would be necessary to develop in young people initiative and creativity and revise higher educational programs to enable them to stand on their own feet without undue focus on being a "functionary" of the government. This will be a driving force for education reform in Benin in the twenty-first century.

BIBLIOGRAPHY

Pliya, J. The fundamental reform of education in Benin, with particular reference to basic education. In UNESCO 1978 *Experiments and Innovations in Education, No. 34: Educational Reforms and Innovations in Africa.* Paris: UNESCO, 1978.

Pliya, J. Educational reform and available resources: An example from the People's Republic of Benin. In UNESCO 1979 *Education on the Move, No. 2: Educational Reforms: Experience and Prospects.* Paris: UNESCO, 1979.

BOTSWANA

by
Josiah S. Tlou
Associate Professor of Education
Virginia Polytechnic Institute and State University, U.S.A.
and
Gaontatlhe Mautle
Lecturer in Education
University of Botswana, Botswana

BACKGROUND

The history of higher education in Botswana is relatively recent. The University of Botswana, the premier institution of higher education, is one of Africa's newest universities and received full university standing only in July 1982. Before this time, the university was part of the University of Botswana and Swaziland (UBS), a direct successor of the University of Botswana, Lesotho and Swaziland (UBLS) which had its headquarters in Lesotho from 1964 to 1975, and in Swaziland from 1975 to 1982.

Bechuanaland, as Botswana was known until 1966, shared many of its administrative structures and personnel with Swaziland and Basutholand (now known as Lesotho). The three countries were protectorates and did not have means to develop a national system of their own. While the idea of a university was a logical outcome of the need for higher education in Bechuanaland, it was recognized that a separate university was economically impracticable. For many years only a few fortunate students went abroad for university training. Fort Hare University College in South Africa became one of the major centers for Bechuanaland students to obtain training in higher education. However, the South African government's 1952 imposition of university entrance restrictions for foreign black students and the adoption of the apartheid system made education in South Africa intolerable, undesirable, and unacceptable to many Africans.

When the University College of Rhodesia in Nyasaland was established, the question was raised in the Botswana government of a possible link with this new university. However, for historic reasons, the obvious answer lay in cooperation among the High Commission Territories of Basutholand, Bechuanaland, and Swaziland which were administered by a British High Commissioner resident in South Africa until 1964.

The opening of the University of Basutholand, Bechuanaland, and Swaziland (UBBS) in January 1964 was an outcome of the agreement reached in mid 1962 between the High Commission Territories and the Oblates of Mary Immaculate of Pius XII Catholic University, Roma, Lesotho. On 13 June 1963, a deed of cession and indemnity was signed by the Oblates and the High Commissioner of Basutholand, Bechuanaland, and Swaziland. The new university, with funds from the Ford Foundation and the British Government, purchased the assets of the Roma Campus for half its value in exchange for guarantees of a continuing Catholic presence on the campus.

Thus, UBBS became UBLS (the University of Botswana, Lesotho, and Swaziland) in 1966, on the independence of Botswana and Lesotho. The new university conferred its first degrees in April 1967, after a transitional period during which Pius XII College students continued to take University of South Africa degrees. UBLS offered its own four-year degrees and diplomas in arts (including economics and administration), science, and education, with law students following a five-year degree including two years tuition at the University of Edinburgh. Other specialized degrees in medicine and engineering were sought from other universities in cooperation with the UBLS where students completed the first two years in science and then transferred.

UBLS was equally funded by the governments of Botswana, Lesotho, and Swaziland and had comparatively little presence in Botswana and Swaziland during the first phase of this collaboration (1964-70).

Relations between the central UBLS administration and the Lesotho government were strained after student unrest at Roma. As a result of these strained relations with the government of Lesotho, the Roma Campus was precipitately withdrawn from the UBLS and reconstituted as the National University of Lesotho (NUL) on 20 October 1975. This move by the Lesotho government gave rise to the establishment of a national university in each of the three countries. Students from Botswana and Swaziland were immediately withdrawn from the Roma Campus upon the nationalization of the UBLS. As a result of this devolution of the UBLS University College, the Botswana and the Swaziland governments created a new University known as University of Botswana and Swaziland (UBS) with two constituent colleges of Botswana and Swaziland (UCB and UCS), respectively. The constituent colleges of the UBS grew and developed rapidly from 1976 to 1982. By 1982 each constituent college of UBS established a separate National University on 1 July 1982.

PRIMARY AND SECONDARY EDUCATION

Primary schooling in Botswana consists of a seven-year cycle. It is a joint responsibility of the Ministry of Education (MOE) and the Ministry of Local Government and Lands (MLGL). The MOE is responsible for determining the primary education curriculum, for providing teachers, and for supervising teaching throughout the educational system using education officers. The MLGL is responsible for providing school buildings and equipment through financial support to district and town councils. An inter-ministerial committee on primary education coordinates the two ministries. Most of the schools are funded by district or town councils. There are also some government aided church schools and some private English medium and Setswana medium primary schools.

Children start school at the age of six and one-half when they enter standard one. Promotion is automatic except that repetition is allowed in standard four based on some form of an attainment test. At the end of standard seven, pupils take the primary school leaving examination, which is the basis for selection to secondary education. Setswana is the medium of instruction for standard 1-4 and there after, English.

Primary education has experienced rapid expansion and development in the last ten years. At the beginning of 1989 (Republic of Botswana Education Report, 1987-88) there were 568 schools with a teaching force of 7,704 teachers and an estimated enrollment of 248,823 who accounted for about 90 percent of the school going age children. Botswana has adopted a policy of education for all in the form of a nine-year basic education. This nine-year education program is intended to require that all Botswana children at least have nine years of basic education. This development in education expansion is in accordance with the priorities set by the National Development Plan 6 (1985-1991) which were as follows: achievement of universal access to primary education during the plan period; increase of access to postprimary education particularly at secondary and technical/vocational; growth of university enrollments related to the nation's manpower needs; improvement of the quality of education with particular emphasis on science education; and expansion of non-formal education activities to complement formal education.

Currently, the system comprises seven years of primary schooling, three years of junior secondary, and two of senior secondary. This 7-3-2 structure will be modified to 7-2-3 and eventually will become 6-3-3 with universal access proposed for the first two levels (i.e. nine-years of basic education).

Secondary school education in Botswana is provided by the government and boards of private organizations either jointly or independently. This results in the categorization of secondary schools into government, government aided, and private. Government secondary schools are owned, financed, and managed by the central government. Government aided secondary schools are church owned (various Christian denominations) and receive government aid mainly through payment of teachers' salaries. The third type is privately owned, financed, and managed. (However since the 1980s, a larger proportion of private secondary schools and community junior secondary schools have come, at least in practice, under government control). This leaves only one secondary school in the country which is truly private.

The curriculum followed at all secondary schools in Botswana, except at one private secondary school, is basically the same. The junior secondary school curriculum prepares students for the Junior Certificate (JC) examination and the senior secondary school curriculum prepares students for the Cambridge Overseas School Certificate examination (COSC). For the COSC examination, the subjects are divided into seven groups: English language (compulsory); general subjects (history, geography, literature, etc.); languages (Setswana, French, etc.); mathematical subjects (mathematics, additional mathematics, etc.); science subjects (biology, physical science, etc.); arts and crafts (art, woodwork, needle work, cookery, etc.); technical and commercial subjects (commerce, geometrical and mathematic drawing, principles of accounts, etc.).

Students must take at least six subjects including English. Students entering senior secondary school follow either an arts or science curriculum depending largely on their aptitude as indicated by their performance on the JC examination. For the arts stream, English language, English literature, mathematics, and biology are compulsory subjects. Three other subjects are required to be selected. One from languages (Setswana, French); two from general subjects (development studies, geography, history); and one from science subjects or arts and crafts. For the science stream, English language, mathematics, biology, and physical science are compulsory subjects. Three other subjects are required to be selected: one from languages (Setswana, French); one from general subjects (English literature, geography, history, development studies); and one from science (agricultural science) or arts and crafts.

Students with an outstanding ability in physical science are encouraged to register for physics and chemistry as separate subjects and the Ministry of Education (MOE) recommends that two extra afternoon periods be arranged for such students. Schools may teach subjects, such as religious education but such periods must fall outside the required forty periods per week.

Duration of secondary education is five years. (Formerly it took three years junior secondary and two years for senior secondary). Presently the system is going though a transition period which started in January 1986 and is scheduled to last until the mid-1990s. During this transition period, junior secondary education takes two years and senior secondary takes three years. By the mid-1990s secondary schooling will take six years: three for junior secondary and three for senior secondary.

The academic year begins in the middle of January and ends early in December. It is divided into three segments called terms, one of which is usually thirteen weeks and the other two twelve weeks each. The first term begins in the middle of January and ends by the middle of April, the second term begins in the middle of May and ends by the middle of August, and the third starts at the beginning of September and ends by the middle of December.

The one private secondary school follows basically the same COSC curriculum. Its students do the COSC curriculum in four years. The school also has a two year Advanced Level curriculum.

At the Advanced Level, students are allowed to study only three subjects which they have passed well (obtaining grade A or B) at Ordinary Level. For advanced level students, the school takes mostly its own students but it also takes a few from government or government-aided secondary schools.

The main purpose of the JC examination is to select students who can proceed to senior secondary school because of the limited places available at that level. Throughout the whole educational system, places become more limited as curricula become more advanced. Less than one third of the students who enter the first JC class progress to the first COSC class. After writing the JC exam, students are awarded the Junior Certificate in the first, second, or third class. Those who fail are not awarded a certificate. Only those who obtain first or second class can be sure to get a place in a senior secondary school. For example, out of 7,075 students who enrolled for form one (beginning JC class) in 1982 only 2,250 enrolled for form four (beginning COSC class) in 1985. Therefore, for the majority of students, JC is terminal.

Except for the subject Setswana, the COSC examinations are set and marked under the arrangements made by the Cambridge Exam Board. The exams unit of the Ministry of Education only receives papers, makes arrangements for the exams to be written, mails answer sheets back to Cambridge, receives the exams results and passes them on to the Department of Secondary Education for publication. The Setswana examination is set and marked by the examiner identified by the Ministry of Education and scores are sent to the Cambridge Board to be incorporated in the rest of the exam results before the individual candidate's results are classified. Students who pass the COSC examinations are awarded the COSC in the first, second, third, or fourth classes. Those who fail the examination are not given a certificate.

Fees for secondary education were abolished in 1987 and education now is generally free in Botswana with a few exceptions at tertiary level and at private schools. Tuition, boarding facilities in the case of boarding schools, and meals are paid for by the government. The only secondary school related expenses that parents incur are cost of school uniform, transportation fare, and pocket money for the students. All secondary schools (like primary schools) require school uniforms largely because the uniform has been associated with schools since the colonial days but there is no government regulation requiring uniform. Parents, even the poor ones, always struggle to provide a uniform for their children. However Botswana government regulations would not allow a school to expel a student because he or she has no uniform.

Medium of instruction in secondary schools in Botswana is English which is the official language. In fact, it is the medium of instruction throughout the educational system, except during the first four years of schooling when Setswana is the language of instruction.

Access to secondary education is somewhat limited. Less than 50 percent of students who complete the primary school enter secondary school. For example, of the 27,659 students who completed standard seven (last primary school grade) in 1984, only 10,265 were in form one, the following year. However, government projections show that 70 percent of students finishing standard seven in 1990 will be in form one in 1991. As we have noted above, access to senior secondary schools is even more limited and less than 30 percent of those completing JC enter form four. Government projections indicate that 5,257 students out of 11,712 completing JC in 1988 will enter the beginning COSC class in 1989, which will be just over 50 percent.

There are two main factors that limit access to secondary school places. The first is the small number of secondary schools (about ninety-two of which twenty-two are senior secondary schools) as compared to that of primary schools (about 600) even though secondary schools tend to be much larger than primary schools. The second factor is the distribution pattern of secondary schools which favors large villages and urban centers.

The allocation of the limited form one places is based primarily on performance in the Primary School Leaving Examination (PSLE). Certificates based on this examination are awarded in the "A", "B", "C", & "D" classes based on the aggregate scores. Only students with "A" certificates can be sure of form one places. Among the "B's", there are "high" and "low" classifications and the former stand better chances of being admitted. A very small number of students with a 'C' certificate are admitted into secondary schools. Those with 'D' certificates have in reality failed the examination and are never admitted to secondary schools.

Most secondary schools are located in urban areas and large villages (villages with over 1,000 people) and as a result, applicants from these places have better chances of gaining secondary school places, especially as day students. Applicants from places with no secondary schools have almost zero chance of being admitted as day students.

Very few (approximately less than 1 percent) foreign students are enrolled in government secondary schools. Most of them are children of foreigners working in Botswana. A large number of foreign students attend school at the private secondary school.

Teaching staff is selected, appointed, and administered by the Unified Teaching Service which is a department of the Ministry of Education. At present there is a shortage of secondary school teachers. For example, in 1984, out of a total of 1966 secondary school teachers only 941 had been professionally prepared (422 were expatriates), and 1,025 were qualified to teach their subjects but were not professionally prepared.

Most of the expatriate teachers come from the US through the Peace Corps Voluntary Service and from the UK through the British Council. But there are also expatriate teachers from other countries, notably India, Denmark, Australia, Norway, Sweden, and some African countries. When a serious shortage is anticipated, the Ministry of Education usually sends officials to other countries on recruiting missions. Expatriate teachers are employed on two-year renewable contracts. Teachers who are citizens are tenured after satisfactorily serving two years of probation.

HIGHER EDUCATION

Institutions

Apart from the University of Botswana, higher education institutions (tertiary) consist of five teacher training colleges, one polytechnic, one agricultural college, and a national health institute. Currently, only the University of Botswana and the agricultural college award degrees. The polytechnic is still seeking degree awarding status. Other institutions provide only diploma certificates.

Teacher training is conducted at four primary teacher training colleges: Francistown Teacher Training College; Lobatse Teacher Training College; Serowe Teacher Training College and Tlokweng Teacher Training College. These four teacher colleges prepare teachers for primary schools. Currently it takes two years to prepare as a teacher with a Junior Certificate plus at least two years teaching experience. Plans are underway to upgrade these colleges to have a minimum entrance requirement of the Cambridge School Certificate or its equivalent. With those qualifications, the colleges will offer a diploma in primary education which will take three years to complete. Molepolole College of Education prepares junior secondary teachers and the minimum entrance qualification is the Cambridge Overseas School Certificate. It takes three years to complete a diploma in education. The graduates of the program are employed in junior high schools (years 7-9). Plans are also underway to start work on the Tonota College of Education which will have the same function as the Molepolole College of Education preparing junior secondary teachers.

Botswana Agricultural College (BAC) in Sebele, is a constituent college of the University of Botswana and offers Bachelor of Science degrees in agriculture. It also offers certificates in animal health, community development, and agriculture, and offers diplomas in agriculture and animal health. Botswana polytechnic is seeking affiliated status with the University of Botswana and is currently working on upgrading itself to be a degree awarding institution of the University of Botswana as a faculty of engineering. The National Health Institute (NHI) with its main campus next to the Princess Marina hospital in Gaborone and with four branches in Francistown, Lobatse, Serowe, and Molepolole is charged with the training of nursing and paramedical personnel in Botswana. It became an affiliated institution of the University of Botswana in 1985. To date there have been three graduation ceremonies at which the University of Botswana qualifications have been awarded to students who successfully complete NHI programs. The application agreement with the NHI is overseen by a board of affiliation. This board is advised by an advisory council. The university senate is the final authority for the award of certificates and diplomas and the appointment of external examiners.

The University of Botswana is composed of four faculties: education, humanities, science, and social sciences. Academic programs within the faculties are offered at certificate, diploma and degree levels. In addition to these four faculties, the National Institute for Research and Documentation (NIR) is also located within the university.

The university is governed by the university council. This university council is made up of leading figures nationally and from the university community. The council as a governing body of the university has broad powers to make statutes, lay down policy, approve programs, and determine any governance procedures for the university. Academic matters are handled by the university senate, composed of senior members of the academic staff and student representatives. The senate has the responsibility for general control and direction of teaching and research activities, examinations, and conferment of degrees.

The chief academic and administrative officer of the university is the vice-chancellor who is the chairman of the senate and is responsible to the university council. He is assisted by a deputy vice-chancellor. The registrar is responsible for academic appointments. The deans of the faculties, the director of NIR, and senior administrative staff, are responsible directly to the vice-chancellor. In the British Commonwealth university structure adopted by many former colonies, the chancellor of the university is usually the head of state. In this case the head of the government of Botswana is the chancellor and the chancellor's position is a titular one.

Undergraduate Studies

The University of Botswana offers undergraduate degrees in arts, commerce, education, science and law. Most bachelor degree programs take four years but professional programs like law take five years.

Duration of the academic year at the University of Botswana is two teaching semesters of not less than fifteen weeks each. The year begins in August and ends in May. Semester one starts in late August ending in early December. Semester two begins in early January and ends in mid-May. The two semesters have each a week's short break. The medium of instruction is English.

Admission into a bachelor's degree program at the university requires either a first or second class pass in the Cambridge Overseas School Certificate (an aggregate of at least twenty-five has to be scored with credit in English language and a credit in mathematics if the student wishes to enrol for a B.Sc. or B.Com. degree) or a General Certificate of Education (GCE) provided that the candidate has taken examinations at the Ordinary Level in at least six subjects in not more than two sittings, obtaining minimum grades of "B" in two subjects and "C" in four other subjects. One of these subjects must be English language (and another must be mathematics for students who wish to enrol for a B.Com. degree). Completed applications must reach the university before the first of April of the academic year for which admission is sought. Student enrollment in the academic year 1988-89 was 2,937, of whom about 7 percent were foreign students.

For applicants who do not have the above qualifications, another admission criterion, The Mature Age Entry Scheme, is used. Candidates who qualify for admission under this scheme must be at least twenty-five years old. These candidates must have at least a minimum qualification of a Junior Certificate or its equivalent to enter the university under the Mature Age Entry Scheme. Candidates must usually have been working for at least two years. They must have completed their full-time school or college education at least five years before the beginning of the academic year for which admission is sought. They should also show that they have attended extramural classes or have undertaken a course of study at an institution recognized by the university.

Extracurricular activities available to university students are manyfold. These various activities are run by a student government called the Student Representative Council (SRC). Various sporting clubs, and social and cultural groupings are organized and aided through the SRC. Over twenty clubs and societies are in existence in areas varying from jazz to political forums. The University of Botswana also offers a competitive intramural program for men and women and co-recreational programs in about fifteen areas including soccer, softball, boxing, athletics, karate and netball.

Halls of residence are situated on campus. More space is being developed and sought for building more of these halls. Students who cannot find accommodation on campus are paid an "off-campus allowance."

University charges a tuition fee of P2,000 for natives and P4,000 for foreign students. Accommodation costs an additional P1,200. Expenses for books, notebooks, personal laboratory equipment, and personal needs are additional. Most students (citizens and foreign students) are sponsored by their respective governments. Very few students are sponsored by either their parents or private organizations. The university does not make loans of any nature to students.

Advanced Studies

The University of Botswana offers master's degrees in arts, education and science. Offerings at the doctoral level are in the planning stage.

Admission to the postgraduate degree programs is severely restricted at present. It is dependent upon staffing and availability of research facilities. Admission to a program leading to a master's degree must be approved by the senate. Permission to pursue a masters' degree program as a part-time student is granted to persons who can show that they are able to devote a reasonable proportion of their time to the work prescribed.

The normal minimum entrance requirement is a bachelor's degree of this or any other recognized university or institution. Applicants should have passed with at least a second-class second-division or its equivalent. The applicants should have studied in their first degree to the level of a "major" in the subject for study in the master's program. Other applicants may be admitted if they satisfy the senate of their potential.

Normally the master's degree is completed or is earned by course work and dissertation. Each student will successfully complete a minimum of four full-courses or their equivalent, before starting formal work on the dissertation.

Candidates may register for the degree by thesis alone, provided they have shown or demonstrated to the department, faculty, and senate their ability to conduct research by submitting to the department concerned a comprehensive research proposal in the approved form. A minimum of second-class first- division in the first degree is normally an additional requirement. The senate may require the candidate to audit certain courses.

The normal period of study for course work is the equivalent of two semesters for full-time students, and four semesters for part-time students unless otherwise specified in the faculty or departmental special regulations.

The dissertation is normally submitted within one year of completion of course work. An extension of six months may be approved by the faculty. The dissertation is a report of original work and/or a review of progress to date in the chosen area of study.

In the case of a degree by thesis alone, the thesis must be submitted within twenty-four months but not in less than twelve months. An extension of six months may be approved by the faculty. Extensions beyond the limits expressed in the regulations may be permitted by the senate on the recommendation of the faculty.

Teaching Staff for the university is recruited internationally. There are, however, some organizations which help to recruit the teaching staff for the university and they include Association of Commonwealth Universities; Association of African Universities, Ghana; Economic Commission for Africa; Techno Impex, Harare; and the University of Yugoslavia.

The university also has agreements with certain universities and institutions in the Netherlands, Canada, U.S.A., and U.K. Through these agreements, these organizations may provide staff to the university, or have the university send some members of staff for training at these institutions or may send some teaching staff and supplement their salaries. Selection of staff is based on academic qualifications, experience and records of research and publications.

ISSUES AND TRENDS

Since independence, the educational system in Botswana has expanded tremendously. Currently, over 90 percent of school going age are enrolled in primary schools. Secondary and higher education is also becoming increasingly available to the Botswana population with 41 percent of school age population now in junior secondary and 19 percent in secondary schools. Along with this rapid expansion in educational opportunities and a population which is becoming increasingly more educated, there is a considerable change in the economic and social climate in Botswana.

Botswana has made extraordinary progress since independence economically. Its economic growth, measured by Gross Domestic Product (GDP) has averaged 12.8 percent per year since 1965. In the past five years, the country experienced growth in the GDP at a much faster rate than anticipated. This growth is attributed to diamond exports, which is now eight times what it was in 1965. The government policy is to diversify its economic activities. The high population growth rate is being reduced (3.8 percent in 1981 to estimated 3.3 percent in 1990). Infant mortality rates are down from 69 per thousand in 1981 to an estimated 56 in 1990). Health conditions are improving. Clinics or health facilities are provided in most communities in rural Botswana. Literacy is on the rise (51 percent in 1981 to 84 percent in 1990). In all these major changes, education is having a critical impact on the development of the people of Botswana. Equally, as the economy diversifies and grows in complexity, there is a corresponding increase in the demand for educated and trained people.

Botswana is committed to providing nine years of basic education to all Botswana of school going age. The government of Botswana has decided that education must respond to social needs of the people such as employment opportunities. Therefore, such basic education should be relevant to employment. This is not to argue for vocationalization of the educational system, but for prevocational skills and attitudes and values that are desirable in basic education.

It is hoped that in this next planning period (the National Development Plan VII 1991-97), the emphasis on basic education should make students who graduate with the nine-year schooling, value the dignity of work, self-reliance, action orientation, optimism, organization of task, efficient use of time, and working with others to achieve a common goal. They are values that emphasize understanding and problem solving in education, rather than rote learning. The role of basic education as envisioned by Botswana is that the basic curriculum should prepare students for the world of work and for further education or training. A basic education curriculum that relates more directly to the economy and prepares school leavers, after nine years of school, to enter the workforce with little or no major problems, helps reduce unemployment, and helps meet the increasing demand for more skills while providing literacy to people at all levels. This type of curriculum should become a step ladder to senior secondary and tertiary education.

The projected University of Botswana policy is to support the government emphasis on rural development and job creation. During the National Development Plan 7 (NDP7) period there will be great challenges facing the university and all tertiary education levels. As the development and expansion of the basic education for the majority of Botswana children progresses, the pressure to expand the secondary level education mounts, and in turn presses demands for higher education at the tertiary level. The university, therefore, plays a pivotal role in training higher level manpower for rural development needs.

The university has just undergone a review by an international review team. There are likely to be new departments added to the university programs, and these may be in home economics education, special education, physical education, health and recreation, educational technology and guidance, and counseling. Plans are also afoot to develop and expand the computing capability at the university by establishing the computer center in order to provide skills in computer literacy.

The university plans to expand enrollments to 5,000 students by the end of the planned period. This type of expansion will require both physical development and faculty increases. There will be need to ensure quality links between expansion on one hand and services provided on the other. The university should place an increased emphasis on the improvement of teaching and research in higher education both at the university itself and at other postsecondary institutions, including teacher training colleges, throughout Botswana. This can be done through, among other things, affiliatory arrangements.

BIBLIOGRAPHY

Botswana, Republic of. *A Career for Secondary Schools*. Gaborone: Government Printer, n.d.

Botswana, Republic of. *National Policy on Education*. Government Paper No. 1 of 1977. Gaborone: Government Printer, 1977.

Botswana, Republic of. *Report of the National Commission on Education: Education for Kagisano*. Gaborone: Government Printer, 1977.

Botswana, Republic of. *Follow Up Report of the Presidential Commission on Localization and Training in the Botswana Public Service, 1977*. (Reviewed 1979, Re-reviewed 1981). Gaborone: Government Printer, n.d.

Botswana, Republic of. *National Development Plans*. 1970-75; 1976-81; 1981-86; 1986-91 and proposed 1991-96. Gaborone.

Botswana Ministry of Education. *The Development of an Intermediate School: A Report of the Committee to Consider Guidelines for the Curriculum for New Expanded Junior Secondary Schools.* Gaborone, 1983.

Institute of Development. *Botswana Primary School System.* Gaborone: University of Botswana, n.d.

Kann, Ulla, and Nelson, Mokgethi. *An Educating Broadening, Maturing Experience.* Gaborone: Government Printer, 1981.

Pesci, F. B., and See, J. H. *Future Development of Higher Education in Botswana.* USAID Contract No. AFR-C. 1457 with the Overseas Liaison Committee of the American Council on Education. Gaborone: USAID, 1979.

Picard, L. A., and Endresen, K. *A Study of the Manpower and Training Needs of the Unified Local Government Service (1982-92).* Volume 1. Gaborone: Institute of Development Management, n.d.

Townsend-Coles, E. K. *Education in Botswana.* Gaborone: Government Printer, 1986.

Turner, John D. *The Role of the University in Meeting National Manpower Requirements.* Gaborone: Botswana Society, 1983.

World Bank. *Supervision Report, Third Education Project in Botswana.* 1983.

USAID. *Botswana Education and Human Resources Sector Assessment.* Gaborone: USAID and Ministry of Finance and Development Planning, 1984.

BRAZIL

by
Alírio F. Barbosa de Souza
Associate Professor, Faculty of Education
Federal University of Bahia, Brazil

BACKGROUND

Till about the beginning of the nineteenth century, Brazilian students seeking higher education had to leave for Europe, going to universities in Portugal and France. There were no colleges or universities in Brazil. At the end of 1807, the Portuguese royal family left for Brazil pushed by the French invasion of Portugal ordered by Napoleon. Brazil became the seat of the Portuguese throne and that epoch saw the birth of higher education in the colony. Higher education institutions were created in order to provide necessary training to those entering public service. Several institutions and programs came into existence between 1808 and 1818: Royal Academy of Navy, Royal Military Academy, Surgery Program, and Surgery and Anatomy Program. The evolution was in the direction of isolated colleges of medicine, law, and engineering (polytechnic school).

With the advent of the republic system in 1889, there were five colleges in Brazil: two colleges of medicine (Bahia and Rio de Janeiro), two colleges of law (Recife and Sao Paulo) and a college of engineering in Rio de Janeiro. The lack of a college of liberal arts made the colleges of law and medicine, centers for studying philosophy.

In 1915 an educational reform authorized the organization of a federal university, which was accomplished in 1920. From that time on, universities were organized according to specific national legislation. Despite being a theme of cogitation since the Empire's creation, the Brazilian university was born from circumstances; and, in almost in its totality, it emerged from the simple union of isolated institutions of higher education which were primarily professional colleges. Thus, professional preparation was the key note.

Some characteristics of contemporary university development in Brazil are directly linked to its origin: (1) the elitist character, (2) the prestige of professional colleges, (3) the great emphasis on teaching, and (4) the almost forgotten research and extension functions. The elitist character of higher education is due essentially to the small number of institutions and to the maintenance of certain mechanisms of admission such as the entrance examination *(vestibular)* and the requirement of an academic secondary education. When vocational and academic secondary education were equated, a great barrier remained due to the paucity of available places. Colleges and universities had an interesting characteristic until the beginning of the 1960s: a great demand for places at professional colleges but a surplus of offerings in the humanities (Brito and Carvalho 1978).

The prestige of professional colleges is based on historical and economical factors. They were the only colleges at a time when the demand was absolute. The few graduates were elite people or they were socially promoted. Education was a privilege (Teixeira 1957). The political, economic, and social success of physicians, engineers, and lawyers, reinforced in the public mind the feeling that a bright, wealthy, and successful future was linked to those professions. Nobody thought of attending a "university", but specifically a college of medicine, law, or engineering. Cultural conditions tended to reinforce that image because there were only few primary and secondary schools. In 1920 approximately 65 percent of the population was illiterate (Simonsen 1974).

The Brazilian institutions of higher education were highly influenced by the French system where research was omitted from universities and colleges because research was developed separately through institutes of research. Research could occur as the will of some bright spirit. Even in the twentieth century, emphasis continues to be on teaching. Research made some contribution in the area of public health where tropical diseases were studied at colleges of medicine.

A historical distortion in the student body of public institutions was created by the fact that most of the students were members of the upper or middle classes. According to Anision Teixeira (1976), the weapon that elites founded to avoid admission of the lower classes to colleges and universities was the requirement of an academic secondary education. Once that requirement was eliminated, there remained stiff competition for the few places at prestigious colleges, and again, the quality of secondary education remained a decisive factor in *vestibular* performance.

In 1977 a national survey (Veja 1977) showed that 80 percent of college students could afford their studies and only 20 percent deserved a tuition-free higher education due to economic disadvantage. However, 45 percent of total college students were attending tuition free institutions. Another observed aspect was that students who needed to work were attending private institutions which had evening programs.

PRIMARY AND SECONDARY EDUCATION

Primary education in Brazil is organized into eight years divided in two levels of four years each with the first level corresponding to elementary school (the first four years). Elementary school is developed in classes by age group and grade, under the responsibility of one teacher for each classroom. At the second level (5-8 grades) class assignments are distributed by teachers with specialized knowledge in their fields (Portugese language, history, sciences, etc.), and by the number of week-hours for each discipline. Nowadays the school year is required to have at least 180 class days or 720 hours, yearly. But, the Ministry of Education intends to push it up to 200 days or more or 900 hours yearly. Primary school provides only basic education. Students must initiate the first grade when they are seven years old.

There is no public preschool and this kind of education has been developed by the private sector. Primarily it is the middle class and wealthy families who sponsor preschool type education for their children. Usually student groups who attend preschool are those who continue to attend private schools and higher education institutions. The lack of more widespread preschool education could be one of the causes for high dropout and repetition rates at the first grade level of elementary school.

Teachers who are trained at "normal schools" (secondary education) can teach at elementary schools. If they get additional training they can teach till the sixth grade. To teach at seventh and eighth grades it is necessary to have university training.

Secondary education is developed in three years and students may follow an academic or professional stream. Both streams give students the right to apply for admission to higher education institutions. Even the professional curriculum present one year of general education (usually the first year). Diplomas or certificates awarded by professional schools confers the titles of "technician" to students.

The length of the school year is the same as in the primary school: 180 class days or 720 hours. For professional certificates an internship or training in the specific activity is required.

Teachers who work at the secondary schools must have a university degree. The reality is that schools which are in urban centers, big towns, and cities have teachers with appropriate qualifications, as specified but inland-schools do not always have that privilege and at secondary level these schools may have teachers with only "normal school" training. In rural areas, all grades of the primary have one classroom schools with only one teacher in-charge of students of different age-groups.

Public primary and secondary schools are funded and administered by the municipalities and/or the state government. Principals are appointed from among teachers and the appointments may depend upon political affiliations. Although teachers must be contracted through public contest, it has not always been the case in the past.

HIGHER EDUCATION

Institutions

Higher education institutions in Brazil are organized under government law and chartered by the Federal Council of Education, a normative organ of the Ministry of Education. They can be organized as colleges or universities. The initiative may be private or public (state). Public institutions are funded by the public treasury and tuition is free. Private institutions are maintained by private foundations or associations. Legally colleges and universities are non-profit organizations.

The most common way of organizing a university has been through the agglutination of colleges. In the past most of the universities were organized in this fashion. Even today that practice can be used by colleges which intend to join together existing programs in specific areas of knowledge like health, humanities, technology, etc. Before, due to this agglutination process, a university had to have at least five colleges. In reality "colleges" in the traditional sense are not needed since the organizational chart can accommodate several programs in "centers" like "center of health sciences", "centers of humanities", etc. This kind of organization is a real revolution because the Brazilian tradition is one program, one college: College of Medicine, College of Nutrition, College of Dentistry, College of Law, College of Pharmacy, College of Economics, etc.

The start of a college or a university must be authorized by the Federal Council of Education which will provide supervision in order to grant accreditation. Without accreditation, the institution cannot issue legitimate diplomas. The transformation of colleges into a university is a long transitional process. At first, the colleges become an "association" or "federation" while some specific requisites are met. Finally, after the completion of all requirements, the university charter is issued.

As the normative organ of higher education, the Federal Council of Education may intervene directly or indirectly in the running of colleges and universities when academic quality is lacking, when administration is poor, or when specific legal requirements are not observed.

Educational legislation in Brazil has changed over the years. Norms and requirements for starting new higher education institutions have been modified. But, since the organization of the first university in 1920, the federal government has created at least one federal university for each state. And the organization of universities has been influenced by several factors like political pressure, popular request, and development strategy, etc.

In the 1930s there was a movement in the direction of creating modern universities. In 1934 the University of Sao Paulo was created and in 1935 it was time for the University of the Federal District. Both were connected to the idea of universities prevailing in the United States and in some European countries, based on rational organization and a research orientation. Due to political unrest, the University of the Federal District was closed in 1937. The University of Sao Paulo survived, with some orientation. The University of Sao Paulo became, for a long time, the best university in the country. At the beginning, several foreign professors participated. At the University of Sao Paulo a College of Philosophy, Sciences, and Letters was created, and it was the first one in Brazil. After 1940 the number of universities began to grow. By 1954 there were sixteen universities, which increased to thirty-seven in 1964 (Cunha 1983). In the 1960s universities and colleges faced many problems including pressure for more places. Admissions were made through entrance examinations *(vestibular)* but the number of successful candidates were greater than the real number of places available. Other problems were related to the old functional structure in higher education institutions, like enrollments on an annual basis instead of on semester and discipline basis. Also students' involvement in politics was active. Law no. 5540 of 28 November 1968 brought about reforms in university education by changing admissions policy to a "classification" basis, reorganizing universities and colleges into institutes and departments, and permitting enrollment by disciplines.

Institutions of higher education may be located in a single campus or may consist of several campuses. The University of Sao Paulo was the first one to have colleges in different towns of the state. Presently, several state universities are also organized on the multi-campus basis, agglutinating already existing colleges and by creating new ones.

According to data from the Brazilian Ministry of Education (1987) Brazil has 853 institutions of higher education, of which 82 are universities and 771 are individual colleges and college federations (integrated colleges).

In the Southeast region, the richest part of the country, there are thirty-five universities and 516 colleges. In the South region which also represents a high level of economic growth, there are eighteen universities and 126 colleges. The Northeast region which is the poorest, is in third place with twenty universities and eighty-one colleges. Centerwest region has five universities and thirty-six colleges. The Northern region, which has the Amazon river and the jungle, has four universities and twelve colleges.

Of the total number of higher education institutions mentioned above, 28 percent are public institutions. Of the universities, 65 percent are public institutions. The biggest universities in the country are public universities.

Governance

Each university is administered by a board of trustees usually known as the university council. The board composition may vary from one institution to another. Generally this board consists of the university rector, deans of colleges, faculty representatives, employees, students, and community members. The university council nominates, from among university professors, six names, for the selection of the rector. In the case of public universities, the rector is chosen by the president of the republic from among the names submitted. In the case of state universities the selection is made by the state governor. In private universities, the board chooses the rector. In the case of Catholic universities, the list may be submitted to the cardinal (or bishop) acting as the university chancellor.

In federal universities, there is also the council of coordination composed of the rector; vice-rector; adjuncts of rector for administration and planning, undergraduate teaching, research and graduate studies, and extension; and representatives of various university programs. It is the university's highest body for solving academic and administrative problems. Usually the council of coordination is divided into chambers: chamber of undergraduate teaching, chamber of extension, and chamber of research and graduate teaching.

The colleges are administered by deans and heads of departments. While the dean is more involved in administrative tasks and in facilitating the institutional flow of information, the academic administration of courses is a departmental responsibility. At federal universities, programs may come under a collegiate body with a coordinator.

Rectors and deans have a mandate for four years. One cannot serve two consecutive mandates. Department heads are elected by peers for two years and one re-election is permitted. The same applies to program coordinators.

Teaching Staff

Teaching staff at Brazilian universities is hired on a full-time or part-time basis. At public institutions it is easier to find people to be hired on a full-time basis. At private colleges and universities a part-time contract is common. In 1987, 42 percent of professors were working with full-time contracts (Ministry of Education, 1987). On the average, the professor-student ratio is 1:7.

The process of higher education reformation initiated in the 1960s generated a significant growth in the number of students in higher education, and resulted in a demand for new professors. New colleges were opened. Universities created new programs or increased enrollment. As a result, many professors were appointed. The Law 5540 annulled the function of *"professor catedratico"* and established a career plan (*"catedratico"* was a powerful professor). Currently the categories of professors are: full professor, associate professor, assistant professor, and auxiliary professor. Although appointment of professors is through public examination, many professors received appointments on a provisional basis due to expansion of education and later they received permanent positions.

Most of the new professors had only undergraduate diplomas. The lack of a strong policy on graduate education in the country resulted in the creation of the program *"Plano Intensivo de Capacitacao Docente* (Intensive Plan for Professor Improvement)" or PICD in 1976, for the upgrading of professors and implementation of a new policy of graduate studies in the country.

The objectives of the PICD were to send out of the country professors for master's and doctoral programs particularly in areas needed by the country or for programs not available in Brazil. As a result, many professors left their universities or colleges to attend graduate programs in foreign countries, mainly in the United States, France, England, and Germany. Others preferred to stay and look for places in the few existing doctoral programs. There was also the efforts to strengthen graduate programs and research at higher education institutions.

The present norms and regulations require public examinations for selection of professors to public universities and colleges. While an undergraduate degree is adequate to become an auxiliary professor, the assistant and associate professors require a master's degree. In order to apply for full professor, a doctor's degree is required. Statistical data from the Ministry of Education (1987) show that 13 percent of the professors hold doctorates, 21 percent have a master's degree, 34 percent have "specialization", and 32 percent have only the undergraduate diploma.

Undergraduate Studies

In Brazil, all undergraduate programs are professional ones, although it is very difficult for students in some programs like the B.A. in philosophy to get a job. Programs vary in length from four to six years: medicine (six years); law (five years); engineering (five years); teacher education (four years); business administration (four years); nursing (four years); and dentistry (five years). Physicians do not receive a doctorate; instead they get a medical degree. Engineers get the degree of engineer. Lawyers, nurses, economists, sociologists, etc., are bachelors. Teachers are licentiates, etc.

The university calendar is organized in two semester-terms with the possibility of summer courses. Courses are structured according to the number of hours (45, 60, 75, etc.) and credits which can be theoretical or practical ones. Student evaluation is done by the professor in charge of the course. The evaluation may consist of tests (written or oral) or final assessment or final paper.

Admission to higher educational programs is based on an entrance examination *(vestibular)* which is given once a year. Students must finish the second degree (senior high school) in order to apply. Entrance examinations cover the following subjects: language (Portugese), humanities (history, geography, social studies), natural sciences (biology, chemistry, physics), mathematics, and one foreign language.

In 1987 there were 447,345 places open in higher education institutions and about 67 percent of these places were offered by private institutions. To get into a university or college is a big "battle". While finishing the senior high school, usually during the last year, students undertake private lessons *(cursinho)*. *Cursinho* is very important because it reviews all subjects during the academic year in a very specific manner, training students for answering questions in the entrance examination. All over the country there are famous *cursinhos*.

The practice of taking private lessons favors upper and middle class students whose family can afford expensive fees. The *cursinhos* industry is so profitable that many private senior high schools have changed the traditional way of academic functioning of the last year, in order to act like a *cursinho,* thereby avoiding loss of students.

At the beginning of the academic year (March) a commercial struggle occurs via billboards, television, radio, newspapers, trying to recruit "customers" for *cursinhos.* In 1987 there were 2,193,861 candidates for 447,345 places in higher education, meaning that a clientele for *cursinhos* is assured, because one can apply for an entrance examination at any time during his life, without restriction.

This process facilitates the admission of students who attended private schools, not only in the number of candidates admitted but also with regard to entrance into prestigious colleges or programs like medicine, engineering, law, etc. Public school students in general belong to the low economic strata. They cannot afford *cursinhos.* The quality of teaching at public schools is something questionable. These students are generally admitted in a small number, and primarily in programs which will not assure a compensatory social and financial reward.

There is no athletic tradition in Brazilian higher education. Nowadays students are obliged to attend classes in physical education. The great tradition is student involvement in politics. All academic programs must organize, according to law, a student association. At a university there is also a central association of students. The associations are important political instruments due to their ability to organize and agglutinate students. Association presidencies are highly contested by rightist and leftist groups. It is very common almost every year for students to find enough reasons to protest: "against the privatization of education", "against the federal policy on education", "against the university rector", etc.

In 1987 the total student enrollment in Brazil was 1,470,559, in public and private institutions of higher education (Ministry of Education, 1987). There are about ten students in higher education for every 1,000 citizens.

Advanced Studies and Research

Graduate studies are done through master's and doctoral programs. Research can be done by any professor who must submit the proposal to his department for evaluation. Financing can be a challenging task for the researcher or for the institution. Through graduate programs all over the country it was created "thematic lines of research" in specific subjects like "higher education", "tropical diseases", "illiteracy", etc. These "thematic lines of research" have better chance of getting financing. Subjects of these "lines of research" are developed by professors and students and also by postgraduate students in their thesis and dissertations.

The Master of Arts degree programs take a maximum of three years. Besides the theoretical credit-courses, a dissertation is required. The doctor's degree, with a maximum of five years length requires a thesis besides the theoretical credit-courses and the qualifying examination. According to CAPES (Ministry of Education), by 1989 there was in Brazil 925 master's programs and 399 doctoral programs, most of them in the South and Southern regions, the best developed part of the Country.

ISSUES AND TRENDS

Higher education in Brazil faces significant issues, many of which are a function of the social environment. First of all the illiteracy rate in the country is still very high and is around 25 percent in the most developed urban areas and 40-60 percent in rural areas. The new Brazilian Constitution aims at eliminating illiteracy in ten years. But given the fact that many other similar commitments in the past have not seen much results, the prospects of wiping out illiteracy are in question. Second, the public primary school continues to be a priviledge. According to official information of the Brazilian government, there were about eight million school age children out of school at the beginning of the school year 1989. Besides, high drop out at the junior high school level is a serious problem. Third, the secondary school or senior high school within the public system is not sufficient to accommodate all students. At this level the "lion's share" belongs to private secondary schools, generally *vestibular* oriented, but very expensive and not affordable for public school leavers. The passage between junior and senior high school is a major hurdle which eliminates most of the students from the formal educational system.

There are also problems involving financing, expansion, improvement, and politics.

Financing of higher education in Brazil follows two single lanes: the public treasury for public institutions, and tuition and fees for private institutions. The Ministry of Education claims to allocate around 80 percent of its budget to higher education. The practical result of that way of financing is not unpredictable. Public colleges and universities are already feeling the tightening of resources. Other social needs are pressuring the government, and the treasury has not been able to help everybody. But even knowing and observing the behavior of public funds, public colleges and universities do not have skills to look for money in other places. There are no fund raisers, there is no alumni association, and contracts for services and research do not have a reliable flow which permits the institution to make longterm decisions.

In general, colleges and universities funded with public resources are free of tuition and fees, or the charges are mainly symbolic. However, because of difficult financial times, the possibility of fees is looming over the horizon.

On the other hand, private colleges and universities try to survive only with tuitions and fees. The result is very well known. The only university function developed is teaching, with professors working part-time on contract. There is no research or extension. There is no ability to get money from other sources. And in times of financial crisis, the public treasury may be called upon to help a private institution to avoid chaos. Research and other services could help a university budget but there are some complications. Although included among new industrialized countries, most of the Brazilian business enterprises are branches of multinational organizations seated in developed countries. Normally these organizations are used to contracting research and services at universities in their own countries. A developing country is a dependent country, specially in the area of technology. The genuine local Brazilian enterprises do not know how to use university research. Also colleges and universities are not yet good negotiators.

Presently the principal agencies for financing research, like CNPq (National Council of Research), CAPES, INEP (National Institute for Pedagogical Studies), FINEP (Financing Studies and Projects), FIPEC (linked to the Bank of Brazil), derive their funds from the government.

At this moment (1989) the federal government is refraining itself from creating any new institutions. The actual legislation is also very restrictive. However because state governments are making investments in higher education, some expansion is taking place, though at a slower pace. Private associations are also creating new colleges. The critical challenge for these new institutions is to be able to engage in all higher educational activities (teaching, research, services, etc.) as the general tendency is just to do the teaching. In spite of the many constraints, the economic growth, population increase, and the need for university cadres in society continue to activate the expansion of higher education.

Improvement of higher education is directly linked to improvement in the quality of teaching staff. The Ministry of Education is continuing the PICD (Intensive Plan for Professor Improvement) program but still there is a long way to go in achieving desired results: only 21 percent of professors have a master's degree and just 13 percent have a doctor's degree (1987), indicating that 66 percent of professors have only a B.A. or equivalent.

Not all university professors have access to masters and doctors programs, and those few programs that exist are in the South and Southeast regions. For many, it is a real sacrifice to leave town or the country for some years to attend a graduate program. Incentives in the academia are also not strong enough to influence candidates. For example, if an assistant professor gets a doctor's degree, automatically (in federal universities) he or she will be promoted to associate professor but the obstacles for becoming a full professor are many fold. The candidate has to wait for a public contest which is initiated at the Ministry of Education level and write a thesis specifically for this examination. And the contest is open to anybody who has a doctor's degree in the relevant subject. In spite of the fact that many professors work on a full-time basis, a large number also consider the act of teaching in higher education institutions a secondary job.

In the 1980s higher education saw the addition of another variable, politics, to the gamut of problems. The phenomenon is not very clear yet. One hypothesis is that during the dictatorship, the political participation through the legal parties was artificial. But politics being a natural part of life, there occurred a politicalization of institutions and organizations in general including higher education institutions. The tradition was student involvement in politics. Usually the student representation was a branch of leftist parties which were illegal until 1985. However, towards the end of the dictatorial period, faculties at colleges and universities organized themselves into associations and started acting like worker's unions.

The first consequence was strikes for improvement of wages. Later, political strikes also took place protesting against the process of choosing a new rector. Instead of the appointment of the rector by the president of the republic, the professors' association, employees' association, and students' representation decided to elect the rector through direct vote, with proportional weight by category, related to the number of voters. The choice of a name other than the one for whom most voted generated several long strikes in many universities, causing an open confrontation with governmental authority.

The crisis of authority is a generalized fact in Brazilian society these days, and it is reflected in higher education and in the total educational system. If democracy prevails in Brazil as a social and political system, many other problems will take priority before attention focuses on the needs of higher education. After twenty-one years of dictatorship it is a tremendous effort to implant a democratic way of life, as the tendency is to think totalitarian.

BIBLIOGRAPHY

Brito, L. N., and Carvalho, I. M. *Condicionantes Sócio-Economicos dos Estudantes de Universidade Federal da Bahia.* Salvador: CRH/UFBA, 1978.

Cunha, L. A. *A Universidade Crítica.* Rio de Janeiro: Liv. Francisco Alves Editora, 1983.

Kelly, Celso. *Política de Educaçao.* Rio de Janeiro: Reper Editora, 1969.

Kotschnig, W., and Prys, E. *The University in a Changing World.* London: Oxford University Press, 1932.

Ministry of Education. *Sinopse Estatística do Ensino Superior: Graduacao.* Brasilia: Service de Estatística da Educação e da Cultura, 1988.

Miranda, M. C. T. *Educaçao no Brasil.* Recife: Imprensa Universitaria, 1966.

Paim, Antonio. *História das Idéias Filosoficas no Brasil.* Sao Paulo: Ed. Grijalbo Ltda, Ed. da Universidade de Sao Paulo, n.d.

Pinheiro, Francisco. *As Teses da Faculdade de Medicina.* Salvador-Bahia: UFBA, 1976.

Ribeiro, Darcy. *A Universidade Necessária.* Rio de Janeiro: Ed. Paz e Terra, 1975.

Simonsen, M. H. *Brasil 2002.* Rio de Janeiro: Apec Editora, 1974.

Teixeira, Anisio. *Educaçao Nao E Privilégio.* Rio de Janeiro: Cia Editora Nacional, 1957.

Veysey, L. R. *The Emergence of the American University.* Chicago: The University of Chicago Press, 1974.

BULGARIA

by
Tzeko I. Tzekov
Professor and Chairman, Department of Criminal Law
Sofia University, Bulgaria

BACKGROUND

Higher education originated in Bulgaria in the nineteenth century, soon after the dismemberment of the Turkish feudal empire that had been established in the Balkans since the fourteenth century Ottoman invasions.

Three basic factors have influenced the development of higher education in Bulgaria: (a) the tradition of national enlightenment and literature brilliantly developed in the early Middle Ages by the Preslav, Ohrid, and Turnovo schools of learning; (b) the higher educational experiences of the U.S.S.R, Czechoslovakia, Hungary, etc., and of the West European countries, systematically brought over to Bulgaria by Bulgarians who studied in these countries since the eighteenth century; and (c) the global scientific and technological progress and the related worldwide trends in higher education.

Higher educational policy in Bulgaria is determined by the state. The state through its bodies (the Ministry of Culture, Science, and Education; the Higher Academic Council; and the Council for Higher Education) formulates the goals and tasks of education, and establishes the structure and content. It regulates territorial distribution and professional specialization of higher schools; decrees nomenclature of professional study branches and specialities; and exercises overall pedagogic, methodic, and financial guidance and control over them. This involves the opening and closing down of some higher schools, as well as bearing the entire cost of their upkeep.

The Council for Higher Education is composed of prominent educationists and scholars, and of the representatives of the cultural establishments, enterprises, associations and departments for which higher education staff are trained. The council performs its day-to-day activity through specialized permanent services. Education at the district level is administered by a district educational council. Each school has its board which oversees the affairs of the school.

SECONDARY EDUCATION

Primary education is realized in two stages: elementary with a duration of four years and basic with a duration of eight years (inclusive of elementary). Elementary education lays the foundation for the physical, moral, and intellectual development of pupils. Basic education grants the theoretical and practical background for continuation of education, and open possibilities for entering the job market.

The overall duration of training in unified secondary polytechnical schools, *technicums* (technical high schools) and secondary vocational-technical schools is 4-5 years after the primary eight year training school.

The duration of the study year for all secondary schools is thirty study weeks. In the last year, the students sit for a school-leaving exam *(matura)* in Bulgarian language and general culture. Those graduating from secondary school can apply to any higher school provided they have the required minimum marks. Secondary education is free.

There is competition when students seek admission to specialized secondary schools *(gymnasiums)*, such as the foreign-language and mathematical *gymnasiums*. The current transition to compulsory secondary education is certain to increase the contingent of university and higher school applicants.

HIGHER EDUCATION

Institutions

Depending on the speciality and the character of professional training, there are several kinds of higher schools with each group having a common administrative body (council of rectors, etc.): universities (in Sofia, Plovdiv, and Veliko Turnovo); higher technical schools (in Sofia, Varna, Gabrovo, and Rousse); higher schools of technology (in Sofia, Plovdiv, and Bourgas); higher pedagogical schools (in Shoumen and Blagoevgrad); higher schools of medicine (in Sofia, Plovdiv, Varna, Pleven, Tolbukhin and Stara Zagora); higher veterinary, medical, and agronomy schools (in Plovdiv and Stara Zagora); higher schools of art (Academy of Pictural Arts, Conservatoire, Academy of Theater, etc.); and higher ecclesiastical seminary (in Sofia), etc. The trend is for increasing the number of higher educational institutions.

The councils of rectors meet periodically to consider the main aspects of academic training for university students; research work and postgraduate training of specialists holding diplomas from the respective group of schools; setting up and functioning of inter-school laboratories and centers; and the use of unique research facilities.

Higher schools have research stations and training facilities at their disposal, and also they may have small enterprises for research and development work performed by their study and research teams. Besides regular study and research teams, the higher schools also have adhoc teams such as program collectives, research groups, and centers for interdisciplinary studies.

Administration of higher schools is carried out by elected and periodically replaceable autonomous bodies. The highest collective autonomous body is the general assembly of the higher school. It comprises all professors of academic rank, and representatives of assistant professors, postgraduate research workers, and students, as well as delegates of enterprises and organizations which employ the specialists trained by the higher school. It elects an academic council for a four-year term; discusses and adopts plans and reports of the higher school; and takes decisions on the organization's basic issues, curriculum content, research work, economic activity, etc.

The academic council elects a rector and vice-rectors for a four-year term, with reelection limited to two consecutive terms. It handles day-to-day business on academic, research, administrative, and other questions; takes decisions on the selection of lecturers for the higher school; and bids for participation in with higher schools and organizations in the country and abroad.

The rector is the chief executive officer and reports to the general assembly and the academic council, as well as to the Ministry of Science and Education.

The faculty's supreme body is the general assembly of the faculty. It comprises all academic rank professors and representatives of assistant professors, postgraduate research workers, students, and enterprises (which employ the specialists trained by the faculty). The general assembly elects a dean for a four-year term, with reelection limited to two consecutive terms. It also elects faculty councillors.

The faculty council elects the dean's assistants, administers regulations affecting the defence of scientific degrees, and votes on conferring the titles of associate professor and full professor. It elects and promotes assistant professors. The dean manages faculty activities and reports to the general assembly, the faculty council, and the rector.

The basic collective autonomous body of a department (chair) is the department's council. It reviews annual plans, research, and postgraduate studies and nominates candidates for head of the department. The head of the department oversees educational programs, research, and postgraduate activities related to the disciplines of the department.

The student body participates, directly or through its delegates, in all the management bodies of higher schools. It makes suggestions on improving curricula and study programs; on the organization of the study process and examination sessions; on improving standards of teaching; and on the opening of new disciplines of learning, special courses, and the like. It helps in organizing extramural activities, takes part in managing the training and education process through training and educational committees, and participate jointly with teaching staff or independently in the research work done at the school. It has at its disposal the means earmarked for youth activity, and it controls the use of these resources. It grants accommodation to students in student hostels, on the basis of pre-established criteria (under a ranking system) and see to it that life in the hostels is properly organized. It also helps students with some of the administrative services.

Programs and Degrees

There exists three educational and training levels: first qualification level, with a duration of 4-6 years; second educational and training level with a duration of up to two years; and a third educational and training level (postgraduate work) of a duration of three years (regular) and four and one half years by correspondence.

The first educational and training level corresponds to the first degree offered by many universities around the world (bachelor's degree).

Candidates for higher schools are recruited from holders of secondary school diplomas through a competitive process, including an examination. Two selective limitations are imposed with the purpose of taking a more accurate account of the candidates' intellectual capacity and creative potential: a minimum average grade in the diploma and minimum marks for disciplines of the respective speciality; and sufficient level of achievement at the competitive exam.

The structure of the first educational and training level consists of three stages. During the first stage (up to two years) the student undergoes fundamental training for a definite professional orientation but a common theoretical foundation is laid for several specialities. For that reason, the curriculum includes general theoretical and general education disciplines, as well as courses of an interdisciplinary character.

By the end of the first stage, a comprehensive evaluation is made of students' abilities, preferences, and interests, and they are accordingly assigned to specialities, or redirected to other professional fields or to schools of lower rating.

The second stage of the first educational training level ensures broad-profile special training for a definite speciality, including technological, economic, and managerial knowledge and practical skills and abilities. The students then expand and master the broad-profile professional conceptual training and widen and deepen their professional know-how. Theoretical and practical professional training are organically linked and interdependent.

The third stage of the first educational and training level is organized both in higher schools and in the environments of material production or research work. Theoretical and practical training bear the character of complete professional directionality and are closely linked with the respective specialization. The tuition content is determined by the higher schools in consultation with enterprises and associations which employ (consumers) higher-diploma holders. Much significance is attached to students' participation in the production or research process at respective enterprises or scientific organizations where they will start work. The students acquire knowledge about the economics, organization and management of the enterprise, labor safety, environmental protection, etc.

The duration of training depends on the character of the future profession. Medium of instruction is Bulgarian. One academic year has thirty study weeks. After completion of training the students must pass a state examination or defend a diploma paper.

Acquiring a professional license in some fields requires a separate probationary period served in the speciality (for example, law graduates must serve one year of probationary period in the courts and under a prosecutor).

The second educational and training level trains staff of a higher rank (in comparison to the mass higher-diploma specialists): managers of various manufacturing and other activities, constructors, designers, specialist doctors, etc. The duration of training is up to two years of thirty weeks each. The roster of specialities is defined by the higher schools on a contractual basis with the interested enterprises and departments. To qualify for admission, the candidates must have shown abilities for research work as university students or displayed creative potential in practical work.

Training ends with the defence of a thesis or diploma paper of a scientific or applied science character. Those who graduate receive a diploma of second level higher education and training. In the framework of second level training, the trainees acquire additional theoretical and practical skills, broadening the scope of their qualifications and deepening their professional specialization.

All specializing students get state or departmental grants which are higher than the amount of grants given to first level trainees. No fees or tuition expenses are paid by the trainees.

The third educational and training level (postgraduate training) is intended for elite staff to fill the needs of research institutes and industry. Three forms of training are used: regular postgraduate work, correspondence work, and postgraduate independent training. The first two forms require winning in a competitive selection process. The number of vacancies usually depends on research and production organizations' needs of elite staff (purpose oriented postgraduate work). The postgraduate trainees undergo theoretical and practical training in the speciality and acquire necessary foreign language and methodological knowledge before passing several examinations. The duration of the academic year is of thirty weeks. Regular postgraduate work takes three years, while work by correspondence takes four and one half years.

After the second year of training, the postgraduate students can engage in teaching and participate in the work of research teams at a more prominent level. The training ends with the defence of a dissertation paper for (winning) the scientific degree of "doctor of the respective sciences."

Regular postgraduate students receive state grants which are substantially higher than the ones for the first two educational and training levels. They get hostel accommodation and receive meals in student canteens.

There exist three forms of instruction at the first level of education and training: regular, by correspondence, and evening tuition. The first form is the most usual; it also gives the best professional training, and it provides the most favorable conditions for success. All three forms follow identical curricula and programs, and the students enjoy equal rights and opportunities for professional fulfillment.T h e most independent and financially secure students are the ones who take correspondence courses.

The organization of training is effected in line with and on the basis of curricula and instructional programs, which determine the ratios of fundamental, general-theoretical and special training; theoretical and practical work; and students' intramural and extramural work. The curricula spell out on an annual basis as well as for the full duration of training the share of compulsory, selectively compulsory, and optional study subjects; the lecture courses; and the special seminars. There is a clear tendency to increase the share of selective-study disciplines and students' independent work. More weight is attached to seminars as well as practical and laboratory work, at the expense of lectures. The process of democratization of higher education is gathering momentum. In some schools, students trained for the teacher's profession can simultaneously graduate in first and second teachers' speciality, provided their marks after the first year demonstrates the required intellectual capacity. Top ranking students with proven intellectual powers can simultaneously graduate in two higher educational specialities, provided they are in a kindred professional field.   Classes are conducted in the framework of a 5-6 day working week, with 24-28 hours of lectures and practicals. Compulsory independent students' work is not less than 20 percent of the weekly intramural classes. The academic year consists of two semesters, each with two examination sessions, and 4-5 exams per session.

The respective faculties and the academic councils play a decisive role in the drafting of curricula and programs for each higher school. Students as well as representatives of enterprises and associations (for which the students are trained) also participate. Even schools of the same type have necessary flexibility to adapt curricula to their individual needs.

Organization of instruction at second and third educational and training levels is characterized by strong individualization and organic links with scientific research. It is effected through special courses and seminars, independent practical lab work, and participation in research, and other creative activity. Instruction at third educational and training level is closely linked to the postgraduate student's scientific research.

All expenses for tuition and research work for maintenance of the material base and facilities; for employment of professors, lecturers, administrative, and auxiliary personnel; for international contacts; for training of students abroad; and for professional development of teaching staff are borne by the state. The state provides the bulk of student grants as well as necessary means for building and maintaining student hostels. The state budget funds most of the expenses of student canteens, and the cost of textbooks and teaching aids. The students pay no tuition fees or any other taxes. The rent for student hostels is low, as they are heavily subsidized by the state.

Although the major source of financing for higher education is the state, higher educational institutions also receive grants on a contractual basis from enterprises, associations, departments, and scientific organizations for which higher diploma staff are trained. These entities may also donate machines and equipment to meet the needs of study or research programs. There is a trend for increased support from enterprises, associations, departments, and firms.

Higher schools plan their activities on the basis of (a) state directives; (b) contracts concluded with enterprises, associations, departments, and firms; (c) international, national, sectoral, and territorial programs for the development of the spiritual sphere of life; and d) international agreements and cooperation accords.

Foreign students are trained under the same curricula and programs as Bulgarian students. They sit for the same examinations, and they live and are catered for in the students' hostels and canteens. There exist three modes of financial assistance for foreign students: (a) grants from the Bulgarian Government or Bulgarian scientific and cultural organizations; (b) grants from their own country; (c) their own means. The latter group of foreign students has shown faster growth in comparison to the other two. Preliminary language training and introduction into the speciality is provided to all foreign students during the first year, at the Foreign Students Institute and at the departments.

The academic staff consists of salaried professors, docents (associate professors) and assistants (who form the bulk of academic staff); honorarium-paid professors; and guest- professors. Staff professors are appointed through public competition and election by the respective scientific council. The teaching staff perform systematic research and collaborates with scientific teams of other countries. Periodically they are entitled to creative (paid) leave for conducting research on certain themes.

ISSUES AND TRENDS

Some of the issues and trends in the sphere of higher education in Bulgaria include the development of higher schools into training and research complexes for further consolidation and promotion of the competition in the educational process; increase of the share of fundamental studies and training; provision of incentives for teaching staff and students to improve standards of their training; expansion of the network of research, and joint ventures with the associations, corporations and territorial and communal bodies; promotion of the trend towards broad-profile qualifications and training; stepping up of foreign language training; intensification of the interdisciplinary character of educational and scientific research work; broadening of the economic, organizational, and statutory prerequisites for the individualization of education and training; development of autonomy in higher schools; and expansion of higher education's role in environmental conservation.

After recent changes in government, the Bulgarian education is undergoing radical changes. Democratization of educational institutions and programs is at the forefront of the political agenda.

BIBLIOGRAPHY

Tsekov, Ts., et al. *Qualifying Characteristics of Higher Diploma Specialists.* 1983.

Tsekov, Ts., et al. *Characterization and Peculiarities of the Three-stage Structure of Higher Education in Bulgaria.* 1985.

Tanev, St. *The Socialist Upsurge of Bulgarian Higher Education.* 1987.

BURKINA FASO

by
Norbert Nikiema
Associate Professor, School of Liberia Arts
University of Ouagadougou, Burkina Faso

BACKGROUND

Higher education in Burkina Faso started with the creation of the Higher Institute for Pedagogical Training *(Institut Supérieur de Formation Pedagogique)* in Ouagadougou, the capital city, in October 1965. This teacher training institute became the Center for Higher Education *(Centre d'Enseignement Supérieur)* in 1969. With the creation of this center, it was possible for students to get a *licence* (bachelor's degree) in the humanities (French, English, history, geography, etc.). The opening of other schools led to the transformation of the center into a university in 1974 when it was designated as the University of Ouagadougou.

The University of Ouagadougou is thus a state university. It is under the responsibility of the minister of higher education and scientific research. The totality of its budget comes from government funding. The rector and the vice-rector of the university are full professors or associate professors appointed by the government. However, the directors of the various schools as well as their associates are faculty members elected by the faculty of each school for a three year period.

The budget of each school, the programs of study, the creation of new disciplines, and the recruitment of new teaching staff must have the approval of the university council *(assemblée de l'université)* presided by the rector or the minister of higher education and scientific research.

The university council is composed of the rector, vice-rector, secretary general, directors of the various schools, representatives of the teaching staff of each school, and representatives of student associations.

PRIMARY AND SECONDARY EDUCATION

It is useful, when talking about primary education in Burkina Faso, to distinguish between informal and formal education. Informal education deals with literacy programs meant for adult (15-65 year old) illiterates. Courses are conducted in the local languages of the country and aim at eradicating illiteracy among the working class citizens. Formal education is the familiar, highly competitive, and selective European-type education. We shall only deal with the latter in this discussion.

Primary school lasts six years and is divided into three two-year cycles known as *cours préparatoire* (C.P.), *cours élémentaire* (C.E.), and *cours moyen* (C.M.). Theoretically, it is compulsory and accessible to 7-8 year old children. Public school is "free" to the extent that no tuition fees are charged. However all other expenses (for textbooks, school supplies, transportation, etc.) must be paid by parents. The few private schools which one finds in the major cities of the country are allowed to charge no more than 15,000 CFA francs (about US$50) for tuition.

Courses are conducted in French (the official language of Burkina Faso) right from the start. The end of primary school diploma is the *certificat d'études primaires élémentaires* (C.E.P.E.). It does not necessarily get students into secondary school as they have to score high enough at the national examination and be among the top 2,000-3,000 pupils who are selected each year for form six (the initial grade in secondary school).

Two levels must be distinguished in secondary education: the first level *(premier cycle)* consisting of sixth through third forms and the second level *(second cycle)* consisting of second form through "terminal". There are also two branches of study: general education and technical education. The first four years of study in the first level are devoted to acquiring basic knowledge in selected areas. The following courses are compulsory for all students in the branch of general education: French, English, history, geography, and mathematics. Instruction is carried out in French which is the official language. The national examination to be taken at the end of the first cycle is the *brevet* (BEPC). The technical branch of studies is vocation oriented. Although such courses as French and English remain compulsory, the mastery of specific techniques in specialized fields receive more credit. The terminal national exam in the first cycle of vocational schools is the *certificat d'aptitude professionnelle* (CAP).

The second level of secondary school lasts three years. The student must choose to specialize in one of the twelve branches or "series": A - philosophy, languages, and literature; B - economics and social science; C - mathematics and physics; D - mathematics and natural sciences; E - mathematics and techniques; F - mechanics; G - management and business administration. The first four series (A through E) may be selected by students who started secondary school in the general education branch. Those coming from vocational schools take the other series.

The diploma awarded at the end of the second cycle of secondary school (high school) is the *baccalauréat* degree. It takes the name of *baccalauréat du second degre* in series A-E, and that of *baccalauréat de technicien* in series F and G. The *baccalauréat* is considered as the first college level qualification. Thus, university professors participate in the *baccalauréat* exam as jury members and presidents although they do not teach at secondary level.

Only those who pass the end of primary school exam and are awarded the *certificat d'études primaires élémentaires* (CEPE) may have access to secondary school. Students who score high enough at the CEPE or the BEPC exams have access to public school. Students whose parent's income is deemed too low (about US$1,200 per year or less) get scholarships and do not pay tuition fees. The other students have to seek a place in private schools where tuition has been fixed by decree at 35,000 CFA francs (about US$140) and 45,000 CFA francs (about US$180) in the first and second cycles respectively.

Foreign students generally attend private schools. Diplomats, international officials, and Europeans in general send their children to special schools that are virtually inaccessible to nationals because of the high cost of tuition.

HIGHER EDUCATION

The university of Ouagadougou is the only university in the country. It is composed of twelve schools and institutes.

- Law: *Ecole Supérieur de Droit.* Major disciplines:public law, judiciary law, commercial law.
- Economics: *Ecole Supérieur des Sciences Economiques.* Major disciplines: development (planning, management), business administration.
- Medicine: *Institut Supérieur des Sciences de la Santé.* Major discipline: medicine.
- Social Sciences: *Institut des Sciences Humaines et Sociales.* Departments: history and archeology, geography, philosophy, sociology, psychology.
- Languages and literature: *Institut Supérieur des Langues, Lettres et Arts.* Departments: linguistics, French language and literature, modern/living languages: (English, German).
- Chemistry: *Institut de Chimie.* Major disciplines: physical, mineral, organic, analytical chemistry.
- Mathematics and physics: *Institut de Mathématiques et de Physique.* Major Disciplines: mathematics, physics.
- Natural Sciences: *Institut des Sciences de la Nature.* Major disciplines: biology, geology, agronomics, natural sciences.
- Rural development: *Institut du Développement Rural.* Major disciplines: agronomy, farming, forestry.
- Management: *Institut Universitaire de Technologie.* Major disciplines: management, secretaryship.
- Teacher Training: *Institut des Sciences de l'Education.* Major disciplines: education, professional training.
- Linguistics and literacy: *Institut Burkinabe de Linguistique et d'Alphabétisation.* This institute has just been created and is not operative yet.

Each school or institute is headed by a director who is assisted by a director of studies and an administrative head. The department councils of each school, composed of the teaching staff and of elected student representatives, are responsible for curriculum development. Major decisions and proposals made by the department councils must have the approval of the *assemblée d'école* (composed of the director, director of studies, department chairpersons and student representatives) before they can be submitted to the university council or to the minister of higher education and scientific research. Each school or institute is autonomous vis-a-vis the others and there is no interaction between them, excepting at the university council where the various heads of institutes meet to discuss matters of mutual concern.

Courses are taught by instructors *(assistants)*, assistant professors *(maîtres-assistants)*, associate professors *(maîtres de conferences)* and full professors *(professeurs titulaires)*. Only holders of at least a doctorate *(doctorat de troisième cycle)* or of a Ph.D. degree may be recruited as faculty members.

Access to higher education requires passing the *baccalauréat* examination in one of the series indicated earlier. However, every year, the University of Ouagadougou organizes what is know as a "special examination" that allows non-holders of the *baccalauréat* diploma to compete for limited places in most schools or institutes.

Admission to specific schools or institutes also crucially depends on the decision of an orientation commission *(commission d'orientation)*. Candidates make three choices ranked by order of preference (say mathematics, chemistry, physics; or law, geography, linguistics). The decision to send a candidate to a given school or institute for a given discipline is made on the basis of considerations that include the performance (scores) of the candidate in the discipline(s) or "series" followed in secondary school, the availability of places, and the priority given by the schools to the "series" chosen by the student.

Specialization begins very early and, as a rule, the line of demarcation between schools is kept sharp. One graduates and continues postgraduate work in the discipline(s) one started in as a freshman.

University studies fall into three cycles or levels. The first cycle lasts two years and is marked by the award of the *diplome d'études universitaires générale* (DEUG) diploma. The second cycle consists of two additional years with a *licence* awarded at the end of the first year and a *maîtrise* at the end of the second year. The third cycle lasts three years and leads to the *diplome d'études approfonde* (after the first year) and the doctorate of the third cycle, in the third year, *(doctorat 3e cycle)*.

While the DEUG probably has no direct equivalent in the American system, the *licence* degree obtained at the end of the first year of the second cycle is generally accepted as equivalent to the bachelor's degree. The first three years of university training may thus be taken to correspond to "undergraduate studies" in the American system. The other diplomas that follow can be considered "graduate or postgraduate" degrees.

It should also be mentioned that the *doctorat 3e cycle* is not the highest diploma one can get. The highest degree is the *doctorat d'état*. It is the only doctorate awarded in the medical school (at the end of the seventh year of studies). In other schools or institutes, the *doctorat d'état* is obtained after several years of research culminating in a second, higher level dissertation. Also, not all schools/institutes of the university of Ouagadougou offer all the degrees mentioned above. Even within the same school, some departments or sections may offer third cycle level diplomas while others only offer the end of first cycle diploma.

The language of instruction is French at all levels except in the department of Modern languages where courses are conducted in English or in German according to the specialization of the student.

The academic year runs from October to mid-September. Courses are offered from the beginning of October to the end of May or the beginning of June.

Each course lasts a minimum of one hour and must meet at least twenty-five times a year.

University charges a modest tuition from nationals, who pay between 6,000-10,000 CFA francs a year at registration (approximately US$24-40); foreign students are charged between 125,000-200,000 CFA francs (US$500-800) a year. Tuition is generally higher in the sciences than in the humanities. The government usually provides scholarships to nationals under twenty-three. The monthly allowance is 32,500 CFA francs (US$150). Parental assistance is often indispensable to students in order to cover the costs of higher education.

Postgraduate studies and research begin essentially with the second year of the "second cycle", when the student is required to write and defend a master's thesis. The student in the third cycle is freed from courses per se. The first year is devoted to seminars in which the student participates by reading papers. The last two years of the third cycle are entirely devoted to the preparation of a dissertation and thus to research.

Research is also an important activity of college professors. Those who have a doctorate of the third cycle actively engage in the preparation of a dissertation for the *doctorat d'Etat*. Team research is encouraged, particularly when the research is not degree oriented. Outside of the university, research work is coordinated primarily by the *Centre National de la Recherche Scientifique et Technologique* (National Center for Scientific and Technological Research). Researchers there are not college professors; they work full time on research projects initiated and funded by the center.

Foreigners who wish to conduct research in Burkina Faso must request a research permit from the Ministry of Higher Education and Scientific Research and also from the Ministry of Territorial Administration. Such a permit is more easily obtained if the person is going to be affiliated to some institution of the Ministry of Higher Education and Scientific Research.

ISSUES AND TRENDS

The most recent comprehensive assessment of the educational system of our country, to our knowledge, is the study made by the planning directorate of the Ministry of National Education in the mid-1970s. *(La reforme de l'éducation. Dossier initial)*. This study, focused on primary and secondary education diagnosed some key issues and problem areas:

-        The "non-democratic" nature of education in the country, revealed by the fact that very few children have access to school. The 1985 census shows that only 19.9 percent of children who reach school age do have access to primary school.

-        The high percentage of wastage in the educational system. The study found that 38 percent of primary school children abandon or are kicked out of school and become illiterate again. Only 17 out of 1,000 pupils who start primary school together do get the *baccalauréat* (end of high school) degree.

-        The high cost of education. Twenty-five percent of the national budget was invested in education at the time of the study. It is also shown that the cost of educating a student is four times higher because of students repeating grades.

    -      The maladjustment of the present educational system to the country's needs and the necessity for a deep and thorough reformation of the system. As a matter of fact the present educational system is largely a legacy of French colonial education.

    The same (or very similar) problems characterize higher education. There are more students who seek to pursue higher studies than the university can take. The 1985 census revealed that only 2.72 percent of the country's literates (who represent 12.1 percent of the entire population) are in higher education institutions. The award of government scholarships has not kept pace with the increasing number of students. On the other hand, it is a paradox that many students who get a college degree are unable to find a job (or one corresponding to their qualifications).

BIBLIOGRAPHY

Ministère de l'Education Nationale (MEN). *Statistiques scolaires 1984-1985.* Ouagadougou: MEN, 1985.

Ministère de l'Education Nationale et de la Culture (MENC). *Réforme de l'Education. Dossier Initial.* Ouagadougou: MENC, 1976.

Ministere de l'Enseignement de Base et de l'Alphabétisation de masse (MEBAM). *Education de base pour tous au Burkina Faso.   (Situation et perspectives).* Ouagadougou: MEBAM, 1990.

Sanou, Fernand. "Politiques éducatives du primaire du Burkina Faso." *Annales.* Vol. 1. 1988. Serie A: Sciences Humaines et Sociales. Universite de Ouagadougou, 1988.

Université de Ouagadougou. *Guide de l'étudiant 1987.* Ouagadougou: Imprimerie Nationale, 1987.

BURUNDI

by
Domitien Nizigiyimana
Director General
Ministry of Higher Education and Scientific Research, Burundi

BACKGROUND

The history of higher education institutions in Burundi dates back to 1960, when Jesuit fathers established an institute in Bujumbura with twenty-nine students. Soon after, an institute of agronomy and a faculty of science were started and in 1963-64 they were combined with the institute established by the Jesuit fathers to form the Official University of Bujumbura. Anxious to diversify the training opportunities and to meet immediate manpower needs, the government created the *Ecole Normale Superieure* (teacher training school) in 1965 and the *Ecole Nationale d'Administration* (school of administration) in 1972. These two institutions were later grouped together with the Official University of Bujumbura and the University of Burundi in its present form came into existence.

In the area of primary and secondary education, no postprimary teacher training institutions existed in Burundi till about 1940. The education provided at primary schools, at that time was confined to a few classes in reading, writing, arithmetic and above all religion. Then in 1940 and 1941 two schools were established to provide a three-year training to teachers. Several other schools followed and also from 1958 the training period has been increased to four years.

In general, secondary education in Burundi saw the beginning of its development only in the last decade of the colonial era (1950-60) with the establishment of the *College du Saint-Espirit* in 1952 and the *Athenee Royal* in 1955. Between 1955 and 1960, a few other secondary schools came into existence but the real expansion in secondary education came only after independence (1960). In a similar fashion, technical and professional education was practically nonexistent till about 1950. One technical school and a few trade schools opened between 1950 and 1960, followed by a tremendous growth in this area after independence. Now in 1989, there are seventeen lycees, fifteen colleges, twenty-four teacher training schools and seventeen technical schools under the direction of the Ministry of Primary and Secondary Education. In addition, there are eleven technical schools under the ministries of agriculture, health, transport, and communications. Private sector is also very active in secondary education and manages twenty-three schools (general, technical, and professional) and eight seminaries belonging to the Catholic church.

PRIMARY AND SECONDARY EDUCATION

Educational policy in Burundi at primary level is designed to assist young children in adapting to the real life environment and has three principal objectives: ruralization and Kirundization (Kirundi is the local language); universal education; and gradual transformation of traditional primary schools into community schools. Implementation of many aspects of the policy has been stalled due to practical difficulties, particularly the lack of suitable terminology in Kirundi to use the language as the medium of instruction. The national conference on primary and secondary education which met in August 1989 has introduced French as the language of teaching from the first year of primary school.

Children start primary school generally at the age of seven years. After six years of studies, the students take a competitive national exam, success at which is a prerequisite for continuing to the middle secondary school. Students are examined in several major courses (French, Kirundi, mathematics, and environment study) and some minor courses (music, sports, religion, home economics, and practical agriculture). A key objective at this level is to provide schooling to all children. To achieve this objective, a double shift system has been introduced in the schools since 1982-83 with one group of students attending the morning sessions and a second group attending the afternoon sessions. It goes without saying that conditions under which primary school teachers work are tiresome.

Secondary education, both general and technical, aims at not only producing middle level manpower to meet socioeconomic needs of the country but also preparing students for higher education. Admission to secondary schools is based on a national competitive exam.

The duration of studies in the general secondary schools is seven years, at the end of which the successful students receive the *certificat homologue des humanites*. Technical and professional schools award diplomas after four, five, or eight years depending on the nature of the program. Students take (internal) exams every three months and at the end of the academic year, based on which they are promoted. French is the language of instruction. To be promoted from one secondary cycle to another, students must pass a nationally conducted examination. Duration of the academic year is nine months. Majority of the secondary school students reside in school boarding houses and pay FBU 6,000 (US$1 = FBU155). Students who do not reside at school pay FBU 1,500. Teaching appointments at secondary schools require a *licence* (first degree) or an equivalent diploma.

HIGHER EDUCATION

Institutions

Higher education in Burundi presently aims at achieving several objectives, most significant of which are to produce the highest level of manpower to meet country's needs; to adapt educational programs to suit national realities with emphasis on practical training; to provide integrated and interdisciplinary programs; to develop inter-university cooperation; to promote Burundization of faculty positions; and to initiate postgraduate (third cycle) programs on an experimental basis. Also efforts are now underway to integrate higher education institutions organized by other ministries, into the system managed by the Ministry of Higher Education and Scientific Research, so as to optimize utilization of resources.

University of Burundi is the premier institution of higher education, and the only university in the country. It is a public institution coming under the Ministry of Higher Education and Scientific Research. The university is an autonomous body governed by a council of administration with a rector at its head, supported by a vice-rector. A consultative rectoral council assists the rector. The university consists of faculties and institutes, each of which has a faculty or institute council with the dean of the faculty or institute functioning as the president of the council. The dean is appointed by the council of administration. The faculty or institute council is made up of teaching staff as well as student representatives. The government is the major provider of funds for the university. Students pay subsidized fees and bear their living costs. The government has a scholarship scheme to assist students.

In addition to the university there are several other higher education institutions with emphasis on technical and professional education. The Higher School of Commerce coming under the Ministry of Higher Education and Scientific Research provides a two-year training program in accounting and management areas, leading to a diploma. The Higher Technical Institute of Urban Studies provides a four-year course in areas related to urban development, and awards the degree *diplome d'ingenieur,* equivalent to a first degree at the university. The Higher Institute of Agriculture, coming under the Ministry of Agriculture and Animal Husbandry provides a four-year course in fields related to agriculture and awards the degree *diplome d'ingenieur,* equivalent to a first degree at the university. Other institutions include School of Journalism coming under the Ministry of Information; Higher Military School run by the Ministry of Defence; and National Police School coming under the Ministry of Interior. The two latter institutions train officers for the military and police respectively.

Programs and Degrees

The programs of studies offered at the University of Burundi lead to the *licence* (first degree), *diplome d'ingenieur* (engineering degree) and doctorate in medicine (faculty of medicine). The faculties of law, letters and humanities, economic and administrative sciences, science, and psychology offer a *licence* after four years of studies. The Faculty of Agronomy awards the *diplome d'ingenieur* in five years. The Faculty of Medicine requires six years of studies for the degree of the doctorate in medicine. The Faculty of Applied Sciences awards an engineering degree in five years. The Institute of Physical Education offers a *licence* after four years. The Institute of Pedagogics has a two year program leading to a university diploma. The Higher Technical Institute offers a *diplome d'ingenieur* degree in three years.

University students receive a small scholarship of US $40 per month from the government. This award helps them to pay for meals (US$17 per month), lodging (US$3.40 per month), medical care, and other expenses, including the registration of US$14 per year. In essence, the tuition, lodging and meals are paid by the government.

Admission to undergraduate studies require the secondary school completion certificate *certificat homologue des humanities* or an equivalent. Qualifications from foreign institutions are acceptable provided they are equivalent to this certificate. Selection to different programs is based on the needs of the country (in a given area of studies), abilities of the candidate, preference indicated by the candidate, and availability of places. French is the medium of instruction. The academic year lasts nine months.

There are a number of student organizations (within the university), in which students take an active part (*Circle Central des Etudiants de Rumuru, Union des Femmes Burundaises, Association des Etudiants Rwandais, Jeunesse Estudiantine Chretienne,* etc.). In addition, the university also has an administrative body that organizes various extra curricular activities as well as student board and lodging on campus.

The teaching staff consists of (in order of importance): *assistants, maitres-assistants, charges d'enseignement, charge de cours, professeurs associes, professeurs,* and *professeur ordinaires.* The conditions of employment are governed by a government statute. The *assistants* and *maitres-assistants* are appointed by the Ministry of Higher Education and Scientific Research on the recommendation of the council of administration. They are required to have a minimum of a *license* degree (or a doctorate in medicine for medical fields). The rest of the teaching staff is appointed by the president of the republic. They are required to have a doctorate (or at least two years of specialization after the medical degree, for medical fields).

Postgraduate programs (master's or Ph.D.) are not yet available at the University of Burundi. The government awards scholarships to selected candidates for study at foreign universities for postgraduate degrees. In the area of research, a director of research oversees a service providing documentation assistance for research activities.

ISSUES AND TRENDS

Although the country is well on its way to achieve many of its educational objectives, some notable shortcomings exist. At the primary level, for example, the office in charge has not regularly evaluated the use of didactic material. The use of Kirundi language had been planned before developing appropriate technical terms. As a result, the books used by the teachers and students are still in French, where as the lessons are delivered in Kurundi. Quality of education has been another issue which has been a matter of concern to the educators. It is believed that quantity has been favored at the cost of quality. This appears to be the case not only at the primary level but also at both secondary and higher education levels.

As a matter of fact, the present educational system may be in need of a thorough evaluation in order to assess its content and quality. This implies the evaluation of students, teachers, curricula and methods, school organization and so on. Other issues of importance include improvement of libraries, and adaptation of higher education to meet the needs and realities of the country's economy and the population.

BIBLIOGRAPHY

Commission Nationale pour l'UNESCO. *Evolution de l'Enseignement au Burundi,* 1896 a 1984. Bujumbura, 1984.

Ministère de l'Enseignement Supérieur et de la Recherche Scientifique. *Les Institutions d'Enseignement Supérieur au Burundi.* Bujumbura, 1987.

Ministeère de l'Enseignement Supérieur et de la Recherche Scientifique. *Politique Sectorielle au Ministère de l'Education Nationale,* Bujumbura.

Universite du Burundi. *Vade-Mecum de l'Etudiant.* Bujumbura, 1989.

CANADA

by
Frank D. Oliva
Professor and Dean, Faculty of Education
University of Calgary, Canada

BACKGROUND

Canadian education has developed out of a struggle between "the twin strains of internal differences and external pressures" (Stamp 1971). The internal differences arose when it was agreed by the nation's fathers that education, under the terms of the Federal Constitution would be the responsibility of the provinces. Thus section 93 of the British North America Act (BNA) states: "In each province, the legislature may exclusively make laws in relation to education". Today, there exists similar but unique educational systems in each of the ten provinces and a further two found in the Territories.

The external influences originated from both the Jesuit colleges of pre-revolutionary France and the nineteenth century British grammar schools. Later, in the 1930s, the American progressive education movement has continued to influence Canadian education particularly in the curriculum area (Kach and De Faveri 1987).

Up until the 1960s higher education was provided almost exclusively through the universities, most of which had originated as private religious colleges particularly those in the maritime and central provinces. In the four western provinces the universities were established as public institutions supported in the main by the provincial governments (Munroe 1976). During the 1960s two issues arose which directly affected Canadian higher education. The first related to equality of opportunity and the second was concerned with the coordination and funding of this level of education. The first concern reflected the external pressures of the traditional or "European" philosophy of a quality education gained through elitism versus the American democratic approach to education (Nash 1961). The second concern reflected the funding needs of higher education facing a combination of the above first concern and the anticipated increase in enrollments due to the "baby boom".

The federal government does not have direct responsibility for the administration of Canadian education, apart from Native education, prison education, and schools for overseas servicemen. The responsibility for education is assumed by each of the ten provinces. There has been a trend towards the establishment of two separate provincial departments of education, one of which is responsible for coordinating the funding and developing policies relating to higher education in that province. The Federal-Provincial Fiscal Arrangements and

Established Programs Financing Act of 1977 currently governs the funding of higher education through a fiscal transfer as well as cash payments from the federal to the provincial governments.   In 1987 the total expenditure on higher education in Canada, including research, amounted to C\$11 billion (Cameron 1987). Universities and colleges receive approximately 83 percent of their operating costs from federal and provincial government sources and the remainder from fees, endowments, and other sources.

In the areas of curriculum development, administration, and control, Canadian higher education institutions enjoy a large measure of autonomy. The Association of Universities and Colleges of Canada, (AUCC) of which all tertiary institutions are members, acts as a self-governing coordinating body. Due to the emphasis on teaching and research in higher education, extensive relationships also exist with commerce and industry.

In 1987, 792,000 full-time students (or 24.5 percent of the population of 18-24 year olds) attended the 266 Canadian higher-education institutions and received instruction from 59,300 faculty (Encyclopedia Britannica Year Book 1988:569). A further 286,000 part-time students were engaged in higher education studies (Fillon 1987).

ELEMENTARY AND SECONDARY EDUCATION

Canadian elementary and secondary education reflects the similarities and differences of approach to education which have arisen due to the uniqueness of the provinces. However, the similarities far outweigh the differences. Canadian education can be described as a decentralized system coordinated at the provincial level by a minister of education (Walker 1972) and administered by a deputy minister, who is a civil servant. At the local level, school boards with elected trustees administer both elementary and secondary levels of education.

Provincial School Acts also allow for a dual educational system based on denominational lines. The Separate School Boards in most provinces include the Roman Catholic orientation while the Public School Boards include all Protestant denominations. This situation is reversed in provinces such as Quebec where the religious orientation of the majority is Roman Catholic. In the two Territories there are no school boards.

The language of instruction in Canada is English or French depending on the first language of the students. Teachers are trained in the faculties of education of Canadian universities. Upon graduation they are hired by local school boards and appointed to the schools under their jurisdiction.

Foreign students may study in Canadian education institutions at any level provided they are prepared to pay additional tuition fees, or obtain a student visa. Student visas are not issued unless the student's parents obtain "landed immigrant" status.

The school year is 180-200 school days and is divided into two semesters: from September to December and from January to June. There are 15,512 elementary and secondary schools in Canada at which 273,190 teachers provide instruction to a total of 4,959,000 children (Encyclopedia Britannica Year Book 1988).

Secondary schools in Canada are of several types varying from the single classrooms in remote rural areas to large urban composite high schools of over 3,000 pupils. In some provinces secondary education is divided into middle schools or junior high schools for students in grades 7-9 and senior high schools for students in grades 10-12. Secondary education has been traditionally academic in nature in Canada although there is an increasing trend towards composite secondary schools offering academic, commercial, and technical classes. Because free, compulsory schooling exists in all provinces and territories of Canada, all students participate at some level of secondary education. In the Northwest Territories compulsory schooling extends to age twelve while the provinces require students to attend until they are fifteen or sixteen years of age (Holmes 1983).

The curriculum includes academic, vocational, fine arts and special interest activities such as physical education, music and drama. The first two years of secondary education are general and exploratory in nature allowing the students to specialize at the senior high level. Most students are required to take core compulsory courses around which they build the program credits required for graduation at the certificate or diploma level. Pupils aiming for university entrance focus on "academic" courses such as English, mathematics, science, history or geography, languages, economics, et cetera. Except for Newfoundland and Quebec where secondary education ends at grade eleven, students in all other provinces graduate from high school after successfully completing grade twelve. Ontario provides an optional grade thirteen. Compulsory examinations set by the provincial authorities are required for graduation now only in Newfoundland, Quebec, Alberta and, in certain circumstances, Saskatchewan. In all other provinces the student's assessment is based on the secondary school record, performance in school-based examinations, and teachers' assessments (Holmes 1983).

Elementary education in Canada is free and compulsory in all provinces. The starting age is six in Alberta, Nova Scotia, Ontario, and Quebec; and seven elsewhere. Elementary schools provide an interdisciplinary approach to a basic education for children from grade one to grade six or eight depending on not only the province but on the discretion of individual school boards. Most provinces utilize some system of continuous assessment and such innovations as open plan schools, flexible timetabling, the non-graded school, individualized programmed instruction, and computer-assisted education are becoming more widely encouraged by local school authorities (Holmes 1983).

HIGHER EDUCATION

Institutions

As a result of the development of a mass higher educational philosophy, there was established a non-sectarian publicly supported coordinated system of higher education made up of universities, community colleges, institutes of technology, and technical and vocational institutions. As a result of the structural changes, three higher educational systems can be identified among the Canadian provinces (Campbell 1975): the binary system, the ternary system, and the unitary system. Of the 266 higher education institutions, there are 68 degree-granting universities, 12 of which are in federation or affiliation with another university (Fillon 1987).

The binary system, as found in the province of Ontario, consist of two higher educational sectors, one comprising the universities and the other, the colleges of applied arts and technology (CAAT); each sector has developed independently of the other. The binary system also exists in the Atlantic provinces and Manitoba. However, the Manitoba colleges have more trade or vocational schools rather than community colleges and rely heavily on the demands of Canada manpower (Oliver Report n.d.).

The ternary system includes three components: the universities, community colleges and the institutes of technology, and other specialized agencies managed directly by the Department of Advanced Education and Manpower. This system is found in Alberta, British Columbia, and Saskatchewan. In Alberta the college system, classified as a combined development model (Worth Report 1972) provides for differentiation between and among types of institutions while, at the same time, facilitating coordination and transfer of credit to the university (Worth Report 1972). In Saskatchewan the ternary system is unique in that the community college unit extends through community organization the services of the universities, institutes of technology, the provincial library, and other government agencies (Campbell 1975). In British Columbia the ternary system resembles that of Alberta in structure although there are several distinct differences in that the colleges enjoy a close allegiance to school-district boards; local taxation supports the colleges and one Department of Education administers all levels of education (Campbell 1975).

The unitary system is confined to Quebec, where the community colleges (*Colleges d'enseignement general et professionel* or CEGEP) are the third level of a four-tiered provincial system of education. Only in Quebec must students enroll first at a college as a prerequisite for entrance into a university. The CEGEPs offer transfer as well as terminal courses, but are less autonomous than other similar Canadian higher educational institutions (Campbell 1975). As Canadian higher education philosophy moved from an elitist stance to a more democratic stance, the proliferation of a diversified array of institutions developed (Pike 1975). This has now stabilized due to a fall in postsecondary enrollments (Sibley 1979).

Teacher education in Canada is conducted at university faculties of education, except in the province of Nova Scotia which operates a teachers' college for the preparation of teachers. Even though teaching positions are far fewer than in the 1960s large numbers of students continue to enter the faculties of education in the hopes of entering the teaching profession.

The private religious postsecondary institutions is an often overlooked sector of Canadian postsecondary education. These range from the Bible College and Bible Institutes, of which there are approximately 120, to the two and three year affiliated colleges, as well as some private religious degree granting institutions.

Undergraduate Studies

There are two types of higher education institutions in Canada: degree granting and non-degree granting. Generally degree granting institutions are covered by the Universities Act in each province and consist, in the main, of the universities. However, there are some private affiliated degree granting colleges.

In the 1960s, when the focus of Canadian higher education changed to a democratic stance leading to "mass higher education" there was a rapid expansion of degree granting higher education institutions. Students were selected on the basis of their performance in grade twelve, either in external examinations or later, internal secondary school assessments. In Quebec, however, students are required to have completed a two year course at a CEGEP after grade eleven. Today Canadian universities offer undergraduate degrees in a wide range of disciplines including fine arts, humanities, social sciences, science, arts and the professional degrees such as engineering, medicine, architecture, education, law, dentistry, nursing, et cetera. A degree in arts or science is normally an entrance requirement into the faculties of architecture, law, medicine, business administration, and theology. Engineering and education are given as first degrees in some universities and second degrees in others. Most undergraduate degrees allow the student to major in one or two areas of specialization. Of the 37.4 percent of the population over the age of twenty-five years who, in 1981, had attended higher education institutions, 102,300 graduates hold a four-year degree, 15,480 a master's degree and 2,070 a doctorate (Marsh 1988).

Course work towards a bachelor's degree generally takes 3-4 years, although professional degrees and honors degrees usually take longer. The academic year begins in September and ends in May, with spring and summer sessions sandwiched between the 12-13 week fall and winter semesters.

The language of instruction in most Canadian universities is English. However, a small number, notably the University of Ottawa and Laurentian University in Sudbury are bilingual. In Quebec the language of instruction in universities is French.

By comparison with American universities tuition fees are moderate averaging C$1,000 per year in the faculties of arts, science, law, business and engineering and C$1,500 per year for Medicine (Fillon 1987). Many students finance their university education by working at part-time jobs during the spring and summer and often during the academic year. Also some provinces, through federal grants, provide student loans for tuition, books, and living expenses up to C$20,000 per program some of which is repayable upon graduation. Students from upper middle class families are often supported financially throughout their university program by their parents. Scholarships are also available to those students who qualify.

Most Canadian universities provide residential facilities for single and married out-of-town and foreign students. However, these facilities cater to only a small proportion of the enrolled students at both the undergraduate and graduate levels. Canadian higher educational institutions open their doors to a significant number of foreign students. Generally most of these students come from the USA,

Africa, and South East Asia to complete both undergraduate and graduate degrees. However, all such students are required to pay an additional differential fee for tuition of about 50 percent of the normal fee.

The minimum academic qualifications required to teach in a Canadian university is the master's degree. However, in practice, due to declining enrollments and budgetary restraints over the last decade, few appointments have been made with less than a doctorate. Faculty also must have a proven publications record and often extensive experience in their field.

Advanced Studies and Research

Canadian universities offer a range of graduate degrees from graduate diplomas to the Ph.D. covering all disciplines. Admission requirements are based on an acceptable grade point average achieved at the completion of the previous degree. Many Canadian universities, particularly those in the western provinces, have adopted the American oriented course based graduate degrees. These degrees require the student to successfully complete a prescribed number of courses as well as successfully defend a thesis. Some universities have a unitary Faculty of Graduate Studies while others have decentralized much of the decision-making to even the department level. Generally a master's degree takes from one to two years to complete while the completion time for a Ph.D. ranges from three to five years.

Students can finance their graduate studies in a variety of ways. Besides using their personal savings and/or assuming personal loans, they can receive, in some cases, research and/or teaching assistantships as well as a limited number of academic scholarships or bursaries. In some professions, such as education, sabbatical leaves are provided to employees to complete graduate degrees required for promotion to administrative positions.

Tuition fees range from approximately C$1,000 to C$2,000 per year. In cases where students are awarded research and teaching assistantships, these fees may be remitted in part or in whole. Foreign students enrolling in graduate programs must pay a fee differential and must be in possession of an appropriate employment authorization obtained through the immigration department before they can hold a graduate teaching assistantship.

Postdoctoral programs are carried out at most Canadian universities. For this purpose, annual fellowships, postdoctoral fellowships, visiting fellowships, and visiting research fellowships are awarded on a competitive basis to those seeking to further enhance their area of specialization. Financial assistance through government agencies and a variety of other sources are also available on a competitive basis to faculty wishing to engage in research projects. Research institutes, centers, and groups exist in each Canadian university. These specialize in narrowly defined areas, examples of which are the Canadian Energy Research Center, the Petroleum Recovery Institute, the Center for Gifted Education, et cetera.

ISSUES AND TRENDS

In elementary and secondary education, the current trend in declining enrollments has created an oversupply of teachers. This is expected to ease during the next five years as the number of teacher retirements increases. The development of computer-assisted education along with other innovative teaching strategies such as individualized instruction, the integrated day, et cetera will be, it is expected, developed on a wider scale as Canadian education enters the last decade of the twentieth century.

The Southam Report, published in 1987, indicated that 24 percent (4.5 million) Canadian residents eighteen years and older are illiterate in either English or French. As a result of this survey and other political forces, the federal government is devoting considerable effort and funding to programs designed to upgrade the level of national literacy.

From an international perspective, Canada ranks among the top countries with regard to the proportion of national wealth spent on education. In 1979/80, C$20,170,000 was spent on education. This figure rose to C$33,336,000 in 1986/87 (Fillon 1987). Compared to the USA, slightly fewer children who enter grade school complete their secondary education. However, social background factors indicate no significant difference between the two countries regarding students' progress through all levels of the system (Pineo and Groyden 1988).

Issues which continue to pose problems in Canadian higher education are indicated in the questions which follow. Who should be served? What mix of general and specialized courses should be offered by the universities and colleges? How can good teaching be assured? What constitutes the desirable balance between teaching and research? How should the costs of education be shared between the student and society? What are the respective roles and responsibilities of the higher education institutions and the governments? How should cooperation between higher education and the corporate world be encouraged (Marsh 1988)?

Some authorities have indicated other concerns facing the universities as they prepare to enter the twenty-first century. These include political interference in the autonomy of the universities, ineffective funding formulas, lowering of university entrance standards, declining grading standards, and a debased curriculum (Bercuson, et. al. 1984). However, similar concerns are being voiced regarding North American universities in general. Overall, the standards of Canadian universities are comparable with that of any higher educational system in the world. Johnson's 1986 evaluation still holds true:

"While the United States may point with pride to some of the finest universities in the world, it also has some of the poorest. Canada's are closer to the norm. We have no Harvard or MIT but for none of our institutions do we need to be overly apologetic" (Johnson 1968).

BIBLIOGRAPHY

Bercuson, D. J., Rothwell, R., & Granatstein, J. L. *The Great Brain Robbery: Canada's Universities on the Road to Ruin.* Toronto: McLelland and Stewart, 1984.

Campbell, G. "Some Comments on Reports of Post-Secondary Commissions in Relation to Community Colleges in Canada." *Canadian Journal of Higher Education.* Vol. V, No. 3 (1975): 55-60.

Encyclopaedia Britannica. *1988 Britannica Book of the Year.* Chicago: Encyclopaedia Britannica Inc., 1988.

Fillion, J. *The Canadian World Almanac and Book of Facts, 1987.* Toronto: Global Press, 1987.

Holms, B., ed. *International Handbook of Educational Systems,* Vol I. New York: John Wiley & Sons, 1983.

Johnson, F. H. *A Brief History of Canadian Education.* Toronto: McGraw-Hill, 1968.

Kach, N., & De Faveri, I. "Recent Secondary School Reviews in Canada." In *Changing Patterns of Secondary Education: An International Comparison,* edited by R. F. Lawson. Calgary: The University of Calgary Press, 1987.

Munroe, D. *The Organization and Administration of Education in Canada, 7.* Ottawa: Secretary of State, Education Support Branch, 1976.

Nash, P. "Quality and Equality in Canadian Education." *Comparative Education Review.* Vol. 5, No. 2 (October 1961): 118-129.

Oliver Report. *Post Secondary Education in Manitoba,* Report on Task Force. Manitoba, n.d.

Pike, R. M. "Excellence or Equality. A Dilemma for Higher Education." *Canadian Journal of Higher Education, 19.* Vol. V, No. 3 (1975).

Pineo, P. C., and Goydeu, J. "The Growth of the Canadian Education System: An Analysis of Transition Probabilities." *Canadian Journal of Higher Education.* Vol. VXIII. No. 2 (1983).

Stamp, R. M. "Canadian Education and the National Identity." *Journal of Educational Thought, 9.* Vol. 5, No. 3 (December 1971).

Tomkins, G. S. "Tradition and Change in Canadian Education: Historical and Comtemporary Perspectives." In *Precepts, Policy and Process: Perspectives on Contemporary Canadian Education, 3,* edited by Stevenson, H., and J. D. Wilson. Ontario: Alexander Blake and Associates, 1977.

Worth Report. *A Choice of Futures.* Report of the Commission on Educational Planning, Edmonton. Alberta, 1972.

CENTRAL AFRICAN REPUBLIC

by
Theophile Touba
Dean, Faculty of Letters and Humanities
University of Bangui, Central African Republic

BACKGROUND

The first formal schools came into existence in *"Oubangui Chari"*, the present Central African Republic, in about 1930. These schools were the primary organs of the Catholic church (brought to the country by the Catholic missionaries) and whenever a church was established, a school followed. By 1932, every parish had a church school. After 1937, the so called government education came into effect with the development of programs to educate the young *Oubanguiens* (Central Africans) and education, though still private, came under the control of the French government (which was colonizing the country, at the time).

After the Second World War, the demographic explosion that occurred in the young population favored the growth of both private and government schools. Thus, by the time the country won independence, there were 125 education institutions for young boys and twenty-seven institutions for young girls. Private as well as government schools functioned side by side with the government playing an increasing role in subsidizing private schools.

In February 1963, the situation changed and the Council of Ministers issued an order abolishing private schools, making government the sole authority over education, based on a law enacted earlier, the Act No. 62/316 of 9 May 1962. However, certain provisions of the government order leaves the door open for the establishment of private schools, on the condition that the government does not have to maintain them and the education provided by these schools is for the benefit of foreigners and is based on their (foreigners') systems. By 1975, the population of school going age children had grown to such an extent, the government, on its own, was no longer able to meet the demand. Private establishments stepped in to fill the void but the schools that came into existence lacked proper facilities, thus putting pupils to study under difficult conditions.

The present educational system of the Central African Republic is governed by the Act No. 84/031 of 14 May 1984 which defines the general principles as well as organization. The system consists of four main categories: nursery education, primary (fundamental) education, secondary education, and higher education. The medium of instruction at all levels of education is French, which is also the official language (national language is *Sango*).

Nursery schools initiate children of 4-6 years to the education process, awakening their talents and preparing them to enter the level one primary (fundamental) school. Nursery education in the country, like all other levels of education, is the responsibility of the Ministry of National Education but the management of nursery schools is somewhat complicated due to the fact that some of these schools come under the authority of several other ministries (Ministry of Defense, Ministry of Public Health and Social Affairs), Catholic missions, and private owners with each party having its own agenda.

PRIMARY AND SECONDARY EDUCATION

Primary education aims at overall development of children by giving them an educational base, both general and practical, and by laying groundwork for the development of their potential. It is organized at two levels: primary one and primary two. Primary level one begins at the age of six or seven and continues for five years for children who have had the opportunity to complete nursery eduction. For other children, primary one conducts a preprimary year, in which case the primary school lasts for six years. There is continued assessment of children. The exam that marks the end of primary level one selects students for entry to primary level two or for vocational education. Primary level two begins at the age of eleven years and continues for four years under three streams: general education, technical and professional education, and agricultural and craft education. A diploma (specifying the stream) is awarded at the end of the primary level two. There are 969 primary schools in the country.

Secondary education consists of two types of schooling: general secondary education, and technical and professional secondary education. Secondary schooling continues for three years. In general, the first year is considered as an "observation" period and the curriculum is designed to deepen the students' grasp of the education they received at the primary school as well as to ascertain their aptitudes. Students who satisfactorily pass the continuous assessment in the first year are admitted to one of the three streams depending on their aptitudes: letters and humanities, experimental sciences, and exact sciences. The *baccalauréat* exams held at the end of secondary education opens the door for higher education.

In technical and professional secondary education, the emphasis is on training the students in subject matter relevant to industry, commerce, rural economy, and various crafts. Technical and professional education has two streams: short and long. The short stream, referred to as the professional and craft stream, prepares students for proficiency certificates in various trades like building construction, mechanical technology, and welding. The long stream, referred to as the technical secondary education, prepares students for the technical *baccalauréat* examination with different specialization such as secretarial studies, administration, mechanical construction and civil engineering.

There are fifty-one institutions of secondary education in the country.

HIGHER EDUCATION

University of Bangui is the center of national higher education and consists of eight units, of which four provide professional training, three are academic faculties covering a variety of fields of studies, and one is primarily engaged in research.

The professional training units consist of the faculty of health sciences which trains medical doctors, nurses, and allied health professionals; the Teacher Training School *(Ecole Normale)* which trains teachers for elementary and secondary schools; the Higher Rural Development Institute which educates professionals in the areas of agriculture, forestry, and animal husbandry; the University Institute of Business Management which trains management personnel for local enterprises.   The academic faculties consist of the Faculty of Law and Economics, the Faculty of Sciences and Technology, and the Faculty of Letters and Humanities.   Minimum admission requirement to the University of Bangui is the *baccalauréat.*

Study programs are organized by cycles (first cycle, second cycle, etc.) in the case of academic faculties, with a diploma (degree) awarded at the end of each cycle. The end of the first cycle (two years) is marked by the award of the general diploma of university studies (DEUG). The master's diploma *(maitrîse)* is awarded at the end of the second cycle (two years after the first cycle) but at this time only the Faculty of Letters and Humanities grant the master's. Steps are being taken now to extend the degree programs offered at other units as well.

In the case of professional training units, studies are defined by the year (first year, second year, etc.) and different diplomas are awarded depending on the level of attainment. In the Teacher Training School, three years of studies lead to a certificate of teaching for first cycle. The certificate of teaching for secondary education as well as for primary education require two years. Teachers who receive further two years of training (generally associated with internal promotion) can receive a certificate for primary education inspection. The Higher Institute of Rural Development awards a diploma in engineering *(diplôme d'ingénieur)* after four years of study and a higher technical certificate after two years. The degrees awarded by the Faculty of Health Sciences fall into three categories: Doctorate in medicine after six years of studies; higher technical diploma after four years of studies; and a diploma in nursing (and allied health fields) after three years.

The University of Bangui enjoys considerable administrative and financial autonomy. The minister of higher education functions as the chancellor of the university but the administrative and academic head of the university is the rector (vice-chancellor). The council of administration is the supreme organ (of the university) which authorizes funds and defines the general policies relating to functioning of the university. It consists of representatives from various ministerial departments and is headed by the minister of higher education. This council meets once a year.

The council of the university, presided over by the rector, carries out the implementation of policies and programs approved by the council of administration and coordinates with the council of administration, in matters relating to functioning of the university.   The scientific council of the university is responsible for promotion of research and culture.

ISSUES AND TRENDS

Like all other newly independent young African states south of Sahara, the Central African Republic has made a strong commitment for the education of its citizens and for elimination of illiteracy.   The result of the commitment is noteworthy: some 40 percent of rural children and 80 percent of urban children have benefitted from schooling.

This phenomenal growth in schooling, although was a necessary element in the development of the country, had however, not been based on a coherent plan, thus resulting in a lack of preparation to meet associated problems.   For example, the effect of demographic explosion on the demand for educational infrastructures or on the training of teachers had not been given serious consideration.   As a result, there has been a lowering of the quality of education, which in turn has had an adverse effect on science education.   In fact, for every 1,000 students who received *baccalauréat* diplomas (at secondary level), only about 150 had taken the science stream.

Given this unsatisfactory situation, the government has placed immediate emphasis on the development of science and technical education which is considered essential for economic development of the country.   More specifically, the government has now established two science *lycées: Lycée Cecile Digo* and *Lycée de l'Ecole Normale Supérieur.*   It is hoped that this action will help reverse the undue importance given to non-science education up to now.

In the area of higher education, the present emphasis is on promoting programs of short duration.   In addition, pressure is on the higher educational sector to professionalize education by providing programs related to the real needs of the employment market.

BIBLIOGRAPHY

Faraj, A. H. *International Yearbook of Education.*   Paris: UNESCO, 1988.

"Reorganization du Système Educatif en R.C.A."   Décret No. 84/031 du 14 Mai 1984. *Journal Officiel* (1984).

"Réunification de l'Enseignement en R.C.A."   Décret No. 62/316 du 09 Mai 1962. *Journal Officiel* (1962).

"Statuts de l'Université de Bangui."   Décret No. 85/264 du 22 Aout 1985. *Journal Officiel* (1985).

CHILE

by
Jorge Alegria A.
Jose Fuica F.
Ricardo Yevenes M.
Professors
Faculty of Education, Humanities and Arts
University of Conception, Chile

BACKGROUND

As in almost all Ibero-American republics, Chilean society is formed of a mixture of Spanish and native people. The Spanish conquest of Chile brought with it certain feudal and religious values. The settlement of the early religious communities also gave rise to the process of formal education in the country. During Garcia Hurtado de Mendoza's government (1556-59), the first basic school was established and by the end of the sixteenth century several high schools were also opened, such as the Dominicos High School and San Miguel High School of the Jesuits. In this period, the outstanding students and the richer class received education in Lima, Peru; upper echelon women received education in nun's schools; and the common people, both men and women, got no proper education.

The seventeenth century saw further expansion in institutions of education and by the eighteenth century, the parish schools as well as government schools were offering gratuitous basic education to more of the population, particularly to those who lived in the capital. Another significant event of this period was the establishment of the first university in Chile, the San Felipe University, in 1757. With the advent of the nineteenth century, higher education became even more important. Several higher education institutions came to be established: University of Chile (1842), Normal Teachers' School (1854), Catholic University (1888), Pedagogic Institute (1889). In the sphere of technical education, schools of art and trade, and agriculture were founded in 1842.

In spite of the expansion in schools during the nineteenth century, the availability of education to the mass of the people was still limited. There were only six public high schools or *lyceums* and not more than fifty primary schools. The curriculum was rudimentary. Only about 3,000 students or less than 2 percent of the potential student population had access to schools. There were virtually no preschools (Vega 1954).

From 1925-70, education became an important preoccupation of the government and several new schools and study programs were established, including technical and professional schools to provide manpower for economic and social development of the country. During this period, the Conception University and

159

State Technical University as well as several regional higher education centers were established. The educational reforms of 1965 further broadened the accessibility of education to the Chilean population.

PRIMARY AND SECONDARY EDUCATION

Primary (Basic) Education

Basic education in Chile has its roots in the most ancient past of the country, dating back to the Spanish conquest and the evangelical efforts at that time. Today, this level of education has the highest enrollment of students, possesses the most amount of building facilities, employs the largest number of teachers and other staff, and has benefited from the biggest allocation of government funds. It is also the qualitative and quantitative base on which the whole educational system is based. Basic education lasts eight years consisting of two cycles of four years each. It includes regular multigrade schooling, evening and night programs for older children (over fifteen years), and programs for handicapped children.

Students in the basic education level are normally in the age group 7-14 years. About 15 percent of the total population or 1,998,134 students were enrolled in 1988 in this level and 6 percent of the students were enrolled in paying schools. The dropout and repetition rates are quite high: only about 70 percent of the students complete the first cycle of four years, and not more than 50 percent complete the full eight years (cycle one and two). Major reasons for the low success rate at the basic level include poor socioeconomic conditions of the family, children entering workforce early, conditions of nutrition and health, lack of adequate school facilities, a system of teaching that offers little motivation, and curricula that do not focus on students' interests.

Majority (60 percent) of the basic level schools are municipal schools, 33.4 percent are subsidized schools and 6.6 percent are private schools. Statistics indicate that from a performance point of view, the municipal schools have not fared as well as the others.

The organization of the basic education level is based on the Decree 4002 of 20 May 1980. The curriculum of the first cycle consists of thirty hours of classes (each class forty-five minutes) per week in the areas of verbal expression, numerical expression, experimentation, plastic arts, dynamic expression, and development of social attitudes. Each area comprises a grouping of courses which include Spanish, mathematics, geography, history, natural sciences, religion (optional), plastic arts, technical/manual education, music, and physical education. The curriculum of the second cycle is somewhat similar excepting for the addition of a foreign language from the fifth year.

In practice, the number of class hours is often reduced as a majority of the municipal schools function on double session. On the other hand non-municipal schools, particularly the private ones are in quite a different situation, being able to have even additional academic programs or activities which, in essence, explains the superior performance of these schools. Thus, although the Chilean system provides opportunity for all to access education, not all receive the same benefits.

To overcome the problems facing basic education and to strengthen the technical-vocational aspects of education, a pilot project is now in place. The project consists of three elements: the first is aimed at making the curriculum more flexible by including technological courses that would prepare students to be productive; the second strives to equip the schools; and the third aims at transforming institutions with science-humanities programs into polytechnic type institutions which will carry technical-vocational programs, in addition to their regular curriculum. However, Chile needs more profound and sustained efforts to solve the multiple problems facing basic education; particularly it is vital to improve the standard of the teachers whose labor receives little reward.

Secondary (Middle) Education

Till about the 1960s, secondary education in Chile, known as the middle education since the educational reforms of 1965, focussed on preparing students for entry into higher education at university level. Thus, this sector of education depended on the University of Chile and not on the Ministry of Education.

From the beginning of 1965, the system underwent a fundamental reform, changing its character from an elite one to a system that serves the masses. As a result, the enrollment in secondary education grew from 148,144 students in 1965 to 735,701 students in 1988. The enrollment in 1988 represented 60.2 percent of the 15-19 year age group, as compared to only 17.5 percent in 1965. According to the Ministry of Education, the percentage of students in secondary education shows even a higher number at 81.7 percent, if a base of 14-17 year age group is considered. Of the students who completed secondary education (1988), 34 percent or 43,616 entered universities and other professional institutes. If the students who entered technical training centers (postsecondary) are also considered, the percentage entering higher education, rose to 67.4 percent.

Secondary education offers the two classical streams to students who complete the basic (primary) education: science- humanities, and technical-vocational. The duration of studies is four years. There are a variety of schools (government, municipal, private, and state subsidized) providing education in each of the two streams. The technical-vocational stream offers further options in commercial, technical, industrial, agricultural and polytechnical areas.

The present secondary educational system in Chile is governed by the Decree 300 of 30 December 1981, which brought about significant changes in the structure and curriculum of the system. Conforming to this decree, the science-humanities stream now consists of two cycles of two years each. While the curriculum in the first cycle is common to all students in this stream, the second cycle incorporates a mixture of common and optional subjects, with twenty-one hours per week of common subjects and nine hours per week of elective subjects (three courses of three hours per week). The law requires elective courses in technical/artistic subjects (music, plastic, arts, and technical-manual education), foreign languages (English or French), and religion. Courses in physics and chemistry fall in to the category of electives.

Article 17 of the above mentioned decree allows the technical-vocational stream also to adopt the same curriculum as the science-humanities stream for the first two years, which keeps the possibility open for basic education to be extended to ten years, with streaming occurring afterwards. Although adoption of this alternative was optional for the technical-vocational schools, the law is clear that the technical-vocational stream starts in the second cycle of secondary education (last two years). This provision was of great importance as students were not required to prematurely select between the two streams. They were able to postpone the selection till the tenth year of studies. However, from the beginning of 1989, based on ministerial directives, the technical-vocational schools incorporated vocational courses from the first year of secondary education, leading to a substantial difference between the two streams and eliminating the common first cycle as existed earlier. (At the same time, physics and chemistry courses in the science-humanities stream ceased to be electives as they were incorporated to the common plan of the second cycle).

On completion of secondary education, irrespective of the stream, students receive the *licencia* which is a basic requirement for admission to higher education institutions.

As defined by Article 1 of the earlier mentioned decree of 1981, secondary education has several objectives: providing a systematic and regular education to produce persons who will have a commitment to their families, to their fellow citizens, and to social and cultural development; ensuring that students acquire knowledge and skills that would permit them to play an active role in the society both materially and spiritually and to become participants in continuing education; ensuring that students are trained to think freely and reflexively; developing students' comprehension of the world in which they live and the problems facing humanity; developing knowledge and an appreciation of our historical and cultural heritage as well as today's realities; and imparting fundamental knowledge that would enable students to continue their education and to participate in the world of work.

HIGHER EDUCATION

Until 1980, higher education in Chile was synonymous with education provided by the universities which consisted of eight institutions. Much of the higher education was dependent on the state. The University of Chile, established in 1842 and directly dependent on the state, was the institution that regulated other universities. The State Technical University which grew out of the earlier *Escuela de Artes y Oficios* was also dependent on the state. Catholic church also played an important role in university education and had established several universities: Catholic Pontifical University of Chile, Catholic University of Valparaiso, and University of the North. Other universities have a regional character and are largely private institutions and they include the University of Conception, Federico Santa Maria Technical University, and the Austral University of Chile.

These eight universities were the only higher education institutions but their capacity was not totally sufficient to meet the demands of higher education given the geographical characteristics of the country. As a result, the more established universities began creating regional centers primarily offering training leading to professional careers, depending on the needs of the regions and in fields that did not require a sophisticated infrastructure (education, social work, nursing, various technical fields, etc.).

A look at the characteristics of higher educational development in Chile show that, until 1964 the university served more or less for youngsters coming from economically advantaged homes. From 1968, talented students coming from economically disadvantaged families were given more opportunities to join the mainstream of higher education through a policy of scholarships and financial assistance. From 1970, with the advent of the concept of "university for all", there was an explosion in demand for university education which resulted in the creation of numerous programs hitherto unknown in the country but promising to lead secondary school leavers to a variety of careers. As the military government came into power, the "normal schools" which trained primary school teachers were closed and this activity was entrusted to the universities, broadening the field of education.

The economic recession of 1975 forced the universities to revise their plans and many of the new programs initiated by the universities were virtually abandoned. Legislation enacted in 1981 brought about a revolutionary change in the concept of higher education. The professional institutes and centers of technical training were made part of the higher educational system and the establishment of private universities was authorized. The latter provision resulted in a tremendous increase in the number of this type of institutions, mainly in metropolitan areas.

From the point of view of degree programs, the universities can award bachelor's *(licenciado)*, master's *(magister)*, and Ph.D. *(doctor);* and have the exclusive responsibility of granting certain titles (advocate, architect, biochemist, dental surgeon, engineer agronomist, civil engineer, commercial engineer, veterinarian, physician-surgeon, etc.). Most of the undergraduate degree programs last five years, excepting dentistry and engineering which take six years and medicine which requires seven years. The professional institutes can award some titles, with the exception of those awarded by the universities. Students who complete their studies at the professional institutes can also enrol in postgraduate programs in the universities, in accordance with criteria established by the universities for their programs.

The higher educational system now consists of a great variety of institutions. The heterogenous nature of the institutions is very much reflected in the diversity found in the quality of education, organizational structures, the number and nature of programs offered, and academic functions. By 1987 the number of private institutions registered with the Ministry of Education increased to twenty-seven professional institutes and nine universities. The growth continued and in 1989 these numbers have risen to thirty-five private professional institutes and fifteen private universities, thus creating a massive number of institutions which fall into the realm of higher education.

Also by 1987 the number of centers of technical training authorized by the Ministry of Education had risen to 114. These centers, according to regulation in force, are institutions of higher education whose ultimate objective is the training of technical people. They are not required to be accredited or evaluated by any institution other then the Ministry of Education, which also oversee their performance.

In reality, it is difficult to speak of a system of higher education, as there is no transfer or exchange of students among different institutions or from one level to another given the differences in their focus. Specially universities, because of their higher level research, stand apart from the rest of the higher education institutions.

The universities and professional institutes coming under the Council of Rectors (a coordinating body of all higher education institutions which are supported by state funding) require the candidate to take a common academic aptitude test, which serve as a barometer for admission. Generally, about 25 percent of the candidates who take this test get admission. Frequently, questions are raised on the fairness of the aptitude test, particularly in the case of candidates who are at the marginal level, or who come from middle or lower socioeconomic levels. However, inspite of the critics, it is absolutely necessary to have some system of selection given the fact that the demand for higher education is much higher than the number of places available.

Until 1980 education at state universities was provided practically free of charge and the institutions were largely supported by direct state funds. Legislation enacted in 1981 brought about substantial changes in the financing of higher education institutions. State contribution to higher education diminished and self-financing including fees became increasingly important. To give relief to students coming from lower socioeconomic levels, a system of higher educational loans was established.

Self-financing, which includes fees and charges for various services provided by the universities as well as grants received by institutions, has been increasing since 1982 forming about 24 percent of an institution's budget. However, self-financing has not been popular among the teaching staff or the students. Teachers who had been used to their traditional academic functions now had to think about selling their services, and students with insufficient economic means and not benefitting from fiscal credit faced the prospect of abandoning school as the cost of their university education increased. By 1986 fees amounted to 55.6 percent of the total self-financing.

Universities in Chile have been traditionally governed, conforming to the Latin concept, by elected officials. The rector and deans or directors of academic units have been elected to office by faculty members. The reformist movements of 1968 then brought in students and staff representatives to participate in the governance of the institutions but this experiment did not seem to have had a very positive effect on the development of academic activities of the university. With the coming into power of the military government in 1973, appointed rectors became the norm and these persons, at the beginning, were active or retired members of the armed forces. In the recent years, there has been a move towards the designation of administrators by committees which can propose three names to the president of the republic, for the post of rector. It must be emphasized that opinion is crystallizing for returning to the system of electing the rector by faculty members.

ISSUES AND TRENDS

As the population in Chile grows from the estimated 13 million in 1990 to about 15.7 million in the year 2000, the basic education level (primary) will have a heavy burden to bear, considering the fact that even now the illiteracy rate is as high as 10 percent.

As pointed out by Cariola and Cox, the principal dilemma of the system of education at secondary level relates to the future effects of strict distinction between general and vocational education: "The question confronting a society striving for equality of opportunities is at what point in secondary education and in what form should the system specialize the education it imparts, given the demands of the society; specialization which in fact cannot be dissociated from the power and prestige between different occupations."

It seems that the critical problem of the Chilean educational system is to find a mechanism for coordinating and integrating differing viewpoints so that a national policy can be formulated giving consideration to opinions of all those involved in education. This will be an answer to the continuous argument of educators against policies that are based on financial criteria but are lacking in social context.

BIBLIOGRAPHY

Cantro Eduardo. *Análisis Crítico de la Reforma de la Educación Media Chilena.* Stgo. de Chile: P.I.I.E., 1982.

Cariola, Leonory Cox C. "La Educación de Los Jóvenes - Crisis de La Relevencia y Calidad de la Enseñanza Media." In *Cuadernos de Educación.* No. 188 (1989).

Cox, Christian, and Jara, Cecilia. "La Educación Media: Crisis de Calidad y Relevancia." In *Cuadernos de Educación.* No. 188 (1989).

Cox C., and Jara C. *Datos Básicos para la Discusión de Políticas en Educación (1970-1988).* Santiago de Chile, 1989.

Mineduc. "Planes y Programas de Estudio" *Revista de Educ.* No. 79.

Vega, Julio. *The Rationalization of Our Teaching.* Santiago: Universitaria S. A., 1954.

PEOPLE'S REPUBLIC OF CHINA

by
Zhongwen Huang
former Professor and Chairman
Department of Foreign Languages and Literature
Nanjing University, P.R.C.
and
Yong Mao
former Vice-Director
Research Institute of Higher Education
Nanjing University, P.R.C.

BACKGROUND

The Constitution of the People's Republic of China adopted in 1982 defines the framework of Chinese education thus: "Citizens of the People's Republic of China have the duty as well as the right to receive education. The state promotes the allround development of children and young people, morally, intellectually, and physically. The state undertakes the development of socialist education and works to raise the scientific and cultural level of the whole nation."

It is basically the government that administers and funds most of the schools. Over the past forty years, with the exception of the cultural revolution period of 1966-76, China has scored great successes in developing and reforming education. In 1985 the central government issued the "Resolution Concerning the Reform of the Educational System" and the State Education Commission was set up. A special day, 10 September, was declared Teacher's Day in honor of teachers. The Resolution affirmed that "education should be geared to modernization, to the whole world, and to the future".

According to 1985 statistics, China had close to one million schools of all types, with an enrollment of over 200 million students, consisting of 832,300 primary schools with 133,700 million pupils; 105,000 secondary schools, with 50,900 million students; 1,016 regular colleges and universities with 1.7 million students; and 1,400 schools of higher learning for adult education with 1.9 million students. The 1985 government expenditure for education was 18.3 million Chinese Yuan or 10 percent of the government budget (2.7 percent of the national income).

From 1979-85, the number of graduates from regular colleges and universities totalled 1,767,100: 33.29 percent in teacher training, 31.49 percent in engineering, 10.36 percent in medicine, 6.89 percent in agriculture and forestry, 6.47 percent in science, 5.38 percent in liberal arts, 3.99 percent in finance and economics, 0.85 percent in physical culture, 0.74 percent in political science and law, and 0.50 percent in arts.

From 1977-87, the government sent about 50,000 students or staff abroad for further studies and research in seventy-six foreign countries. During this period, the Nanjing University for instance, had sent 880 persons abroad for periods over one year, and more than 300 persons for short-term visits or international conferences (the school has a teaching and research staff of 2,431). The school at the same period recruited 816 foreign students and scholars (for periods over one year) and received 1,026 foreign students for Chinese language programs varying from four weeks to five months.

PRIMARY AND SECONDARY EDUCATION

Primary education lasts six years with children entering primary school at the age of six. All cities and about 60 percent of China's counties have primary education facilities. Primary education is universally free.

Secondary education consists of two types of schools. The first type, ordinary middle school, takes three years at the junior high school and another three years at the senior high school. The curriculum comprises Chinese, mathematics, foreign languages, politics, physics, chemistry, biology, physiology, history, geography, physical culture, music, arts, and labor skills.

The second kind is secondary specialized schools (including vocational and technical). Length of schooling is 4-6 years. There are junior specialized middle schools as well as senior schools.

The government has decided to establish universal compulsory public education through grade nine by the year 1990 (six years of primary, and three years for junior high). On finishing the grade nine, students are channeled to ordinary senior high, or to secondary specialized senior high schools, or to training programs that prepare them for employment.

HIGHER EDUCATION

Higher education in China consists of three categories: specialized undergraduate programs lasting 2-3 years; undergraduate programs lasting four years; and postgraduate programs including two-year non-degree graduate studies, master's programs that take 2-3 years, and Ph.D. programs that require 3-4 years.

In addition to regular colleges and universities, the country has developed successfully a very good higher educational system for adults which is commonly called "the five big" schools: universities for workers and staff; radio and television universities; correspondence universities and colleges; evening universities; and higher education examination system for people studying on their own, commonly called self-study (students may pass exams course by course and when all required courses are passed, university diplomas are awarded).

In recent years, various higher educational institutions have been recruiting annually an average of about 600,000 regular college students for undergraduate programs, and about 40,000 candidates for graduate studies (master's and doctor's degrees).

Admission to undergraduate studies is based on a highly unified national entrance examination, conducted in early July. Recruitment committees handle the processing of applications for admission to both undergraduate and graduate programs. For undergraduate liberal arts programs, the students must take the exam in politics, Chinese, mathematics, history, geography, and a foreign language. For sciences, engineering, agriculture, medicine and others, the subjects consist of politics, Chinese, mathematics, physics, chemistry, a foreign language, and biology. Some military academies, art colleges, film institutes, broadcasting institutes have special exam requirements.

Admission to graduate studies is based on a separate unified national examination conducted in January or February.

All over China, schools begins in early September. There are two terms (semesters) in the academic year, but some schools are experimenting on a three term academic year. The fall session is from September to January, and the spring term is from February to early July. Each term is 20-22 weeks long and classes are held on every day of the week excepting Sunday.

The comprehensive universities have two groups of departments: departments of liberal arts and humanities; and departments of sciences. They are usually centers of both teaching and scientific research. Recently, as educational reform deepens, some comprehensive universities added many new disciplines and interdisciplinary specializations, and are trying to link basic sciences with applied sciences and technology, while specialized colleges are setting up departments of liberal arts.

In order to raise the quality of teaching and scientific research, the education authorities in China selected (1981) ninety-six schools as key universities or colleges. In general, these key universities and colleges are well known institutions with a long history, superior staff, and greater resources. They include Beijing University, Qinghua University, Chinese People's University, Fu Dan University, Jiaotong University in Shanghai, Jiaotong University in Xian, Nankai University, Nanjing University, Beijing Teachers' University and Beijing Medical University (Encyclopedia of New China 1987).

The Presidents of colleges and universities are appointed by the State Council or the State Education Commission.

The State Education Commission issues guidelines for various programs, in the form of catalogues. Each catalogue defines the disciplines (specializations), the length of schooling, the objectives and aims of the training, requirements and standards for graduation of students, and the core courses (compulsory courses) which the students in each discipline must complete. Based on these catalogues, the schools, departments, teaching and research groups design their curricula and organize courses as well as the teaching plans.

Majority of the Chinese students do not pay tuition fees and live in the school dormitories free of charge. The government also provides free medical care. A small percentage of students are sponsored by institutions or enterprises that pay the tuition as well as other expenses of the sponsored students. Some students also attend colleges or universities at their own cost.

The government provides subsidies for those who cannot support themselves, irrespective of their academic performance. The system has been gradually replaced now by a scholarship or grant system that makes awards to students based on their performance. Scholarships for undergraduates are divided into grades A, B, and C with annual awards of 350, 250, and 150 Chinese yuan respectively. Those who are not entitled to get scholarships, but have financial difficulties can apply for student's loans, not exceeding 300 Chinese yuan in a year. The interest-free student's loans are required to be paid back upon or after graduation, either by the borrower or by the units which employ the graduates.

The state prepared an overall plan of work assignment (job vacancies) for graduating students. The graduates indicate their preferences, the school makes some adjustments and provide recommendations, and finally the employers (work units) select and accept the graduates.

In 1980 the central government issued regulations governing the granting of academic degrees and by the end of April 1986, 558 schools had been authorized to grant the bachelor's degrees (B.A. or B.S.), 320 colleges and universities and 105 research institutes had been authorized to grant master's degrees (M.A. or M.S. or M.D.), and 155 colleges and universities and 41 research institutes had been permitted to grant doctor's degrees.

The master's and doctoral degree candidates receive financial support from the schools or from their own work units. Some are supported by their future units (employers). Most of them live on campus and accommodation is free.

About 100 Chinese colleges and universities receive foreign students. Since 1950 they trained over 20,000 students from 122 countries or regions. In addition, more than 22,000 foreign students took Chinese language programs in 1978-87. For admission to undergraduate programs, the foreign students are required to be high school graduates aged below twenty-five. Liberal arts candidates are exempt from entrance examinations. Applicants in science, engineering, agriculture, and medicine, have to take examinations (in mathematics, physics, and chemistry) which are conducted by the Chinese embassies in foreign countries.

Foreign students with an academic record of two years of studies in a given field in foreign universities and below thirty-five years are admitted to pursue the same field in China. In addition, foreign students are also admitted to pursue graduate studies (master's and doctoral degrees).

Short-term training programs (classes) are also available to foreign students in areas such as Chinese language, literature, calligraphy, economics, architecture, law, traditional Chinese medicine, Chinese arts, physical culture, etc.

The tuition fees charged from foreign students at undergraduate level is US$1,200 per year for liberal arts programs and US$1,600 for science and professional areas. Board and lodging cost vary from US$75 to US$200 per month depending on the type of accommodation. Graduate foreign students pay somewhat higher tuition fees.

ISSUES AND TRENDS

There are several key factors affecting the development of education in China: the nation's population is too large, the country is economically backward, and the government has not spent and is unable to spend enough on education. The situation is indeed a complex one.

According to a report made by He Dongchang, vice-chairman of the State Education Commission, on 25 June 1988, there are three major problems facing China's education. First, not enough funds are available. Second, salaries of the teachers are low. Third, education is still divorced from practice and reality, and the education of morality and ideology is neglected.

The enormity of the problems facing the educational system is reflected in the number of candidates taking the national collegiate examination which is being held at the time of writing this article (1988). After the preliminary selection, 2.7 million appeared for the exam (33.8 percent for liberal arts and the rest for science, engineering and other areas) but the regular colleges and universities plan to admit only 682,000 or about 25 percent.

BIBLIOGRAPHY

China Education Handbook. 1982-1984.   Changsha, Hunan Province (PRC): Hunan Education Publishing House, Changsha, n.d.

The Great Chinese Encyclopedia (Education Volume). Beijing (PRC): The Great Chinese Encyclopedia Publishing House, n.d.

Guidebook for Study in China. Beijing (PRC): Beijing Languages Institute Pres, Beijing Language Institute, n.d.

CHINA (TAIWAN)

This text is based on information provided by Dr.
Hsin-han Liu, Dean of the Graduate School of
Education, National Chengchi University, Taiwan and
data obtained primarily from *Education in the Repub-
lic of China 1990* (Ministry of Education, Taiwan).
Other reference sources are listed in the bibliography.

BACKGROUND

Educational policy in Taiwan is guided by Dr. Sun Yat-Sen's Three
Principles of the People — nationalism, democracy and the people's livelihood. "In
the spiritual sense, they are freedom, equality, and universal love. As guided by
these principles, education in Taiwan aims at educating the people and reforming
society." (Education in Taiwan Province 1974).

The origins of the present educational system goes back to the system that
existed in the mainland China prior to 1949. "In our education, common courses
shall be based on the teachings of Dr. Sun Yat-Sen and on the eight Chinese moral
virtues, i.e., loyalty, filiality, mercifulness, love, faithfulness, righteousness, harmony,
and peacefulness. Technology courses shall be offered not only to equip students
with the earn-a-living skills but to upgrade labor productivity. Social sciences shall
introduce: (1) international affairs to enhance the sense of nationalism, (2) rural and
urban socio-economics to better our national livings, (3) government organization
and operation to pursue democracy, (4) environmental knowledge to conserve such
properties as forests, parks, and public works, and (5) human behaviors to
encourage mutual cooperation....College and technical education shall be focused
on applied sciences so that students can be equipped with practical skills and
technical knowhows needed in their serving the society....Education for women is
concentrated on cultivation of healthy personality and motherhood....Physical
education is designed to pursue better national health at school or through various
social education programs. Senior high schools and colleges shall offer basic
military training. Agricultural education shall bear an aim to improve the living
standards in the rural area by renovating agricultural techniques, disseminating
technical know-hows, and strengthening farmers' organizations." (Education in the
Republic of China 1990).

The Constitution of the Republic of China on Taiwan (1947) proclaims, in
Chapter 13; "All citizens shall have an equal opportunity to receive education. All
children of school-age from six to twelve years shall receive fundamental (compulsory) education free of tuition. Those from poor families shall be supplied with
textbooks by the government. All national citizens above school age who have not

received fundamental education shall receive supplementary education free of tuition and shall be supplied with textbooks by the government. Governments at all levels shall set up scholarships to assist students of good academic performance and good conduct who lack financial support to continue their advanced education. All public and private education and cultural institutions in the country shall, in accordance with law, be subject to supervision of the State."

According to Chapter 10 of the Chinese Constitution, Powers of the Central and Local Governments, the central government has the power of legislating and administering national education, or delegating the administrative power to the provincial, special municipality, county, or city governments. The provincial government has the power of legislating and administering provincial-level educational systems, or of delegating the administrative power to the special municipalities and county governments. Likewise, the county governments may delegate their administrative powers to the city governments.

At a national level, policies and regulations are prescribed by the Ministry of Education of the central government. In addition, each province has a Department of Education, special municipalities have Bureaus of Education, and each county or city has a Division or Bureau of Education.

The law in Taiwan requires the central and provincial governments (as well as counties/municipalities) to contribute a certain percentage of their revenue, towards education. All government higher education institutions are supported with these funds and students pay for only a fraction of the cost of their education. Private institutions, on the other hand, are largely supported by student tuition and contributions from various government and private sources.

A basic nine-year education plan was implemented in 1968 and since then the number of education institutions, both government and private, grew rapidly. This plan consist of six years of elementary school and three years of junior high school. Increasing emphasis was placed on vocational education, from the 1970s, prompted by the need to meet the demands of a rapidly industrializing economy. With the new extended compulsory education, the number of junior high students rose by over 82 percent within two decades from 617,225 in 1968 to 1,125,238 in 1989, while the elementary school students had shown little growth: 2,383,204 in 1968 and 2,384,801 in 1989 in 2,484 schools. The number of junior high schools grew from 487 in 1968 to 691 in 1989. The total number of students attending schools rose from 3,406,233 in 1967-68 to 5,212,521 in 1989-90. The expansion in educational opportunities was supported by an increasing expenditure on national education, an expenditure which grew from less than NT$20 billion (NT$25.89 = US$1)in 1971-72 to NT$200 billion in 1988-89. Educational expenditure as a percentage of GNP rose from about 0.5 percent in 1971-72 to 6.5 percent in 1988-89.

In the area of higher education, there was one university, three independent colleges, and three junior colleges in 1950, with an enrollment of 6,665 students. Subsequently, three national institutes (Taiwan Institute of Technology, Institute of The Arts, and College of Physical Education) and one private institution (Chang Gung Medical College) were established between 1974 and 1987. By 1989 furthur expansion in higher education had taken place with the addition of several more institutions including the Chang Gung Institute of Nursing and the Chin Min Junior College of Technology in 1988 as well as Chung Cheng University, Yuan-Tse Memorial College of Engineering, Ilan Institute of Agriculture and Technology, Kao Yuan Junior College of Technology, Fortune Junior College of Technology, Ging Chung Business College, and Tz'u-Chi Junior College of Nursing. The student population in higher education had risen to 535,064 in 1989.

Private sector plays a significant role in education, particularly at junior college level. Government encouragement of private sector participation has resulted in a fivefold increase of private funding for education in the past ten years. In 1989, the private sector accounted for 18.7 percent of the total educational expenditure.

PRIMARY AND SECONDARY EDUCATION

According to the Statute of Compulsory Attendance, all children of 6-15 years of age must receive free compulsory education. Children enter elementary school at the age of six years and follow a six-year course that prepares them for admission to junior high school. On completion of three years of studies in the junior high school, students have the option of pursuing higher secondary studies in the academic or vocational streams, each of which lasts three years leading to a high school diploma. The senior high schools emphasize developing the student's personality and conceptual skills while strengthening basic citizenship education. The senior vocational schools provide the youth with knowledge and skills that will permit them to engage in productive work after graduation and these schools specialize in seven areas: agriculture, industry, commerce, marine products, nursing and midwifery, home economics, and opera and arts.

Elementary and junior high schools are mainly established and operated by the government (county/city/municipal) but high schools may by run by the private sector or the government. Special schools (for blind, deaf, physically handicapped, and mentally retarded) are mostly operated by the government. Admission to high schools require an entrance examination.

The development of curricula as well as the compilation of textbooks for elementary and secondary schools are centralized under the Ministry of Education (and the National Institute of Computation and Translation) through various committees which include curriculum specialists, educationists, teachers, and education officials. For senior high schools, textbooks may be compiled by private sector publishers according to the prescribed curriculum, excepting for subjects such as Chinese, civics, history, and geography. Bookstores are generally contracted to do the printing, publishing, and distribution of textbooks for junior and senior high schools. The medium of instruction is the Chinese language.

Elementary school subjects include civics and ethics, health education, Mandarin, mathematics, social studies, natural science, singing and playing, physical education, music, and fine arts. Junior high school curriculum includes civics and ethics, health education, Chinese, English, mathematics, history, geography, natural science, physical education, music, and fine arts. Senior high school curriculum includes Chinese, English, civics, Three Principles of the People, history, geography, mathematics, basic science, and a selection of two science courses (physics/chemistry/biology, earth science), physical education, music, fine arts, industrial arts or home economics, military training and some electives.

Students are required to pass end of year examinations, for promotion to the next grade. Selection for higher education is made by a competitive entrance examination which students take at the end of their secondary schooling.

Non-formal education include non-formal elementary and secondary education programs, extension services, and programs offered through television and radio.

Teachers are trained at two kinds of institutions: teachers colleges which train teachers for elementary schools and kindergartens, and normal universities which trains teachers for secondary schools. Students at these institutions complete a four-year course after senior high school diploma and an additional year of practical dtraining. There is a uniform pay standard for all teachers in government schools, on the same basis as for civil service employees. Private schools are free to adopt their own pay structure but they too generally follow government scales.

HIGHER EDUCATION

There are four types of higher education institutions: junior colleges, independent colleges, universities, and teacher training institutions. Junior colleges primarily offer courses in applied sciences, training students to become qualified technicians. These colleges are of two types: five-year colleges which admit junior high school graduates; and two-or three-year colleges which admit senior high school graduates. Independent colleges and universities focus on advanced study to train specialists. A university is defined as an institution that is composed of at least three colleges. Universities and colleges offer a broad range of fields of studies including arts, agriculture, architecture, commerce, engineering, law, mathematics, medicine, natural sciences, social sciences, and veterinary science. Teachers colleges and normal universities train teachers for elementary and secondary. Colleges and universities may be established and operated by the private sector or the government. However all teacher training institutions are established and operated by the government. In addition, all tuition and boarding costs at teacher training institutions are paid by the government and students receive an essentially free education.

The duration for undergraduate study in most areas at universities and colleges is four years at the end of which students receive a bachelor's degree. Students in law departments and medical colleges spend from five to seven years at study, including internships (six years for dentistry and seven years for medicine).

For domestic students, admission to undergraduate programs in universities and four-year colleges is limited to candidates who have completed the senior high school and who pass the joint entrance examination. Foreign students' applications are screened by a special committee (given the fact that foreign students are not required to sit for the entrance exam). Entrance requirements for teachers' college and normal university admission are the same as for other universities and colleges. While a junior high school diploma is adequate for admission to five-year junior colleges, the two-and three-year junior colleges require a senior high school diploma.

Master's degrees are offered by the graduate schools and they generally take two years of advanced studies beyond a bachelor's degree. The candidates are required to successfully complete a written and oral examination conducted by a committee invited by the university or college. Doctoral programs generally require an additional two years and students defend a dissertation on completion of research work. Admission to graduate degree programs require successful completion of a bachelor's degree and passing of an entrance examination.

Financial assistance is available to students in the form of scholarships based on merit and grants based on need. The Ministry of Education also awards special fellowships to graduate students.

The administrative structure of universities and colleges consist of a president, university council, council of studies, deans, and chairpersons of departments. The president is the highest academic and administrative officer of the institution and is responsible for the overall functioning of the institution. The president is nominated by the Ministry of Education and endorsed by the Executive Yuan. The formal appointment is made by the President of the Republic. The university council which consist of the president, deans, chairpersons of departments, and representatives of the teaching staff oversees the key affairs of the university. The council of studies which includes deans and chairpersons of departments oversees the curriculum. The teaching staff consists of professors, associate professors, instructors and assistants. For senior appointments, a doctorate as well as accomplishments in research, publications, and teaching are all important.

Each college of a university is headed by a dean appointed by the president. A college consist of several departments, each headed by a chairperson, nominated by the dean of the college and appointed by the president. Graduate research institutes are formed within departments and are headed by directors who may concurrently be professors or chairpersons of departments. The president is assisted generally by three key administrative departments (studies, student affairs, and general affairs) each headed by a dean. Administrative deans are selected from among professors of the institution, by the president.

As of 1989, Taiwan had 21 universities, 20 independent colleges and 75 junior colleges enrolling 535,064 students, including 19,549 graduate students (15,750 at master's level and 3,799 at doctoral level) and 222,311 undergraduate students (at universities and colleges). Majority of the students or 33.5 percent majored in engineering, followed by 22.3 percent in business administration, 8.7 percent in medical science, 6.2 percent in humanities, 4.7 percent in education, 3.8 percent in social sciences, 4.2 percent in mathematics and computer science, 2.9 percent in agriculture and 2.7 percent in natural science (1989 data). The number of foreign students in higher education institutions in Taiwan has grown significantly in the recent years. In the school year 1989, there were 6,260 foreign students from 59 nations and nearly 94 percent of the foreign students were enrolled in the humanities.

BIBLIOGRAPHY

Education in the Republic of China, Taipei, Taiwan: Ministry of Education, 1990.

Education in Taiwan Province, Republic of China. Taiwan: Department of Education, 1974.

Educational Statistics of the Republic of China. Taipei, Taiwan: Ministry of Education, 1990.

Lin Ching-jiang. "Current trends and needs of higher education in the Republic of China." *Proceedings of Six American Seminars on Higher Education.* Taipei: National Taiwan Normal University Press, 1980.

Lin Ching-jiang. "Education in the Republic of China." In: Thomas R. M. Postlethwaite T. N. (eds.) *Schooling in East Asia: Forces of Change.* Oxford: Pergamon, 1983.

Wei-fan Kuo. *Education in the Republic of China 1911-1981,* Vol. 1. Taipei: Kuang-Wen, 1981.

COLOMBIA

by
Enrique E. Batista Jimenez
Professor and Dean, Faculty of Education
University of Antioquia, Colombia

BACKGROUND

Education in Colombia was modeled after Spain's — incomplete, deficient, and church-controlled, and this influence is still felt. In 1564 the church established the first schools to teach reading, writing, and the Catholic faith. In early seventeenth century the first universities were created, some of which are in existence today. In the late 1700s, the state assumed responsibility for primary schools and just after independence in 1819, primary education was reorganized. Education was conceived as the basic instrument of moral development, essential to keep the nation free, and as the basis of political institutions of the new nation. In 1886 the Catholic church reassumed full control of education. Six years later, a national unified system was created; a model that is still present, swinging doubtfully between the national control of policies and the local administration of school teachers.

PRIMARY AND SECONDARY EDUCATION

The five grades of primary education cover 3.5 million students, 7-11 years old. The access of general population to primary schools has increased steadily over the past twenty years. Repetition and dropout rates are, nonetheless, high, and quality has not attained the desired level for cultural and economic development. To reach current goals in primary education it is necessary to increase retention, improve quality of teaching and learning, make curricula pertinent to the local needs of the communities, increase the population of teachers, and distribute textbooks and teaching aids in sufficient numbers. In 1985 Colombia had a secondary-school-age population (ages 13-18) of 4.1 million of which 2.1 million (52 percent) were actually attending school. The rate of growth has been diminishing in the last twenty-five years although it had a 24 percent annual average growth in the period 1965-75 (due mainly to the introduction of the double shift). The annual growth was only 5 percent in the decade of 1975-85. The ratio of students to teachers doubled in between 1960 and 1980 increasing from eleven to twenty-one. Currently there are nineteen students per teacher, a ratio which is somewhat higher than in most Latin American countries (Rodriquez 1987). Rural areas have a marginal participation in the access to secondary education: only 15 percent of secondary school students belong to rural zones.

There has been a lot of concern in the last twenty years about the pertinence and the quality of secondary school education in Colombia. Efforts have been made to diversify by enlarging the curriculum of traditional science and humanities secondary schools ("academic" high schools, as they are called) with the addition of other curricular options including industrial, commercial, agricultural, pedagogical, arts, and social work. In spite of the diversification efforts, eight out of every ten student choose the traditional "academic" emphasis, followed by the commercial option (Velez and Rojas 1989). Most of the students at this level have interest in a college education. In fact the "academic" curriculum focuses on basic knowledge to pass a college entrance exam.

Private institutions compete among themselves to rank high on the mandatory national secondary school exam, the results of which are accepted by universities to admit students. As it has occurred in the past in many other countries, a severe educational distortion has occured as school rectors and teachers emphasize preparation for the state exam in detriment of more important educational goals. The distortion is encouraged by the same national exam as it measures aptitudes and basic knowledge in some areas disregarding values, attitudes, and important skills. In addition, the exam ranks schools and students according to mean performance of the respective group and not according to what students should actually know (and school should have taught).

Students following a curriculum in sciences, humanities, industry, and agriculture perceive that they do not get prepared to do a decent job upon finishing high school. Most students, independently of their curricular emphasis, wish to study, even though a significant proportion of them will combine (and actually do it) work and study. Those who only wish to work are the older students, with curricular emphasis on social work and agriculture. High school graduates that do get into the university are the younger ones, whose fathers have higher levels of educations and incomes (Velez and Rojas 1989).

Secondary school students have been found to value positively what schools do for them, but are not as positive about the teaching abilities and styles of their educators. They also have positive perceptions of the different courses they take, but resent the lack of cultural activities that may allow them a better formation on values. They value discipline as good and necessary but see their teachers weak, confused, and fearful to implement it properly.

Diversified (vocational-technical-comprehensive) high schools were created in Colombia in the 1970s. Recent evaluation studies have shown no optimistic results with respect to their goal of creating a qualified manpower pool according to the country's production needs (Psacharopoulos, Velez and Zabalza 1986). The INEM (as these comprehensive high schools were named) were created to help in the democratization of secondary schooling, and to form middle-level technicians. They have shown no success in their economic and occupational goals. The traditional "academic" high school formation continues to be seen as (and in fact it is) the main educational means of social and economic progress (Puig 1989). Substantial changes will have to be made in order to adapt the educational system to the needs of the country and to enter, with better prospects and reasonable hope, into the third millennium.

Entrance to secondary schools is open to students who pass the primary education cycle. A new development in the preparation of students at the primary level is the *Escuela Nueva* (the New School, literally) which has proven to be an alternative to rural education in areas of low population density; it is also a way to offer primary education to all children. The *Escuela Nueva* has been characterized as one of the most important educational innovations in Latin America.

Even though there were one-teacher schools since the 1960s ("unitary schools", they were called), *Escuela Nueva* was initiated as a government project in 1975. The project sought to have a broader coverage of educational needs in rural areas. Ninety percent of the teachers evaluated *Escuela Nueva* as better than the traditional rural schools *(Ministerio de Education 1988)*.

In 1987 there were 8,000 schools attended by 320,000 children, with 15,000 teachers. It is expected that by 1990 *Escuela Nueva* will be expanded to all of the 26,000 rural schools in the country. Sixty percent of them will have, for the first time, the five grades of the primary school cycle (Colbert 1987).

HIGHER EDUCATION

Colombian universities put a strong emphasis on the preparation of students for traditional careers; this is a basic archaic orientation that precludes cultural, scientific, technical, and community development. The ideals of university goals (teaching, research, and social extension) is seldom seen. The bulk of investment and faculty time goes to teaching in the traditional blackboard and chalk ways.

Public universities are funded by the national government. Income generated by the universities themselves is less than 7 percent of total expenditures. Ninety-five percent of their budgets go to salary and operational costs; very little is left to modernization of physical plants, laboratories, faculty development, and other fundamental equipment required as science and technology progresses. In the years from 1973 to 1981 student enrollment grew 88 percent, but central government monies grew only 71 percent; per capita expenditure was down 9 percent. There are ten students for each faculty member, but internal efficiency is low: between 60-75 percent of students drop out (Icfes 1984).

Only few universities guide their efforts toward the needs of the region in which they are located. Very few of them try to create development (even in cases where important industrial, mining, or agricultural projects are in the region). A significant number of universities are outdated in their curricula as well as in the goals and objectives they must reach. Apart from these obvious inadequacies, new teaching methods and technological innovations are required as inequity is built into the system with most universities located in the big cities (Icfes 1984).

Most students enroll in five groups of professions: economics, engineering, education, law, and medicine. There has been an increasing demand for university admission: enrollment grew from 23,000 in 1960 to over 400,000 now. The growing need for university certification has led to the creation of many low quality universities and technological institutes, many of which offer night courses of questionable quality. Unemployment of university graduates has been much lower

(6.5 percent in 1985) than that of the general population (15 percent for men and 19 percent for women in the 20-29 age group).

In the 1980s there was a substantial development in distance education. This development helped to increase the participation of marginal regions in university programs; labor force has been trained in those regions avoiding an exodus to metropolitan centers. Distance education, however, has centered on low cost programs, mainly education, and some six-semester technological programs (Morato and Londono 1986).

A comparative study of students' achievement (distance vs. on campus) in eighteen different courses (same professor, same content, same evaluation) showed nine significant differences in favor of on-campus courses; the other nine comparisons showed no significant differences (Restrepo 1986). Even though there are good programs, distance education still lacks credibility and quality.

In spite of all these limitations common to a great number of countries (Diaz, Mantilla, Malagon, and Correa 1987), there have been important recent developments that allow us to foresee more optimistically the future. There is a growing number of research centers dealing with national and local problems in areas such as economics, education, ecology, tropical agriculture and biology. Universities are developing low-cost, but effective, indigenous technologies that are helping to solve important local problems in many communities. Universities are also working with national and local authorities to undertake solutions to public health problems, especially in rural and urban marginal zones. Basic and applied research led recently to the development of the first vaccine to prevent malaria, a devastating disease in the world.

Internal reforms have been undertaken by a considerable number of universities to improve their administrative and financial models, as well as to introduce new modern technologies and teaching methods. There is an increasing interest on curricular reforms centered around local and national needs. There is plenty of room for improvement, and important efforts are been made in the right direction.

To be admitted to a higher education institution students must have the high school diploma, take the state examination, and in some cases pass an examination defined by each institution.

Two-year undergraduate programs lead to the degree of "professional technician", with emphasis on practical competencies. In the three-year programs emphasizing adaptation or creation of technologies, the "Technologist" degree is awarded. Degrees for the professional take four (nursing, social work, education), five (economics, engineering, biology, law, dentistry), or seven years (medicine). In all cases the program leads to the title of the respective professional (nurse, economist, social worker, etc.). Postgraduate degrees are offered by a few institutions at three levels: specialization, master's, and doctoral programs.

Tuition is paid according to the annual income or wealth of parents. In public universities, the median cost of tuition per semester is about US$42 (about half a month's minimum salary). In private universities the cost is around US$360.

ISSUES AND TRENDS

A most significant hope in future is to be placed in education. Hopelessness appears frequently as a response to the immense problems to be solved and to the lack of adequate alternative solutions and resources. Obviously, claiming to be in crisis, and declaring bankruptcy and hopelessness is not a solution to get a better educational system. We cannot add cultural and spiritual poverty to economic poverty. Solutions belong not only to the realm of international cooperation and economic development, but also to actions within the country: democratic governments, economic reforms to ensure equity, better distribution of wealth, employment, and a higher rate of national savings for development. Main issues are discussed here.

Insufficient Funding of Educational Programs

Less economic resources for the nation, and consequently less resources for education have created a difficult situation for educational development. In fact, given the actual circumstances, we cannot foresee that our country will have significantly more economic resources for education. From here, it is obvious, that new strategies will have to be experimented. The question is now to do more (and better) with less. New political, economic, and managerial strategies in education will be required. At present there is one fact that is difficult to accept: solutions with more resources are not realistic (Oliveira 1989).

Distortions in Internal Distribution of Resources

The whole system can be very well characterized by its inadequate internal distribution of resources for education. In comparison with higher education, primary school level has received less financial resources; this fact led to a distortion that has to be amended. More resources ought to be given to the bulk of the population so that their basic educational needs are satisfied. As far as regions are concerned, funds have been allocated in those geographical sectors with higher concentration of population, instead of allocating monetary resources according to the needs of the population without schooling. Contrary to equity, the state has subsidized to a greater extent the middle and higher income groups (Yepes 1987).

Salary and Investment Imbalance

Teachers are not well paid, and a better payment is a requisite for both attracting better qualified candidates and retaining them in the system. Given the lower budget for education (due among other things to external debt, lower prices for commodities, and defense expenditures), the paradox is evident: higher salaries lead to less amount of money to undertake solutions to other problems in the educational system. Our country invests about fifty times less money in other crucial aspects of schools (books, laboratories, teaching aids, continuing education for teachers) than the most developed countries.

Inadequate Control of Education

Educational issues have turned out to be not a matter of public concern, but mainly a matter of negotiations between the Ministry of Education and the educator's labor union. There is the need to get education and its quality, to be a matter of public concern. Strategies for control of education by a central government does not work and it has proved to be inefficient: bureaucracy becomes the means and ends of education due to the voracious clientele generated by politicians. Partisan and personal interests predominate over national interest. A greater degree of control by local communities will do much to improve control of education and its quality (particularly, control of teachers' efficiency).

Oliveira (1989) has indicated that it is not that important if the school system is centralized or decentralized. Resources have to be allocated to schools. Schools should also have a somewhat permanent structure and the means to carry out successful programs to improve the quality of education. He adds, "From a historical perspective, the structures put in place to manage educational matters represent the natural evolution of a colonial tradition. This legacy includes four interrelated elements: a multilevel administrative hierarchy; legal concepts based on notions of how people ought to behave rather than on how they actually do behave; personalism, or given loyalty to a person; and particularism, or placing the interest of a special group or political party above the interest of the whole" (Oliveira 1989).

Too Little Schooling for Too Many People

Colombia has a population close to 30 million people and is in a process of rapid urban development. Over 60 percent of the population live now in urban centers. The total population growth has a declining annual rate: in 1960-65 the average annual rate per 100 inhabitants was 3.1 percent while in 1985-90 it is 2.1 percent (UNESCO, 1989).

The poorer sectors of the population have little schooling. Even though 90 percent of all children in urban areas (70 percent in rural zones) have access to primary school, internal efficiency is not that good. In urban areas, children attend on the average 3.8 years, and desertion reaches the level of 40 percent and repetition 15.7 percent. In rural areas the average school attendance is only 1.7 years; 50 percent of schools do not have at least five grades; 13 percent of children of 6-12 years of age never attend school; and 20 percent of the children attending first grade and 70 percent of those in fifth grade are repeating it. In urban areas 60 percent of students finish the primary cycle (five grades); in rural areas only 20 percent of the students finish it. Seven out of ten schools in urban areas, and four out of ten in rural areas have the five grades of the primary school cycle (Dane 1989). A complete coverage of all the schooling needs will require 20,000 additional teachers and a considerable amount of money to be invested in physical plants and in all the necessary materials required by schools and teachers (Yepes 1987).

About 25 percent of Colombia's total population is having formal education, another 4 percent receive non-formal education, and 12 percent of the population (fifteen years of age and older) are illiterate. Due to serious educational limitations, the functional illiterates could reach five million people (Rodriguez 1987).

Erroneous Assumptions about Teaching

Quality of education and the administration of the school system have been negatively affected by erroneous suppositions that guide actions in schools:

a).   A high school diploma with some courses on pedagogy qualifies for teaching at the pre-school, primary, and secondary levels. In fact, the "Normal Schools", where teachers are trained, rank very low (sixth among seven high school curricular options) in the general quality of secondary education, as measured by the Colombian general examination (Velez and Rojas 1989). The best students do not enter the teaching profession and those who do enter do not get into "Normal Schools". New strategies for professional training of teachers should be stimulated, as the "Normal School" is insufficient. Emphasis on in-service training and continuing education has proven to be successful (Londono, Velasquez, Urrego and Cadavid, 1988; Vidal, Dussan, Arias and Signore, 1986). The proportion of teachers with higher education diplomas, nevertheless, has tripled in the last few years, increasing from 5 in 1965 to 14 percent in 1984 (Dane 1989). But the proportion is still low at 15 percent. In 1950, 64 percent of all primary school teachers had only primary school education. In 1965 this figure was down to 8 percent while in 1984 it was only 1 percent (Dane 1989).

b).   What a teacher knows is enough to teach. It has been assumed that the sum of a teacher's knowledge accounts for successful education, disregarding other important qualities teachers must have to provide a proper education. There is a lack of common goals and a lack of integration of teachers around a common educational project of great social and political impact. However, a recent pedagogical movement created by the Colombian Federation of Educators has made important advances in this direction (Martinez and Rojas 1984; Escobar and Suarez 1987; Gantivar 1987).

c).   Those hired as teachers have a life right to the job and are not accountable. This supposition has created in Colombia serious difficulties for the improvement and renewal of schools and school practices. Inadequate centralized government supervision and a strong labor union have created a situation where stability on the job is guaranteed even in the face of continuous evidence of ineffective teaching. A recent law of 1989 intends to find answers to this problem by transferring the administration of school teachers to the popularly elected mayors of each municipality in Colombia. The law, however, has serious shortcomings (see Bayona 1989).

d).   What a teacher earns is sufficient for a decent living. As said before, teachers are underpaid. The monthly salary of a Colombian teacher in 1989 ranges from US$95 to US$370, with a mode around US$140 (a decent living for a family with two children require a minimum of US$350-400). This salary in constant pesos decreased through the decade of the 1980s. Teachers usually work in alternate shifts in private schools to ensure additional earnings for a decent living; it is a tiring effort of 10-12 hours a day that has a negative effect in the quality of education.

Too Little Time for Schools to have an Effect

Children in primary education in Colombia must go to school forty weeks (200 days) a year, or a total of 1,000 hours. Due to a considerable number of holidays, teachers strikes, teachers meetings, teachers' or students' absenteeism, the total number of days effectively worked comes down to 140-160 (700-800 hours). This time, however, is reduced even more as teachers spend a considerable amount of it in activities not directly related to teaching. An additional negative factor is given by the double-shift schedule. Students attend school 4-5 hours daily, either in the morning or in the afternoon. The double-shift schedule was an emergency decision taken twenty-five years ago, but has become permanent, adversely affecting the quality of education, the school administration, and the possibility of introducing innovations. A growing public distrust in the quality of public education due to wastage of time has led to a very strong private sector of education. Sixteen percent of all primary students attend private school. In secondary schools this percentage was estimated at 40 percent for 1986. In Bogota, the capital city, this percentage is 85 percent. Forty percent of university students go to private institutions (Velez and Rojas 1989).

Reaching the goals of high internal efficiency and better quality education calls for concrete action in the following areas:

a). Increasing internal efficiency by creating cultural environments responsive to student and community needs and favorable to the goals of education. Special attention has to be paid to pertinent curricula and to the introduction of innovations in the methods of evaluation and promotion of students. In the school year of 1988 a central government decree put into effect the automatic promotion of all students in primary education. This strategy seeks to lower drop-out and retention rates and to change the practice of evaluation. Some positive results are already discernible in this direction (Yepes 1987; Batista, Morato, Martinez, Sannicolas and Londono 1989).

b). Improving the quality of teaching by the introduction and experimentation of new didactics, teaching strategies, teaching methods, and soft or hard technologies. There is a significant amount of evidence that the introduction of appropriate textbooks in less developed countries contributes significantly to improve teaching and learning (Farrell and Hayneman 1989). There are also many innovations that have shown evidence of working well in developing countries (Thiagarajan and Pasigna 1989; Schiefelbein 1989; Restrepo, et al. 1985; Henao, Jimenez, Restrepo and Zuluaga 1988). Experience has shown that improving teaching and learning in Colombian schools, even within current financial constraints is a possibility open to innovative teachers.

c).   Increasing school time. Two main actions are suggested: One is to gradually reduce the numbers of schools with double shifts, so that students can attend school 6-7 hours daily, including here the remediation work for those in need of it, and educational activities different from classroom teaching. This option will be difficult to implement due to the resistance of teachers and to the higher cost it implies, but as the population growth index decreases, the viability of this proposal will improve. The other action has to do with the training of teachers to make a more efficient use of time.

d).   Establishing better relations between schools and their surrounding communities. The integration of parents and community leaders to school life has been everywhere an effective means to monitor and improve the quality of education. In Colombia, with the exception of high-class private schools, parents and community leaders do little for the schools in which their children receive education. As pointed out before, in Colombia, educational matters have gradually become a point of controversy or negotiation between the central government and the educators' union. In rural *Escuela Nueva* and in some other places there have been important advances in this regard (Colbert 1987; Schiefelbein 1989). The Ministry of Education has written a project to make education more pertinent to communities, and communities more participative of school's life (Yepes 1988). At this moment there is no published evidence of its educational or social impact.

BIBLIOGRAPHY

Amar, J. *Los Hogares Comunales Del Nino. Teoria y Experiencias*. Barranquilla: Ediciones Uninorte, 1986.

Batista, E., Morato, C., Martinez, A., Sannicolas, C. and Londono, A. *Escuela y Promocion Escolar*. Medellin: Universidad de Antioquia, 1989.

Bayona, J. "Reflexiones sobre descentralizacion y la ley 24." *Educacion y pedagogia*. No. 1 (1989): 21 - 32.

Diaz, C., Mantilla, M., Malagon, A., and Correa, S. "La crisis de la educacion." *Estudios Educativos*. No. 26 (1987): 7 - 40.

Florez, R., and Batista, E. *El Pensamiento Pedagogico de Los Maestros*. Medellin: Copiyepes, 1982.

Gantiva, J. "El movimiento pedagogico en Colombia 1982-1987." *Educacion y cultura*. No. 12 (1987): 52 - 60.

Herrera, S., et al. *Renovacion Curricular en el Departamento de antioquia. Educacion Basica Primaria*. Medellin: Universidad de Antioquia, 1987.

ICFES *Diagnostico de la educacion superior 1973-1983. Analisis cuantitativo de variables*. Bogota: ICFES, 1989.

Ocampo, J. "Empleo, desempleo e ingresos de la fuerza de trabajo universitaria, 1976-1985." In *Crisis de la Educacion Superior,* by Fundacion para la educacion superior. Bogota: FES, 1986.

Oliveira, J. *Educational Reform in Latin America: Toward a Permament Agenda.* Washington: World Bank (mimeo), 1980.

Psacharopoulos, G., Velez, E. and Zabalza, A. *Una Evaluacion de la Educacion Media Divesificada en Colombia.* Bogota: Rojas-Eberhard, 1986.

Restrepo, B., et al. *La Innovacion en Educacion.* Medellin: Universidad de Antioquia, 1985.

Rodriquez, A. "La educacion colombiana; datos y cifras." *Educacion y Cultura,* No. 12 (1987): 5 - 14.

Schielfelbein, E. "Siete estrategias para elevar la calidad y eficiencia del sistema de educacion." In *Seminario Latinoamericano Sobre el use de Tecnologias en la Educacion y la Capcitacion: Un Punto de Vista Economico.* Vol. 1. Medellin: Universidad de Antioquia, 1989.

Thiagarajan, S. and Pasigna, A. "Proyecto Bridges. El empleo de las tecnologias de aprendizaje blandas para la educacion primaria de los paises en via de desarrollo: una revision bibliografica." In *Seminario Latinoamericano Sobre el uso de Tecnologias en la Educacion y la Capacitacion: Un Punto de Vista Economic.* Vol. II. Medellin: Universidad de Antioquia, 1989.

UNESCO. *Statistical Yearbook for Latin America and the Caribbean.* Santiago de Chile: UNESCO, 1989.

COSTA RICA

by
Jesus Viquez
Professor and Dean, School of Education
University of Costa Rica, Costa Rica

BACKGROUND

The origin of higher education in Costa Rica can be traced back to the establishment of *Casa de Ensenanza de Santo Tomas* (School of St. Thomas) in April 1814. It had a religious character but its curriculum included mathematics, writing, and reading. Ten years later the government assumed funding of this institution. By 1843, it began conferring degrees primarily in literature (in addition to conducting studies in medicine). The year 1843 also saw the creation of the University of St. Thomas by an executive decree issued under the direction of the Chief of State Don Jose Ma. Alfaro and the Minister of State Don Jose Ma. Castro Madriz. This university, regarded as the predecessor of the present day higher education, continued operation only till 1888 when it was closed by the order of the then government of President Bernardo Soto.

Interest in the development of national education resurfaced in the middle of the last century as evidenced by declaration of free and compulsory education, government funding of education (1859), and the establishment of the first center for higher education (1860). These efforts were further strengthened in the seventies and the eighties with the liberal educational reforms heavily influenced by the contributions of Mauro Fernandez. Specifically, three centers of higher education came into existence, of which two had teacher training sections, one was for women and the other was for men. (*Lice de Costa Rica* in 1887, and *Colegio Superior de Senoritas* in 1888). This epoch also marked the strengthening of primary and secondary education.

After the closing of the University of St. Thomas in 1888, there were no opportunities for university education in the country till 1940 when the University of Costa Rica was established. During this period, Costa Rican students attended universities in other parts of the world (primarily in Nicaragua, Guatemala, South America, and Europe). The development of the University of Costa Rica was synonymous with the development of state supported university education in Costa Rica as it was the only university. The seventies then saw the creation of three other universities. University development in Costa Rica has gone through at least four stages: search for strength and autonomy from 1940-49; attempts by the university and the state for endorsement of funding etc. between 1949 and 1957; movement for reform of universities between 1957 and 1967; and formation of university without walls leading to regionalization of education between 1967 and 1976.

The Constitution of the country (1949 and recent amendments) guarantees university autonomy and state funding for state education institutions. A coordinating commission consisting of the ministers of home affairs, education, and planning as well as a representative from the Office of Higher Education Planning and the rectors of the four state universities oversee the funding for higher education. The rectors of the four state universities also form the National Council of Rectors which is attached to the Office of Planning (government). This structure provides for coordination, planning, and decision making with regard to policies affecting state universities in the country.

Within each institution, various internal organs and subdivisions (university council, faculties, schools, regional centers, institutes, and research centers) handle necessary coordination (according to their spheres of activities) with the government, with other institutions in the country, and with the chambers of commerce and industries. The organizational structure of university institutions generally consist of university assemblies, university councils, area councils (based on the fields of studies), faculties, schools, regional centers, institutes, departments, and sections.

Private universities are governed by specific provisions of the (state) law. The National Council of Higher Education oversees approval, planning, and coordination related to private institutions. There are also a variety of para-university institutions of higher education (*colegios universitarios* and *institutos*) formed under the provisions of Law No. 9541 of 1980. They are both state sponsored and privately organized, and provide shorter periods of training for the purpose of producing technical manpower. These institutions are overseen by the Higher Council of Education.

In general, it can be said that the system of education in Puerto Rico is structured into two major segments: formal education and non-formal education. The first is regulated, continuous, complete, integrated, coherent, flexible and diversified. This segment is represented by preschool education, general basic education, diversified education, and higher education.

The non-formal segment provides an open system for Costa Rican citizens to enhance their knowledge and skills. Included are programs such as alphabetization, and basic as well as secondary education for mature people. Among the institutions which merit special mention is the National Apprentice Institution. Informal education is also imparted through written communication mediums (newspapers, magazines, and other publications), radio, and television. In television, there is a special cultural and educational channel with focuses on informal education.

Essentially, the educational system in Costa Rica has eight important characteristics: relationship among the human being, family, and the society; constant search for continuing education; relationship among education, work, and production (output); relationship between education and democracy; preoccupation for knowledge in and for the use of science and technology; humanism; culture and education; and promotion of education as an important factor in the development of the country.

PRIMARY AND SECONDARY EDUCATION

Children enter school at the age of six years and six months (as of the first of March of the year, which is the date schools begin the academic year). However based on special testing or attendance at preschool programs, age requirement may be waived by three months. Since 1972, based on the National Plan for Educational Development under executive directive 3333E, students are given a general basic education for nine years, consisting of three cycles of three years each. This education is compulsory and free of charge (funded by the government). The first two cycles correspond to primary education in the traditional sense and a certificate is awarded on completion of the studies. The third cycle corresponds to the initial years of secondary education.

After nine years of general basic education, students commence diversified education which lasts two years in the academic and artistic stream, and three years in the technical stream. Recent developments (1988) require students to take an examination on completion of the diversified education to obtain the diploma of *bachiller* in secondary education, which is a prerequisite for admission to university. Moreover in two of the higher education institutions (University of Costa Rica and Technological Institute of Costs Rica) an admission test is a requirement. In the technical streams, students obtain the *tecnico medio* (mid-level technician) diploma which permits them to practice a vocation. The diversified cycle of education is also free but not compulsory. The academic year for both the general basic education cycle and the diversified cycle lasts nine months, from March to November.

There is no restriction on the enrollment of foreign students. In fact there are many foreign students attending school in Costa Rica, particularly from Central American countries.

Teachers are trained in the universities and appointments are based on competitive recruiting conforming to statutes of the civil service.

HIGHER EDUCATION

Institutions

Higher education institutions in Costa Rica fall into several categories: state universities, private universities, and para-university institutions (both state and private). In addition, there is one non-university institution.

In the category of state universities there are four institutions: University of Costa Rica established in 1940 with its central campus in San Jose and regional campuses in Guanacaste, San Ramon, Turrialba and Limon; National University established in 1973 with its central campus in Heredia, and regional campuses in Perez Zeledon and Liberia; State University at Distance, (distance education) established in 1977 with its central campus in San Jose and thirty-one academic centers around the country serving as a vital alternative to conventional higher education; and the Technological Institute of Costa Rica established in 1971 with its central campus in Cartago and regional campuses in San Jose and Santa Clara. Private sector consists of six institutions: Autonomous University of Central America created in 1975 comprising twelve colleges; International University of the Americas founded in 1985, offering ten areas of studies; Adventist University of Central America established in 1986 offering three fields of studies and belonging to the Adventist church; Latin American University of Science and Technology founded in 1987 offering studies in four areas; Pan American University established in 1988 with three colleges offering studies in four areas; and a few university centers of higher education in specialized fields (e.g. Central American Institute of Business Administration in collaboration with Harvard).

Para-university institutions offer courses lasting short periods of time for careers in the service sector, and they consist of four institutions: University College of Cartago established in 1976 with a campus in Santa Cruz; University College of Alajuela established in 1978 with its campus in Alajuela; University College of Puntarena created in 1980 with its campus in Puntarenas, and Central American School of Ganaderia established in 1978 with its campuses in Balsa and Alajuela. The first three are state institutions while the last one functions under an agreement between Great Britain and Costa Rica.

An institution of higher education that falls into the non-university category is the Center for Research and Training in Technical Education established in 1976 with its campus in Alajuela, and it comes under the Ministry of Public Education. This institution trains teachers of technical education (industrial and agricultural).

The activities of state universities are coordinated by the Advisory Council of Rectors (supplied by the Office of Higher Education Planning) comprised of rectors of the four state universities. One of the rectors preside over this council, on a rotational basis (presidency rotated every year). Each state university has a university assembly, overseeing the activities of the university. The assembly is comprised of professors, a student representative, and certain other members depending on the institution. Each university is headed by a rector elected by the academic community of the institution, for a period of four years. Deans of faculties, vice-deans, and directors of departments are also elected by the faculty members and the students (25 percent of the votes) of each academic unit (faculty, department, etc.).

Programs and Degrees

Higher education institutions offer undergraduate programs leading to a variety of qualifications. Certificates are usually awarded to mark the completion of short courses of training. Courses of a somewhat longer duration (2-3 years) but not up to degree level lead to diplomas. The *bachillerato* (bachelor's) in specific fields is awarded only by the universities and takes four years of studies. The *licenciatura* in a given field is awarded for one or two years of studies beyond the *bachillerato* and require completion of a thesis. A variety of fields of study are available: sciences, letters, social sciences, arts, philosophy, engineering, etc.

State universities in Costa Rica are also responsible for training of teachers and the three state universities play an active role in this regard. Students can obtain the title of *professor* (teacher) after two years of training at the university. Two more years lead to the *bachiller* degree in education. The *licenciatura* degree in education can be obtained after a further period of two years of studies (with specialization in educational administration, preschool education, primary education, teaching curriculum development, etc.).

Candidates desiring admission to the University of Costa Rica and the Technological Institute of Costs Rica are required to pass an entrance examination. In addition, some fields of studies have special requirements. The National University and the State University at Distance have an open admissions policy.

Fees are charged at higher education institutions but all institutions have a system of scholarships. Although students and their families have to finance their studies, the National Commission for Educational Assistance offers financing for study in priority subject areas.

Foreign students may seek admission to any of the higher education institutions provided admission requirements are met. The universities also receive students and teachers under various agreements with foreign universities, particularly institutions in the United States of America.

Graduate studies leading to master's and doctoral degrees are available at the University of Costa Rica in a variety of fields including biology, microbiology, philosophy, philology, law, medicine, public administration, education, etc. Admission requires a high level of achievement in previous academic work. Standards required are comparable to those of North American universities with regard to the number of necessary credits, duration, and other requirements for graduation.

Research at the universities is conducted at the research centers, institutes, or laboratories. Research activity may form part of the degree requirements for graduate students. Research is conducted in a number of fields including social sciences, law, statistics, psychology, agronomy, biology, medicine, education, etc.

ISSUES AND TRENDS

The educational system as a whole began to see growth in the early 1970s, under a plan of development adopted in 1972. Between 1978 and 1982, a process called regionalization of education was promoted which resulted in community participation in education, thus awakening a high level of consciousness among the people. This gave rise to an adapted curriculum which is still in use in some classes.

Beginning in 1982, a series of actions were taken to improve the quality of education and output including restructuring of study programs, training of personnel in charge of technical areas in the Ministry of Education, and training of the instructors. Between 1986 and now these actions have been further strengthened by the introduction of computers in schools, emphasis on sciences, and tests on academic achievement at the *bachillerato* level.

In the field of higher education, the current tendencies include continued emphasis on regionalization leading to democratization of education; strengthening of postgraduate studies; and pressure to provide increased opportunities for privatizing higher education. Increased emphasis on privatization has led to an increase in the number of private institutions, in the recent years.

In spite of the progress made in education in the recent years, Costa Rica faces several key issues and problems. The internal efficiency of the school system is low and reflects a high percentage of dropouts. This contributes to an increase in functional illiteracy, in absolute terms. The content of the general basic education cycle, in spite of improvements, have not shown to be adequate to meet the needs of the rural areas and to prepare students for integration into productive activities. The diversified cycle, except in the case of technical schools, has been excessively bent on preparing students for higher education for the attainment of a degree, and it lacks flexibility for allowing movement of students into other parallel opportunities, thus leading to disequilibrium between output from education and needs of the market place.

Equal distribution of educational opportunities is restrained by the marked social stratification that is still existing in our society. The socioeconomic origins of the students condition their access to the system and eventual success. There are inequalities in the regional distribution of educational facilities at all levels of the system, which accentuates regional disequilibrium in national development. The system of education does not have sufficient participation of the community that receives the education. Stress is on the transfer of scientific and technological models coming from more developed countries and there is a lack of encouragement for critique of these models and search for own solutions. There is a high demand for teachers as a result of the growth in education propelled by the democratization of education and population increase. However, the teachers lack any economic incentive as they are grossly underpaid compared to other professionals.

BIBLIOGRAPHY

Consejo National de Rectores, OPES. *El Sistems de Educación Superior de Costa Rica. Características, Problemas y Algunas sugerencias papa su Mejoramiento.* San Jose, Costa Rica, 1979.

Consejo Nacional de Rectores, OPES. *Las Instituciones de Educación Superior Públicas de Costa Rica.* San Jose, Costa Rica, 1979.

Consejo Nacional de Rectores. OPES. *El Balance de las Ocupaciones y las Disponibilidades de Recursos Humanos de Nivel Superior hacia 1985.* San Jose, Costa Rica, 1979.

Consejo Nacional de Rectores. OPES. *Leyes, Decretos y Convenios de la Educación Superior Pública en Costa Rica.* San Jose, Costa Rica, 1980.

Consejo Nacional de Rectores, OPES. *Estadística de la Educación Superior, 1980.* San Jose, Costa Rica, 1987.

Consejo Nacional de Rectores, OPES. *Posibilidades de Estudio en la Educación superior Universitaria Estatal de Costa Rica.* San Jose, Costa Rica, 1988.

Costa Rica, Consejo Superior de Educación. *Reglamento General de E tablecimientos Oficiales de Educación Media.* San Jose, Costa Rica, 1965.

Ministeria de Educación Pública. *Regionalización y Mediorizacion Educativa en Costa Rica.* San Jose, Costa Rica, 1979.

San di M. M. *Legislación Educativa.* Vol 2. San Jose, Costa Rica: ENED, 1979.

Ugalde V. J. *La Formación de los Educadores en Costa Rica.* San Jose, Costa Rica, 1968.

CUBA

by
Elvira Martin Sabina
Director
Center for the Study of
Higher Education
University of Havana, Cuba

BACKGROUND

The beginning of higher education in Cuba dates back to January 1728 when the Order of the Dominicans founded the *Universidad de la Habana*. For the next 200 years, this institution continued to be the only university in Cuba. The establishment of the *Universidad de Oriente* in 1947 and the *Universidad Central de Las Villas* in 1952 added new flavor to university education in the country. Some private universities also came into existence but most of them were of questionable quality.

Public universities in Cuba before the revolution of 1959 enrolled only about 15,000 students. Educational programs were primarily in the humanities, with little emphasis on sciences; curriculum and teaching methods were highly traditional and obsolete; and scientific research, excepting in a few isolated instances was practically non existent.

January 1962 saw the proclamation of university reforms which heralded the most important historical development of that decade, in the field of higher education in Cuba. The reforms consisted of, among other things, changes in governance to include participation of teaching staff and students, reorganization of university structure, development of scientific research, creation of a large number of study programs and pedagogical institutes, implementation of a system of scholarships, changes in the structure of degree programs to match the needs of the country, and establishment of a link between studies and work.

In the early years of the 1970s, new forms of study-work programs were created in the higher educational system so as to apply Marxist principles and combine theory with practice, combining school with life and education with production. After a rigorous process of analysis, the Law of Social Service was promulgated in 1973, under which university graduates would render their services, during the first three years of their professional life, in places considered most important to the nation's needs.

Along with the changes in the structure of education, additional centers of higher education were also established. In 1972, the *Universidad de Camaguey* was founded. By the middle of the decade, there was a whole network of higher education centers with the number rising to twenty-eight in 1976-77. Also in July

1976, the Ministry of Education was established with the responsibility for implementation of educational policy and for management of the education institutions. Today (1988-89) the network of higher educational institutions has expanded to thirty-five, spread throughout the country.

Education has been an area of primary importance to the revolutionary government since the very beginning of its undertaking of social transformations in Cuba. Thus, the "Law of Nationalization of Education" was passed on 6 June 1961, establishing following key principles: Education is a responsibility of the revolutionary state and it is a function that cannot be delegated or transferred; Education shall be imparted free of charge for guaranteeing all citizens the right to receive education without distinction or privileges; Education at all levels shall be oriented, through an integrated system, to fully respond to cultural, social and technical needs of the country's development.

The Campaign for National Literacy undertaken in 1961 was a vital element in the expansion of education in Cuba and involved the challenging task of bringing together massive participation of people capable of teaching and those who needed learning. As a result of this campaign more than 700,000 illiterates learned to read and write in one year and the illiteracy rate came down from 23.6 percent to 3.9 percent. By 1981, the illiteracy rate was 1.9 percent among the population aged 10-49 years.

After the implementation of the Plan of Improvement in the late 1970s, the national system of education now consist of several subsystems: preschooling; general; polytechnical and labor education; special education (education for the handicapped); technical and vocational education; pedagogical education (teacher training); adult education; and higher education. There are three levels in the structure: elementary, secondary, and higher education.

The Plan of Improvement required, as a principle, continuous evaluation and adaptation of curriculum and study programs at all levels of the educational system. The implementation of the plan is making it possible to achieve the objective of raising education to a level to make international standards. In the academic year 1987-88, 100 percent of the age group of 6-11 year old children received schooling and the rate was 98 percent for children between the ages of 6-14 years. Enrollment in the educational system consisted of 39.5 percent in primary, 48.2 percent in middle (secondary), and 12.3 percent in higher education. The number of scholarships offered reached over one million. The allocation for education in 1988 is more than 1,700 million pesos.

In essence, the educational system has seen a great transformation in both quantity and quality, responding to the social and economic needs of the country. In addition, the educational system provides assistance to developing countries in the form of scholarships for study in Cuba and supply of teachers and teaching material. On the other hand, the assistance received for Cuban education from the Soviet Union and the East European countries has been very significant. There have also been fruitful exchanges and cooperation arrangements with numerous countries, specially in Latin America and the Caribbean, which have made a very positive contribution for education in Cuba.

PRIMARY AND SECONDARY EDUCATION

Primary education is preceded by a year of preschool and consists of two cycles: the first or preparatory cycle (entry age is six years) with grades 1-4 and the second cycle with grades 5-6 in which specialized subjects are introduced. General secondary education begins in grade seven and continues to grade twelve with two levels: basic secondary (grades 7, 8, and 9) and pre-university (grades 10, 11, and 12). Both primary and secondary education form part of the general polytechnic and labor education sub system, which operates in a manner that all students are provided the opportunity to get a complete general education and to access technical and vocational education, teacher training programs, and higher education until they become trained in a vocation, profession, or speciality. Completion of the twelve year education in this cycle is a requirement for admission to any higher education institution.

Technical and vocational education has the mission of training technical personnel required for the national economy including skilled workers and mid level technicians. The training is provided at polytechnic schools with courses lasting one to four years. Admission to the programs require completion of the ninth grade. The shorter programs (1-2 years) are for skilled workers and the longer (3-4 year) programs are for middle level technicians.

Teacher training programs are available at both middle and higher levels. The middle level pedagogical schools train teachers for primary school, librarians, and special education teachers. Admission requires completion of grade nine and the program leads to completion of grade twelve. The higher level training prepares students who have completed grade twelve, for teaching positions in secondary schools (with specialized training in languages, technical and vocational education, etc.).

Adult education aims at providing workers and adults with a basic general education that could ultimately help them to acquire other qualifications or excel at work. Adult education consist of three levels: worker-farmer education; secondary worker-farmer education; and worker-farmer faculties. These three levels correspond to primary, basic secondary and preuniversity respectively in the general education system.

The academic year lasts from the beginning of September to the middle of July with four terms in the case of primary schools, and two semesters in the case of basic secondary and pre university schools. Technical and vocational schools also have two semesters but they include practical work.

HIGHER EDUCATION

Institutions

Higher education institutions in Cuba fall into three major categories: universities, higher polytechnic institutes, and university centers. The origin for this diversity lies in the necessity to have a flexible system of institutions to meet the development needs of various regions of the country.

The universities have the responsibility of providing an academic education primarily in natural sciences, mathematics, social sciences, humanities and economics. The higher polytechnical institutions train professionals in technical areas. The higher institutes train professionals in specific fields of science such as pedagogy, agricultural sciences, medical sciences, and arts. The university centers train professionals in various branches. There are other branches and units (attached to different higher educational institutions) and located in various parts of the country providing courses for workers. The quantitative increase in the number of institutions in the academic years 1975-76 and 1976-77 was due to reorganization of the higher educational subsystem. For example the *Universidad de La Habana* created four new institutions at higher levels of specialization: Higher Institute of Medical Sciences; Higher Pedagogical Institute; Higher Institute of Agricultural Sciences; and Higher Polytechnical Institute.

Majority of the higher education institutions (fourteen) come under the Ministry of Higher Education; twelve institutions are overseen by the Ministry of Education; and four institutions come under the Ministry of Public Health. The higher institutes of arts, physical education, international relations, industrial design, and nuclear science and technology are attached to organizations that have fundamental responsibilities in these areas of activities.

Governance of Cuban education institutions is through a head (rector) of the institution who is vested with the authority and responsibility for administering the institution. He is assisted by collective organs which includes administrators at other levels of management as well as representatives of students and unions. The administrative structure at the higher level consists of vice-rectors, directors, departments and sections. Faculties form units of teaching, research and administration. A teaching department *(cathedra)* is a component of the faculty and constitutes the basic cellule in the academic structure of the institution and is responsible for academic activities including course development, scientific research, etc. The scientific council is a collective body consisting of elected members from the departments and plays an important coordinating role in the scientific activities of the institution.

The teaching staff at Cuban institutions of higher education consist of four principal categories, two complementary categories and three special categories. The principal categories in order of rank are the professor (titular), associate professor, assistant, and instructor. The complimentary categories are assistant instructor and teaching assistant. Special categories are professor emeritus, visiting professor, and adjunct professor.

Undergraduate Studies

Cuban institutions of higher education offer a variety of degree programs. Candidates who complete studies in sciences, technology, and agricultural fields receive the degree of *ingeniero* (engineer). Architecture programs lead to the degree of *arquitecto* (architect). Studies in medicine, and veterinary sciences lead to the degree of *doctor* (physician). Studies in natural sciences, mathematics, social sciences, humanities, economics, education, and arts lead to the *licenciado*.

In general, the duration for the first degree is five years and the academic year is divided into two semesters with about 14-18 weeks of classes and three examinations for each semester. The curriculum provides about fifty courses and 4,000-4,500 total hours, not including practical work at centers of production and other services required (as part of the professional training) or the time required for preparing the final thesis. About 50 percent of the time is spent for basic and general courses. The educational program is designed to train broadly educated persons, who have the capability to function in a variety of jobs and, once graduated, they can receive specialized training by serving a period of apprenticeship for 2-3 years in an industrial or other enterprise.

Admission requirements for regular full-time programs are different to that for part time studies. There are provincial commissions of admission at pre-university schools as well as in the higher education institutions and these commissions have the responsibility to select the candidates according to established procedures and to arrange orientation programs to facilitate the selection process. The basic requirement for admission to full time programs is the graduation from a preuniversity school (twelve years of studies). In addition, now there is an admission test. This recently (1988-89) imposed additional requirement of the admission test (when combined with academic achievement at school) is expected to give a better measure of the students' capabilities independent of the level of the preuniversity schools from where they graduate. The admissions test is given in three subjects: mathematics and two others depending on the candidate's field of study. Applicants for admission are allowed to indicate up to five alternate fields of study for their degree programs.

Admission to part time programs (courses for workers) is offered to persons engaged in labor, and who have completed preuniversity schooling requirements. It is necessary that the candidates establish a match between their work background and the desired field of study. Also the candidates have to sit for an examination in mathematics and Spanish. Results of the exam are combined with other requisites to develop a grading scale for selection of the candidates.

In 1985, about 54 percent of the students in full time programs received student housing which in Cuba is free of charge. Housing is considered a student right for those whose homes are situated outside the territory of the institution or whose economic situations justify. All students including foreign students who receive student housing are also entitled to free meals, medical facilities, and the benefits. In addition, these students are given a non-reimbursable stipend to assure a minimum level of personal expenses. Part-time students also receive a variety of benefits including a certain number of free days at work.

Advanced Studies

Graduate studies in Cuba provide training both for graduate degrees and for professional development. Graduate degree programs are very similar to those in many other countries and are open to candidates with high academic or professional achievement. Two degrees are available: *candidato a doctor en ciencias* (equivalent to a Ph.D.) and *doctor en ciencias*. The latter degree is awarded to candidates who successfully defend before a scientific council, a scientific work (thesis) that makes a very unique contribution in any field of science. Graduate studies for professional development offers opportunities for candidates to follow courses or undertake training. Candidates can take courses in their professional areas to improve their performance at work or to specialize in any given field. Graduate training is usually based on a specific topic (work) and is given for a specific time in an institution of higher education. In the recent years, the capacity of the institutions to provide graduate professional development has exceeded 30,000 places per year for over 1,500 courses. It must be mentioned that a special effort has been made to improve the qualification of teaching staff in higher education and for this purpose a system of graduate training has been established for them since 1978 including opportunities for basic training, for specialization, and for obtaining graduate degrees.

ISSUES AND TRENDS

The present era marks the beginning of a new stage in the development of higher education in Cuba. It is characterized primarily by a desire to improve the quality of professional training and the effectiveness of higher education as a whole to meet the needs of the current stage of socioeconomical development.

The strategy for development of higher education in the coming years will include preparation of graduates with a broad education, who will receive their specialized training at work, conforming to the needs of the economy. The training will also include graduate education within the higher educational system as well as at enterprises.

The network of centers of higher education would have reached a stable level in number and the emphasis would be in improving their specializations. The structure of programs of study would attempt to accommodate, to a large measure, scientific and technical progress as well as the demand for professionals to satisfy the economic and social needs of the country.

In the very near future, enrollment is expected to increase in the sciences and mathematics. The system of admission to higher education institutions will continue to be an area for study and improvement.

Areas for continuing study and improvement would include the system of admission to higher studies, graduate education, and development of teaching staff as well as scientific activities in the centers of higher education.

BIBLIOGRAPHY

Consejo Nacional de Universidades. *Conclusiones del Primer Seminario de Evaluacion de las Universidades Cubanas.* La Habana: Consejo Nacional de Universidades, 1965.

Consejo Superior de Universidades. *La Reforma de la Enseñanza Superior en Cuba.* La Habana: Consejo Superior de Universidades, 1962.

CRESALC-UNESCO. *La Educación Superior en Cuba.* Monografia. Caracas, 1985.

Martin, Elvira, y otros. *Aspectos socioeconomicos de la preparacion de especialistas con educación superior en Cuba.* La Habana: Ediciónes ENPES, 1986.

Ministerio de Educación, Cuba. *Anuarios Estadísticos.* La Habana: MINED, n.d.

Ministerio de Educatión, Cuba. *Estudio diagnóstico: Análisis cuantitativo y cualitativo, sistema universitario; periodo 1959-1971.* La Habana: MINED, 1972.

Ministerio de Educación, Cuba. *Proyecto para la Organización y Desarrollo de la Educación superior.* La Habana: MINED, 1976.

Ministerio de Educación Superior, Cuba. Direccion de Desarrollo. *Estudio Diagnostico del Desarrollo de la Educación superior; periodo 1959-1980.* La Habana: MES, 1982.

Vecino Alegret, Fernando. *Tendencias en el desarrollo de la educación superior en Cuba; significado del trabajo didactico.* La Habana: MES, 1983.

DENMARK

by
Thomas W. Webb
Professor, Sociology of Education
Roskilde University Center, Denmark
and
Jorgen Nielsen
Chairperson, Institute for Communication Studies,
Educational Research and Theory of Science and
Associate Professor Roskilde University Center, Denmark

BACKGROUND

Over the last twenty years, the educational system in Denmark has been thoroughly changed and modernized. Efforts have been made to link the educational system to development of the socioeconomic system in order to meet the changing demands for qualifications. During this period Danish higher education was transformed from a stable narrow elitist system to a mass educational system, as in many other technologically advanced countries. Mass education can thus be seen as a product of trends of which urbanization, economic development, and industrialization are central components. Within the last two decades the number of students admitted to institutions of higher and further education has risen by over 70 percent and so have the costs of education. In 1988 the number of admissions corresponded to approximately 30 percent of the age cohort.

Until the end of the 1970s the educational changes occurred within a framework of greater democratic opportunities for students. Changes in curriculum were based on critical analysis of the relation between the content of studies and their practical and professional application; organization of teaching-learning processes involved students in group projects focused on problems requiring theories and methods from a variety of disciplines. Criticism of the traditional examination and grading system resulted in new ways of assessment.

In Scandinavia and in several other European countries school reforms can be conceived within the framework of the Welfare State as stressed by the Swedish educational scholar T. Husen. In most Western European countries, the Welfare State, materialized through an increasingly complex apparatus of governmental responsibility and redistribution of wealth, has grown throughout the twentieth century, especially after World War II, against a background of sustained economic growth up to the mid 1970s. The primary function of the Welfare State is to ensure for all citizens a minimum level of protection against social risks. Even though there has been a broad consensus in many European countries regarding the necessity of the Welfare State since the 1950s, the definition of an adequate minimum has been open to discussion. Collective responsibility has gradually expanded to cover the whole spectrum of life: birth and child bearing, health, education, job and income protection, and finally retirement and death. Social Democratic parties, explicitly or tacitly, have based their programs on the idea of redistributing economic surplus into extended and improved social services. Growth has been seen as the path to classlessness. The general idea has been that growth, conceived as stimulated by a modernizing policy, would also give better room for greater liberty for individuals.

Structure of Education

The Danish system of education as it is emerging on the threshold of the 1990s may be characterized as a loosely coordinated network consisting of two sectors: a formally organized system of schools and educational programs differentiated into three successive levels; and a rather loose, less integrated pattern of organized offerings within adult education. Thus four sub-systems may be identified as follows:

a). A first level of compulsory education with a common curriculum for all children of ages 7-16; this is provided in the comprehensive local community schools (Folkeskolen) comprising grades 1-9 and covering what is usually identified as primary and lower secondary education;

b). A second level of upper secondary education for youthof ages 16-19 which is differentiated into a variety of alternative yet parallel forms of schooling or streams which emphasize different combinations of balance between general education preparatory for higher and further education, and terminal vocational education.

c). A third level of tertiary education which is somewhatmore sharply differentiated into two sectors: universities and other colleges of higher education with somewhat longer programs (6-8 years) leading to a first as well as more advanced academic degrees; and schools of further education with somewhat shorter programs (2-4 years) qualifying for what might be considered as semi-professional occupations.

d). A fourth level of "adult education" which consists of a variety of forms of programs providing for supplementation, renewal, and extension of a wide spectrum of qualifications for people after they have left the system at some point following the completion of compulsory education.

The system, besides having the above structure, may also be thought of as having at least the following characteristics:

1). Its maintenance represents a commitment to the need to provide resources to ensure that all children have the opportunity to attain a rather high level of general qualifications that provide a capacity and competence to contribute to the common good in a highly technical society. This commitment comes to expression in the maintenance of compulsory education up through the ninth and tenth grades of the comprehensive local community schools *(Folkeskolen)*.

2). Responsibility for the provision of arrangements to ensure a high level of general qualifications and a wide range of specialized qualifications is neither up to individuals nor specialized interests groups but is a collective concern which is delegated to the state. However, special interest groups are thereby not prohibited from organizing parallel arrangements. The state is responsible for organizing the system.

3). Basically a publicly financed system, where the finances are obtained over taxes and distributed through the annual budgets of national, county, and local authorities.

4). There is a possibility of leaving after each of the first three levels with a certification of qualifications based on nationally supervised examinations.

5). More and more flexibility in students' progression through the system; opportunities for shift between the academic and practical/applied branches; and basic or ground courses at higher education at levels so that students delay their choice of specialization as long as possible.

6). There is increasing centralization of planning, policymaking, and supervision. Within this framework, there is decentralization of rights and responsibilities to use resources in the way that is seen fit locally.

7). Tendencies towards increased influence of students, teachers, and parents in the primary and secondary schools. At the level of higher education, participation of students and technical/administrative staff in the governing bodies of the individual institutions.

PRIMARY AND SECONDARY EDUCATION

At the primary and lower secondary level (ages 7-16),education is obligatory, not schooling. Parents may arrange education in various ways. A majority of them send their children to schools provided by the local community authorities. This form for school, known as *Folkeskolen,* provides nine years of compulsory education for approximately 90 percent of the children in this age group. While the proportion of children attending other school forms provided by private (and in some cases, religious) groups has been increasing in recent years, it appears to be stabilized at present at about 10 percent. These alternative school forms can obtain recognition from the state and receive support for approximately 80 percent of operating costs with the rest being paid through tuition.

This school form provides the same curriculum for all children: Danish (the national language), arithmetic and mathematics, and physical education at all grade levels; and English from the fifth grade. In addition, they have history, geography, and biology, which in the eighth to tenth grade are integrated into contemporary or social studies *(samtidsorientering).* From the seventh grade they have physics/chemistry. From the seventh grade through the tenth, they can choose from among a number of elective subjects, including German and French. At the end of the ninth or tenth grade, pupils take the Leaving Examination of the *Folkeskole (Folkeskolens Afgangsprove).* This unified structure of *Folkeskolen* has been in force since 1976.

At the upper secondary level, streaming into a general and a vocational branch first begins formally when students are sixteen or seventeen years of age. Approximately 40 percent continue with a general course of studies which prepares them for higher education and close to 45 percent embark on a terminal vocational education. Among those who leave the formally organized system of education, about 5 percent attend one or another of the adult education programs for youth. And roughly 10 percent enter the ranks of unskilled workers.

In the general or academically oriented branch of upper secondary education, the most sought school form is the three-year *gymnasium*. In addition to providing a general education, it has traditionally been academically oriented and provided the preparation necessary for continuing into the third level of the system: the universities and other schools and colleges of higher education. After a reform in the middle of the 1980s, these *gymnasiums* are placed under the authorities in the thirteen counties into which Denmark is divided. There are also a few private ones.

In the *gymnasium* program, there are two main lines: languages and mathematics. Increasingly, larger proportions have been choosing the mathematics line (in 1984, close to 63 percent). Some subjects are required of all students, regardless of the line: Danish, history, mathematics and two foreign languages. Some of the subjects are obligatory to the line: a third language in the language line; and mathematics, physics and chemistry in the mathematics line. In addition, a wide range of electives give the students the possibility of toning their program in the direction of classical studies, music, social studies, commercial, or high-tech studies. These programs all end with the Upper Secondary School Leaving Examination *(Studentereksamen)*. It is also possible to prepare for this examination by following a two-year course *(Studenterkursus)*.

Since 1967 there has been an alternative but parallel two year course of studies which also gives admission to institutions of higher education This is known by the name of its concluding examination, "The Higher Preparatory Examination" *(Hojere Forberedelseseksamen - HF)*. The intention behind the creation of this school form has been to provide opportunities for persons who, having done practical work for some years after completing the years of compulsory education, want further education. In order to complete the examination, the students must pass all the subjects in a common core plus some of the elective subjects which can be freely combined.

Since the middle of the sixties, a considerable growth has occurred within a third alternative for an examination at the upper secondary school level, the "Higher Commercial Examination" *(Hojere Handelseksamen - HH)*. Similar to HF, it is a two-year course of studies which is more vocationally oriented than the other two examinations. It can be taken at a commercial school or one of the commercial gymnasiums. Entrance to this type of course of studies requires one of the Leaving Examinations from either the ninth or tenth grade of *Folkeskolen,* plus the basic first year of one of the "basic vocational education" *(erhvervsfaglige grunduddannelser)* programs which combines theoretical and vocational courses together with shorter periods of practical training.

In the vocational or occupationally oriented branch of upper secondary education, school studies are combined with practical training periods. In contrast to the organized apprenticeship programs, the "basic vocational education" programs have organized vocational education not around a single occupation or trade but for a group of related areas (for example, food industry, construction and building trades, agriculture, metal trades, etc.).

While neither the "basic vocational education" programs nor the organized apprenticeship programs give the possibility for automatic or direct entrance to the universities and other schools and colleges of higher education, they can, if supplemented by other qualifications, provide the opportunity for entrance to some of the shorter, relevant study programs in institutions of further education that are more oriented to practical occupations.

Adult education, the fourth area of educational programs, is perhaps best thought of as having developed both in opposition and as supplementary to the other three levels, with regard to offering opportunities for supplementing, renewing, extending, and providing alternatives to the qualifications they provide, both in the form of general liberal education and vocational education. Here are included a wide range of different educational forms: folk high schools; evening schools; freer forms of lower secondary education including youth schools and residential continuation schools; Danish university extension *(Folkeuniversitetet);* a variety of vocational and occupational programs; and educational programs in the form of single subject courses preparatory for examinations at all levels of the system ranging from lower secondary to higher education in the form of Open University.

Folk high schools, evening schools, and the Danish university extension have neither examinations nor give formal credits. Historically these institutions, which go back more than 100 years, have been established by social movements interested in the enlightenment of the population. Due to the Danish social liberal tradition, they are (though run and organized by private organizations) financed with public funds supplemented by fees from the participants at about one third of the costs.

HIGHER EDUCATION

Institutions

Approximately 30 percent of a cohort continue into formalized tertiary education in the form of credit-giving studies that lead to academic degrees, diplomas or certificates. In Denmark, these studies are provided by a large number of institutions which can be classified into two distinct subsystems: twenty-four institutions of higher education including three universities, two university centers, and nineteen other institutions (schools or colleges) of higher education, which provide a series of academic degrees and qualifications for higher-order professions; and a larger number of institutions (schools or colleges) of further education, which provide higher level education for semi-professional occupations.

All of the institutions of higher and of further education come under of the Ministry of Education, with the exception of a few which are under the Ministry of Cultural Affairs. For all institutions of both types, the ministry responsible determines general regulations for curricula, admissions, awarding of degrees, and appointment of academic staff, and the expulsion of students. These two types of institutions are different from each other in that the former, (the institutions of higher education) grant academic degrees. In addition, the teaching staff is not only entitled but also required to devote a significant portion of their time (40 percent in 1989) to carry out research to ensure an adequate foundation for their teaching. In contrast, the educational programs at the colleges of further education lead to diplomas or certificates. The teaching staff has no official right to do research. While universities prepare teachers for the general or academically oriented upper secondary schools, colleges of further education prepare teachers for *Folkeskolen* and other school forms.

For centuries, the University of Copenhagen was the only university in the country, having been established in 1479. It has five faculties: theology, social sciences, medicine, humanities, and natural sciences. The University of Aarhus, founded in 1928 has faculties in the same five areas. The University of Odense, established in 1964, has three main functional areas: a) humanities and social sciences, business administration, economics and modern languages; b) natural sciences; and c) medicine and physical education. Roskilde University Center and Aalborg University Center, opened in 1972 and 1974, respectively, have three main functional areas: humanities, natural sciences, and social sciences.

The other nineteen institutions are specialized schools and colleges of higher education and include The Technical University of Denmark; The Danish Academy of Engineers (The Engineering Academy of Denmark); The Royal Dental Colleges of Copenhagen and Aarhus; The Royal Danish Veterinary and Agricultural University; The Royal Danish School of Pharmacy; The Copenhagen and Aarhus Schools of Economics, Business Administration, and Modern Languages; Academies of Music in Copenhagen, Aarhus, Esbjerg, Aalborg, and Odense; and the Royal Danish Academy of Fine Arts; the Royal Danish School of Educational Studies; and the Danish School of Journalism.

The institutions of further education are more numerous than the twenty-four higher education institutions mentioned above. But they tend to have smaller enrollments and they are spread throughout the land. Included here are eighteen colleges for education of *Folkeskolen* teachers; nineteen colleges for education of preschool teachers and leisure time counsellors; eight colleges for technical engineers; a number of schools for training of personnel within the field of health; six colleges for physiotherapists and occupational therapists; a school of library science in Copenhagen, with a branch in Aalborg; four schools of social work; and a number of local schools of commerce.

Governance

The administration of the system of higher education has been consolidated since 1974 in The Directorate for Further and Higher Education *(Direktoratet for de Videregende Uddannelser)*. While the autonomy of the individual institutions has been reduced in a number of areas, there has been, at the same time, a tendency to decentralize decision and policy making from the ministry to the individual institutions and various advisory committees in which they are represented collectively. As part of the restructuring of the administration of higher education in the mid 1970s there were established five national planning committees to advise the ministry. In addition, there is a planning council for research with six research committees assisted by a permanent secretariat to advise on research activities. The growth of enrollment in the universities and colleges together with the tighter economic situation has meant that the Ministry of Education and the Directorate have been more actively involved not only in planning in the field of higher education but also in controlling and supervising the implementation of policies.

The law of 1970 on the administration of the universities has been amended and revised in 1973, 1976, 1980, and 1981. It now applies to all of the institutions of higher education under the Ministry of Education. This law, considered a democratic innovation, provides greater control over academic affairs to collegiate bodies at lower levels within the individual institutions of higher education. It also gives students as well as technical and administrative staff, elected representation in these bodies. But in recent years it has been criticized for, among other things, weakening the capacity of the institutions to ensure education and research of high quality. It explicitly gives the minister of education the right to lay down and supervise regulations for admission to studies, courses of study, acquisition of advanced degrees, the appointment of academic staff, and the expulsion of students.

Each institution is governed by a rector (president) in cooperation with a number of collegiate bodies. The rector is elected from the academic staff by the members of these bodies. Since 1970, the membership of each of these bodies consists of at least 50 percent representatives elected from and by the academic staff, and of at most 50 percent representatives elected from and by students and technical/administrative personnel.

First Degree Programs

The academic year runs from the beginning of September through June. January and June are reserved as examination periods for the fall and spring semesters.

Some first degree programs lead directly to careers in public administration or the private sector. For some professions such as secondary school teaching, medicine, and law, certification to practice requires additional courses or supervised practical training to provide a perspective for the application of academic studies to professional practice.

The most common first degree program ends with the examination known as *kandidateksamen,* found in the traditional university faculties (theology, social sciences, medicine, humanities, and natural sciences). Another, somewhat more scholarly, degree program is the *magisterkonferens,* provided in certain fields of the humanities, social sciences and natural sciences. First degree programs of both types are prescribed to take from 5-6 years; however, due to circumstances such as employment while studying, etc., it has not been unusual for students to take up to eight years to obtain their degrees.

In addition to the universities, most of the other schools and colleges of higher education offer *kandidat* degrees in their fields of specialization: engineering, veterinary medicine, forestry, horticulture, dairy science, dietetics, agriculture, pharmacy, dentistry, commercial science, commercial language, etc. This type of degree is also offered in education or pedagogics at The Royal Danish School of Educational Studies, but entrance here requires practical experience as a teacher in the primary school *(Folkeskolen)*. Many of these institutions also have programs leading to other kinds of first degrees. Some of them are of the same length (for example, degrees in architecture, fine arts, art education, art restoration, music, music education, etc). Others are of shorter duration, such as those in various commercial subjects and foreign languages. During the 1970s, the two university centers in Roskilde and Aalborg introduced innovations both in the reorganization of the teaching-learning process and in the restructuring of degree programs. In contrast to traditional forms of organizing students' work around attending lectures, they have placed emphasis on groups of students organizing their study efforts around projects, through which they learn theories and methods from pertinent academic disciplines (transdisciplinarity) as they use them as tools to investigate relevant problems. They have also restructured the degree programs by starting with one year (at Aalborg) and two year (at Roskilde) programs of basic studies *(basisuddannelse)* in each of the three functional areas: humanities, natural sciences, and social sciences. These broader, transdisciplinary introductions provide admission to the more specialized parts of the *kandidat* degree programs in traditional areas as well as in a number of new fields. This way of structuring study programs allows a delay of choice of specialization; this is in contrast to the traditional structure in which such a choice must be made upon entry into the university, and where a decision to change fields has required that the students start their studies from the beginning with little or no possibility for transfer of credit. A variation of this new structure is also found within recent years at other institutions of higher education. It takes the form of a one-or two-year ground program *(grunduddannelse)* for a number of closely related subjects followed by two, three, or four years of specialization. This structuring of programs has been incorporated into the reform of the humanities in 1985.

This recent reform in the humanities, as well as that planned for the natural sciences in 1989, is part of a more inclusive reform being planned to harmonize studies and degrees with those found in other countries, especially those in the European Community. This internationalization seems to conform to recent tendencies in Europe which are inspired by the American university tradition. The reform of 1988-89, instituted a new first degree at universities and colleges of higher education, the bachelor's degree in arts and sciences (B.A. and B.S.), which can be earned after three years. This degree is part of a general effort to shorten the long university studies and gives students the option of completing a degree in a shorter period time. This should help to reduce the dropout rate, which is rather high in some degree programs (up to 75 percent). Students also have the option of continuing their studies for two years to the next degree level to earn either the *kandidat* degree, which is available in the same range of fields as before, or the *magister* degree which now is only available for fields within the humanities

Advanced Studies and Research

At the postgraduate level the Danish Ph.D. degree is earned through the *licentiate* program. Permission to work for this postgraduate degree requires at least a *kandidat* degree in the same subject. The prospective student formulates a proposal for a study project which must be approved by the faculty concerned. A counsellor is appointed to supervise the student's work, which may take two or at the most three years. This degree can be earned at all of the institutions of higher education that offer the *kandidat* degree.

The highest academic degree awarded in Denmark is the *doktorgrad*, the Danish doctoral degree or doctorate. It is awarded by various institutions of higher education where research is conducted. There are no course requirements. Instead the applicant must present a doctoral thesis *(disputats)* which requires several years of independent and highly qualified original research. Permission to submit a doctoral thesis can be granted to those who have completed a *kandidat, magister,* or *licentiate* program within a closely related academic area. After the doctoral thesis is accepted by an examination committee appointed by the faculty, the candidate defends his thesis at a public hearing. This degree is rarely awarded outside of a few areas such as medicine.

Research forms an important part of university activities and the members of the academic staff are required to devote 40 percent of their time to research. They are free to choose the problems they will investigate. Universities themselves have very limited budgets to support research.

There is a planning council for research with six national committees which develop programs of priorities that focus on centrally important problem areas. With the budgets they have available, they support individuals or groups of scholars who apply for funds to implement research projects that otherwise would not be possible within the budgets of the universities. Scholars also have the possibility of contract research with private funding sources. A new institution, The Danish Research Academy *(Forskerakademiet),* was established in 1987 as part of the government's action plan to further Danish research and development.

Admission Requirements

Admission requirements for entry to Danish universities and other colleges of higher education vary somewhat but the most common basis for acceptance is one of the following three Danish examinations: a) the Upper Secondary School Leaving Examination *(Studentereksamen);* b) the Higher Preparatory Examination *(Hojere Forberedelseseksamen);* or c) the Higher Commercial Examination *(Hojere Handelseksamen).* Danish applicants with other qualifications may be admitted after assessment of their qualifications.

Acceptable foreign university entrance qualifications specifically mentioned in the admission regulations of the higher education institutions include examinations taken in countries with which Denmark has bilateral agreements on the recognition of university entrance qualifications, and in some cases, university entrance examinations taken in these countries. This applies to all the countries in the European Community, the Nordic countries, the other Council of Europe countries, and a number of Unesco member countries. Programs such as medicine, dentistry, pharmacy, agriculture, civil engineering, etc., however, are subject to specific admission conditions (the "special ties with Denmark" criteria).

Since Danish is the language of instruction, a knowledge of written and spoken Danish is necessary if foreign students are to profit from their studies.

Supplementary tests may have to be taken in subjects required for the studies chosen. For some courses of study (e.g. in the conservatories), there are entrance examinations or work has to be submitted for assessment (The Royal Danish Academy of Fine Arts).

With regard to the Ph.D. degree, a foreign applicant may gain admission if he has a university education which can be assessed as equivalent to a Danish *kandidat* degree, which is judged to be at a level somewhat above a master's degree. He must also be deemed to have the necessary general academic background to enable him to complete the program he has proposed. Similarly, foreigners who apply for the right to submit a *disputats* to earn the Danish *doktorgrad* must include a curriculum vita, documentation of a degree equivalent to a Danish *kandidat* degree, a list of scholarly publications, and a statement on their motivation to deliver a *disputats* to earn the degree.

Until 1977, admission to the institutions of higher and further education was, with few exceptions, open. Enrollment of new students more than doubled from 1960 to 1975, and it was felt necessary to regulate admissions formally. On the basis of a law passed by the parliament in 1976 a general policy came into effect in 1977, affecting the longer degree programs under the ministries of education and of cultural affairs. Quotas for maximum numbers of admission are fixed for each group of disciplines. The criteria for selection among qualified applicants take into account the grade average of the entrance examination and study-relevant work experience.

The size of yearly quotas takes into consideration estimates of future trends of employment and unemployment in the labor market, the capacity of the institutions, and the geographical distribution of applicants. For foreign students there is a specific quota below 10 percent (it is generally 2-4 percent).

Through a national coordinating office, applicants submit a rank ordered list of up to eight degree programs.

Student Facilities

Student accommodation is not provided by the individual universities and colleges of higher education; however, there are a large number of halls of residence *(kollegier)* administered by national and local authorities. These and similar student accommodations may be applied for by foreign students on an equal footing with Danish students. Rent for a room in a hall of residence amounts to approximately US$150-200 per month (1989). While students also need to consider expenses for board, transportation, books, and other study materials, they pay no tuition fees at present. This applies for both Danish and foreign students. The costs of education are financed through general taxes and distributed to the institutions through the annual national budget.

Government educational assistance in the form of state educational support *(statens uddannelsesstotte)* is granted to Danish citizens under specific regulations. Foreign students are also eligible if they have been residents of Denmark and employed full time for two consecutive years immediately prior to application for assistance, or if they have special ties with Denmark. Students (both Danish and foreign) may take jobs while they are studying without any special permission from the university or college; this may, however lead to a reduction of any state educational support they may be receiving. Foreign students are required to have a work permit issued by The Directorate for Foreigners *(Direktoratet for Udlaendinge)*.

ISSUES AND TRENDS

In spite of the growth of the Welfare State through the decades since the 1930s, relative inequalities have continued to be strong in all advanced capitalist societies. The capitalistic system with its market dominance has produced competition among individuals. A result of this competition has been inequality as well as constant innovation and change. As a result of these mechanisms it has been impossible really to do away with inequality in the schools. The sorting related to streaming as well as the selection of who continues to higher levels of education has therefore, in all Western countries, been skewed among the social classes. Of great importance, however, is the question of, at which grade level the differentiation of students through streaming begins. After the school reform of 1976, streaming in Denmark now first begins not after the seventh grade but in reality after the ninth and tenth grades.

After the election of 1988, the conservative prime minister has continued as head of a three-party conservative led coalition. Since 1982, when the Social Democrats had to give up control over the government and let the conservatives come into power, the political and ideological scene has changed considerably in Denmark. The Social Democrats have been driven into a defensive role, and attitudes in opposition to the politics of the last generations have come to characterize the political scene. In all spheres of Danish society, demands for restructuring are being raised. Concepts such as modernization and privatization are gaining ground in the political terminology. The public has also become increasingly more concerned about the economic situation, governmental budget deficits, the balance of payment, and the serious high rate of unemployment (about 10 percent of the work force is without jobs). Politicians as well as the general public express growing concerns about the necessity for austerity in public expenditures.

From many sides it is stressed that funds for social welfare and educational endeavors are not limitless. Within the frame of the "Scandinavian Model", high priority has been given to policies regarding health, social welfare and education. That active form of politics has contributed centrally to the creation of a unique form of societal harmony and consensus; and this policy has for a long time been considered by economists and social scientists to promote economic growth. But since a social and economic crisis has lasted for more than fifteen years, a shift in paradigms has taken place and it is now the general opinion that, first and foremost, there is a need to stimulate the private sector of the economy. Consequently austerity is demanded within the public sector. The opinion today in Denmark in relation to education seems to be that if the private sector falters, so will the schools. In extension of such a private business oriented argumentation, it is said that if Denmark is to be competitive in the international realm, Danish business and industry must be given incentives for retooling and modernization. In addition, it is said that the educational system needs to be more closely geared to providing relevant qualifications for carrying out these tasks.

BIBLIOGRAPHY

Andresn, Arne, ed. *The Danish Folk High School Today - A Description of Residential Adult Education in Denmark.* Copenhagen: The Folk High Schools' Information Office, 1985.

Central Council of Education. *U-90: Danish Educational Planning and Policy in a Social Context at the End of the 20th Century.* Copenhagen: The Danish Ministry of Education, 1978.

Dixon, Willis. *Education in Denmark.* Copenhagen: Centraltrykkeriet, 1958.

Dixon, Willis. *Society, Schools and Progress in Scandinavia.* Oxford: Pergamon Press, 1970.

Husen, T. *The Learning Society Revisited - Essays.* Pergamon Press, 1986.

Jakobsen, Kim M. "Adult Education in Nordic Countries". In *Nordic Democracy - Ideas, Issues, and Institutions in Politics, Economy, Education, Social and Cultural Affairs of Denmark, Finland, Iceland, Norway, and Sweden,* edited by Erik J. Friis. Copenhagen: Det Danske Selskab, 1981.

Mohr, Dr. Birgitte, and Ines Liebig, eds. *Higher Education in the European Community, Student Handbook: A directory of courses and institutions in 12 countries.* 5th edition. London: Kogan Page, 1988.

OECD. *Reviews of National Policies for Education - Denmark.* Paris: Organization for Economic Co-operation and Development, 1980.

Pedersen, Mogens. "Universities and Other Institutions of Higher Education". In *Nordic Democracy - Ideas, Issues, and Institutions in Politics, Economy, Education, Social and Cultural Affairs of Denmark, Finland, Iceland, Norway, and Sweden, edited by* Erik J. Friis. Copenhagen: Det Danske Selskab, 1981.

The Danish Ministry of Education. *Education in Denmark. The Educational System.* Copenhagen: The Danish Ministry of Education, 1985.

The Danish Ministry of Education. *Further and Higher Education in Denmark.* Copenhagen: The Danish Ministry of Education, 1989.

Thomsen, Ole B. *Some Aspects of Education in Denmark.* Toronto: University of Toronto Press, 1967.

UNESCO. *World Guide to Higher Education - A Comparative Survey of Systems, Degrees and Qualifications.* 3rd edition, Paris: The UNESCO Press, 1989.

EGYPT

by
M. Helmy El-Meligi
Professor and Dean Emeritus, Faculty of Education
University of Alexandria, Egypt

BACKGROUND

Education in Egypt, like in many other parts of the world, has historically been closely associated with religious creeds. Over 5,000 years ago, higher education in ancient Egypt took place in temples which could be considered the universities of that age. At those Pharaonic universities of temples, sciences such as physics, astronomy, solid geometry, geography, mathematics, measurements, and medicine were taught. Furthermore, those temples were interested in teaching other branches of knowledge, such as ethics, music, painting, drawing, sculpture, etc. Many great ancient scientists and philosophers such as Plato, the Greek philosopher, attended the famous university of "Eon" in Ein Shams, Cairo, for sometime. Higher education was given in many other temples like the famous temple "Karnak" in Thebes. Its huge and fascinating buildings still exist at Luxor in Upper Egypt.

During the Ptolemaic Age (323-300 B.C.) the Greeks ruled Egypt for about three and one-half centuries and disseminated their culture in Egypt, aiming at mingling both Egyptian and Greek cultures. Alexander of Macedon, the Greek invader, founded the city of Alexandria where education flourished. The University of Alexandria in conjunction with the library of Alexandria and its museum constituted a fruitful foundation and a rich source for higher education and research. The remarkable progress of Alexandria University during the Ptolemaic system produced many great scientists such as Archimedes (287-212 B.C.) and Eukleides (300 B.C.).

After the Islamic conquest of Egypt in year 642, it took Egypt about three centuries to assimilate the Islamic culture and to be transformed into an Arab country. In 972, Gowhar El-Siquelly, the Islamic ruler of Egypt who founded Cairo, established the famous mosque Al-Azhar. He was aiming at using Al-Azhar as a center for disseminating the ideology of his religious sect. Later on, however, Al-Azhar was turned from a center for teaching his sect's ideology into a university. There, higher education of several branches of human knowledge took place. Students from the Islamic countries came to Al-Azhar in Cairo so as to study not only Islamic religion but also logic, philosophy, astronomy, Arabic language, grammar, mathematics, etc.

Al-Azhar provided free education for all students with no discrimination due to social class, race, or nationality. Moreover, it provided free meals and accommodation for foreign students. Afterwards, under the rule of Salah El-Din El-Ayouby, education flourished and was highly developed. He introduced the school system in Egypt and encouraged students by paying them salaries. Many professors from Al-Azhar went to these new schools. Hence higher education became widespread and was no longer limited to Al-Azhar.

Egypt then passed through a dim period of over five centuries under the rule of the Mamelukes (1250-1517) followed by the Turks (1517-1798) and suffered from feudalism and slavery. The inevitable consequences were a state of intellectual rigidity and a stagnant life in all its aspects: economic, social, political, educational and cultural. The role of education, till the end of the eighteenth century, diminished to serve only the social needs for the study of language and the preparation of spiritual leaders and religious men.

At the beginning of the nineteenth century, Mohamed Ali, the ruler of Egypt declared Egypt free and independent of Turkey. Mohamed Ali's main interest was higher education which he conceived as the sound basis for a strong nation and a necessity to defend his regime against Turkey. Therefore, he started by sending educational missions to Europe to study various specializations needed for the implementation of his plans. He established a new educational system that differed in curriculum from that of Al-Azhar. Thus he managed to establish higher military schools (1816, 1822, 1823, etc.) including a marine school (1831), and schools of medicine (1827), pharmacology (1829), veterinary medicine (1829), industrial chemistry (1831), arts (1831), irrigation (1831), agriculture (1834), engineering (1834), metallurgy (1934), gynecology and obstetrics (1837), languages (1837), accountancy (1837), and administration (1840). But this rapid rate of educational and military development was considered as a threat by Turkey and some European countries and Egypt was forced to enter into a treaty that reduced Egyptian military forces and correspondingly Egypt's education plans suffered a serious set back.

The development of higher education began to accelerate again at the beginning of the twentieth century. In 1908, the first national university was established in Cairo with private funds. In 1925 it was transferred to the government under the name of the Egyptian University and formed the predecessor of the present day prestigious University of Cairo.

The University of Cairo comprises faculties of arts, law, economics and political sciences, commerce, science, medicine, pharmacology, dentistry, engineering, agriculture, veterinary medicine, Arabic language, information, archeology, and statistical studies as well as institutes of African studies and research, cancer, and nursing. In 1942, the University of Alexandria was established. Today, Egypt has thirteen public universities, all having somewhat the same academic structure. The American University in Cairo is the only private university.

The Ministry of Education is responsible for policy formulation, planning, and coordination of preuniversity education at a national level. The governorates (Egypt is administratively divided into twenty-six governorates, each headed by a governor) administer the plans and operation of the schools. The minister of education oversees the Supreme Council of Universities which is responsible for planning and policy making for university level education. The Ministry of Islamic

Affairs administers the Al-Azhar University and associated schools. Various educational and training activities are also undertaken by different organizations and ministries, in areas relevant to their activities.

The system of education consists of four stages: preschool stage for 4-6 year olds; basic education stage beginning at age six and continuing for eight years (primary school for five years followed by preparatory school for three years); secondary school stage for three years, generally for ages 14-17; and tertiary stage (university). Education in Egypt is free at all government schools and institutions.

PRIMARY AND SECONDARY EDUCATION

Primary Education

According to the Egyptian Constitution, primary education is free and compulsory for all children. Primary education is the first stage of "basic education" and is considered the essential foundation of the ensuing preuniversity stages. It lasts for five years beginning at age six. It is followed by the final stage of basic education, the preparatory school, which lasts for three more years, up to the age of about fourteen years.

Primary education aims at physical, social, moral, and emotional development of children. Another goal is to give the students necessary knowledge and technical skills needed for a successful practical life. This should be either to work soon after attaining vocational training or to enter the next educational stages.

Secondary Education

Since the Ptolemaic Age and through the rule of Mohamed Ali, in the first half of the nineteenth century, secondary education was restricted to a selected class. Its objectives were limited to the preparation for higher education or for working as employees in governmental departments. These objectives, however, improved later. According to the Egyptian Secondary Education Act of 1953, the objectives of secondary education fall into three categories: to provide the students with a broad and a deep general culture; to prepare the students for continuation of their higher education; to provide the students with opportunities for gaining experience through various activities which are relevant to their interests and aptitudes.

The general secondary education emphasizes compulsory courses for all students in the first two years. Specialization starts in the final year and is optional. The student has to select one of three specializations: arts, science and mathematics. The selection depends on the student's desire, interest, and the field of study he wants to continue in higher education. The medium of instruction in public schools is Arabic language but some foreign language use can be found in private foreign schools.

Internal examinations are held monthly in schools for the first two years. A national examination is held annually for the final year students of secondary schools. Successful students receive the Certificate of General Secondary Education which is the main requirement for admission to universities.

Teachers are often the primemovers for extra curricular activities. Usually they guide the activities for which they have an interest or expertise. A wide range of social, cultural, athletic, scientific, and artistic activities are open to students.

Free education has led to a rapid increase in enrollment in all stages, including secondary education. This expansion was beyond the capacities of schools. The inevitable result was crowded classrooms. The case is however different in private schools. Private schools charge tuition and have limited enrollment. Foreign students may attend schools on the same basis as Egyptian students.

Teaching positions at public secondary schools require a university degree and the postgraduate General Diploma in Education.

Various educational and training activities are also undertaken by different organizations and ministries other then the Ministry of Education. Several specific schools and training centers have been established. Their objective is to prepare skilled technical laborers in order to meet the needs of a productive society. The study in these schools and centers is below the university level. The study extends for three years after the preparatory educational stage. These schools give a technical diploma equivalent to that of the industrial secondary schools. Nevertheless, their curricula and their methods of training are different from that provided by the schools of the Ministry of Education.

The fields of study in these vocational type schools include health education, nursing and first aid, transportation, mining, industrial education, communication, electric power, and construction and building. The ministries who finance and supervise these schools and training centers include the following ministries: manpower, industry, construction and housing, electric power, agriculture, defence, interior, tourism and civil aviation, culture, and social affairs. From the private sector, numerous companies and philanthropic societies have also been enthusiastic in establishing such technical schools or training centers.

HIGHER EDUCATION

Institutions

There are thirteen state administered universities in Egypt, including the most ancient university, Al-Azhar. The only private university is the American University in Cairo which differs from the Egyptian universities in that it is based on the departmental and credit-hour system. The role of universities in Egypt essentially fall into three categories: preparation of graduates for the world of work; development of scientific research that serves the community and contributes effectively to the development of the various fields in Egypt including solution of economic and social problems confronting Egypt's development; and general cultural and intellectual activities.

In addition to the universities, a variety of other institutions provide higher educational opportunities. The National Institute for Higher Administration in

Cairo is sponsored by the Ministry of Scientific Research and provides training programs on administration for various levels of inservice personnel in different fields. The trainees come from all ministries and organizations. The programs focus on technical problems of administration and on making use of developed technology. It emphasizes also the necessity of acquisition of information in order to keep pace with the scientific progress of the twenty-first century and to realize the prosperity of the society. The duration and the type of courses of the training programs vary according to the professional level of the trainees.

The English for Specific Purposes Center in Alexandria provides postgraduate studies in linguistics and translation. The duration of the study is one academic year for full-time students or two academic years for part-time students. Successful graduates are granted a diploma either in linguistics or in translation.

The Higher Institute of Technology is a new technological institution established in Banha in October 1988. It is sponsored by the Ministry of Education and it is at the same level as universities. It provides various specializations in technological fields.

The International Center for Inspection and Control Studies in Alexandira provides training programs for a limited number of university graduates from Egypt, Arab and African countries. The main training program lasts one academic year and aims at producing professional expertise in the field of inspection and control. This includes quality or quantity control on imported or exported industrial equipment, machinery, chemicals, agricultural products, etc.

Faculty structure at the universities consists of a dean who is responsible for all the academic, administrative, and financial issues in his faculty. He is the head of the faculty board which is comprised of the vice-dean for educational and student's affairs, vice-dean for higher studies and research, chairman of academic departments, representatives of the teaching staff, and two or three members invited from outside the faculty and whose specializations are relevant to the faculty programs. Associated with the dean's office are the departments of public relations, statistics, and follow up. Academic departments come directly under the faculty dean.

Teaching staff at universities are generally required to hold a doctorate. The selection is made by the board of the relevant department and approved by both the faculty board and the university council. An additional requirement for appointment is satisfactory attendance in an educational training program on educational and psychological principles of teaching or an equivalent exempting qualification. The training programs are held annually for three weeks in the Faculty of Education. The selection committee consists of three members: two professors of the same specialization and the third is a professor of education, curriculum or educational psychology.

The Permanent Scientific Committee affiliated to the Supreme Council of Universities oversees the promotion of members of university teaching staff. The promotion criteria is heavily based on the originality and quality of the candidates research work. The teaching staff consists of lecturers, associate professors, and professors. A lecturer has to spend five years of teaching before he is considered for promotion to an associate professor. Similarly, an associate professor has to spend another five years before being considered for promotion to the rank of professor.

Governance

The Supreme Council of Universities is comprised of university presidents, representatives of university professors, various specialized members and is headed by the minister of education. The council forms planning committees for various educational sectors of the universities. Each committee consists of the deans of similar facilities. These committees are responsible for studying and investigating the following:

1.   Educational plans of the university and the general strategy for scientific research that contribute to the economic and social development of Egypt. This includes curriculum development in university departments and postgraduate studies.

2.   Determination of academic departments and specialized institutes, and suggestions for establishing new departments or institutes and new specializations in response to developmental needs and world scientific progress.

3.   General principles of coordination between study systems, their standards, and the examinations of similar faculties, taking into consideration the variety of scientific subjects and their methods.

4.   Presentation of opinions on other issues referred to them by the Supreme Council of Universities.

The Supreme Council of Universities forms other committees for the study of certificates and diplomas and their foreign equivalents granted to undergraduate and postgraduate students. The recommendations of the appropriate committees are received by the Supreme Council of Universities for final decision.

The university president directs all academic, administrative and financial aspects of the university within the limits of the policy of the Supreme Council of Universities and the council of his university, and in accordance with the country's law and relevant regulations. Where the law necessitates a decision to be made by the country's president or the prime minister, recommendations of the Supreme Council of Universities are submitted to them through the minister of education.

Thus, although the funds for all educational institutions are provided by the government, the processes of goal formulation and strategy formulation are worked out within the universities and the Supreme Council of Universities through their planning committees.

Undergraduate Studies

The number of years required for obtaining the first university degree vary depending on the field. It is usually four years in faculties of humanities and social sciences. It is five years in faculties of engineering, dentistry, veterinary medicine, pharmacology, and the department of anatomy and physiology. The Faculty of Medicine requires six years including the preparatory year and an additional one year of internship. The duration of the academic year is thirty working weeks.

The medium of instruction is Arabic language in most faculties, especially in humanities, social studies, education, law, commerce, economics and political sciences, information, social service, and tourism and hotels. English language is widely used in the faculties of medicine, science, pharmacology, dentistry and engineering.

Admission to universities for undergraduate studies is controlled by a Central Orientation Bureau. Students make their application to the Central Bureau indicating their preference for faculties or universities they wish to attend. The bureau makes the admission decision by matching the students' qualifications and interests to the availability of places and programs at the higher educational institution.

The minimum requirement for admission to undergraduate programs is the General Secondary Education Certificate. In addition, the selection process takes into consideration the geographical distribution of students according to their residential regions. This admission procedure is believed to ensure justice and equal opportunity to all students countering any variations in the facilities available in different regions. Also some faculties or departments may require besides the minimum qualifications, one or more of the following provisions: a)An entrance examination; written, oral, or both (e.g. departments of English and French languages). b)An interview (e.g. faculties of education, and tourism and hotels). c)High grades in qualifying subjects (e.g. faculties of medicine and pharmacology, and some science departments emphasize biology and chemistry as qualifying subjects. Faculty of Engineering emphasizes physics and mathematics).

The majority of university departments require students to take "major" compulsory courses along with a few optional courses. For example, students of the English department can select French, German, Spanish, etc. as the second foreign language. In the Faculty of Science, students of Chemistry Department, for example, select either botany or zoology as a minor course.

Specialization starts in the first year in most departments, as in the case of departments in the Faculty of Education. However, in some departments like the Department of Sociology specialization may not start till the third year.

Examination systems in the faculties vary according to the field of specialization. For instance, final exams in the faculties of education and arts are held at the end of the academic year. Meanwhile in the Faculty of Agriculture, the academic year has two semesters. Each semester ends with a final exam. Nevertheless, besides these final exams, there is continuous assessment throughout the year in both the systems. This assessment covers practical teaching, science laboratories, phonetics, essays, research, field studies, workshops, etc. The nature of assessment (written, oral, clinical, practical, etc.) depends on the field of specialization.

As mentioned before, education in Egypt is free at all levels, for all Egyptians, at state higher educational institutions. Foreign students are required to pay modest tuition fees.

Universities provide hostels for the accommodation of Egyptian students coming from rural regions far away from university locations and who are in real need of financial assistance. Meals, medical care, and social services are also provided to them. Students' board and lodging are heavily subsidized costing only about US$3 per month. Separate hostels are available for female and male students.

A natural result of free education facilities is the increase in university enrollment, and of society's demand for the expansion of universities. The rapid rate of growth in enrollment far exceeds that of the universities' development, capacities, and budget. These problems are challenging the educational system's ability to provide adequate higher educational opportunities without weakening the quality of education.

Advanced Studies and Research

Candidates desirous of registering for master's and doctoral degrees are generally required to attend a preliminary diploma course of at least one year duration. The diploma course provides training of either academic or applied nature in a specific field of study (statistical studies and research, higher studies in cancer surgery, public health, dentistry, science, engineering, economics, law, social sciences, oriental studies, applied linguistics, etc.). Master's degree requirements include at least two years of work and a thesis. Registration for the Ph.D. requires a "good" grade in the master's degree.

After a period of at least two years of research study, the student is required to submit a thesis in his field of specialization. This thesis as well as the master's degree thesis have to be defended in public. Master's and doctor's degree candidates in all faculties are also required to attend weekly seminars arranged by their departments under the supervision of their professors. Also, they may be appointed as demonstrators in their faculties. Hence the university becomes responsible for providing the expenses of their research. On the other hand, other students who want to continue postgraduate studies so as to obtain diplomas, (M.A., B.Sc. or Ph.D.), minimum tuition fees are required.

The most prominent feature in research activities of Egyptian universities is the organization of research in a framework that encourages applied research relevant to Egypt's development. Projects and programs are oriented towards developing the efficiency of prominent centers of research in the Egyptian universities. Problem solving research in areas of high priority to Egypt is encouraged and supported.

The collaboration of universities of developed countries with the Supreme Council of Universities generates fruitful research programs. These programs aim at increasing the research capability of Egyptian universities and faculty members. An excellent example of this collaboration is the "University Linkage Project" which is a joint Egyptian-United States activity, designed to engage Egyptian faculty members in applied research relevant to Egyptian development. The project links Egyptian and United States universities under the direction of the Foreign Relations Coordination Unit of the Supreme Council of Universities.

ISSUES AND TRENDS

The most significant trend in education today is the new educational policy to confront the challenges of technological development in Egypt. This is reflected in all stages of the educational system. Thirty percent of students who successfully finish the preparatory school in basic education pursue technical education. Technical secondary education (industrial, agricultural, and commercial) has become now an open system to the university, for bright students. A Higher Institute of Technology has been established in Banha city, in October 1988 and students of industrial secondary schools have the privilege of enrolling in this institute.

A frequently debated important issue is the possible establishment of a national non-governmental university. Proponents of this idea believe that this kind of university will be more flexible in providing programs to quickly respond to the needs of the students and the changing society. Moreover, it will provide opportunities to those who could not enroll in public universities. Such a university could be a fee paying institution.

Another current issue is the growing university enrollment that exceeds the universities' capacities and overextends the government budget. A study for the establishment of an open university, as a possible solution, has been carried out. This university is expected to be beneficial to students who have failed or could not enroll in regular universities. In addition, it will be useful for people living in distant areas such as oasis, desert, and rural regions.

Expansion of cultural and educational exchanges with developed countries is also a priority for the universities. Exchange of university staff members, establishment of scientific channels for joint research with institutions of excellence in the developed world, and increase of scholarships for advanced studies and research leading to doctorates are considered vital.

BIBLIOGRAPHY

El-Meligi, M. Helmy. "The Democratization of Education in Response to Societal and Environmental Needs in Egypt." Paper presented at the World Assembly of the International Council on Education for Teaching, Sidney, Australia, July 18-22, 1988.

El-Meligi, M. Helmy. "New Educational Policy to Confront the Challenges of Technological Change in Egypt." Paper presented at the World Assembly of the ICET, Eindhoven, The Netherlands, July 20-24, 1987.

El-Meligi, M. Helmy. "Distance Teaching and Learning: A Case Study." Paper presented at the World Assembly of the International Council on Education for Teaching, Vancouver, Canada, July 22-26, 1985.

Educational Policy in Egypt. Cairo: Ministry of Education, 1985.

"The Educational and Training Efforts of Ministries and Organizations Outside the Scope of the Ministry of Education". *The Specialized National Councils Magazine.* No. 14. Cairo.

Shafshak, M.A., et al. *History and Educational System in the United Arab Republic.* Cairo: The Anglo-Egyptian Bookshop, 1969.

ETHIOPIA

by
Makonnen Yimer
Associate Professor and former Dean, Faculty of Education
Addis Ababa University, Ethiopia

BACKGROUND

Though modern education in Ethiopia was introduced some eighty years ago by Emperor Menelik II when he opened the first government school in Addis Ababa (the capital) in 1908, there existed a highly elaborate, largely status-oriented system of education of the Ethiopian Orthodox Church, and of the Koranic schools, which produced clergymen and mullahs to serve their respective institutions. The system confined literacy to the very few members of the religious oligarchy and to the imperial chroniclers.

Higher education in Ethiopia started about forty years ago when the first higher education establishment, the University College of Addis Ababa (UCAA), was opened in 1950 and as such higher education does not have a long history, though it is among the earliest in the Sub-Saharan Africa. During the first decade, higher education institutions were established in rapid succession but were scattered and operated independently by various government agencies and manned almost wholly by expatriates. This phase may be characterized as a period of total dependence on foreign influence as well as a period of non-uniform policy of academic standards in such areas as admission, promotion, and graduation. Due to this undesirable state of affairs, most of the higher institutions were brought under a centralized university administration by establishing the then Haile Selassie I University (presently Addis Ababa University) in 1961 which pursued a vigorous policy of Ethiopianization. Slowly, more and more Ethiopians assumed leadership roles and efforts were made to Ethiopianize the curriculum and also to make higher education more responsive to the needs of the country.

Since 1961 several other faculties were established and the university has grown both vertically and horizontally. Moreover, other tertiary level institutions have come into existence depending on manpower requirements with specialized training which gave rise to the same undesirable state of affairs of the 1950s. Consequently it necessitated the creation of an educational authority in 1977 (the Commission for Higher Education) to oversee the growth and establishment of tertiary institutions. But as of 1987, by government decree, the power vested in the Commission for Higher Education has been transferred to the Ministry of Education (MOE) and the commission has now become a department under the MOE. In general, the function of the Ministry of Education with respect to higher education, among other things, is to coordinate the administration of the existing higher education institutions so as to facilitate the exchange of information among them regarding their respective operations with a view to avoiding duplication of functions and to meet the country's manpower requirements by way of a planned and coordinated reorganization of higher education institutions.

By the end of 1987-88 school year there were a total of over 9,700 schools with an enrollment of 3,830,700 (not including church, mission, and Koranic schools that do not follow government prescribed curricula) of which 75.3 percent, 22 percent and 0.4 percent were enrolled in primary, secondary, and post secondary sectors respectively. In fact, the enrollment figure has increased over the past fourteen years since the onset of the Ethiopian Popular Revolution of 1974 by an annual growth rate of 9 percent, 11.4 percent, and 11.6 percent for the primary, junior secondary, and senior secondary levels respectively. However, enrollment in higher education institutions (postsecondary), as a percentage of the concerned age group (18-24 year olds) in the country was only 0.35 percent and was too low compared to most African countries.

In addition, to date some 17 million people have successfully participated in the Literacy Campaign which has increased the literacy rate from 7 percent in 1974 to 71 percent in 1988.

Education in Ethiopia is mostly financed from central government budgetary allocations with substantial local community inputs especially for non-government schools in the form of labor support and infrastructural investment, the magnitude of which has not been estimated to date. In addition, Ethiopia has been benefiting quite a large sum of capital investment from foreign sources mostly for infrastructure development. A serious problem which reduce the efficiency and increase the real cost of education is the excessively high wastage ratio resulting from high dropout and high repetition rates in all education cycles especially for grades 1-11 that range from 29 percent for grade one to 19 percent for grade eleven.

Since national growth is greatly dependent on highly trained and intellectually agile manpower, the Ministry of Education has, as a long term measure, reorganized the entire educational system in Ethiopia to focus on polytechnic education with more emphasis on practical application of educational training.

PRIMARY AND SECONDARY EDUCATION

Formal schooling in Ethiopia covers twelve grades and is divided into primary, junior secondary, and senior secondary. The age range for each level is from 5-13, 11-15, and 13-19 years for the primary, junior secondary, and senior secondary grades respectively. There is a national curriculum which all elementary and secondary school children follow. All schools have to follow the syllabuses, textbooks, and teachers guides that have been developed by the Ministry of Education. In general, at the end of each phase (i.e. primary, junior secondary, and senior secondary) students get a centrally issued certificate showing the grades they scored in the national examinations given at the end of each phase. The examinations are usually administered in June for the primary and junior secondary levels, and in March for the senior secondary level.

The preuniversity national examinations play the key role of selection and elimination of students, as they progress through the system. For instance, the school leaving national examinations usually eliminate at the primary level about 20 percent of the students, at the junior secondary about 35 percent and at the senior secondary about 80 percent (depending on openings available in higher institutions for qualified secondary graduates).

Elementary and secondary education is free except for those individuals who enroll in mission or foreign community schools such as the English and Indian Community Schools. The enrollment in non-government schools is about 10 percent, 9 percent, and 2 percent of the total school going children in the primary, junior secondary, and senior secondary grades respectively.

The requirement for a teaching position is the completion of grade twelve coupled with one year's training in a teacher training institute (for primary teachers), a diploma from one of the teacher training colleges or institutes (for junior secondary teachers), and a bachelor's degree (for senior secondary teachers).

During the primary cycle, twelve subjects are taught. These subjects are Amharic (the national communicative language), English, mathematics, political education, physical education, science, agriculture, social science, handicrafts, art, music and home science. All subjects except English are taught in Amharic and at the end of grade six students have to sit a national examination that is centrally set and administered by the Ministry of Education.

At the junior secondary level except for minor syllabus changes, the same subjects continue to be taught. The minor changes occur where social science is replaced by history and geography taught as separate subjects while handicrafts is replaced by productive technology, and commerce is added as a new subject. Presently, textbooks and instruction for mathematics, history, and geography are in English while for the rest of the subjects, textbooks and instructions are in Amharic. At the end of grade eight, students sit for a national examination to move to the next grade (grade nine). Currently, the grade eight examination is set in Amharic for some subjects such as political education and the rest in English for subjects such as science and mathematics.

In the senior secondary schools in grades nine and ten, most pupils follow an academic course while few follow a vocational course by dropping history and geography in order to devote more time to productive technology. The subjects offered in grades nine and ten are the same with the junior secondary level with the exception that science is divided into physics, chemistry, and biology. Subject loading is at its highest during grades nine and ten since pupils study as many as twelve and fourteen different subjects in the vocational and the academic streams, respectively. During the final two years however, loadings become lighter and courses more specialized although the common core of five compulsory subjects (Amharic, English, mathematics, political education, and physical education) are maintained. It is in these grades (grades eleven and twelve) that pupils in academic courses stream into academic science which offer physics, chemistry and biology in addition to the common core subjects, and into academic arts which offer history and geography on top of the common core subjects. Pupils in the vocationally oriented courses branch into three streams: commercial stream which offer bookkeeping and economics courses; home-economics stream which offer biology, chemistry, and home economic courses; or productive technology stream which offer a range of technical subjects such as metal, wood, and electricity. The general goals of the education and training system as elaborated in the Ten Year Indicative Plan of 1984 envisage that by 1994 the present structure of 6-2-4 (six years of primary, two years of junior secondary, and four years of senior secondary) will phase out and be replaced by a general polytechnic education with a structure of 8-2-2 (eight years of general polytechnic education, from grades 1-8, two years of higher general polytechnic education for grades 9-10, and two years of extended polytechnic education for grades 11-12). The polytechnic education will stream students to academic science or arts or to two years of extended technical and vocational education offering courses in industrial and civil engineering, agriculture, commerce and home-economics. The extended technical and vocational training program has been extended to three years for the presently sixteen full-fledged schools that have been instituted throughout the country offering twenty-one specializations in the technical vocational areas.

In order to realize the goal of general polytechnic education, the Ministry of Education is working on curriculum reform and on the development of improved materials for preuniversity schools along with the experimentation of general polytechnic education in seventy sample primary schools as of 1980. At the end of grade twelve, students have to take a national examination and successfully pass to join tertiary education. Since space at the tertiary level is limited, the competition is very stiff. Presently grade twelve national examination is offered in fifteen subjects arranged in eight groups: Amharic and English, mathematics and commercial mathematics, physics and chemistry, general science and biology, geography and history, economics and book-keeping, Geez and French, and political education. Candidates may sit for as many subjects as they choose except mathematics and commercial mathematics where a candidate has to take only one of the subjects. The minimum number of subjects required for entrance to higher institutions is five including the compulsory subjects (English and one of the mathematical options).

HIGHER EDUCATION

Institutions

Three universities form the nucleus of higher education in Ethiopia: Addis Ababa University, Asmara University and Alemaya University of Agriculture. Among the three universities, Addis Ababa University, formerly Haile Selassie I University, is the oldest and largest university in the country with twelve faculties and colleges having over eighty departments as well as a School of Graduate Studies and Continuing Education Division. Fields of studies offered include agriculture, education, languages, law, library science, medicine, pharmacy, social sciences,

sciences, technology and veterinary medicine. In addition, a number of research institutes form part of the university.

The Asmara University has a College of Social Science, Faculty of Science, and an Institute of Language Studies. Several research institutes are also attached to the Asmara University. The Alemaya University of Agriculture specializes in agricultural fields.

The highest governing body within the universities is the senate with the president as the executive officer who is generally assisted by two vice-presidents, one for academic affairs and the other for administration and development. In the case of autonomous colleges, the dean acts as the executive officer assisted by one or two assistant deans and the highest governing body within the college is the academic commission which is also true for faculties and colleges within a university administration. The university senate comes directly under the Commission for Higher Education.

The members of the highest governing body, the senate, for example in Addis Ababa University, consists of the president (chairman), vice-presidents, university officers (such as planning officer, research and publications officer, and registrar), deans, directors of research institutes, elected faculty/college representatives, and representatives from the Ministry of Education, Office of the National Committee for Central Planning, Ethiopian Trade Union, Ethiopian Peasant Association, Addis Ababa Urban Dwellers Association, Ethiopian Teachers Association, Revolutionary Ethiopian Youth Association, and the Workers Party of Ethiopia. It is to be noted that through this structure, both the government and the party (WPE) have direct influence on the policies of the universities or colleges in the country.

Programs and Degrees

At undergraduate level, the higher education institutions in the country presently offer diploma and certificate programs as well as programs that lead to B.A./B.Sc., L.LB., M.D., and D.V.M. degrees. Diploma or certificate programs generally take 2-3 years and bachelors degrees, require four years excepting for professional programs. Engineering, law, pharmacy, and similar professional programs take five years. Medicine is the longest with a six-year duration.

Higher education in Ethiopia from its inception till 1986-87 has produced about 44,000 individuals in its undergraduate and graduate programs. All these graduates of higher education occupy important positions in both the public and private sectors of the economy in the country and in other African countries as well as outside African countries. It is important to note that the current graduate output of the Ethiopian Higher Education Institutions is about 5,000 of which about 57 percent is at the diploma level.

The academic year for all programs runs from September to June, divided into two semesters, September to January and February to June, with the exception of the medical schools which run from early September to February and from March to August. Each semester has a minimum of sixteen weeks. The long vacation falls between July and September.

Eligibility for undergraduate higher education is determined on the basis of the candidate's grade point average (GPA) calculated from his or her five best subjects taken at the grade twelve national examination (including the scores in English and mathematics or commercial mathematics as the case may be). Due to the annual increase in the number of candidates taking the grade twelve national examination and the limited number of spaces available in higher institutions of the country, the eligibility criteria for access to degree and diploma courses have increased in terms of GPA's for admission to all colleges and universities under the supervision of the Commission for Higher Education. (e.g.from 2.0 in 1978 to 3.0 presently on a 4 point scale, for admission to degree courses). It is to be noted that the specialized institutions also follow the general guidelines of the Commission for Higher Education's admission requirements.

Admission to undergraduate programs is also granted on the basis of five passes in other foreign school leaving or matriculation certificates. Foreign secondary school certificates may be granted equivalence by the Commission for Higher Education in individual cases.

Selection of candidates to higher institutions for both the postgraduate and undergraduate levels is made once a year in the month of August and applications must be submitted generally before the end of March each year to the Commission for Higher Education for the undergraduate program and to the concerned university for the postgraduate program. But, applications for advanced standing admissions must be submitted to the college or the university concerned during the month of November and April each year.

Ethiopian nationals who successfully join tertiary level education in the regular day program get free education including free room and board at the undergraduate level while at the postgraduate level only individuals who are sponsored by a national agency or university or college get free education. Non-sponsored individuals pay 50 Birr (equivalent to US$25) per credit per semester where a credit is considered as one lecture recitation or two to three hours of laboratory work for the duration of one semester (sixteen weeks).

Foreign nationals at the undergraduate level pay tuition fees in the amount of 7,000 Birr, 8,100 Birr, and 5,800 Birr per year for science and technology, medicine, and social sciences respectively with a registration fee of 40 Birr payable in hard currency. For postgraduate study, foreign nationals pay a tuition fee of 100 Birr per credit per semester in hard currency.

In addition, Ethiopian nationals who pursue their education at the undergraduate level through the extension program are required to pay 48 Birr per semester per three credit course in the social science areas, and 60-90 Birr per three credit course in the science and technology areas. The amount indicated will be doubled for foreign nationals and must be paid in hard currency.

The minimum duration of training for a Bachelor of Arts or Bachelor of Science degree is four years in the regular program while it is about 8-10 years in the extension or summer program.

In the postgraduate programs, the master's degree and the certificate of speciality require a minimum of two and three years respectively of full time study where a total of 9-12 credit hours per semester is normally regarded as typical full load for a full time candidate. In addition, the Ph.D. degree requires a minimum of three years for graduation.

Regular (full-time) students that follow the day program must register each semester for 15-18 credits and continuing education students must register for 8-12 credits each semester. Though the minimum graduation requirement for a bachelor's degree is 130 credits (and for a diploma 65 credits) the number of credits required for graduation may vary according to the programs offered by the concerned college or department. All the three universities offer undergraduate programs. In addition, nine other specialized institutions including four military training institutions grant degrees and diplomas.

Postgraduate education in Ethiopia was launched in 1978 to satisfy the manpower requirement of higher education institutions and other government agencies as well as to train research personnel in various fields of social science, science, agriculture, education, technology, and medicine. To date there are thirty-eight approved postgraduate programs of which five are at the Ph.D. level, seven at speciality certificate level in medicine, twenty-five at M.A./M.Sc. or M.Ph. level, and one at diploma level.

With respect to postgraduate programs, the master's programs require course work between twenty-four and thirty credits depending on departmental requirement, while the Ph.D. programs require course work and dissertation or dissertation alone. Where the graduate program requires a thesis or dissertation, it is mandatory that it is defended during an oral examination before a committee. Both the thesis and the dissertation are written in English.

At present, there are two universities, Addis Ababa University and Alemaya University of Agriculture that offer postgraduate programs.

Research in higher education is conducted in the faculties or colleges and research institutes. The focus of research in the departments by and large follow disciplinary lines where the staff conduct studies on problems of interest to the department as well as to the individual researcher. Relevance for national development is also an important consideration in approving projects. The general purpose of the research institutes is to conduct multidisciplinary research of national concern. To accomplish their mission, the research institutes draw researchers according to their needs from relevant departments in accordance with the requirements of a given project. Moreover, all the research institutes in higher education are attached to higher education institutions.

The criteria that are followed at all levels in assessing research proposals for funding include the relevance of the proposal to national and university/college/-faculty needs; the timeliness of the proposal; the soundness of the methodology; and the feasibility of accomplishing the project with respect to the capability of the individual as well as the availability of equipment, tools, supplies, etc. in the relevant universities or colleges.

Continuing Education

As it presently exists in the country, continuing education does not have any dedicated institutional facilities but uses the facilities of the institution that offer regular or diploma programs. A large number of institutions offer extension degree/diploma programs through evening study and/or summer programs. The admission requirement for degree or diploma programs in the extension division is the same as the regular day program. In fact, since the level of the course offerings is the same as that of the regular program, the same examinations are given in all programs to ascertain the equivalence of the degree/diploma with the day program. A substantial number of individuals follow continuing education programs. For instance in 1987-88 academic year, there were about 13,000 evening extension students and about 3,000 summer session students as compared to about 17,000 full-time day students registered in all higher education institutions (about 48.5 percent of the regular program).

Moreover, there are various short non credit training programs offered at various institutions. These cover a wide spectrum of subject matter and are offered at basic and more advanced levels. Such short courses are offered in areas including administration, accounting and book-keeping, technology, agriculture, health, law, librarianship, and research methodology.

ISSUES AND TRENDS

As already observed, since the Ethiopian Popular Revolution, student enrollment has grown more than fourfold though it is accompanied by deterioration of the quality of education, particularly in elementary and secondary schools. The main reasons for this unhappy situation include a sharp decline in the quality of staff during the last fourteen years primarily on account of brain drain and a very insignificant expansion of the physical capacity in terms of classrooms, laboratories, libraries and the like relative to the student population.

It is envisaged, as discussed earlier, that an eight year work-oriented general polytechnic education will be provided to all school-age children while secondary education will be expanded with the aim of fulfilling the country's manpower requirement for middle-level professionals. In order to translate these general goals and objectives into specific action programs, the Ministry of Education has already launched a curriculum reform and has developed and is developing improved materials for all schools to build an educational training system which will enable the youth to actively participate in production, science, and technology.

Moreover, the present sixteen full fledged Extended Technical and Vocational Education and Training Schools that offer three-year courses in industrial and civil engineering, agriculture, commerce, and home economics (after the completion of tenth grade) will be increased to forty-two in ten years time by converting existing Comprehensive Secondary Schools. It must be noted that emphasis is put in subject areas that have direct bearing on the promotion of scientific and technical knowledge, attitudes and competencies in science, mathematics, productive technology, and agriculture in all grades of the formal school system.

In full recognition of the problem, the Ministry of Education has instituted an action program to alleviate the crucial shortage of teachers by planning to open a technical teachers' college with capacity to train 564 diploma and 240 degree students (at Nazareth about 100 km. east of Addis Ababa), and a science teachers' college enrolling about 800 for diploma programs and 400 for degree level courses (at Jimma about 346 km. southwest of Addis Ababa).

Furthermore, work on the establishment of three additional regional universities is progressing. These would provide higher education opportunities to qualified residents of the region without having to uproot them. These institutions will also enable individuals to conduct research on the problems of the region and act as "centers of excellence" for some selected fields of study. The creation of such regional universities would involve the clustering of higher educational institutions in a region of the country under a central university administration located in the region. Hence, the northwestern, southern, and western zones are considered convenient and ripe to act as university centers for the three additional universities.

Since the highest concentration of the best trained scientific and technological manpower is normally found in institutions of higher learning, it is quite evident that institutions of higher education occupy a very special place in developing countries like Ethiopia to foster the general economic, social, political, and cultural development of the country. In view of the fact that Ethiopia is one of the least developed countries, she lacks the institutions and the resources necessary to train its own scientists and technologists. However, the Ministry of Education is faced with the challenge of redoubling its efforts to have a supply of trained manpower to be available in the required quantity and quality for meeting the planned national development needs of the country. It is toward this end that efforts are being exerted to strengthen the existing institutions and to create critically needed new ones, with the limited resources available.

It is hoped that education in Ethiopia will move for self-sufficiency by supplying its own teachers, and researchers, by training its own leaders, and by building its own institutions to establish the conditions of universal education in which all individuals will have access to education.

BIBLIOGRAPHY

Aregay, Waktola. "The R & D Environment in Institutions of Higher Education." Paper presented at the First National Conference on S & T Policy Formulation, Science & Technology Commission, Addis Ababa, June 1988.

Central Statistical Authority. *Ethiopia Statistical Abstract.* Addis Ababa, 1986.

Commission for Higher Education. "Preliminary Study on the Formation of North-Western, Western and Southern Regional Universities in Ethiopia." Commission for Higher Education, July 1987.

Commission for Higher Education. "High-Level Manpower Training Program and the Role of Science and Technology." Paper prepared for the First National Conference on S & T Policy Formulation, Science & Technology Commission, Addis Ababa, June 1988.

Commission for Higher Education. "High-Level Manpower Training Program and the Role of Science and Technology." Paper prepared for the First National Conference on S & T Policy Formulation, Science & Technology Commission, Addis Ababa, June 1988.

Commission for Higher Education. *An Overview of Higher Education in Ethiopia.* Addis Ababa: Commission for Higher Education, 1988.

Commission for Higher Education (CHE). *Designing a Strategy for Development of Higher Education in Ethiopia.* Proceedings of the Retreat at the Koka Ras Hotel, Feb. 14-16, 1986. Addis Ababa: CHE, 1986.

Ministry of Education. *Basic Education Statistics.* Planning and External Relations services, MOE, 1988.

Ministry of Education. *Education: Challenge to the Nation.* Report of the Education Sector Review. Addis Ababa: MOE, 1972.

Ministry of Education. *Education Research of General Education System in Ethiopia.* Curriculum Division, MOE, 1986.

Shibru, Tedla. "Nine Years of Graduate Education at Addis Ababa University (AAU), (1978-1987): A Comprehensive Report." School of Graduate Studies, AAU, June 1987.

Tesfa Mariam, Tekie. "Education for Development of Science and Technology." Paper presented for the First National Conference on S & T Policy Formulation, Science and Technology Commission, Addis Ababa, June 1988.

Thompson, K. W., et al, eds. *Higher Education and Social Change.* Vol. 2. New York: Praeger Publishers, 1977.

FIJI AND THE ISLANDS OF BRITISH OCEANIA

by
Robert Stewart
former Professor and Head of the School of Humanities
University of the South Pacific, Fiji
in collaboration with
Robert Stewart, Cliff Benson, Narottam Bhindi,
Henry Elder, Akanisi Lewaravu, Colin Meek,
Konai Thaman, Ruby Va'a, Ian Johnston, and Trevor Rees

BACKGROUND

This paper covers the politically independent small island states in the South Pacific with historic links to Britain. These are Cook Islands, Fiji, Kiribati, Nauru, Niue, Solomon Islands, Tonga, Tuvalu, Vanuatu and Western Samoa. It also includes one New Zealand dependency, Tokelau. All eleven comprise the member states of the Regional English speaking University of the South Pacific (USP).

The University region encompassing these countries spreads over an ocean area three times the size of Europe, and the eleven nations comprising several hundred islands have a total land mass the size of Denmark. There are about 1.5 million people in the USP Region, with Tokelau having the smallest population and Fiji the largest with 720,000. The countries range over Polynesia, Micronesia and Melanesia.

The paper first reviews the University of the South Pacific (USP), the most extensive higher education institution in the region, and briefly covers some of the other regional institutions. It then presents the structure of education at various levels in each of the eleven countries.

The Regional University of the South Pacific

The first students to USP were admitted in February 1968, and the university's Royal Charter and statutes were presented personally by Queen Elizabeth in 1970. The Regional University of the South Pacific was established in 1970 with the mission of disseminating and advancing knowledge by teaching, consultancy, and research; and providing education and training to meet the needs of the communities of the South Pacific. The university has grown enormously over the last twenty years, and now has a campus in Western Samoa as well as in Fiji, and centers in ten of the member countries. At the time of writing, there were about 2,000 students on campus and about 7,000 studying via distance education through extension.

Finance to operate the university is provided by the eleven member nations. However, the governments of Australia, New Zealand, United Kingdom, Canada, United Nations agencies, and the European Economic Community have provided funds for buildings and facilities.

The university has four schools which run its main teaching programs, both on-campus and via distance education. It also has seven institutes involved in research, consultancy, and training. On a regular basis, internationally known external assessors in each discipline monitor the work in all areas across the university.

The School of Agriculture based on the Alafua Campus, Western Samoa, teaches programs for the Bachelor of Agriculture degree, trains teachers of agriculture, and runs diploma programs in agriculture and agribusiness.

The School of Humanities consists of the Department of Education and Department of Literature and Language. The school conducts programs leading to bachelor's degrees in arts, and certificates and/or diplomas in education. The Pacific Languages Unit, based in Vanuatu, conducts courses in Pacific and Metropolitan languages.

The School of Pure & Applied Sciences comprises the departments of biology, chemistry, physics, home economics, mathematics and technology. Studies lead to bachelor's degrees in science and technology. The school also conducts diploma courses in tropical fisheries, computing, and statistics; and offers a certificate of earth science and marine geology as well as some courses toward a medical degree.

The School of Social & Economic Development includes departments of accounting, economics, geography, history/politics land management and development, management and public administration, population studies and sociology. Studies lead to arts degrees, and to certificates and diplomas in accounting and administrative studies, community health, and development. Legal studies are taught at certificate and diploma level by the Pacific Law Unit based in Vanuatu.

Postgraduate degree programs across the university include a variety of certificates and degrees: Advanced Certificate in Teaching (agriculture), Postgraduate Certificate in Applied Science, Postgraduate Certificate in Teaching (secondary teacher qualification), Postgraduate Diploma (area of specialization to relate to the particular student's individual four-course program at the postgraduate level), Master of Agriculture, Master of Arts, Master of Science, Master of Philosophy and Doctor of Philosophy. Areas available for postgraduate study depend on staff availability and extend across the full range of the university's disciplinary coverage.

The seven institutes involved in research, consultancy, and in training consist of the following: Institute of Education, Institute of Marine Resources, Institute of Natural Resources, Institute of Pacific Studies, Institute for Research Extension and Training in Agriculture, Institute of Rural Development, Institute of Social and Administrative Studies, and Atoll Research and Development unit.

The university has an extension services section concerned particularly with creating and strengthening the university presence in the region. University centers operate in ten of the eleven USP member countries. The extension studies section works with the schools to provide materials for off-campus students studying via distance education. Most extension students are over twenty-one years of age and are in some form of employment. Some take only one or two courses out of personal interest, whereas others are aiming for completion of a certificate, diploma, or degree program. The university has established a reputation for working on the frontier of distance education technology. A multi-media approach is used which includes printed correspondence materials, audio and sometimes video cassettes, and a two-way voice communication system using satellite technology.

Students who wish to enroll for on-campus studies at the university apply by 30 December of the previous year. (The two semester university year runs from late February until late November). The university sets the criteria for admission for foundation year, certificates, diploma, undergraduate, and postgraduate degrees, in terms of the level of previous performance. Most on-campus students at USP are sponsored on scholarships awarded through their own governments as members of the USP Region, but there are a number of private students. Most students studying via extension fund their own studies.

As of 1989, full time on-campus students who are studying in the university are charged the following tuition fees; 1,484 Fiji dollars per year (for citizens of USP member countries) and 5,000 Fiji dollars per year (for non-citizens of USP member countries). Additionally there are nominal additional fees for Student's Association (40 Fiji dollars), and refundable caution deposits for on campus studies and residence. Room and board cost for the full year is 2,352 Fiji dollars. Textbooks cost approximately 350 Fiji dollars per year for degree studies.

Students from outside the university region are welcome and well accepted at the university. Some come on their own, while others come via exchange programs. In particular the university participates in various international exchange programs (USA, Papua New Guinea, Japan, etc.).

Other higher educational institutions include three regional theological schools or seminaries. These are the Catholic Pacific Regional Seminary (PRS), Protestant Pacific Theological College (PTC), and Assemblies of God South Pacific Bible College; all in Suva, Fiji. (In addition to these, there are thirteen national theological training institutions). The curricula of most schools includes the following: biblical, theological, and historical subjects; preaching; pastoral counseling; and Christian education. A few include philosophy, anthropology, sociology and psychology. The Protestant Pacific Theological College was the first to grant bachelor's degrees and in 1987 commenced a Master of Theology (M.Th.) degree in church history with a strong focus on the Pacific.

The Telecommunication Training Center based in Suva trains students for the telecommunication industry.

A regional Board, the South Pacific Board for Educational Assessment, commenced operations in 1982 to assist South Pacific island nations to respond to changing patterns of assessment that became evident in the 1970s. The board develops and maintains appropriate school assessment instruments at a national level; the work relates mainly to the secondary level, but also includes tests of achievement at the primary school level, as well as training for relevant people.

Members of the board are Cook Islands, Fiji, Kiribati, Solomon Islands, Tokelau, Tonga, Tuvalu, Western Samoa and the University of the South Pacific.

Cook Islands

Modeled on the New Zealand system, Cook Island's education is compulsory, free, secular, and coeducational. Six years of primary schooling, classes 1-6 (grades 1-6), is followed by a further six years of secondary schooling forms 1-6 (grades 7-12), after which many students leave school or continue tertiary schooling overseas, mainly in New Zealand and Fiji.

The secondary school curriculum leads to the Cook Island School Certificate, which students attempt in form five (grade eleven). Some students proceed to form six (grade twelve) or go overseas. There are eight secondary schools, four on Rarotonga and one each in Aitutaki, Atiu, Mangaia, and Mauka. Some primary schools in the northern islands also offer classes up to form four (grade ten). The medium of instruction is English although Maori is not uncommon.

There are very few opportunities for higher education in the Cook Islands. A local teachers' college has been largely responsible for training primary school teachers since the 1950s. Secondary teachers receive training overseas, mainly in New Zealand and Australia, and at the University of the South Pacific. Many students from the Cook Islands make use of several teacher education programs, many leading to in-service awards, available through Cook Islands USP Extension Center.

Fiji

Like most Pacific Island nations, Fiji's first schools were established by missionaries. The Indian laborers who arrived in 1889 saw salvation in education and were instrumental in establishing and managing a large number of schools.

Out of the approximately 850 schools in Fiji only about 4 percent are financed and controlled by the government. The majority are managed by "committees" (religious, ethnic, charitable, private, or community based). There is in reality a partnership in existence between the government and the committee schools. Financing of buildings, the purchase of equipment, and the general physical development of schools are the responsibilities of the committees. School fees and levies approved by the Ministry of Education and a wide range of fundraising projects assist committees in funding their school programs. Government involvement through the Ministry of Education takes many forms: a) provision of and payment for government trained teachers; b) subsidizing primary education by paying 12 Fiji dollars per student to committees; c) subsidizing 80 percent of the salary of non-government teachers; d) award of grants on a "needs" basis for the construction of school buildings; e) organization of curricula and provision of advisory services; f) national administration and coordination of educational services.

Secondary education in Fiji is neither free nor compulsory. Junior secondary schools, forms 1-4 (grade 7-10), are situated in rural and island locations receiving graduates from class six (grade six), most of whom would have passed the Fiji Intermediate Examination. The Fiji Junior Certificate Examination is taken at the end of form four (grade ten). This by and large determines whether further secondary education is undertaken in one of the 110 secondary schools available.

Secondary schools are fed from three sources: a) from class six (grade six) graduates who enter form one (grade seven); b) from class eight (grade eight) graduates most of whom would have passed the Fiji eighth year examination and who enter form three (grade nine); c) from graduates of junior secondary schools or fourth formers of secondary schools who enter form five (grade eleven).

The Fiji Leaving Certificate Examination is taken at the end of the sixth form and the level of pass determines entry into the foundation year of the University of the South Pacific, the technical and vocational institutions, and into employment in the government and private sectors.

Technical and vocational education is provided by several institutions. Some of the larger, better established secondary schools also have technical and vocational courses for senior students. Various government institutions provide training to meet local manpower needs: Fiji Institute of Technology, Fiji College of Agriculture, Fiji School of Medicine and Teacher Training Institutions (one government and two private). There is an apprenticeship scheme at the certificate and diploma levels jointly sponsored by the Fiji National Training Council (FNTC) which has a coordinating and supervisory role, the Fiji Institute of Technology which undertakes training, and the employers who provide the students and furnish the funds. The government conducts two year vocational courses at centers throughout the country for school leavers at the form 4-6 (grades 10-12) level.

The main campus of the University of the South Pacific is located in Fiji, in Suva. Full-time and part-time courses on the campus as well as extension courses allow many to improve their academic and professional qualifications while in employment. The university has an arrangement with the government of Fiji School of Medicine whereby the university provides some of the courses and awards the medical degree. Scholarships and in-service awards sponsored by the government and the private enterprises, although limited in number, are provided annually.

Current trends, as seen from the policy statements of the minister of education include focus on greater access for all preschools, and primary and secondary schools; greater quality in the training and retraining of teachers at all levels and in the supply of basic equipment and books; and improving relevance of school curricula through regular reviews, modification, and expansion (the current intermediate and year eight examination are both due for thorough assessment).

Kiribati

As elsewhere in the Pacific, formal schools in Kiribati developed from the early efforts of the churches. However in the early 1950s the Protestant church withdrew from primary education. In 1977 Catholic primary schools were amalgamated with the government system. The churches continue to contribute the denominational content of teaching.

The school population in 1988 was 16,152 students attending 113 primary schools, seven academic secondary schools, one postprimary church school, and three tertiary institutions. Overall, there are 614 teachers at the primary, secondary, and tertiary schools (of this number, fifty-seven are expatriates, mainly at the secondary and tertiary levels).

At the secondary level, about 350 students sit for the Kiribati Junior Certificate Examination at the end of form three (grade nine). Selected from this is a smaller group who will attend the government secondary school; the majority will attend Mission Secondary School. At the end of form five (grade eleven), children sit the Kiribati National Certificate Examination. A further selected few, enter form six (grade twelve) and take the Pacific Senior Secondary Certificate Examination. At this point, there are scholarship opportunities to enter the University of the South Pacific, University of Papua New Guinea, or universities elsewhere.

Students who do not wish to continue a postsecondary academic education have the option of entering a technical or vocational institution: Tarawa Technical Institute (13-42 week courses in typewriting, carpentry, engineering, English, accounting, etc); Tarawa Teachers College (two year course to train primary teachers); Marine Training School (for youths 16-25 years, marine training as able seaman, qualified steward, etc.); and School of Nursing (run by the Ministry of Health and Family Planning). In addition to the above, the extension services of the University of the South Pacific maintains a center in South Tarawa.

Nauru

Education is free and compulsory for Nauruan children of age 6-17 years. In 1983 the government had five infant schools, one primary school, and a secondary school.

Scholarships are available to enable children to attend secondary boarding schools in Australia and New Zealand. There is generous provision of scholarships for higher education and training. There is a teacher training center in Nauru but opportunity for training is also offered in Australia.

The trade school offers trade training to school leavers of age sixteen years and over, to prepare them for occupations in industries. While there is still little change in the general attitude towards the social status of technical education, there is an increase in the intake into the school. The school offers an increasing number and range of courses from trade to sub-professional level. There are fourteen trades offered at the school and these include motor mechanics, electrical technology, radio electronics, air conditioning, refrigeration, carpentry and joinery, drafting, panel beating, plumbing, boiler making, fitting, and machining.

At the postsecondary level, Nauru students have been enrolled for the extension courses of the University of the South Pacific since 1980. This was coordinated by the Education Department. In 1986 a Center of the University of the South Pacific was established, which now offers a range of courses available from the University.

Niue

There is one coeducational high school in Niue, with a total enrollment of about 300 students. Students follow the same requirements as for New Zealand secondary schools because of the need for students to sit the various external examinations (which New Zealand has now discontinued). There are a few Niuean students attending secondary schools in other parts of the Pacific, including New Zealand. Most of the teachers are local, although there are a few New Zealanders, mainly in the high school.

Except for a Center of the University of the Pacific, there is no institution in Niue that offers postsecondary programs for school leavers. Most of them go abroad for further education, especially to New Zealand. Some attend the Solomon Islands Technical Institute and many go to Fiji, where they attend various institutions including the University of the South Pacific, the Fiji Institute of Technology, and the Fiji School of Nursing.

It is likely that Niue will continue to look to New Zealand for assistance as far as education and other things are concerned. The fast rate of depopulation of Niue is a major concern both to Niueans on Niue as well as the New Zealand government. As far as higher education is concerned, the number of Niuean students attending the University of the South Pacific, for example, has decreased, as more students tend to go to New Zealand both for secondary and tertiary education. This trend is likely to continue in the future.

Solomon Islands

Under the devolved system of government in the Solomon Islands, both the national government and the provincial governments share the responsibility for education. The national government is responsible for national education policy, curriculum development and materials, teaching service conditions, national institutions (e.g. national secondary schools, and Solomon Islands College of Higher Education), external aid, staff development and training, and national examinations. The provincial governments (and Honiara Town Council) are responsible for preschool education, provincial secondary schools, community education, advisory services to primary schools, in-service training of primary school teachers, and recruitment and transfer of primary teachers.

The Solomon Islands has a dual system of secondary schooling. The twelve provincial secondary schools, operating under the jurisdiction of the provincial education boards, offer a vocationally based curricula for forms 1-3, at the end of which there is a national examination for selection to national secondary schools.

The eight national secondary schools (six are church owned and two are government schools) offer an academically oriented program for forms 1-5 (grades 7-11), and in some cases up to form six (grade twelve). They operate under the jurisdiction of the national education board. Like provincial secondary schools, the pupils of national secondary schools also sit the form three national examination for selection into higher forms. At the end of form five (grade eleven) they sit another examination. Those proceeding to form six (grade twelve) are prepared for preuniversity work. They take the new Pacific Senior Secondary Examination at the form six level.

Because of the limited number of secondary schools in the country, there is a vigorous competition for admission into these schools. The dropout or "missout" rate at the end of class six (grade six) therefore is high and there is pressure on the provincial secondary schools to provide a more academically oriented program like their national counterpart.

Upon completion of secondary schooling, students proceed to either the employment sector or for tertiary studies at the Solomon Islands College of Higher Education (teacher training, marine studies, technology areas). Many students who successfully complete form six (grade twelve) also go to the University of the South Pacific and the University of Papua New Guinea. Also several students study for extension courses offered through the USP Center, Honiara.

Current educational development activities in education focus on the qualitative improvement of primary and secondary education and improving access to secondary education in the different provinces of the country. Priorities in the primary sector cover improvement of classroom teaching, provision of teaching materials and equipment, and teacher upgrading. In the secondary education sector, financial assistance from the World Bank and the Australian government is enabling the Solomon Island government to concentrate on establishing and improving the quality of lower secondary schools in the country.

Tonga

As in the case with most Pacific Island countries, schooling was introduced to the Tongans by early Wesleyan missionaries in the early part of the nineteenth century. In 1876, following the granting of a Constitution by King George I, primary schooling was made free and compulsory. Today, every Tongan child between the age of six and fourteen is required to attend school.

Most primary school leavers find a place in a secondary school, and a unique feature of Tongan education is the relatively low rate of dropouts. Unlike primary education, most secondary schools in Tonga are run by non-government organizations; of the fifty-three secondary schools in the country in 1987, government administered only eight. The main island, Tongatapu, has thirty-one secondary schools, Ha'apai has seven, Vava'u nine, 'Eua two and the Niuas four. Most students attend schools run by the Free Wesleyan Church (about 29 percent of the total). The other main ones are run by the government, the Roman Catholic Church, and Latter Day Saints.

The secondary school curriculum is largely "academic" although recent attempts have been made to introduce more vocationally oriented subjects. This has resulted in the following new subjects becoming the focus of attention at the national curriculum development unit (in addition to the more traditional subjects): home economics, industrial arts, commercial studies, accounting, economics, and agricultural science. Curriculum development work during the past five years, however, has focussed on the preparation of new high school leaving qualifications, following the phasing out of external (New Zealand) examinations at the form five (grade eleven) and form six (grade twelve) levels. These two examinations have now been replaced by a local Tongan Secondary Leaving Certificate (more commonly known as the Tongan School Certificate) and a regional form six (grade twelve) certificate.

A number of postsecondary opportunities are now available to Tongon school leavers. A Community Development and Training Center was established by the government in 1985, and offers a wide range of postsecondary training courses in both vocational and non-vocational subjects. The institution is also responsible for coordinating all postsecondary activities in the kingdom; part of the government's deliberate intent to rationalize and consolidate national training resources and new developments. Such postsecondary facilities include the Teachers Training College (which offers a three-year diploma in education program in both primary and secondary teaching), the Tonga Maritime Polytechnic Institute, the trades training of the Ministry of Works, the research division and extension training of the Ministry of Agriculture, Forestry and Fisheries, Hango Agricultural College (administered by the Wesleyans), and the St. Joseph's Business College (a commercial school for girls).

There are also a number of institutions within the government that are loosely affiliated to the Community Development and Training Center. They include the Queen Salote School of Nursing, the dental and para-medical training programs of the Ministry of Health and the computer division of the Tonga Defence Services. Other postsecondary facilities are available at "Atenisi Institute", a private non-profit institution consisting of a high school as well as a university division. The university division offers diploma, degree, and master's programs in selected fields including Tongan language and culture. Staff and students also engage in research and consultancy activities. Sia'atoutai Theological College, located about eight miles from the main town, also offers programs at the diploma and degree (B.Div.) levels and is administered by the Free Wesleyan Church.

Most Tongan students who are undertaking university level studies in Tonga are doing it through the distance education mode. Several are available, but the majority of students enrol in the University of the South Pacific's Extension Studies programs, available through its Tonga Center at 'Atele.

A large number of Tongan students go abroad for tertiary studies. In 1987, about 200 government sponsored students were studying overseas, under a number of awards. More than half of these were at the University of the South Pacific's two campuses (in Fiji and Western Samoa). Others were in New Zealand, Australia, Papua New Guinea, United Kingdom, U.S.A., Canada and Japan. A large proportion of Tongan students studying overseas are supported by their own families.

Much of the future planning in education in Tonga is focussed on postsecondary education, with recent talk of establishing a national university. However, for now, the Tongan government will continue to send all undergraduate students overseas in order to "expose them to the best there is available in the larger world in each chosen area of study, to make them familiar with other values and world views, and to experience other life styles. It is expected that these extracurricular activities will contribute as much to their education as their formal studies". (Taufe'ulungaki 1989).

Tokelau

Schooling, from preschool to junior secondary (year eleven) level is free and available to all. Tokelauan is the medium of instruction in the schools, with English taught as a second language.

At the end of form four (grade ten) year, pupils sit the Tokelau National Examination. This involves eight subjects, including English. The other seven subjects are taught and examined in the Tokelauan language, a unique feature for a South Pacific country at the time of writing. The medium of instruction was gradually changed from English to Tokelauan between 1987 and 1989. Each atoll has a school which takes children from preschool to form four (grade ten). Thirty to fifty percent of the students are selected at form four (grade ten) for senior secondary education outside Tokelau. The remainder complete a form five year in Tokelau. From 1990, all students will do their form 5 year at a central location in Tokelau and will be selected for further training from that level. A total of twenty-nine Tokelauans were studying in various tertiary institutions in 1986-87. Of these, twelve were in Fiji, thirteen in Western Samoa, and four were studying in New Zealand.

The Tokelauan educational system has been strongly influenced by that of New Zealand. It has a rather ambivalent, dual goal of preparing children for life in Tokelau, and for continuing education in a different country. In addition, many Tokelauana spend considerable periods living in New Zealand, to which Tokelau have free access (although the Tokelau Resettlement Scheme, which led to hundreds of Tokelauans moving to New Zealand, was suspended in 1976).

Tokelau is an active member of the University of the South Pacific Council, with several extension and some full-time students studying at the University of the South Pacific. In addition, Tokelau is a member of the Suva-based South Pacific Board for Education Assessment.

Tuvalu

Education is predominantly government financed and managed, but there has been greater community and church involvement in recent years.

The Government sponsors about sixty-five technical and tertiary students in overseas countries each year, and about another 240 are privately funded.

Motofoua is the only secondary school, and it offers academic courses that can lead to further education. The school is jointly sponsored by the Church of Tuvalu and the government. School fees are charged to help cover some of the costs (approximately 10 percent of the total cost). A new Tuvalu School Certificate has been established at year twelve.

Children are sent for private education to other Pacific Islands (Fiji, Tonga, Samoa) and to a lesser extent, to New Zealand and Australia. About 240 Tuvaluan students are privately funded for overseas studies; about 20 percent of their peer group.

The majority of students must travel overseas for higher technical or tertiary training. Some courses can be taken in-country through the Tuvaluan Maritime School and the University of the South Pacific Extension Center. About sixty-five students are provided with scholarships each year to study in areas such as health, education, fisheries/agriculture, construction and administration. Priority is given to attendance at the University of the South Pacific in Fiji, but scholarships ar also provided for students attending institutions in Australia and New Zealand.

The Tuvalu Maritime School opened in 1979 and has eighteen courses available for training youth from the ages of 17-22 years. There is an entrance test in written and oral English and on general knowledge. Graduates are usually employed on foreign merchant vessels.

Vocational training was introduced with the creation of the Community Training Center in 1982. The goal of the Center is to create more intensive skills training appropriate to rural living. A longer term objective is to use the Center for adult training courses. For ILO study conducted in 1988 suggests that the concept of CTC education be revised with post year 10 education to be continued on four islands (not Funafuti). This plan has yet to be accepted by the parliament.

The University of the South Pacific Extension Center in Tuvalu has been operating since 1980. It offers courses available via this center's headquarters in Suva, Fiji.

The Tuvalu government, in conjunction with overseas aid donors hopes to implement improvement in education at all levels. The study "Education for Life - A Review of the Manpower, Education and Training needs of Tuvalu", being considered at the time of writing by the Parliament, is likely to have a significant influence on Tuvaluan education.

Vanuatu

Pupils selected for admission into the junior secondary schools follow a four year cycle of studies from form one to form four (grades 7-10). A unified curriculum for both the English and the French medium schools are prescribed. Because of the pressure for secondary school places there has been a concerted effort, with assistance from the World Bank, to create additional provisions in the existing secondary schools and to create new secondary schools on selected islands.

At the end of form four (grade ten), pupils sit for the year ten examination for entry into upper secondary schools. From this stage, the English-medium schools follow a three-year cycle of studies and prepare students for the Cambridge School Certificate examination. On the other hand, the French-medium students prepare for the French *baccalaureate* examination.

While the students completing the French *baccalaureate* can obtain entry into a tertiary institution, those completing the Cambridge certificate spend an additional year in New Zealand or Australian schools or go to the University of the South Pacific for preuniversity foundation studies.

For higher qualifications and in training in agriculture, accounting, law, engineering, etc. students proceed under scholarship awards to the University of the South Pacific, University of Papua New Guinea, and institutions in Australia and New Zealand.

Vocational training skills in the rural areas are provided by some church sponsored institutions for primary school leavers and out of school youths. The Technical Institute in Vanuatu (INTV) provides training in areas such as automotive mechanics, carpentry, and secretarial studies. Several students also take advantage of non-credit programs, and extension courses provided by the University of the South Pacific through its center in Port Vila. The university center also houses the University's Pacific Languages Unit and Pacific Law Unit.

The improvement of the quality of primary education is the key government priority. This is hoped to be achieved through teacher upgrading, better teacher advisory services, provision of teaching materials, improvement in the examination and assessment system, and the development of a "common" curriculum. In the secondary sector, the emphasis is on the provision of more secondary schools and recruitment and training of good quality teachers willing and able to serve in the rural areas.

Western Samoa

In 1980 the aims of education for the country were formulated and in 1986, after wide consultation with the public, a further policy statement was released. In 1987 the action plan was begun, but in 1988, a change in government saw controversial proposals to return to the old system. Educational leaders had thought that the old system was too selective and curricula too academic, catering for only a minority, and it was felt that the country needed a wider, vocational-oriented curricula to provide a greater range of opportunities for the children. At the time of writing (February 1989), it is understood that the new system is being followed in the primary schools while the secondary level has reverted to the old system, reportedly until the completion of preparation of curriculum materials.

There are two main providers of education, the government and church missions.

In the old system there were fourteen years of schooling, seven primary, two intermediate, and five secondary. For years 9-11 (junior high), locally developed curriculum materials have been produced and are nearing completion. Years 12-13 (senior colleges) will continue to follow New Zealand curricula for the preparation of students for the two examinations: New Zealand School Certificate (form five) and New Zealand University Entrance (form six). At the time of writing, it is planned that this situation will be changed within three years, when local examinations will be used.

Language of instruction is English although at the junior levels teachers may use Samoan to further clarify some difficult concepts. In addition to the usual subjects such as English, math, sciences, history, geography, accounting, economics, the Samoan language and culture is compulsory for all Samoan children attending government schools.   In the junior high schools, vocational subjects such as agricultural studies, woodwork, and domestic science are included.   Physical education, art, and music are taken as recreational rather than for serious study.

The new systems examination consist of Samoan Junior Secondary Certificate (year eleven, sat by junior high students); Western Samoa School Certificate (year twelve, sat by students from government senior colleges and some mission schools); Form six Certificate (year thirteen sat by students in the absence of NZUE, and until WSSC is ready).

Language of instruction is mainly Samoan but there are some English speaking classes in the central government primary school (Apia primary) and also in some mission schools, particularly Catholic and Latter Day Saints.   The national end of primary examination (form two or grade eight) of the old system is being replaced by a system of checkpoints (one at year six and another at year eight) and a system of internal assessment.

There are 142 primary, 23 junior high and 3 senior high schools.   All primary schools except one, are funded by the local community with teachers' salaries being met by the government.   The one exception is Apia primary which is totally funded by government, with some support from school fees charged.   Junior secondary schools are mostly funded by government with some support from the local communities while the senior colleges are entirely government funded.   School and stationary fees are charged.

Teachers for primary schools are recruited from the Primary Teachers' College and for junior high from the Secondary Teachers' College and some volunteers (e.g. Peace Corps).   Teachers in senior colleges, are mostly degree holders (locals and expatriates on contract).

In addition there are eighteen primary, three junior high, and sixteen senior high schools run by five mission establishments (Catholic, Congregational, Methodist, Latter Day Saints, and Seventh Day Adventists).   Administration of these are by their own boards, each headed by a director.   Funding comes from tuition fees and donations from church members and for some, e.g. Latter Day Saints and Seventh Day Adventist, receive grants from their overseas headquarters. Policy decisions for mission instructions are made by church committees of members drawn from congregations/parishes.   Another private primary school has also been established recently.

Twelve institutions offer post secondary education: six are government controlled, two are mission sponsored, two others are private, and two establishments form part of the Regional University of the South Pacific.

Government institutions consist of the Western Somoa Technical Institute offering two-year courses in trade and commerce with a secretarial component for those who have completed form four; Primary Teachers' College providing a two-year course for graduates from junior and senior high school; Secondary Teachers' College, conducting a three-year course for graduates of senior high schools and teachers already in service; Toloa Marine Training School, training for shipping jobs; School of Nursing to prepare registered nurses; and Le Iunivesite Aoao o Samoa, also known as the National University of Samoa.

The National University of Samoa was established in 1984 and is independent of the Education Department, but the minister and director of education are both on the university council. Other council members include representatives of local mission education establishments, the vice-chancellors of the University of the South Pacific and some other New Zealand and Australian Universities. Administration is through the registrar who is directly responsible to the vice-chancellor.

There are two faculties; science and social science. Currently there are two programs being taught; the pre-degree (university preparatory year) and a two year degree in education (Bachelor of Education). Courses in Samoan studies have been boosted by the creation of a chair for this department, within the Faculty of Social Sciences. A Bachelor of Arts program has been started.

Entry requirements for the university preparatory year is a pass in the form six (grade thirteen) examinations. Courses in this program mostly follow those offered by the University of the South Pacific, and at the time of writing, much of the course materials are from the Extension Services Section of the University of the South Pacific. Full time tutors provide further tuition and guidance. Students are all Samoans and are awarded a living allowance under the government scholarship scheme. There are no residential quarters either for students or for staff. Graduates of this program are sent to overseas universities including the University of the South Pacific for degree studies.

Mission establishments consist of two theological colleges (Congregational and Methodist) and a seminary (Catholic). Students are usually mature persons, often drawn from the work force. A pass in a rigorous entrance examination (academic and moral) is the prerequisite. Graduates obtain a diploma and either move on to study at the Regional College in Fiji or other overseas theological colleges, or are drawn into working for congregations or parishes.

Western Samoa is also the location of the second main campus of the University of the South Pacific including the School of Agriculture and Institute for Research Extension and Training in Agriculture.

Current trends indicate that educational programs focussing on primary and secondary education will continue to be vocational oriented and less academic. National University of Samoa is understood to be slowing down its development. Western Samoa Technical Institute will be expanded to cater for a wider range of studies.

BIBLIOGRAPHY

Asian Development Bank. *Vocational Training and the Labor Market in Vanuatu.* Report of the ADB/ADAB Joint Technical Assistance Team, 1987.

Brice, C. P., and Lawson, G. M. *A Proposal for the Vanuatu/New Zealand Cooperation in Education Development.* Wellington: Department of Foreign Affairs, 1987.

Crocombe, R. C., and Meleisea, eds. *Pacific Universities: Achievements, Problems and Prospects*. Suva, Fiji: Institute of Pacific Studies/The University of the South Pacific, 1988.

Currin, C. B. *Report of Teacher Utilization and Incentives in Solomon Islands*. Honiara: Ministry of Education, 1978.

Department of Education, Government of Western Samoa. *Education Policy and Development: Looking Toward the 1990s*. 1986.

Government of Tuvalu. *Education for Life: A Review of the Manpower, Education, and Training Needs of Tuvalu*. Funafuti, Tuvalu: Government of Tuvalu, 1989.

Implementation and Planning Unit, Ministry of Education, Solomon Islands. *Education Sector Plan 1990-1994*. Honaira: Ministry of Education, 1988.

Johnston, J. *A Project to Help Improve the Quality of Primary Education in Vanuatu*. Australian Assistance Bureau (ADAB) Report No. 36. 1987.

Ministry of Education, Tonga. *Report: For the year 1987*. Nuku'alofa: Government Printer, 1989.

Ministry of Education, Kiribati. *Digest of Educational Statistics*.

Republic of Vanuatu. First National Development Plan 1982-1986. Port Vila: National Planning Office, 1982.

Solomon Islands Government. *Education Statistics (Statistical Bulletin) No. 38/34*. Honaira: Statistics Office, 1984.

Taufe'ulungaki, A. "A Conceptual Framework for Higher Education in Tonga." Ministry of Education, Government of Tonga: Unpublished paper, 1980.

Thomas, R. M., and T. N. Postlethwaite, eds. *School in the Pacific Islands*. Oxford: Pergamon Press, 1981.

Whitehead, C. W. "Education in Fiji: A Study of Policy, Problems and Progress in Primary and Secondary Education, 1939-1973." Diss., University of Otago, New Zealand, 1975.

The World Bank. *Staff Appraisal Report Solomon Islands Secondary Education Project*. Washington: The World Bank, 1986.

FINLAND

by
Jouko Kari
Professor and Director, Institute for Educational Research
University of Jyvaskyla, Finland

BACKGROUND

The origin of higher education in Finland can be traced back to 1640 when the first university was established in Turku, at the initiation of the Swedish governor-general of Finland, Count Per Brahe. The count also played a key role in fostering national awareness of the Finns. He encouraged Swedish nobility to learn Finnish and had the entire Bible translated into Finnish. During the period that followed, a growing feeling of national independence took root in the academic circles in Finland.

When Finland was annexed by Russia in 1809, the Russians met a nation that was fully aware of its national independence. Alexander I turned Finland into a large autonomous principality in which the Finnish language and the old Swedish constitution remained valid. Finland had its own government, formed by Finnish citizens. After the autonomous grand duchy was founded, the University of Turku was moved to Helsinki. This was the origin of the "Emperor Alexander University of Helsinki" founded in 1828. After Finland became independent in 1917, this university was given the name "University of Helsinki". Before the beginning of this century it was the only university and today it is the largest in the country. During the first decades of the twentieth century, the Finnish university system started to develop quickly, especially in technical and economic fields.

In 1919 another Swedish speaking university, the new Abo Academy, was founded. Turku also received a Finnish university in 1922. When the Academy for Social Sciences, which was originally founded in Helsinki in 1925, was moved to Tampere in 1960, it signified a considerable expansion of the Finnish higher educational system into rural areas. This academy was upgraded to a university in the 1960s. Also in Jyvaskyla, in central Finland, an academy for pedagogy was founded, which became in 1966 the University of Jyvaskyla. In 1958 the University of Oulu was founded in Northern Finland. As a result of this decentralization, the Finnish higher education and the university system became evenly distributed throughout the entire country. The higher educational system continued to expand with the addition of a large number of new universities and academies, in addition to the existing institutions.

PRIMARY AND SECONDARY EDUCATION

Finland too, as many other Western nations, has reorganized its educational system during the recent decades and job training has been an important aspect of the reforms. Today general education in Finland takes nine years (7-15 year olds), followed by an intermediate (secondary) level consisting of either three years of upper secondary school with emphasis on general education, or 2-6 years of various aspects of job training. The basis of this reform was the 1978 Law and the subsequent ordinances. In the fall of 1988 this reform was implemented throughout the entire country. In the curriculum of the lower level (of the comprehensive school) the essential factor is that teaching, at least in grades 1-2, is organized according to the integrative instruction principle.

The basic purpose of upper secondary education has always been to prepare students for their studies at universities and colleges. Upper secondary schools operate on a course system with mandatory classes. The Finnish upper secondary curriculum includes a great number of school subjects, with emphasis on languages. In further education and working life, languages play a significant role. Mathematics and sciences are given relatively low importance. An upper secondary that operates without a defined class and grade system is also being tested now. At the end of upper secondary education, students have to pass a standardized high school diploma examination *(Abitur)*. The exam is supervised by an examination commission appointed by the Ministry of Education. Successful completion of the exam generally entitles students to continue their studies at universities and colleges.

A significant structural change which has taken place in the area of job training is the consolidation of the numerous job training fields into twenty-five basic areas. Each basic training area requires a general period of study and a period of special training. The purpose of this reform was to make the transition from job training to higher education easier. Altogether there are more than 220 special fields. In addition to traditional goals, upper secondaries have also been given a new responsibility to provide students with a basic education that may not necessarily lead to strict academic credentials.

HIGHER EDUCATION

Institutions

There are twenty academies and universities that provide a full range of higher educational opportunities in Finland. The University of Helsinki with its origin going back to 1640, is the oldest and the largest with an enrollment of nearly 25,000 students. The Universities of Turku (1922), Tampere (1925), and Oulu (1958) have enrollments varying from 8,000 to 9,500 students. The Helsinki University of Technology (1908) has an enrollment of about 8,700. Other institutions have lesser enrollment of students. Total enrollment in all the twenty institutions was about 94,000 in 1986.

Only 1 percent of the students in higher education are foreigners but it is increasing. Approximately 2,000 Finnish students study abroad, and 25 percent of that number in Sweden. In 1986, 51.2 percent of the students were women. The enrollment of women varies greatly depending on the field of study. In humanities and education the percentage of women today is 70 percent as compared to technical science fields where the enrollment of women is only 30 percent.

The institutions of higher education are under the direct supervision of the Ministry of Education. They are all state institutions, but each of them has an internal administration with complete autonomy in internal affairs. The traditional model of university administration has been developed towards a more democratic model so that not only professors but also other teachers and other staff as well as students are allowed to participate in the administration. In the new administrative system, the internal administration of an institutions of higher education is in the hands of the university council and/or the administrative council, the rector, the administrative office, the faculty councils, and the department councils. The most important matters concerning teaching and studies are dealt with my faculty and department councils.

Particularly active in research is the Finnish Academy *(Suomen Akatemia)*, which especially finances theoretical research. There are also a number of national research institutes. The Institute for Educational Research *(Kasvatustieteiden Tutkimuslaitos)* which is the national institute active in pedagogics and educational research operates as part of the University of Jydvaskyla. The funding for research and development projects in 1986 amounted to FIM 5,864,000 (US$1 = FIM4) of which about 20 percent was spent in universities and academies. While research activity increased by 30 percent from 1971-85, funds devoted by universities and academies for their own research and development projects increased only by about 10 percent. However, funding by external sources increased rapidly.

Higher education in Finland is free of charge, i.e. there are no tuition fees paid to the institutions of higher education. However, the membership fee for the student union is compulsory for all students aiming at the basic degree; postgraduate students may join the union if they wish. The annual membership fee varies from about FIM 300-450, and it must be paid each academic year.

Under the new, reformed system, higher education is governed by nineteen decrees concerning degrees, one for each field of study. The decrees define the overall objectives; the extent of basic degree programs and the relative shares of general studies, specialized subjects, and advanced studies; and some basic features of postgraduate studies. The basic degree in Finland is the higher university degree, which in an international context, roughly corresponds to an M.A. It is still possible to take some lower academic degrees (in law and social sciences).

Programs and Degrees

Under the new degree system, the education in each field of study has been arranged into programs leading to a basic degree. There are about 150 different degree programs. The extent of the degree programs vary between 160 and 220 credit units. These are called "study weeks" in Finnish because a credit unit corresponds to an estimated forty hours of independent and guided work. Professional study fields such as medicine and engineering have the same structure for degree programs, but have much more practical work than other study fields. A basic degree has been designed to make it possible for a full-time student to take it in 4-5 years (in medicine six years), but in practice it may take considerably more time.

The total number of students who complete a qualification at one level or another in higher educational institutions in Finland is about 10,000 per year of which about 360 receive licentiate degrees and about 300 receive doctorates. In 1985-86, about 30 percent of the students took sciences, 12 percent took humanities and 7 percent took medicine. The participation of women was 51 percent in all programs and 28 percent in doctoral programs.

The dropout rate is 5-20 percent, depending on the field of study. In addition, some 10 percent of students change fields or institutions. Dropout is most frequent during the first years. For example, in the natural sciences some 25 percent of students transfer to the medical or engineering fields. Delayed graduation differs from dropout in that it concerns older students. Basic degree studies take 6-7 years on average but there are fields in which they may taken even ten years. One purpose of the higher education reform was to cut the time of studies to 5-6 years. The reason for delayed graduation is usually that the students have a part-time or full-time job or study a great number of secondary subjects. The reasons vary depending on the field of study.

Postgraduate studies in Finland have traditionally consisted of two degrees: the licentiate and the doctor's degree. The lower of these degrees is the licentiate. The preparation of an extensive scientific thesis is a requirement for this degree. Previously, the licentiate was a prerequisite for obtaining the doctor's degree, but in the new system, the doctor's degree may be obtained without first having to take the licentiate. The requirements for the doctor's degree include writing a doctoral dissertation and defending it in a public debate. According to the new statutory orders, a postgraduate student is required, in addition, to familiarize himself extensively with other research in his field of study and with the general scientific theory. The organization of this instruction is presently being planned in most institutions of higher education. On the average, the age of students defending their doctoral thesis was 39.7 years (1946-86). For women, the average was 2.4 years more than male students. In forestry the average age of Finnish students who have defended their thesis is about three years less.

Finnish educational policy aims at securing further studies for all students graduating from the comprehensive and upper secondary schools in vocational training or in higher education. Approximately one fifth of these openings are in institutions of higher education. As a rule, students are selected on the basis of their matriculation and school-leaving certificates and the entrance examination (and in some fields, an aptitude test). Each institution of higher education determines its own selection criteria and methods. Faculties of a given field may cooperate in the selection process. Measures have been taken to secure admission to higher education also for non-matriculated students. At present they represent about 1.5 percent of all enrollment. The number of non-matriculated students coming through vocational training to higher education is expected to grow in the near future.

Teacher Training

The training of teachers in the Finnish general educational system is an old tradition. In 1983, Jyvaskyla celebrated its 120th anniversary of its Training Institute for Elementary School Teachers. As in many other North European countries, the education of high school teachers is different from the education and training of elementary school teachers. The training of upper secondary school teachers dates back to the founding of the pedagogic seminar at the Abo Academy in 1908.

After the traditional parallel school system was abolished and the new standardized school system introduced, efforts were made to reform the education of teachers. The *lyceums* were replaced by new training schools which are affiliated with universities. In agreement with the teacher education law of 1971, the training of teachers was moved to the universities of Helsinki, Jyvaskyla, Oulu, Tampere, Turku, the Academy of Joensuu, and the Swedish teacher training facility at the Abo Academy. Consequently, in 1979 the Rovanicmi College with its teacher training unit was founded in Lapland. According to the teacher education ordinance, the teacher education units consist of the education departments or faculties of the above listed universities and academies and their affiliated training schools.

In 1973, the Committee on Teacher Training compiled new teaching guidelines and plans which were to be realized in these new education units. These new plans were of great importance to a high quality education for homeroom teachers in Finland. The "homeroom teacher" has to instruct in almost every subject from grade 1-6 in elementary schools. Students studying for this job are encouraged to acquire master's degree which would enable them to proceed to the licentiate degree (educational level between a baccalaureate and the doctorate) and to the Ph.D. degree. A university education was expected to provide teachers a thorough knowledge of their subjects, a good balance of teaching skills, and ability to do research. On the whole, the examination reform of the teacher education programs brought about a greater similarity between homeroom teachers and special subject teachers in the remaining school system because pedagogic studies and practical training became more and more important to the education of subject teachers. In addition, the entry examinations for teacher education programs have been improved and standardized.

Admission to homeroom teacher training programs is competitive and depends on the student's grades in their upper secondary diplomas. The emphasis is not on academic subjects but on competencies of importance to the profession of a teacher, i.e. art, music, etc., and on the scores of the admission examination. The basic elements of a study program consist of general subjects, special subjects, specialized intensive studies, and practice in the classroom. As indicated earlier, the effort and work devoted to one study element is measured in Finland by one "study week" (SW). One "study week" represents forty hours of work. Homework varies for each element, depending on the type of classes. For example, for lectures one can assume a ratio of 1:1, i.e. the student has to put in two hours of research and homework for a two hour lecture. For seminars and teaching practice more time is involved. Due to course load, practical training and examinations, it is not uncommon that a part of the course load is carried over into the fifth year. Traditionally Finnish academic year lasts from the beginning of September till the end of May.

The Finnish teacher education program does not require an actual final exam. Students do write a master's thesis at the end of their study program and it is read and evaluated by two professors but there is no oral examination. The system is a continuous evaluation and learning process with numerous written examinations. The students receive their certificates after they have met all the requirements of their study program. Special subject teachers follow university level study in at least two subjects until they have met all the requirements for the first "academic phase", after which they concentrate on their major. Sometimes the pedagogic training begins simultaneously with the academic education. In many cases, the students are introduced to the field of teacher training in their second year and must take an aptitude test before they can start with pedagogics. The training programs for special subject teachers include general subjects (similar to the training of homeroom teachers); special subjects (the major and second subject together require eighty SWs); intensive specialized studies beginning with the third year; and studies in pedagogics including classroom training (this together requires forty SWs). Although 180 SWs are specified for this education program, the length of study in humanities and sciences on an average exceeds five years. For both teacher education programs (homeroom and special subject) the main subjects are evaluated individually. For future employment, the grades of the final training are of particular importance.

ISSUES AND TRENDS

The Finnish educational system has undergone considerable reform during the past few decades. However, schools still needed basic reforms in pedagogics and approach to teaching, based on national and international research. The government development plan of February 1987 is expected to provide a favorable foundation for improvements for the years 1987-92.

It seems reasonable that in a country like Finland with a relatively small population and limited resources, research in education must be coordinated and conducted in a balanced manner, with effective cooperation among institutes that examine and evaluate the various phases and programs in education, without all of them trying to solve the same problems. This concept, developed by the Department for Research in Education, by the YPP Group (Social Politics and Services) has become the framework for organizing research work at most of our institutions. The report also suggested the creation of a Department of Education at the Academy of Finland and the conversion of the Institute for Educational Research of Jyvaskyla into a central unit for long-term research projects in education. Several research projects have been financed in the recent years with an increase in the number of researchers and an improvement of the quality of research projects.

Since basic education as well as the fast growing continuing education of teachers will be the responsibility of universities, teacher education units at these institutes are becoming increasingly important for conducting research and for publishing important research findings. But most pedagogic faculties and departments are still young, and the professors and researchers have only recently started to develop research programs. Only the oldest units have established traditions in research. It is important for the development of pedagogic research that the teacher education units educate researchers within a scientific study program, while encouraging them to maintain direct contacts with the schools.

BIBLIOGRAPHY

Ehdotus koulutusohjelmien muodostamisperusteiksi ja koulutusvastuun jaoksi kasvatustieteellisellä alalla. Tampere: Kasvatusalan tutkinnonuudistuksen ohjaus - ja seurantaprojekti, 1976.

Heinonen, V., and Kari, J. "Finnish Doctoral Theses on Pedagogical Themes in a Production-Time Perspective." *Scandinavian Journal of Educational Research* 34, 3 (1990): 205 - 214.

Higher Education in Finland, Guide for Foreign Students. Helsink, 1982.

Isosaari, J. "Seminaarilaitoksen Syntymästä 120 Vuotta." *Kasvatus,* (The Finnish Journal of Education) 14, 2 (1983): 69 - 78.

Kari, J. "Näkökhtia opinoijen kestosta ja keskeyttämisestä." *Kasvatus,* (The Finnish Journal of Education) 17, 1 (1986): 41 - 45.

Kari, J., and Seidenfaden, F. "Hochschulen und Lehrerausbildung." In *Finland* by Hrsg. V. Corner, A., & Seidenfaden, F. Giessen: Verlag de Ferberschen Universitätsbuchhandlung, 1984.

Korkeakoululaitoksen katsaus. Helsinki: Opetusministerio, Korkeakoulu - ja tiedeosasto, 1987.

Korkeakoulujen perustutkintojen suoritusaika ja opintojen kulku. Helsinki: Kordeakouluneuvosto, 1985.

Opettajanvalmistuksen opetussuunnitelmatoimikunnan mietinto. Helsinki: Valtion painatuskeskus, 1986.

YPP - työryhmän koulutustutkimuksen jaoston mietintö. Helsinki: Valtion painatuskeskus, 1981.

FRANCE

by
Francine Best
Inspector General
Ministry of National Education, France

BACKGROUND

In France, like in the rest of the Western world, the emphasis of any discussion on education tend to be biased towards universities, *grandes écoles,* and post secondary training institutions. Why? Because these are the well structured and sought after institutions that guide to employment opportunities in recognized professions valued by the society. A higher education qualification (degree) remains a very important asset in France: standing of the qualification (degree) has a very direct relationship to the level of professional and social life one can attain. In other words, there are very few "self-made men" in France. The schools, specially in the higher education sector, are the key or "sesame, open the door" for the highest levels of professional opportunities.

More and more, the educational system is judged by the "high quality" and by the avenues it promises and promotes in real life. The high level committee *Education-Economie* created in 1985 by the Ministry of National Education had made numerous studies all of which concluded that elevation of the level and quality of education in the French society was a necessity. Based on these studies, it has become a primary objective of the French educational system, to get at least 80 percent of the young generation qualified to *baccalauréat* level or equivalent. It is an objective that reflects the demands placed on the educational system by the society (employers, parents, economists, intellectuals, and politicians).

Why is everybody almost unanimously endorsing this? The French economy is in need of creative talents to prepare itself for the integration of Europe in 1993, and to generate new employment opportunities through high technology as a means of solving economic crisis and unemployment. The young generation, growing up in an environment of employment crisis, is convinced that acquisition of a higher educational qualification (degree) is an investment for the future.

Then, is the situation a satisfactory one? Will the French universities and *grand écoles* become institutions for study and professional training accessible to at least 80 percent of each younger generation in France born between 1978 and 1988? The situation is far from being simple. The democratization, understood as the mechanism providing equal opportunities to every one to access the educational system, has made significant progress between the years 1960-70, but it is far from being a total reality; it has somewhat regressed, drifted, and produced failures upstream of the *baccalauréat.*

263

PRIMARY AND SECONDARY EDUCATION

One of the well recognized successes of the French educational system is its nursery school, *école maternelle*. Although this pre-elementary stage does not form part of the compulsory education (education is compulsory for ages 6-16 years), it receives young children aged 3-6 years (sometimes 2-6 years. Student success rate is impressive: 99.7 percent of five-year olds; 98 percent of four-year olds, 94 percent of three-year olds and 30 percent of two-year olds.

Majority of the nursery schools are public schools. Teaching staff come under the government and are trained for two years at the teacher training schools *(écoles normales)*. Thus, in France, the children of ages 2-6 years are already students.

Primary schooling *(école élémentaire)* in France lasts for five years and caters to children of 6-11 years. Promotion from one year to the next is based on examinations and teacher assessment. Those who do not reach the required standard have to repeat their classes. Studies show that only 1 percent of the students who repeat the first degree of primary school reach the *baccalauréat* level; however, about 11-13 percent of every generation of children repeat those classes.

Often it is the same students who repeat classes several times at the primary level and then at the secondary before becoming dropouts at sixteen years without a diploma. A number of sociological studies have shown that statistically a majority of the students who repeat classes (ages 6-16 years) are the children of the workers and the unemployed. It seems as if the "selection process" in education is a reflection of social inequalities and the hierarchy in employment status of parents.

The middle school in France, now known as "college" is a four-year school which receive students at the age of eleven years. There are 4,810 such colleges in the public sector and 1,846 in the private sector for students of age 11-16 years.

At college too, the repeat phenomenon continues. Very often weak performers are encouraged to pursue technical education streams, after two years at college. In addition, the transition from primary school to middle is a rough one for the students. During the recent years, the establishment of technological classes, whether in colleges or professional lycees, has resulted in a clear improvement to the system as students are now more attracted to continue their studies, prompted by their interest in technology related subjects. However, still, children have to leave middle school when they reach sixteen years, whether they have obtained the final certificate *(certificat d'aptitude professionnelle* or *brevet d'études professionelles)* or not.

The *lycée* is the highest rung (second cycle) of secondary education and from *lycée* onwards, education is not compulsory. There are 1,114 public *lycées* and 1,189 private *lycées* where students continue education from eighteen years of age till twenty.

The professional *lycées* lead to *brevet d'études professionelles* or various certificates of professional aptitude in a variety of fields. More recent changes have made it possible for these students to sit for a "professional *baccalauréat*". This recent improvement is significant as it increases the likelihood of France achieving its goal of educating at least 80 percent of the young people to *baccalauréat* level by the year 2000. However, the problem of "selection" as discussed earlier, at the primary and middle levels, is still a formidable hinderance.

Here too, like in the case of primary schools, some hope of progress is there. A concept of "differentiated teaching" *(pédagogie différenciee)* has been successfully tried out by Louis Legrand and the *Institut National de Recherche Pédagogique* with the objective of improving the system, by taking account of the heterogenous nature of students' educational abilities while aiming towards a common goal.

The teaching staff at colleges are recruited by the government. There are regional inspectors who oversee the schools.

In reality, about 38 percent of the young generation of France obtain the *baccalauréat* at present. The improvement is significant (compared to 11 percent in 1960) but still it is a long way from the desired 80 percent by year 2000.

The education provided at French *lycées* are of a high standard. Studies conducted by the National Educational Research Institute (INRP) and the Ministry of Education demonstrate that contrary to a popular myth, the "level" of the *lycée* students has not gone down. In certain subjects like mathematics and physics, the "level" has in fact increased.

Majority of present day students are serious and hardworking even though life in most *lycées* is not a particularly enjoyable one. The students, under pressure to obtain the *baccalauréat,* and having to follow classes up to thirty hours weekly and charged with homework (three hours per day), possess very little time for leisure. The transition from *lycée* (where a strict regime was followed) to the university (where students are free to organize themselves) is often seen as a difficult one.

In 1990 about 38 percent of youngsters in France obtained the *baccalauréat* *(baccalauréat d'enseignement général,* about 190,000; *baccalauréat de technicien,* about 93,000; and *baccalauréat professionnel,* about 1,800). Of the students who leave *lycée,* with or without *baccalauréat* about 32 percent enter higher education (this number is growing). But, to show interest exclusively on higher education, is to ignore 68 percent of the population; hence, the remarks made at the outset of this article.

The *baccalauréat* diploma is almost "sacred" in France; yet at issue is the entrance to the university which is "open". No sooner a minister (like Mr. Devaquet) attempts at controlling the entry to the university, whether this control is in the form of financing or another, he encounters enormous resistance (e.g. student demonstrations of 1986). The fact is that there is really no need to put any new obstacles to control university entrance; the entire education system in France, from the age of seven years, is geared to select the best students. Only the *baccalauréat* diploma holders can enter the university. They get there after a continuous selection process.

HIGHER EDUCATION

Universities form the nucleus of higher education in France but, in reality, the system is a dual one: on one side about forty universities along with an array of university institutes of technology; and on the other side, the *grandes écoles* or professional schools.

Grand Ecoles

These are prestigious institutions that train engineers and other staff personnel for industry and commerce. The most famous ones are the *Ecole Polytechnique, Ecoles Normales Supérieures, Ecole Centrale des Arts et Manufactures, Ecole Nationale d'Administration,* and *Ecole des Hautes Etudes Commerciales.* This category also includes a great variety of engineering schools, *(école d'ingénieur),* and higher schools of business *(école supérieur de commerce).*

All the *grand écoles* recruit students through highly competitive exams. Very often entering students have already followed two years of university studies *(diplôme d'études universitaires générales),* although this is not a requirement. The schools that are most difficult to enter are the schools most sought after. The originality of *lycée* system in France, in fact, can be traced back to the rigorous standards set by *grandes écoles.* In general, preparatory classes for entry to *grandes ecoles* is a fact of life at *lycée (lycée d'enseignement général)* as post-*baccalauréat* programs may last two years. The programs require hard work (many hours of classes), oral and written exercises, and lot of homework. Only the best of the *lycée* teachers are chosen to conduct these programs.

At the *grand ecoles* students follow three years of studies for *ingénieur* or other diplomas that open the door to high level positions. The social recognition given to these schools is tremendous. The alumni associations are powerful lobbying organs that help graduating students to find attractive jobs. In 1987-88, the preparatory classes had 41,208 students and engineering schools had 23,290 students. Here are the 60,000 most powerful citizens of France! By all counts, it is not a big number.

Universities

If we follow the course of a French student who has progressed through *école élémentaire,* college, and *lycée* and obtained the *baccalauréat,* after which he has opted to enter the university, he should, in two years, obtain the *diplôme d'études universitaires générales* or DEUG. This diploma marks the end of the first cycle of university studies.

The educational program in the first cycle is based on a system of "units". Each unit corresponds to a specified number of courses, directed assignments, and practical work throughout the academic year (October to June). Grading for each unit is based on continuous assessment by the professor as well as by a final exam. The academic load for each unit is determined by the teachers in the teaching and research unit *(unité d'enseignement et de recherche* - U.E.R.) relevant to the student's academic discipline and approved by the university council. The creation of new "units" require approval of the Ministry of National Education, which regulates the funding (for new teaching positions etc.).

The diploma DEUG requires twelve units, (some compulsory, some optional) and generally takes two years of studies. A good number of students do not proceed beyond DEUG. Often frustrated by the effort required and the difficulties of supporting themselves financially, many students enter working life after the first cycle. (Scholarships and grants are few and are awarded to students whose parents do not have adequate income). Students who continue their studies enter the second cycle that leads to the *licence* after one year or *maîtrise,* after two years.

Students with the *maîtrise* may enter the third cycle to continue studies and research leading to a doctorate (of the third cycle) taking about three years, and eventually a state doctorate *(doctorat d'état)* that takes much longer time. Both doctorates require thesis to be defended in public but the state doctorate marks the completion of a strong body of research and publications compared to somewhat limited research effort for the doctorate of the third cycle.

Studies leading to medical and pharmacy degrees go by the years rather than cycles. The first year in both cases is very competitive and functions as preparation for the exam that selects students for the second year. Medical degree takes seven years and in case of specialization, an additional three years. However, within this period, medical students undergo several practical training programs at university hospitals.

Hospital administrators are trained at *Ecole Nationale de la Santé Publique,* one of the *grand écoles.* The nurses are trained at nursing schools attached to the university hospital centers. Admission to all these schools is by competitive exams.

Training of teachers for elementary and nursery schools is done at special teacher training schools *(écoles normales)* which take in students who have passed the university diploma, *diplôme d'études universitaires générales.* Secondary school teachers are trained at the university.

With regard to administration of universities, France is divided into twenty-seven academies each roughly corresponding to government administrative regions. Each academy has at least one university and, in some, there are several universities as in the case of the Paris region where there are thirteen.

At the head of each academy is a rector responsible for administration of education from preschool to university and functioning as the chancellor of the universities. The rector, who is generally a person of high standing, has authority over educational matters in the academy: the distribution of teachers, including university staff, budgetary control, etc. However, each university is managed by a president elected by a university council. The university council is also an elected body having representatives from a number of electoral colleges, with each college representing a separate group: teachers, students, and local political or business personalities.

At the universities, the teaching staff comprises four categories: *professeurs,* who hold state doctorate and are well versed in research; *maîtres de conférences; assistants;* and *chargés de cours* (often *lycée* teachers holding certification, *agregé,* who give lectures supplementary to their regular work). In 1986-87 there were 11,750 *professeurs,* 17,769 *maîtres de conférence,* 11,339 *assistants* and 4,951 *chargés de cours* or others.

As the student population keeps getting bigger, teaching facilities are strained: lecture halls are overcrowded and not enough places in the laboratories. As the teaching staff at the *professeur* level ages, *maîtres de conférence* and other teaching staff see their promotion prospects blocked.

The university teachers, in general, maintain a high standard of teaching and research. Along with the researchers of the National Center for Scientific Research *(Centre National de Recherche Scientifique),* the National Institute of Medical Studies and Research *(Institut National Scientifique d'Etudes et de Recherches Medicales)* and similar research institutes, they form the core of scientific research in France.

Research work at the universities are done, more and more, in cooperation with industry. However, public institutions and private enterprise are still very much separated. The "sponsoring" of universities (university activities) is not very common. Of course, there has been a significant improvement since 1984. The high level national committee, *Education-Economie,* and the ministries have encouraged higher education institutions to establish a close link with industry and to gear the educational programs to meet professional needs of the industry.

Returning to the "dual character of the French educational system," it must be noted that institutions providing professional education (post-*baccalauréat)* including *grandes écoles* educate about 300,000 students per year compared to the university output of about 800,000. In reality, the system is a hybrid one consisting of a "selective" sector and a "non-selective" sector. The selective sector comprises *grand écoles,* and other professional schools like *écoles normales* and nursing schools that more or less guarantees professional employment opportunities. On the other hand, the "non-selective" sector comprises the universities which receive over 800,000 students but the education offered gives students no assurance of employment. This is a major educational problem which needs to be resolved.

ISSUES AND TRENDS

Higher education in France is expected to be heading for significant transformation in the coming years. The signs are already there: some 10,000 additional students have been seeking university education every year for the last four years. The financial burden that this influx of students has placed on government resources is without precedent.

The French youth, particularly high school students (*lycée* students), have come to recognize the value of higher education for achieving their professional and personal goals. The economy too demands qualified manpower, thus giving rise to a convergence of individual and collective interests. At the same time, professional and technical education, which has been stagnating for a longtime, has shown a new dynamism prompted by strong initiatives of the State Secretariat of Technical Education. The *baccalauréat professionnel* created in 1985 is expected to be in considerable demand in the future. The study programs that alternate periods of study at schools and periods of work experience in industry *(stage en entreprises)* have been very well received both by students and by enterprises.

The growth of the European Common Market and the vibrant interest of the French youth in other countries of Europe put the activities of French universities and the higher educational sector as a whole, in an international perspective. Undoubtedly, the future of French universities seem to be closely linked to international cooperation, East-West and North-South.

BIBLIOGRAPHY

Bienayme, A. "La mesure du problème universitaire français" *Chroniques SEDEIS -* Tome XXXVI No. 3 (1987).

Collège de France. *Propositions pour l'enseignement de l'avenir.* Documentation Francaise, 1985.

Dandoy, D., et P. Monteil - INSEE *Tableaux de l'économie française.* Ed. INSEE, 1988.

Favret, J. M. *Consultation reflexion nationale sur l'école.* Ministère de l'Education Nationale, 1984.

Legrand, L. *Pour un collège démocratique.* La Documentation Française, 1982.

Lesourne, J. *Education et Société - Les défis de l'an 2000.* La Decouverte/Le Monde, n.d.

Prost, A. *Les lycéens et leurs études au seuil de XXIème siècle.* Ministère de l'Education Nationale, n.d.

GABON

by
Lazare Digombe
Director of Higher Education and University Affairs
Ministry of Higher Education and Scientific Research, Gabon

BACKGROUND

Gabon became a French Colony in 1839 and was evangelized by Catholic missionaries: the Holy Ghost priest, Father Bessieux, who later became the First Apostolic Vicar of the Vicarage of the Two Guineas, led the mission and founded in August 1844 the St. Mary's Catholic Mission of Lebreville, now the Archiepiscopacy. The arrival of the missionaries heralded the opening of the first primary and professional schools in Gabon.

Later on, the year 1875 saw the initiation of a secondary school in the context of *Ecole des Latinistes*, a junior college for priests, but it was only at the end of World War II that secondary education institutions were established. First it was the *Collège Catholique Bessieux* in 1949, and then the *Collège Public Moderne* that was later on renamed *Lycée Felix Ebone* and now known as *Lycée National Leon Mba*. When the country became independent in 1960, the need to train at home its university cadre brought about the setting up of the first national university and institutions of higher learning.

On the whole, the development of primary, secondary, and university education has been characterized by national policy of a free and compulsory education for all children of the age group 6-16 years. This has considerably bridged the gap that formerly existed between the school attendance of boys and girls.

PRIMARY AND SECONDARY EDUCATION

Schooling in Gabon is compulsory and free up to sixteen years of age. A good infrastructure of primary schools exist throughout the country with 860 schools enrolling over 150,000 students. The student population is equally divided between males and females, a fact rare in Africa. Free and compulsory schooling coupled with the good infrastructure of schools has resulted in one of the highest literacy rates (90 percent).

Primary education continues for seven years and leads to the *certificat d'études primaires et élémentaires*. Secondary schools are accessible to students who pass the entrance examination for admission to lycees and colleges, (whether they hold the *certificat d'études primaires et élémentaires* or not). Secondary education provides three streams: teacher training, technical, and general.

Teacher training at secondary level is undergoing some reforms now and will be offered at the *écoles normales d'instituteurs* under a four year program leading to the *certificat d'aptitude pédagogique d'instituteurs.* Technical secondary education is provided at the lycees and colleges and is intended to produce specialized tradespeople and technicians. In the professional cycle, the technical colleges offer a four-year program leading to the *certificat d'aptitude professionnel* with options in several technical fields (mechanical technology, building construction, metal work, maintenance, etc.). Various other technical programs *(brevet d'études techniques, brevet de techniciens, etc.)* are also available at technical secondary schools. In the non-professional cycle, the technical lycees offer programs leading to the technical *baccalauréat,* (offered in mathematics and techniques, mechanical construction, electronics, electromechanisms, and civil technology) which provides access to higher education, in related fields. General secondary schools consist of lycees and colleges and studies take seven years leading to the general *baccalauréat* (offered in three branches: literary, scientific, and administrative) which is the basic qualification for admission to higher education.

HIGHER EDUCATION

Until 1970, no higher education institutions were available in the country and students had to be sent to foreign universities. In less than twenty years, Gabon has developed a solid structure of higher education institutions and now almost all the undergraduate needs are met. Only the postgraduate students (for doctorates, etc.) go to overseas institutions. During this period, two universities and several non-university institutions have come into existence. The initiatives of the government in the past and in the present are a bright indication of the future.

The first university to be established is the Omar Bongo University, (established in 1971 as the National University of Gabon, and renamed in 1977 after the head of the state). It has a student population of 2,460 (1987-88) in three faculties: Faculty of Law and Economics; Faculty of Letters and Humanities; and Faculty of Medicine and Health Sciences. The faculties provide a general education spread over three cycles, with the award of a diploma at the end of each cycle. In general, each cycle is of two years duration excepting in the case of medicine.

The Faculty of Law and Economics award the *diplôme universitaire d'études juridiques* or the *diplôme universitaire d'études économiques* at the end of the first cycle (two years). Studies in the second cycle lead to *licence* (third year) or *maitrise* (fourth year). The Faculty of Letters and Humanities, consisting of eight departments, awards the *diplôme universitaire d'études litteraires* at the end of the first cycle (two years). Studies in the second cycle lead to *licence* (third year) or *maîtrise* (fourth year). The Faculty of Medicine offers a short cycle (three years) which prepares for certain careers in allied health fields (laboratory, nursing, etc.) and a long cycle (seven years) in medicine which leads to the Doctor of Medicine degree.

In contrast to the education offered at the faculties, the professional schools *(grand écoles)* of the university provide training that directly lead to a career. In general, access to these schools is through an entrance examination. The *grand écoles* consist of: *Ecole Normale Supérieure* which provide teacher training in two cycles, upper and lower, with the lower cycle (three years) leading to the *certificat d'aptitude de professorat de collèges* and the upper cycle (two more years) leading to the *certificat d'aptitude a l'enseignement secondaire; Ecole Normale Supérieure d'Enseignement Technique* providing teacher training in technical areas with a three year short cycle leading to the *certificat d'aptitude au professorat des collèges d'enseignement technique* and a five year long cycle leading to the *certificat d'aptitude au professorat des lycées techniques; Institut National des Sciences de Gestion,* providing short (two years) and long (four years) program in accounting, finance, marketing etc; and the *Ecole Nationale Supérieure de Secretariat,* providing a three year program in secretarial work leading to a diploma.

The second university to be established in Gabon is the University of Science and Technology at Masuku (1986). It has a student enrollment of 415 (1987-88) and consists of the Faculty of Sciences offering the first cycle (two years) leading to the *diplôme universitaire d'études scientifiques;* and the Polytechnic School offering the first cycle (two years) leading to the diplome de *technicien supérieur* in civil engineering, electrical engineering and a few other fields, as well as a second cycle (five years) leading to the *diplôme d'ingénieur* degree in civil and electronic engineering.

The non-university professional institutions consist of nine *grandes écoles* which come under the Ministry of Higher Education and Scientific Research, and some other state ministries or organizations. About 1,040 students (1987-88) attend these institutions. The programs offered at the non-university institutions vary greatly but in general the training is specialized (administration, forestry, telecommunications, finance, data processing, etc.), varying from 1-4 years (both technician and degree level) and leads to careers in the government.

The Ministry of Higher Education and Scientific and Technological Research is the central authority responsible for universities as well as the national center for scientific and technological research. Each university is governed by a rector assisted by a vice-rector (for education and research) and a secretary general overseeing administration. At the head of each faculty is a dean assisted by a vice-dean (for education and research) and a secretary-general overseeing administrative activities. The *grand écoles* are headed by a director assisted by a director of studies and a secretary-general. The supreme organ responsible for overall governance and policy making within the universities is the university council.

Admission requirement to universities is the *baccalauréat* obtained at the end of secondary studies or an equivalent qualification (working persons over twenty-two years may enter the university by passing a special entrance examination). Local students pay only a very nominal registration fee of US$40 but foreign students are required to pay a tuition of US$600-720 per year. Exemption from tuition is accorded to foreign students, in certain cases (children of expatriate teaching staff, diplomatic personnel, etc.). About 10 percent of the student body, about 2,700 (in 1987-88), consisted of foreign students (Cameroon, Benin, Zaire, Senegal and Congo had the highest number out of over twenty-three countries represented).

Universities are funded by the government. They also receive aid through international cooperation arrangements and from certain large scale enterprises (petroleum and mineral processing companies etc.) within the country. However, higher education institutions in Gabon have serious shortages of scientific literature (reference books, periodicals, etc.), and equipment. In 1988, the government spent 41 percent of the national budget (13,362,983 million of CFA francs) on higher education. Of this expenditure, 83.3 percent went for operating expenses with only 11.7 percent going for capital investment on facilities.

The academic programs (and curriculum) developed by different units of the university require approval of the university council. They are expected to meet three general objectives: provide a university level education; ensure that degrees offered by Gabonese institutions are recognized internationally; and the education is adapted to national (or African) needs, in line with development priorities of the government. In today's environment, it has also become very important to take into consideration the need to orient the programs towards employment with priority to the education of scientific and technical personnel. In addition, it has become imperative to include research as part of the academic curriculum, towards the end of the second cycle of studies (by requiring a research memoir for the award of the degree).

Stemming from the French system, higher education in Gabon does not specifically draw a line between undergraduate and postgraduate levels. The first postgraduate degree (the master) is considered to be the last degree of the second cycle made up of *licence* and *maîtrise* degrees. The other postgraduate degrees form what is normally called the third cycle composed of *diplôme d'enseignement supérieur specialisé (D.E.S.S.), diplôme d'études approfondies (D.E.A.)* and the *doctorats.*

Appointment of teaching staff is governed by a government decree (1981) and the candidates are required to have the *diplôme d'études approfondies* (advanced studies diploma) or *agrégation de l'enseignement secondaire,* for the level of *assistant; doctorat de troisième cycle* for the level of *maître assistant* (assistant professor); and *doctorat d'etat* under the old scheme or *agrégation de l'enseignement supérieur* for the level of *maître de conférences* (associate professor) and professor. In 1986-87, there were a total of 364 university teachers, of whom 44 percent were Gabon citizens. In the same period, the National Center for Scientific and Technological Research had fifty-five researchers, of whom 95 percent were Gabon nationals.

Research

Scientific research, like higher education itself, is of recent origin but more and more effort is being put into this area now to promote it as a tool for socioeconomic and technological development of the country. Scientific research in Gabon takes place within the framework of three types of institutions: university laboratories, laboratories of the National Center for Scientific and Technological Research, and various other research institutions. University laboratories include the Department of Parasitologie where significant research work is being done on disease control, National Archeological Laboratory which is exploring a large number of ancient archeological sites, and the research stations at the *Ecole Polytechnique de Masuku* which study engineering and technology application to local situations. The National Center for Scientific and Technological Research consists of institutes of traditional medicine, humanities, technological research, agronomical and forestry research, and tropical ecology. Other research institutions include two which have received international recognition: *Centre International de Recherches Médicales de Franceville* which studies infectious diseases, reproduction and sterility; and *Centre International des Civilisations Bantu* studying various aspects of Bantu civilization.

Problems in the area of research fall into three categories: First, the main obstacle to progress in research is the absence of an efficient national coordinating body to avoid wastage resulting from duplication of work by different organizations that receive research funds from the same source, the ministry in charge of scientific and technological research. Second, the manner in which funds allocated to universities are managed does not encourage research work to be carried out locally; rather it is more conducive to acquisition of scientific material and for work done abroad (analysis of samples, etc.). Third, lack of involvement of local research institutions in the conception, planning, and implementation of development projects.

ISSUES AND TRENDS

Gabon is a country that has a carefully developed extensive primary and secondary education through a policy of a free and compulsory education for all children of the age group 6-16 years. On the other hand, this seriously contrasts with the existing scanty higher education institutions. The overall orientation has been towards general and literacy studies. The problem now is the passage from a system of general and literacy education that breeds unemployment to a more technical and scientific system that the country direly needs for its economic development. This new orientation is more likely to satisfy firms and industries that are called upon to help absorb the more increasing job seekers.

With regard to higher education, the present preoccupation to resolve the foregoing disparity is also accompanied by the anxiousness to promote quality training that is a sure guarantee for African and international recognition of our national degrees. However, scientific research that has known progress in certain fields like medicine, pharmacopea, archeology, etc. needs to be given more emphasis through a more efficient planning effort, a more developed financing system, and a less bureaucratic management of funds allotted to researchers.

BIBLIOGRAPHY

Digombe, L., et Mombo, J. B. *L'Enseignement supérieur au Gabon, 1970-1987.* Paper presented at the UNESCO seminar, Dakar 4-8 Mai 1987.

Digombe, L. "Le C.I.R.M.F.: 1979-1988. Neuf ans de recherches scientifiques biomedicales." *CIRMF Gabon,* Franceville, 1989.

Hemptine, H. de, et Daguin, J. Y. *République du Gabon. Politique scientifique et technologique, Organisation actuelle et perspectives.* (Technical report) Paris: UNESCO, 1979.

Hemptine, Y. de. *Gabon, services consultatifs dans le domaine des politiques scientifiques et technologiques. Analyse de la situation et des structures actuelles.* (Technical report) Paris: UNESCO, 1987.

Hemptine, Y. de. *Annuire Statistique l'Enseignement supérieur, Année universitaire 1987-1988.* Ministry of Education and Scientific Research, Gabon, 1989.

FEDERAL REPUBLIC OF GERMANY

by
Wilfried Hartmann
Professor, Department of Education
University of Hamburg, FRG

BACKGROUND

Higher education in Germany developed during the medieval times parallel to the establishment of universities in other European countries like Italy and France. The first German university and the first university north of the Alpine mountains was founded in Prague in 1348-49. The first university within the boundaries of today's Federal Republic of Germany was in Heidelberg, founded in 1386. Usually, they were the rulers (very often the emperor or the pope himself) who granted the right to establish a university. The first universities founded by the citizens themselves were the universities of Frankfurt in 1914 and Hamburg in 1919. During the last twenty-five years twenty new universities came into existence, adding new facets to the colorful tapestry woven by institutions of long history and manyfold traditions and connections.

For centuries, the usual program for the students had emphasis on grammar, rhetoric, dialectics, arithmetic, geometry, music, and astronomy. Over the years, the number of subjects and faculties grew, and more and more fields were granted the honor of being subjects at universities. The ideal of having every student studying every subject got lost under Napoleon, when the right of the universities to offer courses in any field suffered a set back with the promotion of the idea to grant individual universities only the right to teach in a limited number of fields as part of the nation-wide imperial university.

When Wilhelm von Humboldt founded a post Napoleon university in Berlin in 1810, he created a model that determined the basis of the German university for more than a century. Humboldt saw the main task of the German university as research and education of a limited number of students. The task of qualifying young people for a profession was only secondary. As the society became industrialized placing a great demand on higher education to train professionals, new types of institutes came into existence and the traditional ideal of the universities underwent a change. The reforms that ensued (even as late as 1968) replaced the traditional faculties by departments *(Fachbereiche)* each of which covers fewer fields of study than the faculties, limiting the chances of professors and students to interact with university members from other fields. Nevertheless, at most universities all students still have the right to sit in any lecture, course, or seminar that is offered, provided room is available.

Today the responsibility for legislation on structure and role of the institutions of higher education lies with the governments of the individual states *(Lander)*, though a federal ministry has the right to ensure a certain common framework. Universities receive funds mostly from the states in which they are located, though the federal government contributes for university construction and expensive research projects of national or international importance. Faculty members and clerical staff are civil servants or government employees of the states. Private and public funding agencies, like the Donators Association of the German Industry or the German Research Society also give grants for research work done by individual scholars and scientists as well as groups. The funding from organizations and industry, though up to now mostly have been distributed through foundations, can be accepted by scholars and scientists only with the approval of their faculty council.

Private universities are an exception. The first (besides the church owned ones that educate priests) was founded as recently as 1982 in a small town called Herdecke in Westphalia and, in 1986, there were altogether 227 students registered at this institution.

PRIMARY AND SECONDARY EDUCATION

In Germany, school attendance is compulsory for twelve years, i.e. 9-10 years (depending on the state) of full-time schooling at general schools, and the rest at least part-time attendance at vocational schools. As all children start primary school at the age of six (after some years of voluntary kindergarten and one year of optional preschool) they are part of the educational system up to the age of eighteen, very often much longer, due to retention and grade repetition or due to an apprenticeship.

All children attend primary school together. There is no differentiation by sex, tracks, or intended careers. Usually 20-30 children are in a class and the classroom teacher teaches most of the subjects.

After four years of primary education, children have the possibility to choose either secondary education at a comprehensive school or a two year probation and observation phase, after which they are placed in one of the three parallel tracks: lower secondary, which is the academically least demanding one *(Hauptschule)* leading to a school leaving certificate after three more years (altogether nine years of schooling); the medium track *(Realschule)* leading to an intermediate certificate after four more years *(Realschulabschluss);* and the highest and most prestigious one *(Gymnasium)* leading to the *Abitur,* the highest type of school leaving certificates which is the qualifications required to enter a university.

Due to the federal structure of the Federal Republic of Germany, the different states have their own ministries of education, issuing their own regulations and curricula, and deciding about the procedures for school leaving examinations. Comparability is ensured by a so-called standing conference of ministers of education and cultural affairs *(Kultusministerkonferenz).* Therefore, no matter how diverse single aspects may seem, the following traits are observed in all the eleven states: The academic year has a duration of about thirty-nine weeks; Courses are normally held in the mornings between about 8A.M. and 2P.M. (Therefore, there are no school   meals offered. The students with the exception of those in some of the comprehensive schools or schools trying to work according to new models, spend their afternoons at home, doing homework for several hours); No tuition fees are charged and practically no boarding schools exist; The language of instruction is German; Students whose mother tongue is not German are taught in their mother tongue (if that is possible) during a transition phase of up to two years.

All teachers are civil servants, appointed by the state's Ministry of Education. Teachers are required to have four years of higher education, two additional years of practical training in schools under the supervision of experienced teachers, and additional courses in methods under the responsibility of the respective ministries of education. They are also required to pass a second state examination after writing a second thesis.

HIGHER EDUCATION

Institutions

In the Federal Republic of Germany, there are 343 institutions of higher education that are called *Hochschulen.* They are of different types.

The universities, including technical universities and other institutions of equivalent standing provide educational programs leading to academic degrees including doctorates (and postdoctoral work) and conduct research. Popular fields of study are economics, medicine, laws, Germanistics, mechanical and process engineering, education, politics and social sciences, biology, electrical engineering, chemistry, physics, astronomy, computer science, mathematics, history, and languages. About 69 percent of all registered students are studying in one of these fifteen fields.

The teacher training institutions *(Padagogische Hochschulen)* train students to become teachers at primary, lower secondary, and special schools. Sometimes these institutions are integrated with universities or departments, where teachers for higher secondary and vocational schools are trained.

The institutes of higher education specializing in certain fields *(Fachhochschulen)* are less research oriented and offer shorter degree courses qualifying professionals to work independently by providing them a practical education with the necessary skills and knowledge. Their graduates usually take up employment but may as well continue studying at academic universities. The fields most popular with the students (96 percent) of these institutions are mechanical and process engineering, economics, electrical engineering, social welfare, architecture and interior decoration, administration and management, constructional engineering, design, computer science, chemistry, survey, horticulture, agricultural science, nutrition and home economics.

The comprehensive universities *(Gesamthochschulen)* combine the functions of all institutions mentioned so far and include schools of art as well. They were newly established in some states or formed by regrouping existing higher education facilities, in the early 1970s. They offer four year academic degree programs as well facilities, in the early 1970s. They offer four year academic degree programs as well as shorter vocational type programs of at least three years duration. Also falling into this category is an institution (located in Hagen, Westphalia) that offers correspondence courses (the only institute to offer such courses). This institution was opened in 1975, and by 1986, the enrollment had reached 18,000 with twenty regional study centers all over the country.

Schools of Art and of Music offer degree courses in artistic and music fields, respectively.

Governance

All institutions of higher education have the right of self-administration. That does mean in practice, that they have the right to decide how to disburse the financial contributions from the state; to develop suggestions from their internal structure, curriculum, and examination regulations; and to hire their own personnel. As state legislations differ among the states of the FRG, and as rights that developed over the years are dealt with in different ways, one cannot easily give a description that fits all institutions of higher education.

In general, however, on top of the structure there is a president or a rector who is responsible only to the minister for education, science, or cultural affairs in that state of the republic where the institution is situated. He is elected by a university council for a fixed number of years (4-8). Re-election is possible in most states. Historically, it used to be a tradition that the rector held the office honorarily and continued with his teaching and research commitments but nowadays most rectors and presidents do their job full time. Usually a vice-president or a vice-rector, elected for a shorter period (one or two years) from among the professors, acts as substitute, whereas a government official, in most cases a life-time civil servant, sometimes called chancellor *(Kanzler),* is the head of the administration. The president or rector on one hand has the right to make his own decisions on certain matters and take responsibility for such action. On the other hand, there are other matters where he has to translate into action the decisions made by elected bodies, like the senate or the council of the university.

This setup, a balance of power and a sharing of responsibilities in academic self-administration between an elected chairperson and an elected council, is repeated with minor changes, but with decreasing independence of decisions, at other levels of the institution such as departments, schools, or faculties, headed by a dean *(Dekan)* or speaker *(Fachbereichssprecher);* and at the institutes, chaired by a director *(Direktor).* Depending on the state, there are variations in the regulations governing the eligibility of members of different groups (professors, lecturers, assistants, clerical staff, and students) for election to various bodies. However, due to federal law, the professors are in majority in different councils. Cooperation between the universities is ensured by a body called *Westdeutsche Rektorenkonferenz* (standing conference of university presidents or rectors in the FRG).

Undergraduate Studies (First Degree)

The basic requirement for admission to German universities is the *Abitur* which is obtained after thirteen years of primary and secondary schooling (certificate of graduation from the *Gymnasium*). The basic requirement for admission to non-university institutions of higher education is called *Fachhochschulreife*, obtainable in different ways (e.g. after ten years of schooling and two years of specialized instruction, or after school, an apprenticeship, and one year of additional schooling). As mentioned earlier, courses at institutions of higher education last at least three years of studies. Therefore the lowest degree obtainable as a rule takes longer than the bachelor degrees from many other countries.

In Germany, the basic idea behind all courses of study is the development of an attitude enabling the students to make the best use of their individual freedom. This begins with the decision on which field to study, and what path to take if one is faced with the choice of waiting for a place or choosing another subject, and continues throughout the course of studies, when students are free to select courses that best meet their plans.

Students desiring admission to universities have to check the latest list of admission restrictions, as entry to certain fields for which there is a great demand (like medicine and dentistry) is centrally coordinated by a Central Clearing House for Admission to Higher Education. Here, the places available for these fields are offered on a competitive basis taking into account not only the average grades achieved during the school leaving examination but also the age, the time that passed since the first application for admission, special social reasons and hardships etc. For medicine, there are additional tests and interviews.

For other subjects like economics, computer science, and law, there is no such restriction but a distribution system guarantees all interested students a place at a German university, but not necessarily in the town of their choice. Only the remaining subjects are under the responsibility of the individual universities' offices of admission.

The academic year at most German universities consists of two semesters of about fourteen weeks of course work each. Remarkable exceptions are the two universities of the armed forces which conduct courses in blocks of three trimesters annually. The students spend the first four semesters in a stage I *(Grundstudium)* consisting of foundation studies. This stage ends with an intermediate examination, called *Vordiplom* in scientific, engineering, and economics subjects and *Zwischenprüfung* in those courses leading to a master's degree or a state examination for the teaching profession. One has to keep in mind that these intermediate examinations are not considered to be degree examinations. They are nothing but proof obtained by sitting in a written *(Klausur)* or oral examination or handing in evidence that one has participated in enough activities of the required types.

With the exception of the courses of study and of the examinations in the medical subjects, which are regulated by a federal law, all other regulations are based on state *(Lander)* legislation.

During the following four or more semesters, the students acquire the necessary knowledge to sit the final examinations. Here again, the academic freedom of choice is the most important feature. Normally nobody will ask a student to register for the final examinations. It is totally up to the students to determine whether they will consider themselves able to pass the examinations. Nobody is pushing them; so you can find students studying in their twentieth semester, though this is not the rule. For all scholarships and bursaries an upper limit of the duration of assistance is defined normally by adding two or three semesters to the shortest time given in the curricula for the completion of studies. The average time students spend at a university is about 6.9 years, with a maximum of 13.1 years for students studying computer science as part of their training as teachers for higher secondary school, 7.8 years for medicine, and down to 3 years for students studying administration at *Fachhochschulen*.

German students take two types of final examinations and consequently receive two categories of degrees. One is called state examination in fields like law, medicine, and teaching. It is given by a board of examiners consisting of professors and state officials from the respective fields like lawyers, members of the school board, or the medical administration. The exam consists of two parts. The first is academic in nature and is followed by a second state examination after a period of about two years of practical in-service training under the guidance of professionals experienced in the relevant field: teachers, lawyers, judges or doctors, etc. It is only this examination that entitles the students to work as fully qualified professionals.

The second type is a master's examination or a diploma: master's degree is given normally in the case of humanities; and the diploma in the case of scientific and engineering studies, economic sciences, psychology, social sciences, and education.

All types of examinations require the students to write an undergraduate thesis in their major subject, sit written examinations under controlled conditions (lasts about five hours), and take part in oral examinations in all their fields of studies (includes practical tests in fields like arts, music, and home economics).

By writing a thesis, the students prove their ability to work independently in a scientific or scholarly subject. During the written parts of the examination, the students are asked to deal with a problem in a limited amount of time, apply the appropriate methods, and suggest a solution. The oral examinations test the students' overall command of their subject and very often the deeper insight in a special field. The exact regulations governing the examinations differ not only from state to state but also from university to university. The language of instruction, as a rule, is German.

Higher educational institutions do not charge any tuition fees either from German or from foreign students. The students have to prove that they have a valid statutory health insurance. They are also required to pay a fee as contribution to cover part of the costs of the student self-government (practiced through a student parliament and a general student council *(Allgemeiner Studentenausschuss)* and the student welfare contribution of about US$20 per term.

Accommodation in halls of residence was never very common in Germany. Today about 10 percent of the students live in dormitories, very often far away from the campus or the inner city area where most of the university buildings are located. Traditionally, students sublet rooms. During the last twenty years, it became more and more common that students rent a flat together and share the expenses.

The costs for board and lodging as well as those for books, writing material, and other material used during their studies (like computer disks or chemicals) are to be paid by the students and amount to about US$350-380 per month (1986).

German students whose parents cannot afford to pay for the costs of their children's studies are generally financed wholly or partially under the Federal Education Promotion Act *(Bundesausbildungsforderungsgesetz)*. They can draw benefits on loans of up to about US$350 per month, which they have to pay back at the end of their studies in monthly instalments. Certain reductions of the debt are granted to students who finish their studies faster or obtain top level grades. In 1986, a total of 244,858 students in higher education received money on this scheme. The average monthly loan for this group amounted to about US$270.

Advanced Studies and Research

As the work for a master's or diploma degree as well as that for a first state examination is considered to be undergraduate work, most of Germany's graduate students are working on their doctoral thesis. One has to keep in mind that at German universities there are no compulsory or prescribed courses for doctoral students. You might even study at home or where you are working for your profession. You will not find a prescribed or recommended program. While working for your doctorate you will experience the loneliness and challenges of academic research. Nevetherless, there will be a professor to give you some hints or discuss the matter with you, but this person is under no obligation to dedicate a specified amount of time to your needs or read a draft, though some of them do that. Normally, it takes between two and four years to complete a doctoral thesis.

The title *Doktor* is conferred on completion of the doctorate. There are four conditions to be fulfilled. First, a minimum time of study of eight semesters altogether, after receiving the school leaving certificate, but at most German universities this is not enough and the successful completion of an undergraduate course with one of the earlier mentioned three degrees (state examination, M.A., diploma) is required. An equivalent degree granted by a foreign university is also accepted. Second, a thesis in which the candidates show that they are able not only to carry independent research but also to develop new approaches, to gain new insight in their fields and contribute to advancement in their subjects. The thesis must receive at least the grade of *Ausreichend* which literally translates as "sufficient" and means "passed" by at least two professors and very often by a jury of up to six or eight examiners. Normally, this dissertation has to be written in German, though on special application, the use of another language that is justified by the topic can be used. Third, an oral examination to defend the thesis and to answer questions related to the candidate's field of studies. Fourth, the publication of the thesis in such a way that the interested scientific or scholarly community will have easy access to the findings.

Living conditions for doctoral students don't differ from those for undergraduates. A limited number of research assistantships are given to students for about three years. Research assistants are required to assist professors in their work for about twenty hours per week for which they will be paid and use the remaining time for work on the dissertation. There are some scholarships offered to those with very high grades.

Postgraduate work can also be undertaken to qualify in additional fields, such as building a connection between two or more different fields of study like law and psychology, biology and medicine, Islamic studies and education, just to mention a few.

Teaching appointments at universities require an additional examination, called *Habilitation* based on a thesis. This thesis must not only give new insight into the field of research but also push forward the boundaries of the land of knowledge, methods and understanding, into the ocean of learning, in such a way that others will be able to work with their research and doctoral dissertations on that reclaimed land. The thesis has to be discussed with scholars and scientists from related faculties and departments. Researchers who have successfully passed this examination are, on application, honored with the title *Privatdozent* and gain the right to teach at the university, even when they are not gainfully employed university members.

Research in the Federal Republic of Germany falls into three areas: universities, non-university research institutions, and industry.

At most of our universities, the professors are independent researchers. Research work is part of their duties and rights. It is totally at their discretion whether to form research groups with others or to work on their own. Neither the directors of the institutes nor the deans of the faculties have a legal right to prescribe the direction of research. In the basic law *(Grundgesetz)* of the Federal Republic (equivalent to a constitution), it is stated that the fine arts and all scholarly research and teaching is free. Nevertheless limits are established due to financial restraints, as institute and faculty councils have to decide on the distribution of the annual budget, and set priorities. In contrast to the situation in many other countries, there is no obligation to publish results regularly and nobody will control the amount of research work actually done. The personal sense of responsibility is the only guide-line for the researcher. No personal allowance or increase of the salary depends on published work. But the chances to receive additional money from foundations or from the restricted funds of institutes or departments are better for successful researchers.

As expensive and long-range research undertaking cannot be handled by part-time researchers, there is a second area to be looked at. For these tasks, often in the natural sciences, one cannot manage without teamwork and large scale equipment. Therefore the federal government funds institutions doing scientific research work on nuclear energy, aerospace, medicine, molecular biology, etc. (and to a smaller extent work in the humanities). In addition, the Max Planck Society for the Advancement of Science with sixty-three research institutes of its own, support work in science and humanities. The third area is industrial research in large enterprises as well as in medium sized companies.

Altogether about 395,000 people are working and 2.8 percent of the total Gross Domestic Product is annually spent for research.

ISSUES AND TRENDS

Up to the end of the 1950s and the beginning of the 1960s, only 8-12 percent of an age cohort did successfully finish higher secondary education. And not more than about 6-8 percent decided to study at universities. Under the heading *Bildungskatastrophe* (disastrous situation of learning, culture and knowledge), a campaign was started to allow more students from all social groups to gain access to better education and better chances in life. The results have been very significant: students at universities and other institutions of higher education increased to about 20 percent (data from 1986); female students rose from 27 to 40 percent (at universities from 34 to 44 percent) between 1960 and 1986; and students from working class families rose from 4 percent in 1952 to 17 percent in 1985. By 1986, there were 1,053,595 students at universities and colleges (including 63,159 foreigners) and 311,007 students at specialized institutions (including 14,215 foreigners).

As demonstrated by the hefty increase of female and wage earner family students, the campaign for democratization of the higher education was very successful but the success also led to three serious consequences. First, the critics claim that not all the students now admitted to the academically more demanding tracks of secondary education or to universities are really capable of studying with the necessary intensity resulting in a decrease in the standard of education. Though there is no evidence for this assumption, it plays an important role in political discussions, especially in connection with the suggestion to make the comprehensive school as the only school type. Second, there are the problems connected with increased enrollment. Third, the students who have successfully passed their final university or college examinations are faced with a situation of unemployment as there are not enough vacant positions available for professionals. Today statistics show up to 60,000 unemployed teachers in Germany and the trend indicates that the other professions will encounter a similar situation in the near future.

After the changes that took place in the German Democratic Republic it is difficult to foresee the further development. On one hand, there is a high demand for cooperation and information in the field of education. Most schools and higher education institutions are interested in partnerships and the exchange of ideas and personnel. That might be a chance for unemployed professionals from West Germany. On the other hand, many of the East German institutions from kindergarten to universities and research academies are overstaffed and suffer from forty years of information restriction and lack of technical support. Therefore it is hard to imagine that all these professionals will be able to compete and keep their jobs and it seems more likely that many of them will add to the number of unemployed.

BIBLIOGRAPHY

Boehm, L., and Muller, R. A. *Universitäten und Hochschulen in Deutschland, Österreich und der Schweiz.* Dusseldorf, 1983.

Der Bundesminister fur Bildung und Wissenschaft, Grund-und Strukturdaten 1987-88. Bonn, 1987.

Deutscher Hochschulfuhrer 1982. 52nd ed., Stuttgart, 1982.

Deutscher Akademischer Austauschdienst (DAAD). *Studies at Universities.* Bonn, 1982.

Deutscher Akademischer Austauschdienst (DAAD). *Academic Studies in the Federal Republic of Germany.* Bonn, 1986.

Eggers, P., Lichtenberg, P., and Burckhardt, J., eds. *Hochschulgesetze des Bundes und der Länder.* Bad Honneff, 1972.

Vademecum deutscher Lehr-und Forschungsstätten. *Handbuch des Wissenschaftlichen Lebens.* Essen, 1977.

EAST GERMANY

(former German Democratic Republic)

by
Jurgen Knoop
and
Eberhard Mannschatz
Professors, Department of Pedagogics
Humboldt University, East Germany

(Author's note: Since this article was first written, Germany has undergone dramatic political changes. The reunification of the two Germanies became a reality in 1990 and the educational system will consequently undergo change, following the example of West Germany. The forty-year endeavors by the German Democratic Republic will be part of history. Time will tell which positive factors in the development of the educational system will prevail and what needs to be discarded. This article, however, will be of interest as a historical discourse. The German Democratic Republic phase cannot be eliminated from history).

STRUCTURE OF EDUCATION

The present structure of education in the German Democratic Republic (G.D.R.) is based on the Education Act of 1965. The ten-form (ten year) secondary school providing general and polytechnical education is compulsory for all children in the country. Children enter the ten-form secondary school at the age of six, after three years in the preschool (creche).

There are several options open to students who complete the ten-form school: a vocational training of mostly two years leading to qualification as skilled worker (about 80 percent of the students take this route); the two-year extended secondary school which is completed by taking one's "A" level (Abitur) which is a prerequisite for admission to university level studies; vocational training coupled with "A" level studies, which enable the students to qualify as a skilled worker as well as attain the academic standard required for university entrance (this course of training lasts three years and is chosen especially by those young people who want to study in a technical field later); attendance at technical schools where nurses, medical laboratory assistants, creche educators, nursery school teachers, teachers for forms 1-4 and librarians are trained within three or four years.

The educational system offers students many possibilities of moving from one stage to another, thus avoiding dead ends, and ensuring a close relationship between general and vocational education. At the same time, there is enough diversity in the system to take account of society's needs as well as individual capabilities and talents.

All education establishments in the country are state run. Essentially they come under the jurisdiction of four government bodies: the Ministry of Health (creches); the Ministry of Education (kindergartens, schools providing general education, adult education centers, schools for the training of nursery school teachers); the State Secretariat of Vocational Training; and the Ministry of Higher and Technical Education. There are no private schools in the G.D.R. Churches and religious communities have no influence on the educational system. The associations of the church are active in the care of handicapped children (Protestant priests are educated at state universities and nurses for hospitals of the church are trained at medical schools).All education and training activities are based on government policy and guidelines applicable nationwide. Education is free at all levels. As in the case of ten-form schools, teaching curricula, teaching programs, textbooks, and teaching aids are prepared by pedagogic scientists, teachers, and educators of various fields. These must, however, be approved by the Ministry of Education, before implementation nationally. At present, a new system of teaching curricula is being prepared for all classes and subjects and will be introduced by 1990. The new curricula aim at improving students' abilities to master the basic knowledge challenging their intellects to find creative solutions to problems, and enhancing moral development.

The Ministry of Higher and Technical Education is responsible for all activities related to colleges and technical schools. It directs and coordinates planning, staffing, admissions, training, research, employment of students who graduate, and funding. There are uniform regulations applicable nationwide, covering contents of courses for various fields, duration of the courses, and examinations. All institutions follow the standard academic year from September to August. Pedagogical research that guides curriculum development and other areas is carried out by the Academy of the Pedagogical Sciences, the Central Institute of Vocational Education, the Central Institute of University Education, the Institute of Technical School Education as well as by universities and colleges. The funding for education comes from the national budget, and it has consistently increased over the years.

PREUNIVERSITY STUDIES

Basic prerequisites for university or college studies is the "A" level (Abitur) or a certificate equivalent to the "A" level. The proportion of pupils who enter from the ten-form secondary school to establishments leading to the "A" level or (corresponding level) is based on the needs of the economy. This approach guarantees that the right to education and the right to work are guaranteed. Special attention is paid to measures which serve to achieve coherence between social requirements and personal interests, wishes and capabilities of the applicants. Advice and information are provided to students abundantly during their middle and upper level classes at the secondary schools and later as well. Approximately 16 percent of the pupils go for the "A" levels immediately after having completed the tenth form. The ratio of the number of applicants seeking admission to universities to the number of places available is about 1.4.

About 65 percent of the students who want to get their "A" level attend the two year extended secondary school after having completed the tenth form. This is the main route to acquiring the academic standard required for university entrance. Another 25 percent complete a three-year vocational training connected with the "A" level. This takes place in the "A" level classes of the vocational schools, and while getting their "A" level the pupils pass simultaneously an examination as skilled workers. This kind of combination of vocational training and preparation for college or university studies is possible for eighty-six professions. This form of education aims at preparing young people for careers for which a combination of university studies and technical training are particularly helpful as in the case of instructors in vocational training, agricultural sciences and economic subjects. In the course of the three years at school, 40 percent of the lessons are apportioned to subjects providing general education, 12 percent to theoretical vocational subjects and 48 percent to practical vocational training.

Other avenues open to students to acquire their "A" level include preparatory courses at colleges and classes of the adult evening programs. There are also special schools that are oriented towards mathematics or scientific subjects, languages, music, dancing, sports, and performing arts.

The educational establishments which prepare students specifically for university entrance ("A" level) have a uniform curricula. This general education is aimed at developing and consolidating the basic capabilities of the young people to acquire knowledge independently and to extend and stabilize basic knowledge and skills in important subjects including German language and literature, Russian and one other foreign language, mathematics, physics, chemistry, biology, civics, and sports. Practical work take a special place in the curriculum. At the same time, the lessons in optional subjects are intensified and the extra curricular activities are utilized to the farthest possible extent, to give the pupils, the broadest range of education.

The practical scientific work at extended secondary schools has proved to be a very effective preparation for university and college entrance. On the basis of the needs of different branches of national economy small groups of pupils work at tasks that are part of the science and technology plan of the respective enterprise to which the pupils are assigned. Activities are supervised by qualified staff of the enterprise. This subject is a continuation of the polytechnical lessons at the ten-form schools but represents a higher level.

State scholarships and grants are awarded to students (after their sixteenth birthday) towards meeting their living costs. Since 1981 improved regulations have been in force. A new regulation awards financial support for all pupils of "A" level classes: 110 Marks in the eleventh form and 150 Marks in the twelfth form, monthly. The pupils of the "A" level classes of the vocational schools get a trainee's pay between 120 and 200 marks monthly.

HIGHER EDUCATION

Institutions

The highest educational establishments in the G.D.R. are the universities, colleges, medical academies, schools of engineering, and technical schools. These educational establishments consist of two categories: universities, colleges and academies; and engineering and technical schools.

The first category, universities, colleges, and academies comprise fifty-four institutions: nine universities (three of which are technical universities) with a wide range of disciplines; five technical colleges, and eleven schools of engineering; three medical academies; two agricultural colleges; two colleges teaching economic sciences; one academy of political science and jurisprudence; nine pedagogical colleges; eleven cultural and artistic colleges; and one college of physical education and sports. The enrollment in these institutions is about 130,000 students. As important centers of science, research, education and culture, they train qualified staff to meet the needs of the society, provide continuing education to those who are already employed, and produce new generations of academics. The universities and colleges also have at their disposal a relatively large proportion of the entire research potential of the GDR. In their research work, the universities and colleges cooperate with institutes of the Academy of Sciences as well as with public enterprises.

Some of the universities and colleges have many years of eventful history: the Karl Marx University of Leipzig founded in 1419, the Ernst Moritz Arndt University of Griefswald, founded in 1456, the Freidrich Schiller University of Jena, founded in 1558, and the Humboldt University of Berlin founded in 1810. The education in technical fields and in the field of coal and steel industry began to develop outside the universities. The mining college of Frieberg (1765) is the oldest college of the world in the field of coal and steel industry. The Technical University Dresden of today was founded in 1828 as a "technical education establishment".

The basic unit of organization at the university or college is the department. The department oversees a group of individual disciplines in a given field of studies. All teachers, scientific collaborators, students, workers, and employees are equal members of each respective department and have equal obligations. The department is headed by a director elected from the circle of professors and formally appointed by the vice- chancellor for a five year term of office.

The head of the institution is a vice-chancellor (rector) who is elected from among the professors by the scientific council of the establishment and confirmed by the Ministry of Higher and Technical Education, for a period of three years. The scientific council consists of members of the teaching staff, scientific collaborators, and students elected by the assemblies of the departments for a period of three years.

The Ministry of Higher and Technical Education empowers the universities and colleges, the degree granting authority and the requirement for the award of degrees are established by law. The first degree is a master's (diploma) and is followed by a doctor's degree in a given field or Doctor of Science.

The second category of higher education establishments include the schools of engineering and the technical schools. These are establishments which (usually in shorter programs of studies) produce specialists with application-oriented scientific knowledge, for putting scientific, technical, technological, economic and social findings into practice. Contents and design of the studies at technical schools are very closely related to practice.

The schools of engineering and technical schools continue a tradition that began already in Germany in the eighteenth and nineteenth centuries when industrial development required technicians and engineers who were educated and trained at these schools. They emerged from former trade schools, mining schools, building and construction, agricultural as well as spinning and weaving schools. Even today, there is a continuing need for specialists having a higher level of qualification than a skilled worker but not necessarily a person graduated from a university or college. These specialists are called "mid-level" staff. The students of technical schools start their education either after having successfully completed the tenth form (medical and pedagogic schools) or after having completed a vocational training (economic and technical schools). As a rule, the direct studies last three years (for lower school teachers four years). Approximately 170,000 students are studying at the 239 technical schools at present. The studies at a technical school are completed by an examination, one part of which is a final thesis which has to be defended. The person having completed a technical school is entitled to bear the professional designation awarded by the state, e.g. engineer, economist, dental technician, secondary school teacher, etc. The schools of engineering and technical schools are managed basically in the same manner as universities and colleges.

Admission Requirements

Minimum requirements for admission to first degree programs at the universities is the "A" level (Abitur). There are a number of fields of study that require a basic practical knowledge. For this reason, all students who want to study n the fields of medicine, agricultural sciences, and technical, economic, and other disciplines are required to complete a one-year practical course at the beginning of the studies if they have not already completed a vocational training program. Approximately 80 percent of the young people who have done the "Abitur" are admitted to take up the studies they had chosen as their first preference. There are no entrance examinations, except in very few fields such as artistic ones.

The number of university/college places (for new students) in various fields are planned based on the needs of the national economy. A commission consisting of college and university teachers, members of youth organization, and representatives of trade unions oversee the selection of candidates, taking into consideration, students qualifications, structure of the population, social needs, and the number of openings. There are more than 270 disciplines of university/college studies to which applicants may be admitted.

The decision is always based heavily on the overall quality of the applicant: the results so far achieved at school, the social activities, talents that have become noticeable, and other characteristics. Admission decisions attempt to ensure that no social class or strata is put at a disadvantage. For decades, about 55 percent of the students studying at colleges and universities have been children of workers or peasants.

Programs and Degrees

Depending on the discipline, the period of study for the first degree lasts 4-6 years. The contents of education, in essence, are characterized by three elements: general basic education covering a broad range of subjects; subject related basic education in one basic discipline; and special education according to the special aims of the respective field of study. The studies start with a relatively wide basic education followed by a more and more increasing specialization.

In all fields of study, the students complete their philosophical, economic, and political as well as ideological education by a systematic study of Marxism/Leninism. Two foreign languages and sports are also compulsory for all students. A student decides, mostly during his third year of study, for a scientific specialization. Later on, it is in this field that he writes his master's thesis under the supervision of university teachers or scientific collaborators of the university or college.

In order to guarantee principles such as the unity of teaching and research, and of theory and practice, the students are encouraged to do independent scientific work as early as possible and they are more and more included in the research tasks of their teachers. Practical courses, some of which are held outside the institutions (in industrial or agricultural enterprises and in various pedagogic, social, or cultural establishments, or in hospitals) provide opportunities for the students to show their knowledge and abilities. Research tasks fulfilled by groups of students have also proved to be of significant benefit.

The basis of the master's degree (diploma) is a written scientific work. By this thesis, the student has to prove that he is able to fulfill a task independently and that he can tackle theoretical and practical problems scientifically and without assistance. The master's thesis is defended in public before a committee of experts. Study at a university or college is completed by the state examination or by the master's degree. The person having graduated from a university or college is thus entitled to bear the thus acquired professional designation.

The study community is organized by grouping the students in seminar groups. Normally, there is a number of seminar groups for each field of study every year. Each group gets a seminar adviser. Pedagogically experienced collaborators, university teachers and lecturers of the respective discipline are charged with this task. Otherwise, the students deal with their affairs themselves. They send their representatives to all university committees and boards. They are included in consultations on development and research affairs and affairs concerning college or university life. They run their halls of residence and clubs themselves.

In the G.D.R. the students live in social welfare. Studies are free of costs. All receive a monthly grant of at least 200 marks, that need not be paid back. In addition, students can earn extra scholarships based on good results. Since the prices of basic food, services, and tariffs have remained stable and low for decades it is not customary to have a job besides the study. A student hostel room costs 10 marks per month (this refers to 75 percent of all students); the maximum price of a canteen lunch is 1 mark; social insurance and medical care are free; and an additional child allowance of 60 marks per child per month is given. The students of all disciplines have at their disposal reference and specialist books for all basic fields of study for which the state provides extensive subventions. The constant improvement in the studying and living conditions is demonstrated by the fact that about 85 percent of all student taking up direct studies complete them successfully.

The medium of instruction at all educational institutions in the G.D.R. is German.

Foreign citizens are admitted to studies in the G.D.R. through delegation by their home authorities. Basis of the distribution of university and college places are international agreements as well as agreements with social organizations of other countries and international organizations. Individual applications are accepted only from those foreign citizens who have their permanent residence in the G.D.R. The applicants for a university or college study must have a certificate that would entitle them to university studies in their home country. As education at universities and colleges is imparted in German, foreign students who do not have a sufficient command of the German language and who cannot learn it in their home country are provided preparative language courses (one year).

Adult Education and Advanced Studies

The continuation of education after school and vocational training is a constantly growing social need. Institutions, enterprises, scientific societies as well as organizations make available a variety of opportunities in this area. Most of the enterprises have established their own "works academies" the courses of which are designed to meet the interests of the employees as well as that of the enterprise. Every year, more than 1.6 million workers and employees continue their education in such courses which are offered free.

Universities and colleges have introduced special courses accessible to all citizens and offered free of charge. Lectures are held on Sundays where important scientists report on their research work and there are evening courses for students of all disciplines as well as for the public. At some universities "veterans' universities" were established considering the educational interests of older citizens.

The highest form of adult education is a correspondence degree course at a university, college, or technical school leading to the graduation or technical school leaving certificates. Also, an already completed study can be extended by postgraduate studies. This form of education is accomplished by the employees while continuing their employment. For this purpose their respective enterprises render generous assistance, e.g. up to forty-eight study days at full pay per year and exemption from work for several weeks for the elaboration of final theses or written works. Postgraduate programs consists of research, short courses, intensive courses, and scientific lectures or seminars. The universities and colleges have the special burden of educating specialists with higher academic degrees and producing the new generation of academics. The traditional form of research assistantship, has been supplemented with additional research positions. Moreover, every citizen who has passed the required examinations and who fulfills the preconditions required for doing a doctorate has the right to submit the results of his independent research work to the scientific council and to apply for the opening of a regular doctorate procedure.

Normally, research studies towards a doctorate starts immediately after the completion of the regular study and lasts three years. Each student doing research studies gets a basic grant of 500 marks. The applicant must submit his doctor's thesis to the scientific council. By this thesis the author establishes that he is able to carry out a socially and scientifically important task at a high theoretical level. As a rule, the thesis is judged by three experts. If the majority of the reports is positive, the scientific council decides on the acceptance of the thesis and appoints a commission for the public defence of the thesis. Public defenses of theses represent an important part of the scientific life of the universities and colleges. The scientific council decides on the award of the doctor's degree on the recommendation given by the commission for the public defence.

Similar to this is the procedure for awarding the third academic degree, the Doctor of Sciences, which corresponds to qualifying as a university lecturer. Here, an essentially higher standard of scientific qualification has to be established. Both dissertations are requirements in a university lecturer's career.

ISSUES AND TRENDS

The standard of general education and professional qualifications which has been achieved has led to an education potential which is of great importance for the development of the modern productive forces. More than 85 percent of all working people in the G.D.R. are vocationally qualified: 21 percent of them have graduated from a technical school, university, or college; 64 percent are master craftsmen or skilled workers. The permanent unfolding of the intellectual powers of the people is the only inexhaustible reserve of progress of all productive forces of the society. Man still remains the main productive even in an age of microelectronics. The orientation of education and vocational qualifications to the practical requirements of modern productive forces and to the ideal of an all round development of personality do not conflict with one another but represent a dialectical unity. In the eighties, the task of the best possible development of the aptitudes and capabilities of every young person came into the center of educational policy. In the educational system too, trends of development that had been characteristic of a mainly expansive economic growth were succeeded by trends directed towards intensive production. For this reason, the structure of qualifications which has evolved in the G.D.R. will change only gradually in the foreseeable future.

There is however a demand on colleges and universities to develop their position and role as the centers of science, high-standard education and culture in an all-round way. A change in the structure of performance and achievements is taking place in the direction of high standard research. The ability of higher and technical education to adapt and react to the dynamic, differentiated and changing requirements of the social, economic, scientific, and technical development has to be augmented especially by a more profound theoretical, methodological, and subject-specific education. And high theoretical demands has to be linked to the shaping of abilities and capabilities in practical application and utilization of scientific findings. This implies an intensified differentiation of education in the courses of study. In order to meet the requirements resulting from the development of science and technology, more than 1,200 teaching programs were revised and introduced, from 1981 to 1985. Microelectronics, automation engineering, biotechnology, and data processing are increasingly included in the education system.

BIBLIOGRAPHY

Hoffman, A., and G. Mehlhorn. *Ich bin Student.* Berlin: VEB Deutscher Vergal der Wissenschaften, 1983.

Klingberg, L., et als. *Zu Erfahrungen und Problemen des Unterrichts in der Abiturstufe.* Berlin: Volk und Wissen Volkseigener Verlag, 1975.

Kraus, A., et als. *Hochschulbildung in der DDR.* Berlin: Hausverlag der Deutschen Staatsbibliothek, 1978.

Schulz, H. J., et als. *Das Hochschulwesen der DDR - ein Überblick.* Berlin: Deutscher Verlag der Wissenschaften, 1980.

Schulz, H. J. *Die Hoch-und Fachschulbildung in der DDR.* Berlin: Institut für Hochschulbildung, 1981.

Statistisches Taschenbuch der DDR 1988. Berlin: Publishing House: Staatsverlag der DDR, 1988.

GHANA

by
Nathaniel K. Pecku
former Dean, Faculty of Education
University of Cape Coast, Ghana

BACKGROUND

Education in Ghana before the fifteenth century was wholly traditional and informal. The young were taught the skills necessary for survival in the environment: parents and other adults achieved this through observation, verbal instruction, and imitation. Formal education started in the early sixteenth century with the arrival of European traders (Portuguese, Dutch, and English) on the coast. Schools were initially opened in the castles on the coast for *mulattoes* (children of Europeans, and African women) to train them as interpreters and clerks for their trading activities. Schools were then small, uncertain and intermittent. The situation improved in the nineteenth century when the missionaries (Basel, Wesleyan, Bremen, and Catholic) got involved in education as a means of evangelism. They expanded primary education from the coast to the rural communities in other regions of the country.

Government participation in education developed slowly from 1852. Government set up a Board of Education in 1852 to administer grants-in-aid to the missions. This inaugurated co-operation between the government and the missions. A revolution occurred in education when Governor Gordon Guggisberg, the then colonial governor promulgated his famous "Sixteen Principles of Education" which emphasized teacher training, technical education, and the establishment of the first state secondary school in the country. Another significant influence on educational development was the visit of the Phelps-Stokes Committee which suggested education related to the environment. Secondary education was started by the Basel and Wesleyan missionaries. By 1930 three secondary schools of note were being run by the government, and Wesleyan and Anglican churches. Many privately owned secondary schools sprang up in different parts of the country by 1935.

Demand for secondary education increased and government paid grants-in-aid to some of the schools. 1951 marked another milestone in educational development. An accelerated Development Plan was then introduced by an all African cabinet which had assumed reins of power then. It expanded educational facilities and made primary education free and later compulsory. The plan also restructured the rest of the elementary school. Secondary education was also expanded to take account of the growing numbers from primary schools. Curriculum in both primary and secondary schools was highly academic.

Higher education in Ghana is usually referred to as tertiary education. The development and expansion of higher education is a recent phenomenon in the country. Higher education commenced with the establishment of some few undergraduate programs at Achimota Secondary School in Accra in the early 1940s. Some science courses (undergraduate level) were then offered at the school. The majority of those eligible for higher education studied overseas, mainly in Europe.

The British colonial government set up the first university institution, the University College of the Gold Coast (now University of Ghana), in Ghana (then Gold Coast) in 1948. Two other universities, the University of Science and Technology and the University of Cape Coast, were founded in 1952 and 1965 respectively. They both began as institutions of higher learning and became universities in 1961 and 1972 respectively. Other tertiary institutions sprang up rapidly as and when the need arose: the Institute of Journalism, the Institute of Professional Studies, the Ghana Institute of Journalism, the Institute of Professional Studies, the Ghana Institute of Languages; five polytechnics; and five diploma awarding colleges for higher qualifications in education (below the degree level). Most of these institutions of higher education were established after 1952 when an all Ghanian cabinet took over the reins of government in the country. More progress was made in the provision of higher education after the country had gained independence. Progress was made because the country then had adequate financial resources to support educational expansion.

Government control of the universities is exercised through the university councils which are chaired by government appointees. A university council is composed of government nominees (3), representative of the academic staff (1), university convocation (1), university supporting staff (1), and students (1). The council constitute the governing bodies of the university. The vice-chancellor, the senate, and the academic boards decide on academic matters but they seek approval of their
university council.

PRIMARY AND SECONDARY EDUCATION

Primary Education

Primary education in Ghana lasts for six years: primary 1-6. Pupils start school at the age of six and most of them finish at the age of eleven years. The dropout rate is high. Many of the schools are managed by the churches but the state pays all salaries and supplies equipment to the schools. Pupils also pay nominal fees for books which are supplied by the government. Primary education is expected to be compulsory but the government is unable to enforce this regulation because schools are not available everywhere. Local languages are used during the first three years of primary schools but English language becomes the medium of instruction in the fourth year and after. Some schools are run by private entrepreneurs who are able to provide better facilities in most cases. From the primary schools some pupils do additional two years in middle school before transferring to a secondary school. Most pupils from primary school continue for four years in middle schools to complete their elementary education. Middle school education is terminal for most pupils. Some may continue in technical, business, and other vocational institutions. Primary education is now part of a nine-year basic education program.

Secondary education

Secondary education in Ghana is a five year cycle (form 1-5); a few schools run a two year university program known as the sixth form. Entry to the secondary schools is by a national examination known as the Common Entrance Examination. Normally less than 25 percent of pupils who take the examination gain admission although more than double that percentage would have passed the examination. The academic year starts in September and ends between the end of June and mid-July. Each year is divided into three terms with school breaks for short holidays during Christmas and Easter.

All secondary schools have a very similar curriculum. A few secondary and technical schools offer both general and technical education. Some schools (a small number) have an extended program that includes technical drawing and other technical subjects. The common curriculum for most schools include arts and science subjects. There has been a trend in the last ten years or so to add a business education option in some schools. Lack of facilities for adequate science education compels many schools to emphasize arts subjects.

Students are required to study all subjects during the first three years (form 1-3) and start specialization in the four year (form four). Course content (syllabus) for the first three years may not be uniform at all schools but all schools follow a common syllabus for the last two years in preparation for the General Certificate of Education (G.C.E.) Ordinary Level examinations. It is often argued that the curricula of secondary schools in the country are dictated by the examination syllabuses of the West African Examinations Council (WAEC), the examining body for English-speaking West Africa. The two year preuniversity course (sixth form) beyond the fifth year, prepares students for the G.C.E. Advanced Level examinations.

Most of the schools are state schools where tuition is free and teachers are paid by government. Students pay nominal fees for books and parents pay about 90 percent of the board and lodging fees. These fees are controlled by the state, and school authorities consider them inadequate. Current government policy is to discourage having board and lodging facilities at schools. Fees are high in the few privately owned secondary schools in the country. Most of the schools which were originally founded and managed by religious bodies are now under state control.

The medium of instruction in the schools is English Language. French is compulsory in some schools and some students study local languages such as Twi, Fante, Ga, Dagbani and Ewe. Teachers generally hold a first degree but diploma holders (qualification just below the degree) also teach the lower forms. Teaching is usually not an attractive profession because the conditions of service are somewhat poor. Science and mathematics teachers are scarce. The universities sometimes have problems filling all vacancies in science subjects.

A secondary school is usually under the administration of a headmaster or headmistress who is assisted by two assistant heads, one for administration and the other for academic affairs. Residential houses are supervised by housemasters or housemistresses who administer the day to day affairs of the house. A form master or mistress appointed for each class in the school supervises the non-teaching activities for the class. Each school has a governing board which oversees the administration of the school. Each school has a number of subject departments which are supervised by the heads of departments. Overall control over secondary schools is vested in a director of secondary education at the headquarters of the Ghana Education Service. Decisions affecting schools in each administrative region is taken by the regional director of education who has an overview of all school in a given region.

Although one may complain about educational opportunities, standards and facilities in the country, Ghana's system is one of the best on the African continent. The nature of secondary education in Ghana will start changing by September 1990 when the new senior secondary schools are established. Access to secondary education will increase and a more diversified curriculum will be available. Residential secondary schools will also be reduced in number.

HIGHER EDUCATION

Institutions

The higher education institutions in Ghana consist of universities, polytechnics, diploma awarding colleges, and professional institutions. The universities constitute the highest level of education in the country. There are three universities in the country each with a specific mission. The University of Science and Technology (UST), initially Kwame Nkrumah University of Science and Technology (1961-66), specializes mainly in theoretical and professional courses in science and technology. Situated at Kumasi in the heart of the forest zone, the University of Science and Technology also has courses in fine arts and social sciences to compliment the science and technology faculties. In all, the university has seven faculties, a school devoted to medical sciences, three institutes, and a board of graduate studies. In addition it has centers for land administration research, technology consultancy, and cultural studies. The faculties are for agriculture, engineering, architecture, pharmacy, science, social science and art. The institutes specialize in mining engineering, renewable natural resources, and technical education. Most department of the university offer four-year degree programs. They also offer diplomas and certificate courses which are below degree level and which last 1-3 years, depending on the program. The Faculty of Social Science and the School of Medical Sciences provide three- year degree programs in social science and human biology respectively. Many departments offer two-year graduate programs. Doctoral programs are at the planning stage. The University of Science and Technology has many professional programs in various fields. The Consultancy Center is recognized nationally for its contribution to industrial development in the country.

The oldest university in the country is the University of Ghana (UG) situated at Legon, a suburb of Accra. It is a liberal arts and science university with professional courses in law, medicine, business administration, and nursing. There are faculties of science, arts, law, social studies, and agriculture. In addition it has three schools: School of Medicine, School of Administration, and School of Performing Arts. The institutes of the university include the Regional Institute for Population Studies, the Institute of African Studies, the Institute for Social Statistical and Economic Research, and the Institute of Adult Education.

The youngest and smallest university institution in Ghana is the University of Cape Coast (UCC) which has sole responsibility to train teachers and educational administrators for schools, training colleges, and administrative institutions in the country. UCC has four faculties: science, social science, arts and education. It is proposed to establish a Faculty of Agriculture in the near future. The university has two institutes (the Institute of Education and the Institute for Educational Planning and Administration) and the Center for Development Studies which is engaged in development research. Each faculty offers courses taught in the preuniversity institutions so as to equip students for their future role in the schools and colleges. All students attending UCC study education as a subject and acquires practical teaching experience as part of their course requirement. It is the only university in the country that offers degree programs in commerce and secretaryship; these courses are therefore heavily subscribed.

Almost all the higher education institutions were established by the government which continues to finance all of them through annual subventions. The universities receive their grants direct from the government but the polytechnics and other postsecondary institutions are funded through the relevant government ministries (for example, institutions for health education receive their grants from the Ministry of Health and those for education receive theirs from the Ministry of Education). Although government provides funds for higher education it does not dictate or impose curricula on these institutions. Curricula for the universities are approved by the academic boards and senates of individual institutions. In the case of postsecondary institutions, the institutions themselves as well as special committees of the respective ministries workout curricula. However, the government, through the appropriate ministries decides on the subject areas to be emphasized. The universities have the right to propose relevant areas of study for their study programs.

Administration of these institutions is the responsibility of the heads of individual institutions: vice-chancellors in the case of the universities; and principals and directors in the case of polytechnics and other higher institutions. The vice-chancellors are assisted by the academic boards and senates in the universities. The non-university institutions have their own committees and boards which assist the heads of the institutions.

Faculties in the universities are headed by deans who are elected by the academic staff of the faculty from among the heads of departments and professors of the faculty. The dean is the chairman of the faculty board which regulates teaching, study and research within the faculty. The faculty boards are made up of heads of departments and elected members from the departmental boards of the faculty.   Each department of a faculty is under the direction of a head of department. He is advised by a departmental board comprising the academic staff of the department. In essence the academic structure at the university rises from the departmental boards through the faculty to the academic boards and the senate, with the final approval coming from the respective councils. Academic work is also regulated through university-wide committees such as the academic planning committees and committees on higher degrees or boards of graduate studies.

Administratively, the university registrar is the head of the administration and advises the vice-chancellor on administrative matters. The registrar is assisted by a team of deputy registrars for academic affairs, administration and other functions as appropriate; and assistant registrars who are responsible for various aspects of administration such as admissions, municipal services, academic affairs, transport, and personnel. Although the administrative structure is the same for all three universities, the administrative sections or units may differ from one institution to another.

The universities use the committee system to manage various aspects of university life. Representatives from various faculties/departments and sections of the institutions are elected or appointed under a chairman. Examples of such committees are transport, health services, and housing. The university councils also sometimes operate through committees such as appointments and promotions board, finance committee, development committee and tender board. Faculty teaching staff comprises assistant lecturers, lecturers, senior lecturers, associate professors, and full professors. Majority of the faculty members are in the lecturer and senior lecturer grades. Very few are professors.

Undergraduate Studies

The University of Ghana awards B.A. degrees in the Arts Faculty and in a few other departments (psychology, sociology, geography) of the Faculty of Social Studies; B.Sc. in the Faculty of Science, in most departments of the Faculty of Social Studies, and in the School of Administration; LL.B. in the Faculty of Law, and M.B. and ChB. in the School of Medicine. Most faculties award B.A. (general) and B.Sc. (general) degrees when students study a combination of subjects from various departments and B.A. (honors) and B.Sc. (special) degrees when students specialize in specific fields. Most of the courses at the University of Ghana take three years to complete.

Honors degrees in the sciences and agriculture take four years. The degree in Medicine takes five to six years depending on whether the candidate takes a premedical course. The University of Cape Coast awards B.A., B.Sc., B.Com., B.Sec. and B.Ed. degrees which take four years to complete. Degrees are awarded in all arts, social science, and science subjects. Honors degrees are also awarded. Every student also earns a Diploma in Education. At the University of Science and Technology, degrees awarded are B.A. in social science and art; B.Sc. in engineering, science, mining engineering, architecture, and agriculture (and human biology), B. Pharm. in pharmacy, M.B. and Ch.B. in medicine. Medical degrees are offered to students who spend three more years after the B.Sc. (human biology). Most of the courses take four years but B.A. (social science) and art take three years. It should be clear by now that all the professional degree programs last four years because they include practical (on-the-job) training. All basic courses take three years and medical courses take five to six years.

In the recent past all three Universities did run a three term year. The year started in late September or October and continued to July with three to four weeks break at Christmas and Easter. Universities stay in session for at least thirty weeks. Currently the University of Science and Technology, and the University of Cape Coast have changed to the semester system. They each do two semesters in a year, each semester lasting for sixteen weeks. The change is complete at UST but has reached only the second year at Cape Coast. It is important to note that the academic year does not always run smoothly. The year may be interrupted by unforseen circumstances which may call for adjustment of the academic year. Student disagreement with the government or with university authorities could lead to such a disruption. For instance the 1987-88 academic year was disrupted by such a disagreement with the government over student feeding allowances.

Almost all undergraduates in Ghana's universities live in residential halls. Each hall of residence constitutes a community with varied facilities. Students are assigned to the halls on admission and constitute the junior members. They elect their own officers to manage residential hall affairs. Faculty staff who are assigned to the halls as tutors (counsellors at Cape Coast) and fellows constitute the senior members of the hall. Each hall has a governing council comprising both junior and senior members. The hall master or hall warden heads each hall. Students are accommodated in cubicles and are sometimes paired in the cubicles. Such halls of residence at the University of Ghana and the University of Science and Technology are autonomous with their own dining halls but central dining halls serve students at the University of Cape Coast.

Tuition and accommodation are free for Ghanian students. The government has recently changed its policy of subsidizing student feeding to one of student loans which the students are expected to pay later after the course. The loans are also meant to support books and cater for other expenses. This new policy puts more financial responsibility on parents and guardians. A scholarship scheme has been suggested for academically superior undergraduates and graduate students. Foreign students are expected to pay full fees for university education. Tuition fees at UCC and UG are US$2,500 per year. At UST tuition fees are US$7,500 per year. Board and lodging fees vary from about US$2,100-3,000 for the academic year. Other expenses for book, examination fees etc., may require an additional US$500-800 for the academic year.

Staff of the universities are well qualified people. The minimum qualification for appointment is a second degree with a good first degree but a doctoral degree is an advantage. People with a first class or second upper first degrees may be appointed directly. All the universities arrange to train their lecturers to attain necessary qualifications. Many staff members of the universities have been trained that way. New appointees serve a probationary period of two years. Appointments are on contract basis which range from two years to six years for each contract. The appointments are made by the relevant appointments and promotions board which interviews applicants. Interviews are also arranged for applicants outside the country. Foreign students are rather few, with the majority coming from African countries. There are very few Western European or American students.

Admissions are based mainly on the G.C.E. Advanced Level examination. At least two Advanced Level passes and at least five passes at the Ordinary Level are required for admission; an applicant with three Advanced Level passes has an advantage because of the keen competition for admission. Admission boards also consider the quality of passes. U.C.C. insists on minimum pass of grade 'D' in two subjects; Legon admits people with three passes or two passes with at least grade 'C'. All three Universities require a pass in the English Language at the G.C.E. Ordinary Level (form six) and some departments insist on a pass in mathematics as well. Legon now requires a pass in science at the G.C.E. Ordinary Level.

Candidates for diploma courses need lower qualifications for admission: The University of Ghana requires G.C.E. Ordinary Level passes in the English Language and four other subjects and postsecondary qualification in either education or agriculture or veterinary science. U.S.T. requires five G.C.E. Ordinary Level passes including a pass in the English Language.

Mature students (that is, candidates who are at least thirty years old) are admitted to degree programs after passing an entry examination and an interview. U.C.C. and U.G. consider a very good pass at diploma level an equivalent to G.C.E. Advanced Level. It is important to note that faculties and departments have their own additional requirements which must be satisfied.

There are a number of polytechnics which offer full-time and part-time courses in engineering (mechanical, electrical, motor vehicle, building and civil), advanced crafts, institutional management, fashion, business, and laboratory techniques. Most of the full-time courses last for two years and part-time courses last for an additional year. Entry requirements are mainly the appropriate G.C.E. Ordinary Level passes including a pass in English Language for full-time courses but some part-time courses require middle school (elementary) leaving certificate.

There are a number of diploma awarding colleges which run courses in various subjects. Diploma certificates are slightly lower than the degree. Some of these colleges award a Diploma Certificate in Education. These colleges specialize in Ghanian language, music, physical education, agriculture, home science, technical education, and education. To gain admission, candidates should possess Teachers (Professional) Certificate 'A' and a minimum of four G.C.E. Ordinary Level passes. They should also have at least three years teaching experience. These courses last three years in each case.

The Ghana Institute of Journalism runs a two year program leading to a diploma in either journalism or public relations. Minimum entry requirements are two G.C.E. Advanced Level passes and five G.C.E. Ordinary Level passes.

Advanced Studies and Research

All postgraduate programs at the universities offer master's degrees. Legon and U.S.T. offer Ph.D. courses but the University of Cape Coast is yet to develop doctoral programs. Cape Coast awards M.A. and M.Sc. degrees in the faculties of arts, social science and science, and the Faculty of Education awards M.Ed. degrees. The University of Science and Technology awards M.A., M.Sc., M. Pharm., M. Phil (based on research), M.Tech., Ph.D. and D.Sc. degrees while the University of Ghana awards M.A. (communication studies, population studies), M.Phil. (adult education, African studies, archaeology, geography, arts subjects, psychology, sociology, music, population studies, Russian), Master of Business Administration, Master of Public Administration, M.Sc. in agriculture (animal science, crops, soil, agricultural extension, agricultural economics) and M.Sc. (nutrition, psychology, food science, biochemistry, and other science subjects). Legon has Ph.D. programs in many subjects including history, geography, philosophy, population studies, study of religions, food science, nutrition, and zoology. The M.A. program at the U.G. takes one year but the M.Phil. and the other masters programs at the other universities take two years to complete. U.C.C. insists on course work during the first year and a dissertation based on research for successful candidates during the second year. U.S.T. awards master's degrees based on research, taught course and partly research and partly taught course. U.G. and U.S.T. also award postgraduate diplomas in various fields. Specializations are offered in the various fields of study indicated above. Some programs have core courses to be taken by all students.

Admission to postgraduate degrees is open to candidates with good first degrees. Preference is given to those who obtain a first class or a second class (upper division) pass at the bachelor's level; holders of second class (lower) degrees may be considered. Interviews are normally held to select suitable candidates; the University of Ghana sometimes holds entrance examinations where necessary. Candidates with master's degrees are eligible for Ph.D. degrees.

As stated earlier, the academic year is divided into two semesters at U.C.C. and U.S.T., and courses may be offered during the long vacation (July - mid September). Legon (U.G.) still runs a three term academic year. The medium of instruction is English which is the administrative and commercial language of the country. Local languages are used but not officially. Graduate students also live in halls of residence on campus. Graduate students study mostly on government scholarships/bursaries; they also receive government loans for books. Some students pursue studies under study leave granted by their employers. Such students receive their normal salaries in lieu of bursaries and other loans. Such recipients are expected to return to the services of their employers. Some graduate students help with teaching on part-time basis and are remunerated for periods taught. Parents, who could afford, supplement the needs of their wards where the need arises. Teaching staff are experienced and qualified faculty who are approved by the department and faculty boards.

Regular postdoctoral programs are very few or non-existent. Academies conduct their own private research. Research at the universities are conducted by individuals or sometimes on departmental and faculty basis. The universities provide funds for research through departments or their various research committees. The universities have special units for research. The Institute for Social, Statistical and Economic Research (ISSER) and the Center for Development

Studies (CDS) at the University of Ghana and the University of Cape Coast respectively are specialized research units. At the national level, the Council for Scientific and Industrial Research coordinates research activities of various research institutes in the country. Examples of such institutes are the Food Research Institute, Animal Research Institute and the Water Resources Research Institute. Funds for research at universities are usually meager. Lack of funds is a major obstacle to development of research activities.

ISSUES AND TRENDS

Ghana is currently undergoing educational reform in content and administration. A junior and senior secondary school systems have been introduced. The new reform proposes a six-year primary course, a three-year junior secondary course, a three-year senior secondary program (6-3-3 system) and a 4-5 year university program as compared to the old system of six years primary, four years middle, 5-7 years secondary program and 3-4 years university course. The aim of the reform is to reduce the period of secondary education from seventeen to twelve years. The curriculum is also being reviewed to include vocational and technical subjects; the aim is to replace the predominantly academic curriculum with a more diversified one. It is hoped that many more children of school going age will have access to education and the needs of students with varied talents would be served. Every child is expected to have nine years of free education. Textbooks have been produced for the new programs but the provision of workshops has been rather slow in many places. Staffing, especially for technical subjects, has been a problem. The abolition of the sixth form (Advanced Level) marks a major educational change.

Cost effective and cost recovery measures are being implemented to reduce expenditure on education but at the same time provide quality education. Reform at the university and other tertiary levels is also being anticipated. A rationalization committee has studied the tertiary level education and has made recommendations. Courses at the universities and polytechnics are being streamlined to meet the manpower needs of the country. Efforts are being made to expand access, improve facilities, and increase staffing by employing cost effective methods. Suggestions have been made to upgrade some teacher training colleges to colleges of education.

The education reform program aims at increasing access, relating programs to social and manpower needs, improving facilities, encouraging cost-effectiveness, and increasing community involvement and participation in education. It will ensure that all children have at least nine years of basic education (grades 1-9). Secondary education is being brought within easy reach of most rural communities which have adopted the reform program wholeheartedly. When the problem of qualified teachers in certain subjects for the junior secondary school is solved, a tremendous stride in education would have been made.

Studies have just been completed to evaluate the "Experimental Junior Secondary School Program" launched in 1975. It is to be hoped that the findings of the evaluation would be used to improve the current junior secondary schools. The current junior secondary schools have also been evaluated by teams that toured the whole country. In response to the government's intention to discourage residential secondary schools which are now very expensive, the Institute of Educational Planning and Administration of the University of Cape Coast has conducted a study of the boarding school system in Ghana.

BIBLIOGRAPHY

Foster, P. *Education and Social Change in Ghana.* London: Routledge and Kegan Paul, 1967.

Graham, C. K. *The History of Education in Ghana.* Accra: Ghana Publishing Corporation, 1976.

McWillian, H. O. A., and Kwamena-Poh, M. A. *The Development of Education in Ghana (New Edition).* Hong Kong: Commonwealth Printing Press Ltd., 1975.

Ministry of Education and Culture. "The Educational Reform Program Policy Guidelines." (Unpublished paper).

Ministry of Education and Culture. "Overview of Educational Reform Program." (Unpublished paper).

Universities Rationalization Committee. *Report.*

GREECE

by
Michael Kassotakis
Professor of Education
University of Athens, Greece

BACKGROUND

Modern Greece became an independent state in 1830 after the victorious revolution of 1821 against the Turks who occupied the country for about 400 years. The long period of Ottoman occupation, the disastrous fights for independence, and the following wars for the expansion of the new Greek state as well as the various sociopolitical upheavals delayed the development of the country. Until the beginning of the 1950s, Greece was a developing agricultural country with low industrial activity. After that period, an acceleration of socioeconomic development started. The country gradually converted into a developed European country. Greek economy, however, still has some structural weaknesses and faces problems.

Once modern statehood was attained, Greece attempted to organize systematically her educational system, the main sources of which were the western educational practice, the tradition of ancient Greece and Byzantium, and the culture of the orthodox religion.

Greek higher education, on which the present study is focused, has developed in a fashion which reflects the socioeconomic evolution and the cultural tradition of the country. Its history goes back to the period soon after independence. The first Greek university was founded in Athens in 1837 under the auspices of King Othon and it was named after him. Later on it was called the National and Kapodistrian University. During the same period a school called "Polytechnic" was established in Athens (1836-37). This school was recognized in 1879 as a higher level institution. It was granted university status in 1914 and it developed later into the National Metsovio Technical University in Athens. Also, the origin of the School of Fine Arts dates back to this period (1836).

In addition, during the nineteenth century and the first decades of the twentieth century various non-university level institutions, known as *Didaskalia*, functioned in Greece. These institutions aimed mainly at educating primary school teachers.

However, the development of Greek higher education in the nineteenth and the beginning of the twentieth century was poor. The socioeconomic conditions of the newly developed Greek state, the lack of infrastructure and teaching staff, as well as efforts pertaining to the expansion of the state prevented the fast development of higher education. An increased rate of development appeared in the period of 1920-30 during which some new higher institutions were established and some others already functioning were legally authorized. The establishment of the University of Thessaloniki in 1925 is considered as the most important event in this period. During the following decade, the primary teacher training colleges called "pedagogical academies", the college for the training of teachers for physical education (E.A.S.A.) which replaced the corresponding *Didaskalia*, and other schools like the schools for industrial studies in Piraeus and Thessaloniki were established.

But the need for substantial development of higher education became more important since the end of 1950s. The acceleration of the economic growth of the country and the changes brought about in the Greek society required a large number of highly skilled workers and scientists. Therefore, the Greek higher education institutions undertook the task of educating the relevant staff. An indication of this educational growth is the fact that about 50 percent of the Greek highest institutions, known as AEIs, were established in the period 1964-85.

In addition, changes also took place at the non-university level institutions for the training of preprimary and primary school teachers. The higher technical and vocational education, however, remained underdeveloped until the beginning of 1970, since the slow industrial development of the country did not create a high need for technical and vocational personnel. One could say that the only institutions worth mentioning before that period were the SELETE (School for Training of Technical and Vocational Education Teachers) which began running in 1959, and the schools for sub-engineers *(scholes ypomichanikon)*.

The establishment of the centers for technical and vocational education, the so-called KATEE, was decided in 1970 when the need for middle level technical and administrative staff augmented. Their creation was supported financially by the World Bank. Five of these centers started functioning in 1974 and their number increased later.

Despite the accelerated growth in higher education, the prevailing views during the last few decades were that higher education has been in a state of crisis. The structural and organizational framework of higher education was viewed as anachronistic and the quality of studies was considered not satisfactory. Therefore, the need for a general reorganization of higher education was gradually becoming greater. To this end, many efforts were made and several proposals were submitted, none of which brought substantial reforms in higher education until the beginning of the 1980s. Only some partial changes of minor importance took place in the organization of studies and legislative framework.

In the autumn of 1981, the socialist party (PASOK) came into power. The newly elected government enacted the laws 1268/82 and 1404/83, which now form the basis on which all higher educational institutions operate. The changes introduced by the reform aimed mainly at democratizing administrative framework of higher education, upgrading studies, and bringing tertiary education on par with the socioeconomic development of the country. Despite the progress made in several sectors, weaknesses and problems still persist. Before discussing the recent changes and other aspects of higher education, we estimate that a brief description of the structure and fundamental characteristics of the preceding educational levels (primary and secondary) is necessary to be made in order for the problems associated with the transition from secondary to higher education to be clarified.

PRIMARY AND SECONDARY EDUCATION

Basic Characteristics

Education in Greece is the responsibility of the state. It is offered completely free by state educational institutions at all levels. Private primary and secondary schools are allowed to operate under the supervision of the Ministry of Education and Religion. They are obliged to follow the national program of studies. The number of private schools is limited. In 1989-90 only 2.6 percent of the preprimary schools, 4.9 percent of the primary schools, 4.1 percent of the *gymnasia* (lower secondary schools), and 4.9 percent of the lycea (upper secondary schools) were private.

Greek primary and secondary educational systems has been from its start very centralized. It also inflicted a rather latent uniformity in curriculum, the texts, the appointment and promotion of teachers, as well as the funding and the administration of the schools. The Ministry of Education and Religion with its regional agents is the central authority overseeing education in the country. Efforts have been made to decentralize the system in the context of recent reforms (1985), but they have not produced satisfactory results yet.

To a great extent, Greek education, especially its secondary level, has been oriented towards offering general education with emphasis on humanistic culture and preparing students to enter higher institutions rather than helping them to acquire marketable skills. Technical and vocational education was very little developed until the middle of 1970s. In spite of the efforts made in the 1970s for increasing the number of students oriented to technical and vocational education, little progress was made. The majority of Greek students dislike technical and vocational schools and prefer to study in a general lyceum despite the fact that they have only limited possibilities of obtaining a job in case they fail to enter a higher institution. On the other hand, the openness and flexibility of the social structure in Greece, the existence of a free education at all levels, and the high social status and the social privileges university graduates enjoy have been some of the important factors favoring the orientation of secondary students of all social classes towards higher education. However, the limited educational efficacy of the existing institutions and the inability of the country's economy to absorb a large number of highly qualified workers have been obstacles in responding to the social demand for higher education.

Structure

Under the present system of education which is based on the Educational Act of 1985, elementary education comprises a) a two- year preprimary school, which is not compulsory; and b) a six-year compulsory primary school. Children aged three and one-half years can register at a preprimary school. Entrance to primary school takes place at the age of 5 1/2-6 years.

Primary school is followed by three years of lower secondary school, called gymnasium, which is also compulsory. At the age of 14 1/2-15 , Greek children enter upper secondary school into one of the four streams: general lyceum, technical and vocational lyceum, comprehensive lyceum; and technical and vocational schools. Education in all lycea take three years and technical-vocational schools take two years. Entrance to the lyceum is not based on examinations. A small number of secondary schools run evening classes.

In 1989-90 the following schools were in operation: a) 5,555 preprimary schools with 8,008 teachers and 141,248 pupils, b) 8,070 primary schools having 38,872 teachers and 846,498 students, c) 1,802 gymnasia with 26,479 teachers and 432,439 students, and d) 1,057 general lycea, with 16,451 teachers and 250,228 students, 25 multi-branched lycea with 1,621 teachers and 19,466 students, 255 technical and vocational lycea with 6,107 teachers and 87,334 students and 260 technical and vocational schools (lower and intermediate level) with 3,242 teachers and 43,569 students.

In addition, there are several kinds of non-formal education which offers supplementary education to children (e.g. music, dancing, foreign languages, etc.) as well as a variety of programs to adults and young people. Technical and vocational training is also provided through apprenticeship programs which are sponsored by the Organization for Employment (OAED) and other bodies. Some other vocational schools operate under the supervision of various ministries other than the Ministry of Education.

Transition from Secondary to Higher Education

The number of students entering higher institutions is limited *(numerus clausus)*. Until 1963 each institution decided on its own the number of students that it could accept and organized its own entrance examinations. This system was abolished in 1964 and ever since the number of students entering higher institutions is defined by the Ministry of Education on recommendations made by individual institutions.

The selection of students for higher education is based upon highly competitive entrance examinations which have been held on a national level since 1964. The selection system, however, has undergone successive reforms and the present system has the following features. The subjects taught in the third year of the general lyceum and the comprehensive lyceum have been divided into a) subjects of general education and b) "preparatory subjects" required for entering higher institutions. The latter are divided into four sets of options called *desmes*, each of which comprises four subjects. Each *desmi* leads to a certain category of higher institutions. Students are examined in the preparatory subjects on a national level. The selection is based upon the total performance in the subjects of the selected *desmi* provided that each candidate has received at least a pass mark in the subject which is considered basic for the field of studies he wishes to follow. The higher education candidates are allowed to sit for examinations several times and education candidates are allowed to sit for examinations several times and also keep the marks they have received in any one subject in the previous examination.

The students of the final class of the technical and the vocational lycea can attend the "preparatory subjects" except the ones leading to humanities, and participate in the examinations for entrance to higher education.

Candidates for some institutions like certain departments of technical universities, faculties of fine arts or physical education, departments of foreign languages, etc., have to sit for examinations in specified subjects (i.e. foreign languages, design) or demonstrate abilities in relevant areas.

A percentage of places at the non-university level institutions of technological education is reserved for the technical and vocational lyceum graduates as well as for those coming from the technical and vocational branches of the comprehensive lyceum (EPL). These graduates are selected on the basis of both their performance in certain subjects which they have taken during the final year of their secondary studies and the mean marks of the lyceum certificate.

A number of places are also reserved for special groups of candidates (i.e. foreign candidates, Greek immigrants, handicapped children and distinguished athletes, etc.). Foreign candidates and Greek immigrants are subjected to a selection criteria, while admission of handicapped persons is not selective. In addition, distinguished athletes may enter the department of physical education without examinations.

The above system for entrance to higher institutions is presently under review.

HIGHER EDUCATION

General Characteristics

Higher education in Greece is exclusively public since the creation of private higher institutions is prohibited by the country's Constitution. It is also completely free. Even a number of basic scientific textbooks is given free to the students. Some private college-level institutions (e.g. Deree-Pierce College) and private postsecondary centers for professional studies *(kentra eleftheron spoudon)* operate, but the degrees they offer are not accredited in Greece. The creation of private higher institutions, however, has recently become a topic of discussion.

Although higher institutions are autonomous and self-governing bodies, they are under the supervision of the Ministry of Education. The Ministry of Education plays a significant role in the formulation of the general educational policy to be followed by higher institutions and controls all financial matters and the procedure for entrance examinations. Higher education is funded to a large extent from the national budget.

Institutions

The present system of higher education comprises institutions falling into two categories: university and non-university. There are also various institutions offering in-service training courses to teachers but as they do not fall within the higher education context, they are not discussed here.

Until 1988 the university level institutions, known as AEIs *(anotata ekpedeftika idrymata)*, comprised a) universities, b)technical universities called polytechnics, and c) 6 highest schools *(anotates scholes)* oriented to certain scientific areas only (economics, political and social sciences, business administration, agriculture, fine arts). In 1989 the aforementioned *anotates scholes*, except for the School of Fine Arts, have been named universities, but they keep their scientific orientation. Some higher military schools are also considered as equivalent to the university level institutions.

The non-university level institutions include a) technological institutions called TEIs originating from the aforementioned KATEEs, and b) various vocational schools.

The non-university level schools for the training of primary and preprimary school teachers, were abolished in 1988-89. They were replaced by university level autonomous departments of preprimary and primary education, which have been functioning since 1984-85. The non-university level schools of physical education were also abolished and were replaced by university departments of physical education. Recently the Charokopios School of Home Economics was also granted the university level.

Governance

A characteristic of Greek higher education as regards its functioning in the past is the stagnation of its organization and the maintenance of the same legislative framework for a long time.

Until 1911 the University of Athens operated according to the regulations which were established in 1837. In 1911 a new legislative framework was approved by the Parliament and it remained valid until 1932, year in which it was replaced by the law 5343. This law determined the way higher education functioned until 1982, when it was replaced by the blueprint law 1268/82. The main innovations introduced by this law are as follows:

a.   The old faculties are divided into departments. Each department corresponds to a scientific area (i.e. mathematics, physics, sociology, history, etc.).

b.   The chair system, which was the focus of the past organization of AEIs is replaced by the "scientific sector" *(tomeas)*. The "sector" is responsible for implementing the basic policy of teaching and research, which must be approved by the general assembly of each department.

c.   All policy decisions related to various levels are taken in the general assemblies of the respective sectors, departments, faculties, or university. These general assemblies consist of all the members of teaching staff and an important number of undergraduates and graduate students.

d.   In the electoral bodies which choose the administrative heads of the university, undergraduate students have the same representation as the members of the academic staff.

e.   Teaching staff at all levels form a single body graded on scales. The main levels of academic staff are: lecturer, assistant professor, associate professor, and professor. Possession of a doctorate is an indispensable prerequisite for access to all levels. In addition, teaching experience in a higher institution and/or research experience of 2-6 years as well as original scientific work are required for the professor's levels. Two years' working experience in a higher institution or research center and at least two publications are required for applying for the grade of lecturer. The academic staff of the two upper ranks possess permanent positions. The appointment and promotion of the teaching staff is done by special electoral bodies, which meet together with the general assemblies of the departments. Also new categories of auxiliary teaching, technical and administrative personnel were created.

f.   Each university is administered by the president supported by two vice-presidents, all three of whom are elected for a period of three years by the university general assembly; the chancellor's council, which comprises the president, the two vice-presidents, one representative of students and one representative of administrative personnel; and the senate consisting of the president and the vice-presidents, the deans of the university faculties, the heads of the autonomous departments, one representative of the teaching staff and one undergraduate student from each department, one representative of the administrative staff and some representatives of the graduate students of the university. The senate is considered as the top administrative agent of the university. Each faculty consisting of related departments is administered by the dean who is elected for three years by the general assembly of the faculty; a council which comprises the dean, the heads of the departments and one undergraduate student from each department; and the general assembly of the faculty which consists of the general assemblies of the departments. Each department is administered by the head, who is elected for two years; the administrative council which comprises the head, the directors of the departmental sections and representatives of students and the technical and administrative personnel; and the general assembly of the department. The director of each sector, who is elected for one year, and the general assembly of the sector are the sector's administrative agents.

g.   Undergraduate studies have been reorganized into "semester courses" and a basic structure for the promotion of graduate programs has been set up.

The organization and the functioning of the TEIs are based on law 1404/1983, the presidential decrees, and the ministerial decisions which were issued in connection with this law. TEIs are differentiated from AEIs in terms of their purpose, function, qualifications and hierarchy of the staff, duration of courses, and absence of postgraduate courses. However, their organization and operation is similar to that of the AEIs. The TEIs are oriented towards the implementation of recent technological knowledge and practice, while AEIs are more science and research based institutions. For this purpose, TEIs have direct links to various productive enterprises where most of the practical work of the students are carried out. Over 10,000 students spend at least six months in different public or private services each year.

TEIs are self-governing bodies enjoying full academic freedom. They are divided into schools and departments as in the case of AEIs. In general TEIs have schools specializing in graphical arts and fine arts; health and welfare; food technology; agriculture technology; administration and economy; and applied technology. However, some TEIs do not have all of the above mentioned types of schools.

Programs and Degrees

Undergraduate degree programs offered at higher educational institutions normally last for four years (eight semesters). The studies in schools of agriculture, schools of dentistry and in technical universities last for five years (ten semesters), while undergraduate studies in the school of medicine last for six years (twelve semesters). The degrees *(ptychia)* are awarded by various departments of the faculties.

However, in the higher technical and vocational schools (TEIs) the duration of studies is three years (six semesters). Exceptionally, the studies in the department of food technology and graphics and fine arts last for seven semesters. One semester of practical training is obligatory for acquisition of the TEI degree. The academic year extends from about the beginning of September to the end of June. All higher institutions function five days a week.

The Greek universities award doctorate degrees and some university departments also award other postgraduate degrees in some specialties. The acquisition of a doctorate degree requires the submission of an original thesis to a committee of academic experts.

Until recently there were no systematically organized postgraduate programs in Greece. The thesis was prepared by the postgraduate student under the supervision of one professor. The new comprehensive law (1268/82) provided for the establishment of a postgraduate school independent of the other departments of the universities. However, this school never started operating due to opposition from academic staff and students. For this reason, new regulations of postgraduate studies were introduced by the law 1566/1985. Each department could develop, within its scientific orientation, programs of postgraduate studies which had to be sanctioned by the senate and the Minister of Education. The law also opened the possibility of organizing inter-departmental or inter-university programs of postgraduate studies. Another law (1771/88) provides for the establishment of a scientific committee for research and postgraduate studies at the Ministry of Education for coordinating the development of postgraduate programs and the creation of research institutes within university departments. In spite of the legislative provisions, little progress has been made towards the systematic organization of postgraduate studies. In most departments little change has taken place.

The selection of postgraduate students is done by the relevant department. A committee consisting of three members of the academic staff nominated by the department supervises the students' work. Postgraduate students have the same rights and facilities as the undergraduate students.

A small number of scholarships for postgraduate studies called EMY *(Eidiki Metaptyxiaki Ypotrofi)*, are available in all universities. These scholarships are awarded based on candidate's success in an advertised examination. Its duration is one year and may be renewed for five years according to the candidate's progress. The scholars are obliged to engage in auxiliary teaching and research work at the departments for few hours every week. Scholarships are also awarded by the Greek Scholarship Foundations (IKY), Onassis Foundation, Bodossakis Foundation, and some other scientific and social organizations. The scholars must have successfully passed examinations which are advertised each year, or they are selected according to their university performance. A small number of scholarships is awarded to foreign students.

Student Population

The growth of student enrollment was proportional to the rate of development of the institutions. The increase is especially spectacular after the 1960s. The student population of university level institutions (AEIs) increased from 25,658 in 1960-61 to 72,269 in 1970-71 (increase of 182 percent), and to 116,412 in 1989-90 (increase of 354 percent). In a similar fashion, the enrollment in higher technical and vocational educational institutions grew even more rapidly from 5,840 in 1965-66 to 13,682 in 1974-75 (increase of 134 percent) and 77,169 (including students in vocational-ecclesiastical institutions) in 1989-90 (increase of 1221 percent), (OECD, 1980 and unpublished data NSSG, 1990). As a percentage of population aged 20-24 years, the enrollment in higher educational institutions rose from 3.8 percent in 1960 to 28.0 percent in 1990. If we add the Greek students studying abroad this percentage will exceed 30 percent.

Of the total student population, 49.9 percent were male and 50.1 percent were female. The female student population noticed considerable growth recently, increasing from 32 percent in 1965 to about 50 percent in 1989-90. The participation of women in tertiary education is higher in Greece than in most countries of the European Community (UNESCO statistics, 1989): Belgium 47 percent (1987), Greece 49 percent (1986), Luxembourg 34 percent (1984), Ireland 43 percent (1985), Italy 47 percent (1986), Netherlands 42 percent (1986), United Kingdom 46 percent (1986) and West Germany 41 percent (1986). The increase of female student population is the result of the democratization of education and the socioeconomic changes that have taken place in Greece in the recent years. The changes in the university entrance selection system have been regarded as having positively contributed to this increase.

In the middle of the 1960s (according to a study conducted by OECD), Greece had the highest percentage of students following law and social sciences and the lowest in the technology among OECD members (OECD 1971, Tsoukalas 1975). During the recent years this imbalance has diminished significantly although humanities, law, and social and economic sciences still attract the majority of students. In 1986 the distribution of student population among the different fields of studies indicated that 20.9 percent of students had registered in humanities, fine arts, and education; 24 percent in social, economic, and legal sciences; 26.7 percent in sciences and technology; 19.2 percent in medical studies; and 9.2 percent in other fields (UNESCO 1989). Several factors have been responsible for these changes: the creation and development of higher technical and vocational institutions (KATEEs, which converted into TEIs later on); the establishment of new universities and new branches of studies in the existing universities; and the socioeconomic development of the country which modified the needs that higher education must satisfy.

Almost 6 percent of the students registered in the higher educational institutions in 1981-82 were non natives. 63 percent among them were from Cyprus. The rest came from several countries in Asia, Africa, North America, and Europe (NSSG 1987).

ISSUES AND TRENDS

The Demand for Higher Education

As discussed above, the demand for higher education in Greece has always been high due to social and economic reasons. Some surveys show more than 80 percent of the general lyceum students wish to enter higher educational institutions (Kassotakis 1979, OECD 1979, Psacharopoulos 1978, Dimitropoulos 1985, Pappas 1989). However, the number of available places in tertiary educational institutions which rose from 7,965 in 1961 to 42,846 in 1989 has always been inferior compared to the number of candidates which grew from 28,140 in 1961 to 127,430 in 1989. In the last five years (1985-89) those entering higher institutions represented only about 32 percent of the number of candidates applied. Consequently, high competition exists among the candidates. This, in conjunction with the fact that many schools fell short of preparing students fully for entrance examinations, led to the growth of private schools, the so called *frontistiria*, which prepare pupils for entering higher institutions.

According to data from recent studies about 70 percent of lyceum students, especially those from the last class attend private preparatory schools or take private lessons at home (Polydorides 1985, Kassotakis 1989, Pappas 1989). Attendance in *frontistiria* creates a serious expense to Greek families, goes against the government's formal educational policy of free public education for all, creates fatigue in students, and has a negative impact on the performance of secondary school teachers who are tempted to offer private lessons. In order to cope with this problem and to improve the equality of educational opportunities, the Greek government established in 1983 the postsecondary preparatory centers *(Metalykiaka Proparaskevastika Kentra)*, offering free tuition to all secondary school graduates who wish to prepare themselves for entrance to higher educational institutions. The postsecondary preparatory centers however did not decrease substantially the number of private preparatory schools *(frontistiria)*. The abolition of these centers is under consideration.

The general lyceum graduates who have failed to enter universities are not competent enough to practice a profession (except for employment as office clerks) since they lack marketable skills. Some of them return to the *frontistiria* and continue their preparation for entering universities and retake entrance examinations for a second, and/or a third time. Some follow public or private technical or vocational schools, whilst others seek (often in vain) a white-collar post. Thus, when such posts are advertised the competition is very high.

Student Emigration

A great number of students who have failed to enter a higher institution in Greece go abroad for studies. According to UNESCO statistical data, Greece has one of the highest student emigration rates. In 1982, the number of Greeks studying abroad was 44,465. This number represented 32.3 percent of the student population in Greece. In 1983 the above number became 44,046 and decreased afterwards. In 1986 for instance, it amounted to 27,085 students and represented about 14 percent of the student population in Greece.

Furthermore, the delayed development of postgraduate studies reinforces student emigration. Many Greeks go abroad in order to pursue their postgraduate studies. In 1986 there were 6,287 postgraduate students abroad thus representing about 23 percent of the emigrant student population. Among them a small number held scholarships from the Greek state or grants from other sources.

The emigration has a detrimental effect on the country both because of the loss of scientific manpower (many good scientists eventually remain abroad) and monetary exchange. According to the recent statistical data, the exchange for the expenses of Greek students abroad multiplied by fifteen between 1960-80. In 1983 it was 11,711 million drachmas, while the total current expenditure for the higher education was 12,768 million drachmas (Pesmatzoglou 1987). It is hoped that the increase of higher education opportunities in Greece will significantly eliminate the student emigration.

Inequality of Opportunities for Access to Higher Education

In Greece, like in many other countries, the opportunities for lower social strata origin students to enter higher education are lower than for those coming from upper social strata. In 1981-82 students whose fathers were professionals, managers, and higher level administrators had three times as many chances to enter higher institutions as those coming from "working class" background (farmers and blue-collar workers). However, it is worth mentioning that according to an OECD comparative study, the social inequality as regards access to higher education was among the lowest observed in the OECD countries around 1960 and 1970 (OECD 1975, Psacharopoulos Grand Kazamias A. 1985). The low level of social inequality of entrance to higher education and the flexible structure of social formation in Greece explain the importance of the role that higher education has been playing as a mechanism for upward social mobility.

Insufficiency of Educational Funds and Infrastructure

In 1985, the share of educational sector in Greece formed 2.9 percent of the gross national product (UNESCO 1989). It is very low compared to other countries of Western Europe (this share is about double in several European countries). The problem becomes more serious in the higher education sector because about 75-80 percent of the total educational expenditure go to primary and secondary levels.

The insufficiency of funds for higher education worsened during the last years due to the creation of new universities and other institutions, and the general growth of enrollment. As a result, the infrastructure necessary for efficient functioning of higher institutions and for upgrading of the quality of studies has not received attention. This problem appears to be more acute in the provincial universities *(perifereiaka)*. Several departments in these universities are located in different cities or localities for political and economic reasons, and the associated increase in their operating expenses does not help the situation.

Besides, the limited educational funds have damaging effects on research, the underdevelopment of which is an important weakness of the Greek AEIs. In 1987 only 0.33 percent of the GNP was allocated for research activities in Greece compared to 0.45 percent in Portugal, 0.47 percent in Spain, 0.92 percent in Ireland, 2.5 percent in France, and 2.7 percent in West Germany. Moreover only a part of this small amount is offered to the universities for research. The low research activity has adverse consequences on postgraduate studies. Thus increased allocation of funds is considered a prerequisite for improvement of Greek education.

Socioeconomic Efficiency of Higher Education

Until now Greek higher education was mainly oriented towards the production of clerks and staff for state services. According to some estimates, 90 percent of university graduates have been employed by state services, banks, and public enterprises (Pesmatzoglou 1987). The involvement of higher education in the productive processes has not been satisfactory and its socioeconomic efficiency is considered low. The efforts aimed at developing cooperation between the technological institutions (KATEEs/TEIs) and enterprises has not borne the expected outcomes (Glambedakis 1989). The limited capabilities of the small size Greek enterprises and the use of old-fashioned methods and means of production did not favor such cooperation.

Recently, in view of the integration of the European Market in 1992 and the expected competition, extensive efforts have been made towards the reorganization of the industrial sector in Greece and the increase of economic productivity. These efforts have also led to increasing cooperation between higher education institutions and industry.

Employment Problems

A few years ago unemployment in Greece was almost non- existent among university graduates. However, in recent years unemployment has increased even among university graduates. According to a survey conducted by the National Statistical Service of Greece in 1987, there were 46,400 unemployed higher institution graduates constituting 16.2 percent of the total unemployed population. The respective percentage among unemployed individuals of 25-29 year age group was about 29.8 percent. (NSSG 1988).

If one adds to the problem of unemployment the under employment and especially the common phenomenon of being employed in positions which do not directly relate to one's scientific training and specialization, then the problem of employment of graduates seems even more serious.

Prospects

Despite the existing problems, the prospects of further development of Greek higher education are good. The elimination of existing weaknesses has started and it is hoped that in due course the existing problems will be gradually eradicated. The ongoing socioeconomic development of the country, the planned integration of the European Market countries in 1992 and the specific role Greece is challenged to play in improving links between the European Community and the countries in the Balkan Peninsula or the neighboring Arabic countries, are expected to open new horizons for Greek higher education. Also the participation of many Greek higher institutions in European research projects and in teacher and student exchange programs is expected to have a positive impact on Greek higher education.

Moreover, the possibility of establishing new public and private universities (assuming the constitutional article relevant to private institutions gets modified), the change of the system of appointment for posts in public services, the abolition of the *numerus clausus,* and the reform of the existing system for admission to universities have been considered recently. These possible changes will open new perspectives on Greek higher education in the near future.

A better distribution of student population by areas of specialization is expected especially with the development of TEIs and the adoption of new directions of studies in the universities. Emphasis must be placed on new technology and sciences. Furthermore Greece, due to its classical historic heritage, must give more attention to classical studies, thus becoming a world center for the study of ancient Greek civilization.

We think that higher institutions should become more autonomous; their dependency upon the state budget should be limited and the formation of links between them and productive units should be fostered. It is also hoped that the upgrading of undergraduate programs and the promotion of graduate studies and university research will enhance the quality of studies, and improve the socioeconomic efficiency of higher education.

BIBLIOGRAPHY

CEE/Eurydice Unit. *The Greek Educational System,* Brussels/Athens, 1988.

Dimitropoulos E. et al. *Educational and Vocational Decisions of the Last Class of Lyceum Students* (in Greek). Thessaloniki, 1985.

Dendrinou-Antonakaki, K. *Greek Education.* New York: Teachers College, Columbia University, 1955.

Glambedakis, M. *Economy and Education: The Contribution of Higher Technical Education to Industrial Development and the Integration of its Graduates in the Industrial Sector* (in Greek). Athens: Ed. Ion, 1989.

Kazamias, A. *The Educational Crisis in Greece and its Peculiarities: A Historical, Comparative Approach* (in Greek). Athens: Academy of Athens, 1983.

Kazamias A. & Kassotakis, M. The Educational Reforms in Greece: Efforts, Impasses, Perspectives *(in Greek). Rethymnon.* 1986: 20-44

Kassotakis, M. *Le dévelopement économique et le problème de l'orientation scolaire et professionnelle en Grèce.* Athènes: Université d'Athènes, Laboratoire de Pédagogie Expérimentale, 1979.

Kassotakis, M. The Technical and Vocational Education in Greece and the Attitudes of Greek Youngsters Towards It. *Journal of the Hellenic Diaspora.* (1981): 2-3.

Kontogiannopoulos-Polydorides, G. et al. An Evaluation of the System of Entrance Examinations for Higher Education (in Greek). Athens: Ministry of Education/Ministry of Industry, 1985.

Kintis, A. A. *The Higher Education in Greece* (in Greek). Athens. Ed. Gutenberg, 1980.

Koutsoumaris, G. *Higher Education and Economic Development,* Athens Institute of Industrial Development, 1980.

Massialas, B. *The Educational System of Greece.* Washington, D.C.: U.S. Department of Education, 1981.

National Statistical Service of Greece (NSSG), *Statistical Yearbook 1987.* Athens, 1988.

National Statistical Service of Greece (NSSG), *Statistics of Education 1981-1982.* Athens, 1987.

National Statistical Service of Greece (NSSG), *Manpower Labor Survey (Employment) 1987*. Athens, 1988.

OECD. *Educational Policy and Planning: Educational Reform Policies in Greece*. Paris, 1980.

OECD. *Individual Demand for Education, General Report and Case Studies: France, Germany, Greece, United Kingdom*. Paris, 1979.

OECD. Education, Inequality and Life Chances. Vol. 1 and 2. Paris, 1975.

Pappas, G. The Plans for Higher Studies of the Students of the last Lyceum Year. In Varvakios Graduates Union: *The Transition From Secondary to Higher Education*. Athens, 1989.

Psacharopoulos G., and Kazamias, A. *Education and Development in Greece: A Social and Economic Study for Higher Education*. Athens: National Center for Social Research, 1985.

Pesmatzoglou, St. *Education and Development in Greece 1948-1985* (in Greek). Athens: Ed. Themelio, 1987.

UNESCO. *Statistical Yearbook*. Paris, 1989.

Vrychea, A., & Gavroglou, K. *Attempts to Reforming the Higher Education in Greece 1911-1981* (in Greek). Athens: Ed. Synchrona Themata, 1982.

GRENADA

by
Roy Rathan
Chief Education Officer
Ministry of Education, Culture, and Fisheries, Grenada

The basic educational system in Grenada includes preprimary education (ages 3-5), primary education (ages 5-16), secondary education (ages 16 +), and tertiary education.

PRIMARY AND SECONDARY EDUCATION

Primary education has following objectives: to make every child in the state literate and numerate; to provide a sound education for the 5-16 year old children of the country; to lay a base for further education; to provide the kind of education that will equip students for the world of tomorrow and for the job market; to help each child develop socially, emotionally, culturally, and physically; to develop in every child an appreciation of the democratic system of government; to enable the children to think critically so that they may examine evidence before coming to conclusions; and to foster in each student healthy work attitudes and a sense of national pride.

The primary schools are commonly referred to as "all-age" primary since they cater to the educational needs of pupils of ages 5-16 + . There are fifty-seven schools distributed as follows: government (16), Anglican (9), Roman Catholic (25), Methodist (4), Seventh Day Adventist (2), and Presbyterian (1). At the end of the 1988 school year, there were 750 teachers and an enrollment of 19,988 pupils. Apart from the public and denominational primary schools there are eight private schools with a total enrollment of over 1,000 pupils.

Pupils normally pass from the primary school into the secondary through the Common Entrance Examination. This examination is usually taken by pupils who reach at least junior level (ages 10-13 +). Some pupils therefore have as many as four chances of sitting this examination. Between 1976 and 1989 the percentage of primary pupils who were awarded places at secondary schools moved from 8.1-45.4 percent.

The subject areas of the Common Entrance Examination include general knowledge (history, culture/sports, commerce/economy, geography, and politics of Grenada and the Caribbean); natural science (animals, plants, physical science, health science, and earth science); language arts (spelling, grammar, punctuation, reading, vocabulary, alphabetizing, using the dictionary, using the encyclopedia, etc.); mathematics (concepts, skills, and problem solving); and mental skills. In addition to academic subjects, the curriculum also includes arts, crafts, music, drama, sports, athletics, and other social activities.

The students who do not succeed through the Common Entrance Examination in going to secondary school, continue their education at the all-age primary school until the age of sixteen plus. At this final year in school, they sit the School Leaving Examination. They are required to pass in English language, mathematics, and in at least three optional subjects. The pass mark for the compulsory subjects is 40 percent while that for the optional subjects is 34 percent. An overall average of 40 percent is required for passing the examination.

Pupils who pass this examination can be classified into three categories: pupils who are awarded scholarships to secondary school; pupils who are awarded bursaries to join the technical and vocational institute; and students who join the labor market. The subjects of the School Leaving Examination are agricultural science, art, business education, English language, geography, health science, history, home economics, mathematics, needlework, science (integrated), Spanish, and woodwork.

The main objectives of secondary education in Grenada include education of children for responsible citizenship in a democratic society; propagation of attitudes and values conducive to the development of the individual and the community; education and training of manpower to meet the needs of the nation in order to promote social economic development; and development of identity and pride in national heritage.

There are nineteen secondary schools of which six are government, one is private, and twelve are denominational. The government appoints (and pays the salaries of) all teachers except those in the private school. At the end of the school year 1988, the enrollment was 6,477 with 327 teachers.

The curriculum of the secondary school, like that of the primary school, includes not only academic subjects but also cultural and sporting activities. The subject areas include English language (or language A), English literature (or Language B), mathematics, principles of business, Spanish, French, geography, history, social studies, physics, chemistry, biology, agricultural science, human and social biology, accounting, commerce, economics, office practice, computer science, woodwork, metal work, technical drawing, sociology, religious studies, fashion and fabrics, food and nutrition and a general paper.

The external examinations are the Cambridge General Certificate of Education (G.C.E.) and the Caribbean Examinations Council (C.X.C.) examinations. The former examination was the recognized one for many years. However, the C.X.C., being a regional examination, is believed to be more relevant. As a result, students are only allowed to sit G.C.E. in subjects which are not offered at this point in time by C.X.C.

Secondary education is a five year course and students sit external examinations at the end of the fifth year. A student who passes in at least four subjects including English language is qualified for completing secondary education.

HIGHER EDUCATION

The Grenada National College which provides tertiary education was formally opened in September 1988. It incorporated the following former tertiary institutions: Grenada Technical and Vocational Institute (G.T.V.I.), Institute for Further Education (I.F.E.), Grenada Teachers College (G.T.C.), Grenada National Institute of Handicraft, Domestic Arts Institute, Mirabeau Farm School, School of Pharmacology, School of Nursing (to join at a later date), and Adult and Continuing Education Programs. The college provides first year university courses and associate degrees. It aims at fulfilling the manpower needs of the nation. At present there are some 832 full-time and 1,500 part-time students with a teaching staff of seventy of which 61 percent are males.

The college is a department of the Ministry of Education but it is hoped to turn it into a statutory body in due course. At present it is administered by a principal assisted by director of studies, registrar, and two deans.

The college is divided into the following three divisions: Division of Professional and Technical Studies (training of primary school teachers, pharmacy training, technical programs, Certificate in Para-legal Studies, Certificate in Agricultural Science, and hotel and tourism courses); Division of Arts, Science, and General Studies (Cambridge Advanced Level, Certificate of Further Education, associate degrees, secretarial science, craft programs in art, bamboo craft, handicraft and pottery); and Division of Adult and Continuing Education (training in typewriting, electronics, and a variety of skills and remedial programs, mainly to give a second chance to people who drop out of the primary and secondary schools).

ISSUES AND TRENDS

Despite the many problems and difficulties facing educational activities in Grenada, efforts are being made to ensure that graduates of the system will have the social, moral and technical skills which are necessary for the development of the country and of each person.

Significant issues and problems include the following: teachers for the most part are untrained and lack subject matter competence; the curriculum is not sufficiently related to the needs of the students and the country (tending to promote unfavorable attitudes towards manual labor); inadequate supervision; low internal efficiency with many students dropping out of school or having to repeat; inadequate building facilities, libraries, equipment and furniture; poorly maintained physical plants; lack of clearly defined and widely published goals and objectives in overall educational plans; and insufficient teachers.

GUATEMALA

by
Rigoberto Juarez-Paz
Dean, School of Humanities and founding Vice-President
Francisco Marroquin University, Guatemala

BACKGROUND

The University of San Carlos founded in 1676 and its forerunner, the Colegio de Santo Tomas, were the first institutions of higher education in Guatemala. In the historical development of the State University of Guatemala, there are two fundamental changes that are worth recording. First is the introduction of new scientific criteria near the end of the eighteenth century. The name of Fray Antonio de Goicoechea is associated with this reform movement, which is also known for its General Studies Program, common to all professional careers. Second, in 1944 the *Universidad de San Carlos* became autonomous, in the sense that it acquired the constitutional right to organize itself. Previously, all over Latin America, university authorities were appointed and removed by the ministries of education.

At this time, right after the overthrow of General Ubico, the *Universidad de San Carlos* adopted the "democratic" organization which had resulted from the *Reforma Universitaria of Cordoba*, Argentina, in 1918. According to the reform, university authorities would now be elected by students, professors, and alumni, with each group having the same number of votes. It also implied the freedom to establish curricula, graduating requirements, etc.

PRIMARY AND SECONDARY EDUCATION

Guatemalan children enter primary school at the of 6-7 years. Many of those who attend private elementary schools (specially those in the capital city) have had the benefit of one or two years of kindergarten in which they learn to read and write.

Primary school lasts six years, excluding kindergarten. The curriculum is built around Spanish, social sciences, and mathematics. Besides, they receive physical education, music, and handicrafts. At the completion of the sixth grade, students receive a diploma which is a prerequisite to enter secondary schools.

Secondary education in Guatemala originated in 1875. Soon after the election of Dr. Juan Jose Arevalo in 1944, there was an educational conference in Santa Ana, El Salvador, in which it was decided that Guatemala's secondary schools would have a three year program. It was a common program for both normal schools (training elementary school teachers) and schools dedicated to the training of students who would go on to pursue university studies.

By 1952, the three-year basic core curriculum was extended to every type of high school. During their stay at high school, students study Spanish, mathematics, social studies, natural sciences, English, industrial arts, home economics (for girls), physical education, and esthetic education (music etc.). Most of these courses meet daily from Monday to Friday. English courses meet four times a week. Physical education, music education, and home economics meet twice a week. The school year is from January to October. Each school, whether public or private, does its own evaluation, but there is a set of requirements established by the Ministry of Education that must be met.

In the capital city of Guatemala more than half of the secondary schools are private, and the tuition fees in a good many of them are as high or even higher than the tuition that students have to pay at the universities. They all charge more than the *Universidad de San Carlos*, but many do charge as much as most private universities. Public high schools are free.

The diplomas awarded by Guatemalan secondary schools are as follows: Baccalaureate of Sciences and Letters (two years beyond the basic curriculum); Elementary School Teacher (three years beyond the basic curriculum); Kindergarten Teacher (three years beyond the basic curriculum); Teacher of Musical Education (four years); Teacher of Home Economics (three years); Teacher of Physical Education (three years); Industrial Baccalaureate (two years); Computer Science Baccalaureate (two years). Thus, including the basic curriculum, secondary education lasts 5-7 years with children entering secondary level at the age of 12-13 years.

HIGHER EDUCATION

Institutions

Higher education in Guatemala is provided by the state-financed *Universidad de San Carlos de Guatemala* and four other private universities. Private universities are independent both financially and academically and the degrees awarded stand on an equal footing with those conferred by the state university. However, *Universidad de San Carlos de Guatemala* is the sole institution authorized to recognize degrees of foreign universities. The universities are generally organized into faculties or "schools" such as law, medicine, and economics.

The *Universidad de San Carlos de Guatemala* has been an autonomous institution since 1944 but it is totally dependent on the government for its finances. As a matter of fact, the Guatemalan Constitution requires that 5 percent of the ordinary national budget is to be allocated every year to the state university.

Guatemalan students pay less than US$50 per year; students from other Central American republics pay US$300; students from the rest of Latin America US$550; and all of the others must pay US$1,000 a year to attend the university.

Tuition fees at private universities are considerably higher. The *Universidad Francisco Marroquin* which has the highest fees in Guatemala, charges US$1,000 a year, whether the students are Guatemalan or not. But in the Medical School, Guatemalans pay US$1,290 a year; Central Americans pay US$1,700; and the rest must pay US$3,100. These fees are for the first four years of study. Afterwards the fees increase by 20 percent.

The oldest of the private universities is the *Universidad Rafael Landivar*, and it was founded in 1961. *Universidad de Valle de Guatemala* and *Universidad Mariano Galvex* were both founded in 1966. The *Universidad Francisco Marroquin* (of which the author is one of the founders) came into being in August 1971.

Universidad Rafael Landivar, named after an eighteenth century Jesuit poet, is a Catholic university run by the Jesuits. Offerings at the *Universidad del Valle* are mostly in science (both natural and social sciences) and mathematics. It also has an extensive program for training secondary school teachers.

Universidad Mariano Galvez, named after a nineteenth century progressive president of Guatemala, is called "the Protestant University" but neither are its authorities Protestant ministers nor is any Protestant church in charge of it excepting that most of the founders and the present higher authorities of the university are in fact Protestants.

Universidad Francisco Marroquin was named after the first bishop of Guatemala and founder of Central American education. It is dedicated to academic excellence and to the teaching of the fundamental values of Western civilization. Besides trying to offer the best professional training in different fields of studies, it teaches the (economic, political, juridical, and moral) principles of a free society. It has no religious affiliation. Another distinctive mark of *Universidad Francisco Marroquin* is that it is the only institution of higher education in Central America that has a correspondence school. In its organization, clues were taken from Britain's Open University and similar institutions in South Africa, Israel, and Spain.

Programs and Degrees

Only *Universidad del Valle* and *Universidad Francisco Marroquin* award B.S. and B.A. degrees after four years, without a thesis. The first professional degree in all of Guatemala's universities is the degree of *licenciado,* which requires a thesis and which can be obtained in architecture, agricultural science, business administration, dentistry, economics, law, medicine, psychology, social sciences, theology, public accounting, computer science, civil engineering, education, history, philosophy, veterinary medicine, chemistry, chemical engineering, and few other fields.

Except for medicine, which is a six-or seven-year program, most other specialities require a four-to five-year program for the degree of *licenciado.*

Only *Universidad del Valle* and *Universidad Francisco Marroquin* require a differential aptitude test as a requirement for admission. The other universities have no such requirement. The academic year is usually between February and November. All teaching is in Spanish. There are practically no residential facilities for students. The students either live at home or rent a place to live. There is a very small residence (forty students, perhaps) for students who come from the provinces. The Universidad de San Carlos also has a small residence.

Even though the tuition fees for Guatemalan students are extremely low, the *Universidad de San Carlos* has a scholarship program. On the other hand, private universities award loans to students who are unable to pay all of the fees. The loans are expected to be paid back upon graduation.

A good many degrees (including medicine, dentistry, and engineering) require supervised practical training in towns and villages before graduation.

The Universidad de San Carlos de Guatemala also has several programs of postgraduate studies in engineering (sanitary engineering), hydraulic resources, food science and technology, ophthalmology, public administration, and higher education. These are very intensive programs. In order to obtain the M.A. degree in one year, students dedicate sixty hours a week to their studies. A less effort will require them to spend more than two semesters.

Postgraduate students of public administration (twenty-nine months) have their fees paid directly to the university by the Institute for Public Administration, a government institution. They also get paid US$180 a month.

Postgraduate students of food science and technology must take an entrance examination besides being holders of the *licenciado* degree. The degree is an eighteen month program, and all students are on scholarships.

The Universidad Francisco Marroquin has a M.A. program in business administration, computer science, psychology, social science, internal medicine and ophthalmology. In most of these programs there is no financial aid, and they last approximately two years.

Both the *Universidad de San Carlos* and *Universidad Francisco Marroquin* have doctoral programs in their schools of humanities, but the great majority of graduate students are enrolled in M.A. programs.

Universidad del Valle has a M.A. program in educational evaluation.

ISSUES AND TRENDS

Over one half of the population of Guatemala is illiterate, in spite of the fact that for a long time there have been costly campaigns aimed at solving that problem. Intimately connected with it is the fact that there are several native languages spoken in the country. A large percentage of illiterates are native Americans who speak one or more languages neither of which are found, nor is likely to find, its way into the political institutions of the country.

It is obvious that all of the literacy campaigns have failed. The situation today in that respect is just as bad or worse than in the past. And the reason for it is not hard to find. Literacy is meaningful when it is a necessity; and this happens only in countries that have attained a certain level of development. In underdeveloped countries one can live without reading or writing. The real enemy is economic underdevelopment; illiteracy is just one of its effects.

At the university level, there is concern about offering courses of study that will relate to economic development. Many university leaders take for granted that economic and industrial development will come when the country has enough university graduates in technical fields. I myself do not share that assumption, which also underlies anti-illiteracy campaigns. I believe it is exactly the opposite: there will be technical education and literacy when industrial development demands it.

BIBLIOGRAPHY

Gavidia, J. Mata. *Fundación de la Universidad en Guatemala, 1548-1688.* Universidad de San Carlos de Guatemala.

Lanning, John Tate. *The University in the Kingdom of Guatemala.* Cornell University Press, 1955.

Menendez, Luis Antonio. *Hacia un nuevo concepto de enseñanza media.* 1975.

Ministerio de Educación, Guatemala. Consejo Nacional de Planificacion Económica. *Plan Nacional de Educación, Ciencia y Cultura.* 1975-1979.

Orellana, C. Gonzalez. *Historia de la Educación en Guatemala.* 1970.

Ramirez, A. Carrillo. *Evolucion historica de la educación secundaria en Guatemala, 1831-1969.*

GUYANA

by
Alan Persico
Dean, Faculty of Education
University of Guyana, Guyana

BACKGROUND

The 1960s and the 1970s saw significant strides and changes in the organization and the structure of the educational system in Guyana. this was the period in which British Guiana became independent Guyana. One of the immediate major tasks, educationally, was to ensure that citizens were equipped with adequate skills to meet the needs of the new nation, and to do so while nurturing values that were consistent with the goals and objectives of Guyana.

Some of the national goals, in which a restructured educational system was expected to play a leading role, included the building of an egalitarian society; furthering the development of Guyana through self-help and the medium of cooperatives; ensuring rapid growth in the agricultural sector; facilitating Caribbean unity in political, social, and economic matters; and, with respect to international affairs, maintaining a position of non-alignment.

The emphasis on meeting the educational needs of the nation manifested itself in many ways: the "taking over" of all schools by the government (most secondary schools at the time were government-aided, or wholly private, with only a few fully government schools); the provision of additional teaching materials and equipment; the expansion of teacher education; the construction of new schools, including multilateral schools; the implementation of the secondary schools entrance examination; and the inclusion of new subjects/disciplines in the schools' curricula. Technical and vocational education, for example, received special attention. This was also the period during which "guidance" was formally introduced into education in Guyana. The early 1960s also saw the establishment of the University of Guyana and the initiation of a formal and more structured nursery education program.

Education in Guyana is the responsibility of the government and comes under the jurisdiction of the Ministry of Education. The ministry, headed by the minister, has the responsibility for formulation, endorsement, and execution of educational policy. The permanent secretary of the Ministry of Education is the central administrative authority for pre-university education. The professional staff of the Ministry of Education is headed by the chief education officer and consists of several other education officers at different levels. Since 1987, a professional inspectorate system is in place with the responsibility for ensuring quality and standards at schools. Education in Guyana is free from nursery to university.

Various agencies, institutions, and groups have inputs into the policy formulation and curriculum development process. This is done through meetings and consultations, directly and indirectly, between officers from the central administration and representatives from several groups and institutions including national subject committees, educational specialists, teachers associations and unions, the University of Guyana, Test Development Unit, Curriculum Development Center, and practicing teachers.

A major characteristic of the educational system is its attempt to create and maintain links with business, industry, and the world of work in general. This is perhaps most clearly noticeable in the functioning of the ministry's Prevocational Unit, and its program of technical and vocational education. The Prevocational Unit aims at providing students with appropriate learning experiences in agriculture, home economics, business education, and industrial arts; both theory and practice. The program for technical and vocational education seeks, among other things, to ensure that persons who graduate from the technical institutes, the Industrial Training Center, the Burrowes School of Arts, and the Carnegie School of Home Economics, can enter directly into industry and perform with a minimum of further orientation. Also, it endeavors to create and strengthen linkages with industry and commerce, to assess their needs, and to adjust course content and subject areas to satisfy the needs. Indeed, "craft" has become an important activity in respect of self-employment, business, and creativity.

PRIMARY AND SECONDARY EDUCATION

Pupils enter nursery school at the age of 3-4 years. The nursery education program aims at providing the children an opportunity for self-initiated activity while developing a sense of patriotism and learning to accept each other irrespective of differences in social, economic, religious, or ethnic backgrounds. After two years at the nursery school, children proceed to the primary school. The primary school curriculum is designed to provide basic literacy and numeracy skills as well as to develop attitudes to self, family, community, and nation. After six years of primary school, children may enter the secondary school. Placement in the secondary school program is based on performance at the secondary school entrance examination, in which the student's verbal and mathematical skills and knowledge are tested. Details of the secondary and tertiary education are treated later in this essay.

Secondary education is basically of two types. There is the traditional (general) secondary program which is broad based. After about five years, candidates write the exams offered by the Caribbean Examinations Council, or the General Certificate of Education (usually of London). Students may enter the world of work on the basis of these examinations or begin university education, either locally and abroad. Students can also continue beyond this level for a further period of two years in one of the six "sixth form" schools in the country. Students who complete the additional two years are expected to write the General Certificate of Education (Advanced Level) examination. The traditional secondary schools offer courses in English language, literature, Spanish, French, history, geography, social studies, mathematics, science, technical drawing, agriculture.

The other type of secondary program is offered in the community high school. After three years in this program, students write the Secondary Schools Proficiency Examination (SSPE). On the basis of the SSPE (taken usually after three years) students who demonstrate that they could benefit from a more academically oriented program could seek transfer to the traditional secondary school. Students who remain in the community high school for the fourth year, specialize in prevocational subject areas. The community high school provides both academic and prevocational training (arts, national sciences, social sciences, industrial arts and crafts). The community high school attempts in particular to provide training in occupational skills.

In 1985, a school of excellence, known as the "President's College" was established to educate children who did extremely well at the Secondary Schools Entrance Examination (SSEE). The objective of the "President's College" is to ensure that students who have shown intellectual promise are prepared academically and technically to assume leadership roles in their respective fields and that they also develop a high degree of socialist consciousness and patterns of behavior. This college offers an even wider range of courses (subjects) and experiences, including electronics, computer sciences, swimming, horse-back riding, in addition to subjects traditionally offered by other schools.

The institutions that offer technical and vocational education are The Government Technical Institute, the New Amsterdam Technical Institute, Guyana Industrial Training Center, Burrowes School of Art, and Carnegie School of Home Economics. The courses offered by the technical institutes and the Industrial Training Center include building and civil engineering, electrical and mechanical engineering, business studies, science, land surveying, plumbing, masonry, welding, carpentry, and agricultural mechanics. These courses lead to the Ordinary Technical Diploma, which also qualifies the students for admission to the University of Guyana. The Carnegie School of Home Economics offers the household management course, which is a two year course and is intended for students of 14-17 years of age. Classes include food preparation and service, nutrition, art and craft, garment making, laundry work and textiles, consumer education, and family life education. The Institute for the Blind and the David Rose School for Handicapped Children provide education to handicapped children.

Teaching staff is appointed by the Teaching Service Commission. It is not necessary to be a formally trained teacher to begin teaching in schools in Guyana. However, there is a time limit by which such persons must present themselves to be trained. Salary is based in part on professional training and experience. The Teaching Service Commission approves and may also initiate promotion, transfers, and termination of service. There is one teacher training institution for non-graduate teachers. It offers programs and certificates for nursery, primary, and secondary school teachers. Programs are of two years duration at both the secondary and primary levels. Admission to the teacher training institution is normally based on satisfactory performance in secondary level examinations offered either locally or overseas. After graduating from the Teacher Training College, students may be admitted to the Faculty of Education, University of Guyana to study for the Bachelor of Education degree. They may also pursue any other bachelor's degree program, in which case, they may follow it with the Postgraduate Diploma in Education offered by the Faculty of Education. The Bachelor of Education is a five year part-time program, but first year exemption is granted to trained teachers. The Diploma in Education is a two year part-time program.

HIGHER EDUCATION

Institutions

The University of Guyana is the only university in Guyana. The officers of the university are the chancellor, the pro-chancellor, the vice-chancellor, the registrar, the bursar (financial controller), and the deans of faculties. Responsibility for the general administration of the university lies with the vice-chancellor. The governing body of the university is the university council which consists of persons from both within and outside of the university community.

The university's academic board consists of the vice-chancellor, deputy vice-chancellor, deans and assistant deans of faculties, all full professors, heads of departments, directors of institutes associated with the university, the chairman of the board of graduate studies, the librarian, one representative from among the teaching staff of each faculty not included among those already listed, an academic member of the University of Guyana Staff Association, the director of the Office of Planning and Development, and normally, two representatives of the students' society. The academic board has the academic authority of the university.

A committee of deans serves as an informal coordinating body that advises the academic board on matters such as examinations, prizes, bursaries, scholarships, and other such awards. This committee may also deal with such matters as may be necessary for the efficient running of the university, should the vice-chancellor and deputy vice-chancellor, for whatever reason, be not in a position to perform their functions.

Each faculty has a faculty board comprising principally of staff from within the faculty, a representative from each of the other faculties and the library, and representatives from the office of the registrar. The chairman of faculty board is the vice-chancellor, if he is present. Normally the dean functions as the chairman. Subject to the approval of the academic board, the faculty board regulates the teaching and the study of the subjects assigned by the faculty. The faculty board also makes recommendations to the academic board for the award of degrees, diplomas, certificates, faculty prizes, as well as the rules and regulations governing these. Within each faculty, there is a faculty coordinating committee which may take decisions on behalf of faculty board, in between meetings of the board (the board normally meets once a month).

Other committees include the finance and general purposes committee which exercises the powers of council in all matters relating to finance and any other matters so delegated to it by the council; and the appointments committee which, on behalf of the council and subject to the general policy decisions of the council, determines among other things, matters pertaining to staff appointment, promotion, study, sabbatical, and vacation leave. The academic ranks consist of professor, reader, senior lecturer, lecturer II, lecturer I, and assistant lecturer.

Undergraduate Studies

The University of Guyana offers undergraduate programs in the faculties of arts, agriculture, education, health sciences, natural sciences, social sciences, and technology. The bachelor's degree program is normally of four-year duration, while certificate and diploma programs are normally two or three years duration, depending on the speciality. The Faculty of Health Sciences recently (1985) introduced the Bachelor's Degree in Medicine, which is innovative in the sense that it is problem-based and community oriented. It consists of four years academic, clinical, and community health care training, followed by two years of internship.

Admission requirement for a bachelor's degree program is normally five subjects at the General Proficiency Examination of the Caribbean Examination Council or at the General Certificate Examination or equivalent. Mathematics, English language, and other subjects relevant for the selected program are usually required. For some programs, applicants also have to write the University of Guyana Open Entrance Examination. Applicants must be at least sixteen years old. For some programs, for example, the Diploma in Pharmacy, and the Diploma in Radiography, applicants must be at least eighteen years of age. For most courses, the final grade the student receives is based on a combination of course work and final examination (usually in June-July). Typically the ratio is 50 percent for course work and 50 percent for final examinations. However there are variations. Some courses in the Faculty of Education, for example, require 40 percent of the grade for course work, and the balance for the final examination. There are other courses that make use of the continuous assessment method. For these, there is no final examination. Although the academic year is September - May (with examinations in June and July), some courses (for example in the Faculty of Agriculture) run from September to January, and January to July. The language of instruction is English.

As pointed out earlier, education in Guyana is free from nursery to university, so the major expenses for students are those related to accommodation and transportation. The University of Guyana does not have living accommodation for students. Only a limited number of foreign students (less than 10 percent) are enrolled at the university at the present time. Recent changes in regulation may require foreign students to pay tuition fees in foreign currency.

Categories of academic staff include assistant lecturer, lecturer I, lecturer II, senior lecturer, reader, and professor. Promotion criteria include excellence in teaching, research, public service, and contribution to the university. Initial appointments are made by open competition.

Advanced Studies and Research

Postgraduate programs leading to the master's degree are offered in the faculties of arts, natural sciences, social sciences, and education. There have not been any doctoral programs so far. Master's programs are usually of two years duration, and involve both course work and thesis. Research projects are expected to have as much relevance as possible to the urgent needs of the Guyanese society while meeting required standards of scholarship. With respect to financing of graduate studies, the university gives priority to graduate students in the selection of instructors, tutorial or research assistants, and research fellows. Admission to graduate programs require a bachelor's degree from the University of Guyana with at least a "credit" pass or an equivalent qualification. The full-time teaching staff in graduate programs are required to have at least a master's degree.

Staff members who wish to carry out research may apply to the Research and Publications Committee of their own faculty, or to the University Research and Publications Committee for funding. However, they are encouraged to seek funding from agencies outside the university. If the committees believe that the research proposed is appropriate, worthwhile, and feasible, the project usually receives either full or partial funding from the university (provided funds voted for the purpose have not been exhausted). As in the case of undergraduate studies, the number of foreign students at the graduate level is quite small. Foreign students however are very welcome and are encouraged to apply for admission.

ISSUES AND TRENDS

One of the major developments taking place in education in Guyana, at the present time, is the movement towards the implementation of distance teaching. The geographical layout of Guyana makes it difficult for some citizens to attend university, Teacher's College, and some other institutions which are situated in the capital, Georgetown. Distance teaching, therefore, has become very important. The Institute of Adult and Continuing Education of the University of Guyana is expected to participate actively in the coordination of this effort.

Attempts are also underway to improve effectiveness and efficiency of the educational system. Some of the measures seriously being considered at this time include upgrading of information storage and retrieval systems; reinforcement of the school inspectorate system; publication of more teacher guides and student materials; introduction of standardized tests on a wider scale; reorganization of the community high schools to allow for greater participation of the communities in which these schools exist; implementation of a more formalized system for the in-service education of teachers; establishment of national subject committees; greater assistance for the disabled and for other children and youths with special needs; and decentralization of the administration and management of school finance.

BIBLIOGRAPHY

Baird, C. L. "Growth Points in Education: A Decade in Change." In *Guyana: A Decade of Progress*. Georgetown: Ministry of Information and Culture, 1974.

Bynoe, Jacob. ed. *New Tasks for Guyanese Education: Readings in the Philosophy of Schooling*. Turkeyen: Faculty of Education, U.G., 1973.

Digest of Educational Statistics. 1980-1981. Georgetown: Ministry of Education, 1982.

Ministry of Education and Social Development: *Annual Report 1987*.

Ministry of Education: *Brief Account of Stages in Education System of Guyana*. Georgetown: Ministry of Education, 1983.

State Paper: On Educational Policy 1988-1993. Georgetown: Ministry of Education.

University of Guyana - Bulletin 1988-1989. Georgetown: Guyana National Printers, 1988.

University of Guyana: 25 Anniversary Year, 1988. Georgetown: Guyana National Printers, 1988.

HAITI

by
Charles-Poisset Romain
Dean
Haiti Institute of African Study and Research, Haiti

BACKGROUND

Five distinct periods are identifiable in the development of education in Haiti: colonial education (1492-1796), post-independence period (1797-1842), creative period (1843-1896), consolidation of public education (1896-1976), and the current period with new educational reforms (1976 to present) (Tardieu 1990). In general, critics of Haitian education link the origins of education to country's independence. However, there are others who consider that well defined educational programs existed during the colonial period.

After independence, Jean Jacques Dessalines, the father of the liberation movement and the leader of the newly independent nation made provision for education in the first Haitian Constitution. Subsequently, King Henri Christophe who ruled part of the country called upon the British to establish schools in his kingdom. At this time, the country had been broken up into two parts: one part, a monarchy, ruled by King Henri Christophe; and the other, a republic, under President Alexandre Petion. President Alexandre Petion, however, followed a different philosophy and educational policy. Under his regime, a number of primary schools came to be established without any state control. The government, on its part, imported the books as well as curriculum and established the Alexandre Petion Lycee and a public library. Jean-Pierre Boyer who succeeded Petion was not a promoter of education. He is thought to have believed in the policy "to sow the seeds of education is to sow revolution".

The year 1843 was a turning point in Haitian education. A revolution rocked the government. There was popular public demand for education and primary education became an electoral issue. By the middle of the nineteenth century, the government inaugurated a new three pronged policy on higher education: putting in place a vast program for manpower training, granting resources to foreign teachers, and putting public education under the charge of parishes and parish priests. In 1860, Haiti signed an agreement with the Vatican which aimed at the creation of a coherent and centralized system of education through the intermediary of the Catholic Church and the financial backing of the government of Haiti. From the time of inception up to now, Haitian education has faced numerous problems and several reforms have been attempted.

The broad objectives of Haitian education can be outlined as follows: provide all (citizens) a solid and broad education with equal opportunities for

343

specializing at different levels and for developing individual aptitudes; provide opportunities to all Haitians to participate in the life of the community in a conscious, responsible, competent and productive manner; and impart an education that would make it possible to change physical, material and spiritual conditions of the students. The Constitution of 1987, (Edition Scolha 1987) in its articles 32, 32.1 and 32.2, stipulates: "The state guarantees the right to education and oversees the physical, intellectual, moral, professional, social and civic education of the population. Education is the responsibility of the state and its territorial organs, which must provide schooling free of charge and must oversee the training of teachers for both the public and the private sectors. The state has the primary responsibility for providing mass schooling (for the nation)".

Two successive legislations govern the system of education in Haiti: the Law of 28 September 1979 and the presidential Decree-Law of 8 May 1989. The Law of 1979, in essence, give three mandates to the Ministry of National Education: to modernize administration of the department, to ensure a good coordination, and to reinforce the planning and evaluation functions. The present Ministry of National Education, Youth, and Sports is governed by the Law of 1989. The articles 1 and 2 of the law gives the ministry the authority to administer and govern Haitian education. The ministry develops the national educational policy at all levels of education, sets objectives for both formal and non-formal education, and oversees their implementation. The ministry also oversees the implementation of national higher educational policy and engages in curriculum development and production of teaching material.

Education in Haiti is subsidized by the state. Based on data from USAID (1987), the annual cost of a student in public school is shared by parents (US$26), government (US$44), and financial aid organizations (US$33). In a similar fashion, the cost of a university student (excepting students in the faculty of medicine) is shared by parents (US$138), government (US$430), and financial aid organizations (US$171). On the other hand private higher education in Haiti costs the students' parents (US$592), government (US$372), and financial aid organizations (US$220).

PRIMARY AND SECONDARY EDUCATION

Primary Education

The Constitution of Haiti requires primary education *(enseignement fondamental)* to be compulsory and free of charge. Under the present educational system, primary education consist of the earlier seven-year primary school of two cycles plus a third cycle which covers the first three years of the secondary school *(lycée* and college). Children enter primary school at the age of six years. The objective of the primary level is to provide children with a general education and to develop their skills to a level that would enable them to either pursue secondary education or to enter the world of work. This new approach allows democratization of education, permits use of flexible pedagogical techniques, and links the school with the community.

The curriculum aims at providing instruction in a variety of fields with an interdisciplinary perspective and based on a rational distribution of time among different subjects. Teaching is focussed on languages (Creole as the mother tongue and French as the second national language); mathematics (which include reinforcement of reasoning, capacity, and application of mathematical logique to the solution of everyday problems); social sciences (particularly history, geography, and economics as building blocks to train students to become full citizens of tomorrow); experimental sciences (preparing students to progressively master technical know-how and to understand the scientific phenomena); aesthetic education (to assure the broadest development of students as they leave school); introduction to technology and productive skills; physical education and sport (for improvement of the physique, maintenance of good health, and development of community and competitive sport).

The third cycle studies at the primary school (lasting three years) is termed as the *cycle d'orientation* and provides either a general education (science and humanities) or technical and vocational training leading to a diploma (with classical or vocational option). Student enrollment at primary level (cycles one and two) has grown annually at an average rate of 6.9 percent between 1979 and 1987. Growth of enrollment in the private sector is somewhat higher at 8.6 percent. However, the internal efficiency of primary schools is low. Of every 1,000 children who enter primary level, only 439 succeed in reaching the seventh year (end of second cycle). In 1986-87, there were 612,200 students enrolled in primary cycles one and two (ages 6-12 years) and they represented 61.2 percent of the total 6-12 year old population, compared to 40 percent in 1979-80. During the academic year 1988-89, the enrollment in primary schools had increased to 741,605.

Secondary Education

Before the new reforms, secondary education consisted of seven years of studies divided into two cycles. The first cycle was of three years duration and the curriculum focussed on general studies. The second cycle consisted of three streams: section A (Greek and Latin), section B (Greek and Latin) and section C (science and languages). After six years of studies (in the first and second cycles), students receive the first certificate of secondary studies *(baccalauréat première partie)* on passing the state examination. After one additional year students could obtain the second certificate of secondary studies *(baccalauréat deuxième partie)*. Qualifying exams for the *baccalauréat* were conducted by the government. During the course of their secondary studies, students have the option of selecting normal primary schools (teacher training), commerce schools, nursing schools, and similar vocational schools.

However, the new reforms of education are changing the character of Haitian schools with the traditional primary school being replaced by the "fundamental cycle" in which the primary school include the first three years of the secondary school, thereby reducing the secondary school to three years.

Secondary education in Haiti is offered at public schools named lycees or colleges. The lack of sufficient public schools have led to a proliferation of private establishments. These days it is common to hear in Haiti of the "flourishing industry of private education". Student enrollment at secondary level has grown from 98,570 in 244 schools in 1981-82 to 173,700 in 372 schools in 1985-86. In 1981-82 government schools or lycees enrolled 16 percent of the total students but in 1985-86 only 12.2 percent of the students were accounted in lycees. On the other hand, enrollment in private establishments has grown annually by about 16.5 percent with a 1985-86 enrollment of 152,500 students. In summary, public sector involvement in secondary education has diminished for the benefit of the private sector. Private sector now operates over twelve times the number of schools as the public sector. As regards internal efficiency of secondary education, the statistics indicate that only 36.3 percent of the students who enter secondary level complete the secondary education diploma. In the academic year 1987-88 the enrollment in secondary schools had risen to 155,067 of whom 127,811 or 82 percent were in private schools.

Technical and vocational programs require three years of studies at technical schools which admit students who complete the primary school. These programs are administered by the National Institute of Vocational Training (*Institut National de Formation Professionnelle*) which come under the jurisdiction of the Ministry of National Education, Youth, and Sports and works in close collaboration with the Pilot Center for Vocational Training. Institutions falling into this group can be classified into several categories: schools for technical and vocational education, centers for vocational training, public vocational education schools, agricultural training schools, private vocational education schools which are subsidized by the government, and schools for commercial education. Programs at these institutions vary from *baccalauréat d'aptitudes professionnelles* to technical diplomas (university level studies). There were over 3,521 students in these schools in 1987-88.

HIGHER EDUCATION

Institutions

Higher education in Haiti has its roots in the earliest years of the country's independence. Laws for the creation of three schools of health were promulgated as far back as 1808. In 1815 the King Henri Christophe founded the Royal Academy of the North which consisted of a school of medicine, surgery, and pharmacy; a school of arts and crafts; and a school of agriculture. The faculties of medicine and of law in Port-au-Prince are the two oldest university institutions in Haiti. The University of Haiti itself was created under the Decree Law of 23 December 1944 by the government of Elie Lescot. This university later became the State University of Haiti on 16 December 1960.

The mission of the university was outlined in the presidential decree: "The State University is created in place of the old University of Haiti for the purpose of imparting higher education, both theoretical and practical, in its faculties, schools, and institutes; and for stimulating and organizing scientific research. The State University of Haiti is the central organization responsible for higher education and research". The constitution of 1987 gives it the status of an autonomous institution and states "Education is free for all degree programs and access to higher education is open, uniquely on the basis of merit and equality of opportunity". The law makes it an obligation for the state to finance the functioning of the State University of Haiti and public schools of higher education. As regards the private sector, private higher educational institutions require authorization from the State University of Haiti to function.

There are two categories of university institutions in Haiti. The first category consists of public institutions which come under the State University of Haiti. The State University of Haiti is headed by a rector who is the president of the university council formed by deans and directors. There are seven faculties (medicine, odontology, science, agronomy and veterinary medicine, ethnology, humanities, law and economics), four schools (nursing, teacher training, pharmacy, and medical technology), five institutes (development science, psychology, African studies, Afro-American studies etc.) and a center for applied linguistics. The second category consist of twenty-four private institutions including universities, faculties, schools, institutes, and seminaries. The State University of Haiti has given recognition to some of these institutions and for the diplomas awarded by them.

Programs and Degrees

Higher education institutions in Haiti offer degrees at three levels: (a) the first degree, *licence,* after three or four years of studies, for which some institutions may require presentation of a memoir before a jury; (b) the *maîtrise* after two or three years of studies beyond the *licence,* also requiring presentation of one or more rigorous studies; and (c) the *doctorat* which requires several years of work beyond *maîtrise* including completion of a dissertation based on an original contribution in the field.

Majority of the faculties, schools, and institutes (agronomy, applied sciences, humanities, linguistics, African studies, accounting, administration, economics, education, theological studies, etc.) do not offer programs beyond the first cycle of studies (university diploma or *licence*). The Faculty of Ethnology offers programs at all the three levels: *licence* in anthropology and sociology, *maîtrise* in humanities, and *doctorat* in humanities. The Faculty of Medicine and Pharmacy offers the Doctor of Medicine degree after six years of studies.

In 1987, according to a study conducted by the ex-Rector Jean Baptiste Romain (Romain 1987), higher education institutions in Haiti enrolled 7,500 students, of whom 5,187 or 69.2 percent were in public institutions with the rest 29.8 percent being enrolled in private institutions. In 1986-87 there were 1081 teachers employed in higher education institutions, including 14.3 percent females. The teaching staff consisted of 73.8 percent holding *licence* or equivalent, 18.1 percent holding *maîtrise* and 8.1 percent holding doctorates. Full-time teachers formed only 7.0 percent of the teachers, with the rest functioning on part-time basis. In 1989, the enrollment at the state university was 6,278 and the higher education institutions in the private sector accounted for 3,000 students.

Students in higher education work under difficult conditions with no university restaurant facilities, no health services, no organized transport, and inadequate laboratories and library facilities. For example, the library of the faculty of agronomy has only 5,276 books and the Institute of African Studies and Research of Haiti has only 2,000 books. The building space available for the faculties and for student facilities are extremely limited. For example, the building space per student, for the last seven years had been 21.5 square meters in the Faculty of Agronomy and Veterinary Medicine and 3.22 square meters in the faculty of humanities.

In Haitian higher education, organized research is practically non-existent. Nevertheless on rare occasions, university teachers engage in scientific research activities on their own. Some faculties may require the students to prepare a research memoir to be presented before a jury. Publications are rare.

The problems facing higher education are a reflection of the problems facing the Haitian society as a whole. As indicated by the former rector of the State University of Haiti, university education requires, "in-depth reforms covering autonomy and learning centered simply on books, improvement of the condition of teaching staff, restructuring of programs to meet the needs of the country, equivalency of university degrees, decentralization, betterment of student life, and student participation in university activities" (Romain 1987).

ISSUES AND TRENDS

Over the last decade or so five educational plans have been unveiled in Haiti. First, the five year plan for 1981-1986, then the biennial plan for 1984-1986, supplemented by the annual plan for 1985-1986. These were followed by the biennial plan for development for education for 1986-1988 and finally the national plan which is in the process of being implemented. In Haiti, as in many other countries, education has become one of the most remarkable phenomena of this century. What Marie-Roger Biloa pointed out is very much relevant to Haiti's situation, "In all countries, there exist two categories of human beings: those who have the knowledge and those who don't.... Those who have the power and those who dominated. And the magic bridge that allows a person to move from one condition to the other (the better one) has a name, called school" (Jeune Afrique n.d.).

For a long time, the school has been the object of a "veritable collective cult". In the recent years it has lost some of its magic force, in the face of underdevelopment. Paulo Freyre spoke of "the education of the oppressed" and Ivan Illich dreams of "a society without schools". In Haiti, the system of education has been questioned. During a seminar on improvement of education (1967, Haiti's primary school certificate has been described as, "A heavy weight ... hardly homogenous ... a dress too tight for anybody to wear". Many other critical opinions have been expressed on the distressful situation of the system of education in Haiti.

As pointed out by H. Wiesler, "Hardly 5 percent of the school teachers have university degrees and only about 10 percent of the teachers have a diploma from a teacher training school. There is only a 3 percent probability that a student who enters school continues his or her schooling, and the average schooling per child is only 3.6 years" (Weesler 1973).

As all weaknesses in the early education of a child ultimately result in the quality of higher education, the debate from the very beginning has been on the improvement of primary and secondary education, which still remains a desired yet unachieved objective.

The educational reforms which have been undertaken in Haiti, in spite of their shortcomings, are going to bring about many changes of pedagogical significance. The reforms provide for greater participation, search for knowledge, linking school culture with real life and the community, and setting up of measurable objectives and indicators.

BIBLIOGRAPHY

Bilboa, Marie-Roger. "Dis, maman, à quoi ça sert, l'école?" *Afrique* No. 1503 (October 1989): 6.

Editions Scolha. Constitution de la Républic d'Haiti. Port-au-Prince, Haiti: Impressions Nagiques, 1987.

Locher Uli. Nalan, Thierry, et Pierre-Jacques, Charles. "Evaluation de la Réforme Educative en Haiti." (Rapport Final de la mission éducative en Haiti). Geneve, 1987. Mimeo.

Rodrigue, Jean. *Crise de l'Education et Crise du Developpement.* Port-au-Prince, Haiti: Imprimerie des Antilles, 1987.

Romain, Dr. J. B. *Situation de l'Enseignement Supérieur en Haiti.* Port-au-Prince, Haiti: Imprimerie des Antilles, 1987

Tardieu, Charles. *L'Education en Haiti (de la période coloniale à nos jours).* Port-au-Prince, Haiti: Imprimerie Henri Deschamps, 1990.

Weesler, H. *Scolarisation en Haiti.* Port-au-Prince, Haiti, 1973.

World Bank. "Premier Projet d'Education." Port-au-Prince, Haiti, 1982. Mimeo.

World Bank. "Rapport d'Evaluation. Deuxième Projet d'Education," March 1985, Mimeo.

HONDURAS

by
Irma Acosta de Fortin
Rector
Jose Cecilio Del Valle University, Honduras

BACKGROUND

The origin of formal organization of education in Honduras can be traced back to the reforms initiated by the 1881 Act of Education. For the first time, this Act provided public schooling and organized a national university. The system underwent important reforms in the late 1950s and in the beginning of the 1960s. Subsequently, in 1972, all levels of education underwent another round of reform.

The organization, direction, and development of education come under two authorities: the secretary of public education in the case of primary and secondary schooling; and the National Autonomous University of Honduras, in the case of higher education. Primary schools are located throughout the country but the secondary schools are found only in regional centers and in some of the important cities. The universities and other higher education institutions are located in the capital and in three cities in the north of the country. In 1988, Honduras allocated 20 percent of its budget to education. The biggest allocation, 42 percent, was for primary education. Secondary education received 32 percent and higher education got 19 percent (17 percent for National Autonomous University of Honduras and the remaining 2 percent for the Higher School of Teacher Training). At this level of expenditure, the investment for one student in the National Autonomous University of Honduras was equal to that for ten students attending primary school.

PRIMARY AND SECONDARY EDUCATION

At the primary level, 93 percent of the children between seven and thirteen years enter school (Banco Central, 1986-88). However, all the six grades, as specified, are offered only in 55 percent of the schools due to shortage of teachers and other limitations. Teachers who work in primary schools have had only twelve years of schooling which means that they have not received an education beyond secondary level. Their training in mathematics and natural sciences is weak and thus, their ability to formulate programs that would lead the students to careers requiring a science background is very limited.

Towards the end of the 1950s, the secretary of education implemented a reform in secondary education that resulted in two cycles: a common general cycle or lower secondary, and a diversified second cycle or upper secondary. The objective was to provide a terminal education to qualify those who wanted to enter the labor force and to prepare others for programs in higher education. In 1972, the National Autonomous University of Honduras changed their admission policy to accept all those who completed secondary education irrespective of their subject areas.

At the end of the common first cycle of three years, a youth can follow studies leading to the academic *bachillerato* in sciences and letters (two years), nursing, or secretaryship (one year); industrial *bachillerato* in agriculture or forestry, business administration, or accounting (three years); diploma of agricultural technician or teacher of primary education (three years); and technician's diploma in industrial electricity, agricultural mechanics (four years).

The academic year is of nine months duration with a minimum of 200 school days. Academic assessments are conducted two or three times per year. There are no general country wide exams. Each individual school conducts its own exams based on continuous assessment; only the dates and frequency of exams is determined by the secretary of education. Admission to the common first cycle requires completion of six years of primary education. Successful completion of the common cycle is required for continuing education in the diversified cycle.

Teachers for secondary schools are trained at the *Escuela Superior del Profesorado* (Higher School for Teacher Training). Given the fact that this is the only training school of this kind in the country, only about 24 percent of the teachers in the 474 schools are trained for their jobs (UNESCO, 1984). Of the 177 teachers trained in 1988 at the school, 48 percent were in social sciences, 41 percent were in exact sciences, and 11 percent were in humanities (Banco Central, 1986-88).

At the secondary level, there are 162 private schools, some of which are bilingual (Spanish-English and Spanish-French). Fees at these schools vary from US$12-150 per month. Students who were enrolled in secondary studies in 1988 constituted only 21 percent of the age group 14-19 years (Banco Central, 1986-88), indicating that only a small percentage of the children who enter primary schools continue to secondary level. Lack of enough schools in all the cities is obviously a contributing factor.

HIGHER EDUCATION

Institutions

The founding of the National University in 1847 through the collaboration of the Catholic church and the government heralded the beginning of higher education in Honduras. A century later, in 1941, the first non-university center of higher studies in agriculture, the Pan-American School of Agriculture, was established. In 1905 the first military school, the Francisco Morazan Military Academy, was founded.

The initiatives for establishing more centers of higher education increased since 1975 and resulted in the founding of the first private university, Jose Cecilio del Valle University in 1978. Between 1975 and 1988, the number of higher educational institutions increased significantly and today there are four universities and ten non-university institutions of higher education. Ten of the institutions are supported by state funds and the rest are financed by student fees and donations.

The public institutions consist of the National Autonomous University, Higher School for Teacher Training, National School of Agriculture, National School of Forest Sciences, Francisco Morazan Military Academy, Military Academy of Aviation, National Police Academy, Staff (Military) School, School for Police Officers, and the Center for Naval Studies. Public institutions are fully funded by the government. The private institutions consist of the Jose Cecilio Del Valle University, St. Peters University, Technological University of Central America, and the Pan-American School of Agriculture.

The National Autonomous University is an autonomous institution since 1957 and the governance is effected through councils consisting of equal numbers of representatives from students and professionals (professors, administrators, and alumni). This mode of organization gives strong participation to students in the formulation of country's educational policy on higher education.

In 1988, higher education institutions enrolled 38,560 students of whom 85 percent were in the National Autonomous University, 3 percent in the other universities, 9 percent in the Higher School for Teacher Training, 2 percent in the agricultural schools, 0.5 percent in the military schools and the rest 0.5 percent in the National School for Forest Sciences.

About 84 percent of the teaching staff engaged in higher education are employed by the National Autonomous University and 64 percent of this staff are on full-time employment. The rank of titular professor requires minimum of five years experience. Academic achievements as a measure for position classification is used only at the Jose Cecilio Del Valle University.

The National Autonomous University, given its size, organization, and character, is the central leader of the higher educational system. However, the coordination of its activities is somewhat weak and there is much room for improvement in its administration and in the role it plays relating to the development of the country.

Undergraduate Studies

In Honduras, as in all Latin American countries, the first degree offered at universities is the *licenciado,* which requires 242 credit hours including in some cases, remedial courses in mathematics and Spanish.

The reforms initiated in 1962 at the National Autonomous University has resulted in the creation of departments of exact sciences and humanities, modification of curricula, and a program of training for professors. The reforms led to the establishment of *bachillerato universitario* (bachelor's degree) at first by the National Autonomous University and subsequently by the Jose Cecilio Del Valle University, Pan American School of Agriculture and the Higher School of Teacher Training. There is no difference between the *bachillerato universitario* and the *licenciado* with regard to admission to master's degree programs in foreign universities; the difference lies in the number of credit hours required. The curriculum requires an average of 12 percent of courses in general subjects, up to

63 percent of courses in the area of specialization and the rest in optional subjects. All courses are taught in Spanish excepting in Jose Cecilio Del Valle University and Pan American School of Agriculture where English is used sometimes when students' backgrounds permit such use.

The fees charged by the National Autonomous University are practically insignificant (only US$25 per semester). The fees at other institutions vary from US$450 per semester at the Jose Cecilio Del Valle University to US$825 per semester at the Technology University of Central America. The Pan American School of Agriculture charges US$6,000 per year including board and lodging. Educational costs at the National Autonomous University and at the Higher School of Teacher Training are subsidized by the government.

Graduation requirements include development of a project known as *integrado*. In the Pan American School of Agriculture, this project takes the form of a program of scientific investigation. The School of Medicine (of the National Autonomous University) requires one year of hospital internship and one more year of (social) service.

Advanced Studies and Research

Postgraduate programs at the master's degree level are offered at the National Autonomous University and the Technological University of Central America. Visiting foreign professors participate in offering these programs. Postgraduate qualifications are also offered in social work at the National Autonomous University, as part of a Central American integration effort. The National Autonomous University also offers a doctorate in administrative law but it cannot be said that these postgraduate programs approach the level of postgraduate offerings available in the United States, Europe, or some of the other Latin American countries. Specialization in medicine consist of a combination of courses and practical work requiring three years after the six years of undergraduate studies.

ISSUES AND TRENDS

The characteristics of development, growth in population, and the regional problems facing the country since the 1970s have been impediments for the development of an efficient system of education to meet the country's needs.

Primary education remains at the forefront of priorities of the state, as this sector of education is weak and incomplete: the level of student success is low, and of those who complete the primary education, just a small percentage continue to the next level. Only 7.8 percent of the age group of 20-24 years are in higher education.

The country needs to exploit its natural resources, become more productive in the agricultural sector, and initiate industrial development. For this, the country had in 1988 only the following personnel for every 100,000 habitants: physicians and surgeons - 58; veterinarians - 3; economists - 10; lawyers - 49; civil engineers - 31; architects - 5; agronomists - 55; pharmacists - 19; primary education teachers -

1,615; professional nurses - 24; and mechanical, electrical and chemical engineers - 9.

Productivity improvements in the agricultural sector can be pursued only if the rural population is organized and trained to modify the work methods. Moving from an agricultural economy to an industrial economy, as other countries in the third world have done, is going to be a very difficult task if our educational system is not improved to match developments in modern societies and to adapt to present day technological advances.

BIBLIOGRAPHY

Banco Central, Honduras. *Honduras en Cifras.* 1986-1988.

UNESCO. *Desarrollo de la Educación en un Contexto de Limitación de Recursos, Honduras.* 1984.

HONG KONG

by
Cho-Yee To
Professor and Director, School of Education
Chinese University of Hong Kong, Hong Kong

BACKGROUND

Hong Kong, a city of 388 square miles with a population of over five million, has developed one of the most complicated, eclectic, and yet functional systems of higher education anywhere. Established upon a multiple-track elementary-secondary system, Hong Kong's three universities are the University of Hong Kong, a British model institution using English as its medium instruction; the Chinese University of Hong Kong, whose proclaimed mission is the perpetuation of the Chinese cultural heritage and the promotion of intercultural and international academic integration; and the newly founded Science and Technological University of Hong Kong.

In addition, there are two British model polytechnics, three British-American combined model postsecondary colleges, four British model teacher training colleges, A British-American combined model college of performing arts and several Taiwan model colleges, all with programs ranging from two to four years beyond secondary education. These universities and colleges subscribe to different educational ideals; they design their own curricula, represent different standards, appeal to different audiences, and admit students of different aspirations and abilities. They differ significantly from one another in enrollment and resources. Often they compete with one another, and yet at the same time they supplement one another, providing a variety of programs to meet the educational needs of their society.

Hong Kong became a British colony in 1842. For a full century thereafter higher education did not show much development. Before World War I, there was only one small university, one teacher training institute, and one technical college. But beginning in the 1950s, higher education in Hong Kong developed rapidly and soon evolved into a fascinating arena for academic competition among the various educational institutions. As a result, one can find a specimen of almost every kind of English postsecondary institution in Hong Kong.

The system of education in Hong Kong is decentralized, and permits diversity and differences. This diversity and the multiplicity originated in the city's colonial days. When the colony was founded, the government and the Western missionaries were concerned only with the development of English education. The local people who could not qualify for the government-supported English education, or who did not want to follow the British pattern of education, had to find ways to meet their own educational needs. They did so by establishing various private schools whether classical or modern, academic or vocational, open or exclusive. The colonial government's policy was to let them struggle for their own survival. It did not take responsibility for their support; it financed only the English schools operated by its Education Department and the recognized church groups. The government treated the other private schools or colleges not as educational institutions but as businesses.

Thus the competition characterizing higher education in Hong Kong has not been fair; government and government-aided institutions have clearly been in privileged positions. But the competition has at least been open: all institutions exercise their creativity and ingenuity, mobilize their resources, and summon their courage to attain their goals. Many have failed and disappeared, becoming only a paragraph in the educational history of Hong Kong. But others such as the Chinese University of Hong Kong, have managed to overcome their difficulties and eventually emerged as sound and vigorous institutions.

In the late 1950s, three private Chinese-language colleges, unrecognized by the Hong Kong government, decided to consolidate their resources to form a stronger institution, a new university with a Chinese cultural identity. Support was won first from the international academic community and finally from the local colonial government. Thus, in 1963, the Chinese University was established and recognized. Despite continuous discrimination and bias against its non-British four-year curriculum in Chinese, and doubt about its academic standard, the university gradually built a strong faculty holding some of the strongest academic credentials in Southeast Asia. It has made excellent use of local talents and attracted some of the best scholars from Taiwan, North America, England, and Australia. A number of its graduates have become internationally recognized scientists and scholars. Its Department of Chinese, the largest academic unit on campus, emphasizes classical as well as modern learning. The university graduated its first class of physicians in 1986. Its School of Education founded the Hong Kong Educational Research Association in 1984 and has since assumed a crucial leadership role for the improvement of the whole educational system of Hong Kong. The institution which, not long ago, was so uncertain about its future, has become a uniquely Chinese university outside of China enjoying international standing. It is celebrating its 25th anniversary this year.

The advancement of the Chinese University broke the monopoly on local higher education held by the University of Hong Kong. Faced with the challenge of the younger university, this well-established British-model university, always very proud of its uncompromising elitism, launched a series of programs to revitalize and redevelop itself. Professional faculties such as dentistry, law, architecture have since been added or expanded in recent years. The constant comparisons and contests between these two universities have been a source of academic tension. They have also helped to generate superior academic achievements by the teachers and students of both campuses. Among the benefit of this competition to Hong Kong has been the provision of outstanding university graduates to the teaching, research, and administrative staffs of other higher education institutions in the city.

The Hong Kong government has never had a futuristic, deliberate plan for ambitious and comprehensive development of higher education. The educational patterns in existence are a historical accident, the result of continuous adjustment and adaptation to the constant change of the Hong Kong society. All these different types of universities, colleges, polytechnics, and schools are but the outcome of direct and indirect responses to the educational and cultural needs of the people.

The development of higher education in Hong Kong can be summarized as follows: (1). A system of higher education with a multiplicity of categories emerged within a laissez-faire government to meet the demands and needs of different and sometimes conflicting interests of the people. (2). The system has been undergoing continuous adjustment and revision. Unproductive and untimely categories disappeared, and categories useful to the educational, cultural, political, or economic sectors of the society survived. (3). The transformation from a colony to a special administrative district with considerable autonomy will certainly accelerate the process of political maturity. The multiple system of higher education, an unplanned by-product of the past, has become a tradition that is being deliberately maintained.

PRIMARY AND SECONDARY EDUCATION

The school system in Hong Kong encompasses six years' primary education (ages 6-11). The primary schools are not much differentiated by curriculum. Apart from small groups of schools which adopt curricula influenced by British or American models, the majority follow a common curriculum. Primary schools are also more or less homogeneous in their choice of language of instruction. In most of the schools, the students' mother language, Chinese, is used in instruction with English taught as a second language. English is used in only about 5 percent of the primary schools. Most primary schools operate on a bisessional basis offering morning and afternoon sessions. However, the government has announced a plan to convert them to whole day operation. There is a centrally-planned system through which primary and junior secondary places are allocated. Which secondary school a primary six leaver will join depends on the primary school's internal assessment scaled by a centrally-administered aptitude test and the choice made by the parents.

Hong Kong's secondary educational system receives students who have completed six years of primary schooling. There are four types of secondary schools serving different educational purposes. They are the Anglo-Chinese secondary schools, the Chinese middle schools, the secondary technical schools, and the prevocational schools. There are differences in curriculum, medium of instruction, number of years of studies and the kinds of public examinations prepared for the sixth form students. The following is a brief description of these four types of schools.

In the Anglo-Chinese schools, the medium of instruction is English. They offer a five-year secondary program in a broad range of academic and cultural subjects leading to the Hong Kong Certificate of Education examination. Beyond the five-year program, these schools offer a two-year curriculum leading to the Hong Kong Advanced Level examination, which serves as the matriculation examination for the University of Hong Kong.

In the Chinese middle schools, students also take courses leading to the Hong Kong Certificate of Education examination at the end of their fifth-year of study. In these schools, instruction is mainly conducted in Chinese. English is taught as a second language. The Chinese middle schools offer a one-year sixth form program leading to the Hong Kong Higher Level Examination, which is the admission examination of the Chinese University of Hong Kong. Students from the Anglo-Chinese schools who complete the first year of their two-year preparatory program may also take this examination to gain admission to the Chinese University of Hong Kong.

Secondary technical schools prepare their students for the Hong Kong Certificate of Education examination with special emphasis on technical and commercial subjects. Students can continue their studies in the sixth form in technical institutes. They can also apply for admission to other higher education institutions if they can fulfil the academic requirements.

Prevocational schools are secondary schools which provide students with a general education as well as basic training technical skills upon which further vocational studies may be based.

In 1986, about 19 percent of the population had received upper secondary education and another 18 percent had received lower secondary education. About 33 percent had received primary education but 20 percent of the population had received no schooling.

By the mode of financing, there are three main types of schools: government, government-aided, and private. Among the primary schools operated in 1988, 81 percent were aided, 12 percent were private and 7 percent were government operated. Concerning the secondary schools, 71 percent were aided, 20 percent were private, and 9 percent were government operated. In the government operated and government-aided schools, no tuition fees are charged at the primary and junior secondary levels and for senior secondary and sixth form levels, only nominal fees are charged. Private schools charge fees at all levels except those places subsidized by the government. For the government schools, capital and recurrent expenditures are fully financed by the government.

Aided schools have full support for their recurrent costs and 80 percent support for their capital costs from the government, the other 20 percent being financed by the schools' sponsors. Most private schools are profit making and the government does not meet any part of their operating costs. However, because there is not enough junior secondary places for the implementation of the plan of free junior secondary education, the government buys places, i.e. pays tuition fees for students, at some of the better-run private secondary schools, and limited recurrent aid is given to the non-profit making schools.

HIGHER EDUCATION

In recent decades, higher education in Hong Kong has been undergoing considerable change and expansion. It is a consequence of population growth and economic development of the city. Changes in the structure of the labor market and the rise in living standards have resulted in increasing demand for various types of higher education. Postsecondary institutions such as universities, polytechnics, approved postsecondary colleges, colleges of education, technical institutes, and private colleges attract a very large number of applicants every year.

There are three universities in Hong Kong: the University of Hong Kong, the Chinese University of Hong Kong, and the Hong Kong University of Science and Technology (which will start admitting students in 1991). All the universities in Hong Kong are self-governing, drawing their income mainly from grants made by the Hong Kong government. Competition for university places has always been fierce. Students entering the universities are, without exception, those who fare the best in the entrance examinations. The following is a brief description of the two universities in Hong Kong.

The University of Hong Kong was founded in 1911. It is the oldest higher educational institution in the city. The structure and the governance of the university are modelled after the British system. A court, a council, and a senate govern the university. The court is the supreme governing body of the university. The council administers the property and manages the affairs of the university. The senate regulates matters relating to education in the University. There are nine faculties: arts, architecture, dentistry, education, engineering, law, medicine, science, and social sciences. Each faculty offers both undergraduate and postgraduate programs. Besides awarding bachelor's, master's, and doctoral degrees, the university also offers programs leading to various professional diplomas and certificates.

The Chinese University of Hong Kong was founded in 1963. It is a federal university with four constituent colleges. The governing and executive body of the university is the council which manages and controls the affairs, purposes, and functions of the university. The senate controls and regulates instruction, education, and research. The principal medium of instruction is Chinese. However, the majority of the teaching staff are bilingual, i.e. Chinese and English. The university has six faculties: arts, business administration, science, social sciences, medicine, and education. In addition to bachelor's degrees, master's and doctoral degrees are conferred through twenty-nine graduate divisions of its graduate school. The University also offers postgraduate diploma programs in education, social work, family medicine, etc.

The Hong Kong Polytechnic and the City Polytechnic of Hong Kong are the two polytechnics in Hong Kong. Both are relatively new institutions. The former was established in 1971, while the latter was established in 1984. They are fully funded by the government. They offer a great variety of professional and occupational programs to meet the city's needs of manpower in commerce, industry, and community. Every year, there are a large number of secondary school graduates entering the two polytechnics.

The Hong Kong Polytechnic has twenty-five teaching units. They are grouped under seven divisions: Division of Applied Science and Textiles, Division of Business and Management Studies, Division of Communication, Division of Mathematical and Computing Studies, Division of Construction and Land Use, Division of Engineering, and Division of Health and Social Studies. There are programs that lead to the awards of bachelor's degree, master's degree, associateship, professional diploma, higher diploma, diploma, postregistration diploma, postregistration certificate, endorsement certificate, higher certificate, and certificate of proficiency.

In the City Polytechnic of Hong Kong, there is a rapid build-up of student population and diversity of specializations. During the academic year of 1988-89, thirty-six specializations were offered. Diploma, higher diploma, professional diploma, bachelor's degree, postgraduate diploma, and master's degree are conferred upon successful completion of the studies. More new programs will be offered in the coming years.

There are two approved post-secondary colleges: the Shue Yan College and the Lingnan College. These colleges offer university level courses but have not achieved full university status. However, government financial assistance is available for their students.

Besides the three universities and the two polytechnics, the Hong Kong Baptist College which was established by religious groups is also fully funded by the government. The college has twenty departments grouped under three faculties and one school: the faculties of arts, social sciences, and science, and the School of Business. The college offers degree programs, honors diploma programs, as well as post-advanced level diploma programs.

The Hong Kong Shue Yan College has three faculties: arts, social sciences, and business. Only diploma programs are offered. Some of the college's programs are financed by public funding.

The other approved postsecondary college is Lingnan College. The college has three faculties: arts, business, and social sciences. These faculties conduct two-year postsecondary programs, higher diploma programs, and honors diploma programs in various fields. Government financial assistance is granted except for the honors diploma programs.

In Hong Kong, there are four colleges of education, with one of them specifically for the training of technical teachers. These institutions are financed and staffed by the government's Department of Education. Colleges of Education are responsible for the preparation of teachers for the local primary and junior secondary schools. The Technical Teachers' College offers courses for future teachers of technical subjects in secondary and prevocational schools. It admits students who have completed either technical or commercial subjects at secondary level. The other three colleges of education offer two to three years teacher education programs in a wide range of specializations.

There are eight technical institutes in Hong Kong. They provide training programs in craft and technical subjects at postsecondary levels. These institutions are also operated by the Education Department of the government. Most of their curricula have been validated by the Business and Technician Education Council of the United Kingdom.

There are a few private colleges in Hong Kong. Among them, the Chu Hai College and the Hang Seng School of Commerce are two which have made considerable contributions to higher education.

The Chu Hai College offers four-year degree programs in arts and social sciences. The degrees awarded are recognized by the Government of the Republic of China (Taiwan). The Hang Seng School of Commerce provides two-year programs in commercial and business training for secondary school graduates.

In 1987, there were 113,651 students enrolled in higher education comprising universities (15 percent), approved post-secondary (7 percent), polytechnics (28 percent), colleges of education (4 percent), and technical institutes (46 percent). About 3 percent of the population in 1986 had obtained degrees and another 2 percent had non-degree tertiary education.

Undergraduate Studies

For admission to undergraduate programs of the University of Hong Kong, students must first obtain satisfactory results in an approved Advanced Level examination. In Hong Kong, this means that they have to finish seven years of secondary education. In the university, most undergraduate programs are of three year's duration, such as bachelor's degrees in arts, science, computer studies, biochemical science, engineering, architectural studies, social sciences, and laws. Exceptions are the curricula for Bachelor of Architecture, Bachelor of Dental Surgery, Bachelor of Medicine and Bachelor of Survey degrees, which require five years of study for completion. The Bachelor of Science in Quantity Surveying requires four years of training. All courses, apart from some in the department of Chinese, are taught and examined in English. Student housing of the university accommodate about 25 percent of undergraduate students.

The Chinese University of Hong Kong admits students through the "Provisional Acceptance Scheme" and the Hong Kong Higher Level Examination for which the applicants should have finished sixth form study, or through the Hong Kong Advanced Level examination. A wide range of full-time undergraduate programs are also offered at the Chinese University of Hong Kong, leading to bachelor's degrees in arts, science, social sciences, business administration, and medicine and surgery. A new program leading to the Bachelor of Arts in Primary Education has just been introduced.

In the past, programs at all the faculties are of four years duration, except that of the Faculty of Medicine, which requires six years of studies. However, starting from the academic year 1991-92, the university will adopt a credit unit system which will allow students to complete their degree requirements in three years time. The university emphasizes bilingualism. Students have to be proficient in both Chinese and English on admission and both languages are used in teaching. About half of the undergraduate students live on campus in university dormitories.

Advanced Studies and Research

The University of Hong Kong grants a wide range of higher degrees. During the academic year of 1987-88, higher degree enrollment constituted about 16 percent of total student registration. The following higher degrees are conferred: Master of Philosophy, Master of Arts, Master of Science in Engineering, Master of Science in Urban Planning, Master of Social Sciences, Master of Social Work, Master of Business Administration, Master of Education, Master of Medical Sciences, Master of Dental Surgery, Master of Surgery, Doctor of Philosophy, and Doctor of Medicine. For the award of master's degree, candidates of Master of Philosophy have to complete approved schemes of research while candidates of other master's programs have to satisfactorily complete prescribed courses of study. The program of Doctor of Philosophy is a degree by research.

There are also postgraduate diplomas and certificates granted including Certificate in Education, Advanced Diploma in Education, Postgraduate Certificate in Laws, Diploma in Management Studies, Certificate in Medical Sciences and Certificate in Psychology.

There are a number of research centers at the university: the Center of Asian Studies, the Center of Urban Studies and Urban Planning, the Kadoorie Agricultural Research Center, the Social Sciences Research Center, and the Swire Marine Laboratory.

The Chinese University awards the following higher degrees: Master of Science, Master of Arts, Master of Social Sciences, Master of Arts in Education, Master of Social Work, Master of Business Administration, Master of Divinity, Master of Philosophy, Doctor of Philosophy, Doctor of Medicine, and Doctor of Science. There are also postgraduate diploma programs in education and social work. Award of master's degree may be based on performance in course work or research as prescribed by the individual department. The program of Doctor of Philosophy is a degree by research.

The university is strongly committed to research. In addition to research projects conducted in the teaching departments, there are six research centers operating under three research institutes. Under the Institute of Chinese Studies are the Center for Chinese Archeology and Art, the Ng Tor-tai Chinese Language Research Center, and the Research Center for Translation. The Institute of Social Studies consists of the Center for Hong Kong Studies and the Center for Contemporary Asian Studies. The Chinese Medicinal Material Research Center is part of the Institute of Science and Technology.

ISSUES AND TRENDS

Higher education in Hong Kong has recently attracted international attention to its development. This is due to the government's announcement of a drastic plan for rapid expansion in higher education, such that by the year 1994-95, the number of places available will be increased by 80 percent. This will be a measure to ensure the stability and growth of the Hong Kong economy, which faces the threat of losing a large number of professionals through emigration that started in the late 1980s. In a public seminar titled: "Higher Education in the 1990s: Development and Challenges", held in May 1990, speakers from government agencies, higher education institutions, and the business sector expressed their views on the issue of expansion of higher education. The following facts and viewpoints are presented to describe the current situation and trend of higher education in Hong Kong.

With the coming of 1997, when Hong Kong will cease to be a British colony and become a Special Administrative District of China, many of the people who lack confidence in Hong Kong's political future and who can qualify for a foreign visa, will choose to emigrate to other countries. A study of the emigration phenomenon conducted by the Hong Kong Institute of Personnel Management (HKIPM) and the Hong Kong City Polytechnic during 1987 and 1988 shows that there is a high proportion of emigrants with superior educational attainment. This may have a great impact on Hong Kong's economic, industrial, and educational developments. In order to maintain its status as a major international, commercial, financial, and manufacturing center, Hong Kong will need a large number of well-educated and professionally trained people to be managers, engineers, and specialists of different kinds. This need is made more urgent due to the fact that the economy of Hong Kong has been shifting from the labor-intensive to the knowledge-intensive and high-technology direction. A survey completed recently by the Hong Kong government projects that by 1996, the local labor market will require some 50,000 more university degree holders. It is obvious that there is a need to change the current elitist higher education policy, so that more opportunities can be provided for the young people to attend universities and colleges.

There has always been a shortage of university places in Hong Kong. In 1989, there were 6,300 first degree places offered; that is, one out of three matriculants or 7 percent of the relevant age group were able to obtain admission. To meet society's need in the coming years, the government has recently decided to increase degree places to 15,000 by the academic year 1994-95. It is estimated that by then, four out of five matriculants or 18 percent of the relevant age group will be admitted to an undergraduate degree program. With degrees, post-degrees, and sub-degrees offered by institutions of higher learning counted together, there will be an 81 percent growth by 1995. The increase in first degree places will be achieved mainly through accelerated expansion of the three universities and the two polytechnics.

This plan of expansion of higher education is certainly welcomed by students and parents. There is a concern, however, that quality may suffer in such a drastic expansion. University instructors worry particularly about a sudden decline of academic standard of higher education. Clearly there will be a substantial increase in the number of university teaching positions needed in the next several years. The problems of recruiting fully qualified teaching staff is sharpened by the continuous loss of lecturers and researchers through emigration. Actually, the above-mentioned study conducted by the HKIPM shows that during 1987-88, the pace of emigration by educators was higher than that of other professional groups.

BIBLIOGRAPHY

Census and Statistics Department, Hong Kong Government. *Hong Kong Annual Digest of Statistics, 1989.* Hong Kong, 1989.

Education Department, Hong Kong Government. *Education Department - Annual Summary, 1989-1990.* Hong Kong, 1989.

Education and Manpower Branch. *Education Commission Report No. 1.* Hong Kong, 1984.

Education and Manpower Branch, Hong Kong Government. *Education Commission Report No. 2.* Hong Kong, 1986.

Education and Manpower Branch, Hong Kong Government. *Education Commission Report No. 3: The Structure of Tertiary Education and the Future of Private Schools.* Hong Kong, 1988.

Government Information Service, Hong Kong Government. *Hong Kong 1989.* Hong Kong, 1989.

Government Secretariat, Hong Kong Government. *The Hong Kong Education System.* Hong Kong, 1981.

Government Secretariat, Hong Kong Government. *A perspective on Education in Hong Kong: Report by a Visiting Panel.* Hong Kong, 1982.

The Chinese University of Hong Kong. *The Chinese University of Hong Kong Calendar, 1989-1990.* Hong Kong, 1989.

University of Hong Kong. *The University of Hong Kong Calendar, 1989-1990.* Hong Kong, 1989.

University and Polytechnic Grants Committee, Hong Kong Government. "Interim Report for the 1988-1991 Triennium - July 1988 to December 1989." Hong Kong, 1990.

HUNGARY

by
Arpad Petrikas
Professor and Head, Department of Pedagogy
Kossuth University, Hungary

BACKGROUND

The evolution of public education in Hungary since World War II is characterized by several general features. Primary and secondary education are exempt from school fees. Other schooling expenses are mainly paid by parents. In higher education, students pay fees depending on their academic performance. Students in secondary and higher education are provided a wide range of social help. Educational system provides social mobility by offering ample possibilities for moving up from one level to another. Admission to universities and high schools is performance based. Schools are coeducational. Students have the freedom to form student groups or organizations, and are actively involved in the administration of their institutions.

PRIMARY AND SECONDARY EDUCATION

Primary schooling starts at the age of six years and continues until students enter secondary school at the age of fourteen years. The number of children completing their primary school has steadily increased from 67.6 percent in 1950 to 93.1 percent in 1980. Presently about 90 percent of the children complete primary school. At secondary level, students have several options: secondary grammar schools (four years); secondary technical schools (four years); skilled worker's training (1-3 years); and special schools (2-3 years). A recent development is the so-called 4+1 system secondary technical school which enables the student to complete secondary education and at the same time obtain a technician qualification. On completion of secondary education, students obtain the *"maturity"* qualification which is a basic requirement for entry to university level study programs. Education is compulsory for ages 6-16.In the 1960s the idea of making secondary education compulsory came up, but up to now suitable conditions for achieving this could not be provided and the practice in various parts of the country differ a great deal.

Since the middle of 1960s, secondary technical schools have been playing an important part in educating middle level specialists. These schools are controlled by the Ministry of Education in coordination with other relevant ministries. Secondary technical schools provide special training in the field of production (e.g. electrical technology, engineering, mechanical technology, and other

367

branches) and services (e.g. health, cultural, trade branches etc.). An innovation to the program provide the possibility of getting a technician degree with an additional year of training. There has been an effort to bring the educational programs of secondary technical schools and that of the previously shorter termed (2-3 years) skilled workers' training schools closer, so that a uniformed secondary educational system could be achieved.

The number of students enrolled in secondary schools has grown significantly from about 67,000 in 1950 to 130,000 in 1985, a 94 percent increase. Skilled workers' training has been the most dynamic and together with secondary technical education they formed two-thirds of all secondary school enrollment. Secondary grammar school enrollment has decreased and forms now only about 22 percent of the total enrollment. As a result, the most important task of the next school reform would be to increase both the quantity and the quality of grammar school education.

Funding for secondary education has also increased steadily over the years. The 1980 expenditure was 2,225 million florints for skilled workers training, an increase of 330 percent from 1960; and 3,410 million florints for secondary schools, an increase of 385 percent from 1960. Expenditure per pupil in 1980 was 14,521 florints for skilled workers training and 16,328 for secondary schools.

However, parallel with the economic crisis of the country, the growth came to a standstill but efforts are being made to ensure necessary conditions for expanding secondary education. The demographic explosion in the recent past reaches the secondary level from 1989 onwards and it can put further pressure on secondary education.

The administration of the system of public education has a dual pattern. Central policy making is performed by the Ministry of Culture and Education. The ministry controls the planning, development, and theoretical principles of public education. The ministry is a united body, which transfers the government's concept of public education to the middle and lower levels of the education structure. Various institutions, agencies, and experts assist the ministry in this task. The organizational, administrative, and decision making aspects are rather centralized. On the other hand, the county and town institutions oversee and direct activities related to school maintenance.

The Education Act 1 of 1985 is the legal framework governing all levels of education in Hungary and gives the authority to the Minister of Culture and Education to regulate the educational system and functioning of all education institutions including those which come under the supervision of other ministries such as universities of medical sciences (supervised by the Ministry of Health) and agricultural universities (supervised by the Ministry of Agriculture and food).

HIGHER EDUCATION

Institutions

Within the framework of the Education Act 1 of 1985 (as mentioned earlier) and the subsequent decrees, the individual higher education institutions are free to organize their activities independently. They themselves regulate curricula, and admission requirements for students. Although the functional and organizational statutes concerning teaching staffs and researchers as well as the scientific and research activities must be approved by the appropriate minister, higher education institutions are free to disburse their funds, including not only what is allocated to them from the state budget but also what they can earn by means of activities which they conduct under contract for external institutions and enterprises.

All universities, including those founded soon after the War, have a high degree of autonomy as compared to the university level colleges that were established only recently. The essential difference is that universities, in conformity with their own organizational statutes, decide independently on those fundamental questions which determine the content and the efficiency of their educational and scientific work. The supervising minister can veto the decision of a university only if it violates the law or it is in conflict with cultural policies. The case of colleges is different: here decision-making power concerning a variety of questions is retained by the supervising minister.

There are differences in organizational structures as well. The universities function within the traditional system of faculties. Colleges, on the other hand, are managed according to the institute system. This difference arises as a logical consequence of the differing educational objectives of the two types of institutions. Institutions of higher education have the right to express their institutional opinions in all matters, including matters of employment or of dismissal affecting themselves which come within the scope of authority of their respective supervising ministries or of other superior authorities. In addition, institutions of higher education may establish professional bodies or councils to attend to specific tasks, in particular to those related to training, modernization and scientific research.

The composition of the councils and professional bodies active in institutions of higher education, the proportions of elected and appointed members, their functioning, and their scope of authority are set by the statutes of the institutions in conformity with the law.

The councils include the following members: the office bearers of the corresponding units and the elected representatives of the social organizations, the teaching and non-teaching staffs, and the students. Representatives of state authorities who have an interest in the end result of the training offered and eminent figures of professional life also participate, in appropriate proportions, in the councils of the institutions of higher education and in the faculty councils.

In addition to the heads of institutions of faculties, and of independent teaching units, the governing structure includes councils that have authority to make decisions on the content of teaching and of research and in other areas of fundamental importance such as educational efficiency.

Universities are headed by rectors; colleges by directors; university faculties by deans; and college faculties organized at universities, by director-generals. These officials are assisted by deputies in the performance of their duties. University and college institutes and clinics are headed by directors. Teaching units are coordinated by heads (of departments, etc.).

Rectors are appointed from among the professorate by the Council of Ministers; directors of colleges are appointed by the supervising ministers from among university and college professors and assistant professors. Deans are appointed from among university professors and assistant professors; the directors of college faculties at universities, from among university professors; assistant professors and college professors, by the supervising minister. The appointments of the heads of universities, colleges, and college faculties at universities are valid for five years. An appointment can be renewed once.

The appointment of deputy heads of universities, colleges, university faculties, and college faculties at universities, including the appointments of heads of independent teaching units and departments is regulated by the Council of Ministers. Decisions regarding the appointment of heads of institutions of higher education and heads of teaching units must be made with due consideration for the wishes of the teaching units concerned and of the faculty and institutional councils. They must also take heed of the opinions of relevant social organizations.

Undergraduate Studies

In the nomenclature of Hungarian higher education, the term "undergraduate training" designates those studies which lead to a first degree, regardless of the type of course. All training accomplished after the student has taken a degree is included in the term "postgraduate training".

The number of regular students in undergraduate studies more than doubled in between 1960 and 1982. In 1982 there were over 100,000 students enrolled, of which 63 percent were regular students. In 1960, only 4.1 percent of the population of the age group 18-22 years was enrolled in regular courses of higher education. This percentage had reached 9.7 percent in 1983. The growth in the number of students is largely due to the increased demand by the society for specialists with advanced training. The reorganization of the teacher training schools specialized in the training of lower primary school and kindergarten teachers, and the organization in the early 1960s of technological and agricultural colleges also contributed to this growth. In 1982, 35 percent of the regular students were enrolled in technological and agricultural fields, 33 percent in education, and 14 percent in health related areas.

Since 1960, dual-mode training has been successively introduced into higher education. Universities prepare their students to occupy posts including research and development, management, etc., which require deep and extended theoretical knowledge. Colleges, on the other hand (the curricula of which require shorter study periods), prepare their students for more practical tasks in such areas as technology, business administration, and health services. As regards school teachers, those for secondary schools are trained by universities, and those for primary schools, by colleges. Experiments are however under way to develop a so-called "comprehensive model" for the training of teachers. It will be based on common foundations but will branch off corresponding to the current requirements of the different levels of public education.

The respective proportions of university-level and college-level education have changed substantially over the past twenty years. In the past, universities had 75 percent of the total students enrolled in higher education but in 1983, their share was only about 50 percent with the rest receiving education at colleges.

Evening and correspondence courses, developed only after 1945, have played a role of historical significance in Hungary both from a social and an economic point of view. The importance accorded to them was motivated by political and cultural factors as well as economic demands. In many cases, however, the negative consequences of a lower educational level and the need to make corrections afterwards had to be faced. One might have expected that, over the past few years, the widening opportunities for traditional study would have reduced the importance of evening and correspondence courses; however, the opposite has occurred. Between 1960 and 1980, the number of students enrolled in evening and correspondence courses rose in all the sectors of higher education. This rise has continued up to now in all sectors with the exception of those relating to technology and agriculture.

In Hungary, education offered by institutions of higher education is defined by legal provisions and fundamental educational requirements as promulgated by central curricular directives. The directives for long-term development and basic educational requirements for all the fundamental discipline groups of higher education (humanities, natural sciences, technology, agriculture, economics, law, medical sciences, teacher training, the arts, etc.), corresponding to demands of scientific, technological, and cultural progress for the country, were issued in 1984. They were drawn up by the governmental authorities in cooperation with the most highly qualified scientific and educational experts in the respective disciplines. The new directives particularly stress the incorporation of new scientific and cultural achievements into the curricula of higher education.

Hungarian higher education is currently changing over to the modular system. Training units or "modules" completed at one institution can be credited towards a higher ranking one. For instance, modules completed in a technological or agricultural college will be honored for continued study in the corresponding course of a university. Studies begun at teachers' colleges can be continued at universities. Degrees can be complemented by further specialized degrees, etc.

The basic subjects of given professions serve, during the first years of higher education, to lay the foundation for broad professional education. They prepare students to choose specializations and to change them, possibly by making use of those modules already completed, to qualify in another study branch, or another level.

Compulsory general education subjects form an organic part of the education of intellectuals to provide for the systematic, planned broadening of the general education completed in secondary school. Broadening of this sort includes the extension of knowledge of the humanities, economics, sociology, political science, and organization, and the mastery at a high level of a foreign language already learned in secondary school as well as the learning of a second foreign language. Systematic physical education is also included among the required general education subjects.

Subjects leading to professional specialization are designed to qualify candidates for posts requiring highly specialized knowledge. In their mastery, the close unity of theoretical and practical training is particularly stressed in order to provide for the efficient development of professional skills. This stage of the educational process further stresses creative experimentation, the exploration of new methods of learning, the cooperation of teachers and students in the creation of scientific innovations, and the participation of students in research work. The success of these efforts will be a prime necessity for raising the quality of professional education.

Optional complementary subjects are offered to deepen and enlarge student's breadth of learning. The students may freely choose subjects of their choice and attend special lectures including those given at other institutions of higher education. The widening of optional subjects is envisaged in the development plans with a view to raising the level of higher education. It will also be possible to count such optional studies towards the earning of complementary degrees.

From the start of the higher education cycle and particularly towards the latter stages (nearing graduation), departments tend to stress the practical aspects of education, specially creative learning, active participation in experimentation, and research work. The scientific-creative reputation of a given higher education institution is well served if students take part in deliberate planning exercises, and write graduation theses and doctoral dissertations. These exercises, in addition to the usual examination papers, teach students the methods of independent experimentation and research as well as self-education. All these types of creative study and work contribute to the research programs of higher education institutions.

University programs leading to bachelor's degrees generally take five years, with medical studies lasting six years. Universities also offer degrees through correspondence and evening courses which take 3-5 years. These are usually second degrees (not postgraduate). Other schools of higher education provide similar programs. Artistic programs lasting 4-6 years are run by academies which are ranked as universities.

Admission to schools of higher education and universities is based on a point system calculated on the basis of secondary school final examinations as well as entrance examinations.

Student Life

The principal framework for successful study as well as the assertion of the interests both of students and of collective education is the so-called study group, a small community of students who are enrolled in the same year in the same course. The study group, which possesses many competencies, has an autonomous democratic character. It elects its own leaders and representatives. It presents proposals for study support and material assistance (scholarships, meals in student restaurants, accommodations in student residence halls, grants of various sorts, etc.) for its members. It participates in the safeguarding of the interests of students and of their qualifications and participates actively in the organization of their study program.

Simultaneously, the study group plays an important group-role in education. It pays great attention to work, study achievements, discipline, and character development of its members. It organizes group entertainment. It draws its members into significant social events and activities organized by the faculty, the institution, or by other organizations and, according to their specific interests, into scientific, cultural, sporting, and self-education activities. The community life of the study group is an important field of training for intellectual development.

In many institutions of higher education, tutors are assigned to assist the whole study group in its work and to follow the academic and human development of individual students, assisting them with pedagogical advice.

Through their elected representatives, the students participate in the life of the departments, faculties, and institutions in all decisions concerning students, and in the work of the governing bodies of the institutions. According to law, youth parliaments must be convoked at defined intervals by work units and institutions. At these assemblies, young people, through their elected representatives, add their input on problems of public interest and propose measures to be taken. The heads of institutions are obliged to report to these parliaments on their activities relative to youth. At universities and colleges, the Young Communist League, the political organization of Hungarian youth, organizes the public activities of the students. It engages in political persuasion in study groups, in the representative bodies of the students, and in the managerial organs of the institutions. Its social activities foresee the inclusion of students in work activities which correspond to their future professions or in other collective actions intended to promote the public interest (the construction of camps, assistance in agriculture, public education, health, environmental protection, etc.).

Advanced Studies and Research

At the present time, postgraduate education in Hungary is not uniform. Conditions for application, admission, and assistance are not consistent.

Currently, a regulation exists in medicine which makes periodic training to update knowledge mandatory for physicians. In other disciplines and areas, no uniform postgraduate studies are imposed; rather, variable individualized programs are recommended. This latter form will be extended in the future by the organization of postgraduate study centers linked to institutions of higher education, functioning eventually as a part of a university or a college. However, the basic rule will still be valid that a new degree can only be obtained by passing the necessary examination(s) at the appropriate institution of higher education.

Training for research at universities takes place at the postgraduate level and leads to the earning of a university doctorate. This degree now counts as a scientific title. The new Education Act will regulate the postgraduate training. Councils chaired by rectors or pro-rectors and consisting of members representing the "candidates of sciences", "doctors of sciences", and members of the Academy of Sciences serving on the staffs of universities will be organized to deal with matters related to university doctorates. Representatives of the committee of scientific qualifications will also be invited to attend the session of these councils.

Earlier, the title "doctor of the university" was not recognized as a scientific degree; only the degrees "candidate of sciences" and "doctor of sciences" awarded by the committee of scientific qualifications and its specialized scientific commissions were counted as scientific degrees. They were awarded independently of the universities. The intention of recent regulations is to bring the scientific work undertaken at the universities and that undertaken at the institutes of the Academy of Sciences, along with scientific degrees to be earned by such work, closer together. According to the new enactments, the requirements to be met for taking and passing university doctoral examinations are identical to those of the examinations required for the higher-ranking "candidate of sciences" degree. After a degree candidate has passed the university doctoral examination, the doctorate council of the university may propose to the committee of scientific qualifications that the applicant be awarded the degree of "candidate of sciences", if it judges that the scientific value and level of the doctoral dissertation is adequate.

Applicants for the degrees of "doctor of the university" and "candidate of sciences" may participate in the scientific postgraduate training which is organized by the relevant university and may enjoy all benefits granted to postgraduate students. Applicants for the degree of "doctor of sciences" may obtain a one-year scholarship equivalent in value to their average annual salaries.

In the area of research, substantial improvements have taken place in recent decades in the research activities of the universities and colleges, with the total research expenditure forming 7-13 percent of the education budget. According to 1982 statistics, 49 percent of the academicians, 47 percent of the "doctors of sciences" and 36 percent of the holders of "candidates of sciences" degrees are employed by the universities and colleges. However, the growing number of forms and possibilities for postgraduate training has added to the burdens of teaching staffs, resulting in a reduction of the time allotted for research (to both teachers and auxiliary personnel). In 1980, the time allotted to teachers for research was 23.6 percent and that for auxiliary personnel was 35.5 percent.

The accomplishment of research and teaching tasks is inconceivable without international cooperation. Hungary cannot contemplate self-sufficiency either in the field of research or in science education. International scientific cooperation is not only of primary interest to the country but also an objective necessity. Of the 2,700 programs to which Hungary is a signatory, the institutions of higher education participate in 558 involving research, primarily in the area of natural sciences. Also Hungary maintains bilateral inter-institutional relations with eight socialist countries and eleven Western countries. At present, there are no common research links with developing countries.

ISSUES AND TRENDS

The continuing popularity of evening and correspondence courses makes the subject an important issue. From a historical perspective, the popularity has been motivated by many factors, including the extensive industrial growth of the

1970s and the demographic developments that stimulated the demand for technicians and teachers. What became an urgent problem of manpower shortages had to be solved by putting untrained individuals to work and then training them simultaneously. Thus, in those professions most affected by this situation (lower elementary school teachers, for instance), students started to work as soon as they had finished their first year of study, completing the rest by means of evening courses.

Although the situation is different now, correspondence and evening courses must be retained in the interests of the society, on one hand, to respond to the changing demands for specialists, and on the other, to promote social mobility. Moreover, an important function of such courses is to facilitate career changes. Although the latter motive may seem to be based on individual interest (prestige, increased income, development of one's personality to its fullest extent), this motive, taken collectively, is a significant motivating force in the dynamics of social movements.

Evening and correspondence courses will be able to fulfil their potential only if their improvement is given sufficient weight in the development plans of higher education. Improvement will require the introduction of new forms of organization and new methodologies, so as to raise the level of training efficiency. Experiments are under way, for example, to develop special "teletraining" processes, by which students will be prepared for independent learning by special intensive courses and by periodic self-evaluation. In addition to mastering the subject matter via television, students will receive study aids and guides intended to direct their learning processes. Although the cost of teletraining is obviously much higher than that of traditional evening and correspondence courses, its efficiency is unquestionably higher.

Suitable forms of undergraduate work-study have also been stimulated by government measures that give students of evening and correspondence courses financial aid and time off from their employment. Like regular students, evening and correspondence students must only pay tuition fees if their marks are mediocre. Attempts are also being made to interest employers to grant financial aid to regular students in order to ensure the recruitment of graduates. One means for accomplishing this task is the system of what is known as social scholarships which are offered under specific conditions by enterprises and institutions. At present, these scholarships form 12 percent of the total financial benefits given to regular students.

In the area of quality of higher education, efforts are underway to modernize the forms and methods of teaching. Substantial changes are taking place in the methods and proportions of the traditional forms of instruction such as regular and special lectures, exercises, group studies, individual and group consultations, practice and control examinations, etc. The roles of independent and creative work, of small study groups, of lectures which survey the large and essential parts of a given subject-matter, and of consultative lectures are increasing. In order to promote independent, intensified work, the number of compulsory exercises as well as the role of examinations are being reduced. The amount of study time is being raised, and greater emphasis is being placed on continuous and steady work.

The recent political developments in Hungary also promise structural reforms in the system of higher education. The universities and other schools of higher education are expected to have much greater autonomy, including power to make decisions relating to creation of new programs and academic chairs, formulation of procedures for admission of students, and determination of the number of students to be enrolled. Students are expected to have a voice in the selection of professors and other academic staff. Other changes in the educational system could bring classical secondary school education and alternative schooling to come to prominence.

BIBLIOGRAPHY

A tobbszinu kepzesi rendszer fejlesztese Magyarorszagon (The Development of the Educational System with Several Stages in Hungary). Budapest, 1976.

Fukasz, Gyorgy. Adult Education in the Hungarian People's Republic.

Hungarin Central Statistical Office. *Education and Cultural Conditions in Hungary.* 1960-1980. Budapest, 1983.

Kemenes, Erno. *Educational Administration and Management. Structures and Functions at National, Regional and Local Level Dealing with Educational Administration in Hungary: A Case Study.* Paris: Unesco, 1983.

Ladanyi, Andor. *A Magyar Felsooktatas strukturajarol. Statisztikai adatok, problemak, kutatasi feladatok.* (On the Structure of Hungarian Higher Education). Budapest, 1974.

Ladanyi, Andor. "A tanarkepzes tovabbfejlesztese: problemak, feladatok" (Development of Higher Education in the Field of Teacher Training: Problems and Tasks). *Felsooktatasi Szemle.* Budapest. 29, No. 7-8 (1980): 385-393 and No. 9 (1980): 538-543.

Nagy, Jozsef. *L'experience hongroise de l'OOK; un instrument pour le developpement de la technologie educative.* Paris: Unesco, 1980.

Palovecz, Janos. *Tanulmanyok a felsooktatas korebol* (Studies on Higher education). Felsooktatasi Ped. Kutatokozpont, 1974.

Sipos, ed. "System of Admission to Higher Education in Hungary." *Higher Education in Europe.* Bucharest-Cepes, vol. 7, No. 1, (1978): 3 - 4.

Timar, Janos. *L'enseignement superieur et le developpement economique et technique en Hongrie.* Paris: Unesco-IIPE, 1983.

ICELAND

by
Bragi Josepsson
Associate Professor of Comparative Education
Icelandic College of Education, Iceland

BACKGROUND

Icelandic devotion to learning and scholarship can be traced back to at least the eleventh century, following the conversion of the population to Christianity. In the twelfth century, Icelanders were famous in Scandinavia for their interest in history and poetry. In the middle ages and later, literacy appears to have been much more widespread in Iceland than in most other countries of Western and Northern Europe. This can probably be related to the popularity of the vernacular literature, sagas of various kinds, and rimur (narrative poetry based on the sagas or the translations of chivalric romance). It became a common custom on the farm for the entire household to sit with handwork in the winter evenings to the accompaniment of reading and recitation.

The first schools in Iceland were founded at the cathedral establishments, at some church-farms and in the monasteries. Their main purpose was to educate men for the priesthood. The first known regular school of this kind was established at Skalholt by Bishop Isleifur Gissurarson soon after his consecration in 1056. Some fifty years later, the first bishop of Holar, Jon Ogmundsson, started a similar school. Teaching also continued at Oddi and Haukadalur, important farms in south of the country. Between 1133 and 1493 eight monasteries were founded in Iceland.

Following the Lutheran Reformation, the responsibility and authority of the Church in Iceland declined, and the dominant influences on education in Iceland were centered more in Denmark than at home. The shift in decision-making from Iceland to Denmark gradually became a permanent administrative feature. It persisted until early in the twentieth century, when Iceland achieved home rule, and finally disappeared with the country's full independence in this century.

Icelandic society is homogeneous and there are few minorities. In the educational system there is no discrimination. Most schools are run by the state and local authorities or by the state alone, and all education is free from primary school through university. Private and parochial schools must conform to educational standards set by the Ministry of Education and must comply with ministry regulations.

The Icelandic school system is highly centralized under the minister of education. Responsibility for primary education is shared among eight regional authorities. Each authority appoints an education council headed by a superintendent of schools. Each of the eight education regions is divided into school districts, each with a school board appointed by local authorities.

The language of instruction is Icelandic. At the secondary level, and particularly at the university level, textbooks in both English and Scandinavian languages are frequently used. University lectures may also be given in English and Scandinavian languages.

As a rule, the academic year is nine months long in all schools. The school year begins in September and ends in May. In rural areas, primary schools may be operated for a shorter time. Also in the rural areas, schools may be operated for six days a week, but as a rule Icelandic schools observe a five-day week.

The school system of today is based on the School Systems Act and the Primary School Act, both of 1974, and the Law on the University of Iceland of 1979 and the 1988 laws on the Teachers University and Secondary Education. According to the School Systems Act, Icelandic education is organized into three interrelated levels: a primary level represented by a unified comprehensive school of nine grades, providing primary and upper primary education for pupils from seven to sixteen; a secondary level of four years, providing advanced general and vocational education; and a university level. Grade nine is normally required as a condition of acceptance into schools at the secondary level.

According to the Secondary School Act, all secondary education has been integrated into a single system with parallel courses and subject groupings, both theoretical and practical. These ideals, however, had been put into effect in practice as early as 1973 with the passing of a bill on an experimental, comprehensive secondary school which opened in Reykjavik in 1975 *(Fjolbrautaskolinn i Breioholti)*. Important developments are also related to new practices adopted by one of the Reykjavik grammar schools *(Menntaskolinn vio Hamrahlio)* in the early 1970s. This school introduced a course-point system and, furthermore, established a special adult education department, offering all grammar school courses through evening classes. Other schools have now started similar programs.

Until World War II all educational practices were strongly influenced by Danish and German school traditions. The frequent visits of Icelandic scholars to Scandinavia had considerable influence. A number of reports by Icelanders travelling to countries such as Great Britain, France, Germany, the Netherlands, Canada, and the United States also had some effect on school practice. Icelandic Society is extremely cosmopolitan in nature and open to foreign influence. But at the same time the Icelandic tradition is very strong, particularly with regard to the Icelandic language and Nordic culture.

In educational philosophy, the free and liberal trend which generally is related to Sweden, has had strong impact on education. School practices and ideology have also been strongly influenced by those of the United States; the concept of the comprehensive high school is, no doubt, the most notable. Developments in British schools have also had an impact. The open school system is an example of school practices adopted primarily from Britain.

The role of education in development is evident at all levels. At the primary level, schools are urged to relate the instructional program to work and industry; at the secondary level, adult education and retraining programs are provided in towns and villages throughout the country. Research institutes at the University of Iceland are increasingly involved in developmental projects in agriculture, fisheries, earth science, and various other fields, for the purpose of strengthening the nation's economy.

Educational Research is funded by the Iceland Science Foundation, the Science Institute, and the Education Research Institute (a joint establishment run by the Teacher's University, the University of Iceland, and the Ministry of Education). Funds for research are also received from universities, foreign institutes, and international foundations and organizations.

Teachers' salaries range from approximately US$2,600 per month for university professors to approximately US$1,200 for beginning teachers in primary schools.

Primary school teachers, secondary school teachers, and teachers at universities are generally appointed for one year initially, after which they may be appointed permanently. Teachers may work until they reach the age of 65 or until their years of work plus chronological age totals 95. Teachers who retire after working regularly in the school system may receive pensions between 80 percent and 90 percent of the pay they received at the time they retired.

PRIMARY AND SECONDARY EDUCATION

Primary Education

In all towns and larger communities, primary schools comprise grades 1-9 as well as classes for six-year old children. From the fall of 1990, schooling for six-year olds will also be mandatory. In some cases school may include only the first six grades and the six-year olds, or may include grades 7-9 only. Grades 1-6 are commonly distinguished as the first stage and grades 7-9 the second stage. Some primary schools offer a one-or two-year program of additional classes at the secondary level with curriculum corresponding to that offered in the first two years at the comprehensive high schools.

In rural areas, the trend has been toward larger schools, involving boarding schools and/or school busing. In some rural areas a system of "alternate teaching" has been practiced and children spend one or two weeks alternatively in school and at home.

The weekly load of class work in grades 1-9 ranges from twenty-two to thirty-five classes, each class lasting for forty minutes. For every 100 minutes of class work there are to be fifteen minutes break time. In many schools there are no breaks between the first and second classes or between the fourth and fifth, allowing for longer brakes between the second and third classes. Meals are not provided in schools (with the exception of boarding schools), but the government and local authorities are now making plans for providing meals in primary schools, particularly in grades 7-9.

All primary schools have a coordinated syllabus aimed at providing pupils with general education, informing them about the main occupations in Icelandic society, and preparing them for further education. The subjects now taught in primary schools are Icelandic, mathematics, social studies, religion, home economics, arts and crafts, music, physical education (including swimming), science, Danish and English. Foreign languages are now being introduced earlier then before: Danish in fourth grade and English in sixth grade. Science subjects have also been increased in the lower grades. In grades 7-9 pupils may take electives for 10-14 hours per week. Students who have left schools after completing the eighth grade and who have been employed regularly in the labor market, may count this experience towards elective credits when they return to finish their final examinations in primary school. A graded curriculum is issued by the ministry in every subject taught in primary schools.

One principal guideline in primary education is the policy of integration, which means that students are not grouped according to ability. Consequently, supplementary instruction is provided for certain students who attend regular classes, and special education is available for slow learners and students with behavioral problems and other learning difficulties. Mentally handicapped children receive instruction from birth and continue in school for a minimum of two years beyond regular compulsory education at the age of four. In recent years, some of the schools of special education have been discontinued and their programs integrated into the general school system. Today there are special classes for the blind, for slow learners, and the physically handicapped, but special schools are available for those with hearing defects, the mentally retarded, and the mentally disturbed.

Secondary Education

Secondary education in Iceland is provided in grammar schools, comprehensive high schools, and vocational schools.

Grammar schools are four-year schools leading to the matriculation examination. The traditional subjects have consisted of modern languages, classics, physics, mathematics, natural science, and Icelandic literature and history. Recently subjects such as social studies, business studies, and music have been added to the range. The older grammar schools have gradually been adopting a course-point system and other new organizational principles.

Courses to be taken towards matriculation fall into three categories: obligatory subjects, course-related subjects and optional subjects. The weight of each category is approximately 70 percent, 20 percent, and 10 percent respectively. Textbooks and other curriculum aids are rather limited, but individual schools and teachers decide which books and instructional materials are used. The Ministry of Education, particularly through the agency of the Center for Educational Materials, has made provisions for the development of curriculum material for these schools. It is not, however, supplied free to students at the primary level.

Comprehensive high schools have been established in several towns since 1975. In practice they have replaced the old grammar schools which principally prepared students for university entrance at a time when higher education was limited to a few academic fields. In addition to the academic line still maintained by the grammar schools, the comprehensive high schools also offer a variety of technical and vocational subjects. Courses are grouped as follows: (1) Academic studies, with specialization in modern languages, humanities and literature, mathematics, physics, natural science, social sciences, music, and technical education. (2) Health and hygiene studies, offering nursing, health and beauty care, and a variety of programs linked to the health services. (3) Home economics and domestic science. (4) Social services, with special courses for training in physical education and nursery school work, and a general program linked to various social services such as youth work and other forms of community care. (5) Business education. (6) Fine arts. (7) Technical education, with specialized courses such as metal and woodworking, fishing, navigation, marine engineering, and aeromechanics.

The schools operate on a course-point system with courses taking two, three, or four years. Students may transfer from one field of study to another and from one comprehensive high school to another. Courses in each field may lead to a matriculation examination, to a diploma, or an examination which leads to further vocational training.

Vocational and other schools include commercial schools, trade schools, schools of agriculture, nautical schools, schools of music and fine arts, and a variety of other schools.

Secondary education or more precisely passing the matriculation examination entitles students to enter into universities. In 1984-85 there were 15,537 students enrolled in secondary schools and 54 percent of the students were females.

HIGHER EDUCATION

Institutions

Until the latter part of the nineteenth century no higher education could be obtained in Iceland. All Icelandic students desiring higher education had to travel overseas. Most of them studied at the University of Copenhagen, which was founded as early as 1479. In 1847 the Theological Seminary was founded in Reykjavik. Three decades later (1876), the School of Medicine was founded and finally another three decades from then (1908) the School of Law was founded.

In 1911 these schools merged as the three first faculties of the University of Iceland. Until recently the university which is state operated represented the only institution of higher learning in Iceland. Today, university education is provided at six other institutions: Teachers University of Iceland, Technical College of Iceland, College of Agriculture at Hvanneyri, University at Akureyri, Commercial College of Iceland, and Co-operative Commercial College. The first four of these institutions are state operated and the other two are private schools.

The Ministry of Education has primary responsibility for the development of higher education, as well as all other education in Iceland. Certain educational laws have been passed by the *Althing* (Parliament) and are implemented and enforced by the Ministry of Education through its various departments and agencies. With regard to the University of Iceland, the university council is the highest governing body within the university and works to promote the interests and objectives of the university and its research institutes. It presents matters to the Parliament or to the various government ministries for reform considerations and funding purposes.

The university council consists of the rector, the executive head of the university and ex-officio chairman of the council, the dean of the nine faculties, four student representatives, and two representatives of the university teachers' union. In addition, the registrar and the dean of students are non-voting members of the Council. The rector of the university is elected to a three-year term by the faculty, staff, and students. The deans are elected from among each faculty's professors and serve a two-year term. Students have representatives on the university council, the Icelandic Student Services Board, the Students' Loan Fund Board, the University Cinema Board, and the Federation of Icelandic Youth Organization. The day-to-day management of the university is in the hands of the registrar and the dean of studies.

Nearly all the posts held by permanent teaching staff carry tenure. Permanent staff members are officials of the Icelandic State. Formally, the president of Iceland appoints professors, after being advised by the ministers, but *dosents* and lecturers are appointed directly by the Minister of Education. A committee of three representatives is appointed to determine the eligibility of the applicants to the posts of professor and *dosent*. A person may not be appointed professor unless the majority of the adjudicating committee has voted in favor of his eligibility. Also, the opinion of the faculty in question shall be sought regarding the applicants. Student representative groups are often informally formed to determine eligibility of applicants for the posts of lecturers. Each faculty is governed by a faculty board, of which all permanent staff on the faculty are members in addition to representatives of temporary staff and students registered in the faculty.

Approximately thirty-five organizations or research institutions are affiliated with or directly associated with the university. The principal areas are various aspects of medical research, geology, and Icelandic language/sagas/history research. Also in direct association with the University of Iceland is the Reykjavik Pharmacy, the University Lottery, and the University Cinema. The Reykjavik Pharmacy is a commercial establishment which also provides training for pharmaceutical students. Until six years ago the capital funds of the University came from the University Lottery, which was established in 1933 by a law giving the university exclusive rights to run a national sweepstake in Iceland. The proceeds of the Lottery are used for general capital expenditures. Recently, the funds have not kept pace with the rapid expansion of student numbers and research activities, thereby requiring the university to acquire capital appropriations from the state. The University Cinema is used as a movie theatre and as a hall of concerts, conferences, and lectures. The Icelandic Student Services, a financially separate and autonomous organization, is jointly owned by the Ministry of Education and the University of Iceland. This organization is run by students and includes the dormitories, the bookstore, the duplicating center, the Student Travel Office, the Student Day Care Center, and several student coffee shops.

Programs and Degrees

Admission to university education requires, as a rule, the matriculation examination *(studentsprof)*, i.e. the secondary school leaving certificate. Admission to the Technical College of Iceland requires the completion of a preparatory course equivalent to the matriculation exam in science and physics. Certain vocational training is also required. Entry requirements to the B.S. program at the College of Agriculture are two years training in agriculture and the matriculation or equivalent.

All higher education at state operated institutions is free of charge. The University of Iceland has considerable independence, both academically and with regard to financing; the other schools do not have the same independence. All of them, however, are under the administration of the Ministry of Education, with the exception of the College of Agriculture, which comes under the Ministry of Agriculture.

In 1984-85 there were 4,722 students enrolled in higher education in Iceland and 2,262 in universities abroad. Of the total of 6,984 students enrolled in universities in Iceland and abroad, 48 percent were females.

Courses of study are generally based on a credit-unit system where one year of study constitutes thirty credit points. The B.A. degree is based on sixty credits in a major field and thirty in a minor or a total of ninety credit points in one field.

The University of Iceland which is the biggest higher education institution is located in the City of Reykjavik. It has a student population of almost 5,000 and an instructional staff of some 300 full-time professors, associate professors, and assistant professors, in addition to approximately 500 part-time teachers. The university has nine faculties and several research institutes and departments (some are affiliated with the university). The faculties are theology, medicine, law, economics, arts, dentistry, engineering, natural sciences, and social sciences.

The Faculty of Theology offers a three-year program leading to a B.A. degree in theology. This three-year program may be acquired either by taking a two-year major within the faculty and a minor of one-year in another or by completing the course of study in the Faculty of Theology. Students in other fields of study may also take a one-year minor in theology. The faculty also offers a five-year program, leading to the degree of *cand.theol.,* a required qualification for ministers of the Lutheran Church (the state Church). A thesis is required for both degrees.

The Faculty of Medicine offers the following programs of study: 1. A four-year program leading to B.S. degrees, one in medicine (three years of pre-clinical study followed by one year of research), nursing, and physical therapy; 2. A five-year program in pharmacy leading to a degree of *cand. pharm;* and 3. A six-year program in medicine leading to a *cand. med. et chir.* degree, which qualifies the holder to practice medicine in Iceland.

The Faculty of Law offers a five-year program leading to the degree of *cand. juris.,* which entitles the holder to practice law in Iceland.

The Faculty of Economics and Business Administration offers a three-year program leading to a B.S. degree in economics and a four-year program in business administration leading to the degree of *cand. econ.* Students in other fields of study may also take a one year minor in this faculty.

The Faculty of Arts offers the following programs of study: 1. Three-year programs leading to a B.A. degree in Icelandic language and literature, history, philosophy, linguistics, Greek, Latin, Danish, Finnish, Norwegian, Swedish, English, French, German, Spanish and Russian (the last one can only be taken as a minor subject). The B.A. program may be acquired either by taking a two-year major subject and one year in a minor field (within or outside the faculty) or the students may choose to take the whole program in a single major field. A thesis is required in all major fields. Students from other faculties may likewise take a minor in these subjects; 2. A three-year program for foreign students leading to the degree of *Bacc. phil. Isl;* and 3. A two-or three-year graduate program in Danish, English, history, and Icelandic literature leading to the degree of *cand. mag.* A dissertation is required.

The Faculty of Dentistry offers a six-year program in dentistry leading to the degree of *cand. odont.*

The Faculty of Engineering is divided into three departments: civil engineering, mechanical engineering, and electrical engineering. Each department offers a four-year program leading to a final examination in engineering. A thesis is required.

The Faculty of Natural Sciences is divided into six departments: mathematics, computer science, physics, chemistry, biology and geosciences. Each department offers a three-year program leading to a B.S. degree. In the Mathematics Department students may specialize in pure mathematics or applied mathematics. In the Physics Department specialization is offered in theoretical physics, applied physics, and geophysics. Within the Geoscience Department students can specialize in geology and geography, and in the Department of Chemistry they can specialize in chemistry and food science. A thesis is required in geology but is optional in other fields. In addition to this, a two year program is offered both in chemical engineering and engineering physics. These are non-degree programs for students entering degree programs abroad.

The Faculty of Social Science offers a three-year program leading to a B.A. degree in psychology, sociology, political science, anthropology, education, library and information science, cultural anthropology, media studies, and social work (the three last mentioned subjects can only be taken as a minor subject). This program may be acquired either by taking a two- year major subject and one year in a minor field (within or outside the faculty) or the students may choose to take the whole program in a single major field. Following the B.A. degree, students may take a one-year program in education, leading to a teacher's certificate (a qualification for teachers at the secondary level) and a one-year program in social work, leading to the Social Worker's Certificate.

In 1988-89, 170 foreign students, eighty-one male and eighty-nine females, from thirty countries, were enrolled at the University of Iceland. These students were enrolled in the different departments as follows: theology, 3; medicine, 22; liberal arts, 133; economy, 9; engineering, 6; and social science, 8. Most of the students are from the United States (25), Sweden (21), Norway (20), Denmark (17), West Germany (17), Britain (9), France (9), Canada (6), and Spain (5).

Countries represented with less than five students are Australia, Belgium, Bulgaria, China, Finland, Iran, Iraq, Ireland, Israel, Italy, Malaysia, Netherlands, Nicaragua, Philippines, Poland, Somalia, South Africa, Switzerland, and U.S.S.R.

For centuries Icelandic students have studied abroad. In 1986-87 there were approximately 2,700 Icelandic students studying abroad in twenty-five countries. Most of them were in : United States (786), Denmark (684), West Germany (223), Norway (218), Sweden (216), England (166), France (80), Canada (55), and the Netherlands (53).

Countries with less than fifty students were Australia, Austria, Belgium, China, Colombia, Finland, Ireland, Italy, Japan, Mexico, New Zealand, Scotland, South Africa, Spain, and Switzerland.

These students were enrolled in more than 200 different fields of study, including popular subjects such as engineering, economics, fine arts, education, nursing and health education, social sciences, computer science, natural sciences, etc.

Approximately 87 percent of all Icelandic students studying abroad in 1987-88 received study loans in different amounts according to the country of study. For example students studying in the United States received a loan of US$800 per month. Those studying in England received the amount of 460 pounds sterling per month.

The Teacher's University of Iceland is located in Reykjavik. It offers a three-year program in education leading to a B.Ed. degree, which qualifies the holder for teaching in primary schools. (In 1971, the Teacher Training College of Iceland, an upper secondary school founded in 1907, was reorganized as the Teacher's University of Iceland).

In addition to the regular program for primary school teachers, the Teacher's University offers an advanced two year program leading to the degree of B.A. in special education. Finally the Teacher's University provides in-service training for teachers. According to a recently passed legislation in 1988, the Teacher's University may decide to offer advanced programs beyond the degrees of B.Ed. and B.A.

Other higher education institutions in Iceland, namely, University of Akureyri, Technical College of Iceland, College of Agriculture at Hvanneyri, Commercial College of Iceland, and Co-operative Commercial College, offer degree programs in selected fields.

ISSUES AND TRENDS

An unusual feature of the University of Iceland is its great number of part-time instructors. This is not only due to the difficulty of creating new positions, but also because of increased specialization and the small society of Iceland. In other countries the part-time instructors are usually graduate students who are also engaged in research. The University is looking for ways to get part-time instructors to participate in research to a greater extent. There has been growth in research services and outside contracts in recent years.   Statistics indicate that the University's role in research is on the increase.

The increase in study possibilities at the University has been accompanied by a vast increase in the student population entering higher education in Iceland. Still however, most subjects only lead to the B.A./B.S. degree, and most postgraduate studies must still be pursued abroad.   Furthermore, there are still many university level studies which are not taught in Iceland since such a small nation does not possess the means to establish courses in specialized subjects with low attendance figures.   Examples of subjects which must be studied abroad at the undergraduate level are meteorology, veterinary medicine, architecture, and archaeology.

Another concern of the university system is the high dropout rate of the students in higher education, particularly in the first year of study.   Options being considered include a fourth year of study in the programs, thereby allowing the first year to be less specialized; and also improved communications from the university to the secondary level schools concerning the students' necessary preparatory studies.

BIBLIOGRAPHY

Gislason, Ingvar. *University Education in Ireland.* Reykjavik: Ministry of Culture and Education, 1981.

Gudjonsson, Halldor. "University Education." In *Iceland 1986,* edited by Johannes Nordal and Valdimar Kristinsson. Reykjavik: The Central Bank of Iceland, 1987.

Hanson, George. *Icelandic Education: Tradition and Modernization in a Cultural Perspective.* Diss. Chicago: Loyola University, 1979.

Josepsson, Bragi. *Current Laws on Compulsory Education and School System in Iceland.* Reykjavik: Icelandic College of Education, 1986.

Josepsson, Bragi. "Education." In *Iceland 1986, edited by*   Johannes Nordal and Valdimar Kristinsson. Reykjavik: The Central Bank of Iceland, 1987.

Josepsson, Bragi. *Education in Iceland: Its Rise and Growth with Respect to Social, Political and Economic Determinants.* Diss. Nashville: George Peabody College for Teachers, 1968.

Josepsson, Bragi, "Iceland." In *World Education Encyclopedia.* Vol. II, edited by George Thomas Kurian. New York and Oxford: Facts on File Publications, 1988.

Josepsson, Bragi. *The Modern Icelandic School System in Historic Perspective.* Reykjavik: The National Center for Educational Materials, 1985.

Kristjansdottir, Thuridur J. "Teachers Education in Iceland." *Delta Kappa Gamma Bulletin* 45 (1979): 60-63

Ministry of Culture and Education. *The Educational System of Iceland - Summary* (unpublished report), April 1986.

OECD. *Reviews of National Policies for Education, Iceland.* Paris: Organization for Economic Co-operation and Development, 1987.

Ragnarsdottir, Asta Kristrun, and Ragna Olafsdottir. *University of Iceland.* Reykjavik: University of Iceland, 1988.

INDIA

by
T. S. Rao
Professor and Dean, Faculty of Education
Banaras Hindu University, India

BACKGROUND

Universities in India, as compared to those in Europe, are of recent origin and the oldest three (Madras, Calcutta, and Bombay universities) date back only to 1857. But the tradition of higher education has its roots in the ancient history of India: the famous universities of Hindu and Buddhist studies in the very early periods and those of Muslim learning in the medieval times bear testimony. During the colonial era, the British who occupied India were at first inclined only to patronize traditional learning, and the Calcutta *Madrassah* and the Sanskrit College of Banaras represented this way of thinking. But in the early part of the last century, a bitter controversy reigned between those who favored encouragement of traditional learning and others who wanted its replacement with European learning. Many colleges came into existence, primarily due to voluntary efforts. These colleges were started by forward looking Indians such as Raja Ram Mohan Roy as well as some foreigners. Soon missionaries too became active, and by 1857 when the first universities were started, there were already twenty-seven colleges of general learning.

The first three universities, established on the recommendation of Wood's Despatch (1854), were just examining bodies. They were patterned after the University of London. The colleges which already existed were affiliated to these universities, marking the beginning of a practice that in later years came to occupy a prime place in higher education in India. To these three were added a number of other universities, some of which were of mixed type (universities with affiliated colleges as well as teaching facilities, and unitary universities with no affiliated colleges). At the time India attained independence, (1947) the number of universities stood at nineteen. The number of institutions began to expand significantly since independence.

Education was a state subject in India's Constitution till 1978, when by the forty-second amendment, it was made a concurrent subject (of both state and central governments). In recent years the central government has taken an active role in the establishment of central universities as demonstrated by the setting up of Jawaharlal Nehru University in Delhi, the North Eastern Hill University at Shillong, and more recently, one in Assam, all governed by acts of parliament. Apart from these central institutions, all the other universities are "state universities", established by the states. While the central universities may or may not have geographically delimited areas, the state universities, if they are the affiliating type, have well demarcated regions within a particular state and all colleges in this region are generally affiliated to the university serving that region.

A university, as defined by the University Grants Commission (UGC) Act, means a "university incorporated by or under a Central Act, a Provincial Act, or a State Act". Other institutions of higher learning may be deemed to be universities but may not be designated as such. Thus we have a number of deemed universities which have not been established by any act but have been accorded the status of universities under section 3 of the UGC Act. In addition to these three categories, we have the fourth one, which does not fall into the category of universities in any sense, but resemble them in many ways, and like the universities, can award degrees. The Indian Institutes of Technology, the Indian Agricultural Research Institute, the All Indian Institute of Medical Sciences, and a few others are in this category. These are designated as institutions of national importance.

PRIMARY AND SECONDARY EDUCATION

The duration of school education at present is generally ten years, it being further sub-divided into two stages: middle school and secondary. The point of division in general is class eight. This is followed by another stage, the higher secondary stage (or the old intermediate stage) of two years duration, sometimes attached to schools and in a few states in a separate entity called junior college or in still a few other states, in regular colleges.

The structural pattern of education that is now followed, the $10+2+3$ pattern, was the result of sustained prodding by the Union government and the University Grants Commission, after the Education Commission of 1984-86, popularly called the Kothari Commission, made the recommendation for reorganizing the entire pattern of education. While syllabuses for primary and middle stages are prepared by the departments of education of state governments, the syllabuses for secondary and higher secondary stages are generally prepared and prescribed by the more than thirty boards of secondary education. At the middle stage, in most of the states, there is a school based terminal examination. But the secondary and higher secondary stages are followed by common public examinations conducted by the boards. The higher secondary certificate is the qualifying examination for admission to all courses at the higher education stage. Normally an Indian child admitted at the age of five years, in the first standard of the primary stage, completes the higher secondary stage at eighteen years.

There has been a steady increase over the years in the number of schools as well as in the number of students on rolls. The enrollment in 1950-51 in the 13,400 middle schools was 3.1 millions and in 1982-83 in 123,300 middle schools it rose to 22.7 millions, thereby registering a 6.4 percent per year growth in enrollment. The enrollment in classes 9-11 in 1950-51 in 7,300 secondary schools was a 122 million, which in 1982-83 went up to 949 millions in about 50,000 schools, registering a growth of 7.8 percent per year.

There has been, thanks to the Education Commission's recommendation, an attempt at streaming off a percentage of students into vocational streams at different points of schooling. Thus, one section of students will step out at the end of middle school into the vocational stream, and again another section at the end class ten. These vocational courses would be either in the school itself or in separate institutions offering vocational courses. There were 1,600 vocational institutions in 1983-84, but a big percentage of this were in just two states, Tamil Nadu and Maharashtra. This was designed to check the ever-increasing rush for academic courses in institutions of higher education.

HIGHER EDUCATION

Universities

At present there are 11 central universities, 132 state universities, 22 deemed universities, and 15 institutions of national importance, in India.

Universities now rarely limit themselves as examining bodies. Although they are mostly of the affiliating type, some teaching activity is not uncommon. We have in addition federal universities, Delhi being its typical example. All the colleges situated in the Union Territory of Delhi are the constituent colleges of Delhi University. Since all federal as well as affiliating universities do some teaching, the old distinctions have now lost relevance. Most universities in India are multi-disciplined, and have multiple faculties. But we find emergence of single discipline universities like the Roorkee Engineering University. Another institution of this type, the Technological University in Andhra Pradesh (unlike the Roorkee), is an affiliating one with all engineering colleges in the state affiliated to this university. The university at Khairagarh is for fine arts only. Of the 149 universities in 1985-86, 26 were for agricultural and veterinary sciences, 5 were for technical and agricultural sciences and 3 were for technology. While there has been no sexist bias in higher education, universities to foster women's education came to be established, the pioneering one being the S.N.D.T. at Pune, followed by institutions in Andhra Pradesh and Tamil Nadu. The Sampurnand Sanskrit University at Varanasi, developed from the ancient Sanskrit College as nucleus, has grown into a center for fostering Sanskrit and oriental learning. It is also an affiliating university with Sanskrit colleges all over India affiliated to it.

As the majority of universities are of the affiliating type, the total number of universities appear to be small compared to the size of the country. But the fact is that by 1987-88 there were 6,597 colleges affiliated to these universities. Of these, 67 percent offered programs in arts, sciences, and commerce with the rest being professional colleges.

The numbers of both universities and colleges have been continuously increasing within the last three quarters of this century. The peak was in the sixties when forty new universities were started. This rate of growth slowed down only in the seventies. A parallel increase was witnessed in the number of colleges. The number of colleges in 1857 was 27, and by 1947-48 the number had increased to 636 of which 496 offered programs in arts and science, and 140 offered professional courses. While only 278 new colleges were started in 1956-1961, the number added in the third plan was 623. The increase in this number seems not to slacken as published statistics indicate 922 new colleges between academic years 1984-85 and 1986-87, and 85 between 1986-87 and 1987-88.

It must be noted that a University Grants Commission was set up in 1956 with a comprehensive role "to take in consultation with the universities or other bodies concerned all such steps as it may think fit for the promotion and coordination of university education and for the determination and maintenance of standards of teaching, examination, and research in the universities". The UGC slowly came to acquire unlimited powers over the universities although the latter themselves were established as statutory bodies and hence were fully autonomous. The UGC guidelines to states regarding establishment of new universities required that before a state government formulated a proposal for the establishment of a new university, it had to undertake a survey of the existing facilities for higher education in the state, involve the UGC from the very beginning of the proposal and have sufficient data regarding the existing position and justification for the need for an additional university.

This was however not binding on the states, which after all are empowered by the constitution to run their affairs. But the UGC's power lay in its prerogative in disbursing the funds as all central grants to higher education in the states are channeled through the UGC. The 1972 amendment to the UGC Act stipulated: "No grant shall be given by the central government, the commission, or any other organization receiving funds from the central government, to a university which is established after the commencement of the UGC (Amended) Act, 1972, unless the commission has, after satisfying itself as to such matters as may be prescribed, declared such university to be fit for receiving grants".

A university has a number of bodies, the most important one being its senate or the academic council. Traditionally the senate or the academic council has been an all-powerful body symbolizing the autonomous status generally enjoyed by the university. This body frames ordinances for conducting the work of teaching, examining and awarding diplomas and degrees.

Apart from the larger body of senate/academic council, a university has a court which has become inconsequential now, and a syndicate/executive council. The syndicate is the governing body of the university, and consists of a limited number of persons including a few teachers nominated by the government or by the chancellor. The chancellor is invariably the governor in the case of state universities, while in the case of central universities, the equivalent designation is visitor who is normally the president of the country.

The executive head of the university is the vice-chancellor who is appointed by the chancellor/visitor from amongst a panel constituted for the purpose. The vice-chancellor holds office for a term of 3-5 years. It is in the appointment and termination or dismissal of the vice-chancellors that the state governments exercise the greatest control over the universities, and make a farce of university autonomy. For example, Bihar government removed vice-chancellors of all the universities in the state enmasse as many as four times, in 1972, 1977, 1985 and 1988, and a vice-chancellor holds office at the pleasure of the chancellor according to Bihar Universities Act.

The size of universities in India depends on the type of universities. Unitary universities appear to be big since students are enrolled and are taught in them. In the case of the affiliating universities, enrollment generally will be in the colleges. Overall, some of the older universities are very large, with Calcutta leading them. Unitary universities such as the Banaras Hindu University and Aligarh Muslim University have large enrollments ranging from 15,000 to 20,000. Some of the unitary universities have much smaller enrollment like the Jawaharlal Nehru University in Delhi with less than 4,000 students. This university has a large number of faculties and a large campus, but conducts only courses leading to postgraduate and research degrees.

Colleges

Since universities do very little of undergraduate teaching, and mostly concentrate on postgraduate teaching or research, and also because of historic reasons, the system of affiliation is a prominent feature of the higher education scene in India. There is no accreditation as in some other countries but affiliation to a university requires inspection and evaluation of the institution by a team sent by the university. In this, the state government also is involved since the finances of the college are met by the government through the grants-in-aid system.

There is no fixed number of colleges that a university can affiliate: the University of Bombay had 160 in 1984-85, and the Ajmer University has 200. Three out of four southern states had the highest average number of affiliated colleges per university ranging between 90 and 109. The Education Commission had recommended that the number of colleges per university should be thirty.

Though the best colleges lost their preeminence after 1916, i.e. after the universities started establishing departments and research assumed greater importance over teaching, the colleges still hold the scene in higher education. Most of the undergraduate teaching and a great deal of postgraduate teaching is done in the colleges. In 1986-87, affiliated colleges enrolled 87.7 percent of undergraduate students and 56.5 percent of postgraduate students in India. Combined, the affiliated college accounted for 83 percent of the enrollment. The colleges are of varying sizes. Six colleges in Calcutta together had 50,000 students, but most of the colleges have between 200 and 400 students and according to a UGC study, majority of the colleges in thirteen states do not come up to the desired minimum enrollment of 500.

Nevertheless more and more colleges are being set up, and according to Professor Yash Pal, chairman of U.G.C., the Eighth Plan envisages opening of 500 new colleges. Colleges are not started solely to meet the genuine higher education needs, but for a number of reasons other than academic. They are created more for political and regional considerations. Instead of higher education taking upon itself the task of ushering in of a casteless society, the system has tended to reinforce the caste consciousness. Caste-based colleges have grown very abundantly, and many colleges are started and run by caste associations such as the Nair Service Society in Kerala and Khalsa or the D.A.V. Colleges in different parts of North India. Many colleges are exclusive caste institutions, and take shelter as minority institutions under Art. 30 of the Constitution. These are of course the later versions of the earlier missionary institutions which once dominated the higher education horizon. Fortunately, caste consciousness is less in evidence in the central government institutions.

Higher education is mostly a private effort, and most of the colleges are privately managed. The number of colleges run by the government is small, and in fact, the University Education Commission in 1948 had recommended that the government should not run any college. Still all state governments run colleges which are under a director of collegiate/higher education. Private colleges have their own management bodies, and receive most of their funds from either the state government or from the UGC for special purposes. Fees do not form a substantial part of the total expenditure.

Since the system of affiliation of colleges developed over the last century has manifested certain weak spots, there has been a search for alternatives to the system of affiliation and a committee was set up by the UGC to formulate guidelines for granting affiliation to new colleges by universities. Another alternative suggested as far back as in 1966 by the Education Commission was the setting up of autonomous colleges. The commission recommended that outstanding colleges which have shown a capacity to improve be given autonomous status; with powers to frame their own rules of admission, to prescribe courses of study and to conduct examinations. They will however be under the supervision of the parent university which will also confer the degrees. Though this proposal has generated a lot of controversy, the government has gone ahead with the idea, and by the end of 1987-88, sixty-eight colleges had already been given autonomy. According to the chairman of the UGC, it is proposed to convert about 200 colleges into autonomous institutions, and as per the original scheme, 500 colleges are to be made autonomous eventually.

Demand for Higher Education

Higher education in India has seen tremendous growth. The number of students in higher education institutions at the dawn of independence was 21,500, whereas in 1986-87 there were 3.68 million. Between 1955 and 1977 there was great expansion, about 11-12 percent per annum, with the student population doubling every seven years. The growth has come down since the 1970s and now stands at 4 percent per annum.

The heavy demand in the past can be attributed to a variety of reasons. Universities have always followed an open door policy with respect to admissions, and this has resulted in every one passing out of the high school seeking admission to the college or university. Low fee structure in India's higher education compared to very high fees in most of the countries has encouraged even the non-deserving students to try to improve their qualifications. The system has generated a growing demand for higher education, in spite of the fact that there were 16,735,362 educated persons on the registers of employment exchanges according to the Estimates Committee of the Parliament. Of these, 20 percent were graduates. Due to educated unemployment, there has been a rise in the minimum qualifications for all kinds of jobs. The wider base of school education, and provision of facilities for disadvantaged sections of the society have also altered the social base of university entrants, leading always to chronic shortage of seats and further additions to the number of colleges.

With the growing demand from the people, and with more and more colleges being started by the public, and universities being started by the states with or without the concurrence of the University Grants Commission, the higher educational system has grown to be a gigantic one. It is claimed to be the third largest system, next only to those of USA and USSR. While the quality of undergraduate and graduate education has never invited encomiums, the higher educational system in India has carved a place for the country amongst the nations in the area of research and scientific development. India is third in the number of researchers, next only to the United States of America and Russia. Indian researchers alone account for half of the 16,000 research articles from the third world according to a recent survey; an almost scientific research super power of the third world. About 150,000 qualified scientific technical personnel are produced each year, and the total stock of technically qualified manpower now surpasses 2.5 million.

This expansion of higher education is ultimately at the expense of lower levels of education, and when economic development is not in a position to sustain this expansion, higher education becomes a drag on the economy instead of being a significant instrument for social or economic change. Hence the policy has always been to arrest this expansion. This was to be achieved first by giving up the open door access to higher education and second by curbing indiscriminate starting of colleges and universities. Selective admissions even for general courses were advocated in the First Five Year Plan of 1951-56, though it did not find favor, and could not be acted upon. The Education Commission again called for selective admissions, for which purpose the UGC was advised to set up a Central Testing Organization. It has now been included in the national policy on education. The idea was to link enrollments in various courses to the manpower needs. Along with selective admissions by means of admission tests, growth of institutions was also to be controlled.

In India, while "universities never nourished the kinds of invidious distinctions which the European universities had to contend when they began to modernize themselves in the nineteenth century", it is a historic fact that higher education institutions attracted boys and girls mainly from the upper strata of the society, both caste-wise and economically. Eighty percent of seats in higher education were taken up by the top 30 percent income bracket. The bias in favor of the upper strata has been more pronounced in the case of professional courses (as much as 50 percent of the students in professional colleges hailed from homes with white collar occupations) and a study by A. King showed that the proportion from upper income groups has been progressively increasing. Things have changed somewhat since the 1960s, and there has been a wider base at least in non-professional courses with most of the students now belonging to the middle class.

Financing

That the expansion of higher education has been unplanned is evidenced by one fact, and this is the low expenditure on education in India: around 3 percent of the G.N.P. in 1979-80, which is much less than in Sri Lanka, Malaysia, Algeria, Tanzania, and Uganda. The national policy on education, (1986), hoped: "It will be ensured that from Eighth Plan onwards, it will uniformly exceed 6 percent of national income." Higher education was given priority in development plans, with about 25 percent of the total expenditure on education allocated for college and university education. In the words of J. P. Naik, "Higher education has received the highest priority, best attention, and proportionately large allocations of funds. It is also the one sector of education which has expanded most." The ratio has been changing adversely towards lower levels of education. The total annual expenditure of the union and the states put together was Rs. 11,000 crores, and as far as the union budget was concerned, higher education took ninth position in priority. Some states such as Andhra Pradesh have been spending disproportionately on higher education, allocating 20 percent of the annual budget of education for higher education alone. In spite of high illiteracy rate requiring priority for universalization of elementary education, there has been overemphasis on higher education. It does not seem to be waning. The UGC's proposal for the Eighth Five Year Plan commencing in 1990-91 has proposed an outlay of Rs. 3,200 crores for development of higher education, Rs. 2,500 crores being in the central sector and the rest in the form of contributions from the respective state governments.

Programs and Degrees

Most of this discussion pertains to colleges imparting non-professional education. It may be mentioned here that colleges as well as universities share undergraduate teaching amongst themselves, though not necessarily in equal proportions. Undergraduate courses preparing for graduation (bachelor's degree) in arts, sciences, and commerce are now of three years duration as a result of sustained initiatives by the government of India and the UGC, following the general acceptance of the 10+2+3 pattern of education suggested by the Education Commission. The +2 stage after the ten year secondary school is generally designated as higher secondary, but in some states it is called pre-degree or pre-university. This course had its forerunner in the intermediate stage which for long was part of higher education. But after the reorganization of education and upgrading of the two-year first degree into a three-year degree program, this stage was removed from the colleges and now is part of the high school. Students now take admissions to the first year of the degree course, and after the three-year degree can complete a two-year master's degree which also entitles them to be appointed as lecturers or seek admission for courses leading to Ph.D.

Professional courses are conducted in separate colleges or universities or in specialized institutions. Of the 6,597 colleges in 1987-88, 4,428 conducted general courses, 719 focussed on technical and professional courses, 470 were for physical education and education, 62 were devoted to music/fine arts, and 714 were for oriental learning. The professional courses are of varying duration, ranging from 4-5 years. While the colleges of general education are only required to be affiliated to universities, the professional colleges have more than one step to attain recognized status. There are statutory agencies set up by the central government and these agencies regulate the professional courses as well as recognition of the colleges. Medical Council of India, the All India Council of Technical Education, and the Pharmacy Council of India oversee medical education, engineering/technical education, and pharmacy education respectively. It is now proposed to set up a National Council of Higher Education having adequate representation of these bodies to ensure integrated planning in higher education.

But the situation in respect of professional education has become quite complicated due to a new type of college which started coming up around the middle fifties, and which have now swarmed the scene. They are not started with any infrastructure but the government of the state and the university of the area grant recognition/affiliation due to political considerations. They charge heavy "capitation" fees towards capital costs, and do not therefore depend on government grants. Such "capitation" charging colleges of medicine and engineering have become extremely popular, and students who do not get admission in government aided professional colleges because of rigorous and negatively discriminatory (towards upper castes) admission procedures buy seats in them. Students from underdeveloped countries also have found them as an easy path to obtain professional degrees. Many such colleges are not recognized by the professional bodies (Medical Council etc.), and demands have been continuously made for ending the system of "capitation". The UGC had set up a committee to suggest a scheme of accreditation of professional colleges, and this committee's recommendation for setting up a council for accreditation and assessment of professional colleges is awaiting implementation.

Faculty-wise, in 1987-88, 40.3 percent students were enrolled in arts, 19.7 percent in sciences, and 21.5 percent in commerce, and the remaining 20 percent in other faculties including professional courses. It is significant to note that there has been a slight fall in the share of arts, and a significant fall in the case of sciences. This has been to the advantage of commerce in which the enrollment percentage increased from 8.6 percent in 1950-51 to 21.5 percent in 1987-88.

Stage-wise, 88 percent of students were in graduate classes, 9.5 percent in postgraduate classes, and 1.1 percent in research, in 1987-88. These percentages have remained constant during the last few years. At the research level, 86 percent of students are registered in arts, science and commerce faculties.

Higher education means for a majority of students pursuit of two courses, the first one leading to graduation and the second one leading to a master's degree. The bachelor's degree varies in duration depending on the specialization. The first degree in arts, science, and commerce is now of three years duration in all the universities. This is followed by a master's degree of two years duration. The professional degrees are of varying lengths, ranging from one year in the case of teacher training (which can be taken only after graduation) and journalism, to two or three years in law. These professional courses with minimum admission requirement of just a higher secondary course are of longer duration; 4-5 years in the case of medicine and technical subjects. A master's degree in a subject is a requirement for registration for doctoral degrees, the duration of which is two or three years.

Universities in India have very rigid requirements of studies for all courses. In graduation, with examinations coming at the end of each semester or year, a student has to choose three subjects, one of which is a honors subject for intensive study. It is usual in all universities to have two theory papers for each subject in the examination. The master's degree is in a single subject specialization with four or five branches for study in each year. Many universities permit work for a dissertation in lieu of one or two papers. The examinations are all external with teachers who taught the subject having no role to play. A student passes in first, second, or third division; the normal cut off marks being 60 percent, 50 percent, and 35 percent respectively. In professional courses, some universities have introduced the credit system and award of grades instead of marks.

The doctorate degree is awarded after two or three years, and Indian universities do not prescribe any syllabus for this. The student has only to work on a topic approved by the research committee of the subject department. There has been a move in some universities to have a predoctoral course leading to a degree called M.Phil., and this course has all the characteristics of any master's degree course.

Standard of Education

The standard of education in the universities and colleges in general have not always been high, and all structural changes have been aimed at improving the standards. The standard of research also has invited adverse comments, and the Education Commission had noted the low standard of research in some of the subjects. One reason for this was that major portion of scientific research was left to be done outside the university system (the national laboratories were started with the best facilities) and it is only recently that efforts are being made to bring research into the university system. The Government of India adopted a resolution in 1968 to the effect that "institutions of research should function within the fold of the universities or in intimate association with them".

The fact that the standard of teaching and study continues to be poor is evidenced by the poor performance in examinations. The percentages of students who passed different examinations in 1979 were B.A. 54.3 percent, B.Sc. 55.1 percent, and B.Com. 52.7 percent. In Madras University, these were as low as 27 percent for boys and 58 percent for girls in B.A. examinations. The percentages are higher in postgraduate examinations. But many of those who pass do so in either second or third divisions.

One reason for the large percentage of failures is sometimes attributed to the methods of teaching in Indian universities and colleges. Instead of students learning on their own, they depend on class teaching which is predominantly by the lecture method. With large classes, and unfavorable teacher-student ratios, teachers also do not have any other alternative. Moreover the libraries in the colleges are poorly equipped for individual study. Now with only forty-five universities continuing to use English as the sole medium and the rest using Hindi and other languages in which sufficient books of high quality are not available, the scope for in-depth study by students on their own has become severely limited. The UGC in its concern for improving standards has issued guidelines regarding actual teaching days and on teaching methods. This assumes significance if we remember that teaching is generally disrupted due to strikes by either students or teachers.

System of Evaluation

The system of evaluation prevailing in India has attracted perhaps the greatest criticism from all corners. The UGC had long time back commented: "We are convinced that if we are to suggest any single reform in university education, it should be that of examinations". Examinations come at the end of the course and are mostly written examinations. These are also external, in the sense that the teachers who taught the paper would not be involved in setting the question paper and in evaluation. The examinations in universities have become a big headache to administrators with mass copying, walkouts, and violence, and universities are forced to call the law and order machinery of the state for smooth running of examinations. The validity of examinations has never been beyond doubt.

The Education Commission, made a number of recommendations in 1964-66 to improve the state of things. Some of these are adoption of continuous evaluation, internal assessment and grading of examinations results, system of credits, use of semester plan and adoption of question banks. It called for adoption of improved techniques of evaluation. The UGC mooted the idea of setting up of examination reform units in universities, but only ten universities and three deemed universities accepted this suggestion, in spite of the UGC providing financial assistance. The Commission claims that through wide-ranging consultations, it had succeeded in evolving consensus in favor of three important measures of examination reform. These are continuous internal evaluation, creation of question banks, and grading. By 1982, continuous evaluation at different levels has been introduced by forty-four universities, eight deemed universities, and twenty-two agricultural technological universities. The idea of question banks has been accepted by nineteen universities and two agricultural universities. Grading system was in operation at twenty-two universities, six deemed universities and eighteen agricultural/technological universities.

Curriculum

Universities in Asia are replicas of Western universities and in India the first three were patterned after the ones in the U. K. They do not have an ethos of their own, and the fourth regional conference of ministers of education and those responsible for economic planning in Asia and Oceania held in Colombo in July-August, 1978, remarked that "these models do not suit the socioeconomic conditions and developmental requirements of the societies concerned, or the preservation of their cultural identity". The curriculum of higher educational courses has always been the target of criticism, and a committee on general education had suggested introduction of general education courses for all students. But this was never acted upon. The scheme of restructuring of courses was initiated in the Seventh Plan period with a view to making the first degree courses more relevant to the environment and the development needs of the community. Every undergraduate student is to be given a grounding in three areas: (1) a set of foundation courses which are designed to create awareness of broad areas of knowledge; (2) core courses; and (3) a set of courses of an applied nature. Ten universities and 134 colleges had introduced the restructured courses by 1988 and the UGC is very keen in its wider acceptance.

ISSUES AND TRENDS

Growth of higher education in India, though significant by itself, has not been evenly spread over the entire country and over different strata of the society. According to a study covering the decade 1965-1975 conducted by the UGC, Maharashtra and Uttar Pradesh recorded a very large increase in the number of colleges. Some states did not see any new university coming up, and this included Jammu and Kashmir, Madhya Pradesh, Karnataka, Orissa, Punjab, and Rajasthan. Even after another ten years, regional imbalances continued to bog the planners. Some states are backward and Bihar, Orissa, Rajasthan, Uttar Pradesh, and even West Bengal fall into this category. Maharashtra ranks high in the number of universities and colleges, with 13.13 percent of total enrollments in the country in its universities and colleges as against only 9.17 percent of country's population in the state. Another dimension of the regional imbalances is the wide disparity in availability of facilities in rural and urban areas. Only 30.7 percent of institutions of degree standard and above was located in rural areas and enrollment in them was still lower (only 17.3 percent).

The other imbalance is in respect of women's education. Though women began to make a place for themselves almost as soon as the universities came into being and there has not been any tradition of keeping women away from universities as in the West, the women's share of enrollment is still low due to social traditions of the country. In 1985-86, it was only 29.6 percent. Although this was a significant increase from the 10.9 percent in 1950-51, it was still very low. The statistics for 1987-88 show a slight increase to 31.3 percent. The increase in women enrollment over the years has been partly due to a significant increase in the number of colleges meant exclusively for women (802 in 1987-88 compared to 577 in 1979-80). Here too, while Kerala, Punjab, Delhi, Haryana, Meghalaya, and Nagaland were in the lead, Bihar remained at the bottom with women enrollment representing only 15.9 percent of total student enrollment. More and more women are now following postgraduate and research programs as well as non-traditional professional studies such as engineering, and the picture as a whole is bright.

Though the Indian Constitution forbids discrimination on the basis of caste etc., a large percentage of the population continues to be deprived of access to education because of centuries of discrimination and resulting backwardness. The scheduled castes and the scheduled tribes constituting 14.6 percent and 6.9 percent of the population respectively (1981 census) are educationally backward, and this is reflected in enrollment in higher education. Scheduled castes constitute only 7.5 percent of graduate and postgraduate enrollment, and the scheduled tribes just 1.6 percent in undergraduate and 1.3 percent in postgraduate classes. This was in spite of the fact that 15 percent and 7.5 percent of total seats are reserved for scheduled castes and scheduled tribes respectively. In many states the seats reserved could not be filled because a sufficient number of students belonging to these communities did not qualify for admission. The imbalance is particularly marked in professional courses.

Educationally, Muslims who constitute the largest minority group in the country, remain backward in spite of a strong educational tradition amongst Muslims throughout the historical period. But because of the fact that during the colonial period, Muslims did not take to Western education with enthusiasm, their backwardness in secular education became pronounced in the later years. Attempts to improve the situation took the shape of founding of Aligarh Muslim University and the Jamia Millia Islamia, the first one being a central university. There are a large number of colleges managed by Muslims, but even here the percentage of Muslims is outnumbered by that of non-Muslims. The poor percentage in enrollment leads to poor representation in the later years in the professions and services.

Universities in India have been afflicted to an unprecedented degree by campus unrest and violence, and by the end of 1985 more than fifty universities were closed for one reason or the other, ranging from silly to genuine. A major factor responsible for student unrest is the failure of higher education to promote the process of identity formation. Students are not encouraged to develop self-reliance or realize social responsibility. Hence they have no stake in smooth running of the classes. In addition, political parties take active interest in campus politics, and students union elections may be influenced by political parties with funds supplied by them. Many student leaders have in recent years flowered into political leaders and have become ministers and even chief ministers.

The system of education in India seems to have begun well. One observer remarked that when compared with England of the nineteenth century or even later, the universities in India have been far in advance of the society in repudiating social distinctions. Higher education institutions till the dawn of independence were casteless, merit based, open institutions. But there has been a rapid degeneration resulting in emergence of a system where there is rampant encouragement to every separatist tendency. Teachers and students could move easily from one part of the country to another not too long ago. In its place, we now find all sorts of restrictions making it impossible for teachers to be recruited and students to be admitted if they do not belong to a particular region. A perceptive observer has remarked that political, cultural, religious, and other forces have transformed the educational system into a non-functioning anarchy.

But instead of taking a position outside the system and sitting in judgement, if one becomes a part of the system, one sees growth and development all round and feels proud at the pace of development. One can hope that in due course, the higher educational system of today will do for the country what the one it replaced did in putting the country at the pinnacle of glory, as one of the most civilized and advanced countries of that age.

BIBLIOGRAPHY

Chauhan, C. P. S. *Higher Education in India.* New Delhi: Ashish, 1990.

Kaul, J. N., ed. *Higher Education, Social Change and National Development.* Simla: Indian Institute of Advanced Study, 1975.

Ministry of Education. *Report of the Education Commission, 1964-66.* New Delhi: Ministry of Education, 1966.

Ministry of Human Resources Development. *Selected Educational Statistics, 1986-87.* MHRD, 1988.

Ministry of Human Resources Development. *National Policy on Education.* MHRD, 1986.

Ministry of Human Resources Development. *Education in India, 1983-1984.* Volume I. MHRD, 1988.

Singh, Amrik, and G. D. Sharma, eds. *Higher Education in India - The Social Context.* Delhi: Konark, 1988.

IRAQ

by
Kashi Al-Ma'adhidi
Assistant Professor, College of Education
University of Baghdad, Iraq

BACKGROUND

The establishment of first schools in Iraq can be traced back to many thousands of years. Education occupied a prominent place in the ancient society (3,500 B.C.) as civilization flourished. Numerous ruins of schools of ancient times have been found in many cities in Iraq. Besides writing and language, higher education in those early periods included mathematics, music, astronomy, medicine, and law.

When the Arab Islamic State was established later along with the advent of Islam, some of the most famous Islamic schools were founded in Baghdad: Al-Nidhamiyah School in the year 409 and Al-Mustansiriyah School in 630. A number of similar schools were also established in other cities in Iraq, particularly in Mosul, Basrah, and Tikrit. Teaching in these schools were conducted in Arabic.

In recent years, Iraq has devoted a tremendous amount of resources, since the revolution of July 1968, to the development of education through a system of compulsory and free education. Educational facilities have been expanded to provide equal opportunities to all citizens. School and university curricula have been recompiled in line with the central philosophy of the Party, aspirations of the Revolution, and the requirements of the new society.

There are two authorities responsible for education in Iraq. The Ministry of Education is responsible for general education including kindergartens, primary schools, and secondary schools. The Ministry of Higher Education and Scientific Research oversees the universities, technical institutes, and research centers.

The Ministry of Education carries out following functions: sets the educational policy related to the domains of its functions and based on society's needs; sets the educational plans in the light of the prescribed educational policy; secures the provision of human and material resources and technical and organizational requirements necessary for implementation and evaluation of its plans; secures the training of teachers, educational supervisors, administrators and supervisors of general education, and their in-service retraining; forms the administrative and technical organizations necessary for the planning and administration of education; prepares educational curricula for primary, secondary, vocational, and adult education as well as kindergartens; takes care of religious and moral education, physical education, and artistic education; ensures the establishment and management of all schools of various kinds and categories; takes care of school health programs and student nutrition; gives special attention to educational research and experiments aiming at the development of the educational system in the country and boosting its efficiency.

General education in Iraq consist of three stages. Kindergartens for children under six years of age, providing a two year program. The Primary Stage for children over six years of age, and for a period of six years (education at this stage is compulsory for all the children of Iraq). The secondary stage, consisting of two levels: (a) the intermediate stage for a period of three years after primary education; and (b) the preparatory stage lasting three years after intermediate education and having three branches (the scientific branch, the literary branch, and vocational education branch).

Teacher training institutes are of two kinds: (a) institutes that offer a five-year program after intermediate education; and (b) institutes that offer a two-year program after secondary education.

PRIMARY AND SECONDARY EDUCATION

Primary education is compulsory and is free. Primary education is funded from appropriations made by the state, and the Ministry of Local Government is responsible for administration. Instruction in primary education is conducted in Arabic. Children, at the age of six years enter primary schools which are full-time day schools. The schools fall into three categories: schools for boys, schools for girls, and mixed schools. Each class has about 20-40 pupils. Registration of new pupils starts during the month of June each year and instruction in schools begin in mid-September. The children of Arabs and foreigners lawfully resident in Iraq receive the same treatment as Iraqi children.

The weekly study load in primary schools is between thirty and thirty-two hours and the scholastic year has no less than thirty-two weeks excluding holidays. There is continuous assessment of students' performance of daily and monthly classroom tests, midyear examinations and final examinations. Pupils' success depends on their obtaining 50 percent of marks in each subject, but their performance will be regarded incomplete if they obtain less than that in one or two subjects (and have to take the examinations again in the failed subjects). A pupil will fail if he obtains less than 50 percent either in three subjects in the first session of the final examinations or in one subject in the second session of the examinations. The highest mark is ten in the examinations of the first, second, third, and fourth years and 100 in the examinations of the fifth and sixth years.

The Primary Stage ends at the end of six years of studies, with a general ministerial examination for primary education.

The following are the subjects taken by the pupils in primary schools: Islamic education, Arabic language and handwriting, English language (in the fifth and sixth years only), mathematics, civic education, history, geography, biological education, science and health education, and artistic education.

Secondary education in Iraq is the responsibility of the Ministry of Education. The ministry formulates the educational policy to meet the objectives of national development. The ministry sets and approves educational curricula and textbooks, develops the teaching methods, and aids in the methods of assessment and examinations. Furthermore, it is the ministry's responsibility to ensure the proper performance of the educational, scientific, and social activities in these schools, and to exercise educational supervision over them. It also organizes and supervises the examinations. There are separate schools for boys and girls.

Secondary education falls into three categories: general secondary schools with their two stages, intermediate and preparatory; vocational secondary schools (commercial, industrial, and agricultural); and comprehensive schools. Medium of instruction is Arabic.

Pupils who have successfully completed the primary education or its equivalent are admitted to intermediate education provided they submit the primary education certificate accompanied by a special form containing personal information, the civil status card, and a medical certificate stating that they are free from infectious diseases and have been vaccinated against smallpox. Holders of the intermediate education certificate or its equivalent are admitted to general and vocational secondary education provided that they submit the said certificate along with the same documents as required for admission to intermediate education.

The duration of the scholastic year in secondary schools is nine months and studies start in mid-September. Attendance in secondary schools is full-time during which the pupils in the intermediate stage do 30-33 hours of study a week and are taught the following subjects in Arabic: Islamic education, Arabic language, English language, history, geography, civic education, principles of mathematics, algebra, geometry, general science, chemistry, physics, biology, health, artistic education, and physical education and military training.

In the preparatory stage, the weekly hours of study range between thirty-one and thirty-five, and the following subjects are taught (in its scientific and literary branches according to specialization): Islamic education, Arabic language, English language, economics, mathematics, chemistry, physics, biology, physical education and civil defence, artistic education, and national and socialist culture.

There is continuous assessment of students' performance, as in the case of primary school. The general ministerial examinations for intermediate education (three years) and preparatory education (three years) conducted by the Ministry of Education are held at the end of each stage.

Graduates of teacher training institutes or those with equivalent qualification are appointed teachers in primary schools; with a headmaster and one or more assistant headmasters appointed from among teachers based on performance. The headmaster, his assistants, and all the teachers work jointly towards ensuring the progress of the educational process in schools. They are also responsible for organizing extra curricular activities such as sports, arts, and scouting with a view to developing group and cooperative spirit, and democratic and socialist values.

Teachers in the general and vocational secondary schools are generally graduates of colleges or higher institutes. Preference is given to holders of bachelor's degree or higher qualifications and to those who have received pedagogical training.

HIGHER EDUCATION

Institutions

The Ministry of Higher Education and Scientific Research (established in 1970) is the responsible authority for implementation of the educational, cultural, scientific, and technological policy of the state within the framework of official and private educational institutions of the country. The ministry carries out this responsibility through general, systematized central planning and execution.

The ministry oversees universities (University of Baghdad, University of Mosul, University of Basrah, University of Salahuddin, Al-Mustansiriyah University, University of Technology, University of Kufa, University of Anbar, University of Tikrit, and University of Qadisiyah); The Body of Technical Institutes (forty-one institutes); and research centers (six research centers attached to the University of Baghdad).

The law for the establishment of the University of Baghdad was legislated in 1956 and was the foundation stone for building and establishing universities in the country. Later, the law of the University of Baghdad was enacted in 1958. The university now consists of the following colleges: law, education, medicine, pharmacy, engineering, arts, science, agriculture, dentistry, veterinary medicine, physical education, nursing, sharia (Islamic law), fine arts, administration and economics, languages and political science. The research centers attached to the University of Baghdad include: Natural History Museum, Educational and Psychological Research Center, Palestinian Studies Center, Psychological Health Care Center, Urban and Regional Planning Center, Center for the Revival of Arab Scientific Heritage.

Other universities in Iraq are organized somewhat similar to the University of Baghdad with the number of "colleges" varying (and therefore the fields of studies) depending upon the emphasis of the institution.

Teaching staff in Iraqi universities and institutes are appointed by the Ministry of Higher Education and Scientific Research following nomination by the academic department, college, or the university concerned. The teachers must hold a master's degree or a doctorate in the subject of their specialization. Different staff levels include assistant instructor, instructor, assistant professor, and professor.

The Technical Institutes Body is a technical institution attached to the Ministry of Higher Education and Scientific Research and comprises forty-one technical institutes distributed over various parts of the country. Their task is to train intermediate technical personnel for service in various industrial, agricultural, administrative, and commercial institutions of the state. The period of study in these institutes is two calendar years and is equivalent to three academic years when a student's qualifications and marks are assessed for work or for appointment in government offices. There are institutes of technology with multiple technological fields of study such as the Institute of Technology in Baghdad, and others that specialize in specific fields (e.g. Institute of Administration in Baghdad, Institute of Applied Arts in Baghdad, and the Technical Institute of Medicine in Mosul).

Programs and Degrees

The undergraduate programs at the university generally take four years and leads to a bachelor's degree. The period is longer for some professional programs: medicine is six years, pharmacy is five years, architecture is five years, dentistry is five years, and veterinary medicine is five years. Master's degree programs are also available in most fields. Doctorates (Ph.D.) are awarded in the colleges of arts, science, law and agriculture. Medium of instruction is Arabic.

Colleges of medicine: Study is based on theoretical subjects and practical application in hospitals and laboratories where, under the supervision of their teachers, the students apply their theoretical studies to the actual treatment of patients. The practical work also includes dissection and study of human and animal corpses. During the sixth year students spend most of their time in teaching hospitals.

Colleges of pharmacy: Students study a number of subjects similar to those in medical colleges including specialized subjects. The courses of study also require training in drug factories, pharmacies, and field research for a period of five months by final year students.

College of dentistry: Students study a number of subjects similar to those in the colleges of medicine and pharmacy in addition to specialized subjects in dental medicine and surgery.

Colleges of engineering and the University of Technology: Study in most of the departments of the colleges of engineering and in all the departments of the University of Technology is of a practical character. Students make practical applications of the theoretical subjects in laboratories, factories, and projects.

Colleges of education: These colleges contain departments for sciences and departments for humanities. Their basic aim is to train teaching staff qualified for the teaching profession in intermediate and secondary schools according to the latest educational methods.

Colleges of physical education: Admission requirements stipulate that candidates should pass a test for body fitness and must demonstrate that they are free from any physical disabilities. They are also required to be interested in physical education and willing to work as technical trainers or coaches in intermediate and secondary schools. The course of study includes theoretical subjects as well as practical subjects requiring effort and bodily fitness.

Colleges of fine arts: The nature of study and training require a desire for artistic work during and after the period of study. Admission to these colleges require candidates to pass a special interview. They aim at training artistic personnel specializing in various branches of art to work as artistic trainers in intermediate and secondary schools and in teacher training institutes and as technicians in relevant institutions.

Colleges of nursing: The curricula consist of theoretical subjects as well as practical work during which students undergo training in hospitals inside the country and abroad. When appointed, graduates of nursing colleges are granted privileges beyond those enjoyed by graduates of other colleges with similar academic qualifications.

Colleges of arts: Study in these colleges involves theoretical subjects in addition to some applied subjects. Their basic aim is to graduate scholarly persons specialized in various branches of human knowledge to work in institutions related to their specializations. Some of the graduates are appointed to teach in intermediate and secondary schools. Others are prepared for higher studies.

Colleges of administration and economics: These colleges aim at graduating academically equipped personnel specialized in administration, economics, and statistics. They also train teaching staff for vocational (commercial) secondary schools. Candidates for admission to these colleges undergo an interview held at the colleges to ascertain their ability in the English language.

Colleges of agriculture: Study at these colleges has a theoretical as well as an applied nature where some course work is done in the fields, farms, laboratories, factories, and in various agricultural and productive institutions.

Colleges of veterinary medicine: The course of study in these colleges include theoretical subjects as well as practical subjects applied to animal resources.

Colleges of science: The curricula of these colleges include theoretical subjects in addition to applied practical subjects in laboratories. The basic aim of these colleges is to train specialists in various sciences.

Colleges of Sharia (Islamic Law) and Figh (Jurisprudence): The curricula of these colleges include theoretical subjects in addition to applied work in laboratories. The basic aim of these colleges is to train specialists in Islamic sharia and sciences to work in relevant offices and institutions.

Technical institutes: Study at these institutes include practical work in laboratories, fields, factories, and service projects in addition to the study of theoretical subjects. These schools aim at training specialized intermediate technical personnel capable of implementing the plans and projects of the national development plan.

All Iraqi students who have successfully passed the General Secondary Education Examination (baccalaureat) are entitled to be admitted to Iraqi universities and institutes, depending on the availability of places in each field of study provided that the total marks obtained by the candidate is not less than 360. Graduates of vocational secondary schools (industrial agricultural or commercial) ranking first in the examination results are also entitled to apply for admission to colleges related to their specializations. The same applies to graduates of religious secondary schools who are entitled to apply for admission to religious programs. Applications are made through the Central Admissions Department of the Ministry of Higher Education and Scientific Research. Preference in admission is determined on the basis of a student's total marks and his desired field of study.

Admission is open to foreign students who satisfy following conditions: they must hold the Iraqi General Secondary Education Certificate or its equivalent; they must have graduated during the preceding three years; they must submit the relevant application form stamped by the competent authority through which it is to be submitted; the candidates have to pass the prescribed medical examinations as well as physical fitness tests; admission to Arab students residing in Iraq and holding the Iraqi Secondary Education Certificate is governed by the same rules applicable to Iraqi students. Visiting Arab and foreign students graduated from

Iraqi secondary schools receive the same treatment as Iraqi students with regard to the required documents and academic conditions.

The academic year begins in September each year and ends in June of the next year. The academic year is divided into two terms with a mid year vacation of ten days in between. Weekly hours of instruction are 22-30 hours for humanities and 32-40 hours for scientific studies. There is continuous assessment of performance (of students) throughout the year, for which 50 percent of the grades are given. The other 50 percent of the grades are based on final examinations, conducted by the departmental committees. The minimum passing mark is fifty (on a 0-100 scale) provided that a student's general average in all subjects is not less than 60 percent.

Postgraduate studies at the universities strive to revive the national heritage and display its values that are compatible with the requirements of building a socialist unitary society; promote the standard of academic studies and diversify such studies; train the teaching staff members and the researchers needed for the higher education sector and for other state institutions; turn the university into a creative center for the propagation of original Arab-Islamic culture and values; and establish links between higher studies and the needs of the country.

Iraqi universities award the following higher degrees: higher diploma for which the period of study is 1-2 years after the first degree; master's degree for which the period of study is 3-6 terms after the first degree; and doctorate for which the period of study is 4-8 terms after the master's degree or the higher diploma. Admission to postgraduate programs require a first degree or a master's degree in the subject of his specialization or equivalent.

University education at all stages is free. The state covers all the expenses of a student's study, such as, textbooks, educational material, instruments, and laboratory expenses. The university grants Iraqi students who are not government officials, suitable financial assistance or university grants. Government officials who are accepted for higher study are granted study leave with full pay.

BIBLIOGRAPHY

Ma'rouf, Naji. *The Scholars of Al-Nidhamiyah Schools: The Schools of the Islamic East.* Baghdad, 1973.

Ministry of Education, Directorate of Curricula and Textbooks. *Study Plans for the Primary, Intermediate and Secondary Stages.* Ministry of Education, n.d.

Qubain, F. I. *Education and Science in the Arab World.* Baltimore, Maryland: Johns Hopkins Press, 1966.

Taha, Baquir. *An Introduction to the History of Ancient Civilizations: The Civilization of Mesopotamia.* 1955.

IRELAND

by
Daniel G. Mulcahy
Professor of Education
Eastern Illinois University, U.S.A.
(Formerly, Professor and Head of Department of Education
University College, Cork, Ireland)

BACKGROUND

The system of education in Ireland has undergone enormous transformation during the past quarter of a century or so, as investment in education grew from less than 3 percent of GNP in 1961 to over 6.5 percent in 1986. As a result, participation rates have vastly increased and new structures and institutions are commonplace, even though the basic legal and constitutional framework has not changed greatly. Like in all countries, the educational system in Ireland is largely the product of its past, as is Irish society in general. Throughout its history Ireland has had a strong tradition of schooling and learning, a tradition in higher education which dates back to the great medieval monasteries such as that at Clonmacnoise. Today it retains many of its attractions as a center of higher education. It is frequently the host to summer schools for visiting students from many parts of the world and remains a popular center for more prolonged periods of study by overseas students during the regular academic year.

Dublin University, of which Trinity College, Dublin, is the sole College, is Ireland's oldest university. It was founded in 1591. It wasn't until the middle of the nineteenth century, when there were increased demands by Catholics for a university which would be less objectionable to Catholics, that a move to establish a second university achieved any success. In 1845 the Queen's Colleges were established. These ran into difficulties and were replaced in 1879 by the Royal University. By this time, the Catholic hierarchy had established a university of its own in Ireland, namely the Catholic University of Ireland which was founded in 1851, and whose first rector was Cardinal John Henry Newman. Eventually, all of these nineteenth century university institutions ran into difficulties and it was not until 1908 that a second and lasting new university was established in Ireland, namely the National University of Ireland. It was not until sixty years later that the next major expansion in Irish higher education took place. This occurred with the establishment of the National Council for Educational Awards in 1972 and the setting up of a National Institute of Higher Education in Limerick in the same year. (The National Institute of Higher Education has been renamed in May 1989 as the University of Limmerick). Since then, enrollment in higher education and expenditure thereon have grown very considerably and today there is a highly complex network of institutions of higher education stretching throughout the entire country.

While the role of government in the development of higher education in the Republic of Ireland has been crucial, religious considerations have also played a significant part, especially during the nineteenth century. Today the government continues to be the major source of funding for universities and other colleges, even though the universities, and perhaps to a lesser extent the non-university colleges, retain their autonomy especially in academic matters. Thus, while institutions may be prodded or coaxed into certain lines of academic and curriculum development by promises of government support and funding, the decision to develop in one way or another or not at all, rests in the final analysis with the institutions themselves. Furthermore, funding of the colleges and universities does not come directly from any state department but is funnelled through the Higher Education Authority, itself an independent statutory body.

Each individual college has its own administration and some of them, in addition, are owned privately by religious orders. Both formally and informally, a variety of structures exists for inter-relations among the various organizations of higher education and, to a lesser extent, between these organizations and industry and various professional organizations. Thus, for example, there is in existence the Conference of Irish Universities to enable the various university institutions to discuss matters of common interests to them. Likewise, the heads of Irish universities meet on a continuing basis to discuss matters of common interest, and, in addition, the Higher Education Authority is itself composed of representatives from several of the major institutions of higher education. Facilities also exist whereby heads of universities can meet with the minister of education or officials of the Department of Education.

PRIMARY AND SECONDARY EDUCATION

Primary Education

The legal minimum age for entry to school in the Republic of Ireland is four years. Nearly all primary schools (about 95 percent) are officially termed national schools. They are bound by regulations of the state Department of Education, their teachers are paid by the Department of Education, and their curriculum is decided by the Department of Education. National schools are managed by boards of management usually composed of parents, teachers and nominees of the school patrons, usually a bishop of the diocese. The responsibilities of the board relate to appointments and financial matters rather than to educational policy and curriculum.

Even though the curriculum of the national school is decided by the Department of Education, individual teachers have considerable freedom in its implementation. The following are required subjects of study by all students: Irish (Gaelic), English, mathematics, social and environmental studies, arts and crafts, music, physical, and religion. Since the introduction of a new curriculum in 1971 a special emphasis is given to the integration of subjects where possible. The abolition of the primary certificate examination in 1967 put an end to formal state examinations at this level of education and most pupils complete primary education by the age of twelve.

Secondary Education

Secondary education in the Republic of Ireland is offered in secondary, vocational, comprehensive, and community schools and colleges. While the forms of ownership and management of these schools and colleges differ from one another, today they all offer substantially the same type of curriculum. Thus, the secondary school, for example, must offer approved syllabuses in Irish, English, history, geography, mathematics, and civics, with similar regulations applying in the other types of schools. In the early years of secondary education the core of subjects is mandatory for all pupils; in the senior cycle of secondary education there is a greater degree of choice of subjects. In practice, the subjects offered by the schools are also determined by the requirements of the public examinations and the choices of subjects by students are influenced to some extent by whether they plan to proceed to higher education or directly enter work on leaving school. All junior pupils must study Irish, English, mathematics, civics, and at least three other approved subjects. Senior pupils must study at least five subjects, Irish being the only mandatory subject. There are some thirty approved subjects in all available to pupils.

The approved subjects are the subjects which are recognized for the public examinations. The public examinations, and in particular the school leaving certificate examination, exert a very considerable influence, with admission to universities and colleges very much dependent upon performance in the examination. While the public examinations are administered by the Department of Education, and are held in the summer of each year, the leaving certificate is normally accepted by the universities and colleges as the basis for matriculation or admission. Admission, however, will be dependent upon how well one performs in the examination, and different faculties and colleges stipulate different levels of performance before a student can gain admission.

Secondary education normally lasts five years and is aimed at the age group 12-17. Aside from the formal curriculum, varying degrees of provision are made for extracurricular activities, including sporting activities and a variety of other social and cultural activities. Tuition is charged in only a very small number of secondary schools, known as fee-paying schools. Since most pupils live at home living expenses are normally borne by the home. In the small number of boarding schools which exist, yearly fees range from US$2,500-$5,000. In some cases scholarships are available to pupils attending boarding schools or fee-paying schools, though it is normally the family which bears the cost of education in such cases. Access to education in the secondary school is at the discretion of the school authorities. Selection is not permitted in the case of other second-level schools except where demand for places exceeds the number of places available. In practice, all secondary level schools hold entrance tests and various forms of selection are employed when numbers exceeds places available. Foreign student enrollment can normally be arranged without great difficulty, and outside of the major urban centers such enrollments would be few. The normal language of instruction is English in the great majority of schools, though there is a number of Irish language schools where instruction is carried out through the medium of Irish. The selection and appointment of teachers is a matter for the school management authorities but for purposes of incremental salary and certification by the state, basic educational qualifications, normally including a degree and a professional training in education, are required. For the purpose of certification by the state, teachers are also required to pass an examination in Irish.

HIGHER EDUCATION

Institutions

There is a considerable variety of institutions responsible for higher education in the Republic of Ireland. These include the Higher Education Authority, The National Council for Educational Awards, The Central Applications Office, the universities and their various constituent and recognized colleges, the national institutes for higher education in Dublin and Limerick (which were renamed as University of Limerick and City University of Dublin respectively in May 1989), the colleges of education for the education of teachers, the regional technical colleges, the Dublin Institute of Technology, The Royal College of Surgeons, the Dublin Institute of Advanced Studies, and the National College of Art and Design. In addition to these institutions there is also a number of specialist institutions such as the Crawford Municipal School of Art and the Cork School of Music, the Limerick Technical College, the Dun Laoghaire School of Art, the Mater Dei Institute of Education, and the Irish School of Ecumenics.

Of the above-mentioned institutions, the Higher Education Authority, the National Council for Educational Awards, and the Central Applications Office are not teaching institutions. The Higher Education Authority, for example, is the state authority for dispersing most of the monies spent on higher education in the country. This, along with the overall coordination of the various teaching institutions which come within its jurisdiction, is its primary responsibility. The National Council for Educational Awards is concerned with the validation of courses offered in a large number of colleges and institutes which are not associated with the universities. It also awards certificates, degrees, and diplomas to successful students in these institutions. The Central Applications Office has a coordinating role in regard to the admission of students to a large number of the colleges and institutes of higher education.

In addition to the Higher Education Authority, two other institutions, namely, the state Department of Education and the Vocational Education Committees, of which there are thirty eight in all, have a role in the dispersal of monies to institutions engaged in higher education. The Department of Education directly finances the colleges of education for the education of primary teachers and the vocational education committees finance the various regional technical colleges and a number of other institutes and colleges which offer advanced technical education. There is also a small number of private institutions of higher education, of which the Royal College of Surgeons is one. The cost of higher education in these institutions is borne fully by the students.

Turning to the teaching institutions themselves, both the Dublin University and the National University of Ireland are fully autonomous academic institutions having their own chancellor who is head of the university, and their own governing body, which is the senate in the case of the National University of Ireland and the board in the case of Dublin University. The National University of Ireland is a federal university with three constituent colleges, one in Cork, one in Dublin, and one in Galway. Each of these colleges has its own president, who is the chief executive, and its own governing body. In Dublin University there is one college, namely, Trinity College, Dublin, which has its own provost or chief executive and governing board. In each of these university colleges there are faculties of arts, commerce, engineering, law, and science. Other faculties include agriculture, architecture, Celtic studies, dairy and food science, and veterinary medicine. All of the colleges offer courses leading to diplomas, bachelor's degrees, master's degrees, and doctoral degrees.

In the National University of Ireland there are five recognized colleges in addition to the constituent colleges. These include St. Patrick's College, Maynooth, The Royal College of Surgeons, St. Patrick's College of Education, all in Dublin; Mary Immaculate College of Education in Limerick; and St. Angela's College of Domestic Science in Sligo. As with the constituent colleges, the teaching is done in the colleges but the awards are made by the university. Dublin University also has a number of colleges in addition to Trinity College associated with it for the purpose of validation of courses and making of awards. Four of these are colleges of education, namely, the Church of Ireland College of Education, St. Mary's College, Froebel College and St. Catherine's College of Domestic Science. Colleges of the Dublin Institute of Technology also have degrees awarded by the University of Dublin.

The National Council for Educational Awards is the validating and award granting authority in the non-university sector of higher education. The National Council for Educational Awards was established on a statutory basis in 1980, having operated on an ad hoc basis since 1972. It is made up of a council whose members represent different agricultural, educational, industrial, and government interests. Like the universities, the National Council for Educational Awards discharges its responsibilities largely through appointed boards of studies, panels of assessors, and external examiners.

The two former national institutes of higher education, namely, those in Limerick and in Dublin are the two major institutions which came within the ambit of the National Council for Educational Awards. They offer courses in business studies, computer studies, engineering, European studies, science, secretarial studies, and communications. The regional technical colleges, of which there are nine spread throughout the country, also come within the ambit of the National Council for Educational Awards. These colleges offer education of a technical and applied nature which lead to the award of certificates and diplomas as well as degrees. Thomond College of education, which is a college of education for specialist teachers in physical education, trade subjects, rural science, and business studies; and the National College of Art and Design, also have their courses validated and awards made by the National Council for Educational Awards.

Undergraduate Studies

There is a large variety of undergraduate programs leading to bachelor's degrees such as B.A., B.Sc., B.Comm., B.E., B.Agr.Sc. and B.Ed. While basic admission requirements to undergraduate studies are broadly the same in all universities and colleges, different admission standards apply for different degree courses. This, along with the excess number of applicants over places normally available, has led to the emergence of what is called the "points system" of admitting applicants. In this system, points, as determined by each college, are assigned to the examination grades obtained by applicants in the subjects presented for the leaving certificate examination. Entry to medicine and electrical engineering has called for the greatest number of points in recent years, and only students with the requisite number of points are admitted. Admission to the B.A. degree in faculties of arts is normally gained by students with fewer points than those required for most other programs. This, nonetheless, will normally be a standard of above-average in the leaving certificate examination, with successful grades required in the case of the National University of Ireland, for example in three languages including Irish and English, mathematics, and at least two other recognized subjects.

The fields of study available for undergraduate study have already been identified. It is more difficult to address the question of degree of specialization. Normally, undergraduate programs attempt to strike a balance between breadth of knowledge and specialization. In the case of a B.A. degree, for example, students could study four subjects in the first year of the degree program and as few as two subjects for the two remaining years. Degree of specialization is also affected by the structure of a degree program and in many newer degree programs studies may range over many subjects including mathematics and science subjects, engineering subjects, European languages and components in the humanities.

Most undergraduate programs in Irish universities and colleges are of three or four year duration. Courses of study leading to medical qualifications can be of six or seven years duration. The normal duration of the academic year is from September or October to June. In the case of all colleges, a wide range of extracurricular activities is available. These include both intramural and intercollegiate sporting activities, and activities organized by subject societies, student clubs and a wide range of special interest activities. Political clubs also exist on most campuses, and student life is greatly enriched by the continuing flow of guest speakers drawn from academic, cultural, and economic spheres at both national and international levels.

At all colleges and universities, English is the major language of instruction, though some encouragement is given to promote a small number of courses through the medium of Irish in a number of colleges, and especially in University College, Galway, which has been especially designated for this purpose. Tuition fees vary considerably from one degree program to another, though living expenses and arrangements for student accommodation are broadly similar in all institutions. In the academic year 1988-89 in University College, Cork, for example, the annual fee for a full-time student studying for the B.A. degree is US$1,600. In the same college, a student enrolled in the degree program in science or electrical engineering pays US$2,400 per annum and a student enrolled in the medical or dental program pays approximately US$3,200 in fees. Living accommodation for students is, by and large, much the same for students attending any of the colleges or universities. For the most part, students will live at home, if they live in a university town, or live in approved accommodation of a private kind such as private homes and houses surrounding the campuses. Irish universities and colleges have limited residential facilities.

Most Irish students finance their education from private means. There is a system of grants for students but there is a means test for these and many students of middle class background find that the family income is above that which is required to enable them to qualify for a grant. There is a number of scholarships available in most university colleges, though these are very frequently insubstantial. In all, about one third of students benefit from public grants. Foreign student enrollments have been increasing at both the undergraduate and postgraduate levels. This can be expected to increase further with the development of exchange arrangements between Irish students and students from other member states of the European Community under the ERASMUS Program.

The selection and appointment of university teaching staff is largely a matter for the individual colleges. In the case of senior appointments such as professorships in the National University of Ireland, for example, the appointment is made by the senate of the University rather than by the individual constituent college. In such cases, however, the colleges send recommendation to the senate and, with some notable exceptions, these are normally approved by the senate. A development of recent years, one which has lead to the setting up of a teaching development unit in University College, Cork, has been the movement for the continuing education of the staff appointed. Traditionally, faculty appointments are made on the basis of academic qualifications and research, with less attention given to the matter of preparation for the role of lecturer or university teacher.

Advanced Studies and Research

There is a wide range of postgraduate diploma and degree programs available in Irish universities and colleges. These diplomas and degrees are to be found in all faculties and cover a range of specialities which one associates today with a high quality higher education service. The purpose of these postgraduate diplomas and degrees is varied.

Postgraduate diplomas, such as the Higher Diploma in Education and the Diploma in Social Works Studies, and the M.Ed. degree, the M.B.A. degree, and the M.S.W. degree are degrees of a professional nature. On the other hand the degrees of M.A. and M.Sc., for example and the Ph.D. degree which is available in all faculties, are seen primarily as research degrees.

Normally, admission to postgraduate diploma and degree programs is reserved to graduates, usually requiring students to have obtained an honors primary degree. The degree of specialization required in postgraduate degrees varies depending on whether it is a professional or a research degree, and in the case of research degrees such as the M.A. and the Ph.D., a high degree of specialization is required, as students pursue independent research into a particular topic. Postgraduate diploma and degree programs vary in length from one year to a maximum of six years for the Ph.D. degree. The duration of the academic year is the same as for all other degree programs, though it is commonplace for research students to pursue research as fully out of term as in term, and for this reason the facilities of universities and colleges are available throughout the entire calendar year.

As with undergraduate studies, the language of instruction is primarily English. Extracurricular activities are still available to postgraduate students, though customarily postgraduates play a less prominent role than do undergraduate students in such activities.

At the postgraduate level, fees for research degrees for native students tend to be the same in all faculties (around US$1,200 per annum), with postgraduate diplomas in professional areas showing greater variation, and ranging from US$500 per annum up to US$2,300 per annum. Living expenses and living accommodation for students is largely the same as it is for undergraduate students, though many postgraduate students will be married and some may be earning a living while pursuing their postgraduate work on a part-time basis. Other postgraduate students will have the benefit of research or teaching assistantships and scholarships. Thus the financing of postgraduate studies normally leaves students less dependent on parental support and more dependent on their own personal resources, scholarships, and teaching assistantships. The selection and appointment of teaching staff in postgraduate programs is the same as for undergraduate programs, as in almost all cases university teachers engage in both undergraduate and postgraduate teaching. As a proportion of the graduate student body, foreign students make up a higher proportion than is the case with undergraduate students.

The organization of research in Irish universities and colleges, and the amount of funding available for it varies greatly from field to field. The greatest levels of financial support, and accordingly the greatest levels of research output, is normally to be found in the science and technology areas. In recent years, a feature of postgraduate studies and the organization of research has been the establishment of a number of specialist research centers and industry-oriented research concerns.

There exists a number of postdoctoral degrees, such as the D.Litt. and D.Sc. for the award of which research work may be submitted to the university. Honorary doctoral degrees are also awarded from time to time by the Universities.

ISSUES AND TRENDS

The major current trend in higher education in the Republic of Ireland revolves around the severe budgetary condition of the universities, the state initiated measure to institute major curriculum reforms at the primary and secondary levels of schooling, and the issue of the over supply of graduates in many professional areas, such as teaching, medicine, dentistry and law.

Historically, Irish universities and colleges have depended very heavily for financial support upon the state. As part of its efforts to correct its budget deficits, cutbacks of the order of 3 percent per annum have been imposed since 1987 upon the universities by the state. This has led to the initiation of a scheme of early retirements and redundancies and the freezing of vacant academic posts. In the views of some, this is now reaching crisis proportions and there is the fear of a threat to academic standards and quality as well as service to students.

In the case of the curriculum and examinations, the government established in 1988 a National Council for Curriculum and Assessment, a successor to the Curriculum and Examinations Board which was established in 1984. The purpose of these bodies was to review the curriculum offerings of the schools and the examination system. The most concrete outcome to date has been in the introduction of a new examination at age fifteen and the introduction of new syllabuses for seven subjects at the junior cycle of the postprimary school. It is intended that the work of the National Council for Curriculum and Assessment will continue into the future, though concern is being expressed as to the efficacy of its initiatives in the absence of substantial support for the in-service education of teachers.

As with other professional areas, there is a large surplus of trained teachers. The population structure is such that the school population in the Republic of Ireland is expected to decline between now and the end of the century. The age structure of teachers is also such that the average age is approximately forty years. As a result, there is the prospect of a continuing oversupply of teachers in the system, as long as the current pupil-teacher ratios are maintained.

Faced with this situation, the government has agreed to an OECD National Survey which focuses on the question of teacher training and supply. The recommendations and the report of this survey team is awaited with great interest, and even anxiety. Accordingly, the major ongoing study in Irish education is the study being carried out by the OECD survey team. Other studies recently completed include two works in educational policy and a major work analyzing participation in higher education in the country.

Looked at in a comparative perspective, education in Ireland today still bears the imprint of its modern beginnings and early evolution during the period of British rule in Ireland up until the third decade of the twentieth century. During the almost seventy years of native government, the educational system, beginning especially in the 1960s, has expanded very considerably in terms of new structures, institutions, and enrollments. Investment in education has gone ahead at a very rapid rate since the mid 1960s and today the Irish educational system is held in high esteem all over the world, for the quality of both its teaching, and its graduates. In the years ahead, it is likely that the major developments will be in the areas of preschool education and adult and continuing education; areas which have not yet felt the favor of strong government support and funding.

BIBLIOGRAPHY

Clancy, Patrick. *Who Goes to College? A Second National Survey of Participation in Higher Education.* Dublin: The Higher Education Authority (Ireland), 1988.

Commission on Higher Education. *Report of the Commission on Higher Education, 1960-1967.* Dublin: The Stationery Office (Ireland), 1967.

Coolahan, John. *Irish Education: History and Structure.* Dublin: The Institute of Public Administration (Ireland), 1981.

Higher Education Authority. *Progress Report 1974-1984.* Dublin: The Higher Education Authority (Ireland), 1985.

Investment in Education. Dublin: The Stationery Office (Ireland), 1965.

Kenna, A. T. M., ed. *Higher Education: Relevance and Future.* Dublin: The Higher Education Authority (Ireland), 1985.

Mulcahy, D. G. *Curriculum and Policy in Irish Post-Primary Education.* Dublin: The Institute of Public Administration (Ireland), 1981.

Mulcahy, D. G., and Denis O'Sullivan, eds. *Irish Educational Policy: Process and Substance.* Dublin: The Institute of Public Administration (Ireland), 1989.

Program for Action in Education: 1984-1987. Dublin: The Stationery Office (Ireland), 1984.

White Paper on Educational Development. Dublin: The Stationery Office (Ireland), 1980.

ISRAEL

by
Lya Kremer-Hayon
Head, Center for Educational Administration and Evaluation
University of Haifa, Israel

BACKGROUND

The history of education in Israel is fraught with dilemmas and conflicts, some of which are characteristic of any educational system, others stem from specific political, social, and demographic conditions, as well as from educational ideologies. The present Israeli educational system, which is an outcome of this history, was formally established in May 1948 with the declaration of the state. Its roots go, however, a long way into the past. The pre-state period which started in the last decade of the nineteenth century and the post-state period, upon which the essay will focus, are only small segments of a long sequential tradition.

Before the declaration of the state of Israel in 1948, during the British Mandate, schools were under the authority of a central national committee. Kindergartens belonged to private or community organizations. The elementary school system, grades 1-8, was divided into three tracks that were identified with political and ideological orientations: the general track, the labor track, and the religious track, each having different curricular emphasis and entertaining 50.1 percent, 24.8 percent, and 25.0 percent of the general pupil population, respectively. This differentiation was a topic of debate and conflict which was resolved only in 1953 by State Law, according to which the three education sub-systems mentioned above were transferred to the Ministry of Education, and education became compulsory, first for eight years, and later for nine and ten years.

The secondary schools belonged to private organizations. Pupils of relatively high academic achievement were admitted after completing eight years of elementary education for four more years of studies. Upon graduating the high school they had to pass matriculation exams which made them eligible as university candidates. Those pupils who were not interested in pursuing an academic education continued their education in vocational schools, or started working during the day and taking courses in the evening. At the same time, however, most youngsters were affiliated with youth movements. One of the main aims of these movements was to develop strong national and social values. The schools encouraged their pupils to join the youth movements as the latter were in fact complementary educational subsystems. Not to be overlooked is the unique feature of education in the *Kibbutz* settlements, which was characterized by a progressive orientation, with a special focus on individualization of instruction.

421

Higher education was provided in two institutions: The Hebrew University in Jerusalem and the Technion Institute of Technology in Haifa, both granting academic degrees (including Ph.D.). In addition there were a number of teacher education colleges which after two years of study granted teaching certificates.

In the pre-state period, education was characterized by a strong national ethos, of an old nation coming back to its homeland. The new young idealistic settlers came from Eastern Europe in the hope of building a safe and peaceful home, of reviving the Hebrew language, the language of the Bible. Both ideals required strong will and resulted in difficult struggles for life. The aims of education were an outcome of these ideals and strongly related to them. They were well reflected in the declaration of the State Education Law, "...education will be based on the values of the Israeli culture, on love and loyalty to the Israeli state and its people, on training to work, on pioneering, on the wish to build a society based on freedom, equality, tolerance, mutual help, and love of mankind". The contents of this declaration served as guidelines for curriculum development and teaching in the "state period".

PRIMARY AND SECONDARY EDUCATION

The present Israeli educational system is based on the State Law (1949) for compulsory education for ages 5-15, which also provides for free education until the age of seventeen. This system embodies kindergartens, elementary and high schools, teacher education colleges, and institutes for adult education. It is divided into six geographical districts, each headed by a superintendent. The curricula are planned by a central department in Jerusalem. Although some subject matter content is compulsory, a great deal of initiative and autonomy is encouraged.

Several historical landmarks and changes have influenced the development of today's educational system in Israel. The main event which has a great impact on education at the beginning of the post-state period was the vast amount of immigration. The population grew from 600,000 in 1948 to about 4,000,000 in 1989. The educational system had to cope with this growth which occurred very rapidly in the first few years. However, the most difficult problem stemmed from the fact that a large number of the immigrants came from Asian and African countries and brought with them a relatively different cultural heritage. They found it difficult to adjust to the Israeli culture and the Israeli teachers had not been prepared to cope with cultural diversities in their classes. The main aim of the educational system turned to be cultural and social integration. This aim was to be achieved by an educational reform which was proposed by a parliamentary committee, and carried out after a long series of debates and struggles. It is now implemented in about 50 percent of the schools.

The reform introduced new curricula with an emphasis of teaching in heterogeneous classes. It also changed the school structure from 8+4 elementary and high school grades respectively, to 6+3+3 grades in the elementary, junior high school, and high school, respectively. Before this reform, teachers in the first eight grades had to be graduates of teachers' colleges, in which the length of studies was two years after matriculation examinations. The reform system requires teachers to be university graduates, starting with the seventh and eighth grades, thus extending the number of grades which require academic preparation. Another result of this reform was the establishment of a large number of comprehensive schools which offered a variety of study tracks to suit a wide range of individual differences.

An additional major reform, which is still going on, occurred in the teacher education system. This reform concerns the academization and professionalization of teacher education for elementary schools. The number of years of study was prolonged from two to four years, at the end of which the graduates are granted the degree of B.Ed. Teacher training for high school teaching is carried out in universities which, in addition to bachelor's or master's degrees, grant teaching certificates.

HIGHER EDUCATION

Institutions

The history of higher education in Israel is intertwined in the history of Israel, in the growth of its population, in its economy, and mainly in the recognition that its future is largely dependent upon its ability to generate knowledge and to develop new technologies and industries. Consequently, along with teaching, the universities are deeply engaged in basic as well as in applied research. About 30 percent of all research and development in Israel and about 45 percent of the civilian research and developments in the natural sciences, medicine, agriculture, and engineering takes place in the universities. Furthermore, the higher education policy proposes that teaching which is not accompanied by research cannot maintain a proper academic level for any length of time.

In addition, it is the policy of higher education to cultivate the studies in the field of humanities as a means of building a society which is oriented by moral and social values, and it is expected of the universities that they recognize their obligation to contribute, to the best of their abilities, towards the solution of vital national problems.

The state institution responsible for higher education is the Council for Higher Education, which derives its authority from a state law issued in 1958. This council is an independent body coming between the government and the national institutions on the one hand, and the institutions of higher education on the other. The majority of the council's members are university professors. A small minority are professionals of high reputation. The Minister of Education is ex-officio chairman of the council.

The principal functions of the council are the following: to grant permission to open and maintain an institution of higher education; to open and maintain a new unit within a university; to accredit an institution of higher education and to recognize academic degrees; to revoke the accreditation of an accredited institution; to authorize an institution to confer an academic degree; to propose the consolidation, enlargement and improvement of accredited institutions of higher education for academic cooperation; and to present to the government proposals for the development of higher education and for government participation in the budget of higher education.

Higher education in Israel is offered at several institutions: The Hebrew University of Jerusalem, The Technion - Israel Institute of Technology, Tel-Aviv University, Bar-Ilan University, The University of Haifa, Ben-Gurion University of the Negev, The Weitzman Institute of Science and the Open University (the latter grants only bachelor degrees). Four other institutions of higher education are authorized to grant only the bachelor's degree: Bezalel Academy of Arts and Design, The Jerusalem Rubin Academy of Music and Dance, Jerusalem College of Technology, and Shenkar College of Textile Technology and Fashion. Six institutions for the training of teachers have received a permit of accreditation, either for the entire program or for certain segments of the program. In addition, specific academic courses that are accredited by the universities are offered in regional colleges.

Except for the Technion, all universities are headed by a president elected by the institution's board of governors. The main roles of the presidents are of an administrative nature. More specifically, Israeli university presidents are expected to develop public and international relations, and lately with a focus upon fund raising. The academic affairs are run by the universities senates, whose members are professors elected for a period of three years by the university professor population. Senate members may be elected for a period of two additional years, after which they may not be elected for one year. The senate elects its head, the rector, who is in fact the head of all academic affairs. At the Technion, the president acts also as a rector. The senates elect all the academic committees, one of which is the appointment committee. The latter is the committee which receives the recommendations of professional committees, which act as ad hoc committees for the promotion of faculty members. The senate appointment committee decides whether to adopt or reject the recommendation of the professional committee.

Programs and Degrees

A wide variety of fields of study are available in the institutions of higher education. For example, the Hebrew University, Tel-Aviv University, Bar-Ilan University, University of Haifa and Ben-Gurion University have programs in humanities, social sciences, arts, social work, teacher training, mathematics, and natural sciences. The Hebrew University and Tel-Aviv University also offer degrees in law, medicine, dentistry, and para medical studies. The Technion-IIT, Tel-Aviv University, Ben-Gurion University, Jerusalem College of Technology, and Shenkar-Text. & Fash. offer programs in engineering and technology.

Access to institutions of higher education is based on the Israel matriculation certificate or its equivalent from Israel or another country. In addition, each candidate is required to pass the university entrance examinations which have been centralized in one office. Some exceptions have been legally allowed provided that the total number of students otherwise accepted does not exceed 2 percent of all those admitted. Such an admission is based on individual basis. The universities have to report to the Secretariat of the Council of Higher Education on their admission regulations and procedures, follow ups, and all data collected, including data on students who were admitted on individual basis. About 35 percent of the overall number of applicants are admitted. In some departments it is more difficult to get accepted than in others.

Most universities offer preacademic preparatory courses aimed at giving a "second chance" to young people who for some reason have not completed their matriculation exams. Furthermore, students from disadvantaged socioeconomic backgrounds who are considered "worthy of academic advancement" are given financial assistance to cover their tuition. Other kinds of financial aid programs are also available to students: 1. In a tutorial joint project of the Ministry of Education, the universities and the National Union of Students, students who volunteer to devote four hours a week to act as tutors to school pupils are eligible for scholarships. About 11,000 are involved in this project; 2. Loans are available on the basis of a combination of the student's economic situation, marital status, number of members in the family, army service, and home residents (for students residing in developmental areas). The average tuition is 3,900 Israeli shekels per school year (the equivalent of about US$2,000). Some scholarships are granted on the basis of academic excellence, and some are granted on the basis of low income. In addition, boarding facilities are attached to each university. Special scholarships are granted to foreign students.

The student population has been constantly growing from 34,373 in 1970 to 64,190 in 1988. Following is the distribution of students in 1988 in the various universities in percentages: Tel-Aviv University 29.0 percent; The Hebrew University in Jerusalem 24.1 percent; The Technion 13.6 percent; Bar-Ilan University 13.6 percent; University of Haifa 10.2 percent; Ben-Gurion University 8.5 percent; and Weitzman Institute 1.0 percent. An additional number of students (1,800) are affiliated with the Open University. Of the total number of university students in 1988, 45,730 (71 percent) were undergraduate, 14,065 (22 percent) were enrolled for the masters degree, 3,625 (6 percent) for the Ph.D. degree, and 770 (1 percent) for various diplomas.

Out of an entering class of undergraduate students, approximately two thirds complete their studies and get their degree and one third drops out. Approximately 20 percent of those commencing university studies have previously completed a preparatory pre-academic course. Four years is the average amount of time taken for the completion of an undergraduate course of studies, although the official period of time required is three years. Except for professional preparation (engineering, social work, etc.) two major fields of studies are required for the bachelor degree.

Almost all department in all universities, including the Technion, offer master's degree programs. Not all departments are entitled to offer Ph.D. programs. The permission to offer academic programs is granted by the Council of Higher Education, after a thorough and rigorous examination of the proposed curriculum and of the academic level of the staff. Graduate students often act as research assistants, some have full time jobs, others are granted scholarships to help in living costs.

Men and women are almost equally represented in the student population. A characteristic of the Israeli student population is the relatively older age of entrance to the universities. Since at the age of 18, men and women have to join the army for three and two years respectively, they start their studies at an older age than is usually the case in other countries. Consequently, it appears that the Israeli students are very professionally oriented. Upon entering the university, most of them have already made a career choice and try to finish their studies in the shortest period possible.

As mentioned earlier, teacher education is provided both by universities and teachers colleges. While the universities prepare teachers for the junior and high schools, the teachers colleges prepare for kindergarten, elementary, and junior high teaching. The teachers colleges are affiliated with a central department of teacher education in the Ministry of Education. They constitute a relatively large part of the overall Israeli postsecondary education. In 1988, the number of student-teachers was 11,965. They were enrolled in twenty-eight institutions which provide teaching certificates for kindergarten, elementary, and junior high schools. These institutions are going through a process of academization. Some have been authorized by the Council of Higher Education to grant the B.Ed. degree, and it is expected that in the future all of them will grant academic degrees in education. One teachers college offers specialization in physical education and grants academic degrees in this field.

Despite the growth in the number of students, the number of faculty members did not grow because of budget constraints. There were 17,590 research and teaching staff in 1979, and 17,276 in 1986. Of the latter number, 972 were full professors, 966 associate professors, 1,238 senior lecturers, 163 senior instructors, 605 instructors, and about 2,900 research and teaching assistants fulfilling various roles. There are three tracks for faculty positions: The research track starting from the rank of teaching assistant up to the rank of full professor; the teaching rack including the rank of instructor and senior instructor; and the clinical track goes up to the rank of associate professor. Promotion is attained mainly on the basis of research in the research track, on the basis of good teaching in the teaching track, and on the basis of high reputation as clinician in the clinical track. Service to the community and to the university are additional criteria for promotion in all tracks. Tenure is, however, granted only in the research track starting with the rank of senior lecturer.

In order to encourage excellence in research, several allocations have been established. Fellowships for young researchers enable the universities to provide the fellow with initial full time appointments thus ensuring the fellow's absorption into the higher education system. The university undertakes to employ the fellow at the end of three years of fellowship. In addition, there are several funds for the advancement of research, such as funds for basic research; funds for electronics, computers, and communication; the joint atomic energy commission-research fund; the joint Ministry of Defense fund; the United States - Israel Education Foundation funds; as well as special allocations for scientific equipment and research increments.

ISSUES AND TRENDS

An attempt made by the Council of Higher Education to foresee the year of 1995 generated the following picture: The number of students will grow up to 85,000 as a result of developments in the technological areas. The rapid growth of knowledge will bring back a large number of adults who will feel the need for academic refreshment. The growth in the number of adult students will also result from the tendency of people to retire earlier and return to the universities. This tendency is already apparent. Although these students will not necessarily pursue a full-time program leading to a degree, some kind of re-organization of the higher education system is anticipated.

The dilemma of general-liberal education vs. professionally oriented programs of studies for the bachelor's degrees will preoccupy the higher education policy makers. This major dilemma, though not a new one, stems from conflicting needs: one concerns the wish to provide the best professional preparation possible, and the other concerns the wish to widen perspectives and provide a sound general humanistic education. This dilemma will probably become even more acute in view of technological developments which will call for a longer period of professional education.

The future efforts appear to be in the areas of enlarging budgets, of recruiting the best faculty possible, and of constant reconsideration and development of curricula and research with regard to scientific and societal relevance.

BIBLIOGRAPHY

The Council of Higher Education (Israel), The Planning and Grants Committee. *The Higher Educational System in Israel.* Jerusalem: The Council of Higher Education, 1983.

The Council of Higher Education (Israel), *Report no. 1, 1976-1981. Report No. 2, 1981-1986. Report No. 14, 1986-1987. Report No. 15, 1987-1988.* Jerusalem.

The Council of Higher Education (Israel), The Planning and Grants Committee. *Report No. 14, 1986-1987. Report No. 15, 1987-1988.* Jerusalem.

Ormian, H., ed. *Education in Israel.* Jerusalem: The Ministry of Education, 1973.

Zilberberg, R. *The Studies for the Bachelor Degree in the Higher Educational System.* Jerusalem, 1987.

ITALY

by
Diega Orlando Cian
Professor, Department of Educational Sciences
University of Padova, Italy

BACKGROUND

The foundation of present day education in Italy lies in the 1948 Constitution of the republic which guarantees eight years of education for all children (elementary school 6-11 years and lower secondary school 11-14 years) and continuation of higher secondary and university studies based on merit. Administration of education from nursery school (3-6 years) till the end of higher secondary level is overseen by a central Ministry of Public Instruction which ensures a uniform curriculum at all public and private schools. Education is decentralized: the capital of each province has an "inspector of the academy" *(provveditore agli studi);* provinces or departments are divided into districts administered by an inspector; and districts are in turn subdivided into regions under a director. Beginning this year (1990), the universities come under a separate ministry, the Ministry of Universities and Scientific and Technological Research.

The development of Italian universities dates back to the middle ages and is linked to European renaissance after 1000 A.D. This period saw the formation of groups of teachers *(domini)* and students *(socii)* who entered into contractual arrangements for the teaching of specified disciplines. Towards the second half of the twelfth century, the centers frequented by the best known teachers received the standing of *studia generalia* with which they gained the authority from the pope or the emperor to grant degrees *(licentia ubique docendi).* The first universities were born at these centers, and they took the form of corporations of teachers and students who had the tendency to defend their autonomy against civil and religious authorities. From the twelfth to the fifteenth century, the student migrations that occurred gave birth to several different universities in Bologna, Padova, Plaisence, Pavie, Rome, Perouse, Pise, Florence, Turin and Sienne.

PRIMARY AND SECONDARY EDUCATION

Primary and Lower Secondary Education

In Italy, primary schooling is compulsory and free, and is attended by children of the age group 6-11. (Early childhood education is provided at nursery schools, *asilonido,* and maternal schools, *scuola materna*). In 1985 new elementary school programs aimed at children's development and basic literacy were approved, within the framework of the Italian Constitution and of the International Declarations of Human and Children Rights. Unlike in the past, in the new elementary school each class will be taught by more than one teacher. New subjects such as social studies, visual education, musical education, physical education and one foreign language will be offered alongside traditional subjects. Additionally, the handicapped children are enrolled in elementary schools (in the proportion of one handicapped student for every four) would be provided with special education teachers.

Lower secondary education (ages 11-14) consists of a three year program and it is also compulsory. It was instituted in 1962 upon the merging of different types of lower secondary schools into a single one *(scuola media)*. From 1962 to 1977 the curriculum offered both compulsory and optional courses. However, since 1977 Latin is no longer offered while previously optional subjects such as technical education and musical education have been made compulsory. The current school programs have been in existence since 1979. At the end of the three years, students in the lower secondary take a diploma exam *(esame di licenza)*. *Successful students are able to enroll in any of the secondary schools.*

Secondary Education

Efforts at reforming secondary education in Italy go back to 1950, but from a legislative point of view no new developments have yet taken place. However, a number of experiments are being tried out, like the teaching of a second foreign language or introduction of computer related training. The high school diploma *(esame di maturita)* is still being experimented. Thus, the secondary education has in fact reformed itself awaiting the official reforms, which are expected to come to fruition in the very near future.

The fact that secondary education in Italy is in a period of transition makes it very difficult to give a realistic account of the system. Various kinds of experimental projects are being tried to adapt the school system to the changing needs of the society, specially to provide broader opportunities for employment in a national and international context (particularly European, at this time). Given this situation, what is described here could very well undergo some changes in the coming months.

The present system of secondary education is highly differentiated with several types of schools including classical lycee, scientific lycee, artistic lycee, teacher training schools, art institutes, technical institutes, and professional institutes. Certain subjects like Italian, mathematics, and history are taught at all secondary schools but other subjects like philosophy, physics, Latin, vary depending on the school.

The classical lycee (five years of studies) where Greek language is also taught has always been a unique institution, purely educational in character, preparing students for university studies in any faculty without any preoccupation on professional education. The lycee scientific (five years of studies) on the other hand, focuses on scientific disciplines and also prepares students for university studies. Studies at both the classical and scientific lycees lead to a baccalaureate diploma *(diploma di maturita)* at the end of five years of studies.

The teacher training schools (four years of studies) prepare students for teaching positions at elementary and nursing schools. The diploma which the students receive also enables them to enroll in a teacher education *(magistero)* faculty to work towards a degree in education or literary disciplines, or after one more year of studies students become eligible to enroll in any faculty. Today there is a significant number of young teachers who have received the degree. Legislation enacted in 1973 envisages all elementary and nursery school teachers to follow four years of studies at university level but this has not come into force yet.

Technical institutes offer five years of studies in various technical fields and include agricultural technical institutes, industrial technical institutes, commercial technical institutes, merchant marine technical institutes, and technical institute for tourism. Although the primary purpose of technical institutes is to prepare students to enter the job market, a law passed in 1969 allows these students to enroll at the universities. However, their preparation may not always be adequate to pursue professional fields.

The institutions which provide secondary level education in art and music are characteristically different to other schools. The artistic lycees (four years of studies) with a supplementary year leads to a baccalaureate diploma which enables the students to enroll in the Academy of Fine Arts or in the Faculty of Architecture. The institutes of arts offer three years of studies and provide a variety of practical courses.

The professional institutes include some institutions coming under the Ministry of Public Education and offering programs of studies leading to a baccalaureate diploma. On the other hand, schools that provide strictly professional type training are governed by regional administrations and prepare students primarily for working life. In addition, there are many secondary level training programs geared to the training and continued education needs of technical and professional personnel in industry. These are organized by the relevant ministry, the trade unions and various associations and foundation.

Primary schooling is compulsory and free. Books are also provided free of charge. For secondary schools, students are required to pay a registration fee of 10,000 liras (US$1 = 1,454 Liras) and an attendance fee of 25,000 liras per year. This is only a modest expense and in any case, fee remissions are available to needy students.

At the end of the secondary school, students appear for the baccalaureate exam *(esami di maturita)* which is still on an experimental basis, subject to pending reforms. The jury for the exam consists of five members, including a teacher (internal) who is very familiar with the students' work at the school. There are two written exams: a dissertation in Italian and a test specific to the type of the secondary school. An oral examination is also conducted on different subjects. Students graduating from five-year study programs are eligible to enroll in the universities. (Those who follow the four-year programs requires an additional year, at the same school).

HIGHER EDUCATION

Institutions

Italian universities consist of faculties which prepare students for various degrees or diplomas. The "higher institutes", on the other hand, specialize in a given field of studies and these include the University Institute of Economics and Commerce in Venice, polytechnics of Turin and Milan, and higher institutes of physical education. As mentioned earlier, beginning this year (1990) the universities come under the new Ministry of Universities, and Scientific and Technological Research and are expected to undergo restructuring and receive much greater autonomy. However it is expected that the present didactical organization, which has already gone through a series of changes, will continue with faculties in the areas of law; political science; economics and commerce; statistical, demographic and actuarial sciences; letters and philosophy; education; medicine and surgery; natural, physical and mathematical sciences; architecture; sociology; veterinary medicine; and engineering. Recently other faculties have also been created in response to the demands of professions related to environmental studies, new technologies etc. Some others have changed or are changing the faculty designations. For example, the Faculty of *Magistero* is going to be divided into two faculties: the Faculties of Psychology and the Faculty of Humanities.

Under the new reforms, the university organizational structure probably will not undergo much change: the rector as head of the university or higher institute; the academic senate consisting of the rector and the deans of faculties; the council of administration presided by the rector and consisting of pro-rector, representatives of the government and the regions, representatives of local institutions, and representatives of teachers and students (as well as non-teaching staff); and the university commission for inspection of administrative and teaching activities, conforming to the Law of 1980. In fact, since 1980, "departments" have come into existence on an experimental basis (replacing "institutes") to coordinate, among faculties, research work and doctoral courses etc. Also there are research centers linked to the Center for National Research, faculties and regional authorities, interdepartmental service centers, and inter-university research and service centers. In 1980, a new research doctorate was instituted, and the candidates receive a salary while working on their degree which requires several years of course work as well as research (evaluated by a jury of three professors).

Teaching staff comprises two categories and both are selected through open competition: professors whose selection is based on academic qualifications and publication record (professors can become full professors after a three year trial period); and associate professors whose selection is based on academic qualifications and teaching experience. Both ranks are at the same level as regards teaching and research functions but the associate professors are not entitled to administrative posts (rector, dean of faculty, director of department, coordinator of doctoral research, etc.) and there is a difference in the salary. In addition, there are researchers who are also chosen in open competition and who may be required to sit for written and oral tests.

At the universities, there also exist non-governmental schools, which conduct programs and degrees recognized by the government and the teachers at these institutions have the same qualifications as teachers in government institutions. Moreover, universities have many links, more so in the recent years, with local schools, industry, business enterprises, and other institutions, through conventions or associations.

Programs and Degrees

The basic degree programs at the universities take 4-6 years. In 1986-87, there were 246,942 students enrolled in the first year and the staff consisted of 51,081 teachers. Minimum admission requirement is the baccalaureate level exam *(maturita)*. Equivalent qualifications obtained from foreign institutions (included in the approved list of the ministry) are also acceptable. Secondary school qualifications from member countries of the Council of Europe are accepted *de jure*. Students are free to follow lectures, seminars or attend laboratory work and are allowed to re-enroll in the same course, if they are short of grades. If the *licence* is not completed in the specified number of years, students pay an additional fee for every year of delay. When all examinations required by the specific program of studies (approved by the faculty), students are admitted to the "thesis work for degree" which is a written scientific exposition judged by eleven members, each of whom has ten points, and successful students have the possibility of getting a minimum of sixty-six or maximum of 110 points. In addition, work that is of an exceptional nature receives special mention.

Based on 1986 figures, students pay a registration fee of 50,000 liras, annual fee of 120,000 liras, and in the case of specialized schools 250,000 liras per year. Fee exemptions are given to students who demonstrate need or who have obtained full marks (60/60) at the baccalaureate level and pass subsequent years at the university with an average of 28/30 (provided their incomes do not exceed a certain level).

As regards postgraduate studies, the research doctorate *(dottorato di ricerca)* has been in existence since 1980 and it requires a two-year course. It is offered by university institutes and departments. The degree of research doctor *(dottore di ricerca)* is a purely academic one, and its attainment is evaluated within the realm of scholarly research, after the candidate has followed a series of higher courses, and prepared a doctoral thesis whose acceptance is determined by a national commission.

Students have the right to elect representatives to important governing bodies of the university (faculty councils, administration councils, etc.) and to have meetings within the university for scientific and educational activities. University complexes have been expanding in different regions and departments (of the country) and there are sixty-nine of them now. To assist out-of-town students, student housing is provided.

ISSUES AND TRENDS

Italian education, as indicated earlier, is in a period of great transition. A process of continuous fermentation of innovative programs is in place; universities envisage a significant increase in the degrees, (two-or three-year type), specialized courses, and research doctorates offered. These developments could accompany greater collaboration between universities and public institutions as well as the society. In addition, it may no longer be possible to provide in one faculty, all the courses required for a degree program.

University programs are being established for teachers of elementary and nursery schools, lasting three years. It must be noted that the curriculum reforms envisaged by the law of 1980 is in a way already out of date with the developments that are now taking place in the educational institutions. A quick glance through a university statute (e.g. University of Padoua) will show the breadth of specialized programs, for example, in medicine (forty-nine in 1984) which award postgraduate diplomas in different specializations (after a Doctor of Medicine degree) requiring study periods of up to five years (mostly practical in nature).

It appears that the Italian university is beginning to retrace its European roots, with the reforms promoted by the Ministry of Universities and Scientific Research and in alliance with the world of work, schools, and all those institutions that work with today's youth. In particular, the universities will take in to account the many new professional fields that are beginning to appear in the areas of finance, administration, commerce, data processing, robotics, automation, fine arts, etc.

Italian universities are also attracting an increasing number of foreign students. (In Perouse, there is a university specially for foreign students). International collaboration continues to grow, providing increasing mobility to students, particularly within the European community.

BIBLIOGRAPHY

Annuario Statistico dell'Istruzione. Roma.

Statuti annuali di ciascuna universita italiana.

Daniele, N. *L'ordinamento Scolastico Italiano, in Trattato di Diritto Amministrativo.* Padova: Cedam, 1989.

Trivellato, U. and A. Zuliano. *The Determinants of Student Achievement in Italy.* Stockholm: Almqvist and Wiksell, 1979.

Vari, Autori. *La Scuola Secondario: Riforma, Curricolo, Sperimentazione.* Bologna: IL Mulino, 1981.

Vari, Autori. *Riforma Della Scuola Secondaria superiore e L'insegnamento Della Pegagogia.* Brescia: La Scuola, 1988.

IVORY COAST

by
Lancine Sylla
Professor, Department of Sociology
National University of Ivory Coast, Ivory Coast

BACKGROUND

In Ivory Coast, education is the "priority of priorities", as evident from the fact that more than 40 percent of the government budget is allocated to education. Education has attracted the interest and involvement of everybody and every sector of the economy. There are public schools and private schools. While there are ministries responsible for education (Ministry of Primary Education, Ministry of Secondary and Higher Education, and Ministry of Technical Education) many other ministries have also established institutions for training their cadre. In addition, since the setting up of a tax from enterprises for the purpose of "continuing education", the enterprises themselves organize a variety of continuing education programs for their employees. As described in the economic development plan of the country, education is considered as "a means of acquiring material well being, social promotion, and personal growth".

The establishment of the first primary school (in Assinie) in Ivory Coast can be traced back to 1889, five years after the country became a French colony. Then in 1930, the first secondary school was founded in Bingerville. Nearly three decades later and one year before independence, a center for higher education consisting of a school of law, letters, and sciences was established, which in 1964 became the present day national university.

The first decade of independence saw the creation of the Ministry of Technical Education (1970) and Ministry of Scientific Research (1971), passing of legislation to levy a tax from enterprises for the purposes of promoting continuing education of their employees (1977), and enactment of an educational reform law (1977) aimed at removing vestiges of colonialism from education and for adapting education to the realities of Ivory Coast and its development needs. Student enrollment has risen spectacularly from 1960 onwards. In 1985, there were 1,179,000 students in primary schools, a six-fold increase from 1960; 245,000 students in secondary schools, a thirty-fold increase from 1960; and 15,630 students in higher education compared to a mere forty-eight in 1960. (Majority of Ivory Coast students in higher education before 1960 were enrolled in foreign universities).

PRIMARY AND SECONDARY EDUCATION

Primary education is the sector that has grown most rapidly in Ivory Coast, since its independence in 1960. While only 28.5 percent of the children attended primary school in 1960, the rate has climbed to 80 percent in 1980. Primary school begins at the age of six years and continue for six years with a curriculum that prepared the students for secondary education. Completion of primary schooling is marked by an exam which is used for selection of students for secondary schools. Successful students also receive the *certificat d'étude primaire* and scholarships (for most deserving candidates). Students who fail in the exam still have the possibility of entering fee paying private secondary schools.

At the secondary level, students have two options: secondary general education, and secondary technical education. In both cases, the first cycle requires four years of studies followed by a second cycle of three years.

The secondary general education, offers its first cycle of studies in the *collèges d'enseignement général* leading students to the diploma of *brevet d'étude primaires et complémentaire*. On completion of the first cycle, students may proceed to the second cycle of general education, enter the second cycle of technical secondary education (after passing an entrance exam), or join fee paying private schools. The second cycle of general education is offered in the *lycées* and leads to the *baccalauréat* diploma. Students have the option of different streams: Bac A (philosophie and letters); Bac B (economics and social sciences); Bac C (mathematics and physical sciences); Bac D (mathematics and natural sciences). The *baccalauréat* diploma gives access to higher education at the university or (after passing an entrance exam) or higher professional schools *(grandes écoles)*.

The secondary technical and professional education aims primarily at training young people for employment. It is characterized by a great diversity in the fields of training which are geared to meet the manpower needs of Ivory Coast, in its effort to develop and modernize the country. Unlike the general secondary education, it is difficult to neatly categorize technical education in the form of cycles due to the diversity and interrelations that exist among different programs.

However, in very broad terms, the first cycle of technical and professional education can be considered to consist of *unités mobiles* and *ateliers d'application et de production* which train traditional type artisans (with no official diploma awarded); *centres de formation professionnels* which trains students in different trades (agromechanics, mechanical trades, building construction, etc.) and awards the *certificat d'aptitute professionelle,* and *colleèes d'enseignement technique industriel et commercial* which awards either the *certificat d'aptitude professionelle, brevet professionel* or a simple attestation of completion of studies, depending on the nature of the program. The second cycle can be considered to consist of *lycées techniques* and *lycée professionnels* which admits students who possess the *brevet d'études primaire et complémentaire* in the general education stream or the *certificat d'aptitude professionelle,* in the technical education stream. Completion of the second cycle is marked by the award of *brevet de technicien* or *baccalauréat technique* which allows the students to enter working life or to proceed to higher education.

HIGHER EDUCATION

Higher education in Ivory Coast consists of establishments that come under several authorities. The sector of general education is the responsibility of the Ministry of National Education. The sector of professional and technical education, is to a large extent controlled by the Ministry of Technical Education and Professional Training, but several other ministries oversee their own schools of training (public works, agriculture, construction, etc.). In addition, there are a number of institutes and centers of research affiliated to the faculties and professional schools but are coordinated by the Ministry of Scientific Research (which also oversees other autonomous research centers in the country).

Thus in the analysis of higher education in the country, it is useful to look at higher education as consisting of general higher education (university establishments), technical and professional higher education *(grandes écoles)*, and scientific and technological research. Of course, in any account of higher education in Ivory Coast, it is not possible to ignore the contributions made by another sector, the non-formal, which plays a significant role in the continuing education of the masses.

General Higher Education

The University of Abidjan, is the dominant force in the area of general higher education in Ivory Coast. The structure of university education in Ivory Coast has been greatly influenced by the French university system excepting that, in Ivory Coast, it is a single national university which groups together a sizable number of (classical type) faculties and is expected to oversee several other campuses that are being established. The university consists of six faculties (law, economic sciences, letters, arts and humanities, science and technology, and medicine and pharmacy) and an institute of odonto-stomatology. Under each faculty are several departments and specialized laboratories. In addition, there are centers and institutes of research attached to the faculties.

The admission to the university (to different faculties), in general terms, requires the *baccalauréat* diploma or equivalent or a special admission exam. Admission is centrally handled by the *Commission Nationale d'Orientation* under the aegis of the Ministry of National Education. Representatives of other relevant ministries participate in this commission, which directs the placement of students based on their examination results.

The programs of study consist of three cycles. The first cycle lasts two years and leads to the *diplôme d'étude universitaire générale*. The second cycle comprises two additional years with students receiving *licence* after one year and the *maîtrise* after two years. In the third cycle, students spend three years of study and research to receive the *doctorat de troisième cycle*. On completion of the first two years of the third cycle, students receive the *diplôma d'études approfondies*. The highest academic degree is the *doctorat d'état* (state doctorate) or *agrégation* which are based on scientific work and publications (with no specific time limit). Of the students enrolled at the faculties (17,597 in 1988), 30 percent were in letters, 23 percent were in law and economics, 19 percent were in sciences, and 13 percent in medicine. These proportions have remained somewhat stable over the last five years but as indicated earlier, total student enrollment has risen dramatically since independence and has nearly doubled within the last ten years. In 1988-89, the teaching staff consisted of 861 teachers, of whom 85 percent were of Ivory Coast nationals. About 10 percent of the teachers were full professors, with 16 percent associate professors (maitres de conferences). The majority or 45 percent were assistants. The university has awarded from 1963-88, 13,775 *licence* and 7,212 *maîtrise degrees,* and 980 *doctorat* degrees.

Technical and Professional Higher Education

Technical and professional higher education in Ivory Coast is offered at a variety of institutions including professional schools. There is a significant number of professional schools coming under different ministries. The University of Abidjan also offers professional programs and is steering its efforts, more and more, in this direction to provide openings to its graduates, at a time when unemployment is a major problem facing the government. The institutions that offer technical and professional education can thus be grouped into four categories: first, the faculties associated with the university; second, the professional schools *(grandes écoles)* coming under the Ministry of Technical Education and Professional Training (the university comes under the Ministry of National Education); third, professional schools *(grandes écoles)* coming under ministries other then the Ministry of Technical Education and Professional Training; and fourth, the teacher training schools *(ecoles normales)* that train teachers at all levels.

The faculties associated with the university are playing an ever increasing role in structuring programs for providing technical and professional training. For example, certain *maîtrise* programs are now geared to the study of engineering sciences (electromechanics, geology, etc) which offer immediate employment opportunities.

The professional schools *(grand écoles)* coming under the Ministry of Technical Education and Professional Training have been regrouped into a national higher institute of technical education *(institut national supérieur de l'enseignement technique)* which functions more like a polytechnic having as objective, the training of technicians and higher level cadre to meet the technological and commercial needs of the economy. This central organization oversees nine establishments: *Ecole Nationale Supérieur d'Ingénieurs d'Abidjan, Ecole Nationale des Ingénieurs de Specialite, Ecole Supérieure de Commerce d'Abidjan, Ecole Supérieur des Ingénieurs Informaticiens, Institut Supérieur de Compatabilite, Institut de Technologie Industrielle, Institut de Technologie Tertiare, Institut Supérieur d'Informatique,* and *Institut Superiéur de Secretariat.* The engineering schools offer *diplôme d'ingénieur* in six years. Programs offered by other schools include several three year diplomas; *diplôma universitaire de technologie, brevet de technicien supérieur,* and *licence.*

The professional schools *(grand écoles)* run by other ministries primarily train personnel in the employment of establishments coming under these ministries. These types of institutions have grown significantly since 1970 as each ministry is permitted to create schools to train personnel suited to their needs. (For example,

Ecole Nationale Supérieur d'Agronomie trains agronomists for the Ministry of Agriculture). There are sixty-eight such institutions run by twenty ministries. Admission to these institutions is through entrance examinations (candidates must hold *baccalauréat* or equivalent). Some of the institutions offer a full range of educational opportunities, from secondary up to completion of higher education.

The *écoles normales* that train teachers are institutions to which authorities attach a great importance, as it has become vital to train an increasing number of teachers to meet the explosion in enrollment. These institutions also come under several ministries and consist of training schools for preschool teachers, primary teachers, secondary teachers, teachers of technical and professional education, physical education teachers, and teachers for higher educational institutions. The periods of training vary from 2-3 years. For example teachers for *collège d'enseignement général* (first cycle of secondary education) receive three years of training (after *baccalauréat*) leading to the *certificat d'aptitude pédagogique pour les CEG*. Similarly, teachers for *lycées* (second cycle of secondary education) receive two years of training (after *licence* or *maitrise* degree) leading to *certificat d'aptitute pédagogique a l'enseignement secondaire*.

As a result of the spread of educational programs and lack of rationalization, the cost of education in Ivory Coast tends to be high. More than 40 percent of the government budget is spent on education, in addition to the expenditures borne by parents of the students. In 1989, the budget of the National University of Ivory Coast was 5,525,400,000 CFA francs, of which 96.6 percent was provided by the government

Revenues earned by the university, through tuition charges are insignificant compared to the subsidy received from the government. Tuition charges are more symbolic than substantial: 4,200 CFA francs annually for scholarship students; 7,200 CFA francs for non-scholarship students; and 50,000 CFA francs for foreign students. On the other hand, private institutions (all students, local and foreign) charge about 100,000-400,000 CFA francs annually depending on the level of studies (higher costs are for professional/technical programs). However, scholarship students receive a stipend of 45,000 CFA francs per year from the government. Food and lodging costs are about 3,500 CFA francs per month.

Research

In recent years, the scientific and technological research sector has become an important contributor to higher education, for the part they play not only in the education of teachers of higher education but also in achieving development objectives of the country. Recognizing this importance, the authorities have promoted the creation of a number of research centers and institutions, covering fields varying from priority areas like agronomy to other areas like solar and nuclear energy. Three types of research institutions are run today by the Ministry of Scientific Research: centers and institutes of research at the universities, national (non-university) centers of research, and research institutions of an international character (often run in collaboration with foreign or international organizations).

The centers and institutes of research attached to the university have a teaching function as well as a research objective with emphasis on fundamental research. They provide support for teaching, giving the teachers the opportunity to tie research work to courses they teach. They also provide research training to students, and to potential faculty members and researchers who pursue higher level degrees *(maîtrise, doctorat)*. In addition, the centers carry out applied research on contract for external establishments (private, government, and foreign).

The national centers of research primarily focus on applied research aimed at meeting development needs of the country. The order of priority, as established by the Ministry of Scientific Research is as follows: agronomy, sciences, medicine and pharmacy, engineering, social sciences, and humanities.

The research institutions of an international character include the former French run research institutes grouped under *Groupement d'Etudes et de Recherche pour le Développement de l'Agronomie Tropicale, Centre de Recherche Suisse, Néerlandais et Allemand, Institut des Resources Naturelles en Afrique,* and *Centre International Francophone de Recherche pour le Développement.* While the university and national research institutes are intensifying collaboration with their counterparts in foreign countries around the world, Ivory Coast solicits support from international organizations (UNESCO, FAO, etc.) in the area of training in scientific research.

ISSUES AND TRENDS

The evolution, structure, and functioning of the educational system in Ivory Coast have made a remarkable change in direction since the enactment of education reform law of 16 August 1977.

In theory, the reform law has not yet come to fruition as the country has lacked the means to achieve the ambitious objectives set by the law, particularly at a time of economic crisis when the prices of the country's major products (coffee and cocoa) have dropped steeply. However, in practice, the policymakers as well as the practitioners have tried, on their part, to apply the law in bits and pieces and somewhat progressively.

The multiple changes that have taken place in education, changes arising from social pressure and the desire of the policymakers to adapt to the constantly changing realities, seem to be going certainly in the direction of the intended reforms. But the effects of these changes on the socio-educational system, like the massive increases in student enrollment, proliferation of educational programs and structures, unemployment of young diploma holders, have created a situation whereby the reform law itself may be surpassed by the realities of change, requiring yet another reform. In essence, the reform law runs the risk of being overtaken by the evolution of the world and the realities for which it was meant.

Among other things, the reforms aim at adapting the educational system to the new realities and economic needs of the country by implementing methods and programs of teaching developed in a national context. The reforms also emphasize professional education that would open up employment opportunities for the graduates. In addition, the reforms are to promote regionalization (decentralization) of education to respond to geographical exigencies of national development.

All these, and other aspects of the reforms are somewhat at crossroads, faced with many contradictions.

For example, regionalization of education is proceeding but for it to succeed, the regions themselves must undergo development. The city of Abidjan (and the southern region of the country), already has the heaviest concentration of secondary and higher education institutions and decentralization would help to expand these institution to the interior of the country. There is evidence that regionalization is taking place to some extent: two university centers are planned for the central and northern regions, at Bouake and Korhogo respectively; the relocation of some of the higher educational institutions from Abidjan to Yamousoukro is about to be completed; professional *lycées* have been established in several of the interior towns; and the policy of increasing the number of "communes" in the interior of the country along with transfer of administrative power over education has given a new impetus to the creation of schools, colleges and *lycées* at the municipality level across the country. Yet, the key question is: will the government be able to provide "communes" with sufficient funding to implement regionalization objectives?

It appears that the continuing deterioration of currency exchange rates and the precipitous drop in the prices of export products are hampering seriously the ambitions of the reform law of 1977, for the country's development is largely dependent on its major export products (coffee and cocoa). Of course, the efficient implementation of reforms in education is not solely dependent upon funding; it also requires intelligence, imagination and a sense of realism. Imagination and realism not only to master the perverse factors and effects of changes due to social pressure but also to minimize, as much as possible, the costs. In the system of higher education in Ivory Coast (and the reform law does not seem to remedy the situation), the proliferation of educational and training structures, as well as the duplication of programs and teachers result in inutile competition and wastage of scarce resources which, through imagination and realism, could have been avoided. Thus, there seems to be an urgent need, without challenging the fundamental objectives of the reform law, to undertake regrouping (of institutions) and rationalization of the higher educational structure in Ivory Coast.

BIBLIOGRAPHY

Diarrassouba, V. C. *L'Université Ivoirienne et le développement de la nation.* Abidjan: Les Houvelles Editions Africaines, 1979.

Kouassi, N. *Les Etablissements d'enseignement supérieur en Côte d'Ivoire.* Abidjan: Ministry of National Education, 1986.

Ministry of National Education, Ivory Coast. *Enseignement Supérieur de Côte d'Ivoire.* Abidjan, 1977.

Ministry of Technical and Professional Education - ONFP, Ivory Coast. *Annuaire statistique de l'enseignement technique et de la formation professionnelle, 1986-1987.* Abidjan, 1988.

Ministry of Technical and Professional Education - ONFP, Ivory Coast. *Bilan de l'Enseignement technique et de la formation professionnelle.* Abidjan, 1984.

Ministry of Technical and Professional Education, Ivory Coast. *Le Système de formation en Côte d'Ivoire.* Abidjan, 1983.

Raoult, M. *L'Extrascolaire en Côte d'Ivoire.* Abidjan: Centre d'Enseignement et de Recherche Audio Visuels, 1978.

UNESCO. *Cahiers sur l'enseignement supérieur No. 9: La Problematique de la pédagogie de l'enseignement supérieur et de la recherche pédagogique dans la perspective de la réforme globale de l'éducation en Afrique francophone.* Paris: UNESCO, 1984.

UNESCO. *Cahiers sur l'enseignement supérieur No. 13: Structures de fontionnement de la recherche et prespectives de coopération.* Paris: UNESCO, 1986.

JAPAN

by
Akira Arimoto
Professor, Research Institute for Higher Education
Hiroshima University, Japan

BACKGROUND

Early efforts at formalized public education in Japan can be traced back to the Meiji regime which, in 1872, promulgated the Government Order of Education. The system consisted of three stages: elementary school, middle school, and university. The Elementary School Order, Middle School Order, Imperial University Order, and Normal School Order were issued in 1886. Four years of compulsory attendance was enforced throughout the country and tuition in public elementary schools was abolished in 1900. By the beginning of the twentieth century, enrollment in primary education exceeded 90 percent and provided the foundation for growth of enrollment in secondary and tertiary education that took place later.

Establishment of an institution of higher education comparable to those in the West was that of the Imperial University *(Teikoku Daigaku)* which was founded in 1886 based on the Imperial University Order and rearrangement of the former Tokyo University (which was established in 1877) and other institutions. In this period, the introduction of a modern educational system, especially that of higher education, was necessary for building and modernizing the country but, of course, Japan had almost no historical background in this field. There was neither institutionalization of science nor any dedicated facilities and equipment. Responding to this situation became a major preoccupation of the government. Teachers were invited from centers of learning around the world including, for example, the United Kingdom, France, Germany, and the United States. Also many Japanese students were sent to these countries for higher studies. When these students came back after graduation from schools abroad, they became professors at the university, replacing the foreign teachers. The foreign teachers taught in foreign languages like English, French, and German but gradually the academic profession was occupied by Japanese, and Japanese language became the medium of instruction in universities and other institutions of higher education in Japan.

The Imperial University changed its name to The University of Tokyo in 1947 when postwar reforms were made in the higher educational system. The cluster of imperial universities which now include Tokyo, Kyoto, Tohoku, Kyushu, Hokkaido, Osaka, and Nagoya (in order of their establishment) have enjoyed the highest prestige in the hierarchy of academic stratification. When the University Order was introduced in 1918, some private universities including Waseda and Keio, the most prestigious institutions in the private sector, and several other national and public universities were recognized for the first time by the government.

The Ministry of Education, Science, and Culture *(Monbusho)* has had the overall responsibility for control, administration, policy formation, and funding. Boards of education of the prefectures (there are forty-seven prefectures) administer education at local level including supervision of personnel, inservice programs for teachers, and advice to municipal boards of education. The municipal boards of education administer education affairs for municipal schools. The Ministry of Education allocates financial assistance to prefectural and municipal boards.

In 1947, a new constitution was adopted and the constitutional and statutory laws established principles, forms, and procedures of education substituting imperial ordinances which were established in the Meiji period and which worked throughout the prewar period. The Fundamental Law of Education enacted in 1947 was followed by a series of statutes including the School Education Law which deals with organization and administration of the school system, and the Social Education Law which controls outside school education. Japanese education has been operated on the basis of these laws and statutes.

Immediately after World War II, public education was democratized along American lines by the occupation policy-makers and to meet with this decision, major reforms in the Japanese education system were made by recommendations of the United States Education Mission. They included the following: transformation from a multi-track system of school education to a single-track system; equal opportunity of education according to ability; the introduction of the system 6-3-3-4 grade structure; nine years of general education; the establishment of coeducation; and the introduction of university based teacher training.

The organization of the present school system, which is compulsory except kindergarten, is as follows: kindergarten *(yochien)* admit children aged three, four, or five and provide them with one-to three-year courses; general and special education is provided through elementary schools *(sho-gakko),* which admit children aged six and provide them with six-year courses; and the lower secondary schools *(chu-gakko),* which provide three-year courses. Other types of school including upper secondary school *(koto-gakko),* special training school *(senshu-gakko),* technical college *(kotosenmon-gakko),* junior college *(tanki-daigaku),* university *(daigaku)* etc. are optional.

From recent statistics, the enrollment rate by school level is as follows: 99.9 percent in both *sho-gakko* and *chu-gakko;* 94.7 percent (93.6 percent male, 95.9 percent female) in post-compulsory education; and 36.3 percent (35.8 percent male, 36.8 percent female) in higher education. Japanese education expanded so much along with the growth of the economy, especially after the 1960s, the enrollment between 1965 and 1988 in upper secondary education schools grew from 71 percent to over 94 percent and that in institutions of higher education increased from 17 percent to 36 percent. In 1989, enrollment in universities and junior colleges was 2.5 million.

PRIMARY AND SECONDARY EDUCATION

Primary education applies to the first part in the present 6-3-3-4 system where all children at the age of six are obliged to enroll in elementary school *(shogakko)* to study for six years. Most children come to the first grade with some experience of having attended such preschool education as kindergarten *(yochien)* and nursery school *(hoikusho)* for two or three years. In 1989, of all five year old children, 63.5 percent attended kindergartens, and 30.3 percent attended nursery schools.

Elementary schools are run by national, public, and private establishing bodies. In 1989, the number in each category consisted of 73, 24, 608, and 170 respectively. Of the students attending elementary schools, 98.9 percent or 9.5 million were in public schools. The standard subjects studied at elementary school are as follows: Japanese language, social studies, arithmetic, science, music, art and handicraft, homemaking, physical education, moral education, and special activities. Recently both social studies and science subjects are replaced with life environment studies at the first and second grade levels.

Secondary education in Japan is divided into two levels: lower and upper. Children begin the lower secondary schools *(chu-gakko*, ages 12-15 years) on completion of six years of elementary school studies beginning at age six. The prescribed subjects of the lower secondary school are Japanese, social studies, mathematics, science, music, arts, health and physical education, industrial arts and home-making, moral education, special activities, and elective subjects (including foreign languages).

The Japanese school year begins on 1st April and ends on 31st March of the following year. Elementary schools, lower secondary schools and most upper secondary schools adopt a three-term school year: from April to July, September to December, and January to March. Most universities have two terms. Vacations are scheduled in summer, winter, and spring.

All those who graduated from a lower secondary school (after three years of studies) or an equivalent school can be admitted to the public upper secondary school *(koto-gakko)* when they pass a selection process consisting of credentials prepared by the principals of lower secondary schools and the record of entrance examination which is administered by the boards of education. National, private, and technical schools conduct their own entrance examinations. In 1989, the average percentage of lower secondary school graduates who entered upper secondary schools and technical colleges is 94.7 percent (male 93.6 percent female 95.9 percent).

About 70 percent of all upper secondary students are in general courses mainly leading to universities and colleges, while the rest are in specialized vocational courses. The vocational courses include commercial, technical, agricultural, fishery, domestic arts, fine arts, and science-mathematics. A minimum of eighty credits (three years) are necessary for graduation from upper secondary schools. The subjects that all students are required to study regardless of courses are as follows: Japanese language, geography, history, citizenship, mathematics, science, health and physical education, and art. Female students are required to study home economics. Students in specialized vocational courses are required to take not less than thirty credits in specialized subjects. In addition to the above requirements, schools must provide for each grade not less than one school hour (fifty minutes) per week of homeroom activities and club activities to meet extracurricular requirements.

Teachers employed by the national government are "national public officials" and those employed by local authorities are "local public officials". In 1987, about 97 percent of lower secondary and 78 percent of upper secondary teachers were employed in national or local public schools. Teaching appointments require a teacher certificate. Prefectural boards of education appoint teachers of prefectural and municipal schools on the basis of a qualifying examination.

The teacher certificates for kindergartens and elementary schools are awarded on the basis of a common curriculum, while those for lower and upper secondary schools are awarded for specified subject areas. There are two kinds of certificates: the first and the second class. The requirement for a second class certificate to teach in lower secondary schools is sixty-two credits obtained after two years of study at a university. The requirement for the first class certificate for teaching in lower or secondary schools or a second class certificate to teach in upper secondary schools is a bachelor's degree. The first class certificate to teach in upper secondary schools require a master's degree or thirty credits beyond the bachelor's degree.

Recently, the rapid diminution of student population caused by birthrate decline has reduced the demand for teachers and increased competition among candidates desiring to enter the teaching profession, in almost all prefectures. Just as there are *ronins* (literally means a *samurai* who is out of a job, and in modern version means a student preparing for the next entrance examination after failing) at entrance examinations to universities, there is an increasing number of *ronins* for the qualifying examination for teachers. Responding to the decrease in demand for teachers, some universities offering teacher training have cutback on the courses for teacher training, and some institutions have switched their courses and departments to other related fields.

HIGHER EDUCATION

Institutions

After the Second World War, a new national system of higher education started with the promotion of many institutions to the rank of four-year universities and colleges (both called *Daigaku* in Japanese) in addition to the institutions which already existed as imperial, national, public, and private universities. Junior colleges were established in 1949, and technical colleges were inaugurated in 1962, and also special training schools were established in 1976. The university of the air was started in 1983.

At present, higher education consists of four-year institutions (universities and colleges or *daigaku*); technical colleges *(kotosenmon-gakko);* the University of the Air *(hoso-daigaku),* which is usually included in the category of a four year institution; and special training schools *(senshu-gakko)* offering postsecondary courses. Distribution of these institutions by the authority responsible for administration is given below.

Higher Education Institutions and Enrollment (1988)

Type of Institution	Total	National	Municipal	Private
Number of Establishments				
four-year institutions	490	95	38	357
two-year institutions	571	40	54	477
technical colleges	62	54	4	4
special training schools3191 (postsecondary)	3191	172	177	2842
Enrollment (in thousands)				
graduate course	82	52	3	27
undergraduate				
four-year institutions	1994	491	59	1444
two-year institutions	450	19	22	409
correspondence courses	96			96
University of the Air	23	23		
postsecondary				
technical colleges	51	43	4	3
special training schools	699	18	26	655

The number of institutions of higher education grew rapidly, especially after the 1960s. As of 1988, there were 490 *daigaku,* with the total enrollment of two million students. *The Tanki-daigaku* numbered 571 and enrolled 450 thousand students for engineering subjects. The *Kotosenmongakko,* most of which concentrate on technical and engineering subjects, admit graduates from junior high schools and require five years before completion. The final two years of education, fourth and fifth grade, is equivalent to the first two years of higher education. The total enrollment of these institutions constitutes a small part. The *Senshu-gakko,* most of which provide occupational and technical training such as computer programming and foreign language interpretation, is a rapidly growing segment. The postsecondary course *(senmon-katei),* one of three courses offered by *senmon-gakko,* requires a diploma of upper secondary school for admission. Enrollment in this *senmon-katei* segment accounts for almost half a million.

Of the 1,061 institutions in the segment of universities and junior colleges, 79 percent were private sector institutions and 21 percent were under national and public control. About 72 percent of all students attended private sector institutions with the balance in national and public sector institutions. University students were distributed by fields of study, in the following manner: 39 percent in social sciences,

20 percent in engineering, 15 percent in humanities, and 8 percent in education and teacher training. In junior colleges, women represent 92 percent of the total enrollment, while the proportion of women students in universities is 28 percent. The proportion of women students enrolled in universities and junior colleges has been increasing; it rose from 26 percent in 1960 to 48 percent in 1988. Majority of the university level institutions are located in big cities with Tokyo boasting for 22 percent of all such institutions and 18 percent of all students.

The establishment of a university, junior college, or technical college, irrespective of ownership, requires the approval of the *Monbusho,* and the University Chartering Council. All institutions come under the jurisdiction of the *Monbusho,* but each institution is governed by its own governing agency.

Governance

The administrative structure of universities vary. Private institutions have their own organizational structure within the provisions of the Private School Law of 1949. At national universities, important decisions are made by the university administrative council *(hyogikai)* at the institutional level and by the departmental faculty conference *(Kyojukai)* at the departmental level. The autonomy of the universities is ensured through these self-regulating bodies. All administrators and faculty in national institutions are appointed, either directly or indirectly, by the Minister of Education.

In the selection and appointment of faculty, there is no system of *habilitation* as in Germany or *aggregation* as in France. As soon as a vacant post becomes available in an institution it is advertised in academic journals. Faculty personnel recruitment committees review the applicant's personality, ability, achievement, and potential and make recommendations for the appointment. The number of candidates for a post often reaches ten, twenty, or even more than fifty in certain fields. There are many postdoctorals who are waiting for academic posts. Pending availability of an academic post, a postdoctoral may work in a temporary position outside or inside the academic institutions, mostly as part time teachers. Some of them may work as special researchers sponsored by the Japan Society for the Promotion of Science which, under a program established in 1985, assists excellent post-doctoral scholars without jobs.

In the chair system in research universities (which have doctoral courses), the faculty usually consists of a professor *(kyoju),* who is a chair holder, an associate professor *(jokyoju)* or lecturer *(koshi),* and an assistant *(joshu).* The vacant posts of professors are filled by either the candidates who apply from other institutions or candidates who are promoted directly from the junior rank positions in the same chair. The latter case is rather popular among the prestigious institutions, although this custom is sometimes associated with academic nepotism and inbreeding which is thought to create an unfavorable climate for research activities. Recently some prestigious institutions which had traditionally adopted this kind of recruitment custom moved to change it by hiring professors from other institutions. Even so, there still remains a strong trend of inbreeding recruitment among prestigious institutions. Also the exchange of academics among the prestigious research institutions consisting of the former imperial universities is taking place to the extent that the recruitment process tend to exclude the academics from traditionally less prestigious institutions including national, public, and private universities.

When an academic staff member is hired as a lecturer or associate professor in an institution, he or she is substantially guaranteed a tenured position until retirement. Promotion to professoriate is examined on the basis of academic productivity, teaching experience, and seniority. Retirement age depends on the institution; the average age is approximately sixty-three in national and local institutions, and sixty-eight in private institutions.

Undergraduate Studies

For the first two years in a university undergraduate course, students study subjects of general education in the humanities, social science and natural science; foreign languages; health and physical education; and professional subjects. The first diploma (gakushi) is obtained after four years of study. Gakushi is not legally recognized as the first degree thus far in Japan but it is expected to be legally recognized in the near future based on one of the recent recommendations of the University Council.

Students who want to get into a university or junior college for undergraduate studies are required to complete the twelve-year formal schooling as a basic qualification. In the case of national or local institutions, applicants must take the Joint First Stage Achievement Test, JFSAT (Kyotsu Ichiji Shiken) conducted by the National Center for University Entrance Examination (Nyushi Senta) since 1979. It is held at many places throughout the country once a year. There were almost 400 thousand applicants for this test in 1989. In addition to JFSAT they are required to take the second stage achievement tests conducted by each institution. They need not take JFSAT if they want to enter private universities and junior colleges, but they must take the entrance examinations conducted by the institution of their choice. Recently, many institutions regardless of whether they are national, public, or private, are basing their admission decisions on credential reports prepared by the principals of upper secondary schools.

The Monbusho introduced a new test to substitute the JFSAT, in 1990. The new test applies to not only national and public institutions but also private institutions. Many private institutions, however, seem to hesitate to participate in this new test. In 1990, all national and public universities (ninety-five and thirty-nine respectively), and twenty-one private universities (or 5.8 percent of all private universities) are participating.

The JFSAT, which examines scholastic ability in as many as five academic subject areas and seven subjects, required a tremendous amount of hard work and as a result, the number of applicants for this test has decreased over the ten years of its existence. At the same time, the number of applicants for private institutions, which examines few subjects, has been on the increase. Some private institutions located in large cities have become more and more competitive as more applicants came to their own entrance examination, while national and public institutions including even some former imperial universities in local areas have become less competitive. Along with this trend, some change has occurred in the prestige hierarchy among academic institutions. If private institutions participate in the new test together with the national and public sector, they might loose their rising status because they cannot exercise their own entrance examinations anymore. It is probably one of the reasons why the private sector institutions are somewhat hesitant to participate in the new test.

Many fields of study are open to undergraduate students. For example, in the University of Tokyo, there are nine faculties: literature, education, law, economics, science, medicine, engineering, agriculture, and pharmacy. In addition there is a college of liberal arts. Each faculty and college has several departments. The qualification for graduation is regulated by *Monbusho*. The number of credits that students must take in each course of general education, foreign languages, health education, and professional education are specified as 36, 8, 4, and 76 respectively. In Japan it is often said that most students can graduate from undergraduate programs without dropping out because it is not difficult for students to attain the credits required. This may be true in some departments, faculties, and institutions, but not in every field or institution. Probably students may get course credits more easily in the soft disciplines (humanities and social sciences) than in the hard disciplines (science, engineering, medicine, etc.) In this context some *gakushi* diplomas are more difficult to get than others. There are twenty-one *gakushi*s and they include B.Agr. (*no-gakushi*, agriculture), B.A. (*gakugei-gakushi*, arts), B.Econ. (*keizai-gakushi*, economy), B.Ed. (*kyoiku-gakushi*, education), B.Eng. (*kou-gakushi*, engineering), LL.B. (*hou-gakushi*, law), B.Lit. (*bun-gakushi*, literature), B.Sc. (*ri-gakushi*, science).

Tuition fees charged at national universities are uniform throughout the country, those in public universities are not uniform, and those in private universities vary greatly. In general, the average amount of tuition and other educational expenses for university students in 1986 was 371,500 yen (US$1- = 142Yen) in national universities, 404,900 yen in local public universities, and 855,400 yen in private universities. Living expenses for food, housing, etc. were 738,000 yen, 650,400 yen, and 679,600 yen respectively. The cost of a university education has been rising rapidly over the years and the students with meager means are finding it more and more difficult to have a university education, especially in fields like medicine.

Financial aid for students come from the Japan Scholarship Foundation (JSF), the Students' Assistance Association, and many other scholarship agencies. The JSF offers loan scholarships to students with good performance, who demonstrate financial need. In 1987, the monthly amount of an ordinary loan for a student in national and local public university is 26,000 yen (living at home) and 32,000 yen (out of home). Students in private universities received 35,000 yen (living at home) and 45,000 yen (out of home). Of all student awards, 11 percent went to university students and 4 percent went to junior college students.

Advanced Studies and Research

In 1989, graduate students numbered 85,263 which accounted for only 4.5 percent of undergraduate students. As this figure shows, the graduate student population still remains a small segment in Japan.

The graduate school is usually divided into several fields of study. Those who complete an undergraduate course or its equivalent are eligible to enroll in a graduate course. Those who finish schooling in foreign countries are required to have a sixteen-year course and in the case of those who want to enter a graduate course in medicine and pharmacy, an eighteen-year course is required. (Those who are recognized as qualified by the Minister of Education and those who are recognized by graduate school as having the equivalent ability to those who complete the undergraduate course in Japan are also eligible).

Master's degree *(shushi)* and doctor's degree *(hakushi)* are offered in a variety of fields. Master's degree takes two years. The doctor's degree is of two types: one program takes five years, and the other combines the first two years of the master's degree and an additional three years. In 1988, Japanese institutions conferred 25,524 master's degrees and 9,602 doctor's degrees (49 percent of which was in medicine).

The monthly amount of loan scholarships offered by the Japan Scholarship Foundation (in 1986) for a student in the master's course was 69,000 yen and that for a student in the doctoral course was 80,000 yen. Majority of beneficiaries (59 percent) were doctoral students. Students cannot expect to work as teaching assistants in order to earn money for fees and other expenses because the system of teaching assistantship is not sufficiently developed in Japanese graduate schools.

The Japanese Government Scholarship Program, which was started in 1954, invites promising foreign students who wish to study in Japan. Scholarships are offered for two years by the program to graduate students who are under thirty-five years old. The monthly stipend rate for 1987 was 176,500 yen for research students.

ISSUES AND TRENDS

Japan is now engaged in the third education reform after two previous reforms: the Meiji and occupation reforms. There are several major reports and proposals developed within the last two decades. At the level of the national government, the Central Council for Education *(Chuo Kyoiku Shingikai)* called for eliminating uniformity and promoting diversity. In 1970, the Organization for Economic Cooperation and Development (OECD) criticized the centralized control, conformity, institutional hierarchy, and the emphasis on university entrance examinations. In 1975, the Japan Teachers Union proposed an education reform plan. In 1979, the Japan Committee for Economic Development proposed creativity, diversity, and internationalism in education.

More recently, The National Council on Educational Reform *(Rinji Kyoiku Shingikai),* which reports directly to the Prime Minister, (not to *Monbusho*), in its final report (1987), recommended the realization of individuality, fundamental scholastic ability, creativity, ability of thinking, expansion of choice, humanization of the educational environmental, lifelong learning, and internationalization. In the specific area of higher education, the council recommended further diversification and enrichment of university education through reforms of general education; more flexible admission to postsecondary institutions; more frequent mobility of students among institutions and departments; improvement of graduate education and research; closer cooperation between universities and society; and establishment of a University Council *(Daigaku Shingikai)*.

One of the most important issues now facing Japanese education is to reform the "degreeocratic society" *(gakureki-shakai)*. University degrees or diplomas are overvalued to the extent that almost all children are enforced to study at cram schools *(juku)* or preparatory schools *(yobiko)* besides elementary and secondary schools, and parents must incur enormous expenditure for preparing students to join the competition for entry to higher education institutions in search of degrees. In the climate often termed as "examination hells", children are compelled to study hard from their early life stage in order to get into prestigious universities. This climate is said to have resulted in many socially undesirable phenomena: juvenile delinquency, school bullying, school phobia, school violence, and suicide.

As demonstrated by recent international scholastic tests in which the Japanese children obtained the highest or near the highest scores in some fields including mathematics and science, it is an undeniable fact that the quality of primary and secondary education in Japan can be ranked very high. This high quality of education is probably due to many factors: the curricula, the educational tradition which has been cultivated since Tokugawa era, and even social pressure for hard study caused by the degreeocratic society.

However, the quality of Japanese higher education has not kept pace with the international reputation of the Japanese primary and secondary educational system. Even though the national system of higher education has spread throughout the country on a mass scale, the quality has suffered. One of the most important reasons for the drop in quality is the low level of public expenditure on higher education, compared to primary and secondary education. For example, in 1989, the government higher education expenditure was as low as 0.44 percent of G.N.P. of 1986. Also much attention has been paid to entrance examination but on the contrary less attention to the content of education, curriculum and teaching methods, evaluation of teaching, and the development of students once they enter the universities.

Almost all students who are accepted to institutions can graduate (dropout rate is approximately 10 percent). This astonishingly high retention rate might be caused by the high quality of scholastic achievement which students acquire at entrance but not necessarily by sufficient education and teaching during their stay at the university. Reforms must be realized by not only eliminating "examination hell" at entrance examinations but also by improving the content of education and teaching in universities and colleges.

The population of the traditional students, ages 18-22 years, is expected to begin to decrease gradually after 1992 (the population of eighteen-year old children is expected to reach its peak of 205 million and then go down to 151 million). This will result in institutions competing to attract the limited number of students.

Students will look for quality when shopping for a school. Many foreign students as well as adult students other than traditional students will have to be accepted by those institutions and this will need more improvement in education and teaching ability among academics. Especially the number of foreign students has increased in recent years: it was 4,300 in 1970; 6,200 in 1980; 10,300 in 1984; and 32,000 in 1989. This rapid increase has generated pressure and created incentives for more internationalization and improvement of higher education.

Some of the international assessments of academic research activities in Japanese universities say that the quality of basic research is almost at levels equivalent to or more than that of European countries, though it depends on the fields of study. As it is known, research activity in applied areas which mainly takes place in the firms, have marked high quality but research activities in universities need to be improved considerably if Japan is to make more contributions to the development of scientific knowledge and culture of the world. For this purpose, it is indispensable to reform graduate schools; reforms that would result in the improvement of research organizations, the system of research assessment, and the training and education of creative scholars.

BIBLIOGRAPHY

Amano, Ikuo. *Kotokyoiku no Nihonteki-Kozo* (Structure of Japanese Higher Education), Tokyo: Tamagawa Daigaku Shuppanbu, 1986.

Amano, Ikuo, Shogo Ichikawa, Morikazu Ushiogi, and Kazuyuki Kitamura, eds., *Kyoiku wa Kikika* (Is Education in Crisis?), Tokyo: Yushindo, 1988.

Amono, Ikuo. *Kindai Nihon Kotokyoiku Kenkyu* (Study on the Modern Higher Education of Japan), Tokyo: Tamagawa Daigaku Shuppanbu, 1989.

Anderson, Ronald S. *Education in Japan: A Century of Modern Development.* Washington D.C.: U.S. Department of Health, Education, and Welfare, 1974.

Arimoto, Akira. "The Academic Structure in Japan: Institutional Hierarchy and Academic Mobility." *Higher Education Working Paper, No. 27,* Yale University, New Haven, Connecticut, 1978.

Arimoto, Akira. *Daigakujin no Shakaigaku* (Sociology of Academic Profession). Tokyo: Gakubunsha, 1981.

Arimoto, Akira. *Academic Productivity no Joken Nikansuru Kokusai Hikaku Kenkyu* (A Comparative Study on the Conditions of the Academic Productivity), Research Institute for Higher Education. Hiroshima: Hiroshima University, 1986.

Arimoto, Akira. "Merton Kagaku Shakaigaku no Kenkyu: Sono Paradigm no Keisei to Tenkai" (Study on the Sociology of Science) in Robert K. Merton: The Formation and Development of Its Paradigm. Tokyo: Fukumura, 1987.

Aso, Makoto. *Kindaika to Kyoiku* (Modernization and Education). Tokyo: Daiichi Hoki, 1983.

Clark, Burton R. *The Higher Education System: Academic Organization in Cross-National Perspective.* California: University of California Press, 1983.

Cummings, William K., Ikuo Amano, and Kazuyuki Kitamura, eds., *Changes in the Japanese Universities: A Comparative Perspective.* New York: Praeger, 1979.

Dore, Ronald P. *Education in Tokugawa Japan.* London: Routledge & Kegan Paul Ltd., 1965.

Dore, Ronald P. *The Diploma Disease: Education, Qualification and Development.* London: George Allen & Unwin Ltd., 1976.

Kaigo, Tokiomi, and Masao Terasaki. *Daigaku Kyoiku* (University Education). Tokyo: Tokyo Daigaku Shuppankai, 1969.

Ministry of Education, Science and Culture, *Education in Japan: A Graphic Presentation.* Tokyo: Ministry of Education, Science and Culture, 1989.

Narita, Katsuya. *System of Higher Education: Japan.* New York: International Council for Education Development, 1978.

Seki, Masao. *Nihon no Daigaku Kyoiky Kaikaku: Rekishi, Genjo, Tenbo* (University Education Reform in Japan: Its History, Present State and Perspective). Tokyo: Tamagawa Daigaku Shuppanbu, 1988.

U. S. Department of Education. *Japanese Education Today.* Washington, D. C.: U. S. Government Printing Office, 1987.

JORDAN
by
Hani A. Saleh
Dean of Students
and
Ibrahim A. Nasser
Assistant Professor, Faculty of Education
University of Jordan, Jordan

BACKGROUND

In 1921, Jordan inherited from the Ottmans (who ruled the country for more than four centuries), a traditional system of education. This consisted of a limited number of religious schools known as the *Kuttabs*; several primary schools providing three years of study; and some elementary schools providing six years of study. Soon after, many new schools were built and especially in the past two decades, education has received much attention. By 1988, the number of schools from kindergarten to secondary level (both public and private) had risen to 3,565 (from 691 in 1950) with a student population of 963252 (compared to 123319 in 1950) and staff of 42,533 teachers (compared to 12,310 in 1950). In 1988, there were 963,252 students attending schools (kindergarten to secondary) compared to 123,319 in 1950.

The 1964 Education Act defines the educational philosophy in Jordan as follows: Believing in God and the ideals of the Arab Nations; Believing in Arab Unity, its freedom and its personality in the integrated united Arab home; Believing in international understanding on the basis of freedom, equality, and justice; Respect for individual dignity and freedom, and respect for the public interest of society, to an extent where one does not dominate the other; Social justice and providing equality of educational opportunities for all Jordanians according to individual potentialities; Assisting every student to grow physically, mentally, socially and emotionally, to be a responsible citizen for himself and his society; Benefiting from modern technological development, and paying attention at the same time to its repercussions and problems, taking advance measures to avoid problems and to find solutions for them; Respect for freedom and for the democratic system; and Positive participation towards the development of international civilization, in science, arts, and literature.

The Education Act vested responsibility for the administration of education in a highly centralized Ministry of Education. Through its various bodies, the ministry administers all educational activities in the country. There are three levels of control: the national level is the Ministry of Education (centered in Amman, the capital); the regional level administration in the governorates, and districts; and the institutional level of administration in schools.

PRIMARY AND SECONDARY EDUCATION

In Jordan, as in most other Arab countries, the basic educational ladder comprises twelve years, consisting of three stages. A child is admitted to the first grade of elementary school when he or she is six years old. The duration of elementary school cycle is six years. Education is free in the compulsory level which consists of six years at the elementary level and three at the preparatory level. The cycle of secondary education in Jordan lasts three years. There are two types of secondary schools: the general and the vocational. The secondary general schools are intended to prepare students for higher education. The secondary vocational schools are intended to prepare students to take up middle level positions in Jordanian economy. The secondary general schools offer two options or streams: literary and scientific. Streaming occurs at the beginning of the secondary grade.

The curricula and textbooks used in the schools are decided by the Ministry of Education.

The curriculum for elementary (primary) schools consist of social studies (history, geography), general sciences, arithmetic, religion (Islamic in public schools, in addition to Christian religion in some private schools), and Arabic language. English language classes start from the fifth elementary grade in public schools, and from the first elementary grade in most private schools. Some schools teach French as a second language from the first grade.

The curriculum for the preparatory cycle consists of Arabic language, English language, history, geography, chemistry, physics, mathematics, and Arabic society. The curriculum for the first secondary stage corresponds to that of preparatory cycle, but more rigorous and thorough.

At the upper stage also, the Jordanian schools have two streams: literary and scientific. In the literary stream subjects studied include Arabic language, English, history, geography, sociology, religion, Arabic society, logic, and economics. In the scientific stream the curriculum include religion, Arabic, English, chemistry, physics, mathematics, and biology. Vocational, commercial, industrial, agricultural and technical schools have special curricula suited to the programs offered at the schools.

Selection for teaching appointments is made by the Civil Service Commission which takes into account the academic qualifications and teaching experience of the candidates. The names of selected candidates are then sent to the ministry which in turn forward them to the directors of education in governorates and districts. Teachers may have following qualifications (grade of appointment and salary depending on the qualifications): Teacher's Institute Certificate, B.A. or B.Sc. degree, M.A. or M.Sc. degree, Ph.D. degree. According to the civil law, the initial salaries and annual increments of teachers are equal to those of any other professional group possessing the same qualifications. Promotions are based on teaching ability and performance. Teacher training is conducted at the many institutes of teacher training established by the Ministry of Education.

The language of instruction in Jordanian schools is Arabic. English is taught as a second language. There are some private schools teaching other languages such as French, Spanish, German, and Italian.

Beside public (government) schools there are a number of private schools in Jordan. These private schools include national education institutions, and foreign education institutions. The Ministry of Education has the right to supervise all private schools. No private institution is allowed to be established without a license issued by the ministry. Private schools must accept general educational policies and the Jordanian curriculum and must follow the text books issued by the Ministry of Education. If private schools want to teach other subjects, or to use other text books, it is necessary for them to seek the approval of the Ministry of Education.

In addition to the private schools in which Jordanian programs are taught, there are some foreign private schools which teach foreign programs such as American, British and international programs.

HIGHER EDUCATION

Higher education sector in Jordan has undergone rapid growth. Four national universities and a number of community colleges provide a variety of higher educational programs.

Jordan University in Amman was established in 1962. It has 670 faculty members, 16,000 students and consists of the colleges of arts, economics, science, medicine, agriculture, education, engineering and technology, law, nursing, pharmacy, dentistry, physical education, and Sharia (Islamic studies). Yarmouk University in Irbid was established 1976. It has 400 faculty members, 10,000 students, and consists of the colleges of science, arts and humanities, and economic and administrative sciences. Mou'ta University was established in 1981 in Karak. It has fifty faculty members and 1,000 students. It consists of the departments of engineering, science, humanities, administrative sciences, and law. Science and Technology University in Irbid was established in 1987. It has 200 faculty members and 3,000 students. It consists of the colleges of medicine, dentistry, pharmacy, nursing, engineering, agriculture, and science.

The aim of the universities in Jordan is to provide opportunities for general learning and for the study, preservation, and assimilation of Arab Islamic culture and heritage. Its mandate was to promote research and creativity in all branches of knowledge as well as to serve Jordanian society, the Arab Nation, and humanity at large. All the Jordanian universities are public but autonomous institutions of higher education which have assumed a prominent position as centers of learning and culture in the Middle East.

Jordanian universities believe that university education requires not only the highest proficiency and experience in teaching but also a considerable effort in preparation and management. Therefore, a reduced teaching load is assigned to faculty members to ensure sufficient time for academic research.

ISSUES AND TRENDS

The National Conference for Educational Development that was convened in 1987 recommended that the formal education which precedes higher education be divided into two main stages: basic education, and secondary education. The basic schooling under the new plan consists of ten compulsory years of education, attended by students of 6-16 years of age. The secondary schooling consists of two specialized and non-compulsory years, attended by students of 16-18 years of age. The secondary schooling has two main streams: comprehensive stream which is based on general and combined cultural base and specialized academic or vocational education; and applied schooling stream which is based on vocational training and preparation.

Since the implementation of the above recommendations need a transitional period (for planning etc.) the Ministry of Education has drawn up a systematic plan that extends from 1988 to 1994, to effect the change over to the new system.

BIBLIOGRAPHY

Al-Bukhari, Najati. *Education in Jordan* 1973.

Al-Ganam, M.A. "Arab World in 2000 A.D." *New Education Magazine* May-August 1980.

Educational Statistics 1987-88. Ministry of Education, Jordan, 1988.

Salman, A. N. H. "Some Problems in the Educational System of Jordan." Diss. University of London, 1986.

Summary Data on Higher Education in Jordan 1985-1986. Ministry of Higher Education, Jordan, 1986.

REPUBLIC OF KOREA

by
Sung-Yun Hong
Professor and Dean, Graduate School of Education
Chung-Ang University, South Korea
and Gi-Woo Lee
Research Director, Child Research and Development Division
Korean Institute for Research in the
Behavioral Sciences, South Korea

BACKGROUND

The higher educational system in Korea traces its origin to *Taehak* or the Great School which was founded by the Koguryo Dynasty in 372. Its founding was coincidental with the introduction of Buddhism from Chien-Chin China. Another two dynasties, Paekje and Silla, had some form of a higher educational system. In the Koryo Dynasty (918-1392), the earlier institution of higher learning gave way to a new one called *Kugjagam* which was founded in 992. With the advent of the Yi Dynasty (1392-1910), the *Kugjagam* was replaced by the *Sungkyunkwan* which was established in 1398. In the period of the colonial rule (1910-45), the Japanese Government founded Keijo Imperial College in 1926. After the liberation of the country, Seoul National University was founded in 1946 by amalgamating Keijo Imperial College and nine public and private colleges. Since then, universities, both national and private, have mushroomed.

At present, the Education Law provides for the establishment of the following types of schools in order to enable all citizens to have equal opportunity for an education, irrespective of religious faith, sex, or differences in social status or economic means: 1. elementary schools, middle and high schools, and universities or colleges; 2. teacher's colleges, Korea National University of Education, and colleges of education; 3. junior vocational colleges, correspondence colleges, and open colleges; 4. commercial high schools; 5. civic schools and civic high schools; 6. special schools; 7. kindergartens; and 8. miscellaneous schools. Among these, the schools in category 1 constitute the backbone of the educational system in Korea based on the 6-3-3-4 pattern.

All national, public, and private colleges and universities are under the direction and supervision of the Ministry of Education. It is necessary to obtain its approval before institutes of higher education are established or abolished, departments of study are recognized, student quotas are assigned, admissions procedures and curricula outlines are determined, and admission fee/tuition levels for national universities are determined. The minister of education approves appointments to the presidency of private institutes. As such, higher education in

Korea is part of a centralized system of education. However, the system is being liberalized.

The centralized nature of education places a tremendous responsibility upon the Ministry of Education, but at the same time it provides substantial leverage and power for introducing educational reforms at the government's initiative. In recent years, there has been a noticeable trend toward institutions of higher education assuming a greater degree of autonomy in examination, curriculum and system operation, tuition adjustment, and innovative programs. The inauguration of the Council for Higher Education, which provides meeting grounds for the presidents of colleges and universities, marks a great step forward in this direction.

The introduction and strengthening of cooperative relationships among institutions of higher education and the communities that surround them is viewed as essential not only for the improvement of institutions but also for the social and economic development of the regional communities. The Ministry of Education took the lead in promoting such relationships so that higher educational institutions in a given area could provide supportive services to the local society and to regional governmental agencies; and industrial establishments could more easily seek advice and assistance from their local colleges and universities.

PRIMARY AND SECONDARY EDUCATION

Primary education in Korea is given free of charge and is compulsory for children attaining the age of six years. It aims at achieving the following seven specific objectives: to promote the correct understanding and proper use of the national language; to nurture morality, a sense of responsibility, a civic spirit, and a spirit of teamwork through proper understanding of reciprocal relationships between individuals, society, and state; to nurture the ability to make scientific observation and analysis of natural phenomena; to nurture the ability to understand and dispose of quantitative relations necessary in life; to nurture a spirit of industry, perseverance and self-help by promoting a proper understanding of the requirements of daily life; to promote the proper understanding of sanitation and to habituate sanitary practices in order to ensure harmonious development of body and mind.

Educational curricula encompass both the regular curriculum and extracurricular activities. The regular curriculum is made up of moral education, Korean language, social studies, arithmetic, science, physical education, music, fine arts, and crafts. Extracurricular activities include children's homeroom activities, club activities, and school-sponsored activities. Extracurricular activities are introduced in third grade. For the first two grades, some of the nine regular courses may be combined in the light of existing inter-course connections and the developmental state of children. Thus, for the first and second grades, moral education, Korean language, and social studies are combined into "the proper behavior of life", arithmetic and science into "the wisdom of life", (for first grade only), and physical education, music and fine arts into "the enjoyment of life".

Secondary education is provided in three-year middle schools and high schools. The purpose of middle school education is to provide secondary common education on the basis of education received at elementary school. Admission is granted to graduates of elementary schools after six years of compulsory elementary education and those adjudged to be similarly qualified. Tuition is borne by the students.

Entrance examinations for middle schools were abolished in 1969, and all applicants are accepted and allocated to schools within the school district of residence by lottery. Some 99.5 percent of all elementary school graduates moved on to middle schools in 1988. Compulsory and free middle school education was introduced beginning with rural areas in 1985, and will perhaps be extended throughout the nation by the target year of 1991.

Middle school curricula consist of the regular curriculum as well as extracurricular activities. The regular curriculum is made up of twelve courses, i.e. moral education, Korean language, Korean history, social studies, mathematics, sciences, physical education, music, fine arts, classical Chinese, foreign languages (mainly English), and vocational skills and home economics. Extracurricular activities are made up of homeroom activities, club activities, and other school-sponsored activities.

The purpose of high school education is to provide higher common education on the basis of achievements in middle school. High schools are classified into general high schools, vocational high schools, and other (arts, physical education, science, etc.) high schools. Admission is granted to middle school graduates and those adjudged to be similarly qualified. Tuition is borne by the students.

A revised high school entrance examination system was put into force in 1974, according to which entrance examinations are given to all the applicants and they are allocated to schools by lottery within school districts of residence in the order of test results. There are some differences in the implementation procedures between large cities (subjected to the "equalization" reform) and other areas in the country. In large cities allocation is first made to vocational high schools, and in the second stage to general high schools. Some 96.2 percent of all middle school graduates enter high schools.

High school curricula consist of the regular curriculum as well as extracurricular activities. The regular curriculum is divided into general subjects and specialized subjects. The general subjects, classified into common required and elective courses, are made up of thirteen courses, i.e., moral education, Korean language, Korean history, social studies, mathematics, science, physical education, military training, music, fine arts, classical Chinese, foreign languages, and vocational skills and home economics. Extracurricular activities include school militia activities, club activities, and school-sponsored activities.

HIGHER EDUCATION

Institutions

The Institutions of higher education are classified into four categories: colleges and universities offering four-year undergraduate programs (medical and dental colleges are six years); 2-3 year vocational colleges; teacher's colleges; Air and Correspondence University and open colleges.

The purpose of a university and college education is to teach and study the fundamental theories and practical means of application of the various branches of arts and sciences necessary for the progress and development of the nation and the human race, and thereby foster persons capable of leadership. The purpose of junior vocational colleges is to teach and study specialized theories and knowledge in various fields of social activity; to develop one's capability, and to educate competent professional personnel required for national and social development. Teachers' colleges are to train elementary school teachers, while colleges of education are to train middle and high school teachers. The correspondence college and the open college are intended to offer educational opportunities at college or junior college level to those industrial workers who have completed or interrupted school education, as a part of the lifelong education approach.

Under the Education Law and subsequent presidential and ministerial decrees, all higher education institutions, whether public or private, come under the direct or indirect supervision of the minister of education. The Ministry of Education exercises control over such matters as student quotas, qualifications for the teaching staff, curriculum and degree requirements, and general education courses.

The total number of higher education institutions in 1988 is 511 with a combined enrollment of 1,387,170. About 80 percent of them are private. In the case of private institutions, the appointment of members of the boards of trustees and presidents are authorized by the ministry. The minimum qualifications that members of the teaching staff should have are specified by the Educational Public Official Law. Private colleges and universities are financed by foundations, donations, and students' fees, but the Education Law provides for government subsidies to private colleges for activities related to the development of teaching and research in the fields of science and technology.

During the last several years a number of relationships between colleges and universities have developed within Korea and with institutions in other countries. For example, intra-country cooperation at the graduate level has taken place between Chung-Ang, Soongjun, and Inha Universities, making possible a cross-registration program. Students in Korea who have participated in programs of this type will have academic records showing that they have taken course work at another university, but within an integrated program.

A number of U.S. colleges and universities as well as colleges and universities in other countries have established sister college affiliations with colleges and universities in Korea. Examples of this are the sister affiliations of Chung-Ang University with Nihon University in Japan and the University of Alberta in Canada and the University of Wisconsin in the United States. These affiliations involve faculty and student exchanges.

In recent years, a number of U.S. colleges and universities have established joint programs in affiliation with colleges and universities in Korea. There are also private secondary schools established for foreign residents as well as English language centers and programs sponsored by U.S. institutions for U.S. military personnel in Korea. For example, Korea, Ewha Womans, and Yonsie Universities have developed agreements with foreign universities to recognize credits that foreign students earn for summer courses offered in Korea. These three institutions have agreements regarding credit acknowledgement with a number of foreign universities primarily in the United States, Japan, and Australia and are looking forward to developing agreements with institutions in Europe. These summer courses are approximately six weeks in length with six to nine credit hours, and they are primarily concerned with the Korean language, history, and political science. A number of Korean university students will be spending time during the summer vacation period at foreign institutions where credits earned will be recognized by Korean institutions.

Undergraduate Studies

The undergraduate courses in Korea are of four years duration and medical and dentistry colleges include six years of study. A university must have a minimum of three components colleges, of which at least one must be in the field of liberal arts and sciences. There are 104 colleges and universities which offer bachelor's degree in over twenty-five fields or departments, including literature, theology, fine arts, music, jurisprudence, political science, public administration, commerce, physical science, home economics, gymnastics, engineering, medicine, dentistry, oriental medicine, sanitation, nursing, pharmacology, agricultural sciences, veterinary medicine, and fisheries.

The curriculum of undergraduate programs include both general studies and specialization, with required courses as well as electives. It is compulsory to complete the required courses for graduation, while students can select the elective courses in order for them to broaden their academic background in their fields of special interest. It is required that the general study courses represent the humanities; social sciences and natural sciences in a harmonious blend; national ethics; Korean language; and physical education. Regarding the major courses, each student is allowed to take two majors at most. When one major is taken, a student may take minor subjects exclusive of those included in the major.

Except for medical and dental colleges, 140 academic credits must be earned to complete a bachelor's degree. The number of credits to be earned for a semester vary from eighteen to twenty-one points. The credits assigned to the elective courses are limited to less than one-third of the total credits required for graduation, and the general subjects are not to exceed one-third of the required course.

Any applicant for admission to a college or a university is given equal opportunity, regardless of race, religion, sex or social standing and applications are invited through public announcement. A candidate for admission to college must have one of the following qualifications: graduation from an accredited high school; certification from the College Entrance Qualifying examination (given once annually by the Ministry of Education) in case the applicant has no formal schooling; graduation from a school recognized by the Ministry of Education as equivalent to high school; completion of twelve years of school education in a foreign country.

When the number of applicants exceeds the student quota, candidates are selected according to the results of written and oral examinations given by individual institutions. In general, foreign applicants are not affected by the student quota. Admission to colleges of medicine and dentistry is granted to those who have completed a two-year preparatory course.

The academic year commences at the beginning of March and ends at the end of February of the next year. The first semester is from the beginning of March to the end August, and the second semester is from the beginning of September to the end of February. Each college or university is required to have at least 210 school days throughout the academic year (at least 180 days for graduate school).

There are two vacations every year. The summer vacation usually lasts about sixty days during July and August, and the winter vacation extends for about seventy days, starting in the middle part of December and terminating at the end of February.

All students admitted must register with the office of student affairs, and must also pay an admission fee within a specified period. In most institutions, students are required to sign a written pledge, that they will comply with rules and regulations, and to present a written statement from their sponsors, who are responsible for tuition and other school expenses. The sponsor is normally a parent or close relative of the student.

Each semester the student must register through prescribed procedures for the courses he intends to take. Those students who fail to register within a set period may be subject to dismissal. At registration time, students pay tuition and other fees.

The amount of tuition for national universities is determined by the Ministry of Education, for they are financially dependent on the latter. In the case of private colleges and universities, the Ministry of Education, sets the ceiling in a way that narrows the payment gap among them. The tuition at national institutions is lower than those of private ones. The tuition fee payable to the national and private institutions averages 500,000 won (US$735) and 700,000 won (US$1,029) for each semester respectively. The entrance fee averages 80,000 won (US $118). On some courses extra costs may be incurred for such items as field courses, project work, special instruments, or laboratory equipment and materials. There may also be additional fees for any student who has to take an examination and write a thesis associated with pursuing advanced degrees. This fee scale also applies to the graduate schools and vocational colleges.

The required number of credit points varies according to the course of study. Even though the average number of credits which the undergraduate student can earn for a semester is set at twenty points, those students whose grade average in the previous semester was "A" or above may be allowed to earn up to twenty-three points. One whose credit falls short of fifteen points may be subject to dismissal. The minimum credit requirement for graduation from an undergraduate course is 140 points (180 points for medicine and dentistry). Professional qualification courses in education are provided for those who desire to secure a license for secondary school teaching, and credits so earned may be included in the total credit requirement. From 1984, a double-major system was adopted.

Basically there is no difference in tuition fees payable by local and foreign students. The fees comprise an admission fee, tuition fee and laboratory (or shop) fee, all payable to the college (university) accounting office. The admission fee only applies to new entrants and adds to tuition and laboratory (or shop) fees for the first academic semester. Beginning with the second semester, students pay only tuition and laboratory (or shop) fees.

All foreigners who want to study in Korea must have sufficient funds to pay for their studies and living costs. Foreign students cannot assume that they will be able to finance their studies on the basis of part-time work. According to the immigration law, it is illegal for foreign students to hold jobs. Proof of sufficient funding is required of all foreign students before they are issued an admission certificate. Information on scholarships for foreign students is generally available from Korean diplomatic or consular missions abroad.

No university in Korea is fully residential. A few universities have dormitories, but their facilities are severely limited and obtaining a place is highly competitive. The majority of students from out of town live in "lodgings" where a room and meals are included. (It is advisable, when applying for admission to a Korean university from abroad, to apply for university accommodation, for some institutions give foreign students priority in assigning rooms).

The cost of a room and meals in a dormitory is relatively low, ranging from 100,000 wons (US$147) to 150,000 won (US$221) per month (this excludes meals on weekends). The cost of "lodging" is 200,000 won (US$294) per month. Renting a room is another possibility: while it costs more than "lodging", it offers the choice of meals to suit individual tastes, when the room is furnished with kitchen utensils. The cost of renting a room in a private residence varies with the type of room and whether it is furnished or not. The lowest cost of renting an unfurnished room averages 300,000 won (US$441) per month including heating.

Living expenses, including room and meals, transportation and other personal expenses amount to at least 300,000 won (US$441) per month, providing that overseas students live in "lodging". It may vary, though, according to the locality. Living expenses in Seoul are higher than in the provinces due to the concentration of cultural and educational amenities in this area.

Financial assistance takes three forms: tuition exemption, scholarships, and credit loans. Tuition exemption and scholarships are available to applicants who have shown high academic standards. Credit loans are available to needy students if an arrangement can be made to guarantee the repayment of the loan after graduation. Many universities have their own funds for providing this financial aid. At the undergraduate level, it is extremely difficult to be the recipient of a scholarship. Even though some universities may award one, scholarships in general have a limited availability, benefiting only a few students. Apart from this, there are various local organizations which award scholarships. These scholarships generally specify the qualifications of recipients and are awarded on a competitive basis when applicants exceed the number. There is no special provision for foreign students, since foreign students are put on an equal basis with Korean students to compete for financial assistance. Off-campus scholarships are partially available for foreign students, varying in type and amount with universities.

Advanced Studies and Research

Korean postgraduate education, like other segments of postsecondary education, is going through extensive change and growth. The range in the quality of equipment, facilities, and staffing among colleges and universities appears to be quite wide. Most institutions do not have a full-time graduate faculty. Few colleges or universities have an adequate number of full-time staff assigned to this level of education. However, significant improvements have taken place in staffing postgraduate programs in the last several years, particularly in the fields of social science and the humanities.

Because of the rapid increase in student enrollment in the areas of science and engineering, faculty members with experience and advanced degrees in engineering and science are in demand. One of Korea's primary goals for the future is to develop the areas of basic research and high technology. This, coupled with the increased needs of industry for talented scientists and engineers, has placed the postsecondary educational system in these fields under severe stress to recruit experienced faculty. Well-trained and experienced faculty are scarce, enrollments are increasing, and the quality of physical facilities is barely adequate at best. This segment of higher education is receiving high priority for study and improvement by the Ministry of Education and the colleges and universities.

Each year, many faculty and staff members at colleges and universities are sent to other countries to further their education and skills and to pursue advanced degrees. This commitment to professional development has made it possible for Korea to establish a potential for excellence at the graduate level. Within the next ten years a number of Korean programs at the graduate level should rank high in their productivity and quality of research in comparison to other institutions worldwide.

There are 251 schools which offer master's and/or doctoral degrees in the humanities, social sciences, natural sciences, engineering, home economics, education, agriculture, medicine, arts, public health, and environmental studies.

An applicant for a master's program must have one of the following qualifications: graduation from an accredited four-year college with a bachelor's degree; completion of a bachelor's degree program in a foreign country; academic achievements recognized by the Ministry of Education as equivalent to completion of a four-year college program. The student normally has adequate undergraduate preparation for the requested graduate specialized field. If there are deficiencies in this area, background courses will be requested.

The master's degree requires four semesters or two years of full time study but should not take more than three years to complete. Advisory committees are appointed by the college or university accepting the student at the master's level. Prior to receiving a master's degree, the candidate must pass a comprehensive examination, an examination in one foreign language, and complete a master's thesis. A student is required to have a 3.0 grade point average or better to successfully complete the master's program.

Students requesting admission to a doctoral program must have a master's degree or its equivalent, a scholarly background in the field of speciality, some demonstrated research experience, and recommendations from individuals in the master's degree field of speciality. Generally, a doctoral program requires a minimum of sixty credits taken over three or more years. Students must pass a foreign language test to demonstrate proficiency in two foreign languages. They must also pass a comprehensive examination, complete the coursework with a grade point average of 3.0 or "B" or better, submit a dissertation, and have it accepted, and pass an oral examination. An advisory committee is appointed at the doctoral level.

ISSUES AND TRENDS

The following text is based almost entirely on the document entitled The Longterm Prospect for Educational Development 1978-91 issued by the Korean Educational Development Institute (KEDI). The plan discusses the development of high level and technical manpower under six headings, and identifies under each a number of policy tasks.

A.   Strengthening of Education in Basic Sciences.

The following tasks are identified: teaching science as an integrated field at the primary and middle school levels; an interdisciplinary approach at the high school level and above; supply of learning materials at low cost; supplementary programs for the retarded and the gifted; improvement of the in-service training programs for teachers; systematic treatment of environmental problems; increase in the supply of laboratories and equipment; establishment of schools for the gifted in science; revision of the science education promotion law; strengthening research in the basic sciences in the universities and graduate schools; strengthening information exchange activities; and establishing a cooperative network for research in the basic sciences.

B.   Reorganization of the Manpower Development System.

The following tasks are identified: organization of general and specialized courses in vocational education into broad fields to promote flexibility in meeting manpower needs; early identification of aptitudes; extension of school-industry cooperation, in-service training opportunities for employed people; diversification of vocational education system; development of institutions of higher education other than colleges and universities; increasing public investment; more active participation of the private sector in the development of vocational education; and the provision of occupational training for female students to increase their participation in the labor force.

C.   Strengthening of Vocational Education in High Schools.

The following tasks are identified: expansion and regrouping of technical high schools; improving the quality of vocational education teachers; upgrading of agricultural education; intensive development of demonstrative agricultural high schools; enlarging employment opportunities for agricultural high school graduates;

transforming agricultural high schools into centers for rural development; modernizing the commercial educational system and improving the quality of commercial high schools; development of fishery high schools.

D.   Reform of Higher Education.

The following tasks are identified: grouping universities into clusters to include a balanced representation of graduate schools and universities of different kinds in one cluster; limiting enrollment quotas to the establishment of quotas by academic fields; improving criteria for the admission of students to universities; improving the quality of teaching staff; increasing flexibility in requirements for graduation; improvement of curricula; improvement of facilities and equipment; improving the administration of higher education; increasing financial support for higher education, including private universities, expansion and improvement of junior colleges; designation and operation of model institutions; increasing facilities for radio and correspondence colleges; improving student welfare; and expanding the enrollment of women in higher education.

E.   Strengthening of Graduate Education.

The following tasks are identified: providing graduate programs on a bigger scale; developing a cooperative system of graduate schools; reforming the entrance examination system; and quality control of graduate programs.

F.   Promotion of Academic Research and Development.

The following tasks are identified: increasing financial support for research and development; institutionalizing sabbatical leave; reducing teaching hours; increasing opportunities for sharing experiences with other nations; offering scholarships for graduate studies; supporting academic associations; utilizing research findings; establishing an academic research foundation; creating an academic research promotion fund; and establishing an academic research center.

BIBLIOGRAPHY

Gannon, P. J. *The Republic of Korea: A Study of the Educational System of the Republic of Korea and a Guide to the Academic Placement of Students in Educational Institutions of the United States.* American Association of Collegiate Registrars and Admissions Officers, 1985.

Jayasuriya, J. E. *Education in Korea: A third world success story.* Seoul: Korean National Commission for UNESCO, 1983.

Korea Research Foundation. *1986-1987 Study in Korea.* Seoul: Korea Research Foundation, 1986.

Ministry of Education, Republic of Korea. *Education in Korea: 1985-1986.* Issued annually.

Ministry of Education, Republic of Korea. *Statistical Yearbook.* 1988.

Morgan, R. M., and Chadwick, C. B. *Systems Analysis for Educational Change: The Republic of Korea.* Tallahassee, Florida: Department of Educational Research, Florida State University, 1971.

KUWAIT

by
Saad Jasim Alhashil
Associate Professor and Dean, College of Education
Kuwait University, Kuwait

BACKGROUND

The present educational system in Kuwait had its beginning in the 1930s and since then, the system has undergone significant improvement (in the 1960s) to cope with the social and economic changes in the country.

Preuniversity education in Kuwait consists of three stages of four years each: primary, intermediate, and secondary. The state of Kuwait provides free education at all levels, from kindergarten through university. Children start primary school at age six. School attendance through the intermediate level is compulsory for all children. Two governmental bodies, the Ministry of Education and the Ministry of Higher Education, are responsible for providing educational services. The Ministry of Education is responsible for public and private education, as well as for other types of general education. Until 1980, the Ministry of Education had a central administrative system. Since that time, there has been a gradual tendency towards decentralization in administration and management. The recently established Ministry of Higher Education is responsible for Kuwait University and for the Public Authority for Applied Education and Training. The Ministry of Education also provides a free preschool (kindergarten) for Kuwaiti children of ages 4-6 years

SECONDARY EDUCATION

Historically, secondary education consisted primarily of recitation and dictation. However, the educational methods that have recently been adopted comply with contemporary ideas of starting students on the path to applied studies, self-education, and continuous acquisition of skills. The student's means of selection are increased, and educational programs help students enter the world of work or continue their studies at institutions of higher learning.

Both the credit-hour system (which is implemented in a few schools) and the semester system are used in secondary education with continuous assessment of students. In addition, further improvements have been made in secondary education, such as introduction of computers, expansion of disciplines of free activity, addition of more practical studies to the set curricula, introduction of self-education in order to help students pursue their own research, and development of school facilities to meet the requirements of the school curricula. Extracurricular programs at schools include cultural, social, sports, and artistic events, such as competition in reciting the Holy Koran, Arabic grammar contests, free reading, reciting Arabic poetry, newspaper competitions, social studies research projects, school broadcasting and theatrical and musical performances.

Students who cannot pass the intermediate and secondary eduction (general education) examinations are transferred to "parallel education". The course of study in the parallel schools lasts four years, at the end of which the student receives the Vocational Qualification Diploma in his speciality. The parallel school encompasses six speciality programs, namely, offset printing, plumbing, metal welding, concrete carpentry, painting, and decorating. In addition, students study cultural subjects, basic sciences, and general technical subjects.

Kuwait has always been committed to providing educational services to all children, including handicapped youngsters. The first special education school in Kuwait was for the blind. Today, there are thirteen schools for both male and female pupils who have visual, hearing, motor, or mental handicaps. Article 4 of Law 11/1965 concerning compulsory education requires handicapped students with physical or sensory defects to attend special education schools as long as they are able to do so. In 1985-86, 1,881 male and female students were enrolled in special education.

Kuwait has given special attention to the eradication of illiteracy and the further education of adults who were either deprived of schooling or were unable to continue their education. Kuwait has 108 illiteracy eradication centers, of which fifty-six are for males (serving 26,474 students) and fifty-two are for females (attended by 15,013 students), serving a total of 41,487 students. Instruction in the illiteracy eradication centers is in line with the general system applied throughout Kuwait. Student can study up to the secondary stage, which qualifies them to enroll in the university. In a comprehensive drive to wipe out illiteracy in the country, a law was enacted in 1981, stipulating compulsory illiteracy eradication. To encourage students who are pursuing their education at the illiteracy eradication centers, the most successful students are given financial incentives.

Private education in Kuwait began in 1976, to accommodate the desires of increasing numbers of multinational expatriates to educate their children in their native languages. There are currently forty-two Arab and thirty other foreign private schools in Kuwait, including those for the Indian, Pakistani, American, British, Japanese, French, Iranian, and German communities. About 60,000 pupils attend the Arab private schools and 40,000 pupils attend the other foreign private schools.

It is noteworthy that the Kuwaiti government supports the Arab private schools to the tune of about KD 4 million (US$13.6 million) per year, in addition to providing free textbooks to all pupils. Another form of government support is the granting of land required for the construction of schools. The Ministry of Education directly supervises all these schools. The Private Education Department within the Ministry has the authority over their operation.

Foreign students are accepted at public schools if they meet any of the following criteria: (a) the student's father has been working in Kuwait for 20 years or more; (b) the student is the child of a teacher; (c) the student is the child of a diplomat; (d) exceptional cases (as approved by the minister of education).

The Ministry of Education administers a common examination for secondary schools that operate under a two-semester system. Schools operating under the credit-hour system have their own assessment system. When students complete secondary education in either system, they are awarded the General Secondary Certificate (GSC) diploma. This diploma qualifies students (based on their grade point average) to continue their education at either the Kuwait University or the Public Authority for Applied Education and Training.

A center for training teachers and administrators offers a number of educational sessions periodically to teachers and other personnel who work in various departments. Through these sessions, the center acquaints both new and experienced teachers with changes or developments in the school curriculum. The center also trains school principals or headmasters, headmistresses, and vice-principals.

Graduates of the College of Education (at Kuwait University) and the College of Basic Education (at the Public Authority for Applied Education and Training) are appointed as teachers at the general education level. Kuwaiti and non-Kuwaiti graduates of Kuwait University and of colleges other than the College of Education are also selected through interviews. Because there are usually not enough local applicants (Kuwaiti and non-Kuwaiti) to satisfy the demand for teachers, Ministry committees are sent to other Arab countries to recruit additional teachers.

HIGHER EDUCATION

Public Authority for Applied Education and Training

The efforts of the Ministry of Education with regard to technical and vocational education were crowned by the establishment of the Kuwait Institute of Applied Technology in 1976-77. Although the institute was started on the grounds of the former Industrial College, it rapidly acquired new facilities, laboratories, and modern equipment. Recently, the institute joined the newly formed Public Authority for Applied Education and Training, which was created to provide an open-door comprehensive program of education and training. The purpose of this program is to help students develop their potential in occupational areas and by doing so, to help Kuwait develop and upgrade its work force.

The curriculum of the Public Authority focuses primarily on courses that correspond to employment opportunities in industry at the technician level. After obtaining their diploma, graduates can pursue their studies toward a B.S. or B.A. degree, as well as higher degrees in their chosen fields.

The Public Authority encompasses eight colleges, institutes, and training centers, namely, College of Basic Education (males and females - ten sections and specializations), College of Health Sciences (females only - five sections), College of Commercial Studies (males and females - nine sections), College of Technological Studies (males only - twenty sections), Civil Aviation Institute, Telecommunications and Air Navigation Institute, Industrial Training Center, and Water and Electricity Training Center (males and females). These colleges, institutes, and centers provide many types of technical and vocational education and training. In addition to full time training, they offer a number of in-service programs for company employees and individuals.

Programs in the College of Technological Studies include chemical technology (industrial, petroleum), construction technology (building, highways, surveying), electrical technology (electrical machines, transmission, and distribution), electronics technology (biomedical, communication, industrial), and mechanical technology (air conditioning and refrigeration, automotive, marine, power, production, welding).

To qualify for enrollment as a regular student at the Public Authority, an applicant must have successfully completed the general education (secondary level) or equivalent, be able to attend full time, and pass all admission tests. The policy of the Public Authority is to accept up to 10 percent of non-Kuwaiti nationals for each freshman class. Admission tests as well as the minimum grade point average for acceptance are determined by the internal regulations of the college or institute within the Public Authority. Requirements for graduation from a college or institute within the Public Authority include completion of all necessary credit courses as well as specified field training.

The duration of study varies among the colleges and institutes within the Public Authority. The College of Basic Education requires eight semesters (four years in some programs and two years in other programs), the College of Technological Studies requires six semesters (three years), and the remaining colleges and institutes require four semesters (two years). In all of the colleges and institutions within the Public Authority the medium of instruction is Arabic language.

In addition to its role in providing technical and vocational education and training through a wide variety of specialized programs and courses designed to fulfill the country's needs, the Public Authority furnishes social, cultural, and religious care for its students. To encourage Kuwaiti youths to enroll in technical and vocational colleges and institutes, they are offered financial incentives. For example, some colleges give their students monthly grants of KD150 (US$510). No fees are charged from students (Kuwaiti and foreign alike) who are admitted to the Public Authority. This is an extension of the government's policy of free education at all stages.

The Public Authority offers scholarships to foreign students from the Gulf area and to sons and daughters of residents who were born in Kuwait. Two main categories of scholarships are available: those obtained through bilateral agreements between other governments and the Kuwaiti government, and those won by Kuwaiti residents based on their grades in the high school certificate programs and other criteria.

The Public Authority provides housing for foreign as well as Kuwaiti students. A special bus furnishes transportation between students living quarters and the campus.

Kuwait University

Kuwait University was opened in October 1966, five years after the country had achieved independence and full sovereignty. From a modest nucleus of one college (the College of Science, Arts, and Education), thirty-one teaching staff, and 418 students, the University has burgeoned to eleven colleges, a teaching staff of 880, and 17,419 students. The University also includes three centers (the English Language Center, the Community Service Center, and the Evaluation and Measurement Center). A teaching hospital has also been constructed.

The university is equipped with sports facilities, including a swimming pool, a gymnasium, tennis and squash courts, and football fields. In addition, there are two university clubs, one for staff members and employees and the other for students. The university also offers housing accommodation for staff members.

After following the academic-year system for ten years, Kuwait University introduced the credit-hour system in 1975-76. Following its success in the College of Commerce, Economics, and Political Science, the credit-hour system has been extended to all colleges except the College of Medicine.

Kuwait University offers the bachelor's degree in a variety of fields: education, law, commerce, economics, political science, arts, sciences, engineering, medical sciences, and allied health professions. To earn a bachelor's degree, a student must complete the specified number of credit hours (vary from 120 to 144 depending on the program) and pass the required courses. In addition, the cumulative grade point average and the grade point average for courses required in the major must not be less than 3.0 on a 4.0 scale. Engineering degrees take 144 credit hours. Continuous evaluation takes place throughout each semester. Fifty percent of the student's final grade is based on this continuous evaluation, and 50 percent is based on the final examination score. A bachelor's degree generally takes about four years. A medical degree takes three years beyond the preparatory degree of Bachelor of Medical Sciences.

The Language Center at the university is the technical and administrative authority entrusted with teaching all foreign language courses at the university. Foreign language courses are obligatory and constitute part of the general university requirements for graduation. The Language Center and the colleges are responsible for specifying the appropriate objectives and curriculum. The Language Center also prepares and develops teaching materials that are compatible with the requirements of the various colleges. Admission to undergraduate programs is governed by the following criteria: (1) Students must have the secondary school certificate or its equivalent, with a high percentage of achievement at this stage; (2) Secondary school graduates are generally admitted into one of the university colleges, according to their interest and the grade point average at the secondary level (senior high); (3) Persons holding a secondary school certificate from the Kuwait Religion Institute may be admitted to the College of Shari'a and Islamic Studies; (4) Persons holding a diploma from the College of Basic Education (two years after high school) may be allowed to work toward a Bachelor of Education degree; (5) Students holding a diploma from the Commercial Studies Institute (two years after high school) may be admitted to the College of Commerce, Economics, and Political Science.

The university also organizes educational programs on an as needed basis, and may grant certificates or diplomas. For example, the College of Education offers two professional programs (in addition to the undergraduate program) that lead to diplomas in educational counseling and in-teacher preparation. The latter is organized for teachers who come from the Ministry of Education to acquire professional qualifications. Both of these special programs take one and one-half years to complete.

University education in Kuwait is free, but a small registration fee (KD5 or US$17) is collected from students. Scholarship students who study at the expense of Kuwait University or the Kuwaiti government (study-leave students) are exempted from paying registration fees. Scholarship students also receive a monthly allowance as well as book expenses, free room and board, and transportation to and from the campus.

The medium of instruction in the colleges of education, arts, Shari'a and Islamic studies, law and commerce, economics, and political sciences is Arabic. However, in the colleges of science, medicine, allied health, and engineering, the language of instruction is English.

The Student Affairs Office of the university is responsible for extracurricular activities and for making dormitory arrangements for student who need living accommodation.

Kuwait University is committed to allowing students from other Arab countries and overseas to benefit from the country's academic facilities. Scholarships are awarded to foreign students. The proportion of foreign students admitted to the university cannot exceed 10 percent of the total student enrollment. The university provides foreign students with housing accommodation and helps them resolve their social and economic problems.

Faculty appointments at Kuwait University require a Ph.D. or equivalent degree and a record of research publications. In addition to this general requirement, the experience required for faculty members vary depending on the rank: professors require a minimum of fourteen years experience after earning a bachelor's degree or equivalent and a minimum of four years experience as an associate professor at the university level; associate professors require a minimum of nine years experience after a bachelor's degree or equivalent and a minimum of four years experience as a lecturer at university level; instructors require a minimum of nine years experience after earning a bachelor's degree or equivalent qualification.

Applications for faculty appointments are considered by a committee of three: head of the relevant department concerned and two members nominated by the departmental council. The committee presents its recommendations to the dean of the college who in turn refers it to the College Consultative Committee for appointment and promotion. The Consultative Committee forwards the recommendation to the dean who refers it to the vice-rector for academic affairs. The vice-rector presents the final recommendation to the rector.

The College of Graduate Studies

The College of Graduate Studies at Kuwait University was founded by Amiri Decree on August 21, 1977. Following two years of preparation, the first graduate students were admitted in September 1979. The College of Graduate Studies offers a Master of Arts in the College of Arts. A Master of Science degree is available through various units of the university: College of Science (mathematics, physics, chemistry, biochemistry, geology, zoology, botany); Faculty of Medicine (anatomy, pharmacology and toxicology, physiology, microbiology); College of Engineering (mechanical engineering, civil engineering, electrical and computer engineering, chemical engineering). Other graduate programs are expected to begin in the near future.

The academic requirements for admission are as follows: a bachelor's degree or its equivalent from Kuwait University or an academic institution recognized by Kuwait University; a minimum overall grade point average of 2.67 on a 4.0 scale or its equivalent (grade point average in candidate's field of specialization should not be lower than 3.0 on a 4.0 scale or its equivalent). In addition, the candidates must fulfill all additional requirements specified by the department to which they are applying. All applicants are also required to take the Test of English as a Foreign Language (TOEFL) and arrange to submit an official report of the scores to the Office of Graduate Student Programs of the College of Graduate Studies.

In thesis programs, a minimum of twenty-one credit-hours in addition to the thesis is required of each master's degree candidate. The master's thesis should demonstrate the graduate student's ability to carry out research and to present the results in a clear and systematic form. With the approval of the College of Graduate Studies, departments may offer non-thesis programs for the master's degree. In such a case, the graduate student must take a minimum of thirty credit hours in addition to carrying out a research project. Each graduate student must pass a comprehensive written and/or oral examination.

Students need to spend at least two semesters or twelve months from the date of admission to complete all requirements for the master's degree. For full-time students, the normal period for completing a master's degree program is two years of full-time study and research. The maximum time limit for completing all requirements for the master's degree is three years, including periods of withdrawal and interruption of study. For part-time students, the normal period for completing the master's degree program is three years of study and research, and the maximum time limit set for completing all requirements for a master's degree is four years, including periods of withdrawal and interruption of study. In exceptional cases, a student may, with the approval of the program director and the graduate college, be allowed to extend his/her enrollment in the program for a maximum of one or two semesters beyond the four years.

A limited number of teaching and research scholarships are available on a competitive basis, for graduate students.

ISSUES AND TRENDS

Kuwait has made significant improvements to its educational system in the past two decades. It is recognized that education should be linked to the world of work, so as to have educated youths and skilled workers who can satisfy the country's social demands and economic needs. Therefore a comprehensive drive has been undertaken to eradicate illiteracy in the country. One hundred and eight literacy centers have been established throughout the country, and attendance at these centers is strongly encouraged.

Various types of education are provided in Kuwait, including special education, vocational education, and baccalaureate and master's degree programs to encourage students to pursue their interests and to maximize their potential. All education from preschool through university, is provided free of charge. In addition, the Kuwaiti government spares no effort or expense in supporting research and keeping pace with the advanced world.

BIBLIOGRAPHY

Alhashil, Saad, and Odeh, Mohammad. "A Descriptive Study of Teacher Education in Kuwait". Conference paper, College of Education, Kuwait University, 1988.

Arab Information Center. *Education in Kuwait.* New York: Arab Information Center, 1966.

Introduction to Kuwait and Kuwait University. Kuwait: Office of Vice-Rector for Community Service, Kuwait University, 1986.

Ministry of Education. Educational Information Center. *General Annual Report (1985-86).* Kuwait: Ministry of Education, 1987.

Printing Press Affairs Department. *Report on the Development of Education in the State of Kuwait 1984-86.* Kuwait: Ministry of Education, 1986.

LESOTHO

by
Zusi A. Matsela
Associate Professor and Dean, Faculty of Education
National University of Lesotho, Lesotho

BACKGROUND

The school system of Lesotho was started in the late nineteenth century by Christian missionaries from France, mainly by the Paris Evangelical Missionary Society which established the Lesotho Evangelical church, the Catholic church and the Anglican church. All of them worked hard to establish primary schools and to bring literacy to the congregations of their denominations. They also established vocational schools for girls and teacher training colleges to produce their own teachers. It was from these humble beginnings that Lesotho secondary and tertiary education developed.

Higher education in Lesotho originated from the then Union of South Africa (the present Republic of South Africa) of which Lesotho, though a separate political entity, is an enclave. Before 1945 and for some time thereafter, Basotho nationals received higher education from institutions in the Union of South Africa, especially from the University College of Fort Hare, the University of the Witwatersand, the University of Cape Town, and the University of Natal Medical School (at Wentworth). University education in Lesotho started in 1945 when the Catholic University College (later called Pius XII University College) in Roma, was established. The latter college was affiliated to the University of South Africa. By a charter granted by her Majesty Queen Elizabeth II, the college was transformed into the University of Basutoland, Bechuanaland Protectorate, and Swaziland (later called the University of Botswana, Lesotho, and Swaziland), the forerunner of the present universities of Lesotho (National University of Lesotho), Botswana, and Swaziland. The National University of Lesotho was established by Act No. 13.

PRIMARY AND SECONDARY EDUCATION

Primary Education

In Lesotho, primary education lasts seven years beginning at about age six and running to about age twelve. There are in all about 1,200 primary schools with an enrollment of 331,858 and about 6,000 teachers (1987). Over 90 percent of them are church-owned, with the government overseeing curriculum development, instructional effectiveness, examinations, teacher education and salaries for most of the teachers. A primary school leaving examination is given at the end of standard seven and about 40 percent of those who succeed are allowed into secondary and junior vocational schools. However, a large number remain without opportunities for further studies, unless they can use the correspondence facilities of the Lesotho Distance Teaching Center.

At this level, the government has concentrated its attention on curriculum development and evaluation, teacher education and remuneration, and sharing school construction efforts with school proprietors and communities (leaving out maintenance entirely in the hands of the latter groups). Plans are afoot to control levels of school fees and to ensure regular auditing of their accounts. In order to increase the number of trained teachers and to upgrade teachers whose training is not up to standard, the National Teacher Training College and the University have organized in-service education programs.

Secondary Education

Secondary education in Lesotho spans a period of five years, following the seven years of primary education. The academic year for secondary education is two semesters of approximately five months each, and is divided into four quarters. It extends from January to December. The five-year secondary education ends with "Ordinary Level" examinations (Cambridge Overseas School Certificate or COSC and General Certificate of Education examination or GCE) or matriculation-level examination which take place at the end of the fifth year of secondary education. The secondary education curriculum is composed of language (English and Sesotho), mathematics, science, a practical subject (e.g. development studies, bookkeeping and commerce, agriculture, home economics, basic handcrafts, etc.) as the core requirement, and a selection from history, geography, biology, and religious education or bible knowledge. Students may take up to eight subjects of which at least six must be passed at the Ordinary Level for an overall certificate (COSC) to be awarded. A pass in single subjects leads to the award of GCE subject certificates. All secondary schools offer something out of the following extracurricular activities and resources: sports, music and singing, youth organizations, debating and dramatic societies, and the like. Except for the teaching and learning of Sesotho alone, all other secondary school subjects are taught in English which is also used as a medium of communication in the schools during the school week.

All secondary education is paid for jointly by parents, guardians, and the government. The former pay school fees, board and lodging costs, and other student's expenses (books, etc.), while the latter pays teachers' salaries and to some extent also capital expenses for the construction of classrooms, laboratories and workshops. Aside from fees, every secondary school child is also expected to pay a tuition fee of US$12 (25 maloti) per annum to the government. Children whose parents or guardians cannot afford to pay these fees, are not able to attend school, unless they had a sponsor for some or all these charges.

While the largest number of secondary school students in Lesotho are of local origin, about 10 percent in some of the lowland region schools, come from the Republic of South Africa. The 1987 secondary school enrollment stood at 41,138 at 164 secondary schools, with 1,891 teachers. Secondary school teachers are normally recruited by the school management (headmaster, headmistress, or school committees) which make teacher selections and offer appointment contracts initially, and then submit the latter to the Teaching Service Commission in the Ministry of Education for final action.

HIGHER EDUCATION

Institutions

The National University of Lesotho, is the premier higher education institution in Lesotho. It is an academically independent organization, administered by the university council as its supreme governing body. It is associated to the Lesotho government through the Ministry of Education which seeks and guarantees its annual subventions and enactment of its acts, and statutes. The university's chancellor is His Majesty the King of Lesotho who, (head of state) on the advice of the head of government, appoints the vice-chancellor, who is the chief academic and administrative officer of the university. The council, advised and assisted by boards and committees, is responsible for the university's policy formulation. The university senate oversees the development and administration of academic programs of the university. Most of the university's budget comes in the form of the university's subvention from the Government. The Lesotho Government is represented in the university's main governing bodies: board of finance and university council. The management of the university's academic affairs, vests mainly in its senate, while its general administration is the responsibility of the vice-chancellor assisted by the registrar, bursar, faculty deans, librarian, directors of institutes, and the various boards and committees of the university.

The National University of Lesotho (NUL) is the only university in the kingdom of Lesotho. While it has in its council, representatives of the private sector and the general public, appointed by the head of state, the university is generally autonomous in its administrative and academic affairs. It is free to enter into contractual relationships with various organizations and also to establish linkages with whichever organizations or institutions it chooses.

Graduate and postgraduate academic studies are provided by the university in the areas of education, humanities (arts), law, science and social sciences. Lesotho has, aside from the university, several institutions offering tertiary level education: the Center for Accounting Studies (CAS), the Institute of Development Management (IDM), the Lesotho Agricultural College (LAC), the Lerotholi Polytechnic (LP), the Lesotho Institute of Public Administration (LIPA), the National Teacher Training College (NTTC), St. Augustine's Seminary (SAS) and the School of Nursing (SON) soon to become the Lesotho College of Nursing. Three of these Colleges (the LAC, SON, and NTTC) are affiliated to the NUL and offer joint diplomas and certificates between them and the university. The roles of these institutes of tertiary education are varied. The CAS provides professional level training in accounting studies; IDM provides management training at various levels of expertise; the LAC provides certificate and diploma level training in various aspects of agriculture, (animal, plant, soil conservation etc.); the LP trains artisans and technicians in various crafts and engineering studies (civil, mechanical, and electrical); the NTTC trains primary and junior secondary school teachers; SAS provides associate and licentiate level education in philosophy and theology for the clergy, while the SON provides training for nursing staff.

Most of these institutions (except CAS and SAS) are administered by the government, through boards of governors. It is the current policy of the university to phase out certificate and diploma level programs (to be offered through the tertiary institutions), so that it can concentrate as far as possible on undergraduate degrees and postgraduate level education and research. These above-mentioned tertiary institutions offer a variety of certificates, diplomas, and licentiates for the programs they offer. Basic entry qualification is generally the Ordinary Level (COSC, GCE, or matriculation certificate). Their academic staff are generally graded as assistant lecturer or assistant tutor, lecturer or tutor, and senior lecturer or senior tutor. Department heads, deans of studies, and rectors or directors provide administrative and academic leadership.

Undergraduate Studies

The National University of Lesotho offers three undergraduate (bachelor's) degrees in education (B.Ed., B.A.Ed., and B.Sc.Ed.), one in humanities (B.A.), two in law (B.A.Law and LL.B.), one in science (B.Sc.), and two in social sciences (B.A. and B.Comm.). The normal entrance qualification for entry into degree programs is the COSC in the first or higher second class with a credit in English. Science students also require credits in mathematics and a science subject. Equivalent qualifications are also accepted (e.g. G.C.E. or matriculation certificate). Mature applicants (twenty-five years old and over) are selected through the Mature Age Entry Scheme (about 5 percent), with English and mathematics ability tests and interviews. Undergraduate degrees generally take four years. The NUL does not as yet offer degrees in medicine, engineering, dentistry, and the like. But it has planned to open faculties of agriculture, technology, and pure and performing arts within the current Development Plan ending in 1990-91.

The university's academic year extends from August to May with mid-breaks in October, December, and early March. Students' tuition fees are normally (for most students) paid as part of their scholarships from the government or donor agencies. Other fees include board, lodging, book fees, and personal allowances. Government bursaries are granted on loan payable (partially) after degree completion when the graduates are in employment. Students without government or donor support have to be financed by their parents or guardians. The university has accommodation facilities for 1,000 students. The rest of the students enrolled on full-time programs, must find their own accommodation in the nearby village and towns.

While the largest percentage of the students are of local origin, no less than 20 percent foreign students are taken every year, mainly from the Republic of South Africa, Swaziland, Botswana and other States, mainly in the southern and eastern regions of Africa and elsewhere.

Vacancies occurring in the academic and non-academic sectors are normally advertised, and selected suitable applicants are then appointed either on permanent or short term contracts as academic or non-academic staff.

Advanced Studies and Research

Presently postgraduate facilities, mainly at the master's degree level, are available in all the faculties and in the Institute of Southern African Studies (ISAS). The master's degrees offered are M.A. (humanities), M.A. (social sciences), M.Ed. (education), M.Sc. (science and mathematics), M.Comm. (social sciences, proposed) and M.A. (ISAS, proposed). The minimum entrance qualification for courses leading to the master's degrees is normally a high second class pass in the bachelor's degree or equivalent qualifications from other universities. In the case of doctoral degrees, there is a Ph.D. degree common to all subjects and faculties, unless determined otherwise by the university senate. Normal entrance requirement into Ph.D. studies is a good master's degree. The degree of specialization depends on the availability of supervisory as well as library resources, and specialized equipment where necessary.

Master's degrees may be done in one of two ways: either by Mode 1 (which is by course work and by thesis) or by Mode 2 (which is by thesis only). Before a candidate is allowed to proceed with research work on the thesis, the faculty and senate must satisfy themselves on the suitability of the title of the thesis as well as the accompanying statement outlining "how the candidate will follow the research and treat the topic and showing further that the thesis will have suitable academic content and relevance." The Ph.D. on the other hand "shall be a program of supervised research, at the end of which the thesis shall be submitted for examination. In certain cases, to be determined by the Higher Degrees Committee, a certain amount of examined course work shall also be required."

Duration of the academic year for postgraduate studies is normally the same as for undergraduate programs where course work is concerned, otherwise for the whole program of master's degrees a minimum of two years is expected, with a maximum of five years from registration time. For doctoral programs, the duration is a minimum of three years and a maximum of seven years from registration. Curricula depend on areas of specialization and is tailored in accordance with the special needs of the students and the special requirements of the disciplines of study. There are no special requirements in respect of extracurricular activities, except where these may be advocated for special reasons, by the supervisors. Two examiners are normally required for master's degree programs and three examiners for Ph.D. programs, with one of them local (from the university) and the rest external. Except in the special languages, like Sesotho and French where instruction may be in the language concerned, in all other courses at the university, instruction is in English only.

It is the responsibility of the Higher Degrees Committee to recommend to the senate the registration of students for postgraduate studies, basing itself on the submission made by the departments and the faculties; to appoint supervisors to monitor students' progress; to recommend senate's appointment of examiners and to receive and submit their reports to the senate and otherwise to oversee postgraduate programs and report accordingly to the senate. For this to happen smoothly, department heads must receive regular reports from the supervisors concerned.

Tuition fees for master's (and Ph.D.) programs, while currently the same as those for undergraduate programs, are likely to change because of the higher demands on the university for these programs. Here again sponsors (whether staff, government, parent, guardian, or other private donor) are responsible for student's fees (tuition, board, lodging, books, research funds, etc.). However, the university may in a few special cases be able to support some students especially those who are on exchange programs.

Staff who may teach or supervise and examine candidates in a postgraduate study program, are normally holders of senior degrees (Ph.D. and master's degrees), with the added qualifications of expertise in the areas of study concerned and appropriate expertise (senior lecturer or professorial level). So long as students qualify for entry and departmental and university resources permit, there are no territorial limitations to their recruitment. This stipulation might, however, be modified later when local enrollments increase.

The Institute of Southern African Studies may take in postdoctoral research fellows for research purposes in relevant areas, either alone or in conjunction with a relevant faculty. Faculties may also allow research fellows to operate in them with or without the faculties resources. In such cases, these research fellows are expected to present seminar papers from time to time and also to leave copies of their research reports with relevant faculties or institutes, upon conclusion of their research assignments.

ISSUES AND TRENDS

While the $7+5+4$ structural pattern of the educational system of Lesotho seems destined to stay as such for some time, there are various alternative routes now available. A national dialogue in education was held in 1977-78. The dialogue opened the nation's eyes to its rights and obligations in education; for example, the dialogue made it more aware, that the nation had a right to look into or to question the effectiveness of education and to seek alternative strategies for solving the problems of education. The dialogue culminated in the "1982 Education Sector Survey: Task Force Report" embodying policy directives on preprimary, primary, special, vocational, technical, and teacher education. The policies of the document are still being implemented, albeit in modified form as required by varying circumstances.

While in the past all youth in Lesotho schools wanted to matriculate and enter the university, current awareness of the benefits of technical education is succeeding to influence more and more youth to follow a technical education. This is the main trend of postsecondary education in Lesotho today. No effort is being spared to influence youth at all levels of education, to interest them in vocational and technical education. Both the NTTC and NUL produce teachers of vocational and technical education at certificate and diploma levels, respectively. It is also planned to establish faculties of agriculture and technology soon at NUL and to develop the Lerotholi Polytechnic Institution to do more in producing artisans and technicians in the crafts and in basic engineering. The multi-million dollar Lesotho Highland Water Scheme will require a large number of various kinds of engineers as well as social workers, economists, scientists, educators, accountants, and other professional people. This is Lesotho's greatest educational and developmental challenge today and higher education is preparing itself for it.

Lesotho is also giving greater attention to adult and non-formal education more than ever before. There are several institutions (e.g. the Institute of Extra-Mural Studies, the Lesotho Distance Teaching Center, Women's Associations, Lesotho Family Planning Association, the Sesotho Academy, Christian Churches, Community Development Associations, Agricultural and Credit Unions etc.), whose main objective is one or other aspect of national or community development. All of them have training and education listed high among their priorities. Non-formal educational opportunities are being created at all age levels to respond to the needs of non-school goers, school leavers, and dropouts, for example, by means of evening or night schools, correspondence or distance education facilities leading to JC and COSC and short term courses in practical skills development (gardening, fruit production, animal husbandry, and industrial crafts like knitting, dressmaking, and weaving for young women). Attention is also being drawn to business and industrial concerns to have skills training as part of their development plans.

There are tendencies towards a policy of coordinated tertiary and higher education, with the university playing the role of leader, guardian, and supervisor, in one way or another. As new economic development programs are formulated, it is likely that more will be done to train more technicians, scientists, and engineers in conventional as well as newer fields like water engineering. While the Lerotholi Polytechnic and the university are likely to increase their intakes and to diversify into other development-oriented areas of study, it is likely that new institutions will be established to increase the number of students with qualifications at secondary "Advanced Level" for increased intakes into the colleges and the university.

BIBLIOGRAPHY

Lesotho Ministry of Education. *The Education Sector Survey: Report of the Task Force.* Maseru: IMRC, 1982.

An Educational Manifesto Related to the Proposed Five-Year Comprehensive Program for Secondary and High Schools in Lesotho. Maseru: IMRA, 1984.

The Way Ahead into Action. Maseru: IMRC, 1985.

Matsela, F. Z. A. "The Indigenous Education of the Basotho." Diss. University of Massachusetts, Amherst, 1979.

Higher Education Institutions in Lesotho. UNESCO: BREDA Dakar Office, 1987.

LIBERIA

by
Melvin J. Mason
President
Cuttington University College, Liberia
(assisted by W. S. Salifu, S. Naame,
J. Nimley, and L. S. Asanji)

BACKGROUND

The history of higher education in Liberia is traceable mainly through two institutions: the University of Liberia and Cuttington University College.In 1862, the Liberia College, now University of Liberia, was founded and later chartered as a university in 1951. It is a public institution enrolling approximately 6,500 students and operates primarily on government subsidies and appropriations.

Cuttington University College, then known as Cuttington College and Divinity School, was founded in 1889 by the Episcopal Church of the United States of America and the Missionary District of Liberia. It is dependent primarily on tuition and fees, as well as some support from government and donor agencies abroad. Cuttington is the only private, coeducational and church related institution in all of Sub-Saharan Africa that offers a four-year degree program. The institution enrolls 800 students per year.

Liberian higher education includes relatively few institutions thus making the organizational and governance structure easy. Until the proposed National Commission on Higher Education is in effect, these institutions are still largely autonomous from the Ministry of Education which has direct supervisory responsibility for education through the twelfth grade. Each of the degree granting institutions has a charter from the National Legislature and a Board of Trustees appointed under the terms of that charter.

Preuniversity educational structure includes a six-year (grades 1-6) elementary school followed by a junior and senior high school program of three years each. A Bureau of Secondary Education under the Ministry of Education is responsible for overall supervision of educational activities up to grade twelve (end of secondary education).

SECONDARY EDUCATION

The term secondary education in Liberia includes junior high school (grades 7-9) and senior high school (grades 10-12). The Bureau of Secondary Education (under the Ministry of Education) which oversees secondary education has three major goals as indicated in the Ministry of Education report of 1988: to improve the quality of instruction and make the curriculum more relevant to the socioeconomic conditions of the country; to provide the students with greater opportunities and exposure to the world of work; and to increase the number of adequate facilities.

At the junior high level, schools are expected to provide articulation between the elementary and more diversified senior high work; help students explore a variety of work related experiences and identify their abilities and interests; and guide students to information about their country and educational, employment, and training opportunities. At the senior high level, the curriculum is intended to provide a broadly-based program that is geared towards the needs of the national economy, allowing students to move into middle level technical and professional positions; and train students to develop independence and assume responsibility as members of the Liberian society.

The secondary curriculum comprises four major courses: mathematics, social studies, language arts, and science. In addition to these core courses, agriculture, and music are offered in selected schools. Additionally, physical education is required of all schools even if it has to be taught in the classroom due to lack of yard (play) space. Bible is taught, depending on the availability of teachers competent in this area. It should be stated that there is a move to change Bible to religious education when the revised curriculum goes into effect soon. Religious education will include Bible, ethics, and other related content.

Under normal circumstances, the number of years of study should be six. However, there are provisions for repeaters. Students are not allowed to repeat a class for more than two consecutive years.

The academic year runs from March to December with a long weekend for Easter and two weeks in July. Unlike the European system, the long vacation is from mid-December to end of February.

At the end of the ninth and twelfth grades, students take a national examination (in October) administered by the West African Examinations Council (W.A.E.C.) in Liberia in addition to the schools' own examinations which are administered earlier. Grades obtained in the national examination will account for 50 percent of a student's final grade average, with the other 50 percent based on the school's examination.

Extra curricular activities vary from one school to another depending on the interests and needs of the students. Sports such as soccer, volleyball, basketball, and kickball are found in most schools. Some schools have drama, public speaking, and several other extracurricular activities.

Tuition varies greatly depending on the type of school (public, mission, private boarding, or day school). Living expenses vary according to the locale in which the students live. Educational costs for children are generally borne by their parents or guardians.

In Liberia, the medium of instruction is English. There is no discrimination in the access to education. Schools are found all over Liberia. As part of the contract which foreign companies sign with the government of Liberia, they are required to establish schools for children of their employees.

Principals of private and mission schools enjoy the enviable privilege of employing their teachers based on qualification and experience. Teachers for junior and senior high schools are required to have a minimum of a bachelor's degree. Teachers for public schools are employed by the Ministry of Education and assigned to various public schools.

HIGHER EDUCATION

Institutions

As indicated earlier, the University of Liberia and Cuttington University College, the two premier higher education institutions, have similar administrative structures. The president is appointed by the Board of Trustees and is the chief executive officer of the institution. The major line administration divisions reporting immediately to the president are the offices of administration, academic affairs, and comptroller. The academic and administrative offices are headed by vice-presidents at the University of Liberia and deans at Cuttington University College.

The University of Liberia and Cuttington University College have faculty senates with representatives selected from the academic divisions and departments. At the University of Liberia, the faculty senate has the responsibility for all academic policies, including recommendations for faculty promotion and tenure decisions. At Cuttington University College, the faculty senate established in 1987, has still not developed a clear role in college governance.

Faculty appointment, promotion, and tenure procedures are fairly similar on all three campuses. Appointments to academic ranks are made by the president of the institution on the recommendation of the academic affairs office or dean, while initial review for promotion and tenure is handled by faculty committees and forwarded by deans or division chairpersons. The usual criteria of teaching, research, and professional service are listed as the basis for decisions, but teaching is the primary concern.

Some significant structural differences exist between the University of Liberia and Cuttington University College. The University of Liberia includes seven separate colleges, a large Continuing Education Division, a planning and development officer, and operations of three campuses (main campus, Fendell, and medicine). Cuttington University College has no college-type units but operates six academic divisions on the same campus.

The University of Liberia and W. V. S. Tubman College of Science and Technology receive their funding directly from the government of Liberia and nominees to their boards are approved by the president of Liberia. Cuttington University College's charter provides that the Episcopal bishop of Liberia serves as the chairman of the board and appoints its fifteen members from those nominated by the existing board.

Besides the University of Liberia and Cuttington University College, there are nine other tertiary institutions: two teacher education institutions; Kakata Rural Teacher Training Institute (KRTTI), Zorzor Rural Teacher Training Institute (ZRTTI), Ricks Institute (2-year junior college program), W. V. S. Tubman College of Technology (associate degree in engineering technology), Leigh-Sherman Community College (associate degrees in accounting, management, and secretarial science), A. M. E. Zion (associate degrees in accounting, business administration, secretarial science, computer science, book-keeping), Institute of Professional Studies (associate degrees in accounting, secretarial science, certificates in book-keeping and clerk-typing), and the College of West Africa (associate degrees in book-keeping, accounting, economics).

Although some of these tertiary institutes operate with the view of enabling graduates to transfer to the 4-year degree granting institutions, the programs are intended to prepare individuals specifically for the employment market. Like the two leading institutions, the University of Liberia and Cuttington University College, these tertiary institutions are generally autonomous. Although many of the tertiary institutions are privately owned, they have similar administrative structure with a president as the head.

Programs and Degrees

Undergraduate programs are offered at the University of Liberia, Cuttington University College, and the other nine tertiary institutions mentioned earlier.

At the University of Liberia, bachelor's degrees are offered in social sciences and humanities, education, agriculture, business and public administration, science and technology, and law. The duration of the bachelor's degree program is generally four years. Degree in medicine takes five years. A master's degree program is offered in regional planning and takes two years beyond the bachelor's degree. Cuttington University College offers a four-year bachelor's degree in education, humanities, science, nursing, social sciences, and theology.

St. Pauls seminary offer programs in theology, natural and behavioral sciences, and some areas of humanities. Gbarnga School of Theology specializes in theology programs. African Methodist Episcopal Zion Community College offers two-year associate degrees (AA) in business related subjects. College of West Africa also offers two-year associate degrees (AA) in liberal arts, natural sciences, mathematics, and business related subjects. The African Bible College offers bachelor's degrees in bible studies. The Liberia Baptist Theological Seminary offers bachelor's degrees in theology and religious education. The Don Bosco Polytechnic offers two-year associate degrees in business related subjects, teacher education, nursing and several other technical areas. The Liberia Assemblies of God Bible College offers a bachelor's program in theology.

Admission to undergraduate programs is based on the West African Examination requirements, high school credits, and an entrance examination or interview. Individual institutions may have additional or somewhat different requirements.

Tuition for undergraduate studies vary from about US$175 per year at the University of Liberia to US$550 per semester at the Cuttington University College. Tuition for foreign students at the University of Liberia is about US$700-1,000.

Dormitory facilities are available at many of the institutions and board and lodging costs up to US$1,000 per year.

ISSUES AND TRENDS

Current issues in education in Liberia stem from three broad national goals in the Second Four-Year National Socio-Economic Development Plan, 1981-1985: economic diversification, improved income distribution, and Liberianization. The most recent national plan for education, the National Education Plan of 1978-1990, called for expanding access to formal education, improving educational quality at all levels, and strengthening administrative and supervisory capabilities of the Ministry of Education.

The major challenges facing primary education are the improvement of educational quality, teacher quality, instructional supervision, and incentives for teaching. In an attempt to improve educational quality in particular, the Ministry of Education is currently involved in a five-year phased national implementation of the Primary Education Project (PEP). The project is a competency-based instructional system that emphasizes the use of programmed teaching materials in grades 1-3 and professional instructional materials combined with textbooks and supplemental teacher activities in grades 4-6.

Secondary education too has three main issues of great concern: improvement of the quality of the instructional program, ensuring articulation between the PEP and the junior high curriculum, and reduction of the drain on secondary school resources caused by vocational skill tracks that operate in twelve secondary schools.

Higher education which invariably absorbs products of both primary and secondary education also has a number of issues currently under study by policy makers and the institutions concerned: improving the preparation of students entering higher education institutions; financing of higher education including new arrangements by which students can bear more of the cost of their education; improving management and coordination of higher education through the creation of a National Commission on Higher Education; creating an appropriate accrediting system for Liberian higher education; and developing institutions and centers to conduct policy research.

BIBLIOGRAPHY

Harvard Institute for International Development (HIID). *New Directions for Education and Training in Liberia: A Preliminary Survey.* Monrovia: HIID, 1976.

Liberia: Education and Human Resources Sector Assessment. USAID, Bureau for Science and Technology, 1988.

"Report of 1984 National Policy Conference on Education and Training." Cuttington University College, Liberia.

Towards the Twenty-First Century: Development-Oriented Policies and Activities in the Liberian Educational System. McLean, Virginia: Institute for International Research, 1984.

MADAGASCAR

by
Jeanine Rambeloson-Rapiera
President, EESR of Arts (Letters) and Humanities
University of Antananarivo, Madagascar

BACKGROUND

Madagascar was a French colony from 1866 to 1960. The last five years before independence marked the creation of first modern institutions of higher education, with the founding of schools dependent on the French faculties of Marseille, Paris, Bordeau, and Aix en Province. These schools were established in Tananarive, the capital of Madagascar. In 1960, a National Higher Education Foundation (*Fondation Nationale de l'Enseignement Supérieur*) was set up with the Malagasy government sharing the running expenses with the French government which paid the staff salaries. The Malagasy education followed the French system as a model, and an understanding was reached for mutual recognition of degrees.

The purpose of the National Higher Education Foundation was to train executives, good scientists, and skilled technicians, and above all, to train teachers for secondary schools. The Foundation consisted of three faculties (sciences, arts, law); seven higher professional schools; three engineering colleges; three schools of administration; and five research centers.

In 1972, a student movement which widely spread (receiving the support of many people) and struggled for cultural liberation resulted in changes to the cooperation agreement with France and Malagasy educational policy came to be guided by three principles: Malgachization, democratization, and decentralization. These principles were reaffirmed in 1975 by the "democratic revolution". Since 1972 the structure of higher education has remained basically the same excepting for a few modifications.

HIGHER EDUCATION

Institutions

From 1972 till July 1988, higher education in Madagascar was provided by one public university divided into six university centers situated in the main towns of Antananarivo, Fianarantsoa, Toliary, Mahajanga, Toamasina, and Antsiranana. In July 1988, the university centers became six universities. The biggest one is Antananarivo where 75 percent of the students are enrolled. There are no private institutions of higher education. The universities are dependent on the Higher Education Ministry (*Ministere de l'Enseignement Supérieur*) but some higher professional schools are dependent on other ministries and they do not belong to the university. Institutions that fall in to the latter category include *Institut National de Promotion Formation* (INPF), and *Ecole Nationale de Formation Administrative Revolutionnaire* (ECFAR) where civil servants are trained; *Institut Malgache des Techniques de Planification* (IMATEP) for training planners; *Academie Militaire* for training officers; and *Ecole Nationale d'Enseignement Maritime* for training naval technicians etc.

A vice-chancellor appointed by the government is the head of each university. Each university is made up of higher education and research establishments (*Etablissement d'Enseignement Supérieur et de Recherche* or EESR), sometimes called higher schools, which are generally directed by boards of management. These boards elect the presidents of the EESR who are equivalent to deans of faculty. The presidents are helped by "establishment councils". The boards of management consist of members elected from among students, teachers, and administration staff. They do not receive appointments. The higher schools often have heads who are appointed by the Ministry of Higher Education, and in this case, the boards of management are only advisory, or boards are abolished. The EESRs are composed of training departments which are managed by elected leaders. Vice-chancellors, presidents of EESR, higher school heads, and leaders of departments receive small additional allowances and must be native teachers.

There are three types of EESRs and higher schools:

1.   The EESRs where students can register if they have the *baccalauréat* (the final examination of secondary school). Sometimes, there are few further requirements, for example, the students must have obtained, during the examination of *baccalauréat* and during their secondary studies, good marks in the subject they want to study at the university. The EESRs of this type resemble faculties because they give general training, sometimes completed by specialized studies. EESRs of Arts and Human Sciences are found in Antananarivo, Toliary, Mahajanga, and Antsiranana. EESRs of Sciences are located in Antananarivo, Toliary, Mahajanga, and Antsiranana. EESRs of Law, Management, Economics and Sociology are found in Antananarivo, Toamasina, and Fianarantsoa.

2.   The EESRs where native students who want to be registered are selected competitively according to their results in the *baccalauréat* examination. These EESRs give specialized training. The EESRs of medicine are located in Antananarivo and Mahajanga. The EESRs of polytechnic education are located in Antananrivo and Antsiranana (engineering and technology related areas).

3.   The EESRs and higher schools where state competitive entrance examinations are organized. These consist of the EESR of Agronomy in Antananarivo; higher teacher training colleges in Antananarivo, Toliary, Fianarantsoa, and Antsiranana; Higher School of Computer Science in Fianarantsoa; National School of Dental Surgery in Mahajanga; and Higher Training Department of Halieutic Engineering in Toliary.

As indicated above, admission to EESRs require that the students must have passed the *baccalauréat* examination, or have obtained recognized foreign diplomas. One exception is in the EESRs of law, management, economics, and sociology, where students who pass the diploma *capacité en droit* (law diploma), after attending courses in a preuniversity cycle, may enroll in law programs. Before entering university, Malagasy young people must do their national service. Candidates who do not have the diploma of *baccalauréat* may become unregistered students.

There are also research centers linked to universities or to EESRs. Three research centers in Antananarivo (Radio Isotope Laboratory, Art and Archeology Museum, Observatory) are linked to the university. Five other research centers (philosophy, art and archeology, Malagasy, applied linguistics, and anthropology) are linked to the EESR of Arts. These research centers also give specialized courses. There are also other research centers linked to EESRs and universities.

The six universities receive annual government grants. They may also receive donation in kind (books, scientific and pedagogic equipment, etc.). They are members of international university organizations, and are helped by them. They make agreements with foreign universities for teacher exchanges, student training, research, exchange of information, donation in kind, etc. It must be pointed out that the financial resources available to the six universities are inadequate and they are short of scientific and pedagogic equipment.

Programs and Degrees

The primary purpose of higher education in Madagascar is to train good scientists and skilled technicians who are able and ready to contribute for the development of their country. Although the French influence is still evident, great efforts have been made to adjust the programs to suit national needs. Most of the teachers are Malagasy, but the language of instruction remains French. Education at university level fall into two categories: general training, and specialized and professional training.

General training is provided by the EESR of Arts and Human Sciences; EESR of Sciences; and EESR of Law, Management, Economics and Sociology in three academic cycles. The first cycle is composed of first and second years and students obtain the university study diploma, *diplôme d'études universitaires*, when they pass the examinations of the second year. The second cycle is composed of third and fourth years and students obtain the *licence* (bachelor's) at the end of the third year, and the *maîtrise* (master's degree) at the end of the fourth year. The third cycle requires four years at the very least. In the third cycle, students can obtain the advanced study diploma, *diplôme d'études approfondies,* after one year and then can continue to work for 2-3 years towards the first doctorate, *doctorat de troisième cycle.* Several years of furthur work is necessary to obtain the second doctorate, *doctorat d'état* (state doctorate), which is the highest qualification. The object of the first and second cycles is to make students specialists in the disciplines they choose. The third cycle coaches them for research. An academic year lasts twenty-five weeks, usually from November to June, and is followed by two university exam sessions: the July exams and the October resits.

The government formulates the broad outline of the education policy. Sections of the boards of management in the EESR, called *Commissions Pédagogiques,* composed of elected students and teachers, annually review the curricula and propose them to be approved by the vice-chancellor and the minister of higher education. The curricula form the subject of ministerial orders which are published. Each EESR has its own curriculum. In the first and second cycles, courses may consist of lectures, supervised practical work, and field work. From the fourth year (second year of the second cycle) students must write dissertations or thesis and have their viva voce.

The general forms of examinations are proposed by the *Commissions Pédagogiques* and approved by the vice-chancellor and the minister of higher education. But the examination questions are decided confidentially by teachers who also correct the papers. Juries of teachers decide on the exam results. To pass exams and to move up into the next year, students must get 50 percent of the marks at the very least. Dissertations and thesis do not get marks, but are assessed publicly by juries having three or more members. Students are authorized to repeat the first year only once. If they do not pass after repeating, they must change their subjects.

The specialized and professional training category has no common structure, but is drawn up for the purpose of studies. Each higher school or EESR has its own organization and curriculum development, approved by the authorities. In the EESR of medicine, studies last for seven years spread over two cycles followed by one-year of training course. The first cycle is composed of first and second years, and the second cycle comprises third, fourth, fifth, and sixth years. The first year is a premedical program, that strengthens students' knowledge in basic science subjects. Medical studies start really from the second year, and end in a doctoral thesis leading to the award of the Doctor of Medicine degree Practical work is compulsory for medical students. Students may be non-resident students at a teaching hospital after the third year.

In the EESR of polytechnics, training lasts five years and is divided into two cycles. The first year is made of common core syllabus. Students who pass the exams of the first cycle, become higher technicians and obtain university diplomas in technological studies (*diplôme universitaire d'études technologiques*). When they pass the second cycle, they become engineers and receive diplomas of engineering (*diplôme d'ingénieur*). They must write end-of-study dissertations in the fifth year. Third cycle trains for the doctorates (*docteur-ingénieur*). Students go on compulsory training courses in industrial enterprises after the second year.

In the higher teacher training colleges (*Ecole Normale Niveau 3*), training lasts five years and end in the diploma *certificat d'aptitude pédagogique de l'ecole normale* or CAPEN. All students receive grants. Once they receive diplomas, they may join as teachers in the secondary schools or keep studying (in an EESR) to obtain a doctorate. They are authorized to repeat a year, only twice during the whole curriculum development. They must go on pedagogical training courses in the fourth and fifth years, and write end-of-study dissertations in the fifth year. These dissertations consist of research work in pedagogical matters.

In the EESR of Agronomy, training lasts four years and two months. During the two first years, basic knowledge areas are deepened; the rest of the time is devoted to specialized training. The academic year lasts twelve months from the first till the third year, and fourteen months in the fourth year. Studies end in engineer's diploma (*diploma d'ingénieur*) of the EESR of Agronomy. Final dissertations must be written by students who obtain the diploma.

In the Higher School for Computer Science, training lasts four years spread over two cycles of two years each. Students passing the exams of the first cycle become higher technicians and obtain the *diplôme universitaire de technicien supérieur en informatique* or DUTSI. Passing the second cycle, they become engineers. There are competitive examinations for entrance into the first and the second cycles. To have the engineers diploma, student must write a final dissertation. The curriculum also includes training courses in the industry. Students are authorized to repeat a year only once in each cycle.

In the National School of Dental Surgery, training lasts five years spread over two cycles. The first cycle is composed of two years, and the second cycle of three years. Studies end in the degree of Doctor of Dental Surgery. The first cycle deepens basic knowledge of biology. The second cycle is devoted to specialized training. Students are authorized to repeat a year only once in the first cycle. In the fifth year, they have to go on training courses at a hospital. Practical work is compulsory for students during the program.

The Higher Training Department of Halieutic Engineering offers only postgraduate training programs which last one year. The academic year is made of twenty-six weeks of lectures and twenty-two weeks of practical work and training courses in the industry. To obtain the engineer's diploma, students have to pass final examinations and write an end-of-study dissertation.

To sum up, some common points can be brought out regarding specialized and professional training: repeating a year is restricted; practical work and training courses are very important; and to pass exams and to move up into the next year, students must get 50 percent of the marks at the very least. To obtain their diplomas, students have to pass exams and complete dissertations which must be assessed by juries.

All the EESRs and higher schools are also responsible for fundamental and applied research. Research work is performed by teachers and postgraduate students supervised by teachers. There are no official and structured programs. Researchers take the initiative for their work; they have the advantage of being relatively independent but at the same time the independence may result in financial and material difficulties. In particular, the Ministry of Higher Education does not finance research. Everybody has to search for funds and sponsors, and must have the authorization to use them. Researchers lack documentation and contacts with researchers in other countries. Thus, cooperative agreements with foreign universities are very important because they allow access to additional resources. In spite of the shortcomings, Malagasy researchers try hard to make their work known in local and international reviews, publications, symposiums, etc.

Teaching Staff

There are 1,080 teachers in the six universities and 884 of them are Malagasy. Among the 196 foreign teachers, ninety-seven are French. The other are of varied nationalities: Soviet, Canadian, Arab, Vietnamese, German, etc. There are four levels of teachers and university institutions: assistants who are holders of advanced study diploma (*diplôme d'études approfondies*); junior lecturers who hold third cycle doctorate or *agrégation*; senior lecturers who hold state doctorate or *agrégation* in law (for law faculty); and professors and full professors. Holders of other recognized diplomas are also allowed to teach (e.g. *diplôme d'ingénieur*, M.A., Ph.D.). Academics can be helped by *collaborateurs techniques*, who have only *licence* or *maitrîse*. They are not academics, and must carry on their studies to be assistants or junior lecturers.

To be recruited or to be promoted, teachers must have the required diplomas and draw up a file on their curriculum vitae, diplomas, research, work experience, etc. Files are examined by "teacher colleges" which give their recommendations on the candidates both for new recruits and for promotions. The minister of higher education makes the final decision.

The number of teaching hours vary according to the needs of EESR, degrees, and the study program. On average, a teacher has to devote every week three hours for lectures or five hours for supervised practical work. Very often, teachers combine lectures and practical work.

The teaching staff at higher education institutions face several problems. The teachers are few; 1,080 for 35,106 students in 1987-87. So, they have to work overtime. It is hard to get promotion through qualifications to become senior lecturers, professors, or full professors. There are many difficulties in doing research because of the inadequacy of equipment, funds, time, documentation, etc. Moreover, salary increase in being promoted is not very significant. It is the reason why only 6 percent of academics are professors, and only 5.4 are percent senior lecturers. Teachers are short of opportunities and lack contact to participate in exchange programs with other countries.

Student Facilities

There were 35,106 students enrolled in higher education institutions in 1986-87. Seventy-five percent of them were at the University of Antananarivo, 60 percent study human and social sciences, and girls are as almost numerous as boys. Of course, most of the students register at EESRs where there is no competitive entrance examination.

Those who study far off their homes may live in university halls of residence. But rooms and canteens are insufficient and over populated.

More than 50 percent of the students have modest state scholarships. Postgraduate students may obtain loans from the government for work leading to dissertations or thesis. It must be noted that enrollment fees are paltry and duplicated lecture notes are practically free. Admittance to laboratories, library etc. is also free.

In every EESR or school, there are student associations that help in the orientation of new students, defend students' interests, participate in committees in charge of allocating scholarships, and coordinate other student activities. Leisure activities of students (sports, etc), are organized by the University Sport Association and students' associations. Cultural teams take part in national competitions.

ISSUES AND TRENDS

The Malagasy University is inherited from the French, but it has been modified according to the needs of Madagascar history and traditions. Studies are quite selective. For example, at the very most, only 5-20 percent of students pass the exams of the first year (in the EESRs without competitive entrance examinations). But the level of Malagasy higher education is considered good by many countries where Malagasy diplomas are recognized, particularly in France. The Malagasy higher education is at the forefront among African countries situated in the south of Sahara. Of course, there are many problems. In particular, the problem of lack of employment opportunities for holders of diplomas makes it necessary to review higher educational programs for the purpose of structuring them for the introduction of students to professional work related to development needs of the country.

BIBLIOGRAPHY

Evolution de L'enseignement supérieur à Madagascar de 1960 à 1985. Ministry of Higher Education, Madagascar, 1985.

L'Enseignement supérieur à Madagascar - son evolution de 1958 à 1969. Université de Madagascar.

Rajaoson, Francois. *L'Enseignement supérieur et le devenir de la societé malgache.* Diss., 1985.

Razafindrakoto, A. Educational reform and decentralization: An example from Madagascar. *Education on the Move,* Vol. 2. *Educational Reforms: Experiences and Prospects.* Paris: UNESCO, 1979.

MALAWI

by
Ephraim D. Kadzombe
Associate Professor and Principal
Malawi Institute of Education, Malawi

BACKGROUND

Historically, no trace can be made of initiatives by the colonial government to introduce formal education to Malawi. It was in 1875 that the free Church of Scotland opened the first school at Cape Maclear under the leadership of Dr. Robert Laws. Other missionaries followed the example of the free Church of Scotland by establishing mission education all over the country. This trend continued up to 1929. African education was left entirely in the hands of missionaries. By 1940, education was still at primary school level. Secondary education began in 1941 when Blantyre Secondary School opened its doors for form one students. The Catholic Secondary School followed suit in 1943 in Zomba. The first government secondary school to be established was Dedza Secondary School which began in 1950. University education followed much later in 1965 when the University of Malawi came into being.

It should be noted, however, that presently, the provision and control of public education in Malawi is the responsibility of the Malawi government through the Ministry of Education and Culture. The Ministry of Education and Culture (MOEC) has administrative, financial, and academic control of all education institutions (primary, secondary, teacher training, technical, and university levels).

PRIMARY AND SECONDARY EDUCATION

Primary education in Malawi lasts eight years. Pupils enter standard one (grade one) at the age of six years. After eight years of schooling, they write the primary school leaving certificate examination. For the majority of pupils, this is a terminal examination because there are few secondary school places available. A few who pass this exam are selected for secondary school education. There are over 2,500 primary schools but only 80 secondary schools.

The main objective (but not the only objective) of the first four years of primary school program is the attainment of permanent literacy and numeracy, while the major objective of the last four years is the enhancement of literacy and numeracy and an active preparation for life. All eligible children are given access to primary schooling as and when demanded. Under the policy of open access to education, no restriction is placed on the numbers of children who seek to enroll any one year or in any given class.

Since 1988, the primary school curriculum has been undergoing review. The revised curriculum has the following subjects: agriculture, Chichewa (local official language), creative arts, English, general studies, home economics, music, physical education, primary mathematics, religious education, science and health education, and social studies.

After eight years of primary school education, pupils are selected for secondary school education on merit. Secondary school education is of 4-6 years duration. After four years study, a student is awarded a Malawi School Certificate. A further two years would qualify a candidate for a Higher School Certificate in which students specialize in two or three academic subjects plus English. An academic year lasts from October to July of the following year with two weeks breaks each during Christmas and Easter.

Tuition fees are about US$5 per pupil per year while boarding fees are about US$30 per pupil per annum. As can be seen, there is a very heavy government subsidy.

English is the medium of instruction in all schools. Access to education is free in the sense that those who can afford to pay the tuition fees can attend school as day pupils. Students do not reside at the school. Education is as yet not compulsory.

Teaching staff are selected and appointed by a Public Service Commission on merit after passing an interview. Most teaching staff are holders of university diplomas and degrees which are recognized internationally.

Foreign students are normally enrolled but they have to be first cleared by the government.

In 1988, there were 17,601 male pupils and 9,044 female pupils in Malawi secondary schools, giving a total of 26,645 pupils. There were 19,760 students in Malawi College of Distance Education centers made up of 13,936 males and 5,824 females. These were pursuing secondary level studies by distance learning. Secondary school enrollment grew from 15,000 students in 1977-78 to 26,644 in 1987-88.

HIGHER EDUCATION

Higher education is the responsibility of the University of Malawi. The University of Malawi has four constituent colleges: Bunda College which offers diplomas and degrees in agriculture; Chancellor College which has five faculties (Faculty of Education offering diplomas and degrees in education; Faculty of Humanities offering degrees in humanities; Faculty of Law offering honors degrees in law; Faculty of Science offering degrees in the sciences; Faculty of Social Science offering degrees in the social sciences); Kamuzu College of Nursing which offers diplomas in nursing studies; the Polytechnic which offers diplomas and degrees in commerce, engineering, and technical education. (There are three faculties at the polytechnic, namely, applied studies, commerce, and engineering).

A faculty of medicine is on the drawing board and should be operational soon.

The administrative officers of the University of Malawi are the vice-chancellor, registrar, finance officer and assistant registrars, librarian, and the estates development officer. Each college has a principal, vice-principal, registrar, assistant registrar, and deans of faculties. These are the principal administrators at every college. Each subject department is headed by a head of department who work hand in hand with deans of faculties, and they are answerable to the principal of the college.

Several types of undergraduate degree are offered by the University of Malawi: B.A., B.Sc., B.Soc.Sc., B.Ed., LL.B., B.Sc.(Agric.), B.Com.(Accounts), B.Sc.(Eng.), etc.

Admission requirements are at two levels. Level one is for those who have had four years of secondary school education and have been selected on merit. These students spend four years for a degree. Level two is for those who do six years secondary school education and obtain the "Advanced Level" in two or three subjects. These students spend three years in the university and are awarded an honors degree.

An academic year is of thirty-three weeks duration over three terms of eleven weeks long. The first term normally begins in early October and ends about mid-December. Second term begins in the first week of January to Easter. The third and final term starts soon after the Easter break and continues till the end of July. The long vacation is from August to the end of September.

Students pay an annual contribution of US$80 per annum. Board and lodging is paid for by the government. In the academic year 1987-88, the cost of maintaining a student in the university was US$2,800. So university education is very heavily subsidized by the government. Scholarships are also available on a competitive basis. English is the medium of instruction.

Staff are appointed by an Appointments Committee. Those who apply to advertisements are invited and interviewed. If successful they are appointed.

Foreign students are admitted to the University of Malawi but they must be first cleared by the government. They must also provide evidence of financial support while in the university.

At the postgraduate level, both M.A. and Ph.D. degrees are offered by the University of Malawi. These are mostly by research and on a part-time basis. To date, the only taught postgraduate degrees are master's in education (science, mathematics, educational technology, and educational management); M.Sc. (industrial chemistry); and M.Sc. (animal science). These are two year courses. Part time M.A. and M.Sc. degrees run from 3-5 years and Ph.D. degrees are purely by research and take 4-6 years.

There are very wide opportunities for postdoctoral research in education (education at all levels: primary, secondary, and tertiary). The problem, however, is funding. Research institutions exist in the country that encourage research. The University has a Center for Social Research, a Research and Publications Committee and a government institution called the National Research Council. All these encourage research at all levels. A center for education research has just been established (1990) funded by the World Bank. In 1987-88, full time enrollment of the University of Malawi was 2,330. This was made up of 1,837 male and 496 female students. Part-time enrollment at the polytechnic in Blantyre was at 333.

ISSUES AND TRENDS

In both the primary and secondary education, the current trend is increasing enrollments. This trend has created shortages of classrooms, teaching and learning materials, teacher supplies, etc. The Ministry of Education and Culture is responding to these challenges by encouraging communities to build classroom blocks on self-help basis. Some international donor agencies, like the World Bank, UNESCO, World Vision International, and UNICEF are also helping in a considerable way.

The supply of teachers is being tackled in a number of ways. Special programs are under way to train teachers. In 1989, 4,500 school leavers were recruited to undergo a three year teacher training program by distance teaching. The trainees were posted to needy schools after some orientation and briefing. During the summer vacation, they were given intensive training at the teacher training colleges for eight weeks. These eight week sessions will be complemented by distance learning materials which were developed specially for this course.

Some of the teacher training colleges are being expanded so that more students can be accommodated.

One other problem is that there are more school leavers than can be absorbed by the University of Malawi. Although there are technical colleges offering various trades, the places are fewer than the number of candidates wishing to enroll. This created unemployment problems. The University of Malawi has, since 1989, has been admitting non-residential students for degree/diploma studies. This is a very welcome trend because it gives extra learning places to students.

With respect to teaching and learning materials in the primary school, the Malawi Institute of Education in conjunction with the MOEC and with UNESCO/-UNDP funding began to revise the primary school curriculum in 1988. New pupils' books and teachers' guides have been developed for standard one and will be tested in selected schools. The development of these materials will ease the problems of textbook shortages currently experienced in the primary schools.

BIBLIOGRAPHY

Banda, Kelvin N. *A Brief History of Education in Malawi.* Blantyre, Malawi: Dzuka Publishing Co., 1982.

Bude. Odo, and Shaneen Chowdhri. *Improving Primary School Teaching.* DSE - Aga Khan Foundation, 1990.

Holmes, B. ed. *International Handbook of Educational Systems* (Vol 1) New York: John Wiley and Sons, 1983.

Kadzombe, E. D., et al. *Lands and Peoples of Central Africa.* Essex, UK: Longman, 1983.

Malawi Government, MOEC. "Education Service Review - Final Report." MOEC, 1988.

Malawi Government, OPC (1989) *Economic Report.* Zomba: Government Printer, 1989.

Ministry of Education and Culture, Malawi. *Education Statistics.* MOEC, 1988.

Ministry of Education and Culture, Malawi. *Education Development Plan 1985-1995.* MOEC, n.d.

MALAYSIA

by
Isahak Haron
Professor, Faculty of Education
University of Malaya, Malaysia
and
Leong Yin Ching
Associate Professor and Head
Department of Development Education
University of Malaya, Malaysia

BACKGROUND

As indicated in various development plans, Malaysia's educational objectives essentially consist of the following: 1. Strengthening the educational system so as to promote national unity and integration through (a) the implementation, in stages, of the Malay language *(Bahasa Malaysia)* as the medium of instruction at all levels, (b) narrowing the gap in educational opportunities between the rich and poor, and between ethnic groups and geographical regions, and (c) the eventual integration of the education systems of Sabah and Sarawak with the national system. 2. Orientating and expanding the educational and training system to meet national manpower needs, particularly in science and technology. 3. Improving the quality of education in order to reduce wastage and increase its effectiveness in nation building.

The system of formal education in Malaysia basically comprises four levels: primary, secondary (lower and upper), postsecondary or form six, and tertiary. Normally, primary schooling begins at the age of six and tertiary education commences at the age of nineteen. The organizational structure of the educational system consists of four hierarchical levels: federal, state, district, and school. The federal Ministry of Education is the central authority responsible for policy, planning and overall administration. Administrative activities at the state and district level are managed by a director of education and district education officer, respectively. The district coordinates the activities of the district schools, each headed by a head teacher or principal.

PRIMARY AND SECONDARY EDUCATION

Children in Malaysia begin primary education at the age of six and continue for six years. Presently, there are three types of primary schools. While the national primary school uses *Bahasa Malaysia* as the medium of instruction, the national-type Chinese and Tamil schools use Chinese and Tamil respectively as the medium of instruction. The New Primary School Curriculum *(Kurikulum Baru Sekolah Rendah)* with its emphasis on reading, writing, and arithmetic, has been in operation since 1982. Primary education is free, though not compulsory, and pupils progress automatically from one grade to the next. On completion of primary schooling, pupils are promoted automatically to the lower secondary level. While pupils from the national primary schools move directly into form one, those from Chinese-medium and Tamil-medium schools make the transition through a year of "remove class" where they concentrate on improving their proficiency in *Bahasa Malaysia.* The transition rate of enrollment from primary to lower secondary level in government- assisted schools in Malaysia increased slightly from 88.1 percent in 1981 to 90.1 percent in 1986.

As a continuation of the New Primary School Curriculum, the Integrated Secondary School Curriculum *(Kurikulum Bersepadu Sekolah Menengah)* was implemented in the first year of lower secondary schooling in 1988. Following three years of lower secondary schooling, students sit for the Lower Certificate of Education *(Sijil Rendah Pelajaran)* examination. Based on their performance in this examination, students either proceed to two years of upper secondary education (in the academic, vocational or technical streams) or terminate their schooling. The transition rate of enrollment for lower secondary to upper secondary level in government-assisted schools rose from 64.9 percent in 1982 to 67.6 percent in 1986. At the end of two years of upper secondary education, students take the Malaysian Certificate of Education *(Sijil Pelajaran Malaysia)* examination or the Malaysian Certificate of Vocational Education *(Sijil Pelajaran Vokasional Malaysia).*

Students who wish to pursue university education proceed to form six. The transition rate of enrollment from upper secondary to post secondary in government-assisted schools increased from 13.9 percent in 1981 to 15.8 percent in 1986. Following the two year course, students sit for the Malaysian Higher School Certificate *(Sijil Tinggi Persekolahan Malaysia)* examination. In the government's efforts to encourage *Bumiputeras* (Malays and other indigenous people) to take up science, engineering, and medical courses, preuniversity or matriculation classes have been instituted in local universities. Bumiputera students achieving commendable results in the *Sijil Pelajaran Malaysia* can be channelled directly into these classes following which they are eligible for placing in the appropriate courses at the university level. There are alternative educational opportunities for students who do not wish to pursue a university education. Those with *Sijil Pelajaran Malaysia* or *Sijil Tinggi Pelajaran Malaysia* may seek college level education in public and private institutions. College level courses relate to areas such as teacher training, trade, vocational, technial and engineering skills, computer science, accounting, business, and management.

HIGHER EDUCATION

Institutions

Higher education refers to all courses of study above the sixth form level which leads to the award of a degree, diploma or certificate. In the Malaysian context, such courses of study are largely provided by universities and college-level institutions under the control of the Ministry of Education. Private institutions also play an increasingly important role in providing education at the tertiary level.

Prior to independence in 1957, facilities for higher education in this country were relatively limited. At the college level, facilities were largely confined to teacher training and to technical and agricultural fields. Total enrollment at the college level was 2,683 in 1957. With regard to teacher education, various training schemes were formulated to meet the needs of the different school systems. The normal classes, introduced in 1907, conducted training courses during weekends in different language media to prepare teachers for the primary schools and, to a lesser extent, for the lower forms of the English-medium secondary schools. Teachers for the Malay-medium primary schools were trained at the Sultan Idris Training College, Tanjong Malim, established in 1922 and the Malay Women's College in Malacca, set up in 1935. The English-medium residential colleges at Kirkby and Brinsford Lodge in England, established in 1951 and 1955 respectively, and the Malayan Teachers' College in Kota Bharu, Kelantan, set up in 1954, prepared teachers for secondary schools.

Technical education was provided at the Technical College in Kuala Lumpur which began at the Public Works Department's Technical School in 1925. The Technical College in Kuala Lumpur was opened in 1955 and offered three-year courses of study leading to the award of a diploma.

Agricultural education was provided in the School of Agriculture, established in 1931 at Serdang. Its status was raised to that of a college in 1947. The College of Agriculture in Serdang offered a three-year diploma course in 1948 for agricultural personnel in government and quasi-government establishments and the private sector.

The first university in Malaysia, the University of Malaya *(Universiti Malaya)*, was established in Kuala Lumpur in 1962, five years following independence. However, the history and origin of the University of Malaya can be traced to the establishment of the King Edward VII College of Medicine in 1905 and Raffles College in 1929. In accordance with the recommendation of the Carr-Saunders Commission on Higher Education, these colleges were amalgamated to form the nucleus of the University of Malaya in Singapore with full degree granting status in 1949. Ten years later, two divisions were established by the university, one in Kuala Lumpur and another in Singapore. While the division in Kuala Lumpur became the University of Malaya in 1962, the division in Singapore was renamed the University of Singapore, presently known as the National University of Singapore.

With the achievement of independence in 1957, the government began to focus on the development of tertiary education to meet the manpower needs of the country. In 1962, the Higher Education Planning Committee was formed to review tertiary education and to make recommendations for its development. The recommendations of the committee, incorporated in a report in 1967, served as guidelines for the expansion of higher education for the period 1967-85.

The Technical College in Kuala Lumpur and the College of Agriculture continued to be the main centers for technical and agricultural education in the country. As more local teacher training colleges were established to meet the increasing demand for teachers, those in Kirkby and Brinsford Lodge ceased to operate in 1962 and 1964 respectively.

A new institution of higher learning, namely the MARA Institute of Technology *(Institut Teknologi MARA)*, emerged on the local educational scene. Established in 1954 as a center to train Malays in coil and rope making, its functions have expanded over the years to include the provision of sub-professional and professional courses. Some of these courses prepare students for external examinations of institutions such as the Institute of Costs and Works Accountants and the British Institute of Management.

Enrollment at the University of Malaya increased at an impressive rate. The enrollment of 322 students in 1959 increased to 6,672 in 1969, giving an annual growth rate of 197.2 percent. However, student enrollment did not reflect the ethnic composition of the Malaysian population. Of the total student population in 1959, 60.6 percent were Chinese, 19.2 percent were Malays and 20.2 percent were Indians and others. In 1969, the corresponding figures were 52.9 percent, 35.6 percent and 11.5 percent respectively. Furthermore, a majority of the Malay students were enrolled in the arts and humanities (arts, education, and economics and administration) while a majority of the Chinese students were following courses in science and technology (science, engineering, agriculture, and medicine).

A cause of the outbreak of inter-ethnic rioting in 1969 was diagnosed to be the socioeconomic imbalance among the major ethnic groups in the country. This imbalance was perceived to be a consequence of unequal educational opportunities among the different ethnic communities. To rectify this imbalance, greater educational opportunities would be provided for the Bumiputera especially in the area of science and technology at the tertiary level.

In line with the policy of enhancing integration among students in institutions of higher learning, a committee was formed to study campus life at the University of Malaya. In 1971, the Campus or Majid Report contained recommendations which would rectify the ethnic imbalance among the university's student population and enhance the educational opportunities of *Bumiputeras* at the university level. It was recommended that student enrollment should reflect the ethnic composition in the country, not only in relation to the university as a whole but also on a faculty by faculty basis. In admitting students, more weight is to be given to those from the rural areas. In addition, authorities concerned were encouraged to provide more scholarships in the sciences to Bumiputera students. These recommendations, with far-reaching implications for the social mobility of the urban and, in particular, rural Malays through education, were adopted not only by the authorities of the University of Malaya but also those responsible for the administration of universities established in 1969 and after.

Policy changes were also made with the introduction of the Universities and University Colleges Act 1971. Under the Act, the Ministry of Education was made responsible for the general direction of university education and the administration of the Act itself. Further, government control was provided by the 1975 Amendment to the Act when additional heads of government departments or their representatives were appointed to serve as council members of universities. This provision enabled the government to ensure that universities conformed to national policies and decisions made were coordinated.

The period 1970-85 witnessed the restructuring of the educational system in science, mathematics, and technical courses to increase the supply of scientific manpower. MARA Institute of Technology established branch campuses in Sabah, Sarawak, Perlis, and Terengganu to increase its educational and training facilities. Tunku Abdul Rahman College *(Kolej Tunku Abdul Rahman)*, sponsored by the Malaysian Chinese Association and the government, was established to conduct form six classes and sub-professional and professional courses. Apart from the Ungku Omar Polytechnic *(Politeknik Ungku Omar)* established in 1969, four other polytechnics were set up in Kuantan, Alor Setar, Batu Pahat and Kota Bharu. At both certificate and diploma levels, the enrolment of students in science, engineering, technical and commercial courses in colleges and polytechnics was thus increased.

Private colleges and institutions make an important contribution in absorbing the increasing number of school leavers who are unable to find places in tertiary institutions provided by the government. Institutions such as the Goon Institute, Stamford College, Vanto Academy, and the Federal Institute of Technology have been providing young people with training in specific skills relevant to the manpower needs in this country.

As for university education, five new universities together with a number of branch campuses were established. University of Science Malaysia *(Universiti Sains Malaysia)*, National University Malaysia *(Universiti Kebangsaan Malaysia)*, University of Agriculture Malaysia *(Universiti Pertanian Malaysia)* and University of Technology Malaysia *(Universiti Teknologi Malaysia)* were founded in 1969, 1970, 1971, and 1972 respectively whereas Northern University of Malaysia *(Universiti Utara Malaysia)* was established in 1984. Also, the government assisted in the founding of the International Islamic University *(Universiti Islam Antarabangsa)* in 1982. During this period of rapid educational expansion, MARA Institute of Technology and Tunku Abdul Rahman College which hitherto provided only certificate and diploma courses introduced a number of degree level courses as well.

To a significant extent, *Bahasa Malaysia* has replaced English as the medium of instruction in institutions of higher learning provided by the government. This has been accomplished in a series of planned phases whereby large numbers of staff and students have been provided with facilities to learn the national language.

Despite the rapid expansion of higher education, particularly in the 1970s and early 1980s, demand far exceeded supply in terms of the number of places. This has led to a substantial number of Malaysian students seeking tertiary education overseas. The number involved includes both private as well as government sponsored students.

Given the expansion in education institutions, the output from the tertiary education sector also increased. For the decade 1960-70, only 7,357 students graduated from local institutions of higher learning. However, the number of graduates between 1981-85 was 26,800 (55.2 percent in arts and humanities and 44.8

percent in science and technology). The output of local graduates is expected to increase to 52,800 by 1990 (52.6 percent in the arts and humanities and 47.4 percent in science and technology).

As the system of education expanded over the decades following independence, total expenditure increased fifteenfold from 1960 to 1980. The expenditure in 1985 was M$4,493 million (US$1 = M$2.69), an increase of 61.3 percent from 1980. At the tertiary level, the importance of university education is evident from the budget allocation it receives. Expenditure in tertiary education has risen from M$33.6 million in 1970 to M$699.6 million in 1985, registering a twentyfold increase. The proportion of total educational expenditure received by universities increased substantially from 7.1 percent in 1970 to 15.9 percent in 1975 and thereafter, it fluctuated between 13.6 percent and 15.6 percent. Through financial grants and allocations, the government provides over 90 percent of the income of local universities and hence its control of higher education in this country.

Programs and Degrees

In the local public universities, admission to undergraduate programs is based on the performance in the Malaysian Higher School Certificate examination. Degree courses cover a wide range of disciplines including arts, humanities, applied arts, science, technology, applied sciences, and medicine. Course structures and curricula are oriented to meet not only manpower requirements of the public and private sectors but also to instil positive attitudes and values among students.

Joint programs between local private colleges and overseas universities provide yet another alternative for higher education. Although the degrees are awarded by the overseas university, part of the course is conducted locally with the help of academic staff from the university with which the college has a training program. Both undergraduate and graduate courses are available. However, the courses offered tend to be more oriented towards professional areas such as law, management, accounting, economics, and engineering.

Postgraduate studies leading to master's or doctorate degrees are provided by the various faculties of the seven local universities. In addition, postgraduate centers have been established since the late 1970s in universities such as the University of Agriculture Malaysia (Center for Extension and Postgraduate Studies) in 1976 and the University of Malaya (Institute of Advanced Studies) in 1979. Duration of postgraduate courses vary between two years (master's program) and seven years (doctorate program). At both levels, part-time as well as full-time programs are offered.

The development of postgraduate courses in local universities represents a government effort in encouraging more students to pursue these courses in the country. This minimizes the loss of foreign exchange, the outflow of nearly M$1,200 million (US$447.8 million) per year, given the large number of Malaysian students in foreign institutions of higher learning.

Courses at the postgraduate level are conducted in either *Bahasa Malaysia* or English. Dissertations are evaluated both internally by the supervisors and externally by the external examiners. Types of courses and their contents are reviewed continuously to enhance the quality education as well as the employability and marketability of graduates.

During 1985-90, the estimated total number of students pursuing postgraduate studies in local universities is 3,740. Of this total, 1,020 or 27.3 percent will be in the science and professional courses. This is in line with the government's emphasis on managerial, scientific, and technical expertise.

As with undergraduate studies, postgraduate programs come under the purview of the Conference of vice-chancellors. Chaired by the minister of education, the conference comprises not only the vice-chancellors but also the secretaries-general of the Ministry of Education and the Treasury, the director-general of the Public Service Department and the Higher Education Secretariat. Among the functions of the conference is the determination of the type, direction, strategies, and objectives of higher education in the country.

In the area of research, a major portion of the work is undertaken primarily by the academic staff and postgraduate students of universities. Both staff and students are encouraged to engage in research in the various disciplines and areas of their interest, either on an individual or group basis or in collaboration with international agencies. Sources of funding are the universities, private organizations, or foreign institutions and agencies.

With the anticipated shift of the economy towards high technology industries, increasing importance has been given to studies in science and technology under the research and development program of the government. Relative to the fields within science and technology, research in the social sciences and humanities receive limited funding from the government. It has been suggested that the selective allocation of funds marks the beginning of government intervention in the research activities of local universities. In promoting research and development, universities are to establish closer links with the private sector and other established research institutions like the Standards and Industrial Research Institute of Malaysia (SIRIM), the Malaysian Agricultural Research and Development Institute (MARDI) and the Malaysian Institute of Micro Electronic System (MIMOS).

ISSUES AND TRENDS

The social demand for tertiary education, especially university education, is both high and increasing. This is an outcome of the rational behavior of parents and students, given the relatively low direct and indirect private costs of university education and the availability of scholarships to a large proportion of students in the local universities. However, it has been suggested in a study on university education and employment in Malaysia that costs do not appear to be a major explanatory factor. For instance, scholarships were found to be unimportant incentives for pursuing university education. In addition, about 55 percent of Malaysian students in foreign universities in 1985 were privately financed. Even though the total cost of education in an overseas university is higher than that in a local university, students and parents seemed prepared to meet the costs.

Taking into consideration the high educational expenditure at the university level and the fact that demand for education is relatively unresponsive to increases in private costs, it has been suggested that a system of "user charge" for university education with an extensive student loan scheme and with scholarships reserved only for the very deserving students could be introduced. Such measures would increase the internal and external efficiency and equity of university education.

Past experiences indicate that investment in a university education will bring about high returns in the way of good jobs, high socioeconomic status and upward mobility. This outcome, however, may no longer match with present or future realities. A new phenomenon of the "educated unemployed" emerged on the Malaysian scene during the recession years of the early 1980s. While the number of unemployed graduates stood at only 530 in 1978, the total has increased to 40,000 in 1987. At the same time, the number of unemployed graduates has not affected substantively the demand for university education. On the contrary, inability to obtain jobs on leaving school is likely to prompt young people to obtain higher qualifications in enhancing their chances of gaining employment.

In attempting to resolve the dual phenomena of graduate unemployment and the demand for university education, the government has introduced a number of measures. Some of these measures pertain to the request of local universities to increase their intake of new students, the introduction of economic measures to enhance investment opportunities in both the public and private sectors so that more jobs could be created, and the implementation of courses and programs to encourage graduates to become either entrepreneurs or self-employed.

If college and university education is to meet the needs of the Malaysian economy and society more adequately, education and training authorities may have to give less emphasis on manpower projections and more on manpower analysis of the operations of the labor market. It is important for the authorities concerned to ascertain how their graduates fare in the labor market. Such feedback by way of surveys and tracer studies would increase the internal and external efficiency of education and training authorities.

To ensure a better fit between graduates, especially those in non-professional courses, and employment, education and training authorities should consider the adoption of an inter-disciplinary curricula. The provision of a curricula with an interdisciplinary orientation would enable graduates to be trained with flexibility and adaptability in mind. Furthermore, emphasis ought to be given to the development of their affective skills: qualities which are considered to be important by employers.

Another issue which merits concern is private education. Considerable development has been witnessed in the area of private education, particularly at the tertiary level and in the 1980s. Private educational institutions encompass a varied range of instructional programs; from academic, business, computer, and language to secretarial, technical and trade. The present situation in private educational institutions seems to warrant the introduction of measures that will ensure quality education and protect the legitimate interests of students and their parents. However, before any changes are made to the existing regulations or new regulations introduced, it seems necessary that a thorough review of private education be undertaken or, at the very least, a consultative mechanism be established to seek the views of all parties concerned.

A review of the studies, listings, and bibliographies on higher education suggests that research studies in colleges and polytechnics are few and far between. The major portion of research studies has been on university education. In addition, a number of facets of higher education deserve greater efforts on the part of the researchers. Examples of these areas are cost effectiveness of higher education programs and their efficiency, higher education and income distribution, administration and organization of institutions of higher learning, and alternative financing and budgetary procedures in colleges and universities. Resources channelled to research studies in some of these areas could generate information and data to enhance higher education and its contribution to the individual and society at large.

BIBLIOGRAPHY

Fulton, O. "Needs, Expectations and Responses: New Pressures on Higher Education", *Higher Education,* 13(2), (1984).

Higher Education in Malaysia: A Bibliography. Singapore: Regional Institute of Higher Education and Development, 1983.

Isahak Haron. "The Role of the Government in Higher Education." In *The Role of government in Asian Higher Education Systems: Issues and Prospects.* Hiroshima: Hiroshima University, 1988.

Isahak Haron, and Wan Abdul Kadir bin Wan Yusof. "Higher Education and Unemployment in Malaysia", *Jurnal Pendidikan* (Journal of Educational Research), v. 8 (1978-1981).

Malaysia, Fifth Malaysia Plan 1986-90. Kuala Lumpur: National Printing Department, 1986.

Mehmet, O., and Yip, Y. H. *Human Capital Formation in Malaysian Universities,* Kuala Lumpur: Institute of Advanced Studies, University of Malaya, 1986.

Psacharopoulos, G., and Sanyal, B. C. *Higher Education and Employment: The IIEP Experience in Five Less Developed Countries.* Paris: Unesco - IIEP, 1981.

Ungku A. Aziz, et als. *University Education and Employment in Malaysia.* Paris: IIEP, 1987.

MALI

by
Mamadou Traore
Professor
Higher Institute of Applied Research and Training, Mali

BACKGROUND

As Mali gained independence in 1960, it became a preoccupation of the country to search for the most effective tools for socioeconomic development and reinforcement of national consciousness; the search was for a system of education that would respond to the needs of the new environment. It is thus necessary to outline the basis of the reforms of 1962, that established the general structure of the educational system.

Essentially there are five principal objectives that guided the reforms: a quality education that is accessible to the masses; an education that meets the manpower needs of the country in the shortest period and most economically; a standard of education that ensures recognition by other modern countries of educational qualifications offered in Mali; an education that recognizes universal values and is African-centered; and an education that removes the vestiges of colonialism from the minds of the people. Although these ideals, which the reforms sought to emulate were very appealing, implementation has not been easy and has run into many problems.

Structurally, the educational system of Mali consists of primary (fundamental) education; secondary education (general, technical, and professional); higher education; and postgraduate studies.

PRIMARY AND SECONDARY EDUCATION

Primary (fundamental) education in Mali covers the first nine years of schooling, in two cycles: the first cycle includes years 1-6 and leads to the *certificat de fin d'études du premier cycle*; the second cycle follows the first and lasts for three years, leading to the *diplôme d'études fondamentales* and giving students access to secondary education. During these nine years students are not uprooted from their environment. They live with their families and in their communities attending the local village school. While the parents take care of the student's board and lodging and school supplies, the government provides free education. The medium of instruction is French but since 1979, some (experimental) schools teach in national languages (particularly Bamanan).

The reforms also envisage linking the school to real life with the aim of creating dignity of manual labor by harmonious integration of students with the

517

realities of rural work. It is for this purpose that two types of classes are conducted at the fundamental (primary) level: the first type of class where students sit in a class room and receive traditional type instruction; and a second type of class where students learn how to be productive (initiation to activities of a rural, industrial, and artisanal nature). The idea behind this promotion of dignity of labor, to a certain extent, is to create a deterrent to possible exodus from rural areas.

After nine years of primary schooling, students enter secondary education which consists of three types of schools: general and technical, professional, and teacher training. General and technical education is given in the *lycées* where students follow three years of studies leading to the *baccalauréat* which provide access to higher education. Professional education at elementary level takes two years and is marked by the award of *certificat d'aptitude professionelle*, which enables the successful candidates to seek employment as technical workers. At the medium level, the studies take four years and lead to *brevet de technicien*, which provides the students with a higher level *technicien* qualification. Teacher training education trains students to become teachers of the first cycle (at primary level) after two years of studies and teachers of the second cycle (at primary level), after four years of studies.

Mali has seven administrative regions and the "capital" district. Each region has at least one *lycée* and the "capital" district has seven *lycées*. The medium of instruction is French but students may enroll in other language courses (English, Russian, German, Arabic, etc.). There are no boarding schools and students live with their parents. All students who pass the primary school *diplôme d'études fondamentales* are entitled to enter secondary schools, with students below twenty years of age being admitted to general or technical *lycées* and others being directed to professional training schools. School teachers are government employees and at secondary level they are graduates of higher educational institutions specializing in teacher education with a minimum qualification of *licence* in education or an equivalent diploma. Each secondary school is administered by a director.

In the 1987-88 academic year, the general secondary schools had 8,383 pupils with a teaching staff of 1,085, while the technical and professional schools had an enrollment of 5,361 with a teaching staff of 122. The high student to teacher ratio of about forty-four in the technical and professional sector (compared to eight in the general sector) has affected the quality of education in that sector. (The ratio has, of course improved significantly over the last five years).

HIGHER EDUCATION

The reforms of 1962 made a fundamental change in the direction of higher education by deliberately opting for a system of professional schools *(grandes écoles)* over the traditional type of university education. The objectives of higher education in Mali are manyfold: assure training of high level manpower to meet the needs of the country and to provide them continued education; promote development of scientific research; assure continuous adaptation of education to scientific progress and changing life patterns; and diffuse culture.

Higher education is provided in specialized professional schools (*grandes écoles*) and institutes. Access to higher education requires a *baccalauréate* diploma (or equivalent) or passing a competitive entrance examination for those who are employed and having at least three years of experience who do not have the *baccaleauréat*. At present, the majority of high level and medium ranking staff in government employment and in the economy are products of higher education.

The institutions of higher education include: *Ecole Normale Supérieure*, the first higher education institution in the country, created in 1962 for the purpose of training secondary school teachers and presently providing a four year degree; *Ecole Nationale d'Administration*, created in 1963 and providing four year degree course leading to careers in administration, economics, accounting, etc; *Ecole Nationale de Médicine et de Pharmacie*, created in 1968, providing six years training leading to Doctor of Medicine and Doctor of Pharmacy degrees as well as postgraduate specializations (three years); *Ecole Nationale d'Ingénieurs*, created in 1963, awarding four year engineering degrees; *Institut Polytechnique Rural*, created in 1969, providing programs (at both technician and engineer level) in agriculture, animal husbandry, and rural affairs; *Ecole Nationale des Postes et Télécommunications*, providing a four year degree leading to careers in the post and telecommunications department; and *Ecole des Hautes Etudes Pratiques* that trains (two years of studies) junior level staff for private and public enterprises.

Postgraduate education in Mali is provided at the *Institut Supérieur de Formation et de Recherche Appliquee* which offers programs in mathematics, natural sciences, physical and chemical sciences, humanities, and geology. The institute offers a one year postgraduate program leading to a diploma in advanced studies (*diplôme d'études approfondies*) and after a further two years, a doctorate (*doctorat de specialité*). Admission to postgraduate studies is based on a competitive selection process. Since 1973, seventy-eight doctorates have been awarded.

Student enrollment in all the higher education schools in 1985-86 was 6,918, a 32 percent increase from 1979-80. In 1985-86, majority of the students were in the *Ecole Normales Supérieure* (26 percent), the *Ecole Nationale d'Administration* (24 percent), and *the Institut Polytechnique Rural* (17 percent).

Foreign students are admitted to higher education institutions but the institutions themselves do not directly entertain applications. They generally come under government-to-government programs or through sponsorships of international organizations.

All regular students admitted to higher education institutions receive government scholarships to meet their needs including board, lodging, and supplies, although the awards are hardly sufficient to cover full cost. Malian students receive 180,000 CFA francs for the academic year in scholarship money. They also receive an additional sum of 50,000 CFA francs to cover preparation of year-end study memoires. On the contrary, foreign students have to pay tuition fees up to about 250,000 CFA francs per year and their scholarships vary from 35,000-80,000 CFA francs, depending on the country.

Teaching staff at higher education schools is appointed by the government and the minimum qualifications required is a *doctorat de specialité, agrégation, doctoral d'état*, or *diplôme d'ingénieur*. In 1985-86, there were 892 teachers (including part- timers) in all schools, of whom 82 percent were Mali citizens, 11 percent were French and others came from U.S.S.R., U.S.A., and several other countries.

Higher educational institutions come under the authority of the Ministry of Higher Education and Scientific Research. Each institution is headed by a director-general assisted by a director of studies and a secretary-general. Discipline departments within an institution are administered by a head elected by the teachers in a given discipline. The council of professors oversees the examination and evaluation of students. Another council oversees the adaptation of training to employment needs. The educational council addresses matters relating to student discipline.

In general, the academic year begins in October and continues till end of June.

Research at higher education institutions in Mali is very much at its infancy. Educational reforms of 1962 have placed emphasis on training high level manpower to meet country's development needs and as a result resources devoted to research (both financial and otherwise) have been negligible. However, Mali does recognize the importance of research as a basis for education and for various development activities in the country. Thus, some effort at least is being made to require all senior level students to conduct a research project culminating in a report. In addition, the teachers themselves also engage in research activities, though in a limited fashion. In 1986, a National Center for Scientific and Technological Research was also created for promotion of research activities in the country.

ISSUES AND TRENDS

The basis of the educational system in Mali is the 1962 reforms which envisaged rapid education and training of Malian citizens to meet the growing socioeconomic needs of the country. The reforms were intended to be radical: to remove vestiges of colonialism and gear the education system to meet the economic and social realities of a newly independent nation. However, the intended transformation is far from becoming a reality.

The situation today has a lot to be desired. The student population has grown by leaps and bounds but there is a significant imbalance between the demand for education and the availability of facilities. As pointed out earlier, more and more students are going for technical and professional education but teaching staff in this area falls far short of the demand. The reforms also intended to link education to real life. The underlying principle was to create dignity of labor. If this was to be realized, the schools ought to have had facilities for practical work such as workshops but none exist. Excepting in a handful of experimental schools, which have made some headway, the objectives of the reform are far from being achieved. French, which is a foreign language, continues to be the medium of instruction. Only in 1979-80, the use of national languages commenced and that too only on an experimental basis in a few schools.

The professional schools (*grandes écoles*) no longer serve the purpose for which they were established. They have become more like the traditional universities producing large numbers of graduates who now face difficulties in finding employment. A good part of these shortcomings can be attributed, of course, to the serious lack of financing for education. Only 11 percent of the national budget is spent for education at present.

BIBLIOGRAPHY

Coumare, Fode. "L'Enseignement supérieur au Mali - mission, organization, problèmes, défis et dilemmes." Bamako, 1986.

Guedj, P. "L'Enseignement supérieur en Afrique - Instrument de développement ou facteur de desintegration? Une étude de cas - Le Mali (1960 - 1985)" Diss. 1986.

Ministère de l'Education Nationale. *L'Enseignement en République du Mali (Dix ans après la Réforme de 1962).* Bamako, 1973.

Ministère de l'Education Nationale. "Quelle Education pour quel développement? Rapport final de l'étude sur l'education de base." Bamako, 1978.

Ministère de l'Education Nationale. *L'Education au Mali - problèmes, perspectives et priorités.* UNESCO/MEN, Bureau des Projets Education, 1981.

Ministère de l'Education Nationale. *Annuaires des statistiques scolaires du Mali.* Bamako, n.d.

MALTA

by
Charles Farrugia
Professor and Dean, Faculty of Education
University of Malta, Malta

BACKGROUND

Malta has had a long tradition of education. Evidence shows that the country had a state school in the fourteenth century and the origins of the University of Malta itself goes back to the sixteenth century. However, universal primary and secondary education became fully available only at the middle of this century. Now Malta enjoys a comprehensive system of education that spans a wide spectrum of academic provisions, and caters for the majority of the educational needs of its citizens. In spite of its limited natural resources, Malta is endeavoring to provide the highest possible quality education that the small country can afford.

All the administrations, particularly those in power since self-government in 1947, and even more so those following independence in 1964, have invested heavily in education with the strong conviction that such investment enhances the human potential of the population and compensates for the country's lack of material resources. Current educational policy aims to increase the number of young people who attend university, as well as to provide the retraining necessary to improve the skills and competencies of the working population, particularly in the service sector.

Legislation for compulsory school attendance was enacted in 1924, to be improved by the Education Act of 1946 which made schooling compulsory for all children 6-14 years of age. Universal secondary education was introduced in 1970; and the 1988 Education Act has made school attendance compulsory for all those who are between 5-16 years of age. The effective literacy rate is currently at the 87-90 percent level.

Malta has always enjoyed a healthy competition between state and private education especially at the secondary level. At present one third of the school population attend private schools, the majority of which are church run. Tuition in all state schools is free, and the government provides heavy subsidies to private schools so that parents who send their children to private schools are required to pay only nominal fees. Again the state encourages all students to stay on to postsecondary schooling through grants and vacation employment in government and para-statal enterprises. University tuition is entirely free for Maltese citizens, and students receive stipends or allowances during their studies, and wages for vacation work. Since Malta is a small country and students do not have to travel long distances from home to school or university, most students reside with their parents. Low cost accommodation facilities are available for students from Gozo, Malta's sister island, for those students who prefer to live on their own, and for foreign students, who are on the increase.

Structure

The Maltese educational system operates through the following structure: kindergarten, 3-5 years; primary, 6-11 years; secondary, 12-16 years; and post-secondary, 17-18 years; and tertiary, 18+. The secondary schools consist of highly selective academic schools, general area schools, and trade schools. The postsecondary schools include higher secondary arts, science, and commerce schools; vocational schools; and technical institutes.

The Maltese educational system caters also for students with physical, mental, and other special learning needs, and has a built-in system of remedial teaching. In addition, various government departments, para-statal bodies, private industry, the church, and numerous philanthropic organizations provide extensive provisions for informal education.

The Maltese educational system is a highly centralized one with the Ministry of Education providing overall guidance and control. The Department of Education at the Ministry of Education employs the teaching and supportive personnel working in the public sector. The Department also sets curricula, provides teaching materials, school buildings, and the general organizational setup for all formal and non-formal public education.

Legislatively, the Department of Education has jurisdiction also over private education, but in effect these regulate their own academic and organizational affairs. The Education Act of 1988 reinforces and consolidates the beneficial aspects of the previous Acts. For example, it binds the state to provide all types of education, including education for the handicapped. It establishes minimum curriculum requirements for both the primary and the secondary school sectors; it recognizes officially that teachers hold professional status along with the other traditional professions, and sets out a legislative code of ethics for the teaching profession.

Another important innovation in the 1988 Act lays the ground for less state centralization and a higher degree of autonomy for state schools and provides for the establishment of school councils to regulate their non-academic organization and management. In contrast to the highly centralized structure that state schools in Malta have been accustomed to, this provision should prove to be an interesting experiment for local school initiatives, especially as school councils are intended also to act as the forerunners of local civic councils for the wider community.

The Department of Education generally regulates curriculum development through the services of its educational officers who are responsible for different subject areas. However, teachers at the school level are encouraged to develop their own curricula as long as these conform to the general outlines in the minimum curriculum requirements. Specialized curriculum research is carried out by the Faculty of Education at the University of Malta in close collaboration with the Department of Education at the Ministry of Education. Ongoing research takes place in such areas as educational streaming and setting, pedagogical implications of teaching English and Italian as second languages, the effect of nutritional changes on the physical and psychological development of Maltese children, and item analysis of examination scripts.

The monitoring of academic standards is effected through a system of nationality based examinations both at primary and secondary level. At the end of secondary school, students attending state and private schools sit for the "Ordinary Level" of the matriculation examination set by the University of Malta and/or the General Certificate of Education set by British universities. Following two years of higher secondary school, students sit for the "Advanced Level" of the matriculation examination set by the University of Malta and/or the General Certificate of Education set by British universities. Entry to the university and the more lucrative job market depends to a large extent on the level of attainment in the "Advanced/-Ordinary Level" examinations (matriculation or General Certificate of Education).

PRIMARY AND SECONDARY EDUCATION

Children enter formal schooling at age five, and spend six years at primary school. Officially, the objectives of primary school are to provide children in their formative years with basic education and to develop their social skills. In reality, however, many primary schools have transformed themselves into preparatory schools which emphasize rigid formal instruction in readiness for the competitive entrance examinations into the highly selective secondary schools. Children in primary schools learn Maltese, English, mathematics, religion, social studies, science and environmental studies, physical education, arts, crafts, and drama.

At the age of eleven plus, children sit for the secondary schools entrance examination, and depending on the results they achieve, go either to the grammar type state "junior lyceums" and private secondary schools, or to the less academically demanding state "area secondary schools." It should be noted that the Maltese educational authorities are working hard to eliminate the distinctions between the two types of secondary schools.

HIGHER EDUCATION

Institutions

The University of Malta is the major tertiary level institution in Malta. It traces its origins to 1592 when the Knights of Saint John, who at the time ruled Malta, invited the Jesuit Fathers to open a Collegium Melitense in the then newly founded city of Valletta. Later, the college merged with the Kinghts' medical school and with the eventual inclusion of theology and law provided the foundations of the present institution. Over the years, dentistry, arts, science, and architecture were established as additional faculties; more recently education, engineering, and management studies were added to provide a wider range of disciplines to local and foreign students who seek university study in Malta.

The council, the senate, and the faculty boards are the governing bodies of the university. Members of the council comprise representatives of the academic staff, university students, and the Maltese community. The council is the ruling body of the university. It allocates finance, establishes posts, and makes statutes. The senate is responsible for all academic matters, and is composed of representatives from the faculty boards, the institutes, and the student body. The faculty boards coordinate the academic and administrative work of their respective faculties. Members of the faculty boards include representatives of faculty staff, students, and members of the community who have special interests in the academic disciplines catered for by a particular faculty.

The principal officers of the university are the chancellor, who is appointed by the president of Malta; the pro-chancellor, who is nominated by the minister of education; the rector, who is elected by the council; the secretary, who is appointed by the council; and the deans of the faculties, who are elected by the staff of their faculty. The chancellor is the highest official of the university and has the responsibility to ensure that its operations conform with the law. The pro-chancellor deputizes for the chancellor in the latter's absence, and acts as ex-officio president of the council. The rector as the principal academic officer of the university is responsible for its day-to-day administration. He is also the ex-officio chairperson of the senate and the faculty boards. The deans of faculties administer their respective faculties and chair the faculty board meeting in the absence of the rector.

Programs and Degrees

The University of Malta offers undergraduate degrees in the faculties of architecture and civil engineering; arts; dental surgery; economics, management and accounting; education; mechanical and electrical engineering; science; and theology. Faculty of Law offers the degree of Doctor of Law, Diploma of Notary Public, and Diploma of Legal Prosecutor. Faculty of Medicine offers the Doctor of Medicine and Surgery and Bachelor of Pharmacy degrees.

The general entry requirements to degree courses at the university are a minimum of eight matriculation or General Certificate of Education subjects, of which three must be at Advanced Level and five at Ordinary Level. In addition, Maltese candidates must obtain a pass in the local "systems of knowledge" course or must complete successfully the foundation year at the university. In effect this means that students require two years of postsecondary studies following their completion of secondary education at the end of form five, usually at age sixteen. One should note, however, that entry into the medical and dentistry courses is limited and consequently is rendered very competitive so that the entry qualifications are considerably higher. The University of Malta welcomes foreign students and considers equivalent qualifications to the Malta matriculation as suitable for entry into most of its courses.

All faculties offer doctoral degrees in their specific research areas. Furthermore, most faculties offer diploma level courses, often on an interdisciplinary basis. For example, the Faculty of Law, in collaboration with the Faculty of

Economics, Management, and Accountancy runs a diploma course in administrative law. Some courses are offered regularly, others on an ad hoc basis in response to the specific needs of the country, or at the request by any sector of the community.

The most recent development in tertiary education emerge from the rising demands of a more technologically oriented society as well as the need for an increasing number of skilled personnel required by the social policies being implemented. Further major developments are planned for, primarily with the aim of bringing about change to make it possible for more eighteen year olds to attend the university, and to improve in a university context, qualifications for middle-level professions (for areas ranging from medical technology to fish-farming).

A recent important development in the structure of the University of Malta has been the establishment of several institutes able to carry out research and offer degrees and other qualifications in interdisciplinary subjects. The new entities which are independent of the existing faculties, but which work closely with them are as follows: Institute of Health Care, Institute of Energy Technology, Institute of Linguistics, Institute of Anglo-Italian Studies, and Center for Distance Learning.

The duration of courses by the faculties and institutes of the university vary according to their level as well as their historical development. For example, most general and honors bachelor's degrees are of three and four years duration respectively, but those in accountancy and architecture are five years each. The M.D. course is also five years, while the Doctor of Laws program is six years. Diploma courses are of one year duration on a full-time basis or two-years on a part-time basis, except that the Diploma of Notary Public, a full-time program is four years.

A relatively recent important development at the University of Malta has been the setting up in 1986 of the Foundation for International Studies which is devoted to the pursuit of research and training at the international level. In particular, the foundation is interested in promoting and supporting research and training concerning the Mediterranean covering historical, cultural, as well as contemporary socioeconomic and political issues. The foundation's work involves also environmental matters, especially those relating to the common heritage of mankind, marine studies, and human rights. Studies and research on the Mediterranean is a major area of the foundation's concentration.

The foundation is responsible for a number of institutes and centers working in cooperation with it. These include the International Environment Institute, the Mediterranean Institute, and the International Ocean Institute. In addition, the Foundation also hosts the Euro-Mediterranean Marine Contamination Hazards Center set up within the foundation by the Council of Europe, as well as the Mediterranean Social Sciences Network. The International Maritime Institute is also located at the University of Malta.

The university has a special relationship with several Universities in the United States. Since the early sixties it ran a program of Mediterranean studies in conjunction with SUNY Binhamton for students following arts or science courses. American students spend a semester in Malta for which they are awarded appropriate academic credit. A similar program has been run in conjunction with Luther College. Several Maltese have graduated from Luther College which has a

Malta Studies program. At present the university is investigating the possibility of setting joint programs with Notre Dame University. Indeed, during his recent visit to Malta to receive the degree of D.Sc. *(honoris causa)*, Notre Dame's previous president, Professor Theodore Hesburgh advised the university on the setting up of an Institute of Peace Studies within the university. Furthermore, the University hopes to foster links with Georgetown University in connection with the proposed course in diplomatic studies.

Perhaps the most wide ranging contacts that have developed between the University of Malta and American universities have been through the ISEP (International Student Exchange Program) with an average of fifteen American students attending courses at the University of Malta for one or two semesters, and a similar number of Maltese students going to various American universities. Since the commencement of the exchange program in 1983, sixty-three American students have studied in Malta and fifty-six Maltese students have been to the United States. A major contribution to the development and the fostering of such links has been the University of Malta's participation in the Fulbright-Hayes program for the exchange of lecturers. The university has benefited for several years from this program which makes it possible for American professors to teach in Malta, and their Maltese counterparts to experience academic life in the United States.

BIBLIOGRAPHY

Director of Education, Malta. "Report on Education in Malta for the Year 1987." Valletta, Malta, 1988.

Farrugia, Charles. "Malta: System of Education." In Husen T. and Postlehwaite T. N. eds. *The International Encyclopedia of Education.* Oxford: Pergamon, 1985.

Farrugia, Charles. "Challenges Facing the Maltese Educational System." In *The Teacher.* Valleta, Malta: Malta Union of Teachers, 1987-1988.

Farrugia, Charles. "The Professional Development of Teaching Personnel in Small States." In Bacchus, K., and Brock, C., eds. *The Challenge of Scale.* London: Commonwealth Secretariat, 1988.

Ministry of Education. *The Education Act of 1988.* Valletta, Malta: Department of Information, 1988.

Vella, Andrew P. *The University of Malta.* Valletta: University of Malta Press, 1969.

MAURITIUS

by
Surendra Bissoondoyal
Pro-Chancellor
University of Mauritius, Mauritius
and
Devi Venkatasamy
Deputy Director
Mauritius Institute of Education, Mauritius

BACKGROUND

As Mauritius transforms from its colonial past to a modern nation, there is a firm committment to "education for all". Education is considered "*sine qua non*" for greater social, cultural, economic and political equality. There is free education at primary, secondary, and tertiary levels. Fees were abolished for secondary schools in 1979 and for university in 1988. The Ministry of Education, Arts, and Culture is the responsible government authority for policy formulation, planning, and administration related to all educational activities and is headed by the permanent secretary.

The implementation of education policies is undertaken by several parastatal bodies such as the Mauritius Institute of Education, the Mauritius Examinations Syndicate, the Mahatma Gandhi Institute, the Private Secondary Schools Authority, and the Mauritius College of the Air. Theoretically all these bodies are under the umbrella of the Ministry of Education but actually each one is more or less independent, with its own governing body.

PRIMARY AND SECONDARY EDUCATION

Free education is provided for six years of primary schooling, five years of secondary schooling and two years of post secondary schooling. Children begin primary schooling at the age of five.

Access to secondary education is determined by the performance of pupils in the Certificate of Primary Education examination (CPE) which is a national examination held at the end of six years of primary education. The rate of success at the CPE examination is around 55-60 percent. Successful students have access to secondary education; about 25 percent repeat the primary final class and about 25 percent dropout or terminate their formal education.

The CPE examination not only serves as a selection device for secondary education, but also as a streaming device for the selection of pupils for different schools which vary in quality. The five years of secondary education in forms 1-5 lead to the School Certificate and is followed by two years of studies towards the Higher School Certificate. The flow of students in the secondary school is determined by the rates of dropout, repetition, promotion, and the proportion of students who leave secondary education (at the end of form five) as School Certificate holders. On an average, about 15,000 students enter form one, but only about 8,000 pass the School Certificate and about 3,000 complete the Higher School Certificate successfully or pass in two Advanced Level subjects. In other words, only about 20 percent of the student body of form one are the final beneficiaries of higher secondary education.

In Mauritius, primary and secondary education is provided in both state and private schools. The private sector predominates in the provision of secondary education. There are disparities between both types of schools at this level in terms of quality and standards and this is reflected in the result of students in the terminal examinations. With the abolition of fees at secondary level in 1977, the government took over the responsibility of financing secondary education provided in private schools. The Private Secondary Schools Authority was established in 1979 to improve educational standards in the private schools and to act as a paying agent for channelling government funds to these schools. In 1987, about 81 percent of the 125 schools were private. Of the student population of 69,825, 78 percent were in private schools.

The range of government expenditure per secondary pupil is very large; the average ranges from Rs 150 to over Rs 400 per month according to the category of school. On the other hand, secondary education, although free, does have private costs for most students. Students or their families spend much on private tuition. Form five and form six students have also to meet the cost of external examination fees. Such fees are about Rs 1,000 per student on an average. Students who cannot afford to pay the external examination fees, can claim assistance from the Ministry of Social Security. There is a loan scheme for textbooks, and this helps to reduce the financial burden on poor families.

The curriculum in present use in lower secondary schools consists of a core curriculum (English, French, mathematics, integrated science, and social studies), compulsory core activities, and electives. The framework for curriculum for the primary and secondary stages of school education as well as syllabi and instructional and learning materials at the national level, are developed by the Mauritius Institute of Education. The new curriculum framework also highlights the importance of the non-scholastic areas of curriculum such as the development of creative expression, physical education, music, and so on. At present, all students in forms 1-3 take the core curriculum plus electives framework. After form three, they get their preparation in a variety of options offered at the School Certificate and the Higher School Certificate (H.S.C.) examination levels.

The Mauritian society is multicultural. English and French are recognized as the official languages and both are used as mediums of instruction. The dialect in common use is Kreol. Asian language courses (Hindi, Urdu, Tamil, Telegu, Gujarathi, Marathi, Modern Chinese and Arabic) are also available from primary level.

The selection and appointment of teachers for state schools is the responsibility of the Public Service Commission. The secondary school sector employs around 3,500 teachers of both sexes, and academic qualifications are distributed as follows: 10 percent postgraduate qualification holders; 30 percent first degree holders; 26 percent diploma/certificate holders; 15 percent H.S.C. ("A" level holders); 19 percent School Certificate and other qualification holders.

HIGHER EDUCATION

Higher education in Mauritius is provided at the following institutions: the University of Mauritius; the Mauritius Institute of Education; The Mahatma Gandhi Institute; and the Mauritius College of the Air.

The University of Mauritius is by far the most important tertiary institution. It was established in 1965 following a report by Colin Leys. Leys considered that the function of the university should be to aid in national development and that it should concentrate on areas with a quick payoff in terms of economic growth. Three schools (agriculture, administration, and industrial technology) were set up. It is recognized that these original functions are now outdated. While continuing to meet the demand for middle level training, the university is now launching degree courses in areas requiring higher level training.

Following a Visitor's Report on the university in 1987, four schools have been set up, namely, agriculture; engineering; law, management, and social studies; and science (including a Center for Medical Research and Studies). A fifth school, social studies and humanities, is expected to be established in 1990.

It is not strategically desirable to set up a separate Faculty of Medicine for reasons of critical size and therefore the Sir S. Ramgoolam Center for Medical Studies and Research is made to operate within the Faculty of Science. The creation of a School of Social Studies and Humanities has been recommended to provide degree courses in the humanities and to correlate with work in this sector at the Mauritius Institute of Education and at the Mahatma Gandhi Institute.

These developments have given a new orientation to the University of Mauritius which is now offering degree courses in law, economics, the pure sciences, accountancy, computer science, and engineering. Under its multidisciplinary research program and consultancy services, the university is conducting a national survey on a wide range of diseases with special reference to asthma, allergology, and cardiology.

Undergraduate courses at the University of Mauritius are offered at three levels: certificate, diploma, and degree. the courses offered for the academic year 1989-90 include bachelor's degrees in accounting, agriculture, civil engineering, management studies, mechanical engineering, and science. In addition, diploma courses are offered in accountancy, agriculture and sugar technology, building and civil engineering, computer science, land surveying, management studies, occupational health and safety, personnel management, and social work. Certificate level courses are also offered in several technical and business areas.

Since 1968 (the academic year is normally from September/October to June of the following year), only about 10,000 students successfully followed courses at the university, including some non-credit courses and courses for external awards (City and Guilds of London Institute, Chartered Association of Certified Accountants, and Institute of Chartered Secretaries and Administrators). In addition, about 2,500 teachers have been offered courses. The student population in the university is expected to grow rapidly in the future.

The University of Mauritius was set up, as mentioned earlier, to give priority to the training of middle level technical and administrative cadres. Even courses leading to graduate qualifications were not established on a regular basis.

However, in the field of agriculture, both training and research were being carried out even before the setting up of the university mainly by the former College of Agriculture (eventually incorporated in the School of Agriculture of the university) and the Mauritius Sugar Industry Research Institute (MSIRI).

Today students can work for M.Phil. and Ph.D. qualifications not only in agriculture and related disciplines and research, but also in several other fields.

The MSIRI is a research institution of international standing which is primarily concerned with the well-being and development of the sugar industry but has also undertaken worthwhile research in other areas of agriculture. It has also run courses supported by international agencies for students of other countries in areas in which it has great competence.

The university has major ongoing research projects at the Center for Medical Research (studies in allergy, asthma, cardiology, etc.). It has also carried out studies in alternate forms of energy and on a whole range of socioeconomic issues such as nutrition, productivity, and the quality of life in general.

The Mauritius Institute of Education was established in 1973. It is responsible for curriculum development and teacher education, and it performs a vital role in undertaking educational reforms in Mauritius. It has fifteen departments: science education, agriculture education, mathematics and computer education, movement and physical education, home economics and visual arts, design and technology, commerce and business studies, education studies, curriculum studies, English, French, social studies, educational administration and management, and media and teaching aids.

The Institute of Education has played a crucial role in the reappraisal of primary and secondary school curricula and in the development of new curricula at both levels. It is the only teacher training institution in Mauritius and has helped to clear the backlog of unqualified teachers who were working in secondary schools prior to its establishment. Although it has its origins in the training of secondary school teachers, it has since 1983 diversified into the primary and preprimary sectors. Its teacher education courses lead to four levels of certification: teacher's certificate (primary and secondary) generally for G.C.E. "Ordinary Level" holders; teacher's diploma (secondary) for "Advanced Level" holders; postgraduate Certificate in Education (secondary) for degree holders; Bachelor of Education (secondary) for diploma holders. The institute also organizes ad hoc short-term courses at the request of particular ministries.

Following the recommendations of a Commission on Education in 1983 and the government's 1984 White Paper on Education, the institute had to revise its institutional objectives. The responsibility for organizing and conducting examinations was passed on to the newly established Mauritius Examinations Syndicate. The institute is expected to specialize in curriculum development and teacher education including administration courses, and related research activities.

The Mahatma Gandhi Institute was set up in 1970 with assistance from the government of India. This institution concentrates on many cultural activities and courses leading to certificates and diplomas in Indian music and dance, and in Fine Arts. It collaborates with the Institute of Education in teacher education and curriculum development in Asian languages.

The Mauritius College of the Air (MCA) did not originate as a tertiary education institution, but in fact it has been offering supplementary audio-visual education for the primary and secondary schools for the last two decades. It has recently been given the task of using open learning methods to promote the development of education, including that of the tertiary sector. It was established as a corporate body by an Act of Parliament in 1986. The MCA produces educational programs for radio and TV broadcast by the Mauritius Broadcasting Corporation in collaboration with other bodies. To date, the MCA distance learning programs have focussed primarily on cultural, health and child development. Basic literacy programs for other ministries are now under development.

The Mauritius Examinations Syndicate (MES) was set up by an Act of Parliament in 1984 to organize and conduct examinations, award certificates, and cooperate with other bodies. The establishment of the syndicate has made it possible to rationalize and centralize all examinations not falling under the aegis of the University of Mauritius and other external bodies. The long term objective of the syndicate is to Mauritianize the syllabus for many of the examinations which it administers. It has also started to award certificates jointly with the City and Guilds of London Institute in respect of technical and vocational courses.

These higher education institutions tend to work independently of one another, although there are some linkages. Thus, the University of Mauritius and the Institute of Education collaborate in the running of joint courses such as the B.Ed. and in mutual utilization of physical plant and equipment (viz. libraries, laboratories). The work of the Institute of Education and the Mahatma Gandhi Institute is articulated in a certain way. Both institutions work together in the primary curriculum development and in the training of Asian language teachers. The Institute of Education collaborates with the Mauritius College of the Air in the use of distance learning methods, and in radio and television broadcasts and with the Mauritius Examinations Syndicate in examinations.

The higher education institutions depend on the availability of adequate financial resources for their proper operation. Recurrent grants are received from the government every year. The Ministry of Education normally lays down the framework within which annual estimates are prepared. About 80 percent of the current budget of these institutions is for salaries and allowances. About 98 percent of their income is derived from government financial support.

The Ministry of Education, Arts, and Culture has the responsibility for overseeing all the para-statal bodies in higher education. The university is the only autonomous body in this sector. There is no direct control as such over these institutions, which are however expected to implement government policy and follow general government guidelines. Thus the Tertiary Education Commission (TEC) was set up in 1988 to foster the development of tertiary education and training facilities in accordance with the social, cultural, and economic needs of the country. It is also concerned with making optimum use of resources and training available in post secondary education. The four tertiary institutions which come within the purview of the TEC include the University of Mauritius, the MIE, the MGI, and the MCA.

The TEC is expected to act as a mechanism for discussing the main priorities for higher education in Mauritius and for translating these priorities into programs. The TEC is an independent body endowed with adequate powers through legislation, to encourage the institutions to plan their work effectively. The main power of the TEC rests in its control over finance. The TEC is expected to submit periodical reports to the Minister of Education. In this way, the government would be in a position to influence the direction of tertiary education, but would not have direct control over the institutions that undermines their academic independence.

Though the role of research in influencing and shaping educational policies is not always clear in Mauritius, various commissioned enquiries have been instituted to look at issues pertaining to the system of higher education. The Glover Commission on Tertiary Education (1985), the Visitor's report on the University of Mauritius (1987), Dr. Davis's Report on the Mauritius Institute of Education (1988), Lord Young's report Open Learning with reference to the Mauritius College of the Air (1988) are examples of such enquiries. Some of the recommendations from these commissions have been implemented, while others have been shelved and others are still in search of national consensus.

ISSUES AND TRENDS

Certain major issues have emerged within the framework of education in Mauritius and they relate to the role of the tertiary sector, schools, the world of work, teacher education, and the concept of basic education.

The Mauritian system of tertiary education grew up to meet specific needs of the moment without an overall plan reflecting coordination and cooperation in the proper utilization of resources. The time has come for a more coordinated approach to the development of higher education in the island. There is a strong feeling that a restructuring of the organic relationships of the four main participants in higher education, could help revitalize this sector. The National University Act (1982), Manraj Report on the University (1987), Davis Report on the MIE (1988), Young Report on Open Learning and the MCA (1988), all recommend a restructuring of the tertiary system with a view to bringing considerable "economies of scale" in terms of physical and human resources. It is anticipated that the extent and the form of restructuring will acquire new dimensions when the Tertiary Education Commission becomes fully operational or when the new master plan for education is implemented.

Despite the obvious achievements in the education sector in Mauritius, the educational system is subject to some basic weaknesses, one of which has been up to now the lack of technical education facilities. Attempts to reorient the educational system towards technical education failed in the past because they did not match the aspirations of the people. The reconversion of the junior secondary schools with a technical bias to normal state secondary schools was mainly due to this aspiration for academic qualifications. It is now recognized that human resources development should be geared to the growing industrial development of the country.

A recent study Mauritius Towards an Industrial Training Strategy by Bheenick & Hanoomanjee (1988) has put this case succinctly: "In view of the massive economic restructuring that is taking place and its impact on nationwide demand for industrial labor, the gap between the output from the educational system and the requirements of the world of work, which is already very wide, can only widen further in the absence of policy changes." Continuing economic growth will depend upon salvaging the 12,000 annual primary school failures and the 10,000 students who leave the school system at the secondary level, as well as continuing the training of those who are already working. The recently set up Industrial and Vocational Training Board is expected to coordinate and give direction to training in order to optimize human resource development.

It is generally agreed that one of the priorities in educational development is not only to reduce the rate of dropout in the schools but also to ensure that those who dropout, have attained a minimum level of basic literacy and competency. This implies special remedial work, curriculum adaptation, new orientation of teacher education and a reconsideration of the existing examinations. A related priority is to expand and up date technical education and training to meet the challenge of the growing industrial development of Mauritius.

All policies related to upgrading the quality of education involve the improvement of teacher education. The significant social and educational change occurring on the island necessitates a more sustained professional development of teachers. It is also recognized that the heavy investment in curriculum development projects have not brought about substantial changes in classroom practice. There is a strong need to provide in-service training opportunities at crucial points in the teacher's career. This in turn postulates the establishment of a new classification of teacher certificates which would enhance the professionalism and status of teachers and also attract better qualified persons into the profession.

The advent of new information technologies as well as the development of educational technology is having an important impact on the methods of teaching, compelling teachers at all levels to adapt themselves to the needs of learners. The use of open learning methods holds potential for teacher education even in a small island like Mauritius. The main question which arises here is how can distance education be efficiently organized to be an effective supplementary mode of teacher education.

Other issues concerning teacher education relate to the improvement of research in that sector which still remains a sensitive issue, and to the undertaking of more systematic and comprehensive approaches to the evaluation of teacher programs.

Mauritius is progressing in its task of reforming its school curricula at both primary and secondary levels. Both curricula have been reorganized to include a compulsory core and electives which would provide a general basic education to all Mauritian children. Certain general issues have emerged within the framework of basic education. A major issue is the extent of diversification of the curriculum to meet the needs of both average and talented pupils, yet maintaining some uniformity so essential in a pluralistic society.

Another concern is the criteria used for the selection of the essential ingredients within the core curriculum. Do these criteria take into account the kind of skills which should be regarded as basic for the twenty-first century? Should not the concept of core and electives be reexamined to include new curriculum concerns? Other major issues emerge with respect to student achievement. The pertinent issue here is whether promotion should be based entirely on the final external examination at the end of the primary cycle, or as is now proposed, on continuous (course work) assessment. How desirable or practicable can continuous assessment be in a country where paper qualifications carry a great weight and where the public is very sensitive to the selection aspects of some examinations? A continuous assessment project is presently under trial in some selected primary schools in the island.

Questions are also being raised as to the suitability of the present structure of primary and consequentially secondary education. A recently published report by Ramdoyal et al *(Proposal for Structural Reform, May 1990) is proposing the replacement of the present 6-7 year cycle by a seven-year cycle with eight years for slow learners. The report is being studied in the context of the preparation of a master plan for the education sector.*

Many important questions relating to current trends in education have not been touched. The issues raised here are of sufficient importance in the Mauritian context to give priority in this discussion.

BIBLIOGRAPHY

Bheenich, R., and Hanoomanjee, E. *Mauritius: Towards an Industrial Training Strategy.* 1988.

Glover, V. *Report on the Commission of Enquiry on Education 1982-1983.* Port Louis, 1983.

Ministry of Education, Arts & Culture. *A Strategy for Cost Effective Education and Training.* 1984.

Ministry of Education, Arts & Culture. "Extract from National Development Plan (1988-1990), Education." 1989.

Ministry of Education, Arts & Culture. "White Paper on Education." 1984.

MEXICO

by
Ma. de Los Angeles Cavazos
Director, Division of Educational Sciences & Humanities
University of Monterrey, Mexico
in collaboration with
J. A. Guerra, S. G. Guerrero, F. I. Garcia,
L. F. M. Martinez and V. Z. Gonzalez.
Professors at the University of Monterrey, Mexico

BACKGROUND

The Spanish conquest and colonization of Mexico in the early sixteenth century led to the birth of European type institutions of education in Mexico and the consequent demise of Meso-American patterns of education that had existed before. As a result of church and state initiatives in the colonial period, several important institutions of education came to be established. They included *La Real Pontificia Universidad de Mexico* (The Royal and Pontifical University of Mexico) in 1553, *El Colegio Mayor* (The Main College) in 1573, *La Escuela de Grabado* (The School of Engraving) in 1778, *El Colegio de Nobles Artes de San Carlos* (The College of Noble Arts of Saint Carlos) in 1781, and *La Real y Literaria Universidad de Guadalajara* (The Royal and Literary University of Guadalajara) in 1791. Besides these institutions which depended on the viceroy of the New Spain, several other institutions sponsored by the Jesuits also flourished until the Jesuits were expelled in 1767.

The independence of Mexico in 1821 brought many changes in the education institutions of the country. The ideas and efforts of intellectuals and governors of this period focussed on two areas: to make education accessible to the masses; and to enforce the separation of church and state, in activities related to education. Both aspirations were reflected in the laws and public discourses. However, the political instability and financial difficulties prevented the new nation from achieving these ideals.

The present educational structure of Mexico has its foundation in the aspirations of the Mexican Revolution, as synthesized in Article 3 of the 1917 Constitution. Since then, education in Mexico is declared as free and non-sectarian, and is the responsibility of the state. Private institutions are subjected to supervision by the government (Department of Public Education).

The evolution of higher education in Mexico has been conditioned by the inherent characteristics of the Mexican society and its development. Although development of higher education began to receive increasing attention after 1917, it gained social and economic importance only towards the 1930s, responding to population dynamics and the needs of industrialization and urbanization. In 1920, Jose Vasconcelos was named rector of the National Autonomous University of Mexico and since then this institution came to be considered as a model for higher education institutions.

During the period 1940-50, the economic policies of the country influenced the higher educational system to focus on technical education in order to achieve technological self-sufficiency of the country. In these years, the demand for higher education grew, resulting in the establishment of several universities and technological institutes, including the National Polytechnic Institute. Since the 1950s, higher education has experienced further growth at the tertiary level, as citizens have been striving for social mobility. The demand for traditional professions grew in such areas as law, medicine, accounting, administration, and odontology. The growth of higher education took a steep climb in the 1970s with a significant growth in the number of institutions, faculties, and programs. The year 1978 saw the creation of the National Pedagogical University and an elevation of teacher training to degree level. The present economic crisis, however, has had a negative effect on the expansion of higher education and has forced higher education institutions to reorganize their activities.

PRIMARY AND SECONDARY EDUCATION

Primary education is part of the basic education cycle and includes six grades of schooling. It is compulsory and children begin primary school at the age of six years. On completion of primary level, children enter middle education which consist of a three-year secondary school followed by a 2-4 year higher middle school or preparatory level.

Education at secondary school level is offered at several types of institutions: general secondary school, established in 1925, provides general education to students of age 13-15 years, preparing them for higher studies; technical secondary school, established in 1940, provides vocational education to students of age 13-15 years, preparing them for employment; tele-secondary school, established in 1966 on an experimental basis, provides educational instruction through television for students who do not have access to the formal school system, as in remote rural areas; open secondary school, established in 1975 on an experimental basis provides education to adults (over fifteen years of age), with the duration of studies depending on the needs of individual students; and secondary school for workers provides classes similar to those in the general secondary.

The total number of secondary schools in the country in the academic year 1987-88 was 17,640 with an enrollment of 4,347,257 (in all the three years) and a teaching staff of 230,285. The general secondary schools and workers secondary schools together had 43 percent of the total enrollment and the technical secondary schools had 23 percent. The federal government administered 70 percent of the schools, state governments 22 percent, and private sector 8 percent. About 83 percent of the eligible student population attend secondary school. Schooling at primary and secondary levels is free. Courses at secondary level include Spanish, mathematics, physics, chemistry, biology, geography, history, English, artistic education, physical education, and technological education.

The higher middle school or preparatory level consist of three streams: a terminal technical option that trains technicians for positions in farming, industry, and services (graduates of these schools are not admissible to higher education institutions); a technical preparatory option (also called bivalent) that, besides preparing students to continue studies at higher education institutions gives students skills to enter the job market (they receive the *bachillerato* diploma); a propaedeutic option that prepares students to pursue further studies at higher education institutions (the curriculum is general and formative in character, with students receiving the *bachillerato* diploma).

The studies at the higher middle level last 2-4 years and are offered under two modes: structured or open. The structured programs lead to general preparatory, technological, or pedagogical *bachilleratos*. Students who follow structured programs are aged 16-19. A secondary school certificate is a prerequisite. The open preparatory is aimed at those students who have obtained the secondary school certificate but are engaged in work that does not permit them to attend a structured program (regular school). In the academic year 1987-88, there were 1,586,098 students in higher middle schools taught by 101,064 teachers. Of the total enrollment, 23 percent were in the technical option.

There is a great diversity in the curriculum at the higher middle level. However, it has been proposed to create a common core curriculum at a national level for all *bachillerato* programs in order to include a minimum level of achievement in the sciences. The completion of the technical option leads to the title of "middle technician" and the propaedeutic option leads to a *bachiller* diploma. Teachers in the propaedeutic and technical options of the higher middle level are required to hold the *licenciatura* (bachelor's degree).

HIGHER EDUCATION

Institutions

The 1988 statistics published by the National Association of Universities and Institutes of Higher Education of Mexico show 705 higher education institutions in the country distinguishable in three categories: universities which offer a minimum of six professional careers covering three areas of studies, of which at least one is social and administrative sciences or education, and humanities; institutions of technological education which are almost like universities but emphasize engineering, technology and agriculture; teacher training institutions which offer bachelor's and postgraduate programs in teacher training; and other institutions which do not fall into any of the above categories. In 1988, these institutions together had an enrollment of 1,166,674 students at *licenciatura* level, 39,505 at postgraduate level, and 1,192 in teacher training.

The broad objectives of higher education institutions are threefold: to impart higher education, to conduct research, and to disseminate culture. Guided by these objectives, each institution charters its course based on its particular characteristics and capabilities.

Universities are self governing institutions and elect their own administrative organs: university council; rector; and directors of faculties, schools, and institutes. Moreover they are free to establish their internal organizational structures within the provisions of the laws governing universities. The rector is the head of the university and is supported by vice-rectors who together oversee academic and administrative aspects of the institution. In 1971, academic reforms were instituted to restructure higher education in order to increase internal efficiency, improve quality, and meet social needs. In essence, the reforms replaced the schools and faculties with a new structure of areas, divisions, and academic departments. In the earlier system, the faculties operated somewhat autonomously offering degrees in specific areas, while in the new departmental system, the resources are centralized with increased interaction between different areas. At present twelve of the thirty-three institutions which form the subsystem of universities as well as some private universities have instituted the new structure.

Undergraduate Studies

The first degree program offered at higher education institutions is the *licenciatura* and it qualifies graduates to practice a given professional activity. The diplomas which the students receive on completion of first degree studies carry different names depending on the program of studies: in law, the social sciences, and the humanities, the degree is *licenciado*; in the natural science areas, students receive the title of *ingeniero*; in medicine, the title is *medico*; teacher training schools award a *licenciado*; and students in technological institutes receive the title of *technico superior*. In Mexico, there is no intermediate degree between the *bachillerato* and the *licenciatura*. Anyone who abandons studies during the course of the first degree cycle does not receive any qualification and this is one of the problems facing education institutions, particularly the public ones.

The duration of first degree studies lasts 4-6 years, depending on the field of studies and requirements for practical training. In general, the academic year starts in August and runs on a semester basis. Depending on the institution, the exact dates of the beginning and ending of the two semesters vary. There are some universities that function on a quarter basis and they cater primarily to students who desire to complete studies in a shorter time.

For admission to first degree programs, candidates must have completed the higher middle level of secondary education and obtained a *bachiller* or an equivalent certificate. The universities, technological institutions, and teacher training colleges also require candidates to take an admission test, primarily for the purpose of helping students to select appropriate programs of studies.

By law, students are required to perform social services to the community according to their abilities. This requirement must be fulfilled to obtain the degree. Foreign students are exempted from this requirement.

The language of instruction at all institutions is Spanish. However, students are encouraged to use other languages, particularly English and French.

The universities provide ample opportunities for extra curricular activities such as music, theater, dance, painting, sculpture, and sports. The Student Associations provide a focal point for students to interact with the institution's academic and administrative leadership.

Higher education in Mexico is not totally free. The cost varies greatly between public and private institutions. State supported institutions charge a nominal fee which all students can generally afford. The fee is about US$10-50 per semester. On the other hand, private institutions charge from US$400-1,200 per semester for tuition. Fees for foreign students are higher.

It is important to note that almost all institutions of higher education in Mexico are located in the big cities. As a result, very few institutions offer board and lodging facilities, and students generally make their own arrangements. The cost of board and lodging vary depending on the location of the institution, from about US$3,000 per semester in big cities to about US$2,300 in medium size cities.

Both the public and the private sector offer scholarships and financial aid to low-income students based on criteria established by each institution.

Advanced Studies

Postgraduate studies form the fourth cycle of studies in the national educational system and commence after the *licenciatura*. Postgraduate studies are offered at three levels: specialization which focuses on a given field of studies, and is of applied nature with no award of an academic degree; master's degree programs which offer advanced academic training primarily for students interested in teaching and research; and programs leading to a doctorate (the highest academic degree) which is awarded on the basis of advanced knowledge and independent research achievements in a given academic discipline. Most major universities, technological institutions, and teacher training colleges offer postgraduate programs. In addition, there are institutions such as *El Colegio de Mexico* (College of Mexico) founded in 1940, that are exclusively devoted to postgraduate studies and research.

Postgraduate programs are available in a variety of fields: agriculture, health sciences, natural and exact sciences, social and administrative sciences, engineering and technology, education, and humanities. Full-time programs are more prestigious and all students in such programs receive scholarships. Part-time programs are usually pursued by employed persons, who are generally self-financed. Postgraduate programs require completion of a specified number of "credits" but the general duration is about twelve months for specialization, one or two years for a master's degree, and two years for a doctorate (not including time needed for writing a thesis).

Admission to specialization and master's degree programs require the *licenciado* degree or equivalent. Additional requirements may include an admission test, knowledge of a foreign language, and practical experience. Admission to doctoral programs require a master's degree.

The cost of postgraduate studies could vary from US$50 to US$2,000 depending on the institution (public or private).

ISSUES AND TRENDS

The present centralized system of education, implemented in 1917, has become very costly and inefficient. The growth in bureaucracy has made it impossible to control and rejuvenate the system. Centralization cannot deal with problems of the immediate environment, thus, giving rise to a partial vision of education. Moving to a decentralized system would make it possible to better recognize the needs of local communities and would not mean abandoning an integrated approach to national education.

At present there are 4.2 million persons over the age of fifteen who do not know how to read and write. About 20 million adults have not completed primary school and about 16 million have not completed secondary level. Moreover only 54 percent of the 14.6 million students in primary school complete their studies, and only 83 percent of those who complete primary school enter secondary level. Worst affected are the indigenous, rural, and female populations.

Urbanization has generated considerable movement of population and a consequent rise in the demand for educational effort. In areas where population density is reduced, it becomes very difficult to provide education by traditional means.

The Mexican educational system has begun to show scientific and technological stagnation. Local industry is not equipped to provide necessary technology and depends on imported techniques and technology, which are very often not appropriate for the needs of the country. In the face of these challenges, many developments have taken place during the last several years. One such development is the National Institute of Adult Education which is entrusted with the task of eradicating illiteracy among persons over fourteen years of age through non-formal programs and opportunities to complete the basic education level.

The demographic changes, particularly in the mountainous regions, has led to the creation of the National Council of Educational Support, entrusted with the task of taking basic level education to towns with less than 500 citizens. It is a task that has required considerable curriculum and teaching innovation.

The weaknesses of the excessively centralized and bureaucratic system have given rise to a movement for decentralization, seeking participation of state and city governments in the decision making process. This movement, though complex in nature, is producing fruitful results in the administrative, political, and educational spheres.

BIBLIOGRAPHY

Annuies. *Anuario Estadístico: Licenciatura.* (Statistics Annuary: Bachelor's Degree), Mexico, D.F., 1988.

Annuies. *Anuario Estadístico: Posgrado.* (Statistical Annuary: Postgraduate), Mexico, D.F., 1988.

Barron, Toledo, J. *Características del Postgrado en México*. (Characteristics of Postgraduate Studies in Mexico). Anuies, Mexico, D.F., 1981.

Castaneda, Carmen. *La Educación en Guadalajara Durante la Colonia* (Education in Guadalajara During the Colonial Period. 1551-1821). Guadalajara: El Colegio de Jalisco, 1984.

Castejon, Jamie, et al. *Prospectivas del Posgrado 1982-2000* (Prospectives of Postgraduate Education. 1982-2000). Mexico, D.F.: Secretaria de Educacion Publica, 1982.

Nino, M. A., y Otros. "Educación Media Superior, Evaluacion y Alternativas." (Middle Education, Evaluation, and Alternatives). *Educación*. (Journal of Del Consejo Nacional Tecnico de la Educación). Vol. VII. 36 (1981).

Poder Ejecutivo Federal (Federal Executive). *Program Para la Modernización Educativa 1989 - 1994*. (Program for Educational Modernization). Mexico, D.F., 1989.

Prawda, Juan. *Logros, Inequidades y Retos del Futuro Sistema Educativo de México* (Achievements, Inequities, and Challenges of the Future Educational System of Mexico). Mexico, D.F.: Grijalvo, 1989.

Quintero, J. L. " La Decentralización Educativa o el Federalismo Liquidado" (The Educational Decentralization or the Terminated Federalism). Center for U.S. - Mexican Studies, University of California, San Diego. An unpublished investigation report. 1984.

Rangel Guerra, Aflonso. *La Educación Superior en México* (The Higher Education in Mexico). Mexico, D.F.: El Colegio de Mexico, 1979.

Rendon, B., and Dominguez B. A. "Educación Media Basica, Evaluacion y Alternativas." *Educación*. (Journal of del Consejo Nacional Tecnico de la Educacion). Vol. VII. 37 (1981).

Resendiz D. Barnes Dorotea. "Los Estudios de Postgrado en Mexico." (Postgraduate Studies in Mexico). In *Science and Development*. (1987).

Valades, Diego. "La Educación Universitaria." *In Historia de la Educación Publica en Mexico* by Fernando Solana. (History of Public Education in Mexico). (Vol. II). Mexico, D.F.: Fondo de Cultura Economica, 1982.

Vaughan, Mary K. *Estado, Clases Sociales y Educación en México* (State, Social Classes, and Education in Mexico). Mexico, D.F.: Fondo de Cultura Economica, 1982.

MONGOLIA

by
H. Doger
Director,
Scientific Research Institute of Pedagogics, Mongolia

BACKGROUND

The Mongolian revolution of 1921 destroyed the feudal theocratic social order that existed before and created objective conditions for eradication of socioeconomic and cultural backwardness of the country. At the basic stage, it was necessary to eradicate mass illiteracy among the population. In this context, the new Mongolia embarked on the task of creating an integral system of public education.

The campaign to eradicate illiteracy was waged in two directions. First was the extensive enrollment of children in free public schools. Second came the enrollment of adults in an out-of-school educational system. Within one month of the establishment of the people's government, the first primary school was set up and a Department for Public Education attached to the government was created. The establishment of the state system of education was one of the most significant achievements of national education in the Mongolian People's Republic (MPR).

From the first days of the victory of the people's revolution in our country, the social protection and the education of the children became an integral part of national policy. The party and the government of the MPR took a number of basic measures directed at developing establishments for children.

The system of education in the MPR, including preschool education, ensures the unity and continuity of all educational stages. All children can attend school free of charge. After the victory of the people's revolution in 1921, the government of Mongolia adopted the "decree on the development of the elementary school", which is one of the most significant acts. By the beginning of the 1940s, the MPR had attained a uniform system of national education. The number of schools was increased, seven-class schools were opened in the county centers and towns.

From the middle of the 1950s until the end of the 1960s, a developmental process was brought to a close in the course of which the whole Mongolian population had to undergo obligatory elementary training. In the 1950s, ten-class schools were developed which imparted secondary training to matriculation level.

In Mongolia, all schools are state managed and the curriculum is uniform throughout the country. All citizens have equal rights in the acquisition of education. This right is guaranteed by the general eleven-year training of the children as well as by providing opportunities for the young people who wish to continue schooling in institutions of higher education. All children have the right to be trained and have lessons in the mother tongue. They have to enter school when they have reached their seventh birthday. A goal of tremendous social significance is the gradual general education of all school-age children. The compulsory elementary education for children of school-age had been realized in 1970 throughout the country. The efforts then focussed on sending all children through the eight-class school. The public educational system in Mongolia is based on the following principles: the equality of all citizens of the MPR in receiving education irrespective of the origin, social or property status, race or nationality, sex, language, attitude to religion, occupation, residence or other qualifications; universal secondary education and vocational training for the younger generation; state and social control of all educational establishments; free education and full upkeep of school-age children by the state, with allowances and benefits to pupils and students, free issues of school textbooks, and the provision of material aid in various forms; uniformity of the public educational system; unity of education and communist upbringing; cooperation between educational establishments, parents, public organizations and work collectives in raising the younger generation; coeducation; gradual progress of education in step with the latest developments in science, technology, and culture;　and a secular education with no religious influence.

PRIMARY AND SECONDARY EDUCATION

In Mongolia, the schools are of a polytechnical nature and follow the principle of combining education with productive work. At present, education for work and vocational guidance are integral parts of the curriculum.

Apart from the general eight-class and eleven-class schools there are schools which emphasize certain subjects, provide evening classes, or give correspondence courses for working young people. Also there are special schools for physically and mentally handicapped children.

The school curriculum is uniform and specifies the subjects to be taught at schools in different years and the number of hours to be spent for each. The curriculum includes humanities, natural sciences, mathematics, labor training, and is intended to give the children a comprehensive education. The Ministry of Education and the Research Institute of Pedagogy has made some recent (1988-89) changes to the curriculum by including new subjects such as the "fundamentals of information science and computer techniques" course in the ninth and tenth forms, and the "fundamentals of production and agriculture" course in the sixth, seventh, and ninth forms. The following maximum number of school hours per week is established for general secondary schools: first form - 22 hours, second and third forms - 24 hours, fourth form - 25 hours, fifth form - 29 hours, sixth form - 33 hours, seventh form - 36 hours, eighth and ninth forms - 34 hours, and tenth and eleventh forms - 32 hours. Pupils wishing to extend their knowledge beyond the standard subject areas of physics-mathematics, chemistry-biology, social science-humanities, or technical cycle are offered optional courses for which two hours per week are allotted in the seventh and eighth forms and three hours per week in the ninth and tenth forms, over the standard curriculum.

Great importance is attached to the execution of independent work in various fields, exercises in the laboratory, polytechnical lessons, and productive work in order to deepen the connection between the lessons and the practice of socialist construction. Pupils are given a course of labor practice which continues twelve days in the ninth form. Additional time is allotted for socially useful, productive work: three hours per week for forms 7-8, and four hours per week for forms 9-10. Along with the transition to the new curriculum, the quality of lessons in the fundamentals of sciences has been improved. School facilities have also improved significantly over the years. Between 1985 and 1990, school capacity was expanded by 48,000 places. Nearly all centers of agricultural associations and state farms have eight-class schools or secondary schools which lead to matriculation standard. Today, more than 430,000 students receive education at over 600 comprehensive schools staffed by about 13,000 teachers.

Vocational education is also an important segment of the educational system in Mongolia. Every year, 16,000 boys and girls are trained in about 100 vocations important to the national economy. Pupils coming from the eight-class and eleven-class schools can enter vocational schools. The period of training comprises 1-3 years, dependent on the vocation. Both daytime and evening classes are offered. The pupils at the vocational schools are fully maintained by the state. They are provided with clothing, food, lodging, tuitions, textbooks, and teaching aids free of charge.

The main objectives of vocational schools are to train skilled workers to meet the demands created by social, economic, scientific, and technological progress; to educate specialists capable of operating new industrial facilities by mastering and developing new technologies; to educate future workers as conscious and active members of the socialist society; to cultivate respect for Mongolian laws and socialist rules of conduct and to develop an awareness of the necessity to observe them; and to give adequate physical education to improve the trainees' health.

Practical training in industry is conducted at various enterprises, factories, and other work places where modern equipment and facilities are available.

Graduates of vocational secondary schools are issued a secondary education diploma awarding them a grade, class, or category in a particular trade. Those who have distinguished themselves are awarded an honors diploma.

HIGHER EDUCATION

On the tenth Party Congress of the MRPP (1940), the decision was taken to establish a university. In 1942, the first university of Mongolia, the Mongolian State University, was opened. This was followed by the establishment of several other institutions: University for Agriculture in 1958; University for Economy in 1967; the University for Medicine in 1961; Polytechnical University in 1969; Pedagogical University in Khoud in 1979; and the Russian Language Institute in 1979. These institutions are playing the role of training manpower to support the economic and cultural development of the country. Moreover, high schools and correspondence courses have been included in the system of university training since 1962. Since 1973, the universities also offer preparatory courses to young people (with matriculation standard) to prepare them for entrance examinations that lead to university studies.

At present, 16,000 students are trained at Mongolian universities in more than 130 branches of study. The universities also offer continuing education. Teaching staff includes many professors and lecturers from the USSR and GDR. Students and candidates from socialist and other countries are also enrolled. The study period of training at the Medical University is six years, at the Pedagogical University is four years and at the other universities is five years. A quarter of all students live in university hostels.

Graduates of higher education establishments are issued a qualification diploma of the given speciality and a pectoral badge.

All universities have postgraduate courses. The study period is three years. After defending a dissertation, the postgraduate student receives the academic rank of "candidate of science". More than 60 percent of all research activities are carried out in mutual cooperation with the Academy of Science of the MPR, research institutes and their branches, and universities of other countries. A third of all specialists with an academic degree who go in for scientific work in research institutes are university teachers. Three-fifths of all university teachers pursue some form of research.

In addition to the universities, Mongolia also has a system of colleges that offer professional and technical training in specialized fields: railway traffic, civil engineering, agriculture, forestry, water supply, etc. The study period varies depending on the educational level of the students at entry. Students who enter after the eleventh grade take 2-2.5 years, and students who enter after the eighth grade take 3-4 years. The curriculum consists of general (technical) subjects in the first one or two years followed by specialized training. Graduates of these schools receive a specialist diploma and are also awarded a pectoral badge.

BIBLIOGRAPHY

"Materials of the 5th Congress of Mongolian Teachers." Ulaanbaatar, June 1989.

Sanjaasuren, R. and I. Jernisec. *Education in Mongolian People's Republic.* Ulaanbaatar: Publishing House of the Ministry of Education, 1978.

Shagdarsuren, L. *Polytechnical Secondary Education and its Development.* Ulaanbaatar, 1966.

MOROCCO

by
Eirlys E. Davies
Lecturer, Department of English
Sidi Mohd. Ben Abdellah University, Morocco
and
Abdelali Bentahila
Professor, Department of English
Sidi Mohd. Ben Abdellah University, Morocco

BACKGROUND

The origins of higher education in Morocco go back to the ninth century, when the Karaouine mosque was founded in Fez. This soon became a center of learning, and scholars from all over North Africa and the Middle East travelled to study or teach there. In fact, it became known as the first university of the whole region. The major subjects of study were Islamic theology, jurisprudence, philosophy, philology, logic, and literature, and graduates received the title of *Oulema* (Islamic scholar). After the Middle Ages, this university became less important and by the nineteenth century it had no more than a thousand students and had become (Bidwell, 1973), "merely the shadow of the great University which, in the middle ages, had numbered a future Pope among its students; now it was incapable of attracting anyone from abroad". However, this traditional system of higher education still exists today and produces specialists in Islamic doctrine and law.

In the twentieth century, a quite separate modern system of higher education was developed alongside the traditional one. This originated during the period of the French protectorate in Morocco, when Franco-Islamic and Franco-Jewish secondary schools were set up for a very limited elite of Moroccan children. These were based on the system of education used in France, except that classical Arabic (or Hebrew in the case of the Jewish schools) was taught as well as French.

The beginnings of modern higher education came with the founding in 1921 of the *Institut des Hautes Etudes Marocaines* and the *Institut Scientifique Cherifien* which offered studies in social sciences and sciences respectively. These two higher education institutes, both in the capital, Rabat, were attached to the Universities of Bordeaux and Algiers, and it was not until after independence that they together became an autonomous Moroccan institution, Mohamed V University.

In 1975, two more universities were established: Sidi Mohamed Ben Abdellah University in Fez, and Hassan II University in Casablanca. Four years later, in 1979, two other major centers became universities, with the foundation of

Cadi Ayad University in Marrakesh and Mohamed I University in Oujda. In addition, a large number of more specialized higher institutes and colleges have also come into being.

Today all state education in Morocco is administered and controlled by the central authority of the Ministry of Education and its various departments and committees. It is the government which ultimately decides educational policies and controls the budget, and the universities and secondary schools are financed directly by the Ministry of Education, although some scientific and technological institutes may supplement their budgets with earnings from projects associated with industry. Likewise all teaching staff in state education are employees of the state and salaries are paid direct from the central authority. Administration is organized in a hierarchical system.

PRIMARY AND SECONDARY EDUCATION

Primary Education

The first education many Moroccan children receive is at one of the traditional Koranic school, which descend directly from those that existed in the Middle Ages. Children are admitted to these institutions from a very early age, sometimes as early as three. The major aim of the teaching is an initiation into religious knowledge through the learning by heart of passages from the Koran. At the same time the children acquire the skills of reading and writing and some knowledge of grammar. Other children, especially in the modern cities, attend private nursery schools or kindergartens, which have a more westernized approach and may introduce French as well as Arabic.

The compulsory state primary education program does not cater for children until they reach the age of seven. It extends over five or six years and provides training in basic numeracy and literacy skills, the latter is not one but two languages, classical Arabic and French. French is introduced as a subject in the third year of primary education, once the children have become familiar with the Arabic writing system. Examinations are held at the end of each year, and admission to the next class is dependent on satisfactory performance in these. All state schools use the same curriculum and national textbooks compiled in accordance with ministry requirements.

Secondary Education

Secondary education extends over seven years, each academic year lasting from mid-September until the end of June. Admission to secondary school is conditional on success in an entrance examination administered to pupils in the last year of primary education. The secondary program is divided into two cycles, the first lasting four years, and the second three. Some schools offer only the first cycle, others only the second, while in some cases the whole secondary program is provided within one establishment. With the exception of a few special schools which offer what is called original education, which prepares pupils for further studies of the type offered by the Karaouine, with an emphasis on Islamic studies, the vast majority of secondary schools offer what is known as the bilingual program. For instance, in 1987-88, 1,263,340 secondary pupils were following the latter scheme, as opposed to 13,598 in original education.

In the first cycle of the bilingual scheme, all pupils follow a common curriculum, covering subjects such as Arabic language, culture and literature, Islamic studies, French, history, geography, mathematics, science and physical education. In the fifth year pupils are able to choose one of several options, the major ones being mathematics, sciences, and arts. In the case of arts there is a further choice between a modern option (focussing on Arabic, French, and another foreign language, either English, Spanish, or German) and a traditional one (with more emphasis on Arabic). Those who successfully complete the arts courses are equipped to go on to a university course in a faculty of arts or law, while those choosing mathematics or science options may go on to a faculty of science or medicine, or to some of the other scientific institutions.

Another option which has expanded considerably in the last few years is the technical one, which is subdivided into commercial, economic, and industrial sections. Pupils choosing these branches receive training in technology, with some practical work, as well as general background instruction. The number of pupils in this option has increased from only 5,549 in 1971-72 to 16,884 in 1988-89; a reflection of attempts to adapt the secondary system to prepare the technologists Morocco needs. Those who complete the technical option successfully may go on either to some of the higher institutes mentioned earlier or to teacher training institutions offering either two or four year courses. Finally, a limited number of schools offer a specialization in hotel management and catering, and pupils who choose this option may go on to further studies at the *Institut Supérieur de Tourisme*.

During the time when Morocco was a French protectorate, the major language of instruction in secondary education was French, but since then various programs of Arabization have been carried out which have gradually replaced French as a language of instruction by Arabic. Science and mathematics were the subjects to be Arabized last, but now, even these are taught through the medium of Arabic. Nevertheless, special efforts are made to ensure that pupils specializing in scientific subjects achieve a high level of proficiency in French, with special emphasis on scientific French, since French is still the medium of instruction for scientific subjects in higher education.

Successful progress through the secondary education system depends on pupils' performance in the examinations held every school year. Only those who succeed in these examinations are allowed to proceed to the next year, the others being required to repeat the year's courses again before resitting the examination the following year. Those who repeatedly fail these yearly examinations dropout of secondary education altogether. The ultimate goal of secondary school pupils is the school-leaving qualification known as the *baccalauréat*, which is awarded following continuous assessment of pupils' performances during the whole of the last three years of secondary education, when examinations are held at the end of every term. The *baccalauréat* is awarded only to pupils who achieve satisfactory results in all their subjects; for those who do not reach this level of attainment, no national certificate is offered.

The main extracurricular activities offered by schools tend to be sporting ones, with football, basketball, volleyball, athletics, and cross-country running among the most popular pursuits. Some schools also organize cultural activities such as drama and cinema clubs. There are also boarding facilities in some schools for pupils resident in remote areas, who would otherwise have to travel impracticable distances to school each day.

State secondary education is entirely free, although pupils are expected to purchase their own copies of all textbooks needed. However, in addition, private fee-paying schools exist alongside the state schools in most towns. These include the French-run schools of the *Mission Universitaire Culturelle Française*, which follow the same programs as schools in France, and other bilingual Moroccan-run schools which follow the usual Moroccan programs. In 1987-88 there were 69,203 pupils enrolled in private secondary schools *(Le Maroc en Chiffres* 1987).

The teaching staff in state schools are normally required to hold a university degree in the relevant subject, together with a teaching diploma awarded after a one-year postgraduate training course at the Faculty of Education, or alternatively a longer course of professional training at one of the other teacher training institutions. However, in earlier years, where there was an urgent need for more staff, some teachers were recruited with lesser qualifications. These teachers are now being offered the opportunity to pursue further studies to bring them into line with the current requirements. The selection of teachers is in effect carried out before they become teachers, when they apply for places on teacher training courses; those who are admitted to and successfully complete such courses are automatically offered teaching posts through the central appointment system of the ministry of education, which assigns them to schools where staff are needed.

The administration of secondary education has recently been reorganized in an effort to achieve decentralization. This has been carried out through the creation of a number of academies, each responsible for a particular region of the country and working in collaboration with the university in that region. All secondary schools follow the same national curriculum, the subject matter of particular courses being laid down in official texts, but whereas previously a single national examination was held at the end of the secondary school program, now the individual academies are responsible for setting and administering their own examinations though, of course, there is coordination to ensure that these are comparable in content, presentation, and standard.

HIGHER EDUCATION

Institutions

Until 1989, all the higher education faculties in Morocco were grouped into the six independent universities whose names were cited earlier, but now separate university status has been bestowed on the institutions in various other cities which were previously attached to one or other of the original six. Today, then, independent universities also exist in Meknes, Tetouan, Kenitra, and Agadir. Altogether the modern universities comprise between them thirteen faculties of arts and social sciences, eleven faculties of science, and five faculties of law. There are faculties of medicine and pharmacy and of dentistry in Rabat and Casablanca. Rabat also has the only faculty of education. The Karaouine, for its part, possesses faculties of chariaa (Islamic law) in Fez and Agadir, a faculty of Arabic language in Marrakesh, and a faculty of Islamic studies in Tetouan. All these faculties offer first degrees, and some also provide postgraduate courses or research facilities. In the academic year 1987-88, a total of 157,484 students (34.9 percent of whom were female) were enrolled as undergraduates in these universities *(Le Maroc en Chiffres* 1987).

The other major sector of higher education in Morocco is composed of the various more specialized institutes, most of which focus on scientific or technological domains and offer more vocationally oriented courses than most university programs. Among these we might cite (ordered according to number of students) the *Institut Agronomique et Veterinaire Hassan II* (2.023 students), *Ecole Nationale d'Administration Publique* (1,181 students), *Institut Supérieur de Commerce et d'Administration des Entreprises* (681 students), *Ecole Mohammedia d'Ingénieurs* (575 students), *Institut National de Statistique et d'Economie Appliquée* (553 students), *Ecole Nationale de l'Industrie Minerale* (472 students), *Ecole Hassania des Sciences de l'Ingénieur* (411 students), *Ecole National des Postes et des Télécommunications* (403 students), *Institut Royal de la Formation des Cadres de la Jeunesse et des Sports* (369 students), *Ecole des Sciences de l'Information* (324 students), and many more, covering specialities such as architecture, tourism, journalism and maritime studies. All figures are for the year 1987-88, in which the total number of students enrolled in these higher institutes was 8,544. These institutions offer various types of diploma and professional qualifications including postgraduate diplomas.

Finally, we might mention a number of establishments which specialize in preparing teachers for primary and secondary schools. These are the *Centre de Formation des Instituteurs* (2,449 students), the *Ecoles Normales Supérieures* (2,665 students) and the *Centres Pédagogiques Regionaux* (6,551 students). All figures are for 1987-88. It should perhaps also be noted that considerable numbers of Moroccan students are offered the opportunity to pursue their higher education at institutions abroad; in 1987-88, 10,459 grants for study abroad were given, (7,892 for undergraduate studies and 2,567 for postgraduate studies).

Each institution of higher education has its own administrative body. A university is headed by a rector and further divided into faculties, each with a dean and its own administrative staff, and other institutes headed by directors. The director or dean is responsible for exploiting the individual budget of the faculty and its day-to-day running, as well as for academic and pedagogical affairs, while the rectorate coordinates the work of the various faculties. Both rectors and deans are appointed by royal decree. Further down the hierarchy, the faculties are divided into departments for each subject taught. The head of each department is elected by the permanent members of staff in the department for a period of two years. The programs taught in each department follow a basic plan set out in ministerial documents, which outline the subjects to be taught in each year and the number of hours to be devoted to each; however, within this framework there is flexibility with regard to the exact content of each course, which is normally decided by the members of staff who teach it.

Undergraduate Studies

All the faculties mentioned earlier offer first degrees *(licence ès lettres, licence ès sciences, licence ès sciences juridiques,* etc.), while the institutes of higher education offer specialist diplomas. Arts and social science degrees are in a single subject such as Arabic, French, English, Philosophy, History, etc., whereas in science, degrees are given in combinations such as Physics/Chemistry or Biology/-Geology. The faculties of law offer degrees in subjects including political science, economics, and law. The medium of instruction in arts and social science subjects is Arabic, except in the case of degrees in languages, where all instruction is carried out through the medium of the language being studied. Those studying for a degree in an arts or social science subject are also required to follow courses in Arabic, Islamic thought, and a foreign language (if the degree is already in one foreign language, they are required to study a second one). For all science subjects, however, the medium of instruction is French, while in law both French and Arabic medium options are available.

Degree courses normally last for four years, apart from some special cases such as medical degrees which take seven years including hospital training. As in secondary education, each academic year begins in mid-September and finishes at the end of June. For most subjects the only admission requirement is possession of a recent *baccalauréat* in the relevant option; however, admission to certain popular and prestigious courses such as medicine and engineering is dependent on candidates' performance in a competitive entrance examination. Progress through the years follows the same pattern as in secondary education, with admission to each following year of the course being conditional on success in the end of year or end of semester examinations; those who fail being required to repeat the whole year's studies and resit the examination a year later.

There are no tuition fees, and all Moroccan students holding a *baccalauréat* can obtain a government grant to allow them to pursue undergraduate studies for a maximum of five years (this allows for the possibility that they may need to repeat one year of their course). The grants are available to all regardless of personal or parental income, although a distinction is made between those students whose family home is in the city where they are studying and those who have to move to the city from elsewhere; the former receiving smaller grants than the latter. Students are free to choose the subject area they wish to study (provided, of course, that they have the necessary option in their *baccalauréat*), but they are normally required to register in the faculty nearest to their home which offers this subject; thus each faculty has a clearly defined catchment area from which it recruits its students. Cheap residential accommodation is provided in the form of halls of residence offering shared or individual rooms for those students who come from outside the city. There are also student restaurants providing meals at very reasonable prices on production of student tickets. Foreign students are not very numerous; in 1987-88 there were 1,879 foreigners enrolled as undergraduate students in Moroccan higher education institutions.

Members of the teaching staff of higher education institutions are normally recruited following their proposition by the dean or director concerned and approval of this proposition by the Ministry of Education. Various grades of teaching staff are distinguished, with differences in teaching loads, responsibilities and salaries. These are professor, senior lecturer, lecturer, and assistant lecturer. Appointment to a particular grade is dependent on academic qualifications and, in the case of professor, on length of service. Moroccan but not foreign members of staff normally receive tenure after a short period of probation. In 1987-88, there were in all 5,440 full-time university teachers, 21.2 percent of whom were women; these include 300 foreigners (*Statistiques Universitaires* 1987-88; *Le Maroc en Chiffres* 1987).

Advanced Studies

Postgraduate studies are mainly carried out at the older established faculties and institutes. Types of studies, length of courses and admission requirements vary from one institution to another. One recent postgraduate scheme is intended to prepare future university lecturers; this involves rigorous entrance examinations yielding small numbers of students who are awarded grants to allow them to pursue two years of intensive course work. Successful completion of these allows them to be appointed as trainee lecturers and they are then required to submit a thesis within a time limit of three years, after which they are awarded the *diplôme d'études supérieures* and attain full lecturer status. Other postgraduate schemes include a one-year course open to all graduates in the relevant subject; those successful in the end-of-year examinations are awarded the *diplôme d'études approfondies* and may then proceed to write a thesis. Some grants are available for such courses, but most students are self-financed, many holding posts as teachers and pursuing postgraduate studies in their spare time. Higher postgraduate degrees *(doctorat d'état),* obtained by research alone, are also offered in certain subjects by certain faculties and institutes, depending on the particular expertise of their staff. The staff involved in teaching and supervising postgraduate students are normally selected from among the higher grades of university lecturers. The languages of instruction for postgraduate studies are as for the undergraduate courses.

ISSUES AND TRENDS

To put the current state of Morocco's educational system in perspective, it is important to realize the very rapid expansion that the system has undergone. In the years immediately following Morocco's independence in 1956, the numbers of Moroccans having access to secondary or higher education were extremely small; for instance, in 1959-60, there were only 23,000 Moroccans enrolled in secondary schools, and in 1963-64 there were only 7,310 Moroccan students in higher education (Al-Jabiri, 1973). Comparison with the 1987-88 figures of 1,348,670 secondary pupils and 157,484 higher education students *(Le Maroc en Chiffres* 1987), will give some impression of the staggering rate of expansion. To achieve this, vast sums of money are devoted to the establishment of large numbers of new education institutions every year, and the cost of education looms large in the total budget of the country.

For instance, in 1988 the budget for running higher education alone was 13,319 million dirhams, constituting 5.3 percent of the entire national budget, with another 400 million dirhams devoted to investment in higher education (2.5 percent of the total investment budget) *(Statistiques Universitaires* 1987-88). It can thus be seen that education is a very high priority for Morocco and that a great deal of importance is attached to making the system more extensive, more productive, and above all adapted to the current and future needs of the country.

The modern Moroccan educational system is obviously still much influenced by the French system which originally inspired it. Many aspects of its present organization can still be traced to the influence of the period of French colonization (1912-1956) and the close economic and cultural links with France which Morocco has maintained to this day. However, as was noted earlier in this survey, Morocco did have its own tradition of higher education before the coming of the French, and efforts have been made to ensure that the present system is adapted to the special needs of Moroccans.

One of the most notable changes which have been introduced since independence is certainly the process of Arabization. As was mentioned earlier, this has involved the gradual replacement of French as a medium of instruction by Arabic, the national language of Morocco. Thanks to the efforts of the Ministry of Education and specialist bodies such as the *Institut d'Etudes et de Recherche pour l'Arabization,* materials, textbooks, and personnel have been prepared and the Arabization of teaching at the secondary level has now been successfully completed. Nevertheless, great stress is still placed on ensuring that the Moroccan pupils achieve a high level of proficiency in French and where possible in other modern languages as well, so that the advantages of bilingualism can be retained. Now that the links between Morocco and the other North African countries forming the Great Maghreb have been reinforced, we can expect to see greater cooperation between Morocco and its Arabic speaking neighbors in the field of higher education and research.

BIBLIOGRAPHY

Adam, A. *Une enquête auprès de la jeunesse musulmane du Maroc.* Aix-en-Provence: Publications des Annales de la Faculte des Lettres, 1963.

Baina, A. *Le système de l'enseignement au Maroc.* Casablanca: Editions Maghrebines, 1981.

Bentahila, A. *Language attitudes among Arabic-French bilinguals in Morocco.* Clevedon: Multilingual Matters, 1903.

Benyakhlef, M. "Propositions pour une arabisation de niveau." *Lamalif 104*. (Feb. 1979).

Bidwell, R. *Morocco under colonial rule*. London: Frank Cass, 1973.

Bounfour, A. "Le bilinguisme des lycéens: essai de description." *Lamalif.* (April 1973).

Ibaaquil, L. "Le discours scolaire et l'ideologie au Maroc." *Lamalif 95*. (March 1978).

L'enseignement: situation, problèmes, perspectives. Ministère de l'Enseignement et de la Formation des Cadres, 1970.

Le Maroc en Chiffres 1987, 27th ed. Direction du Developpement de la Banque Marocaine de Commerce Exterieur, n.d.

Le mouvement éducatif au Maroc en 1973-74 et 1974-75. Ministère de l'enseignement, 1975.

Recueil de textes relatifs à l'enseignement supérieur. Ministère de l'Education Nationale, Division des Relations Universitaires Exterieures, Service de la Documentation Universitaire, 1978.

Sekkat, A. *La politique de l'enseignement au Maroc: 1956-1977.* Diss. Faculte de Droit, Grenoble, 1977.

Statistiques Universitaires 1987-1988. Service des Enquêtes et du Traitement des Statistiques, Ministère de l'Education Nationale, n.d.

Tazi, A. *Onze siècles a l'universite Quaraouiyine.* Fedala: Imprimerie Mohammedia, 1960.

Tazi, A. "Al-Quaraouiyine, la plus ancienne université du Monde." *Maroc-Magazine 13* (May 1979).

MOZAMBIQUE

by
Sergio Vieira
Director, Center for African Studies
Eduardo Mondlane University, Mozambique

BACKGROUND

The catholic church received the monopoly of African education in Mozambique through the Missionary Law of 1940. Although other religious faiths could have schools, the Africans who attended them were forced to take their exams in the Catholic missionary schools. They were often compelled to accept baptism in the Catholic faith, thus disowning the religion in which they had been educated.

The education at the time was well characterized by the statement of the cardinal archbishop of the colony of Mozambique's capital city (1950s) who stated that the schools had the task of "teaching the negro to read and write and about the greatness of the nation that was educating him". He was defining the task of the missionary schools, to which were entrusted exclusively, by law, the education of "indigenous people".

In lectures given at the Higher Strategic Studies Institute in Portugal at the end of the 1960s, General Kaulza de Arriaga, who was later to become commander-in-chief of the colonial army in Mozambique, was in the same school of thought when he said that it was important to block African access to education while convincing Africans that everything possible was being done.

The colonial reality in Mozambique was one of an absolute barrier against access to education for non-whites. Government statistics for the 1950s, which still showed students' race, tell us that less than 5,000 non-whites were studying in the primary schools. Around 200,000 were in the so called missionary education, reserved for blacks and aimed at providing the rudiments of catechism in Portuguese; at best it produced semi-literates trained to serve the settler administration in lowly positions.

Even at the beginning of the 1960s there was only one secondary school in the whole colony, attended by a few dozen non-whites, and two technical and commercial schools mainly aimed at the more "advanced Africans". Teacher training or higher education was inexistent.

The developments that took place in the mid 1960s and early 1970s were a response to the pressures of the liberation war and of international opinion, that condemned the backwardness of Portuguese colonial education policies.

The education splintered the African off from his culture, and his geographic and historical space. The student born on the banks of the Zambezi river would know absolutely nothing about it, while having to learn by heart every tributary from the right or left bank of every tiny Portuguese river. He learned to thrill at the resistance struggles waged by the Lusitanians against Roman conquest, and to distinguish between the wives and mistresses of the kings of Portugal in the thirteenth century, but he had never heard of the Monomotapa Empire or of the Zimbabwes whose ruins lay in his own country. He knew that Vasco de Gama "discovered" Mozambique and the sea route to India, but he could not learn what took the Portuguese navigator to the East, under threat of reprisals against his family. He was taught eleventh-century Portuguese literature, but the study of his own language or the reading of books written by his compatriots was forbidden.

National liberation, the war against the foreign occupier, altered this situation profoundly.

In the 1970s, in the areas freed by the war, there were already over 25,000 studying in schools, with books prepared and teachers trained by, FRELIMO, the Mozambique Liberation Front (five times the size of the numbers in the official colonial schools). More than 200 Mozambicans were sent abroad on FRELIMO scholarships to complete their higher education, while barely forty blacks managed to enrol in the colonial university.

The post-independence period up to 1980 saw an impressive leap forward in education. Between 1975 and 1980 the numbers in primary school grew 206 percent, and in secondary school 515 percent. By 1980 over 10 percent of the population was attending school, not counting the adults in literacy courses. The illiteracy rate, which at independence had been over 90 percent, fell by more than 30 percent.

These efforts were then jeopardized by the terrorist acts of regression carried out by the armed bandits. The State Department Gersony Report published in 1988 presented many facts about the methodology of aggression.

In education, the results of aggression between 1980 and 1988 have been the destruction of 3,000 primary schools and many secondary schools, teacher training centers, and other institutions. Over 400 primary school teachers have been murdered, mutilated, or kidnapped during this period. Nearly 750,000 children have been deprived of access to primary school, through the destruction of their schools or the prevention of new building work. The cumulative effects of the war and the need to provide assistance to the approximately 25 percent of the population who are now displaced, have forced the government to make significant reductions in the percentage of the budget allocated to education.

Military development in 1988 have resulted in improvements, though still precarious, in the level of order and public security. This situation makes it possible to look at the future of education with some optimism.

The system of National Education in Mozambique presently comprises seven years of primary education, three years of lower secondary education, two years of upper secondary education, and higher education, structured according to the training level of each course. Technical and vocational training is subdivided into elementary, basic and middle levels. Both the general education and the technical and vocational education sectors give access to higher education, either at the university or at the higher institutes.

PRIMARY AND SECONDARY EDUCATION

Primary education is structured in two levels, in accordance with the country's new educational system. The first level is termed level one primary education, and has five classes. The basic subjects taught include Portuguese, mathematics, history, natural sciences, drawing, and physical education. The second level, level two primary education, adds physics to the basic subjects, and has two classes. At the end of this period the pupils are directed towards the different training areas that will lead them to a future specialized education.

At independence in 1975 there were 5,234 primary schools, teaching five-year courses going from preprimary to fourth class, attended by 671,617 pupils. In 1980 there were already 5,730 schools, teaching the same classes, with 1,387,192 pupils enrolled. There are currently 4,382 schools, some of them teaching the two levels of primary education from first to seventh class, with 1,251,391 pupils enrolled.

Secondary school curricula are defined by the Ministry of Education through the medium of the National Institute for Educational Development (INDE), and cover a variety of subjects. At the lower secondary level which lasts three years, the curriculum consists of civics education, Portuguese, English, mathematics, physics, chemistry, biology, history, geography, drawing, and physical education. At the upper secondary level which lasts two years, students have two options: the humanities stream or the science stream. In the humanities stream, the subjects taught are Portuguese, English, history, geography, mathematics, and physical education. In the science stream, the curriculum focuses on the sciences: Portuguese, mathematics, physics, chemistry, biology, drawing, and physical education.

At the secondary level, pupils pay an enrollment fee of MT 2,000 (US$1 = MT1,000) per year, and at upper secondary level MT 3,000. There is exemption for pupils less able to pay, and coming from families whose total annual income is less than MT 16,000 per person. Boarding in Ministry of Education hostels is paid for by the students, and costs MT 1,000 per month at secondary level and MT 1,500 per month at upper secondary level. Students who have exemption from paying enrollment fees are also exempt from these costs. The cost of basic school materials is borne by the student, though the schools administer Social Action funds which give assistance to students who are less able to pay.

Foreign students at secondary level are required to pay higher enrollment fees: MT 5,000 per year for lower secondary and MT 10,000 for upper secondary education.

The school year has thirty-six weeks, divided into two terms: the first runs from 16 February to 30 June, and the second from 20 July to 30 November. Exams for the final classes are in December. The exams are national ones, and are taken at the end of each cycle (ninth and eleventh classes), in every subject except civics education and physical education. In the other classes passes are defined through school-level evaluations for which the teachers are responsible. Diplomas and/or certificates are granted on completion of the exams. The teaching language is Portuguese. Extracurricular activities include sports, cultural activities and practical work, programmed and carried out in accordance with the opportunities and possibilities of each school.

Teachers for secondary education are trained at specially established training centers within middle or higher level institutions, according to the teaching level to which they have been designated. They are trained to teach at least two subjects in the same specialized area.

At independence in 1975, there were twelve secondary schools attended by 17,463 students. By 1980 there were eighty-five secondary schools with a total of 90,041 students. The most recent figures show that there are currently 174 secondary schools with a total of 133,527 students. Access to education is a constitutional right. There are limitations due to the inadequacy of the school network.

Technical and vocational education is divided into three basic areas and into three levels. The levels are elementary, basic, and middle, in the following training areas: administration and accountancy, technical/industrial, and agricultural sciences. General and technical or vocational subjects are taught at each level with sufficient depth to enable the graduate to train in the technical instruments essential to practical execution in each speciality.

The current school calendar for technical education is the same as that for general education. The final exams are at national level, and are held every year.

At independence, technical and vocational education had only twenty-six schools, with 8,891 students. By 1980 there were thirty-five technical/vocational schools with 13,751 students. Current figures show that there are now thirty-four schools with 10,485 students.

HIGHER EDUCATION

The Eduardo Mondlane University was created one year after independence, and is the only university to date. It draws up its own programs for the various courses, appropriate to national realities. Administration and control includes the inter-relations between the various bodies and the productive sector; industry in particular. This is carried out through practical work which is programmed as an integral part of the training process laid down by the curricula for each course. Higher institutes for teaching sciences and for international relations have been created in recent years, with a technical-vocational nature at university level.

Eduardo Mondlane University is organized into faculties, departments, and services. The faculties cover a wide area of training, with various departments overseeing a number of sub-areas of training/research. The services cover a broad range of academic and para-academic activities, including specialized research sectors.

The faculties are grouped into training areas. Thus the area of social sciences and humanities consist of the faculties of economics, law, and the arts. The Faculty of Arts is subdivided into departments of history, geography, modern letters, educational sciences, and teacher training (secondary school). The area of agricultural and biological sciences consist of the faculties of agronomy (which groups agronomy and forestry engineering), medicine, veterinary sciences, and biology. The area of technical and natural sciences consist of the faculties of architecture, mathematics (which is subdivided into pure mathematics and geographic engineering), and engineering and science (the departments of civil engineering, electrotechnical engineering, mechanical engineering, chemical engineering, physics, chemistry, geophysics, and geology).

There are two types of basic university degrees available at the Eduardo Mondlane University: bachelor's degree, programed for 3-4 years; and master's degree, programed for 5-6 years of study.

Admission to the university is open to students emerging from the national educational system, completing the eleventh class at secondary school or technical/-vocational program at middle level in the middle level institutes. Other entrants come from worker-students who have the required or equivalent level; they are sponsored by their work places or they may directly apply at the beginning of the academic year. Foreigners are allowed to enroll if they are residents in Mozambique and do not do any paid work while they are students. Students are selected on the basis of their individual choice of course, taking into consideration their marks in the subjects required for that course.

The program structure for each course is defined in the light of the following main criteria: fundamental course subjects, specific course subjects, and specialized subjects. Defining programs on the basis of this structure does not mean that the course results in being specialized. The objective is to familiarize the graduate for his or her future specialization. All the courses have practical productive work as part of the program. The medium of instruction at the university is Portuguese.

Since 1985 all courses last for five years, at the end of which the graduates receive master's degrees. The only special case is that of medicine which takes six years.

The academic year is forty-six weeks long, subdivided into two terms. Some subject exams are taken between terms, and there are yearly exams at the end of the year for subjects that have one-year programs.

Extracurricular activities include sports and other forms of recreation, including cultural activities.

The university teaching body is made up of an external component, expatriate teachers, and of Mozambicans chosen from among student monitors, who are the best in their first two years and who at the end of their courses do some teaching practice as a way of entry to an academic career.

At university level, students pay an enrollment fee of MT 200 per subject. In the case of worker-students their work place pays their expenses for enrollment and educational materials. The state gives a subsidy to the students who are less able to pay, covering accommodation, food, books, and clothing, totalling MT 268,800 per year. There are currently only four university hostels, and they house 500 students. The students pay the costs, while a subsidy is given for scholarship holders to cover these costs and the cost of study materials. The cost of living in a university hostel is equal to about two-thirds of the subsidy. Foreign students pay

MT 15,000 per term as an enrollment fee, irrespective of the number of subjects they will take, and the course is budgeted as costing US$2,000.

There are currently 2,718 students at the university, of whom 1,093 have scholarships and the remainder are self supporting or have the support of their families or work places. These is a significant number of worker-students.

The UEM does not at the moment give postgraduate courses, for which students have to go to foreign universities. The selection criteria vary, but the general requirement is a master's degree and two years of work experience.

A more recently created institution of technical and vocational training is the Higher Institute for Teaching Sciences opened in August 1986 with only ninety-three students. It is organized into faculties and small scale support services. The faculties are structured by areas of training/research. The main task of the institute (ISP) is to give pedagogical and professional training for the area of secondary school teaching. It thus has the following faculties: languages, history and geography, biology and chemistry, physics and mathematics, and pedagogy and psychology. The teaching calendar is the same as that of the Eduardo Mondlane University.

The Higher Institute for International Relations was also created in 1986, with the task of training professionals for the area of international relations and civil servants for the diplomatic and consular services. Given its specific nature it comes under the Ministry of Foreign Affairs, and offers the master's degree. This institute is organized into departments according to the major areas of specialized study. At the moment it has departments of languages, basic studies, and specialized studies. About 140 students were enrolled in the 1988 academic year, divided among the first three years of the course.

Research activities at Eduardo Mondlane University are divided into work areas. The area of social sciences and humanities has the Center of African Studies, the Mozambican History Archive, the Museum of Colonial Domination, the National Money Museum, and the Archaeology Department. The area of agricultural and biological sciences has the Natural History Museum.

Apart from these institutions, there are several institutes of research in the areas of agricultural and biological sciences, and technical and natural sciences.

BIBLIOGRAPHY

Mawema, M. A. *British and Portuguese Colonialism in African Education.* Columbia: Columbia Univ. Teacher's College, 1981.

Ministry of Education, Mozambique. *Sistema nacional de educacao. Maputo: Ministry of Education, 1985.*

UNESCO. International Yearbook of Education. Paris: UNESCO, 1986.

World Bank. Mozambique: Education and Manpower Development Project. Washington, D.C.: World Bank, 1988.

NEPAL

by
Kedar N. Shrestha
Member Secretary
Council for Higher Education, Nepal

BACKGROUND

Traditional forms of higher education were prevalent in Nepal centuries before the introduction of modern concepts of higher education to the Indian subcontinent. Higher education based on the modern concept of a university is a recent phenomenon whose beginning can be traced back to 1918 when the first college (affiliated to the University of Calcutta in India) was established. The country was ruled for a century by autocratic Ranas who deliberately discouraged the expansion of public education in Nepal. So, up to the end of the Rana regime in 1951, the country had only one college, the Tri-Chandra College, offering courses up to bachelor's level in science and humanities.

The democratic government that came into power in 1951 established several colleges. To keep up with the popular demand for higher education, the government also encouraged the establishment of private colleges supported by government grants. As there was no university in Nepal up to 1959, all the colleges that were established were affiliated to Patna University in India. The College of Education (1957) offering teacher training was the only institution that offered its own degree.

SECONDARY EDUCATION

Nepal has a $5+2+3$ school education structure. The first five years are in primary education, the second two years in lower secondary level, and the last three years are in secondary level. Recently the government has decided to eliminate the lower secondary level and add two more years at higher secondary level, subsequently to adopt a $5+5+2$ system. The school system (1989) consist of 15,893 primary schools, 4,039 lower secondary schools, and 1,894 secondary schools. The number of students in primary, lower secondary, and secondary level are 2,511,025, 325,353, and 338,508 respectively.

Primary education in Nepal is free. The government bears the entire cost of primary education. Textbooks are given free of cost to all the female students and students of remote areas at primary level. Other primary students upto grade three also get free textbooks. To increase the enrollment of girls, 5 percent of the girls enrolled get uniform allowance and monthly allowance. In Nepal, the curriculum in all the primary schools is uniform across the country. The first three grades teach comparatively simple curriculum which includes Nepali language, mathematics, social studies, health and physical education, and handicraft and drawing. In grades four and five, subjects like Sanskrit, English, science, health, and moral education are added. The government has adopted a policy of achieving universal enrollment at primary level by the turn of the century.

The curriculum in secondary school consists of core and selective courses. The courses include English, Nepali, math, history, geography, science, health, vocational studies (home science, agriculture, office management etc.) and optional subjects (social studies, commerce etc.).

The Curriculum, Textbook, and Supervision Development Center is the agency of the Ministry of Education and Culture responsible for the development of curriculum and textbooks. The controller of examinations of the ministry is the agency which conducts examinations at the end of tenth grade and issues the School Leaving Certificate to successful students.   About 130,000 sit this national examination every year. The pass percentage of these students has been 25-35 percent during the last five years.

The secondary schools of Nepal operate on the basis of a partnership between the government and the private sector. The government pays half the salary of the teachers and other half is met by money earned as tuition fees. The monthly salary of a secondary school teacher is about US$75 per month and students pay about US$2 per month as tuition fees. Some schools have properties. But most schools operate only on two sources: government grants-in-aid and student tuition fees.

In general, Nepali language is the medium of instruction in the secondary schools. The government, however, has allowed willing schools to adopt English as the medium. Most of these English medium schools operate boarding facilities as well, and the average cost of boarding, lodging, and schooling per student is about US$450 per year. As more than 99 percent of students go to school on foot and stay with their parents, the cost of secondary education for a student is limited to about US$20 for tuition fees and US$25 for books and supplies. Because of the special characteristics of the Nepalese curriculum, there are no foreign students in the secondary schools in Nepal.

To maintain the quality of secondary education, the government has fixed bachelor's degree as the basic minimum academic qualification for secondary school teachers.   Training is being arranged for the teachers to equip them with pedagogical skills. A teacher service system is being instituted at the district level. There is a "teachers selection committee" for each district. The written examination or interview technique has been suggested. Teachers are selected by the committee, and appointed by the school management committee of individual schools. The service conditions are laid down in the education regulations of the government. Teachers appointed for permanent tenure receive pension and gratuity after retirement.

HIGHER EDUCATION

Institutions

The Tribhuban University, established in 1959, is the premier institution of higher education and has the operational jurisdiction for higher education in Nepal. A second university, the Mahendra Sanskrit University, came to be established later. In 1971, a new Tribhuban University Act was enacted which made it a teaching university with constituent campuses (earlier affiliated colleges). The University Act was again amended in 1987 based on the recommendations of a Royal Commission on Higher Education appointed by His Majesty the King Birendra Veer Bickrama Shah.

Though the total responsibility for planning, policy making and financing is centrally controlled by the government through the Ministry of Education and Culture, the operational functions of higher education are delegated to the two autonomous universities namely Tribhuban University and Mahendra Sanskrit University. In fact, as mentioned before, it is the Tribhuban University which plays the dominant role in higher education in the country. The management structure, funding system, and academic programs of the Tribhuban University are synonymous with the operation of higher education in Nepal.

Tribhuban University and Mahendra Sanskrit University are both autonomous institutions having His Majesty the King Birendra Veer Bickram Shah Dev as the chancellor, and minister of education and culture as the pro-chancellor. His Majesty the King, in the capacity of the chancellor, appoints the vice-chancellor who is vested with the powers and responsibilities to operate the universities. Each university has a rector and an registrar. The former assists the vice-chancellor in academic affairs and the latter in administrative affairs.

Technical education is another area where the government has brought about a major policy change. A Council for Technical and Vocational Education has been recently established with a view to providing (8-10 years of schooling level), training to produce craftsmen, and semiskilled and skilled manpower. At present, the technical institutes of Tribhuban University operate undergraduate courses in technical areas like forestry, medicine, agriculture, and engineering to produce middle-level technical manpower.

Teaching staff at Tribhuban University falls into four categories: professor, reader, lecturer, and assistant lecturer. A minimum of master's degree is required to be eligible for a teaching position in the university except in technical areas like engineering, education, and agriculture where a bachelor's degree has been set as a minimum academic requirement.

Admission requirement for the certificate level is the successful completion of ten years of schooling and the School Leaving Certificate. Entry for bachelor's degree programs requires successful completion of the certificate level or twelve years of schooling. Master's programs require completion of a bachelor's degree.

Another important feature of Nepalese higher education is the size of the campuses and courses offered in the campuses. Because of the lack of easy means of transportation and the difficult geographical terrain, the campuses are very small.

There are a large number of campuses which offer courses only in humanities and each of which has less than 200 students.

Undergraduate Studies

At present, Tribhuban University offers first degree programs in all the institutes and faculties. Admission requirement is either the completion of twelve years of schooling or certificate level related to the intended area of specialization. In technical areas like agriculture, engineering, medicine, and forestry, the Certificate in Science is also recognized as an admission qualification. The bachelor's level in business administration is open to all certificate holders. In general, a candidate should have completed the certificate level (11-12 grade) course to join the bachelor level course. The area of humanities and social sciences is open to certificate holders in either arts or science.

The duration of bachelor's degree vary depending on the subject of study. The undergraduate degree course, in general, is of two years duration in arts, science, business, education, and law. The duration is longer in engineering and medicine, both of which take four years. An academic year consists of ten months. There is an external examination at the end of each academic year. A student need not pass all subjects to study the next year's course. However he will be declared successful only when he will have passed all the courses.

Campuses offering undergraduate degrees are relatively well-equipped. Many such campuses have boarding facilities. Higher education, however, is relatively very cheap. A student pays only about US$50 as tuition fee and about US$350 for board and lodging per year. About 25 percent of the enrolled students in technical institutes receive stipends which cover tuition and books and stationary expenses. About 30 percent of the student get tuition waivers in other faculties of the university.

The undergraduate courses are offered either in the constituent campuses or in the affiliated (private) campuses. The constituent campuses of the university have the teaching faculty appointed by the university. At present, the university regulation has the provision of a "teacher selection committee" which is authorized to select a candidate for tenure service. The affiliated and private campus, however, have been operating the campuses mostly by employing part-time teachers.

Advanced Studies and Research

Almost all the faculties of the university offer postgraduate degrees. But only few campuses offer the courses. Mainly, it is in the central campus where most of the postgraduate teaching is conducted. In almost all cases, a bachelor's degree in the related field is the requirement for admission to the master's level.

The faculties of humanities and social sciences, science and technology, and education offer both the master's and doctoral (Ph.D.) degrees. The faculty of management offers the master of business administration degree. The faculties of humanities and social sciences, education, science and technology, and management have also recently introduced the M.Phil. program on an experimental basis for students preparing for the Ph.D. degree.

There is not much difference in the yearly cost for students of different levels. The tuition fees and other costs are similar to other levels. There are a few regular foreign students enrolled in the university for research.

ISSUES AND TRENDS

Higher education in Nepal has expanded rapidly both in size and variety, over the last few decades. In 1951, the country had only 321 primary schools and 11 secondary schools enrolling less than 0.5 percent school age children. Today, the country operates a fairly comprehensive education system of primary, secondary, technical schools. About two million children are enrolled in the 1249 primary schools with an enrollment of 85 percent of the primary school age group. Similarly about one million students receive education in about 4,000 secondary schools. The literacy percentage has risen to 35 percent. Technical schools are added every year to provide lower level technical manpower. However, Nepalese education faces many issues yet to be addressed.

Primary education has been included as one of the national "basic needs" program of the government. Accordingly, plans and programs have been prepared to universalize primary education by the year 2000. The target is to enroll 100 percent of the primary school age children. At present, the gross enrollment is about 84 percent, the net enrollment is estimated to be only 54 percent (because of the enrollment of a large number of overaged and underaged children). One major problem is the low percentage of enrollment of girls in primary schools. Several strategies are being adopted for the universalization of primary education: free education at primary level, free textbooks, scholarships for girls, and accelerated schooling program for out-of-school children.

At present, Nepal has a $5+2+3$ structure system of schooling. Recently, His Majesty's government has announced its decision to work towards increasing the schooling years from ten to twelve years and adopting $10+2+3$ system. The reasons behind the decision to increase the schooling years are numerous. For example, almost all the neighboring countries of Nepal have twelve year schooling systems. To maintain equivalency and to help students go to the neighboring countries for further studies, the number of schooling years must be increased. Also, because of the growth of knowledge in all fields, there is a need to provide a longer duration of schooling.

Nepal had adopted a policy of having only one university and a unified system of higher education. But the growing demand for higher education and the eventual need for increased funding had led to a new policy. The government has recently established another university for Sanskrit education. The government, also, has encouraged popular initiative by allowing private colleges to be funded by the people. There is a policy even to establish another university.

Nepal has achieved tremendous success in expanding the educational facilities but the quantitative development has taken place at the cost of quality. The government has established the free primary educational system for the whole country. But the rising number of expensive private primary schools and their popularity among the people raise serious questions on their quality. Similarly, the pass percentage in the School Leaving Certificate examination has remained less than 35 percent. More serious is the picture in higher education. Only about 10 percent students complete the certificate level (first two years of college) within the stipulated period of two years. The quality of other levels of higher education has remained unsatisfactory. Lack of adequate research funds and facilities has hampered the quality of higher education in the country. There is a serious need to balance the quantitative expansion with qualitative growth.

Much of what is taught in the classrooms consist of subject matter that has hardly been revised during the last few decades. The curriculum renewal is very seriously needed mainly at the higher education level.

Ever since the programs of expansion of educational facilities started in Nepal, the responsibility to build physical facilities was always given to the people. There was neither planning for the creation of physical facilities nor a program to provide meaningful grants-in-aid for the schools. Hence, almost all physical facilities of the schools are far below desirable levels. As most of the technical institutions have been created either by foreign aid or loans, physical facilities in these schools are superior. The government has recently launched a program to provide partial grants to primary schools to improve the physical facilities in six of the seventy-five districts of the country under the "Primary Education Project". Similar programs are to be developed and implemented to raise the quality of physical facilities of schools throughout the country.

Despite the existence of numerous deficiencies, the real problem is not of quality per se. The question is of efficiency and relevance. Students who complete their education in the Nepalese education institutions are not inferior to the students of the neighboring countries such as India, Pakistan, or Bangladesh by any standard of measure. The problem is that of internal efficiency. More than 50 percent of the first graders dropout before they complete grade five. More than 60 percent of the students fail the final tenth grade examination. Teaching in the campuses, except in the technical areas, has been very irregular. The methods of teaching, and curriculum contents have to be updated.

BIBLIOGRAPHY

National Education System Plan (1971-1976).   Kathmandu: The Ministry of Education and Culture (Nepal), 1971.

Pandey, B. D.   "Higher Education in Nepal."   Ph.D. diss., Southern Illinois University, Carbondale, Illinois, 1981.

Report of the Royal Commission on Higher Education. Kathmandu: His Majesty's Government Press (Nepal), 1982.

Report of the Nepal National Education Planning Commission. Kathmandu: College of Education, Education Press (Nepal), 1956.

Shrestha, K. N. "Higher Education in Nepal." In *Educational Administration in Nepal.* Ed. Institute of Education (Nepal). Kathmandu: Institute of Education, 1982.

Tribhuban University, A Profile. Kathmandu: Curriculum Development Center (T.U.), 1987.

THE NETHERLANDS

by
Jan K. Koppen
Director, Higher Education Research Program
Center for Educational Research
University of Amsterdam, The Netherlands

BACKGROUND

The higher educational system in Holland is currently subject to major changes. These changes are a result of sociocultural developments that have led, among other things, to a massive demand for higher education. German traditions have predominated the organization of higher education in the Netherlands and its relationship with the environment. Since the 1960s the attention of policy makers has been directed towards Anglo-Saxon ideas and structure of higher education. Educational orientation has gradually shifted to a more profession-related system. The Dutch educational system is composed of three main levels: primary education (including special education), secondary education (general, vocational and special education), and higher education (university and vocational sector).

PRIMARY AND SECONDARY EDUCATION

Primary schools provide eight years of schooling, for children of ages 4-12 years. The curriculum has recently been revised under the new Primary Education Act of 1985. Besides basic subjects, it includes English language, health education, creative arts, and training in social competence.

Compulsory education lasts until the age of sixteen. For young workers, a two-year period of partial education is additional. All pupils, therefore, will have to spend at least three years in secondary education.

Recent policy plans are oriented towards creating a "basic training stage" for the 12-16 year old children. Proposals for the content of the curriculum of this basic training period and the way to implement this stage in the existing educational structure are presently under discussion.

Secondary education, intended for pupils aged 12-18, is divided into two main categories, general and vocational secondary education. In addition, there is a relatively separate sector of "senior special education".

There are three different general secondary education types: pre-university education (*voorbereidend wetenschappelijk orderwijs* or VWO), senior general education (*hoger algemeen voortgezet onderwijs* or HAVO), and general secondary education (middelbaar algemeen vormend onderwijs or MAVO) with duration of six, five and four years respectively. In vocational education there are two types of schools: junior (LBO) and senior (MBO) level (with a subdivision), each having a duration of four years.

The first year in all types of secondary education (except for "special education") is a transition year intended for orientation and adjustment, although the effects of tracking are well known. Transfer between categories and types is possible but in this case, moving upwards in the system generally costs an extra year. In many instances, different types are included in comprehensive schools with up to 2,000 pupils, although the combination of all types is rare.

Completion of secondary education is by means of a national examination in curriculum subjects (for each school type), preceded by internal examinations in the subjects throughout the year. In preuniversity education (VWO) a pupil has to pass seven subjects for examination; and six subjects in the other school types. Pupils need to make a choice in these examination subjects, as well as in a number of non-examination subjects. Subjects like Dutch and English language are compulsory.

Through an increased participation of pupils in the school types that give admission to higher education (i.e. VWO, HAVO, and among them pupils from lower income backgrounds), the proportion of graduates form these types has risen to 50 percent of the relevant age group. The remaining 50 percent has certificates from MAVO, LBO, and other vocational branches; special education; or no certificate at all.

The preuniversity education (VWO) gives general access to universities, with certain limiting conditions. The senior general education (HAVO) and vocational secondary education (MBO) give access to the higher vocational sector (HBO). Vocational education comprises short senior secondary vocational courses (KMBO), full-time or part-time, and an apprenticeship system which provides training under an apprenticeship contract in a company. Neither is related to higher education.

Schools are under public (municipal or state) or private administration. The latter includes Protestant, Roman Catholic, and non-denominational schools. All schools are publicly funded, except for a minor share of the private schools' funds.

Tuition fees in secondary education are, in principle, non-existent for the schools under public administration. After the age of sixteen, fees charged amount to about 20 percent of the real expenses per pupil. In the school year 1987-88 the fee is DFL1,030 (approx. US$480). From this age, every student receives a basic grant from the government. The value of the grant is presently under political debate.

HIGHER EDUCATION

Structure

Institutions like the universities of today in Europe developed in the early middle ages around the twelfth century. They originated in clerical groups and convent schools.   Universities of Bologna, Paris, and Oxford were the first institutions to be established.

In the Netherlands the first university, in Leiden, appeared only in 1575. Soon thereafter, two other universities were founded, in Groningen and Utrecht. All other institutions are of relatively modern origin.   The last university was founded in Maastricht in 1976.

The first higher technical school was established in the early nineteenth century (Delft) followed by two others after the second World War.   These technical schools just recently received the status of universities (1986).

The Netherlands has a relatively closed system of higher education funded predominately by the government. The Ministry of Agriculture and Fisheries is in charge of the (small) agricultural sector, the Ministry of Education for the other sectors. All higher educational institutions are listed in the law. New institutions can only be established by approval of the minister of education. The approved institutions are entitled to government funding, and are authorized to grant titles. Their students have the right to financial assistance provided by the central government.

The field of higher education and academic research in the Netherlands today has four distinct subsystems, namely, university education (WO), higher vocational education or professional education (HBO), Open University (OU), university teaching hospitals, and research institutes. The two latter subsystems are not treated here as they do not fall within the scope of this discussion.

In the Netherlands the general objective of university education, according to the University Education Act, is threefold. It comprises (1) independent pursuit of scholarship, (2) preparation for the occupation of professional positions for which academic training is required or desirable, and (3) promotion of the understanding of the fields of science and scholarship as a whole.

For the higher vocational sector, separate legislation was introduced in 1986. The merging of vocational schools with the higher educational system meant the upgrading of the former institutions. The emphasis regarding their objectives is on the training for the practice of professions, on personal development, and on the satisfactory functioning in society, of its students.

Finally, the "Open University" provides higher education through the medium of distance teaching.   Founded in 1984 the Open University offers correspondence courses at both WO and HBO level, in which there is freedom of choice concerning courses and pace.

Higher education is no longer the monopoly of these institutions under government funding. A very small but growing share is held by private enterprise investment in higher education. The more traditional private institutions are the theological institutes, spread over the country. A recent development is the accreditation, by the ministry, of institutions that provide specialized education of a higher educational level. The University for Business Administration at Nijenrode is an example. Other privately funded institutions are found in the area of post graduate education. The Rotterdam-Rochester University is an example. Some of these institutions receive an initial grant from the government.

Except for a few correspondence courses, there are no other privately funded institutes (for adult) higher education.

Higher education has recently come under some dramatic changes in policy. The system in terms of quality, output, success-rates and length of studies (together with rising expenditures) was no longer considered acceptable. In the last decade a strong belief in government planing and control over the system of higher education has been expressed and put into several policy documents. Meanwhile, many policy measures have been taken in the area of staffing, budgeting, and concentration of educational and research activities. The attitudes regarding control have changed from intense to limited government regulations, in favor of more administrative autonomy of the institutions. Nonetheless the government keeps a strong grip on the output of the system through financial regulations.

Today the system is undergoing changes in planning and funding, curriculum development, admission regulations and quality control, in combination with budget cuts. In 1982, a new two-tier structure (first tier for undergraduate education and second tier for postgraduate education) was introduced in the university sector after a long period of political debate and some half-hearted reforms in the 1970s. Implementation of the second tier policy plan is still going on, however, with significant modifications from the original ideas.

The higher vocational sector traditionally possessed a relatively low profile and was entirely separated from the universities. About a decade ago the government, in an effort to upgrade the vocational sector, initiated a policy directed towards integration of the higher vocational education (HBO) into the university system. This policy has later changed in favor of the establishment of a new HBO structure that is not to be integrated in the university sector. Legislation came in 1986 and the HBO system went through major changes. Today the HBO system and the university system are legally equivalent but in fact not (yet) equivalent in status.

The general goals of higher education, based on the principle of "higher education to the many", consist of the following: determination of individual needs of higher education not on social background or purchasing power, but on aptitude conveyed by formal qualifications; respect for individual freedom of educational choice in sector, subject, and institution; and satisfaction of the needs of the society for graduates, both quantitatively and qualitatively.

The attitudes towards control of the educational system are currently changing, as indicated earlier. The government aims towards a "dialogue" with the educational establishment, putting the views of the minister into policy documents that are presented to the institutions, the parliament, and the educational councils.

Relevant authorities in policy formulation include the "Netherlands Universities Association", and the "HBO-Council", "the Higher Education Consultative Committee", and the "Education Council", (which is an important independent advisory board to the minister of education).

Both the university and the HBO sector have a two-tier structure, of which the second tier has not yet been adequately developed. The first tier program is scheduled for four years. Extension of studies for another two years is allowed. Every student is, therefore, entitled to remain enrolled at any higher educational institution for six years. This time restriction, which only recently came into force for the whole of higher education, creates substantial reduction in educational budgets for the government, but limits the students' possibilities of changing degree programs or sectors. First research results indicate that only a small percentage of students are willing and able to finish studies on a four-year schedule.

If a student has used up the maximum enrollment time, he or she may be enrolled as an "auditor" or as an "external candidate". Students in these categories, however, hold a different status in the system. Under certain exceptional circumstances (as judged by the administrative authorities), supplementary entitlement for enrollment is awarded. Some exceptions are indicated in the Law. For example, a student is entitled to three more years of enrollment in a university degree course, provided he or she holds a HBO degree.

For study at the Open University no limitations in the maximum study time are in force.

Graduates of the first tier (four-year program) receive the title of *doctorandus*. This same title was awarded under the former 5-6 year university program and used to be comparable to a master's degree. The level of the new first tier graduate program courses is not yet clear, but in the eyes of many it has generally been lowered. Graduates from HBO programs receive the title of "bachelor". A bachelor can be admitted to a short university program (e.g. two-year program) in order to obtain a doctoral degree. Limited possibilities exist for both WO and HBO graduates to obtain a doctoral degree, comparable to a Ph.D. The Open University awards both the *doctorandus* and the "bachelor" titles.

The numbers of students seeking higher education, as a proportion of the relevant age group, has risen considerably since the 1960s. First year students rose by 40 percent between 1970 and 1986. The participation of women has almost doubled, but not in all disciplines. In engineering, the participation rate is only 10.5 percent, whereas in "language and culture" it is 64 percent. Numbers of part-time students and students over twenty-one years of age are increasing.

The number of first year HBO students is more than twice that of WO students. This figure is decreasing, however, because more and more pupils from the HAVO-branch of secondary education follow VWO, and apply for university entrance instead of higher vocational education. This trend will probably become stronger since measures concerning the maximum enrollment time (six years) are in force, and switching from HBO to WO is hampered by the time restriction. The higher vocational sector is at the moment relatively large in comparison to other countries.

Growth in freshmen and gross numbers has occurred both in HBO and WO sectors, particularly in law, economics, and "language and culture", (and agriculture in HBO), whereas other disciplines are relatively stable. A decline has occurred in the sector of "behavior and society" for WO, and "education" for HBO. In the year 2000, more than 20 percent of the population in Holland will have completed higher education. This trend is obvious in many European countries, more so than in the USA. This is not surprising since the participation rate in higher education as a percentage of the population is twice as high in the USA (5.3 percent) as in most European countries (2.7 percent).

As a result of demographical developments, a decrease of the younger generation group is likely, and the number of entrants into graduate programs is predicted to be 30 percent lower in the future.

The policy on admission to higher education is one of encouragement. Restrictions are as few as possible. Besides a certificate in preuniversity education and a propaedeutic examination in HBO, a *colloquium doctum* examination for anyone who does not meet the requirements and is over twenty-one years of age gives admission to university education. A HAVO or a MBO certificate gives entrance to HBO education. Many disciplines set entrance requirements. For example, without having passed the subject of mathematics I in secondary education, only law and some "language and culture programs" are open. The same holds true for the subject of physics in case of any technical program in HBO.

No specific requirements for admission to the Open University exist for anyone over the age of eighteen.

A *numerus clausus* measure is in force for some degree programs. The programs involved are announced every year. If a *numerus clausus* is set, students are selected by lot, with a weighted draw favoring those with the highest average marks in their school-leaving examination. A *numerus clausus* measure can be taken whenever the number of students is expected to exceed student capacity in a particular program. Discrepancies between the number of candidates and the labor market prospects in a specific field give another reason for restriction of numbers of freshmen. These rules will be strengthened under the new higher educational legislation in order to minimize *numerus clausus* decisions by the minister of education.

The gross number of students enrolled in university education (WO) was almost 169,000 in 1986, of which 38 percent were women. The total number is expected to be much lower in the near future, around 130,000 in the year 2000. The participation of women in higher education is still on a low level, compared to that in other countries.

The student numbers in HBO has risen by about 40 percent in the last decade to a total amount of 200,000 in 1986, of which 44.5 percent were women.

The number of foreign students at Dutch universities is relatively small, only 2.3 percent. Students origin is mainly European, but approximately one-third comes from developing countries, including the former Dutch colonies of Surinam and Indonesia.

Tuition fees are charged from everyone attending higher education. Traditionally this fee was rather low, but has gradually increased (in the recent years at a quickened pace) in order to reduce ministerial deficits. The fee for the 1988-89 academic year will be Dfl.1,750 (approx. US$800) and is equally charged for WO and HBO full-time programs.

Before the introduction of the two-tier structure, median enrollment duration was 7.2 years. Due to the new six year restriction, this figure will decrease, and gross numbers enrolled will come down. The pace of study is also valued differently. Success rates are now considered to be an important performance indicator. The mean percentage of students who graduate used to be around 60 percent of the original entrance group. Institutions attach more importance than before to raising this percentage. A rise by a few percent is likely under the new structure.

The government allocates funds to higher educational institutions on the basis of a funding model, in which fixed norms concerning the relationship between duties and funds are specified. In the Netherlands, approximately 90 percent of the income of institutions is made up of central government grants. Student fees, educational and research contracts, and sponsorship figure on a relatively small scale in institutional budgets. New legislation is being made to increase the share of tuition fees. The cost of higher education per student per year vary from Dfl.3,600 (law) to Dfl.37,000 (veterinary science) (approximately US$1,750-18,000), a little less in the HBO sector. The cost per student decreased considerably after 1975, as the Dutch system of higher education came to be more expensive than the surrounding systems in Europe.

In the near future funding will be more and more output oriented, based on performance indicators of individual institutions or sectors.

Financial assistance to students, and especially to students from low-income families, has been given since the 1960s. In 1986 a new Financial Aid to Students Act came into force which made students financially more independent from their parents. The principle underlying the new system was a basic grant to which every student (from rich or poor background) is entitled. Above this assistance an extra grant can be obtained in some cases, depending on parental income. Extra loans, which are often indispensable, have to be obtained from private banks. The system of grants and loans only applies to students within their six-year enrollment restriction and under twenty-seven years of age.

This system recently became operational and is beset by severe problems such as computerized registration of student claims and the costs involved (budgets have risen to unexpected heights). In addition, recent changes in loan conditions and the involvement of private banks are widely criticized.

Housing for students is traditionally rather problematic because of a shortage of available rooms. Only a very small part of housing is on a campus like basis. Students have to find accommodation in the limited facilities provided by the institutions, or through private organizations (for the most part in blocks of student flats) or in rental flats or rooms in the private market. The latter are sparsely available and expensive, especially in major cities.

There are now six times as many graduates as in the late forties, and graduates under thirty are twenty times more. The proportion of graduates in the social sciences, especially, has increased. Employment opportunities for higher education graduates has also risen considerably. The growth rate has been 4.8 percent per year (against 0.7 percent for the total of the professional labor force) and the share of higher educational graduates in the labor force has increased from 4.4 percent in 1960 to 17.9 percent in 1985. More growth in employment is predicted.

Nonetheless the unemployment figures are high for graduates of some sectors like "behavior and society", "language and culture" (around 14 percent unemployment compared to 7 percent for the total of higher educational sector in 1986). The unemployment is mainly caused by a growing supply of graduates and not by a decreasing demand. The unemployment percentage for women is twice as high as that for men. The unemployment level for graduates has stayed relatively stable in the last few years. An increase in unemployment of up to 25 percent is predicted for the year 2000 under a high demand projection, and a decrease to 4 percent under a low demand projection. A surplus in supply is expected to arise in the sectors of "behavior and society", and "language and culture" whereas in the sectors of "science", "economy", and "engineering" a shortage is expected.

Program designers put a lot of energy into the construction of programs that are up to date and meet the needs of trade and industry. This is a difficult process since employers are very demanding as a result of the oversupply of qualified labor. Programs have to reflect a balance between general qualifications and profession-oriented special qualifications.

Institutions

There are thirteen universities in The Netherlands, nine general universities Amsterdam (Municipal University and Free University), Leiden, Groningen, Utrecht, Rotterdam, Maastricht, Nijmegen and Tilburg), three universities of technology (Enschede, Delft, and Eindhoven) and one university of agriculture (Wageningen). Of these institutions, the Free Universities of Amsterdam (Reformed Protestant), Nijmegen (Roman Catholic) and Tilburg (Roman Catholic) are the only private institutions. The difference between public and private universities is very small (from a student's point of view). All are under government law and funding, but there is a bit more freedom of policy in the privately run institutions.

The Universities of Amsterdam and Utrecht are the biggest, with total enrollments of 26,500 and 23,600 respectively (in 1986). Maastricht is the smallest university, with a total amount of 3,200 students, but with a growing potential.

As indicated earlier, the HBO system consisted of many small scale institutions. Through mergers, an increase in scale was established. There are around eighty-five of these new style HBO institutions, as against approximately 300 a few years ago. Unlike universities, HBO institutions are mainly privately run. Under public funding, they have to fit into the framework of the Higher Education Act.

The HBO institutions differ considerably in size. The largest institution is the High School Rotterdam with 11,700 students (1986), while several institutions have less than 200 students.

The Open University is situated in Heerlen, in the south of the country. In 1986, 30,500 students participated in one or more courses in the Open University.

Higher education institutions in Holland are highly standardized, except for relatively minor differences between institutions in degree programs in a discipline. Institutions are also well matched in quality. Quality control used to be directed towards the lower quality limits, and not to high quality levels. Internationally, the Dutch standards in higher education are highly recognized. Policy, however, is more and more directed towards differentiation between institutions, both on the side of the curricula as on the qualitative level.

Undergraduate Studies (First Tier)

At present, the key concept in government control is the individual discipline. A list of all degree programs is contained in the higher educational legislation. Both universities and HBO institutions need approval from the ministry to establish a new degree program in order to receive government funding. For all degree programs, general requirements, mostly concerning the subjects that have to be part of the core curriculum, are specified by legislation. This rather bureaucratic legislation will be subject to change in the next years, leaving the institutions with more freedom in curriculum planning and establishing new programs. In the 1990s a higher level of government control is being proposed and the concept of "sector" will be introduced instead of the current disciplines. Nine sectors are proposed in the draft bill on higher education that has yet to pass through parliament: education, agriculture, science, engineering, health, economics, law, behavior and society, and language and culture.

According to government policy, this new procedure is meant to allow the institutions to construct curricula that meet the needs of students and community and, therefore, improve the quality of education. Nevertheless, many problems will rise as former disciplines will loose their traditional identity within the new "sectors". Students will need more guidance with compiling their own individual programs.

Presently in university education, a student has a choice of over a hundred separate degree programs. Within the limits set by the possible special require- ments and/or a *numerus clausus* measure, every student has a freedom to enter any program desired. Law and economics offer very popular programs and are by far the largest disciplines. In contrast, "language and culture" offers many small disciplines that do not attract more than a few dozen students nationwide.

All first tier degree programs are divided into two parts. A "propaedeutic" stage covers the first year. This stage is meant for adaptation, orientation, selection, and referral to other programs if necessary. To enter the next three-year doctoral stage, the student has to pass a propaedeutic examination. The first tier program duration is designed to be 6,400 working hours, and is based on the academic year of forty weeks with forty working hours. One week or forty hours work is equivalent to one credit point and all units of a degree program are organized in these credit points. Each unit of the program is followed by an examination for which a board of examiners is responsible.

Many degree programs offer a basic training program after the propaedeu- tic stage lasting about 1-1.5 years, after which a choice is made for a major. Some programs have a wide range of subjects to choose from and in those cases a personal program may be devised. The HBO is subdivided into about thirty branches (like the faculties in university education), with a total of some 300 separate programs.

Part-time study arrangements are possible in a limited but growing number of programs. In HBO, part-time studies are more common. Ministerial approval is necessary for part-time programs. Due to the increase in demand, the number of part-time programs has increased.

The new two-tier structure gave opportunity to offer short programs, e.g. two-year programs. This possibility has not yet developed, probably because labor market demand for graduates from these short programs is unknown.

All institutions do not offer the same range of programs. Big universities like the ones in Amsterdam and Utrecht offer considerable choice, whereas the technical universities have a limited range. Through a process of concentration of disciplines in the past few years, particular programs are now offered at a smaller range of universities. Similarly, through the merging operation in HBO, a particular program can be followed at fewer places in the country than a couple of years ago.

Under the legislative regulations already mentioned, teaching programs are under the responsibility of the faculty councils of the universities and of a corresponding committee under the relevant authority in HBO.

Advanced Studies (Second Tier)

The first-tier curriculum should prepare students for the occupation of professional positions for which a higher educational level is required or desirable. An exception is made for doctors, dentists, veterinary surgeons, and pharmacists, who follow six-year programs. The two-tier structure was intended to provide a wide range of postgraduate courses, including research and vocational courses. Through policy changes, the government withdrew responsibility for all postgraduate courses except for teacher training courses. Together with the uncertain quality of the output of the system, in terms of knowledge and abilities of the new first tier graduate, this has resulted in a rather confusing situation which has not yet been clarified.

Currently, a new terminology is used, i.e. "post-initial education". It comprises several postgraduate training facilities, both in WO and HBO. In WO, only medical courses and the teacher training courses mentioned above are government funded. Provisions are also made for postgraduate philosophy courses. All other courses are the responsibility of the higher education institutions or privatized. The same holds true for the present funding of the second tier HBO.

Possibilities for post-university (continuing adult) education are limited. Firstly, there is a system of postgraduate courses, coordinated by a private organization (PAO and post-HBO) under the responsibility of the institutions. Courses are designed for broadening and renewal of knowledge (refresher course) and favor professionals. They are usually combined with regular job activities, and they have to be paid for. About 45,000 people make use of this kind of course.

Second, there is a new category of trainee research assistants (AIOs). They are employed by the universities for a maximum period of four years, on a salary that is generally considered very low. They teach, receive training, and complete a doctorate (Ph.D.). There are about 2,300 assistants at the moment.

Thirdly, there is a growing number of postgraduate vocational courses, in which trade and industry participate. The ministry is in some cases willing to supply an initial grant to institutions that provide these new vocational courses. About 2,100 students are now involved in these kinds of training courses.

Together with the second tier teacher training courses (1,200 students), the second tier courses for the medical professions (3,500 students) and the second tier HBO (5,500 students) about 14,800 students are involved in post-initial education (excluding the PAO courses and the post HBO courses).

In HBO there is a total of 9,500 students involved in post-initial education, apart from refresher courses. In addition, the industrial sector has an elaborate private system of training courses for workers, without much relationship to the formal education system.

A number of students go on after graduation, in most cases after a considerable lapse of time, to obtain a doctorate (Ph.D.). The production of a dissertation usually takes at least four years. In fields like humanities and liberal arts, the research and the writing of the dissertation is often performed in spare time, as the candidate is employed elsewhere. The number of completed dissertations is growing. The new salary structure for civil servants in educational institutions is probably the reason for this trend as a doctorate degree is necessary for the occupation of higher posts. The output of the AIO system will also lead to more doctorates.

ISSUES AND TRENDS

The spectacular rise in participation in higher education, together with the present economic conditions have resulted in serious financial problems for the government. Changes in the system are necessary for reasons of budget-cuts alone. Higher education is also subject to contradictory trends from demographic and sociocultural developments: a decrease of the relevant age population in the near future together with a rising percentage of that same age group seeking higher education make predictions about enrollments uncertain.

Unemployment among graduates is a relatively new phenomenon. Never before has the labor market influence on educational planning been so strong as today. The professional labor force is both growing and aging. Most people appeal for facilities for recurrent education. Technological innovation will create a demand for highly skilled and specialized labor.

The heterogeneity of the student group as to age, sex, nationality, and type of program (duration, intensity, level, extent of specialization), will increase. This will inevitably lead to a differentiation in educational programs, such as part-time and recurrent education, short courses, centers of excellence, refresher courses, and contract education. The differentiation may also extend to degrees obtained, and probably will result in different quality profiles for institutions themselves due to strategic and market-oriented approach.

The Higher Education and Research Bill, that has not yet passed through Parliament, sets rules for the organization of the degree programs. These rules are meant to ensure a uniformity in course structure. Through this uniformity, individual programs can be offered to students more easily. This so-called "modular system", which is already well known abroad, will be introduced in combination with a uniform system of credit points for blocks of subjects and a voucher system.

More attention will be paid by the institutions to an increase in the success rates of graduates as this serves a two-fold purpose: budgets per students will be lower and the predicted demand on the labor market for graduates from certain disciplines will be met. Higher success rates cannot be realized without increased effort in the field of student guidance. A monitoring system for quality-control of the educational output will be more and more a necessary component of these changes, since all the above mentioned developments create a potential threat to the quality of academic education.

(Note: The research for this report was part of the Research Program of the Center for Innovation & Co-operative Technology at the University of Amsterdam. The program aims at gaining a better insight into the relation between action and cooperative support, both in schools and in the helping profession. The program is headed by Prof. Dr. G. de Zeeuw.)

BIBLIOGRAPHY

Commission of the European Communities, *Higher Education in the European Community. Student Handbook.* London: Kogan Page, 1988.

Koppen, Jan K. *Evaluatieonderzoek Wet Twee-fasenstructuur: Deel B. Onderwijskundig Eindrapport.* (in Dutch) 's-Gravenhage, Staatsuitgeverij, 1987.

Maassen, Peter A. M., and Frans A. van Vught. *Dutch Higher Education in Transition: Policy Issues in Higher Education in the Netherlands.* Culemborg: Lemma b.v., 1989.

Ministry of Education and Science, Directorate General for Higher Education and Research. *Dutch Higher Education and Research. Major issues; Facts and Figures.* 's-Gravenhage, 1988.

OECD. *The Organization and Content of Studies at the Post-compulsory Level: Country Study* - Netherlands. 1987.

Teichler, U. "Government and Curriculum Innovation in the Netherlands." In *Governmental strategies and innovation in Higher Education,* edited by F. A. van Vught. London: Jessica Kingsley, 1989.

Wiegersma, S. *Innovatie van het Hoger Onderwijs.* (in Dutch) Groningen: Wolters Noordhoff, 1989.

NEW ZEALAND

by
William L. Renwick
Senior Research Fellow, Stout Research Center
Victoria University of Wellington, New Zealand

BACKGROUND

The development of higher education in New Zealand falls into three distinct periods. The first covers the century until 1961, during which the University of New Zealand was the dominant institution. The second, 1961-89, was a time of great expansion and diversification. The federal University of New Zealand was replaced by six (now seven) autonomous universities. Twenty-three polytechnics were established, and the eight (now six) teachers colleges became autonomous and broadened their responsibilities. The third period is being inaugurated through comprehensive policy changes which, when fully implemented during 1990-91, will profoundly change the character of all institutions of public education, including higher education.

Historically, the central government has been the essential agency of change and development in higher education. This is certainly underlined in the convulsive changes of policy now in progress. All institutions of higher education have been created through government initiatives and have depended almost entirely on public funding for capital development and current operating costs. And since education has, since 1876, been a responsibility of the central government, policies and funding priorities for higher education have been the continuing subject of public debate and political action at the national level.

Historically too, there has been a strong and widespread public belief that education is a public good which should be freely available to all who could be expected to benefit from it. Until quite recent years, tuition fees were very low. There was also a strong public expectation that the central government should ensure that universities in particular were able to meet the growing demand from suitably qualified applicants. These views drove the expansion and diversification of higher education during the years 1961-89. But during the 1980s they have been subjected to much searching criticism.

The policies of the third phase the system is now entering rest on different assumptions about education as a public good, and about the role of central government in the provision and management of public funds for publicly supported education. In the first two phases, the emphasis was on national policies which, through the intervention or moderation of central agencies, would ensure national uniformity in the administration of higher education. The theory of the policies for the third phase is that, perhaps paradoxically, strong interventions are now needed

585

by the central government to free the system from what the fourth Labor Government perceives to be too great a reliance on centrally driven policies. The role of central government aside, each of the three periods has had a different leitmotif.   In the first, higher education, which essentially meant university education, provided the highest rungs in the ladder of educational opportunity. In the second, educational opportunity broadened to include policy commitments to equality of educational opportunity within a context of national development that saw education as vital to social, economic, and technological advancement. In the third period, equity, efficiency, and accountability are the determining policy concepts.

Concern for equity has increased during the eighties in the light of the evidence that the policies which have sought to achieve equality of educational opportunities have been very unequal in their results. Admission to institutions of higher learning and the successful completion of their courses of study are closely correlated with ethnic background and socioeconomic status. There has been a growing public perception that government policies have been captured by the well educated, more affluent members of the community, the costs of whose higher education was being subsidized by general taxation at the expense of the indigenous Maori, members of various ethnic minorities, and the less well-off. General benefits in the form of bursary assistance and inexpensive tuition fees are being replaced by policies under which students will meet the full costs of courses of higher education, with exceptions based on age (under eighteen) and financial means. Policies aimed at delivering a more equitable distribution of higher education will take the form of scholarships targeted on particular groups in the community associated with bridging courses and other kinds of educational assistance to make good deficiencies in a student's previous formal education.

The drive for efficiency is taking three main forms. There is the underlying belief that the people working within educational institutions will make better decisions than politicians, administrators, and advisers who are planning or managing resources at a regional or national level. Secondly, those who make the decisions must have full control of all resources to be made available to carry them out.   Thirdly, providers of education must be clear about their objectives and priorities, and they must be accountable to their students and to local and national communities of interest.

The result is that most of the administrative apparatus built up during the first and second periods in the development of higher education is being dismantled. The University Grants Committee, which acted as the intermediary with the central government and the universities, will be abolished in 1990. The directive role which the Department of Education exercised in national policies for the polytechnics and teachers colleges has ceased. The governing bodies of thirty-six institutions of higher education will deal directly with the newly created national Ministry of Education. The nature of each institution's responsibilities will be set out in its charter which it will negotiate with the ministry. Charters must include commitments to national policy goals for equity, equal opportunities, and affirmative action, as well as to educational objectives that are specific to each institution's mission. The institutions will be funded by bulk allocations to cover all aspects of their operating costs by means of rolling triennial grants. Their performance will be evaluated in relation to the success they have in achieving the objectives set out in their charters. A new body, the Education Review Office, is responsible for reviewing and reporting on all educational institutions on a regular basis.

Policies for curriculum development are best understood in relation to the authority under which the various qualifications of institutions of higher education are awarded. The greater the control of the institution over the degree, diploma, or certificate, the greater its autonomy in curriculum development. During the second period, university teachers of general degree courses determined what they taught and how they would teach it. The curriculum of professional degrees was influenced to varying degrees by advisory councils comprising practicing professionals and university teachers. Teacher's colleges developed their curricula within broadly written national guidelines and advised by local committees of educationists, practicing teachers, and employers of teachers. The polytechnics developed under policies which included national examining bodies and national awards for which they were to prepare students. Generally speaking, they have had (until now) less local autonomy in curriculum matters. At both national and local levels close links between the various departments of polytechnics and their relevant profession, trade or occupation have been a strong feature.

As part of the restructuring of the educational system, a new body, the New Zealand Qualifications Authority, will set the criteria for all courses of study taught, or proposed to be taught, in the New Zealand educational system. The Vice-Chancellor's Committee of the New Zealand universities will apply these criteria to university awards, and similar bodies will be set up to do the same for polytechnic and teacher's college awards. The New Zealand Qualifications Authority will approve secondary school courses for vocational awards and proposals from providers outside the formal educational system. Initially, at least, only a small number of degree courses are likely to be approved for polytechnics and teacher's colleges.

PRIMARY AND SECONDARY EDUCATION

In New Zealand, all children of ages 6-15 years are required by law to be enrolled in a school. Children may enroll at primary school from the date of their fifth birthday and virtually all do. A very high percentage will already have attended a kindergarten, play center, *kohanga reo* (Maori language nest) or child care center. The formal school system spans thirteen years: eight primary, and five secondary.

The primary years are further subdivided into cycles of primary and intermediate schooling. The first six years, for children of 5-10 years, are the "primary" years. These are followed by two years of intermediate schooling (forms 1-2) which in cities and larger towns take place in separate intermediate schools and in rural districts as the first two years of secondary schooling. There is virtually no grade repetition in New Zealand schools. Children progress through the school system with others of their age. There are no examination requirements for enrollment in a secondary school, and all children make the transition. Virtually all children now remain in school until form six (16 + years). No tuition fees are charged for children of New Zealand citizens or permanent residents.

All secondary schools follow national curricula which are approved by the minister of education on the recommendation of widely representative curriculum committees. The work of the last three years of secondary school courses is strongly influenced by the prescriptions and other requirements of the national qualifications which are awarded at the end of each of those years. The School Certificate, testifies to successful completion of a general course of secondary education. It is usually sat at the end of the fifth form, the third year of secondary education. It includes more than thirty optional subjects which are intended to enable students with widely different subject interest to qualify. Performance in most subjects is judged on the basis of external examinations, but an increasing number of subjects are now assessed partly or wholly, by internal assessment. The Sixth Form Certificate is awarded to students at the end of their fourth year. It is replacing School Certificate as an indicator of a reasonably balanced course of secondary education. It is an internally assessed award. Students may be considered for enrollment in university degree courses, and many are selected for teachers' college or polytechnic courses on the basis of their Sixth Form Certificate results. Most students preparing for university study remain for a fifth year, as do an increasing number whose aim is to be selected for teachers' college or specialist courses in polytechnics. The competitive and academically prestigious university scholarships and bursaries are awarded at the end of the seventh form.

These national awards ensure the maintenance of good academic traditions in secondary schools throughout the country. The fact that New Zealand secondary schools are staffed overwhelmingly by graduates of New Zealand universities means, too, that the ethos of university study exerts a continuing influence on the curriculum policies of secondary schools. But this is tempered by school policies which prevent subject specialization in the early years of secondary education. The requirements for matriculation at the New Zealand universities have been kept deliberately broad over the years. This rests on the policy conviction that successful performance in an institution of higher education is likely to be ascertained more accurately on the basis of a students response to its courses of study than on the basis of entrance examinations.

By no means all the students admitted to courses of higher education (and this applies particularly to the universities) are admitted immediately after the completion of the sixth or seventh form. Historically, there have always been undergraduate students who were older (often much older) than the typical ages of 18-22. The arrangements for part-time study alone mean that courses which can be completed after three years full time study may take at least five for some. Historically, too, the universities have been open to what have come to be called "second chance" students; adult men and women who do not have the usual qualifications for matriculation, but who have life experiences and a strong determination to succeed. Ten percent of university undergraduates comprise such people who are given provisional admission and who may continue their studies so long as they reach the same levels of minimum success as other students.

These features of university admission policies mean that the transition from secondary school to university study is by no means so traumatic in New Zealand as it is in many other countries. Indeed, only about 50 percent of the students who by the end of the seventh form are qualified to matriculate at a New Zealand university choose to do so in the next year. Some, perhaps many, will do so in some later years. Others will proceed to a polytechnic or teachers college.

Despite pressures on accommodation, it remains the case that anyone wanting to enrol in a university and qualified to do so will be admitted to one course of study or another. But students enrolling for specialized professional courses, whether it is medicine, engineering, or computer sciences in the university; or industrial design, or hotel management in a polytechnic, face very strong competition.

It is important in the concept of a balanced secondary education that students take an active part in extracurricular activities. Competitive games are an essential feature of New Zealand national culture. So, too, are a wide range of outdoor recreational pursuits. Students normally need no special encouragement to become actively engaged. Music, drama, arts and crafts, Maori oratory, and other forms of Maori cultural expression are an integral part of secondary school life. English is the medium of instruction. Maori, however, has recently been given the status of the other official language of New Zealand and is taught in an increasing number of schools.

The secondary school year is of thirty-eight weeks duration. Most students attend their local school as day students. Boarding bursaries are available for students who must live away from home. The correspondence school provides excellent distance learning services for students who, through remoteness, illness or temporary residence outside New Zealand, cannot attend a secondary school.

Principals and teachers are appointed by each school's governing board, on which parent representatives predominate. There are increasing numbers of foreign students enrolled in public and private secondary schools. Most are from Pacific Island countries and South East Asia and are sponsored by their home governments or by the New Zealand government under development assistance schemes. The number of foreign fee payment students (most of them from East and South East Asia) is increasing, encouraged by government policies that make it easier for such students to be enrolled.

HIGHER EDUCATION

Institutions

Higher education remains overwhelmingly a public enterprise. There are some private commercial colleges, one private teacher's college, an increasing number of private colleges offering instruction in English as a second language, and an art academy; all of them on a small scale. Some private joint venture colleges for Japanese and, in some cases for other Asian students are in various stages of planning. There are moves within Maoridom to establish tribal *wananga* which are higher schools of learning teaching aspects of contemporary expertise in a context of traditional knowledge and values. The *Wananga-o-Raukawa* of *Ngati Raukawa* is the precursor, some of whose foundation students have now graduated.

The public institutions of higher education fall into four groups: universities, teachers' colleges, polytechnics, and others. Until the present time, only universities have had the authority to grant degrees. That has determined the development and character of all institutions of higher education. The New Zealand universities have at all times been open to part-time students in general degree courses, and this has meant that students could be enrolled concurrently in, say, a teachers' college and a university. Elaborate arrangements for cross-crediting have also been worked out: students, for example, who have successfully completed a New Zealand Certificate in Science or Engineering at a polytechnic can then enrol in a relevant university degree course and be admitted to the second or third year of study. During the second period, too, Waikato, Massey, Otago, and Canterbury Universities introduced Bachelor of Education degrees in cooperation with their neighboring teachers' college. Auckland followed in 1990. These are four year professional degrees for students preparing to teach in primary schools.

As the latecomers, the polytechnics were conceived as institutions that would teach courses of further education for qualifications lower in status than university degrees. Their mission was to provide advanced vocational education for the burgeoning range of occupations of an industrial and post-industrial economy. During the second period, too, the teachers' colleges broadened slightly the range of their courses. Some of them now teach courses in librarianship, social work and in aspects of educational principles and practice for people whose work is educative but not in the institutional setting of schools and colleges. To underline this broadening, the teachers' colleges have changed their names to colleges of education.

In the third period, which the system is now entering, the policy intention is that the university will not have a monopoly on degrees. The theory is that there are "markets" for advanced educational qualifications, that all institutions of higher education should compete for them, and that the possibility of competition, quite as much as its reality, will improve efficiency in the provision of higher education.

Important, too, is the distinction between intramural and extramural teaching and learning. New Zealand has comprehensive arrangements for distance learning in higher education. These are conducted by Massey University, the Open Polytechnic, the Advanced Studies for Teachers Unit of Palmerston North Teachers College, and the Correspondence School. Most of these courses are "mixed mode" in the sense that they combine print, audio, and visual materials with regular contact with tutors and some face to face teaching through block courses on a campus.

Virtually all the public institutions of higher education under the new policy dispensation will be administered under the Education Act and funded by the Ministry of Education. The Queen Elizabeth II Arts Council administers the New Zealand School of Drama and the New Zealand School of Dance.

There are broad similarities in the administration of all public institutions of higher education. Each has an academic and executive head (vice-chancellor, principal, or director) who is appointed by and answerable to a governing body predominantly made up of people elected or appointed from the community, but including staff and student representation. Academic and professional policy for each institution is approved by the governing body on the advice of a committee which is usually chaired by the academic head and is predominantly made up of teaching staff. The universities are organized by faculties or schools comprising the teachers who teach the degree courses for which each faculty or school is responsible. The polytechnics and teachers colleges are similarly organized in schools and departments.

The universities award a wide range of degrees which are ranked as bachelor, bachelor with honors; master's; and doctor's of philosophy, music, literature, laws, and science. They award honorary doctorates to distinguished academics and members of the wider community. They also award diplomas, almost all of which are postgraduate awards. The teachers' colleges award diplomas of teaching which, with additional practical experience, qualify their recipients for registration as a teacher in preschool, primary, or secondary teaching. The polytechnics award an increasing range of certificates, diplomas, and endorsed diplomas.

Undergraduate Studies

University education dates from 1869 when the University of Otago was established. The Scottish universities and the University of London were decisive influences on Otago, on the three other university colleges established in the nineteenth century (Canterbury, Auckland, and Victoria), and on the University of New Zealand. The Scottish model of general bachelor's degrees followed by specialized master's degrees remains to this day. Non-professional bachelor's degrees require three years full time study. They typically comprise one or two major subjects which are studied in each of the three years supported by other subjects each of which may be studied for one or for two years and which are intended to give breadth to the student's course of study. Students are examined or assessed at the end of each semester or academic year and must normally complete successfully one stage or unit of a subject before they can proceed to a higher one. English is the medium of instruction. University teachers, when determining academic policy, face the universal problem of balancing the interests of breadth and depth in undergraduate courses. As the universities have expanded and course offerings have increased, there has been a marked tendency for students to complete bachelor's degrees in which the minor subjects complement rather than contrast with their major subject(s).

Undergraduate courses that are the basis for later professional registration are of not less than four years duration. Some, such as law, combine academic work with experience of legal practice in the later years of the course. Medicine is a six year course, including a hospital intern year. The numbers admitted to the professional faculties are restricted and this makes for much stronger competition for admission than for general arts and science degrees. The competition in medicine and in some branches of engineering is particularly intense.

Teachers' college courses are of three years duration for early childhood education and for primary trainees enrolled for the Diploma of Teaching. Students enrolled concurrently in a teachers' college and their neighboring university for B.Ed. follow a four year course. Courses of secondary training are normally for graduates or people with comparable qualifications and take one year.

Full-time courses in polytechnics range from six months to three years. Some courses, notably those for New Zealand certificates in various technician occupations, are undertaken by cadets as an adjunct to employment. They follow the equivalent of a three-year course spread over five years, with blocks of full-time study interspersing periods of employment and training on the job.

All the universities, most teachers' colleges and some polytechnics have halls of residence or student hostels. Most undergraduate students live at home, in flats, or as boarders. The concept of the fully residential institution has never been part of the New Zealand image of higher education or, for that matter, university education. In that regard, too, New Zealand has followed Scottish rather than English models.

During the second period, successive governments committed themselves to policies for student support which included bursaries for tuition and grants in aid for living purposes. One of the more marked changes of the third period is the abolition of those policies of general entitlement. As from 1990, university students will pay tuition costs and must support themselves during the academic year unless they are judged by criteria of equity to qualify for financial support from public funds. Similar policies apply to polytechnic students but on less stringent criteria. This change of policy is politically contentious. If there is a change of government at the general election in October 1990, the previous policy is likely to be restored.

The academic year comprises twenty-six weeks for most university undergraduates, thirty-six weeks for most full-time students in polytechnics, and 36-37 for teacher college students. In earlier times, students could from their summer earnings save towards their living costs in their next year of full-time study, but high levels of unemployment now make it very difficult for them to do this.

Foreign students comprise 6 percent of the full time students in universities and 2 percent in polytechnics. Most come from Pacific Island countries but numbers from South East Asia and East Asia are increasing.

According to official statistics, the annual tuition costs per student ranged from $NZ8,000-24,000 in 1990 ($NZ1 = US$0.60). Typical estimates were: $NZ8,500 for university undergraduate courses in arts, commerce, law; $NZ8,500 for polytechnic typing/secretarial courses; $NZ9,500 for teacher's college courses for primary teachers; $NZ9,700 for engineering technician courses; $NZ12,500 for teachers college courses for secondary teachers; $NZ14,500 for university undergraduate courses on science, computer science, engineering, agriculture and other applied subjects; and $NZ24,000 for veterinary science. Living costs for students were estimated at $NZ7,000 for the 1990 academic year.

Advanced Studies and Research

The master's degree has traditionally provided opportunities for specialization and for an introduction to original research. In some universities during the second period honors bachelor's degrees were introduced to provide subject specialization without a significant research component. Students with a good honors bachelor's degree would then proceed to a Ph.D. degree and enroll for a research degree.

Honors bachelor's degrees require one year of full time study after the completion of a bachelor's degree. Master's courses were originally conceived as a one year course of full- time study, normally requiring a student to be examined in six papers or in four papers and a thesis. But it is usually only students who present six papers who can complete in one year.

During the second period there was a big increase in the number of postgraduate diplomas. These typically provide an introduction to some field of specialized professional activity and usually require one year of full time study after graduation. Virtually all medical postgraduate education is conducted by the specialist colleges of the medical profession, but university teachers contribute significantly to them. Some teachers' colleges teach one-year advanced diploma courses for experienced teachers in special education and English as a second language.

Doctoral degrees are of three kinds: doctorates in philosophy (Ph.D.); other doctorates in science, law, music and literature; and honorary doctorates. The Ph.D. is a research degree. The typical requirement for registration is a pass with first or second class honors in a bachelor's (honors) or master's degree. Successful candidates produce under supervision a thesis which is a significant contribution to the knowledge or understanding of a field of study. The Ph.D.s take at least two years of full-time work to complete. Doctorates of science, law, music and literature are awarded for substantial published work of a high standard which entitles the candidate to an authoritative standing in his or her field of expertise.

From their inception, the New Zealand universities have fostered research as well as teaching. During the second period, their contribution to research and scholarly publication increased greatly. The expectation is that university teachers will devote about one third of their time to research and publication. This commitment to research is much less well developed in the teachers' colleges and polytechnics which have been thought of as essentially teaching institutions. Under the new policies for publicly funded research now being introduced, teachers in all branches of higher education will be able to compete for funding support. Until the present time the most important source of outside funding has been the Medical Research Council (now the Health Research Council). Many university teachers, particularly in science, engineering, and other professional faculties are regularly engaged in research under contract to outside funding agencies.

During the second period, it was the policy of the University Grants Committee to strengthen postgraduate research in New Zealand universities. Students were encouraged by study awards and the offer of tutoring responsibilities to undertake Ph.D. studies in New Zealand rather than overseas. For those who have successfully completed a Ph.D., postdoctoral fellowships are available in competition for further study or research overseas. Foreign students do postgraduate research in New Zealand, notably under the Commonwealth Scholarship and Fellowship Plan and under Fulbright awards.

ISSUES AND TRENDS

It will be clear from this account that, in 1990, higher education in New Zealand is at a moment of profound change. What is happening in the entire system of public education is to be seen in the context of changes which the fourth Labor Government has since 1986 instituted in the role of central government, with far reaching consequences for the entire public sector and for the society as a whole. The economic crisis which the country has experienced since the first oil shock of 1973 meant that radical changes of direction were needed. The public sector had become too dominant in the expectations of New Zealanders and the economy could no longer sustain all the policy commitments that previous governments had entered into in the fifty years between 1935 and 1984. To this, the fourth Labor Government brought the ideological conviction that, as a matter of basic strategy, the central government should become much less interventionist when seeking to achieve its policy objectives of equity, efficiency, and accountability. It should create the necessary framework of law and regulatory protection, work out (in consultation) the national guidelines within which educational and other public institutions should operate, and then establish conditions under which they can set and review their own objectives and develop their own self-steering mechanisms.

There is a great deal of Adam Smith in all this which gives a warm glow to believers in what is happening and raises cries of despair and disbelief among those who are yet to be persuaded of either its wisdom or its practicality. New Zealanders are being thrust into a brave new world whether they like it or not.

BIBLIOGRAPHY

Administering for Excellence. Report of the Task Force to Review Education Administration (The Picot Report). Wellington, 1988.

Department of Education, New Zealand. *Annual Reports.* (Appendices to the Journals of the House of Representatives). Wellington, New Zealand.

Gould, J. *The University Grants Committee 1961-1986 - History.* Wellington: University Grants Committee, 1988.

Hawke, G. R. *Report of the Working Group on Post Compulsory Education and Training.* Wellington, 1988.

New Zealand's Universities: Partners in National Development (the Watts Report). Report of the Review Committee set up by the New Zealand Vice Chancellor's Committee. Wellington, 1987.

Parton, H. *The University of New Zealand.* Auckland University Press/Oxford University Press, 1979.

Probine, M., and Fargher, R. *The Management, Funding and Organization of Continuing Education and Training.* Department of Education, New Zealand, 1987.

The Treasury, New Zealand. *Government Management Brief to the Incoming Government Volume II: Education Issues.* Wellington, 1987.

Universities Grants Committees, New Zealand. *Annual Reports* 1962-1990. Wellington, New Zealand.

NORWAY

by
Karl Oyvind Jordell
Research Coordinator
Institute for Studies in Research and
Higher Education, Norway

BACKGROUND

In the middle ages, Norwegian students seeking higher education had to study abroad in continental Europe or England. From about 1500, they also travelled to Sweden (Uppsala, Lund) and Denmark (Copenhagen). The first enrollments at the University of Oslo took place a few years after the establishment of the first university in 1811.

A second university was not established till after World War II (Bergen in 1946), but specialized institutions of higher education (such as the Technical University in Trondheim), were in existence since 1900. Before the turn of the century the first institutions in technical education and teacher education also came to be established although these did not become institutions of higher education until the middle of this century.

From about 1965, a major expansion took place in the system of higher education resulting in steep increases in the number of students at the universities in Oslo and Bergen; the establishment of two new universities, one in the very north (Tromso), and one in the middle Norway (Trondheim) through merging the Technical University with other institutions; and the upgrading of vocational schools in fields like teacher education, nursing, and engineering. In addition, district colleges were established offering professional training in fields like business and public administration, and university courses at lower levels.

The government of Norway plays the key role of general policy making and funding for education, through the Ministry of Education and Research. The universities have for a long time had more or less complete freedom in designing curricula, and presently the policy is to delegate more budgetary decisions as well to the institutions. Institutions in other sectors of the higher educational system operate in a somewhat similar fashion but they have to deal with other levels of authority in addition to the ministry: advisory councils, to some extent, influence the curricula in semiprofessional schools for nursing and teacher education; and regional boards of higher education have some influence in budgetary and personnel matters, and may have strong opinions in questions concerning what kind of studies and courses should be offered at the regional institutions.

The role of private organizations and the private sector is limited in Norwegian higher education. Church affiliated organizations have run teachers' colleges and still own a few nursing colleges. The funds for these colleges come, however, almost exclusively from the state. Likewise, the state contributes substantially to three privately owned institutions in the field of theology. In the field of business administration, there are a few private institutions, most notably the Norwegian School of Management in the Oslo area.

During the last five to ten years, public institutions have established stronger links with industry, by establishing science parks etc. It is likely that curriculum development in certain areas, most noticeably in science, will be influenced by this. Likewise, in the humanities, the institutions have become more oriented towards giving shorter courses that will form part of degree programs in fields such as science and economics.

PRIMARY AND SECONDARY EDUCATION

Norwegian children start school at the age of seven, and complete their compulsory education at the age of sixteen. Some children will have participated in preschool activities, or gone to kindergarten, before the age of seven. A lowering of the entrance age for primary education to six years is now being considered.

Compulsory primary education is divided into two sections: grades 1-6 (childrens' school) and grades 7-9 (junior high school). All children now study English from grade four, and students with a non-Norwegian background are offered training in their mother language, in addition to Norwegian. An important characteristic in the Norwegian primary school system is the existence of many small schools: in sparsely populated areas, students are not transported to central schools, but given their education in their local village, at schools which may have less than twenty students.

As there is no streaming in compulsory school, any student who has completed the nine years can in principle be accepted in any area of study in the secondary education, but in certain areas and/or geographical locations students may compete, on the basis of grades, to get into the area of their primary choice.

The curriculum at secondary level consists of ten areas of study: general subjects (formerly the gymnasium), commercial and clerical subjects (formerly the economic gymnasium), technical subjects, maritime subjects, physical education, domestic sciences, social work and health subjects, aesthetic subjects, fishing industry, and agriculture and natural resources.

Students planning to take higher education, normally take three years of secondary education in the general or commercial areas of study. Within the area of general subjects, students, until recently, had to choose a particular branch of specialization after their first year. The most common branches were science, languages, and social sciences. However, the curriculum within these branches was not limited to these specialities. All branches provided a well-rounded general education. Students planning to go into engineering or medicine had to choose the science branch.

Since 1988, two thirds of the curriculum is used for general subjects, and one third for in-depth studies in some of the general subjects, or in specific subjects. The general subjects are Norwegian, social science, history, geography,

English, second foreign language (usually German or French), religion, physical education, mathematics, and science. Areas of in-depth studies include mathematics, physics, biology, chemistry, economy, law, social science, foreign languages, etc. The major change is that students may now undertake in-depth studies in unrelated fields (e.g. mathematics, law, and French). Formerly, students who wanted to specialize in math would also have to take several science courses, and courses they would have otherwised desired (e.g. law and French) could not be taken or could only be taken with difficulty. However, the option of choosing related fields, like in the branch system, is still open. Students planning to go into medical fields and engineering still have to take both math and sciences.

The length of the school year is 185 days, from about 20th August till 20th June with holidays for Christmas and Easter, and in February/March. National examinations are held in the major subjects (like Norwegian, mathematics, and English) and the grades from these examinations are included in the diploma along with the annual averages.

Extra curricular activities in Norwegian secondary schools are more limited than in American schools. For example, students interested in sports generally join clubs not affiliated with the school.

Most students can live with their parents while attending secondary school. No tuition fees are charged, but students/ parents have to buy the books.

Teachers in the general studies area of secondary school are normally trained at universities, and teach two or three subjects. Increasingly, teachers of general subjects in secondary school have started their teaching career in grades 7-9 in compulsory school.

The number of foreign students in secondary education is small; more or less limited to children of foreign citizens living in Norway, and students participating in exchange programs.

HIGHER EDUCATION

Institutions

The system of higher education in Norway is composed of the university sector, the college sector, a few public institutions in the arts and the performing arts, and some private institutions. The university sector consists of four general universities (Oslo, Bergen, Trondheim, Tromso) and six specialized institutions of university status in fields such as business administration (in Bergen), agriculture (at As, south of Oslo), and veterinary medicine (Oslo). The college sector comprises about 110 institutions organized under seventeen regional boards, primarily giving education in the semiprofessional areas. Some of the institutions also give basic university courses. The total number of students in higher education is about 110,000. The University of Oslo is the largest institution, with about 25,000 students.

The institutions in the university sector (and a couple of the private institutions) are heavily research oriented, and give courses and degrees at all levels. Institutions in the college sector are less research oriented, and only a few of them give courses at the higher levels. It is, however, relatively easy to transfer from institutions in the college sector to universities.

Universities are generally divided into faculties, and the faculties are divided into departments (called "institutes"). This structure is less explicit in the college sector where most institutions are small; only a few have more than 1,000 students.

Administration of the university is in the hands of a board, headed by an elected rector. A faculty is governed by a council and a board headed by an elected dean, and a department is overseen by a council and a board headed by an elected department chair. All members of boards and councils are elected within the university, by professors (who hold a majority of the seats), students, and technical and administrative staff. The university director is the secretary of the board and is in charge of administrative offices of the university. Faculty directors and department secretaries have similar functions at lower levels.

All four universities offer degrees in humanities, sciences, social sciences, and medicine. Law is offered at three (Oslo, Bergen, Tromso), odontology at two (Oslo and Bergen), and theology at one (Oslo).

Undergraduate Studies

In the university sector, two types of programs are available: professional programs and degrees of 5-6 years duration (in law, medicine, etc.), or general degree programs in humanities, sciences, or social sciences. In the latter fields, there is a lower degree *(cand.mag.)*, generally of about four years duration and composed of courses in 2-3 different subjects.

In the college sector, students are either offered three year programs, preparing them for the semiprofessions, or study subjects in the humanities, sciences, or social sciences in courses up to eighteen months duration. In a few cases, institutions in the college sector also offer 4-5 year programs (engineering, business administration, special education, etc.).

The general admission requirement for higher education is the completion of secondary school in the general or commercial areas of studies. However, students may also be accepted on the basis of studies in other areas in the secondary curriculum plus a certain number of exams from the general area of studies. This option is more in use in the college sector than in the university sector.

In a few of the fields, admission is coordinated by a central agency. Generally, however, the individual school or faculty handles admission. In most fields, admission is more or less competitive, on the basis of grades rather than on work experience.

One important characteristic of the undergraduate studies in Norway is that specialization is fairly high, especially in the humanities and social sciences. Students normally concentrate on one subject at a time, pursuing it for one year *(grunnfag)*, one and one-half years *(mellomfag)*, or two years *(storfag)*. This trend is somewhat less explicit in the sciences, which employs a credit system (twenty credits per year). In many fields of studies, students are not required to follow classes, but may study on their own till it is time for taking the exam. In the college programs for the semiprofessions, students often take small units in several subjects, alongside supervised practice.

Another important characteristic of the system is flexibility, in the sense that students may include units from several programs in their degrees. Thus, inside the universities, students may not only include units from another faculty in their *cand.mag.* degree (e.g. mathematics or first level of law in their *cand.mag.* degree in humanities). They can also take an interfaculty *cand.mag.* degree, combining units from several faculties (e.g. English, mathematics, and law). This combination may be used as a basis for a higher degree and thus has the same standing as a more "pure" degree.

Diplomas from semiprofessional programs at the colleges, and units in other subjects completed at these colleges, may be incorporated into a "pure" or an interfaculty *cand.mag.* degree. There is also a "regional" *cand.mag.* degree, composed of diplomas/or units from the college system. The regional *cand.mag.* degree, however, does not include preparatory courses in history of philosophy and logic, which are mandatory in almost all university degrees.

To some extent, units from within or outside universities may make up parts of the professional degrees at the universities. Thus, a diploma from a college of engineering gives access to the third year at the technical university. In general, however, flexibility with reference to professional degrees at universities is more limited.

In Norway, all students in higher education plan to complete a degree. Many limit themselves to a diploma from a semiprofessional school. And even if they continue their education, and complete additional courses (e.g. one *grunnfag*), they may not qualify for any degree. Nevertheless, they are considered qualified for their profession or vocation on the basis of a diploma and possible additional courses.

In principle, Norwegian institutions of higher education limit their activity to teaching and giving exams, and bear no direct responsibility for housing, extra curricular activities, etc. Except in nursing, few, if any, institutions are residential. Housing, cafeterias, and to some extent extra curricular activities are the responsibility of semipublic welfare associations for students. Many students have to rent rooms or apartments in the open market. Most extracurricular activities are taken care of by students' associations, with somewhat loose ties to the university. No tuition fees are charged by public institutions and among private institutions too, only a few charge fees.

The cost of higher education for the individual student is thus limited to living expenses and books. A special state bank offers loans at a reasonable interest rate. Students also get small stipends, at approximately 15 percent of the estimated yearly cost. Many students are hesitant to accumulate high debts, and prefer to work part-time. In the universities (more than in semiprofessional programs) this tendency affects the efficiency of the system with many students spending more years at the university than necessary, if the students were doing full-time studies. If studies are prolonged over certain limits, stipends and loans are cut off. Stipends and loans are also provided to Norwegian students who study abroad. Support to foreign students in Norway is limited to certain groups of students from developing countries such as students with refugee status, and students with strong relations to Norway.

In the universities, the classes are offered for about thirty weeks per year. In addition, exams take time as written exams must be graded before oral exams can take place. Thus, a normal academic year consists of a fall semester of four months (approximately 20th August-20th December) and a five month spring semester (15th January-15th June). The latter includes a ten day break for Easter, and some holidays in May/June. Most teaching is in Norwegian, but in many fields several textbooks are in English. In the semiprofessional programs in the colleges and in medicine and odontology, the school year may last till about 25th June, and the Christmas break is shorter.

The typical method of assessment is the written exam at the end of a course. This is graded anonymously by external examiners and teachers from the institution. Take-home exams have been introduced in some fields. At some institutions group exams, written or oral, are used. Grading scales vary considerably.

Professors at universities move from the rank of tenured assistant professor *(amanuensis)* to associate professor (first *amanuensis*) on completion of a doctorate or the equivalent. In many fields, competition for a university position is strong. In these fields most professors have a doctorate when taking a position, and thus start at the level of associate professor. To become a full professor, it is generally necessary to compete for a vacant position at this level. As there are far fewer full professorships than lower positions, many teachers at the university are not promoted to full professors, even though their qualifications may be more than adequate. A few associate professors are given promotion to full professor on the basis of their personal qualifications without having to compete for a vacant position. Before entering tenured positions, teachers normally have gone through a 3-5 years recruitment period, in various types of non-tenured positions. Research accomplishments form the main criteria for appointment and promotion.

In most institutions in the college sector, research qualifications among teachers are less significant. Most institutions, however, have a few professors with high research qualifications using the title *dosent*.

The number of foreign students registered in lower degree studies and in the college sector is about 3,700. Knowledge of Norwegian is a prerequisite to be admitted to most institutions, and courses in Norwegian for foreign students are offered at the larger universities. Admission of foreign students is based on a quota and for students considering study in Norway it is preferable to approach the institution about a year in advance.

Advanced Studies and Research

Students who have completed a lower degree *(cand.mag.)* may continue for a higher degree at a university, by pursuing advanced studies in a selected subject in a two-year program. In these *hovedfag* programs, the writing of a thesis is a major requisite: often more than 50 percent of the time (one academic year) is allocated for this purpose. These *hovedfag* programs are thus research oriented. The field pursued for a higher degree must normally have been studied for one and one-half years for the lower degree. Furthermore, flexibility is more limited when it comes to entering higher degrees programs. A degree, for example in history, from a regional college may not qualify for a *hovedfag* in history at a university, unless certain requirements are met.

Students completing a higher degree get the titles *cand.philol.* (humanities), *cand.scient.* (sciences) or *cand.polit.* (social sciences). A *mag.art.* degree (offered in humanities and social science) is a higher degree which gives the student an opportunity of high specialization within his or her field. In a few cases, two-year *hovedfag* programs are offered at other institutions.

As students for the professionally oriented degrees at universities are not required to complete a lower general degree before taking their professional degree after approximately 5-6 years of study, degrees in theology *(cand.theol.)*, law *(cand.jur.)*, medicine *(cand.med.)*, odontology *(cand.odont.)*, psychology *(cand.psychol.)*, and economics *(cand.econ.)*, etc. are regarded as higher degrees. In general, students pursue disciplines within their field for the whole duration of their program. In some cases (e.g. medicine and odontology) students have clinical practice; in others, the study of other subjects may form part of the professional program.

Professional programs at the specialized universities (e.g. business administration, veterinary medicine) are generally a little shorter than those in the general universities. Entrance to these programs, and to medicine, odontology, and to some extent law, is highly competitive.

Formerly, the Norwegian doctorate was primarily an individual undertaking, with no course work and little or no formal advising system. This was especially true in the "softer" subjects. In science and medicine, the programs were more formalized, at first probably as a consequence of the candidate sharing instruments or patients with the more established researchers.

Over the last few years, however, doctoral programs modeled after American Ph.D. programs are in the process of being established in most fields: *dr.legis* in law, *dr.art.* in humanities, *dr.scient.* in science, and *dr.polit.* in social science. In theology, medicine, and odontology, the traditional degrees *(dr.theol., dr.med., dr.odont.)* have been kept but formalized. In the other fields, it is still possible to complete the "old" *dr.philos.* degree, without following programs and formalized advisory system. Similarly the "older" degrees in law *(dr.juris.)* and economics *(dr.econ.)* have been kept. The specialized universities are increasingly offering structured doctoral programs as well (e.g. *dr.ing.* at the technical university). One institution in the college sector offers a doctorate, *dr.scient.* degree, in special education.

Students are admitted to the "new" doctoral programs if they have completed a higher or a professional degree. Most candidates for the "older" doctoral degrees will likewise have completed a higher or a professional degree in the relevant field. The new programs have a formal duration of three years, with a thesis as the major part.

Students working towards a higher or professional degree get loans and stipends on a similar basis as those studying for a lower degree. Candidates working towards a doctorate do not get loans or stipends from the state bank. They hold regular employment or get stipends from the university or research councils.

Post doctoral programs are not very well developed, but some stipends are available, mainly in the natural sciences and medicine.

Most of the research performed in the higher education sector fall in to the basic research category. Norway differs from most other European countries by having a relatively large sector of research institutes not affiliated with the higher education system, mainly in the technical sector and in the social sciences. Most research activity in these institutes is applied. This is also the case for research activity taking place in the industrial sector.

A total of about 1,300 foreign students are enrolled in higher degrees and doctoral programs.

ISSUES AND TRENDS

Norwegian policies for education were reviewed by OECD in 1987. As for higher education, these experts brought up issues related to improvement of higher education by amalgamation of the many small units of higher education, and establishment of closer links between universities and other institutions. The experts were also concerned with problems of recruitment of students to longer university programs.

These questions and many others were later dealt with by a national governmental commission (1988), which suggested the establishment of the "Norway network", an integrated network of institutions of higher education. Another major issue in the national report was "the restoration of the full-time student", through better stipend and loan schemes for students, and better housing and child care facilities. Other important issues were the research policy of Norway, and reorganization of the administrative structures of the universities.

A new university law passed in 1989 dealt with some issues in the latter group, and a white paper on research policy was also debated in the Parliament in 1989. However many other educational issues, student welfare and closer ties between institutions of higher education, have not been dealt with in any substantial way. Problems in the national economy has made it difficult to give priority to student welfare. Strong regional and, to some extent, professional interests will make any likely amalgamation process in higher education a lengthy one.

Another new development in 1989-90 is the dramatic increase in the number of applicants to institutions of higher education, probably due to high unemployment rates. Admission to many fields of study has become highly competitive.

BIBLIOGRAPHY

Bie, K. N. *Creating a New University. The Establishment and Development of the University of Tromso.* Report of the Institute for Studies in Research and Higher Education Report. Oslo, 1981.

Eeg-Henriksen, F. *The Role of Women in Higher Education. The Case of Norway.* Report of the Institute for Studies in Research and Higher Education Report. Oslo, 1985.

Gundem, B. B. "Trends in Research on Higher Education in Norway - A Tentative Outline and Some Examples." *Higher Education in Europe* Volume VIII (1983): 12-18

Gundem, B. B. "The Case of Norway: State-of-the-Art in ten selected areas of research on higher education." *Higher Education in Europe* Volume XII (1987): 83-90.

Kyvik, S. *The Norwegian Regional College. A study of the establishment and implementation of a reform in higher education.* Report of the Institute for Studies in Research and Higher Education. Oslo, 1981.

Kyvik, S. "Decentralization of Higher Education and Research in Norway." *Comparative Education* 19 (1981): 21-29.

Kyvik, S., and Skoie, H. "Recent Trends in Norwegian Higher Education." *European Journal of Education* 17 (1982): 183-192.

Kyvik, S. "Postgraduate Education in Norway." *European Journal of Education 21* (1986): 251-260.

March, J. G., and Olsen, J. P. eds. *Ambiguity and Choice in Organizations.* Oslo: Universitetsforlaget, 1976.

Med viten og vilje. *Report of the Norwegian Royal Commission on Higher Education.* Norwegian Official Reports. NOU, Oslo: Norwegian Official Reports, 1988.

Midgaard, K. "The Interplay of Local and Central Decisions." In: Daalder, H., Shils, E. eds. *Universities, Politicians and Bureaucrats.* Cambridge: Cambridge University Press, 1982.

OECD. *Review of National Policies for Education - Norway.* Paris: OECD, 1987.

PAKISTAN

by
Manzooruddin Ahmed
Vice-Chancellor
University of Karachi, Pakistan

BACKGROUND

Education in Pakistan reflects the difficult conditions through which the new country is passing since its inception in 1947. The official system of education, which receives state support and patronage, is essentially a legacy from the system that British introduced in the Indian subcontinent in the nineteenth century. It was bequeathed to Pakistan, not only with a specific structure and organization, but also with its contradictions and inconsistencies. In the last forty years of its life, the new country is making every effort to make the system more workable and compatible to its own needs and aspirations. The country has to grapple with educational problems as they persist and devise solutions relevant to its own situation, needs, and aspirations.

Politically, Pakistan is a federation of four provinces with a federal government in Islamabad. According to the Constitution, education is a provincial subject and its administration and supervision is basically the responsibility of the provincial government which has, for the purpose, a department of education headed by the minister of education of the province. Each province is divided into regions for primary, secondary, college, technical, and professional education. The educational network of institutions in each region is administered and supervised by the respective directorate of school education or college education.

The federal government has a Ministry of Education headed by a minister of education with the responsibility to formulate educational policies for the country, and to coordinate educational efforts at the level of the provinces to ensure uniformity of educational objectives, practices, and standards; and to oversee the developmental needs of the provinces pertaining to education. To date, in addition to basic guidelines evolved through deliberations of the First Education Conference in 1947, four major policy documents have been produced by the federal Ministry of Education; each coinciding with a change of government in the country. Apart from the degree and areas of emphasis, there is a continuity and similarity in the four policies in as much as they relate to an identical structure of education and address themselves to a common set of problems. It is ironical that any innovations and deviations sought or attempted by a particular government enjoyed only a short lease of life and ended in failure or came to an abrupt end with the installation of a new government in office. The Ministry of Education formulates policies or plans of action in cooperation and consultation with the University Grants Commission, the Ministry of Finance, and the Ministry of Planning and Development, the Economic Affairs division, and such other agencies as may have relevance to education. The federal ministry also provides funds for university education, and through the University Grants Commission, coordinates the work done in the different universities of the country.

Apart from the official system, the country also has a traditional system of education which consists of *darul ulooms* and *madrassahs* concentrating on teaching Islamic disciplines of learning. This system has persisted independent of government support both before the creation of Pakistan and since then. The feeling is growing in the country to reform and update the curriculum of these institutions and to lessen the present hiatus between the two systems.

ELEMENTARY AND SECONDARY EDUCATION

Structurally, the school education is on a $5+5+2$ basis of which the first five years represent the elementary school stage; the next five years, the secondary stage; and the last two years, the higher secondary stage. The cities in Pakistan have a network of preprimary schools (also special montessori schools) but these are privately run and not a part of the state supported system. The elementary education, though not compulsory, is free for all incoming students. Primary education is a weak link in the chain of the educational system and at present is not able to cater to more than half of the nation's children. The excessive dropout rate from classes 1-5 specially in rural areas, is also a serious problem.

The curriculum at the primary level includes reading, writing, arithmetic, general science, social studies, religious studies, and physical education. A trained primary school teacher should have a "PTC" or "CT" certificate which consists of one year training beyond matriculation and higher secondary stage respectively. Classes begin at 8 *a.m.* and continue till 1 *p.m.* with a fifteen minutes recess in the middle. It is not uncommon for a school to run in two shifts. The education is free in government-run schools, though the text books and copy books have to be bought by the children. In cities, non-government private schools also proliferate where the story is different. They are usually very well provided schools, teaching is much more regular and systematic, the use of audio-visual aids is popular, but the school fee is generally very high. In general, the quality of education in private schools is much higher than the government schools.

Secondary education begins from class six and is organized in three stages. The first stage represents classes 6-8, the second stage comprises of classes 9-10 and the third stage, which is also known as higher secondary, consists of classes 11-12. The curriculum is diversified and has been designed to prepare the students for a vocation or to concentrate on a profession. There is emphasis on science and mathematics and attempts have been made to correlate general education with technical education. The diversification of subjects begins from class nine, when students are allowed the option to pursue specialized education, either in sciences, arts, industrial arts or commerce.

Efforts are being made to further integrate the secondary and higher secondary education, so that they may become a continuous unit rather than separate and independent of each other. Thus the duration of education up to the end of secondary stage will become twelve years instead of the ten as the case has been so far. Teaching at the secondary school level is done by the subject teacher. Here again, there is a difference in the standard and the quality of teaching in the government schools and the private schools. Private schools charge higher fees but the quality of their education is also better. The duration of the academic year is about nine months. In summer there is usually a two month vacation and a twenty day break in winter. Most of the government schools, run in double shifts from 8 *a.m.* to 1 *p.m.* and 1.30 *p.m.* to 5.30 *p.m.* The teaching is done in the national language (Urdu) or the provincial languages. There are also government schools where English is used as the medium of instruction.

In most of the private schools, English is used as the medium for teaching purposes. The qualifications for high school teachers is a B.Ed. degree and the responsibility for selection of teachers rests with the relevant directorate of education. The private schools also try to adhere to the B.Ed. condition but occasionally appointments are made otherwise. Hostel facilities at the secondary level are not too common, but in cities provision of hostels for students can be found. The government- run public schools, cadet schools or other schools maintained by the defence services keep the students full-time on a residential basis. These institutions charge fees, but are heavily subsidized by the government. For academic control and examination purposes, the schools are affiliated to different secondary or intermediate boards of education.

The boards of secondary education hold examinations for the tenth class or both for ninth and tenth classes in the form of annual examinations and successful candidates receive their high school leaving certificate (matriculation) in different divisions or grades along with their transcripts. Similarly, the boards of intermediate education hold examinations for eleventh and twelfth classes and the successful completion entitles the student to receive a certificate for higher secondary or intermediate stage. The boards have also the responsibility of prescribing the curricula, prepared by the bureaus of curriculum in the provinces. They also act as the accrediting agency to determine the equivalence of different high school certificates in comparison to their own. The enrollment of foreign students at the secondary education level is not very significant and is directly dealt by the teaching institutions. Most of the foreign students prefer going to private schools rather than to the mainstream education. A good number of private prestigious schools, in addition to matriculation, also prepare their students for "O" level and "A" level examinations conducted by the University of London or the Cambridge University.

In case of institutions charging a regular fee, it is borne by the parents. However, government sponsored education is heavily subsidized and private schools also have a practice of fee concessions which amount to 15-20 percent of the total fee receipts. At the secondary stage of education both in government and private schools, these is no distinction for fees between Pakistani and foreign students. The school day consists of mainly a curricular program but all schools make an attempt to arrange extracurricular and cocurricular activities. These consist of debates, functions, exhibits, excursions, picnics, etc. The schools also try to encourage sports activity. The provinces also have a directorate and a board of technical education at the secondary and higher secondary level with technical schools and polytechnics which impart technical education in various trades and the successful candidates receive a certificate or a diploma in the specific trade.

HIGHER EDUCATION

Institutions

At the inception of Pakistan in 1947, the new country started with three universities and currently, despite the separation of Bangladesh, the country has twenty-two universities of which twenty are state or government universities and two are privately sponsored and financed. The universities in Pakistan, though exclusively financed by the government are considered autonomous bodies, more or less independent in their academic and research work. For liaison with the government, the chancellor of the university is the governor of the region and in certain cases, the minister of education of the province acts as the pro-chancellor.

For coordination among universities, and to facilitate funding for the universities, a university grants commission was established in 1973. The commission is responsible for disbursing grants provided in the annual development program of the federal government for the higher education and research sector, in addition to funding of a number of approved projects. The commission directs its own program of activities for development and updating of curriculum in the universities, promotion of research, teacher exchange programs and student welfare. What the universities earn from fees comes to even less than 5 percent of the university budget. In a sense, the total university budget is provided by the federal government.

The universities in Pakistan are either general universities or agricultural and engineering universities. In addition, some universities have a special character of their own. Allama Iqbal University as an institution of distance education is based in Islamabad, the capital. Similarly, Islamic University of Bahawalpur and the International Islamic University at Islamabad are mainly devoted to Islamic learning. The Aga Khan Medical University is operating as a private university in Karachi, and Lahore also has a University of Management Sciences which is a private institution. Of the twenty-two universities, twelve are general, three agricultural, four engineering, and three fall under the general category of others.

The general universities have a dual academic function to perform, namely their own undergraduate and graduate teaching and research and the academic supervision and holding of examinations for the affiliated and the constituent colleges. (For example, the total enrollment in the University of Karachi is about 70,000). Each university has a number of affiliated colleges and constituent colleges working under its academic jurisdiction. The general universities have law colleges, medical colleges, and teachers' training colleges as constituent colleges. Professional universities have affiliated or constituent colleges in their own academic area. The constituent colleges are under a university faculty which regulates and supervises their academic program and activities through a board of studies. The university itself has teaching departments under different faculties, institutes, area study centers, and centers of excellence.

The academic and the administrative head of the university is the vice-chancellor who is appointed by the chancellor, generally from among the senior teachers of the university. The registrar, the director of finance, and the controller of examinations, manage the university offices and are responsible for the day to day administration, financial management, and the conducting of university examinations. The chief executive authority of the university is the syndicate, which has a representation of the teachers, students, prominent citizens, and government nominees. With a wider representation and above the syndicate is the university senate, which meets once or twice a year, but its function is mainly formal and ceremonial. The university selection board performs the task of selection and appointment of teaching staff according to the requirements prescribed by the university grants commission. The selection board recommends the appointments to the syndicate for approval and once the approval is received, the registrar notifies the applicant of his appointment. The salaries and grades of university teachers are the same as in the civil services of the country.

For the supervision of academic programs and related decisions, every university has an academic council represented by deans of the faculties, chairmen of departments, directors of institutes, and teachers. All academic programs and curricular provisions which emanate at the level of the departmental board of studies and pass through the board of faculty, receive approval from the academic council, and eventually from the university syndicate. The number of faculties and the teaching departments vary from university to university and each department makes provisions generally of two types of studies. At the undergraduate studies level, honors courses are conducted and M.A. classes are available at the graduate level. Most of the universities are presently run on a semester system, but certain universities, finding the experience not very suitable have decided to revert to the annual system. Diploma courses are also offered but they do not form a regular feature of the teaching program of the departments.

Academic appointments are in the ranks of lecturers, assistant professors, associate professors, and professors. Chairmen of departments are elected from among associate professors and professors usually in order of seniority. Each department has a board of studies to supervise the curricular program of the department. Any desired changes are submitted for approval to the board of the faculty which is headed by the dean of the faculty. Teaching in most of the universities is carried out under a semester system, but the method of teaching most popular is the lecture mode. English and Urdu are used for instructional purposes and students are free to answer their examination papers in either of the two languages. The assessment and monitoring of teaching is done through midterm and terminal tests, and transcripts show a grade point average. Admission to degree programs is on merit based on students' previous grades but a certain percentage of candidates are admitted on a quota basis which allow consideration to teachers' wards, sports and underdeveloped regions.

The university charges fees from the enrolled students but fees charged are nominal as compared to the expenses incurred on a student. Most of the students are day scholars and commute from their residence in the city, but most universities have hostels for out-of-town students and for foreign students. Again, the lodging and boarding in the hostels is heavily subsidized by the universities. All the universities provide for extracurricular activities which are usually carried out through student organizations and through the student union. Sports and games receive considerable attention in the university and each university tries to have teams competing at the provincial, inter-provincial, and national level.

All the universities have a certain number of foreign students, studying in different faculties. Most of them do graduate studies but enrollment for undergraduate studies is also not uncommon. All foreign students before 1986 were treated at par with Pakistani students with respect to tuition fees and other charges, but subsequently the Ministry of Education has increased the fees for foreign students. For general students the fee now is Rs.28,000 (US$2,400) and for students in professional programs (medicine, engineering, pharmacy, etc.) the fee is Rs.38,000 (US$2,900) per year. However, any foreign student applying for a concession receives a sympathetic hearing and is allowed a certain amount of fee waiver. The enrollment of foreign students from the baccalaureate to the Ph.D. level in the universities has been approximately 2,000.

Undergraduate Studies

Undergraduate studies are carried out mainly in colleges which retain an affiliation with the university of their region. A college represents a four-year study program of which the first two years are not concerned with the university but consist of higher secondary or intermediate years and are academically supervised and examined by the Board of Intermediate Education. The higher secondary years are important because the diversification of students into different professional channels begins after this stage. A successful intermediate student is free to compete for admission into a medical or engineering college which are the two main professional streams. The selection is mainly carried out on the basis of overall academic merit. The applicants for professional studies should have physics, chemistry, and biology as their higher secondary subjects for medical degree programs; and physics, chemistry, and mathematics for engineering. The rest of the students carry on their studies through the bachelor's degree program which is diversified into three major academic divisions, namely, arts, science, and commerce, enabling students to work for a B.A., B.Sc., or B.Comm. degree, respectively.

The subjects of languages (Urdu and English), Pak studies, and Islamic studies are compulsory for all students. Rest of the papers in the major area must be relevant to the field chosen by the student but it is possible to have different optional groupings of subjects in the same majoring field. The selection of students is on merit and nominal fees are charged. A system of fee concessions is also operative in the colleges and needy students either receive a half freeship or a full freeship.

College education is generally on an annual system and the teaching is done either in Urdu or in English. In private colleges sometimes they have two different groups of students, one being taught through Urdu and the other through the medium of English. Some colleges are only for boys, some coeducational, and others exclusively for girls. The college usually runs throughout the day. The students in arts finish by early afternoon, but science students have their practicals in the afternoons, and commerce classes are usually conducted in the evenings. Apart from the regular academic program, the colleges have an extracurricular program of activities conducted through the college union which is formed by students through annual elections.

Some of the colleges have residential facilities and out of town students or foreign students seek accommodation in the hostels. The hostels charge a fee but are heavily subsidized by the government. Administratively, colleges are the responsibility of the directorate of colleges which appoints principals for each college from among the teachers, generally based on seniority. Fees which form only a nominal part of college expenditure is deposited in the government treasury and each college is allocated a budget and a specific teaching and non-teaching staff strength, relative to the enrollment in the college.

The selection of teachers is through competitive recruiting and is handled by the provincial Public Service Commission. The service record of each teacher is maintained for purposes of placement and promotion. The rank of the teacher is at par with a junior officer in the civil service. Private colleges also function but, similar to government institutions, they also have to have an affiliated status with the university. Foreign students also enrol but their number is not significant as they usually opt for professional colleges, rather than general colleges.

Undergraduate studies are also available at the universities in the form of honors programs of studies consisting of a three year course with major concentration in a specific subject. Some of the colleges also carry honors programs and there is a feeling that honors programs should be turned over to the colleges, confining the universities to graduate teaching.

Advanced Studies and Research

Research work has its beginning at the M.A. and M.Sc. level, and in each departmental program, students are required to complete a research thesis on a problem related to their area of specialization. The regular research work at the university begins on a more serious basis, beyond the M.A., for M.Phil. and Ph.D. degrees. The research program at this level organizationally is supervized by a board of advanced studies and research in each university. The University Grants Commission, in order to promote research, has initiated a system of stipends and scholarships for research students, thus enabling them to give exclusive attention to research work they undertake. The M.Phil. degree has a normal duration of two years and once the M.Phil. has been completed, the student is allowed to enroll for the Ph.D. degree. The normal period for a Ph.D. degree beyond the M.Phil. is three years. Once a thesis is completed, it is submitted to the department of examination and is sent to two experts, appointed by BASR, for evaluation. On receipt of a favorable evaluation, the candidate has to defend the thesis before a panel comprising of the director, the external examiner, and the dean of the faculty.

The different centers and institutes at the university conduct research work as a major part of their programs in the relevant area of specialization. In addition to research guidance, they also provide library and laboratory facilities for research workers to conduct their work in a congenial atmosphere. The work produced is printed either as a separate monograph or it appears in the professional journal of the institute. Encouragement of research work at the Ph.D. level can be gauged from the fact that the universities allow a special pay to their teachers holding a Ph.D. degree.

There is no organizational set up for postdoctoral research in the universities, but research work is stipulatory for promotion of lecturers to higher teaching echelons. The University Grants Commission and the Pakistan Science Foundation actively help the faculty members in the form of travel grants and financial help to carry out an approved research project. The university also earmarks a certain amount of funds for the promotion of research and publications by faculty members.

ISSUES AND TRENDS

In educational development, Pakistan has had perhaps more than its fair share of problems. Some of these are remnants of the educational legacy which Pakistan inherited at the time of its creation and the others reflect the pangs of the general socioeconomic and political development of the country. The major problem has been of quantity versus quality. With the rise in the number of children every year, it is difficult for the educational complex to keep pace with new demands. Available facilities are heavily over strained and with crowded classrooms and poor resources to match, it is difficult to withhold a lowering of educational standards. Pakistan spends less than 2 percent of its GNP on education and unless the priorities are revised and education receives more input, the problem of quantity versus quality will continue to grow to alarming proportions.

A serious corollary of the overstraining of educational facilities and of the lowering of standards is the growing indiscipline among students and the spread of violence on the campuses. Student activism on Pakistani campuses is a legacy from the days of the Pakistan movement but active interest of political parties in the students, instability of the political process in the country and, more recently, the easy availability of arms and ammunition have given it a diabolical turn. Without rigorous and extreme measures it seems that the situation will continue to remain explosive and unmanageable.

As a system, education in Pakistan does not bear the appearance of a single unified whole operating to serve the educational needs of all sections of its population. There is a basic cleavage between traditional and modern education. Despite the lack of state support, the traditional Islamic system of education has continued to persist with remarkable tenacity. It is mainly directed towards propagation of Islamic faith. Though the system has remained static for years and there is a definite need for its reform and modernization, it still carries appeal for a significant number of people.

Similarly, the official system also has disparities and divisions within itself. The major split is between the so called public schools, cadet schools, and cantonment schools on the one hand; and the network of ordinary schools on the other. In keeping with the legacy from the British days, the government continues to support financially the public schools which cater to the educational needs of the elite of the country. In addition to their apparent prosperity, another feature which serves to further widen the gulf between these schools and the ordinary schools is the distinction of the use of English as medium of instruction in the elite institutions. In contrast, the ordinary schools use Urdu or the vernacular languages, and their quality of education is poor. Thus far, the government has not been able to devise and implement a consistent and long term policy about the teaching of English.

The system of education also suffers from structural deformities inherited from the past. Due to overemphasis on higher education, the country is still without a well established system of primary and secondary education. As a result, not all the school-going children have the opportunity to receive education. The present government has expressed its intention to make a major thrust in this direction and bring about universal compulsory primary education in a matter of years. However, the success of this venture will depend on a number of factors which may not be educational as much as economic and political.

From the days of the British, the selection for entry into higher education was effected through a system of external examinations and, gradually, the principal function of the university became conducting of centralized external examinations for different degrees rather than teaching and creating new knowledge. As a result, students became obsessed with examinations, and this obsession persists even today and the students, instead of learning and receiving education through a regular program of studies, seek to pass the examinations by short cuts and unfair means. They memorize the examination questions, they have guess examination papers to help them in their endeavor, and they use unfair and even violent means in order to have access to the piece of paper known as the certificate or the degree. The boards of education and the universities have been experimenting with different methods and techniques which can make the assessment more objective and free from malpractices but, thus far, the exercises in this direction have not made any significant headway.

Another major weakness which continues to persist in the educational system is the weak relationship between education and national economy. In Pakistan, though a gradual emphasis has been growing on the teaching of sciences and technical subjects, the traditional bias in favor of humanities and liberal arts still remains and the consequent problem of educated unemployment has increased to an alarming extent. Even in producing science graduates, there is no planning to align the process with the manpower requirements of the country, with the result that there is never a certainty of jobs for even science students. The situation is responsible to a great extent for the increasing frustration of the Pakistani youth and for the resultant agitation of students against the system of education and the government. The present government has realized the increasing discontentment of the educated youth and in order to give immediate attention to this problem, a Ministry of Youth has been formed to make sure that there is an expansion of job opportunities for them and to divert their energies into healthier and constructive channels.

Other weak spots of the educational system which have received increasing attention of the government in the recent years include adult literacy, non-formal education, women's education, and special education. Schemes have been devised and some headway has been made in these areas but lasting solutions require long range sustained efforts which ultimately depend on a stable economy and even more so on a stable political process in the country.

BIBLIOGRAPHY

Ghafoor, A. "Financial Management of Education in Pakistan." *Educ.Rev.* 1(5):112-129

Qureshi, I. H. *Education in Pakistan: An Inquiry into Objectives and Achievements.* Karachi: Ma'arif, 1975

PANAMA

by
Ilsa Esther P. de Ochoa
Professor and Head, Department of Educational Administration
Central American Institute of Educational
Administration and Supervision
University of Panama, Panama

BACKGROUND

The origin of higher education in Panama can be traced back to the colonial period of the eighteenth century, when Jesuit Fathers made the first moves to form a higher education center. This institution was established on 3 January 1749, by Bishop Francisco Javier de Luna Victoria y Castro under the authority of a royal proclamation of King Francisco IV of Spain and carried the name Royal and Pontifical University of San Javier.

The programs of study offered at the university, like those at other universities in America at that time, had a predominantly religious character. As pointed out by Professor Francisco Cespedes, "The primary purpose of colonial education was to disseminate faith as a medium to attain salvation. The education essentially followed ethico-social values and goals. The organization, direction, and control were in the hands of the Church and the content of education was mainly religious". The colonial University of San Javier offered bachelor's, master's and doctoral degrees until it ceased to exist in 1767 with the expulsion of the Jesuites by King Carlos II.

In 1824, at the initiative of Francisco de Paula Santander, the vice-president of Colombia, a new center for higher education was founded under the name of College of Istmo with programs of studies in Castilian and Latin grammar, rhetoric, theology, and public and canon law. This university ceased to function with the eruption of the "war of the thousand days" (1900-1903). Then in March 1904, the republic proclaimed the Organic Law of Public Education leading to the creation of the Faculty of Philosophy and Letters which took the form of the University College of Panama. In 1933, the initiatives of the Society for Community Action led to the establishment of the Popular University, which offered courses in law, social studies, arts, and pedagogy. In the same year, the Institute of Pedagogy was formed to train teachers.

The government of Dr. Harmodio Arias decreed in May 1935 the formation of a College of Arts and Sciences which later took the name of the National University of Panama and moved in 1950 to a new campus of its own with an enrollment of 1688 students. At this time the university offered courses in philosophy, letters, education, engineering, architecture, medical sciences, library science, and administration. The university displayed a strong professional character in the early years but has now expanded considerably with many faculties and professional programs.

The 1972 Constitution of Panama places the responsibility on the state to organize and manage national education and to guarantee parents' right to participate in the education of their children. It is the duty of the state to provide freedom for learning and free education at the preschool, primary, and secondary levels and to strive for elevating the cultural level of the citizens. The purpose of education is to train students to develop a consciousness of the history and problems of the country, social justice, and human solidarity; to master sciences, technology, and culture; to develop an aptitude for work; and to participate in the economic development.

The article 97 of the same constitution governs higher education and recognizes the University of Panama as the official university of the republic and grants autonomy to the university. Key players in the education sector in Panama comprise the Ministry of Education, the universities, the Institute for Training and Development of Human Resources, the Panamanian Institute of Special Habilitation, National Institute of Culture, and the National Institute of Sports. Other institutions like the ministries of work, social welfare, agricultural development and the National Institute of Professional Training also oversee certain educational programs.

PRIMARY AND SECONDARY EDUCATION

Elementary (primary) education in Panama is free and compulsory. It lasts six years and is made available throughout urban and rural areas, to children in the age group 6-15 years. It is not only compulsory for children of this age group to attend school but it is also obligatory for the state to provide the opportunities.

The academic plan for elementary school include Spanish, mathematics, natural sciences and hygiene, social studies, religion, agriculture, English, physical education, artistic and recreational activities, and manual activities. In schools where the English subject is not taught, the teacher, in consultation with the director, will devote corresponding period to subjects in which students need reinforcement.

Students who satisfactorily complete elementary school studies are granted a certificate that enables them to enter the secondary school.

Secondary education, commonly known as the middle level studies in Panama is meant for the age group 12-18 years and consists of several types: general, vocational or professional, technical, industrial, commercial, agricultural, and teacher training. Secondary education is organized into two cycles: the first cycle usually lasts three years and is general and exploratory in character; the second cycle provides specialization in specific areas for a further period of three years and leads to the *bachillerato,* which is the requirement for admission to higher educational institutions.

The curriculum for the first cycle consist of Spanish, mathematics, history, geography, civics, sciences, English, religion, physical education, artistic and musical education, and one or two vocational subjects. The number of hours of instruction per week increases over the three year period: thirty-three hours in year one, thirty-five hours in year two, and thirty-six hours in year three. Students can follow one of several streams: the arts and sciences stream, which prepares students for higher studies in the university but offers no vocational training; commerce stream which offers vocational training in areas such as secretarial work and accounting providing the necessary background for higher studies at the School of Public Administration and Commerce; pedagogical studies which enables students to become teachers of primary schools or to enter the Faculty of Philosophy, Letters, and Education to pursue higher education; and industrial stream which prepares students in mechanical, construction, electrical, electronic, and chemical technologies enabling them to enter the world of work in these fields as engineering assistants or to pursue university studies in engineering, architecture, or technical teaching. In addition, students who complete the first cycle also have the option of pursuing several vocational programs of 1-3 years for obtaining qualifications to practice in selected vocations such as agriculture and industrial technology.

In the arts and sciences stream, students take Spanish, mathematics, English and physical education as common subjects during the full duration of the cycle (three years), history and geography in the first two years; artistic and musical education, basic science, and French in the first year; and Panamanian history/geography and history of relations with the USA, in the third year. Starting with the second year, students begin focussing on either arts or sciences. Arts courses include Latin, advanced French, and Latin American history. Science courses include physics, chemistry, and biology. Curriculum for the commerce and industrial streams include Spanish and English for three years and a variety of other courses related to the chosen vocation. The number of hours of instruction per week vary during the three years of studies: thirty-five hours in year one, thirty-eight hours in year two, and up to thirty-seven hours in year three. Teacher training programs consist of courses in Spanish, English, music, ethics and religion, social sciences, mathematics, natural sciences, physical education, agriculture, and pedagogical subjects.

The planning, organization, and supervision of secondary education is the responsibility of the Directorate of Professional and Technical Education and the Directorate of Secondary Education, both functioning under the Ministry of Education.

HIGHER EDUCATION

Higher education at tertiary level is offered in Panama at six institutions which play the crucial role of training professionals and technologists for the country. These institutions comprise University of Panama, Technological University of Panama, University of St. Mary, Nova University, University of Florida, Panama Canal College, and University of Istmo. As these institutions differ from one another in character, each institution and its programs will be discussed separately.

The University of Panama was the only institution in Panama from 1935 (when it was established) to 1965 and is the leading university today both in enrollment and in the variety of programs offered. The university enrolls students in forty-six fields of studies leading to *licenciatura* (first degree) and the fields comprise all major areas: administrative, commercial and juridical sciences (22 percent); social sciences (31.4 percent); science and technology including architecture and agronomy (33.3 percent); and health sciences (12.9 percent). In addition, the university offers a professional doctorate in dentistry and medicine. The *profesorado* (title of teacher) program offered by the university trains students (who have completed the *licenciatura*) for teaching positions in secondary education.

The structure and curriculum of the programs reflect the university's goal of ensuring continuity, development, diffusion, and popularization of the national culture; and the training of socially conscious scientific personnel, professionals, and technologists to strengthen national independence and integral development of the country. The programs are based on semester credit hours with each credit hour being equivalent to one hour of lecture or seminar per week throughout the semester or 2-3 hours of laboratory or practical work. The number of credit hours required for the first degree varies from 135 for *licenciatura* in mathematics, to 217 for *licenciatura* in law and political science or up to 262 for the Doctor of Medicine degree. To obtain the *profesorado* qualification, students are required to complete thirty-three credit hours beyond the *licenciatura*. Other programs leading to intermediate qualifications, such as those for technologists, vary in duration from 4-6 semesters or 60-100 credit hours.

The governance of the university is through various collegial bodies, comprising university council, academic council, administrative council, faculty committees, and committees of the regional university centers. The administrative and academic head of the university is the rector with vice-rectors having responsibility for functional areas (academic, postgraduate studies and research, administration), deans overseeing the faculties, and a director-general in charge of regional university centers (each center also has a director). Within each faculty, there are departments or schools headed by a director supported by departmental committees. The rector as well as deans of faculties and directors of regional university centers are elected by respective governing committees.

The Technological University of Panama is known to be "the highest level institution in the country in the area of science and technology". The university trains high level engineering professionals and technologists necessary for development of the country, particularly in the industrial sector. Generally the studies take five years and leads to *licenciatura* in several fields of engineering (civil, electro-mechanical, industrial, mechanical, etc.). The university also trains middle level technologists in programs which lasts 2-3 years. These programs allow students the access to pursue further studies leading to the *licenciatura*, when they wish to do so.

All study programs at the Technological University of Panama are offered through five faculties in its central campus, seven regional centers, and two extension centers. The university utilizes a credit hour system similar to the one at the University of Panama with *licenciatura* requiring an average of 210 credits and technologist's programs requiring about 100. The administrative structure of the university is very similar to that in the University of Panama excepting that there is a Committee of Regional Technical Institutes which oversee regional centers.

The University of St. Mary is an important higher educational option available to Panamanians, particularly in the middle and higher social strata. It is a Christian institution which trains professionals in scientific, technological, and humanistic areas. It offers seventeen fields of studies leading to *licenciatura* and students enroll in one of the five faculties: administrative sciences (50 percent), natural sciences and technology (25 percent), humanities and religious sciences (12.5 percent), social sciences (8 percent), and law and political sciences (4.1 percent). A small number of programs leading to teaching and technologist qualifications are also offered. Credit hour requirements vary from 177-200 for the *licenciatura* and about ninety for middle level qualifications. The general curriculum is intended to give the student a deep and coherent understanding in the main branches of knowledge, while striving for a good balance between basic professional training and academic culture. The main governing body of the university is the committee of the directors of the university headed by the archbishop of Panama who functions as the chancellor of the university. The administrative and academic head is the rector who is appointed by the chancellor.

The Nova University campus is a branch of the Nova University in the United States of America and it offers master's degrees in business and administration of human resources as well as advanced courses in English. The University of Florida campus is a branch of the University of Florida in the United States and offers *licenciaturas* in business administration, inter-American studies, international studies, and social sciences. The Panama Canal College functions under the authority of the US Department of Defense and offers higher educational programs in arts, sciences and technology for North American residents of the Canal Zone and their dependents. Associate degrees require sixty-four credit hours and bachelor's degrees require 128 credit hours.

The University of Istmo is a private institution established in 1987, with a Christian character and offers programs in several areas of administration, leading to *licenciatura.*

Tuition for full-time students of University of Panama is US$20 per semester (subject to change). In addition, there is a charge of US$10 for laboratories; US$2 for meals service; and US$1 for student card. The cost of books is about US$200 per semester. For students taking odontology, medicine, and architecture, the costs can go up to US$300-400 per semester. Cost at private universities are much higher. For example in Nova University, the students pay US$60-75 per semester credit (each semester must be of eight credits). The cost of books will range from US$90-100 per semester.

Postgraduate programs available at the University of Panama consist of special courses, master's degrees and doctorates. Postgraduate courses may be taken individually or as part of a program leading to a higher degree. Master's degree programs are intended for qualifying university teachers or researchers and for training professionals in specialized fields. These programs require about thirty credit hours and a thesis, which generally takes 3-4 semesters and are available in several fields including mathematics, entomology, education, nursing, and public health. The Technological University of Panama offers only master's degree programs in engineering sciences for which thirty-three credit hours are required. The University of St. Mary offers two-year master's degree programs in industrial administration, engineering economics, and business administration. Other higher educational programs do not offer postgraduate degrees.

Admission to master's degree programs require completion of *licenciatura* or equivalent qualification and a high level of academic achievement in previous course work. Selection criteria takes into account the nature of previous studies and corresponding grade point averages, professional experience, the candidate's field of study, and results of admission tests and an interview. Classes are conducted in Spanish and the cost is about US$10,000 per year for foreign students (including lodging expenses).

BIBLIOGRAPHY

Cespedes, Francisco. *La Educatión en Panamá, Panorama Histórico y Antología.* Panama: Biblioteca de la Cultura Panamericana, 1981.

Comision Coordinadora de la Educación Nacional. *Sintesis del Estudio Diagnóstico de la Realidad Nacional.* Vol. 3. 1983.

Comision Coordinadora de la Educación Nacional. *Raíces Históricas y Filosofia de la Educación.* Vol. 4. 1984.

Mendez, Pereira Octavio. *Desarrollo de la Instrucción Pública en Panamá. Capitulo I: La Colonia.* Santiago de Chile: Imprenta Universitaria, 1912.

Ministerio de Educación Panamá. *Plan Nacional de Educación:* 1969-1983. Edición Revisada. 1979.

Ministerio de Educación Panamá. *Anteproyecto de Ley de Actualización del Sistema Educativo Nacional.* 1987.

Nassif, Ricardo. "Aproximaciones a un Modelo Panameño de Universidad." *Revista Acción y Reflexión Educativa.* (Universidad de Panamá) No. 2. (1978).

Torrijos, Susana Richa de. *La Educación Panameña, Situación, Problemas y Soluciones.* 1989.

Universidad de Panama. *La Educación Universitaria: sus problemas y perspectivas.* 1987.

PERU

by
Benicio Virgilio Gutierrez
Principal Professor
National University of San Cristobal de Huamanga, Peru

BACKGROUND

The history of higher education in Peru dates back to the colonial period (1532-1824) when universities came into existence prompted by the necessity to train theologians and clergymen for the task of evangelizing the natives, and for producing men of law the society needed at that time. The royal and pontifical university, *La Real y Pontificia Universidad de la Ciudad de Los Reyes* (San Marcos) was the first university to be established in South America (1551) and it began functioning (1553) with faculties of theology and arts. Soon after, faculties of canons, law, and medicine were added. This was followed by the establishment (1677) of *La Real y Pontificia Universidad de San Cristobal de Huamanga* with faculties of theology and arts. Later, faculties of law and sacred canons were added. Then in 1692 *La Real y Pontificia Universidad de San Antonio Abad del Cuzco* was founded with a structure similar to other universities. Essentially, these higher education institutions trained citizens for professions that were held in eminence at that time (to become theologians, philosophers, lawyers, doctors, etc.).

After independence (1824) the higher educational structure expanded with the founding of several republican universities. The *Universidad de Santo Tomas y Santa Rosa de Trujillo* and the *Universidad de San Agustin de Arequipa* came to be established in 1824 and 1825 respectively. The school of civil engineering and mines founded in 1875 became the *Universidad Nacional de Ingenieria* in 1955. The national agricultural and veterinary school established in the early part of the twentieth century became the *Universidad Nacional Agraria de La Molina* in 1960. The first private university, *La Pontificia Universidad Catolica del Peru,* came into existence in 1917.

By 1960s, the country had eight universities. Since then the higher educational system has expanded rapidly and today there are forty-six universities, of which twenty-seven are national or public institutions (funded by the government) and nineteen are private fee charging universities. A high concentration of universities is found in the metropolitan Lima area with four public universities (San Marcos, Ingenieria, La Molina, and Federico Villarreal) and nine private universities (including *Pontificia Universidad Catolica de Peru, Cayetano Heredia,* and *La Universidad del Pacifico*).

The Ministry of Education is the responsible authority which oversees education in Peru. Laws and regulations enforced at the ministerial level, under the provisions of the Constitution and the General Law of Education, govern the decentralization, autonomy, and other aspects of education. The National Council of Education functioning within the ministry, studies and reviews functioning of the educational system and helps formulate educational policy. The Council consists of seven members, one appointed by each of the following: president of the Republic; National Assembly of Rectors; presidents of National Academies of Science and Culture; directors of ten oldest secondary education centers; presidents of Associations of non-government schools; Professional College Canistry of Teachers; and presidents of parents associations.

PRIMARY AND SECONDARY EDUCATION

Primary education in Peru is compulsory for children over six years of age and forms the major part of educational effort in the country. Primary schooling lasts for six years and is intended to provide competency in reading, writing, and oral expression; basic knowledge of the history and geography of Peru in relation to the world; understanding of local and national realities; development of cognitive and physical faculties and maturity; and knowledge and practice of ethical, civic, aesthetic, and religious values. The curriculum consists of language, mathematics, physical education, artistic education, natural sciences, social sciences, religious education, and vocational education.

In 1987, there were 3,681,342 students enrolled in the primary schools, of whom 88 percent were in public (government) schools. In addition 82,388 adults were receiving primary education, with 94 percent in public education centers. There were 117,111 primary school teachers, of whom 86 percent taught in public schools. The adult primary education centers had 2,639 teachers, of whom 94 percent were in the public sector. There were 25,730 primary schools of which 88 percent were public, and 689 adult education centers of which 91 percent were public.

Secondary education in Peru is open to students who successfully complete primary education, and the programs aim at furthering the knowledge students have acquired at the primary level and training them in various vocational fields. Secondary schooling lasts five years. The first two years are common to all students and in the remaining three years, students follow one of the following streams: science-humanities, agricultural, artisanal, commercial, and industrial. In addition, secondary education is provided to adults as well. The methods and contents in adult secondary education are designed to suit the interests and experience of adult students. Successful completion of secondary education, irrespective of its content and methodology, offers all students equal opportunity for access to higher education.

In the science-humanities stream, the curriculum consists of an average of forty hours of studies including language and literature, foreign languages (English); geography; religious education; psychology, biology; political economics; physics; philosophy; logic; mathematics; physical education; natural sciences; history; chemistry; and pre-military training. In the other streams of secondary education, variations are made in the curriculum to focus on the vocational areas relevant to each stream.

The duration of the academic year is nine months from April to December. Students are evaluated bimonthly or monthly. Public schools offer free education, where as students have to pay fees at private institutions. The amount of fees vary depending on the institution.

In 1987, secondary schools had an enrollment of 1,523,141 of whom 85 percent were in public schools. In addition, the adult education sector had 209,325 enrolled of whom 95 percent were in public centers. The teaching staff consisted of 69,768 teachers in secondary schools of whom 80 percent were in public schools. The adult education sector engaged 6,505 teachers of whom 94 percent were in the public centers. There were 4,558 secondary schools of which 79 percent were public institutions.

The total student population in the country in 1987 was 6,700,871 and was distributed as follows: 6.4 percent in nursery; 56.2 percent in primary; 25.9 percent in secondary; 8.5 percent in higher education; and 3.0 percent in various other programs. In 1989, the government of Peru spent 285,178 million Intis (US$1-=100,000Intis) or 18.9 percent of the national budget, on education.

HIGHER EDUCATION

Institutions

The universities in Peru, according to Law 23733 of 1983, are dedicated to the study, research, and diffusion of knowledge and culture. They enjoy academic and administrative autonomy within the law.

The fundamental academic, administrative, and economic unit of the Peruvian university is the faculty, which is responsible for academic and professional education, research, promotion of culture, social interaction, and other services associated with the study programs. Within a faculty there are professional schools, a postgraduate section, a research institute, and a center for social interaction (Centro de Proyeccion Social). A faculty commission serves as an advisory body and the academic departments coordinate academic activities in specific disciplines. The school of postgraduate studies is a joint body consisting of postgraduate sections of the faculties.

University administration consist of faculty council and deans of faculties, rector, university council, and university assembly. The supreme governing body is the university assembly. It consists of university authorities as well as representatives of professors, students, and graduates and has following functions: review and reform of university statute; election of rector and vice-rectors; ratification of annual operating plan for the university; and approval of creation, amalgamation, or elimination of faculties or other academic units within the faculty. The university council consists of the rector, vice-rectors, deans of faculties, director of the postgraduate school, as well as representatives of students and one representative of graduates. The rector is the head of the university. The faculty council, headed by the dean, consists of representatives of professors and students as well as representative from graduates.

At the national level, the National Assembly of Rectors, which consists of rectors of both public and private universities, coordinates inter-university activities as well as those affecting university education in the country as a whole.

The forty-six universities in Peru, mentioned earlier, offer eighty-six professional programs ten of which enroll about 60 percent of the students. The ten programs are accounting (43,000), law (35,000), secondary education (35,000), administration (29,000), economics (25,000), industrial engineering (17,000), medicine (14,000), civil engineering (14,000), nursing (12,000), and psychology (10,000).

On a national scale, the professional programs offered at most universities include accounting (34); administration (29); secondary education (28); economics (25); nursing (22); law (21); civil engineering (17); industrial engineering (17); agronomy (16); medicine (12); obstetrics (12); mining engineering (12); biology (12); metallurgical engineering (12); sociology (12); social service (12); fisheries engineering (10); and nursery education (10).

In 1987, higher education institutions had an enrollment of 409,654 students of whom 66 percent were in public universities and the rest were in private universities. There were 23,480 university teachers, of whom 70 percent were in public universities. Of the 312,810 students who took university admission exams in Peru in 1987, only 20.8 percent were accepted for enrollment. In the same year 19,115 students graduated from the universities and 65 percent of them came from public universities. The student population at the universities consisted of 63.5 percent males. Of the teachers, 78 percent were males. The annual growth in admissions to universities, since 1970 is over 6 percent per year. In 1990 the admissions are expected to reach over 490,000.

Universities in Peru offer 575 majors at undergraduate level, eighty-six fields at master's level and forty-four areas for specialization at doctoral level. At master's level, the most popular fields are education, chemistry, economics, administration, and social sciences. At doctoral level, the most popular areas are education, law, medicine, and economics.

In addition to the universities, a variety of other higher educational and post secondary institutions exist in Peru conforming to the education Law 23733. These include *Facultad de Teologia Pontificia y Civil de Lima* which offers bachelor's, master's, and doctor's degrees; the officer training schools of the armed forces and the police: a school of public health providing postgraduate programs; *Escuela de Administracion de Negocios para Graduados,* a private institution awarding master's degree in administration; *Institutos Superiores Pedagogicos,* which train teachers for nursery, primary, and secondary levels; and *Institutos Superiores Tecnologicos,* which provide academic as well as professional training in areas such as accounting, mechanical technology, nursing, secretarial work, etc. In addition, there are also schools for fine arts, *Escuelas Superiores de Formacion Artistica* in Lima and other regional cities, and several music schools (*Escuelas Superiores de Musica*).

In 1989, the government of Peru spent 58,316 million Intis or 3.5 percent of the national budget, on higher education.

Programs and Degrees

The statute of each university establishes study programs, commonly on a semester credit system and with a flexible curriculum. Universities in Peru offer bachelor's, master's and doctoral degrees. These are offered successively, with the first degree (bachelor's) taking a minimum of ten semesters (five years) including an initial basic studies cycle. For completion of the degree, a research memoir is required. The master's and doctor's degrees, each take a minimum of four semesters and require public defense of a thesis based on original research as well as knowledge of a foreign language. Professional studies (*licenciado* or equivalent) which generally takes ten semesters, with the exception of medicine and law which take fourteen and twelve semesters respectively, include an initial basic studies cycle. Practical training and professional exams may also form part of the professional study programs, where relevant.

Education at public universities is gratuitous (public universities are funded by the government) provided students successfully complete degree programs within periods specified by the university statutes. In the case of private universities, students pay fees. Private universities which are subsidized by the government are required to dedicate part of the subsidy, for the award of scholarships and grants based on need and academic achievement. The National Council of Science and Technology also awards scholarships based on academic achievement.

The universities organize many services for the well being of its members: health services, recreational facilities, cultural events, sports, and artistic activities. Majority of the institutions have university restaurants and some provide residential accommodation.

Admission to undergraduate studies (bachelor's degree) require successful completion of secondary education and passing an admission examination which is held twice a year. The number of students admitted in any given year depends on the availability of places, teachers, and economic resources.

Postgraduate studies lead to master's and doctoral degrees. Each level requires four semesters of studies. Admission to master's program requires a bachelor's degree. The structure of each postgraduate program is developed by the relevant postgraduate section of the faculty and all the university-wide postgraduate programs are consolidated by the postgraduate school of the university. At present, majority of the postgraduate programs are offered by a few of the universities: *Universidad Catolica del Peru, Universidad Nacional Agraria de la Molina,* and the *Universidad Nacional Mayor de San Marcos.* To a smaller extent, other universities like *Universidad de Ingenieria, Federico Villarreal, del Pacifico, Trujillo, Arequipa,* and *Cuzco* also offer postgraduate programs.

Cost of postgraduate studies is borne by the institutions which sponsor students or by the students themselves. In the recent years the National Council of Science and Technology has provided significant support to this level of studies as well as for research through scholarships and grants. Postgraduate studies and research also form an important part of the programs for the training of university teachers, and the National Council of Science and Technology has been a strong supporter of this activity.

ISSUES AND TRENDS

For Peru as well as for Latin America in general, the decade of the 1960s has been a period of radical criticism of the focus and development of educational material as well as educational planning and reforms. The decade of the 1970s was different in that the social and political realities pressed for changes that were desired by the Latin American countries and encouraged by research findings in the educational field. By the beginning of the 1980s, it was evident that the initial planning had not lost its vigor, although the almost utopian thinking that had influenced the planners had matured on the face of realities in countries like Peru.

This is how, in the case of Peru, the educational reforms of 1972, were abolished soon afterwards in 1976 but the new law of general education enacted in 1982 almost brought back the system that existed at the beginning of the 1970s.

It is evident that Peru has not yet resolved the many problems affecting the development of its education. The illiteracy rate in the population over fifteen years of age is over 13 percent, with a higher rate among the habitants in the mountain regions. For every 100 children who enter primary schools, only thirty-nine complete their education. Out of the thirty-nine, thirty-five enter secondary education but only twenty-three complete it. These indicate that there are profound structural shortcomings in the educational system (shortcomings that lead to student frustration and under employment) despite the expansion of education since the 1960s. The situation appears even more serious when it is considered that in 1987, more than half the students at the primary level repeated their classes.

At the university level, the expansion of the educational process since the 1960s, has resulted in the evolution of a university education that reflects the social structure of the country. A small number of universities, particularly private ones located in the capital, have made significant progress with the help of private capital, both local and foreign. With a severe limitation on admission quotas, these universities select the best candidates, particularly students coming from the best private institutions. The other universities receive the mass of students coming from public schools, particularly students who could not get admission to more reputed universities. The graduates of these universities gradually discover that they are not going to get either adequate preparation or economic security they were looking for from an occupation, but, their education, apart from little economic benefits associated with it, is only a means to higher social status.

An aspect that overshadows university education is the situation that only 21 percent of the students who attempt entrance to universities gain admission, thus leaving out 79 percent who either seek other educational avenues (Institutos Superiores) or enter one of numerous preuniversity preparation halls, to repeatedly try for university admission. In this respect, the demands of the young people for education cannot be satisfied by the limited university opportunities available now. This is a matter that needs the utmost attention of policymakers.

The fact that mobility in the society depends on social factors rather than on economic criteria gives rise to social discrimination often observed in the employment market place. For example, the secondary school students show a notorious disinterest in manual work, while the graduates of technical schools and from modest social origin see their qualifications as a means of differentiating them from the working class.

Another factor which is most important to the improvement of education is the level and quality of the teaching staff. A persistent problem in Peru as well as in other Latin American countries is the growth in the number of teachers who have not received adequate training (about 35 percent in Peru, at primary and secondary level) primarily due to the rapid expansion of the educational system that required recruiting teachers in large numbers. This problem, however, is not a result of a real shortage of qualified persons as many qualified teachers work in jobs outside of their training because of better remunerations (compared to teaching), more professional development opportunities, and better stability. The situation is aggravated by the reluctance of many teachers to accept appointments in rural areas and small cities. Also the lack of opportunity for educators to participate in the planning and discussion of educational reforms has not only had a negative influence on the implementation of reforms but also led to a virtual divorce between educators and the educational administrators.

Peru is now about to see a new legislation on education. The minister of education has presented the new law to the education commission of the national parliament. The law aims at implementing a flexible system of education, mindful of the changes that have taken place during the last thirty years. The law strives to provide a plan that would educate the whole person, developing his cultural and historical consciousness, and training him for democracy and national development.

BIBLIOGRAPHY

Asamblea Nacional de Rectores Comision de Coordinación Interuniversitaria. *Estructura Académica y Administrativa de las Universidades Publicas y Privadas del Peru.* Lima, 1988 (Mimeo).

Bernales Ballesteros, Enrique. *Movimientos Sociales y Movimientos Universitarios.* Lima: Pontificia Universidad Catolica del Peru, 1974.

Blat Gimeno, Jose. *La Educación en América Latina y el Caribe en el Ultimo Tercio del Siglo XX.* Paris: UNESCO, 1981.

Cariola Barroilhet, Patricio, et.al. *La Educación en América Latina.* Mexico: Ed. LIMUSA, 1981.

Chiroque, Sigfredo. "Mapa de la pobreza educativa en el Peru". *Autoeducación* (1988).

Galdo Gutierrez, Virgilio. *La Educación Universitaria: Diagnóstico y Perspectivas.* Ayacucho: UNSCH, 1981.

Gall, Normal S. *La Reforma Educativa Peruana.* Lima: Mosca Azul Editores, 1976.

Gonzalez Carre, Enrique., and Galdo Gutierrez, Virgilio. "Historia de la Educación en el Peru." In *Historia del Peru. Procesos e Instituciones.* Tomo X, edited by Juan Mejia Baca. Lima, 1980.

Instituto Nacional de Estadística. *Peru: Compendio Estadístico 1987.* Lima: Dirección General de Indicadores Económicos y Sociales, 1988.

Ministerio de Educación. *Reforma de la Educación Perúana. Informe General.* Lima, 1989.

Peru: Estadísticas Universitarias 1960-1986. (Boletin Informativo No. 10) Lima: DID, 1988.

PHILIPPINES

by
Alicia S. Bustos
President
Baliuag College, Philippines

BACKGROUND

The present Philippine educational system evolved from developments dating back to the Spanish and American colonial periods. During the Spanish era, instruction began as an instrument of Christianization and continued largely under religious auspices. A landmark of educational history under Spanish rule was the Educational Decree of 1863 which established a uniform course of study for elementary schools and the training of teachers. Secondary schools remained in private hands while collegiate programs were left to institutions already established by religious orders. By the turn of the twentieth century, the process of basic educational development was well underway.

When the American colonizers took over, the Philippine Commission (the "Commission") was established to govern the country. The Commission, in line with its democratization policy, formulated a comprehensive system of free public education administered by a Department of Public Instruction, later known as the Department of Education.

Adopting English as the medium of instruction, teachers were initially members of the American armed forces until over a thousand professionally trained teachers and administrators were brought in from the United States. Reliance on American nationals continued until teacher training institutions were created to prepare Filipinos for teaching. In 1901, the Philippine Normal School, now the Philippine Normal College, was established for the purpose of teacher training. This was later followed by the establishment of the secondary normal course in provincial high schools. In 1908 the University of Philippines was established. By 1941, children were being taught by Filipinos in schools predominantly administered by Filipinos.

Schools established during the early period of American rule followed the pattern of American education. And higher education, following its American precedent, had been developed with a wide range of courses and colleges under an open-door policy. As a result, there was a rapid expansion of educational institutions.

A number of private secondary and tertiary schools were established and incorporated under the Corporation Law of 1906. To maintain standards in the increasing number of private schools, governmental recognition and supervision of private schools became obligatory under the 1917 Private School Law. For this purpose, the Bureau of Private Schools under the Department of Public Instruction was created. By 1946, when Philippine independence was granted by the United States, about 46 percent of secondary and about 98 percent of higher education enrollments were in private institutions. Since then, government schools at the secondary and tertiary levels have also been established. As of school year 1987-88, 39 percent and 73 percent of all secondary and tertiary schools were private, respectively.

Since the establishment of the educational system by the Americans, the government has always been concerned with quality issues as evidenced by the succession of government commissioned studies seeking ways to improve the country's educational system, starting with the Monroe Survey of 1925 and ending with the 1969 Presidential Commission to Survey Philippine Education (the "PCSPE Report"). The findings and recommendations of the PCSPE Report, a milestone in Philippine education, provided the impetus for the implementation of major educational reforms in the 1970s and 1980s.

Since the attainment of Philippine independence in 1946, Philippine education has slowly rid itself of a colonially imposed system. It has taken the direction of providing an educational process that will eventually produce Filipinos who are Filipino in orientation, purposes, attitudes, and outlook without being parochial, but rather national and universal; who are literate and productive, motivated by civic conscience, and social awareness; and who are morally upright and nationally patriotic. These objectives are now explicitly provided in the 1986 Philippine Constitution which states as follows:

"All educational institutions shall inculcate
patriotism and nationalism, foster love of humanity,
respect for human rights, appreciation of the role
of national heroes in the historical development of
the country, teach the rights and duties of
citizenship, strengthen ethical and spiritual values,
develop moral character and personal discipline,
encourage critical and creative thinking, broaden
scientific and technological knowledge and promote
vocational efficiency". (Section 3, Article XIV)

In the pursuit of these objectives, the 1986 Constitution mandates, among other things, that the state shall undertake the following:

(1) Establish, maintain, and support a completely integrated system of education relevant to the needs of the people and the society; (2) Establish and maintain a system of free public education in the elementary and high school levels; (3) Establish and maintain a system of scholarship grants and student loan programs; (4) Recognize the complementary roles of public and private institutions in the educational system; (5) Exercise reasonable supervision and regulation of all educational institutions; (6) Take into account regional and sectoral needs and conditions and encourage local planning in the development of educational policies and programs; (7) Assign the highest budgetary priority to education; (8) Guarantee academic freedom in all institutions of higher learning; and (9) Give priority to

research and development, invention and their utilization, science and technology education, training and services.

The 1986 Constitution further guarantees the right of all citizens to quality education and the accessibility of such education to all. The Education Act of 1982 set the framework for the establishment and maintenance of an integrated system of education relevant to the goals of national development. Executive Order No. 117 provides the basis for the present reorganized structure of the Department of Education, Culture and Sports (DECS):

"DECS shall be primarily responsible for the formulation,
planning, and coordination of the policies, plans,
programs and projects in the areas of formal and non-
formal education at all levels, supervise all education
institutions, both public and private, and provide for
the establishment and maintenance of a complete, adequate,
and integrated system of education relevant to the goals
of national development". (Section 4)

The DECS assumes its responsibilities through four main units, namely the department proper; the department services; the bureaus; and the regional offices. The department proper consists of the office of the secretary which is assisted by five undersecretaries, each in charge of the following functional areas: (a) elementary and secondary education; (b) non-formal and vocational/technical education; (c) higher education, culture and foreign-assisted projects; (d) administration and management; and (e) legal and legislative affairs. The department services comprise of the following five offices, each headed by an assistant secretary: (a) Office of Planning Service; (b) Office of Financial and Management Service; (c) Office of Administrative Service; (d) Office of the Human Resources Development Service; and (e) Office of Technical Service.

The six bureaus, each headed by a director, are in charge of elementary education, secondary education, technical and vocational education, higher education, non-formal education, physical education, and school sports. The bureaus are engaged in staff functions such as the formulation and evaluation of guidelines and standards for curricula, instructional materials, physical plant and equipment, and general management. The fourteen regional offices, each headed by a director, are responsible for formulation and implementation of the regional plan proposals based on the DECS' national plan and oversee the administration of schools. As front-line managers, the regional directors report directly to the secretary. About 50 percent of DECS' 4,000 work force are in the regional offices.

With the current enrollment of about fifteen million students spread over thousands of schools in various levels and non-formal educational programs the DECS has to manage, the magnitude of the tasks facing the DECS is enormous.

PRIMARY AND SECONDARY EDUCATION

Elementary and secondary education in the Philippines comprise the first ten years of schooling: six years of elementary and four years of high school. In its organizational structure, the educational system includes three levels of instruction:

elementary, secondary, and tertiary. Also considered as a program of the formal system is preschool education. Although preschool education is not a prerequisite to enter the first grade of elementary schools, a number of private institutions and public schools offer it as part of the elementary education level. Under the 1986 constitution, funding of secondary education is nationalized; at the same time providing for free education for all youth.

Elementary education primarily aims at enabling every Filipino child to acquire the basic skills, knowledge, habits, attitudes, appreciations, and ideas to make him an efficient and intelligent citizen in a democratic society. Secondary education, on the other hand, is primarily concerned with continuing basic education but expanding it to include the learning of gainfully employable skills. Through the years, the curricula of these two levels of education have been revised from time to time to cope with the challenges of the times. The latest revisions of these curricula were the offshoots of the PCSPE Report.

Following the PCSPE Report, the government implemented two development programs in basic education: (1) the Program for Decentralized Educational Development ("PRODED"); and (2) the Secondary Education Development Program ("SEDP"). PRODED was a ten-year program in elementary education which began in 1981 to institute reforms aimed at raising quality, efficiency, and accessibility in educationally deprived areas. The SEDP is a five-year development program in secondary education aimed to complement PRODED whose first graduates entered high school in 1989. Both programs are expecting increased participation rates and decreased dropout rates in formal schools, with the institution of a new curriculum and the provision of teacher-training, facilities, equipment, and textbooks. These new programs expect to raise the achievement levels of students in basic education.

The new curriculum in elementary schools focuses on the development of basic literacy, numeracy, thinking, and work skills which will enhance not only learning capabilities but also civic and social values, particularly a sense of humanity and nationhood. This new curriculum reorients elementary education to national development requirements. It is composed of the following major learning areas: (1) character education activities; (2) communication arts in Filipino; (3) communication arts in English; (4) mathematics; (5) civics and culture for grades 1-3 and history/geography/civics for grades 4-6; (6) science and health; (7) arts and physical education; and (8) home economics and livelihood education. The new revised secondary curriculum provides for more in-depth learning for academic excellence, values development, and productivity skills. These three main areas are translated into the following seven subject area curriculum components: (1) English and Filipino; (2) mathematics; (3) social studies; (4) science and technology; (5) home management and technology education; (6) physical health and music education; and (7) values education.

HIGHER EDUCATION

Tertiary level of education in the Philippine system refers to all post-secondary schooling of which there are two types: technical-vocational education and higher education. Technical-vocational education include non-degree programs leading to one, two, or three year certificates in preparation for a group of middle-level occupation. Higher education includes degree programs in a specific profession or discipline and is geared towards the achievement of the following objectives: Provide a general education program that will promote national identity, cultural consciousness, moral integrity and spiritual vigor; Train the nation's manpower in the skills required for national development; Develop the professions that will provide leadership for the nation; and Advance knowledge for improving the quality of human life and responding effectively to changing societal needs and conditions.

Institutions

Higher education in the Philippines is composed of multi-sectoral institutions. Within the public school subsystem are the state colleges and universities which have their own charters, the non-chartered colleges, and the community colleges operated by local governments and supported and maintained principally through public funds. Within the private school subsystem are the sectarian and the non-sectarian institutions which are further classified as stock or proprietary and non-stock corporations. Private schools are principally supported by tuition fees paid by students while non-stock schools can accept fees from other sources (e.g. donations).

Chartered state colleges and universities are established by specific law. Pursuant to their charters, these educational institutions each have a governing board vested with the authority to formulate policies covering all areas of their operation. The DECS secretary, or his duly appointed representative, sits as chairman of the board. These chartered schools receive their budget through congressional appropriations.

Non-chartered colleges are established by law, and the regulation and supervision of these are vested with the DECS. Their programs and courses of studies are subject to DECS recognition. As educational institutions offering collegiate programs and being principally public in character, community colleges are also treated as non-chartered schools. Non-chartered colleges and community colleges receive their budgets from the DECS.

Only two chartered colleges and universities were originally chartered as universities: the University of the Philippines (UP) which remained the only state university for many years, and Mindanao State University (MSU), created in the early 1960s to respond to the needs of Muslim Mindanao.

Many of the present state colleges and universities were former high schools, which maybe regular or vocational, agricultural, nautical and maritime schools. Many of these schools were created by an executive order or presidential decree issued by the president of the Philippines, although a majority of these were created by statute.

As has been mentioned earlier, the founding of the earliest institutions of higher education dates back to the early period of Spanish rule. These schools which had been established by Catholic religious orders were the forerunners of a number of private sectarian colleges and universities in the country today. Among these schools are the University of San Carlos established in 1595, the University of St. Thomas in 1611, and the Ateneo de Manila University in 1859. The majority of sectarian institutions of higher education were established at the turn of the twentieth century by Catholic religious orders and other religious denominations, particularly the Protestant missionaries.

Religious education institutions have indeed made a large and significant contribution to higher education in the Philippines. The majority of the colleges and universities with the largest enrollment, however, are proprietary schools classified by the government as "non-sectarian".

As of 1987-88, there were 782 higher educational institutions in the country with a total enrollment of 1,204,000, both public and private. Within the country, the National Capital Region (Metro Manila Area) leads in terms of the number of schools located in its area, with 169, of which 157, are private schools with a total enrollment of 456,456.

The administration, supervision, and regulation of all higher education institutions at the system level are vested in the DECS. Such functions of the DECS, however, are conducted without prejudice to the charter of any state college or university which extends to it considerable autonomy. The Bureau of Higher Education (BHE) is the central staff unit of the DECS for higher education. Its functions include the following: Development, formulation and evaluation of programs, projects, and educational standards for the various disciplines or profession within the area of higher education; Provision of staff assistance to the Board of Higher Education in the policy formulation and advisory functions, and provide technical assistance to encourage development programs and projects in tertiary educational institutions; and Compilation, analysis, and evaluation of data on higher education.

To improve the quality and efficiency of policy-making in higher education, Education Act of 1982 mandates the creation of a board of higher education to serve as the overall policy-making body in the area of higher education. Its membership is composed of an undersecretary of DECS and four other members who have distinguished themselves in the field of higher education either in the public or private sector. To provide the necessary expertise in various fields of specialization or discipline that are not normally available in the bureaucracy, the DECS has created technical panels composed of experts serving in a consultative, advisory, and recommendatory capacity on matters relating to their specific disciplines or fields of specialization.

The internal governance of state colleges and universities is vested in governing boards which adopt policies, enact rules and regulations within the law. Each school is headed by a president who is responsible to the board. The composition of the board is uniform for all these schools. They are composed of the DECS secretary as chairman, the president as vice chairman, a representative of the National Economic Development Authority, and two prominent citizens.

Like state colleges, the internal governance of private institutions is vested in governing boards. For proprietary schools, the members of the board of trustees are elected by the stockholders. For non-stock schools, which are church related schools, the board of trustees is elected by the governing board of their respective religious orders.

The curriculum for each higher education program or course of study in every college or university is designed and formulated with the involvement of concerned sectors of the educational community to harmonize the content and objectives to individual and national needs and aspirations. The minimum standards for any program are set by the DECS for schools under its supervision.

The minimum educational qualification required for a teaching position in higher education institutions, as stipulated by DECS, is a master's degree for undergraduate programs, and a doctoral degree for the doctoral programs. For second degree programs, such as law and medicine, the teaching staff must be holders of appropriate professional degrees.

Although a graduate degree is set as the minimum requirement for undergraduate teaching, the colleges, especially in the provinces, are not always able to meet that requirement. As incentives for the faculty to pursue graduate education, colleges provide faculty development opportunities through scholarships and study leave.

Teaching personnel of higher education institutions are assigned academic ranks based on a merit promotion criteria. Their ranks from lowest to highest are: assistant instructor, instructor, assistant professor, associate professor, and professor. While employed on a probationary status which is normally three years, new teachers are assigned to the academic rank of assistant instructor. However, a new teacher may be appointed to a higher academic rank or as a lecturer on the basis of his qualifications. Faculty members of colleges and universities serve on either full-time or part-time basis. Specially for highly technical or specialized courses, teaching of the courses in done mostly by full-time faculty.

The qualifications, rights, responsibilities, and privileges of all teaching personnel in the state colleges and universities are set forth in the Magna Carta for Public School Teachers. For private school teaching personnel, such provisions are stipulated in the DECS Manual for Private Schools, as well as in collective bargaining agreements between faculty and management in schools where there are faculty unions.

Undergraduate Studies

As a general rule, the DECS prescribes certain general subjects for the undergraduate curricula of degree programs. These general subjects are offered in the first two years. Categorized areas for general education are English, Filipino, mathematics, natural sciences, and social sciences.

Higher education schools in the Philippines offer diverse undergraduate degree courses. The number of years students are required to study depends on the courses they enrol in. The degree programs offered in Philippine colleges and universities can be grouped into several broad categories: arts and sciences; teacher training and education science; engineering and technology; medicine and health related programs; commerce and business management; agriculture, fisheries, forestry and veterinary medicine; law and criminology; and religion or theology.

The highest enrollment areas were in business (32 percent), engineering and technology (22 percent) and arts and sciences (15 percent).

Consonant with the provisions of the Constitution, the Filipino language is to be used as the medium of instruction in the following subject areas: social studies, social science, character education, work education, and health and physical education.

Although not fully implemented, the use of Filipino as medium of instruction is rapidly gaining momentum in Philippine colleges and universities.

The entrance into many professions after graduation from degree programs is controlled by government examinations which inevitably influence the collegiate programs, although the examining boards are not supposed to set curricula.

To be eligible for admission to a collegiate course, students have to pass the National College Entrance Examination (NCEE) administered by the DECS. This is a general scholastic aptitude test designed to serve as an indicator of the individual's potential to successfully do college work. High school graduates from Philippine and foreign high schools have to qualify in the NCEE if they wish to enrol in college courses requiring four years of study or more. The NCEE is administered twice a year: the regular NCEE around September or October and the Special NCEE on the last Sunday of June of every year. In addition to the NCEE requirement, there are colleges and universities which administer an entrance examination as basis for selecting the students they are to admit. There are also specific entrance requirements to each professional course which are embodied in the standards set by DECS.

In the case of foreign students seeking admission to any college program, prior authority to enrol has to be secured from the DECS.

As of the school year 1988-89, there were 5,394 foreign students enrolled in various fields in higher education institutions representing various nationalities. Jordanian and Thai students formed the majority consisting of 24 percent and 23 percent respectively. Pakistanis, Americans, and Koreans each represented about 6 percent of the foreign student population.

To assist indigent but deserving college students in their studies, various forms of financial assistance are extended by the government pursuant to the mandate of existing laws. Such assistance take the form of study grants and loans.

Annually, the National Scholarship Center selects among high school graduating classes, the "state scholars" who are granted scholarships in the sciences, arts, and letters. Their expenses including tuition, matriculation, textbooks and equipment, board and lodging, clothing, and travelling expenses are defrayed from government funds. Student loans in the Study Now Pay Later Program are also made available to students who are eligible as per DECS requirements based on their NCEE rating, high school record, and family income.

Other forms of assistance are the National Integration Study Grant Program, the Study Grant Program for Southern Philippines, and the Ethnic Groups Educational Assistance Program. Effective school year 1989-90 the government established two additional assistance programs: the Private Education Student Financial Assistance (PESFA) program for college students; and the Educational Service Contracting (ESC) program for high school students. The PESFA grant covers 90 percent of tuition and other school fees not to exceed P3,500 (US$1-=P21.10) per year, plus an allowance of P2,000 for each student who qualifies for the grant. In the ESC program, students who cannot be accommodated in public high schools of a particular community are enrolled in private high schools with their school fees defrayed from government funds. In addition to these government assistance programs, individual colleges, both public and private, also offer assistance in the form of scholarship grants, student loans, graduate assistantships/-fellowships, and part-time jobs in school. Scholarship grants are also available from various industrial corporations and non-governmental agencies.

Advanced Studies and Research

There are two levels of graduate education programs offered in Philippine colleges and universities: master's degree programs and doctoral programs. In general, the curricula for these programs contain a minimum total of thirty-six units for the master's program and sixty units for the doctoral program, with most curricular subjects offered as three-unit courses equivalent to at least fifty-four hours per semestral term. Fields of specialization offered by graduate schools vary widely depending on the existing undergraduate programs and the human and financial resources capabilities of the school offering the program.

A typical doctoral program includes a minimum of forty-eight academic units, and twelve dissertation units, and a written comprehensive examination on completion of all course requirements.

Graduate programs are diverse within each sector. There are a number of fields offered by the state colleges and universities of which the University of the Philippines has the largest graduate and research components. A number of education institutions, particularly the unchartered institutions have heavy non-degree components in their graduate programs. Within the private sector, graduate programs and research opportunities are limited by the inadequacy of fees that private schools charge to cover the high cost of graduate education, especially research. Since private schools do not receive government funds, their concentration is more on undergraduate teaching.

ISSUES AND TRENDS

As the educational system of the country continues to exert efforts to provide the Filipinos, particularly the youth, the best in educational services, many issues have been raised. Of late, educators have focused their attention on three vital issues in higher education: quality, equity, and efficiency.

The quality issue is attributed to the meager investments in teaching staff and physical facilities due to limited financial resources. Graduate education is not pursued by many faculty members since they have to cover the cost of their own training, thus, resulting in the non-fulfillment of the DECS requirement of a master's degree for college teaching. School investments in laboratory equipment, library books, and materials, and other quality related facilities are minimal due to their cost. In addition, both public and private institutions are dominated by undergraduate teaching programs focused on job oriented fields.

While well intended, the government's practice of subsidizing colleges and universities often fails to promote social equity in higher education. Poorer students cannot get access to subsidies if they do not attend public educational institutions. Income bias increases at the best public institutions, for most of their students come from above the national average income level.

The issues of quality, equity, and efficiency have called for rationalization of higher education, primarily on the following basis:

1.   Encouragement of voluntary accreditation. Under the present system of voluntary accreditation, a tested mechanism has been mounted by schools, colleges, and universities to bring about desired results. Accreditation, mainly a private and voluntary process designed to encourage academic institutions to meet higher than DECS minimum standards of quality, has received considerable encouragement from the government and has brought considerable amount of prestige and autonomy to accredited institutions.

2.   Proposed implementation of the flagship approach. Conceived for the purpose of upgrading standards and increasing the effectiveness of schools, the flagship concept contemplates the categorization of institutions into national, regional, and provincial levels, and calls for the production of quality manpower in each institution using its own resources and competence. The schools having graduate research and development capabilities and facilities are assigned the flagship role which simply means assumption of an educational task as a source of direction for growth and of assistance to other schools in the "fleet". Institutions designated on the national level may offer graduate degree programs that compare favorably with the best in other countries. Those on the regional level may initially offer courses at the professional level, and could likewise proceed to graduate programs if circumstances warrant. And those on the provincial category may only be allowed initially to offer special technical/technological programs.

3.   Encouragement of consortium arrangement among institutions. Higher education institutions are encouraged to enter into a consortium arrange-ment among themselves for purposes of becoming more potent instruments for change, innovation, and relevance to their respective constituencies. A consortium arrangement is an inter-institutional cooperation calling for the pooling together of member institutions' manpower and physical resources to enhance the capabilities of these institutions to provide quality education and public service, and to participate more effectively in the attainment of national developmental goals.

4.   Moratorium on the opening of schools and courses. In the belief that the existing number of institutions and courses are more than what is necessary, the DECS has declared a moratorium on the opening of new ones to be in effect after the manpower supply and demand for every region would have been determined.

5.   Government assistance to private school students and faculty members. Republic Act No. 6728 which was passed by the Congress on June 16, 1989 provided for government assistance to students and teachers in private education and instituted deregulation procedures for school financing requirements.

6.   Technical Panel Approach. The involvement of experts in their respective disciplines as members of ad hoc bodies/technical panels in the formulation and recommendation of policies and program standards, leaves more time for the Bureau of Higher Education to take care of implementing DECS policies.

BIBLIOGRAPHY

Bureau of Elementary Education, Philippines. *1987 Annual Report.* Bureau of Elementary Education, DECS.

Bureau of Higher Education, Philippines. *1988 Annual Accomplishment Report.* Bureau of Higher Education, DECS.

Bureau of Secondary Education, Philippines. *Primer on the Secondary Education Development Program (SEDP).* Manila: DECS, 1988.

Bureau of Secondary Education, Philippines. *Secondary Education Development Program (SEDP): Curriculum Focus.* Manila: DECS, 1988.

Carson, Arthur L. *The Story of Philippine Education.* Quezon City: New Day Publishers, 1978.

Constitution of the Philippines. Republic of the Philippines, 1986.

DECS Statistical Bulletin, School Year 1987-1988. Manila: Department of Education, Culture and Sports.

Federation of Accrediting Agencies of the Philippines. *Towards Quality Education.* 1988.

Government of the Philippines. "Education for National Development: New Patterns, New Directions." In *Report of the Presidential Commission to Survey Philippine Education.* Manila, 1970.

Guingona, Serafin. ed. *Standards and Viability: Crises and Responses in Higher Education.* Manila: Phi Delta Kappa Philippines Chapter, 1987.

Guingona, Serafin. ed. *Issues in Philippine Education.* Manila: Phi Delta Kappa, Philippines Chapter, 1982.

Guzman, Raul. "Report on State Universities and Colleges in the Philippines." In *Report of the Task Force to Study State Higher Education.* Vols. 1-III. Manila, 1987.

Lacuesta, M., et al. *Historical, Philosophical, and Legal Foundations of Education.* Quezon City: Philippine Association of Teacher Education and Katha Publishing Co., Inc., 1986.

"National Strategies Facilitating Access to All Types and Levels of Education in Rural Areas." In *Proceedings of the UNESCO-DECS Sponsored Conference on Rural Education,* Manila, July 13-17, 1987.

POLAND

by
Karol Poznanski
Professor, Institute of Pedagogy
Maria Curie-Sklodowska University, Poland
and
Ryszard Kucha
Professor and Head, Institute of History of Education
Maria Curie-Sklodowska University, Poland

BACKGROUND

The traditions of higher education in Poland go back to the fourteenth century, when King Casimir III the Great founded (in 1364) the University of Cracow with three departments: law, medicine, and liberal arts. The Universities of Bologna and Padua served as the organizational patterns for the Cracow University. In 1400, Ladislaus II Jagiello gave a new foundation act to the university. This time, the University of Paris functioned as the organizational pattern. In addition to the three departments mentioned before, one more department was also introduced with intent to strengthen the religion (Christianity) as well as the education of the clergy.

The best times of university development occurred in the period of the Renaissance in Poland (15th-16th centuries). The academy enjoyed an excellent reputation thanks to the high level of education in liberal arts, law, mathematics, and astronomy and the brilliant scholars who drew students from neighboring countries as well as from Scandinavia. The manuscripts of the Cracow scholars were known in Paris, Oxford, Vienna, and Leipzig. One should mention the fact that Nicholas Copernicus studied there in the years 1491-95. The geographical discoveries and the works of Ptolemy caused the development of geography.

The history of the Cracow University was deeply connected with the history of Poland. It went through ups and downs with the evident decay in the seventeenth century and a renaissance in the years of the National Education Commission (1773-95), the first Ministry of Education in Europe. After its reformation, the National Education Commission functioned as the Main School (*Schola Principes Regni*) and superintended all elementary and secondary schools in the Kingdom of Poland (1777-83). It was the main center for teachers' education. In 1795, Poland lost its independence and the Austrians who occupied Cracow started to Germanize the university. In 1809, Cracow was annexed to the Duchy of Warsaw. It became free in the years 1815-46. The university got the name of Jagiellonian University and enjoyed full autonomy. Yet, being isolated from the other parts of Poland, it also got a provincial character. In the 1860s when Galicia was given autonomy, Joseph Dietl (the rector) started the process of re-Polonization of the university which lasted till 1870.

In 1873, another higher institution was founded in Cracow. It was the Academy of Sciences, the highest scientific institution, which attracted scholars from Galicia and the Prussian and Russian zones. Soon Cracow became one of the leading university centers in Central Europe, specially related to Slavistic studies and linguistics. This was a period of development for other disciplines too (classical and Polish philologies, medicine, and geology, etc). The Cracow History Department became very famous for its scholars (Joseph Szujski, Michal Bobrzynski, etc.). On the eve of World War I there were ninety-seven departments, professor's chairs, and research centers at the Jagiellonian University. There were almost 3,000 students in the university.

Other universities which played an important role in the history of Polish education were the two higher schools of Vilna and Lvov. The former was founded by King Stephen Bathory who raised the Jesuit College in Vilna (1578) to the level of an academy which consisted of two departments: the Department of Theology, and the Department of Liberal Arts and Philosophy. It reached the height of its development in the mid-seventeenth century and after the World War II, came under Lithuanian territory. The University of Lvov was founded in 1661 as a result of raising the Jesuit College (1606) to the level of an academy. The three departments (theology, philosophy, and law) were established under the foundation act of John Casimir, the king. In 1772, when Austria captured the whole south part of Poland, Lvov became the capital of the province called Galicia. A year later, the university fell down as a result of the abrogation of the Jesuit Order. In its place the Austrian authorities organized *Collegium Theresianum* and then, *Collegium Medicum* at the lycee level. This was the base of the university founded by Emperor Joseph II in 1784. After the restoration of independence, the university got the name of John Casimir.

Polish higher education suffered a great loss during World War II. About 40 percent of the professors were killed. The Warsaw University lost 162 scholars, the Jagiellonian University lost 109 scholars, and the Poznan University lost about 60 scientists. Of the laboratories which existed before the war, only three survived and 356 of them were completely destroyed. The Germans demolished most of the university buildings. The property of the Poznan University and of the Commercial Academy was almost completely devastated. Lots of scientific equipment, furniture, books, and apparatus were stolen.

The Polish higher education started its quick and intense development as soon as the World War II finished. Apart from the Catholic University of Lublin, the governmental university of Maria Curie Sklodowska in Lublin, and some departments of Warsaw Polytechnic came into existence. Most of the private schools were nationalized. Tuition fees were abolished and many students who needed financial help were given scholarships as well as subsidized accommodation and meals.

New scientific and education centers were established in Gdansk, Szczecin, Wroclaw, Lodz, and Torun as the need arose for trained specialists for the reconstruction of different branches of national economy and culture. By 1948, higher education in Poland surpassed (quantitatively) the achievements of the period between the wars. Twenty-three higher education institutions had been established: seven universities and six polytechnics, nine higher non academic schools, and sixteen artistic schools. There were 162 departments in all and 78,000 students.

The change of the political system which appeared after World War II found its reflection in the organization of education and higher schools. According to the decree of "the organization of education and higher schools" (28 October 1947) one can see the clear tendency to abridge and reduce the autonomy of higher schools as well as to centralize and subordinate them to the new sociopolitical situation of the country. Under the Act of 26 April 1950, all higher schools were subordinated to the Ministry of Higher Schools and Science which meant leaving the patterns which functioned before the war. A month later, higher education was reorganized in accordance with the Russian models. Universities lost their autonomy. The whole system of management was based on a single authority's responsibility and control.

As a result of deep political changes which took place in the years 1980-81, the whole system of higher education underwent another round of change based on new regulations of 4 May 1982, which were again renewed on 25 July 1985. In October 1987 the Ministry of National Education took the function of the Ministry of Education and the Ministry of Science and Higher Education. The revised act of higher schools (4 May 1982) is the main document regulating the present structure and the organization of higher education. Main tasks outlined in this act, for higher education institutions, include the education of highly skilled specialists with independent thinking and creative abilities, development of academic staff, research, cultivation of all national cultures, and practical use of art and science for the benefit of society.

Every higher education institution has the right to establish its own statute, to choose collegial organs, and to determine its internal structure and organization in accordance with the principles mentioned in the act. Under the act, higher education institutions are also empowered to plan the programs of research as well as study curricula; confer scientific degrees and determine the number of first year students; dispose the finances and the property of the school within the bounds of the law; employ staff and stipulate qualifications for employment; organize cooperation with higher schools and scientific centers abroad; and carry on other activities necessary for functioning of the university. The minister of higher education formulates education policy at a national level and also coordinates the activities of higher education institutions coming under other ministries. The schools run by the Ministry of Home Affairs and the Ministry of the National Defence as well as higher papal schools and higher seminaries do not come under the act.

Today in Poland there are eleven universities and eighty-one higher schools (eighteen technical, nine agrotechnical, six economics, ten pedagogical, six physical training, seventeen arts, eleven medical, and four others).

PRIMARY AND SECONDARY EDUCATION

The traditions of primary and secondary education in Poland is old and go back to the beginning of the thirteenth and the sixteenth centuries respectively. In the years 1918-39 (the period between wars), the secondary level took eight years for students coming from the four-year primary schools. The secondary school was divided into a three-year gymnasium, and a five-year higher secondary.

The gymnasium was differentiated by curriculum and it involved three departments: mathematics - sciences; humanities; and classical studies. Each covered five classes with a thirty hour teaching load per week (150 in all). The graduates of the higher gymnasium took a final exam which entitled them to compete for admission to higher schools. No other secondary school provided such qualifications. These schools enjoyed a high reputation in the society and their teachers constituted majority of the intelligentsia.

In 1932, the whole educational system was reformed. The primary schools got three different organizations levels (four, six and seven years). On the base of the six year primary school there appeared a six-year secondary school (of general education) which was divided into a four-year gymnasium and a two-year lycee, differentiated (in curriculum) under two departments: mathematics - sciences, and humanities and classical studies. The curriculum of the gymnasium (from 1934) emphasized development of responsibility and duty consciousness among young people and had, as an objective, the preparation of pupils for higher studies and self-realization. In October 1939, all secondary schools were closed as the German invaders occupied Poland and there started to function the Underground Organization of Teachers (TON) which organized underground teaching in the regions of the so called "*General Guberniya*" (province).

After the liberation of Polish lands in 1944-45, the secondary schools renewed their work immediately. First, it functioned on the basis of the pre-war organizational structure. From 1948 the gymnasium was included into the lycee and the whole educational cycle was shortened to four years at secondary level on the base of a compulsory eight-year primary schooling. The lycee prepares students for higher studies. The curriculum includes languages (Polish, Russian, and West European), social sciences, mathematics, sciences, music, and gymnastics. Each year the secondary schools (lycees) admit about 20 percent of the primary school leavers.

Students who do not succeed in entering lycees are directed to vocational schools which consist of several types: the basic vocational schools (ZSZ) with a three year cycle of learning for students who completed primary school (8 + 3); the secondary technical vocational schools and vocational lycees with 4-4.5 years of schooling for students who completed primary school or three years of schooling for students who completed the basic vocational school (8 + 3 + 3); the secondary technical-vocational schools and vocational lycees for students who completed the second class of lycee $(8+2+3)$; and the two year teachers' studies. About 50 percent of the primary school leavers attend the basic vocational schools, 20 percent attend vocational technical secondary schools and 5 percent attend the vocational lycees.

HIGHER EDUCATION

Institutions

Higher education in Poland is offered at several types of institutions and majority of them function under the Ministry of Education. The Ministry of Education oversees ten universities (nine governmental), eighteen technical higher schools, five economics academies and schools, ten pedagogical schools, and nine agricultural academies and schools. The Ministry of Health and Social Welfare is responsible for eleven medical academies and the Center for Post Diploma Education. Ministry of National Defense runs seventeen higher military schools. The Marine Economy Board is responsible for two higher schools of navigation. The Ministry of Culture and Arts oversees eight musical academies, six higher schools of art, two theatre schools and one school of film, television and theatre. Several other authorities are responsible for schools in their spheres of activity. In 1987, about 50,000 students graduated from higher institutions (including 340 foreign students). The administration of all higher education institutions in Poland must conform to government acts and regulations.

The academic senate is the highest body at most of the higher schools in Poland. The senate includes president (rector); vice-presidents; deans of faculties; representatives of professors, lecturers, and other workers of the university; and representatives of students' organizations, military department, political parties, and teachers' unions. The president often invites other advisers to take part in the senate's meetings. The senate may constitute various boards as necessary.

At the level of the faculties, there are faculty councils headed by the deans of the faculties. Similarly, at the institutes, there are institute councils, headed by the directors. The key officials of the university (president and vice-presidents, deans and vice-deans, directors of the institutes and vice-directors) are elected for a period of three years. Also the collegiate bodies remain elected for a period of three years.

Teachers are selected on a competitive basis and are required to have a minimum of a good master's degree or diploma at entry level. They undergo one year's training before starting to work as assistants. During the following eight years, they are required to publish their research in scientific journals and defend a doctoral dissertation. Contracts of candidates who do not complete these requirements are not renewed. To be promoted to the "adjunct" level (the highest rank of professor's assistant), candidates must present good knowledge in a foreign language and complete a six-month training period at another institution.

Programs and Degrees

Graduation from university is marked by the award of master's diploma, technical master's diploma, and other degrees such as diplomas in medicine. The duration of studies vary from 4-6 years depending on the program of studies. Most higher education institutions in Poland provide study opportunities for both resident and non-resident students.

The curriculum of studies at the universities is a broad one. The regional needs of the national economy are reflected in the programs offered at various institutions. First degree programs last 4-6 years depending on the program and require preparation of a "master's dissertation". The academic year is nine months and consists of two semesters beginning in October. The obligatory plans of studies are generally for the average students. Those who are specially talented can tailor their own programs by choosing extra courses and by participating in research. They also have the opportunity to accelerate their studies and to complete the programs in a shorter period with the approval of the department council. The medium of instruction is Polish excepting in foreign philology and advanced language classes where use of a foreign language is a necessity.

The minimum requirement for admission to higher education institutions is a pass in the final examination at a Polish gymnasium. Candidates for first degree programs (master's or diploma) compete for admission on the basis of the results of an entrance examination consisting of the main subjects and one foreign language. The candidates who are winners of the "central school subjects competition" are accepted without examinations. The medical academies conduct an integrated test in biology, chemistry, physics, and a chosen language. At the musical academies the test includes musical subjects. At the higher schools of arts, the candidates have to first present their work and if accepted must sit for an examination which includes a practical test (painting etc.). Admission to higher marine schools and higher military schools require good results in the main subjects (mathematics, physics, chemistry), a foreign language, and a practical test in physical abilities. Competition for entry to higher education institutions is severe. Students are required to do well in the entrance examination. Only one in about seven are accepted.

All government higher education institutions in Poland are free. Of course, this has resulted in a shortage of funds for investment in labs, equipment, and libraries. This is also the reason for the limited number of places in student hostels and the worsening of living conditions of students. Scholarships are available to students based on need and performance. The maximum amount of a scholarship can be as high as the monthly salary of a beginning teacher at the university. Students' families may also receive assistance. In general, the main expense which a Polish student has to bear is that of books and supplies. Out-of-town students who do not get a place in the university hostel must rent outside rooms which are very expensive; so they have to depend on their parent's support.

The graduates with master's and doctor's degrees can participate in the realization of research projects (central, local, university, or their own research) in accordance with the needs of the national economy. The results of their works are published simultaneous with the process of preparing their dissertation for *docent (habilitation)*, the degree which gives the right to be ultimately appointed as a professor. The "adjuncts" have to complete this dissertation in a nine-year period (from the date of receiving the doctor's degree). They may receive scholarships and special leave. On receipt of the *docent* degree (habilitation) they are promoted to the group of independent academic teachers and given, this way, the right to supervise doctoral work and to direct research groups. Then, on the basis of their overall achievements, they may win the two successive titles of associate professor and full professor. These are the highest ranking scientific titles in Poland. Unfortunately, the formalized procedure of receiving the scientific degrees and titles pose many obstacles and administrational barriers for prospective teachers. According to statistics, the master's degree is received at the age of 23-25; doctorate, at 33-34; *docent* title after the age of 40; and professor's at 50 or older.

In 1987 there were 38,227 academic teachers (including 2,137 assistants) for 261,951 students in higher education. The student population included 3,447 foreign students from 38 countries.

ISSUES AND TRENDS

The contemporary system of education in Poland is a reflection of national and cultural traditions, and the sociopolitical environment. It functions under the conditions of a deep economic crisis while the whole society has been looking for new ways of improving the social and political pluralism. While the emphasis has been on quantitative improvements, it is now becoming increasingly important to focus on the qualitative side. Improving this situation requires the shortening of preschool education and commencing primary school at the age of six years. The education would last for nine years with this school becoming a nine-grade one. Introduction of pedagogical and vocational guidance in the grades eight and nine are also planned. This school would provide a solid base for the general secondary school.

There is also a tendency towards broadening vocational education and preparing the pupils of general schools for professional fields. Reform is needed in the system of postsecondary schools so that they do not constitute "a blind alley". Such reforms will require many changes in the higher schools too, like giving up the idea of "the master's degree for everybody"; the development of alternate programs; and the introduction of changes in enrollment procedures for the first year of study at universities.

The policy of financing higher education also needs change. Even countries which are more prosperous than Poland cannot afford to cover the full cost of higher education entirely from government funds. Allocations from industry, social organizations, and from people themselves may need to be considered.

The year 1990 marks the beginning of complex reforms in higher education in Poland, based on the global program of the National Council of Education. The present educational system in Poland inherits both advanced and conservative elements of the educational experiences of the Poles. Its bureaucratic and centralized structure which originated to a great degree in the Stalin period, blocked and limited the reformative tendencies and the innovative work of the educators. Although the system played the role of democratizing education after World War II (about 1.6 million people got diplomas from higher schools in the years 1945-88) it needs much modification to meet the educational and cultural aspirations of present day Poles.

BIBLIOGRAPHY

Araszkiewicz, F. W. *Szkola srednia ogolnoksztalcaca w Polsce w latach 1918-1932*. Wroclaw: Ossol, 1972.

Informator Nauki Polskiej 1987-1988, Vol. 1-2. Warszawa, 1987.

Informator dla kandydatow na studia dzienne w szkolach wyzszych na rok akademicki 1988-1989. Warszawa, 1988.

Kozakiewicz, M. *Skolaryzacja mlodziezy polskiej*. Warszawa, 1976.

Pecherski, M. *System oswiatowy w Polsce Ludowej na tle porownawczym*. Wroclaw, 1981.

Siwinski, Cz. *Zmiany strukturalno-organizacyjne w szkolnictwie zawodowym PRL*. Poznan: UAM, 1981.

Skubala-Tokarska Z., and Tokarski Z. *Uniwersytety w Polsce*. Warszawa: Wiedza Powszechna, 1972.

Tymowksi, J. *Organizacja szkolnictwa wyzszego w Polsce*. Warszawa: PWN, 1975.

PORTUGAL

by
J. A. Esperanca Pina
Rector, New University of Lisbon, Portugal
in collaboration with
M. F. Loureiro Dias
Jurist, New University of Lisbon, Portugal
and
Virginia S. Guerreiro
Economist, New University of Lisbon, Portugal

BACKGROUND

Portugal has an old university tradition. The country's first university was established in Lisbon in 1288. During the last 700 years, universities have tried to respond to the needs created by human intelligence and imposed by the development of knowledge itself within the varying conditions of each succeeding epoch by teaching, learning, researching, and providing services to the community. The present system is thus the result of a combination of those traditional elements as well as modern innovations which together enable it to play a decisive role in building the future.

Ever since Pope Nicholas IV gave his formal recognition in 1290 to the teaching ministered by the first Portuguese university (in Lisbon), university education has closely followed the trends developed by other European universities. Higher studies underwent profound reforms particularly in the eighteenth century. The university in Lisbon by then had been transfered to Coimbra. The prestige of the higher studies (as university education was then called) at Coimbra increased so significantly that two new "higher schools" were founded in Lisbon and Oporto to meet the growing demand for higher training. Expansion of higher education continued vigorously in the twentieth century and in 1973, eight new universities were established within the scope of a higher education policy of expansion, diversification and regionalization. More recently, the new universities of Madeira and Macau were founded.

The political constitution which came into force in Portugal in 1976 guarantees freedom of education and the provision of an educational system organized by the state. It also recognizes private and cooperative education and paved the way for the formulation of the *Lei de Bases do Sistema Educativo* (Educational System General Law) by the government. The aims of this law were to regulate and systematize various types of higher education institutions and thus provide a definition of the parameters for the degrees to be awarded by each institution.

In Portugal, the state is considered responsible for upholding the constitutional principle by which every citizen has the right to education, culture, and learning as well as to equal opportunities for attaining school success. Consequently, the Ministry of Education is the government department which promotes and coordinates all policies related to higher education through the secretary of state and the director-general for higher education, i.e. the two authorities which link directly with the universities in all matters concerning national policies for education, science and culture.

Activities developed within Portuguese universities are coordinated by the Council of Rectors of the Portuguese Universities which is consulted by the Ministry of Education on matters related to activities of the schools. In this context the government and the universities are jointly considering at present, legislation which will allow the ministry to introduce a system of continuous evaluation of university activity, as stipulated by the university autonomy decree of 1988.

PRIMARY AND SECONDARY EDUCATION

The educational system starts in Portugal with the nursery schools. Nursery education is for the children whose parents want them to have it. Nursery schools are for children aged 3-6 years. The nursery schools cover the period before the primary school begins. The primary school corresponds to the first stage of compulsory education. The preschool education is administered, either by the public system, or by private entities. Its main purpose is to ensure the conditions that favor a global development of the child and to correct discriminatory effects caused by social and cultural conditions in the access to the educational system. Afterwards, children have the so-called "basic education", which is non fee charging and compulsory until they are fourteen years old. It lasts for six years and has two forms: primary and preparatory.

The primary school lasts for four years and is divided into two stages of two years each. Its purpose is the acquisition of basic knowledge and the development of capacities and behavior, which may enable further studies and a better integration of the student into society.

The preparatory school can be directly taught through television, or intensely administered in the evening. It lasts for two years and aims at giving the students the necessary tools that enable them to make intellectual progress. It aims at developing in the student the capacity of perception and the sense of responsibility so that they may become dynamic agents of transformation in their milieu, society, culture, and in the world.

The secondary education lasts six years and is divided into two stages: general secondary education and secondary complementary education. The general secondary education, at present is not compulsory, but will become so after 1992-93. It lasts three years. It is concerned with general studies administered either during the day or in the evening. The first two years have a common branch of ten or eleven main disciplines (mathematics, Portuguese, two foreign languages, history, social studies, natural sciences, physics, chemistry, manual works, and crafts. The terminal year integrates, besides the common branch, a discipline of vocational character, which can be chosen among thirteen options.

The secondary complementary education is not compulsory and lasts three years. It consists of complementary studies, technical-professional studies, and teachers' studies. These studies are organized into five main areas: natural sciences; technological sciences; social sciences; humanities; and visual arts. Each one of these areas, besides possessing a common set of disciplines of general education also have a component of vocational education.

HIGHER EDUCATION

Institutions

The Portuguese higher educational system has two main components: universities and polytechnic institutes. In total, there are at present 102 public higher education institutions (ninety-six of which are directly dependent on the Ministry of Education) and thirty-two private and cooperative higher education institutions, including the *Universidade Catolica* (Catholic University). During 1988-89, 135,000 students were enrolled in higher education institutions and the number is expected to increase to 200,000 in 1989-90.

In the last few years, universities have absorbed approximately 85 percent of the students attending higher education institutions. However, the recently created polytechnic institutes have been showing, as expected, a sustained increase in enrollment. At the same time, since the recognition in 1986-87 of several private institutions, the weight of the private higher educational sector is also increasing.

University autonomy, was legally instituted only towards the end of 1988. Its introduction has given universities a normative framework within which the institutions are now able to get their own statutes with real independence and responsibility. In this context, universities are legally recognized collective bodies which enjoy statutory, scientific, pedagogic, administrative, financial, and disciplinary autonomy. They collaborate with the government in the formulation of educational, scientific and cultural policies and are entitled, through the Council of Rectors of the Portuguese Universities, to make pronouncements on any proposed legislation with regard to matters of direct concern to them.

Scientific autonomy afford universities the freedom to define, plan, and carry out research and other scientific and cultural activities. Pedagogic autonomy allows universities to set up, suspend, and abolish courses; to prepare study plans and curricula; to define teaching and evaluation methods; and to try pedagogic experiments. Within the terms set by law, universities are also empowered to take disciplinary action against and apply punitive sanctions to students, teaching staff, and other categories of staff. As far as administrative and financial autonomy is concerned, universities can make use of their assets, and freely administer not only the allocations attributed to them every year by the state but also their self-raised tax free funds. The state guarantees the availability of required operational funds which are allocated upon approval of budget proposals based on short and medium term development plans as well as previous year's activities.

The exact concept of "university autonomy" can be extracted from the principle which underlies the institution itself: "...universities should guarantee freedom for scientific, cultural, and technological creativity, ensure diversity and free expression of orientations and opinions, promote the participation of all university sectors in academic life and ensure the observance of democratic methods in their management."

Portuguese universities have been developing extremely useful exchange programs between themselves and with foreign higher education institutions in the pedagogic, scientific and cultural fields. In more recent years, they have been intensifying and extending their cooperation with industry and the community in general, providing services and cultural extension as well as training and research facilities. Cooperation links with foreign institutions have included the participation of Portuguese universities in European, EEC, and international programs for scientific, pedagogic, and institutional exchanges.

Cooperation with European countries is paving the way for the integration of the European Common Market countries planned for 1992. At the same time, Portuguese universities have also been maintaining increasing cooperation with those countries outside Europe which are linked to Portuguese culture and language.

University education aims at "ensuring the acquisition of solid scientific and cultural knowledge which together with the provision of technical training enable professional and cultural activity and the development of conceptual and analytical capacity". On the other hand, polytechnic education aims at "providing solid cultural and high level technical training; developing innovative and analytical capacity; and imparting scientific knowledge of a technical and practical nature applicable to professional activity".

At the moment, there exists in Portugal fourteen universities located in different cities: Lisbon *(Universidade de Lisboa, Universidade Tecnica de Lisboa, Universidade Nova de Lisboa)*, Coimbra, Porto, Aveiro, Braga, Evora, Covilha, Vila Real, the Azores, Algarve, Madeira, and Macau. The universities in Lisbon, Coimbra, and Oporto are internally decentralized into units (faculties and/or institutes) interconnected via a central service called *reitoria* (vice-chancellors's office). The other universities, established in smaller urban areas, have tended to adopt a multidisciplinary internal structure of a departmental nature.

The administrative structure of a university generally includes the assembly, the rector, the senate, and the administrative council. The internal administration consisting of faculties is decentralized and each faculty or institute is responsible through its governing board for its policies (scientific, pedagogic, and administrative), and their articulation within the main policy lines established by the university. In the universities where internal structure is based on departments, there is an effective interdisciplinary relationship between the various departments which share and have access to common equipment, facilities, and services. Although administratively they are more centralized, the departments are autonomous and are responsible for their activities.

University and polytechnic teaching staff form part of the Portuguese Civil Service, but their careers are structured according to specific legislation, i.e. the

Estatuto da Carreira Docente Universitaria (career statutes for university teachers) and are divided into following categories: *assistente estagiario* (junior lecturer), *assistente* (lecturer), *professor auxiliar* (assistant professor), *professor associado* (associate professor), and *professor catedratico* (full professor). In the polytechnic system, career categories are as follows: *assistente* (lecturer), *professor adjunto* (assistant professor), and *professor coordenador* (professor coordinator). Institutions can also offer teaching contracts to both nationals and foreigners of proven and recognized merit.

Programs and Degrees

University education in Portugal offers courses in a variety of fields including arts, law, social sciences (including economics and management), exact and natural sciences, engineering, health sciences (including medical, pharmaceutical, and dental sciences), agrarian and marine sciences (including veterinary sciences), and physical education. Universities are also responsible for the training of secondary and higher education teachers.

Universities award the degrees of *licenciado* (bachelor of arts and of science with honors), *mestre* (master of philosophy), and *doutor* (doctor of philosophy), academic titles, honorary degrees, and other certificates and diplomas for short courses (special and postgraduation short courses). The degree of *licenciado* is awarded after successful completion of a 4-6 year course of study. The degree of *mestre* is awarded after successful completion of a postgraduate course of 3-4 semesters duration (beyond the *licenciado*) and the approval of a dissertation. The degree of *doutor* (doctoral degree) is awarded after the presentation of a written thesis and the "viva" examination. The thesis must be based on original research and must reveal general knowledge and capacity in the subject area within which the doctorate is awarded.

Reference should also be made to the *escolas superiores de belas artes* (higher schools of fine arts) which are not integrated in universities or institutes but are directly dependent on the Ministry of Education (via the Directorate-General for Higher Education) and award degrees equivalent to *bacharel* and *licenciado*.

Polytechnic institutes award the degree of *bacharel* after successful completion of a three-year course of study and also diplomas in *estudos superiores especializados* (specialized higher studies) which are equivalent to the degree of *licenciado* for professional and academic purposes. These diplomas are awarded after post-*bacharel* studies are completed. The polytechnic institutes also award other certificates and diplomas after successful completion of short courses.

Access to higher education in Portugal is limited, that is to say, it is conditioned by virtue of the *numerus clausus* system. The number of available places in higher education institutions is fixed each year according to available capacity and needs. Selection of candidates is dependent upon grades obtained in assessment tests, set at national level. In order to sit the national assessment tests, candidates must have successfully completed their twelfth year of schooling. Candidates who have obtained their qualifications abroad need to possess a certificate of eligibility proving that they would have been able to enroll in the country from where the qualification was obtained, in a course comparable to the one they wish to follow in Portugal.

In the area of postgraduate studies, the master's and doctoral degrees aim at giving a deeper knowledge in a specific scientific field and at developing capacities for research. The studies are organized in credit units. The acquisition of these degrees covers, in the Portuguese universities, a great number of areas in the fields of science and human knowledge. The progression in the academic career also depends on it.

The doctorate is labeled after the corresponding area of knowledge according to the main fields in the school that confers it. The specialization chosen for the dissertation can be added too. When a trainee assistant obtains this degree he can proceed in his career and make a contrast as assistant professor.

The postgraduate programs (master's degree and doctorates) as well as programs and contracts for research in which students and academic staff collaborate, provide the opportunities for scientific research through which lecturing maintains itself up to date and penetrates the world networks of scientific knowledge. This is carried out either in university departments, institutes, or centers, some of which are supported by state institutions (National Institute of Scientific Research, National Council of Scientific and Technological Research, etc.). Recently the government has created a "science" program, through which universities are invited to become engaged in the modernization and international-ization of scientific infrastructure of the university system. An important goal of this program is to finance new structures and to increase the human resources dedicated to scientific and technological development of the country.

Courses are taught in Portuguese. The academic year which starts in October and ends in July is normally divided into two semesters.

Cost of fees in the public higher education sector is symbolic (1,200 escudos per year). However, in the future, universities may alter this policy.

There are a number of student support services which provide financial support, lodgings, meals and also assist in exchange programs with foreign institutions of higher education.

ISSUES AND TRENDS

Higher education in Portugal is now going through a decisive phase. As in most European countries, universities need to reflect upon their future development. The challenges which can be anticipated in the scientific, technologi-cal, and pedagogic fields, in terms of efficiency, efficacy, and excellence are of vital importance. In this process, higher education in Portugal will play several important roles: trainer of qualified labor; source of updated knowledge maintained through continuous scientific research; abode of experts for the promotion of culture; and the provider of advisory support.

Recognizing the significance of the roles that universities play, the government has tried to stimulate their potential, by conferring upon them great autonomy and responsibility. It must be remembered here that the main financial support for the universities comes almost exclusively from the national budget and for this reason, the development of the universities depend upon the funds which are allocated to them.

The ceilings on public expenditure imposed by the government create difficulties to the universities particularly in the recruitment of qualified staff, thus making, in economic terms, career prospects in Portuguese universities appear unattractive and little stimulating.

The objectives which need to be achieved by the mid-1990s, with regard to the number of students in higher education (23.3 percent of 18-22 year old youth) and the setting up and development of university based scientific research, require the collective efforts of the universities as institutions, and of their teaching staff as agents of the whole process.

The adaptation and restructuring needed in the higher educational system should be directed to respond to present training requirements and to the rapid changes produced by the requirements themselves without generating excessive financial burdens. The aim is to create a more modern, flexible, and efficient system that would allow flexibility in the use of resources (human, physical, and financial); swift reaction to changing needs; reduction of the dependency on government funding; increased cost-effectiveness; diversification and enlargement of sources of finance; and introduction of changes in teaching methods and in the curricula of some courses.

As far as students are concerned, it is anticipated that the following concrete objectives would be achieved: the reappraisal of the process by which students pass from secondary to higher education; increase in the number of students gaining access to higher education; and increase in the social and financial support accompanied by changes in the types and nature of student support (grants, subsidies, loans, halls of residence, refectory facilities, etc.).

In summing up, it can be said that several predominant trends are noticeable in the Portuguese higher educational system: improvement of the internal and external efficiency of the system; development of science and technology, particularly through the development of scientific research; improvement of the quality of output; and modernization of teaching processes and content. The support for these trends is found in the profound motivation felt by the universities to collaborate and push forward a far reaching reform of Portuguese society as a whole with a view to ensuring active participation of Portugal in the European Community and in the larger context created by the recent political changes in the continent.

BIBLIOGRAPHY

Gracio, R. *Educaçao e Processo Democratico em Portugal.* Lisbon: Livros Horizonte, 1981

Ministério da Educaçao, Portugal. *Guia do Acesso ao Ensino Superior - 1993.* Ministério da Educaçao, 1990.

PUERTO RICO

by
Jose A. Acosta Ramos
Associate Professor, Faculty of Education
University of Puerto Rico, Puerto Rico
and
Jaime Ortiz Vega
Director-Dean
Catholic University of Puerto Rico at Mayaguez, Puerto Rico

BACKGROUND

The 1952 Constitution of Puerto Rico guaranteed free elementary and secondary education to its citizens and made primary education compulsory until the age of fourteen. The constitutional provisions also put primary and secondary education under the responsibility of a secretary of public instruction, while guaranteeing the existence of private education. This last aspect has facilitated the creation of private schools of religious and secular nature throughout the state. Although since 1948 the official language in public education has been Spanish, there are various private schools which provide instruction in English. The state manages public education through a centralized organization directed by the secretary of public instruction who determines the policies related to the state's elementary and secondary education. Since the secretary is a member of the Council of Higher Education, he or she also participates in determining the policies which govern public and private higher education in Puerto Rico.

During the academic year 1988-89, public schools had an enrollment of 661,576 students consisting of 30,788 in preschool education; 344,068 in elementary education (grades 1-6); 273,409 in secondary education (grades 7-12); and 13,311 in special education. Of the students in secondary education, 153,806 were in intermediate schools (grades 10-12). During the academic year 1986-87 public schools employed 32,361 teachers.

The development of higher education in Puerto Rico is a phenomenon particular to the twentieth century. Under Spanish rule (1508-98), there was no university as such. All attempts to establish one during this period in history were unsuccessful, because the island could not sustain the economic burden of an institution of this nature. Besides, there was a dearth of native professors to fill the required positions. Among the attempts made were the courses taught in 1532, by an order of the Dominicans, in the Saint Thomas of Aquino Convent in San Juan.

In 1888, the Institution of Higher Education of Puerto Rico was founded, in the facilities housing the Puerto Rico Literary Association (ATENEO), under the direction of the University of Habana, Cuba. In 1891, by royal decree, two normal schools (teacher training schools) began functioning. One prepared males, and the other prepared females for teaching positions in the country.

When Puerto Rico came under the rule of the United States of America, the new government founded a normal school in 1900 which later developed into the University of Puerto Rico with the enactment of the University Law of 1903. The university was directed by a board of trustees, which included among its members, the country's governor, and the commissioner of education. According to the law, the commissioner of education became the president of the board of trustees as well as the rector of the university. This law, with slight modifications was in force until 1942. In 1942, the University Reform Law was passed creating the Council of Higher Education, to take the place of the board of trustees. This council became the rectorate of the University of Puerto Rico. Its members were named by the governor, for a period of ten years. The council was entrusted with the responsibility to carry out six basic functions: 1) consider and approve the rules of the institution; 2) name the rector; 3) approve the budget; 4) confirm or reject appointments made and submitted by the rector; 5) enlarge or organize colleges, schools, faculties, departments or other dependent agencies required; and 6) articulate the goals of the university to those in public education and society.

In 1966 the Puerto Rican legislature approved another university reform act. The act created several academic units, and put the administration of the university under a presidency. In addition, it authorized the establishment of regional colleges to avoid over population of the Rio Piedras Campus, while providing opportunities for university education to those residing outside the metropolitan area.

The new law granted autonomy to the College of Agriculture and Mechanical Arts of Mayaguez, which was founded in 1912 as a branch of Rio Piedras, specializing in engineering and agriculture. The college later became the Campus of Mayaguez. In addition, the School of Tropical Medicine created in 1924 (which had become the School of Medicine of the University of Puerto Rico in 1949), acquired the status of a Campus under the University Reform Act of 1966 to become the campus of Medical Sciences of San Juan.

During the twentieth century, Puerto Rico's education has made great progress, making it possible for all citizens to receive an education regardless of their social or economic status. As Puerto Rico changed from an agricultural economy to an industrial one in the second half of the twentieth century, enormous growth has taken place in vocational and technical education, as well as in higher education.

PRIMARY AND SECONDARY EDUCATION

Elementary school education in Puerto Rico is composed of kindergarten and grades 1-6. The General Education Law, enacted in July 1990, made the kindergarten a part of education in every elementary public school of the country. This law divides the elementary education in two levels: from kindergarten to third grade, and from fourth to sixth grade. The law also changes the name of the Department of Public Instruction to Department of Education. The Department of Education is planning, in the long run, to offer preschool education to four-year old children. Preschool education is not offered on a compulsory basis. Elementary schools are spread all over urban and rural areas of the island.

Secondary education is composed of the intermediate level (grades 7-9) and high school (grades 10-12). Some private schools operating under plan 8-4, have the secondary level, consisting of grades 9-12. Depending on the organization of the secondary school, the years of study can be six or four, six being the most common. The academic year begins in August and ends in May. Upon completion of the secondary level, students who have met the requirements satisfactorily receive a diploma. The General Education Law contemplates that in order for the students to be promoted from one educational level to the other they must pass an academic competencies test. These tests shall be applied at the end of the third, sixth, ninth, and twelfth grades. Those students who do not pass the tests will receive supplementary education before they can take the tests for the second or third time. When the students pass the twelfth grade test, they are awarded the diploma.

The secondary level consisting of grades 9-12, allows students to follow different curricula depending on their interests. There is a general education curriculum designed to prepare students who plan to enter institutions of higher education. The vocational curriculum is designed to prepare students who plan to enter the work force. In addition, students can follow a combination of both curricula.

The elementary school curriculum consists of Spanish as the native tongue, English as a second language, mathematics, social studies, science, fine arts, and physical education. The time devoted to each of the main subjects (Spanish, English, math, social studies, and science) varies from grade to grade, and one organizational level to the other, but the minimum amount of time is 300 minutes per week. The curriculum at the junior high school consists mainly of Spanish, English, mathematics, social studies, science, industrial arts or home economics, and physical education. The minimum time given to each subject is 300 minutes per week. There is more variety in the high school curriculum. the students study three years of Spanish and English, two years of mathematics and science, one year of history of Puerto Rico, one year of history of the world, and one-half year of history of the United States. Also, there are a number of other optional subjects available to students. The vocational education schools have a varied curriculum according to the occupational needs of the regions where they are located.

Education is free in state schools. In private schools, students pay fees which vary from one institution to another. Public secondary schools (with some exceptions) are not boarding schools. Each municipality of the island has at least one high school. Some private schools are boarding schools.

In public secondary schools Spanish is the medium of instruction, but there are numerous private schools in which English is used.

Teachers of public schools are required to have certification from the Department of Public Instruction. As established by law, the certification requires a minimum of high school preparation with a speciality in the academic area which pertains to the subject to be taught, and a teacher's certificate granted by the state, through the Department of Public Instruction. Private secondary schools too use the same criteria when recruiting teachers.

It is not customary to enroll foreign students in the public secondary schools, unless they are residents.

HIGHER EDUCATION

Institutions

The University Reform Act of 1966 resulted in three autonomous units, each directed by a rector: Campus of Rio Piedras, Campus of Mayaguez, and School of Medical Sciences. In 1971 the administration of regional colleges of the University of Puerto Rico was brought under the direction of a rector. The principal objective was to organize and manage the regional colleges of the University of Puerto Rico, institutions whose purpose was to award two year associate degrees and to provide the students the opportunity of pursuing the first two years of a baccalaureate program which can be completed in the campuses. The University Reform Act of 1966 also created the Council of Higher Education. This body, besides formulating policies for the university of the state, is in charge of evaluating and authorizing private institutions of higher education. The council in fact is the accrediting agency for private institutions.

The state provides funds for private institutions of higher education to meet the needs of specific areas, but not to the same extent as for state institutions. The United States Federal Government provides funds for private institutions as well as for public ones through various programs. These funds are used for many purposes including construction of student housing, improvement of the faculty and libraries, and curriculum development.

Some institutions are affiliated with religious groups. The Catholic University of Puerto Rico, the *Universidad Central*, and the *Universidad del Sagrado Corazon* are institutions affiliated with the Roman Catholic Apostolic Church. The Antillian University is affiliated with the Seventh Day Adventist Church. The Evangelic Seminar of Puerto Rico has as its main function the preparation of ecclesiastic personnel for various evangelical denominations in Puerto Rico and in the Caribbean and Spanish speaking countries. In addition, there are institutions which have some type of affiliation with other organizations. The Technological Community College is sponsored by the municipal government of San Juan, the School of Fine Arts is affiliated with the Puerto Rican Cultural Institute, and the technological institutes are affiliated with the Department of Public Education, among others. The Mutual Assistance Society *(Sociedad de Auxilio Mutuo)* sponsors the School of Anesthesia in the Mutual Assistance Hospital.

In Puerto Rico there are thirty-eight institutions of higher education certified by the Council of Higher Education and they offer academic degrees ranging from an associate degree to a doctorate. Several of these institutions have a great number of autonomous or quasi autonomous sub units. One example is the University of Puerto Rico, which has a total of eleven units, four of these being completely autonomous. Another specific example is the Inter-American University of Puerto Rico, which is governed by a highly centralized system, composed of eleven units.

Governance

Higher education governance varies among institutions. The most common structure, used by the biggest and the most complex institutions, consist of an executive board of directors, a president, chancellor or rector, deans, and department heads. Also, there are other governance bodies, such as academic councils or boards and academic senates. The executive board of directors selects the president and establishes the policy to be developed and implemented by this officer. The president is the main executive officer of the whole institution. He or she administers, coordinates, and supervises various academic, administrative, student, and financial activities of the institution. The chancellor or rector coordinates and supervises a definite campus or academic unit in the areas of academic, administrative, student, and financial affairs. The deans are in charge of specific areas at the different campus, colleges, faculties or schools; such as academic, administrative, or student affairs. The directors, or heads of departments are in charge of the same areas but at the academic department level. The procedure to select this personnel differ among the institutions. In some institutions the faculty and the non-academic staff participate in the consultation process. In other institutions (mainly in the private ones), the governance bodies select the administrative personnel.

The academic councils or boards analyze, discuss and recommend possible solutions to general problems that effects the academic institution. It is an advisory body composed mostly of administrative personnel.

The academic senate is the official body representing the faculty or academic community. It is composed of certain administrative personnel, the faculty representatives elected by the faculty, and the students representatives elected by the student body. Usually, the senate is presided by the chancellor or rector. The senate analyzes, discusses, and puts into practice solutions to problems affecting the faculty and student bodies. The members suggest solutions to problems and make recommendations to superior authorities.

Undergraduate Studies

Of the thirty-eight recognized institutions of higher education, twenty-nine offer undergraduate studies leading to associates degrees in arts and sciences; and bachelor's degrees in liberal arts, sciences, business administration, and divinity.

Candidates seeking admission to undergraduate studies are usually required to take the aptitude test given by the College Board (an independent organization which conducts the test for the use of institutions of higher education in Puerto Rico, as well as in the United States). Each educational institution establishes the level of the score required for admission. This varies from institutions which require high scores to those which only require the test to be taken as a placement requisite, regardless of the score obtained. The first case is common at the University of Puerto Rico, for which the admission is selective, due to the high number of students soliciting entrance compared to available openings. The university also requires superior academic achievement in high school. In general, the level of the aptitude test score is not an important factor for admission to institutions which offer associate degrees. Some institutions have separate admission criteria for non traditional students, who are not required to take the aptitude test.

Undergraduate programs generally require 60-72 credits to complete an associate degree and a minimum of 120 credits for a bachelor's degree. The academic year may consist of semesters, trimesters, or four quarter terms. The programs are designed in such a manner that a student who studies full time can complete an associates degree in two years, and a bachelor's degree in four years. Studies have shown that the actual average to complete a degree in Puerto Rico is three years for the associate's degree and five for the bachelor's degree.

The major fields of studies at the undergraduate level, available at majority of the higher education institutions are social sciences, education, natural sciences, humanities, languages, fine arts, general studies, business administration, nursing, the different branches of engineering, and different technical specialties.

In most of the institutions of higher education, instruction is in Spanish. The Inter-American University of Puerto Rico has a system called "double track" by which courses are given in Spanish as well as in English, depending on the student's preference.

The tuition cost for an undergraduate student in institutions of higher education can fluctuate from US$15 per credit in the University of Puerto Rico, to US$75 or more per credit in private institutions.

Only a few institutions provide residence facilities to students. Among these are the following: University of Puerto Rico, Rio de Piedras Campus; University of the Sacred Heart; Catholic University of Puerto Rico in Ponce; and the Interamerican University, San German Campus. About 95 percent of the students in institutions of higher education pay the cost of their studies with the help of financial aid from both the state and the federal government, or entirely from the federal government. Students in the public university system benefit from scholarships provided by the Puerto Rican government. Students in private institutions pay the cost of their studies mainly through Pell Grants (US government). In addition, the federal government provides funds for work study programs and guarantees bank loans that students may obtain from private banks. Also the state government grants universities a legislative scholarship fund, which the private institutions can utilize for providing financial aid to their students. The basic criteria used by the institutions in providing financial aid to students is their level of family income and financial need. The majority of students who enroll in private institutions come from social classes of lesser income, and they require financial aid to pay the cost of their studies.

The criteria for selection and retention of faculty are established by the institutions in their faculty procedures. A master's degree is required by institutions of higher education, although it is common to recruit teachers with a bachelor's degree for institutions which offer associate degrees and certificates. This situation may also arise in institutions offering bachelor's degrees in areas for which there is a scarcity of teachers (computer sciences, nursing, food technology, etc.). In some institutions the recruiting of candidates is initiated and highly influenced by the already constituted faculty and in others, the recruiting is done by the administration, with little or no input from the faculty members.

Institutions of higher education in Puerto Rico have traditionally been open to foreign students, mostly from the Caribbean Basin, Latin America, Africa, and Asia. Foreign students pay a fee of US$1,000 per semester for the bachelor's program, and US$1,500 per semester for postgraduate programs at the state/public institutions.

Advanced Studies and Research

Postgraduate studies are offered at the following institutions: Rio Piedras, Mayaguez, and Medical Sciences Campuses of the University of Puerto Rico; San German and San Juan Campuses of the Inter-American University of Puerto Rico; Catholic University of Puerto Rico; University of the Sacred Heart; Metropolitan University; University del Turabo, Ana Mendez Foundation; Caribbean Center of Postgraduate Studies; Center of Advanced Studies of Puerto Rico and the Caribbean; Dowling College (Caribbean Graduate Residence Center); Graduate School of the South; New Hampshire College San Juan Center; New York University (Puerto Rico Residence Center); University of Phoenix; Ponce School of Medicine; St. John's Baptist School of Medicine; Central University of the Caribbean; and Puerto Rico Institute of Psychiatry. There are four schools of medicine: Medical School of the University of Puerto Rico at the Medical Sciences Campus; St. John's Baptist School of Medicine; Central University of the Caribbean; and Ponce School of Medicine. Three university institutions have law schools: Catholic University; Inter-American University, San Juan Campus; and University of Puerto Rico, Rio Piedras Campus. The Inter-American University has a School of Optometry at the San Juan Campus.

Generally, the admission to postgraduate studies are based on a general aptitude test and several specific tests related to the chosen area of studies, academic performance in previous studies, academic performance in courses related to the speciality to be studied, and an interview with the members of the faculty in the chosen area of studies.

Master's degree is offered in a variety of fields including educational administration and supervision, teaching of English as a second language, elementary and secondary education, educational technology, psychology, social work, business education, special education, speech pathology, library science, pedagogical research and evaluation, hispanic studies, criminal justice, public health, hospital administration, nutrition, economic planning, pubic communication, architecture, bilingual education, natural sciences, rehabilitation counseling, economics, public administration, business administration, nursing, medical technology, and agricultural administration.

Specialities available for doctorates include educational administration and supervision, curriculum and instruction, educational planning and evaluation, teaching of English as a second language, law, marine sciences, chemistry, biology, physics, psychology, hispanic studies, odontology, medicine, nutrition, and counseling.

The structure of the master's and doctoral programs vary depending on the department, faculty, and school. Usually the period of study and research last from 3-7 years. The academic year lasts from August to May, and summer sessions are available. The medium of instruction for most specialities is Spanish, but a majority of the texts used are written in English. The schools of medicine tend to use English as their language of instruction.

The cost varies from US$45 per credit in state institutions to about US$160 per credit in private institutions. Schools of medicine have a fixed cost by semester, regardless of the number of credits taken by a student. Postgraduate students reside outside the institutions, excepting those who are in specialties which require residence within the institution.

Postgraduate studies are financed in various ways: scholarships, financial aid, bank loans guaranteed by the federal government, study leave with pay granted by the institutions which employs the student, teaching assistantships, and financial support from the student's family.

ISSUES AND TRENDS

The institutions which prepare technical personnel have introduced changes in their curricula with the objective of enriching them with field experiences that will demonstrate application of the theory they learned. In addition, cooperative programs with businesses, industry, and banks are under preparation. Cooperative partnerships are developing between the country's institutions, and institutions in other countries. Technology is being integrated into university curricula; utilization of computer capabilities in university courses is a case in point.

Adult education has taken a new turn. Adults return to institutions of higher education to further their knowledge and skills for advancement in their careers. In addition, they engage in educational pursuits in other areas of knowledge and occupations that interests them. This has resulted in an increase in the afternoon, evening, and Saturday classes at many institutions. The institutions have expanded their services to communities far from the traditional centers, giving rise to a new proliferation of educational centers all over the island. New specialities such as geriatrics and training of medical emergency technicians (paramedics) have been added. The tendency of the institutions of higher education is to respond to the social and economic demands of the society, and to the needs of the immediate communities which they serve.

BIBLIOGRAPHY

Aponte Hernandez, R. *The University of Puerto Rico: Foundations of the 1942 reform*. Unpublished doctoral dissertation, University of Texas, Austin, TX, 1966.

Benitez de Avila, C. *A study of the administrative development of higher education in Puerto Rico from 1957 to 1973*. Unpublished doctoral dissertation, Lehigh University, Bethlehem, PA, 1982.

Benner, T. E. *Five years of foundation building: 1924-1929*. Rio Piedras, PR: Universidad de Puerto Rico, 1965.

Castro, A. *Higher education in Puerto Rico, 1898-1956*. Unpublished doctoral dissertation, Lehigh University, Bethlehem, PA, 1975.

College Entrance Examination Board. *Acceso a la educacion superior en Puerto Rico*. Hato Rey, PR: CEEB, 1974.

College Entrance Examination Board. *Study of student aid in higher education in Puerto Rico*. Hato Rey, PR: CEEB, 1971.

Cotto, R. *The regional college movement in Puerto Rico*. Unpublished doctoral dissertation, Lehigh University, Bethlehem, PA, 1973.

Hansen, M. *Problems of a university in a small country*. Rio Piedras, PR: University of Puerto Rico, 1974.

Lopez Yustos, A. *Historia documental de la educacion en Puerto Rico (1503-1970)*. San Juan, PR: Sandeman, Inc., 1985.

Negron de Montilla, A. *Americanization in Puerto Rico*. San Juan, PR: Editorial Edil, 1971.

Osuna, J. J. *A history of education in Puerto Rico*. Rio Piedras, PR: University of Puerto Rico, 1949.

QATAR

by
M. Monir Morsi
Professor and Director, Educational Research Center
University of Qatar, Qatar

BACKGROUND

In common with all the other Arab countries, Qatar has known the classical pattern of religious non-governmental education represented in the *Katateeb*, (one room schools and mosques), for a very long time. It was not until 1952 that the government started to shoulder some responsibility for education by establishing the first public primary school. Since then the school system has witnessed steady expansion. Para "C" of article 8 of the second chapter of the Provisional Basic Law of the State of Qatar stipulates that the goal of education is to create people who are strong in body, mind, intellect, and personality; who believe in God and in virtuous conduct; who have pride in their Islamic Arab heritage; who are equipped with knowledge; and who are conscious of their duties and aware of their rights.

The Ministry of Education and Instruction supervises the entire public educational system, at all levels, including national, private, foreign, and non-government kindergarten schools. It also issues permits for the establishment of such schools. At the local level, Qatar is at present divided into three educational zones, with each zone having a director who is responsible to the minister for the progress of education and its management in that zone. There is also a body that is responsible for technical orientation and guidance, which includes male and female inspectors whose function is to guide teachers and ensure the proper functioning of the educational process.

Expenditure on education is funded from the allocations that are set in the state general budget, as is the case in all other Arab Gulf States. The budget sets forth, in addition to the general expenditure, the monthly bursaries and grants and other allocations to meet the cost of text and writing books, transport, and other services that are offered free of charge to pupils. The education budget has been growing steadily in recent years which reflects the growing interest on the part of the state in this vital sector.

The share allocated for education is approximately 10 percent of the general budget, which is comparable to allocations in the other Gulf States. Similarly, the average cost per pupil per year in Qatar is US$5,600 which is considered to be one of the highest averages in the world.

Public education in Qatar is organized according to the recommendations of the charter of Arabic cultural unity which divides public education into three stages: a primary stage of six years for children of ages 6-12; a preparatory stage of three years for ages 12-15; and a secondary stage of three years for ages 15-18. At secondary level, the schools are diversified into academic, technical, commercial, and industrial schools.

There are no government kindergarten schools in Qatar. All kindergarten schools belong to the national or private sector which includes, in addition to individual efforts, the contributions of the cooperative societies and the Qatari Public Petroleum Foundation. But it is expected that the increasing participation of women in the work force and the educational and social evolutionary trends would induce and eventually dictate the establishment of government kindergarten schools to cater for the children of these working women, as has happened in other Arab States.

Similarly, there is no compulsory system of education. Yet in Qatar, education in all stages is free of charge for all those who wish to receive it. Besides government education, there is a parallel religious system of preparatory and secondary education. There are also foreign and local private schools, all of which are subjected to government supervision. There are no coeducational government schools at any educational stage in Qatar. But in the private non-government sector all kindergarten and most of the primary schools are coeducational, according to 1985-86 statistics.

PRIMARY AND SECONDARY EDUCATION

Primary Stage

Primary stage is the basic stage on the education ladder and caters for children of ages 6-12 years (lasts six years). This stage is manifesting a progressive quantitative growth in enrollment with the number of pupils in government schools reaching approximately 32,000 pupils in 1985-86. Of this number, 56 percent are Qataris, and the remaining pupils are of different Arab and non-Arab origin with Palestinians and Jordanians leading the of list of Arab nationals, making about 14 percent of the total number of pupils. Girls constitute about 48 percent of the total number of pupils of this stage. There is an end of year exam for each grade, but the general primary school certificate exam was abolished in 1979. Pupils who fail are given a second chance and can sit for a supplementary exam which is usually held a few weeks after the first.

A field study conducted by the inspectorate of primary education, found that the rate of failure at the primary stage, in 1986, was 25 percent. This means that one fourth of all pupils do not pass successfully their exams. This is regarded by educational authorities to be an exceptionally high failure rate that does not justify the immense effort and money spent on holding such exams (about 13 million Qatari riyals or about 3.5 million US dollars).

The study pointed out that the main causes underlying this high failure rate can be attributed to low performance of teachers; lack of continuous evaluation; difference in pupils age range within the upper two grades of the primary stage; weakness of the syllabuses; and the absence of parallel education to absorb unsuccessful pupils.

Preparatory Stage

This is the intermediate stage between the primary and the secondary stages and extends over three years for ages 12-15. It primarily serves to extend the primary stage objectives.

The number of students in the preparatory government schools according to 1985-86 statistics is a little over 12,000 students, of whom 63 percent are Qataris; the rest are made up of different Arab and non-Arab nationalities with Palestinians and Jordanians making up 17 percent of the total number of pupils. Girls make up 49 percent of the number of all students.

The 1985-86 official statistics point to a high rate of failure among boys in this stage which is a lot higher than the rate of failure among girls. Thus, from 6,276 students who took the exam, 1,324 students, or 21 percent of all students, fail to pass the exam. This rate drops to about 9 percent in the case of girls. These failures are regarded by many to be just a waste of effort and money and need urgent remedial policy.

At the end of the school year, an exam is held for each grade, and there is a second session exam to give those who failed a second try. The general preparatory exam which used to be held at the end of the stage was abolished in 1987. A quick glance at the results of 1984-85 preparatory stage exams shows that the rate of success in both the first and second sessions among Qatari students has been decreasing systematically in the three grades. This phenomenon is manifested in both boys and girls schools and extends to the general preparatory school certificate exam, which is seen by educators to be an extension of the same phenomenon and ought to be thoroughly investigated and remedied.

Secondary Stage

The secondary stage lasts three years and caters for students of the age group 15-18 years. It is of two kinds: academic and technical.

In the academic secondary stage, study in the first year is general, at the end of which students are divided into two specialized sections: scientific and literary. Students have the option to choose one. The principal objective of this stage is to prepare the student to resume his tertiary education in one of the various specialized fields it may offer. The number of students in this stage was estimated at 7,500 students in 1985-86, of which 61 percent were Qatari students. Palestinian and Jordanian students represent over 22 percent of the total number of students in this stage. The number of girls is about 57 percent or more than half the entire school population of this stage. This peculiar phenomenon has its explanation in that this is the only kind of education which girls can take and that this high rate represents the number of all girls doing secondary education, in contrast to boys who have other kinds of secondary education they can undertake. In fact if we add the number of boys in religious and technical education to the number of students in the academic secondary education the above 57 percent would drop to about 48 percent which is its normal average as in the other stages.

Exams are held at the end of the year for each grade, and there is also a second session exam for those who fail the first. The secondary school certificate exam is held at the end of the stage.

It is noticed that in the secondary stage, as is the case in the preparatory stage, there is a high rate of failure among boys of about 18 percent, but this rate is reduced in the case of girls to about 7 percent which implies that the standard of achievement of girls is higher than the standard of boys in this stage which qualifies them to enrol in higher education. In actual fact there is a common complaint about the low achievement of boys in this stage which has prompted the University of Qatar to offer courses below university standards to reinforce students who have been accepted to pursue tertiary education. It is indeed a peculiar situation for a university to take upon itself the task of correcting the shortcomings of the secondary school. There is a tendency toward reviewing the organization of this stage, in the light of the experiences of other sister Arab States in the comprehensive and credit hour system, with a view to application of these improvements in Qatar.

In fact Qatar needs to reorganize its entire educational system to eradicate existing dualism between religious and public education for unifying the basic structure of the different kinds of secondary education in one comprehensive school system.

The technical secondary stage consists of two streams: commercial and industrial. Commercial secondary education is given in the Commercial Secondary School, and lasts three years after the preparatory stage. It is the only school of this type in Qatar and has about 100 students, all of whom are boys. Industrial secondary education is given in the Industrial Secondary Boys School and lasts three years of study. The school has a population of less than 200 students. Until 1975 the period of study in that school was six years after the primary stage, but in an attempt to raise the cultural standard of its pupils, admission rules were modified, restricting acceptance to the preparatory school leavers.

It is noticed from an analysis of the exam results of both the commercial and the industrial secondary schools for the year 1985-86 that the number of successful students was as low as 25 percent of the total number of the commercial school students, and 29 percent of the industrial school students who did the exams, which points to a substantial loss in effort, money, and time in these two types of schools. Technical education in Qatar is shunned by Qatari youth and those who decide to take it come mainly from culturally and materially deprived social classes. In an attempt to encourage Qatari students to enroll in technical schools, the educational authorities offer a variety of rewards and other privileges in the form of monthly grants, higher grade positions after graduation, and better opportunities to join tertiary education. But all these solutions are like soothing tablets that relieve the symptoms but do not cure the disease. The real solution lies in the reconstruction of the basic system of secondary education as a whole, with all its different specialized branches and kinds, in one unified school as done by some other Arab and Gulf States.

There are numerous national and private schools at nursery, kindergarten, primary, and secondary levels. Some of them are operated by national or cooperative societies while the others belong to the Qatari General Petroleum Company or certain individuals. There are also foreign schools that are supervised by their national embassies. All these schools are bound by the regulations and conditions laid by the Ministry of Education and Instruction which has a special section that assumes all supervision of national education in conformity with the National Educational Law of 1967 which permits national Arab agencies to establish primary and preparatory schools only. Foreign schools are permitted to have all the three stages of primary, preparatory, and secondary education.

The ministry provides free books and some furniture to the national private schools and exempt them from the payment of any dues on electricity consumption. School fees are fixed by a ministerial order which also determines the minimum salary range of teachers.

Teaching Staff

The State of Qatar has always relied on expatriate teachers from different Arab countries. There has been no system for teacher preparation in Qatar until 1962-63, when just one teachers' institute at secondary level was established. The preparation of women teachers was not introduced until five years later with the establishment in 1967-68 of a second teachers institute for the preparation of women teachers.

The two institutions were under the supervision of the Ministry of Education. These two institutes were, however, liquidated following the establishment in 1973 of the Faculty of Education at Qatar University and the creation of a special program for the preparation of primary school teachers. In fact, in recent years, the educational policy in Qatar has been orientated toward raising the scientific and professional standard of teachers' preparation through the unification of all patterns of teacher preparation within the framework of the university. In fact Qatar is regarded as one of the first pioneers among Arab Gulf States with regard to the preparation of primary stage teachers within the framework of the university.

The Faculty of Education qualifies students to teach in primary as well as preparatory and secondary schools.

The number of teachers working in all three stages of public primary, preparatory, and secondary education is a little over 4,000 of whom 2,400 or 60 percent are females according to 1986-86 official statistics. This means that more than half the teachers in Qatar are women. This is due in the first place to the large numbers of university female graduates who find their best job opportunity in teaching, on one hand, and the disinclination of male Qatari youth to enter the teaching profession, on the other. This explains the presence of the high number of female teachers. In fact the number of male Qatari teachers as a whole is insignificant. Thus we find that in the secondary stage, there are only seventy-five Qatari teachers, eleven in the preparatory stage and sixty-four in the primary stage, which is clear evidence of the negative attitude of Qatari men to make a career in the teaching profession, even if they are graduates of the faculties of education.

The 1986-87 official statistical data point out that a high rate of all teachers in all stages of public education are professionally unqualified and that their rate increases as we move up the education ladder. Thus we find that in the primary stage 37 percent of teachers are professionally unqualified and that higher education graduates represent only 21 percent. Similarly, in the preparatory stage we find that approximately 32 percent of teachers are professionally unqualified and that their rate in the secondary stage is as high as 50 percent, which means that half the teachers in the secondary stage are not qualified to teach. This situation points out to the existence of a serious gap in the professional standards of teachers. It should be noticed that there is actually a rehabilitation program for such teachers which the Faculty of Education at Qatar University readily offers. There are also the in-service programs which the educational authorities make available to them.

Since the beginning of education in Qatar, the training of working teachers was the responsibility of technical inspectors. Each technical inspectorate had the task of organizing training programs for teachers under its jurisdiction. But with the increase in the numbers of teachers and the content of the training programs, the Ministry of Education and Instruction decided upon the establishment of a special training section in 1976-77. This section undertook the organization of long and short term rehabilitation and renewal programs.

HIGHER EDUCATION

Institutions

A brief description of the development of the University of Qatar would help one to understand higher education in Qatar. This is simply because the university is the only institution for higher learning at the tertiary level. Historically, tertiary education started in 1973, with the establishment of two faculties of education; one for males, the other for females. The university was inaugurated in June 1977 by proclamation of a state law. It stipulates that the University of Qatar is a public academic and cultural institution with an independent structure and budget, and that the university would be concerned with all aspects of learning and scientific research, with the preparation of specialized manpower, and the preservation, and nurture of Islamic and Qatari cultural heritage.

Despite the relatively short history of the university, it has gained wide recognition at the regional and international level. It enjoys membership of the Association of Arab Universities and the International Association of Universities.

There are certain principles underlying university education in Qatar, which may be summarized as follows: University education should aim at the preservation and development of Arab and Islamic culture, preparation of highly qualified manpower, the advancement of knowledge,and the development of the community in general; University education is provided free and no tuition fees are charged; Separation of male and female students should be ensured in every aspect of university activities; Academic freedom at the university is guaranteed within the Arab and Islamic traditions; Arabic should be the medium of instruction when and where possible; Guaranteed employment of Qataris after graduation is ensured; and As a state university, it is financed by the government from public funds, within the general budget of the state.

Since its establishment (first as the College of Education in 1973), the University of Qatar has grown in size and structure. At present, it consists of six faculties and four research centers. The university faculties are organized on lines similar to those common in faculty organizations in many universities of today. Each faculty is subdivided into departments. The four faculties are education (nine departments); humanities and social sciences (seven departments); science (seven departments); Islamic studies (four departments); engineering (four departments); and administration and economics (four departments).

Each faculty is headed by a dean, who is elected by the faculty council from among the faculty professors. His formal appointment for a four-year term of office is by Emiri Decree, on the recommendation of the university council. The dean is an ex-officio member of the university council and also presides over his faculty council, which consists of all heads of the faculty departments as well as some other staff members.

The research centers of the university consist of the Educational Research Center, Scientific and Applied Research Center, Research Center for Humanities and Documentation, and Research Center for Sirat (biography of Prophet Mohamed) and Summat (saying and deeds of prophet Mohamed). In addition, the university has an oceanographic research vessel.

Each research center is headed by a director, who is appointed for a period of four years by an Emiri Decree, on the recommendation of the university council. All directors of the four research centers, like deans of the faculties, are ex-officio members of the university council. Each research center has a governing board, headed by the president of the University. The board is composed of members from the university, representing their respective disciplines, and outside members, representing interested and concerned bodies.

The Emir, who is the ruler of the state, is the supreme head of the university. At the top of the administrative echelon of the university is the president, who is appointed by an Emiri Decree.

The university council constitutes the final link in the chain of the decision making process and is the highest governing body of all academic, administrative, and financial matters relating to the university. In general, decisions taken by the council are final. Only in policy matters of high significance, are the council decisions subject to the approval of the highest authority, the Emir.

The main functions of the university council are to formulate, supervise, and direct the general policy of the university. In addition to the assistant president, vice-president, and secretary-general, the university council consists in general of the deans of the faculties and directors of the various research centers, as members from the university. There are also members from outside the university, who represent interested and concerned bodies.

The board of the university was formed in 1977. As suggested by the name, it is a consultative body with the responsibility to review, evaluate, organize, and assign priorities, in regard to the objectives and present policies for the development of the university. It also recommends policies for the further development of the university and gives advice on the quality of education, in order to meet internationally recognized standards.

This board, which has the president of the university as its chairman, consists of members, who represent higher learning institutes in developed countries such as U.K., U.S.A., and France, in addition to members representing Arab universities.

The Higher Council of Education, which was formed in 1974 as a bridge between the university and the Ministry of Education, is presided over by the minister of education. It includes the president of the university, university professors, and other members from the Ministry of Education. Its main function is to coordinate educational matters, which are of interest to both the university and the Ministry of Education.

Programs and Degrees

The requirement for admission to degree programs at the university is a minimum of twelve years of primary and secondary education. A precondition is the Certificate of General Secondary Education (GCE). (The last two years of secondary education are divided into two sections: the literary section and the scientific section. Both prepare students to receive the GCE). However, while the certificate awarded to those in the scientific section is accepted for admission into all the faculties, that received by the students in the literary section is accepted only for admission into the literary faculties, i.e. education, humanities, and Islamic studies. This is generally the case in universities of the Arab world.

Programs and courses offered by the university are varied and diversified in order to meet different needs and requirements. The major full-time university program, in which most students are enrolled, prepares them to specialize in one of the fields of specialization previously mentioned. As the university programs are organized on the basis of the credit hour system, a total ranging from 138 credit hours to 162 credit hours is required in order to graduate. Students who successfully complete this program are granted the degree of B.Sc. or B.A. in their field of specialization.

The other programs are regulated on a part-time basis and are offered by the Faculty of Education exclusively. One specially tailored program is offered to primary school teachers employed by the Ministry of Education, in order to help them pursue their studies for the B.Sc. or B.A. degree. The requirements for graduation are similar to those for the major program mentioned earlier.

Another program is offered to post primary (i.e. preparatory and secondary) school teachers employed by the Ministry of Education, to qualify them as teachers. A qualified teacher in the Arab educational system, as in many other systems of the world, would mean one who is professionally prepared as a teacher in a special educational institute. Hence, those teachers with B.Sc. or B.A. degrees only and no teacher's education are not considered qualified teachers. Of course, the reason for employing unqualified teachers are obvious and most common in many school systems of today. This part-time education program for teachers calls for 36 credit hours in order to graduate. Students who successfully complete the course are granted the General Diploma in Education, which is similar to the Post Graduate Certificate of Education (PGCE) in U.K.

The third part-time course, which is also offered by the Faculty of Education prepares students for higher studies in education. Twenty-two credit hours are required to graduate. Students who successfully complete the course are awarded the Special Diploma in Education. This Diploma, which is similar to the Academic Diploma in Education in the U.K., is a partial fulfillment for further studies in education, such as M.A. or Ph.D., which are not yet available in the University of Qatar.

Plans are already under way to start courses for the master's and Ph.D. degrees in the near future.

The academic year is divided into two semesters, namely, fall and spring. Each semester extends over a period of sixteen weeks. Some summer courses are provided in different areas of specialization.

The academic achievement of students can, on the whole, be matched with recognized standards of university education in the world in general, and in the Arab world, in particular. this is partly evident from the fact that many graduates are presently studying successfully for their master's and Ph.D. degrees in the U.S.A., U.K., and Arab countries. It is noteworthy that recent research has shown the academic achievement of female students at Qatar University, to be higher than that of their male counterparts. This is partly due to the fact that many of the best male students who have completed their secondary education, have the opportunity to study abroad in their fields of specialization which are not yet available in the University of Qatar. Such a chance for girls, especially at the undergraduate level, is very remote. Recent research has shown also that the levels of academic achievement of both males and females are on the decline from one year to another. It is hoped that this alarming situation is likely to change with the new policy of admission which requires higher standards of achievement.

The total number of students has risen considerably from about 328 in 1973 to about 5,281 in 1988. Approximately two thirds of the university students are female and 66 percent of the students are nationals. Majority of the students (47 percent) were enrolled in education courses. Humanities had 9 percent, Islamic studies 8 percent, and sciences 6 percent.

The government awards scholarships to foreign students to pursue their studies at the university. In addition to airfares, these scholarships cover board and lodging and text books.

The number of students who have graduated from the university has increased from 117 (thirty-eight male and seventy-nine female) in the year 1977 to 889 in 1988, of which 30 percent were non-Qatari students. Females constituted 36 percent of the graduating students in 1988.

National graduates are employed mostly by the government. Selecting those with the "right academic qualifications for the right job" is not the case in the Arab States of the Gulf Region. With the high demand for highly educated nationals to be assigned to key and important jobs in administration and the various positions in the government, almost any graduate, regardless of his field of specialization, can be easily employed. Statistical data on manpower show that the vast majority of nationals occupy administrative and non-technical jobs.

In fact, the country depends heavily on expatriates to fill those posts involving highly professional and semi-skilled jobs. Though the university has faculties of science and engineering, the disinclination on the part of the national students to join these two faculties means that this situation is not likely to change in the near future.

Teaching Staff

The total number of teaching staff at the university has also risen from about thirty-two in 1973 to 290 in 1988. The student-teacher ratio has also increased considerably from 10:1 in 1973 to 18:1 in 1988. Most of the staff are expatriates or non-nationals from various Arab universities, employed on secondment or contract basis. At the moment, only thirty-seven Qataris are staff members, i.e. 13 percent of the total number of the teaching staff.

The university also depends on visiting professors from different universities, who are invited to teach for short periods, usually two months. It may be argued that this kind of arrangement may account for a degree of staff instability. However, the number of permanent staff members is increasing steadily. This does not mean that the problem will soon be solved or even eased. With most, if not all nationals, who get their Ph.D. degrees and join the university staff, assigned to high administrative jobs, this situation is unlikely to change for some years to come.

All staff members are Ph.D. holders. Many of them have obtained their degrees from universities in advanced countries like the U.S.A., U.K., France, and Germany and are qualified to international standards.

One way Qatar is building up the national teaching staff is by appointing only Qataris as graduate assistants. After spending a year at the university, they are usually sent to study abroad for their master's and Ph.D. degrees. In 1988, there were 116 graduate assistants, of whom sixty-nine or 60 percent were female. Of the graduate assistants studying abroad in 1988, 57 percent were in Egypt, 23 percent were in U.S.A., and 18 percent were in the United Kingdom.

ISSUES AND TRENDS

The educational system of Qater is undergoing significant changes especially on the levels of secondary and tertiary education. The introduction of the two-semester school year system to replace the old system of secondary education is already underway. The feminization of the staff of primary schools, now on a limited scale, is likely to continue for good reasons: the influx of university women graduates on one hand and the disinclination of men graduates to work as teachers on the other.

New additional burdens on the educational system include the accomodation of the children of thousands of Kuwaiti families who fled Kuwait after the Iraqi invasion.

Reminiscent of the diehard old practices is the duality between the system of general education on one hand the the two seperate systems of religious and technical education on the other. The low standard of education, the exceptionally high cost per pupil, and the acute shortage of Qatari male teachers are major persistent problems for years to come. Also in-service education programs for teachers and other professional personnel of the Ministry of Education seem to be inefficient and need more attention and careful considerations. The improvement of the content and methods of these programs is of paramount importance. This has been suggested by evidence from recent Ph.D. research supervised by the author of this paper on the evaluation of in-service training programs and suggested reforms.

There is a general dissatisfaction with the standard of secondary school graduates who are admitted to the university. Measures taken by the university in the past years to improve the academic standard of the fresh students proved unsuccessful. In recent attempts, the university authority decided to raise the standard of admission beginning from the year 1990-91. Yet the problem is likely to continue because the roots of the problem are deeply entrenched in the system of public education. In fact, research evidence suggest that the standard of the university students has been deteriorating continuously from one year to another. There is a strong tendency, at the policy level, to have university education geared to the development of the Qatari society. There is also a growing tendency to give university education an orientation towards technological education and a technological college has already started this year (1990-91). Though it is too early to give an ecaluative account, past experience in technical secondary education and science university education cast doubt on its future success.

BIBLIOGRAPHY

Arab Education Bureau of the Gulf States. *Education Statistics in the Gulf Arab States for the School Year 1985-1986.*

History of Education in the East and West. Cairo: Alam Al Kuttob, 1986.

Islamic Education: Its Origin and Evolution in the Arab Countries. Cairo: Alam Al Kuttob, 1983.

Ministry of Education, State of Qatar: *Annual Reports on Education* 1980-1990 (in Arabic).

Morsi, Mohamed Monir. *Contemporary Higher Education: Its Orientation Issues.* Doha, Qatar: Dar Al Thakafa, 1987.

Morsi, Mohamed Monir. *Education in the Arab Gulf States.* Doha, Qatar: University of Qatar, 1990

Public Education in the Arab Countries. Cairo: Alam Al Kuttob, 1986.

Sadeq, Hissa. "A Study on the Evaluation of In-service Training Programs in the Qatari Ministry of Education and Suggested Reforms." Ph.D thesis in Arabic, the Faculty of Education, Ain Shams University, Cairo, 1990.

University of Qatar, Educational Research Center. "Research Papers on Public and University Education 1980-1990" (in Arabic).

SENEGAL

by
Abdou Sylla
Assistant Professor, Fundamental Institute of Black Africa
University of Cheikh Anta Diop, Senegal

BACKGROUND

At the time of its independence from France in 1960, Senegal inherited an educational system which the French initiated in the beginning of the nineteenth century. This "modern" system operated side by side with the traditional education of the country and the Islamic system of Koranic schools. Influenced by the active role of Arab intellectuals and cultural associations (e.g. Federation of Islamic Associations of Senegal) and often funded by Arab countries, the Islamic system also developed a vast network of education institutions around the country, infact posing a significant competition to the "modern" system. In the traditional system of education, children received instruction from their parents and families in the village. This mode of education is still continuing, but today it has taken an informal character. Senegal, thus, has three parallel systems of education but what is described here is the "modern" system as it provides education to majority of the children; it is better organized; and it is funded and managed by the government.

The first school under the "modern" type of education was founded in Senegal in 1816 at Saint-Louis by a French missionary, Jean Dard. Public education, at first, was initiated by the Church in France, through its missionaries. Later on the French government played an active role and by 1860 the French colonial government had established ten schools in major population centers. By 1960, the total number of schools had increased to 636, with 389 of them in rural areas. Majority of the increase took place after 1957, when the country was beginning to enjoy a greater degree of economy, on the eve of independence in 1960. The development of a school system in Senegal during the colonial period was taking place at a very slow pace, primarily because the colonial masters did only what was necessary to achieve the objective of providing limited training as necessary to continue their rule.

The education, given in French, was aimed at getting people to relegate their indigenous culture, to embrace a new culture, and to convince the young Senegalese of their shortcomings; the inferiority of being black, the "barbaric" acts of their ancestors, the "tyranny" of their chiefs (and of course the benefits of being a colony); all of which were being used as a rationale for colonial occupation. As a result, many of the countries in West Africa, at the time of their independence, did not have a cadre of trained nationals for the task of governing. It was only towards 1950 that the French government established any form of higher education in Senegal.

The colonial system of education continued without any significant changes even during the first ten years of independence with heavy influence by and dependence on the French educational system. Then, initiated by student movements of 1968-69, major reforms took place with the promulgation of Education Law 71-036 of June 1971 that has now become the basis of the present day education in Senegal. The reforms aimed at developing the cultural and technical level of the masses, abolishing inequalities created by historical events in the country, promoting contributions of African culture to world civilizations, and producing a younger generation needed for economic development of the country.

In the reformed educational system, the government (the Ministry of National Education) recruits, trains, assigns, pays, and manages all staff engaged in national education. In the actual administration, the country is divided into thirty departments in ten regions. The academic year as well as vacations and holidays are set by the government, each year. But alongside public schools, a system of private schools also exist. Private schools follow the same guidelines as public schools (as defined by the Ministry of National Education) and the government grants subsidies. Since 1983, the government has declared a policy of free supplies for all Senegalese students at elementary, middle, and secondary level. In Senegal, education at all levels (primary, secondary, and university) is free.

ELEMENTARY, MIDDLE, AND SECONDARY EDUCATION

Elementary education in Senegal begins after three years of nursery education (entry age to nursery is about three years). It is the most developed and widely available form of schooling in Senegal. The objectives of elementary education, as defined by law, includes unfolding of children's spirit and mind to permit evolution of their aptitudes; ensuring physical, intellectual, and moral development of children, and cultivating initiative and a critical mind; providing a foundation of knowledge that will form the basis for future education; and reinstating manual work as a factor in the development of intelligence and future participation in the economic life of the country through close liaison between school and life. Elementary education lasts six years and leads to the *certificat d'études primaires élémentaires* and an entrance examination for admission to middle school. Over the years, only about 17-20 percent of elementary students have succeeded in getting admission to middle school, to the limited number of places available every year (as determined by the government). In 1988-89, about 16,000 out of 115,000 elementary students got admitted to middle school. About 25 percent of the students entering middle school go to private schools where parents bear the tuition and other costs. Education in government schools is free. Of the 98,000 students who do not enter middle school, 35 percent repeat the exams, 10 percent enter private work, and the other 55 percent may not receive any further schooling.

The middle school receives children aged 12-13 years and provides a four-year curriculum leading to the *brevet de fin d'études moyennes*. The middle school is essentially a preparation for secondary education and includes a technical and a general stream. In 1986-87 there were 231 middle schools (of which 108 were private) with an enrollment of 107,024 students, an increase of nearly 70 percent from 1977-78. This increase has put considerable pressure on the schools (affecting the quality of education and extending the school day), as the facilities have not kept pace with the growth in enrollment.

The secondary school caters for children who complete the middle school and succeed in the *brevet de fin d'etudes moyennes*. Children enter secondary school *(lycée)* at the age of sixteen years and continues for three years. The objectives of secondary education, as outlined in the law (1971) is: "On the one hand to train middle level staff for both the public and private sectors of the economy and on the other hand to prepare the pupils for higher education".

Secondary education consists of three streams: general, technical, and professional. General secondary education is the most developed and students may select one of the several streams: letters and humanities, social science and economics, sciences, medicine and pharmacy, technical and commercial, etc. On successful completion of secondary education, students receive the *baccalauréat* diploma which provides access to university education. The *baccalauréat* exam is conducted by the University of Dakar. In 1986-87 there were forty-six *lycées* offering general secondary education, with an enrollment of 30,005 students; twelve technical secondary schools with an enrollment of 4,093; and sixteen professional secondary schools with 1,403 students. The country has seen a sevenfold increase in secondary school enrollment, during the period 1978-88.

HIGHER EDUCATION

The history of higher education in Senegal dates back to 1918 when France established a school of medicine in Dakar to train students from its colonies in West Africa to become "African doctors". Then in 1938, the *Institut Français d'Afrique Noire* as well as an Institute of Advance Studies came into existence. Later, in February 1957, France established the University of Dakar, and played a dominant role in the functioning of this university for over a decade after independence.

In 1971, the Senegalese government promulgated the Law 71-036, which is now the basis of higher education in the country. The law stipulates: "The mission of higher education is the transmission of knowledge at an advance level as well as development of research, with the objective of producing men and women qualified at medium and higher levels and adapted to the African context, conscious of their responsibility towards their fellow citizens and serving them with devotion. Parallely with this mission, the higher education institutions, like other forms of schooling, must participate in the task of continuing education....They must engage themselves in the global strategy of development and work towards achieving national and regional objectives". All aspects of higher education in Senegal including funding, administration, and control come under the responsibility of the government. Higher education is free as mentioned earlier and there are no private institutions.

Higher education system in Senegal consists of the University of Dakar (which, in 1987, became the University Cheikh Anta Diop of Dakar) and of several other higher education schools coming under the Ministry of Higher Education and other ministries. The rector of the university who heads the university assembly is also the director of higher education with the responsibility for coordination of higher education at the national level.

The University Cheikh Anta Diop of Dakar consists of autonomous faculties of juridical and economic sciences, medicine and pharmacy, science, and letters and humanities. ; a research institute *(Institut Fondamental d'Afrique Noire Cheikh Anta Diop); a* school of engineering; and two teacher training schools. In addition, there are a number of institutes attached to the university or to the faculties. The institutes attached to the university (university institutes) have a great degree of autonomy (financial, administrative, and organizational) compared to the faculties, but at the same time they work in close collaboration with the faculties. These include institutes of applied tropical medicine; social pediatrics, psychological, and social studies; and research on the teaching of mathematics, physics, and technology. Institutes attached to the faculties are dependent on the faculties and are administered by them. These include institutes of meteorological physics, odontology and stomatology, environmental sciences, and earth sciences, as well as centers of applied economic research, biological research (leprosy), and Afro-Ibero-American studies.

Institutions coming under the Ministry of Higher Education but not attached to the university are autonomous bodies and include schools of applied economics, schools of social workers, centers for administrative training, centers for English language, and the National Institute of Rural Development. Higher education establishments under various other ministries include national schools *(écoles nationales)* of administration, customs, military health, military training, architecture, artistic education, hotel management, maritime training, post and telecommunications, and physical education.

Admission to university (undergraduate) studies require the *baccalauréat* diploma or equivalent. Placement in different faculties and institutes associated with the University of Dakar is centrally coordinated by the *Commission Nationale d'Orientation.* Adult candidates and others who have not attended secondary school and do not possess the *baccalauréat* or equivalent qualification may seek admission through an entrance examination. Foreign qualifications are considered for admission after equivalence is established by the university. While admission to traditional studies, as offered in the faculties require only the *baccalauréat,* the admission to professional type schools *(écoles nationales* and *écoles normales)* have the added requirement of a competitive exam due to heavy demand for a limited number of places.

The faculties offer traditional type of university education, at three levels. In the first cycle, students receive the *licence* after three years of studies. In the second cycle, they may study for two more years towards a *maîtrise.* The third cycle, which generally take three more years, lead to the *doctorat de troisième cycle.*

The highest qualifications in higher education is the *doctorat d'état* (state doctorate) in the case of humanities and sciences and *agrégation* in the case of law, economics, medicine, and pharmacy. The preparation for these latter degrees has no specific time periods. The *écoles nationales* and *écoles normales* offer programs of two, three, or four years that prepares students for professional careers.

Initiation to research, in the Senegalese system of education takes places in the second cycle of university studies, in the form of a research memoire for the *maîtrise* degree. Students continue this research work in the third cycle. Research and teaching are dialectically linked with the teaching staff actively engaged in research, often in preparation for a higher degree *(doctorat d'état* or *agrégation)*. Both fundamental and applied research are conducted at the university.

University education in Senegal is entirely funded and managed by the government, which exercises its authority through the Ministry of Education and the rector of the University of Dakar who is the director of higher education. The rector is appointed by the president of the republic for a period of three years, renewable twice. The hierarchy consist of deans of faculties, faculty assemblies, heads of departments (within faculties) and department assemblies. Faculty assemblies consist of elected representatives from teachers, students, and other staff. Dean is elected by the faculty assembly. University assembly is made up of elected representatives from faculty assemblies.

The institutes, centers, and schools are managed by directors, assemblies or councils of the establishment, and heads of departments. Projects, programs of studies and research, curriculum exams, budgets, regulations, etc. are conceived and developed at the very basic level of the hierarchy and after review at various higher levels (assemblies, deans, etc.) are submitted to the government for approval and promulgation by decree.

Teaching staff at the university consists of many nationalities, as the university has always had a regional character. Essentially, there are three categories: Senegalese, who now form the majority, other African nationals (Mali, Guinea, Togo, Benin etc.); and French nationals. Along with gradual Senegalization of higher education and the increased number of Senegalese students, the proportion of Senagalese staff has been growing. Proportion of African staff as a whole increased from 51.8 percent in 1979 to 86.4 percent in 1989 in the faculties and from 33.4 percent in 1979 to 73.5 percent in 1989 in the institutes.

There are several categories of staff: professors, *maître de conférence* (associate professors) and *chargés d'enseignement,* all of whom are required to have the *doctorat d'état* (state doctorate); *maître-assistants* (assistant professors) and *assistants* who are required to have the *doctorat de troisième cycle;* and *attachés* who are holders of the *diplôme d'études approfondies* (advanced studies diploma). Academic qualification requirements may also be met by acquiring the *agrégation* qualification at the appropriate level, where relevant (e.g. *agrégation* in medicine and pharmacy at *doctorat d'état* level and *agrégation* in secondary education at the *doctorat de troisième cycle* level). After two years of experience, teachers may receive tenure in their grades and in the following year, they are considered for promotion to the next higher grade.

Thus an *assistant* recruited with the *doctorat de troisième cycle* may receive tenure as an *assistant* in two years and in the following year he can present himself to be considered for promotion to *maître assistant,* at which grade he could continue his research work leading to the *doctorat d'état,* the qualification necessary for the next higher position *maître de conférence.* Promotion to the professor grade is based on scientific work and publications. Promotion is determined by the African and Malagache Council for Higher Education, a regional body, which has the responsibility for examining credentials and determining promotions. All teachers are government appointees, selected on the basis of recommendations of various units in the university.

At the inception of the university (1960), only about 33 percent or 1,000 students were Senegalese, with the rest being French and African. The composition of the student body changed significantly over the years and by 1976, 71 percent of the students were Senegalese, 22 percent came from African countries, 4 percent were French, and 3 percent came from other countries. Today, the university has an enrollment of 15,000-20,000 students, of whom about 87 percent are Senegalese. Majority of the students (90 percent) were enrolled in the faculties: 29 percent in juridical sciences and economics; 24 percent in letters and humanities; 20 percent in sciences; and 17 percent in medicine and pharmacy.

Students take an active part in extra curricular activities at the university. Many cultural, educational, religious, and sportive associations are run by students. Popular sports include judo, karate, football, handball, basketball, and athletics. Condition of student life at the university is largely dependent upon the means made available to it by the government including funding of university operations and scholarships to students. Shortage of funds and facilities coupled with the growing student population has resulted in student agitation and strikes that have often paralysed the university during the last ten years or so.

ISSUES AND TRENDS

In its study of educational systems in sub-Saharan African countries, the World Bank (1988) made a rigorous analysis and came to certain conclusions. These findings, we believe, are very pertinent to the Senegalese situation and are worth mentioning.

The Bank determined that during the colonial period, access to education was very limited (in 1960, only 36 percent of the children had access to primary education). From a quantitative point of view, achievement in education since independence is spectacular (between 1960 and 1983, the number of students increased fivefold). But, education in sub-Saharan African countries has now reached a crisis situation as a result of demographic explosion in the number of school age children while the schooling facilities remained very limited; superfluity in classes; and a severe shortage of teaching material. This crisis has resulted in a decline of the growth of student enrollment in the recent years (growth between 1980-83 was only 4.2 percent per year compared to 8.9 percent per year between 1970-80) and a deterioration of the quality of education.

With regard to higher education in Africa, the Bank outlines that the institutions offer too many degrees whose usefulness is doubtful. The quality of students has deteriorated, the cost is very high, and the manner how education is financed is socially inequitable and economically inefficient.

In Senegal, the crisis in education reached its peak in 1979-80 and coincided with the political changes in the country when President Leopold Sedar Senghor was replaced by his prime minister, Abdou Diouf, who initiated in 1981, a reform of the educational system. This global reform directed by the *Commission Nationale de Réforme de l'Education* is being implemented since 1985. The reform is not simply a plan developed by a few experts or technocrats in the secrecy of their offices. It is a program having the benefit of being conceived and developed over a period of four years (1981-84) by a broad spectrum of Senegalese (teachers, researchers, representatives of political, and social groupings etc.) for Senegal with the purpose of creating a system of education that is national, democratic, and popular.

BIBLIOGRAPHY

Commission Nationale de la Réforme de l'Education et de la Formation (CNREF). *Rapport Général et Annexes (Tomes 1 a 6).*

Ministère de l'Education Nationale, Direction des Etudes, des Ressources Humaines et de la Planification (MEN/DERP). *Demande et Offre d'Education Dans d'Enseignement Elémentairs en Zone Rurale.* Dakar, 1989.

Ministère de l'Education Nationale, Direction des Etudes, des Ressources Humaines et de la Planification (MEN/DERP). *Tableau de Bord, Annee Scolaire et Universitaire 1986-1987.* Dakar, 1989.

Sylla, Abdou. *L'Ecole Future, Pour Qui?* Dakar: ENDA, 1987.

Sylla, Abdou. *L'Ecole Sénégalaise en Gestation, De La Crise à La Réforme.* Dakar: NEA, 1990.

SIERRA LEONE

by
Chris J. Renner
Planning Officer, Planning Unit
University of Sierra Leone, Sierra Leone

BACKGROUND

Sierra Leone was settled by freed slaves in 1787. The freed slaves were to be compensated with the introduction of Western civilization. Sierra Leone was thus fortunate to become the experiment in the application of "European enlightenment" in anglophone West Africa. Thus, formal education started in Sierra Leone in 1787 by the first settlers who opened schools to teach their children and the children of their illiterate brothers.

By 1793 some 300 children were registered in schools. The early schools endeavored to educate persons who could fill white-collar jobs as clerks, civil servants, clergymen, teachers, lawyers, and physicians. The goals were so well achieved that Freeton, the capital city of Sierra Leone, became known as the "Athens" of West Africa.

PRIMARY AND SECONDARY EDUCATION

The present formal education based on the British system is comprised of six years of primary education starting at age six, and 5-7 years of secondary education followed by teacher training and/or university education. Primary education is the base of the educational system in Sierra Leone. The Sierra Leone government, through the Ministry of Education is in partnership with voluntary agencies, and Christian and Islamic missions for the maintenance of the system. In the matter of building new schools, the Ministry of Education provides 60 percent costs while the voluntary agency or mission provides the rest. Government meets the cost of all primary teachers' colleges and their instructional centers. Policy, planning, and administration of primary education rests with the Ministry of Education. Government meets the salary of all teachers in the system. At the end of primary education, there is a selective entrance examination for entry into secondary school. This examination consists of tests in English and mathematics, verbal aptitude, and quantitative aptitude. After the first five years of the secondary school cycle, students sit the West African Examination Council (WAEC) Ordinary Level ("O" level) examinations. Exit points are available at the end of the third and fourth years for entry into a three-year course in trade schools and a two-year certificate course in agriculture at Njala University College. A small number of successful students at the "O" level examinations may continue for another two years in the lower and upper sixth forms to prepare for the Advanced Level ("A" level) examinations in order to qualify for admission into the second year of a 4-6 year degree program in one of the constituent colleges of the University of Sierra Leone or for study overseas.

Four options are also available for other successful candidates at the "O" level examinations depending on their level and number of passes at these external examinations: entry into university for 4-6 year degree program or a three year higher technician's diploma; entry into one of the six teachers' colleges for either the teacher's certificate or higher teacher's certificate; entry into a technical Institute for a two year course leading to the ordinary technicians' diploma; and seeking employment in the public or private sector in competition with those who did not pass the examinations.

The Ministry of Education is charged with the responsibility of directing and coordinating all educational programs in the country.

HIGHER EDUCATION

Institutions

Higher education in Sierra Leone is synonymous with the University of Sierra Leone, the only university in the country, which at present consists of three constituent colleges: Fourah Bay College, College of Medicine and Allied Health Sciences in Freetown, and Njala University College at Njala. In addition to the three colleges, the university consists of three off-campus institutes: the Institute of Education, Institute of Library Studies, and Institute of Public Administration and Management. All three institutes are located in Freetown. Each university college is headed by a principal while the University of Sierra Leone has a vice-chancellor as its overall administrative and academic head.

Fourah Bay College, the oldest institution of higher learning in black Africa was founded by the Church Missionary Society (C.M.S.) in 1827 for the purpose of training Africans as school masters, catechists, and clergymen. In 1876, when its scope was enlarged to allow for the admission of other students, the college was affiliated to the University of Durham. The University of Durham was chosen because of its strong theological background. However, the college started providing a more liberal education as its curriculum was diversified to include Latin, Greek, Hebrew, Arabic, history, geography, comparative philosophy, some branches of natural science, French, and German. With the affiliation to Durham University, the college embarked upon a phase of gradual development. Degree courses were instituted in arts, economic studies, and science; and diploma courses in civil, electrical, and mechanical engineering.

The college gradually moved towards university college status. In January 1960, a royal charter constituting Fourah Bay College as the University College of Sierra Leone was granted. The affiliation with the University of Durham continued and degrees in arts, sciences, economic studies, and postgraduate diplomas in theology and education, were awarded by the university. Degree courses in civil, mechanical, and electrical engineering were started in 1965. In September 1968, the college became a constituent college of the University of Sierra Leone which itself was constituted under the University of Sierra Leone Act of 1967. The teaching departments in the Fourah Bay College are now grouped into five faculties: arts, economic and social studies, engineering, law, and pure and applied science. In addition, there are the institutes of adult education and extramural studies, African studies, and population studies located at the college but not under the umbrella of any faculty. The Institute of Marine Biology and Oceanography on the other hand is within the Faculty of Pure and Applied Science.

After the attainment of independence and Sierra Leone's eventual participation in the Addis Ababa Conference of African Ministers of Education in 1961, the government of Sierra Leone decided to improve agricultural and teacher education in the country. A survey team from the University of Illinois, under contract with the United States Agency for International Development (USAID), was invited by the government of Sierra Leone to assess the needs of the country in agriculture and education. Acting on recommendations of the survey team's report, the government decided to establishing a major collegiate institution at Njala some 125 miles from the capital city of Freetown.

In August, 1963, the University of Illinois entered into a contract with USAID, under the terms of which the university and USAID provided technical and other assistance for the development of Njala University College. The College was incorporated by an act passed in the Parliament of Sierra Leone in 1964 and it became a constituent college of the University of Sierra Leone. Njala University College has two faculties, agriculture and education, and offers courses at both degree and certificate levels in agriculture and education. The university senate has given approval for the establishment of a third faculty, Faculty of Environmental Sciences, which was established in October, 1990.

The third constituent college of the University, the College of Medicine and Allied Health Sciences, was established in 1987 and commenced teaching in October, 1988.

The new college has two faculties: Faculty of Basic Medical Sciences consisting of the Division of Science of Pathology and the Division of Human Biology and Behavior; and the Faculty of Clinical Sciences consisting of the Division of Community Health Care, Division of Dental Care, and the Division of Hospital Care. The two faculties cover the traditional fields of anatomy, physiology, biochemistry, pharmacology, histopathology, microbiology, parasitology, hematology, and chemical pathology. The college also teaches pharmacy, nursing, radiography, and medical laboratory technology.

The college offers six-year integrated degree programs. At the end of the first three years of their courses, students of medicine and dentistry receive the B.Sc. Health Science degree, after which they will pursue clinical programs for three years. Those opting for medicine will gain the MBBS and those for dentistry, the Bachelor of Dentistry degree at the end of their clinical years. The pharmacy and laboratory science courses will last for three years at the end of which students receive the B.Sc. health sciences (laboratory sciences) degree.

The Faculty of Clinical Sciences (at the moment) provides teaching at both graduate and undergraduate levels. It prepares students for the certificate in

The Faculty of Clinical Sciences (at the moment) provides teaching at both graduate and undergraduate levels. It prepares students for the certificate in community health (three months), diploma in community health (six months), and M.Sc. degree in community health (two years). The division also monitors preventive health programs and conducts as well as coordinates research in a number of areas relating to health problems in Sierra Leone.

The Institute of Education was set up by the court of the university in 1968. Government's sanction to the establishment of the institute was given in the 1970 White Paper on Education Policy. As an arm of the University of Sierra Leone, the functions assigned to the institute are as follows: the provision of in-service teacher training program, curriculum development, pre-service teacher education, and education research and evaluation.

Approval for the establishment of the Institute of Public Administration and Management as one of the arms of the University of Sierra Leone was given by the university court in 1980. The institute offers courses in professional accountancy (A.C.C.A. and A.A.T.), banking, public administration and general management, human resources management, and computer science. The institute concentrates on improving the quality of management of those already in employment. The bulk of the training consists of in-service and sandwich courses. The clientele catered for include senior and middle level government officials, comparable staff in the para-statal organizations, senior and middle level managers from commerce and industry and managers of various types of agricultural organizations.

Library education activities in the university started with Fourah Bay College Library's program for the training of para-professionals as a means of satisfying the needs for special conditions and regulations governing promotion of junior library staff. The provision for in-service training certificate courses for junior staff was therefore established in 1962, but abolished in 1968 when a decision was taken that junior members of the library staff should be encouraged to take the City and Guilds of London Institute Library Certificate Examination.

In recent years, the need for training at a higher level than the City and Guilds Certificate has been realized and in October 1986 the senate and court gave approval for the commencement of a two-year course for the Diploma in Library Studies of the University of Sierra Leone alongside the City and Guilds Certificate course.

As these courses continue to attract more students (locally and internationally) the need to train trainers at postgraduate level (master's degree in library studies) and for the university to take the lead in developing professional library study programs was apparent. In view of the above, the senate and the university court gave approval for the establishment of an Institute of Library Studies in the university.

Programs and Degrees

The degree programs offered by the university (through the constituent college) are primarily at the undergraduate level. Bachelor's degrees in arts, sciences, agriculture, home economics, and education generally take four years with the requirement of an additional year for the honors degrees. Engineering and medicine take five and six years respectively. Students who possess at least two Advanced Level passes (at the West African Council Examination) may take one year less for the first degree. Master's program is a 1-2 year full-time (or 2-3 years part-time) degree awarded by thesis or written examination or both. Doctorate takes three years of full-time work and requires a thesis and an oral examination. A number of diplomas and certificates are also awarded at undergraduate level, and the duration varies from about six months to three years.

Admission to degree courses in all the faculties is on a two-tier basis: preliminary and intermediate. Applicants with five "O" levels including English language at acceptable standards and other approved subjects are admitted into the preliminary (first) year. Applicants with five "O" levels and two "A" levels at acceptable standards in approved subjects are admitted into the intermediate (second) year. Preference is however given to applicants with the required "A" level qualifications.

Entry to the undergraduate diploma and licence courses is based on the possession of "O" level qualification, usually in four subjects. Entry to certificate courses available in the university is based on departmental arrangements.

Candidates who lack the stipulated entry qualifications may be allowed to matriculate provided they pass a special examination conducted by the university at various centers located in Sierra Leone. Admission to degree programs at the College of Medicine and Allied Health requires "A" level passes in specified science subjects along with five "O" level passes.

Local students pay an annual tuition fee of about Le600 (US$1 = Le50) for undergraduate programs, and Le1,000-1,500 for higher degree programs. Board and lodging cost is about Le8,400 per year. Students require an additional Le1,000-5,000 per year to cover registration, and other costs. Foreign students pay higher rates and in foreign currency.

ISSUES AND TRENDS

In the 1983-84 school year, the Sierra Leone government adopted major changes in the primary school system: a gradual increase in pupil/teacher ratio starting with 35:1 in 1983-84 school year and aiming at 45:1 by 1991-92; an increase in the school entry age from five to six years; and a reduction in the duration of primary school education from seven years to six years. The primary curriculum has also been transformed in a bid to make it meaningful and relevant to the needs, especially of rural communities.

The secondary education sector is currently being reviewed by a task force set up by the Ministry of Education. The final report of the task force awaits government's approval. However, an overview of the report indicates that positive suggestions and recommendations have been made to restructure secondary education and abolish the GCE "O" and "A" level examinations. The new structure recommend adoption of a 6-3-3-4 educational system (six-year primary education, three-year junior secondary school, three-year secondary school, and four-year at the tertiary level).

The adoption of a six-year secondary cycle (three-year junior secondary and three-year senior secondary school) instead of the current five-year cycle, and the inclusion of technical, commercial and other vocational courses in order to make junior and senior secondary school leavers immediately employable will have very serious implications for teacher preparation. A number of crucial factors in the training of teachers for secondary education would have to be given careful consideration by the tertiary sector. Issues that need to be addressed include the availability of the manpower resources both quantitatively and qualitatively to meet the new demands; and the availability of facilities in the institutions (that train teachers for the secondary level) to provide the type and quality of teachers required.

BIBLIOGRAPHY

A methodological synopsis of the role of village/community schools in the Development of Rural Areas in Sierra Leone. Ministry of Education, 1987.

Government of Sierra Leone. *White Paper on Educational Policy.* 1970.

Renner, Chris. "The Implication of New Developments in Secondary Education for Teacher Preparation in Sierra Leone." Position paper presented at the International Conference on Current Developments in Educational Policies and Systems in Anglophone West African Countries, Lagos, Nigeria.

SOUTH AFRICA

by
M. C. J. Mphahlele
Professor and Dean, Faculty of Education
University of the North, South Africa

BACKGROUND

The South African system of education is as complex and as unique as its history and politics. The first white (European) settlers arrived in the Cape in 1652 and ever since the country has been plagued and bedeviled by the so-called "race problem", alternatively "native question". This policy of separation, popularly and officially known as apartheid since 1948, has dominated all facets of life in South Africa. It has adversely affected education, religion, sports, and the socioeconomic life of all the inhabitants of this beautiful part of the world. The first school to be established in South Africa was, ironically, a "slave school", that is, a black school. This was in 1658. The first school for whites was opened in 1663.

From that time, 1663 to 1953, the state was never directly involved in black education. That became the responsibility of the missionaries. With the passing of the notorious Bantu Education Act in 1953, all black education became a direct state responsibility. The government of the day was suspicious of the goals and philosophy of missionary education and wanted to control it and thus be able to implement its policy of separate development.

White education has also an unfortunate history. It has been bedeviled by friction and rivalry between the Afrikaans (Dutch) and the English sections of the white population. This Boer-Briton friction has affected, among many other things, education and politics adversely. In the first place it caused the Great Trek of 1935-1936, which led to the establishment of the Boer Republics in the interior. Secondly, it led to the establishment of many private schools.

This separation of white schools along language or cultural lines, has persisted to today. From the preprimary school level up to the university, there are Afrikaans and English medium schools or institutions. If a child's home language is Afrikaans, for instance, he or she attends a Afrikaans medium school.

At the university level, the emphasis on language differences is less pronounced. Of the twenty odd universities in the country, including the so-called independent states, four are English (white), five are Afrikaans (white), seven are black, two are dual medium (Afrikaans and English), one is Indian and one is colored (brown or mulatto).

The differences between these universities are deeper than one can imagine, it is something more than language or cultural differences. The difference is more in philosophy, politics, and ethos. Among the Afrikaans universities, for instance, there is a difference, depending on whether a university is *verlig* (enlightened) or *verkramp* (conservative). Staff and students who apply to a known *verlig* university like Stellenbosch, are known or expected to be liberal and progressive in attitude.

On the whole, white universities and technikons get everything of the best in terms of resources, votes, donations, facilities, and manpower. This is understandable in a country in which the white sector monopolizes political, economic, and military power. The wealth of the country is in the hands of the whites. Eighty-seven percent of the land belongs to them. When apartheid is applied in such a country, the have-nots are bound to suffer. Separation will always mean inequality.

In South Africa, this system of "separate but equal" is extremely wasteful. There is a lot of duplication. For the blacks (Africans) alone, there are eleven Departments of Education, each with a cabinet minister, secretary or director-general, personal secretary, driver, staff, office, expensive car, and decent accommodation. The whites, Indians, and coloreds have each a Department of Education, more expensively run than those for blacks.

The "black national states" (those which opted for independence) were handsomely rewarded, each with a package of a "national stadium" where celebrations would be held, a university or university college which shortly thereafter attained autonomy, and gallows for anybody found guilty or treason; like challenging or undermining the newly acquired status of the "national state" or in any way found guilty of insulting the person or office of the "president".

PRIMARY AND SECONDARY EDUCATION

Structure

In all South African schools, primary or elementary education starts at the age of six and lasts for seven years. Secondary education starts at the age of thirteen and lasts for five years. For white children education is free and compulsory for a period of ten years, from six to sixteen years of age. This has been the case since 1953. For the coloreds (brown children), education has been compulsory since 1980 and for the Asians since 1979. For the blacks, education at all levels is still a luxury for which the parents must pay from their meager earnings. This should account for the lower enrollment per total population with blacks than with the other social groups.

All Departments of Education seem to favor, in principle, the following structure or format: three years of junior primary school; three years for the senior primary school; three years for the junior secondary school; three years of the senior secondary school; and three years for the junior degree. This usage of the multiple of three is simple and appears to be ideal. The practice or reality, however, as mentioned above, is a period of five years for the secondary education. It starts at standard six and ends at standard ten.

Examinations

The most unfortunate feature of the South African education is the system of examinations. The most important examination is the matriculation or senior certificate examination which is written at the end of the twelfth year of each child's schooling. This is the first and the last public or external examination. In a very real sense it decides the child's future and fate. Those who fail have no future because for all professions and careers in both public and private sectors, a matriculation certificate is the minimum requirement.

All subjects are classified as either higher or standard grades. The former is more difficult than the latter. Those who take all subjects at standard grade, obtain a "School Leaving Certificate". Such a certificate does not qualify one for university education. Those who seek university entrance certificates take all or some key subjects at higher grade. Those subjects are not taken at random. There is streaming and grouping of subjects. There are three streams on the whole. They are science, commerce, and general.

For the purpose of the matriculation "exemption" certificate the subjects are grouped. A candidate must pass his or her home language higher grade (first language), a second language, a science subject, and a subject from the general group. These four subjects satisfy the four groups as specified. Thereafter the candidate has a choice where to pick up two or three additional subjects. The total number of subjects taken is six or seven at most.

What is most disturbing is the number of the matriculation examinations. There are almost as many examinations as the Departments of Education. For the whites alone each province has its matriculation or senior certificate examination, namely Cape, O.F.S., Transvaal and Natal. Most of the blacks write the "National Senior Certificate" examination. A few schools enroll for the Joint Matriculation Board (J.M.B.) Examination. The coloreds and Indians have their own examination bodies. In principle that should be the case with "independent homelands". The Transkei is the first to have its own matriculation examination, whose standard is recognized by the J.M.B. The others still write the examinations set by the Department of Education and Training.

Until all the matriculation pupils in the country write one and the same examination, controlled by the same Department of Education and marked under similar and strict conditions, there will always be arguments about standards and suspicion that one is easier than the others. The South African Certification Council was founded according to Act. 85 of 1986 in order to control the standards of subject matter and examinations. The main objectives of the council is to ensure that all certificates awarded by different examining bodies are of the same standard.

Of the four population or race groups, it is the Africans who experience the highest dropout rate and the highest failure rate. The whites have the highest pass rate, followed by the Indians. It is not uncommon for a number of white candidates to pass all subjects with distinctions. The argument for that is usually that white pupils have the best teachers, the best facilities, higher per capita expenditure, and low teacher pupil ratio. They use home language as medium and lastly, that they can anticipate questions.

Curriculum

Although there are numerous Departments of Education in South Africa, the curriculum for all of them is more-or-less the same. There is what is known as the "core curriculum", from which adaptations are made to suit the peculiar needs of each and every department. The different syllabuses are drawn from this core curriculum. For virtually every subject there are two syllabuses: one standard and the other higher grade. The curriculum and syllabuses are designed by the state. In a sense South Africa has a centralized system of education.

At an ordinary secondary school, the subjects taken are usually the following: English (as first language or as second language), Afrikaans (as first language or as second language), African language (N. Sotho, S. Sotho, Zulu, Xhosa, Tswana, Tsonga or Venda), foreign language, mathematics, physical science, biology, agricultural science, economics, business economics, accountancy, commercial law, history, geography, biblical studies, home economics.

In addition to the ordinary secondary schools there are agricultural high schools, technical high schools, and commercial high schools, that teach subjects relevant to their respective areas of specialization. These are of recent development in black education.

With Whites, the medium of instruction is either English or Afrikaans from the grades to the doctorate. Almost all Indians prefer English and many of them use it as home language. The majority of coloreds use Afrikaans as first language but are abandoning it in favor of English as medium of instruction for political reasons. Afrikaans is seen and regarded as the language of oppression, or of the oppressor.

All Africans in rural areas, urban areas, and "independent national states" have opted for the usage of English as medium of instruction in senior primary and secondary schools. For the initial four years of schooling, the mother tongue is used as medium of instruction, that is, in Grades A and B, and standards one and two.

As a rule, community schools are built on the "R for R" basis. That is the community pays half the cost and the state pays the other half. Where privately paid teachers are hired, pupils pay towards their salaries. From 1986 there is a free supply of books. But they are never enough and remain the property of the school. In addition to all these, there are uniforms to be bought. Bursaries and loans are very difficult, if not impossible, to come by. The extended families come together and raise funds to help where possible.

Teaching Staff

Although education is generally regarded as an "own affair" and therefore managed by separate departments of education for each social group, the minister of national education is responsible for "registration of teachers" and for "salaries and conditions of employment of staff".

Whereas in white education it can be safely assumed that nearly 100 percent of the teachers are professionally qualified, having at least standard ten and higher academic qualifications, the situation is different in black (African) and colored education. In 1988 there were 6,000 professionally unqualified teachers in black education, for instance. In colored education there were about 1,000.

This makes the recruitment, selection, and appointment of teachers problematic. Colleges of education and universities are inclined to take anybody who qualifies; that is in possession of a matriculation or standard ten certificate. No aptitude tests are written. When it comes to the teaching of the natural sciences and mathematics, the situation is really critical. Most of the teachers offering those subjects to matriculation classes have themselves not proceeded beyond standard ten.

HIGHER EDUCATION

Origins

It is difficult to be precise about the origins of higher education in South Africa. The main problem is that what was regarded as higher education was actually "secondary" education. Many educationists and historians regard 1829 as the beginning of university or higher education in South Africa. In that year the South African College was established.

According to Justice J. Van Wyk de Vries Report, however, the origin of higher education was in 1858, when "the first step towards the introduction of university education in Southern Africa was taken with the creation of a board of public examiners". This led to the founding of new colleges to supplement the work already being done in existing academies, such as the one of 1829.

The main characteristic or feature with almost all the South African universities but two, namely VISTA and Rand Afrikaans University (RAU), is that they started as colleges of education or university colleges. Almost all of them were at one time or another constituent members of the University of South Africa, popularly known as UNISA.

The origins of all these universities are treated in the typical South African tradition, style, or fashion; that is racially or ethnically. Afrikaans universities include universities of Stellenbosch, Pretoria, Potchefstroom, and Orange Free State; and the Rand Afrikaans University. English universities comprise universities of Cape Town, Witwatersrand, and Natal; and Rhodes University. Dual-medium institutions are universities of South Africa and Port Elizabeth. Black universities include universities of Fort Hare, Transkei, North, Western Cape, Durban, Westville, Bophuthatswana, and Venda as well as Zululand University and Medical University of Southern Africa.

Universities

In South Africa there are enough universities, twenty-one in number, for a relatively small country of thirty-six million inhabitants (26.5 million Africans, 5 million whites, 3.5 million coloreds, and 913,000 Asians). Some critics already talk of a "proliferation of universities". This is true when compared with the rest of the continent of Africa, south of the Sahara, where on the average there is only one university per country. The total number of university students in South Africa in 1987 was for instance, 258,370.

Most of the South African universities are omnibus, they do not specialize. The Medical University of Southern Africa is perhaps an exception. In accordance with the South African tradition, it should in reality be a Faculty of Medicine attached to an autonomous or independent university. The others offer all fields of study under respective faculties. Taking the famous Witwatersrand University (WITS) as an example, it has the following faculties: architecture, arts, dentistry, medicine, social sciences, natural sciences, law, education, commerce, and engineering.

It competes with Cape Town as the two leading English universities in a variety of fields of study. It is world famous for anatomy, archaeology, mining engineering, metallurgy, and the nuclear physics research. It also has a Department of International Affairs, School of Music, and a school of Dramatic Art. It is anticipated that student numbers at the entire university will increase to 24,000 by 1990. Such growth is possible because the university has funds. Its total expenditure in 1989 amounted to R137 (US$1 = R2.78) million.

The Afrikaans universities are well known for disciplines such as agriculture, theology, and education. They also offer a variety of courses or programs. The universities for the blacks (Africans, Asians, and coloreds) are so small in number of students (about 6,000) and engage in so little research, that by American standards they should be called colleges. They do not have schools of medicine or faculties of architecture and engineering.

Technikons

That there is a chronic shortage of technikons in South Africa, especially for blacks, is historical. Both whites and blacks have developed a negative attitude towards "technical" or "vocational" education. Every parent's wish is to see his or her child at a university. That is why there is such a terrible imbalance between universities and technikons. There are twenty-one universities compared to only twelve technikons; eight for the whites, one for the coloreds, one for the Asians, and two for the Africans.

When some of the homelands became independent, they clamored for "university" education instead of technikons for development. This was done irrespective of the costs involved and in spite of the numbers of pupils who would qualify or satisfy the university entrance qualifications. It is very difficult to change this negative attitude towards technical and vocational education because it is associated with low intelligence and blue-collar jobs. But the country needs such people: people who can work "with their hands".

It is most heartening to notice a change of heart and attitude in respect of technical education among the whites. In 1986 there were 35,047 white students at eight technikons. Of these technikons, the most well known is the Technikon RSA at Braamfontein, in Jahannesburg. It comprises the so-called six schools: School of Management (one year); School of Accounting and Computer Data Processing (three years); School of Natural Sciences (three years); School of Economic and

Behavioral Sciences (three years); School of Police Administration and Law (three years); and School of Government Administration (three years). For the 26.5 million Africans there are only two technikons: the Technikon Northern Transvaal near Mabopane in Pretoria, and Mangosuthu Technikon in KwaZula, Natal. In 1986 the total enrollment at both technikons was 949 students, as compared to 1604 in 1985.

Colleges of Education

Almost all colleges of education in South Africa are state institutions. The state is responsible for the erection of the buildings, the development of curricula and syllabuses and the general maintenance of facilities and funding of programs as well as the payment of the staff salaries.

Most of the white colleges of education are affiliated to universities. The general principle is that a college affiliates to a university nearest to it geographically. Fortunately, white colleges relate more or less one to one in numbers to the white universities. This is not possible with black colleges, because they outnumber the black universities by far. In the Lebowa homeland, for instance, there will be 12 colleges to only one university in 1990.

Whereas white colleges conduct four-year degree courses, black colleges conduct three-year courses. This means a difference in salaries as well. Black education is experiencing serious problems, characterized by shortages. It is also plagued by a huge percentage of underqualified or even unqualified teachers. As a result, colleges in black education are compelled to undertake massive upgrading programs.

In 1987 there were 126,475 African teachers in the field, of whom 24,322 were unqualified and 41,687 were under-qualified. Only 4,774 held university degrees. The total African pupil enrollment in that year was 6,644,859 which is projected to double in ten years, that is grow to 12,019,900 in 1997. (R.I.E.P. 1987: 3).

Administration

All South African universities are quasi-autonomous institutions. The government has a part to play, though indirectly, in the administration of these tertiary institutions, because of the subsidy system described above. It is obvious that the real control is in the hands of the one who sits on the money box.

Of all the three types of universities in South Africa, the black universities are the ones that rely more on and receive almost 100 percent subsidy and consequently, must dance to the tune called by the state. They are followed by the Afrikaans universities, which, however, have the advantage that the government is theirs. The English universities are the most fortunate, because the bulk of the country's wealth is in English hands. They can afford to survive for some time without government subsidy. They can afford to be defiant, if that means independence.

When it comes to administration, all universities are supposed to be managed by councils, partly elected and partly nominated. At black universities an overwhelming majority of councillors are nominated by the state president and the homeland governments. At white universities, councillors represent a great variety of interests; economic, cultural, social, educational, and even political.

Taking the University of the North as a typical black university, the composition of its council is as follows: the rector (vice-chancellor) and vice-rector (deputy vice-chancellor); not less than four persons appointed by the state president; three members of the senate elected by the senate; two persons elected by convocation; one person nominated by each of the self-governing territories or national states; and one person elected from among the donors on account of donations made to the university.

At its first meeting, the council elects one of its members as the chairman. For smooth functioning, the council also appoints committees and it assigns any of its powers and functions to such committees. The most important joint committees of the council and the senate are the finance committee, the personnel committee, and the planning committee.

Because all South African universities are quasi-autonomous, the council may not do certain things without ministerial approval. According to the "Universities Act, No. 61 of 1955, as amended", no university in South Africa can "sell, exchange, or otherwise alienate its immovable property or grant to any person any real right therein or servitude there on; and the University shall not borrow any money". The rector or vice-chancellor, as the chief functionary or head of the institution, sees to the day-to-day administration of the university, assisted by the executive committee of the senate and other minor committees. Otherwise it is the council that runs the university.

The senate is made up of all the heads of departments. They are normally professors, and senior lecturers, who are acting-heads of departments and therefore members of senate. At black universities all associate professors are also members of the senate. The main function of the Senate is academic. It formulates rules and regulations governing academic programs, content, duration of courses, credits, examinations, tests, admission to a degree or diploma course, and graduation ceremonies.

Undergraduate Studies

The commonest undergraduate degrees taken by most students in South Africa are B.A. (Bachelor of Arts); B.Sc. (Bachelor of Science) and B.Com. (Bachelor of Commerce) in that order. There is no university which does not offer all these degree programs. Another set of common or popular degrees is that of career or professionally oriented directions. They are B.A. (Education), B.Sc. (Education), B.Com. (Education), and B.Agric. (Education) for the teaching professions; B.Proc. (Procuration), B.A. (Law) and B.Juris. for law; B.Pharm. (Pharmacy); B.Optom. (Optometry); B.Bibl. (Library Science); B.Theol. (Theology); B.A. (Social Work); and B.A (Fine Art). The duration of these degrees is four years. The fourth year is devoted to practical work or professional training.

A relatively small number of students at black campuses enrol for degrees such as B.Agric., B.Pharm., B.Theol., B.Admin., and B.D. (Bachelor of Divinity).

A relatively small number of students at black campuses enrol for degrees such as B.Agric., B.Pharm., B.Theol., B.Admin., and B.D. (Bachelor of Divinity). At white universities the students have a much greater choice of subjects, courses, and degrees to follow. In addition to those mentioned above, they take degrees in faculties such as engineering, medicine, dentistry, land survey, business administration, and architecture. They are more demanding in all respects and take five to six years to complete. The failure rate in these fields, even for white students, is very high. Ironically, the more difficult and expensive the course or degree is, the more relevant it is to the economic, scientific, and technological development of the country.

Because these all-important and rare degrees are not offered at black universities, many black students apply to the so-called "open" (English) universities. They get admitted on ministerial approval. Gradually and sometimes grudgingly and reluctantly the Afrikaans universities are beginning to open their doors to other racial groups. Racial prejudices in the country are too deep, especially with the Afrikaners.

All junior or bachelor's degrees stretch over a period of three years. In those three years, a student has a specified number of "courses" to pass each year. For Bachelor of Arts degree for instance, the total number of courses is ten, made up as follows: first year, four; second year, four; and third year, two. The Bachelor of Science students take fewer courses, normally nine, whereas Bachelor of Commerce students take more, sometimes fourteen.

Universities differ when it comes to the actual structure of curriculum. One common feature is that each student must take at least two subjects, called major subjects, in the three years of study. Depending on the choice of those majors, certain ancillary subjects may be compulsory. The normal combinations for the majors are: English and Afrikaans, history and geography, sociology and psychology, zoology and botany, physics and chemistry, et cetera. Faculties are not water-tight compartments. Some students straddle them. They would, for instance, take courses in two or three different faculties. The academic year at most South African universities is very short, stretching from March to October. Since strikes and boycotts of lessons are endemic at all Black campuses, the number of days actually used for academic programs is normally far less than the number set aside for lecturing.

Two languages, English and Afrikaans, are used as official languages for communication and as media of instruction at all tertiary institutions. Obviously the Afrikaans universities make use of Afrikaans and the English universities use English as medium of instruction. Two white universities are dual-medium, they are the University of South Africa (UNISA) and the University of Port Elizabeth (UPE). The University of the Western Cape, for the brown or so-called "colored" people is also dual medium. Some students are English speaking and others, the majority, have Afrikaans as home language. In all the black (African) campuses, English is the medium of instruction and communication.

Admission Requirements

Entrance qualifications to any university or Technikon in South Africa is the matriculation or Senior Certificate Exemption Certificate. Although each province conducts its own matriculation examination for whites, and the other departments also conduct their own examinations for the other racial groups, an attempt is made to retain a norm or common standard nationally to select those who qualify for tertiary education. Until recently the Joint Matriculation (J.M.B.), which ran its own matriculation examination, was responsible for granting "exemption" to those who satisfy all the requirements.

Hostel accommodation

For the white universities, the number of students in residence is very small. Only about 20 live in hostels. In contrast, African, colored, and Indian students are almost all boarders. The problem is that their institutions were established in remote places, away from cities, towns, and even townships. The position is worse with the African campuses. They are about thirty kilometers from the nearest town or township and contrast sharply with the immediate environment. That is why they are referred to as "bush" colleges.

The obvious problem with such a situation is when many cannot afford the high boarding and lodging fees. At the University of the North, lodging alone was R1,125 per student in 1989 and boarding may amount to more than the lodging fee per annum. As a result, and out of desperation, some students lodge in the small neighborhood or commute some 40 km. one way daily from the nearest black township of Seshego, West of Pietersburg.

Advanced Studies and Research

In South Africa, a three year bachelor's degree is usually followed by a one year honor's degree or its equivalent, for full-time students. It is the honor's degree that qualifies one for the master's degree. In rare cases some students jump from the honor's degree to the doctorate (Ph.D.).

As could be expected, white universities offer a far greater variety of master's and doctoral degrees than black campuses. At the latter, senior degrees are normally in the faculties of arts and education and occasionally in science and commerce. On the average, there is one master's degree conferred annually and one Ph.D. degree conferred every other year at black universities. At white universities, those receiving senior degrees become so many that a special ceremony for them, normally in Spring, September or October, is arranged.

The nomenclature of the senior degree may not be exactly the same for the same disciplines at all the universities. But the differences are slight. The following are the types of master's degrees offered at most white universities: M.A., M.A. (Dramatic Art), M.A. (Clinical Psychology), M.A. (Fine Arts), M.A. (Social Work), M.A. (Audiology), M.A. (Speech Pathology), M.A. (Translation), M.Mus. (Music),

M.B.A. (Business Administration), M.M. (Management), M.B.L. (Business Leadership), M.Ed., M.Com., M.Econ.Sc., M.So.Sc. (Social Science), and M.Acc. (Accountancy). There is no M.Phil. as found in Great Britain, for instance.

In the field of the natural sciences the following master's degrees are offered: M.Sc., M.ScDiet., M.Sc. (Dentistry), M.Dent., M.Sc. (QS) i.e. Quantity Surveying, M.Sc. (TRP) i.e. Town and Regional Planning, M.Sc. (Building), MEP. (Environment Planning), M.Sc. (Occupational Therapy), M.Sc. (Medicine), M.Sc. (Engineering), and M.Sc. (Land Surveying).

All these master's degrees are followed by Ph.D. (Doctor of Philosophy). As a rule Ph.D. is senior to D.Phil. in as much as D.Litt. et. Phil. is regarded as having greater status than D. Litt. For D.Ed. some universities admit anybody with a master's degree even if the individual has never done a course or degree in the subject or discipline education. He or she is qualified if he or she has a teacher's diploma or is actually engaged in the profession. This reduces the status of the degree. D.Sc. is regarded as by far more important than Ph.D. in any science subject. For a person to qualify for D.Sc. he or she must have contributed to the discipline in many ways, not just applied research. The other well-known doctoral degrees are D.Com., LL.D. and D.D. All these are also regarded as senior to Ph.D.

Master's programs normally take at least one year for full-time students and two years for the part-time ones. For the doctoral (Ph.D.) students it is usually two and four years respectively. All "M and D students", as they are called, are literally at the mercy of the supervisor, sometimes called promoter. He can motivate or discourage and even frustrate his students.

At most white universities, students have the option of either doing the master's degree by course work or by research. Even those who choose course work are obliged to conduct a mini research and come out with a "research paper" or "extended essay". In South Africa, a master's piece of work is called a "dissertation" and a doctoral (Ph.D.) one a "thesis", instead of the other way round.

At black universities, all senior work is still by research. Some are preparing to introduce course work as early as 1990 for the "M" degrees. For the Ph.D. degrees all universities demand serious research. For both "M" and "D" theses and dissertations, at least two external examiners are appointed by the senate to adjudicate on the work. These are experts in the field. There is, however, no public defence of the thesis or dissertation as is the practice in the Western world. Post doctoral programs are virtually non-existent.

Senior degrees are very expensive to enrol for. At black campuses, students pay about R6,000 for boarding, lodging and tuition. At white universities it is double the amount. Because of the costs involved many students apply for bursaries or grants. About 80 percent of the applicants get them. The main sources of such bursaries are the government sponsored CSIR (Council for Scientific and Industrial Research) and HSRC (Human Sciences Research Council), both located in Pretoria and, until 1989, both presided over by brothers Chris and Johan Garbers. They sponsor individual, departmental, and even national research projects. Besides these two national giants, there are many other smaller donors.

ISSUES AND TRENDS

The recently created Department of National Education has announced that new educational institutions are to be established which would combine university education, teacher training, and technikon education. According to the director general, Dr. R. Venter: "The new institutions would be racially based, and controlled by the ministers responsible for education. The new colleges would be adapted to the needs of a particular area and need not necessarily contain all three elements of tertiary education" (Race Relations Survey 1988: 144).

There is no indication, unfortunately, that the present government will abandon the idea that education is an "own affair". The present state president, Mr. F. W. deKlerk, was himself minister of national education, and he is the chief advocate of this philosophy or policy, of "own affairs" and "general affairs". The latter affects everybody in the country and the former affects particular "groups" in certain "group areas".

In conformity with this tendency, the minister of education and development aid (black education), has announced last year (1988) that the government was committed to placing control of African education in the hands of an African minister of education. According to this minister, his replacement by "an effectively operating African executive decision-making minister as soon as possible", was a high priority (Race Relations Survey 1988: 114).

The minister, Dr. Gerret Viljoen, did not envisage a single ministry or department of education in South Africa, in spite of the clamor and demand for it, especially from the African section of the population.

The problem is that, as long as there are numerous departments of education, there will be disparity and differentiation in as far as per capita expenditure is concerned. For a very long time, the ratio of that expenditure per white and black child was 10:1 in favor of whites. It has recently narrowed down to 8:1.

In as far as education in general and black education in particular is concerned, the future appears bleak. Appointment of a black minister of black education is wrought with problems. Ministers are politicians who belong to the ruling party, the Nationalist Party, and of necessity are whites voted into office by a white electorate. For any African to accept such an appointment will not only be foolhardy but illogical and suicidal. Of the thirteen ministers of education in the country, he will be the only one without a mandate of any type or size from his constituency.

A single ministry of education also has problems. In the first place, it will make nonsense of the policy of the government, namely apartheid or separation. Secondly, it would imply equalization of expenditure and parity of everything. This, the economy of the country at this stage can ill afford. For equalization or parity to be achieved, the standard of white education must be lowered and that of black education raised. To the white community this is not negotiable, according to the resolution of the *Volkskongres* (National Congress) held in 1982 in Bloemfontein.

For the education of whites, the government has decided, in 1988, to establish four "provincial education councils" to advise the minister of education and culture (white own affairs) on all educational matters. The councils, one per province, would represent the teaching profession, organized parent bodies, tertiary education, private schools, technical colleges and schools for special education. In the words of the minister responsible, Mr. Piet Clase: "These high level councils are not political bodies, but will function in accordance with our policy of bringing education as near as possible to its users and, by so doing, guarantee diversity within unity" (Race Relations Survey 1987-88: 144).

By implication, the blacks, coloreds, and Indians will also have their own councils at either regional or national level. Contrary to diversification, the universities have decided to have unity in diversity. The two separate university principals' councils have merged to have one called "Council of University Principals" (CUP). The vice-chancellors of black and brown universities are no longer junior partners with observer status at university principals' meetings. They are full members. This trend is most welcome and is a healthy pointer for the future.

Because of the serious economic decline in the country, the universities have embarked on "rationalization". This means maximal utilization of funds available. In effect it means phasing out non-viable courses or subjects and reduction of others or amalgamation. Those years are over when a university could decide unilaterally what courses to offer and when to create or disestablish departments. For the future, universities are grouped regionally. Identified courses like pharmacy, agriculture, land survey, library science, geology, etc, can only be offered by one identified university in each region. This saves money and improves the quality of instruction. This arrangement is cost-effective.

As a result of sanctions and boycotts, the South African universities have been made aware of their plight and shortcomings. They desire more funding and exchange of experts and academics. Staff members suffer from isolation, they want to belong to and attend international conferences and symposia. The frustration experienced by cultural, educational, and economic boycotts has made academics more conscious of the need for speedy political solutions within the country. The present government of President F. W. de Klerk appears determined to end apartheid and thus make the country acceptable and attractive to the outside world.

South Africa is a beautiful country with great potential, but it suffers from this chronic disease called apartheid. This disease affects the country economically, socially, educationally and, of course, politically. The abolition of this system will immediately lead to normalcy, to peace and prosperity at home, and to dignity and acceptance abroad. This implies the creation of a single, unfragmented, united, democratic, and non-racial country. This should be preceded by the unbanning of all political organizations and release of all political prisoners. The immediate benefits would be the return of foreign investments, inflow of foreign capital, the ending of sanctions and boycotts, exchange of professors and academics, and admission of foreign students.

With the economy stimulated and booming and capital available, our universities and technikons would be able to flourish and even export their products and expertise to the neighboring states which depend so much on South Africa for growth and support. No country, no matter how powerful, can survive and thrive in isolation. All countries rely to a greater or lesser extent on foreign capital and foreign investment. In the final analysis, money is the panacea to many problems, especially in education.

BIBLIOGRAPHY

Ackerman, G. J., and Bouwman, P. J. *Education at Tertiary Level in Time Perspective.* UNISA, 1989.

Brooks, E. H. *Report of the Commission on the University of South Africa.* Capetown: Government Printer, 1947.

De Villiers, F. J. *Technical and Vocational Education.* Pretoria, n.d.

Department of National Education. *A Qualification Structure for Universities in South Africa.* 1987.

Department of National Education, RSA. *The Development of the System for the Provision of Eduction Following the White Paper on the Provision of Education in the Republic of South Africa, 1983.* Dept. of National Education, 1985.

Dreijmanis, John. *The Role of the South African Government in Tertiary Education.* Johannesburg: South African Institute of Race Relations, 1988.

Dube, E. F. "The Relationship Between Racism and Education in South Africa". *Harvard Educational Review* Vol. 55 No. 1 (1985).

Holoway, J. E. *Verslag van die Kommissie van Ondersoek oor Afsonderlike Universiteitsopleidings Geriewe vir Nie-Blakes* (1953-1954). Pretoria: Government Printers, 1955.

International Handbook of Education Systems in Africa and the Middle East, Vol. 2. New York: Wiley and Sons, 1983.

Jooste, J. P. *Die Geskiedenis van die P.U. vir C.H.O.* Koers Deel XXV, 1957.

Mphahlele, M. C. J. *Emphasis and Relevance in Black Education.* University of the North, 1981.

Pells, E. G. *300 Years of Education in South Africa.* Juta & Co., 1938.

South African Institute of Race Relations. *Race Relations Survey: 1987-1988.* Johannesburg, 1988.

Van Wyk De Vries, J. *Main Report of the Commission of Inquiry into Universities.* Pretoria: Department of National Education, 1974.

SPAIN

by
Colomer Viadel Vicente
Rector
University of Cordoba, Spain

BACKGROUND

The Spanish higher educational system originated in much the same way as those of neighboring European countries which were co-heirs of the same basic macrocultural unit, namely the Roman Empire. It dates back to the last centuries of the Middle Ages (11th-14th centuries) and arose from the medieval concern of monks with arts and sciences. The universal coding vehicle of this concern was Latin, a true *lingua franca,* whose mastery opened the door to the ecclesiastical and civil powers in many fields, and to knowledge in virtually every area. The Universities of Salamanca and Alcala attained worldwide recognition, and alongside other "comprehensive studies" born in the bosom of cathedral schools, prepared the Spanish transition to European modernity through the Renaissance incubated in Italy. The Spanish Constitution of 1978, which ended forty years of military dictatorship, and the entrance of Spain and Portugal to the European Economic Community knocked down old barriers of isolation and fostered our involvement in European projects and workgroups devoted to science, culture, and higher education. The joint European efforts for economic, industrial, technological, and social progress leads us to believe that we have turned over a real page of our university history and that radical changes are in store for the future. From a higher educational point of view, the forthcoming enforcement of the Only European Act (in January 1993), will mark the birth of an academic Europe and pave the way to the long-dreamed United States of Europe. Everything seems to indicate that the die has been cast for the next few decades, in which the Spanish University will be compelled to coexist and compete with its European counterparts.

The Spanish university system is virtually state-run: thirty public compared to four private universities (all private universities are owned by the church). The government, through parliament bills, is entitled to regulate the creation, functioning, and management of the universities; an aspect that is indispensable to ensure national and international inter-university ratification. However each autonomous region (and its Education Council in the case of regions to which full transfers have been made in education matters) has some decision-making power over its universities.

State-run universities are basically supported through proportional allocations from the state's general budget, in addition to their income from registration fees, or contracts for research or services provided to public or private

711

enterprises, or to various foundations. In this sense, some universities (e.g. Madrid or Cordoba) are joint partners of university-enterprise foundations which foster this type of cooperation.

The Spanish university can be said to be in the final stages of a reconstitution period which started with the historic, social, and political transition to democracy and Europeanization under the auspicious of the new democratic system prevailing in Spain since 1977. The Law of University Reform (1983), currently in effect, has following features:

(a)   It has created the University Council, composed chiefly of university rectors and education officers from the autonomous regions, and personalities from the scientific, economic, and cultural world elected by the congress and the senate. The council insures nationwide coordination of university teaching and the participation of all universities in the formulation of national university policy.

(b)   It has substantially increased the autonomy of the universities, each of which has its own statutes within the aforesaid legal framework.

(c)   It has committed considerable budgetary support from the state for enhancing the academic status of all university teachers by 1992.

(d)   It has created a social council in each of the universities. This council is to foster a linkage between the university and the society (economic development, financial sources, agreements with enterprises, etc.).

(e)   It has brought about significant reforms in the curricula of all university studies and an increase in the number of diplomas and degrees offered. The Royal Decree 1497 of 27 November 1987 establishes the guidelines for the curricula and university degrees which are to be valid throughout the country.

PRIMARY AND SECONDARY EDUCATION

The primary school in Spain (known as the basic general school) takes 8 years and caters to children ages 6-14 years. The primary curriculum includes basic subjects such as social science, Spanish language and literature, biological sciences, mathematics, and physics. There is continuous evaluation of students instead of a year-end exam. Primary schooling is free and compulsory.

On completion of primary education, students enter secondary school, which comprises two alternatives: vocational training (first and second cycle) and academic education. The first alternative, as implied by its name, opens the doors to professional work opportunities that do not require a university education; it also allows those concluding their second-cycle vocational studies to access further university studies related to their professional speciality.

The second alternative, the *bachillerato* (roughly equivalent to the General Certificate of Education, U.K.) is chosen by students wishing to access university studies and this program takes four years: three of *bachillerato* proper plus one year for "COU" (university guidance course, the spanish counterpart of high school). The basic subjects making up the curriculum are Spanish language, foreign language (plus the local language in bilingual regions such as Galicia, the Basque country or Catalonia), mathematics, social studies, natural sciences, ethics or religion, physical and artistic education, and philosophy. The COU offers optional subjects suited to the students' future university or professional studies. At the end of the third year of *bachillerato,* students are granted the *bachiller* diploma (note the marked formal difference with the English term bachelor) which is an essential prerequisite for starting COU.

The academic year starts early in October and ends in mid-July throughout the country. The *bachillerato* examinations are taken at the student's school, whether public or private, while COU examinations and those scheduled for granting access to some university studies (university access tests) are coordinated by the university rectorate of the district to which the school in question belongs. The marks obtained in the access tests and the average of those making up the student's academic record form the basis for admission to different university institutions.

Each institution is entitled to program its own extracurricular activities freely. These, depend to a great extent on the willingness and enthusiasm of parent associations and the school council in which parents also take part. Sports, artistic activities of all kinds, trips and journeys, field activities, etc., form part of extra curricular activities that help students acquire a comprehensive human education. Unlike in the case of universities, the private sector plays a significant role in secondary education by running many secondary schools, both half-board and full-board. Public schools do not charge tuition (apart from a US$80 for COU) but fees in private schools vary from US$500-2,000 per year).

The official language is Spanish (Castillian); however, in some bilingual regions, lessons can be taught in the national and the local language (Catalonian, Basque, Galician). There are also some international schools (e.g. the German and the Italian schools), with a bilingual curriculum.

The Ministry of Education and Science provides students with substantial grants and subsidies. As a result, a conscientious student rarely lacks the opportunity of pursuing studies.

The teachers for public secondary schools are selected by public merit competitions from among university graduates and receive appointments as civil servants. They are provided with teacher training. In addition, psycopedagogical services are also being increasingly provided by public centers.

Foreign students can enroll in private secondary schools without restriction. However, there may be constraints in getting admission to those public schools that have admission policies based on priority criteria such as nearness of the student's residence to the school, number of siblings, domestic income, etc.

The pan-European agreements scheduled to be signed soon will make the secondary school certificate obtained in any country of the EEC valid to gain access to any European university.

HIGHER EDUCATION

Institutions

There are five basic types of university institutions in Spain:

1. Faculties, where different bachelor's studies usually requiring five academic years are provided. (The University Council is currently revising all curricula of existing and new degrees, most of which will require four years in the future).

2. Higher technical schools, which conduct engineering programs that also usually require five academic years.

3. University schools, which have programs known as "first cycle" studies (three years), many of which enable students to access the "second cycle" in order to obtain a bachelor's or engineer's degree leading to completion of full professional training.

4. University colleges (private or state-run), which also cover the "first cycle" curriculum only and enable students to continue their studies in another town or institution (usually in one of the "faculties" mentioned earlier).

5. Tele-teaching university institutions, which make up a centralized remote teaching system (the UNED or *Universidad Nacional de Ensenanza a Distancia*) with national and international coverage. Their studies and degrees have value identical to those granted by any other state university.

The thirty Spanish universities are Alcala de Henares, Alicante, Balears, Barcelona (Autonomous), Barcelona (Central), Barcelona (Polytechnical), Basque Country, Cadiz, Cantabria, Castille-La Mancha, Cordoba, Estremadura, Granada, La Laguna, Leon, Madrid (Autonomous), Madrid (Complutense), Madrid (Polytechnical), Malaga, Murcia, Oviedo, Las Palmas (Polytechnical), Salamanca, Santiago de Compostela, Seville, Valencia, Valencia (Polytechnical), Valladolid, Zaragoza, UNED (Rectorate in Madrid). These universities are comprised of 622 institutions, thirty-six of which are owned by the church.

The faculties offer some or all of the following study programs (only the largest universities offer most of them): arts, canon law (only at private, ecclesiastical universities), computer science, economics and managerial science, fine arts, geography and history, information sciences, law, medicine, pharmacy , philology, philosophy and teaching sciences, political and sociological sciences, psychology, biology, chemistry, geology, mathematics, physics, theology (only at private, ecclesiastical universities), and veterinary sciences.

The higher technical schools may offer programs in the following areas: aeronautical engineering, agricultural engineering, architecture, chemical engineering (only at private universities), civil works engineering, forestry engineering, industrial engineering, mining engineering, naval engineering, and telecommunication (electronic) engineering.

The first-cycle studies (three academic years) offered by university colleges include the following: computer science, library and document keeping, management, nursing, optics, physiotherapeutics, school teaching (primary education), social work (since 1987-1988), statistics, technical architecture and technical engineering.

The *Universidad Nacional de Educacion a Distancia* (National Tele-Teaching University) offers following studies: economics and managerial science; geography and history; industrial engineering; law; philology; philosophy; political and sociological sciences; psychology; chemical, mathematical and physical sciences; and pedagogical sciences.

In the last few years, both the UNED and other public and private universities have increased their offer of specialist professional programs (usually termed "master's") for university degree holders (whether diplomas or bachelor's degrees). The legal regulation of these postgraduate degrees (a very flexible panacea which is now being discovered in our country with a view to facing the current vertiginous changes in the work market) lies in Article 28 of the earlier mentioned Law of University Reform (1983) and in the subsequent Royal Decree 185/1985 of 23 January. This development could be of great interest to those seeking postgraduate qualifications in the next few years, on account of the steady development of this type of studies, aimed at serving the demand that supports them. The degrees, granted independently by each university, do not provide professional competence and are not officially sanctioned; rather, they are guaranteed by the university that grants them and their greater or lesser prestige depends on their acceptance by the society and the labor market.

Governance

The functioning of a university is controlled by its governing council (*junta de gobierno*), vice- rectors, secretary of the university, the deans and directors of faculties and colleges, and some students. Each university has a *claustro,* a major body formed by a variable number of members depending on the statutes of that university. Majority (60 percent) of its members must be professors, while the rest consist of students as well as administrative and service staff (most often, 30 percent are students and 10 percent are administrative and service staff members). The *claustro,* which oversees, the creation, modification and renovation of the institutions statutes, is also entrusted with the major function of electing the rector through a secret ballot. The rector, who can only be dismissed by the *claustro* before the scheduled mandate of four years is elapsed, chooses the vice-rectors, secretary general, and manager of the university, with whom he or she makes up the managing team of the institution.

Faculties and colleges within a university are headed by deans or directors, respectively, who are elected from the teaching staff. Ordinary affairs are dealt with by the dean or director and his/her vice-dean or vice-director team. The Law of University Reform organizes the university around departments, that usually oversee an area or related areas of knowledge and research. The departments can be inter-faculty (i.e. covering various institutions irrespective of the faculty or college where they are actually based). Students are entitled to take part in department, faculty/school, and university meetings through their representatives elected according to the statutes of each university

University lecturers hold doctorate degrees and are selected through public competitions judged by a five-member jury (two professors proposed by the university and three chosen by lot from among those who are specialized in the relevant subject area). All university teachers working full-time must give a scheduled number of lectures per week and announce their student tuition hours publicly.

Types of Degrees and Diplomas

Apart from the postgraduate professional specialization diplomas that each university may grant, there are three basic degrees of official recognition throughout the country, namely; graduate (granted after three years or first cycle studies); bachelor (granted upon completion of first and second cycles of studies, i.e. after 5-6 years); doctor (sanctioning third cycle studies, which usually last two years and entail the realization of research work materialized in a thesis).

Accordingly, the degrees obtained upon completion of the different studies are as follows:

(a)   The faculty studies lead to the degree of bachelor (at the end of second cycle studies) or doctor (upon completion of third cycle studies and passing a thesis) in fine arts, law, medicine, etc.

(b)   Studies performed at the higher technical schools lead to the degrees of architect or engineer (at the end of the second cycle) and doctor architect or doctor engineer (after passing third cycle studies and a doctoral thesis).

(c)   The university schools grant the following degrees: graduate (in nursing, library keeping, optics, social work, etc.), technical architect, and technical engineer (aeronautical, agronomical, etc.).

Undergraduate Studies

It is anticipated that soon (in two or three year's time) the study programs currently offered will be broadened with the introduction of new curricula (Royal Decree of November 1988). Likewise, the reorganization of *bachillerato,* with the scheduled extension of compulsory schooling until the age of sixteen (i.e. the first cycle of secondary education), may also affect the preuniversity education of students.

Curricula are currently organized by subjects: each subject is taught three hours a week throughout the academic year, although there are also some (usually optional) subjects which are of four month duration. The new study programs are organized around credits (one credit is equal to ten lecturing hours) for university studies.

As stated earlier, most university studies take five years for the first degree (with the exception of medicine and, some engineering specialities) which take longer, with two further years for the doctorate. At university schools, the "first cycle" typically takes three years. The academic year starts in early October and ends in mid-July.

Access to university faculties, higher technical schools and university colleges requires passing COU (university guidance course) and selection examinations consisting of two parts: one intended to determine the students' intellectual maturity and general knowledge, based on compulsory COU subjects; and another aimed at establishing the consistency between the students' knowledge and the specific university studies which they wish to follow, based on the compulsory and optional subjects they have studied at secondary school. Entrance to university schools is usually gained by passing COU, though priority is given to students passing the selection examinations. Nevertheless, secondary vocational training students (specialist technicians) are entitled for direct access to schools related to their speciality without the need to pass the COU. In addition, people over twenty-five, irrespective of their educational background, can access university studies by passing the tests organized yearly by each university.

Spain has traditionally welcomed foreign students (particularly Latin American, Arabian, and North African) and offered Spanish philology courses for North American and European students. Spanish universities are currently very sensitive in general to the foreseeable increase in enrollment of foreign students from European countries once academic studies are ratified by the EEC in 1993. Whenever a given academic institution cannot take in all the students who requested entrance, the vacancies available are allocated according to academic merit (marks obtained in the selectivity examinations or average marks of the secondary school record if the former are not required for access to the institution in question). Hence, in filling out their enrollment request, students must provide a priority list of studies in case their original choice cannot be met. All institutions with a limited number of vacancies reserve a certain quota for foreign students.

Foreign students wishing to follow university studies in Spain should take into account several considerations: they must be proficient in Spanish, which can be learnt even at the universities themselves; they should enquire at the Ministry of Education of their country of origin whether there is a cultural agreement between both countries (such agreements offer favorable conditions for studying in the other country); like Spaniards, foreigners over twenty-five can access any of the studies offered by the *Universidad Nacional de Ensenanza a Distancia (UNED),* so that they can have a Spanish university degree without leaving their country; prior contact with the cultural attache of Spain in their countries is essential to gather valuable information on specific practical aspects, including information on degree ratification agreements; and they should consider the inter-European mutual student exchange programs (e.g. the ERASMUS program).

The vice-rectorate of each university deals with students' problems (by the vice-rector for student affairs) and with the organization of extracurricular activities (by the vice-rector of university extension). Sports, musical and theatrical teams, and cine forums, parties, trips, and lectures on topical subjects are a vital, picturesque, and highly educational aspect of Spanish universities.

The medium of instruction is Castillan (known as Spanish abroad) except in bilingual regions (Catalonia, the Basque country, Galicia and Valencia) where some teachers give lectures in the local language.

The fact that most universities are public (state-run), makes university studies quite affordable. Thus, the annual fees in university institutions usually range (depending on the study program) from US$400 to US$600 per year. A student's full board and lodging is rarely less than US$550 per month. The universities usually have more or less formal student guidance services which provide information about reliable residences, hotels, and families that offer accommodation. Apart from their parents' support, students are offered a range of grants and occasional jobs to finance their expenses.

Advanced Studies and Research

The legislation governing third cycle university studies (doctoral curriculum, postgraduate courses, doctoral theses, etc.) is basically contained in the Royal Decree 185 of 1985, modified by the Royal Decree 537 of 1988. According to the legislation, the doctoral curriculum takes a minimum of two academic years and consist of a thesis as well as courses (four credits each) and seminars (two credits each) (one credit is equivalent to ten lecturing hours); and the programs organized by university departments are aimed at the scientific and professional specialization of students in research and teaching. A maximum of five years is allowed between the admission to a doctoral program and the delivery of the finished thesis (this deadline can be exceptionally extended by the rectorial doctorate committee at the request of the department concerned).

Each course or seminar for the doctoral program lasts two hours per week. Lectures usually start by mid-November and end in May. Candidates are usually admitted on the basis of merit taking into account such factors as their academic record, professional experience, research work, knowledge of foreign languages, importance of their doctoral project, etc. The average fees for doctoral programs is about US$1,000 per year. Specific grants for research and postgraduate studies are given every year by the Ministry of Education and Science. Priority is frequently given to cooperation programs with Latin America and various European countries. The Ministry also issues grants covering stays of foreign teachers in Spanish universities. These grants are publicly announced through the BOE, the State's official bulletin. We should emphasize the long tradition of several Spanish universities in the establishment of joint agreements with foreign universities (particularly with institutions in the United States) whose students are provided the opportunity to follow undergraduate as well as postgraduate courses in Hispanic philology here.

ISSUES AND TRENDS

The arena of education in Spain confronts a number of important issues and trends. The most significant ones are outlined here.

- The high juvenile unemployment in Spain (highest in Europe) has led to an artificial increase in university enrollment, turning the university into a sort of storehouse of unemployed youth. There is a lack of true devotion to studies in many students who are compelled to follow the courses they did not choose even as their last option.

- The accelerating imbalance between the social demand from the university as a postsecondary or tertiary teaching institution and the actual training it can provide to students poses a significant challenge to the institutions.

- There is a need for a somewhat radical dialogue between social institutions devoted to young people and adult education (life-long education), political decision-makers, and university officers on new and imaginative ways of allocating scientific research tasks.

- The institutionalized pedagogical deprofessionalization of university teachers, some of whom are brilliant historians, mathematicians or surgeons, but utterly bad teachers is one of the critical problems to be tackled in any realistic attempt at improving the quality of university teaching.

- There is a pressing need in Spain as well as in several European countries for the integral human education of teachers and students. We are "making" powerful executives and producing students with brilliant academic records but with little ability to overcome the smallest personal problems or to succeed in interpersonal communications.

- The lack of involvement of the Spanish (and European) private sector in the creation and support of universities contrasts with the American tradition. Historical reasons apart, we should consider formulas for non-state social participation.

- Universities now are setting themselves free from the old handicaps of bureaucratization, a task in which our European partners, and the Americans, are ahead of us. The dilemma of the practice of guaranteed lifetime employment for state teachers, with the unavoidable risk of generalized lethargy, has encouraged the search for objective indicators of academic quality of the teaching staff.

- The university is now placing increasing emphasis on functionality-rationality criteria by including in syllabuses, topics related to professional training, rather than pure scientific knowledge.

BIBLIOGRAPHY

Benjumea, Cabeza de Vaca, et al. *Guía de Salidas Universitarias. Círculo de Progreso Universitario.* Madrid, 1985.

Ediciones Tecnos. *Legislación sobre Enseñanza. Normas Generales: Educación General Basica, Formación Profesional, Bachillerato.* Madrid: Tecnos, 1987.

Ediciones Tecnos. *Legislación Universitaria 1. Normativa General y Autonómica.* Madrid: Consejo de Universidades-Tecnos, 1986.

Ediciones Tecnos. *Legislación Universitaria 2. Estatutos de las Universidades.* Madrid: Consejo de Universidades-Tecnos, 1986.

Ministeria de Educación y Ciencia. *Las Enseñanzas Universitarias en España y en la Comunidad Económica Europea.* Madrid: MEC-Consejo de Universidades, 1986.

Ministerio de Educación y Ciencia. *La Reforma de las Enseñanzas Universitarias.* Madrid: MEC-Consejo de Universidades, 1987.

Ministeria de Educación y Ciencia. *Estudios en España. Nivel no-Universitario.* Madrid: MEC-Secretaría General Tecnica, 1985.

Ministerio de Educación y Ciencia. *Estudios en España. Nivel Universitario.* Madrid: MEC-Secretaría General Tecnica, 1985.

Riviere, Angel, et al. *El Sistema Educativo Español.* MEC-CIDE, 1988.

SRI LANKA

by
G. B. Gunawardena
Director of Research
National Institute of Education, Sri Lanka

BACKGROUND

Education in Sri Lanka has flourished from 300 B. C. and it was shaped over the centuries by Buddhist traditions and ideology. The rich traditional system met the needs of both the Buddhist monks and the lay elite. The dominance of the Europeans from about the sixteenth century brought a halt to the growth of the indigenous system till the country became independent in 1948. Though the present system has its roots in colonial education, modifications in the system resulting from enactments of successive governments since independence has radically altered the character of education in Sri Lanka. With a literacy rate of 87 percent and a relatively high level of participation in schooling, the education base is well established. The present social problems resulting mainly from sharp ethnic divisions and low economic growth have prevented the achievement of quality and relevance, the two main educational objectives of independent Sri Lanka.

The beginning of the educational system in Sri Lanka can be traced to the introduction of Buddhism into the country in the third century B.C. An indigenous system with the village school *(Gurugedara)*, temple school, and centers of oriental learning *(Pirivena)* provided education at different levels. This system was destroyed during the period of Western dominance which lasted for nearly 400 years.

The roots of present day education in Sri Lanka lie in the colonial educational system that the country inherited from the British. The British developed a system to meet the two major needs of colonial rule: the creation of a Western elite with a Christian ethos patterned on the metropolitan model and the preparation of personnel to develop the infrastructure of colonial administration. The British system of education was accepted by the local Western educated as a determinant of progress and the middle class which agitated for reform towards Ceylonization did not question the inequalities on which the educational system was based. The Buddhist and the Hindu reformists, however, later attacked the denominational system of education.

The introduction of universal franchise and the change in political structure in 1931 permitted the formulation of a national educational policy. This policy formulated in mid-1940s attempted to democratize education and also to improve relevance and quality in education. This resulted in a number of notable achievements. The most significant of these are the introduction of free education from kindergarten to university, the use of the mother tongue as the medium of instruction at all levels, and a unified national school system.

The special thrust on educational opportunity for all resulted in a spectacular quantitative growth in terms of literacy, number of schools, teachers, and enrollment of students in the formal system. Since independence, the number of schools has increased from 5,915 in 1947 to 10,212 in 1987. The number of students in primary and secondary levels grew from 1,025,836 in 1947 to 3,952,745 in 1987 and number of teachers rose from 28,210 in 1947 to 146,408 in 1987.

By early 1970s the policy makers diagnosed the prime need of that time to be the qualitative improvement of education by increasing its relevance. The 1972 curriculum reforms made an ambitious attempt to achieve relevance. Again in 1981, the white paper essentially based on the findings of the Educational Reforms Committee of 1979 provided a basic framework for reforms in the 1980s. In the implementation of these proposals, high priority was given to increasing access and equity, increasing curriculum relevance, improving efficiency and accountability in management, minimizing the mismatch between education and employment, and effective allocation and utilization of existing resources.

From a perspective of national development, the university system is another important sector. Centers of higher education and advanced training like *Mahavihara* had flourished very early in the history of the country but the early institutes of the present system started with the Ceylon Medical College established in 1870 and the Ceylon University College in 1921. The University of Ceylon established in 1942 followed the British model and today there are nine universities with a total of 24,761 internal students and 13,516 external students. The number of universities and the intake increased rapidly with the change in the medium of instruction to national languages and a consequent greater demand for university education. Another significant change was the restructuring of the pattern of university administration and the appointment of the University Grants Commission under a new Ministry of Higher Education which is responsible for the governance of universities in Sri Lanka.

Structure and Administration

The Ministry of Education, Cultural Affairs, and Information under a state minister of education is responsible for the design and management of general education. The Ministry of Higher Education set up in 1978 is responsible for university education as well as technical and vocational education.

The minister of education is assisted by the secretary who is responsible for the implementation of all educational policies and the supervision of the ministry. He also functions as the director-general of education in relation to provincial departments of education and programs conducted by the directorate of the ministry. The secretary is assisted by additional and assistant secretaries and three deputy director- generals and directors in charge of programs conducted from the center at national level. There are three other departments (examinations, educational publications, and colleges of education) under the ministry headed by three commissioners.

The National Institute of Education (NIE) established in 1986 by an act of Parliament, took over the divisions under the Ministry of Education which were engaged in professional activities and it came to be regarded as the professional arm of the ministry, performing an advisory role in curriculum design and development, professional training, evaluation, and research functions at national level. Five institutions under the NIE (Staff College for Educational Administration, Institute of Teacher Education, Institute for Distance Education, Higher Institute of English Education, and the Institute of Aesthetic Education) perform the function of training administrators, principals, and teachers. In addition, there are four other areas of activity: curriculum development, educational research, educational technology, and evaluation. NIE is headed by a director-general assisted by directors who are in charge of different divisions. The governing body of the institute is the council headed by the secretary of education and twelve members appointed by the minister.

At sub-national level, the management reforms of 1984 for administrative decentralization and the thirteenth amendment to the Sri Lanka Constitution in 1987 for political decentralization have restructured the organizational setup of the system. The reforms created eight provincial departments of education, each one consisting of a number of divisional offices. Each division will consist of 10-15 clusters of schools which were established on the recommendation of the white paper of 1981. A cluster of schools was to cover a geographical area conducive to rational planning and development of education on an area basis and consisting of about ten schools, both primary and secondary. Each cluster has a core school with a cluster principal who should supervise the other member schools and ensure rational utilization of the available resources. With the transfer of power from the ministry to departments and from provincial officer to divisions, a new structure and organization has started to operate. The system is managed by three service cadres of the Sri Lanka Educational Administrative Service (SLEAS), the Principals' Service, and the Teachers' Service.

The Ministry of Higher Education is headed by the Minister of Higher Education and Scientific Affairs and is assisted by a state minister. The secretary of this ministry is the chairman of the University Grants Commission (UGC) which was created by the University Act of 1978. The main functions of the UGC are planning and coordination of university education conforming to national policy, the apportionment of funds voted by the Parliament to higher educational institutions, the maintenance of academic standards, the regulation of administration in higher educational institutions, and the regulation of admission of students to higher education institutions. The universities are made up of faculties, each comprising several departments and they offer a variety of courses at undergraduate and postgraduate level.

The technical education division which was earlier under the Ministry of Education came under the Ministry of Higher Education in 1978 and is headed by a director. In addition, the Ministry of Labor and the Ministry of Youth Affairs, through the National Apprenticeship Board and National Youth Services Council, share the major responsibility for middle level technical training.

PRIMARY AND SECONDARY EDUCATION

Children enter primary school at the age of five and there is no state organized preschool education. The preschools which number about 200 are voluntary and entirely private, mostly located in urban areas and charge fees prohibitive for the majority of the people. Participation at primary level is high with an enrolment ratio of 103 and nearly half the school population, about 2 million, are in the primary level. As many as 96 per cent of the schools have primary classes and only 21 per cent have only primary classes.

An integrated curriculum was introduced to the primary schools in 1972 with an emphasis on creative activity. Teachers were expected to integrate teaching around themes such as, our homes and people, things we wear, and the world around us. This approach did not mean that the formal basic skills in reading, writing, arithmetic, grammar, and syntax were ignored. The students have time allocated to subject disciplines, mother tongue, mathematics, environmental studies, and creative and aesthetic activities in the first three years and beginning science, physical education, and English are added from grade four.

Textbooks are distributed free and they occupy a significant place in the teaching and learning process at this stage. A scholarship examination held at the end of year five, provides the child an opportunity to go to a better secondary school and also provides financial assistance to able but needy children. But this examination, which schools and parents consider as very important, promoted mechanical drilling with model papers and private tuition and thus tends to defeat the objectives of the primary curriculum.

With the extension of the span of schooling to thirteen years, the resulting structure of secondary education has become 3:3:2. Five years of primary education is followed by three years of junior secondary (6-8), three years of senior secondary (9-11) and the new phase of a two-year collegiate education (12-13). It was felt that the delimitation of a junior secondary phase of three years as the first segment would permit those who leave the system early to obtain an elementary education which will equip them with adequate adaptations to life situations and also provide those who remain, with a sound foundation for further secondary education. It was also envisaged that this arrangement would facilitate the provision of compulsory phase in schooling.

A common curriculum of nine subjects is used for this phase and the subjects are, first language (Sinhalese or Tamil), religion, mathematics, English, science, social studies, aesthetic studies, life skills and health, and physical education. The logistics of the common curriculum rested on the premise that at the termination of this program, the children would be equipped with the knowledge, skills, and attitudes that are basic and fundamental to the concept of general education. At the end of junior secondary level, a grade eight examination has been proposed. The test is to consist of written tests and continuous in-course assessment, where appropriate, and it is to be conducted at the level of the school cluster.

The senior secondary level (years 9-11), the phase two of the secondary, continues to use the common curriculum with some subjects given a degree of specialization. It is done with the transition to the world of work and the needs of those who are intending to proceed beyond this level in mind. At this stage, technical subjects will replace life skills. An array of optional technical subjects such as woodwork, metal work, language, mathematics, science, and social studies are given greater allocation of time as they appear to demand greater concern than the other subjects. Science, mathematics, and social studies, which have emerged by a clustering of different but related traditional subjects, were conceptualized as disciplines leading to the growth of the child than as examination subjects.

Evaluation at this level had been primarily carried out by means of a written examination. It was observed from the beginning of the 1980s that while the double role, certification and selection, has received legitimacy, it has tended to diminish the value of education and to subvert the educational process. To remedy this, it was attempted to evaluate pupil performance in two ways: continuous in-course assessment, and end of course examination. Due to resource constraints, however, this has failed. The General Certificate of Education Ordinary Level (GCE-O.L.) examination is held at the end of year eleven and is the national certificate examination and also the qualification examination for entry to the collegiate level of the school.

The collegiate level (years 12-13) which is the post-general segment of the school, provides education in specialized fields leading to a General Certificate of Education Advanced Level (GCE-A.L.) that will take the pupils not only to higher studies, but also to avenues of employment relevant to their fields of study.

Three curricular streams are available at this level: arts, science, and commerce. A large number of subjects is available and those who do arts will select four subjects related to humanities or social studies while those who do science will select four subjects from physical or biological sciences. All these courses are academically oriented and are designed exclusively for those entering university. During the last two decades it was proposed on two occasions, (in 1972 and 1981), to change the highly academic nature of the curriculum by reconstituting it into two parts: (a) a common core consisting of four subject areas (cultural heritage and the socio-economic environment of Sri Lanka, first language, second language, and work experience through community oriented projects), and (b) the traditional group of subjects from one of the streams. This reform was, however, never implemented. The present course leads to GCE (A.L.) and the selection of students to universities are based on their performance at the above examination and each candidate is permitted two attempts. Selection to universities is highly competitive as only about 5,000 find places in universities, though nearly 30,000 attain the level specified for entry to universities.

HIGHER EDUCATION

Institutions

The present system of university education has its origin in the Colombo Academy which was affiliated to the University of Calcutta in 1859. The external examinations conducted by the above Academy did not meet the demands of higher education and during the last decades of the nineteenth century, a movement to establish a university was started. A subcommittee of the Legislative Council felt that it should be the responsibility of the state and as a result, in 1921, a University College was established affiliated to the University of London. By 1928, a commission was appointed to investigate the issue of transforming the University College into a national university but due to the constitutional reforms of 1931, the establishment of a university was postponed till 1942. By the Ordinance No. 20 of 1942, the University of Ceylon was established by amalgamating Ceylon University College and the Ceylon Medical College.

The University of Ceylon built on British traditions with a restricted intake of students, started to change from the mid-fifties. The declared policy of the government that all those who qualify at the entrance examination had a right to university education and the change in the medium of instruction from English to national languages, Sinhala and Tamil, were the two major factors that influenced the change. Along with this, the government, by an act of Parliament (No. 45 of 1958), elevated two centers of traditional Buddhist learning, "Vidyodaya" and "Vidyalankara" pirivenas to university status.

A significant change in the governance of the universities also occurred with the Higher Education Act No. 20 of 1966, which changed the already existing informal influence of the state over certain aspects of university education to state control. This act introduced a common governing system to all universities. The state control thus exerted was further strengthened by a subsequent act in 1972, which amalgamated all universities into a single university, University of Sri Lanka, reducing the existing ones to the status of campuses.

A change of government in 1977 led to the restoration of the earlier traditions and practices associated with the University Ordinance of 1942 and by the Act No. 16 of 1978, a University Grants Commission (UGC) was created with a chairman and four members. The Ministry of Higher Education could direct the UGC in pursuance of national policy in matters such as finance, university admissions, and medium of instruction; order all or any of the activities of the administration of universities to be investigated; and intervene in the event of a breakdown in university affairs.

Within a period of five decades, the number of universities has increased to nine: University of Colombo (1942) with faculties of arts, science, law, education, and medicine; University of Peradeniya (1942) with faculties of arts, science, engineering, medicine, and agriculture; University of Kelaniya (1959) with faculties of humanities, social sciences, and science; University of Sri Jayawardenapura (1959) with faculties of applied sciences, arts, and management; University of Moratuwa (1972) with faculties in engineering and architecture; University of Jaffna (1979) with faculties of arts, sciences, and medicine; University of Ruhuna (1984) with faculties of humanities, social sciences, medicine, and agriculture; Eastern University (1986) with faculties of agriculture, management, science, and cultural studies; and Open University with faculties of humanities, social sciences, and engineering technology. Student enrollment (1987) varied from 312 in the Eastern University to 12,550 in the Open University. Total student enrollment (1987) in the universities was 35,438, of which 37 percent (mostly the Open University students) were external students. Also 45 percent of the total student population at the universities were females.

Undergraduate Studies

The universities offer two types of first degree courses: first, a general degree of three years where students read three subjects and second, a special degree of four years in one specialized subject. For some special degrees, students have to offer a subsidiary subject. Medicine and engineering offer only one type of course and the duration is five and four years respectively. Most of the degrees are taken in two parts. The academic year of the Sri Lankan universities starts in October and is of three terms ending in June or July.

The academic staff in the universities are graded on the British pattern. Those recruited to the lowest grade as assistance lecturers should have a first degree with a class and are confirmed when he/she obtains an approved postgraduate qualification in the relevant subject area. All the staff have a probationary period of three years but once they are confirmed, they have tenure until the age of retirement, which is 65. The vacant posts are advertised in the local press and there is a University Services Appeals Board, independent of UGC, which acts as a final body of appeal against decision on disciplinary matters and in the redress of grievances with regard to appointments and promotions. All emoluments are tax free and all academic staff are entitled to sabbatical leave on full pay on the basis of one year for twenty-one terms or seven years of service.

The student admissions became a political issue from the 1970s when the government introduced an admissions policy based on the standardization of marks by medium and district quotas based on population. This scheme was later given up. The scheme now followed is for the top 30 percent of the students to be placed on an all-island merit list based on the aggregate of marks attained. This is followed by a second category of 65 percent on a district quotas based on population percentages, and a third category of 5 percent for specified underprivileged areas. When admissions are determined on the second and the third categories, the aggregate of marks vary from district to district but within the district the criteria is merit based on the marks obtained.

University education is free and as such no tuition fees are charged. There is now a scheme of scholarships awarded by the state *(Mahapola Scheme)* on the basis of merit to those who are in need of financial assistance. Nearly half the number of students receive these scholarships. The earlier idea of residential universities is now not encouraged by the state.

Two issues, one related to the establishment of a degree awarding institution by the private sector leading to a privatization of higher education and the other, a restriction of student unions in the recent past have threatened the functioning of universities since 1987.

Advanced Studies and Research

All the universities conduct courses at postgraduate level and award higher degrees and diplomas. The universities of Colombo and Peradeniya offer most of the courses at master's and doctoral levels in a number of subject areas including arts, science, law, education, commerce, business administration, agriculture, engineering, and medicine. The other universities which were established later are also building up courses at this level and offer courses in a restricted number of areas according to the facilities available to them. Generally the instruction is on an individual level and all courses usually call for a dissertation or thesis in addition to set papers in the selected area of study. A recent innovation is to work on structured courses at this level and this is being experimented within the provision of courses in agriculture and medicine.

The applicants for higher degrees must normally hold an appropriate first degree with at least second class honors from a recognized university. Those with a good master's degree in the relevant field are also allowed to proceed to doctoral studies. The average duration of a master's degree is two years and doctoral studies require three years full-time. Most faculties now allow candidates to follow higher degree courses as part-time or external candidates taking a longer period of time as required by the individual faculties.

A significant feature at this level is the establishment of postgraduate institutes to meet the needs of high-level manpower. Three such institutes, the Institute of Postgraduate Medicine at the University of Colombo, the Postgraduate Institute of Agriculture in the University of Peradeniya and the Postgraduate Institute of Management of the University of Sri Jayawardenapura, offer facilities for postgraduate training and research. Buddhist and Pali University established in 1982 also offers higher degrees with the main objective of promoting Buddhist studies both in Sri Lanka and abroad. The language of instruction and examination are Sinhala, Tamil, or English.

Diplomas are also offered and they are of nine to twelve months duration and the students are expected to attend lectures and seminars.

At postdoctoral level, D.Litt and D.Sc. are awarded by the Universities of Colombo, and Peradeniya, and the Buddhist and Pali University on published work of conspicuous merit in the areas of arts, science, and Buddhist studies.

Research in education in Sri Lanka has been conducted in the past by universities, private research organizations, and individual scholars. Most of this research were products of postgraduate study. Though the need to establish an organization to conduct and promote research in educational theory and practice with a view to improving the methods of teaching was recognized as early as in 1947 (Ordinance No. 26 of 1947), there is little evidence that the intention of the legislature in providing for educational research had been carried out.

Research was not a function of the Department of Education or the Ministry of Education until the establishment of the National Institute of Education in 1986 with a research division was started to achieve the major objectives of conducting and promoting studies on education. Establishment of this unit served to meet a long felt need for a research body acting in coordination with the educational system, providing a scientific information base for well-informed decision making at all levels of education namely, policy making, planning, and implementation.

Training and Vocational Education

Technical and vocational education is provided by a number of agencies under the control of different ministries and departments in the country and the programs can be broadly classified under three headings: professional engineering education at degree and postgraduate levels, technical education for technicians, and technical/vocational education at craft level.

Universities of Peradeniya and Moratuwa offer degree courses in engineering and technology. Intake for these courses are only from GCE (A.L.) qualified candidates with science and mathematics. The Engineering Faculty of the Open University offers distance education programs in engineering leading to the award of degrees in technology with specialization in civil, electrical, computer, and mechanical engineering. These courses are open to those employed in engineering with a diploma or equivalent qualification. The Institute of Engineers conduct certificate courses equivalent to degree courses in the non-formal mode.

Twenty-four technical colleges, controlled by the Ministry of Higher Education offer diplomas and certificate courses in a number of disciplines including engineering, business studies, agriculture, commerce, and stenography. Vocational training at craft level is provided by a large number of ministries as one of their functions and in addition, cooperative bodies, *Sarvodaya Shramadana Sangamaya*, and private agencies also offer courses. These courses vary very mildly in terms of their aims, duration, level and also mode of training. The National Apprenticeship Board (NAB) provides a training scheme which can be distinguished from general or in-service vocational training described above.

Teacher Education

According to the 1986 school census, there were 143,390 teachers in Sri Lankan schools. Out of this, 32,867 were graduate teachers and 110,529 non-graduates but only 13.5 per cent of the graduate and 74.5 per cent of the non-graduate teachers were professionally trained. This indicates that nearly 40 per cent of the teachers have not undergone any professional training.

This situation is a direct result of the practice of appointing teachers without any training to schools and providing them the initial training after they have taught for sometime. Selection to the limited number of places in teachers' colleges and universities were done on the basis of their seniority in service.

Three universities (the University of Colombo which has a Faculty of Education and the Universities of Peradeniya and Jaffna with Departments of Education) provide postgraduate teacher education courses. The output of both the one-year full-time and the two-year part-time courses of all three universities is very low. The Bachelor of Education degree, the only pre-service teacher education course that was conducted by the University of Colombo and the University of Peradeniya was discontinued in 1982. At present, therefore, there is no provision for pre-service training of graduate teachers in Sri Lanka.

The rapid increase of graduate teachers recruited in the 1980s made it necessary to expand the provision of teacher education for graduate teachers. This led to the introduction of a Diploma in Education course by the Open University which is conducted by the distance mode and which uses regional centers for contact sessions and the organization of teaching practice. At present the intake is 700 per year. The National Institute of Education, in response to the above need, inaugurated a Postgraduate Certificate in Education (PGCE) course of one-year's duration equivalent to the Diploma in Education. A mixed strategy of distance material, contact sessions in the regional centers, and school-based teaching practice is used. The present intake is 1400 per year. The arrangements made in both the above courses benefited the school system as teachers were not released full-time and they were now able to follow the courses while continuing to teach in their respective schools.

By 1984, as an outcome of a clear policy on teacher recruitment, it was decided to appoint only those with three GCE (A.L.) passes as non-graduate teachers. Along with this, colleges of education were established to provide a two-year pre-service teacher education course. Seven of the ten proposed colleges have already been started and they conduct a three-year course for both primary and secondary school teachers. The first two years are in the college and are residential. All expenses of board, lodging, and tuition are met by the state. In the third year, the trainees are appointed to a school on internship and are paid a stipend. The curriculum consists of four broad areas of professional education, an area of specialization, general components, and teaching practice. Both written examinations and continuous assessment are used in the award of the certificates which are of two levels, merit and pass.

ISSUES AND TRENDS

The attempt to enforce universalization of primary education in Sri Lanka is one of the major concerns today. The principle of universal education is built into the constitution and the chapter of Directive Principles of State Policy and Fundamental Duties assures the right to universal and equal access to education at all levels. Major factors hindering the achievement of universalization are the non-enrollment and dropping-out, the latter partly caused by the high rate of repetition. The policy objectives of the Ministry of Education for achieving universalization of primary education are positive discrimination in favor of disadvantaged areas in the provision of facilities, enrichment of the primary curriculum, rationalization of the school network to optimize resources, development of the management capabilities of the school heads, and employment of non-formal modalities.

Another trend is the stress laid on continuing education. Although provision of education has widened, varying economic and social factors continue to keep a portion of school-age children out of school. School-based non-formal education units for skill development have been started for those who have not benefited from formal school and an island-wide network of "open schools" for those who have left the formal system has also been proposed. The content and objectives of the skill development program is geared to train the young in skills required for the local labor market and self employment.

A continuing trend is programing education for the "world of work" and projects have been repeatedly introduced during the last three decades. "Work experience" in the 1960s, "prevocational studies" in the 1970s, and "life skills" in the 1980s as compulsory components in the secondary curriculum, attempted to achieve a vocational orientation of education at the secondary level and to prepare the child more purposefully for life and work in society.

A recent trend is to provide a longer period of secondary education. The restructuring has resulted in an eight-year school with a 3:3:2 pattern. The delimitation of the junior secondary phase of three years would, it is felt, permit those who leave the system early, to obtain an elementary education which would equip them with adequate adaptation to life situations, and also provide for others who remain at school a sound foundation for continuing education. It was implied that this phasing would also facilitate provision of the compulsory phase in education. In addition, the decision to extend general education till year eleven, and to have a separate collegiate phase implied an emphasis on general education which was to be provided for a large majority as against the segment for collegiate education which was to be more academically oriented and to which only a minority would have access.

When the impact of scientific and technological progress is considered, the need to pay special attention to the development of educational communications technology has been recognized in Sri Lanka. The two main types used are audio-visual technology such as radio, television, and video; and information technology, particularly, computers. A division for education media has been set up in the NIE and a beginning is made to use broadcasting and television for the benefit of GCE (A.L.) students. An attempt has also been made to bring in modern technology to schools with the introduction of computer assisted learning (CAL). A new project unit has been set up at the NIE and 160 schools were selected to be included in a new computer education program.

Another noteworthy trend in Sri Lanka is the increasing emphasis placed on science education. As there was a dearth of scientifically and technically qualified personnel, science education was increasingly perceived as the means of social mobility and economic success. The stress on science education has made its impact felt even at primary level as in grade four and five, a new area of study, "beginning science," has been introduced. At the secondary level, science came to be taught as an integrated subject of the common curriculum and it was envisaged that the new approach would permit the child to grasp patterns and generalizations and to form a sound foundation for the study of science at a greater depth subsequently. At higher levels, centers of excellence have been proposed which would function as centers of national research. One such center, the Arthur C. Clarke Center for Modern Technology has already been established.

The most significant trend during the recent past towards improving efficiency and participation of management is the decentralization of educational administration. While the management reforms of 1984 attempted to decentralize at regional and sub-regional levels by creating structures and delegating functions, it is with the thirteenth amendment to the constitution in 1988 and the setting up of provincial departments, that several functions were devolved to the regions. It is believed that, through decentralization, regional disparities in education can be reduced more effectively as it will allow closer monitoring and supervision of programs. Linked to this, a training program for administrators and school principals has been started and an attempt is being made to get the parents involved in school management by their participation in School Development Societies and in proposed School Boards.

In the present context of the efforts towards development, the future challenge of education is represented by a number of concerns. In order to achieve the goal of equality in educational opportunity, it becomes vital to improve the capabilities of the poor to participate in education. To ensure equity and social justice in education, a continuing challenge is posed for mobilization of resources to give greater priority to the needs of the underprivileged. A formidable challenge which demands urgent attention is to use education as a means of creating national unity and solidarity by integrating different ethnic groups into the mainstream of national life by a common system of education to achieve unity in diversity. Further, bringing about a fit between the values and belief systems embedded in the indigenous culture and modernity generated by science and technology, has also become crucial. The challenge here is to develop the capacity to critically appraise tradition and modernity to draw out what is best and relevant in both for growth and development. A final challenge is posed by the need for a development-oriented management style in place of the bureaucratic style that had persisted without responding to the demands of the changes and reforms.

BIBLIOGRAPHY

Ariyadasa, K. D. *Management of Educational Reforms in Sri Lanka.* Paris: UNESCO, 1976.

Asian Development Bank. *Sri Lanka Education Sector Study.* Manila, 1988.

De Silva, W. A., and Gunawardena, C. *Educational Policies and Change after 1977.* Colombo: National Institute of Education, Sri Lanka, 1986.

Government of Ceylon. Sessional Paper I of 1962. *Interim Report of the National Education Commission.* Colombo: Government Press, 1962.

Gunawardena, G. B. *National Study on Secondary Education in Sri Lanka.* Colombo: National Institute of Education, Sri Lanka, 1988.

Jayasuriya, J. E. *Education Before and After Independence.* Colombo: Associated Educational Publisher, 1976.

Jayaweera, Swarna. *Educational Policies and Change from the Mid-Twentieth Century to 1977.* Colombo: National Institute of Education, Sri Lanka, 1988.

Lofstadt, T. S., S. Jayaweera, and A. Little. *Human Resources Development in Sri Lanka: An Analysis of Education and Training.* Stockholm: SIDA, 1985.

Ministry of Education, Sri Lanka. *Proposals for a National System of Education.* Colombo: Government Press, 1964.

Ministry of Education, Sri Lanka. *Education in Ceylon: A Centenary Volume. Part I-III.* Colombo: Government Press, 1969.

Ministry of Education, Sri Lanka. *Towards Relevance in Education: Report of the Educational Reform Committee.* Colombo: Government Press, 1979.

Ministry of Education, Sri Lanka. *Proposals for Reform.* Colombo: Government Press, 1981.

Ministry of Education, Sri Lanka. *Report of the Management Reforms in The Ministry of Education.* Colombo: Government Press, 1984.

Nystrom, Kjell. *Schooling and Disparities: A Study of Regional Differences in Sri Lanka.* Stockholm: Institute of International Education, University of Stockholm, 1985.

The World Bank. *Education and Training Sector Memorandum.* South Asian Projects Department, Education and Human Resources Division, World Bank, 1986.

SWAZILAND

by
Robert A. Sargent
Dean, Faculty of Education
University of Swaziland, Swaziland

BACKGROUND

Formal education in Swaziland commenced with the advent of Christian missions in the nineteenth century. Previously the Swazi people utilized a traditional informal approach to educating the younger generation (Nxumalo 1976; 1989). However, with the stimulus of Christian missionary work, and the wide acceptance of Christianity, the development of formal education was popularly accepted. By 1906 the first national school was created for elementary education. Prior to the 1940s, however, secondary and higher education had to be sought outside the country. After 1950 there was a sharp proliferation of missionary, national, government, and private secondary schools. By 1975, seven years after independence, there were sixty-eight secondary schools with a total enrollment of 16,198 pupils (Education Statistics 1986). The expansion of secondary and high school education continued rapidly, and by 1986 there were 100 secondary and high schools with a total enrolment of 30,589 students. This rapid expansion continues and can be projected well into the future (Sargent 1986).

PRIMARY AND SECONDARY EDUCATION

Students normally enter primary school at age six and follow a seven-year program leading to the standard five examination at the end of primary education. Success in this examination, allows the student to apply for admission to secondary school. The secondary program is three years, leading to the Junior Certificate Examination. Success at this level allows students to seek admission to the two-year high school program leading to the Cambridge Overseas School Certificate (COSC) Ordinary Level examination. For the first three years of primary school, the medium of instruction is Siswati except for a few English medium schools, but thereafter all education takes place in English.

The government policy supports universal primary education (Magagala and Putsoa 1986: 41), although at present only 80 percent of all primary school-age children attend school (Sargent 1986). Efforts are being made to provide universal primary education, and discussions are presently under way to implement a program of nine years of basic education for all. Education is an expensive item in the family budget as each child is charged school fees right through primary, secondary, and high school. Fees vary slightly from school to school, depending upon resources and development plans. For example, over and above the set rates for school fees, parents may be expected to contribute to school building funds, and other special costs. Also, each child must be provided with a school uniform and books by the parents. Thus, education becomes a major expense for many families. The National Education Review Commission (NERCOM) has recommended that the first four years of primary education should be made free (NERCOM 1985) but even the implementation of those recommendations will only provide partial relief to parents. As regards enrollment, the 1986 statistics showed following: primary school-142,206; secondary school-24,271; high school-6,218; and total enrollment-172,695.

HIGHER EDUCATION

Institutions

The University of Swaziland as it is presently constituted, evolved from the system operational under the administration of the High Commission Trust for Territories of Basutoland, Bechuanaland, and Swaziland. The opening of the University of Basutoland, Bechunaland, and Swaziland (UBBS) in January 1964 led to the establishment of the main campus at Pius XII College in Roma, Lesotho, with an enrollment of 188 students. The UBBS became the University of Botswana, Lesotho, and Swaziland (UBLS) in 1966 with the independence of Botswana and Lesotho; and by 1970 it had an enrollment of 402 students. The first degrees were conferred in April 1967. Expansion of higher education continued into the early 1970s, particularly with the founding of the Faculty of Agriculture at the Luyengo campus in Swaziland in 1972.

However, on 20 October 1975 Lesotho suddenly withdrew from UBLS and established the National University of Lesotho. After the 1975-76 academic year, Botswana and Swaziland reconstituted the institution as the University of Botswana and Swaziland (UBS), which remained in operation until 1982. The two countries realized from the outset that in the long term the two national colleges of UBS would eventually develop into independent national universities. The 1975-85 administrative agreement recognized these national aspirations, and with the eventual rise in student numbers justifying two national universities after the 1981-82 academic year, two separate institutions came into existence: University of Botswana and University of Swaziland. Cooperation continues, however, particularly in the areas of agriculture and postgraduate training, but the two universities are basically committed to training nationals for the individual human resource needs of each country.

The COSC Ordinary Level examination results establish the criteria for selecting students for admission to higher education in the university and in colleges. The standard of admission in the 1980s demand at least a second class pass in order to even qualify for consideration for any of these institutions (Sargent 1988). Swaziland has only one university, which includes the Luyengo campus which houses the Faculty of Agriculture, and the Kwaluseni campus which includes the faculties of education, humanities, social science, and science. In 1989 there were at least two applicants for each vacancy in all first-year programs at UNISWA. Given the constraints imposed by the shortage of hostel space, classrooms, laboratories, and other physical restrictions, the potential for growth is rather limited. Only 436 students were admitted to the first year of the full-time two-year diploma and four-year bachelor's degree programs in 1989.

In addition to the full-time programs, the university offers, on a part-time basis, various certificates (in pre-vocational agriculture, accounting and business studies, and adult education) and diplomas (adult education, and primary education). A postgraduate diploma in education is also available.

Currently there are five affiliated colleges within the structure of the Ministry of Education but under the umbrella of the university. The Board of Affiliated Institutions, chaired by the vice-chancellor of the University of Swaziland, is the governing body for these colleges and controls admissions, curricula, and examinations in the colleges. The five colleges comprise William Pitcher Teacher Training College (TTC), Nazarene (TTC), Ngwane (TTC), the Swaziland College of Technology (SCOT), and the Institute of Health Sciences. Programs are generally of two or three years duration, depending upon training requirements. The majority of school teachers are products of the Teacher Training Colleges. For example, in 1986 less then 1 percent of the 4,290 primary school teachers were university graduates, and only 35 percent of all secondary/high school teachers had a degree qualification (Ministry of Education 1986). Thus with only a small cadre of degree trained teachers graduating from UNISWA each year who generally assume positions in the TTC's or as headmasters of schools, the situation in schools will persist well into the future. The SCOT trains commercial education teachers to certificate level, and offers a wide variety of vocational courses. The certificate and diploma programs currently offered by the institutions affiliated to the university include certificates in home economics and commercial education; and diplomas in teaching, nursing, midwifery, and health inspection.

The university is primarily funded by a government grant under subvention from the Ministry of Education, but retains its semi-autonomous status in financial and academic matters. It is accountable to the nation through the minister of education and to the chancellor, His Majesty King Mswati III. Through tuition and residence fees, the university also helps to meets its recurrent costs, but financial constraints have forced serious cutbacks from the university development plan (1987-91). Some capital development projects have been funded by international donors, including recent donations by the European Economic Community (EEC) for classrooms, laboratories, and other basic infrastructural requirements. The government is providing funds for an expansion of the refectory. Recently the university also received a generous donation of much needed land from His Majesty King Mswati III. This land is now being incorporated and utilized for planned physical plant expansion as and when capital funds become available.

Undergraduate Studies

As previously indicated, admission to the university is based upon the COSC Ordinary Level examination results. This examinations is administered by the Cambridge Overseas Syndicate, (U.K.) and is normally written in November/-December. The results are released in March when students begin to apply for university entrance. The minimum requirement for entry to degree programs is Cambridge Overseas School Certificate in the first or second division with credit in English language. Individual programs may specify additional requirements. For example, the Faculty of Science demands credits in "hard" sciences and mathematics in addition to the prescribed minimum. The Bachelor of Commerce program also requires a credit in Ordinary Level mathematics. The competition for entry to these two programs is particularly intense, as many of the best high school graduates are competing to study science or commerce at UNISWA. Other faculties and programs in the Faculty of Social Science have lower cut-off points, but the minimum requirements specified in the university regulations are by no means assurance of admission to any degree program.

The entrance requirement for the full-time diploma programs at UNISWA is a Cambridge Overseas School Certificate in at least the third division. Here again, the number of places is limited and recently it has been largely the second division passes which have been admitted to the university and colleges.

The closing date for all applications is 1st April. All applications received prior to the deadline are ranked by the individual faculty tutors, and the information is prepared for final deliberations by the admissions committee. Applicants are informed in writing, by the registrar, of the decisions as soon as possible, particularly for programs which have a pre-entry requirement.

Two programs, Bachelor of Science and Bachelor of Agriculture, require students to take a pre-entry course preceding the normal academic year. The applicants for these programs are usually considered by the admissions committee in the first week of April, and the successful students enter the science pre-entry course (SPEC) or the agriculture pre-entry course (APEC) in late April. These courses run until late July and provide basic foundations in practical science and agriculture, upgrade knowledge in both areas, and generally prepare students for the degree programs in the two faculties.

All students, including those who have taken the pre-entry course, register in the third week of August for the four-year degree program. The academic year runs for thirty-two weeks divided into two sixteen-week semesters. All students who register for first-year studies are required to take a full course in academic communication skills offered by the Department of English. This is basically a remedial program designed to bridge the large gap between high school education and first year university work. It is a compulsory course, and no student may proceed until academic communication skills has been passed.

The degree students at UNISWA currently follow a double major program within a particular faculty. Thus, a student in the Faculty of Science in the second year of study, will select two science majors from the departments of physics, chemistry, biology, geography, and mathematics. Students in the Faculty of Social Science can select from economics, political science, administrative studies, sociology, accounting and management, or statistics as their majors. The Faculty of Humanities offers majors in history, English, African languages, geography, and theology and religious studies. The programs in education, agriculture, and some social science courses (e.g. law) follow a slightly different format. In the Faculty of Education, students are offered a double major in education and one other school teaching subject. Students in agriculture and law take courses directly related to those specialities.

In the early 1990s, UNISWA plans to add an optional single subject major for Part II students (third and fourth year). The best students in Part I (first and second year) will have the option to select a single subject major and to follow a specialized course in only one content area. Prospective students for the single subject major will have to maintain at least a 60 percent average through Part I. New courses are planned to be offered in the areas of computer studies, French, and communication studies. These will come on stream in the early 1990s provided budgetary constraints are overcome.

In general, Swazis interested in postgraduate studies pursue master's and doctoral education abroad in countries such as Britain, Canada, and the U.S.A., on completion of their first degree at UNISWA.

All full-and part-time, diploma and degree students pay annual tuition fees which vary from US$400-450 for local students and US$1,550-1,600 for foreign students.

Swazi students are usually funded by the Scholarship Board for tuition, books (US$110 per year) and residence fees (US$830 per year). Given the restricted number of hostel spaces, however, only about 80 percent of the total student body at UNISWA is housed on campus. This creates some problems because there is only very limited capacity in the surrounding community to absorb off-campus students. This problem of housing has reached a critical stage. It also effects the ability of the university to attract non-Swazi students. The quota of 5 percent foreign students has in recent years not been completely filled. The foreign students who are accepted and who register are usually funded by agencies such as the United Nations Commission for Refugees, or Commonwealth organizations. There are very few privately funded students in any of the institutions of higher learning in Swaziland.

Student welfare is administered by the dean of student affairs. The student representative council (SRC) has the prime function of representing student opinion on campus, providing an official channel of communication between students and university officers, and encouraging social and sporting activities.

Unfortunately, only limited sporting, social, and recreational facilities exist on campus, and in most cases sports equipment and other recreational facilities must be provided by the students themselves. The SRC and the administration recognize twelve sporting clubs on the Kwaluseni campus and eight at Luyengo, which provide a variety of sports: football, athletics, boxing, chess, darts, hockey, karate, volleyball, tennis, table tennis, softball and basketball. Other recreational pursuits are also limited, and may include ballroom dancing, traditional dance, debates, and so on. Facilities include three football fields, six tennis courts, four volleyball courts outdoors, and a large multipurpose hall which can accommodate indoor basketball, volleyball, and other sports and recreational activities. Booking demands for the hall have increased, and some activities must be scheduled after midnight or very early in the mornings if they are to be accommodated. Films are organized by the Kwaluseni Film Society and shown biweekly. However, the limitations on recreational and sporting activities are quite serious, particularly as common room facilities in the hostels have been taken over as dormitories to house students, and the use of the multipurpose hall increases.

Both Kwaluseni and Luyengo campuses have a health clinic run by qualified nurses, together with weekly visits by the university doctor. Students and staff can also obtain medical attention at the Luyengo Government Clinic or the Raleigh Fitkin Memorial Hospital in Manzini, a town about twelve kilometers from the Kwaluseni campus. The University runs a refectory which serves meals to all students.

Advanced Studies and Research

The University of Swaziland is on the verge of entering into a new era where master's degree education will become fairly widespread across all programs. The Faculty of Education has, for a number of years, offered a Master in Education (M.Ed.) degree, and this has recently been revised and expanded to better meet the needs of the country. Additionally, the Department of Economics is presently structuring an M.A. program which it hopes to launch in the early 1990s. Currently, most students seeking postgraduate training must proceed overseas. At present a number of opportunities for research in all areas of potential study are very rich and varied. But it should be noted that research in all areas in Swaziland is coordinated by the National Research Council which was established by the Cabinet in 1988. The Council operates a number of subcommittees which provide approval of all research applications in the various subject areas. Thus, the education subcommittee, chaired by the permanent secretary of the Ministry of Education, scrutinizes and approves all proposed research in educational matters. The other subcommittees operate in the same way. Also there are a number of institutions and agencies that conduct and assist with research in the country. These include the Swaziland Institute for Educational Research, Swaziland Educational Research Association, Social Science Research Unit, Economics Association of Swaziland, and the Rural Development Research Project.

Teaching Staff

Within the five faculties of the university there are (in 1989) 166 academic posts, which includes staff in the library and the Division of Extramural Services, and a number of projects provide another ten supernumerary positions within the University. These projects include the Science Pre-Entry Program and the Social Science Research Unit. The central administrative functions are performed by a staff of sixteen in the Bursary and Registry bringing the total academic and administrative staff population to 182.

The university follows a policy of localization, aiming for an 80 percent local staffing situation by the early 1990s. Local staff are recruited as staff development fellows or teaching assistants after their first degree, and spend between one and two years in their department before proceeding for postgraduate studies overseas. As of 1988, approximately 60 percent of all academic and administrative posts have been localized. Advertisements for lecturers, senior lecturers, assistant professors and professors are published locally and internationally. Currently academic staff include representatives from approximately fourteen different countries including Canada, U.S.A., England, Belgium, Holland, India, Ghana, Uganda, Tanzania, Nigeria, Zambia, Malawi, Ethiopia, and Swaziland.

ISSUES AND TRENDS

There are a number of issues and problems facing education at all levels in Swaziland. These are somewhat interlinked and generally relate to expansion of education, "brain drain", examinations, and training for employment.

Expansion of Education and the "Brain Drain"

The demand for educational places at secondary, high school, and tertiary education has definitely outstripped the supply. The inability of the various sectors and institutions to service the needs of the country in several areas has become increasingly apparent. The growing demand for education has generated a response from communities through the construction of both secondary and high schools throughout the country. In 1988 sixteen new secondary/high schools were opened, which require the Ministry of Education to provide qualified teachers. However, the shortfall in the training of teachers has created serious problems in the provision of secondary and high school education. Swaziland in 1989 is short of qualified teachers, and in desperation has turned to the recruitment of form five (high school) graduates to fill many of the vacancies because, in part there has been a rapid net outflow of educated personnel from the school system and tertiary institutions; a process that seems to be accelerating. The problem is compounded by the regional disparities in wages and conditions of service which result in an exodus of qualified personnel away from Swaziland.

Localization of Examinations

There is a powerful movement operating in Swaziland at the moment, initiated by the National Examinations Council, towards localization of all important examinations, particularly the Ordinary Level examinations. This is coupled with the development of a nine-year basic education program (Bishop 1981), which would ultimately remove standard five examinations, and offer locally constructed and administered examinations at the end of the nine years, to replace the present Junior Certificate Examinations. The high school structure will be of two years duration with a localized Ordinary Level examination; a development which is linked to the localization of the curriculum content in high school for all subjects. This move would require intensive training of local examiners, in-servicing of teachers, and development of new curriculum materials, textbooks, etc.

Education and Training for Employment

Concerns are frequently expressed by the public and in the Parliament about the problems of unemployment for school leavers in Swaziland. This is a growing problem especially as employment opportunities remain rather limited. Academic programs for high school students are presently not tailored for future employment opportunities. This has led to the development of prevocational and vocational education at secondary and high school levels, initially on a restricted basis. Interestingly enough, university and college graduates do not at present experience similar problems in finding employment. Over the past three or four years only one tertiary program, law, has produced graduates who have had difficulty in finding jobs.

BIBLIOGRAPHY

Bishop, G. D. *The Status and Development of Education in the Kingdom of Swaziland*: Education and Training Sector Review. Mbabane: Ministry of Education, Economic Planning and Statistics, 1981.

Dlamini, M. *The Philosophy, Policies, and Objectives of Imbokodvo National Movement*. Mbabane, n.d.

Magagula, C. and B. Putsoa. "Educational Policies in Swaziland -An Historical and Critical Appraisal." Unpublished paper. UNISWA, 1986.

Ministry of Education. *Education Statistics in Brief, 1968-1986*. Mbabane; Government of Swaziland, 1986.

Ministry of Education. *Reform Through Dialogue, National Educational Review Commission Report*. Mbabane: Government of Swaziland, 1985.

Nxumalo, A. M. "The Indigenous Education of the Swazi and Its Implications for Modern Educational Development." Unpublished paper presented to the Boleswa Educational Research Symposium, University of Botswana, Gabarone, 7-11 August, 1989.

Sargent, R. A. "Projections and Policies in Swaziland's Education System." *Swaziland Institute for Educational Research Bulletin*. No. 7 (1986).

Sargent, R. A. "Predictive Value of O-Level Results for University Admission: A case study of the faculty of Humanities at UNISWA." *Swaziland Institute for Educational Research Bulletin*. No. 9 (1988).

SWEDEN

by
Urban S. Dahllof
Professor of Education
Uppsala University, Sweden

BACKGROUND

As in so many other European countries, the present Swedish system of education represents a merger between two quite different traditions. The oldest one started in the medieval ages with cathedral schools (or grammar schools) serving as preparatory institutions for higher learning which in the beginning took place in Paris and other continental universities. But in 1477 the pope consented to give a charter to a Swedish university in Uppsala, the first one in the Nordic countries, founded two years before that of Copenhagen in Denmark. The subsequent development of higher learning in Sweden with universities at Dorpat (the present Tartu in Estonia-1632), Turku in Finland (1640), Greifswald in Northern Germany (incorporated during the thirty-year war) and Lund (1668) was closely connected with Sweden's expanding political power. When the present southern provinces had been taken from Denmark, it was explicitly stated that the new university of Lund was erected in order to facilitate the "Swedization" of the new provinces by training clergy and civil servants loyal to the Swedish crown.

Later on, the curricula of the grammar schools were widened to meet the needs of science and the demand for practical skills in trade and industry. By about 1905 the grammar school was formally divided into two separate sections, *realskolan* (the lower secondary school) and *gymnasiet* (the upper secondary school), each ending up with a certificate. The upper secondary school certificate *(studentexamen)* provided the right to study at a university.

With respect to the schooling of the general population, it was first the duty of the parish clerk and organist to see to it that everybody could read well enough to study the bible, but in 1842 the first act of compulsory elementary schooling was introduced. After 1905 the lower secondary school curricula was built upon grade three of the primary school, but from 1928, transition to secondary schooling could be made either after grade four or grade six. Since the primary school lasted for six years (after 1936, a seventh grade became compulsory) the two systems were running parallel to each other for three or four years. The increasing social demand for secondary education as well as ideological arguments called for the abandonment of the dual system with parallel primary and secondary schools and the prolongation of compulsory schooling to nine years. In 1950 a principal decision was taken about a nine-year comprehensive school common for all Swedish youth which after an experimental period was introduced nationally from 1962.

743

Structure

In Sweden, formal schooling does not start until the age of seven, and the comprehensive school finishes at the age of sixteen. The certificate from grade nine does not have the status of any formal exam, but marks in all subjects are required for entry to the upper secondary school or high school. Also the upper secondary school was later reformed into an integrated high school with academic as well as vocational training programs organized in a system of study lines, each oriented towards a certain competence base (from 1971). At the post-compulsory level, education aims at serving the four-fold purpose of providing continued general education for most of the population with an emphasis on schooling for citizenship; promoting social equality in the enrollment in upper secondary and higher education; training professional and other skilled manpower for the labor market; and preparing students for research.

The consensus among political parties, employers, and labor unions about industrial rationalization has lead to a heavy emphasis on the principles of life-long learning and recurrent education, from programs for vocational retraining to specific schemes for adults in higher education.

From an international point of view, the educational system has several interesting features: Transfer from high school to college does not take place until the age of nineteen; The common curriculum core is broad both at high school and at university; There are no private colleges or universities, and almost no private high schools; Tuition is free; Credits from full study programs can be generally transferred between colleges and universities; There is no general rank-order between universities and the informal status of an institution varies with the subject field and the department; Most programs for a basic degree take 3 years; Certain master's programs are offered only in certain subjects and only to students from countries outside Sweden; and The norm for a doctoral program is four years, one and one-half years for course work and two and one-half years for the dissertation.

PRIMARY AND SECONDARY EDUCATION

All Swedish youth from ages 9-16 belong to the comprehensive school, run by municipal school boards (the state pays the teachers' salaries). A national curriculum guide prescribes the overall objectives and the allocation of teaching time to subject fields.

Up to now, the primary part of the new comprehensive school may be said to have encompassed the first six grades, since the pupils have been taught by class-teachers trained to teach all subjects in the grades 1-3 and 4-6, called the lower and the middle section respectively. The upper section from grade seven corresponded most closely to lower secondary education since the teachers were trained only in 3-4 subjects. The sharp break from a one-teacher system in grade six to sometimes more than five new teachers in grade seven did, however, create problems. So now an "overlapping" teacher system is introduced with two teacher categories, one for grade 1-7 and one for grade 4-9 in the comprehensive school.

A certain portion (12 percent) of the time in grade 7-9 is required to be devoted to thematic studies, and another portion (11 percent) is optional, between either a second foreign language or any other type of study provided by the local school. English is compulsory from grade three or four throughout the comprehensive school. Those who chose a second foreign language have an option between German and French. Thus, before entry to high school, every pupil has to take a total of twenty-one weekly hours of English distributed over five or six years, which means 3.5-4 hours per week every year or a total of about 650 lessons. The corresponding amount for those who take the second foreign language for three years is eleven weekly hours or 340 lessons of German or French in grade 7-9.

About 90 percent of the comprehensive school leavers go straight to high school but they have to apply and gain entry to the various study programs on the basis of marks from the final grade nine, on a normalized scale 1-5. Standardized achievements in Swedish, English, and mathematics provide the basic information about the general performance level of each class.

The high school is organized in five three-year academic programs and fifteen vocationally oriented two-year programs. The former are directly preparatory for entrance to colleges and universities with an emphasis on humanities, social studies, natural sciences, technology, and economics respectively. The latter two lead also to labor market competence as a middle level engineer or economist. Most of the two-year programs aim at a broad vocational competence rather than a specific vocation. All study programs have a common core of subjects aimed at strengthening the competence for citizenship (e.g. by more studies in Swedish and civics).

A third foreign language, chosen among a wider set of options, can be studied in high school. Otherwise, the common curriculum core within each study program is quite strong, so all high school leavers have a quite broad common competence from one of the twenty programs.

HIGHER EDUCATION

Institutions

Since 1977 all postsecondary education has been integrated into one system of state universities and colleges, most of which are university colleges. However, a number of undergraduate programs in nursing and health care are run by municipal colleges, accounting for about 12 percent of all new students.

The universities differ from the colleges in that the former have a permanent organization for research and postgraduate studies. There are six university complexes with more than one faculty area and two of these have deep historical roots (Uppsala, founded in 1477, and Lund in 1668). Another two are big city universities, founded in the late 1800s (in Stockholm, the capital, and in Goteborg, on the West coast). The remaining two are the consequence of a more recent regionalization policy (Umea in the north, and Linkoping in mid-Sweden). Such a policy was also behind the creation of a seventh research center, an institute of technology, and a university college at Lulea, just south of the polar circle.

The university colleges are distributed around the country in different counties. They offer programs for both undergraduate degrees and so-called single courses in certain subjects mainly as further education for adults. Some research is also carried out here in specific projects and by the teachers as part of their professional development. Most of the undergraduate programs at the university colleges are in the areas of arts and sciences, education, and social science. Some two-year programs in different areas of technology are also offered at these colleges more often than by universities. Finally, a few colleges offer specialized programs with a nationwide enrollment such as the School for Librarianship in Boras.

All universities and colleges get most of their funds from the state budget through the Ministry of Education, but the Ministry of Agriculture is responsible for the Swedish University of Agricultural Sciences. Under the Ministry of Education, the National Board of Universities and Colleges (NBUC) headed by the chancellor, common for all universities and colleges, has a coordinating responsibility for budget claims, and planning and evaluation in the areas of teaching and staffing, while four state research councils allocate resources for research projects after specific applications and peer reviews. At the local level, the president is chairman of the highest decision-making body, the senate, in which laymen appointed by the government but nominated by the university are in majority (from 1988). In Uppsala there are eight such laymen, four professors (including the president), and three students in the senate. From 1977 six regional boards with a politically elected majority coordinated budget claims and some resource allocation at the undergraduate level for colleges and universities within each region, but that extra level of governance was abandoned in 1988.

At the faculty level, all permanent staff elect a dean among the professors or the lecturers. They also elect representatives to the faculty board that also has some external members representing employers, unions, and other societal interests. In addition, most departments have a board with elected representatives for teachers, students, and technical staff. The head of the department is nominated by the department board but appointed by the president.

The academic year is divided into two semesters: fall (September to January) and spring (January to May).

Undergraduate Studies

Two parallel ways of study are offered at the undergraduate level in most faculty areas:

1. Study lines leading to a professional competence, reached through a series of courses in a predetermined order with some but few options and sometimes demanding a small piece of independent work as the final part of the exam. A student who gains entry to such a study line is guaranteed a study place through the whole program.

2. Single courses, most often corresponding to one semester's study in a discipline or problem area otherwise defined. Several such single courses may be combined, but the student has to make a new application for every semester. After three year's study (120 credits) such a program may now qualify for a basic degree

(*fil.kand.* corresponding to a B.A. or a B.Sc.) provided that at least three semesters' study (sixty credits) in one of the disciplines is included, which also is the general requirement for entry to a postgraduate program.

The credit system is based on twenty units for each semester, i.e. one credit for one week's full-time study. Single courses are most common in the faculties of the arts and sciences including the social sciences, to which access was free before 1977 for everybody who had matriculated from the academic streams in high school. Credits for completed full courses are generally transferable between colleges and universities as well as between single courses and professional study programs when a course is part of such a program.

The principle of single courses has been introduced as a means of providing opportunities for adults for upgrading and for further education as part of an overall system of recurrent education. A great number of the single courses are offered on a part-time basis as afternoon or evening classes or as part of a distance education scheme, in order to suit the needs of full or part-time employees. Decentralized single courses are also offered at places outside the university or college town.

Each study program is divided into sub-courses that follow each other in a sequential order of time-blocks. Thus, a student most often takes only one sub-course at a time. Examinations are held for one or two sub-courses at a time consecutively during the year, sometimes combined with a final in which the different sub-courses are integrated. Many of the single courses are offered at a "slow-pace", i.e. a one semester's full-time program is distributed over two semesters to facilitate participation by people in the work force.

The course system implies an uneven work load for the teachers. During some weeks they have many class-hours, but in other periods they may have few or none, which gives some room for concentration on planning, research, etc.

Undergraduate teaching is made in Swedish but some of the literature is often in English. Students from abroad can attend special courses in Swedish sometimes offered also in the summer.

Entry to professional full-degree programs is strictly regulated by a national computerized point-system, according to which a candidate gets credit both for the mean of marks from high school and for work experience. A certain minimum number of study places are reserved for students qualified only through their high school marks. For the remaining places, seats are made available to different groups of students in direct proportion to the number of applicants in each of the following five categories: students with high school certificates as their only qualification, students from high school with additional work experience, students with a diploma from a "folk high school" (people's college), adults twenty-five years of age or older with at least four years of certified work experience (the 25:4 scheme), and students from other countries.

A student may compete for a study place in more than one category. Applications to these programs are made twice a year to the National Board of Universities and Colleges in Stockholm in October and April. Entry to single courses is gained on the same basis after application to the local college or university, but their admission boards give priority to the students who have demonstrated the most need to study a certain course. In general, it is easier to gain entry to a single course than to a full-degree program.

Accommodation for students is not under the direct responsibility of the university or college, but student housing is provided by separate organizations; most often by a foundation in which the university or college, the student union and the local municipality are represented. Many student houses do also contain small flats for families. In Uppsala and Lund club-like associations of students from a certain province provide some housing. But many students have to rent a room or an apartment in the open market.

In order to cover living expenses, students have access to a financial scheme which at present gives them about 4900 Swedish kronor (US$800) a month. Of this, 30 percent comes as a scholarship, while the rest is a loan that has to be paid back provided the student reaches a certain level of income. Students from abroad may apply for specific scholarships through the Swedish Institute.

Advanced Studies

Up to 1969 most faculties offered two postgraduate degrees: the Licentiate of Philosophy, expected to take about three years of study including course work and a thesis; and the doctor's degree for which "only" a dissertation was required on top of the licentiate's degree. The dissertations for the doctorate was most often an extended licentiate's thesis. It took an average of four years to complete that dissertation (also published in printed form). Thus, students often took at least seven years to complete the doctorate after a bachelor's degree. According to the 1969 reform, the present "American" type doctorate was introduced, with a normal study time of four years after the bachelor's. About two years of this time is expected to be devoted to dissertation work.

Postgraduate students receive special scholarships *(utbildningsbidrag)*, presently amounting to 8150 Swedish kronor per month, (US$1350). In addition, a limited number of the candidates may get a salaried position (with social security benefits) as a *doktorand,* which gives them about 10,000 Swedish kronor (US$1650). After graduation, a doctorate holder can apply for a position as an assistant researcher *(forskarassisteent)* for a maximum period of four years. A doctorate holder can also get a salaried time-restricted post as a project leader on research grants. In order to get a tenured post, one has to apply again for a position as a senior lecturer or professor.

The Swedish system of postgraduate studies and research has a heavy emphasis on medicine, technology, and the pure sciences which together account for 77 percent of all professorships. However, the doctoral programs in the humanities and the social sciences also award a significant number of doctorates partly because a good amount of this research is organized in project groups funded by state or private research councils.

In general, postgraduate studies and research have been made an exemption from the budget cuts in the public sector, since research is regarded as a strategic investment in Sweden's future.

ISSUES AND TRENDS

Among the issues most commonly discussed are the consequences of the comprehensive school reform in terms of the quality of standards held by high school leavers, due to the abolition of streaming and ability grouping at the secondary level of schooling (Dahllof 1971; Ahlstrom & Jonsson 1980). Part of the cost for the reform has been paid in terms of a lower amount of teaching in the second and third foreign language.

At the graduate level, the 1977 reform has been criticized both for the strong occupational orientation of most full-degree programs in the areas of arts and sciences and for the bureaucratization of the decision making processes (for surveys see Dahllof 1977; Premfors & Ostergren 1978).

The most burning current issue concerns the further dispersion of facilities for research outside the present seven university locations (Goteborg, Linkoping, Lulea, Lund/Malmo, Stockholm, Umea and Uppsala). Several university colleges have started research parks and projects of their own, prompting the government to stress the need to concentrate permanent facilities for research and postgraduate training to the present seven locations.

BIBLIOGRAPHY

Abrahamsson, K. *Adult Participation in Swedish Higher Education.* Stockholm: Almqvist & Wiksell International, 1986.

Abrahamsson, K. ed. *Implementing Recurrent Education in Sweden. On Reform Strategies of Swedish Adult and Higher Education.* Stockholm: Swedish National Board of Education, 1988.

Dahllof, U. *Ability grouping, content validity and curriculum process analysis.* New York: Teachers College Press, 1971.

Dahllof, U. *Reforming Higher Education and External Studies in Sweden and Australia. Uppsala Studies in Education 3.* Uppsala: Acta Universitatis Upsaliensis-/Almqvist & Wiksell International, 1977.

Dahllof, U. "An educational magpie: Student flow analysis and target groups for higher education reform in Sweden." In *Premfors* (1984): 114-135.

Husen, T. and Boalt, G. *Educational Research and Educational Change. The Case of Sweden.* Stockholm: Almqvist & Wiksell and New York: John Wiley & Sona, 1967.

Husen, T. and Kogan, M. eds. *Educational Research and Policy. How Do They Relate?* Oxford: Pergamon Press, 1984.

Lane, J-E., and Fredriksson, B. *Higher education and public administration.* Stockholm: Almqvist & Wiksell International, 1983.

Pike, R.S., McIntosh, Naomi E.S., and Dahllof, U. *Innovation in Access to Higher Education.* New York: International Council for Educational Development, 1978.

Premfors, R., and Ostergren, B. *Systems of higher education: Sweden.* New York: International Council for Educational Development, 1978.

Stenholm, Britta. *The Swedish school system.* Stockholm: The Swedish Institute, 1984.

Willen, Birgitta. *Distance education at Swedish universities. Uppsala Studies in Education 16.* Uppsala: Acta Universitatis Upsaliensis/Almqvist & Wiksell International, 1981.

Wittrock, B. and Elzinga, A. eds. *The university research system. The public policies of the home of scientists.* Stockholm: Almqvist & Wiksell International, 1985.

SWITZERLAND

by
Esther Garke
Staff Officer, Division of Higher Education
Federal Office of Education and Science, Switzerland

BACKGROUND

Swiss education before 1800 developed along much the same lines as that of Central Europe and education was first the task of the monasteries, before municipal schools were founded. In the fifteenth century the first university of our country was founded by the city of Basle (in 1460), while elementary education continued to remain in private hands for several more centuries. Along with the political changes brought about by the French Revolution, education expanded to a broader base. Pedagogists like Pestalozzi gave a decisive impetus to education by opening up primary schooling for a wider strata of the population. A new stimulus to develop higher education manifested itself in the nineteenth century, when liberal political forces gathered to create the Swiss Confederation. This was the time when most of our universities were founded, although the origin of some of them (e.g. Geneva, Zurich) can be traced back to the theological academies founded during the Reformation.

In the second half of the nineteenth century (and also in the twentieth), the secondary schools, the vocational schools, and the universities underwent important reforms mainly influenced by the psychological research of that period. The structural changes in society and industry since World War II has further brought about continuing change in the Swiss educational system. In the 1960s and the early 1970s secondary and higher education enjoyed high priority at the national and the cantonal levels, thus resulting in a phase of quantitative expansion. This phase of almost unlimited growth has come to an end, mainly, but not exclusively, due to the prevailing financial and economic regression. Similarly, the endeavors of several cantons to create new institutions of higher education have been stymied.

PRIMARY AND SECONDARY EDUCATION

As the twenty-six cantonal school systems differ greatly, only a broad description of the significant features of the main stages is given here. In Switzerland, children enter kindergarten at ages varying from four to six according to the canton and the local district and continue until they are six or seven. Preschool education is optional but nevertheless state-run.

Compulsory schooling begins at the age of six or seven depending on the canton, and extends over a period of usually nine years. Primary school lasts five or six years, again depending on the canton. Then the classes are split into two or three streams, into which the pupils are classified taking into account their academic success on one hand, and vocational aims on the other. Thus, secondary schools open up different streams for vocational or higher training. The curriculum includes at least one foreign language (one of the national languages), mathematics, history, geography, biology, art, and several other subjects.

Pupils, who leave school at the age of sixteen (without continuing on to university studies), usually move on to a practical apprenticeship with a firm, hospital, post office, or local government administration, attending compulsory vocational schools part-time (on the average two days per week). Those who do not take up an apprenticeship can enter a full-time vocational school leading to a commercial diploma, or they enter a teachers' training college for infant or primary teachers. The courses at these schools last about four years.

Upper secondary schooling takes place in the grammar schools which require 2-4 years preparatory schooling at secondary level. The actual grammar school courses last four or five years, bringing the school leaving age of their pupils up to about nineteen. In order to obtain the school leaving certificate *(maturity)* the candidates have to pass a final examination which comprises eleven subjects. The Swiss *maturity* regulations distinguish five main types of grammar school training; type A stressing Latin/Greek plus mother tongue, one or two modern languages, mathematics, natural sciences, history, geography, art; type B offering Latin and modern languages (instead of Greek); Type C which emphasizes mathematics and natural sciences; type D with modern languages; and type E offering commercial subjects. The *maturity* certificates are not only the leaving certificates of the grammar schools but they give access to any discipline in the universities. The above mentioned types of *maturities* are officially recognized by the confederation, thus setting a comparable standard for access to universities. This explains why the Swiss system does not hold additional entrance examinations for admission to universities.

The principles of compulsory school attendance and of religious tolerance are laid down in the federal constitution; but the specific aims of education are not defined either in the federal, or the cantonal constitutions. These aims are usually mentioned in the prefaces to the various cantonal school regulations. In principle, the aims of the different schools are comparable. There is a great variety and diversity in the details. Generally speaking, all the statements defining educational objectives stress development of mind and character, improvement of knowledge and ability, and promotion of physical culture and healthy living. Whereas in the nineteenth century primary education was founded on the principle of making good democratic citizens, this aim later receded in view of the increasing subject matter to be mastered due to the fast development of science and technology. Today there is a tendency to revive civic and political education and to imbibe in young people a sense of responsibility towards society and a spirit of international understanding and cooperation.

Educational responsibilities at the primary and secondary levels are devolved in varying degrees to cantonal and local authorities. There is no national authority or institution which could claim extensive responsibility for educational structure, organization, or reforms. Each canton has in its administration a department of education responsible for its schools, for its university, and for further education. Any attempt in the nineteenth century to create a strong central board of education was rejected by the Swiss people for fear of too strong a central control being imposed upon them. Thus it is hardly astonishing that only a few clauses relating to education have been incorporated in the federal constitution. Clause 27 states that the cantons will provide for adequate primary education, which is to be entirely under state control (cantonal or local). It is compulsory and free of charge in all publicly maintained schools and open to members of all denominations without encroaching upon their freedom of faith and conscience. The organization, direction, and supervision of compulsory schooling remain the concern of the cantons, though the confederation contributes to scholarships and other grants. It can also supplement arrangements made by the cantons initiating or supporting measures to further education by means of scholarships and grants. In all cases, cantonal autonomy in educational matters at these levels is to be respected.

The cantonal department of education can devolve power to a great extent to the local authorities, especially in the sphere of preschool and primary education. Thus, in accordance with the Swiss political system, school administration is built up democratically from the bottom upwards.

Cooperative forms of administration prevail: The directors of the cantonal education departments meet regularly in conference, setting up recommendations for harmonizing the various school systems on a regional if not national basis. The lack of a legislative body empowered to implement educational planning on a national scale highlights the importance of the contacts established on a goodwill basis among the Swiss professional associations such as the Teachers' Association, study groups, and intercantonal committees. In this connection mention must be made of the Swiss Educational Documentation Center at Geneva and the Swiss University Documentation Center in Berne, both being joint federal-cantonal institutions.

HIGHER EDUCATION

Institutions

Switzerland ranks among countries having the highest university density, with one university for every 650,000 inhabitants. There are ten institutions of higher learning. Four of the cantonal universities (Basle, Zurich, Berne, and the Graduate School of Economics in St.Gall) and the Federal Institute of Technology (Zurich) are situated in the German-speaking part of Switzerland, which has twenty cantons and about 78 percent of the population. The other four cantonal universities (Lausanne, Geneva, Neuchatel, and Fribourg) and the Federal Institute (Lausanne) are situated in the French-speaking part, which has six cantons and about 22 percent of the population. Italian-speaking Switzerland does not have a complete university of its own. This wealth of universities is a consequence of the historical evolution of Switzerland.

Each university is financially and administratively under the department of education of its particular canton. However, from an academic point of view, considerable autonomy is conferred to the university by law. Only the two institutes of technology are wholly maintained by the confederation. Their academic autonomy too, is assured under the law.

Clause 27 of the federal constitution authorizes the confederation to establish or maintain institutions of higher learning. Until now it has twice made use of this competence; in 1854, when it created the Federal Institute of Technology in Zurich, and again in 1968, when it took over the Polytechnical School of Lausanne. For the last 150 years or so it has been urged repeatedly by some cantons and pressure groups to create or take over a university; but so far, the cantons have insisted on their prerogative to provide higher education, rejecting any attempt to centralize cultural and educational affairs. The increasing financial squeeze has turned the universities into a burden for the eight cantons and as a result those cantons without a university have begun to share the costs in proportion to the number of their own students in the cantonal universities. To this effect the cantons have signed an agreement concerning the financing of the cantonal universities (1981).

Although each university has its own characteristics, their structure is basically the same. They consist of faculties: theology, law, economics and social sciences, arts, natural science, and medicine. Fribourg and Neuchatel offer the basic medical courses only, and St. Gall specializes in economics and law. The two federal institutes of technology produce highly qualified engineers, architects, and natural scientists.

Programs and Degrees

Swiss universities offer both basic studies leading to specialization as well as postgraduate programs. Considerable differences exist between various universities and between fields of studies with regard to the length of study and the structure of the courses. The first academic degree, a *licence* or a diploma require at least four years of study or eight semesters.

A *licence* or diploma with good grades is a prerequisite for access to postgraduate studies leading to a doctorate. Doctoral degrees are awarded on the basis of academic research (thesis) carried out independently and having an original quality, as well as completion of the examination requirements. The topic of a thesis is determined in coordination with the professor who directs and follows the research work. The thesis must be published. The duration of postgraduate studies is not regulated but depends on the chosen topic, the accessibility to sources of documents for consultation, laboratory experiments, and research methodology. In general, a thesis requires three to five years work.

Alternatives to higher education at the tertiary level are provided by the twenty-three advanced technical colleges (HTLs), and the commercial and management colleges. The training at these vocational colleges takes three to four years, and can, as the case may be, lead to studies at the federal institutes of technology. Teachers' training colleges also offer higher educational programs.

Continuing Education

For lack of a more concise term, "quaternary" education may stand for any form of organized learning after a first period of (compulsory or higher) learning and after entering an occupation or profession. It thus includes not only further and recurrent education, postgraduate specialization, and "recycling", but also the various forms of adult education. Professional and vocational education and "recycling" are regulated by federal and cantonal laws, while adult education in general is undertaken by the cantons (cantonal laws on the promotion of adult education and culture) or private associations (e.g. "popular universities"), churches, political parties, workers'unions, broadcasting and television corporations etc. Privately organized courses by correspondence are offered in fields such as commerce, languages, and arts. The confederation grants financial assistance to some of these mostly cultural associations through its *Foundation Pro Helvetia*. An Open University as such does not exist.

Educational Administration

Although the constitution authorizes the confederation to set up a federal university in addition to the federal institutes of technology, it has so far declined to do so. While the confederation is giving preference to financing its institutes of technology, some of the universities with slimmer cantonal resources encountered increasing difficulty in meeting the requirements of a modern Swiss society. The process of catching up proved particularly difficult for cantons with modest or average financial resources, such as Fribourg. A discrepancy between the progress of technical studies at the federal institutes and the classical studies at the universities became evident in the early 1960s. Since university development is in the national interest, an appeal to the confederation for financial aid led to implementation of the Federal Act (concerning the financial assistance to the universities) of 28 June 1968 (amended in 1971, revised in 1988). The scheduled aid consists of two types of subsidies: "basic grants" for operating costs and "investment grants" to help with new construction, conversions, building purchases and rentals, equipment, scientific instruments, libraries, etc.

In the past, the institutional framework of higher education was character-ized (among other factors) by a certain spirit of competition between neighboring universities, by a fair amount of autonomy in the development of each faculty, and by the regional character of each institution. With the rapid economic, financial, social, and scientific changes of the present day, universities need to be coordinated and rationalized, in order to properly respond to national and international developments, and to maximize utilization of resources. To this end, the cantons without a university of their own must also share the responsibility.

A number of bodies are actively engaged in promoting this aim on a national scale. The Conference of the Directors of the Cantonal Education Departments, is responsible for primary, secondary, and (together with the department of economy) technical schools. The Conference of Swiss University Rectors maintains inter-university contacts in order to coordinate the curricula, syllabuses, and examination rules, for various academic degrees as well as to promote uniformity in the conditions of admission. It promotes exchanges of students and teaching staff here and abroad. The Swiss University Conference is responsible for bringing about cooperation among the universities and implementing major reforms relating to academic studies and to the structures of higher education. The conference participates in examining the cantonal requests for federal subsidies. It is a coordinating organization rather than an authoritative body and represents a forum where the conflicting forces in the university sector can reach a compromise on centralist and cantonal interests. One of its committees promotes the harmonization of the cantonal multi-year university plans. The Swiss Science Council constitutes the advisory body to the federal government in matters of science policy.

The Federal Office of Education and Science is part of the federal administration (Department of the Interior). It was created in 1969, when the federal act for financial assistance to the cantonal universities was implemented. It serves as the executive branch of the government in the field of science policy (education as well as research). The office constitutes the administrative counterpart of the advisory bodies, (the Science Council and the University Conference). Based on the recommendations of the advisory bodies, the Federal Office of Education and Science formulates proposals to be submitted to the government (the Federal Council), and prepares bills for approval by the two houses of parliament. It also assures the implementation of the resulting decisions. To this extent, the federal office participates (in collaboration with the advisory bodies) elaborating concepts, directives, and guidelines of the Swiss science policy.

Admission Requirements and Enrollment

The minimum age for admission is eighteen. All faculties are open to students of both sexes. Those wishing to enrol must produce a state recognized Swiss matriculation certificate or a foreign certificate of equivalent value. All Swiss university level institutions are autonomous in the recognition of foreign secondary school-leaving certificates. Even in the case of foreign certificates recognized in principle as equivalent to the Swiss matriculation, the faculties still reserve the right to determine admission. In all cases, adequate knowledge of the language of instruction is a prerequisite for admission.

There has been a marked increase in enrollment at Swiss universities in the 1970s. Since 1970, the total enrollment has doubled, from about 40,000 to 83,000 (1990). So far all applicants who have complied with admission requirements have been granted entry to a university. With the growing number of students, the institutions get increasingly overcrowded, requiring further expansion. Medical students have to accept transfers to a different university than that of their choice, if study places are not available there.

Compared to other European countries, the proportion of foreign students at Swiss universities has always been particularly high; it equals about a fifth of the total student force. The rate varies from one university to the other: foreigners are especially numerous in the French speaking universities (e.g. 35 percent of the total enrollment at Geneva). Female students account for some 36 percent of the total enrollment, representing a large increase over the last few years. In this aspect too, the share is larger at the French speaking universities of Switzerland than at the German speaking ones. The breakdown of students by branch of study indicates that over the last decade an increasing percentage of students were studying arts (mainly languages, history, and psychology). Law and economics are gaining popularity. Alongside the official students' unions at the individual universities, there are political, scientific, and cultural societies for students at every university.

Financial Assistance

At most universities, foreigners pay the same fees as the Swiss, i.e. between 300-1000 Swiss francs annually. In comparison with the general living expenses, the study fees themselves are relatively insignificant.

Swiss universities do not provide accommodation for their students. Students generally live in private rooms or boarding houses in the city. There is now a movement to provide more students' hostels, subsidized by the state. Most university towns have students' restaurants.

Scholarships are allotted by cantons, local authorities, private organizations, and the confederation. Each canton has its own scholarship system. Scholarships, usually intended for the entire normal duration of studies, are granted only to those students whose parents' financial situation is deficient. Every year some one hundred new multi-annual grants are offered by the Swiss confederation to foreign students.

For postgraduate studies, particularly for the writing of a thesis, new sources of financing must be sought; ordinarily, the Swiss National Science Foundation gives subsidies for high-quality research projects (at present roughly a third of those working on scientific projects subsidized by the foundation are foreigners).

ISSUES AND TRENDS

The Swiss system of education is marked by a fair amount of diversity and autonomy. The educational policy, especially as far as university studies are concerned, has always followed the principle of social demand, providing study-places according to individual request. So far the universities have been in a position to rationalize or expand their capacity and staff in order to meet the needs stemming from the rapid growth of the student body in the 1960s and 1970s. There has been no real surplus production of academics leading to overqualified skilled staff or to a considerable number of redundant graduates. On the contrary, there is at present a certain shortage of engineers and computer experts.

At the Swiss universities, teaching and research are complementary and are carried out freely. One of the main challenges in the years to come will be the increasing need for "recycling" and recurrent education, which the state-run universities will have to meet alongside (even in competition) a growing number of private institutes. Furthermore, higher education will become more and more diversified with more tertiary institutions offering specific courses with a vocational rather than academic outlook.

Endeavors continue within the present constitutional and legal base in order to improve the educational system and its organization; to redefine the tasks and responsibilities of the universities; and to strengthen the management of the institutions. Present-day developments require each institution of higher education to plan their activities, staffing, and finances in the light of both national and international needs. In political terms, this calls for a concerted effort by the confederation and the cantons. Thus, though not stipulated explicitly in the constitution, education is de facto a joint federal/cantonal task with the cantons concentrating on education at most levels and the confederation sharing the responsibility and the cost, specially at the tertiary level.

Here, in conclusion, it must be emphasized that a national educational policy cannot be devised in isolation. Switzerland therefore cultivates international relationships at multiple levels: between governments, institutions, academic communities, and individual researchers. Switzerland is a member of numerous international organizations such as the Council of Europe, OECD, and UNESCO. Though not herself a member of the European Economic Community, Switzerland follows the developments in the community, and endeavors to promote European and international understanding by academic mobility.

BIBLIOGRAPHY

Association Suisse pour l'Orientation Universitaire et al. *Schweizer Studienführer/-Guide des Etudes en Suisse.* Bern: Paul Haupt Publishers, 1988.

Egger, Eugen. *Education in Switzerland.* Bern: Swiss Conference of the Directors of Cantonal Education Departments, 1984.

Garke, Esther. Higher Education in Switzerland. Bucharest: UNESCO/CEPES, 1984.

OECD. *Reviews of National Science Policy: Switzerland.* Paris, 1989.

OECD. *Reviews of National Education Policy: Switzerland.* Paris, 1990.

Schweizerischer Wissenschaftsrat (Swiss Science Council). *Berichte über den Ausbau der schweizerischen Hochschulen.* Bern, 1989.

Schweizerischer Wissenschaftsrat (Swiss Science Council). *Hochschulbildung, Arbeitsmarkt, Beschäftigung.* Bern, 1981.

Schweizerischer Wissenschaftsrat (Swiss Science Council). *Die Dienstleistungsfunktion der Hochschulen.* Bern, 1986.

TANZANIA

by

Herme Joseph Mosha
Professor and Dean, Faculty of Education
University of Dar es Salaam, Tanzania

BACKGROUND

Tanzania's educational system is heavily centralized and uniform. By act of Parliament, an "ordinance to make provision for a single system of education" was passed in 1961. It ordered the hitherto racially organized schools to form one integrated school system in which children of all races, creeds, and classes would be schooled together, in identical facilities using the same curriculum. Furthermore, despite financial and managerial constraints, the educational system is directed and controlled centrally by a Ministry of Education in Dar es Salaam. So, although school terms may differ from one region to another, the pupils follow a single curriculum which is centrally set and inspected. The training of teachers and their terms of service are centrally determined by a government sponsored and controlled commission called the Unified Teaching Service. Thus, while all syllabuses for academic schools and teacher training institutions are, in principle, prepared by a single governmental structure (the Institute of Curriculum Development) the control of school quality is vested with the directors of education in the ministry and the inspectorate. At regional and district levels, there are education desk officers for the same purpose.

With the winning of independence in 1961, egalitarian policies were introduced in Tanzania. Education was made free for every citizen. School fees were first abolished for secondary and higher education in 1963. It was argued that school fees discriminated against the poorer children, thus mostly against Africans. Rich parents were sometimes expected to pay part of the costs of their children's education, but only non-citizens paid fully for the education of their children.

A nominal fee for primary education (especially for boarding schools) was retained until 1973 when all school fees for government primary schools were abolished except for the current nominal contribution of 200 Tanzanian shillings (US$1) per child. Thus, theoretically, all children of sound academic ability could acquire education at public expense from primary school to university. This was also consistent with national socialist policies. However, the payment of some school fees at secondary school level were reintroduced from 1984 following recommendations of the Presidential Commission Report (1984). There are also plans to charge fees at other levels for it has been found that free education was an unworkable myth.

759

PRIMARY AND SECONDARY EDUCATION

Primary Education

Primary school education in Tanzania aims at enabling pupils to read fluently and write well in Swahili and to perform basic mathematical operations (Ministry of Education 1984). The pupils are also supposed to acquire basic civic and ideological values necessary for the appreciation of their government and its ideology (of socialism and self-reliance), and culture of society in general. Children enter primary school at the age of 6-7 years and continue for seven years.

Primary schools are supposed to prepare the majority of students (about 90 percent) for lives in the community. Ishumi (1984) and Ishumi et al (1985) have, however, lamented that schools were far from achieving this objective. Hence Nyerere's (1967) proclamation that education at all levels must be complete and terminal, remains to be a mere political platitude propounded by idealists.

Primary schools are also supposed to prepare a part of the student population (about 10 percent of the primary school leavers) for secondary school education and for other tertiary and vocational education institutions. Today educators have found it difficult to blend the twin objectives of preparing students for life in the community as well as preparing them for further education. Since primary education is still academically oriented and places for further education are limited, students often struggle for few places in secondary schools. A majority of them are not selected for secondary education; hence, end up being frustrated.

The primary school curriculum has undergone several changes since independence but the most fundamental ones include abolition of practical subjects (agriculture and handcraft) for political and sentimental reasons geared at enhancing equity among races, as only African children were engaged in agriculture prior to independence. This was a very unfortunate move indeed since "education for self reliance" places emphasis on the same notion of merging theory and practice or preparation for life in rural and urban communities. The price involved in reintroducing them in 1983 and the gap already created by a lack of such skills over two decades may take a long time to bridge.

Switching from English to Swahili as a medium of instruction in all grant-aided primary schools effective November 1969 also had far-reaching effects on the quality of spoken and written English, which was and is still the medium of instruction at secondary levels. Students now lack the language foundation that primary education used to establish.

Finally, although the earlier two tier primary education school system was abolished by converting each school into a full seven-year primary school system between November 1970 and November 1972, it did, however, pose a serious problem. Even academically poor students were allowed or pushed through seven years of schooling without testing their competence; hence the problem of illiterate primary school leavers. Standard four examination was, however, reintroduced in 1984 and now those who fail, normally repeat. Plans are also underway to revert to the eight-year primary education system.

Secondary Education

Selection into secondary schools in Tanzania is very restricted. Only 10 percent of the primary school leavers (ages 13-14 years) are selected for secondary education. There are 152 public secondary schools in Tanzania with a student enrollment of 55,178. Various institutions like religious organizations and private communities used to provide secondary education in Tanzania until 1969 when all schools were nationalized. The nationalization of private and denominational secondary schools was in accordance with the Arusha Declaration which called for state control of all the commanding heights of the economy.

This was an unfortunate move indeed for it resulted in the government bearing the burden of financing an educational system that was previously supported by private agencies. Hence, the expansion of secondary education stagnated as the little resources that the government had were used to support the nationalized schools.

The social demand for more secondary school education, and the government's inability to cope has led, of late, into allowing the mushrooming of private secondary schools since 1975. The private secondary schools now outnumber the public ones: 209 (registered) against the government's 152 (1990).

According to the Long Term Plan (1981 to 2000) efforts are underway to increase enrollment in secondary schools from 1.6 percent in 1981 to 15 percent in 2000 through establishment of four day public secondary schools in each of the country's 120 districts; encouraging communities to open more private secondary schools while the government provides them with support of trained teachers and basic teaching materials; and adapting the current one session secondary school system in urban centers into a double session system in order to be able to use available resources more efficiently.

Selection into public secondary schools is normally based on good performance in the standard seven (end of primary) school leaving examinations. All standard seven leavers in a region are ranked according to sex and selected on merit criterion, until regional quota is filled. The quota system aims at correcting inequalities of opportunity according to region and sex.

Secondary school curriculum is vocationalized. Each of the 152 public secondary schools offer vocational courses in agriculture, technical subjects, home economics, or commercial subjects. There are schools offering courses in more than one vocation.

At independence, the goals of secondary education were to prepare skilled middle and high level manpower for all positions in the public and private sector and replace the skilled expatriate staff. Secondary schools, therefore, offered a traditional academic curriculum. Since provision of public secondary education was strictly meant to prepare graduates for work in specific economic sectors, its expansion was permitted only as much as the projected growth in demand for educated and skilled manpower allowed. Following the introduction of education for self-reliance in 1967, secondary school curricula were subsequently streamlined in order to play down the distinction between education and work.

There are two modes of assessment: continuous assessment and final examinations. The "education for self-reliance" castigated among other things "ambush type of exams" and called for a more objective mode of assessment (Nyerere 1967). Continuous assessment involves administration of monthly terminal tests that constitute 25 percent of the final examination grade. Each student's character is also evaluated by a panel of teachers and the overall grade in character determined. The grade in character assessment has an overwhelming influence on the nature of the certificate to be awarded to a student for one with excellent classroom performance but poor character can never be awarded a first class certificate. He or she has to excel in both. Upon completion of secondary education, students sit for a national form four (Ordinary Level) and form six (Advanced Level) examinations which mark the completion of their lower secondary (four years) and senior secondary (lower secondary + two years) education. Those who obtain first and second class passes in relevant subjects at form four level are normally selected for senior secondary while others proceed to other tertiary institutions, direct employment, or remain unemployed.

Two categories of teachers normally teach in secondary schools: diploma holders and university graduates. In a well staffed secondary school that offers courses up to Ordinary Level, the teacher ratio is 50:50 diploma and degree holders. Only holders of a bachelor's or a master's degree are supposed to teach in senior secondary schools.

Insignificant number of foreign students are enrolled in public secondary schools. Children of expatriate staff are normally enrolled at either the Dar es Salaam or the Arusha International Schools.

Teacher Education

There are forty-one teacher training colleges in Tanzania with an annual intake of about 4,500 teachers. Teachers of different grades are trained for different levels of the education system. Primary school teachers are trained in various teacher training colleges existing in the country. There are two types of pre-service programs for primary school teachers (grade A and grade B). Under the grade B program selected students who have completed primary schools (seven years of education) spend four years in a teachers' college. The first two years are used in raising their academic abilities by offering them courses equivalent to form one and form two of secondary education. The final two years are spent on teaching courses. In the grade A program, trainees are selected from those completing four years of secondary education. The minimum requirement is for the student to have two credits and two passes in their Ordinary Level examinations.

Sumra (1988) maintains that the most important aspect of teacher training programs for primary schools was the distance training program initiated in the wake of party's decision in 1974 to introduce universal primary education by 1977. Introduction of universal primary education required training of nearly 40,000 new teachers over a period of three years. The program involved on the job training supplemented by supervised correspondence courses and radio broadcasts. The training took three years and ended with students spending six weeks residential seminar in a Teachers' College. Nearly 40,000 teachers were trained under the scheme (nearly half of the current total teacher population in primary schools). During the same period, only 8,000 teachers were produced through the normal program in teachers' colleges. Secondary school teachers are trained either in diploma colleges or at the University of Dar es Salaam or Sokoine University of Agriculture. Entry to these training programs require completion of form six (Advanced Level).

Adult Education

Six major programs are offered to adult learners. Sumra and Bwatwa (1988) maintain that the most widespread adult education activities are the literacy classes. The primary and secondary school in the country, community centers, and government offices act as adult education centers where teachers from the school conduct literacy classes. The extent to which illiteracy has been eradicated is assessed by means of a periodic National Literacy Test. Achievement is measured according to defined levels.

The Folk Development Colleges Program (FDC) launched in 1975 (Mosha 1985) was and still is intended to give graduates of literacy classes the opportunity to acquire further knowledge and skills. The colleges, which were modeled on the Swedish Folk High Schools, offer courses for village leaders (chairpersons, secretaries, bookkeepers, and village shop managers); leaders of women's organizations; various groups engaged in implementing various self-reliance projects; and assistant field officers.

In practice, most of the students attending FDCs are those who have completed the full literacy school program and those who have completed seven years of primary education. Village leaders are responsible for the selection of the students. Two types of courses are offered. Core courses include agriculture, technical education, domestic science, and accountancy. Optional courses include political education, economics, culture, and philosophy of adult education. Length of courses vary between those less than six months to those of nine months or longer. By 1986, there were 24,186 students enrolled in fifty-two FDCs staffed by 420 tutors, half of whom had some teacher training.

Swedish interest in the development and operation of the FDCs has been high. The initial planning was assisted by consultants from Sweden, and in the early stages tutors were provided. Sweden has also been providing funds to run these colleges. In 1975-76 its contribution was four times that of the Tanzanian government, whereas in 1985-86 it was only one sixth of the Tanzanian provision.

Two institutions in the country offer correspondence education (Sumra and Bwata 1988). One is the National Correspondence Institute (NCI), which is a department within the Institute of Adult Education based in Dar es Salaam with branches in all the regions of the country. NCI offers courses in four areas: mass education; secondary education; professional studies including teacher training, management, and administration; and a special program for disabled students. Mass education, which includes primary education, is open to those who have completed the full literacy school program. Other courses are offered to those who have completed primary or higher education. Enrollments peaked at about 7,000 in the mid-1970s and are now around 2,500. Far fewer women than men have enrolled in correspondence classes, and most of those enrolled are from urban areas and have completed primary education. The other institution responsible for correspondence education is the Cooperative Education Center (CEC), a sister institution of the Cooperative College Moshi.

HIGHER EDUCATION

Institutions

There are two universities (University of Dar es Salaam and Sokoine University of Agriculture) that offer undergraduate and postgraduate degree programs. In addition, there are twelve other higher education institutions that offer diploma courses, with each of these offering 2-3 year programs in a few specialized areas. These diploma level institutions produce technicians, professionals, and lower secondary school teachers. It is relevant to note that institutions of higher education rely on a very small pool of about 3,100 students and the somewhat uncoordinated proliferation of institutions leads to capacity underutilization.

Development of University Education

The development of higher education in Tanzania has taken place in an environment of changing national policies. Four periods can be identified in which the objectives of higher education have altered. These are the colonial era (pre-1961); the post-independence era (1961-67); the post-Arusha Declaration (1967-74); and the post Musoma Resolution period (1974-present).

It was during the post-1961 period that the first of the higher education facilities, namely the University of Dar es Salaam and the Dar es Salaam Technical College were established. Education for self-reliance as a corollary policy to the Arusha Declaration called for radical changes from provision of an elitist education laden with a foreign value system, to an educational system which was responsive to the country's needs and value system. The Musoma Resolutions of 1974 demanded for more changes in entry qualifications and examination system at university level. To qualify for university entry, students had to complete form six (Advanced Level) with at least minimum university entry requirements, participate in a one year national service (military) training program, work for at least two years before joining the university and demonstrate commitment to serve the people in the course of their work.

Female students were exempted from the two-year work requirement following the Lindi Resolution of 1976 in order to compensate for the social and educational disadvantages suffered by the Tanzanian women in the past. Engineering students were also exempted in order to ensure that expensive technical equipment and teaching capacities at the university were fully utilized. The two latter requirements were scrapped off in 1984 following recommendation of a study by Omari and Galabawa which established that a majority of the best students were not joining university after the two years of work and there was no direct linkage between work performed during the two years and subsequent studies at the university. Hence it was felt that such experience could be gained while on training through fourth term practical attachment in places of work that were related to future careers. Although all faculties introduced a scheme of "Fourth Term Practical Field Attachment", the scheme was subsequently abandoned in most faculties except medicine, engineering, and education due to financial constraints.

The ruling party, CCM (formerly TANU), is responsible for formulation of policy that guide the course of higher education in Tanzania. The aforementioned policies ("education for self reliance" and the Musoma Resolution) were formulated by the party. The government on the other hand gives party policy its legitimacy through enactment in Parliament. Government also oversees the implementation of party policy. Universities often train party functionaries and government bureaucrats who eventually are responsible for formulation and implementation of policy. On rare occasions, direct technical advise is sought from university dons either in the process of policy formulation or its implementation.

University curricula are normally developed by course specialists in the respective departments. Once the course programs are drawn up, they are tabled, discussed, and approved by the respective faculty boards and the university senate before they are adopted for use in classrooms. Each course outline contains delineation of the specific goals/objectives, content, and recommended readings. Modes of assessment are also spelt out. Each student is supposed to attend 95 percent of lecture/seminar sessions, perform satisfactorily in course work assessments that at times constitute 20-60 percent of the final examination grade. The ratios differ by departments and faculty but must have prior approval by faculty board and senate.

Medium of instruction is English except in special language courses (Swahili, French).

Governance

According to Para 7 of the University of Dar es Salaam Act 1970, the president of the United Republic of Tanzania (URT) is the chancellor of the University of Dar es Salaam. The 1984 Sokoine University of Agriculture (SUA) Act similarly stipulates that the president of the URT should be the chancellor of the university but he used his discretion to appoint the CCM chairman and the former president Mwalimu Julius K. Nyerere as chancellor of SUA. According to the act, the chancellor is the head of the university and confers all degrees in the name of the university.

A vice-chancellor appointed by the chancellor is the principal executive officer of the university and is responsible to council for the implementation of the decisions of council. Under him is the chief academic officer (or the pro-vice chancellor for SUA) and the chief administrative officer (or registrar for SUA) who are appointed by the chancellor after consultation with the vice-chancellor. The vice-chancellor and the two chiefs normally hold office for such a period and on such terms and conditions as the chancellor may determine.

Under the chiefs are faculty deans and directors of institutes who are normally elected from among senior members of staff (senior lecturer, associate professor, and professor) by the electoral college consisting of all academic members of staff in the faculty (70 percent), student representatives (15 percent), and support staff (15 percent). Names of the top three candidates are discussed in faculty board, senate, and council; and recommendations sent to the chancellor for the appointment of one candidate. The period of tenure for deanship is three years, but is renewable to a maximum of two terms or six years. Under the deans are the heads of departments who are elected from among senior members of staff in the department (and appointed by the vice-chancellor). The composition of the electoral college and the period of tenure is similar to that of deans.

The university council administers the properties, funds and other assets of the university; receives gifts, donations, grants or other moneys on behalf of the university; and makes disbursements therefrom to the faculties, institutes, constituent colleges or to other persons or bodies.

The senate is responsible to the council for the control and general regulation of instruction, education, and research within the university and in addition satisfies itself regarding content and academic standard of any course of study offered by any faculty and make by-laws.

Faculty boards and committees have powers from time to time to undertake the following functions subject to the general or specific direction of the senate: (1) to review and make recommendations to the senate in respect of control and regulation of instruction, education, and research within the faculty; and (2) to make recommendations to the senate on any matter pertaining to the faculty.

Teachers for the two universities are appointed from graduates who excel in their academic and professional fields (at least an upper second honors degree with a GPA of 3.8). They are then enrolled into a master's degree program and employed on a temporary basis as tutorial assistants. Upon the presentation of satisfactory performance in the master's program and a good report on classroom teaching, they are employed as permanent members of the staff. Each member of the staff is supposed to complete doctoral studies and publish regularly. Performance of each member of the staff is reviewed in an annual staff review exercise.

Undergraduate Studies

Bachelor's degree programs (B.A., B.Sc.,etc.) are offered at the University of Dar es Salaam, in the areas of arts, commerce and management, law, sciences, and pharmacy. Doctor of Medicine and Doctor of Dental Surgery degrees are also available. The Sokoine University of Agriculture offers bachelor's degrees in agriculture, agricultural engineering, veterinary science, forestry, and food science. Bachelor's degrees generally take three years with some programs (education, pharmacy, and engineering taking one additional year). Medical and dental degrees take five years of studies and one year of internship.

Admission to undergraduate programs require the Certificate of Secondary Education (C.S.E.E.) Ordinary Level or equivalent, with passes in five approves subjects obtained prior to the sitting of the Advanced Certificate of Secondary Education examinations (A.C.S.E.E.) or equivalent and two principal level passes (in appropriate subjects) in the A.C.S.E.E. or an appropriate equivalent diploma or certificate of not less than second class level. Mature age candidates (in-service) are considered provided they pass the entry examination and have a favorable recommendation from the employer. Additional faculty requirements may also apply, as in the case of faculties of medicine, engineering, and law which normally select students with best scores and end up with a higher cut-off-point due to demands of a higher degree of excellence in the professions.

Student Facilities and Finance

The University of Dar es Salaam provides ample facilities for extracurricular facilities for sports activities such as football, basketball, netball, volleyball, table tennis, lawn tennis, badminton, and swimming. There are also facilities for athletics, boxing, javelin, and shot-put. There are also regular film shows organized either by the students' organization "MUWATA" or the teachers' association "UDASA", video shows, drama, and dance. Excursion trips to nearby national parks *(Mikumi)* or historical sites *(Bagamoyo)* are often organized either by students or staff at the two universities. There are two social clubs on campus, one for students and the other for academic members of staff that sell refreshments and snacks to its members. The social clubs also serve as forums where exchange of ideas takes place on academic and other social, political, or economic matters.

The universities (Dar es Salaam and Sokoine) provide accommodation for about 80 percent of the students in the halls of residence. The rest of the students, particularly students who are married; students with parents, guardians, or close relatives in town; and students who prefer to live off campus are allowed to do so and are paid an off-campus allowance equivalent to the lodging and meals' fee. The money for accommodation is paid by the government or by the sponsors of foreign students. Students wishing to stay on campus during vacation pay for their upkeep privately.

Except for foreign students, university education is free for those who qualify. The cost of maintaining one student at the university is 640 times more than the cost of primary education (Nyerere 1980). The government is, however, thinking critically about introducing fees at higher institutions of learning due to the decline in the proportion of the national budget spent on education from 19.6 percent in 1962 to 5.2 percent in 1988-89. About 33 percent of the total national budget is spent on servicing the debt.

The total cost of an undergraduate program (including board and lodging) is about TShs250,000-325,000 per year (of which board and lodging cost represents about TShs50,000) depending on the program and the institution.

Through the Inter-University Exchange Program, the university admits about 100 students from East African countries, annually. It also admits students from other African countries and a few from Europe, America, and Asia. Most foreign students receive bursaries from their respective countries, and are self sponsored or are beneficiaries of scholarships offered by international organizations or private organizations. All foreign students must meet entry qualifications, provide a guarantee of adequate funding, and satisfy the country's visa entry requirements.

Advanced Studies and Research

Both the University of Dar es Salaam and the Sokoine University of Agriculture provide postgraduate degree programs

Although there are minor variations across faculties, the general requirement for a master's degree is a good bachelor's degree (lower second honors with a G.P.A. of 3.0) or its equivalence and some experience on the job (one year or more). A minimum qualification does not automatically guarantee admission. Applicants with lower qualifications than those approved by the faculty board are sometimes considered if they had scored an average grade of "B" and above in areas they would wish to specialize, or had gained extra qualifications since graduation.

Master's degree programs at the two universities (available in most fields mentioned under undergraduate studies) consist of course work and a dissertation for full time students. Part-time students write a thesis. Students who follow the thesis route undergo two stages of registration. Stage one consists of identification of a researchable topic, preparation of a synopsis of the proposal, payment of fees, and assignment of supervisors. Such candidates are normally considered to be provisional until they develop a defensible research proposal and until their supervisors are satisfied that the candidate is ready for fieldwork. It is at this juncture that the candidate's registration status is elevated to second stage registration. The duration of master's programs is about two years.

All Ph.D. programs at the two universities are by thesis. The duration ranges from three to six years after which candidates are discontinued unless they have genuine reasons for being granted an extension. However, there have been exceptional cases where one candidate completed a Ph.D. program in statistics in one year, whereas another candidate in law took seventeen years to complete his studies.

All local students are sponsored by their employers. Very few are privately sponsored, while a few manage to obtain scholarships from international organizations. Foreign students must provide a guarantee of adequate sponsorship before they are admitted into the program. The two universities are yet to evolve a system of assistantships. Total cost of following a postgraduate degree program is about TShs120,000 per year (of which board and lodging cost is about TShs50,000).

Facilities exist in most departments and faculties for postdoctoral work. The universities, through the Office of the Director of Postgraduate Programs and Research, process applications for research associateship, sabbatical leave, short visits, exchange programs under link arrangements, or part-time teaching and research endeavors. Candidates for postdoctoral programs must provide evidence of adequate sponsorship before being granted entry visa. On very rare occasions the universities offer part-time teaching to foreign post doctoral fellows particularly in fields where a local staff member is on leave of absence or secondment.

ISSUES AND TRENDS

The most pressing problems facing the educational system in Tanzania today include emerging mismatch between policy and reality. Nyerere (1988), Mosha (1988 and 1990), Ishumi and Cooksey (1986) have all indicated that the goals of education for self-reliance policy were far from being realized.

Omari and Mosha (1987), Malima (1988), and UNESCO (1988) have clearly demonstrated that the quality of education at all levels was declining. The major contributing factors were the lack of adequately trained professional teachers, declining expenditure on education from around 19 percent of the total government budget in 1961 to around 5.9 percent at present (1990) which in turn lead to inadequate teaching/learning facilities, textbooks, materials, and equipment. Issues of relevance of the curricula and problems related to exorbitant costs of implementing a practically oriented curricula in diversified secondary schools (Psacharapoulos and Loxley 1985) constitute another set of problems facing the educational system in Tanzania.

The problem of primary school leavers also seem to be unresolved (Ishumi et al 1986) and neither the post-primary technical centers nor reintroduction of practical subjects such as agriculture seem to have provided the right solutions to these problems.

These problems should not, however, camouflage the country's tremendous success particularly in providing universal primary and adult education to over 85 percent of eligible citizens, promoting equality of opportunities among sexes, and building respect for human dignity. Productive activities at school have also enabled students to reduce upkeep cost and to learn some useful practical skills. Institutions of higher learning also strive to produce the stock of manpower required to man various sectors of the economy.

BIBLIOGRAPHY

Ishumi, A. G. M., G. A. Malekela, P. Biswalo and Y. Bwatwa, "The Problem of Primary School Leavers in Tanzania" Report to the President's Office, Government of Tanzania, Dar es Salaam. 1985.

Ishumi, A. G. M., and B. Cooksey. "A Critical Review of Policy and Practice in Tanzanian Secondary Education" (mimeo), 1987.

Mosha, H. J. *The Progress and Impact of Folk Development Colleges on National Development: The Tanzanian Experience.* Dar es Salaam: Ministry of Education, 1985

Mosha, H. J. "A Reassessment of the Indicators of Primary Education Quality in Developing Countries: Emerging Evidence from Tanzania". *International Review of Education,* Vol. XXX (1988): 17-45.

Mosha, H. J. "Management and Administration of Education in Tanzania" A paper presented at a World Bank Education Seminar held in Dar es Salaam-November. 1988.

Mosha, H. J. "Twenty Years After Education for Self-Reliance: A Critical Review". *International Journal of Educational Development,* Vol. 10, No. 1 (1990): 59-67.

Nyerere, J. K. *Education for Self-Reliance.* Dar es Salaam: Government Printer, 1967.

Omari, I. M. and H. J. Mosha. *The Quality of Primary Education in Tanzania.* Nairobi: Man Graphics, 1987.

Psacharopolous, G. and W. Loxley. *Diversified Secondary Education and Development: Evidence from Columbia and Tanzania.* Baltimore: John Hopkins Press, 1985.

Sumra, S. A., and Y. Bwatwa. "Adult Education, Literacy Training and Skill upgrading in Tanzania." *Alberta Journal of Educational Research,* Vol. XXXIV No. 3 (1988): 259-268.

United Republic of Tanzania. *Basic Facts About Education in Tanzania.* Dar es Salaam: Ministry of Education, 1984.

UNESCO. *Sector Review: Financing of Education in Tanzania.* Paris: UNESCO, 1988.

United Republic of Tanzania. *Basic Education Statistics in Tanzania (BEST) 1983-1989.* Dar es Salaam: Ministry of Education, 1990.

THAILAND

by
Nopadol Tongsopit
President
Khon Kaen University, Thailand

BACKGROUND

The history of modern Thai education can be traced back to the reign of King Rama V (1868-1910) when the monarch tried to modernize his kingdom. Threatened by the advance of Western colonialism which had been rampant in the Far East, the king decided to bring about reforms both in government and in education. It was widely recognized then that if Thailand was to survive the advance of the so-called "neo-colonialism" of the nineteenth century which was swallowing Thai territory bit by bit, Thais had to learn to live with the ways of Western people. That was the compelling reason for educational reform of 1898.

However, for the sake of understanding the development of Thai education it is necessary to take a brief look at the history of Thai education prior to the reform of 1898. For well over eight centuries, education and training for Thai masses were based on Buddhist teachings. During the Sukhothai period (1178-1369), Buddhism had become a major force in shaping the life of Thai people that there gradually developed a system of education characterized by two distinct but parallel programs, i.e. education for the masses of laymen on the one hand, and for the monks on the other. The lay education offered an opportunity for the youth to learn from the learned monks, basic arithmetics, and Pali and Thai languages. The students also received instruction on the codes of conduct based on Buddhist teachings. When they came of age, the men entered the monkhood and spent at least three months in the monastery studying in greater depth, the teachings of the Lord Buddha. Returning again to a layman's life, most of the men assumed the role of the leader of his own family. Only a gifted few were recruited into government service. For those who did not work for the government, continuing family's tradition of livelihood was the norm of the day. Male members of the family learned the family trade from their father. The girls were shut out from the world of learning of the men as there was no avenue for the girls to become a monk's pupil. They were, however, taught Buddhist codes of conduct and skills that women required to prepare themselves to be good mothers.

In 1897, King Rama V spent a few months visiting several capital cities of Western and Central Europe. One of the objectives of the royal visit was to observe firsthand the educational systems of Europe in order to find the most suitable system that could be adapted to the Thai situation. It was after this royal tour of Europe that a concrete plan for a new educational system was finalized in

June of 1898. The plan called for three levels of schooling for all Thai youth, male and female alike. It also called for four major objectives, namely, "to enable the children to read and write, to do arithmetic, to work to support one's self, and to conduct one's behavior properly". However, due to limited availability of funds for educational purposes, King Rama V was able to create only primary and secondary education for his subjects during his reign. At the same time, the government operated several teacher training schools to produce new teachers to satisfy the increasing demand for more teachers. These newly set up primary and secondary schools were all located within the compounds of Buddhist monasteries. This was due to the government's policy of saving money and having children study under the influence of Buddhism. Under the new plan, all Buddhist monks throughout the kingdom were assigned the special task of teaching and training young students with Buddhist codes of proper conduct several hours a week. Therefore, the Thai youngsters of this early period had learned the elements adapted from Western culture, at the same time they were also taught Buddhism so that they wouldn't deviate from the traditional Thai way of life.

The task of continuing and expanding the education of the kingdom was passed on to King Rama V's heir, Rama VI (1910-1925). During the reign of Rama VI, the number of schools multiplied. In 1921, when the government felt confident that there were enough schools to implement compulsory education, a law was decreed. Henceforth, all children of ages 7-14 years had to attend primary school for at least four years.

In 1916, King Rama VI created the first university, the Chulalongkorn, named after his royal father. This newly opened university offered courses at diploma level in medicine, political science, engineering, arts, and science. In 1928, the first bachelor's degree programs were inaugurated. Following the establishment of Chulalongkorn, other institutions (Thamasart, Kasetsart, Silapakorn, Mahidol, Khon Kaen, Chiangmai, Songkhla Nakarin, and Srinakarinwirot) were founded in the ensuing years.

The tradition of private schools in Thailand has a relatively shorter history compared to that of government schools. Private schools started with the coming of the American missionaries during the reign of King Rama III (1824-51). Although the major objective of the missionaries was to convert the Thais to Christianity, they had nevertheless introduced some new knowledge of science to the people, such as Western medicine, astronomy, and geography. The first missionary school for boys was founded in 1852 in the vicinity of Bangkok, and the first school for girls was founded twenty years later, also in the suburb of Bangkok. Following the example of these first missionary schools, other missionary schools were soon founded and expanded in other parts of the country. Other private Thai citizens, inspired by the success of missionary schools, began to engage themselves in the enterprise. Numerous private primary schools, secondary schools, and vocational schools gradually emerged in almost every part of the kingdom. Some of these forerunners of private schools are still in operation today.

Structure of Education

The Thai government has always taken an active role in the organization and control of education in the country. There are two authorities in policy planning: the Ministry of University Affairs and the Ministry of Education. The Ministry of University Affairs is in charge of curriculum development in order to maintain high educational standards at all the universities, state and private institutions alike. In addition, the ministry also oversees the administration of personnel affairs of all the state universities. Although all the state higher education institutions operate under a separate charter of each institution which allows them some freedom of administration, the final power rests with the minister of university affairs. State institutions receive their annual operational funds almost 100 percent from the central government through the ministry. There is a Board of University Rectors in which rectors of all state universities meet regularly to discuss and decide matters which concern their common interests.

Education below the university level is under the strict control of the Ministry of Education. The ministry is sub-divided into several departments with each department overseeing different levels of education. The Office of the National Primary Education Committee is in charge of administration of all primary schools in the country. The Department of Normal Education controls all secondary schools. It appoints the principals and teaching staff, allocates budget, develops curriculum, and supervises all affairs of the schools. The same holds true with other departments within the Ministry of Education. The Department of Vocational Education is responsible for the administration of all vocational schools scattered around the country. The Department of Technical and Agricultural Colleges oversees all technical and agricultural colleges. The Department of Physical Education is in charge of administration of all physical education colleges, while the Department of Teacher Training Education is in charge of administration of all teachers' colleges. It should be noted that the technical and agricultural colleges and the physical education colleges all grant a higher level vocational diploma only, while the teachers' colleges offer training programs leading to a higher level educational diploma and a bachelor's degree as well.

Primary education is also provided by the municipality of each city. Therefore there are two types of primary schools; those under the control of the Office of the National Primary Education Committee and those under the municipality. There is an Office of the Private Education Committee within the Ministry of Education entrusted with the responsibility of overseeing and cooperating with all the private kindergarten, primary, secondary, and vocational schools throughout the country.

PRIMARY AND SECONDARY EDUCATION

Primary school children are required to attend school for at least six years according to the existing compulsory education law. Normally the children start going to school at the age of six and remain there until they are twelve. There is no tuition fee as such at public primary schools (state and municipal), but students are required to pay a small school fee, buy their own textbooks, and pay for the cost of extracurricular activities.

The primary school curriculum is prescribed by the Department of Educational Techniques and the Office of the National Primary Education Committee. All state, municipal, and private schools are required to follow the curriculum strictly, although they are allowed some freedom in the selection of elective courses. The 1978 curriculum content is made of five integrated groups of skills (Thai language and arithmetics), life experiences (science, social and moral education), characteristic and habit building (physical and health education), basic vocational education, and special experience (foreign languages). From the beginning of the 1991 school year, there will be some change in the special experience group in which each local school is allowed greater freedom to incorporate any topic of study regarding local culture, history, etc., into the group.

The secondary schooling lasts six years. The academic year begins early June and is concluded in mid-March with a semester break of half a month during the second half of October. Students normally study seven hours a day, five days a week.

The secondary school curriculum is prescribed by the Department of Normal Education of the Ministry of Education. Both state and private schools must follow the curriculum strictly, although they are allowed some freedom in making minor adjustments. Curriculum content usually consist of the following areas: mathematics, science, Thai language, civic and ethics, social studies, and physical activities. English is a compulsory second language. There are numerous elective courses depending on the needs and potential of the school. The schools are empowered to conduct midterm and final examinations for their students. Teachers make up their own exams and assign grades according to their own criteria. Passing grade is D on the $A = 4$ scale. Successful students with a grade point average (G.P.A.) of 1.0 or better at the end of their sixth year are awarded certificates of completion by the school.

At each school, students are encouraged to join academic, social, religious, and sports clubs. There is a student council in which students elect a council president. The council operates under the guidance of an appointed advisor and final approval for all kinds of activity rests with the head master.

Students in state secondary schools are not charged tuition; they do have to, however, pay a minimal amount of fees which cost about US$40-50 annually. The tuition and fees at private schools are much higher. In general it could cost the students about US$120 per semester. Almost all of the secondary school students live with their families and rely on their parents or guardians for living expenses and costs which could amount to about US$100 per month for an average student.

During the past twenty years, numerous secondary schools have been constructed and now there are more seats than the number of students entering secondary schools each year. This is partly due to the fact that Thailand has been successful in its birth control plan in keeping population growth rate down to 1.7 percent (and it is planning to still lower the rate to 1.5 percent). The other factor which contributes to the decreasing percentage of primary graduates going on to the secondary level is related to economic consideration on the part of the parents. Many parents cannot afford to send their children to school beyond primary school. They prefer to keep their teenage children home to work or to seek employment in order to bring in some income. The result is that only about 45 percent of the primary school graduates continue on to the first year of lower secondary school (grade seven in American system). Of those who continue on to lower secondary school, only about 54 percent continue on to upper secondary level (grades 10-12).

The government sets no barriers against citizens of other countries from enrolling in either state or private schools. In spite of that, the enrollment of foreign students in Thai secondary school has been very minimal. Those who have enrolled are either exchange students or children of temporary foreign residents who spend a short time in Thailand on business assignments.

Teaching staff in state schools are selected on merit. They have to pass a selection examination before being appointed government employees. And once they are appointed they remain employed until they reach retirement age of sixty years.

HIGHER EDUCATION

Institutions

There are both state and private universities, professional colleges (teachers' colleges, colleges of physical education, technical colleges) and polytechnic institutes. While a graduate of a technical college may be allowed to attend a polytechnic institute to continue on for a bachelor's degree, such access is not readily available for him to attend a university. State universities offer courses and degree programs in a variety of fields. Private universities and colleges, on the other hand, tend to be more oriented to technological/vocational education.

The laws governing state and private universities and colleges stipulate for each institution an institution council in which a prominent scholar or a recognized person is customarily appointed president of the council, and the rector or president of the institution is vice-president of the council. The university/college council oversees policy planning and regulates the affairs of the institution on almost every aspect. The colleges for vocational and technical training do not have such governing councils, but are directly controlled by the Ministry of Education.

Undergraduate Studies

All applicants for admission to state institutions of higher education for bachelor's degree programs must compete in an entrance examination administered by the Ministry of University Affairs, Ministry of Education, or institutions themselves. The selection criteria is based on the scores made in the exam. However, there are two open universities which admit unlimited number of students with G.P.A. 1.0 or better in various fields.

Fields of study available at the universities include accounting, agriculture, architecture, banking and finance, business administration, dentistry, education, engineering, foreign languages, humanities, laws, medicine, nursing, science, social sciences, pharmacy, public health, technological science, veterinary science, etc. For four-year degree programs, students normally take 135-145 semester credits before being awarded a bachelor's degree. Credits are spread to cover basic requirements, core courses, and electives. For five-and six-year programs, students normally have to take thirty-five credits or more per year in addition to the 135-145 credits earned during the first four years of study. Duration of the academic year is nine and one-half months, from early June till mid-March, with a break of about half a month during the second half of October. Medium of instruction is Thai.

The institutions encourage students to participate in a variety of extracurricular activities: cultural activities, community development, religious activities and sports. At each institution, there is a student government organization which has considerable freedom of operation concerning student affairs. Students are also free to hold seminars or conferences on any issue. There is an annual university game event in which athletes of all the universities meet and compete in variety of games during the semester recess.

Tuition is about 50 bahts (US$1 = 25.70Bahts) per credit and fees are around 1,500 bahts per semester. Whenever possible Thai university students prefer to live with their parents to save expenses. An average student studying in a major city requires at least 2,500 bahts per month for room, board and transportation, excluding personal and miscellaneous expenses. In small towns, the expenses can be cut down to about 1,800 bahts per month. Most of the provincial universities provide living accommodation for their students at a minimal cost. A few institutions in Bangkok areas provide limited spaces for their students and the charges are quite expensive.

Most Thai university and college students rely on their parents for financial support. There are some scholarships available for needy students. However, the selection criteria for granting a scholarship is highly competitive.

There are a few foreign students enrolled in Thai university and college campuses. Occasionally exchange students come for short stays. Each institution has its own regulations regarding the admission of foreign students.

Selection and appointment of university and college teaching staff are on a merit system. Each applicant must have a master's degree or higher and is required to pass a written examination and an oral interview before being appointed to the institution. Members of university and college teaching staff are appointed permanently until they reach the compulsory retirement age of sixty years.

Advanced Studies and Research

Most institutions require a bachelor's degree and a G.P.A. of 2.5 for admission to master's degree programs. Some institutions require working experiences in addition to an acceptable G.P.A. Each applicant has to pass a written examination and an oral interview. There are many fields of study offered at most of the state universities and colleges. In most cases the fields of graduate studies offered coincide with those offered at undergraduate level by the same institution.

For a master's degree, students normally have to finish thirty-five semester credits plus a thesis. That makes graduation within two or three years possible. For a doctoral degree, 30-40 semester credits are required beyond master's degree, plus a dissertation. Normally it takes at least three years after a master's degree to finish a doctorate. Duration of the academic year is nine and one-half months, starting from early June till mid-March, with a half month break during the second half of October. Medium of instruction is Thai language but some programs are offered in English at the more prominent graduate institutions.

Graduate students are entitled to the same opportunities as the undergraduates, to participate in extracurricular activities. However, due to their heavy load of study they tend to abstain from taking active roles in student activities. As a result, the president of the Student Government Organization has always been an undergraduate.

Graduate tuition is about 250 bahts (US$10) per semester credit and fees are around 1,000 bahts per semester. Tuition and fees for foreign students can be much higher, depending on each institution's policy.

As most graduate students are employed by the government or some other agencies, they are usually granted a leave of absence to further their education. They canXreceivetheir salaries regularly while attending school. Some students may work part-time and at the same time receive partial aid from their parents. Most graduate schools offer some scholarships and research grants, but these are not sufficient to cover a student's full cost.

Graduate teaching staff generally are appointed from among undergraduate staff provided that they hold a doctoral degree or are associate professors. As a member of graduate teaching staff they receive no additional salary or allowances.

Postdoctoral programs are almost non existent in Thailand at the moment. However, as the country is moving toward becoming a new industrialized nation and the economy is booming, it is conceivable that higher education will be expanded to embrace postdoctoral research in the near future. The National Research Council located in Bangkok is the main organizer of research activity. It provides handsome funds for research in almost every field annually.

ISSUES AND TRENDS

There have been several issues under discussion and debate among educators and those responsible for education planning. The most vital ones include expansion of compulsory education from 6-9 years; greater role for private sector in every level of education; and priority status for science and technology oriented fields of study.

There have been plans to examine the educational structure and problems of the country. Several studies have been carried out by the National Board of Education and many other ad hoc committees during the past few years. The results of the studies have often been used for improvement of education.

The educational system of Thailand is very much like the Western model in terms of structure, content, and grading system. While the country strives for academic excellence along Western lines it also puts emphasis on the conservation and transmission of national heritage (history, culture, social values, religion, etc.). Only future can tell whether the country's attempt will be successful or not.

BIBLIOGRAPHY

Mowat, Susanne. *Education and Urban Migrant, A Comparative Analysis of Case Studies in Bangkok, Manila and Jakarta.* Bangkok: UNESCO Regional Office for Education in Asia, 1977.

Roy Singh, Raja. *Education in Asia and the Pacific, Retrospect: Prospect.* Bangkok: UNESCO Regional Office for Education in Asia and the Pacific, 1986.

Sukontanangsi, Sawat. *Development of Thai Educational Bureaucracy.* Bangkok: National Institute of Development Administration, 1968.

Thailand Ministry of Education, Departments of Elementary and Adult Education. *Education in Thailand, A Century of Experience.* Bangkok, 1970.

Thailand Ministry of Education, Educational Planning Office. *Current and Projected Secondary Education Programs for Thailand, Report of the Research Committee on Secondary Education and Human Resources Development in Thailand.* Bangkok, 1966.

Thailand Ministry of Education, Office of National Primary Education Committee. *A Study for Quality Development of Primary Education B.E. 2525-2534.* Bangkok, 1983.

Thailand Ministry of Education. *An Evaluative Study of Primary School Efficiency in Thailand: The Determinant of Primary School Efficiency.* Bangkok: Office of the Prime Minister, 1982.

UNESCO Regional Office for Education in Asia and the Pacific. *Education for Development - Challenges: Dilemmas, 10th Anniversary Lectures.* Bangkok: UNESCO, 1985.

Wirochsiri, Xantharid. *Design Guide for Secondary Schools in Asia.* Bangkok: UNESCO Regional Office for Education in Asia, 1977.

Watson, Keith. *Education Development in Thailand.* Hong Kong: Hinemanu Asia, 1980.

Wyatt, David K. *The Politics of Reform in Thailand; Education in the Reign of King Chulalongkorn.* New Haven: Yale University Press, 1969.

TOGO

by
Date Fodio Gbikpi-Benissan
Director, National Institute of Educational Sciences,
University of Benin, Togo

BACKGROUND

The educational system which Togo inherited from the colonial period underwent significant reform in 1975 in the process of adapting the system to real needs of the Togolose society. The reform outlined several objectives: democratization of education; making education more effective; adapting education to development work; producing a healthy and well balanced generation of people; and preparing students for integration into working life.

Two ministries are responsible for education in Togo: the Ministry of National Education and Scientific Research; and the Ministry of Technical Education and Professional Training. The former controls general education while the latter oversees technical and professional education. Educational policy is formulated by the Higher Council of National Education and the Higher Council of Technical Education which are organs of the ministries. About 82 percent of the funding for education come from the government which allocates, for this purpose, about 25 percent of the national budget. Bilateral and multilateral agreements provided another 15 percent with the balance 3 percent contributed by parents.

The structure of education consists of four levels: nursery and primary (first degree); first cycle secondary (second degree); second cycle (third degree); and higher education (fourth degree). Each level (degree) of education comes under the administration of a separate director at the Ministry of National Education. Inspectors from the ministry supervise the functioning of schools and curriculum development.

PRIMARY AND SECONDARY EDUCATION

Primary education lasts for six years and consists of three cycles of two years each: preparatory cycle, elementary cycle, and middle cycle. The certificate of the first degree (CEPD) awarded at the end of the primary education enables students to enter the second degree schools (first cycle of secondary education).

Secondary education comprises seven years of studies at two levels: second degree and third degree. The academic year extends for ten months from beginning of September to end of June. The medium of instruction is French.

The schools that provide second degree level of secondary education are of two types: colleges of general education (CEG) and colleges of technical education (CET). The schooling starts with the "cycle of observation" which lasts for two years and is followed by the "cycle of orientation" for two more years. Promotions from one class to another is based on school examinations. At the completion of the second degree secondary studies, students appear for one of the two national exams: certificate of the first cycle (BEPC) for students at colleges of general education, or certificate of professional aptitude (CAP) for students at colleges of technical education.

Study at the third degree secondary level, which lasts for three years, is provided either at the general education lycee or at the technical education lycee. Admission to these institutions is based on a competitive examination (for candidates who have completed the second degree). At the end of the second year, the students appear for a national exam, the *baccalauréat 1,* the success at which enables students to proceed to the final year (to one of the sections of literature, science, mathematics, and technology). At the completion of the third degree studies, students appear for the *baccalauréat 2* national exam which is the qualifying examination for admission to universities.

Teachers are recruited by the Ministry of Work and Public Service, on the basis of a competitive exam and are assigned to their posts by the Ministry of National Education and the Ministry of Technical Education. Some staff may be recruited directly by private institutions.

Students take part in a variety of extra curricular activities including athletics, football, basketball, handball, folk dance, theatrical performances, and orchestra.

Fees charged at secondary schools vary from FCFA2,500 (US$1-=FCFA319) at public schools to FCFA40,000 at private establishments. Excepting in the case of students who receive scholarships, the cost is borne by the parents. Foreign students have the option of enrolling in either the Togolese schools on the same basis as Togolese students or entering private institutions that follow foreign programs such as the French primary school, and the lycee. (The fees are FCFA360,000 per year for French students and FCFA540,000 for non-French students).

HIGHER EDUCATION

Institutions

The University of Benin, which is the only university in Togo, was created by presidential decree in September 1970. Its predecessor was the Higher Education Institute of Benin founded in 1965 jointly by Togo and Benin (known at that time as Dahomey) with a school of letters at Lome (in Togo) and a school of sciences at Porto-Novo (in Benin). (In 1970, Benin also formed its own national university). The second higher education institution to be established (in 1968) was the *Ecole Normale Supérieure d'Atakpame* (ENS), which trained teachers for primary and secondary schools (first cycle). Since 1983, with the opening of two other training schools *(Ecoles Normales d'Instituteurs)* this institution now trains only the teachers for secondary schools (first cycle) who undergo a three year program (after *baccaleauréat*) leading to the *certificat de fin d'études normales.*

The University of Benin is 92 percent funded by the government and the balance 8 percent comes from the university's own resources. The "Supreme Council of the University of Benin" is the highest governing body that defines policy and general guidelines for the university. It is presided over by the minister of national education and scientific research and meets once a year. The university council presided over by the rector is the organ that executes the decisions of the supreme council and the educational policy of the government. It oversees organization of education, study programs, study regulations, mode of student evaluation, establishment of titles and diplomas, and the university library. The council reviews the budget and allocates funds.

The rector is appointed by decree of the president of the republic on the recommendation of the minister of national education who selects the candidate from among teaching staff holding the "professor" rank (Togolese nationals). The rector is the administrative and academic head of the university and is supported by a vice-rector, secretary-general, and other administrators. Twelve establishments form part of the university: faculties of law, economic sciences and management, medicine, sciences, letters and humanities; schools of engineering, agronomy, biological sciences, medical assistants, and administrative secretaries; institutes of educational sciences, and management technology. At the head of each institution is a council presided over by the dean (of faculty) or director (of school or institute). The deans and directors are appointed by the minister of national education and scientific research on the recommendation of the rector. The councils of individual institutions are responsible for implementation of decisions made by the university council and control of activities of the institution.

Teaching staff is recruited on a competitive basis by the Ministry of National Education and appointments generally require a doctorate. The rector assigns the staff among different institutions within the university.

Programs and Degrees

The University of Benin offers traditional type university programs that lead to *diplôme d'études universitaires générales* (DEUG) in two years, *licence* in three years, and *maîtrise* (masters) in 4 years, in a variety of literary, scientific, juridic, and economic disciplines. Other programs offered by the university include three-year technology programs in civil engineering, electro-mechanics, administration, and health; five-year diploma in engineering; and a seven-year Doctor of Medicine program.

In addition, the professional training institutions (schools and institutes) award professional diplomas like the three-year university diploma in technology, five-year diploma in engineering, and seven-year Doctor of Medicine degree. Most of the degrees awarded by the university are recognized by the African and Malagache Council of Higher Education, which is the inter-African body that regulates higher education programs.

Admission to the university is open to candidates who possess the *baccalauréat* or an equivalent qualification or who pass the special university entrance examination. The academic year is nine months from beginning October to end June. The language of instruction is French.

The tuition and other fees are FCFA129,250 per year for literary, juridic, and economic studies; and FCFA164,250 for sciences and medicine. Togolese students pay only the registration fee of FCFA4,500 whereas foreign students are required to pay the full tuition and fees. Board and lodging costs are about FCFA75,000 per month, but students who are entitled to subsidized facilities at the university (housing, meals, medical assistance, etc.), spend much less. The government awards scholarships and financial aid to deserving students. The students are often supported by parents. They can also engage in part time work. All students in the master's year (fourth year) receive financial assistance for the preparation of a research document.

Students at the University of Benin take part in a variety of extra curricular activities. All forms of sports are popular: athletics, football, basketball, hand ball, martial arts, etc. Groups engaged in theatrical performances, folk dancing, musical activities (orchestra) are very active.

Research

The teaching staff at the University of Benin has the dual role of being teachers and researchers. Research work and publication of research results are important ingredients for career advancement. The African and Malagache Council for Higher Education reviews research and teaching records of staff, for promotional purposes. Research work of the staff is published in international scientific journals as well as in the *Annales de l'Université du Benin* published by the university periodically. Research activities fall into two categories: at the master's level *(maîtrise)*, students prepare a research document which is intended to initiate students to scientific research; and the teachers conduct their own research programs as preparation for doctoral degrees *(doctorat d'état,* etc.) and as part of research projects sponsored by the government or international organizations. The Directorate of Academic Affairs and Scientific Research oversees all research work of the university.

ISSUES AND TRENDS

In the recent years there has been a strong trend in Togolese education towards diversification with emphasis on professional education. This was due to difficulties faced by degree holders in integrating into the world of work. The Ministry of Technical Education and Professional Training, created in 1984, now directs the establishments of technical and professional training institutions at both secondary and higher levels, based on the employment needs of the national economy.

At the university, the accent on professional education is reflected in the establishment of new programs (cycles) with emphasis on professional education even in institutions that are traditionally academic. For example, the Faculty of Economic Sciences and Management, now has a one year management training program for master's degree holders *(maîtrise)* in any field of study. The Faculty of Science has professional training programs at post-*maîtrise* level. The Department of Mathematics offers programs in applied mathematics related to data processing. The Department of Physics has begun a program in applied electronics. The Faculty of Letters and Humanities plan to establish language programs at post-*maîtrise* level for training translators and interpreters. Several other departments and institutes have initiated similar programs.

Thus, the dynamics of the employment market is having a significant influence on educational policies requiring institutions to adapt themselves to the changing training needs. The traditional outlets in the public service for those who receive higher education are now saturated. The University of Benin which during its twenty years of existence has produced more than 6,000 degree holders (of which 4,000 were Togolese) and contributed for the indigenous development of the country, will focus now more and more on programs that promote professional education and create self employment.

BIBLIOGRAPHY

Ministère de l'Education Nationale et de la Recherche Scientific. *Statistiques scolaires 1988-1990.* Lome: MENRS, 1990.

Ministère de l'Education Nationale et de la Recherche Scientific. *La Réforme de l'enseignement.* Lome: MENRS, 1975.

Ministère de l'Education Nationale et de la Recherche Scientific. *Les politiques et les strategies de l'enseignement et de la formation postsecondaires au Togo.* Lome: MENRS, 1989.

Ministère de l'Education Nationale et de la Recherche Scientific. *Societés en crise et education. Contribution du Togo aux travaux préparatoires a la conférence mondiale sur l'éducation pour tous.* Lome: MENRS, 1989.

Ministère de l'Education Nationale et de la Recherche Scientific. *Rapport National du Togo sur le développement de l'éducation.* Lome: MENRS, 1990.

Université du Benin. *La Réforme de l'enseignement de 1975 au Togo: Perception de l'INSE quatorze ans après.* Lome: INSE, Université du Benin, 1989.

TRINIDAD AND TOBAGO

by
Edrick H. Gift
Senior Lecturer, Faculty of Education
University of the West Indies, Trinidad & Tobago

SECONDARY EDUCATION

Secondary education in Trinidad and Tobago is provided to students who are selected on the basis of the Common Entrance Examination which the students take after five years of primary schooling, when they are in their eleventh year. Students are tested in English, mathematics, science, and social studies. Parents are asked to choose four schools in order of preference. Students are then assigned on the basis of achievement and availability of places.

The academic year for all schools starts in September and ends in July, with three weeks of vacation at Christmas and two at Easter. School examinations are usually held once every term, while secondary school leaving examinations are conducted during the final term of the school year. The number of years of study in secondary school vary according to the type of school.

Schools in Trinidad and Tobago can be classified according to the agencies responsible for running them. There are government and government assisted (denominational) schools where no fees are paid. However, there are also private schools which are run by individuals or organizations, such as church bodies. These cater for students who might not have been satisfied with their Common Entrance placing, or by those who have failed to secure a place and do not have another chance to sit the examination.

The secondary level can be divided into two sectors: a traditional sector and a new sector. The traditional sector comprises forty-six schools, twenty-eight of which are assisted (denominational) and eighteen government. These schools offer the traditional, academic secondary school programs leading to the General Certificate of Education and the Caribbean Examination Council examinations. The Caribbean Examination Council is a regional body which administers a terminal examination to all secondary schools in the Caribbean. This examination is taken after five years of secondary schooling. After the successful completion of this examination, students can either enter the world of work or proceed to prepare for university entrance. Some of the traditional schools offer two additional years of study leading to the Advanced Level (university entrance) examinations. These examinations are external and are offered by Cambridge University. Students study three subjects of their choice which they will continue at university.

The Ministry of Education holds national examinations to certify competencies in the technical and vocational subjects. Successful candidates are awarded the National Craftman's Certificate.

Secondary education in the new sector, obtained at the junior secondary, senior secondary, senior and comprehensive schools is provided in two cycles. The first, Cycle one at the junior secondary or orientation level provides a broad program of eleven subjects: English, mathematics, general science, social science, Spanish, agriculture, industrial arts/home economics, art and craft, music, physical education, religious education, and electives. At the second cycle or senior secondary level, the principal aim is the diversification of the curriculum. The curriculum is conceived in terms of three categories of programs: an academic, a pre-technician, and a specialized craft. In the academic and pre-technician areas, a core of five subjects is compulsory for every student (English language, mathematics, science, Spanish, and social studies).

Composite Schools are newer secondary schools offering, five years in some cases and seven years in others, of general education including some technical-/vocational courses in the five year program. Two sixth form Schools for day students pursuing two years of pre-university studies exist. One is run by the government, other by the Extra-Mural Department of the University of the West Indies. There are also evening programs for students repeating secondary examinations and for others pursuing studies at pre-university level.

The school week is made up of thirty-five class periods, each of forty-five minutes duration. In the academic and pre-technician areas, a core of five subjects is compulsory for every student (English language, mathematics, science, Spanish and social studies). An additional elective is also required.

Most schools in this nation have adequate facilities for extracurricular activities. There are Boys Scouts, Girl Guides, and a paramilitary organization (cadets). Literary and debating societies and drama clubs are very active. Sports include judo and karate, cricket, netball, basketball, football, badminton, and table and lawn tennis.

Teachers in secondary schools are selected by the Teaching Service Commission, an independent body appointed by the government. The minimum qualification is a bachelor's degree in a specialized subject area. In the technical and vocational areas, the requirements may differ. The salaries of all teachers are paid by the government.

Public secondary education is free. All schools are day- schools, so there are no living expenses, but parents must bear the cost of books, uniforms, and transportation, though efforts are made to help the most needy. Foreign student enrollment is limited to children of diplomats and those employed at transnational corporations and international agencies.

HIGHER EDUCATION

Institutions

The University of the West Indies, which is the only university in Trinidad and Tobago, is supported by and serves fourteen territories in the West Indies. They are Antigua, Bahamas, Barbados, Belize, British Virgin Islands, Cayman Islands, Dominica, Grenada, Jamaica, Montserrat, St. Kitts, Nevis, Anguilla, St. Lucia, St. Vincent, and Trinidad and Tobago. In addition, Guyana is a full participant in the Faculty of Law, and by agreement, has a limited number of students in the professional faculties. The institution came into being as the University College of the West Indies under a royal charter on January 9, 1949, and was granted university status under the Royal Charter of Incorporation which passed under the Great Seal of the Realm on April 2, 1962. In Trinidad, the university campus is located on St. Augustine, some eight miles east of Port of Spain, where the Imperial College of Tropical Agriculture was once situated.

Up to 1962, degrees were not awarded by the University College, which by special arrangement with the University of London, taught for degrees of that university using syllabuses modified to meet local needs. From 1962 onwards however, when the University College became an independent university, students began to read for degrees of the University of the West Indies.

A number of institutions are affiliated with the university. The Licentiate of Theology and the degree of Bachelor of Arts (theology) are awarded to students of the following affiliated colleges: Codrington College, Barbados; The United Theological College of the West Indies; St. Michael's Seminary, Jamaica; and St. John Vianney, Trinidad. The Institute of International Relations, Trinidad, and the Caribbean Meteorological Institute, Barbados, are the other affiliated institutions. In the 1988-89 academic year, the university had a total enrollment of 4,209 students of whom 48 percent were women.

The Department of Extra Mural Studies provides adults and adolescents with opportunities for intellectual and cultural activities throughout the Caribbean. It forms an integral part of the university. The Director, with responsibilities covering the whole Caribbean area, is assisted by staff tutors in creative arts, social work, adult education, methods, radio education, and trade union education. Resident tutors are situated in those territories which contribute to the university. Resident tutors and representatives of the department perform administrative and public relations functions, conduct examinations, and disseminate information on the university. They are also responsible for organizing cultural activities, seminars, work-shops, and academic courses of interest to the various islands with the help of resource persons from the campus countries. The department is the outreach arm of the university. Courses are designed to meet some felt need in the community, and to provide an effective medium through which the university is taken to all the contributing territories.

Funding for the university comes from several sources, one of which is central funding. Through a university grants committee, the fourteen contributing territories make allocations (to the central budget) which are proportional to the number of students they have attending the university. In addition to allocations from the university grants committee to the central budget shared by each of the three campuses, there is a campus grants committee, which is charged with determining the level of funding to be provided to the university by the Government of Trinidad and Tobago. A third source of revenue is project funding. This includes allocations for special programs which the government requests the university to implement; funds from international aid agencies and foundations to support terminal projects and grants from the industrial and manufacturing sectors to support research projects which will be of benefit to these interest groups.

Teaching vacancies are advertised internationally. Applications are received and processed by the faculty concerned. A short list of candidates is presented to a selection board which then recommends to the university that an appointment be made. Candidates may or may not be interviewed.

Undergraduate Studies

The bachelor's degrees (B.A., B.Sc., etc.) are similar to those obtained in Britain and involve three tears of full time study from Advanced Level entry. The medical course lasts for four and one half years and leads to the M.B.B.S. degree. Graduates of teachers' colleges are allowed to do a special B.Ed. Students who enter the preliminary year (natural sciences or agriculture) spend an extra year and may transfer to other faculties. Degrees can be obtained from the following faculties at the St. Augustine campus: agriculture, arts and general studies, education, engineering, law, medical sciences, natural sciences, and social sciences.

Only students who will have attained the age of 17 years on 31st December of the year of admission will normally be eligible for admission. However, applicants below this age who satisfy the normal (Advanced Level) matriculation requirements are also eligible. In addition, candidates for direct admission to some degree courses are required to have obtained qualifications in certain specific subjects at specified levels.

The following are eligible for matriculation for admission to degree courses provided their qualifications include a GCE Ordinary Level pass in English Language or the equivalent: persons who have passed all examinations for a degree of any university recognized by the senate for this purpose; holders of General Certificate of Education (or the approved equivalent) satisfying scheme A or scheme B (scheme A requires passes in five subjects of which at least two must be Advanced Level or equivalent and scheme B requires passes in four subjects of which at least three must be at an Advanced Level or equivalent). Students whose native language is not English are required to perform satisfactorily in an approved English language test. The TOEFL test has been approved for this purpose but a special paper may be set if the Matriculation Board considers this desirable. Students registered at another university may follow courses here by special arrangement for credits at their own university.

With regard to tuition, the university, in the interest of maintaining its international character, allows a limited number of students from territories not supporting the university to be admitted at special tuition fees instead of charging the real cost. The quota fixed for such students is 3 percent of the overall registration. Annual tuition fee for the first degree vary from US$2000 to US$3000 for most programs. Law program costs US$4500. The highest charge is for medicine, costing US$12,000 per year. The cost is nearly half for higher degrees.

The University administers, in addition to University Scholarships, a number of other scholarships and awards from individual governments, private donors, and organizations. These awards are available to students who are nationals of territories in the Caribbean which contribute to the university's Budget and who are accepted to pursue full-time degree courses.

St. Augustine has three halls of residence; one for men and women in separate blocks, one for women, and one for men. Accommodation on campus is severely limited. Only 20 percent of the full-time students have places in halls of residence. The remainder live at home or in lodgings. Annual board and lodging (for 31 weeks) is US$1,800 for meals and US$800 for residence.

Advanced Studies and Research

Applicants for admission to master's degree programs are normally required to hold at least a second class degree from an approved university. Master's degrees are awarded on the basis of course work, written examinations, and a research paper, the length of which varies depending on the program. Admission to the M.Phil. normally requires a fist or upper second class degree. Candidates for research degrees are expected to have the capacity to conduct independent research. Applicants to the Ph.D. program are required to submit in writing to departments, a detailed proposal of the research they wish to undertake, within six weeks of notification by the registrar. Applicants for the admission to the Ph.D. who do not hold a master's degree are normally required to register for the M.Phil. in the first instance. Applicants may then have their registration transferred to the Ph.D. on providing evidence to their department of their ability to undertake independent research.

Postgraduate students registered at other universities may apply to work at the university for purposes (and periods) approved by their own university. While at this university the student will be subject to the rules and regulations which apply to students registered at UWI.

The language of instruction is English. Applicants whose native language is not English are required to take an English proficiency test in their country of origin, before they are admitted.

ISSUES AND TRENDS

One of the burning issues in secondary education at present is the dismantling of the shift system, whereby one school plant is utilized by two school populations. One set of students attend from seven-thirty in the morning until noon, and the other from twelve-thirty in the afternoon until five o'clock. It is widely felt that children attending these schools are at a severe disadvantage, since part of the day spent out of school is not wisely utilized. A gradual de-shifting has started, and it is hoped that soon enough places will be available for all students at the secondary level.

It is felt by some educational planners that the goals of schooling should be realigned to satisfy manpower needs and to alleviate a growing unemployment problem. This has triggered curriculum reform geared towards the achievement of this goal. This is evident in many of the programs in continuing education mounted by the government and other organizations in an effort to fill the gaps that might have been left by traditional academic courses.

Another area of concern is the role of education should play in the fight against substance abuse and other related social ills which threaten and destroy adolescents in today's society. Over the past decade, there has been a phenomenal improvement in the quantitative aspect of education. Physical plants increased by over 100 percent and access to secondary education by 150 percent. During this period, however, insufficient attention was paid to qualitative development. To correct this anomaly, the university and the government have joined forces to undertake a massive training program aimed at producing the range of personnel equipped with the necessary expertise to effect qualitative improvement.

As a developing country, provisions made for access to education at certain levels of the system far exceed those in many developing countries. For example 100 percent of pupils of primary school age attend school and 80 percent of the secondary age cohort are in school. Secondary school graduates from Trinidad and Tobago have no difficulty in gaining admission to universities in any part of the world. Graduates of the University of the West Indies maintain their high level of scholarship wherever they seek to do postgraduate work or join the work forces of developing countries.

BIBLIOGRAPHY

Loubser, J. J., R. C. Hughes, Z. Ali and C. Bourne. "Report of an Institutional Review of the University of the West Indies." Prepared for the Canadian International Development Agency, Ottawa, Canada, 1987.

Moses, Edward. "Report of the Cabinet Appointed Committee to Consider Measures to Alleviate Shift Systems at Schools." Port of Spain, Ministry of Education, 1975.

Outlines of a Plan for Educational Development in Trinidad and Tobago 1967-1983. Port of Spain: Ministry of Education, n.d.

Republic of Trinidad and Tobago, Ministry of Education. Education Plan, 1985-1990. Port of Spain: Ministry of Education, 1986.

Trinidad and Tobago Educational Planning Unit. Draft Plan for Educational Development in Trinidad and Tobago. Port of Spain: Government Printery, n.d.

UNESCO. "Educational Planning Mission: Trinidad and Tobago, March - June 1964."

Williams, Eric. *Education in the British West Indies.* New York, 1968.

TUNISIA

by
Mohamed Maamouri
Professor, Faculty of Letters of Manouba
University of Tunis, Tunisia
and
Kacem Ben Hamza
Director, Bourguiba Institute
University of Tunis, Tunisia

BACKGROUND

Traditional education in Tunisia in the nineteenth century and up to the 1950s was based on an informal two-level system made up of the *kutaab* (the Koranic school) and *Jaami az-Zitouna* (The "Olive Tree Mosque University"). The *kutaab* is probably the oldest form of primary schooling in the country dating back at least to, if not before, the year 732, which is the founding year of The Zitouna, the counterpart of the famous *Al Azhar* in Egypt. The *kuttaab - Zitouna* educational structure was financially provided for under a form of religious trusts called the *waqf* system which persisted until the 1960s. Its curriculum was limited to the memorization and explanation of the Koran and other religious texts but it also prepared for the legal profession which is based on Islamic law or *sharia*. All in all, this traditional form of education produced comparatively few literates in the urban areas and even fewer in the predominantly rural parts of the country. These alumni have represented ever since the core of the Arabic-centered elite.

Kheireddine Pacha was the first reformer who dared challenge this strong and powerful structure. He founded the *as-Saadiqiyyah* (College Sadiki) in 1875 which, along with Arabic studies in the early grades, introduced instruction in Turkish, Italian, and French. The first Sadiki alumni continued the same reform movement by establishing in 1896, *Jam'iyyit al-Khalduniyyah* whose aim was to provide a complete school curriculum which explicitly included the sciences in Arabic. This was the first reaction to the cultural and linguistic invasion of the French language after the beginning of the French protectorate. It was soon followed by the founding of still another educational organization in 1905, *Jam'iyyat Qudaamaa as-Saaadiqiyyah* (The Association of the Sidiki Alumni) which clearly stated its aim as the dissemination of Arabic among the graduates of French secondary schools. The French occupation brought with it a new form of schools for the natives, the *écoles franco-arabes* (referred to in the singular as *maktab*) where French was the favored language of instruction as against a "modernized" form of the old Koranic schools (referred to in the singular as *madrasa*) where Arabic still prevailed.

793

In the 1950s, it was clear that the Tunisian system of education was greatly modelled after the French one. French was its medium and the key to social promotion but it was almost completely inaccessible to the wide majority of Tunisian children who, if and when they had access to a primary school education, had no extramural opportunities for practicing it.

At the end of the struggle for independence in 1956, a bold ten-year plan which came to be known as the "Messadi Reform" committed Tunisia to the principle of "free schooling for all" and to the expansion of bilingual education; two traits which were to plague the whole educational structure ever since their implementation, affecting its growth and ruining its quality. The first major reshuffling of the whole educational scene in Tunisia is now about to take place (September 1989) after thirty years of what was no more than a modified pyramidical structure. It concerns what is known as *l'école de base* (which translates best as "The basic school") which is going to cover the first nine years of schooling (the actual six years of the primary and the first cycle of the secondary). The main objectives of "the basic school reform" are to bring about an effective decrease in the very high dropout rate which characterizes the whole system of education, and to take precautionary measures to prevent school children from falling back into illiteracy. This reform which makes schooling compulsory for children of 6-15 years does not question in the least, the validity of the principle of "free and democratic schooling for all".

The first important step towards a long-term policy of development of a solid and reliable system of national education was the promotion in 1958 of a unified system of higher education which clearly opted for a westernized, French-oriented university model. This option consecrated the break with the traditional and more conservative religion-supported *Zitouna* model which was thus led to disappear. The decree of 31 March 1960 creating the University of Tunis structure defined the university's role as the training of all future high-level civil servants and employees for state and private institutions in the fields of education, administration, health, industry, agriculture, trade and banking. This was certainly a highly courageous decision taken by the leaders of independence and more specifically Habib Bourguiba himself, who wanted to get rid of the archaic, millenary structure of the "old Islamic university" which had always been a rallying point for all those opposing the modernization of the country.

Structure

We must state from the very beginning that despite the attempts at reform mentioned earlier in the introductory paragraphs, the Tunisian educational system is still very much patterned after the French system at all levels. This means that like the French one, it is entirely controlled and run by the state and more specifically by two ministries: the Ministry of National Education (for primary and secondary school systems) and the Ministry of Higher Education and Scientific Research (for undergraduate and graduate programs and for postgraduate research whenever and wherever it exists in the institutions which are under the administrative supervision of the ministry). The splitting of what used to be one single ministry took place at the end of the 1970s when it became clear to the Tunisian government that the problems of higher education, and especially those of the riotous and restless university students, were becoming a huge political headache.

The university became the scene of recurring political trouble and it needed an independent administrative structure capable of handling the problem and of giving by the same token, the necessary attention to the prestige sensitive area of "research" which has always had the shorter end of the stick. The splitting of the educational system which lasted until very recently, except for a short two-year period (1985-1987), is, according to most educators and other observers, a very detrimental decision when it comes to implementing fundamental and structural reforms in the system of education. Indeed, it separates the three levels of what should be considered a whole into two administrative units making it almost impossible to ensure the necessary continuity between the beginning (basic schooling) and the end product (university training).

A very few primary and secondary schools find themselves outside of this centralized structure. They are of two types. The first type consist of the French "mission" schools which are reduced, at the present time, to half a dozen primary schools all over the country, and two major *lycées* (high schools including grades 7-13), all under the supervision of the Educational and Cultural Services of the French Embassy in Tunis. They are open essentially to the children of French and other foreign residents in Tunisia but Tunisian students who prefer to register in non-governmental schools can also enter these schools. The second type comprises private primary and secondary institutions which cater almost exclusively to those students who have been rejected by the government schooling system before reaching the high-school graduation year which would have enabled them to take the only entrance exam to higher education in Tunisia, the national *baccalauréat* exam.

There are six universities in Tunisia, which together are responsible for the academic organization of all higher education programs in the country even when the institutions which provide them do not belong to the MESRS. It is the government, in the person of the minister of higher education (with the backing countersignature of the prime minister), who has the final decision when it comes to creating a new degree or reorganizing an older one. The decision becomes a dual one when the institution is under the authority of two ministries. For example in the case for the medical sciences, the decisions usually concern the minister of higher education and the minister of health.

It is in fact the director of higher education under the Ministry of Higher Education and Scientific Research (MESRS) who is directly responsible for the general coordination of all the institutions of higher education in the country. This situation is about to change with the creation of the universities and the nomination of six university presidents (rectors) to head them. In the latest reform of the higher educational structure which is due to appear in the spring of 1989, the general coordination of the university activities will most probably remain in the hands of the director of higher education within the MESRS. The university presidents will certainly be in charge of all the other aspects of both the academic and administrative management of their respective institutions.

PRIMARY AND SECONDARY EDUCATION

Primary Education

Primary school education starts at the age of six and covers six grades with a national entrance exam in the final year which enables pupils to pass into the secondary school system (the *examen d'entrée en sixième* or the *sixième*). Only 40 percent of the schoolchildren on an average pass the exam and enroll in the secondary school system. The other 60 percent usually turn into unskilled laborers who fall back into complete illiteracy in a very short time and are left to join the ranks of the unemployed. The ministry is aware of the seriousness of the dropout problem and is trying to keep these students in school for another two years, (seventh and eighth grades) in which they are initiated to manual activities to help them integrate into agriculture and the small trades labor market.

The six years of primary school education cover the basic language skills, that is to say, oral expression, reading, and writing in Modern Standard Arabic (MSA), which is the national and official language of the country. A second language, French, is added to the curriculum as of the third year in what appears to be a national alternative solution to replace the pre-independence French-dominated situation. MSA is the vehicular language of the other subjects in the school program which include calculus, history, geography, introduction to natural sciences, civics, and Islamic education.

In 1988-89, there were 1,326,150 schoolchildren enrolled in the government primary school system in Tunisia of which 45.1 percent were girls. They were trained by 43,921 schoolteachers (25,766 male teachers and 18,155 female teachers) in 3,676 primary schools which total 43,466 classrooms. This represents an occupancy rate of 30.5 children per classroom and 30.2 children per teacher. The average density of a primary school in Tunisia in 1988-89 represents 361 schoolchildren with a first year primary school enrollment of 94.5 percent of all Tunisian children having reached the age of schooling (97 percent for boys and only 91.9 percent for girls).

Secondary Education

The national *sixième* exam is the first important obstacle faced by the Tunisian schoolchildren who must pass it to continue their education. Once they pass it, they are channeled according to their exam grades into one of the two main streams of the secondary school level: a three-year professional education cycle or a three-year general education cycle. After enrolling for three years in professional education, students who are capable of securing a "professional certificate" may go into the labor market or choose to continue for a "technician diploma". Once they obtain it, they may go to work or choose to attend a seventh year which, if successfully completed, would allow them to attend one of the technical institutions of higher education.

As for those enrolling in the "general education" cycle, they follow a common core curriculum taught in MSA (for arts and humanities) and in French (for mathematics and scientific subject matters). The average weekly hour load is 25-30 hours per week. At the end of their third year, students are channelled into one of the three "specialities": *section lettres* (arts); *section math-sciences* (sciences) and *section math-techniques* (technology). Then, they spend four years before taking the national *baccalauréat de l'enseignement secondaire* exam. When passed, the *baccalauréat* gives them access to a university level education in one of the three major afore mentioned areas. Another channel which is not included in the previous description concerns the teacher training sections which are open to those who, at the end of the three-year common core, choose to become primary school teachers and enroll at the *écoles normales d'instituteurs* for a four-year training period.

The ministry authorities are thinking about introducing a series of minor reforms in the secondary school system as of the coming school year (1989-90) but no official steps have been taken to this date. These reforms mainly concern the splitting of the *section math-sciences* into a *section math* and a *section sciences* and the postponing of the "specialization year" from the end of the third to probably the end of the fifth year. A third reform might concern the use of MSA as the medium of instruction in the first three years for all subjects including the scientific and technological matters with or without the implementation of the "basic school" reform project.

In 1988-89, there were 477,795 students in the secondary representing 266,616 boys (with an additional 2,599 girls in the teacher training programs) in 485 secondary schools representing a total 14,411 classrooms. This represents an occupancy-rate of 33.2 students per classroom and an average enrollment of 985 students per school, of whom 44 percent were girls. There are 23,300 secondary school teachers divided into 14,676 male teachers (including 191 teachers in teacher training centers) and 8,624 female teachers (including seventy in the same centers) which represents an overall ratio of 20.5 students per teacher.

HIGHER EDUCATION

Institutions

Created in 1960 around a small nucleus which included the science departments of the old *Institut des Hautes Etudes de Tunis,* the new higher educational structure soon developed to include a *Faculté des Lettres* (School of Arts and Humanities), a *Faculté de Droit* (Law School) and the *Ecole Normale Supérieure* (School of Education for teacher training purposes only).

Today (1989) the Tunisian higher educational structure includes six universities with forty-three institutions of higher education and a total of 50,947 students, all under the supervision of the Ministry of Higher Education and Scientific Research to which we must add twenty institutions of higher education which depend on other ministries and include 3,519 students. Out of a grand total of 54,466 students there are 20,596 female students and 1,602 foreign students. Majority of the students (69.9 percent) are located in the Tunis area. This is the result of historical development of higher education institutions mostly in the capital city around what used to be generally called the "University of Tunis" or the "Tunisian University" (the Arabic name is responsible for that ambiguity). It is only towards the mid-1970s that institutions such as the *Faculté des Sciences de Sfax,* the *Faculté de Gestion de Sfax,* the *Faculté des Lettres de Kairouan* or the *Faculté de Médecine de Sousse* were created but always under the general heading of "University of Tunis". This situation lasted until 1986 when the two universities of Sfax and Sousse-Monastir were officially recognized as separate multidisciplinary entities, later to be called respectively the University of the South and the University of the Center.

As for the university of Tunis proper, it was divided in 1987, along speciality lines, into three separate universities: University of Tunis I for humanities and social sciences; University of Tunis II for basic, technical, and medical sciences, and University of Tunis III for law, economy, and management. A fourth university, The Zitouna University, was created in 1988 by presidential decree. This re-creation or revival of the famous ancient Islamic institution is more of a political decision meant to please the religious-centered "integrist movement" in the country some months before the first presidential and legislative elections of the new "November 7th" regime. This university concentrates on the theological subjects but will slowly open up to the humanities in general.

Other faculties and institutes located in different parts of the country are organized in five specialization areas: fundamental or basic sciences in Bzertr *(Ecole Normale),* Monastir, and Sfax; humanities in Manuba, Sousse, Kairouan, Sfax; medical and biological sciences in Sousse, Monastir, Sfax; social sciences in Sousse, and Sfax; technical sciences in Nabeul, Monastir, Ksar-Hellal, Sfax, Gabes, and Gafsa. In addition, there are ten institutions which deal with agriculture and related fields and another group of higher institutes in the fields of education of the blind, music, physical education and sports, civil aviation and aeronautics, theater studies, postal services and telecommunications, tourism, and labor.

Governance

Tunisian higher education institutions are run by a 1973 decree which determined the functions and duties of each and every member of the administrative and faculty structure. Elected deans head the faculties, and the ministry appointed directors head other institutions. Deans and directors are officially appointed by the president of the republic for a three year term at the end of which they can go for another term. Each institution has a secretary-general who helps with all general organizational matters and with the administrative (secretarial) and working (cleaning) personnel. The secretary general is in charge of organizing the overall course time table, the student enrollment procedure and paperwork, and the organization and filing of all exams. He is responsible for delivering records, exam transcripts, diplomas, and all other study certificates. He is an MESRS appointed civil servant.

Another body which plays a very important role in the administrative structure of higher education institutions is the scientific council *(conseil scientifique)*. It is an elected board which represents the various ranks of the teaching staff (four elected representatives from the "college A" which includes professors and *maîtres de conférences* and four elected representatives from the "college B" which is composed of *maîtres-assistants* and *assistants*), and four elected representatives of the student body. It is chaired by the dean or director and includes, sometimes and whenever needed, members of the professional, industrial, or cultural world. It is chaired by the dean or director and it includes, sometimes and whenever needed, members of the professional, industrial, or cultural world. This scientific council decides on all academic questions and helps the dean or director in the formulation of policy matters or in program and curriculum development. It is in front of this council that all academic reforms are discussed. It also has an important control authority on all the teaching staff and decides on the promotion of the teaching staff members in the first two ranks (college B). It also decides on the opportunity of granting members of the teaching staff their sabbatical leave or other leaves of absence.

The Tunisian university teaching staff is divided into two groups: group A consist of the categories of *professeur* (full professor) and *maître de conférences* (associate professor); and group B consist of the categories of *maître assistant* (assistant professor) and *assistant* (assistant). All four positions come with tenure, and promotion within each group is considered on the basis of published research and quality of teaching. Entrance in group B is possible if the candidate has successfully completed at least a postgraduate diploma (the *Diplôme de Recherches Approfondies* or D.R.A.) which is usually accepted as the equivalent of two years of postgraduate work with a thesis. Entrance in group A requires a *doctorat d'état* or an equivalent degree. The American type Ph.D. is barely accepted in most Tunisian academic circles as equivalent to the Tunisian or French doctoral degree since it usually represents, according to them, less in terms of years of research and in the "quantity of written pages".

There are 3,901 faculty members in Tunisia in 1989 with 2,125 assistant professors and 519 professors and associate professors. This figure includes 699 medical professors and 558 faculty members who come from the secondary school system or from other professional domains. All the faculty members of a higher education institution are gathered by field of specialization in departments and they elect their head or director for three year terms. The head of the department is responsible for all academic matters and activities.

Within the MESRS, the director of administrative and financial affairs is responsible for all personnel matters including appointments, salaries, and other administrative problems.

The recruiting and promotion of the teaching faculty is however, left to the care of the director of higher education who sets up various specialized commissions with national and international high-ranking faculty members who are asked, whenever needed, to study the files of the applicants. These files usually include, along with official degree papers and theses, all the research production of all the candidates who might be asked to attend an interview and, in some cases, teach a model lesson on a subject chosen by the committee. Following this procedure the opinion of the committee members is submitted to the minister for his final decision.

While some disciplines already register an excess in the available Tunisian faculty members (e.g. chemistry, natural sciences, or history), others suffer from a severe shortage which has a damaging impact on the quality of the teaching provided by the university as a whole (e.g. English language and literature, and some of the engineering specialities).

Undergraduate Studies

The general bulk of Tunisian higher education is centered around the *maîtrise,* a four-year degree which is common to all institutions of the MESRS independently of the area speciality with the exception of the medical sciences and engineering which have a five-year diploma.

The *maîtrise* is structured around four nine month academic years with a teaching load which varies immensely from institution to institution (from as much as 10-15 weekly hours in the faculties to 25-30 weekly contact hours in the highly specialized institutes and schools). An hour-a-week course represents 25-30 hours per year. There is no credit system in Tunisian institutions of higher education.

Courses (that is to say the academic content) are of three types: *cours magistraux* (lecture courses); *travaux dirigés* or T.D. which is comparable to the seminar form but in much bigger groups; and *travaux pratiques* or T.P. which applies best to the laboratory experimentations and work in the scientific branches. It is clear that this hierarchy-based division of courses is not observed any more in the social sciences and in the humanities where all courses are taught on the basis of a mixture of *cours* and T.D.

All courses included in a given year program are compulsory and all students enrolled in that year have to take all of them. There are some optional courses, of course, but they are few in number. The *maîtrise* is composed of two two-year "cycles" in which it is obvious that the first cycle is a very important one for the student who is going to acquire during those two years the basic prerequisites of his specialization.

The exam systems vary from one institution to another and even though a few institutions have already adopted the semester system with regular testing, the majority of institutions of higher education in Tunisia still follow the two-session end of year exam system with a first session in May-June and a re-make session in September-October of every academic year. In order to go from first year to second year, students have to successfully complete their set of exams for that year. They can repeat the year if they do not reach the minimum passing grade average (ten out of twenty) but they cannot spend more than two years in any single year at least in the first cycle. Once they reach the second cycle, students can spend as many years as they please to finish their degree and leave the university. The *redoublement* system is wasteful and expensive. It gives students the possibility to spend as many as eight years to complete a four-year degree and it cannot penalize those who seem to enjoy their student life so much that they become "professional students".

Out of the 54,466 undergraduate students registered in Tunisia for 1988-89, there are 45,931 in MESRS institutions while 3,323 are in institutions coming under other ministries.

The final exam results of the academic year 1987-88 show that a total of 5,204 students graduated with 4,436 of them within the MESRS. The percentage of women graduating varies between 39.2 percent for the total and 44.4 percent for the ministry institutions. The total number of graduates can be divided as follows: 2,296 *maîtrises;* 743 engineering degrees; 541 medical degrees; and 1,624 various technical degrees. The combined success rate for the 1988 graduating class in the whole of higher education in Tunisia is 76.2 percent.

As far as scholarships are concerned, the MESRS granted 23,970 scholarships for the academic year 1988-89 up to January 16,1989, which represents an important 44 percent of the total student body in the country . Of the Tunisian students who got financial help, 23,301 were undergraduates while 318 were in graduate programs. There were also 313 foreign undergraduate students and thirty-eight foreign graduate students on Tunisian scholarships. Students who are not eligible for a scholarship can apply for a university loan. This student financial assistance program is quite new and shows that the government seems to be finally deciding to cut down gradually the level of scholarship assistance which had benefited more than 80 percent of the student body in previous years.

Advanced Studies and Research

Postgraduate studies in Tunisia are just developing and extend from the very restricted nucleus of the three major Tunis faculties (humanities, sciences, and law) to many other institutions. This development is very slow because of the obvious problem of shortage of high-ranking faculty members to direct the candidates' research. Another problem is the very reduced number of graduates who go for a second and third degree.

Tunisian postgraduate studies are organized around two degrees, namely the *diplôme de recherches approfondies* (D.R.A.) which can be obtained two years after the first graduation and after that, the *doctorat d'état.* There is no time limit for this final degree. The *doctorat* is still seen as a consecration in itself even though its prestigious image is slowly changing because of the changing nature of the degree which bears the same title in France. Apart from these two degrees but along the same line, there is a third one which only applied to the scientific fields; it is the *diplôme d'études approfondies* (D.E.A.) which takes usually one year after the first graduation. For matters of easy equivalency with foreign degrees, the MESRS authorities follow the measuring principle of *baccalauréat + 2* for the first cycle of undergraduate studies; *baccalauréat + 4* for the first graduation; and *baccalauréat + 6* for the second graduation. The third graduation is "final" and time is not therefore, taken into consideration.

Another higher education degree, *concours de l'agrégation,* exists for humanities and some of the social sciences, for legal sciences and economics and also for medical sciences. Originally used to recruit the best teachers in the French system of education mainly for secondary schools, this highly selective exam is used in Tunisian higher education either as a second or third degree. It is a third degree equivalent in the legal sciences, economics, management, and medicine, which enables its holder to reach the highest professorial ranks (full professorships and *maître de conférences* positions). As for the humanities, the *agrégation* is just a second degree which competes with the D.R.A., because of its selective nature. It is slightly more prestigious than the latter but that image is rapidly fading away. Both degrees have the same value at the level of the *fonction publique* (which is the central civil service authority which is responsible for the national salary scale).

Entrance requirements for registration in a second degree vary also from one institution to another and sometimes from one field to another. While it is easy to register for a D.E.A. in the sciences or in law after the *maîtrise,* students in the humanities and in some social sciences (history, geography, philosophy, psychology, sociology, Arabic, English, and French), find themselves obliged to study for a one-year degree which is officially part of the undergraduate cycle. This degree is called the *certificat d'aptitude a la recherche* (C.A.R.). Registration for a *doctorat d'état* is only open to D.R.A. holders. No tests, exams, or courses are required before the final presentation of the dissertation which can be written either in French or in Arabic according to the nature of the area specialization and the medium of instruction used in the department concerned. It must be written in English in the case of the English departments.

The MESRS provides a small number of scholarships for graduate students. In the academic year 1988-89, 356 graduate scholarships were granted to 318 Tunisian graduates and 38 foreign exchange graduate students. The dissertations which were successfully defended in 1987-88 amount to a total of 111 divided as follows: eighty D.R.A. thesis and thirty-one *doctorats d'état.* It is interesting to note that the three Tunis universities share together 90 percent of that grand total with more than 50 percent of it for just the University of Tunis II (sciences, technology and medicine).

In principle, the faculty members of all higher education institutions are asked to contribute to fundamental and applied research in order to be promoted. Research and teaching have always been closely connected in the vision that Tunisian higher education authorities have had of research and they have always presented two arguments to back their choice. The first one, according to education authorities, is that quality teaching depends heavily on serious and continuous research, while the second has to do with the ever increasing needs of the institutions of higher education for teaching staff members, hence, their reluctance to lose the teachers to research centers. Because of this situation, it is very difficult to separate the postgraduate research structure from the general structure and organization of undergraduate studies which has dominated for the last thirty years or so all the attention and efforts of the Tunisian higher education authorities.

There are five research centers in Tunisia: The National Institute of Scientific and Technical Research (INRST) which includes the scientific fields of geology, physics, chemistry, and biology; The Sfax Biotechnological Center; *The Center for Economic and Social Research* (CERES); a new center for the legal and political sciences, economies, and management; and the CNUDST which is a national university center for scientific and technical documentation. It is possible that in the near future a new research center will be added for "re-writing" of the contemporary history of Tunisia in view of introducing some necessary corrections and rehabilitations.

These centers are totally funded by the MESRS. The total 1988 funding of this official research unit amounts to 856,000 Tunisian dinars (about a million US dollars). To that 1988 amount, we should also add TD1,147,920 (about US$1,250 million) which represents about a hundred research projects (presented by university institutions research teams) which have been granted contractual funding by the DRST of the MESRS. Most of these projects are in engineering, medicine, biology, geology, and agriculture. The humanities and the social sciences are hardly present in this structure representing about 11.5 percent of the above total.

The DRST takes advantage of bilateral cooperation programs mostly with French research institutions such as the CNRS or INSERM (for medical sciences) with seventy projects in 1988-89. But there are also some joint programs with West Germany, Sweden, Italy, and Canada. Some of the research programs receive some financial help from the EEC, UNESCO, and other United Nations agencies, the ACCT (Cultural and Technical cooperation Agency for French speaking countries), the AUPELF (Association of French Speaking Universities) and other non-governmental organizations such as *Le Laboratoire du Monde* which is located in Italy. The total budget for postgraduate research in the country within and outside of the structure of higher education amounts to not more than 0.2 percent of the national Tunisian GDP.

ISSUES AND TRENDS

Tunisian higher education has been beset by various problems ever since the inception of the "University of Tunis" immediately after independence. Such problems have not abated yet as the university system matured in the last thirty year period but rather, they became more and more acute. The main cause for this critical situation seems to be the high progression of the number of students reaching the university from the secondary school level each year as a result of the democratization of the educational system or what has been known as "the democratic choice". This "free education for all" policy which allows all secondary school graduates to enter an institution of higher education was probably a good and necessary principle in the sixties and early seventies when the number of high school graduates was still rather low, when the country needed all its graduates in all fields of knowledge and when the government of ex President Bourguiba prided itself for spending on an average basis the third of the national government budget for education. This situation is not the same anymore. About 21,000 new *baccalauréat* holders are expected to reach university in 1989-90 making the total student population 63,000. By the year 2000, the projected number of students will be tripled to reach a total of 150,000 students.

In order to prepare for the incoming waves of students, the Tunisian government must take immediate action. It must necessarily increase its intake capacity to accommodate the projected number of students. This can only be done at the extremely heavy cost of about 100 million US dollars over a period of ten years. But if the question of the needed new buildings and equipment can be materially answered at least in theory, the "impossible problem" seems to be the preparation of the required faculty members. If we try to project the needs of the year 2000 by using the 1989 standards, we figure that it would take us 8,000 new teaching staff members in all specialities and especially in the scientific and technological fields where the demand is increasingly higher. This is an impossible challenge to meet in ten years time even at the highest costs.

Other problems include the noticeable demoralization of the Tunisian university students. They live through what should have been an exciting experience with total disenchantment and no high expectations at all. A slogan which appeared in the mid-seventies "with or without education there is no future" reflects the state of mind. Most students lack motivation because the "orientation system" is perceived by them as a barrier separating them from what they would have "really" liked to do if they have been free to choose. These students usually blame the system for their failure in a speciality which does not match their estimated capacity.

It is certainly true that the "orientation system" is not absolutely perfect and does not seem to be based on previous short-term, medium-term, or long-term planning by the Directorate of Planning and other concerned ministries. It is also true that a good number of students have to accept to be registered in specialities which in no way are in line with their school grades or academic profile, if they want to stay within the "free" university structure. It is finally not less true that a yearly total of about 2,000 *baccalauréat* holders or more are below the passing grade average and can never match the institutions' acceptance criteria but are still enrolled at the university where they inevitably end up in the dropout statistics. All these facts combined give the Tunisian higher education system a very high attrition rate of about 75 percent or more for the whole undergraduate studies cycle. The wasteful nature of the whole system of higher education in Tunisia and its unbearably high costs are certainly important facts that the new government of President Zine-El Abdin Ben Ali have to consider with a great deal of seriousness in the near future.

There largely exists a feeling that the university did not accomplish its "developing mission" and that its whole credibility is endangered if it does not prove rapidly that it has the capacity to change and to overcome its shortcomings. An impressive number of reform reports have been stacked at the MESRS but action is slow to come.

The reasons are very simple. It is obvious that the first one is the economic situation of the country which does not permit any more expenditure than what is already allocated to education in general and to higher education in particular. The gist of the matter is that all possible reforms of the educational system in Tunisia centers around one major and very touchy problem which is that of costs. If the government is not capable of bearing the total cost of the educational effort anymore, it becomes obvious then that something has to give and that the principle of a "free university education for all" would have to be seriously looked at and probably even questioned. However, let us immediately say that we very much doubt that any government or political party can at present, openly implement the only solution to the issue being discussed which is charging the students and their families, when they can afford it, an important share of their higher education costs. Other steps which can lead to less emphasis on higher education must also be taken.

The "basic school reform" seems to be one of them since it shows the will of the present government to continue with a minimum adequate schooling for all the Tunisian children in an effort to eradicate illiteracy, while at the same time, increasing the professional and vocational training sectors of education to answer the needs of the industrial and agricultural structures. This last major reform which will be financed with a loan of 100 million US dollars from the World Bank should lead to a less important student enrollment in the secondary school system. This may represent a slight improvement in the realm of higher education which would still need daring and drastic reforms to leave the danger zone.

BIBLIOGRAPHY

Ben Dhia, Abdelazia. *L'Université Tunissiene, Le temps des questions, l'age de nouvelles options.* Tunis: MESRS, 1985.

Chettaoui, Abdelaziz. "Le bilinguisme dans l'enseignement primarie en Tunisie." In *Bulletin de Psychologie,* 335 (1978): 521-535.

Foster, Pablo. "Education in Tunisia." Unpublished manuscript, 1973.

Maamouri, Mohamed. "Literacy in Tunisia." In *Maghreb Digest,* Vol. 5, No. 1 (1967): 61-75.

Maamouri, Mohamed. "The Linguistic Situation in Independent Tunisia." In *The American Journal of Arabic Studies,* 1 (1971): 50-65.

Maamouri, Mohamed. "Illiteracy in Tunisia: An Evaluation." In *Language and Literacy: Current Issues and Research,* edited by Thomas P. Gorman. London: International Institute for Adult Literacy Methods, 1977.

Ministère de l'Education, de l'Enseignement Supérieur et de la Recherche Scientifique, Tunisia. *Academic Year 1988-1989 Statistics.*

Messaoudi, Mohamed M. "Crise de l'université: le cas Tunisien". Actes du Colloque de Montpellier (15-18 Septembre 1987). In *Pedagogiques* Vol. 8, No. 2 (1988): 15-22.

Payne, Richard M.   "Language Planning in Tunisia."   In *Studia Gratularia: Homenaje a Robert A. Hall, Jr.,* edited by D. Feldman.   Madrid: Playor, 1977.

TURKEY

by
Ziya Bursalioglu
Professor and Chairman
Department of Educational Administration and Planning
University of Ankara, Turkey

BACKGROUND

The origin of Turkish education goes back to the foundation of the Turkish Republic on 29 October 1923, when the Grand National Assembly accepted the republican form of government and elected Ataturk as the first president. Among Ataturk's daring reforms in the social, political, and economic arenas, foremost was educational reform. He considered educational reform as the basis of Turkish national unity and the foundation of a secular society. In his view, not only political independence but also economic prosperity of the nation were closely related to educational development. Thus, he considered education as an instrument of modernization. The only way to achieve this end was the unification of all education institutions. With the abolition of the Caliphet and the implementation of the Law of Unification of Instruction in 1924, secular education took the place of religious education at schools, all of which came under the Ministry of Education.

The first attempt for educational reorganization was the invitation of John Dewey to study the Turkish public education in 1924. The Dewey report indicated that the main objective of the Turkish educational system was to provide a framework for developing Turkey to be an independent and lay republic in line with the contemporary world (John Dewey Report 1960).

Next step was the project prepared by the Belgian expert Omer Buyse to organize a network of technical education. Following these, a series of educational legislation was promulgated covering primary, secondary, and higher education. One result was a marked increase in the number of education institutions. Also the introduction of the Latin alphabet in 1928, resulted in a rapid development of public and adult education (Bursalioglu 1965). The present Turkish school system is not different to any centralized system on the Continent except that the total duration of schooling is somewhat lesser with students spending five years in the primary, three years in the junior high, and three years in the senior high schools. With the exception of girl's vocational schools, all others are coeducational.

SECONDARY EDUCATION

In the academic year 1988-89, there were 5,072 junior high and 1,401 senior high schools in general education, and 768 junior high and 1,436 senior high schools in vocational and technical education. Instruction in all institutions of secondary education is given in accordance with the curricula developed by the Ministry of National Education. The duration of studies in junior and senior high schools is three years. Vocational senior high schools require four years of studies.

Academic calendar is determined by the Ministry and requires no less than 170 work days. Academic achievement is evaluated on the basis of written, oral examinations, homework, and projects. Final diploma score is the average of the annual achievement scores. With the exception of some private schools, instruction is in Turkish and is free of charge. Opportunities to benefit from scholarships and boarding facilities are provided to those students who take exams for such purposes. Foreign students are accepted in any of these schools provided they meet the requirements for admission. Extra curricular activities are planned and conducted by students under the supervision of the teachers.

In the academic year of 1988-89, the government expenditure on secondary education was 702,890 liras (US$1 = 2,059 Liras) per student in the general education stream and 1,906,139 liras in the vocational and technical stream. The 808cost for the family was 229,630 and 240,127 liras for vocational and technical streams respectively. The cost of a boarding student for 1990 was estimated at 1,173,530 liras per year. Secondary school teachers are trained in faculties of education, and are selected based on a competence examination conducted by the ministry. They are then selected (by drawing lots) to work in one of the five regions, on a rotational basis.

HIGHER EDUCATION

The Turkish University in Retrospect

After the Turkish Republic had been founded in 1923, Istanbul Darulfunun was transformed into Istanbul University in 1933. The reasons for this reformation was declared by the minister of education at the time, Dr. Desit Galip, as the lack of coordination among faculties and other units in scientific activities; inefficient education and instruction; and lack of scientific research and publication due to outside personal activities of instructors.

The Law 4936 passed in 1946 at the beginning of the multiparty system, and subsequent laws enacted in 1960 after the military revolution aimed at introducing institutional autonomy and academic freedom into the Turkish university. The 1961 constitution ensured autonomy and it was claimed that because of this constitutional autonomy, universities were placed outside any effective supervision and evaluation except by self-elected administrators. Therefore, universities did not adhere to plans and programs envisaged by the State Planning Department and the Parliament. The persistent decisions of university senates to keep enrollments down, and the high concentration of full and associate professors in metropolitan cities (Istanbul, Ankara, Izmir) in contrast to high vacancies in the countryside are pointed out as some of the drawbacks of this autonomy (Council of Higher Education 1988).

After the second military intervention in 1970, the "Law of Universities, No. 1750" was passed in 1973; and although a Council of Higher Education (CHE) was established by this law, Ankara University took the case to the constitutional court and had it overruled on the grounds that representatives of the government in the council outnumbered those of the universities. After the third military intervention in 1980, the new constitution granted only scientific autonomy to universities (with no administrative autonomy) and the new "Law of Higher Education No. 2547" was enacted in 1981 implementing this limited autonomy.

Originally, the Turkish university was organized after the German model under the influence of the German scholars who took refuge in Istanbul University and later in Ankara University during the two world wars. Following American aid and influence, new universities were established later. But the classical university maintained its organizational structure and administrative tradition within the framework of the general university laws. Four university laws have been passed since the establishment of the republic, and the contrast between the last two has been the most controversial. Academic, bureaucratic, judicial, military, and lay circles vary distinctly in their evaluations. For comparative purposes, some organizational and administrative dimensions of these two laws are explained below.

The new law significantly reduced the size of the university senate and the faculty council which are authorized to make academic decisions. The senate lost one third of its participants, due to only one senator being allowed from each faculty (plus the dean) instead of the two earlier. Formerly the faculty council was composed of full and associate professors whose number sometimes exceeded two hundred as in the case of the Faculty of Letters or Medicine. Presently the council consists of one assistant, two associates, and three full professors plus department heads. In order to limit the size, some faculties of social sciences were reduced to three departments of specialization. This formal but not functional limitation aroused justifiable criticism. But the academic administrators already displeased or unhappy with large scale decision organs welcomed the spirit of the principle in general.

The administrative council of the university and that of the faculty remained almost the same in size, but changed in function. First, they are considered as organs assisting or supporting the president and the dean respectively. Second, most of the functions of the faculty council are transferred to the administrative council. Therefore, the academic administrator who previously avoided calling the former to meet frequently because of the difficulties in getting a quorum is now obliged to meet this organ twice a semester and can work through a smaller body with ability for making quick decisions.

The new law envisaged the transfer of authority from councils to administrators. The president and the dean are now equipped with more authority which previously belonged to the senate and the faculty council. Even the department head who used to be a symbol in the department is now charged with full authority and responsibility for departmental decisions and their implementations. The centralization of authority involved both academic and administrative functions, like the new authority of the dean to compose a jury for assistant professorships or to direct disciplinary punishment for a student (after due investigation) without taking such matters to the council concerned. Similarly, much authority of the senate is now centralized on the president.

For the administration of higher education, a Council of Higher Education (CHE) was established by the new law. One third of its members is appointed by the chief of state (president of Turkey), one third by the Council of Ministers, and the last third is elected by the Interuniversity Council. The new law also provided another Council of Supervision for Higher Education whose members are elected by the Council of Higher Education.

A most significant and controversial change introduced by the new law was the replacement of elective procedure by appointive procedure. Previously, the president of a university was elected by full and associate professors of that university. The dean was elected by the faculty council composed of the same academics. The new law requires an administrative team. Now the president of a university is appointed by the chief of state from among four nominees, including outsiders, presented by the CHE. Similarly, the dean is appointed by the CHE from among three nominees presented by the president. The department head, previously elected by the faculty council, is now directly appointed by the dean. In arguing their case, the proponents of this procedure gave examples of the disadvantages of the exchange theory attributed to the elective system. The opponents, in turn, concentrated on the cases of political infiltration particularly into the appointive system. Both parties missed the quality factor. In other words, without clear-cut specifications of the qualities of the academic administration at every echelon, each approach would entail its own probable risks. The procedure does not follow the basic principle of administration that a superior should at least have a voice in the selection of his subordinates, if not a direct right. There were cases when a senate did not elect the candidate of the president as his vice-president.

A review of university presidents appointed by the CHE under the present law shows that about one third came from medical science, the speciality of the CHE president, and one fifth from Hacettepe University, the former university of the CHE president. Some university presidents were in place before the law and maintained previous organizational balance, but in some universities there was a rapid turnover of presidents within six years which proved that all appointments were not judicious after all. The mobility in case of deans was even higher, and appointments took place without much regard to administrative success or competence. Inexplicably, of twenty-two faculties of education, only two have professors of education appointed as deans by the CHE.

According to the former law, promotion to full professorship required the evaluation of a candidate through a jury organized by the faculty council, and the approval of the jury evaluation by both the faculty council and the university senate. The new law authorizes the president to organize a jury for the candidate and the jury reports are evaluated in the university administrative council which legally is not an academic organ.

Due to excessive inbreeding, the academic cadre of old universities have been unnecessarily larger. On the other hand, the new universities have always been in need of academic support. The new law stipulated three years service in another university as a prerequisite for promotion to full professorship. Also full professors with less than eight years of service would be subject to rotative service, under certain conditions. The first stipulation was removed in 1988. The second has been a case of informal agreement between the president and the dean.

As far as the academic load is concerned, it is at least ten hours a week for full and associate professors. The relative weights of the elements of this load, such as instruction, practice, advising etc. are determined by the CHE. Presidents and deans are exempt from academic load. Their assistants and department heads are charged with half of this load.

A permanent characteristic of the CHE has been its composition and recomposition usually with members drawn from one half of the political spectrum. This trend generally has been reflected in the appointment of academic administrators. Although during the initial term a few impartial ones were considered harmless, such was not the case later. After the 1983 elections and the reestablishment of the civilian government, this trend expanded as a result of the Eastern and somewhat religiously oriented policies. Therefore, any critical evaluation by the press, academics, or professional circles were reacted to through ideological role defense.

Undergraduate Studies

In the academic year 1987-88, student population in Turkish universities was 495,101 representing 10.3 percent of the age group. Acceptance to undergraduate programs requires diploma of senior high school of any kind and success in the two stage entrance examinations coordinated nationwide on the same day and time. Last year about 825,000 high school graduates took the first one which aims at a general evaluation and 51.5 percent became eligible to take the second about two months later. At the end of the second exam which is more specialized (natural or social sciences) 23.5 percent obtained admission to undergraduate education. Degree programs are offered in a variety of fields: natural sciences, social sciences, medical sciences, agricultural sciences, veterinary sciences, technology, engineering, languages, literature, fine arts, etc. With the exception of medical sciences which require six years, duration of first degree programs is four years. Again, with the exception of the Middle East, the Bilkent, and the Bosphorus Universities, instruction is in Turkish.

Tuition for medical sciences is 200,000 liras, for natural sciences and engineering 130,000 liras, and for social sciences 90,000 liras. The minimum monthly expenditure of a student who lives in a state dormitory is about 250,000 liras. There are about ninety-six state dormitories which generally offer bed and breakfast. The main source of student financing is the family. A federal organization offers monthly credit of 100,000 liras. Various private and federal organizations and foundations provide scholarships free or in return for compulsory service. Some students also work on part time basis. Some faculties require graduation thesis, but most research is conducted at the graduate level. In 1989, there were about 7,500 foreign students in Turkish universities. Medical care and extracurricular activities are provided by the department of health and sports in every university. Music, drama, excursions, and similar activities are also organized by this department.

Advanced Studies

Admission to advanced degree programs require a good first degree plus proficiency examinations in a foreign language and in the field of specialization. The entrance and achievement score for master's candidates is sixty-five, and for doctoral candidates is seventy-five and above. In 1989, there were about 18,000 candidates in the master's programs and 8,900 candidates in the doctoral programs. Main fields of specialization are very similar to those in the undergraduate programs. Graduate instruction is organized by the institutes of social, natural, and medical sciences, but carried out by the departments of the relevant faculties. Academic year is composed of two semesters with sixteen weeks of instruction. Master's programs require twelve courses in two semesters and a thesis which takes two additional semesters. Doctoral programs also require twelve courses in four semesters plus a thesis which take four extra semesters. With the exception of the three universities mentioned earlier, instruction is in Turkish. Postgraduate students are exempt from tuition, but they are not granted federal scholarships. In 1989, about 150 professors taught in postgraduate programs. Conventional field or library research is required in partial fulfillment of the degrees mentioned above.

ISSUES AND TRENDS

The basic issues of Turkish education have been and will be the reorganization of the educational system, the desired student flow from general to technical education, the renewal of contents of instructional programs, and the integration of formal and adult education. In addition, a very controversial issue has been the unplanned increase of *imam-hatib* (mosque priest and minister) junior and senior high schools from 7 in 1951 to 718 in 1988. These schools graduated about 425,000 students between 1961 and 1987, in contrast to the volume of mosques in the country which number only 63,000. It is feared that this trend will create a society with religious bias in contrast to Ataturk's vision of a secular state. It is further claimed that this trend has reflected itself in staffing universities after 1980 military intervention (Adem 1990).

In the arena of higher education, the dominant issues have been the ones relating to the implementation of the new Law of Higher Education 2547 of 1981 as compared to the provisions of the earlier Law 1750.

The new law aimed at the integration of higher education not only of universities (including the two with special status) but also of all institutions of higher education, although most of them were already within the jurisdiction of the

Ministry of National Education. As a result, all teacher training institutions with three-or four-year instructional periods have been hurriedly transferred and attached to universities closest to them, without giving sufficient time for orientation. The philosophy of this quick transition was not only to raise the standards of teacher training, but also to free teacher training enterprises from political infiltration and ministerial violations. As a result, twenty colleges (faculties) of education and twenty-two junior colleges of education were created out of previous teacher training institutions. Such a structural and administrative integration has long been indispensable in Turkey particularly for secondary education which consists of about twenty types of secondary schools. A true integration at the level of higher education will probably force secondary education, although a reverse development, in the same direction.

The new law has banned membership in and activity on behalf of any political party by academic staff and student body. With the exception of public service, membership in any association is subject to authorization of the president upon approval by the dean. Nevertheless, if any academic is called to serve in the Council of Ministers, the Parliament, or other public institution (without being attached to any party), his right to return to his university at the end of such service is reserved.

The new and legalized trend in the Turkish university administration for moving from decentralization to centralization has been perceived differently by the affected institutions and individuals according to their frames of reference. Those involved in political activity were the most unhappy because of the alleged state control at the cost of academic freedom. Those who taught few hours a week and spent the rest of their time in moonlight jobs were displeased. Those who sincerely and candidly believed that university administration should be different from that of a normal public institution were in a state of anticipation of further evaluation of prospective implementation. Those who worked full time and were too conscious to evade their professional duties were glad because of the legal constraints and probable justice.

One of the most controversial issues in the university has certainly been the academic freedom, which has evoked more controversy under the new law. The opponents of the new law have persistently held that this freedom was reduced if not entirely eliminated. Under the initial impact of the new law, the authorities conducted disciplinary investigations of the academicians who criticized the law or its implementative consequences. Some academic administrators conducted or requested such investigations under false pretenses. Some of these requests were rejected by the Council of Higher Education, some others were overruled by administrative courts, and some resulted in punishment; but all caused psychological pain for academicians.

A public opinion poll conducted by the Milliyet newspaper showed that 73 percent of those consulted believed that universities did not have academic freedom (Milliyet 13 April 1986) whereas academic freedom is the indispensable element for a healthy generation of science and technology, as pointed out by Kemal Kafali, the president of the Technical University in Istanbul (Kafali 1987). Due to this lack of freedom, universities which used to think and react before the law have been silent now (Yaylacioglu 1987). Therefore, while political interdictions pursued by the earlier military administration have slackened, academic ones were still in effect (Kepenek 1988). The article 7/1 of the law states, "Those who act against the objectives, principles, and order envisaged in this law shall be transferred to another institution of higher education for reevaluation, or shall be discharged upon the request of the university president, or directly within normal procedure". This veiled threat over the head of the academician has rendered all optimistic interpretations of academic freedom dubious.

The last reorganization of the Council of Higher Education by a government decree divided this organ, still with ten bureaucrats, into two: the General Council composed of twenty-four members, and the Executive Council composed of nine members. This structure will probably produce a more closed system of strategic decision making in higher education.

From the very beginning, the Council of Higher Education has suffered from a lack of balance in terms of representing primary university disciplines in the composition of the CHE. This entailed the amusing contrast that no professor of education has been elected to the Council of Higher education. It might have originated from the misconception that every university professor is a specialist in education. As a result, educational planning remained at an amateur level. Some of the members were former academic or bureaucratic administrators and the leadership is considered to be autocratic. The Council of Higher Education has also been a scapegoat for whatever that has gone wrong in universities, because it had centralized the most trivial aspects of authority, with little discretion left to presidents, and almost none to deans. The repetitive criticisms of journalists, academicians, and politicians serve as prima facie evidence of the insensitivity of the educational authorities in power.

Power without opposition is neither infallible nor enjoyable. The two dilemmas of leadership behavior are that either the leaders believe in their undisputable success or their close followers make them believe so, which is more detrimental. The truth is usually discovered and accepted at the very end.

The critical evaluations documented in this article do not imply the denial of the contributions and sacrifices made so far. Nevertheless, given the unquestionable support of the state President Kenan Evren, the vast legal and administrative authority, and the favorable resources devoted to higher education, some advancement may have certainly been made. This evaluation is intended to indicate that a great deal more could have been achieved, as stated in the report of the World Bank, through more efficient administration. What else remains to defend if the present minister of national education of the party in power qualifies our educational system as not being contemporary (Guzel 1988).

Any educational innovation should be evaluated in terms of new contributions to students and society. The significance does not lie in new system structures, but in new relationship between the system and its environment. Structural innovations should follow the innovations needed for such relationships. Much speculative material has been written and uttered on the new structure and administration of Turkish higher education. But there has hardly been any research effort to carry out a proper evaluation.

Initial data derived from a study conducted by one of the author's doctoral candidates appear to justify the incessant criticism directed at the present law and its implementation. The study compared the two laws of Turkish higher education (the new law 2547 and the previous law 1750) from the viewpoints of organizational structure and administrative process by means of a statistically valid survey of full and associate professors (who had served at least five years under each law governing higher education) of all the twenty-seven Turkish universities. From a potential survey population of about 2,500 individuals, one fourth responded. Based on the survey, the collective perception of the majority was that the previous law and its implementation were more professional and rational than the one now enacted (Baskan 1989).

Since enactment of the present law governing Turkish higher education, the virtues of the organizational structure and administrative process it prescribes have been persistently and stoutly defended by state educational authorities without recognizing its many inherent shortcomings. Not the least of these shortcomings is the low regard that the new law enjoys among key members of the academic community as demonstrated by this study. If the prescriptions of the current law were sound, then these academic critics would be the strongest proponents of the law instead of being its opponents.

BIBLIOGRAPHY

Adem, Mahmut. "Ulusal Eğitimimizin Öncelikli Sorunlari". *Cumhuriyet,* 14 April 1990.

Baskan, Gulsun. "A Comparison of the University Law numbered 1750 and the Higher Education Law numbered 2547 from the viewpoints of Organizational Structure and Administrative Process." Doctoral diss., University of Hcettepe, Ankara, 1989.

Bursalioğlu, S. Z. "The Changing Character of Education in Successive Reformation Periods of Turkish History." Unpublished Ph.D. diss., University of Illinois, Urbana, 1965.

Council of Higher Education, Turkey. *1981 Yükseköğretim Reformu ve Alti Yillik Uygulama Sonuclari.* Ankara: CHE, 1988.

Guzel, H. C. "Eğitim Sistemi Cağdas Değil." *Sonhavadis,* 21 Mark 1988.

Kafali, Kemal. "YÖK Yeniden Düzenlenmeli." *Cumhuriyet,* 2 October 1987.

Kepenek, Yakup. "Bilimsel Yasaklar Sürdürülüyor." *Cumhuriyet,* 25 February 1988.

Millî Eğitim, Bakanliği. Test ve Araştirma Bürosu. *The John Dewey Report.* Ankara, 1960.

"Üniversiteler Özerk Değil." *Milliyet,* 13 April 1986.

Yaylaclioğlu, Ahmet. "YÖK, Üniversitelerimiz ve Ülke Sorunlari." *Milliyet,* 21 March 1987.

UGANDA

by
J. P. Ocitti
Professor and Dean, Faculty of Education
Makerere University, Uganda

BACKGROUND

Education in its broadest sense, as a process of learning which enables each individual to acquire completeness as a human being within the framework set by the society, predates the introduction of Western style school education, largely by the Christian missionaries, towards the end of the nineteenth century. That education is variously referred to as "socialization", "enculturation", "traditional", or "indigenous" education. It enabled individuals to become full and effective members of their society through incidental, informal, and formal acquisitions of practical knowledge, skills, and values. In that sense, indigenous education was a truly basic education; a package for successful and acceptable living for every member of society set against a largely rural environment.

The indigenous forms of education, however, do not appear to have had well-developed formal modes of higher education during the pre-colonial period, apart from the training of traditional specialists (for example, craftsmen like blacksmiths, royal potters, and makers of bark-cloths and musical instruments) through a long period of apprenticeship, herbal medicine men through private tuition, and political and military leaders mostly within the royal enclosures.

Thus higher education as we know it today in Uganda began with the establishment of Makerere College in 1922 basically to train talented "natives" for subordinate positions in the colonial civil service. From 1922 up to the mid 1950s, Makerere College was the only center of publicly funded higher education for the whole of the Eastern African region. By 1970, it achieved the status of a fully fledged university. Today, Makerere University has a student population of some 7,000 with a staff-student ratio of 1:15. It comprises the faculties of arts, science, engineering, agriculture and forestry, social sciences, law, commerce, veterinary science, and medicine; the School of Education and Fine Arts; the Center of Continuing Education and the institutes of environmental science, computer science, statistics, and applied economics and of social research.

Besides Makerere University, there are nearly fifty other institutions of higher education in Uganda, most of which were set up after 1962 when Uganda achieved political independence from Britain and there was a great need to train sufficient manpower to fill the vacant posts previously occupied by the white colonial administrators.

PRIMARY AND SECONDARY EDUCATION

Today, Uganda has a network of Western style education institutions spread throughout the country. The medium of instruction at all levels is English. The first cycle of education lasts seven years. It enrolls about 2 million pupils of which 43 percent are girls. The gross enrollment for this level of education is about 55 percent of the age group 6-13.

Due to limited resources, education at the second cycle is restricted to less than 20 percent of the pupils who complete the first cycle. It is carried out in about 600 schools with a total enrollment of some 200,000 pupils of which 33 percent are females. It takes thirteen years of schooling for a bright student in Uganda to enter any institution of higher learning i.e. seven years of primary education ending with the Primary Leaving Examination (P.L.E.): four years of ordinary level secondary education leading to the Uganda Certificate of Education ("O" level); and two years of advanced or higher secondary culminating in the Uganda Advanced Certificate of Education ("A" level).

Most preuniversity institutions follow a largely academic curriculum including among others, mathematics, physics, biology, English, French, German, Swahili and Luganda languages, geography, history, religious education, political education, agriculture, and commerce. There are extracurricular activities in all schools, the commonest being sports, games, and cultural activities.

Like the first cycle of education, secondary education is, indeed, the rich man's harvest. Parents have to pay heavily, relatively speaking, to have their children educated. The government meets mainly the cost of buildings, equipment, and teachers' salaries. One-third of the secondary institutions are boarding schools but apart from being prohibitedly expensive, these have very limited access due to heavy competition. The majority of the teaching staff in secondary schools are graduates and over 60 percent are professionally trained.

HIGHER EDUCATION

Institutions

In Uganda, the term higher or tertiary education is used to refer to the system of advanced education undertaken in post - "A" level institutions. That is to say, a student must have successfully completed six years of secondary education before he or she gains admission to any higher education institution.

Higher education institutions in Uganda are either publicly or privately supported and controlled. Those which are publicly financed are furthermore subdivided into three types: universities which are autonomous; institutions under the Ministry of Education; and institutions under the Public Service Commission.

Publicly funded institutions which are autonomous and regulated by their own acts of parliament include the Makerere University and Mbarara University of Science and Technology.

Tertiary institutions falling directly under the Ministry of Education comprise the following: Institute of Teacher Education, Uganda Polytechnic, National College of Business Studies, technical colleges (four in number), colleges of commerce (five in number), and national teachers' colleges (ten in number).

Government departmental training institutions which fall under the overall control of the Public Service Commission and which appropriately fall in the category of higher education include Institute of Public Administration (mainly for postgraduate studies), Uganda Law Development Center (mainly for postgraduate studies), School of Radiography, School of Medical Laboratory Technology, and School of Physiotherapy. Other Public Service Commission institutions which are partially tertiary (since they admit students from both "O" and "A" levels) include agricultural colleges (four in number), Fisheries Training Institute, veterinary training institutes (two in number), Kigumba Cooperative College, and Soroti Flying School, and other paramedical schools (ten in number).

Privately funded institutions of higher education include Islamic University in Uganda, national seminaries (three in number - Catholic), Bishop Tucker Theological College (Anglican), Bugema Adventist College, College of Tertiary Studies (Anglican), Chartered Institute of Bankers, and Nkumba College of Commerce.

Makerere University was established by an act of parliament (Makerere University Act, 1970) making it autonomous in both academic and administrative matters. Under this act, the university has the following functions: provision of instruction to all those admitted to the university; advancement, transmission, and preservation of knowledge; stimulation of intellectual life in Uganda; preservation and fostering of the university's right to determine the qualification of who may teach, what may be taught, how it may be taught and the requirements to be fulfilled in order to be admitted to various disciplines; planned development of higher education in Uganda, (working with other appropriate bodies) and in particular to examining and making proposals to the government for new faculties, new departments, new degree courses, or new subjects of study; and award of degrees, diplomas, and other certificates provided for by the statutes.

The Islamic University at Mbale and the Mbarara University of Science and Technology, although new, are equally autonomous in academic and administrative matters as guaranteed under their separate charters.

Unlike universities, other public institutions of higher education which may have statutes but not full charters have their academic and professional development and administrative operations greatly curtailed by their mother government ministries. Thus, tertiary institutions under the Ministry of Education, such as the Institute of Teacher Education, Uganda Polytechnic, Uganda College of Business Studies; colleges of commerce and national teacher's colleges have their policies, structure, and operations controlled by that ministry. Similarly, the Ministry of Agriculture determined the objectives, structure, and administration of its agricultural colleges. The same is true with the other tertiary institutions under the ministries of health, cooperatives and marketing, labor, public service and cabinet affairs, and justice.

Although registered with the Ministry of Education, private institutions of higher education which are mainly theological or concerned with business education are controlled much more by their financiers (owners) than by the government. And for those private institutions which prepare their students for external degrees, their academic programs as well as development and management are usually influenced by the awarding institutions as well.

Governance

In theory, the Ministry of Education, in consultation with the Ministry of Planning and Economic Development and Finance, is responsible for formulating policies and strategies for developing tertiary education in the country as a whole, usually in accordance with the recommendations of an education commission. Other ministries which have tertiary training institutions are also responsible for formulating some policies, to some extent, for the establishment and development of such institutions, but in strict adherence to their manpower requirements. The proposed policy is normally submitted to the Cabinet of Ministers for discussion and subsequently presented to the National Legislature (Parliament) for final approval.

At the institutional level, the development of universities are guided by their respective plans which are normally initiated by the faculties, discussed at length in the senate, and finally approved by the supreme organ, the university council. The implementation of such plans, of course, will vary largely depending on the willingness of the government (in the case of public universities) to release more funds.

For other non-university institutions which do not have charters of their own, the plans are made by the institutions' governing boards in consultation with the ministry relevant to their institutions. In turn, their ministries are required to have the clearance of the ministries of planning and economic development, public service and cabinet affairs and finance, before any implementation is undertaken (that is, if the institution concerned is publicly funded).

Institutions of higher education, especially the universities, are expected to have three main outputs: teaching, research, and public service. Given the financial support, institutions of higher learning in Uganda have set up administrative structures and created atmospheres which are generally conducive to the achievement of the three goals.

Makerere University, for example, faced with a bewildering variety of academic programs, research agendas, and community services is able to manage all this diverse work because it has a system of governance that can be described as complex. Its structure basically comprises central, faculty, and departmental administration. The central administration, through its major organs like the council and the senate together with their associated committees, is charged with the responsibility of carrying out coordination, planning, and operation of different faculties, departments, and general administration. The supreme organ that runs the university is the council, whose membership consists of representatives from the government, university community (staff, students, and workers) and members of the public. The council has several committees to deal with specific issues such as finance, appointments, and other administrative issues. Academic affairs of the university are under the guidance and supervision of the senate, most of whose members are drawn from the university community such as deans, heads of departments, students, and academic staff. Like the council, the senate has many working committees on matters related to activities of the university such as library, research, publications, and student affairs.

The head of Makerere University as that of Mbarara University is the chancellor who is also the head of state. But the executive head of each institution is called the vice-chancellor (in the case of public universities) or rector in the case of the International Islamic University at Mbale and in some private tertiary institutions like the Catholic National Seminaries. Each faculty or school is headed by a dean while departments and institutes have heads and directors respectively. Faculty boards are the highest organs in the administration of the faculties, schools, or institutes and there are also departmental boards which take care of teaching, carrying out research, curriculum development, and student administration issues.

Non-university tertiary institutions, on the other hand, have got administrative structures which are fairly simple. Most are headed by principals or directors who manage their institutions in accordance with policy guidelines which are formulated by their respective governing bodies called boards of governors.

In most institutions of higher education, particularly the universities, the use of the committee system is popular for several reasons; it ensures thorough work thus achieving efficiency and it encourages wider participation by members of the institution making the process democratic. Together with the existence of staff associations, workers committees, and student unions, each institution of higher learning is able to be in harmony with itself on the one hand, and with the larger society outside its campus, on the other.

In general, the largest share of revenue for public higher education is contributed by the government. This accounts for nearly 100 percent of the expected revenue. Students who are nationals do not pay anything. Instead they are supported financially by the government which meets their transport and pocket money requirements as well as their boarding expenses. Besides, the costs of staff salaries, instructional materials, physical facilities, infrastructural materials and other requirements of an academic nature are all met by the government. And because the bulk sources of finance comes from the national budget, each of the public institutions of higher education is required to present its estimates to its ministry which examines the budget and submits it to the Ministry of Finance. The funds from the national budget cover both recurrent and development expenditures including salaries for the staff and the maintenance costs of students.

At Makerere University, the unit cost per student is about 80,000 Uganda shillings (US$500) per annum. The overall recurrent expenditure averages about the equivalent of US$12 million per year. Research activities account for about 5 percent of the recurrent expenditure and money spent on library requirements is 3 percent.

National universities (Makerere and Mbarara) enjoy the virtue of academic freedom, but because their finances are provided by the government, their autonomy is partially curtailed. For the same reason, other public institutions of higher education have even lesser independence partly because they have no charters of their own. In contrast, private institutions of higher education, although registered in the Ministry of Education, enjoy a much wider degree of both management and financial autonomy.

Undergraduate Studies

Undergraduate fields of study at Makerere University may be categorized into degree, diploma, and certificate programs. Certificate courses include adult studies and librarianship (lasting one year). And diploma courses are offered in librarianship, music, dance, and drama (for two years).

First degree courses are offered in professional fields such as education, medicine, dentistry, veterinary, agriculture, engineering, commerce, forestry, law, social work, and statistics as well as in the following academic subjects: philosophy, comparative religion, geography, history, languages (Luganda, Kiswahili, Lingala, English, French, German, and Russian), linguistics, political science, public administration, sociology, economics, music, dance, drama, fine art, physics, chemistry, zoology, botany, geography, mathematics, environmental science, and computer science.

At the Islamic University in Mbale, fields of study leading to bachelor's degree awards include Islamic studies, education, and medicine. On the other hand, the new Mbarara University of Science and Technology prepares students for first degree awards in development studies, education, medicine, and applied science.

The Institute of Teacher Education at Kyambogo admits teachers with diploma qualifications for a two year B.Ed. degree. Other candidates, with "A" level passes admitted to national teachers' colleges are trained as lower secondary school teachers for two years and awarded the Diploma in Education by the institute.

Other tertiary institutions, especially those for technical and commercial subjects such as agriculture, fisheries, veterinary science, and paramedical work train their students for certificates and diplomas with the duration of the courses ranging between two and three years.

With the exception of medicine and veterinary science which are studied for five years each, and engineering for four years, first degree programs in Uganda normally last three years. The academic year runs from 1st October to 30th June or to 30th August for four term courses. During the first year of degree study, all candidates are required to take and pass three subjects before being allowed to proceed to the second year of study. Supplementing the academic programs which include lectures, tutorials, library studies, and practicals, undergraduate students have facilities for social relaxation, chaplaincies and health care, numerous sporting activities, and other recreations including participation in students' government.

Undergraduate studies are free for Ugandans, with the government meeting the total costs. However for the few foreign students, accounting for about 1 percent of the total enrollment, a sum not exceeding US$6,000 is charged per year.

The Advanced Certificate ("A" level) conducted by the Uganda National Examination Board (UNEB) or its equivalent is required for admission to diploma or degree programs. Besides, some programs of study may require the candidates to pass an oral interview in addition to the possession of both "O" and "A" level secondary school certificates. Other variables for determining admission depend on the type of program. For example, paramedical courses require knowledge of biology and chemistry, engineering needs passes in mathematics and physics, and commerce or statistics requires good performance in mathematics.

At the universities, there is, besides the direct entry based on "O" and "A" level passes, a provision for admission of students who might have stopped their formal school education five or more years before applying for admission to various courses. The candidates who must be over twenty-five years of age sit for a special examination under the Mature Age Scheme and if successful, are admitted to diploma or degree courses.

A limited number of Uganda students are encouraged to go abroad if the courses they wish to take are not available locally. For instance, under the East African Inter-University Student Exchange Program, forty Uganda students are admitted to universities in the neighboring countries of Kenya and Tanzania each year. In addition, limited annual scholarships are offered to Uganda by friendly countries and organizations under which some students gain admission to universities and institutes abroad.

Similarly, there are foreign students at Makerere University, sponsored by their home governments or the United Nations High Commission for Refugees, or other funding sources including the Inter-University Student Exchange Program. At the Islamic University in Uganda at Mbale, according to its Charter, 50 percent of students must be foreign, principally from the English-speaking African countries.

All in all, the criteria for determining the number of students in higher education institutions include the physical capacity available in the institutions; the manpower requirements of various government ministries and institutions; and, above all, the finances the government is prepared to release to maintain the students and to run the institutions.

Advanced Studies

Postgraduate studies, leading to awards of higher degrees and postgraduate diplomas are confined to Makerere University. The programs are open to graduates of Makerere University or of other recognized universities.

The minimum requirements for a postgraduate diploma is a bachelor's degree in a subject or subjects relevant to the course sought. For a master's degree, the admission requirement is a bachelor's degree of at least upper second class. Applicants with lower qualifications who feel that they can cope with higher degree work must satisfy the relevant department that they have acquired academic maturity, for instance, by evidence of research and publications. In some departments, a qualifying course is given.

For the Ph.D. degree, possession of a master's degree is a must. However, first degree candidates who wish to register for a Ph.D. may register for a master's first and after a year or two of satisfactory progress, apply for upgrading of their candidature to Ph.D. For M.D. and Ch.M. degree, any Bachelor of Medicine and Surgery (M.B.Ch.B.) degree of not less than three years standing constitute the minimum entry requirements.

Makerere University awards the following categories of postgraduate qualifications: postgraduate diplomas in education, computer science, librarianship, medicine (obstetrics and public health) and statistics; master's degrees in specialized subjects of education, arts, fine art, social sciences, laws, agriculture, forestry, veterinary medicine, human medicine, surgery, statistics, environmental science, and other science subjects; and doctoral degrees in the same disciplines as in the master's degree program.

Whereas postgraduate diplomas are done by course work and practical work, all higher degree courses involve a great deal of individual and original research. Candidates work on their own under the guidance of supervisors. Some degrees, however, begin with full-time course work lasting for one academic year. Upon successful completion of the course work, the candidate goes on to research.

The duration of postgraduate studies vary. Diplomas last one academic year; master's degree takes two calendar years (three years if it is undertaken on a part-time basis); and medicine takes three years. On the other hand, the Ph.D. and M.D. degrees last five calendar years. With permission, these periods may be extended to five for master's and seven years for doctoral degrees. The period of study for a higher degree largely depends on the nature of the subject and the candidate's own preparedness for it. For instance, a hardworking and good candidate who registers on full-time basis may be allowed to submit a master's thesis one year after registration and a doctoral thesis two years after registration.

For Ugandans, fees for tuition, research, and accommodation are completely free. But candidates who are not Ugandan citizens are required to pay annual fees of US$5,000 for study by research and dissertation, and US$7,000 for full-time study by course work plus dissertation. These figures do not cover, research and accommodation expenses which, if taken into consideration, will double the above figures.

Teaching Staff

The administrative procedures followed in the recruitment, appointment, confirmation, development, promotion, and disciplining of teaching staff in all types of public institutions of higher education in Uganda are generally similar. For university teaching and administrative staff, the recruiting and appointing authority is vested in their respective appointments boards. However for staff of other higher education institutions, the recruitments and appointments are undertaken by the Teaching Service Commission (for staff teaching in institutions directly controlled by the Ministry of Education) and the Public Service Commission (for staff teaching in other tertiary institutions attached to government ministries).

Private institutions of higher learning have their appointing bodies as well but all in all, the minimum academic qualification required of any person who wishes to be appointed to teach, particularly in universities and other degree-granting institutions is a good master's degree. As part of staff development, in-service training seminars and workshops are organized from time to time to retrain or refresh the teaching staff including the supporting staff, especially the technicians who assist in practical work.

Apart from training which a few of the staff who may pursue during the postgraduate diploma course in education (geared to secondary school teaching), appropriate pedagogical education to give initial teaching skills to those who intend to teach in institutions of higher education does not exist. However, it is hoped that with the opening of the Department of Higher Education in the Makerere University School of Education, appropriate programs would soon be developed and the much needed pedagogical training instituted, for teaching staff in higher education institutions.

Opportunities for postdoctoral studies, study leaves, sabbaticals, and secondments to other universities both at home and abroad under the staff exchange programs, do exist. Staff members are encouraged to avail themselves of such opportunities in order to increase the level of exposure to new ideas and the access to modern teaching aids and research methods.

ISSUES AND TRENDS

With the opening of more universities and colleges of higher education, Makerere University, which is the oldest institution of higher education in Eastern Africa, is gradually assuming the full role of academic, professional, and research leadership in Uganda. One noticeable trend in higher education in the country is reflected in the efforts being made to redesign curricula in order to bring them in line with recent academic needs and innovations on the one hand, and to meet the national development priorities on the other.

It is also becoming apparent that there is a gradual move from rigid academic structure to more flexible programs. e.g. through the introduction of the credit system; through modern technology; and through interdisciplinary programs, courses and optional subjects.

There is the public call for the democratization of higher education through widening of admission avenues to ensure equality of opportunity especially for women and the handicapped; introduction of part-time and evening classes for working persons; strengthening of the counselling and information services for the students; and diversification of higher education by expanding existing and new institutions partly to facilitate the introduction of new disciplines.

In general, all types of higher education in Uganda are confronted with the double-edged problem of inadequate qualified manpower, and financial resources required for their efficient and effective operations and development. The future lies in exploring other alternative sources of revenue to supplement government efforts for higher education in Uganda. Currently, financial and material contributions by the private sector is very insignificant, as reflected in the case of Makerere University, by occasional sponsorship of professional and other posts, and donations of teaching materials and books. The other possibility to pursue is the sharing of higher education costs between the government, the parents, and other beneficiaries.

There is a move in official circles to introduce the student loan system under an arrangement of cost-sharing formula so that the students and their parents meet the non-pedagogical costs. There is also the call directed at the private sector, especially the large industries, to contribute more meaningfully to the financing of higher education in the country.

Other challenges facing higher education in Uganda include maintaining education excellence partly through adequate financial allocations to higher education; strengthening the revenue generating capacity of universities and other tertiary institutions; and creating greater efficiency and effectiveness in the administration and management of higher education institutions so that their manpower, research, and public service outputs have the highest quality.

BIBLIOGRAPHY

ESAURP. *The Inventory of Universities and Selected Tertiary Institutions in Eastern and Southern African Countries.* Dar es Salaam, Tanzania: Eastern and Southern African Universities Research Program, 1983.

ESAURP. *The Development of Higher Education in Eastern and Southern Africa.* Dar es Salaam, Tanzania: Eastern and Southern African Universities Research Program, 1985.

Goldthrope, J. E. *An African Elite: Makerere College Students, 1922-1960.* London: Oxford University Press, 1965.

Macpherson, M. *They Built for the Future.* London: Cambridge University Press, 1964.

Wandira, A. *The African University in Development.* Johannesburg, South Africa: Ravan Press, 1977.

UNION OF SOVIET SOCIALIST REPUBLICS

by
A. Ya Savelyev
Director, Moscow State Research Institute
for Higher Education, U.S.S.R.

BACKGROUND

The history of higher educational development on the territory that currently is the U.S.S.R. goes back to ancient past. An important role was played by the Georgian Colchis Higher Rhetorical School established in the fourth century, as well as the academies founded in the eleventh and the twelfth centuries (Ikatoyan, Germian, and Gelatian). The Gelatian Academy (near Kutaisi) became a center of both secular and clerical education offering a variety of subjects: arithmetic, geometry, astronomy, philosophy, grammar, rhetoric, and music.

Teaching in medieval institutions of higher education was of scholastic nature; the goals of education were to protect church and theological postulates and to propagate religion. Natural phenomena were viewed through religious dogmas. At the same time these institutions, in spite of the church domination, played an important role in creating an intellectual foundation for the medieval society, and a foundation for the development of science. Their activities were aimed not only towards giving knowledge of theory, but also towards creating a tradition of abstract and logical thinking.

The development of capitalism, accompanied by the rapid growth of productive forces and the advancement of theoretical (mathematics, mechanics, astronomy) as well as experimental (metallurgy, chemistry, applied astronomy, medicine, etc.) sciences contributed to the liberation of institutions of higher education from the influence of the church. Educators and humanist writers such as Vitgorio da Feltre, E. Rutherdame, L. Vivey, F. Rable, and M. Montel spoke out against clergy's control of education and against domination of scholasticism in higher education. They laid a foundation of new methods of education for the youth, based on development of independent thinking, memory, skills, and meaningful study of the laws of nature.

Invention of printing in the fifteenth century was of exceptional importance. Educational process at the universities and academies improved. Experience was been generalized, and the use of experimentation expanded. Outstanding scholarly achievements during the Renaissance period were reflected in the works of the most prominent Slavic educator Ya. A. Kamensky who proposed a well-structured successive multileveled system of education with academy as a final level. Formation of centralized states in the fourteenth and the fifteenth centuries contributed to increased influence of the secular authorities over institutions of higher education.

By the end of the sixteenth century, after a long struggle with the clergy who dominated higher education, secular authorities drove the latter out of the universities and a system of secular education began to take root. In 1579 the Vilnius Academy was established. It had the rights and privileges of a university, yet it mainly served the interests of the Catholic Church (in 1803 it was reorganized as a university).

In 1632 the first Russian-Ukranian institution of higher education, the Kiev-Mogiliov Academy, was established where Slavonic, Latin, and Greek languages, and seven liberal arts (grammar, rhetoric, dialectic, arithmetic, geometry, astronomy, music, and theology) were studied. The Kiev-Mogiliov Academy became a major center of Southern and Southwestern Russia at that time. Many prominent figures of culture and education worked and studied there (Epithany Slavinetsky, Simeon Polotsky, Theophan Prokopovich, etc.). In 1661, the University of L'vov was established. In 1687, the Slavic-Greek-Latin Academy was organized in Moscow. The Academy contributed to the spreading of general education in Russia. Many prominent leaders of the seventeenth and the eighteenth centuries came out of it (F. P. Polikarpov-Orlov, K. Istomin, V. K. Trediakovsky, P. V. Postnikov, L. F. Magnitsky, and the first professors of the Moscow University, N. N. Popovsky and A. A. Barsov). Another of the oldest institutions of higher education is the Tartu University, whose history goes back to 1632 when Gustavian Academy was established in Tartu. In 1755, Moscow University was established. In 1773, a mining school was opened in St. Petersburg (now Leningrad Mining Institute). Other institutions established at that time include the School of Land-surveying in Moscow, and the Academy of Medicine and Surgery in St. Petersburg.

Higher education flourished in the nineteenth century. Governments needed more and more officials and administrators, engineers, and doctors. The number of universities and specialized higher education institutions grew to meet the demand. Among them were technical, agricultural, and medical schools. Establishment of new institutions increased the number of people with not just specialized education, but with general education in natural sciences as well.

In the second half of the nineteenth century, Russia entered a period of steep advance in capitalist industry. The consequence of this was the increasing necessity for engineers and other specialists. Employers as well as statesmen understood the necessity of further development of higher education, particularly in technical areas. In 1895, there were already 11 higher technical education institutions (Kharkov's Technological Institute in 1835, Ekaterinoslav's Mining Institute in 1889, and others). Also new kinds of institutions, the polytechnical institutes, were created. These institutions were to be technical universities, preparing a wide spectrum of specialists in applied knowledges. Polytechnical institutes were opened in Kiev (1898), Petersburg (1902), Novocherkassk (1909), and in Tomsk (1900). Pedagogical higher education institutions were also established in Petersburg (1903), and in Moscow (1911).

However, the scale of development of higher education in Tsarist Russia was incommensurate with the real necessities of social and economic life and the potential for growth. The Russian Empire with a population of 180 million had only 105 higher education institutions in 1914-1915 and they were situated in the European part of the country and had an enrollment of only 127,000 students. The chauvinistic policy of the autocracy restrained the development of higher education in outlying parts of the country. On the territories of contemporary Byelorussian, Azerbaijan, Armenian, Kazakh, Lithuanian, Kirghiz, Tajik, Turkmen and Uzbek United Republics, there were no institutions of higher education at all. Essentially education was seen as a privilege, dominated by feudal aristocracy.

The beginning of the nineteenth century saw a radical change in the development of higher education, following the establishment of the Soviet state. The resolutions and decrees of the Soviet People's Commissions, initiated by Lenin in 1918, opened education to the masses regardless of nationality, sex, class or creed. Education was made accessible to the working class, with the establishment of worker's faculties attached to higher education institutions. Payment for education was abolished. A system of financial support for students from peasant and working class backgrounds was established. By 1925-26, students in worker's faculties formed 40 percent of all persons admitted to higher education institutions.

In 1918, on Lenin's initiative, the Academy of Mines with three faculties (mining, geological survey, and metallurgy) was opened in Moscow. Universities in Tbilisi (1918), Dnieprope-trovsk (1918), Ickutsk (1918), Voronezh (1918), Yerevan (1920), and in several other regions were established. By 1921-22 there were 272 higher education institutions with 222,000 students. These included seven in Byelorussia, five in Azerbaijan, four in Uzbekistan, one in Armenia, and one in Kazakhastan. In the 1930s, sectoral institutions were established on the base of the larger higher education institutions. For example, institutes of oil and peat, steel, non-ferrous metals, and gold were established within the framework of the Academy of Mining and Geological Survey. In 1938, uniform regulations were enacted, governing the structure and working of higher education institutions. By 1985, the number of higher education institutions in the U.S.S.R. reached 894 with an enrollment of 5.2 million students, and a pedagogical work force of 0.5 million. Training is now given in more than 400 specialized areas and over 240 towns have higher education institutions. Equality is provided by free education at all levels.

The main goals of higher education in the U.S.S.R. are to train students as ideologically convinced, physically healthy active builders of the society with high moral qualities and as patriots ready to protect the socialist motherland; to develop in students responsible and creative attitudes, self disciplined and conscious approach to work, and a sense of social duty; to carry out scientific and research work promoting social, economic, scientific, and technical progress; to train scientific and pedagogical personnel and other specialists for the national economy; and to develop text books and training aids.

Administration

The system of administration and control of education has undergone several changes since the establishment of the Soviet state. During the first decade of the revolution, all education institutions, including higher education institutions came under the people's commissariats of the union republics. Subsequently, after several reorganizations, the Ministry of Higher Education of the U.S.S.R. was formed in 1959, which later became the Ministry of Higher Specialized Secondary Education with supreme authority over higher education. Its functions included development of educational plans; determination of types of institutions and organizational forms; approval of text books, regulations, and methods of training; state inspection of institutions; and coordination with each republic's Ministry of Higher and Specialized Education as well as other ministries having jurisdiction over higher educational institutions.

In 1988, a further reorganization took place and the Presidium of the Supreme Soviet abolished the ministry and established the State Committee of the U.S.S.R. for National Education centralizing management of all systems of education. The reorganization aimed at creating continuity for every level of education with universal secondary education for youth; improving management of the system of education by abolishing inter-departmental barriers and promoting democratization; and integration of education, science, and industry. For higher education institutions, this development heralded increased autonomy and broadening of academic freedom.

PRIMARY AND SECONDARY EDUCATION

There are two types of schools in the U.S.S.R.: ten-or eleven-year secondary schools with children entering school at the age of seven years. The government introduced universal primary education (8-12 year old children) in the 1930s, universal eight-year education (7-15 year old children) in the 1950s, and universal secondary education (7-17 year old children) in the 1970s. Most children who complete the eight-year school continue their studies at general secondary schools, secondary vocational schools, or specialized secondary schools. The ten-year secondary school is gradually changing to a eleven-year school with a "zero form" being added for the six year olds.

All general secondary schools in the U.S.S.R. offer a work oriented polytechnical curriculum that is identical. Students attend school six days a week. Four lessons (forty-five minutes each) are taught per day in the first three forms (junior form) and five to six lessons are taught in the higher forms. Students take thirty hours per week of compulsory subjects, and the balance in optional subjects. In 1984, with the enactment of the law on "Reform of the General and Vocational Schools", school curricula for the senior forms have been revised with the addition of new subjects such as fundamentals of production and choice of profession, ethics and psychology of family life, and fundamentals of information and computer technology. The law also established closer links between secondary schools and industry to acquaint and train the pupils in industrial trades. The trend is towards universal specialized secondary education by which every pupil will learn a trade. The examinations marking completion of general secondary education is uniform across the U.S.S.R. Successful candidates receive the high school diploma. There are nearly 44,000 general education schools in the U.S.S.R. with an enrollment of

44 million students. The enrollment at vocational training schools and specialized secondary schools is significantly smaller with about 9 million students.

HIGHER EDUCATION

Institutions

There are three types of higher education institutions in the U.S.S.R.: universities, polytechnical institutes, and specialized institutes.

The Soviet universities, the biggest education and scientific centers in the country, train specialists, researchers, and teachers in almost all branches of social and natural sciences and in humanities including mathematics, physics, chemistry, biology, geography, geology, philology, history, journalism, philosophy, economics, law. Universities exercise a significant influence on the organization of higher education in the whole country by the very fact that they train a large number of the teachers in general scientific fields (mathematics, physics, chemistry, etc.), to meet the needs of all higher education institutions. There are sixty-eight universities in the country, with an enrollment of over 610,000 students.

The polytechnical institutes are the main centers that train students in engineering fields. These institutes also offer facilities for broad scientific training and research and have the capability to develop programs in new branches of technical knowledge. There are over sixty polytechnical institutes spread over different regions of the country.

The specialized institutes generally provide training in a single specialized field such as machine building, mining, metallurgy, chemical technology, building, law, economics, pedagogy, transport, communications, theater, and arts. The specialized institutes have the advantage of being able to build a strong scientific and laboratory base in a given field as well as to establish close links with the corresponding branches of the national economy. there are over 700 specialized institutes.

In addition to the institutions that offer regular full-time programs in higher education, there exists an extensive network of institutions and branches of faculties that provide evening and corresponding courses. These include higher technical schools organized for workers at large industrial enterprises, where work and studies are rotated with six months of day time studies and six months of work combined with evening studies. Students at these institutions have the advantage of being already adapted to the industry and of receiving an allowance for their study days as well as a wage for their working days. Correspondence and evening courses also provide the opportunity for people to continue their education without leaving their jobs or families. These courses duplicate full time day programs and forms a vital part of higher education in the U.S.S.R.

All higher education institutions are public state establishments that have similar organizational structures, generally following common standards. They operate under the jurisdiction of different ministries but are under the administrative umbrella of the State Committee of the U.S.S.R. for National Education. Also the scientific and pedagogical collectives of the institutions play an important self governing role (in managing the institution).

At the head of each higher education institution is a rector appointed by the relevant ministry and he is assisted by several pro-rectors each having the responsibility for a functional area (teaching, research, administration, etc.). Branches of the institution are headed by directors. The key educational, scientific and administrative unit within the university is the faculty. Each institution has several faculties which consist of one or more chairs (departments) and laboratories in related fields. The faculty oversees the training of both undergraduate and postgraduate students. In order to bring educational centers near to the place of work, specially in industrial areas where there is a large student population, general technical faculties have been formed to provide general scientific and engineering training covering the first three years of university study.

Each faculty is headed by a dean chosen from the senior faculty members (for a three year term) by secret ballot of the academic council. The academic council is the main governing body of the institution. The council is headed by the rector and includes pro-rectors, deans, department heads, representatives of the teaching staff, as well as representatives of social organizations, enterprises, and establishments operating in the same field. The basic organizational unit is the department (within a faculty) which oversees educational and research activities in a given discipline or several related disciplines.

Programs and Degrees

Higher education institutions in the U.S.S.R. follow common standards in the award of degrees. They utilize educational plans and programs developed by leading specialists in the country and approved by the relevant institution's councils. Training is offered in more than 400 areas of studies. The first degree, diploma of higher education, takes from 4-6 years of full time study depending on the speciality. For persons entering with top grades the period may be reduced by 6-12 months, in some specialities. The academic year consists of two semesters with an examination at the end of each semester. In many fields the studies are closely linked to practical work.

The program content during the first two or three years consist of a number of subjects that are common to all higher education institutions e.g. political economy, philosophy. Correspondence and evening programs have identical curriculum and lead to identical qualifications but they require additional time (generally one additional year). About 45 percent of the students in higher education follow correspondence and evening courses. Teaching at most higher education institutions is done both in Russian and in national languages (of the republics). Russian language provides a medium of communication between different nationalities. Students are guaranteed jobs, on completion of their studies.

Admission to higher education institutions require completion of secondary or specialized secondary school education. Applicants for admission must take an entrance examination in three subjects: Russian language and literature or student's native language, and two other subjects according to the schools' speciality (e.g.

mathematics and physics or chemistry for engineering fields, and history of the U.S.S.R. for humanities).

Postgraduate studentships provide opportunity for students to engage in research leading to advanced degrees. The "Candidate of Science", a degree comparable to a Ph.D. may be obtained after three years of advanced studies and research in any field, including a publicly defended dissertation. This degree is offered by many higher education institutions, which have necessary research facilities and staff for advanced work. Moreover, The Academy of Sciences also offers the "Candidate of Science" degree at its research institutes designated for this purpose. The highest degree is the Doctor of Science which is awarded usually to senior scholars, on the basis of advanced original contribution to the candidate's field of study as demonstrated by a dissertation. There is no requirement for following a specific study program.

Teaching Staff

One of the remarkable achievements of Soviet higher education institutions is the training of an impressive force of national scientific and pedagogical staff in the union republics. The higher education institutions today employ over half million of professors, instructors, and other scientific workers who form about one third of the total work force engaged in Soviet science. For example, prior to 1917, the middle Asia republics had no higher education institutions, where as today over thirty thousand scientists and instructors are in the work force with one third of them having academic degrees. In addition, women have been provided the opportunity to gain their rightful place among the educated and now about 60 percent of the professionals are women.

Professors are the highest ranking teachers of the institution and this title is accorded to the most distinguished scientists and teachers who play a leadership role in their field. At present there are over 17,000 professors working at higher education institutions. Other teaching staff include readers, lecturers, and instructors.

The faculties of professional improvement at leading higher education institutions provide refresher programs to teaching staff for enhancing their skills. These programs last 4-6 months. Sabbatical programs provide opportunities for the teaching staff to spend time at industrial and agricultural enterprises, and other leading higher education and research institutions.

Student Facilities

Attention to material, social, and cultural needs of youth engaged in education is one of the main guarantees of right to education in the U.S.S.R. Education is provided free of charge and board and lodging costs are heavily subsidized. Most higher education institutions have student hostels and in big cities, well appointed student towns have been built. Students pay only about 2.5-3 percent of their allowances for lodging. Medical care is also provided free of charge. Students' councils manage many of the activities at student residences.

Students have the opportunity to take part in a variety of extracurricular activities and sports. Higher education institutions also receive significant financial assistance for student welfare from trade unions, including support for state social insurance and for accommodation at sanatoriums and vacation resorts. Majority of the students (about 75 percent) in higher education institutions receive a state allowance to cover their living expenses. Students who receive excellent grades receive a 25 percent increase in their allowances and those who fail have their allowances suspended temporarily. Almost all postgraduate students (working for the "Candidate of Science" degree etc.) receive allowances and they get twice the amount given to first degree students. Allowances are determined by individual institutions and vary in value.

Foreign Students

There are more than 70,000 foreign students (1987) from 149 countries studying at over 500 higher education institution in the U.S.S.R., including many at the Moscow State University, the largest university in the country. Foreign students receive benefits similar to Soviet students with free education and scholarships including awards under bilateral agreements. Students who are not proficient in Russian have the opportunity to follow a preparatory course (one year) in the language.

ISSUES AND TRENDS

As the Soviet Union moves towards a radically new economic and social environment under "perestroika", restructuring of the educational system, particularly the higher education is undergoing examination.

When the new presidential decree (October 1990) comes into force, universities and higher education institutions are expected to have greater autonomy with more control over budgets, curriculum, methods of teaching, and faculty appointments. Higher education institutions will have greater flexibility in developing contacts with industry and various branches of the national economy. There is also a trend for conversion of polytechnic institutions into technological universities thus giving the students and teachers of these institutions some additional privileges.

A recent interesting proposal that the government is now considering and which is supported by many Soviet citizens, is to replace the traditional general studies degree program (which takes 5-6 years) by a two-tier system: a basic higher education level lasting four years, leading to the award of a degree comparable to the bachelor's degree; and a higher level professional studies program that would take 1-2 years beyond the basic level, leading to a qualification comparable to the master's degree or a professional diploma ("engineer", "economist", etc.). Such a system would bring qualifications offered by Soviet institutions to a common level with degree programs in most countries, thus facilitating interaction (students, faculty, etc.) with international institutions.

The move in the direction of a decentralized market economy will make it difficult to sustain the state system of job allocation (for students who graduate from higher education institutions). In its place, a national system of employment of specialists is expected to be introduced. There are some suggestions to have the potential employees sign contracts with students.

Changes are also expected in the way higher education institutions are funded. While basic higher education may receive funding from state budgets (through the tax system), professional education may require support through contracts and agreements with industrial enterprises and businesses. The possibility of charging fees from students has also been discussed, of course, without much support for the move, so far.

BIBLIOGRAPHY

Anthology of Pedagogical Thinking in the Ancient Russia (in Russian). Moscow, 1985.

Higher Education Statistical Yearbook (in Russian). Moscow, n.d.

Savelyev, A. Y., V. M. Zuev, A. I. Galagan. *Higher Education in the U.S.S.R.* (in English and Russian). Moscow, 1990.

UNITED ARAB EMIRATES

by
Muhyieddeen Sh. Touq
Dean, College of Education
United Arab Emirates University, U.A.E.

BACKGROUND

Since its independence, the United Arab Emirates has considered education as the main vehicle for development. Thus, schools were established in an unparalleled pace and money was poured into educational endeavors. In 1988, 14 percent of the overall government budget went for education. Teachers were brought in from other Arab countries to make up for shortages of teaching staff among the citizens of the country. There was phenomenal growth in the number of schools, classrooms, students, and teachers. In the academic year 1987-88 there were 431 public schools with a staff of 15,864 and an enrollment of 209,184 students representing an increase of about 17 percent in the student population from 1985-86 (with a corresponding increase in student facilities). In addition, there were 192 private schools with a teaching staff of 5,350 and an enrollment of 80,519 students.

In the area of higher education, the UAE University was inaugurated in 1977, and soon after, many colleges, two-year institutions, and technical colleges were established to provide advanced training for the citizens.

Education in the UAE aims at promoting "good citizenship" among its population; thus producing citizens with well balanced and integrated personality equipped with proper abilities, skills, values, and positive attitudes that help them participate in the national development. More specifically, the key objectives that the educational system strives to achieve can be stated as follows: comprehending Islam as a religion and a way of life; mastering language as a means for communication, and a vehicle for thought and expression of culture; reinforcing national unity and developing patriotism (patriotic to the country, the Arab World and the Islamic Nation); developing cognitive powers and thinking abilities of students and encouraging their creativity; acquiring knowledge and comprehending science and technology; perceiving the importance of arts and developing artistic abilities of students and encouraging their free expression and appreciation of beauty in life; developing proper attitudes and wise exercise of freedom, democracy, work, and production; recognizing the individual's right to education, equal educational opportunities and life-long education; and increasing national income through proper education and diversified training so as to meet individual needs as well as requirements of national development.

The Ministerial Cabinet Order 1 of 1987 governs the administration of the educational system in the UAE. The order regulates the specific duties and responsibilities of the Ministry of Education which is organized into three levels: central level, educational zones, and schools. Furthermore a high committee for educational policies has been set up under the chairmanship of the minister of education. The committee includes the ministers of information, planning, finance and industry, and labor; the university chancellor; and two distinguished members. The specific duties of this committee are to develop policies of the Ministry of Education; follow up and evaluate the ministry's policies; coordinate between the Ministry of Education and other ministries with regard to activities carried out by the ministry. A committee for administration, organization, and development has also been established. This committee lays down the details of educational policies and the requirements needed to carry them out properly and efficiently. The ministry is committed to decentralized management of educational zones and offices. The undersecretary of the ministry is the executive head and he is assisted by assistant undersecretaries in the areas of planning and evaluation, educational affairs, central activities, and administrative affairs. Zones and offices are authorized to supervise education in schools in their respective areas. The directors of education of the zones report directly to the undersecretary and they have two assistants: one for planning and administration and the other for educational affairs and activities. This arrangement facilitates coordination between educational zones and administrative units of the ministry.

An important feature of the educational system is that schools receive their instructions and directives directly from educational zones. This facilitates contacts and decision making. Each school has a principal and a vice-principal, overseeing the staff.

The education budget is part of the national budget. This budget is dedicated to the construction of schools, and the education of nationals as well as expatriates living in the U.A.E. This budget has grown rapidly over the years and is DHS1,828,491,000 in 1987 and represents a 12 percent increase from 1985 (US$1 = DHS3.68). The education budget represents 13.2 percent of the national budget. Salaries and wages consisted of 77 percent of the budget. Salary costs are high because the majority of teachers are expatriates and they are provided with free housing and annual air tickets to their home countries.

The educational system in the U.A.E. comprises three stages: kindergarten, basic (primary and preparatory education), and secondary education. There are also private schools, vocational institutes (e.g. for secretarial training), and schools set up by women's associations to teach girls sewing, embroidery, home economics, and child welfare. Due to the importance of the first years in the building up of a child's personality, the U.A.E. has set up kindergartens and has expanded them. Children join these kindergartens at the age of four and spend two years there. Here children are prepared socially and psychologically in a way that develops their aptitudes and qualifies them for the primary stage. Attending kindergarten is not compulsory.

PRIMARY AND SECONDARY EDUCATION

Education in the U.A.E. is undergoing important reforms in order to improve its quality and adaptability to the challenges of the future. Elementary and preparatory stages are being combined together in one basic education stage. Children begin the basic education stage at the age of six and continue for nine years. The objective of this stage is to develop the abilities and aptitudes of children and supply them with Islamic ethics and values. They are also provided with knowledge and scientific and professional skills that correspond with the environment. Students who finish this stage are able to continue their education on to the academic secondary stage or go for job oriented training.

Secondary education is comprised of three years. Students who finish basic education stage successfully are admitted in secondary schools. Education in this stage is free for the nationals but not compulsory. Expatriates pay nominal fees. Secondary education is diversified so as to satisfy the needs and interests of the students and the needs of the society at large. All stages of education, including secondary education, is under the control and supervision of the Ministry of Education.

Education in the secondary stage is specialized and is based on a broad basis of general education. There are five major types of secondary schools: academic, religious, technical, commercial, and agricultural schools. The overwhelming majority of students join the academic secondary school which is also divided into literary and scientific streams. The division takes place in the second and third years, while the first year is unified.

Major changes are taking place in secondary education as part of the educational reform plan. The academic secondary school will be divided into five branches: islamic studies, languages, social sciences, sciences, and mathematics and computer science. Vocational and technical schools will be further developed and linked to major businesses and industry in order to attract more able students.

According to the new curricula, the students will have to take forty class periods per week (each class period is forty-five minutes). Approximately 50 percent of the time will be allotted to general education while the rest of the time will be for specialized subjects. All instruction is in the Arabic language. General education courses for all branches consist of Islamic education, Arabic language, English language, vocational (or family) education, physical education, math and computer science, and science. The specialized and supporting courses consist of Islamic studies branch (Arabic language, Islamic education, Islamic history); languages branch (Arabic language, English language, third language); social sciences branch (sociology, economics, history, geography, philosophy etc.); science branch (mathematics, physics, chemistry, biology, geology); and mathematics and computer science (physics, chemistry, biology, mathematics, computer science). In each branch two periods will be allocated for extracurricular activities (art, music, handicrafts, etc.).

School year is divided into two semesters; the first semester starts in mid-September and ends in mid-January, and the second semester starts in early February and ends in mid-May. The total number of school days per year is now

185 days but according to the reform plan, the number will be extended to 210. The third secondary school year ends in a general secondary school examination conducted by the Ministry of Education. Those who pass the examination successfully are awarded the secondary school certificate which is a prerequisite to enter the university. Nationals of the country are not charged any fees or tuition. They are provided free bus transport to school and textbooks. Expatriates pay nominal tuition.

Many expatriates and few nationals attend private schools where they have to pay rather high fees and tuition. Approximately 25 percent of all students in 1987-88 were attending private schools. Expatriates who are government employees or employees of public institutions have the right to send their children to government schools. Some employees of the private sector, particularly those in the oil companies and big businesses, get education allowances. Many ethnic groups have their own schools, but they are all supervised by the Ministry of Education.

Teaching Staff and Teacher Training

The demand for teachers in the UAE increased rapidly since independence. Due to population growth and expansion of educational services, the country has witnessed an annual growth of about 10 percent in the number of teachers. The teachers and administrators who numbered 9611 in 1980, rose to 21,214 in 1988.

Education in the UAE is primarily segregated. In the 1988-89 school year, 204 schools were male, 199 were female, and 54 were coeducational. The coeducational schools are mainly the kindergartens. Among teaching and administrative staff about 56 percent were females.

The majority of teachers (UAE nationals) have secondary school certificates and have attended a teacher training program. This program is mainly conducted by the Ministry of Education for one or two years. The second largest group of teachers (UAE nationals) are those who have a university degree but without teacher training. Fifteen percent of all teachers (UAE nationals and non-nationals) had a secondary school certificate or less. Thirty-six percent have attended a teacher training institute or some form of post secondary institute. Forty-eight percent had the first university degree, and 1 percent had a higher university degree.

A unique feature of the teaching and administrative staff in the UAE and in other Arab gulf states is their heavy dependence on expatriate teachers coming from other Arab states such as Jordan, Egypt, and Syria. Twenty-one percent of the teaching staff in the academic year 1988-89 were nationals of the country and 79 percent were non-nationals. Among all teaching, administrative, and technical staff, nationals comprised 27 percent, while 73 percent were non-nationals. Nationals comprised 23 percent of all teaching staff in the elementary stage and 14.6 percent in the secondary stage. The nationals of the country outnumbered the non-nationals only in administrative staff where they constituted 61 percent of the overall staff. There are two parallel teacher education systems in the UAE. The first system is a pre-service teacher training program organized, conducted and supervised by the Ministry of Education. The second system is a pre-service teacher education program totally conducted by the College of Education at the UAE University.

The Ministry of Education program is of two years duration and is comprised of seventy-two credit hours, out of which twelve hours are devoted to cultural studies, twenty-seven hours to professional teacher education courses, twenty-three hours to specialized academic subjects, and ten hours to student teaching. Entry requirements consist of obtaining at least 60 percent in the General Secondary School Exam conducted by the Ministry of Education on the one hand, and passing a written test to assess some personality dimensions, readiness, and language abilities on the other hand. A personal interview is also conducted.

The graduates of this program become kindergarten and elementary school teachers. Secondary school teachers have to have a university degree. Entry into the profession is contingent upon the successful completion of the program. Neither the ministry nor the professional teacher association have any licensing procedures or certification. The graduates of this program are awarded an intermediate diploma. The Ministry of Education as of September 1989 has limited its program to areas such as family education, art education, physical education, music, and secretarial training.

HIGHER EDUCATION

Institutions

Tertiary education in the UAE dates back to 1977 when the United Arab Emirates University (UAEU) was established as the sole and only national university in the country. In the mid-eighties several other higher education institutions were established as the need for further education grew rapidly. Several private and government institutions with programs lasting 2-4 years were established. The United Arab Emirate University, however, remains the only government university in the country.

The UAEU which started with 502 students and five colleges in 1977 developed rapidly in the last few years to become a leading higher education institution in the area. Situated in the city of Al-Ain, a desert oasis, the UAEU is comprised now of eight colleges with a total enrollment of about 9000 students. It offers only the first university degree since graduate studies have not yet started. It offers bachelor's degrees in arts, sciences, law, engineering, education, administration and political science, agriculture, and medicine.

One unique aspect of UAEU is that education is totally financed by the federal government. Students don't pay fees or tuition. They also get free books, housing, and meals. This applies to nationals as well as non-national students. There is also free transportation once a week for female students to and from their Emirates (home state). All students are accommodated in dormitories and are provided with excellent opportunities for extracurricular activities.

There are currently over 400 faculty members in the teaching staff, nearly half of them are on secondment (leave) from other Arab universities while the rest are on personal contracts. In 1989 approximately 10 percent of the teaching staff were nationals, 85 percent were from other Arab countries, and 5 percent were from foreign countries.

Faculty members are recruited from all over the world and are offered four year renewable contracts. Beside the salaries, each faculty member is provided with free housing and utilities. They are also given a furniture allowance and a yearly ticket for self, spouse, and three children.

Several other government and private higher education institutions exist in UAE. The Higher Institute of Technology and the Ajman College of Science and Technology are the two most important ones.

The Higher Institute of Technology (HIT) ia a government owned three year postsecondary education institution. It provides intermediate diplomas in office management, medical secretaries, business accounting, business administration, and electronics. The HIT is headed by the chancellor of the UAEU and has six campuses in different emirates, three for males and three for females. The colleges maintain strong ties with business and industry. All instruction is carried out in English. Students/ staff are treated as UAEU students/staff as far as privileges are concerned.

The Ajman College for Science and Technology (ACST) is a privately owned four-year college. It provides university-equivalent degrees in electronics, communication, civil engineering, electrical engineering, management and informatics, computer science, English, French, and methods and techniques in basic education. The ACST offers some graduate diplomas and graduate studies. The ACST maintains strong ties with some Arab and international universities which provide the college with some of its teaching staff. Most of the college students are non-nationals and have to pay heavy fees and tuition.

There are also other smaller colleges which are affiliated with other Arab universities mainly in Egypt and Saudi Arabia. These colleges are Police College in Abu Dhabi, Police College in Dubai, Dubai's Medical College for women, Zayed Military College, Dubai's College for Arabic Language, Dubai's College for Islamic Studies, Communications College in Sharjah, and College of Islamic Studies in Ras al Khaimahe.

Programs and Degrees at the UAE University

Admission requirements have varied slightly over the years and differs between nationals and non-nationals and between different colleges. A student who is admitted to the university has to pass the General Secondary School Examination (GSSE) with a minimum of 60 percent marks to enter colleges of arts, sciences, education administration and political science, and agriculture. To enter the colleges of engineering and medicine the student has to show superior performance (80% marks). Expatriates (non-nationals) have to have much higher GSSE grades to enter the university. Nearly 15 percent of the student population is from other Arab and Islamic countries. Nationals who score less than 60 percent in the GSSE are admitted as special students for one or two semesters before they are transferred to regular student status depending on their successful completion of several courses of compensatory education. All students who score less than 70 percent in Arabic, English, and mathematics in the GSSE have to take a placement test in the three areas. Students who fail to pass those tests have to take remedial courses.

Students are admitted in one of the eight colleges according to their choices and GSSE grades. By the end of their first year in college they are counseled to choose their major area in the college. There is however, an ample degree of freedom for transfer between colleges and within departments in the same college.

The university offers forty-three fields of study leading to B.A. or B.Sc. degrees. The fields are grouped under eight colleges: arts and humanities, sciences, education, administration and political science, Sharia and law, agriculture, engineering, and medicine and health sciences.

Because of the low participation rate of nationals in teaching, and the tremendous need for teachers, the university geared its admission policies to meet this demand, and the college of education was restructured accordingly.

The new structure is comprised of eight undergraduate programs, and two diploma programs. Heavy emphasis was put on the academic subject component of the study plan, as well as on the practical training. To further enhance the role of the college in the development of the educational system, a center for research, development, and educational services was established. The present programs of the college (in the academic year 1985-86) at the first university degree level include kindergarten education, elementary, intermediate, and secondary education, psychology, family education, special education, physical education, art education, and subject areas (languages, social sciences, sciences etc.). At the post B.A. or B.Sc. level the college offers two diploma programs: one in general education, and the other in educational administration and supervision.

UAEU follows a credit-hour system as the academic basis for its organization, where the student has to finish a certain number of credits before graduating. With regard to administrative structure, the university is divided into colleges and colleges are further divided into academic departments. There are eight colleges and thirty-six departments. The academic year is divided into two semesters; the first one starts at the beginning of September and ends in mid-January, and the second one starts at the beginning of February and ends at the beginning of June. Each semester class is 17-18 weeks long where the students have to meet in classes at least for fifteen weeks not including exams. A bachelor's degree generally takes four years of studies. Engineering and law takes five years. Medical degrees take seven years (including two-year premedical).

In 1987, five research centers were established to enhance research productivity and to provide services for the country. These centers are Desert and Marine Environment Research Center, Educational and Psychological Research Center, Development and Services Center, Administration, Financial and Economics Research Center, Technology and Energy research Center, and the Remote Sensing Center.

ISSUES AND TRENDS

Education in the UAE is undergoing careful reexamination and evaluation in order to improve its efficiency, effectiveness, and adaptability to rapidly changing conditions. Reform efforts cover the total educational system including higher education.

A reform committee was set-up by the Ministry of Education in early 1989 to study the educational system of the country, analyze its characteristics, identify its weaknesses and problems, and suggest improvements. Based on the country's heritage and past experiences on one hand, and the developments in education, science, and technology on the other hand, the committee started its work by making a thorough analysis of the educational systems of other countries which have made substantial educational progress. Field visits were conducted to Japan, South Korea, W. Germany, England, Jordan, and Tunisia. As a result of these visits, and extensive evaluation of reform efforts in other parts of the world, the reform committee is working on a new plan to develop education in UAE. The objectives of the reform plan include diversification of secondary education and improvement of the quality of the teaching-learning process by improving curriculum, improving textbooks, up-grading teaching qualifications and certification, introducing new pre-service and in-service schemes for educational personnel, improving the quality of educational administration and supervision, incorporating modern instructional aids and materials into the teaching-learning process, improving measurement techniques and educational evaluation, and enhancing the role of extracurricular activities in the educational process.

In the higher educational sphere, the UAEU is also conducting an evaluation of its programs. Utilizing highly qualified international external evaluation teams, the UAEU has been making a serious endeavor since early 1989 to improve its curricula, teaching methods, evaluation techniques, research capabilities, and services to match international standards. This process will last for three years after which a comprehensive development scheme is expected to be completed and put into effect.

BIBLIOGRAPHY

Arab Bureau for Education for the Gulf States. *Guidebook for Higher Education in the Arab Gulf States* (in Arabic). Riyadh, Saudi Arabia, 1988.

Ministry of Education. *Annual Statistical Report 1979-1988.* Abu Dhabi, Dubai: Ministry of Education, 1989.

"Recent Developments in Education in the United Arab Emirates." A report submitted to the 41st session of the International Bureau of Education, Geneva, 1988.

Touq M. Sh. "Teacher Education in the United Arab Emirates: A National Case Study." Paper submitted to UNESCO and ICET interregional seminar, Cairo, 1989.

UNITED KINGDOM

by
Michael T. Williams
Professor and Dean, Faculty of Educational Studies
University College of Swansea, U.K.
and
Gareth E. Jones
Professor of Educational Research
University College of Wales, Aberystwyth, U.K.

BACKGROUND

The system of education in the United Kingdom is distinguished by its disunity. In Scotland and Northern Ireland there are legally autonomous systems which share some of their principal structural characteristics with the system of education in England and Wales. Foreign readers about education in the United Kingdom must approach generalizations with caution and pay close attention to the sources of statistical data to be certain that they refer to the particular national systems.

There is an additional source of disunity in that, traditionally, the administration of education has been largely devolved in England and Wales to local education authorities, the educational wings of administrative shire counties and metropolitan counties, and to bodies instituted by royal charter. The borderlines between state institutions and private institutions may appear to be hazy and these lines are currently being redrawn as new arrangements for funding education at all levels come into existence following the passing of recent legislation by central government.

PRIMARY AND SECONDARY EDUCATION

Primary and secondary education in England are under the aegis of the Department of Education and Science, a major department of state located in London. In Wales they are administered by the Welsh Office, located in Cardiff. Education in Scotland and Northern Ireland is run by the Scottish Office and the Northern Ireland Office respectively. The latter systems of secondary education are administered under separate legislation.

In England and Wales the primary and secondary education systems operate under a series of acts of parliament, culminating in major legislation passed in 1988. Education is compulsory for pupils of ages 5-16 years. Pupils normally enter primary school during the year in which they reach the age of five, though substantial numbers will have had some kind of voluntary nursery education before this. There are normally two stages of primary education: infant schools for ages 5-7 years, and junior schools for ages 8-11 years. Pupils then transfer to a secondary school. There are some notable exceptions to this pattern. Within the state system some counties still operate "middle schools" as a stage between primary and secondary education and the private sector operates its own system of preparatory education prior to a "common entrance" examination. Pupils are free to leave school at the age of sixteen if they wish or continue into further or higher education. Many proceed to the sixth forms of secondary schools for a further two years, but there is a growing tertiary sector in which students aged 16-18 study in the same institution as those of more mature age.

Across England and Wales the majority of pupils are educated in state comprehensive schools. In 1986-87 in the United Kingdom there were 5,091 secondary schools and 2,544 non-maintained or private schools of all types, but the total proportion of pupils in private secondary education is not substantial, amounting to about 7 percent of the total. Of the secondary pupils in the state sector, the great majority (85.8 percent in England, 98.5 percent in Wales in 1986-87) are in comprehensive schools which accept pupils by catchment area rather than by ability, or ability to pay. The state has chosen not to interfere in the administration of the private, fee-paying schools, some of which, confusingly, are known as public schools.

In the state sector, full implementation of the 1988 legislation will revolutionize the control and curricular organization of the schools. The main thrust of this legislation concerns organization and the curriculum. Each secondary school has a body of governors which controls that schools's budget, allocated by the local education authority in a lump sum according to a government-approved formula. In effect, therefore, the governors, some nominated by the local authority (county or metropolitan borough councils), some elected by parents, and some co-opted by existing governors, control the appointment and dismissal of staff and the day-to-day running of the school. Secondary schools are permitted to seek to avoid even this degree of involvement with the local authority. If a sufficient number of parents, in successive ballots, wish to opt out of the local system, they may seek to acquire their block grant direct from the Department of Education and Science or the Welsh Office. They would then buy in those services normally provided by the local authority.

The curriculum of those schools in receipt of public funds is now to be determined by the state. The legislation of 1988 laid down the subjects which must be taught in the secondary schools. These fall into two categories: core subjects and foundation subjects. In England the core subjects are English, mathematics, and science. The foundation subjects are history, geography, craft, design and technology, music, art, physical education, and modern languages. Religious Education, with a Christian (though non-denominational) basis is compulsory, though is not designated a core or foundation subject. In Wales, the situation is slightly more complicated because of the existence of the Welsh language which, according to the last census of 1981, was spoken by just under 20 percent (about 500,000) of the people of Wales. The result is that, in some schools in Wales, five or more subjects are taught through the medium of Welsh. In such schools Welsh is to be a core subject, enjoying equal status with English. All other secondary schools in Wales, unless very exceptionally they are allowed exemption, must teach Welsh as a foundation subject.

The "matters, skills, and processes" (essentially the syllabus content) of each of the subjects of the curriculum is in the process of being determined by government-appointed committees. When this process has been completed, as at the time of writing it has been for the core subjects, and a consultation process completed, the essentials of the subject curriculum become law and have to be taught. A National Curriculum Council superintends the general implementation of this process in the schools.

Another nominated body, the Secondary Examinations and Assessment Council, superintends the way in which this curriculum is assessed and certificated. Each phase of education is designated a key stage. In the primary phase, there are two key stages, relating to pupils aged 5-7 and 8-11. In the secondary phase, there are two key stages: key stage three relating to pupils aged 11-14, and key stage four to pupils aged 14-16. Assessment of each stage of the curriculum is by a combination of teacher assessments and centrally-devised standard assessment tasks which are taken towards the end of each key stage. When this system is fully operational pupils will be assessed on a variety of attainment targets within each core and foundation subject. All these attainment targets are specified at ten levels and pupils will be graded accordingly. At present the first external certification in the secondary schools takes place at age sixteen, by means of the General Certificate of Secondary Education (G.C.S.E.). It is administered by five examination boards in England and one in Wales and is available in all school subjects and in a variety of combinations of these. Grades are awarded on an alphabetical scale but grades A to C inclusive have a particular significance in that they provide a qualification, in combination with Advanced Level examinations, for university entrance. It is not clear at the time of writing exactly how the newly-designed assessment procedures at key stage four and the G.C.S.E. examination will mesh but G.C.S.E. will remain the certification for the great majority of school leavers. At present in England under 10 percent of pupils leave school at sixteen without any kind of examination certificate; the proportion is slightly higher in Wales. Pupils wishing to further their academic studies can do so either in school or college. Others undertake further training through youth training schemes.

The academic year in secondary schools is divided into three terms of varying length, but each averages fourteen weeks duration, including half-term breaks. There are holiday periods over Christmas, at Easter, and in high summer. Teachers are required to be on the school premises for 1,265 hours per year. All schools, both state and private, have strong sporting traditions, though the trend in the state schools in recent years has been towards more individual than team games. The private sector tends to sponsor more esoteric forms of sport, such as lacrosse and rowing, as well as the traditional forms of sport. Despite these features, there is still a strong presence of competitive team sport both within and between schools. Such sports as association football (soccer), rugby football, and cricket are the major team sports for boys, while hockey and netball dominate girls' team games. Athletics, in the summer term especially, are ubiquitous, as is tennis for girls.

There is an enormous variety of other kinds of extracurricular activities, but music, both choral and instrumental, is the most significant in that public concerts and musical events provide one of the main ways in which secondary schools relate to their communities.

Secondary education in the United Kingdom is provided free in the state sector. In the private sector fees are charged and vary from a few hundred (British) pounds a term for pupils in relatively low-status day schools to a few thousand (British) pounds a term for pupils in the highest-status boarding schools. In the state sector, people resident in the country, whether British citizens or not, in effect, have to send their children to school, though it would be possible to meet the legal requirement by educating them to a satisfactory standard at home. Pupils who attend school are provided with free tuition, books, and (normally outside a three-mile radius) with free transport. If school uniform is worn, pupils' families are responsible for providing it, as they are for providing clothing for physical education lessons. There is a strong tradition in the U.K. for providing instrumental music lessons, and instruments are lent to pupils free of charge. Education visits outside school, for example to a museum, can only be undertaken if parents volunteer to meet the cost.

In all the countries of the United Kingdom, English is the normal language of instruction in schools. The main exception to this is the minority of schools in Wales in which Welsh is the language of instruction.

Teaching staff in the secondary sector are normally graduates in the subjects which they teach, though in some subjects, for example mathematics, this can be more an aspiration than a reality. In other subjects, such as history, most teaching at secondary level is done by specialists in that subject. Teachers in secondary schools train in two ways. First, they can attend an institute of higher education or one of the few free-standing colleges responsible for training only teachers, where they take a three or four year course, specializing academically in one or two subjects, interspersed with periods of teaching practice. Such courses have to be approved by the Council for the Accreditation of Teacher Education, a body nominated by the government. Those students who take the university route to teaching do so by means of a three-year degree course in the subject of their choice, then apply separately to enter a course leading to a postgraduate certificate in education. Such courses are available in both public-sector institutes, alongside concurrent teacher-training courses, and, more commonly, in university departments of education. These one-year training courses are also externally approved. They are of thirty-six weeks' duration and include roughly similar proportions of work in the university and teaching in the schools. Under the 1988 Education Act, teachers, including headteachers, are appointed by school governors, though employed by the local education authority. In response to a currently worsening teacher supply situation, the government has introduced other avenues into teaching, to apply to mature age teachers and others who are labelled accredited and licensed teachers, though it seems likely that this will affect only a relatively small minority.

HIGHER EDUCATION

Institutions

Of the forty-six universities in the United Kingdom the oldest are Oxford and Cambridge which were founded in the twelfth and thirteenth centuries and they were followed by the Scottish universities of St. Andrews, Glasgow, Aberdeen, and Edinburgh founded from the fifteenth to the sixteenth centuries. As Britain prospered economically in the nineteenth century the new centers of population became the sites for universities. By 1945 there were seventeen universities and then came a period of expansion leading to the current figure of forty-six.

It is important to emphasize that universities see themselves as institutions independent of government, despite the fact that they derive the great majority of their funds from the central government. Until the passing of the Education Reform Act of 1988, public money was distributed to the universities by the University Grants Committee which had been appointed by the secretary of state for education and science (the title of the senior government official who would be called a minister of education in many other systems). The Act of 1988 legislated for the replacement of the University Grants Committee by the Universities Funding Council and this symbolized a change in the financial arrangements for universities.

The Universities Funding Council allocates block grants to each university, including funds for capital expenditure and to support research and teaching. It engages in monitoring the research and teaching work of each university. In 1989, universities went through the second round of a research selectivity exercise at the end of which each department in every university was given a research rating which is used for the allocation of research funds. Universities are currently engaged in introducing schemes of staff appraisal and course auditing in response to central initiatives. In addition, a new system of bidding for student numbers will be introduced in 1992.

A highly controversial issue which, at the time of writing (February 1990), is proceeding through parliament is legislation for the introduction of "topping-up" student maintenance loans. In recent years students who have been successful in the competition to enter universities have had their university fees paid as mandatory awards and, in addition, they may have been awarded maintenance grants to cover accommodation and other expenses; the size of award being dependent on a means test of the student's family.

Universities have been encouraged by politicians and others to seek funding from sources other than central government. Industrial sponsorship of undergraduate students, external funding of research equipment and research activities, and joint university-industrial teaching arrangements are parts of this alternative funding.

Universities award their own degrees and are entirely responsible for their teaching and examinations. They select their students by competitive entry and select their own teaching and non-teaching staff. They are administered by councils composed of academic and lay members and their day-to-day administration and management is the responsibility of a senate chaired, usually, by a vice-chancellor who is usually a distinguished academic.

Matters of immediate academic concern, academic initiatives, and students' academic and examination concerns are normally discussed in relevant faculties which report to the senate. All academic staff or departments within, for example, the Faculty of Arts or the Faculty of Applied Science are normally members of the relevant faculty, the chair of which is the dean.

Within each faculty there is a variety of departments or schools, for example, the Department of History or the School of Biological Sciences. Individual department members decide their own teaching and research programs and priorities in collaboration with the head of department, an academic who has in the past normally been a professor but is more frequently now an elected member of the senior staff. Department academic staff may be lecturers, senior lecturers, readers (a title awarded for research distinction), and professors. All are appointed by committees composed of senior academics within the relevant institution except that, in the case of professorial appointments, external assessors are also involved.

The universities constitute one arm of the higher educational system. The other arm is made up of public sector institutions which, in England (though not in Wales), were freed by the 1988 Education Reform Act from control by local education authorities. Public sector higher education comprises polytechnics and colleges of higher education. Many of the latter grew out of former colleges of teacher education which diversified their course provision in the late 1970s and early 1980s. Funding of the public sector institutions had come from central government sources mediated by local education authorities. Funding of polytechnics and colleges in England is administered by the Polytechnics and Colleges Funding Council.

Students entering public sector institutions to follow courses similar to or identical with undergraduate courses in universities were eligible for mandatory awards to cover course fees and, subject to a means test, the award of a maintenance grant.

Public sector institutions relied on external arrangements for the validation of their awards. The Council for National Academic Awards validates and accredits a national structure of diplomas, undergraduate and postgraduate degrees and other awards.

An essential principle underpinning the recent evolution of higher education in the United Kingdom was enunciated in the report of the Committee of Higher Education (the Robbins Report) of 1963: places should be available in higher education for all who have the ability and willingness to benefit from them. This principle was accepted by the government of the day and the opposition parties. From 1963 one can trace the response of higher education to an expansion in student numbers, an explosion in knowledge and an increase in the expectations of young people for extended education. These are reflected in the establishment of new universities and public sector institutions, the introduction of new fields and subjects for study, the arrangement of new types of courses and greater concern with curriculum development. Symbolic of the new courses and types of study was the establishment of the Open University which began its first courses in January 1971 and by July 1976 was enrolling 50,000 students.

In 1987-88 there were 968,000 students in higher education and some 15.5 percent of these aged 18-19 years participated in higher education. In 1979 the equivalent figure was 12.5 percent. Although there is a forecast that the number of eighteen year olds will fall by approximately 30 percent between 1985 and 1995 the age participation rate is expected to exceed 20 percent by 1995. Evidence for this potential growth was evident in the numbers entering universities and public sector institutions in the Autumn of 1989 when a release of central government control on higher education targets witnessed significant increases in numbers of first year undergraduates. Between 1975-76 and 1985-86, student enrollment at the universities increased from 351,000 to 430,000, an increase of 22.5 percent. In the same period, enrollment at the polytechnics and colleges of higher education increased from 243,000 to 383,000, an increase of 57.6 percent.

Undergraduate Studies

Conventionally, young people wishing to register for higher education leave school at the age of eighteen years and, having been successful in (Advanced Level) examinations in three subjects at school, they enter a university, polytechnic, or college of higher education.

In 1987-88, specialist subjects studied by students at the polytechnics and colleges of higher education included education (12.8 percent); medicine (3.8 percent); engineering and technology (15.2 percent); agriculture (0.7 percent); science (14.5 percent); business and social studies (25.6 percent); professional and vocational (7.3 percent); languages (2.8 percent); and other arts, music, drama, and design (17.0 percent). Students at the universities were distributed somewhat differently: education (3.8 percent); medicine (11.1 percent); engineering and technology (13.0 percent); agriculture (1.9 percent); science (24.5 percent); business and social studies (23.7 percent); professional and vocational (1.9 percent); languages (11.9 percent); and other arts, music, drama, and design (8.0 percent).

These students would follow their courses leading to undergraduate awards usually based on three academic years of full-time study. The academic year in universities is usually divided into three terms (Michaelmas, Lent, and Summer) each of approximately ten weeks duration. Increasingly a fourth year is being added to enable students to obtain industrial, commercial and other experience which constitutes part of the study program. At the end of their courses, successful students are awarded a bachelor's degree. For some professional qualifications, e.g. medicine, dentistry, and architecture, a student is required to study for a period of more than three years. Thus a medical student will follow a program of study yielding two degrees (one in surgery and the other in medicine) which are the minimum requirements for a doctor.

Degree courses are organized by subject departments usually headed, in universities, by a professor to whom teaching staffs are responsible. Departments have one or more professors depending on their size. Departments are grouped into faculties which provide the frameworks for teaching and research, playing a significant role in the arrangement of course examinations. Faculties link together cognate subject departments, carrying titles which include science, engineering, arts, medicine, education and social science. The academic management ladder is based on the sequence senate, faculty, department. A similar structure is found in public sector institutions.

Vocational and professional degrees are used by external professional bodies as qualifications for entry to their respective professions. This leads to the accreditation of awards by bodies such as the Council for the Accreditation of Teacher Education, the British Psychological Society, the Engineering Council, and an array of similar agencies in such fields as architecture, law, accountancy, and dentistry. Higher education institutions in the U.K. have been encouraged to innovate in terms of course organization and structure. This encouragement has come from governmental, industrial, commercial, and academic sources. The innovations can be seen not only in curriculum revision of traditional courses, i.e. in the revision of course aims and objectives, content, teaching methods, and modes of assessment. It is also evident in the introduction of part-time degree programs, the widening of access to include disadvantaged groups, and the design of credit transfer arrangements. It is particularly striking in the distance education programs introduced by the Open University which include the use of national broadcasting media. It is also noticeable in the development of continuing education programs which include post-experience vocational education.

Reference to the Open University serves to highlight one eccentric feature of British higher education. However, even a brief visit to a selection of British institutions would reveal that each had its own idiosyncrasies. Uniformity is found only in the most general of senses. The universities vary in size of student enrollments from the very large to the very small. There are two substantial federal universities (Wales and London) and a number organized on a collegiate basis e.g. "ancient" Oxford and Cambridge and "new" Lancaster and York. There are technological universities, such as Loughborough, Aston, and Salford, which were created from former colleges of advanced technology. Each university, polytechnic, and college has its distinctive ethos for study and recreation. A feature of British higher education is the provision by the institutions of residential accommodation in the form of halls of residence and student villages which include self-catering and catering accommodation. Students have athletic and students' unions which include in their responsibilities the provision of a rich array of recreational facilities. Clubs and societies abound and, traditionally, Wednesday afternoons are kept free of teaching to enable students to participate in their activities. The mixing of students from different sociocultural, ethnic, and foreign backgrounds is regarded as an important ingredient of higher education. The attraction of study in Britain remains strong for undergraduates drawn from a large number of foreign countries. Part of this attraction lies in the sharing of the English language by foreign students with their British counterparts.

Undergraduate tuition fees for session 1990-91 are 1,675 British pounds for home students who receive a mandatory grant and 675 British pounds for students from countries of the European Economic Community and British students not in receipt of a grant. For students not in these categories the fees are, typically, 4,560 British pounds in arts subjects and 6,050 British pounds in science subjects. A very rough indication of the living expenses is provided in the following section.

Advanced Studies and Research

Both universities and public sector institutions of higher education mount postgraduate courses, including degree courses. There is a great variety of such courses, both full-time and part-time. Successful completion also earns a variety of degrees, such as Master of Arts, Master of Science, Master in Education, Master of Letters, and Master of Philosophy. The nomenclature of the postgraduate doctorate is common to all subjects, that is the Doctorate of Philosophy. The degrees of Doctor of Letters, Doctor of Science, etc. are awarded either for outstanding contributions to knowledge on the basis of published work or as honorary degrees.

The main route into postgraduate work for domestic students still tends to be by means of study immediately after completion of the initial degree, at least in the university sector. Departments require a good first degree, first or upper second class honors, but a major criterion is a student's ability to obtain a grant to cover fees and living expenses. Fees for home students for postgraduate study at a university are, typically 1,985 British pounds per annum in 1990-91. For overseas students the fees are 4,560 British pounds in arts, rising to 6,050 British pounds per annum in science. The fees for part-time postgraduate students are typically 500 British pounds per annum. Admission to a postgraduate course depends on the level of the individual student's education in his/her home country and also on preferences of fields of study. Home applicants are normally interviewed while applications from abroad can be dealt with by correspondence. It is impossible to put a precise figure on the amount of money required to live in university halls or lodgings. However, some indication might be that the full grant for undergraduate students outside London, exclusive of fees, is currently just over 2,100 British pounds per annum, a sum which students find inadequate. Hall fees, when they include half board, are about 1,500 British pounds per annum. In sum, the competition for research grants from research councils, British Academy, or the universities themselves is very considerable. The standard of living enjoyed by most postgraduate students dependent solely on grants is not high, although students sponsored by industry tend to be in a rather more favorable position.

The approach to master's degree courses varies from university to university and even from department to department within each university. In the University of Wales, for example, it is possible to take a master's degree purely by personal research, the result of which is the presentation of a thesis. If accepted by the examiners, this results in the award of the degree of M.Phil. Other master's degrees (of science, arts, education) can be gained either by successful completion of taught courses or a combination of such courses with the submission of a dissertation which may not necessarily involve any original work. The degree of Ph.D., on the other hand, can only be awarded on submission of a thesis which constitutes an original contribution to learning in that subject.

Higher degree courses are available on a full-time or part-time basis. Full-time master's courses are usually of one year's duration, though the dissertation is sometimes scheduled for completion in the succeeding year. Part-time master's courses normally take three years' study though up to five years is allowed for completion in, for example, the University of Wales. Full-time Ph.D. students take a minimum of three years to complete their studies, though most take longer. Part-time doctoral students sometimes complete after five years of study but most take longer. The "year" in question is the academic year which runs from 1st October to 30th June in British universities, with the exception of the Open University which operates a calendar year and which is based primarily on distance learning, though it also operates a substantial postgraduate program.

Both full-time and part-time postgraduate work is based at the host institution which has the research teams and necessary equipment and library facilities. Each student is assigned to a supervisor who directs the student's program and maintains regular contact. The language of tuition is English and most universities put on courses for those potential postgraduate students wishing to improve their English. We have seen that most full-time students rely on grant aid from a variety of bodies, both public and private, to sponsor their research and to provide them with a maintenance grant. Such funding is by no means adequate in all cases and students take a variety of measures to augment their incomes. Some take part-time jobs but the only really satisfying of these is part-time teaching or demonstrating in the host department. Such employment is less in evidence since the cuts in university funding of the 1980s.

Postgraduate students naturally enjoy all the facilities which universities have to offer and these are extensive: artistic, sporting, and social. They have access to what are still, despite recent underfunding, the flagship educational institutions in Great Britain. While not all departments are equally prestigious, none has yet been relegated to the status of teaching-only group of staff. All university staff are still contracted to pursue original research in their subjects, which means that their students have access, through supervisors and their colleagues, to the latest scholarship in their respective subjects. Foreign students are welcomed and in some subjects form a substantial section of the research student body. Universities cultivate them and any student from abroad wishing to study at a British university has merely to write to those institutions which interest him or her. Basic details, addresses, organizations, names of staff, etc. are provided in the *Commonwealth Universities Year Book*. The relevant individual departments would provide details of any postdoctoral work.

ISSUES AND TRENDS

The 1980s have witnessed a dramatic change in the profile of education in Britain and in the way it is administered and organized. Government policy towards education has been mainly responsible for this.

In university education, the 1980s have been dominated by government attempts to make universities more accountable for their stewardship of public funds and to make them more susceptible to market forces. To this end there has been considerable redistribution of funding based on two research exercises which have attempted to classify departments within universities on the basis of their international and national research reputations. No similar exercise has been undertaken for teaching ability and reputation. A series of "rationalization" exercises was undertaken in conjunction with the research ratings led to closure of some departments and merging of others. These policies were pushed through by the University Grants Committee (replaced by the Universities Funding Council). The average age of university dons is high and salaries are uncompetitive. Some foresee a crisis of staffing in the 1990s, though this will be unevenly spread both geographically and between subjects. There has been much talk of designating some universities as "teaching" universities which will not be funded for research, but this now seems less likely as the government relies on market forces to determine more specifically the ranking of universities. The larger southern universities, on the whole, are profiting.

In schools in England and Wales, the last decade has seen a yet greater revolution. In 1980 the vast majority of primary and secondary schools in England and Wales were, in effect, administered by the local authorities and had considerable freedom to decide their own curriculum. At the beginning of the 1990s larger primary schools have considerable freedom to run their own affairs in financial and administrative terms. Secondary schools have an additional potential for financial independence in that parents can choose to opt out of the local authority system altogether and receive a block grant from the Department of Education and Science. Such freedoms are offset by the implementation of a greater degree of government control of the curriculum of the schools than has ever been the case. By 1995 all pupils in all state, though not private, schools will have to study core and foundation subjects (their content determined by government appointed working parties) by law. It remains to be seen how this will affect standards and the teaching of non-statutory subjects. It is also not clear how far it will change styles of teaching in primary schools from topic-based work to subject-based work.

At the top of the school age-range, the major issue is the degree to which pupils aged 16-18 should be as specialized in their fields of study as is presently the case. Those who wish to take Advanced Level, the main criterion for university entrance, generally take no more than three subjects, usually falling into arts or science categories. Attempts to broaden this base were recently substantially rejected by the government, though the issue is by no means dead. However, it is likely that the main thrust of educational research in the next decade will be concerned with the implementation of the national curriculum and, especially, the tests being devised for the pupils. The central issues will be those of standards, the effectiveness of standard assessment tasks, and the way in which these marry up effectively to the levels of attainment identified for the various subjects of study. Since these levels have not been empirically verified, the relationship will have to be investigated after their implementation.

BIBLIOGRAPHY

Ball, C. *Aim Higher: Widening Access to Higher Education.* London: Royal Society of Arts, 1989.

Gosden, P. H. J. H. *The Education System since 1944.* Oxford, 1983.

Lowe, R. *Education in the Post-War Years. A Social History.* London, 1988.

Maclure, S. *Education Reformed.* London: Hodder and Stoughton, 1989.

Simon, B. *Bending the Rules. The Baker "Reform" of Education.* London, 1987.

Universities Central Council on Admissions. *UCCA Handbook.* London: UCCA, 1989.

UNITED STATES OF AMERICA

by
Paul V. Bredeson
Associate Professor of Educational Administration
Pennsylvania State University, U.S.A.
and
Donald J. Willower
Distinguished Professor of Education
Pennsylvania State University, U.S.A.

BACKGROUND

With volumes of well documented historical analyses of education in the United States, there is obviously a danger of over simplification in any abbreviated overview of the American educational structures, their organization, and operation. Given this caveat, the current educational enterprise is a product of the unique history of this nation. This historical experience has resulted in a fundamental paradox of great diversity amid remarkable sameness across fifty states and over 15,000 local public school governing units. This diversity results, at least in part, from regional variations with respect to size differences (large urban to very small rural school districts), control structure (public or private, elected or appointed), and fiscal support (high wealth to financially deprived districts). Despite the lack of a centrally controlled federal system of public education, there is a noteworthy similarity reflected in organizational structures, teaching modalities, instructional materials, curriculum content, and common school experience for most American youth. High rates of population mobility among educators and students, the influence of major publishing companies and state-wide adoption of educational materials, collaboration among professional organizations and state school officers, the use of standardized tests, and a highly developed system of communications have all tended to minimize the range of substantive differences in public education.

Education in Colonial America

Formal education in colonial America was largely controlled by religious denominational interests. Based on the experiences of primarily British immigrants dispersed among thirteen original colonies on the eastern coast of this vast nation, early schools (grammar schools and colleges) were often financed privately through religious support. Over a century and a half, the new immigrant population migrated further west across the new territory. In the New England colonies of Connecticut, Massachusetts and Rhode Island settled by church dissenters, the colonists found it necessary to enact legislation for the organization and support of

857

public education. The mid-Atlantic and southern colonies generally retained and supported church sponsored and privately supported schools. Though the fifty state systems of public education have unique histories, the New England colonial experience became the dominant model for the establishment of public education across the United States. Out of these colonial experiences with early school legislation dating to 1635, two basic principles evolved: (1) the state could require children to be educated, (2) the state could require towns to establish schools and use mandatory taxes to support teachers and to build schools. As a result, local education evolved into a governmental function rather than a religious one. Private religiously sponsored schools continued to exist and be important institutions, but the notions of compulsory and fiscally supported public schools were legitimated. Thus, when the U.S. Constitution was adopted in 1787, strong traditions for locally supported and publicly funded schools already existed.

The Role of the Federal Government in Education

Visitors to the United States are often surprised that there is no federally controlled and administered school system. In fact, the U.S. Office of Education was not established until 1867. The U.S. Constitution makes no specific mention of education. Thus, under the Tenth Amendment, public education was included among those responsibilities which "are reserved to the states, or to the people." Despite this reserved constitutional status, education was a priority among the early revolutionary leaders. Thomas Jefferson writing from Paris in 1787 stated: "Above all things, I hope the education of the common people will be attended to; convinced that on this good sense we may rely with most security for the preservation of a due degree of liberty." James Madison added, "A satisfactory plan for primary education is certainly a vital desideration in our republics. A public government without popular information or the means for requiring it is but a prologue to a farce or tragedy, or perhaps, both."

The federal government through presidential initiatives and congressional legislation has had major influence, primarily through targeted federal monies to support particular programs and the achievement of nationals goals, on the educational systems and policies enacted across the states. Major legislative initiatives have included the Northwest Ordinances of 1785 and 1787; the Ohio Enabling Acts of 1802 and 1803 (which operationalized support for public education and for higher education); the Morrill Land Grant Acts of 1862 (which provided 30,000 acres of public lands to support mechanical and agricultural arts, a major source of support for the large public research universities); the Smith Hughes Act of 1917 to support vocational training in public schools; the National Defense Education Act of 1958, a major federal push to upgrade curriculum and educators; Elementary and Secondary Education Act of 1965 (massive entitlement programs); and Public Law 94-142 for the education of children with special needs and/or handicaps.

Another major arena in which the federal government has greatly influenced education has been through the federal courts. Despite the lack of specific constitutional language governing public education, the courts have invoked clauses contained in various constitutional amendments, especially the first, fourth, tenth, and fourteenth, to decide legal issues in education involving freedom of speech for students and teachers, separation of church and state by prohibiting the establishment of religion in public education through fiscal support, curriculum content or policy, equal protection and due process for all participants in schools, state legislative control over local administrative school districts, racial integration of schools, equitable financing across local administrative units within states, and contractual agreements and laws for employees and their governing bodies. The breadth of these issues and the importance of public schools as institutions for accomplishing specific social goals reinforce the assertion of a popular journalist who noted that sooner or later the problems of the larger society which are not satisfactorily resolved in other social arenas come to rest at the steps of the school house door.

ELEMENTARY AND SECONDARY EDUCATION

The reserved constitutional status of public education has resulted in the fifty states establishing, governing, and supporting education within their boundaries. Because of the geographical size of these states, the typical pattern is that the state, through a state department of education, delegates authority for the operation of schools to local school districts, political subdivisions of the states. State Departments of Education generally are agencies that gather educational data for the legislature and for local school districts, provide services and assistance in meeting regulations, and complete various forms and reports on local, regional, and state educational outcomes. Currently there are some 15,500 operating local public school districts in the United States. The geographic size and the population of a state often dictate the number of local administrative school districts necessary to operate schools efficiently and effectively. Hawaii operates one school district while Texas and California each delegate education to over one thousand local administrative units.

Each state, through legislative mandate, establishes guidelines for the development and daily operations of curriculum at the local school district level. Generally these guidelines, operationalized and monitored by the state department of education, are minimum standards which must be met in terms of the number of hours in a school day, the number of school days per year, and the minimum units of study in particular curricular areas such as mathematics, social sciences, biological and physical sciences, language arts, and the arts. In addition to the mandated curricular offerings, the school day is typically enhanced by a rich assortment of extracurricular activities which includes athletic teams, musical and fine arts programs, scholastic competition teams, special interest clubs, and student government groups. Recognizing the tremendous diversity that is likely across thousands of local school districts, a typical school day is 6-7 hours and a typical school year is 180 school days. Although urban school districts are beginning to experiment with different patterns for a school year calendar, most districts, urban, suburban, and rural, continue to follow a deeply ingrained historical tradition of beginning classes in early September and finishing the school year soon after the end of May.

Each state education department is vested with the responsibility to certificate school professional staff, teachers, administrators, and support staff. Minimum qualifications for teachers include a four year baccalaureate degree from a college or university along with specific preparation in content teaching areas and pedagogy. Administrators usually must have had a minimum number of years classroom teaching experience and a post baccalaureate graduate program of studies to qualify for certificates as school principals, superintendents, and/or educational specialists.

Private schools operate under general state legislative mandates for public education but each is chartered separately, finances operations without state or local tax monies, and governs its own curriculum and educational policies. Private schools continue to play a noteworthy part in education in the United States; however, the numbers of schools and students enrolled in them remains less than 15 percent of the total pupil population.

Between the state department of education and the local school district, some states have intermediate service units, variously named. The primary purpose of these units is to provide special services to school districts within a given region of the state. Programs to meet the needs of exceptional/handicapped children, professional development activities for local teachers and administrators, and special educational services, which individual school districts can not afford to offer because of lack of economies of scale, are among the primary activities of these intermediate service units.

The general pattern for accreditation of schools is that the state department of education in all fifty states reviews and officially endorses schools and their programs. Since states provide on average 50 percent of the operating revenues for public schools, they have considerable leverage to enforce standards for granting or renewing charters for schools and for licensure of professionals in those schools. The term accreditation more commonly refers to regionally based and privately organized and operated consortia of institutions such as, the North Central Association of Colleges and Schools. Though strictly voluntary, accreditation from such bodies has a profound impact on local and state confidence in the quality and operation of institutions.

Currently there are 40.3 million students enrolled in nearly 58,000 public elementary schools and over 21,000 secondary schools. Another 5.7 million attend private schools, 15,300 elementary schools, 2,400 secondary schools, and 7,800 other schools with combined grades and structures. The schools are staffed by over 2.6 million public school teachers and 400,000 private school staff. Financial support for public schools totals approximately US$185 billion per year, about 7 percent of the gross national product. Though the figures vary across the states and school districts, the distribution of revenues to operate schools averages 6.7 percent federal, 49.4 percent state and 43.9 percent local. These revenues are raised primarily from taxes on individual and corporate income and local property taxes. Average expenditure per pupil is approximately US$3,600 per year. Private schools are not supported by public monies and thus rely on student tuition fees and private monies, often from church sponsorship.

At the local district level, each district has a governing board which is usually elected by the voters. This governing body has ultimate responsibility for the governance of the local schools. The tradition of local control is deeply embedded in the history of schools. The school board vested with delegated powers from the state and within legal and state legislative parameters, oversees the business of education in its locale. The hiring of professional and support staff, determining the most appropriate local curriculum, and developing and approving a budget to carry out educational programs are major responsibilities of these local governing bodies. Typically the board of education employs a superintendent of schools who is the chief executive officer at the local level. Depending on district size, the superintendent and the central office staff, made up of assistants and clerical personnel, carry out the daily managerial and operational aspects of education. At the building level (local school level), the school principal carries out the administrative responsibilities.

The typical organizational pattern for schools, elementary and secondary, is that of a graded school. Students are grouped by age primarily and move through primary levels, kindergarten through grade six at ages 5-11, and then move on to secondary school, grades 7-12. Public education is compulsory for all children, generally until age sixteen, although this varies across the states. Over 70 percent of all students continue their education to complete twelve grades and graduate with a diploma or its equivalent. There are no tuition fees for students who attend public schools. Fees for unusual curricular offerings are rare and nominal if they do exist.

Since the local school district is the delegated authority for public education, students attend schools in their attendance area or district. Because of inequities across attendance areas which have resulted in poor educational opportunities, racial discrimination, and/or schools which may be unresponsive to parental and student needs, some states and regions are beginning to experiment with expanded attendance areas where students have greater choice in selecting educational programs and the schools which offer them. Some states, such as Minnesota, have attempted to address problems created by rigid local school district boundaries and have expanded individual educational choice to the boundaries of the state itself.

Three types of schools commonly make up the public school experience for children: elementary, middle or junior high, and the high school. For all levels of schooling, students live at home. There are very few residential public schools across the country. Only in very remote areas where daily transportation to and from school would be prohibitive do such residential schools exist. Despite the fact that public schools are local, over 36 million students are transported to schools on a daily basis at public expense. This expenditure alone amounts to over US$5.7 billion per year.

The primary or elementary school is usually kindergarten through grade six. This school is generally a neighborhood school and reflects in many ways characteristics of the local environment. The middle school or junior high school is perhaps the most flexible in terms of graded structure. Students attend these schools anywhere from grades five through nine. Demographic, fiscal, and physical realities of available classroom space tend to play more of a role in determining the structure of these schools and the groupings of students housed there than do pedagogy or developmental theories. The culminating public school experience is the high school, grades nine through twelve.

HIGHER EDUCATION

Institutions

Institutions of higher education developed from two major European traditions, the Parisian concept of university and the collegiate model of residential study from Great Britain. From these two traditions colleges and universities emerged in the United States. The earliest institutions of higher education were established to study religion and to prepare clergy for the new colonies. Among the first colleges established were Harvard 1636, William and Mary 1693, Yale 1701, The University of Pennsylvania 1740, Princeton 1746, Kings College Columbia 1754, College of Rhode Island-Brown 1764, Queens-Rutgers 1766, and Georgetown 1789. Given their charters and purposes, they were theocratic in focus. By 1775, on the eve of the American Revolutionary War, the combined total of all bachelors degrees conferred by these nine colleges was only 152.

In the post-Revolutionary War era 1776-1862, the expanding new nation required the development and growth of many more institutions of higher learning, both public and private. Many of these colleges tended to model themselves after the earliest New England colleges. Between 1840 and 1850, schools dedicated to agricultural needs were established and in subsequent decades many more "Common Schools", designed to provide one year of training for elementary teachers, were founded. The Morrill Land Grant Act of 1862 provided support from the federal government through the appropriation of 30,000 acres of land to establish and support schools dedicated to mechanical and agricultural arts. In the early 1900s, the major growth area of postsecondary education was in the two-year community college. By 1990 there were over 1,300 of these types of institutions.

Admission to an institution of higher education is autonomously governed by each college or university. Though weighted and evaluated differentially by each institution, the general criteria used to determine admission include successful completion of high school, grades 9-12; high school grade point average and class rank; minimal course of studies in areas of English, mathematics, and sciences; and results from standardized tests such as the SAT (Scholastic Aptitude Test) and the ACT (American College Testing Program's battery of achievement and advanced placement examinations).

There are three major tracks which students follow beyond the high school experience. The first is the technical institute, which consists of approximately 8,000 schools, both public and private (proprietary and nonprofit) institutions, whose primary purpose is to train students for particular occupations in technical, service, and professional areas usually within one to three calendar years depending on the field. Certificates and/or associate degrees awarded in these areas are generally recognized for acceptance into certain positions in government, business, or industry, but the curriculum is primarily vocational and thus most credits are not transferrable to the other two postsecondary tracks.

Junior or community colleges, primarily two year institutions which grant associate degrees or branch campuses of larger four year colleges and universities, are the fastest growing segment in postsecondary education with over 1,300 institutions and 38.4 percent of the total student enrollment in higher education. Two thirds of these institutions are public. These two year colleges have made postsecondary education much more accessible to students because of lower costs, convenient locations near major population centers, and flexible curriculum structures which meet the needs of part-time students. Though each four-year institution has its own policy for acceptance of transferred student credits, credits and courses taken at these two-year institutions are normally applicable to requirements for a four-year bachelor's degree.

The third major track in postsecondary education is the four year undergraduate degree program offered at specialized, general baccalaureate, comprehensive, and doctoral institutions. The typical bachelor's degree awarded at a four-year college includes approximately 120 credits hours with specific requirements for major and minor courses of study. Sixty credits are common to complete the major field. A minor support area and general studies in other disciplines and colleges make up the remainder of the credit requirements for the bachelor's degree. The bachelor's degree is typically a pre-professional degree. Post-baccalaureate professional degree programs are required in areas such as law, medicine, and dentistry.

Over six million students attend these institutions. Specialized institutions are those which emphasize one academic field of study, such as business or engineering. General baccalaureate colleges are primarily concerned with providing general four-year liberal arts or undergraduate degrees. Comprehensive institutions have diverse undergraduate and post-bachelor's programs but do not engage in significant doctoral level education. Doctoral institutions have varied programs offerings and research activities and grant the highest academic degrees available.

At present there are a total of about 3,400 colleges, universities, and branch campuses. Somewhat more than half of this total are private with control vested in religious denominations, professional organizations, and/or private foundations. Even with the large number of private higher education institutions, 78 percent of all college students attend public institutions. The majority of colleges, both public and private, are located in states which have the largest populations. New York and California have 308 and 299 institutions respectively while sparsely populated states such as Nevada and Wyoming have only nine institutions each.

In institutions of higher education, regional, national, and professional accrediting agencies have great influence on program status and often on professional licensure for particular professional groups. These accrediting bodies include a range of consortia as varied as the professional fields themselves. The American Psychological Association, the American Medical Association, and North

Central Association of Colleges of Teacher Education are examples of these powerful professional accrediting agencies.

Higher education in the United States is also characterized by diversity in terms of institutional size, type, control, program emphasis and climate, and population served. Coeducation is the norm in higher education. Though many of the colleges were originally established to prepare just males or just females, fewer than 200 single sex institutions remain in operation.

Governance

The history of higher education organization and governance reflects many of the same deeply ingrained principles of decentralization and local control that guided political government in colonial times. Strong affinities for local and state control rather than federal control were the norms. The United States' federal constitution legally vested individual states with authority over education, public and private. Private colleges apply for charters from the state. Public colleges are often created by separate articles in state constitutions or by legislative action creating statutory institutions. Once a charter is granted, legal liability and governance is placed in the hands of a governing body such as a board of directors, trustees, or regents. The notion of a "lay governing board" again grew out of early colonial experiences in the governance of sectarian controlled and operated colleges. The governing board engages a president or chancellor, who serves at the pleasure of the board, to administer the institution. The president then delegates authority to other officials, vice-presidents, deans, and academic chairpersons, to carry out the institution's major purposes. Most institutions have two major organizational dimensions: the administrative organization, responsible for budgeting, physical plant, purchasing, and daily logistical operations and services; and the academic program in charge of program content, admissions, and the rules and traditions governing these areas. This organizational bifurcation of responsibilities results in a blend of at least three models of organizational practice. They are in part bureaucratic or hierarchical in terms of decision making and authority, collegial in terms of shared responsibilities among a community of scholars, and political in that there are various self-interest groups vying for support within the institution and thus there is a need to focus on conflict resolution processes.

Student enrollment varies tremendously across these public and private institutions with the smallest numbering about 200 full time students to institutions with more than 65,000 students. These institutions employ about 900,000 instructional staff, 73 percent male and 27 percent female. Higher education faculty in the United States has been underrepresented by women and minorities. Despite affirmative action efforts and active institutional recruitment of women and minorities, their numbers remain low. Given the fact that only 22 percent of the total number of 12.5 million students in higher education attend private schools and there are more private colleges and universities than there are public, over 80 percent of private postsecondary institutions maintain enrollments between 200 and 3,000 students. Only three private universities have enrollments over 30,000 students while there are over 30 public universities with enrollments over 30,000. Thus, public institutions tend to have somewhat larger student enrollments with 85 percent of the institutions ranging in size from 1,000 to 20,000 full time students.

Higher education in the United States has become increasingly accessible to graduates of high school. The traditional cohort group, ages 18-22, is still the largest age group by percent represented across college campuses. However, there is a trend to bring in older students for associate degrees, graduate studies, and for professional development and training. The growth of local junior/community colleges and branch campuses has greatly increased access to higher education for all segments of the population. The convenience of campus location and the availability of financial aid through government loans, grants, and private scholarships have helped to attract and support many students who would not otherwise have been able to pursue a postsecondary education.

Undergraduate Studies

The programs and major fields of study in postsecondary education are as varied as are the types of institutions. With some 12.5 million students, the range of studies is obviously quite broad. Within the last two decades there has been a trend toward major fields in undergraduate studies which are occupationally focused so that students are not only immediately employable but placed in financially rewarding jobs. Given the increased personal costs for a four-year degree, this trend is not surprising. In the early 1980s only 7.4 percent of the undergraduate degrees were awarded in majors such as English, literature, foreign languages, history, mathematics, and physics. The real growth has been in the fields of business, management, engineering, computer sciences, and health professions, which accounted for 41.8 percent of bachelor degrees awarded. These data have a number of significant implications for particular occupational areas. In education, for example, the current and projected demands for teachers far exceed the number of students in preparation programs. With over 50 percent of the current national teaching force eligible to retire by 1992, the prospect of understaffed K-12 schools is a critical issue in the United States.

Undergraduate degree granting institutions also provide a range of pre-professional courses of study. Graduates of these four year institutions move into a variety of professional occupational areas. However, many professions such as law, medicine, and dentistry require post-baccalaureate studies. These professions have extensive certification/licensing processes which are generally state regulated and not necessarily transferable from state to state. Though preparation requirements may be similar among the states, individual state licensure is required to practice. Most candidates for professions attend state, regional, and nationally accredited programs/institutions and thus have the benefit of professionally accredited standards of preparation. Entry level examinations and requirements for on-going professional development for educators, doctors, and attorneys are common.

In 1985-86 there were 988,000 bachelor's degrees conferred in the United States. These were almost evenly divided between males and females. However, women have increased their percentage by 19 percent in the last decade while males have declined by 4 percent. Of the 288,000 master's degrees, half were awarded to women. Differences between males and females appear in terms of degree conferrals in first professional degrees, dentistry, medicine, and law with males receiving nearly three times as many degrees as females of the 72,000 degrees awarded. Males also received twice as many doctoral degrees of the 33,000 conferred.

International students, approximately 340,000, represent less than 2 percent of the total number of students in higher education. These foreign students tend to specialize in programs which emphasize sciences and mathematics. In engineering, for example, in 1983, 43 percent of the total number of degrees conferred were awarded to international students. Thirty-six percent of the degrees in mathematics and computer science went to international students.

Ease of access to higher education is an important tradition and commitment to all segments of the population in the United States. If diversity is a salient characteristic of higher education, then the cost to attend particular institutions mirrors this diversity. Cost for one year of full-time residential study typically include tuition and fees, room and board, and additional fees for activities, books, and supplies. Though access is important, costs clearly make a difference in individual choice of which college to attend. At the less expensive end of the cost continuum, that is, a residential state supported community based college, total costs for one year would be as low as US$110 for tuition, US$2,600 for board, and US$400 for books and supplies. At an elite private liberal arts college, the costs are significantly higher with tuition US$15,700, room and board US$3,300, and US$1,000 for additional costs. Between these two extremes the average costs at a four-year state supported college are tuition US$1,700, room and board US$2,400, and US$400 other fees and supplies. (While private institutions charge the same rate of tuition from both the state and out-of-state students, state supported institutions require out-of-state students to pay a higher rate. International students fall into the category of out-of-state students). It should be noted that none of these average costs include individual spending money for extras. Despite the enormous differences in costs, most institutions, public and private, provide student financial assistance based on sliding scales of individual family wealth and ability to pay. Such financial aid is given to individual students in the form of scholarships, grants, work assignments for pay, and student loans.

Given the increased costs for delivering higher education, college administrators spend a major portion of their time garnering resources to support students, programs, and their institutions in general. Competition for dollars from public and private sources is fierce. Current fund revenues for all higher education institutions is approximately US$100 billion: US$65 billion for public and US$35 billion for private colleges. There are major differences between public and private institutions and their sources of revenue. At public institutions, student tuitions and fees account for 14.5 percent of the total while at private institutions the percentage is approximately 38.6 percent. Another major difference occurs in state funding. Public institutions receive on average 45 percent of their revenue from the state government while private institutions receive less than 2 percent. Thus in terms of their total operating budgets, private colleges and universities rely much more on federal grants and contracts (16.5 percent), the solicitation of private gifts (9.3 percent), as well as monies from endowments and sales/services (27.7 percent) to support their operations. Over the past twenty years the most dramatic change in terms of sources of revenue from private gifts has occurred in public institutions, which recently have become more aggressive in seeking these monies. Today public and private institutions share nearly evenly private contributions, which reverses a trend that saw the private institutions enjoying a greater proportion of such support.

Advanced Studies and Research

Graduate studies and research are primarily carried out in 408 comprehensive four-year colleges and universities and in 167 doctoral degree granting institutions, public and private. Graduate programs are often organized to prepare students for work in a specific professionally certificated occupation such as medicine, law, or public school administration. Three levels of graduate studies are common: a typical master's degree program consists of thirty graduate credits in a major field over a 1-2 year course of studies; professional certificate programs are usually designed to prepare students for external examination and licensure in state certificated occupations; and doctoral programs, generally of 3-5 years, grant degrees such as the Ph.D. (Doctor of Philosophy, the highest degree awarded in most institutions), M.D. (Doctor of Medicine) and D.Ed. (Doctorate of Education, a professional degree).

Admission standards for graduate studies are very rigorous and intended to select a limited number of candidates to study and prepare for advanced degrees and professional careers. Performance measures from undergraduate degree programs, results from standardized tests such as the Graduate Record Examination (GRE), and letters of recommendation are commonly used to select students for advanced study.

Though not exclusively, major funded research (applied and basic) is carried out in doctoral research institutions. Research and development centers and institutes parallel doctoral studies and often provide the financial support for faculty and students to continue their studies. Though teaching and service activities are important dimensions of faculty workloads, emphasis on incentive systems designed to reward original research and publications is the norm at research institutions.

ISSUES AND TRENDS

Both public and private education in the United States have been responsive to social, economic, and political changes and the new demands accordingly placed upon schools. From early colonial times to the present, education has been reshaped and reformed in terms of its fundamental purposes, organizational structures, desired outcomes, and populations it serves. These changes are rarely, if ever, made without a great deal of debate and public attention at the local, state, and national levels. Though there are many factors which have and continue to influence educational reform, demographics is a useful construct for understanding many of the current educational reform issues.

Shifts in the numbers and backgrounds of school-age populations have generally required concomitant adjustments in education institutions at all levels. As massive waves of immigrant populations greatly influenced the curriculum and structures developed for public education in the late nineteenth century and most of this century, current demographic realities are forcing educational stakeholders to rethink again and then reform the structure, content, and imperatives for public education. As the United States moves into the twenty-first century, demographers cite dramatic changes in the school-age population. Over a third of all pupils coming to schools will be from racial minority backgrounds, primarily black and Hispanic Americans. Since substantial numbers of these future students currently live in poverty, the challenge to educate these children and to insure their success in schools is of critical importance to achieve desired social, economic, and educational outcomes.

Perhaps the most influential publication affecting education in the last several decades is *A Nation at Risk* (1983). Though many publications have been critical of education, this report brought focus and greatly intensified interest in perennial educational issues and debates. As a result, the education sector, business and industry, professional associations, and federal, state, and local levels of government have all contributed to unprecedented levels of involvement, commitment, and interest in education. A review of current journals and publications in the United States would highlight issues such as children at risk, effective schools, school improvement, educational choice, teacher empowerment, educational equity, restructuring schools, funding public and private education, reform of teacher and administrator professional preparation programs, roles of business and industry in education, and enhanced use of technology (computers, interactive video, and distance education structures).

In addition to the wide-ranging level of concern and the development of policy initiatives in education from political, economic, and social arenas, research in education is a major activity in this country; one carried out chiefly in the universities. Educational research is published in numerous professional and scholarly journals. Some important reviews of major research topics and findings are found in *The Handbook of Educational Research* (1982), *Handbook of Research on Educational Administration* (1988), and in the annually published *Review of Research in Education* of the American Educational Research Association.

BIBLIOGRAPHY

Boyan, N. J., ed. *Handbook of Research on Educational Administration*. New York: Longman, 1988.

Digest of Education Statistics. National Center for Education Statistics, Washington, D. C.: United States Government Printing Office, 1988.

Mitzel, H. E., ed. *Encyclopedia of Educational Research* 5th ed. New York: Macmillan and Free Press, 1982.

National Commission on Excellence in Education. *A Nation at Risk: The Imperative for Educational Reform.* Washington, D. C.: United States Government Printing Office, 1983.

Wittrock, M. C., ed. *Handbook of Research on Teaching.* 3rd ed. New York: Macmillan, 1986.

VENEZUELA

by
F. Javier Dupla
Director, School of Education
Catholic University of Andres Bello, Venezuela

BACKGROUND

The origin of education in Venezuela goes back to 1721 when King Philip V of Spain decreed the creation of a university. The university had a pontifical character and incorporated the activities of the former Seminary of Santa Rosa. It offered theology, law, medicine, and art, but theological training was the dominant activity. After the country gained independence, this institution became the Central University of Venezuela in 1826.

During the nineteenth century three more universities were established: the University of Merida in 1810, now known as the University of Los Andes; the University of Maracaibo in 1891, now known as the University of Zulia; and the University of Valencia in 1892, now known as the University of Carabobo. The latter two universities stopped functioning after a few years of their opening, due to political reasons but they were reopened later; University of Zulia in 1946 and University of Carabobo in 1958.

PRIMARY AND SECONDARY EDUCATION

In Venezuela, as in almost all other countries, the system of education consists of four levels: preschool, primary (basic education), secondary (middle level), and higher education. Preschool education generally lasts for one year; primary education consists of nine grades (or years); secondary education lasts two or three years depending on the area of studies; and higher education takes a minimum of two and one half years. Only the primary education is compulsory.

Secondary education, diversified and professionally oriented, consists of seven distinct areas of studies: sciences, humanities, art, agriculture, social work, commerce, and industrial studies. The majority or 53 percent of the students completing secondary education pursue sciences; 12 percent humanities; only 0.1 percent arts; 7 percent agriculture; 2 percent social work; 10 percent commerce; and 15 percent industrial studies.

The academic year lasts from October to July and is divided into three terms: October-December, January-March, and April-June. There is an exam at the end of each term and final exams are held in July with a repeat exam scheduled for September. School vacations last approximately two months (August and September). On satisfactory completion of the two or three years of secondary education, students receive the diploma of *bachiller* indicating one of the seven areas that the candidate had chosen to follow. About 73 percent of the students are enrolled in government run schools *(liceos)* while 27 percent are in private institutions, usually known as colleges.

Public schools are free (a small fee is charged for matriculation etc.) and the private schools charge fees varying from 100 to 1600 bolivars (US$1 = 14.50 Bolivars) per month. About 400 private Catholic colleges serve economically underprivileged population and up to 80 percent of their cost of operation is subsidized by the government.

Living expenses of the students are borne by the families. In 1987, the government assisted 105,000 students with over 100 million bolivars, giving emphasis to rural, native, and frontier population. In addition, the government awarded over 102,000 scholarships to students who lacked adequate resources, at an expenditure of 240 million bolivars.

Teaching appointments at the secondary level require a degree from a school of education in a university. The salary of a full time secondary school teacher is about 7,000 bolivars per month.

HIGHER EDUCATION

Institutions

In 1958, after the fall of the dictatorial government of Perez Jimenez, the new democratic government decreed a law governing the functioning of universities. This law gave autonomy to universities to establish their own standards (organizational aspect), to plan and execute research programs (academic aspect), to elect and appoint staff (administrative aspect), and to administer their funds (economic and financial aspect). This level of autonomy is enjoyed by the universities of Los Andes, Zulia, and Carabobo, and the Central University of Venezuela, which are not only the oldest universities in the country but also the institutions which, together, account for over half of the student population enrolled in higher education. The structure of these national autonomous universities consist of faculties and schools, headed by deans and directors respectively.

There are also experimental national universities which have been established by the government to try out new academic and administrative structures. These institutions also enjoy autonomy within the limits of their mission. There are twelve such universities, the oldest one being the University of the Orient founded in 1958. In all these universities excepting in the University of the Orient, the administrators are appointed by the Ministry of Education or the president of the republic. The academic structure of the experimental universities consist of departments and programs.

The next category of higher education institutions comprise private universities, which can only open faculties and schools approved by the National Council of Universities. There are nine private universities, of which the two oldest are the University of Santa Maria and the Catholic University of Andres Bello.

In addition to the universities, there are university institutes that train teachers, polytechnics, technological institutes, university colleges, institutes that train officers for armed forces, institutes that train clergy, and special institutes of research and postgraduate studies. These institutions function under special regulations enacted in 1974 and generally specialize in one or two branches of knowledge or in one program.

The university institutes for teacher training prepare instructors for preschools, primary schools, and secondary schools. They provide general training as well as training in specific areas such as languages, social sciences, mathematics, biology, etc. At present there are six public institutions and one private one of this type. The six public institutions form the Experimental Pedagogical University.

The polytechnical institutes trains engineers in various fields, and the structure of studies is somewhat similar to that of the universities. There are four polytechnical institutes: Barquisimeto (1962), Guayana (1971), Luis Caballero Mejias (1974) and one for the national armed forces.

The university institutes of technology offer short term career training programs in technology, agriculture, commerce, construction, administration, informatics, etc. They award the title of higher technician. There are fourteen public institutes of this type, and seventeen private ones.

The university colleges were established to offer the basic education cycle of some universities which could not fully meet the heavy demand imposed on them by the increasing student population. They are similar to university institutes of technology. There are fifteen such institutions, of which eight are public. They award the diploma of higher technician.

The government, by decree No. 42 of March 1979, effected integration of the subsystems of higher education. The National Council of Universities consisting of rectors of all the universities and representatives of the government coordinates and regulates functioning of universities. There is a separate body (similar to the National Council of Universities) overseeing the functioning of institutes and university colleges, but in practice it has not functioned.

Universities depend totally on the government for funding their operation. The government allocates a block grant to the National Council of Universities, which makes the distribution among the universities. Funding for institutes and university colleges also come from the government based on recommendations of the Ministry of Education. About 80 percent of a university's expenditure is for salaries of teaching and other staff.

Historically, allocations for higher education increased 7.5 times between 1972 and 1981. This increase is well reflected in the number of new institutions that have been established during this period (the number of institutions increased from twenty-one to eighty-four). The growth includes creation of eight public universities and four private ones; two public and one private pedagogical institutes; two polytechnical institutes; and twenty-three public institutes and university colleges, and twenty-three private ones. Between 1981 and 1985, allocations for higher education stagnated, stabilizing at about 5,300 million bolivars per year, in the face of the country's fiscal crisis due to low oil prices. The period 1985-88 saw a return to the growth mode in funding for universities and allocations nearly doubled within this period. This strong increase is not due to a corresponding increase in the enrollment but primarily due to increases in salaries and socioeconomic benefits for staff, provision of social security for students, and improvement of student services. A small part of the increased funding also went for improvement of libraries and development of research.

Undergraduate Studies

Undergraduate studies in Venezuela are of two types: short programs leading to the diploma of higher technician which take two and one-half to three years (5-6 semesters), and long programs leading to the title of *licenciado* or equivalent which take 5-6 years (10-12 semesters). The short programs are offered at the institutes and university colleges. The long programs are offered at the universities, pedagogical institutions, and polytechnics. The main programs offered in various institutions are as follows: basic sciences, engineering, architecture, technology, agricultural and marine sciences, health sciences, education, social sciences, arts and letters, and military science. The basic sciences which include chemistry, physics, mathematics and biology are offered at the Central University of Venezuela, Simon Bolivar University, University of Zulia, University of Los Andes and the University of the Orient. In the areas of engineering, architecture and technology, over twenty-five long programs and thirty-nine short programs are available at various institutions spread across the country. In the area of health sciences, six long programs and eight short programs are available across the country. The education field provide opportunities for twenty-one long programs and six short programs at a number of institutions. In humanities, arts, and letters opportunities exist for pursuing twelve long programs. In social sciences, there are twenty-one long programs and thirty-six short programs. Studies in military sciences offer four long programs at four institutions.

The basic requirement for admission is: a *bachiller* diploma (secondary school completion) obtained in Venezuela or an equivalent qualification. Not all holders of *bachiller* diploma get selected. As the demand for places is higher than what is available, the Office of University Planning is entrusted with the task of assigning available places. The procedure for selection is set by the National Council of Universities and since 1984, the concept of *numerus clausus* apply. Applicants are assigned to each institution based on the availability of places at the institution, in the applicants' field of studies, and a point system under which candidates are assigned points for their performance during the last four years of secondary schooling and at aptitude exams (those who receive the highest points have the best opportunity for admission to the institution and to the field of their choice). Some institutions have additional requirements such as admission tests.

The academic year extends from October to July. The semester system is very common in Venezuelan educational institutions, with the academic year divided into two semesters from October to February and from March to July. When annual system is in force, university laws do not permit students to be promoted if they do not pass the year end exam. There is some provision to carry over one subject to the next year; however, failure in two or more subjects results in repeating the entire year.

The extracurricular activities most significant in the campuses consist of student representations (in various bodies) and sports. Students are represented in all academic councils. All institutions of higher education have student welfare offices, which help the students to obtain scholarships and concessions in books and supplies, to arrange transport, and to find board and lodging as necessary. Student housing managed by the Department of Student Relations help keep students' costs low. Students also take an active part in inter-university sports championships in athletics, baseball, football, volleyball, etc.

Education is tuition free in public universities and institutions of higher education (a very small fee is charged for registration every year and at graduation etc.). At the private universities, the tuition charges vary from 1,000 to 4,000 bolivars depending on the institution. Students coming from families that lack adequate financial resources tend to study in fields that allow time for part-time work such as social sciences and education. On the other hand, courses which require full dedication, like engineering or health sciences, tend to be taken by students with adequate resources. Some universities provide subsidies (reduced fees etc.) to needy students. Budget allocation for student services is about 1.3-4.6 percent of the total budget of a given institution.

Foreign students seeking admission are required to possess either the Venezuelan *bachiller* diploma or a foreign equivalent or must be following a course of studies at university levels in the student's country. University to which admission is sought determines the equivalency.

Advanced Studies and Research

In 1988, Venezuelan higher education institutions offered 571 postgraduate courses of studies, of which 250 were at "specialist level", 262 were for master's degree and 59 were in doctoral programs. There are twenty-eight higher education institutions offering postgraduate courses and of these, six institutions offer 74 percent of the courses as follows: Central University of Venezuela (235 courses), Simon Bolivar University (43 courses), University of Los Andes (42 courses), University of Zulia (4 courses), University of the Orient (31 courses), and Catholic University of Andres Bello (30 courses).

Postgraduate studies in Venezuela dates back to 1941 when the Faculty of Medicine of the Central University began to offer courses for specialization. In hardly fifteen years, postgraduate programs have seen an explosive growth. In 1980, there were 18.6 postgraduate students for every 100,000 inhabitants and consisted of 13 percent of the total enrollment in higher education. Venezuela rose to the fourth place among Latin American countries with regard to the number of postgraduate students (6,200 in 1980), after Mexico (31,000), Brazil (12,000), and Colombia (7,500). Postgraduate studies have grown at such a rapid pace that 80 percent of the postgraduates in 1980 had been trained within the prior ten years.

The general qualification for admission to postgraduate studies, at specialist, master's, or doctorate levels is somewhat similar but selection criteria depend on the speciality. A first degree is a necessity, possibly in the area of specialization. Other criteria include academic record of the candidate: teaching and research activities in the selected field; knowledge of a foreign language, preferably English; presentation of an outline of proposed research or scientific project; references; interview with the director of the program; and a curriculum vitae. The duration of postgraduate courses is 1-3 years; master's degree takes a minimum of two years and the doctorate takes three years. In general, master's and doctoral degrees require presentation of a thesis. Areas for which postgraduate programs are available include administration and management (thirty-four); biology, agronomy, and zoology (twenty); applied sciences (twenty-six); education (twenty-two); law (fourteen); economics (eleven); history (eight); informatics and computation (six); engineering (forty-two); mathematics (fifteen); planning (fifteen); medicine (eighty); and other areas such as architecture, communication, statistics, pharmacy, philosophy, literature, and transportation.

Enrollment for postgraduate programs takes place at the beginning of the semester (September, January, and June). Many of the programs admit only once a year. Cost of postgraduate programs vary in both public institutions as well as private institutions from about 300 bolivars per unit of credit to over 1,000 bolivars per unit of credit. Each course requires 2-3 credits, which implies 2-3 hours of class per week for that course. The total number of credits required is about thirty for "specialization", thirty-six for master's degree, and forty for the doctorate. Between 1974 and 1983 the government supported 32,295 students for postgraduate studies in Venezuela as well as in foreign countries through a program developed by the *Fundacion Gran Mariscal de Ayacucho*. At present, fiscal difficulties have tightened the availability of funds. In 1987 the government awarded 123 postgraduate scholarships and 1,461 educational loans.

ISSUES AND TRENDS

Current issues and problems in Venezuelan education can be outlined as follows:

1. Reduction in the quantitative growth of the educational system due to a decrease in the birth rate among the higher and the middle classes of the population and a strong reduction in immigration as a result of economic difficulties faced by the country since 1983. The reduction in the birth rate is reflected in the low levels of enrollment at the primary education level, while in the higher levels, the pressure for access to education continues. The annual rate of growth in primary school enrollment has been reduced from over 3 percent in the 1970s to an average of 2 percent in the 1980s, although in 1986-87, the rate has risen to about 4 percent.

2. Reform of the system of education based on the Organic Law of Education promulgated in 1980. Before this law, the compulsory primary education consisted of six years, followed by secondary education which continued for 5-6 years, divided into two cycles. At present, the compulsory basic education embraces the old primary plus the first cycle of secondary education (nine years in total). The curriculum has been revised along with the abolishing of year-end

exams, and the grades are now calculated taking averages of achievement levels at the end of the three terms (of the year). The qualitative results of these reforms are not yet known given the fact that the changes have only been made recently.

3. Necessity to improve the quality of education. There is a general feeling among experts and students of education that the system of education lacks quality. Of the students who enter primary (basic) education, only about 33 percent or only one in three complete compulsory education. Thus two out of three students leave school without any intellectual preparation to face life. Those who stay in the school end their education without obtaining the full benefits of the education they received, as illustrated by the grades obtained at the *bachiller* diploma level. According to Arturo Uslar Pietri, "64 percent of the students who held the *bachiller* diploma in 1984-85 had an average of only 10-12 points (on a scale of 0-20) and only 9.8 percent had 15 points or more."

4. Changes in the administrative structure of the Ministry of Education. The Ministry of Education is a gigantic and complex organization which employs 88,000 teachers in basic education grades 1-6; 61,000 teachers in basic education grades 7-9 and secondary education; 25,000 teachers in higher education; and over 50,000 other employees. Conforming to the tradition of strong central control that exist in Venezuela since colonial times, all the important decisions are taken in Caracas (seat of the ministry). The country is divided into administrative regions but in practice only the routine actions are taken in the regions. The excessive interferences of political parties in the appointment of staff and unnecessary bureaucracy in the ranks of the ministry lead to a heavy overhead in the Ministry of Education. As an example, the Ministry of Education in Venezuela has more supervisors than its counterpart in France.

BIBLIOGRAPHY

Congreso Nacional de Educación. *La Educación Superior.* Caracas: CNE, 1989.

CNU-Núcleo de Directores de Desarrollo Estudiantil. *Proposiciones sobre políticas de desarrollo estudiantil.* Maracaibo, 1988 (mimeo).

CNU-OPSU. *Oportunidades de estudio en las instituciones de educación superior de Venezuela.* 1985.

Ministerio de Educación, Venezuela. *Memoria y Cuenta.* Caracas: ME, 1987.

Morles, Victor. "Los estudios de postgrado en América Latina: vision panoramica." *Inteyciencia.* (Jan-Feb. 1983).

Pietri, Arturo Uslar, et al. "Informe que presenta al Presidente de la República Dr. Jaime Lusinchi la Comision presidencial del Proyecto Educativo Nacional." Caracas, 1986.

VIETNAM

by
Hoang Duc Nhuan
Acting Director General
National Institute for Educational Science, Vietnam

BACKGROUND

The reunification of Vietnam became a reality in April 1975 and about four years later, in January 1979, the Politbureau of the Communist Party of Vietnam issued Resolution No. 14/NQ/TW on education reform aimed at developing a uniform educational structure for the whole country. The content of the resolution was institutionalized in the Decision No. 135/CP of the Council of Ministers (27 March 1981) on the official adaptation of the twelve-year primary and secondary education consisting of two levels: the basic general education level lasting nine years (five-year primary and four-year lower secondary); and the secondary (or upper second) level for three years. In general the objectives of education and training are "to train the young to become new socialist citizens having character, dynamism, creativity, and will to push their country forward and to develop talent to meet the requirements of the socialist economy".

The Ministry of Education and the Ministry of Higher and Vocational Education are responsible for all educational activities in Vietnam. The Ministry of Education administers the general school education including preschool and adult education as well as handicapped children's education. Most of the colleges and universities are administered by the Ministry of Higher and Vocational Education. Some colleges and vocational training schools are managed by the Ministry of Higher and Vocational Education and the related ministry. But, the teacher training colleges and teacher higher schools are mainly directed by the Ministry of Education. The minister is assisted by the vice-ministers, ministry-council, and other councils. The board of the ministry is divided into three areas: the State Administrative Area with eleven sectors each overseeing a fundamental area; the Scientific Research Area composed of the National Institute for Educational Science of Vietnam with its sixteen sub-institutes and research centers; and the Production and Business Area consisting of educational publishing house, printing factory, and school equipment enterprise. The Ministry of Higher and Vocational Education administers thirty-four colleges including Hanoi University. The planning for education is done by two financial and planning departments from the Ministry of Education and the Ministry of Higher and Vocational Education on the basis of the general plan of the State Planning Committee and taking into consideration the economical and social goals of the provincial planning committees. National expenditure on education in 1980 was about 69 percent of the national budget.

PRIMARY AND SECONDARY EDUCATION

Primary education is compulsory and consists of five grades (1-5). Children enter school generally at the age of six and continue for five years.

The curriculum includes seven subjects: Vietnamese language, math, ethics, social and natural studies, work art (includes music and painting), physical education, and hygiene. The Vietnamese language and math subjects make up 61 percent of the total class periods. The work subject includes handicraft work and simple technical work appropriate to their age level. There are 2.5 average class periods per week. Each class period lasts thirty minutes, except the Vietnamese language and math subjects for grades 2-5 and the social and natural studies for grades 4-5 which last forty minutes. At present, there are 8 million primary school children in Vietnam.

The lower secondary education consists of four grades (6-9). Students follow twenty-eight class periods per week, in thirteen subjects including one collective activity period per week.   Each period lasts forty-five minutes. Curriculum includes Vietnamese language, a foreign language, literature, civics, physical military training, technical subjects, history, geography, mathematics and the sciences. During the practical periods, vocational guidance is introduced. At present there are over 13,000 lower secondary schools in the country, with an enrollment of 4 million pupils.

Upper secondary education comprises three grades (10-12). The reformed grade ten will come into effect only in the academic year 1990-91. It is intended to adopt divided sections at the reformed upper secondary level.   There may be sections such as math-physics; physics-chemistry-biology; literature-history-geography; foreign language; and "general". The section division will not be carried out simultaneously and all schools may not have all sections. The classes comprise 26-27 periods per week for the "general section" and 27-30 periods per week for other sections. There are four types of upper secondary education: the common or ordinary secondary education, the technical upper secondary education (linked to factories, and enterprises on state farms); the specialized upper secondary education (for gifted students); and the study and work upper secondary education. The last type is set up by the people. The first three types are set up by the government, depending on local requirements.   At present there are about 1,030 upper secondary education schools with an enrollment of 1 million students.

In addition to basic general and secondary education schools there are nearly 100 centers for practical experiments serving each cluster of basic general education schools, and nearly 100 centers for polytechnical education responsible for production work education, vocational guidance, and training aspects of secondary general education schools.

Teaching Staff

In the past decades, the training of teachers and educational managers has been improved and expanded. Before the August Revolution in 1945, there were about 5,500 teachers for the whole country. Now there are 74,700 kindergarten teachers, 398,000 teachers for basic general education, 40,900 teachers for secondary level, 11,800 teachers for vocational secondary schools, and 19,800 teachers for colleges and universities. There are 183 teacher training schools in the country. Teacher training schools recruit graduates of general secondary education and train them for 2-5 years. Two year training is for kindergarten and primary level teachers. Teachers for lower secondary schools receive three years of training and those for upper secondary level receive 4-5 years of training.

In addition, the teaching staff of general education schools is being provided with graduates and engineers from Hanoi University, Polytechnic College, Agriculture University and Forestry University. During the past two decades, teachers have been provided further or follow-up training on a regular basis, under various forms, either full-time or in-service. This type of training has enabled many teachers to achieve higher educational qualifications including master's degrees. The training of educational managers and principals is carried out at two central management training schools and other similar institutions in provinces and cities.

Vocational Education

At present there are 293 vocational secondary training schools with a total of 117,000 students from different sectors such as agriculture, forestry, industry.

There are three types of vocational secondary schools: schools that recruit graduates of basic education schools, training them for about three years; schools that recruit graduates of secondary level, training them for about two years; and schools that recruit graduates of secondary schools, training them for three years. The first two types train secondary and primary level skilled workers. The third type produces senior technicians. In addition, there are about 300 vocational training schools that produce technical workers.

HIGHER EDUCATION

Higher education in Vietnam can be traced back to the eleventh century. Quoc Tu Giam, the first university, was set up in 1076. The main areas of learning were poetry, literature, ritualism, and philosophy. Since the thirteenth century, examinations on mathematics and law were organized. The great work *Dai Thanh Toan Phap* on mathematics was written by Luong The Vinh in the fifteenth century. The first school to train the art of fighting called *Giang Vo Duong* was established in 1253, under the Tran Dynasty. In post Le Dynasty, the Trinh and Nguyen families organized master's and doctoral examination on the art of fighting.

The University of Hanoi (Indochinese University) was established by the French in 1917. The teaching staff of the university was entirely French. The university consisted of the following divisions: School of Medicine and Pharmacy (which became the Faculty of Medicine and Pharmacy in 1941); School of Law and Administration (which became the Higher School of Law in 1933 and the Faculty of Law in 1942); Higher School of Pedagogy; Higher School of Agriculture and

Forestry; School of Public Works; and School of Commerce. In 1924, the Higher School of Fine Arts, and in 1941, the Higher School of Sciences were added.

All schools of the university were located in Hanoi, and a student dormitory was built in the suburbs of Hanoi in 1943 to accommodate some 300 students who came from the provinces. The enrollment was 700 in 1939, and 1,538 in 1944. In 1940, the Institute of Advanced Legal and Social Studies was added. Also the School of Midwifery and the School of Dental Surgery were attached to the Faculty of Medicine and Pharmacy. Right after the August Revolution of 1945, all universities were reorganized. Today, Vietnam has 100 higher education institutions with 116,700 students of whom 33.7 percent are girls. The institutions specialize in following areas: industry (13), agriculture and forest (8), economics (12), medical-sport and game (12), teacher training (40), culture and art (8) and basic science (7).

The duration of first degree programs vary: teacher training colleges (science), four years; University Polytechnical College and Foreign Language Teacher Training College, five years; and Medical University, six years. Vietnamese language is the instruction medium for all subjects. Of the teaching staff at higher education institutions, about 7,000 hold the doctoral degrees. Postgraduate programs are also conducted in some institutions.

ISSUES AND TRENDS

The 1989-90 plans for educational development focus on several activities:

(a)   Continuing to stimulate all forces in order to eliminate the laboring people's illiteracy and to accomplish universalization of primary education.

(b)   Increasing the number of students who graduate from one level of education to the other: 60 percent from the primary to the lower secondary schools; and 25-30 percent from the lower to the upper secondary schools in the national school system. At the same time, encouraging and supporting the opening of people-founded schools (schools built by the people) with a view to develop citizen's continuing education.

(c)   Creating favorable conditions for 15-20 percent of the preschool children to enter into creches, and 30-35 percent to enter into kindergartens (including the national school system and the people-founded schools).

(d)   Consolidating the system of vocational schools and vocational centers at districts and stimulating the private vocational schools; increasing the quality of in-service training courses at colleges; expanding the training modality for students who fail in the national entrance examinations but wish to continue their studies; and continuing to implement the establishment of the Postgraduate Training Council.

BIBLIOGRAPHY

General Statistics Department, Vietnam. *The 1987 Statistics Yearbook.* Hanoi: Statistic Publishing House, 1989.

Le Van, Giang. *The History of Higher Education in Vietnam.* Hanoi: Institute of Higher Education, 1985.

Ministry of Education. Education in Vietnam. Hanoi: Vietnam Courier and the Ministry of Education, 1982.

Ministry of Higher Education. "The Three Working Programs of the Higher and Vocational Education 1988-1990". *Higher Educational Review.* Hanoi: Higher Education Publishing House, 1988.

Ministry of Education. "The Drafted Rules of the Objectives and Training Plan in Secondary Schools". Hanoi, 1989.

Ministry of Education. *Program of Education Development 1987-1990.* Vol I. Hanoi: Ministry of Education, 1987.

Vo Thuan, Nho et als. *The Thirty Years of the General Education Development.* Hanoi: Education Publishing House, 1980.

ZAIRE

by
Nyango Mpeye
Professor, University of Kinshasa and
Inspector General of Higher Education
and Scientific Research, Zaire

BACKGROUND

It was not too long ago (40-50 years) that a debate reigned in the country whether to send Congolese students to Belgium or to establish higher education institutions locally in Zaire (known as Congo at that time). Some brought forth the argument that Africa did not have the social and cultural fabric to support local higher education institutions. However, good sense prevailed and overshadowing many obstacles, the first university level institution *Centre Universitaire Congolais de Lovanium* came into existence in 1947 which in February 1956 received the title of a university by decree. This institution was the forerunner of the present day University of Kinshasa. The establishment of the Lovanium center followed two earlier institutions (medical assistants' school in 1925 and agronomy assistants' school in 1932), in affiliation with the Catholic University of Louvain in Belgium.

The second university, *Universite Officielle du Congo Belge et du Rwanda-Urundi* established in 1955 in the Shaba region later was renamed University of Lubumbashi (in Lubumbashi). It was principally supported by the universities of Bruxelles, Liege, and Gand. The third university, the University of Kisangani, was established in 1963 (in Kisangani) at the initiative of European and North American Protestants.

The three universities, irrespective of the differences in their origin, had a common trait; they were modeled after Belgian universities. Since 1948, as the number of secondary school graduates increased and as the country geared up development, university education grew rapidly. Student enrollment rose from 567 in 1960-61 to 8,059 in 1970-71.

Parallel with the establishment of universities, the development of higher institutes *(instituts superieurs)* took place even more rapidly. International organizations like UNESCO, USAID, and Ford Foundation played a key role in the formation of these institutes. The number of students in pedagogical higher institutes increased from about twenty in 1960-61 to 2,238 in 1970-71 and higher technical institutes experienced a growth from 176 students in 1960-61 to 1,367 in 1970-71.

The evolution of higher education took another major turn in 1971. The government combined all the three universities and the higher institutes into a highly centralized one single university and issued the Decree 71-75 of 6 August

1971 creating the National University of Zaire. The former institutions became separate campuses of the national university.

Governed by a council of administration, the National University of Zaire was administered by a rector assisted by a general administrator. At the head of each university campus was a vice-rector whereas the higher institutes were managed by a director-general or a director. The centralized operation of higher education in this manner, proved to be too ineffective and there was another reform in 1981 which decentralized the administration granting autonomy to each of the institutions. The campuses again became universities. However, certain aspects of the 1971 reforms were retained: the state's sovereignty and control over the entire system of education; a set of regulations common to all institutions with regard to academic, scientific and administrative personnel in higher education; abolition of ideological rifts harmful to national cohesion; and a set of admission and academic standards common to all institutions.

PRIMARY AND SECONDARY EDUCATION

The objective of primary education is to provide children with a basic level of general education covering physical, moral, civic, and intellectual development. In particular, primary education is expected to prepare all children to integrate themselves usefully into the society and to train those who have the capacity, to undertake higher studies. Primary schooling in Zaire consist of six years of study divided into three levels: elementary level, intermediate level, and terminal level. Children enter elementary level at the age of six years. A regular school year has at least two hundred days of class attendance and a minimum of 900 hours of class work.

The history of secondary education in Zaire goes way back to the period when the country was under the colonial rule of Belgium. From 1908 to 1958, within a period of fifty years, a dense network of over 26,000 primary schools and 5,000 secondary schools came into existence and the enrollment rose to more than one million students.

Secondary education in Zaire comprises two categories: technical and professional education, and general education. The studies at secondary level last six years for the "long cycle" and four or five years for the "short cycle". The successful completion of the "long cycle" is marked by the award of a state diploma, whereas students who complete the "short cycle" receive a certificate *(brevet)* of professional aptitude.

For pragmatic reasons, the emphasis has been on the development of technical and professional education. The "long cycle" has several options: agricultural option including agriculture, food technology, and veterinary work; dressmaking section; and industrial section including mechanical trades, industrial design, construction, electrical technology and similar areas. The objective of this "long cycle" is to train students to assume technician level positions in industry. Students receive an education in both theory and practice. They are also trained to plan and organize their activities. In the "short cycle", the focus is primarily on the practical aspects of a given profession or trade and candidates have two options: agricultural option, and industrial option.

For students who do not succeed in the "long" or the "short cycle", specialized training is available at the *Centre de Specialisation Professionelle* which provide programs of a shorter duration (10-24 months) to produce persons skilled in various trades (masons, electricians, plumbers, etc.).

Other professional type secondary education that produce technician level persons include "long cycle" programs in commerce, plastic arts, tourism, teaching, and meteorology.

The general secondary education consists of two categories: literary, and scientific (mathematics and physics, chemistry and biology). The objective of general secondary education is to prepare students for higher studies.

Public secondary education is funded by the government but parents are also required to pay part of the cost.

HIGHER EDUCATION

Institutions

Higher education institutions in Zaire comprise three universities, nineteen higher technical institutes, and fourteen higher pedagogical institutes. The mission of each category is well defined by the political leadership.

The universities are responsible for formation of persons with the broadest range of knowledge and conceptual capability. To achieve this end, the universities provide programs that are favorable to the blossoming of new ideas and for the development of professional aptitude. Universities also have the task of conducting both applied and scientific research oriented towards solving problems specific to Zaire, taking into account worldwide developments in science and technology.

The higher technical institutes aim at producing staff with specialized training in the sciences, and applied technology. They also have the task of conducting research related to adaptation of technology and techniques to local conditions, and promoting artistic talent.

The higher pedagogical institutes have as their mission, the training of teachers of the highest calibre, awakening their conscience to the nobleness of the teaching profession. These institutions are also responsible for research in pedagogy to improve the quality of primary and secondary education, and to propagate the results of research by developing necessary teaching manuals.

The overall coordination of higher education is done by the Department of Higher (and University) Education and Scientific Research through which the government exercises its authority. Under the department, there are three councils of administration corresponding to the three types of institutions: universities, higher technical institutes, and higher pedagogical institutes. The councils are the governing bodies. By the authority vested in them for decision making and budget appropriations, they exercise control over the institutions coming under them. The councils have the authority to define objectives and policies for their institutions; decide on the establishment of new faculties, programs, and research centers;

control finances; approve budgets and present them to the government; approve regulations relating to activities at the institutions; and authorize capital acquisitions.

Each institution has its own university (or institute) council, management committee, rector or director-general, councils of the faculties (or sections) and departmental councils. Faculties are headed by a dean.

Recruitment, promotion, and other conditions of service for teaching staff are governed by government regulations (Law No. 025/81 and 81/160 of October 1981). Staff at the *assistant* and *charge de pratique* level are recruited by the council of the university or the institute. The appointment and promotion of staff at higher levels are done by the (government) Commissioner of Higher Education, on request from the councils of administration at the universities or institutes. Salaries of teaching staff at higher education institutions come from the government budget. Over the years teachers' salaries have decreased in real terms affecting motivation although teachers are better paid than most other public service staff.

Programs and Degrees

Studies at different universities and higher institutes are structured in a similar manner. The first cycle takes three years of studies and leads to the diploma of graduation. However, in certain fields of studies, the first cycle takes only two years, in which case the diploma awarded is the *capacitaire*. Before undertaking studies in some faculties, a preparatory year may be required or recommended.

The second cycle consists of two years of studies and leads to the diplomas of "licensee", "pharmacist", "dentist", "engineer", etc., depending on the field of studies. In the faculty of medicine and veterinary medicine, the second cycle takes three years (of which the final year is an internship) and leads to the Doctor of Medicine or Doctor of Veterinary Medicine, respectively.

In the third cycle, the first two years are spent in studies leading to the Diploma of Advanced Studies (DES). The program consists of a certain number of courses and seminars (with a scientific and a pedagogic component) as well as presentation of a dissertation. On completion of the DES, students can proceed to prepare a doctoral thesis. The culmination of the third cycle of studies is the doctorate which may take 5-7 years. It must be noted that during this period, the candidates are often employed either at the institution or elsewhere. At the Faculty of Veterinary Medicine, the diploma awarded at the end of the third cycle is the *agrege de l'enseignement superieur en medicine veterinaire*. In the Faculty of Medicine the third cycle is much longer. Doctors first spend 3-4 years specializing in a given field and obtain a specialist diploma, following which they then spend some more time to obtain the diploma of *agrege de l'enseignement superieur en medicine*.

Basic entrance qualification to the first cycle of any higher education institution is the completion of secondary education. In addition, the following conditions apply: the candidates must have a state diploma or equivalent; within the regional quota system, priority is given according to the marks obtained at the state diploma (secondary); candidates who obtain 70 percent or more marks at the state diploma examination can select a field of their choice; candidates must pass an admission examination for entry to Polytechnical Faculty, Faculty of Science, Higher Institute of Applied Technology, and Institute of Building and Public Works; admission to the second cycle in the higher institutes of technology require a graduation diploma (first cycle) and two years of work experience; admission to the second cycle in the higher institutes of pedagogy require passing an admission test; and admission to studies for the Diploma of Advanced Studies (DES) require a second cycle diploma.

The government awards scholarships to students who meet specified criteria and the awards vary from 2,500 to 4,000 Zaires per month. On-campus students' housing is available but conditions have deteriorated due to overcrowding. Withdrawal of government subsidized meals has resulted in poor nourishment of students.

ISSUES AND TRENDS

Two important issues facing education in Zaire can be highlighted:

(a)   The social demand for higher education remains at a very high level in spite of the many difficulties facing the country. A vast number of students who complete secondary education want to pursue higher education, essentially because of two factors: the desire for social mobility through education; and the structure of secondary education does not adequately emphasize professional avenues.

(b)   Financial constraints have adversely affected the entire public sector. Since 1984, the government allocations no longer reflect the real needs of the institutions. Often budget provisions are reduced during the course of the year, resulting in curtailment of planned expenditures. Also the funds available to higher education institutions have not kept pace at all with the rising cost of living.

BIBLIOGRAPHY

Vanderlinden, J. et als. *Du Congo au Zaire 1960-1980: Essai de Bilan.* Brussels: CRISP, 1981.

Verhagen, B. *l'Enseignement Universitaire en Zaire: Du Lovanium a l'UNAZA, 1958-1978.* Paris: l'Harmattan, 1978.

ZIMBABWE

by
C. E. M. Chikombah
Senior Lecturer and Dean, Faculty of Education
University of Zimbabwe, Zimbabwe

BACKGROUND

Zimbabwe was a colony of Great Britain from 1890 to 1980. The changes that have taken place in education since independence in 1980 have not been able to completely obliterate the philosophy that influenced the structure, content and administration of education in the pre-independence era. However, a new thinking is starting to prevail at each level.

The Education Act No. 5 of 1987 divides the formal educational system in Zimbabwe into four levels: infant, primary, secondary, and higher education. The organization of infant education is just starting and it is found mostly in the urban areas. Infant education is a private enterprise and the Ministry of Primary and Secondary Education encourages those interested in organizing infant education. In reality, a majority of the children in Zimbabwe starts schooling at primary school level. Details of education at each level will be discussed later.

Higher education, defined as that activity in education undertaken after secondary education (grades 4-12), started in Zimbabwe in about 1956 with the creation of the University College in Salisbury (1956) which is now the University of Zimbabwe. Subsequently several other institutions were established: Heany Training College (1956), Gwelo Teacher Training College (1964), and Salisbury Polytechnic College (1965). Teacher training colleges were there long before the identified dates but could not be classified as higher education institutions because entry qualification was below the level of form four (twelfth grade). The (Salisbury) Harare Polytechnic and other technical colleges, until recently still had some departments where entry qualification was below five "Ordinary Level" passes at the secondary school exam.

With regard to the role of government in higher education, as previously described by Chikombah, "The truth of the matter is that the Zimbabwe Government like other governments, either directly or indirectly, positively or negatively, has a role in university education. This role in university education can be played through one or more of the following: planning, funding, control, expansion, coordination, and change" (Chikombah 1988). This statement about the role of government in university education still applies to higher education. The Zimbabwe government through funding determines policies, curricula, and programs particularly those in polytechnics, teachers' colleges, and agricultural colleges. The polytechnics, teachers' colleges, and agricultural colleges administratively come under the government. The University of Zimbabwe, however, is governed by a university council through the university senate and faculty boards.

The University of Zimbabwe plays a supervisory role in higher education, particularly with regard to teachers' colleges and polytechnics. All syllabuses in teacher education colleges (Chikombah 1988) are approved by the University of Zimbabwe before they are implemented. This is done under the University of Zimbabwe and teachers' colleges associateship program which started in the mid-1950s. Under this scheme, the university, through the Associate College Center (ACC) professionally supervises teacher education college activities. This scheme has been extended to the polytechnics (for the degree programs only).

The government creates all teachers' and technical colleges, and determines who teaches in them. Except for teacher education colleges, all other higher education institutions have a very strong long standing relationship with industry. Agricultural colleges have a well defined relationship with the farming industry. Polytechnics have relationships with trade and commerce, and manufacturing industry. The university by the nature and spread of its programs has a clear relationship with all sectors. There is even an "Industry-University Committee" whose activities are directed at monitoring the needs and interests of both the university and industry, covering programs and manpower requirements.

SECONDARY EDUCATION

The Zimbabwe secondary school system can be divided into three stages: Zimbabwe Junior Certificate, the Cambridge Certificate ("O" level) and the "A" level. Each of the stages require two years of study. The academic year is nine months from January to December, and consists of three terms with vacation periods of about equal duration in between the terms.

The secondary school curriculum covers up to 120 subjects or subject areas. Most of the subjects are offered at "O" level. However, there are some subjects offered at "O" level which are not offered at "A" level and the reverse is also true. The key subjects include English, Shona, Ndebele, Portuguese, French, Spanish, history, biology, mathematics, economic history, economics, ancient history, chemistry, and computing science. English is the medium of instruction.

Extracurricular activities in Zimbabwe secondary schools cover a large spectrum of activities including soccer, tennis, basketball, netball, rugby, athletics, and gymnastics.

Although primary schooling is free, fees are charged at secondary level and the cost depends on the type of school; private or government, group A or B, and boarding or day. At government urban group A schools, fees and levy are US$52 and US$75 per term, respectively. At government urban group B schools, fees are US$52 and levy is almost negligible per term. Private day or boarding schools are very expensive. The charges are as high as US$300 per term for day students and over US$700 per term per child for boarding students (cost includes tuition and living expenses). Most secondary school tuition and other activity fees are the responsibility of the parent. The government policy in this regard is "no child should be excluded from attending classes because parents have failed to pay fees and levy".

Selection and appointment of the teaching staff is done by the Ministry of Primary and Secondary Education. The government policy is that all teachers should be trained and qualified to teach in schools. Unfortunately, as a result of the expansion which has taken place at all educational levels, it has not been possible to have professionally qualified teachers in all the schools.

There are foreign students in both primary and secondary schools in Zimbabwe. They are sons and daughters of visiting scholars, ambassadorial staff from various countries, expatriate teachers in secondary schools, and refugees.

HIGHER EDUCATION

Institutions

There are several types of higher education institutions in Zimbabwe: university, polytechnics, teacher education colleges, and agricultural colleges.

The University of Zimbabwe is the only university in the country. The university has ten faculties and about sixty departments and units. It offers 80-100 degree and diploma programs and at the undergraduate degree level offers degrees in the fields of agriculture, arts, commerce, education, engineering, law, medicine, science, social studies and veterinary science. Postgraduate programs cover certificates, diplomas, and master's and doctoral degrees in several of these fields.

The University of Zimbabwe plays multiple roles: the research role, the training role, the supervisory role and the extension role (Chikombah 1988). The research and training roles are not unique to the University of Zimbabwe. However, the supervisory and extension roles are unique. The extension role of the University of Zimbabwe is manifested in the "vacation school". Every year each university faculty and department designs one or more courses in its area to offer to the general public for two weeks in August. The courses which range from gardening to solar energy, are organized at major centers throughout the country. The supervisory role as has been discussed earlier, is directed at teachers' colleges, technical colleges, and other affiliated institutions of higher learning. The curricula for some programs in technical colleges and all programs at teacher education colleges are approved by the university before they are implemented. This activity is aimed at improving the quality of programs and ensuring uniformity of programs in these institutions.

Polytechnics and technical colleges form another sector of higher education. Zimbabwe has eight polytechnics and technical colleges in or near major centers: Harare Polytechnic, Technical College Bulawayo, Mutare Technical College, Kwekwe Technical College, Gweru Technical College, Kushinga Phikelela Technical College, Masvingo Technical College, and Belvedere National Vocational Training and Development Center (NUTDC). The colleges offer courses in many areas with some of them having more offerings than others. Harare Polytechnic offers courses in ten areas while the Technical College Bulawayo and the Kwekwe Technical College offers courses in only seven and four areas respectively. The fields of studies generally available include automotive engineering, civil engineering and building, electrical engineering, mechanical and production engineering, printing and graphic arts, science, technology, business education, mass communication, computer science, library and information service, commerce, hotel management, and adult studies. The main role of these colleges is to train manpower with appropriate skills for various sectors of the economy.

The technical administrative structure consists of the college advisory council, the college administration, and the college board of studies committee. The college advisory council (CAC) members are appointed by the minister of higher education to advise the principal and the Ministry of Higher Education on the requirements of industry and commerce in relation to manpower needs. It also advises the principal on how best to run the affairs of the college. The college administration (CA) is the administrative organ of the college. It is comprised of the principal, registrar, deputy registrar, and assistant registrar. The college board of studies committee (CBSC) is composed of senior administrative staff of the college administration. This committee is chaired by the principal of the college and is responsible for monitoring study programs and general administration.

The certificates and diplomas granted by these colleges consist of National Certificate (NC), National Intermediate Diploma (NID), National Higher Certificate (NHC) and National Diploma (ND). Teacher education colleges are the largest sector of higher education. There are fifteen teacher education colleges in Zimbabwe (Andrew Louw, Belvedere, Bondolfi, Chinhoyi, Gwanda, Gweru, Hillside, Marymount, Mkoba, Morgan, Morgenster, Mutare, Nyadiri, Seke, and The United College of Education). As in the case of technical colleges, teacher education colleges are situated in major centers of the country. However some centers have more colleges than others. Teacher education colleges offer a wide range of subjects in the fields of arts, languages, mathematics, sciences, social sciences, and other technical and commercial areas. Not all subjects are offered at all colleges every year. Colleges choose their curriculum according to their manpower situation. However, there are some courses that must be offered at every college at all times such as English, mathematics, Shona/Ndebele (African Languages), science, and professional foundations.

Some colleges train teachers for primary schools only, some offer secondary school training only, while others offer both primary and secondary school training. Some colleges like Belvedere prepare teachers both for traditional subjects (English, Ndebele, Shona, history, biology, chemistry, physics, mathematics, geography, etc.) and technical subjects (technical drawing, metalwork, building, woodwork, etc.) This has been made necessary by the introduction of technical subjects at the secondary level.

The main role played by teacher education is that of training and providing skilled manpower for the schools. The certificates granted by these colleges are University of Zimbabwe certificates because of associateship between the University of Zimbabwe and teachers' colleges.

In general terms, all colleges are administered by the Ministry of Higher Education, but because of the special relationship teacher education colleges have with the University of Zimbabwe, the teachers' colleges have a status somewhat different from that of the technical colleges. In addition to the normal administrative structures of a government college, teacher education colleges have an academic board known as the Associate College Center Academic Board. This academic board is composed of all college principals, two or more representatives from the Ministry of Higher Education's teacher education division, and five or more representatives from the University of Zimbabwe. The purpose of the board is to monitor all academic programs and approve pass lists from all colleges.

Undergraduate Studies

The University of Zimbabwe, as mentioned earlier, offers bachelor's degree programs in a wide variety of fields: arts, education, engineering, humanities, law, medicine, sciences and social sciences.

The admission requirements are "A" level passes (Cambridge Certificate) in a specified number of subjects, under a scheme of points. Depending on the area of specialization, some areas may demand more passes than others. For 1989, the cutoff was seven points. Some faculties like medicine, veterinary science, engineering, and law were taking only those with nine points and above. Faculties which usually specify two points were taking only those with seven points and above. There is also the mature entry route for those who are twenty-five years and above and who have five "O" levels but have no "A" level subjects. These students take a test sometime in October. Those who do well in the test are then offered places.

Some faculties stipulate the number of courses a person has to do in order to graduate. For example, in the Faculty of Education the structure for the B.Ed. degree program is two courses in the teaching subject prerequisite, six courses in the teaching subject itself, and one course project. Generally a student is required to select three subjects to study for the duration of the degree program. Most of the degrees at the University of Zimbabwe are three years. however, in areas like medicine, engineering, and veterinary science, the period ranges 4-6 years. The academic year duration is about nine months from March to December spread out in three terms: March-May, June-August, September-December.

As in primary and secondary schools, English is the medium of instruction. Other languages such as Shona, Ndebele, French, and Spanish, are studied as well but they are not used for instruction. The tuition fees and living expenses may vary from one program to another but they are generally about US$700-870 for full time and US$420 for part time programs. Living expenses range between US$360 and US$860. Most of the candidates accepted by the university get grants from the government to cover tuition and living expenses. Some parents bear the cost of their children's education.

The selection and appointment of the teaching staff is done by the university through selection boards chaired by the vice- chancellor or pro-vice-chancellor and composed of dean, deputy dean, and chairman of the department concerned.

There are foreign students in all faculties but most of them are in the faculties of medicine, veterinary science, and engineering.

Advanced Studies and Research

Almost every faculty at the University of Zimbabwe offers postgraduate degree programs. The University postgraduate programs are of two types: course work and thesis, and research only degrees. The master's degrees through course work and thesis lead to M.A., M.Sc., M.Ed., M.B.A., and M.Med. in various areas of specialization. Each faculty grants at least four master's degrees. For example, the Faculty of Education grants M.Ed., in educational administration, curriculum studies, educational psychology and adult education as well as M.Sc. in educational psychology.

The University of Zimbabwe has no doctoral course work. All the degrees at this level are research degrees and are called D.Phil. degrees. As at the master's level, D.Phil. is offered by almost all faculties. The admission requirement for the master's degree is an undergraduate degree in the area of specialization. Admission to D.Phil. programs require a master's degree in the area of specialization. There are some variations beyond these basic requirements. Also the level of passing at the master's level is examined. Only those who pass with a B+ and above are considered.

The structure of a master's degree by course work is different from the M.Phil. and D.Phil. degrees which are by research only. The course work master's degree structure varies from faculty to faculty. Some degrees have a total of ten courses such as those in the Faculty of Education. These ten courses are determined as follows: one research methods course; two courses (dissertation); five courses educational administration; and two optional courses from other areas of interest to the candidate. For research degrees, M.Phil. and D.Phil., the structure requires a candidate to present a complete research study to the Higher Degrees Committee.

Coursework master's degree programs may take 1-2 years full time or 2-3 years part time. The M.Phil. and D.Phil. take a minimum of two and three years respectively, on full time basis.

Duration of the academic year is as described under the undergraduate programs earlier. However, the M.Phil. and D.Phil. programs are organized on an individual basis and therefore there is no fixed starting and finishing dates. Postgraduate studies, like all other levels of studies are conducted in English.

Tuition expenses for postgraduate students vary from US$830 for social studies (M.A.) to US$2,800 for commerce (M.B.A.). Doctoral study costs are somewhat lower. In addition, there is examination fee of US$40-205 per candidate depending on the field of study.

Although the discussion on postgraduate studies has emphasized the master's, the M.Phil., and the D.Phil., there are also postgraduate diplomas in many of the faculties. These are programs in between a first degree and a master's degree. The entrance to these diploma programs require a first degree in the relevant field.

There are very few postgraduate students at the University of Zimbabwe (UZ) who stay in university residence; so they look for their own accommodation outside the campus. Rental rates are very high in Zimbabwe (Harare). A room could go for US$60-150 per month depending on the area. The university does not have accommodation for graduate students. There is an accommodation shortage even for undergraduate students.

Full-time postgraduate students can apply for scholarships. However there are very few scholarships to go round. So the majority of postgraduate students finance their own studies. Most graduate students are married, have children of their own, and expect no assistance from their parents. The use of students as teaching assistants is not common at the University of Zimbabwe. What is common here is for members of staff to register for either M.Phil. or D.Phil. on a part-time basis. Employees of the university can register for a program of study free of tuition costs.

Foreign student population at this level is very low. Definitely, the numbers are lower than at the undergraduate level.

ISSUES AND TRENDS

There are several areas of education from which current issues emerge: expansion of primary and secondary education, tertiary education, teacher shortage, development of science and technology, vocational education, etc.

Since independence, the primary and secondary sectors have expanded by about 205 percent and 538 percent respectively up to 1985 (Chikombah 1988). This expansion has put pressure on teacher education and university programs.

There is need to provide adequate teaching staff for the primary and secondary school systems. For this reason, the enrollment in teacher education colleges, for the same period, increased by 656 percent and the university's enrollment grew by 238 percent. The increased enrollments at both teacher education colleges and the university have led to an increase in the number of teacher education colleges from six at Independence in 1980 to fifteen in 1989 and the setting up of a commission to examine the need for a second university. The commission has recommended the setting up of a second university in the second largest city, Bulawayo, in the south of Zimbabwe.

There is a liaison committee at the University of Zimbabwe in the Faculty of Education composed of people from the Ministry of Primary and Secondary Education, and the Ministry of Higher Education and department chairpersons of the Faculty of Education. The main functions of this committee is to examine education related issues and to recommend to the university and the government, appropriate action.

BIBLIOGRAPHY

Atkinson, N. D. *Teaching Rhodesians: A History of Educational Policy in Rhodesia.* London: Longman Group Ltd., 1971.

Chikombah, C. E. M. *Education Issues in Zimbabwe Since Independence.* Stockholm: Institute of International Education, University of Stockholm, 1988.

Chikombah, C. E. M. ed. *Education in the New Zimbabwe*. Michigan: African Studies Center and the International Networks in Education and Development (INET), Michigan State University, 1988.

Chikombah, C. E. M. *The Associateship Between Teachers Colleges and the University of Zimbabwe: An Evaluation Research Report*. Harare: Faculty of Education, University of Zimbabwe, 1988.

Chikombah, C. E. M. "The National Case Study on Teacher Education in Zimbabwe." Paper submitted to the International Council on Education for Teaching, Washington, 1989.

Gelfand, M. *A Non-Racial Island of Learning: A History of the University College of Rhodesia from its Inception to 1966*. Gwelo: Mambo Press, 1978.